LIVING WITH ART

EIGHTH EDITION

Mark Getlein

Boston Burr Ridge, IL Dubuque, IA Madison, WI New York San Francisco St. Louis
Bangkok Bogotá Caracas Kuala Lumpur Lisbon London Madrid Mexico City
Milan Montreal New Delhi Santiago Seoul Singapore Sydney Taipei Toronto

The McGraw-Hill Companies

Mc Graw Hill Higher Education

LIVING WITH ART
Published by McGraw-Hill, a business unit of The McGraw-Hill
Companies, Inc., 1221 Avenue of the Americas, New York, NY,
10020. Copyright © 2008, 2005, 2002 by The McGraw-Hill Companies, Inc. Copyright © 1998, 1995, 1992 by Rita Gilbert. Copyright © 1988, 1985 by Alfred A. Knopf, Inc. All rights reserved. No
part of this publication may be reproduced or distributed in any
form or by any means, or stored in a database or retrieval system,
without the prior written consent of The McGraw-Hill Companies,
Inc., including, but not limited to, in any network or other electronic storage or transmission, or broadcast for distance learning.
Some ancillaries, including electronic and print components, may
not be available to customers outside the United States.

This book is printed on acid-free paper.

1 2 3 4 5 6 7 8 9 0 DOW/DOW 0 9 8 7 6

ISBN: 978-0-07-110180-6
MHID: 0-07-110180-2

www.mhhe.com

BRIEF CONTENTS

CONTENTS

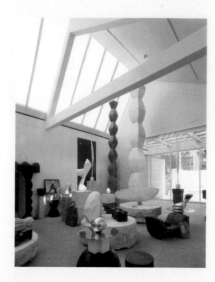

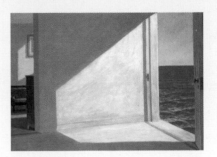

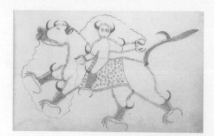

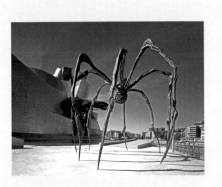

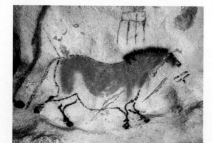

LIST OF ESSAYS

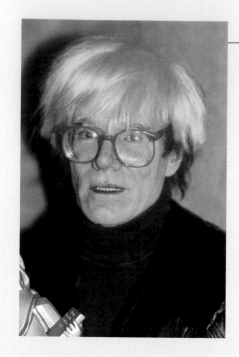

Artists

Thinking about Art

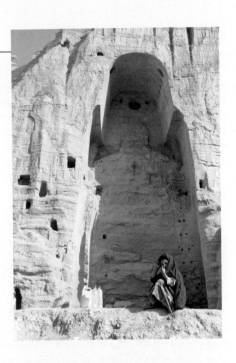

Crossing Cultures

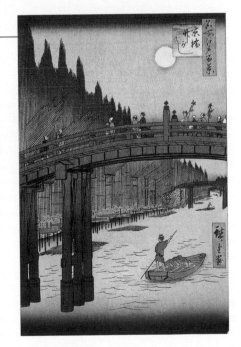

Preface

Living with Art is a basic art text for college students and other interested readers. It offers a broad introduction to the nature, vocabulary, media, and history of visual art, illustrated by hundreds of examples drawn from many cultures and across many centuries.

Organization of the Text

As in previous editions, *Living with Art* is divided into five parts. The chapters of **Part One** provide a general overview of the subject, introduce basic concepts, and explore themes that shed light on the continuity of the artistic enterprise across the immense span of the human experience. **Part Two** takes up the visual elements, first presenting them in detail, then examining how artists have organized them into art and how this organization structures our experience of looking. **Part Three** covers two-dimensional media and devotes a chapter each to the most common categories—drawing, painting, prints, camera and computer arts, and graphic design. In **Part Four** the same detailed coverage is applied to three-dimensional media—sculpture and installation, crafts, and architecture. The chapters in **Part Five** set out a brief but comprehensive history of art, beginning with the overlapping cultures of the ancient Mediterranean, then continuing with the formation of Europe and the development of Western art down to the present day. Interrupting this narrative on the brink of our own modern era are chapters that look at the historical development of art beyond the West in the cultures of Islam and Africa, of India, China, and Japan, and of the Pacific and the Americas.

Illustrations

Living with Art is lavishly illustrated in full color throughout. Every image available in color appears in color. Many images appear a second time in miniature as part of the unique Related Works feature that links the history chapters to the rest of the text. We have made every effort to obtain the best possible transparencies and digital files, and we have reviewed and color-corrected each image during the production process to ensure that the reproductions are as faithful to the originals as four colors of ink on paper can be.

Featured Essays

Brief illustrated essays scattered through *Living with Art* focus on three broad topics. **Thinking about Art** essays serve as springboards for classroom discussion. They examine ways in which cultures have reflected upon, organized, and regulated the universal human activity of making art. They also explore controversies surrounding restoration, censorship, public art, and the removal and display of artworks from tombs. **Artists** essays present brief biographies of noted artists. **Crossing Cultures** essays highlight artistic contact and exchange across history.

Maps, Pronunciation Guide, Glossary, Suggested Readings

As in previous editions, maps are integrated into the history chapters of Part Five. Key cities, sites, and works mentioned in the text are indicated on the maps. The Pronunciation Guide for unfamiliar names (both people and places) is found after the last chapter. Words that appear in bold at their first mention in the text are listed and defined in the Glossary at the back of the book. A list of Suggested Readings provides a bibliography for those who want to read further.

New to the Eighth Edition

This revision acknowledges two important trends in the art of our time. The first is the coming of age of **Internet art** and the increased presence of computer technology in contemporary art making. The second is the ongoing **globalization** of the art world, which enables artists from previously marginalized regions to reach an avid international audience.

Two new **Thinking about Art** essays provide springboards for discussion about issues surrounding cultural property. One examines the debate about whether the British Museum should return the Parthenon marbles to Greece; the other looks at legislation enabling American Indian peoples to reclaim sacred objects from museum collections. A new **Crossing Cultures** essay follows the journey of paper from its invention in China through its refinement in Islamic lands to its arrival centuries later in Europe.

This edition also reaffirms *Living with Art*'s **continuing commitment to contemporary art**. Some 40 contemporary artists appear for the first time in these pages, including Zaha Hadid, Betty Woodman, Polly Apfelbaum, Tim Hawkinson, Yinka Shonibare, Eve Sussman, Matthew Ritchie, Yayoi Kusama, Thomas Ruff, Jodi.org, Chris Ofili, Mona Hatoum, El Anatsui, Gary Simmons, Yang Fudong, Petah Coyne, Surendran Nair, Sally Mann, Andreas Gursky, Raymond Pettibon, Vija Celmins, and Julie Mehretu.

Highlights of the revision by chapter include:

- **Chapter 6: Drawing.** Newly added works by Chris Ofili, Yvonne Jacquette, Julie Mehretu, Raymond Pettibon, and Gary Simmons convey the expanded formal parameters and vibrant presence of drawing today.

- **Chapter 7: Painting.** A new closing section called "Off the Wall" presents artists whose work explores the frontier between painting and sculpture. Polly Apfelbaum and Matthew Ritchie are featured.

- **Chapter 8: Prints.** The closing section has been recast as "Printmaking and the Computer" and includes an Iris print by Indian artist Sayed-Haider Raza.

- **Chapter 9: Camera and Computer Arts.** The new title highlights the increased presence of computer technologies in contemporary art and acknowledges that the digital revolution has created a special link between camera and computer. The discussion of photography has been modified to trace a historical sweep from the earliest daguerreotypes through photographs created entirely on the computer using images found on the Internet. Later, a new closing topic, "The Internet," presents four artists whose medium is computer code and whose work resides on or takes advantage of the Internet. Finally, the film section has been revised in order to emphasize the international character of the medium and to touch on traditional artists' use of it before the advent of video. Filmmakers new to the edition include Georges Méliès, Windsor McCay, Luis Buñuel, Salvador Dalí, Andy Warhol, Jean-Luc Godard, Tsai Ming-liang, and Hayao Miyazaki. New presences elsewhere in the chapter include Thomas Ruff, Sally Mann,

Liu Zheng, Man Ray, Andreas Gursky, Wolfgang Staehle, Ben Fry, and Jodi.org.

- **Chapter 10: Graphic Design.** A new closing section called "Motion and Interactivity" looks at design in the digital world of DVDs, Web sites, and computer programs. Earlier, a project by the artists' collective known as 0100101110101101.org criticizes the ubiquitous presence of corporate logos in the visual landscape by provocatively transforming one into a design for a public sculpture.
- **Chapter 11: Sculpture and Installation.** The section on assemblage has been refreshed by juxtaposing a pair of works in metal by David Smith and Mark di Suvero with a pair of works using organic materials by Ejagham artists and Petah Coyne. Jeanne-Claude and Christo's resplendent 2005 installation *The Gates* has been added later in the chapter.
- **Chapter 13: Architecture.** Zaha Hadid's recently completed museum in Cincinnati, the Lois & Richard Rosenthal Center for Contemporary Art, is a stunning new presence here.
- **Chapter 20: Art of the Pacific and of the Americas.** The chapter now introduces tattoo, the Pacific art form that has become an everyday presence in contemporary American life.
- **Chapter 22: Art Since 1945.** A new closing section called "Opening Up to the World" looks at the globalization of the art world and discusses works by contemporary artists from China, Japan, Africa, Latin America, the Middle East, and India. Yinka Shonibare, Yoshitomo Nara, Yang Fudong, Emily Jacir, Gabriel Orozco, and Surendran Nair are featured.

STUDENT RESOURCES

MyArtStudio available on the Online Learning Center

The student content for the Online Learning Center of this new edition of *Living with Art* has been reorganized and newly enriched. All of the Core Concepts content previously available on CD-ROM has been revised and converted so that students can access the information online. Students can watch videos about various art techniques, access interactive activities designed to strengthen their understanding of art elements and Concepts, and use the guided Research in Action tool to enhance their understanding of time periods, genres, artists, and artworks. We hope that this online availability will not only strengthen student understanding of the concepts, ideas, artists, and artworks covered in *Living with Art* but also spark their own creativity. All of this information is available at www.mhhe.com/lwa8 when you click on the MyArtStudio link.

SUPPORT FOR INSTRUCTORS

Online Learning Center

The OLC boasts extensive password-protected resources for instructors. Each chapter contains an outline that includes an image list for the chapter, sample lecture topics, sample discussion topics, student projects, and video resources. You will also find presentation ideas and discussion ideas in all of the chapters in Parts One, Two, and Five (Chapters 1–5, 14–22). Also, new and improved for this edition, the test bank will include multiple-choice, essay, and image-based essay questions that are assignable to students. Also available on this OLC will be an Information Center that describes what is new to this edition, a note from Mark Getlein, the Table of Contents, a guided demonstration of the Image Vault, a Feature Summary, and an Overview of the new edition and the OLC. A link to the Image Vault will also be included on the Instructor's side of the OLC. All of this information is available at www.mhhe.com/lwa8. To receive a password for this site, please contact your local sales representative or e-mail us at art@mcgraw-hill.com.

The Image Vault

A large percentage of images from the illustration program are available to adopting instructors in digital format in The Image Vault, McGraw-Hill's new Web-based presentation manager. Instructors can incorporate images from The Image Vault in digital presentations that can be used in class (no Internet access required), burned to CD-ROM, or embedded in course Web pages. See www.mhhe.com/theimagevault for more details.

ACKNOWLEDGMENTS

One of the small triumphs of this edition is the inclusion of a mandala, an important world art form that I've been trying to work into *Living with Art*'s narrative for some time. A mandala is an appropriate image for organizing acknowledgments as well. As anyone who has ever worked on a large project for a major publisher knows, a cosmic diagram is just what's needed to envision the vast hierarchy of greater and lesser deities, helpful spirits, fearsome guardians, and friendly bodhisattvas that help to bring a book into being. My first debt is to Lisa Moore. Although as Publisher for English, Art, and Humanities she officially belongs to the ranks of starry and distant deities, she willingly assumed the bodhisattva role of sponsoring editor for this project during a time of transition at McGraw-Hill. In this she was beautifully assisted by Melissa Currier, clearly at the beginning of her own ascent to the higher realms. As of this writing, Lisa Pinto has just settled into the pose of royal ease as my editor, rejoining the project in a new role after having guided its planning stages some eighteen months earlier as Director of Development. Before disappearing (only to reappear again in her new guise) Lisa left me in the capable hands of freelance development bodhisattva Barbara Conover, whose meticulous editing cleared what was cloudy, and whose pointed queries more than once saved me from error.

Moving outward to the surround of protective spirits and fierce guardians, my gratitude lights on Robin Sand, who once again managed the monumental task of gathering pictures and clearing rights. Together, Robin and I even thwarted an art demon or two, malformed and malevolent beings who capriciously tried to refuse us permission. Yoshiko Nihei graciously consented once more to represent us to temples, museums, and photographers in Japan. Many of the images of Japanese art in this book would have been unobtainable without her participation. Susan Trentacosti, our project manager, is best envisioned as a smiling, benevolent deity with a windmill of arms, all of them working on transforming a dog-eared, coffee-stained manuscript into a beautiful finished book. Through her I am grateful to copyeditor Maria Paras and production supervisor Carol Bielski; to Greg Zies, Pat Goley, and the rest of the pros at ProGraphics; and especially to Wanda Lubelska, who poured a long stream of text and images into a finite sequence of elegant pages. Meanwhile, a succession of three marketing fates—Susanna Ellison, Sharon Loeb, and Pamela Cooper—marshaled the spirits of publicity to spread the word about this latest incarnation of *Living with Art*.

A book of this intellectual scope exceeds any single person's expertise, or at least it exceeds mine. I am grateful to artist Paul Johnson, who kindly spared a few hours to help me get my footing in the world of computer and Internet art. You can see his work at Postmasters Gallery, www.postmastersart.com. Joel Rutten of the Bernard Tschumi Studio took time out of a busy day to bring me up to date on the progress of the Acropolis Museum in Athens and the negotiations over the return of the Parthenon marbles. Jim Whittaker and Deanna Greenwood shared their expertise in color proofing technologies, their loupes to help me see what they were talking about, and a wide northern window with cool, even light. Debts carried forward from earlier editions include those to Monica Visonà, Herbert Cole, Marylin Rhie, David Damrosch, and Virginia Budney for matters African, Tibetan, Mesoamerican, and sculptural. The tireless Terry Hobbs again worked patiently through the text, alerting me with unfailing good humor to typos and errors that had somehow made it past many pairs of vigilant eyes. Finally, I thank again, both for the pleasure of the task and for the opportunity to spell their names correctly, Kathleen Desmond and Stephen Shipps, whose CAA Education Committee sessions first gave me the courage of my convictions, and whose engaged and inventive teaching strategies help me to imagine what can be done with the materials set forth in these pages.

Reviewers

This book belongs to it users, whose needs and wishes give it form. I am especially grateful for the suggestions and criticisms of all who have reviewed this edition or responded to a survey in art appreciation for us.

Cecelia Allen; Laura Amrhein, *University of Arkansas at Little Rock*; William Anderson, *University of Wisconsin–Milwaukee*; William Andrews, *Mississippi State University*; Laura Antonow, *University of Mississippi*; Barbara Armstrong, *El Centro College*; Peter Barr, *Siena Heights University*; Christine Bentley, *University of Indianapolis*; Linda Brady, *Norfolk State University*; Blake Carroll, *Jefferson College*; Patricia Cheyne, *Pacific University*; Donna Colebeck; *Southern Polytechnic State University*; Lisa Costello, *Parkland College*; Kathleen Desmond, *Central Missouri State University*; Clifford Davis, *Rivier College*; Michelle Delano, *Richard Bland College*; Danny Drotos, *Ohio Northern University*; Michelle Duran-McLure, *University of Montevallo*; Valerie Eggemeyer, *Casper College*; Christina Fetty, *Pima Community College*; Martha Fenstermaker, *Laredo Community College*; Pamela Flynn, *Holy Family University*; Raymond Gaddy, *University of North Florida*; Don Hall, *Delta College*; Herbert Hartel, *John Jay College, CUNY*; Nancy Hayes-Kitchens, *Georgia College and State University*; Angie Hill, *VSCC & MSCC*; Heather Hollan, *University of North Carolina, Greensboro*; Leah Johnson, *Hinds Community College*; Randy Jolly, *Hinds Community College*; Wonjung Jung, *New River Community College*; Diane Kendrick, *Averett University*; Hideki Kihata, *Saginaw Valley State University*; Pamela Lee, *Washington State University*; Bob Lossman, *College of Lake County*; Susan Luddeka, *ECU School of Art and Design*; Keith Luebke, *Minnesota State University, Mankato*; John Marshall, *Meridian College*; Lynn Metcalf, *St. Cloud State University*; Deborah Milosevich, *Texas Technological University*; Andrew Murad, *McLennan Community College*; Darby Ortolano, *John A. Logan College*; Yvonne Petkus, *Western Kentucky University*; Robert Simile, *West Virginia University Technical College*, Irene Soriano, *Santa Ana College*; Carole Splendore, *Chabot College*; L. Benson Warren, *Cameron University*; Miriam Weinberg, *Montclair State University*; Diane Weintraub, *Cuyamaca College*; Kimberly Winkle, *Tennessee Technological University*; Shelia Wolfe, *Butte College*.

I would also like to thank the readers of the previous editions, whose counsel continues to enlighten the text.

Fred C. Albertson, *University of Memphis*; Antoinette M. Aleccia, *Montgomery College–Rockville Campus*; Judith Andraka, *Prince George's Community College*; Mary Alice Arnold, *Appalachian State University*; Gisele Atterberry, *Illinois State University*; Jean Audigier; *University of San Francisco*; Michelle R. Banks, *Memphis State University*; Ross Beitzel, *Gloucester County College*; Kyra Belan, *Broward Community College*; John Bell, *Blue Ridge Community College*; Catherine Bernard, *City College of New York*; Barbara Bernstein, *Fresno Pacific University*; Arlene Berrie, *Miami-Dade Community College*; David Bertolotti, *GMI Engineering and Management Institute*; Sarah Burns, *Indiana University*; Carole Calo, *University of Massachusetts*; Roger Churley, *Southwestern College*; George Arnott Civey III; Charlotte Collins, *Kennesaw State University*; Brian Conley, *Golden West College*; David Cooper, *Butte College*; Shelley Cordulack, *Millikan University*; Jerry Coulter, *James Madison University*; James Craig, *Columbia Basin College*; Patricia Craig, *California State University, Fullerton*; Catherine Jones Davies, *Kirkwood Community College*; Larry Dellolio, *Camden County College*; Beverly Dennis, *Jones County Junior College*; Christina Dinkelacker, *University of Memphis*; Betty Disney, *Cypress College*; Richard T. Doi, *Central Washington University*; Shirley Dort, *Virginia State University*; Carole Drachler, *Mesa Community College*; Henry Drewal, *Cleveland State University*; Paula A. Drewak, *Macomb Community College*; Steve Eliot, *Broward Community College*; Deborah Ellington, *North Harris College*; Robert N. Ewing, *California State University, Fullerton*; Pat Federinko, *University of Alabama*; Kathy Flores, *New Mexico State University*; Elisabeth Flynn, *Longwood College*; Leonard Folgarait, *Vanderbilt University*; Lynn Galbraith, *University of Nebraska*; Douglas George, *University of New Mexico*; Larry Gleeson, *University of North Texas*; Dwaine Greer, *University of Arizona*; Paul Grootkerk, *Mississippi State University*; Bertha Steinhardt Gutman, *Suffolk County Community College*; Cheryl M. Hamilton, *University of Wisconsin–Oshkosh*; Janis Hardy, *Georgia College*; Terry Hobbs, *Fort Lewis College*; Marleen Hoover, *San Antonio College*; Sharon K. Hopson; Susan Jackson, *Marshall University*; Ralph Jacobs, *Mankato State University*; Penny Jacoby Prince, *Georges Community College*; Andrew Jendrzejewski, *Vincennes University*; Rebecca Jones, *University of Texas–Pan American*; Tim Jones, *Oklahoma Community College*; Soo Yun Kang, *Chicago State University*; Kay Klotzbach, *Camden Community College*; Katherine E. Kramer, *SUNY Cortland*; John Keller, *Harding University*; Karen Kietzman, *College of St. Francis*; Jan Koot, *California State University, Long Beach*; Cher Krause, *West Texas A&M University*; Nell Lafaye, *University of South Carolina*; Leslie A. Lambert, *Santa Fe Community College*; Pamela Lee, *Washington State University*; Anne Lisca, *Santa Fe Community College*; Robert Llewellyn, *Frostburg State University*; Kathleen Lobley, *Butler University*; Carolyn Loeb, *Central Michigan University*; Marie Maber, *Brookdale Community College*; Robert Mansfield, *San Diego State University*; Gayle McCarty, *Hinds Community College*; Walter Martin, *Concordia University*; James May, *University of Nebraska*; Robert McGrath, *Dartmouth College*; Julie McGuire, *Georgia Southern University*; Helaine M. McLain, *Northern Arizona University*; Timothy McNiven, *Ohio State University*; Lynn Metcalf, *St. Cloud State University*; Sue E. Milner, *Eastern Wyoming College*; Joseph Molinaro, *Broward Community College*; Tim Morris, *University of Central Arkansas*; Lois Myuskens-Parrot, *Richland College*; Susan Nelson, *Indiana University*; Jo Anne Nix, *Georgia College*; Percy North, *Montgomery College*; Carola Naumer, *Truckee Meadow Community College*; Christie Nuell, *Middle Tennessee State University*; Pamela Patton, *Southern Methodist University*; Lawrence Rakovan, *University of Southern Maine*; Mallory Pearce Armstrong, *Atlantic State University*; Emma Gillespie Perkins, *Morehead State*.

Mark Getlein

LIVING WITH ART

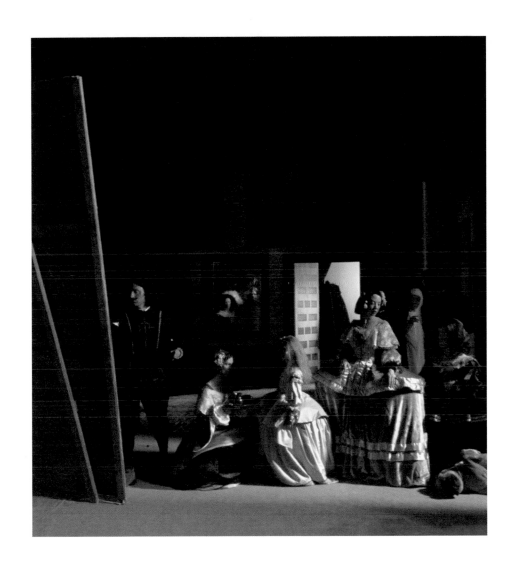

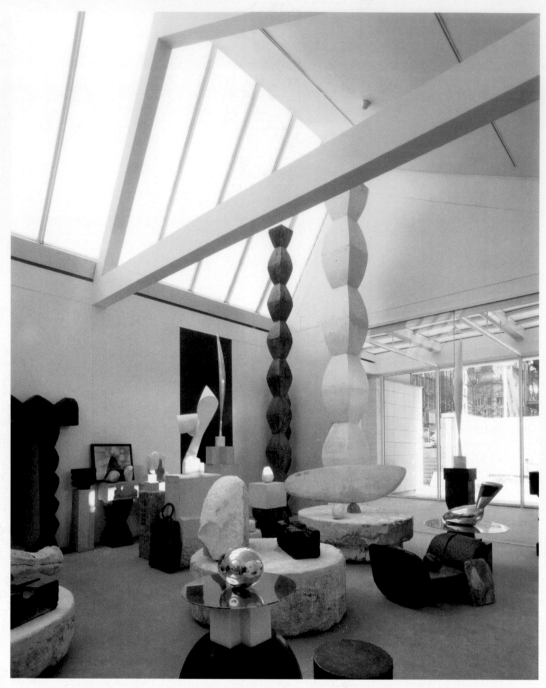

1.1 Brancusi's studio. Reconstruction at the Musée National d'Art Moderne, Centre Georges Pompidou, by the Renzo Piano Building Workshop. 1992–96.

PART ONE
Introduction

CHAPTER ONE

LIVING WITH ART

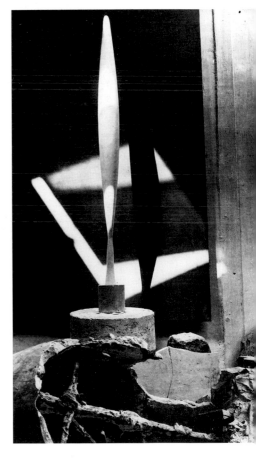

1.2 Constantin Brancusi. *Bird in Space*. c. 1928–30. Gelatin silver print, 11¾ × 9⅜".
Musée National d'Art Moderne, Centre Georges Pompidou, Paris.

Our simplest words are often the deepest in meaning: birth, kiss, flight, dream. The sculptor Constantin Brancusi spent his life searching for forms as simple and pure as those words—forms that seem to have existed forever, outside of time. Born a peasant in a remote village in Romania, he spent most of his adult life in Paris, where he lived in a single small room adjoining a skylit studio. Upon his death in 1957, Brancusi willed the contents of his studio to the French government, which eventually re-created the studio itself in a museum (**1.1**).

Near the center of the photograph are two versions of an idea Brancusi called *Endless Column*. Pulsing upward with great energy, the columns seem as though they could go on forever. Perhaps they *do* go on forever, and we can see only part of them. Directly in front of the white column, a sleek, horizontal marble form looking something like a slender submarine seems to hover over a disk-shaped base. Brancusi called it simply *Fish*. It does not depict any particular fish, but rather shows us the idea of something that moves swiftly and freely through the water, the essence of a fish. To the left of the dark column, arching up in front of a patch of wall painted red, is a version of one of Brancusi's most famous works, *Bird in Space*. Here again the artist portrays not a particular bird, but rather the idea of flight, the feeling of soaring upward. Brancusi said that the work represents "the soul liberated from matter."[1]

A photograph by Brancusi shows another, more mysterious view of *Bird in Space* (**1.2**). Light from a source we cannot see cuts across the work and falls in a sharp diamond shape on the wall behind. The sculpture casts a shadow so strong it seems to have a dark twin. Before it lies a broken, discarded work. The photograph might make you think of the birth of a bird from its shell, or of a perfected work of art arising from numerous failed attempts, or indeed of a soul newly liberated from its material prison.

Brancusi took many photographs of his work, and through them we can see how his sculptures lived in his imagination even after they were finished. He photographed them in varying conditions of light, in multiple locations and combinations, from close up and far away. With each photograph they seem to reveal a different mood, the way people we know reveal different sides of themselves over time.

Living with art, Brancusi's photographs show us, is making art live by letting it engage our attention, our imagination, our intelligence. Few of us, of course, can live with art the way Brancusi did. Yet we can choose to seek out encounters with art, to make it a matter for thought and enjoyment, and to let it live in our imagination.

You probably live already with more art than you think you do. Very likely the walls of your home are decorated with posters, photographs, or even paintings you chose because you find them beautiful or meaningful. Walking around your community you probably pass by buildings that were designed for visual appeal as well as to serve practical ends. If you ever pause for a moment just to look at one of them, to take pleasure, for example, in its silhouette against the sky, you have made the architect's work live for a moment by appreciating an effect that he or she prepared for you. We call such an experience an *aesthetic* experience. Aesthetics is the branch of philosophy concerned with the feelings aroused in us by sensory experiences—experiences we have through sight, hearing, taste, touch, and smell. Aesthetics concerns itself with our responses to the natural world and to the world we make, especially the world of art. What art is, how and why it affects us—these are some of the issues that aesthetics addresses.

This book hopes to deepen your pleasure in the aesthetic experience by broadening your understanding of one of the most basic and universal of human activities, making art. Its subject is visual art, which is art that addresses the sense of sight, as opposed to music or poetry, which are arts that appeal to the ear. It focuses on the Western tradition, by which we mean art as it has been understood and practiced in Europe and in cultures with their roots in European thought, such as the United States. But it also reaches back to consider works created well before Western ideas about art were in place and across to other cultures that have very different traditions of art.

THE IMPULSE FOR ART

No society that we know of, for as far back in human history as we have been able to penetrate, has lived without some form of art. The impulse to make and respond to art appears to be as deeply ingrained in us as the ability to learn language, part of what sets us apart as humans. Where does the urge to make art come from? What purposes does it serve? For answers, we might begin by looking at some of the oldest works yet discovered, images and artifacts dating from the Stone Ages, near the beginning of the human experience.

On the afternoon of December 18, 1994, two men and a woman, all experienced cave explorers, were climbing among the rocky cliffs in the Ardèche region of southeastern France. From a small cavity in the rock they felt a draft of air, which they knew often signaled a large cavern within. After clearing away some rocks and debris, they were able to squeeze through a narrow channel into what appeared to be an enormous underground room, its floor littered with animal bones. Pressing farther into the cave, the explorers played their lights on the walls and made an astonishing discovery: The walls were covered with drawings and paintings (**1.3**)—more than three hundred images as they eventually found—depicting rhinoceroses, horses, bears, reindeer, lions, bison, mammoths, and others, as well as numerous outlines of human hands.

It was evident that the paintings were extremely old and that the cave had remained untouched, unseen by humans, since prehistoric times. The explorers agreed to name the site after the one in their number who had led them to it, Jean-Marie Chauvet, so it is called the Chauvet cave. What they did not realize until months later, after radiocarbon testing had accurately dated the paintings, was that they had just pushed back the history of art by several *thousand* years. The Chauvet images were made about 30,000 B.C.E. and are the oldest paintings we know. The paintings date from a time known as the

Upper Paleolithic Period, which simply means the latter part of the Old Stone Age. Archaeologists have formed some tentative conclusions about how the paintings were done. Pigments of red and yellow ochre, a natural earth substance, along with black charcoal, could have been mixed with animal fat and painted onto the walls with a reed brush. In powdered form, the same materials probably were mouth-blown onto the surface through hollow reeds. Many of the images are engraved, or scratched, into the rock.

More intriguing is the question of *why* the cave paintings were made, why their creators paid such meticulous attention to detail, why they did their work so far underground. The paintings clearly were not meant to embellish a dwelling space. The cave artists must have lived—slept, cooked their meals, mated, and raised their children—much nearer to the mouths of these caves, close to daylight and fresh air. Until the Chauvet cave was discovered, many experts believed that ancient cave paintings were done for magical assistance in the hunt, to ensure success in bringing down game animals. But several of the animals depicted at Chauvet, including lions and rhinos and bears, were not in the customary diet of early peoples. Perhaps the artists wished to establish some kind of connection with these wild beasts, but we cannot know for sure.

As fascinating as these mysteries are, they pass over perhaps the most amazing thing of all, which is that there should be images in the first place. The ability to make images is uniquely human. We do it so naturally and so constantly that we take it for granted. We make them with our hands, and we make them with our minds. Lying out on the grass, for example, you may amuse yourself by finding images in the shifting clouds, now a lion, now an old woman. Are the images really there? We know that a cloud is just a cloud, yet the image is certainly there, because we see it. Our experience of the images we make is the same. We know that a drawing is just markings on a surface, a newspaper photograph merely dots, yet we recognize them as images that reflect our world, and we identify with them. The experience was the same for Paleolithic image-makers as it is for us. All images may not be art, but our ability to make them is one place where art begins.

1.3 Left section of the "Lion Panel," Chauvet cave, Ardèche Valley, France. c. 30,000 B.C.E.

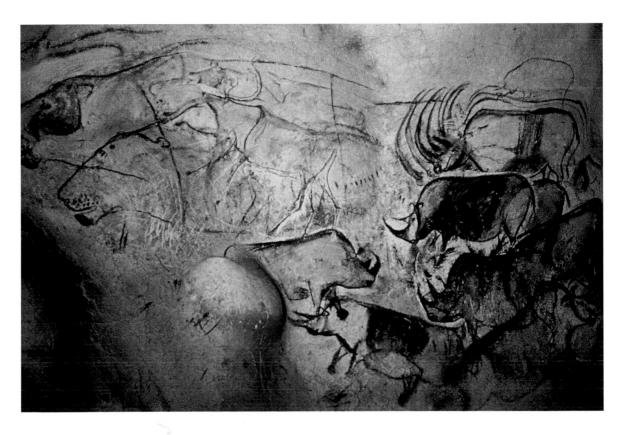

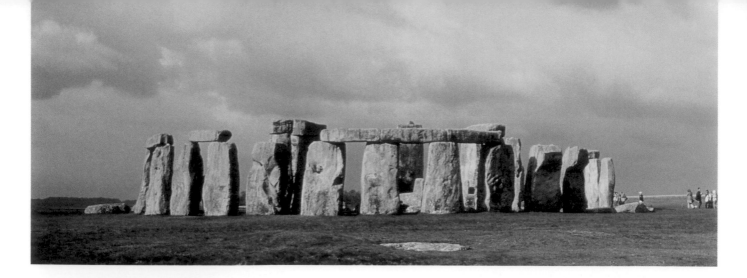

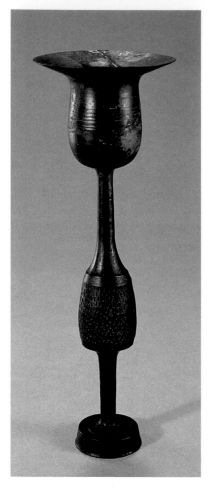

The contemporary British sculptor Anthony Caro has said that "all art is basically Paleolithic or Neolithic: either the urge to smear soot and grease on cave walls or pile stone on stone."[2] By "soot and grease" Caro means the cave paintings. With "the urge to pile stone on stone" he has in mind one of the most impressive and haunting works to survive from the Stone Ages, the structure in the south of England known as Stonehenge (**1.4**). Today much ruined through time and vandalism, Stonehenge at its height consisted of several concentric circles of **megaliths,** very large stones, surrounded in turn by a circular ditch. It was built in several phases over many centuries, beginning around 3100 B.C.E. The tallest circle, visible in the photograph here, originally consisted of thirty gigantic upright stones capped with a continuous ring of horizontal stones. Weighing some 50 tons each, the stones were quarried many miles away, hauled to the site, and laboriously shaped by blows from stone hammers until they fit together.

Many theories have been advanced about why Stonehenge was built and what purpose it served. In the 20th century it was discovered that Stonehenge is oriented to the movements of the sun, and one American astronomer went so far as to propose that the monument served as a sort of calendar, measuring out the year and even predicting eclipses. Most experts remain skeptical of such elaborate theories. It seems likely that the site was used as a setting for public rituals or ceremonies, but beyond that nothing is certain. Perhaps, as Caro suggests, Stonehenge can do no more than stand as an example of how old and how basic is our urge to create meaningful order and form, to structure our world so that it reflects our ideas. This is another place where art begins.

Stonehenge was erected in the Neolithic era, or New Stone Age. The Neolithic era is named for the new kinds of stone tools that were invented, but it also saw such important advances as the domestication of animals and crops and the development of the technology of pottery, as people discovered that fire could harden certain kinds of clay. With pottery, storage jars, food bowls, and all sorts of other practical objects came into being. Yet much of the world's oldest pottery seems to go far beyond purely practical needs (**1.5**). This elegant stemmed cup was formed around 2000 B.C.E. in what is now eastern China. Eggshell-thin and exceedingly fragile, it could not have held much of anything and would have tipped over easily. In other words, it isn't practical. Instead, great care and skill have gone into making it pleasing to the eye. Here is a third place we might turn to for the origins of art—the urge to explore the aesthetic possibilities of new technologies. What are the limits of clay, the early potters must have wondered. What can be done with it? Scholars believe such vessels were created for ceremonial use. They were probably made in limited quantity for members of a social elite.

To construct meaningful images and forms, to create order and structure, to explore aesthetic possibilities—these characteristics seem to be part of our nature as human beings. From them, art has grown, nurtured by each culture in its own way.

1.4 (above, top) Stonehenge. c. 2000–1500 B.C.E. Height of stones, 13'6". Salisbury Plain, England.

1.5 (above) Stemmed vessel, from Weifang, Shandong, China. Neolithic period, Longshan culture, c. 2000 B.C.E. Black pottery, thin biscuit; height 10½".

WHAT DO ARTISTS DO?

In our society we tend to think of art as something created by specialists, people we call artists, just as medicine is practiced by doctors and bridges are designed by engineers. In other societies, virtually everyone contributes to art in some way. Yet no matter how a society organizes itself, it calls on its art-makers to fulfill similar roles.

First, artists *create places for some human purpose*. Stonehenge, for example, was probably created as a place where a community could gather for rituals. Closer to our own time, Maya Lin created the Vietnam Veterans Memorial as a place for contemplation and remembrance (**1.6**). One of our most painful national memories, the Vietnam War saw thousands of young men and women lose their lives in a distant conflict that was increasingly questioned and protested at home. By the war's end, the nation was so bitterly divided that returning veterans received virtually no recognition for their services. In this atmosphere of continuing controversy, Lin's task was to create a memorial that honored the human sacrifice of the war while neither glorifying nor condemning the war itself.

At the heart of the memorial is a long, tapering, V-shaped wall of black granite, inscribed with the names of the missing, the captured, and the dead—some 58,000 names in all. Set into the earth exposed by slicing a great wedge from a gently sloping hill, it suggests perhaps a modern entrance to an ancient burial mound, though in fact there is no entrance. Instead, the highly polished surface acts as a mirror, reflecting the surrounding trees, the nearby Washington Monument, and the visitors themselves as they pass by.

Entering along a walkway from either end, visitors are barely aware at first of the low wall at their feet. The monument begins just as the war itself did, almost unnoticed, a few support troops sent to a small and distant country, a few deaths in the nightly news. As visitors continue their descent along the downward-sloping path, the wall grows taller and taller until it towers overhead, names upon names upon names. Often people reach out to touch the letters, and as they do, they touch their own reflections reaching back. At the walkway's lowest point, with the wall at its highest, a corner is turned. The path begins to climb upward, and the wall begins to fall away. Drawn by a view of either the Washington Monument (as in the photograph here) or the Lincoln Memorial (along the other axis), visitors leave the war behind.

In a quiet, unobtrusive way, the place that Maya Lin created encourages a kind of ritual, a journey downward into a valley of death, then upward toward hope, healing, and reconciliation. Like Stonehenge, it has served to bring a community together.

1.6 Maya Lin. Vietnam Veterans Memorial, Washington, D.C. 1982. Black granite, length 492'.

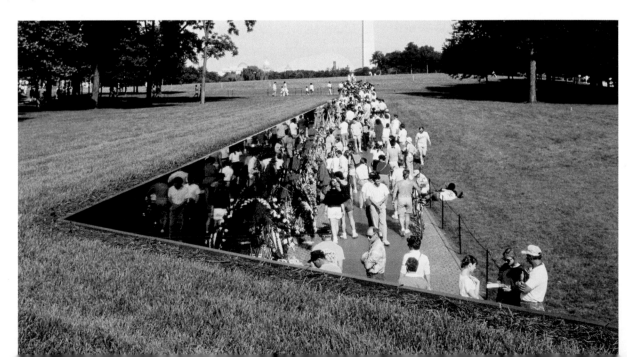

MAYA LIN

b. 1959

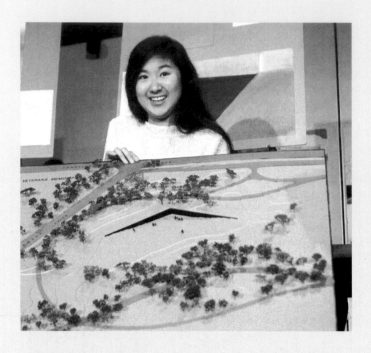

"**E**ACH OF MY works originates from a simple desire to make people aware of their surroundings, not just the physical world but also the psychological world we live in," Maya Lin has written. "I create places in which to think, without trying to dictate what to think."[3]

The most famous of Maya Lin's places for thought was also her first, the Vietnam Veterans Memorial in Washington, D.C. Lin created the design in response to an open call for proposals for the memorial, and it was selected unanimously from the more than 14,000 entries that flooded in. We can imagine the judges' surprise when they dialed the winner's telephone number and found themselves connected to a dormitory at Yale University, where Lin was a twenty-two-year-old undergraduate student in architecture. Like much of Lin's work, the memorial's powerful form was the product of a long period of reading and thinking followed by a moment of intuition. On a trip to Washington to look at the site, she writes, "I had a simple impulse to cut into the earth. I imagined taking a knife and cutting into the earth, opening it up, an initial violence and pain that in time would heal. The grass would grow back, but the initial

cut would remain a pure flat surface in the earth with a polished, mirrored surface, much like the surface on a geode when you cut it and polish the edge." Engraved with the names of the dead, the surface "would be an interface, between our world and the quieter, darker, more peaceful world beyond. . . . I never looked at the memorial as a wall, an object, but as an edge to the earth, an opened side." Back at school, Lin gave her idea form in the university dining hall with two decisive cuts in a mound of mashed potatoes.

Maya Lin was born and grew up in Athens, Ohio. Her father, a ceramist, was chair of the fine arts department at the Ohio University, while her mother, a poet, taught in the department of English there. Both parents had immigrated to the United States from China before Maya was born. Lin readily credits the academic atmosphere and her family's everyday involvement with art for the direction her life has taken. Of her father, she writes simply that "his aesthetic sensibility ran throughout our lives." She and her brother spent countless hours after school watching him work with clay in his studio.

Lin admits that it took a long time to put the experience of constructing the Vietnam Veterans Memorial behind her. While the design had initially met with widespread public approval, it soon sparked an angry backlash that led to verbal, sometimes racist, attacks on her personally. They took a toll. For the next several years she worked quietly for an architectural firm before returning to Yale to finish her doctoral studies. Since setting up her studio in 1987, she has created such compelling works as the Civil Rights Memorial in Montgomery, Alabama; *Wave Field*, an earthwork at the University of Michigan in Ann Arbor; and the Langston Hughes Library in Clinton, Tennessee.

Critics are often puzzled about whether to classify Lin as an architect or a sculptor. Lin herself insists that one flows into the other. "The best advice I was given was from Frank Gehry (the only architect who has successfully merged sculpture and architecture), who said I shouldn't worry about the distinctions and just make the work," Lin recalls. That is just what she continues to do.

Maya Lin with a model of the Vietnam Veterans Memorial, 1980.

A second task artists perform is to *create extraordinary versions of ordinary objects*. Just as the Neolithic vessel we looked at earlier is more than an ordinary drinking cup, so the textile here is more than an ordinary garment (**1.7**). Woven in West Africa by artists of the Asante people, it is a spectacular example of a type of textile known as *kente*. *Kente* is woven in hundreds of patterns, each with its own name, history, and symbolism. Traditionally, a newly invented pattern was shown first to the king, who had the right to claim it for his own exclusive use. Like the Neolithic vessel, royal *kente* was reserved for ceremonial occasions. Rich, costly, and elaborate, the cloth distinguished its wearer as special as well, an extraordinary version of an ordinary human being.

A third important tasks for artists has been to *record and commemorate*. Artists create images that help us remember the present after it slips into the past, that keep us in mind of our history, and that will speak of our times to the future. Illustrated here is a painting by a 17th-century artist named Manohar, one of several painters employed in the royal workshops of the emperor Jahangir, a ruler of the Mughal dynasty in India (**1.8**). At the center of the painting we see Jahangir himself, seated beneath a sumptuous canopy. His son Khusrau, dressed in a yellow robe, offers him the precious gift of a golden cup. The painting commemorates a moment of reconciliation between father and son, who had had a violent falling out. The moment did not last, however. Khusrau would soon stage an armed rebellion that cost him the throne. While the intricate details of Mughal history may be lost on us today, this enchanting painting gives us a vivid glimpse into their vanished world as they wanted it to be remembered.

1.7 (left) *Kente* cloth, from Ghana. Asante, mid-20th century. Cotton, 6'5¼" × 45". The Newark Museum, New Jersey.

1.8 (right) Manohar. *Jahangir Receives a Cup from Khusrau.* 1605–06. Opaque watercolor on paper, 8³⁄₁₆ × 6". British Museum, London.

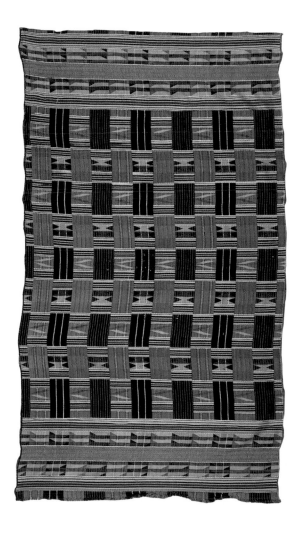

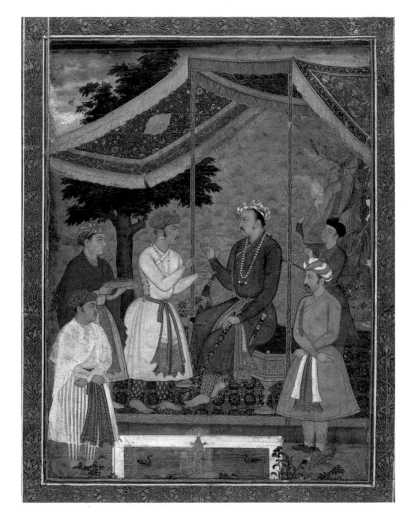

A fourth task for artists is to give *tangible form to the unknown.* They portray what cannot be seen with the eyes or events that can only be imagined. An anonymous Indian sculptor of the 10th century gave tangible form to the Hindu god Shiva in his guise as Nataraja, Lord of the Dance (**1.9**). Encircled by flames, his long hair flying outward, Shiva dances the destruction and rebirth of the world, the end of one cycle of time and the beginning of another. The figure's four arms communicate the complexity of this cosmic moment. In one hand, Shiva holds the small drum whose beat summons up creation; in another hand, he holds the flame of destruction. A third hand points at his raised foot, beneath which worshipers may seek refuge, while a fourth hand is raised with its palm toward the viewer, a gesture that means "fear not."

A fifth function artists perform is to *give tangible form to feelings and ideas.* The statue of Shiva we just looked at, for example, gives tangible form to ideas about the cyclical nature of time that are part of the religious culture of Hinduism. In *The Starry Night* (**1.10**) Vincent van Gogh labored to express his personal feelings as he stood on the outskirts of a small village in France and looked up at the night sky. Van Gogh had become intrigued by the belief that people journeyed to a star after their death, and that there they continued their lives. "Just as we take the train to get to Tarascon or Rouen," he wrote in a letter, "we take death to reach a star."[4] Seen through the prism of this idea, the night landscape inspired in him a vision of great intensity. Surrounded by halos of radiating light, the stars have an exaggerated, urgent presence, as though each one were a brilliant sun. A great wave or whirlpool rolls across the sky—a cloud, perhaps, or some kind of cosmic energy. The landscape, too, seems to roll on in waves like an ocean. A tree in the foreground writhes upward toward the stars as though answering their call. In the distance, a church spire points upward as well. Everything is in turbulent motion. Nature seems alive, communicating in its own language while the village sleeps.

Finally, artists *refresh our vision and help us see the world in new ways.* Habit dulls our senses. What we see every day we no longer marvel at, because it has become familiar. Through art we can see the world through someone else's eyes and recover the intensity of looking for the first time. Ernst Haas'

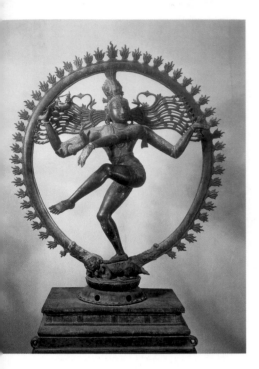

1.9 (above) *Shiva Nataraja.* India, 10th century C.E. Bronze, height 5'1¼".
Rijksmuseum, Amsterdam.

1.10 (below) Vincent van Gogh. *The Starry Night.* 1889. Oil on canvas, 29 × 36¼".
The Museum of Modern Art, New York.

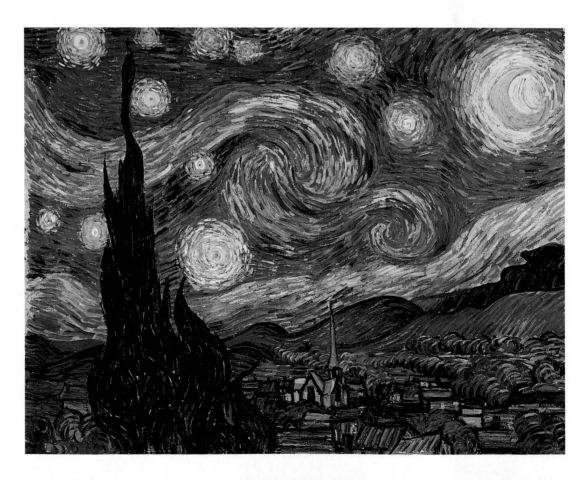

VINCENT VAN GOGH

1853–1890

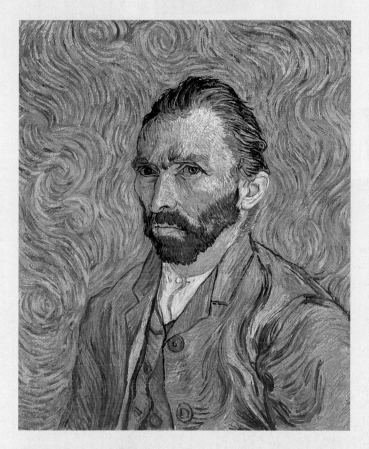

THE APPEAL OF Van Gogh for today's art lovers is easy to understand. A painfully disturbed, tormented man who, in spite of his great anguish, managed to create extraordinary art. An intensely private, introspective man who wrote eloquently about art and about life. An erratic, impulsive man who had the self-discipline to construct an enormous body of work in a career that lasted only a decade.

Vincent van Gogh was born in the town of Groot-Zundert, in Holland, the son of a Dutch Protestant minister. His early life was spent in various roles, including those of theological student and lay preacher among the miners of the region. Not until the age of twenty-seven did he begin to take a serious interest in art, and then he had but ten years to live. In 1886 he went to stay in Paris with his brother, Theo, an art dealer who was always his closest emotional connection. In Paris Vincent became aware of the new art movements and incorporated aspects of them into his own style, especially by introducing light, brilliant colors into his palette.

Two years later Van Gogh left Paris for the southern city of Arles. There he was joined briefly by the painter Paul Gauguin, with whom Van Gogh hoped to work closely, creating perfect art in a pure atmosphere of self-expression. However, the two artists quarreled, and, apparently in the aftermath of one intense argument, Van Gogh cut off a portion of his ear and had it delivered to a prostitute.

Soon after that bizarre incident, Van Gogh realized that his instability had gotten out of hand, and he committed himself to an asylum, where—true to form—he continued to work prolifically at his painting. Most of the work we admire so much was done in the last two and a half years of his life. Vincent (as he always signed himself) received much sympathetic encouragement during those years, both from his brother and from an unusually perceptive doctor and art connoisseur, Dr. Gachet, whom he painted several times. Nevertheless, his despair deepened, and in July of 1890 he shot himself to death.

Vincent's letters to his brother Theo represent a unique document in the history of art. They reveal a sensitive, intelligent artist pouring out his thoughts to one especially capable of understanding. In 1883, while still in Holland, he wrote to Theo: "In my opinion, I am often *rich as Croesus*, not in money, but (though it doesn't happen every day) rich, because I have found in my work something to which I can devote myself heart and soul, and which gives inspiration and significance to life. Of course my moods vary, but there is an average of serenity. I have a sure *faith* in art, a sure confidence that it is a powerful stream, which bears a man to harbour, though he himself must do his bit too; and at all events I think it such a great blessing, when a man has found his work, that I cannot count myself among the unfortunate. I mean, I may be in certain relatively great difficulties, and there may be gloomy days in my life, but I shouldn't want to be counted among the unfortunate nor would it be correct."[5]

Vincent van Gogh. *Self-Portrait*. 1889.
Oil on canvas, 25½ x 21½".
Musée d'Orsay, Paris.

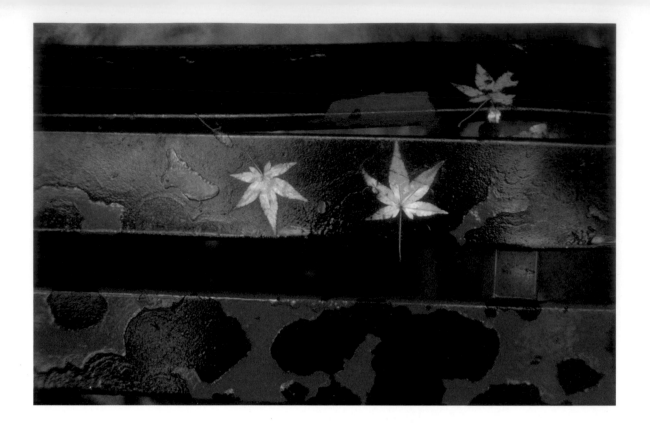

1.11 Ernst Haas. *Peeling Paint on Iron Bench, Kyoto, 1981.* 1981. Kodachrome print.

photograph *Peeling Paint on Iron Bench, Kyoto, 1981* (**1.11**) singles out a small detail of an ordinary day and asks us to notice how rich it is if we really take the time to look. Rain has made the colors shine with fresh intensity, brilliant red against deep black, and the star-shaped leaves could almost be made of gold. After seeing through Haas' eyes, we may find ourselves—if only for a few hours—more attentive to the world around us, which is stranger, more mysterious, more various, and more beautiful than we usually realize.

CREATING AND CREATIVITY

Out walking on a rainy day in Kyoto, Ernst Haas could have noticed the park bench, smiled with pleasure, and continued on his way. Standing in a field over a century ago, Van Gogh could have had his vision of the night sky, then returned to his lodgings—and we would never have known about it. We all experience the moments of insight that put us where art begins. For most of us, such moments are an end in themselves. For artists, they are a beginning, a kind of raw material that sets a creative process in motion.

Creativity is a word that comes up often when talking about art, but what is creativity exactly? Are we born with it? Can it be learned? Can it be lost? Are artists more creative than other people? If so, how did they get that way? Many writers and educators have tried to analyze creativity and determine what makes a person creative.[6] While the exact nature of creativity remains elusive, there is general agreement that creative people tend to possess certain traits, including:

- *Sensitivity*—heightened awareness of what one sees, hears, and touches, as well as responsiveness to other people and their feelings.
- *Flexibility*—an ability to adapt to new situations and to see their possibilities; willingness to find innovative relationships.
- *Originality*—uncommon responses to situations and to solving problems.
- *Playfulness*—a sense of humor and an ability to experiment freely.
- *Productivity*—the ability to generate ideas easily and frequently, and to follow through on those ideas.

- *Fluency*—a readiness to allow the free flow of ideas.
- *Analytical skill*—a talent for exploring problems, taking them apart, and finding out how things work.
- *Organizational skill*—ability to put things back together in a coherent order.

We might bear this list in mind as we look at Tim Hawkinson's *Emoter* (**1.12**). Like many of Hawkinson's works, *Emoter* looks like a do-it-yourself science project that has gotten a little out of hand. The stepladder on the floor houses a black-and-white television monitor tuned to a local broadcast station. Rows of light sensors attached to the monitor's screen react to changes in the moving image, sending signals through a tangle of cords, cables, and wires up to a large photograph of the artist's face. The components of the face—eyes, nostrils, eyebrows, and mouth—move continuously in response to the signals they receive, generating expressions that are as extravagant as a mime's.

Certainly sensitivity made Hawkinson a keen observer of faces, and originality suggested to him that such unlikely material as laboratory experiments monitoring brain waves, or antiquated scientific theories linking specific facial expressions to specific emotions, could inspire a work of art. Playfulness, flexibility, fluency, and productivity set him to exploring ways in which his project could be given form, while analytical and organizational skills allowed him to carry it to completion.

The profession of artist is not the only one that requires creativity. Scientists, mathematicians, teachers, business executives, doctors, librarians, computer programmers—people in every line of work, if they are any good, look for ways to be creative. Artists occupy a special place in that they have devoted their lives to opening the channels of *visual* creativity.

Can a person become more creative? Almost certainly, if one allows oneself to be. Being creative means learning to trust one's own interests, experiences, and references, and to use them to enhance life and work. Above all, it means discarding rigid notions of what has been or should be in favor of what *could* be. Creativity develops when the eyes and the mind are wide open, and it is as important to looking at art as it is to making it.

We close this chapter by exploring what looking creatively might involve.

1.12 Tim Hawkinson. *Emoter.* 2002. Installation (left) and detail (right). Altered ink-jet print on plastic and foam core on panel, monitor, stepladder, and mechanical components; print: 49 × 36 × 4"; stepladder height 27".
Courtesy Ace Gallery, Los Angeles.

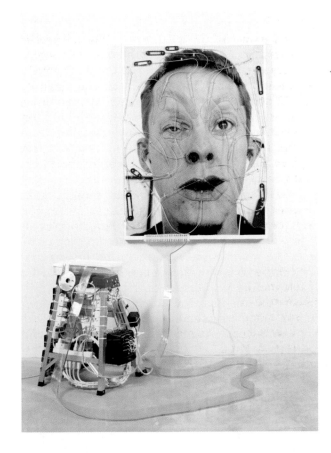 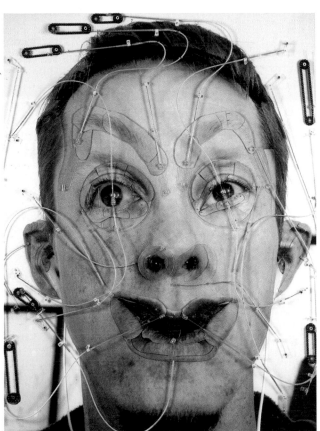

LOOKING AND RESPONDING

Science tells us that seeing is a mode of perception, which is the recognition and interpretation of sensory data—in other words, how information comes in our eyes (ears, nose, taste buds, fingertips) and what we make of it. In visual perception our eyes take in information in the form of light patterns; the brain processes these patterns to give them meaning. The role of the eyes in vision is purely mechanical. Barring some physical disorder, it functions the same way for everyone. The mind's role in making sense of the information, however, is highly subjective and belongs to the realm of psychology. Simply put, given the same situation, we do not all notice the same things, nor do we interpret what we see in the same way.

One reason for differences in perception is the immense amount of detail available for our attention at any given moment. To navigate efficiently through daily life, we practice what is called selective perception, focusing on the visual information we need for the task at hand and relegating everything else to the background. But other factors are in play as well. Our mood influences what we notice and how we interpret it, as does the whole of our prior experience—the culture we grew up in, relationships we have had, places we have seen, knowledge we have accumulated.

The subjective nature of perception explains why a work of art may mean different things to different people and how it is that we may return to a favorite work again and again, noticing new aspects of it each time. It explains why the more we know, the richer each new encounter with art will be, for we will have more experience to bring to it. It explains why we should make every effort to experience as much art in person as possible, for physical dimensions also influence perception. The works reproduced in this book are miniaturized. Many other details escape reproduction as well.

Above all, the nature of perception suggests that the most important key to looking at art is to become aware of the process of looking itself—to notice details and visual relationships, to explore the associations and feelings they inspire, to search for knowledge we can bring to bear, and to try to put what we see into words. A quick glance at Juan de Valdés Leal's *Vanitas* (**1.13**) reveals a careless jumble of objects with a cherub looking over them. In the background, a man looks out at us from the shadows. But what are the objects? And what are the cherub and the man doing? Only if we begin to ask and answer such questions does the message of the painting emerge.

In the foreground to the left is a timepiece. Next to it are two flowers: one in full bloom, the other already dying. Then come dice and playing cards, suggesting games of chance. Further on, a cascade of medals, money, and jewelry leads up to an elaborate crown, suggesting honors, wealth, and power. At the center, books and scientific instruments evoke knowledge. Finally, back where we began, a skull crowned with a laurel wreath lies on its side. Laurel traditionally crowns those who have become famous through their achievements, especially artistic achievements.

Over this display the cherub blows a bubble, as though making a comment on the riches before him. A bubble's existence is even shorter than a flower's—a few seconds of iridescent beauty, and then nothing. Behind the books, a crystal globe resembles a bubble as well, encouraging us to see a connection. When we meet the man's gaze, we notice that he has drawn back a heavy curtain with one hand and is pointing at a painting he has thus revealed with the other. "Look at this," he all but speaks. The painting depicts the Last Judgment. In Christian belief, the Last Judgment is the moment when Christ will appear again. He will judge both the living and the dead, accepting some into Paradise and condemning others to Hell. The universe will end, and with it time itself.

We might paraphrase the basic message of the painting something like this: "Life is fleeting, and everything that we prize and strive for during it is ul-

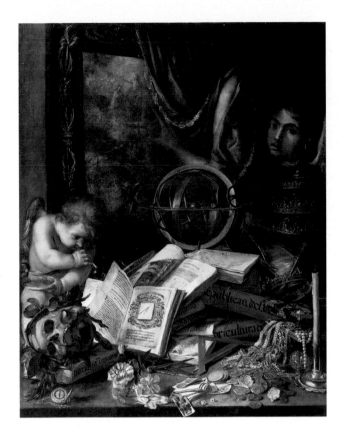

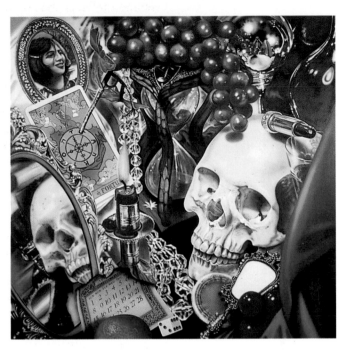

timately meaningless. Neither wealth nor beauty nor good fortune nor power nor knowledge nor fame will save us when we stand before God at the end of the world." Without taking the time to perceive and reflect on the many details of the image, we would miss its message completely.

Vanitas is Latin for "vanity." It alludes to the biblical book of Ecclesiastes, a meditation on the fleeting nature of earthly life and happiness in which we read that in the end, "all is vanity." The title wasn't invented or bestowed by the artist, however. Rather, it is a generic name for a subject that was popular during his lifetime. Numerous *vanitas* paintings have come down to us from the 17th century, and together they show the many ways that artists treated its themes.

Closer to our own time, the painter Audrey Flack became fascinated by the *vanitas* tradition, and she created a series of her own, including *Wheel of Fortune (Vanitas)* (**1.14**). Knowing something of the tradition Flack is building on, we can more easily appreciate her updated interpretation. As ever, a skull puts us in mind of death. An hourglass, a calendar page, and a guttering candle speak of time and its passing. The necklace, mirrors, powder puff, and lipstick are contemporary symbols of personal vanity, while a die and a tarot card evoke the roles of chance and fate in our lives. As in the painting by Valdés, a visual echo encourages us to think about a connection, in this case between the framed oval photograph of a young woman and the framed oval reflection of the skull just below.

Flack may be painting with one eye on the past, but the other is firmly on our society as we are now. For example, she includes modern inventions such as a photograph and a lipstick tube, and she shuns symbols that no longer speak to us directly such as laurels and a crown. The specifically Christian context is gone as well, resulting in a more general message that applies to us all, regardless of faith: Time passes quickly, beauty fades, chance plays a bigger role in our lives than we like to think, death awaits.

Despite their differences, both Flack and Valdés provide us with many clues to direct our thoughts. They depict objects that have common associations and then trust us to add up the evidence. At first glance, a contemporary

1.13 (left) Juan de Valdés Leal. *Vanitas*. 1660. Oil on canvas, 51⅜ × 39 1/16". Wadsworth Atheneum, Hartford.

1.14 (right) Audrey Flack. *Wheel of Fortune (Vanitas)*. 1977–78. Oil over acrylic on canvas, 8 × 8'. Collection Louis K. Meisel Gallery, New York.

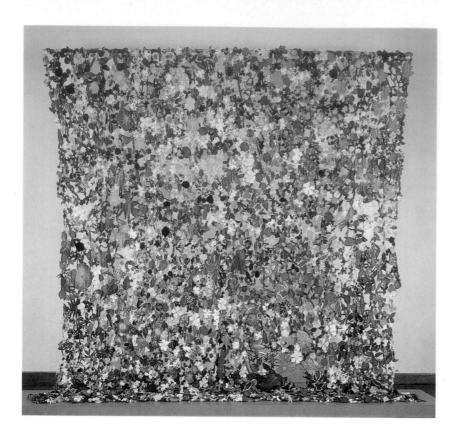

1.15 Jim Hodges. *Every Touch.* 1997. Silk flowers, thread; 16 × 14'. Philadelphia Museum of Art.

work such as Jim Hodges' *Every Touch* seems very different (**1.15**). *Every Touch* is made of artificial silk flowers, taken apart petal by petal. The petals were ironed flat, intermingled, then stitched together to form a large curtain or veil. Yet while *Every Touch* may not direct our thoughts as firmly as the other works, we approach it in the same way. We look, and we try to become aware of our looking. We ask questions and explore associations. We bring our experience and knowledge to bear. We interrogate our feelings.

We might think of spring. We might be put in mind of other art, such as the flowered backgrounds of medieval tapestries (see 12.13) or the role of flowers in the *vanitas* tradition. We might think about flowers and the occasions on which we offer them. We might think about the flowers we know from poetry, where they are often linked to beauty and youth, for all three fade quickly. We might think about petals, which fall from dying flowers. We might think about veils and when we wear them, such as at weddings and funerals. We might notice how delicately the work is stitched together and how fragile it seems. We might think about looking not only *at* it but also *through* it, and about how a curtain separates one realm from another. The man in Valdés' painting, for example, draws back a curtain to reveal the future.

Every Touch is not as easily put into words as the *vanitas* paintings, but it can inspire thoughts about many of the same ideas: seasons that come and go, how beauty and sadness are intertwined, the ceremonies that mark life's passing, the idea of one realm opening onto another, the fragility of things. In the end, what we see in *Every Touch* depends on what we bring to it, and if we approach the task sincerely, there are no wrong answers.

Every Touch will never mean for any of us exactly what it means for Hodges, nor should it. An artist's work grows from a lifetime of experiences, thoughts, and emotions; no one else can duplicate them exactly. Works of art hold many meanings. The greatest of them seem to speak anew to each generation and to each attentive observer. The most important thing is that some works of art come to mean something for *you*, that your own experiences, thoughts, and emotions find a place in them, for then you will have made them live.

WHO BUYS IT?

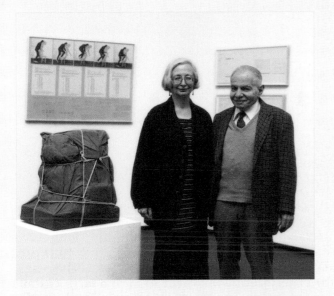

Aᴿᴛ ᴄᴏʟʟᴇᴄᴛᴏʀꜱ ᴀʀᴇ rich. Art collectors are glamorous. Art collectors are members of the upper classes or the nobility, or else they are important business leaders. Everybody knows these facts, but apparently nobody bothered to inform Dorothy and Herbert Vogel of New York City. The Vogels—she a retired librarian, he a retired postal worker—are not rich, and their lifestyle is modest. They are the sort of people one can't help but call "ordinary." One fact about the Vogels is undeniably *extra*ordinary: They have been collecting art on an ambitious scale for more than thirty-five years.

Everybody in the fashionable art world of New York, it seems, knows the unfashionable Herbert and Dorothy. The Vogels attend as many openings as possible, they regularly visit several artists' studios, they study the art seriously—and they buy. Their small Manhattan apartment eventually became crammed to the ceilings with some seventeen hundred original works of art, emphasizing Minimal, Conceptual, and Postmodern artists. This collection was acquired almost entirely on Herbert's salary from the post office. Dorothy's income pays the couple's living expenses.

The odds against two such . . . well . . . *ordinary* people becoming important art collectors seem formidable. Herbert, the son of a tailor, grew up in New York and started working for the post office after high

school and the army. Dorothy, born in Elmira, New York, earned a master's degree in library science and took a librarian's job in Brooklyn. The couple met at a singles' party, dated for a year, then married in 1962. Their plunge into the art world was led by Herbert, who had taken some art courses at New York University, had made friends with young artists, and aspired to become an artist himself. Soon Herbert got Dorothy involved, and the two decided collecting would be more to their taste.

The Vogels began slowly. Rushing from their respective jobs in the evening, they would rendezvous in a subway station, then go off to a gallery to study the art and consider possible purchases. At first, dealers and gallery habitués wondered, "Who on earth *are* those people?" The Vogels do not look like one's usual image of collectors. Soon, however, their informed and persistent buying attracted attention; soon their appearance in a gallery created a stir. As their collection grew, so did their reputation. Artists accept them as friends because their love of the work is so sincere.

No doubt an important factor in the Vogels' success has been their single-mindedness. Dorothy and Herbert have no children, though they have turtles, fish, and cats in quantity. Nearly all their time is devoted to the collection. They are shrewd buyers, stretching their limited budget to the utmost.

The value of the Vogels' collection was demonstrated in 1992, when the National Gallery of Art in Washington announced it would acquire the collection as part purchase, part donation. Once the art was moved out for inventory, the Vogels had their apartment painted for the first time in decades—and went back to buying art.

Most people pretty much live out the lives they were born to, but Herbert and Dorothy Vogel obviously are made of stronger stuff. The postal worker and the librarian—together they invented a special life for themselves, a life with art. Seeing them, talking with them, one cannot doubt they are enjoying every moment of it.

Collectors Dorothy and Herbert Vogel at the exhibition "From Minimal to Conceptual Art: Works from the Dorothy and Herbert Vogel Collection," at the National Gallery of Art, May 29 through November 27, 1994.

CHAPTER TWO

WHAT IS ART?

Art is something that has great value in our society. Across the country, art museums are as much a point of civic pride as new sports stadiums, pleasant shopping districts, public libraries, and well-maintained parks. From daring structures designed by famous architects to abandoned industrial buildings reclaimed as exhibition spaces, new museums are encouraged by city governments eager to revitalize neighborhoods and attract tourists. Inside our museums, art is made available in many ways, not only in the galleries themselves, but also in shops that offer illustrated books, exhibition catalogues, and photographs of famous artworks reproduced on posters, calendars, coffee mugs, and other merchandise. The prestige of art is such that many of us visit museums because we feel it is something we ought to do, even if we're not exactly sure why.

Many artists from the past have left moving accounts of just how much they, too, valued art. For Vincent van Gogh, to be an artist was a great and noble calling, even if the price to be paid for it in life was high. In a letter written to keep up his brother Theo's flagging spirits, he admitted that the two of them were "paying a hard price to be a link in the chain of artists, in health, in youth, in liberty, none of which we enjoy . . ." And yet, he continued, "there is an art of the future, and it is going to be so lovely and so young that even if we give up our youth for it, we must gain in serenity by it."[1] Here as elsewhere he speaks of art in a way that makes it seem greater than any single painting or sculpture, something that exists in an ideal realm.

Van Gogh's world was not so far removed from ours. He bought his paints and brushes at an art supply store, just as we could. He walked out into the nearby countryside and set up his easel at the edge of a field, just as we could. He painted *Wheat Field and Cypress Trees* (**2.1**) . . . and here we feel the comparison ends. Van Gogh was an artistic genius. His vision of the world was so strong, so uniquely individual, that the force of it seems present in every brush stroke. The world itself bends to his intense way of seeing, its colors heightened, its forms undulating and alive: the golden grain, the writhing olive tree, the tumbling blue hills, the ecstatic, cloud-filled sky.

In another letter to his brother, Vincent sounds both prickly and confident about his art. "I cannot help it that my pictures do not sell," he writes. "Nevertheless the time will come when people will see that they are worth more than the price of the paint and my own living, very meager after all, that is put into them."[2] After his death, this prediction came true. Even Van Gogh, however, could not have imagined that in 1990 one of his paintings would sell for 82.5 million dollars, at that time the highest price ever paid for a work of art. We are a long way from the cost of paint, lodgings, and food.

Money, of course, is one way in which we express value. Part of the value today of a painting by Van Gogh lies in the fact that his work had a major influence on artists of the next generation, and so when we tell the story of Western art, he plays an important role. Part of the value also comes from the fact that there are a limited number of paintings from his hand, and there will be no more. But much of the value seems to lie elsewhere, in the connection that the painting allows us to feel with the artist himself, who has become a cultural hero for us, both for his accomplishments and for the story of his life.

We value not only art but also artists. We are interested in their lives. A handful of artists are so well known that even people who know nothing about art can recite their names. Van Gogh is one. Picasso, Michelangelo, and Rembrandt are others. In casual speech, we use them almost as brand names, saying "That's a Picasso" in the same way we might say "That's a BMW." Robert Watts created a work about this phenomenon in *Rembrandt Signature*, which is nothing more or less than the great painter's signature reproduced in neon as a work of art in its own right (**2.2**).

2.1 (below, top) Vincent van Gogh. *Wheat Field and Cypress Trees*. 1889. Oil on canvas 28½ × 36".
The National Gallery, London.

2.2 (below) Robert Watts. *Rembrandt Signature*. 1965/1975. Neon, glass tubing, Plexiglas, transformer, 13½ × 44 × 5⅛".
Courtesy Robert Watts Studio Archive.

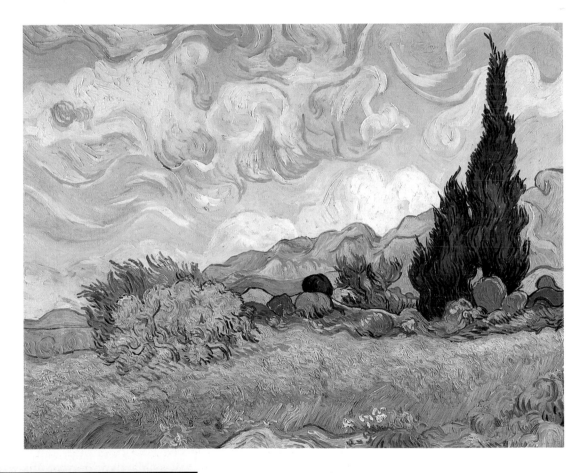

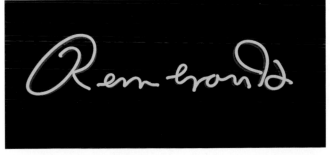

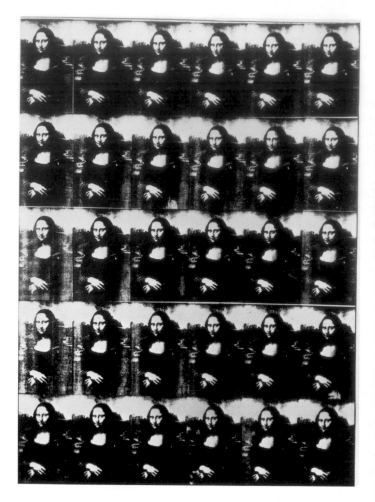

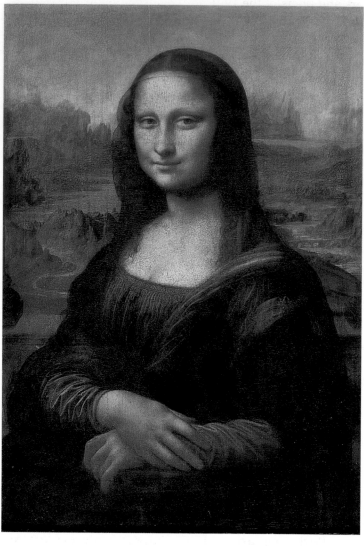

2.3 (left) Andy Warhol. *Thirty Are Better than One.* 1963. Silkscreen ink, acrylic paint on canvas, 9'2" × 7'10½".

2.4 (right) Leonardo da Vinci. *Mona Lisa.* c. 1503–05. Oil on panel, 30¼ × 21". Musée du Louvre, Paris.

Certain works of art, too, have become as famous generally as they are among art lovers. Van Gogh's own *Starry Night* is one of these (see 1.10). Another is the *Aphrodite of Melos,* popularly known as the *Venus de Milo* (see 14.28). But by far the most famous work of Western art in the world is the portrait known as *Mona Lisa.* Andy Warhol paid tribute to her renown in his slyly titled *Thirty Are Better than One* (**2.3**). Warhol portrays the painting as a celebrity, someone whose instantly recognizable image circulates in endless multiples through our mass media. He depicted stars such as Marilyn Monroe and Elvis Presley in the same way, repeating their publicity photos again and again.

Warhol was fascinated by how celebrities have a separate existence as images of themselves. But just as Marilyn Monroe and Elvis Presley were also private individuals with private lives, so of course the *Mona Lisa* is an actual painting with a physical existence and a history (**2.4**). It was painted by Leonardo da Vinci during the early years of the 16th century. The sitter was probably a woman named Lisa Gherardini del Giocondo. Leonardo portrays her seated on a balcony that overlooks a landscape of rock and water. Her left forearm rests on the arm of her chair; her right hand settles gently over her left wrist. She turns her head to look at us with a hint of a smile.

The portrait dazzled Leonardo's contemporaries, to whom it appeared almost miraculously lifelike. The *Mona Lisa*'s current fame, however, is a product of our own modern era. The painting first went on view to the public in 1797, when it was placed in the newly created Louvre Museum in Paris. Writers and poets of the 19th century became mesmerized by what they took to be the mystery and mockery of the sitter's smile. They described her as a dangerous beauty, a fatal attraction, a mysterious sphinx, a vampire, and all manner of fanciful things. The public flocked to gaze. When the painting was stolen from the museum in 1911, people stood in line to see the empty space where it had been. When the painting was recovered two years later, its fame was greater than ever.

Today, still in the Louvre, the *Mona Lisa* attracts over five million visitors every year. Crowds gather. People standing toward the back raise their cameras over their heads to get a photograph of the famous masterpiece in the distance. Those patient enough to make their way to the front find their view obscured by glare from the bulletproof glass box in which the priceless painting is encased. The layer of protective varnish covering the paint surface has crackled and yellowed with age. Cleaning techniques exist, but who would take the risk?

Obviously we do not see the *Mona Lisa* as Leonardo's contemporaries did, before the crowds, before the glass, and when its colors were fresh. Few people know, however, that we don't see as much of it, either. The painting used to be larger. If you follow the balcony ledge out to the left and right edges of the work, you will find two small, dark, curved forms—all that remain of the columns that used to frame the sitter. At some point during the centuries before the portrait went on view to the public, these were cut away. Someone took a saw and trimmed the painting down. Today, with our regard for art and for the genius of Leonardo, this seems unimaginable. Yet it was not so unusual for its time. Paintings might be trimmed down or enlarged, often to fit a favorite frame or to hang in a specific place. Elaborate frames were luxury items as well, and highly prized.

The ideas we have about art today have not always been in place. Like the fame of the *Mona Lisa,* they are a development of our modern era, the period that began a little over 200 years ago. Even our use of the word *art* has a history. During the Middle Ages, the formative period of European culture, *art* was used in roughly the same sense as *craft.* Both words had to do with skill in making something. Forging a sword, painting a picture, cobbling a shoe, carving a cabinet—all of these were spoken of as arts, for they involved specialized skills.

Beginning around 1500, during the period known as the Renaissance, painting, sculpture, and architecture came to be thought of as more elevated forms of art. Their prestige was such that the word *art* gradually attached almost exclusively to them, while other kinds of skillful making became known as craft. During the mid-18th century this division was given official form when painting, sculpture, and architecture were grouped together with music and poetry as the *fine arts* on the principle that they were similar kinds of activities—activities that required not just skill but genius and imagination, and whose results gave pleasure as opposed to being useful. At the same time, the philosophical field of aesthetics came into being and began to ask questions: What is the nature of art? Is there a correct way to appreciate art? Are there objective criteria for judging art? Can we apply our concept of art to other cultures? Can we apply it backward to earlier eras in our own culture?

Many answers have been proposed, but the fact that philosophers still debate them should tell us that the questions are not easy. This chapter will not give any definitive answers. Rather, we will explore topics that touch on some common assumptions many of us have about art. We will look at where our ideas come from and compare them to ideas that were current earlier and elsewhere. Our goal is to arrive at an understanding of art as we find it today, at the beginning of the 21st century.

ARTIST AND AUDIENCE

Claude Monet's *Fisherman's Cottage on the Cliffs at Varengeville* is the kind of painting that almost everyone finds easy to like (**2.5**). The colors are clear and bright. There is no difficult subject matter that needs explaining. We can imagine ourselves on vacation, taking a walk along the cliffs high over a beach below. We've stopped to appreciate the view near a quaint fisherman's cottage. How pretty the orange tile roof looks against the deep blue waters!

Monet belonged to a group of painters we know as the Impressionists. Most of them met as art students in Paris, and they banded together because they shared certain ideas about what art could be. Like Van Gogh, his junior by fifteen years, Monet spent his early adult years in poverty, painting pictures that few people wanted to buy. Unlike Van Gogh, however, he lived long enough to see his art triumph, eventually finding galleries willing to display his paintings to the public, critics able to write insightfully about them, and collectors eager to buy them. Museums accepted his work into their collections. When he died at age eighty-six, his reputation as a great, influential, and original painter was secure. All along he had been faithful to his personal artistic vision, working to express the quality of light on the landscape at different times of day, under various weather conditions, and across the seasons.

Monet's world of art schools, galleries, critics, collectors, and museums is still with us, and artists still struggle to make their way in it. We may think of it as the way things have always been, but to the 15th-century Italian artist Andrea del Verrocchio, it would have seemed strange indeed. One of the foremost artists of the early Renaissance, Verrocchio did not create what he wanted to but what his clients asked him for. He did not work alone but ran a workshop staffed with assistants and apprentices—a small business, essentially, that produced paintings, altarpieces, sculptures, banners, objects in precious metals, and architecture. He did not hope to have his art enshrined in museums, for there were no museums. Instead, displayed in public spaces, private residences, civic buildings, churches, and monasteries, the products of his workshop became part of the fabric of daily life in Florence, the town where he lived and worked.

One of Verrocchio's best-known works is a statue of the biblical hero David (**2.6**). The work was commissioned by Piero de' Medici, the head of a wealthy and powerful Florentine family, for display in the Medici family palace. Piero's sons later sold it to the City of Florence, which had adopted the

2.5 Claude Monet. *Fisherman's Cottage on the Cliffs at Varengeville.* 1882. Oil on canvas, 23⅝ × 31¹³⁄₁₆″.
Museum of Fine Arts, Boston.

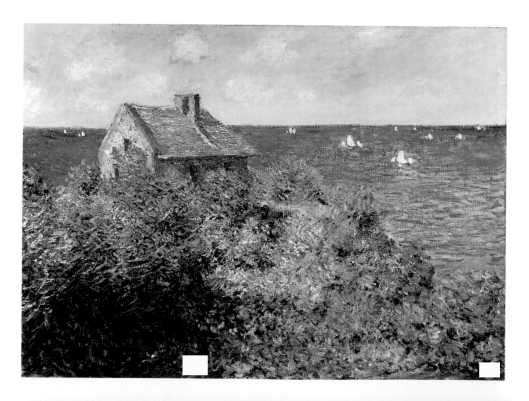

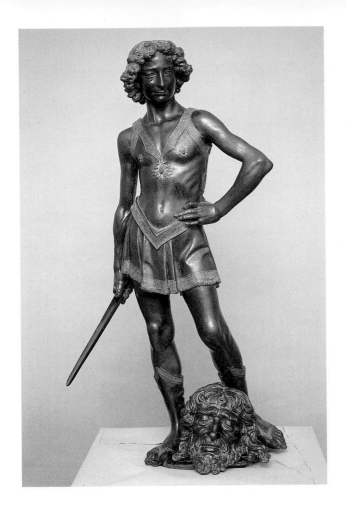

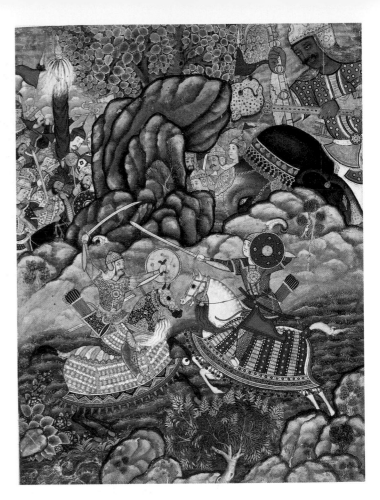

story of David as an emblem of its own determination to stand up to larger powers. Thereafter, the statue was displayed in the city hall.

Verrocchio had learned his skills as all artists of the time did, by serving as an apprentice in the workshop of a master. Boys (the opportunity was available only to males) began their apprenticeship between the ages of seven and fifteen. In exchange for their labor they received room and board and sometimes a small salary. Menial tasks came first, together with drawing lessons. Gradually apprentices learned such essential skills as preparing surfaces for painting and casting statues in bronze. Eventually they were allowed to collaborate with the master on important commissions. When business was slow, they might make copies of the master's works for sale over the counter. Verrocchio trained many apprentices in his turn, including a gifted teenager named Leonardo da Vinci. The *David* may actually be a portrait of him.

Our next three artists had yet another working arrangement and audience. Dasavanta, Madhava Khurd, and Shravana were employed in the royal workshops of Akhbar, a 16th-century emperor of the Mughal dynasty in India. Their job, for which they were paid a monthly salary, was to produce lavishly illustrated books for the delight of the emperor and his court. Akhbar ascended to the throne at the age of thirteen, and one of his first requests was for an illustrated copy of the *Hamzanama*, or *Tales of Hamza*. Hamza was an uncle of the Prophet Muhammad, the founder of Islam. The stories of his colorful adventures were (and still are) beloved throughout the Islamic world.

Illustrating the 360 tales of the *Hamzanama* occupied dozens of artists for almost fifteen years. The painting here portrays the episode in which *Badi'uzzaman Fights Iraj to a Draw* (**2.7**). Prince Badi'uzzaman (in orange) is one of Hamza's sons. Iraj (in green) is a warrior who fights him just to see if he is as brave as he is reputed to be. Looming up in the background is Landhaur, a friend of Hamza's. He is portrayed as a giant on a giant elephant, perhaps because of his role as an important presence behind the scenes.

2.6 (left) Andrea del Verrocchio. *David.* c. 1465. Bronze with gold details, height 47¼".
Museo Nazionale del Bargello, Florence.

2.7 (right) Dasavanta, Shravana, and Madhava Khurd (attr.). *Badi'uzzaman Fights Iraj to a Draw,* from the *Hamzanama.* c. 1567–72. Opaque watercolor on cotton, 26¼ × 19⅞".
MAK—Austrian Museum of Applied Arts/Contemporary Art, Vienna.

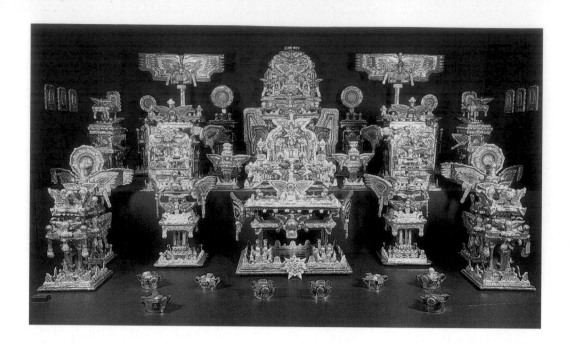

2.8 James Hampton. *Throne of the Third Heaven of the Nations' Millennium General Assembly.* c. 1950–64. Gold and silver aluminum foil, colored kraft paper and plastic sheets over wood, paperboard, and glass. 180 pieces, 105 × 27 × 14½'.
National Museum of American Art, Smithsonian Institution, Washington, D.C.

A single artist would sometimes be responsible for an entire illustration, but more often the paintings were the result of collaboration, with each artist contributing what he did best. Here, Dasavanta created the overall design and painted the lavender rock formation with its billowing miniature mountain. Madhava Khurd was called on to paint Landhaur and his elephant, while Shravana was responsible for the rest of the figures. Like Verrocchio, these artists would have learned their skills as apprentices.

Our fourth and final artist takes us out of the realm of professional training, career paths, and intended audiences altogether. James Hampton had no particular training in art, and the only audience he ever sought during his lifetime was himself. Hampton worked for most of his adult life as a janitor for the federal government in Washington, D.C., yet for many years he labored secretly on an extraordinary work called *Throne of the Third Heaven of the Nations' Millennium General Assembly* (**2.8**). Discovered after his death in a garage that he had rented, the work represents Hampton's vision of the preparation for the Second Coming as described in the biblical Book of Revelation. Humble objects and cast-off furniture are here transformed by silver and gold foil to create a dazzling setting ready to receive those who will sit in judgment at the end of the world.

We do not know whether Hampton considered himself an artist or whether he intended his work to be seen as art. He may have thought only about realizing a spiritual vision. The people who opened Hampton's garage after his death might easily have discarded *Throne of the Third Heaven of the Nations' Millennium General Assembly* as a curiosity. Instead, they recognized it as art, and today it is in a museum collection and on view to the public.

Our modern ideas about art carry with them ideas about the person who makes it, the artist, and the people it is for, the audience. We take it for granted that the artist's task is to pursue his or her own vision of art; to express his or her own ideas, insights, and feelings; and to create as inner necessity dictates. We believe these things so strongly that we recognize people like James Hampton as artists and accept a broad range of creations as art. We assume that art is for anyone who takes an interest in it, and through museums, galleries, books, magazines, and academic courses we make it available to a wide public. Other times and places did not necessarily share these ideas, and most visual creators across history have worked under very different assumptions about the nature of their task, the purpose it served, and the audience it was for.

WHO IS AN ARTIST?

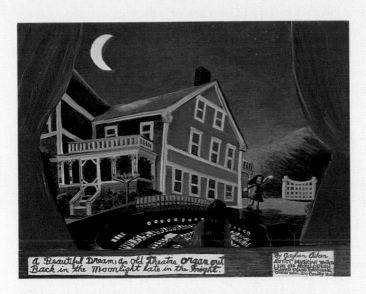

FROM HER GIRLHOOD during the 1940s until her unexpected death in March 2005, Gayleen Aiken made and exhibited puppets, drawings, and paintings such as the one illustrated here. Like many contemporary artists, she drew inspiration from popular culture, comic books, music, and local life—in this case the life of her hometown in Vermont. Aiken became well known, but not simply as an artist. She became known as an outsider artist.

Over the past fifteen years there has been a great deal of interest in outsider art, art by so-called self-taught artists. These artists have little or no formal training in the visual arts and often live far from the urban centers traditionally associated with artistic creativity. With this interest there has been an unprecedented growth in the number of venues that exhibit and sell outsider art. Many outsider artists maintain highly visible careers and have gained impressive followings among collectors and critics. There are even a number of magazines, such as *Raw Vision*, devoted to outsider art.

The term *outsider* has come into common use only recently. *Folk, naive, intuitive, primitive,* and *art brut* (French for "raw art") have also been used over the past century to categorize work by nonprofessional artists. Interest in such work can be traced to the efforts of psychiatrist Hans Prinzhorn, who, from the late 1890s through 1920s, amassed thousands of pieces by schizophrenic patients from psychiatric hospitals around Europe. Prinzhorn's book *Artistry of the Mentally Ill,* published in 1922, greatly inspired many artists and writers. Leading figures of the Surrealist movement, for example, celebrated the art of the "insane," attributing to these artists the most exemplary works of Surrealism. Later some of these same paintings would be used by the Nazis in their infamous Degenerate Art exhibition of 1937 to support their thesis that modern art was "pathological," for it resembled the art of the mentally ill. Many Prinzhorn artists were murdered in Nazi death camps.

Unlike such terms as *Surrealism* or *Impressionism, outsider* does not label a recognizable style or artistic movement. Rather, it attempts to define a group of people and their work as somehow "apart." Questions about what these artists are apart from, where the boundaries are drawn, and what social forces are at work in drawing them have placed outsider art at the center of a hotly contested debate over art's role in reinforcing society's attitudes about such topics as class, race, gender, and human difference. Indeed, the very notion of an artistic "outsider" has been called into question. Since the 19th century at least, critics point out, artists have tended to see themselves as visionaries and outsiders, even as outlaws. Hence, the line between insider and outsider has long been somewhat fuzzy. Paul Gauguin, for example, took great pride in his self-imposed "outsider" status (see 21.9), while the "naive" French painter Henri Rousseau is now considered to have been, with Picasso and Matisse, among the most important artists of the early 20th century (see 3.26).

The popularity of outsider art today is a result of the most progressive aspect of our modernity. The emergence and validation of difference within culture, the collapse of the distinction between "high" and "low," the great proliferation of the popular arts—these are all part of the democratization of culture brought about by modernism.

Gayleen Aiken. *A Beautiful Dream.* 1982. Oil on canvasboard, 12 × 16". Courtesy Grass Roots Art and Community Effort (GRACE), Hardwick, Vermont.

ART AND BEAUTY

Beauty is deeply linked to our thinking about art. Aesthetics, the branch of philosophy that studies art, also studies the nature of beauty. Many of us assume that a work of art should be beautiful, and even that art's entire purpose is to be beautiful. Why should we think that way, and is what we think true?

During the 18th century, when our category of art came into being, beauty and art were discussed together because both were felt to provide pleasure. When philosophers asked themselves what the character of this pleasure was and how it was perceived, their answer was that it was an intellectual pleasure and that we perceived it through a special kind of attention called disinterested contemplation. By "disinterested" they meant that we set aside any personal, practical stake we might have in what we are looking at. For example, if we are examining a peach to see whether it is ripe enough to eat, we are contemplating it with a direct personal interest. If we step back to admire its color, its texture, its roundness, with no thought of eating it, then we are contemplating it disinterestedly. If we take pleasure in what we see, we say the peach is beautiful.

Edward Weston's photograph *Cabbage Leaf* embodies this form of cool, distanced attention (**2.9**). Gazing at the way the light caresses the gracefully arching leaf, we can almost feel our vision detaching itself from practical concerns (good for coleslaw? or is it too wilted?). As we look, we become conscious of the curved object as a pure form, and not a thing called "cabbage leaf" at all. It looks perhaps like a wave crashing on the shore, or a ball gown trailing across a lawn. Letting our imagination play in this way was part of the pleasure that philosophers described.

But is pleasure what we always feel in looking at art? For a painting such as Bellini's *Pietà*, "sadness" might be a more appropriate word (**2.10**). Italian for "pity," *pietà* is the name for a standard subject in Christian art, that of Mary, the mother of Jesus, holding her son after he was taken down from the cross on which he suffered death. Bellini intended the work as a devotional image, which is an image meant to focus and inspire religious meditation. While the subject matter is both sad and moving, as opposed to pleasurable, many people may still find the painting to be beautiful.

2.9 Edward Weston. *Cabbage Leaf*. 1931. Gelatin silver print, 7½ × 9½".
Collection Center for Creative Photography, The University of Arizona, Tucson.

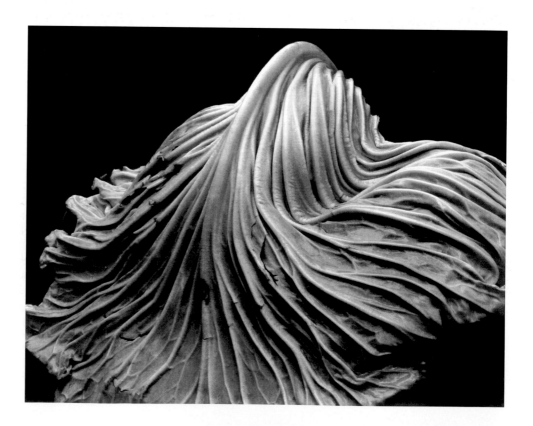

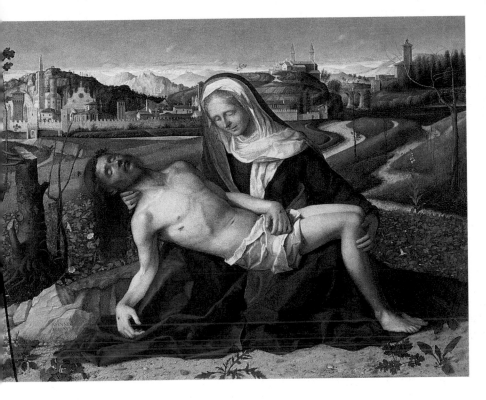

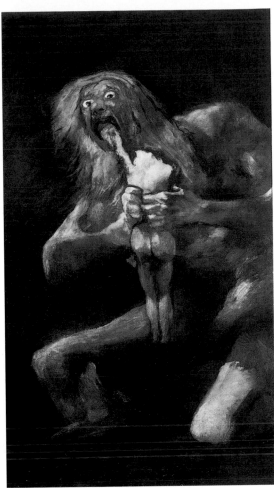

2.10 (left) Giovanni Bellini. *Pietà.* c. 1500–05. Oil on wood, 25⅝ × 35⅜".
Gallerie dell'Accademia, Venice.

2.11 (right) Francisco de Goya. *Chronos Devouring One of His Children.* c. 1820–22. Wall painting in oil on plaster (since detached and transferred to canvas), 57⅞ × 32⅝".
Museo del Prado, Madrid.

Some theories link beauty to formal qualities such as symmetry, simple geometrical shapes, and pure colors. Here, for example, Bellini has arranged Mary's robes so that they form a symmetrical triangular shape. The white of Christ's loincloth is continued in Mary's head covering. The curve of the head covering is echoed by the curves of the roads in the background. The pure blue and violet of her robes are echoed by the paler blue of the sky and matched by the intense green of the vegetation behind her, while the rest of the painting is in subdued but glowing earth colors. If we find Bellini's *Pietà* beautiful, perhaps these are the qualities we are reacting to.

In order to contemplate the formal beauty of Bellini's painting, we detached ourselves from the pitiable subject matter in somewhat the same way that Edward Weston detached himself from any feelings he might have had about cabbages in order to create his photograph. But not all art makes this sort of detachment so easy. An image such as Francisco de Goya's *Chronos Devouring One of His Children* seems to shut down any possibility for aesthetic distance (**2.11**). It grabs us by the throat and shows us a vision of pure horror.

A Spanish painter working during the decades around the turn of the 19th century, Goya lived through tumultuous times and witnessed terrible acts of cruelty, stupidity, warfare, and slaughter. As an official painter to the Spanish court he painted lighthearted scenes, tranquil landscapes, and dignified portraits, as asked. In works he created for his own reasons, he expressed his increasingly pessimistic view of human nature. *Chronos Devouring One of His Children* is one of a series of nightmarish images that Goya painted on the walls of his own house. By their compelling visual power and urgent message we recognize them as extraordinary art. But we must admit that they leave notions of pleasure and beauty far behind.

Art can indeed produce pleasure, as the first philosophers of aesthetics noted. But it can also inspire sadness, horror, pity, awe, and a full range of other emotions. The common thread is that in each case we find the experience of looking to be valuable for its own sake. Art makes looking worthwhile. Similarly, art can be beautiful, but not all art tries to be beautiful, and beauty is not a requirement for art. Beauty remains a mysterious concept, something that everyone senses, many disagree about, and no one has yet defined. Artists are as fascinated by beauty as any of us and return to it again and again, though not always in the form we expect. Often they seek out beauty in new places—in a cabbage leaf, for example.

ART AND APPEARANCES

The son of a painter who taught drawing, Pablo Picasso showed talent as a child and was surrounded by people who knew how to nurture it. Like a Renaissance apprentice, he grew up so immersed in art that he mastered traditional techniques while still a teenager. He completed *First Communion* in 1896 at the age of fifteen, the year he was accepted into art school (**2.12**). After graduation Picasso moved from Barcelona to Paris, then the center of new directions in art. There he experimented with style after style. The one that launched him on his mature path would become known as Cubism, and it began to take form in paintings such as *Seated Woman Holding a Fan* (**2.13**).

2.12 (left) Pablo Picasso. *First Communion.* 1895–96. Oil on canvas, 65⅜ × 46½".
Museo Picasso, Barcelona.

2.13 (right) Pablo Picasso. *Seated Woman Holding a Fan.* 1908. Oil on canvas, 59 × 39⅜".
State Hermitage Museum, St. Petersburg.

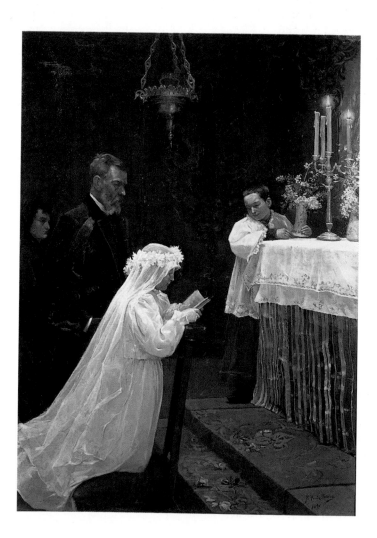

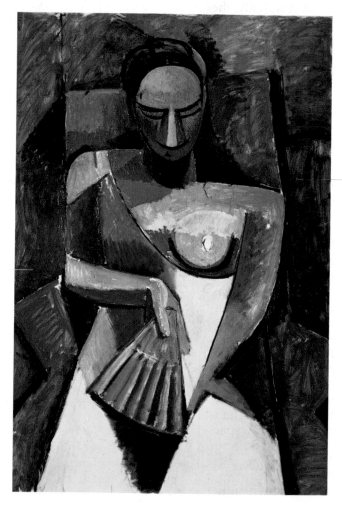

Picasso was part of a courageous generation of artists who opened up new territory for Western art to explore. These artists had been trained in traditional skills, and yet they set off on paths where those skills were not required. Many people wish they hadn't. Many people feel that art should aim at representing appearances as faithfully as possible, that artists who do not do this are not good artists, and that paintings such as *Seated Woman Holding a Fan* are not good art, or perhaps not even art at all.

Where do we get these ideas? The simple answer is that we get them from our own artistic heritage. For hundreds of years, Western art was distinguished among the artistic traditions of the world by precisely the concerns that Picasso and others turned their backs on. The elevation of painting and sculpture to higher status during the Renaissance had gone hand in hand with the discovery of new methods for making optically convincing representations. From that time until almost the end of the 19th century, a period of about 500 years, techniques for representing the observable world of light and shadow and color and space—the techniques evident in *First Communion*—formed the foundation upon which Western art was built.

Why did art change all of a sudden? There are many reasons, but Picasso, when asked, pointed to one in particular: photography. "Why should the artist persist in treating subjects that can be established so clearly with the lens of a camera?"[3] he asked. Photography had been developed not long before the artists of Picasso's generation were born. They were the first generation to grow up taking it for granted. Photography is now so pervasive that we need to take a moment to realize how revolutionary this change was. From the Paleolithic cave paintings until about 160 years ago, images had to be made by hand. Suddenly, there was a mechanical way based on chemical reactions to light. For some artists, photography meant the end of painting, for manual skills were no longer needed to create a visual record. For Picasso, it meant liberation from a lifetime spent copying nature. "Now we know at least everything that painting isn't,"[4] he said.

If the essence of art was not visual fidelity, however, what was it? The adventure of the 20th century began.

Representational and Abstract Art

Both paintings by Picasso refer clearly to the visible world, yet each has a different relationship to it. *First Communion* is **representational.** Picasso set out to represent—that is, to present again—the visible world in such a way that we recognize a likeness. The word *representational* covers a broad range of approaches. *First Communion* is very faithful to visual experience, recording how forms are revealed by light and shadow, how bodies reflect an inner structure of bone and muscle, how fabric drapes over bodies and objects, and how gravity makes weight felt. We call this approach **naturalistic.**

Seated Woman Holding a Fan is **abstract.** Picasso used the appearances of the world only as a starting point, much as a jazz musician begins with a standard tune. He selected certain aspects of what he saw, then simplified or exaggerated them to make his painting. In this instance, Picasso took his cue from the fan. The lower edge of the fan is a simple curve. Picasso used this curve-idea to form the woman's brow, her nose, her breast, and the line of her dress as it swings up to her shoulder. The top part of the fan is an angle or wedge. Picasso used the angle-wedge-idea almost everywhere else: the shadow below the fan, the woman's left hand and the shadow it casts, the arms of the chair and gray space they cut out of the background, and so on.

Like representation, abstraction embraces a broad range of approaches. Most of us would be able to decipher the subject of *Seated Woman Holding a Fan* without the help of the title, but the process of abstraction can continue much farther, until the starting point is no longer recognizable. In *Woman with Packages* (**2.14**), Louise Bourgeois abstracted the visual impact of a standing woman all the way to a slender vertical column topped by an egg-shaped element. *Woman with Packages* belongs to a series of sculptures that the artist called Personages. A personage is a fictional character, as in a novel or a play. Like a writer, Bourgeois created a cast of characters in an imagined world. She often displayed her *Personages* in pairs or groupings, implying a story for them.

At the opposite end of the spectrum from Bourgeois' radically simplified forms are representational works so convincingly lifelike that we can be fooled for a moment into thinking that they are real. The word for this extreme optical fidelity is ***trompe l'oeil*** (pronounced tromp-loy), French for "fool the eye," and one of its modern masters was Duane Hanson. Hanson's sculptures portray ordinary people in ordinary activities—cleaning ladies and tourists, museum guards and housepainters (**2.15**). Like a film director searching for an actor with just the right look for a role, Hanson looked around for the perfect person to "play" the type he had in mind. Once he had found his model (and, we may imagine, talked him or her into cooperating), he set the pose and made a mold directly from the model's body. Painted in lifelike skin tones and outfitted with hair, clothing, and props, the resulting sculptures can make us wonder how much distance we actually desire between art and life.

By opening Western art up to a full range of relationships to the visible world, artists of the 20th century created a bridge of understanding to other artistic traditions. For example, sculptors working many centuries ago in the

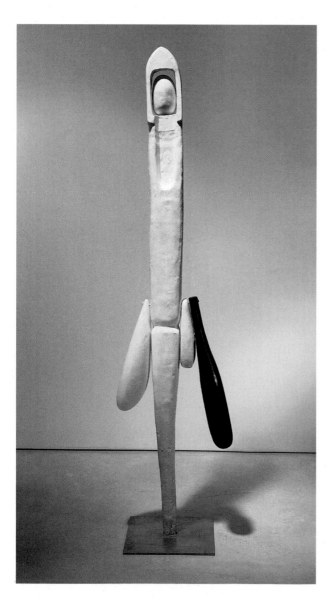

2.14 (left) Louise Bourgeois. *Woman with Packages.* 1949. Bronze, polychromed, 65 × 18 × 12".
Collection the artist.

2.15 (right) Duane Hanson. *Housepainter III.* 1984/1988. Autobody filler, polychromed, mixed media, with accessories, life-size.
Hanson Collection, Davie, Florida.

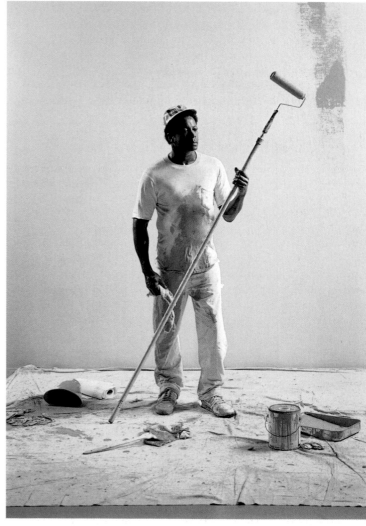

LOUISE BOURGEOIS

1911–

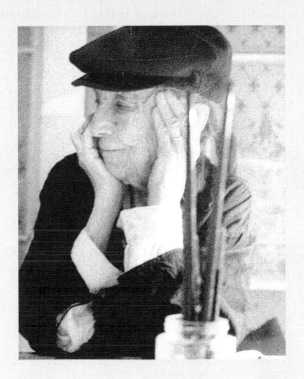

STILL GOING STRONG in her tenth decade, Louise Bourgeois makes art whose unsparing emotional honesty and restless formal inventiveness can leave far younger artists in awe. At an exhibition in 1992 at New York's Museum of Modern Art, the video and installation artist Bruce Nauman, some thirty years her junior and himself on the cutting edge of aggressive new art, paid her the ultimate compliment. Standing before Bourgeois' monstrous, mechanical, copulating *Twosome* (1991), he said simply, "You've gotta watch that woman."

Louise Bourgeois was born in Paris in 1911. Her parents were restorers of antique tapestries, and as a teenager Louise helped out by drawing missing parts so that they could be rewoven. After earning an undergraduate degree in philosophy, she studied art history at the Ecole du Louvre (a school attached to the famous museum) and studio art at the Ecole des Beaux Arts (the School of Fine Arts, France's most prestigious art school). Bourgeois was a restless student, however, and her dissatisfaction with official art education led her to explore alternate paths, most valuably a period of study with the painter Fernand Léger. In 1938 she married Robert Goldwater, a young American art historian who was in Paris doing research. The couple moved to New York that same year.

It was in America that Bourgeois discovered herself as an artist. "When I arrived in the United States from France I found an atmosphere that allowed me to do as I wanted," she told an interviewer.[5] The young couple quickly established themselves in the New York art world. Robert published his groundbreaking work *Primitivism in Modern Art* and began a distinguished scholarly career. Louise exhibited frequently, culminating with her first solo show of paintings in 1945. She exhibited her first sculptures four years later.

Louise Bourgeois' art is deeply rooted in memories of her childhood and adolescence. "My childhood," she writes, "has never lost its magic, it has never lost its mystery, and it has never lost its drama." The drama was not a happy one. When Bourgeois was eleven years old, her father brought a woman to live with them. She was to teach the children English and serve as a chauffeur to their mother. In fact, the woman soon became her father's mistress and lived with them as such for ten years. Bourgeois' fury at her father for this betrayal and her uncomprehending anger at her mother for putting up with it remained at the troubled core of her own adult emotional life. Periods of depression often crippled her, and for several decades she featured only intermittently on the New York art scene.

In 1982 the Museum of Modern Art held a retrospective exhibit of Bourgeois' work, the first such show it had ever devoted to a female artist. The attention the exhibition generated fueled an astonishing late flowering of creativity, and masterpieces have since poured forth from Bourgeois' studio to worldwide acclaim. Through her art, Louise Bourgeois tries to come to terms with a past that she cannot let go of. "My goal is to re-live a past emotion," she has said. "My sculpture allows me to re-experience fear, to give it a physical form so that I am able to hack away at it. I am saying in my sculpture today what I could not make out in the past."

Louise Bourgeois in her studio, 2001.

Yoruba kingdom of Ife, in present-day Nigeria, also employed both naturalistic and abstract styles. Naturalistic portrait sculptures in brass were created to commemorate the kingdom's rulers (**2.16**). Displayed on altars dedicated to royal ancestors, each head was accompanied by a smaller, abstract version (**2.17**). The two heads relate to concepts that are still current in Yoruba thought today. The naturalistic head represents the outer, physical reality that can be perceived by the senses, while the abstract head represents the inner, spiritual reality that can be perceived only by the imagination. Similarly, Louise Bourgeois' *Woman with Packages* could be said to portray the inner essence of the subject, while Duane Hanson's *Housepainter* is about how abstract concepts such as "housepainter" are rooted in the particular details of an individual.

Somewhere between naturalism and abstraction lies stylization. **Stylized** describes representational art that conforms to a preset style or set of conventions for depicting the world. Much of the art of ancient Egypt is highly stylized, as in this depiction of the goddess Hathor greeting the ruler Sety in the afterlife (**2.18**). Notice their hands. The fingers are evened off and set next to each other, like a single finger repeated four times. They curve gracefully and then tip up at the nail. Thumbs are placed on the side of the hand nearest the viewer, with the result that Sety looks as though he has two right hands and Hathor two left hands. For almost 3,000 years, apprentice artists in Egypt learned to draw hands following these conventions. We can imagine their drawing teacher saying to them not, "Look at a hand, observe how it works, and draw it from every conceivable angle," but rather, "This is one way we draw hands; make a row of them to show me you understand."

2.16 (left) *Head of a King*, from Ife. Yoruba, c. 13th century. Brass, life-size.
The British Museum, London.

2.17 (center) *Cylindrical Head*, from Ife. Yoruba, c. 13th–14th century. Terra cotta, height 6⅜".
National Commission for Museums and Monuments, Nigeria.

2.18 (right) *Hathor and Sety*, detail of a pillar from the tomb of Sety I. Egypt, c. 1300 B.C.E. Painted plaster on limestone, height 7'5".
Musée du Louvre, Paris.

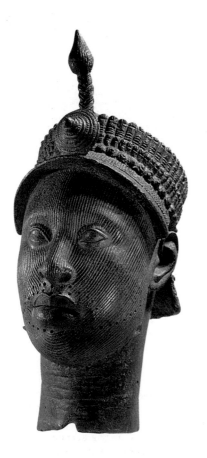

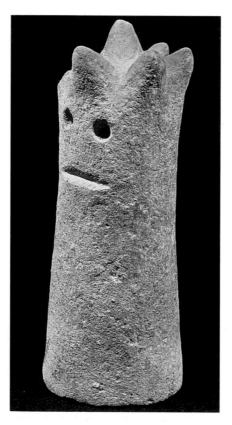

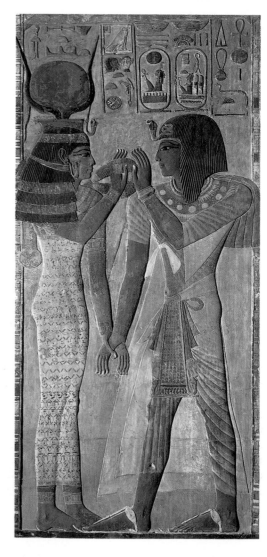

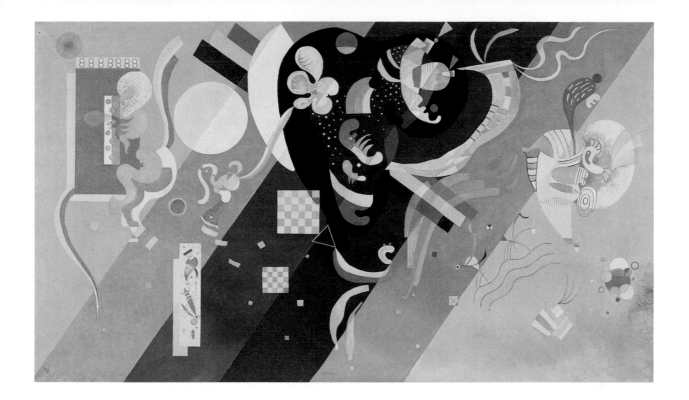

Nonrepresentational Art

While Picasso and others experimented with abstraction, seeing how far art could go without severing its ties to the visible world, other artists at the beginning of the 20th century turned their backs on the visible world altogether as a starting point for art. We call such art **nonrepresentational** or **nonobjective.** Like abstract art, nonrepresentational art developed from the search for art's essence in the wake of the challenge presented by photography.

The Russian painter Vasily Kandinsky was one of the pioneers of nonrepresentational art. Kandinsky often drew comparisons between nonobjective painting and music. Music, he pointed out, does not represent anything outside of itself. It is composed of sounds and pitches arranged over time, and yet it is capable of affecting us deeply. Similarly, paintings such as Kandinsky's *Composition IX* are composed of colors and shapes arranged over a flat surface (**2.19**). The precision of the drawing seems to reflect scrupulous, minute observation—but of what? Dreams from an unknown universe, perhaps.

Like many of his generation, Kandinsky came to the conclusion that art's ability to communicate lay in the very language of art itself, in the elements of shape and form, color and line. His ideas were more than just the result of formal investigations, however. They were linked to a larger philosophy about art's purpose. Kandinsky believed that the role of art in an increasingly materialistic society was to be a channel for the spirit, to allow us to commune with something bigger than ourselves. These beliefs have echoed down to our own day. Contemporary artist Rebecca Purdum finds them confirmed by her own experience with her mentally handicapped siblings. "When you have a special person in your family—and I have two—you begin to see that there is a kind of communication that exists way beyond language," she has said. "And when I paint, when I'm really into it, there is a degree of nonverbal communication that becomes everything—it fills me up."[6] To create paintings such as *Chin Up* (**2.20**), Purdum rubs the paint onto the rough canvas with her hands (protected by rubber gloves), gradually building up layer after layer. The result is intriguingly misty and vague, as though something we could make out were constantly about to take shape, though it never does. Purdum evokes a luminous world that remains forever just beyond our reach.

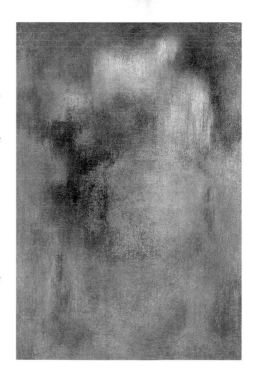

2.19 (above, top) Vasily Kandinsky. *Composition IX*. 1936. Oil on canvas, 44⅝ × 76¾". Musée National d'Art Moderne, Centre Georges Pompidou, Paris.

2.20 (above) Rebecca Purdum. *Chin Up*. 1990. Oil on canvas, 9 × 6'. Courtesy Jack Tilton Gallery.

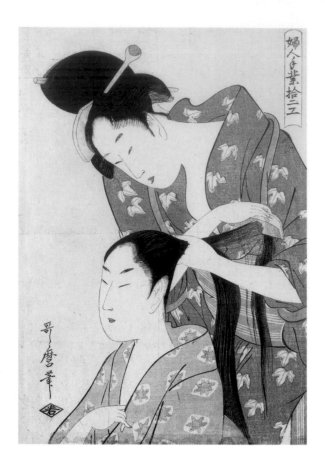

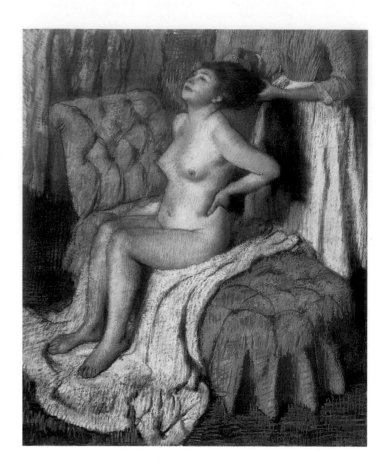

2.21 (left) Kitagawa Utamaro. *Hairdressing*, from *Twelve Types of Women's Handicraft.* c. 1798–99. Polychrome woodblock print, 12½ × 10½".
Art Gallery of South Australia, Adelaide.

2.22 (right) Edgar Degas. *Nude Woman Having Her Hair Combed.* c. 1886–88. Pastel on paper, 29⅛ × 23⅞".
The Metropolitan Museum of Art, New York.

Style

Terms such as *naturalistic* and *abstract* categorize art by how it relates to the appearances of the visible world. A work of art, of course, has a place in the visible world itself. It has its own appearance, which is the result of the artist's efforts. A term that helps us categorize art by its own appearance is *style*. **Style** refers to a characteristic or group of characteristics that we recognize as constant, recurring, or coherent. If a person we know always wears jeans and cowboy boots, we identify that person with a certain style of dress. If a friend who always wears her long hair in braids gets her hair cut very short, we speak of a change in style. If a family has furnished their living room entirely in antiques except for one very modern chair, we would recognize a mix of styles.

In the visual arts as in other areas of life, style is the result of a series of choices, in this case choices an artist makes in creating a work of art. As we grow more familiar with a particular artist's work, we begin to see a recurring pattern to these choices—characteristic subject matter or materials, distinctive ways of drawing or of applying paint, preferences for certain colors or color combinations. For example, now that you have seen three paintings by Van Gogh (1.10, the self-portrait on page 11, and 2.1), you can see certain traits they have in common such as heightened color, thickly applied paint, distinct brush strokes, distorted and exaggerated forms, and flamelike or writhing passages. Each subsequent work by Van Gogh that you come across will fine-tune what you already know about his style, just as what you already know will provide a framework for considering each new work.

One theory of art maintains that style is what distinguishes artists from other skillful makers. Not all people who set out to make art eventually develop an individual style, but all artists do. An enjoyable way to get a sense of the great range of individual styles is to compare works that treat similar subjects, as in these three depictions of a woman having her hair combed (**2.21, 2.22, 2.23**). The first is a woodcut by the 18th-century Japanese artist Kita-

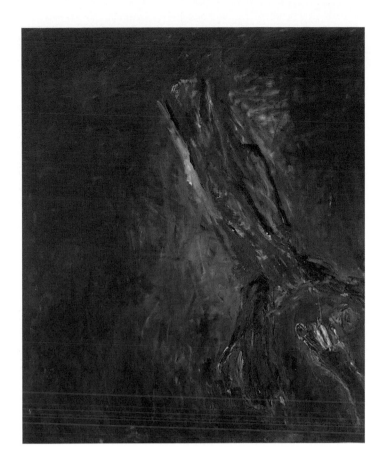

2.23 Susan Rothenberg. *Maggie's Ponytail.* 1993–94. Oil on canvas, 65¼ × 53¼".
Courtesy Sperone Westwater, New York.

gawa Utamaro (2.21), the second a drawing in pastel by the 19th-century French artist Edgar Degas (2.22), and the third an oil painting by the 20th-century American artist Susan Rothenberg (2.23).

Utamaro's women are slightly stylized. They do not strike us as particular people drawn from life, but as types of women drawn from the imagination—the beauty and her hairdresser. Their robes, too, are stylized into a series of sinuous curves. Slender black lines describe the faces and features, the robes and their folds, even the individual strands of hair. We could take away the color altogether, and the lines would still tell us everything we need to know. Color is applied evenly, with no lighter or darker variations. This makes the robes seem flat, as though they were cut out of patterned paper. The background is blank, and gives no hint of where the scene is set.

Edgar Degas works in a naturalistic style. The woman seems like a particular person, probably a model who posed for him in his studio. Faint lines describe the contours of her body and the chair she sits on, but these lines do not have a life of their own, as in the Japanese work. Colors are applied in individual strokes that remain distinct even as they build up in layers. Variations in color depict light and shadow, showing us the roundness and weight of the woman's body and sculpting the deep folds of the ruffles on the upholstered chair. Not all forms are depicted with equal attention to detail. The woman's body is very finely observed, while the outer areas of the image are treated more freely. The background is suggested rather than really described, yet the scene is clearly set in an interior. The composition is quite daring, with the servant's body cropped suddenly at the upper torso.

Susan Rothenberg's style is a unique combination of representational and nonrepresentational traditions. She portrays not complete figures but fragments, bits of representation that seem to surface like memories in a nonrepresentational painting. Here, two arms detach themselves from the red.

Their hands grasp a dark mass—we understand it as hair only when we notice the small ear to the right that indicates a human head. A hand at the lower right offers a ring to secure the ponytail.

Each of these artists formed their style within a particular culture during a particular historical moment. Artists working in the same culture during the same time often have stylistic features in common, and in this way individual styles contribute to our perception of larger, general styles. General styles fall into several categories. There are *cultural styles* (Aztec style in Mesoamerica), *period* or *historical styles* (Gothic style in Europe), and *school styles*, which are styles shared by a particular group of like-minded artists (Impressionist style). General styles provide a useful framework for organizing the history of art, and familiarity with them can help us situate art and artists that are new to us in a historical or cultural context, which often helps understanding. But it is important to remember that general styles are constructed after the fact, as scholars discern broad trends by comparing the work of numerous individual artists. Cultures, historical periods, and schools do not create art. Individuals create art, working with (and sometimes pushing against) the possibilities that their time and place hold out to them.

ART AND MEANING

"What is the artist trying to say?" is a question many people ask when looking at a work of art, as though the artist were trying to tell us in images what he or she could have said more clearly in a few words. As we saw in Chapter 1, meaning in art is rarely so simple and straightforward. Rather than a definitive meaning that can be found once and for all, art inspires interpretations that are many and changeable.

According to some theories of art, meaning is what distinguishes art from other kinds of skilled making. Art is always *about* something. One brief definition of art, in fact, is "embodied meaning." Viewers who wonder what the artist is trying to say are thus right to expect their experience of art to be meaningful, but they may misunderstand where meaning can be found or underestimate their own role in making it. Understanding art is a cultural skill and, like any cultural skill, must be learned.

Four key terms related to meaning are form, content, iconography, and context. We look at each one in turn.

Form and Content

Form is the way a work of art looks. It includes all visual aspects of the work that can be isolated and described such as size, shape, materials, color, and composition. **Content** is what a work of art is about. For representational and abstract works, content begins with the objects or events the work depicts, its **subject matter.** As we experience how form and subject matter interact, we begin to interpret the work, and content shades into meaning.

Two paintings by Henri Matisse allow us to explore the intimate relationship of form and content in art (**2.24, 2.25**). Both begin with the same subject matter, a piano lesson. Both are the same large size. They even depict the same young student, Matisse's son Pierre, and are set in the same place, the Matisse family home, with the piano placed in front of a window looking out onto a garden. Yet their form clearly differs, and thus their content diverges as well.

Piano Lesson (2.24) is abstract. Matisse takes his cue from the metronome, the pyramidal form that sits on the piano. A metronome is a device that disciplines musicians as they practice by beating steady time. The wind-up type Matisse depicts has a slender wand that ticks as it sways back and forth like a windshield wiper. The boy is concentrating so hard that his face is disappearing into this ticking. He is concentrating so hard that almost everything around him is vanishing into grayness. Outdoors, the garden has been abstracted into a green wedge—even nature obeys the metronome! On the piano a candle burns low, suggesting that many hours have passed. In the background a woman sits on a stool, her head turned toward the boy. She seems to be a teacher, and a severe one at that. Actually, she is a painting by Matisse hanging on the far wall. Nestled in the lower left corner is another work by Matisse, a small bronze figure of a nude woman. The boy's muse and inspiration, perhaps, but also another work of art.

Music Lesson (2.25) sets music in a social realm of family togetherness. Again Pierre practices, but he is not alone. His sister stands over his shoulder, watching him play. His older brother sits in a chair, reading, while out in the garden his mother works on a piece of sewing. Instead of a metronome on the piano there is an open violin case with a violin inside. Matisse played the violin, and this is his way of saying "I'm here too." The painting in the background is once again just a painting, its gold frame visible, while the bronze statue has moved outdoors into the garden, where it reclines by a little pond. The austere abstraction of *Piano Lesson* has blossomed here into a relaxed representational style of luscious colors and curves.

We could summarize the difference in content by saying that *Piano Lesson* is about the discipline of music, its solitary and intellectual side; *Music Lesson* is about the pleasure of music, its social and sensuous side. Matisse has expressed each message through a different form; we in turn have interpreted the form to arrive at the content.

We could say more about the form of Matisse's paintings. For example, we could point out that they are made of oil paint applied with brushes to canvas stretched over a wooden frame. Yet these aspects of their form don't seem to change things one way or the other. Oil paint, brushes, and canvas had been the standard materials of European painting for centuries, and Matisse took them for granted—they don't represent important choices he made. Similarly, Rodin probably took white marble and the technique of carving for granted

2.24 (left) Henri Matisse. *Piano Lesson.* 1916. Oil on canvas, 8'½" × 6'11¾". The Museum of Modern Art, New York.

2.25 (right) Henri Matisse. *Music Lesson.* 1917. Oil on canvas, 8'½" × 6'7". The Barnes Foundation, Merion, Pennsylvania.

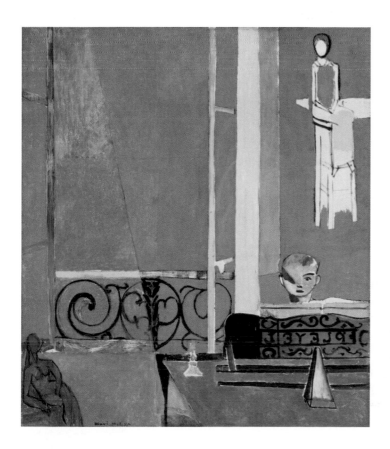

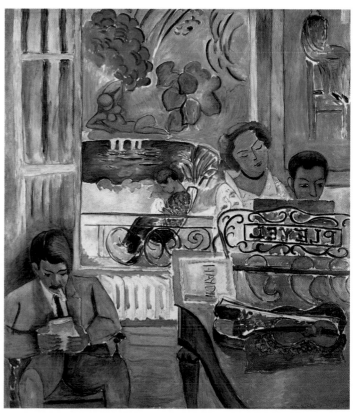

when he created *Kiss,* one of his most famous works (**2.26**). White marble had long been a standard material for sculpture in Europe, and carving was the standard way to shape it.

With Janine Antoni's *Gnaw,* in contrast, what it is made of and how it was made are the first things that grab our attention (**2.27**). The artist has reached far outside of traditional art materials and techniques, and her choices are fundamental to the work's content. *Gnaw* consists of a 600-pound cube of chocolate and a similar one of lard, each gnawed at by the artist herself. The chewed portions of lard were made into lipsticks, while the chocolate was made into heart-shaped, partitioned boxes for fancy gift chocolates. These are displayed in a nearby showcase, as though in an upscale boutique. Chocolate has strong associations with love, as both a token of affection and a substitute for it. Lard summons up obsessions with fat and self-image, which in turn are linked to culturally imposed ideals of female beauty, as is lipstick. *Gnaw* is about the gap between the prettified, commercial world of romance and the private, more desperate cravings it both feeds on and causes. The gnawed blocks of chocolate and lard resemble the base of Rodin's statue after the couple has gone, and perhaps that is part of the message as well. *The Kiss* wants to convince us that love is beautiful, and that we are beautiful when we are in love. Not always, *Gnaw* replies, and the romantic illusions that works like *The Kiss* inspire are part of the problem.

2.26 (left) Auguste Rodin. *The Kiss.* 1886–98. Marble, height 5'11¼".
Musée Rodin, Paris.

2.27 (right) Janine Antoni. *Gnaw.* 1992. Installation view (above) and details (below).
Courtesy Luhring Augustine Gallery, New York.

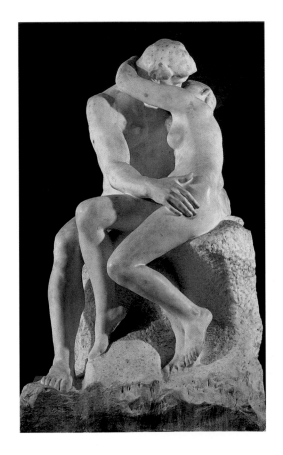

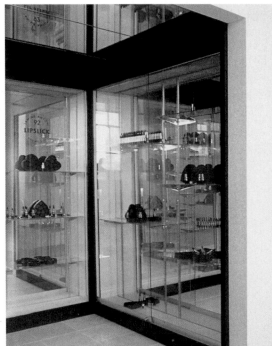

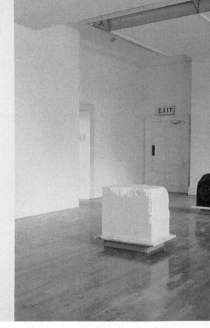

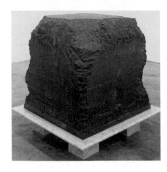

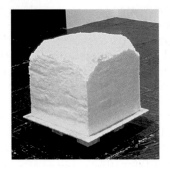

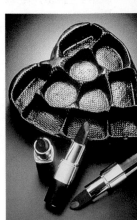

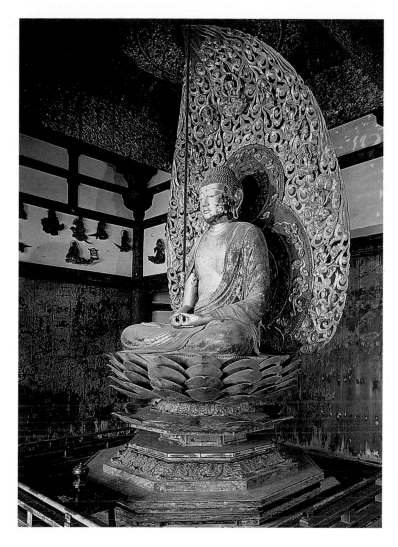

2.28 Jocho. *Amida Nyorai,* in the Hoodo (Phoenix Hall), Byodo-in Temple. c. 1053. Gilded wood, height 9'2".

Iconography

In talking about form and content in Matisse's *Piano Lesson,* we relied on something so basic you may not even have noticed it. In fact, it was our very first step: We recognized the subject matter. We know what a piano looks like, and what lessons are. We expect to see a piano, a student, a teacher. Other objects depicted in the painting required some research to identify. Who was the first viewer to notice that the teacher in the background is actually another painting by Matisse? Today this information is standard knowledge, and almost any description of *Piano Lesson* will include it. But at some point it was newly discovered. One object depicted in *Piano Lesson* even carried a traditional meaning of its own: the candle burning low, which has a long history in Western art of symbolizing the passing of time.

This kind of background information about subject matter is the domain of iconography. **Iconography,** literally "describing images," involves identifying, describing, and interpreting subject matter in art. Iconography is an important activity of scholars who study art, and their work helps us understand meanings that we might not be able to see for ourselves. For example, unless you are schooled in Japanese Buddhism, you would not recognize the subject matter of *Amida Nyorai* (**2.28**). An important work of Japanese art, the statue was created during the 11th century by the sculptor Jocho for a temple called Byodo-in, where it still resides. Its intended audience—Buddhists who come to worship at the temple—understands the statue easily. The rest of us need some help.

Our investigation begins with the most basic question of all, Who is Amida Nyorai? Amida Nyorai is a buddha, a fully enlightened being. The historical Buddha was a spiritual leader who lived in India around the turn of the 5th century B.C.E. His insights into the human condition form the basis of the Buddhist religion. As Buddhism developed, it occurred to believers that if there had been one fully enlightened being, there must have been others. In Japan, where Buddhism quickly spread, the most popular buddha has been Amida, the Buddha of the Western Paradise.

The iconography of the historical Buddha image was established early on and has remained constant through the centuries. Amida is portrayed following its conventions. A buddha wears a monk's robe, a single length of cloth that drapes over the left shoulder. His ears are elongated, for in his earthly life, before his spiritual awakening, he wore the customary heavy earrings of an Indian prince. The form resembling a bun on the top of his head is a protuberance called *ushnisha*. It symbolizes his enlightenment. Sculptors developed a repertoire of hand gestures for the Buddha image, and each gesture has its own meaning. Here, Amida's hands form the gesture of meditation and balance, which symbolizes the path toward enlightenment. He sits in the cross-legged position of meditation on a lotus throne. The lotus flower is a symbol of purity. Rising up behind Amida is his halo, radiant spiritual energy envisioned as a screen of stylized flames.

The iconography of this statue is readily available to us because it forms part of a tradition that has continued unbroken since it first developed almost 2,000 years ago. Often, however, traditions change and meanings are forgotten. We cannot always tell with certainty what images from the past portray, or what they meant to their original viewers. Such is the case with one of the most famous images in Western art, the *Arnolfini Double Portrait* by Jan van Eyck (**2.29**). Painted with entrancing clarity and mesmerizing detail, the work portrays a man and a woman, their hands joined. He has taken off his shoes, which lie on the floor next to him; hers can be seen on the floor in the background. Seemingly pregnant, she stands next to a bed draped in rich red fabric. Overhead is a chandelier with but one candle. On the floor between the couple stands an alert little dog. A mirror on the far wall (**2.30**) reflects not only the couple but also two men standing in the doorway to the room and looking in—standing, that is, where we are standing as we look at the painting. Over the mirror the painter's signature reads "Jan van Eyck was here."

By the time the painting ended up in the National Gallery in London in 1842, it had changed hands so many times that even the identity of the couple had been forgotten. Researchers working from old documents soon identified them as Giovanni Arnolfini, a rich merchant capitalist, and his wife, Giovanna Cenami, also from a socially prominent family. But what was the purpose of the painting? What, exactly, does it depict? One influential theory claims that the painting records a private marriage ceremony and served as a sort of marriage certificate. The men reflected in the mirror are none other than Jan van Eyck and a friend, who had served as witnesses. Moreover, almost every detail of the painting has a symbolic value related to the sacrament of marriage. The bride's seemingly pregnant state alludes to fertility, as does the red bed of the nuptial chamber. The single candle signifies the presence of God at the ceremony, while the dog is a symbol of marital fidelity and love. The couple have cast off their shoes as a sign that they stand on sacred ground.

Another, more recent theory claims that the painting does not depict a marriage but a ceremony of bethrothal, an engagement. It commemorates the alliance of two prominent and well-off families. In this view, the details do not carry specific symbolism, although many of them serve to underscore the couple's affluence. Canopied beds, for example, were status symbols and as such were commonly displayed in the principal room of the house. Candles were enormously expensive, and burning one at a time was common thrift. The shoes were of a style worn by the upper class and were probably taken off routinely upon going indoors. The dog is simply a pet: Everyone had dogs.[7]

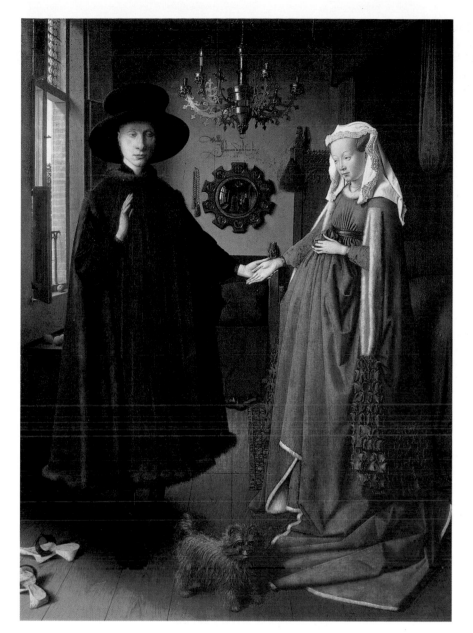

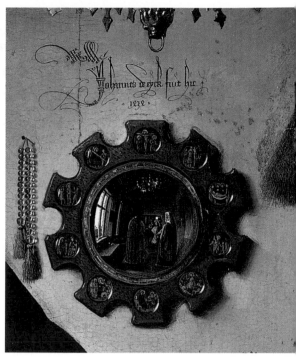

2.29 (left) Jan van Eyck. *Arnolfini Double Portrait*. 1434. Oil on wood, 33 × 22½".
The National Gallery, London.

2.30 (right) *Arnolfini Double Portrait*, detail.

Both of these theories are supported by impressive research and reasoning. Some scholars believe one, some the other. Viewers will continue to find their own meanings in this magical painting, but we may never know just what it signified for its original audience.

Context

Art does not happen in a vacuum. Strong ties bind a work of art to the life of its creator, to the tradition it grows from and responds to, to the audience it was made for, and to the society in which it circulated. These circumstances form the **context** of art, its web of connections to the larger world of human culture.

This chapter has already made use of the kind of insights that context can provide. Near the beginning, passages from the letters of Vincent van Gogh helped set his painting in the context of his life and thought. In talking about Picasso's *Seated Woman Holding a Fan*, the challenge posed by photography was mentioned in order to set the painting in the context of the development of European art.

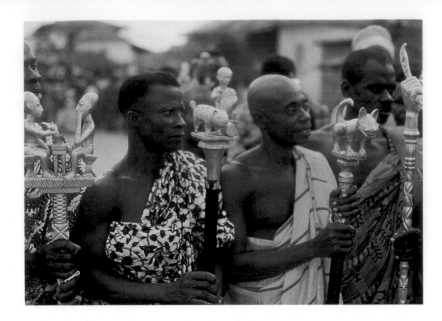

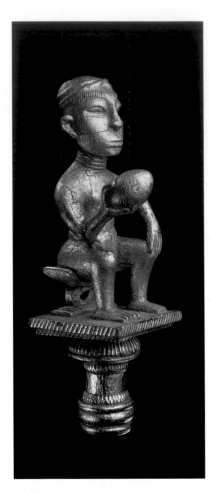

2.31 (above) Finial of a linguist's staff, from Ghana. Asante, 20th century. Wood and gold, height 11¼".
Musée Barbier-Mueller, Geneva.

2.32 (above, right) Akan (Fante) linguists at Enyan Abaasa, Ghana, 1974.

The type of context that especially concerns us here is the social context of art, including the physical setting in which art is experienced. Figure **2.31** portrays a work of African art as we might see it today in a museum. Isolated against a dark background and dramatically lit, the gilded carving gleams like a rare and precious object. We can admire the harmony of the sculpture's gently rounded forms in much the same way that we contemplated the light flowing over Edward Weston's cabbage leaf earlier in the chapter (see 2.9). Yet the sculpture was not made primarily to be looked at in this way. In fact, it was not made to be seen in a museum at all.

Figure **2.32** shows similar sculptures in their original context, as they were made to be seen and used by the Akan peoples of West Africa. The men in the photograph are officials known as linguists. Linguists serve Akan rulers as translators, spokespersons, advisers, historians, and orators. Every local chief employs at least one linguist, and more powerful chiefs and kings may be attended by many. As a symbol of office, a linguist carries a staff topped with a wooden sculpture covered in gold leaf. Each sculptural motif is associated with one or more proverbs, often about the nature of leadership or the just use of power. In the photograph here, for example, the staff at the far left portraying two men seated at a table calls forth the proverb, "Food is for its owner, not for the one who is hungry," meaning that the chieftaincy belongs to the man who has the right to it, not just to anyone who wants it.

In an Akan community, the aesthetic attention that we directed at the sculpture (2.31) would have been the unique privilege of the artist who carved the work and the linguist who owned it. Other members of the community would have glimpsed the figure only during public occasions of state. More meaningful to them would have been the authority that the staffs symbolized and the pageantry they contributed to—a lavish visual display that reaffirmed the social order of the Akan world.

Museums are the principal setting our society offers for encounters with art. Yet the vast majority of humankind's artistic heritage was not created with museums in mind. It was not made to be set aside from life in a special place, but rather to be part of life—both the lives of individuals and the lives of communities. Like the Akan linguist staff, its meaning was united with its use. This is as true for Western art as it is for the art of other cultures. Figure **2.33** shows Titian's *Assumption* in isolation, as we might expect to find it in a museum or an art book. "Assumption" names another standard subject of Christian art, that of Mary, the mother of Jesus, being accepted bodily into heaven at her death. Titian has imagined Mary being borne upward amid a crowd of angels, her garments swirling about her, into a golden glory. Above, God appears to welcome her; below, witnesses marvel at the miracle.

Titian's masterpiece does not reside in a museum, however, or on the white pages of an art book. It towers up behind the main altar of the Church of the Frari in Venice, in the exact location the artist painted it for. Thomas Struth's photograph *Church of the Frari, Venice* captures something of the experience of seeing Titian's work in context (**2.34**). Now we understand that the painting is part of a richly worked, massive stone altarpiece, with fluted columns, marble inlay, and gilded carving. A statue of Christ crowns the ensemble, flanked by two monks. We can see how the tall, arched shape of the painting repeats the pointed arches of the church itself, and we can appreciate how the painting's bold composition projects clearly into the cavernous interior.

But all of these ways of looking are still ways of looking at art. At its unveiling in 1518, the painting was seen through the eyes of faith. We need to imagine the effect it produced when Christianity was the central culture force of Venetian life. Citizens filling the Church of the Frari would have felt the truth of their beliefs through the splendor of the architecture echoing with music, the pageantry of the rituals, and the glorious vision of a miracle made present through Titian's skill and imagination. In Struth's photograph, light falls on a small group of tourists who have paused to look at the famous painting. They have come to look at art, as though the church were a museum. And yet for a moment they seem transfigured.

The museum as we know it today—a building housing a collection of art and open to the public—developed in Europe during the decades leading into the 19th century, the same decades that witnessed the social upheavals that inaugurated our modern era, including the American and French revolutions. Viewed as repositories of the past, newly created museums were filled with

2.33 (left) Titian. *Assumption.* 1518. Oil on wood, 22'7¾" × 11'11⅜".
Church of the Frari, Venice.

2.34 (right) Thomas Struth. *Church of the Frari, Venice.* 1995. C-print, 7'7⅜" × 6'1⅜".
Courtesy Marian Goodman Gallery.

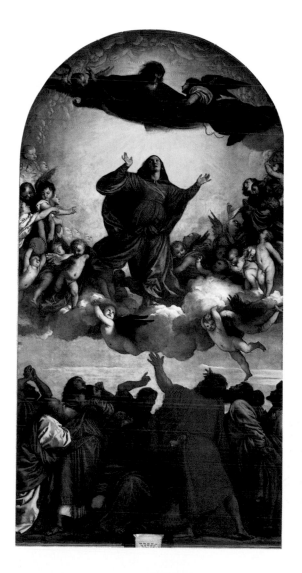

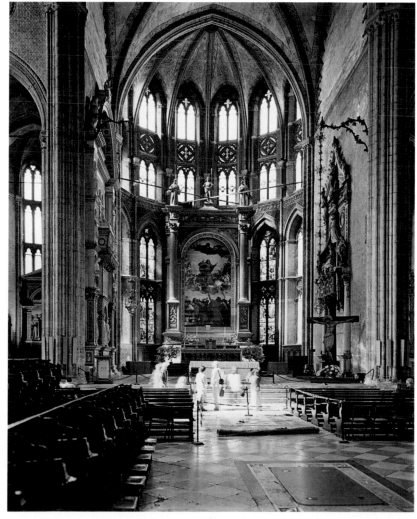

objects that used to belong to the aristocracy or the Church, or to vanished civilizations such as ancient Rome and Egypt. All of these objects were removed from the contexts that originally gave them meaning. Placed in a museum, their new function was to be works of art.

While the first museums were concerned only with the art of the past, many museums now exhibit the work of living artists. Along with galleries that display (and usually sell) art, and a circuit of international exhibitions that survey current artistic trends, they are the principal context for the art of our time. Our artists work with these institutions and spaces in mind, and as viewers we expect to see their work in these settings.

There is a long tradition of artists who have protested this separation of art from the fabric of everyday life. Often they make art that tries to reach outside of this specialized context or to question it. We will look at some of their ideas next. But there is an equally long tradition of artists who have explored what could be done *within* such a context. One such artist is Tom Friedman, whose inventive, labor-intensive works defy categorization. Here, we illustrate a cereal box he made by cutting nine boxes into small squares and then piecing them back together as one (**2.35**). Elsewhere, he has exhibited a pencil processed through a sharpener into one continuous coil of shaving and a life-size statue of himself made of sugar cubes.

Friedman not only intends his art specifically for the quiet, empty, white spaces of contemporary galleries and museums, but even suggests that the things he makes are not quite art outside of such spaces. "I think that after I make it and it goes into the gallery it's in its sort of original context within a body of work," he explains. If a collector buys an individual work from the exhibition, "it becomes historical, more of an artifact, as opposed to the same conveyor of meaning it was originally."[8]

Friedman's remarks underscore the importance of context to meaning, just as his work illustrates how our modern context of galleries and museums opened up new possibilities for what could be seen as art.

2.35 Tom Friedman. *Untitled.* 1999. Cereal boxes, 31¼ × 21¼ × 6⅝".
Courtesy the artist.

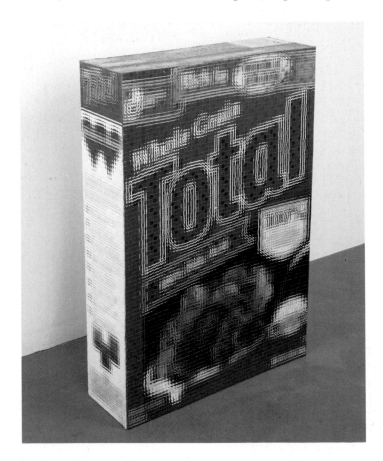

AESTHETICS

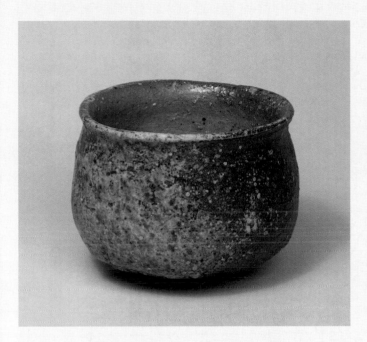

T HE WORD *aesthetics* was coined in the early 18th century by a German philosopher named Alexander Baumgarten. He derived his word from the Greek word for perception, *aisthanomai,* and he used it to name what he considered to be a field of knowledge, the knowledge gained by sensory experience combined with feelings. Like art, aesthetics existed before we named it and outside of our naming it: Just as cultures around the world and across time have created what we now call art, so they have thought about the nature and purpose of their creations and focused on certain words for evaluating and appreciating them.

Exploring the aesthetics of other cultures can help us understand what expressive forms they value and why. For example, the illustration here depicts a tea bowl formed by hand in the Japanese province of Shigaraki during the early 17th century. While we may find the bowl pleasing to look at (or not, depending on our taste), we have no way of talking about it as art. A tea bowl holds no meaning for us. In Japan, however, this small vessel would be the focus of intense appreciation centered on two key terms, *wabi* and *sabi. Wabi* embraces such concepts as naturalness, simplicity, understatement, and impermanence. *Sabi* adds overtones

of loneliness, old age, and tranquility. The two terms are central to the aesthetics that developed around the austere variety of Buddhism known as Zen. They are especially connected with the Zen-inspired practice we know as the tea ceremony. Through its connection with the tea ceremony and with Zen Buddhist spiritual ideals, this simple bowl partakes in a rich network of meanings and associations.

The closest traditional Japanese equivalent to the word *art* (in the sense of visual art) is *katachi.* Translated as "form and design," it applies to ceramics and furniture as much as it does to paintings and sculpture. The Navajo people of the American Southwest, in contrast, do not have a word that separates made things from the rest of the world, for in the Navajo view the two are deeply intertwined. According to Navajo philosophy, the world is constantly becoming, constantly being created and renewed. Its natural state is one of beauty, harmony, and happiness, conditions summed up in the word *hozho.* Yet all things contain their opposites, and thus *hozho* is countered by forces of ugliness, evil, and disorder. The interplay between opposites is what allows creation to perpetuate itself. Day and night, for example, are opposite aspects of an ongoing process. One shades into the other, together they keep creation in motion. Humans do not stand apart from this natural world but rather have a vital role to play: Through harmonious thoughts and actions they radiate beauty into the world, maintaining and restoring *hozho* against the threat of dangerous spirit forces. Many of these actions we would call art—singing, painting, weaving. Yet beauty for the Navajo does not lie in the finished product but in the process of making it. The most famous example of this is sand painting, discussed later in this chapter (see 2.36).

In their different ways, Japanese and Navajo aesthetics challenge and expand traditional Western ideas about art, one by erasing our boundary between fine art and other kinds of skilled making such as ceramics, the other by valuing process over product and by not recognizing a border between art and life.

Tea bowl. Japan, early 17th century. Stoneware, height 3⅜".
r Victoria and Albert Museum, London.

ART AND OBJECTS

During the 20th century, many artists began to feel that something important had been lost when art was separated from life and placed in a separate, privileged realm. Seen in the larger context of consumer culture, where shopping and window shopping are favorite leisure activities, were museums and galleries really so different from department stores and boutiques? Despite the talk of meaning and spiritual value, did the role of the artist in modern society come down in the end to making objects for display and sale?

Sometimes a slight shift in perspective is all it takes to open up new ways of thinking. A painting, for example, is indeed an object. But it is also the result of a process, the activity of painting. In questioning the purpose of art and the role of the artist in contemporary culture, many artists began to shift their focus away from the products of art to its processes, considering how they might be meaningful in themselves.

Looking beyond the West to other cultures often provided guidance and inspiration. The Navajo practice of sand painting, for example, is one of the most famous instances of an art where product and process cannot be separated, for the painting, its making, and its unmaking are all equally important. Sand painting is part of a ceremony in which a religious specialist known as a singer, *hataali*, calls upon spirit powers to heal and bless someone who is ill. The ceremony begins as the singer chants a Navajo legend. At a certain point, he begins making the painting by sifting colored sand through his fingers onto the earthen floor. The photograph illustrated here depicts two Navajo men demonstrating the technique of sand painting for the public (**2.36**). Actual sand painting is viewed as a sacred activity, and photography is not permitted. The painting acts as an altar, a zone of contact between earthly and spirit realms, and together with the chanting it attracts the spirits, the Holy People. When the painting is completed, the patient is instructed to sit at its center. The singer begins to touch first a portion of the painting and then the patient, gradually transferring the powers of healing. When the ceremony is over, the

2.36 (left) Navajo men creating a sand painting. Photograph c. 1939.

2.37 (right) Standing figure holding supernatural effigy. Olmec culture, 800–500 B.C.E. Jade, height 8⅝".
The Brooklyn Museum.

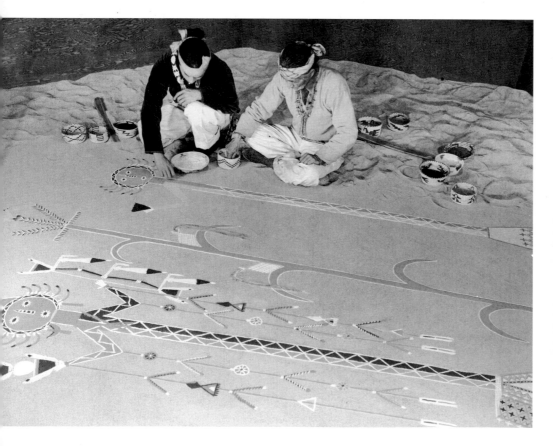

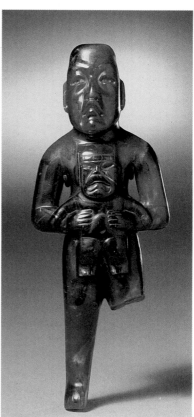

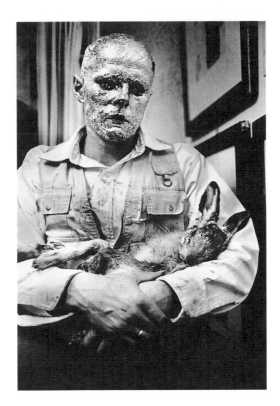

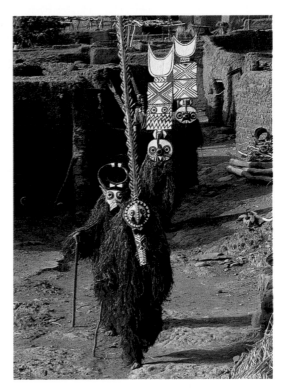

painting is unmade—swept with a feather staff into a blanket, then carried outside and deposited safely so that it does not harm anyone with the sickness it has taken on.

The Navajo *hataali* is a shaman, a type of religious specialist common to many cultures. A shaman is a person who acts as a medium between the human and spirit worlds. A jade carving from the ancient Mesoamerican Olmec culture gives visual form to ideas about the power of shamans (**2.37**). Standing in a pose of meditation, the shaman holds up a small creature whose fierce, animated expression contrasts vividly with his own trancelike gaze. The creature's headband, catlike eyes, snub nose, and large downturned mouth identify him as the infant man-jaguar, a supernatural being mingling animal and human traits. The navels of the creature and the shaman are aligned, as on an axis linking the cosmic and earthly realms. In Olmec belief, the creature probably served as the shaman's contact in the supernatural world.

The person who most directly adopted the idea of the artist as a kind of shaman and art as a tool of spiritual healing was Joseph Beuys. In his 1965 work *How to Explain Pictures to a Dead Hare*, he covered his head in honey and gold leaf and appeared in a gallery cradling a dead hare in his arms (**2.38**). Walking about the room, he spoke quietly and tenderly to the animal as he brought it close to the pictures on display. On the floor in the middle of the gallery was a withered fir tree that Beuys stepped over from time to time, still cradling the hare. Beuys' performances—he called them Actions—did not result in an object at all. They were ritual-like events that, for those who chose to reflect on them, touched on issues of art, society, and nature. Like Kandinsky, Beuys believed that an artist's role in a materialistic society was to remind people of human and spiritual values, but he also thought that artists should be concerned with how these values point to the need for social and political change.

As with other developments in Western art during the 20th century, accepting the idea that art could embrace process and performance helped build bridges of understanding to other cultures. The masquerades of Africa, for example, constitute one of the most varied and compelling world traditions of art in performance (**2.39**). Masquerades serve to make otherworld spirits physically present in the human community. The photograph here shows a

2.38 (left) Joseph Beuys performing *How to Explain Pictures to a Dead Hare*. 1965.

2.39 (right) Bwa masqueraders, Burkina Faso.

procession of nature spirits entering a community of the Bwa people of West Africa. Raffia costumes and carved and painted masks completely disguise the performers' human identities, which are believed to be subsumed into the spirit identities of the masks. Masks are called upon during times when the co-operation of spirits and the natural forces they control is especially needed. For example, masks may appear at festivals surrounding the planting and harvesting of crops, or during the initiation of young people into adulthood, or at funerals when their help is needed to ensure that the spirit of the deceased leaves the human community and takes its place in the spirit world of ancestors. When Western scholars first became interested in African masks, they tended to discuss them formally as sculptures, for this was the standard Western category of art that masks most resembled. Today, our broader understanding of art encourages us to see masks as an element in a larger art form, the masquerade, which is based in performance.

Viewers, too, have a process related to art, the process of experiencing and reflecting upon a work. Artists looking for new directions thought about this process as well. They realized that being in a gallery or a museum is itself an experience, and they began to take this into account in various ways. One result was a new art form called **installation,** in which a space is presented as a work of art that can be entered, explored, experienced, and reflected upon.

The photograph here captures a view of *Mantle,* an installation created by Ann Hamilton in the Miami Art Museum in 1998 (**2.40**). To the left is a 48-foot-long table heaped with cut flowers. Speakers buried in the flowers broadcast the confusion of voices and static arriving over eleven shortwave radios mounted on a shelf overhead. To the right, a woman (Ann Hamilton herself, as it happens) sits in the light of a tall window, sewing sleeves onto a series of coats. She worked quietly and methodically, seemingly unaware of the flowers and the noise behind her. Nor did she take any notice of the museum visitors as they entered and explored.

Hamilton's installations are site-specific, developed for a particular location and not repeated elsewhere. They are also impermanent, and photographs such as this one are all that remain once their time is over. Situated in a museum, *Mantle* referred on the one hand to art of the past. The sewing woman had her ancestors in the quiet, window-lit women of painters such as Vermeer (see 3.24), and the flowers looked back to paintings such as Juan de Valdés Leal's *Vanitas* (1.13). Yet *Mantle* also reached out to the living world outside the museum, drawing its sounds in through the radios and mingling them with the silent flowers. Visitors to *Mantle* found themselves in a place where present and past, inside and outside, sound and silence, and art and life were blurred together.

2.40 Ann Hamilton. *Mantle.* Installation at the Miami Art Museum, 1998. Eight tables, eleven shortwave radio receivers, voice, chair, figure, steel block, sewing implements, 33 wool coats, and approx. 60,000 fresh-cut flowers; overall dimensions 16 × 24 × 72'.
Courtesy Sean Kelly Gallery, New York.

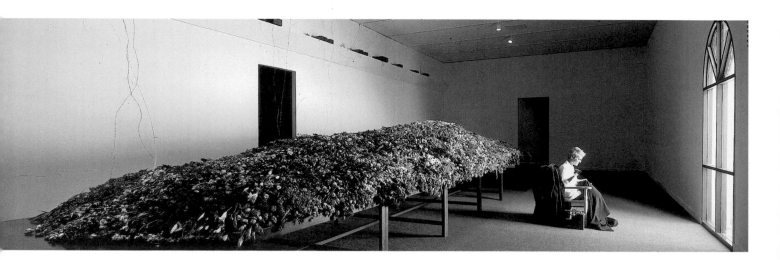

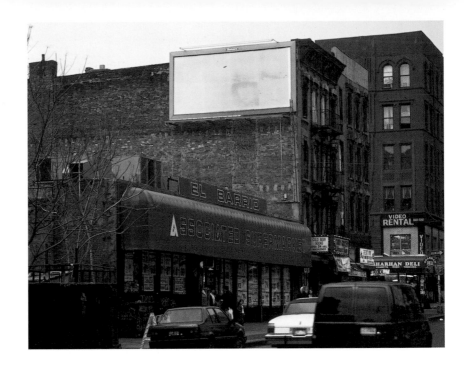

2.41 Felix Gonzalez-Torres. *Untitled.* 1995. Billboard, dimensions vary with installation. Courtesy Andrea Rosen Gallery, New York.

In the works illustrated here, Hamilton and Beuys brought the outside world into the specialized spaces of galleries and museums, insisting on a connection between them. Other artists have worked in the opposite direction, slipping works of art into the everyday visual world. In 1995, Felix Gonzalez-Torres had a black-and-white photograph of a single bird in flight placed on twenty-four billboards around New York City (**2.41**). Nothing told passersby that it was art. No words tried to explain it or take credit for it. The artist presented the image anonymously, hoping only that people might notice, might wonder, might bring their own meanings to this unexpected encounter.

Gonzalez-Torres did not take the photograph himself. It was an image he found. His art consisted in having it reprinted at billboard size, renting the billboard locations, and slipping the image into the clamor of signs, symbols, and advertisements that surrounds us. The collector who bought the work bought both the right and the responsibility to continue this gesture, as often and on as many billboards as desired. The collector, in essence, bought an idea. Insisting that art could reside in an idea was the most radical of 20th-century artists' many moves away from making objects. During the 1960s, idea-based art became known as Conceptual Art—a very intimidating name for so gentle, generous, and hopeful a gesture as Gonzalez-Torres' billboard of a bird in flight.

The questions that artists of the 20th century posed about the nature of their task, and the great formal variety of their responses to these questions, served to map the territory of the word "art." We now understand that art can manifest itself in many more ways than the 18th-century philosophers who invented the category ever dreamed. A painting, a sculpture, a video, an installation, a Web site, a computer program, a concept, a performance, an action—all of these and more may be presented and understood as art.

CHAPTER THREE

THEMES OF ART

There are several ways to approach the study of art. A popular one is to trace its history chronologically, from the earliest cave paintings of the Stone Age to the art of our own time. This method offers great advantages, because it places works of art in the context of the cultures from which they emerged and allows us to follow the development of art over the centuries. Part Five of this book will present a brief chronological survey of art.

The chronological approach has one drawback, however, in that we may lose sight of the characteristics that works made by different cultures have in common. For instance, a sculpture produced today and one produced ten thousand years ago may seem very different, and a chronological approach emphasizes the differences by focusing on the cultural aspects that influenced each. But suppose the two sculptures are images of political leaders; then we would say they have the same *theme*, so we can make interesting comparisons between them. While it is useful to understand how and why works of art differ, it is also helpful to see how much they are alike, even when thousands of miles and years separate them.

A theme is like a thread running through the entire history of art, and there are many such threads. No doubt every person setting out to name the important themes in art would produce a different list. This chapter proposes nine themes, ranging from the arts of daily life to art about art. Each theme allows us to consider the world's art from a particular point of view. Just as a work of art may inspire many interpretations and hold many meanings, so it may also reflect more than one theme. A painting that primarily addresses the theme of the sacred realm, for example, may also have something to tell us about the social order of the culture in which it was made or the artistic tradition it is responding to. As you read this chapter, you may find yourself considering works discussed earlier in the light of the new theme at hand, or thinking about how a newly encountered work also reflects themes discussed earlier. This is as it should be. Themes do not reduce art to neat categories. Rather, they provide a framework for exploring how complex a form of expression it can be.

VISUAL DELIGHT AND THE ARTS OF DAILY LIFE

In many cultures, art and craft are still one concept, and the artistic impulse is expressed as much through objects created for daily use as it is through images and architecture. Often these objects carry meanings far beyond their practical functions. Among the Pomo Indians of California, for example, the art of basketry is highly valued (**3.1**). Legend tells that when a Pomo ancestor stole the sun from the gods to light the dark earth, he hung it aloft in a basket that he kept moving across the sky. The daily journey of the sun reenacts this original event. Pomo baskets are thus linked to larger ideas about the universe and about the transfer of knowledge from gods to humans at the beginning of the world.

Traditionally a woman's art, basket weaving began with the harvesting of materials. This activity, too, was endowed with ritual significance, for it involved following ancestral paths into the landscape to find the traditional roots, barks, and woods. Here, willow and bracken fern root were used to produce a pattern of alternating lights and darks. Feathers, clam-shell beads, and glass beads procured through trade are woven into the surface. Somewhere in the basket the weaver included a small, barely noticeable imperfection. Called *dau*, it serves as a spirit door, letting benevolent spirits into the basket and allowing evil ones to leave. Feather baskets were produced as gifts for important or honored persons, and they were usually destroyed in mourning when the person died.

Like the Pomo, most traditional societies assign some arts to men and others to women. This thinking is part of a larger way of viewing the world in which men and women have complementary roles. Among the Ndebele people of South Africa, a family homestead—a walled enclosure containing several single-room structures—is viewed as a woman's domain. Men and other outsiders may not enter the inner courtyards or the house itself without a woman's permission. Men and women begin constructing the buildings together, setting up a framework of wooden poles, weaving walls of twigs and sticks between them, and laying on a thatched roof. Once this stage is complete, the women continue the work by themselves. Over a period of months they patiently build up mud walls around the woven framework. After smoothing and plastering the walls inside and out, they decorate them with murals (**3.2**).

The illustration here depicts the interior of the home of Selina Masombuka, who painted this set of murals to prepare the house for a family wedding. The bold forms, clean colors, and precise black outlines are typical of Ndebele style. Though Ndebele women draw on a common vocabulary of geometric and abstract motifs, each woman's murals are different and original, an expression of her own unique spirit and creativity.

3.1 (left) Feathered basket. Pomo, c. 1877. Willow, bulrush, fern, feather, shell, glass beads; height 5½".
Philbrook Museum of Art, Tulsa, Oklahoma.

3.2 (right) Living room with wall painting by Selina Masombuka, Pieterskraal, South Africa.
Photograph by Margaret Courtney-Clarke.

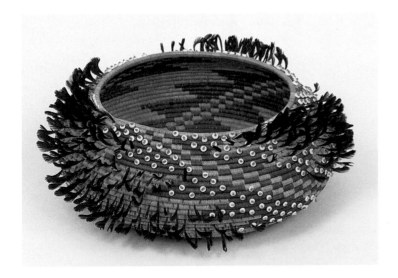

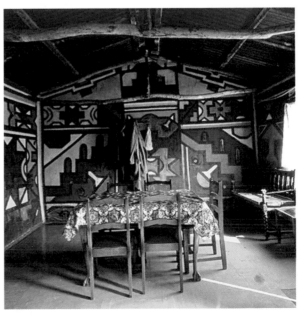

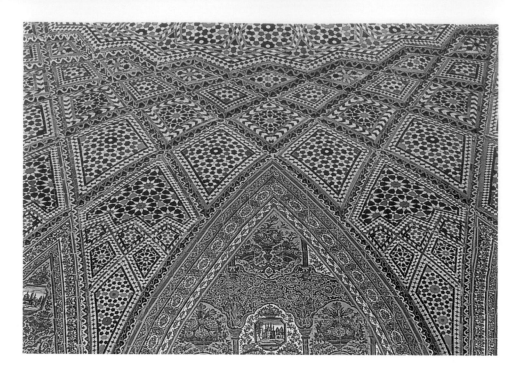

3.3 Interior detail, Nasr al-Mulk mosque, Shiraz. Mid-19th century. Mosaic and ceramic tile.

The photographer whom Selina Masombuka allowed into her home asked many Ndebele women why they painted their murals. "I learned from my mother" or "it is the law of the Ndebele" were typical answers.[1] To be Ndebele is to paint murals. In this way, the arts of daily life often serve to reinforce the identity of a community and make it visible in the world. The Ndebele and Pomo are small, localized communities, but everyday arts can also proclaim much larger cultures. One of the world's most widespread artistic traditions is tilework—the decoration of architectural surfaces with glazed tiles. While tilework has been practiced in many cultures, it was artists in Islamic lands that made tile the focus of sustained aesthetic attention, so that today we think of tilework as a characteristic Islamic art. From its first wave of popularity during the 12th century, the custom spread rapidly through Islamic lands from southern Spain to the borders of India. Palaces, homes, markets, mosques, schools, public fountains, city gates—all were ornamented with glazed tiles, often cut and pieced into intricate mosaics (**3.3**). The illustration here depicts a detail of the interior of a 19th-century mosque in Iran. Intermittently discouraged for religious reasons from representing human and animal forms, Islamic artists have concentrated for hundreds of years on the pure visual delight that pattern and color can provide.

THE SACRED REALM

Who made the universe? How did life begin, and what is its purpose? What happens to us after we die? For answers to these and other fundamental questions, people throughout history have turned to a world we cannot see except through faith, the sacred realm of the spirit. Gods and goddesses, spirits of ancestors, spirits of nature, one God and one alone—each society has formed its own view of the sacred realm and how it interacts with our own. Some forms of faith have disappeared into history, others have remained small and local, while still others such as Christianity and Islam have become major religions that draw believers from all over the world. From earliest times art has played an important role in our relationship to the sacred, helping us to envision it, to honor it, and to communicate with it.

Many works of architecture have been created to provide settings for rituals of worship and prayer, rituals that formalize contact between the earthly and divine realms. One such work is the small marvel known as the Sainte-

Chapelle, or holy chapel (**3.4**). Located in Paris, the chapel was commissioned in 1239 by the French king Louis IX to house an important collection of relics that he had just acquired, relics he believed to include pieces of the True Cross, the Crown of Thorns, and other instruments of Christ's Passion. The king's architects created a soaring vertical space whose walls seem to be made of stained glass. Light passing through the glass creates a dazzling effect, transforming the interior into a radiant, otherworldly space in which the glory of heaven seems close at hand.

The Sainte-Chapelle is a relatively intimate space, for it was intended as a private chapel for the king and his court. In contrast, the Great Mosque at Córdoba, Spain, was built to serve the needs of an entire community (**3.5**). A mosque is an Islamic house of worship. Begun during the 8th century, the Great Mosque at Córdoba grew to be the largest place of prayer in western Islam. The interior of the prayer hall is a vast horizontal space measured out by a virtual forest of columns. Daylight enters through doorways placed around the perimeter of the hall. Filtered through the myriad columns and arches, it creates a complex play of shadows that makes the extent and shape of the interior hard to grasp. Alternating red and white sections break up the visual continuity of the arch forms. Oil lamps hanging in front of the focal point of worship would have created still more shadows.

In both the Sainte-Chapelle and the Great Mosque at Córdoba, architects strove to create a place where worshipers might approach the sacred realm. The builders of the Sainte-Chapelle envisioned a radiant vertical space transformed by colored light, while the architects of the Great Mosque at Córdoba envisioned a disorienting horizontal space fractured by columns and shadows. In both buildings, the everyday world is shut out, and light and space are used to create a heightened sense of mystery and wonder.

The sacred realm cannot be seen with human eyes, yet artists throughout the ages have been asked to create images of gods, goddesses, angels, demons, and all manner of spirit beings. Religious images may serve to focus the thoughts of the faithful by giving concrete form to abstract ideas. Often,

3.4 (left) Interior, upper chapel, Sainte-Chapelle, Paris. 1243–48.

3.5 (right) Prayer hall of Abd al-Rahman I, Great Mosque, Córdoba, Spain. Begun 786 C.E.

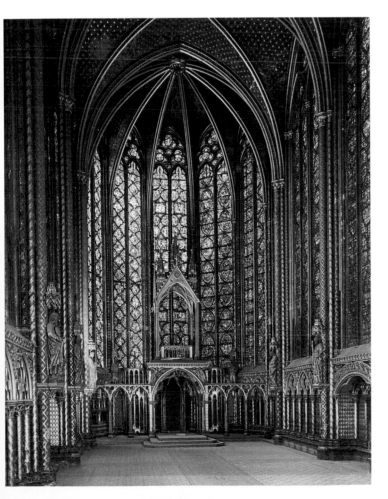

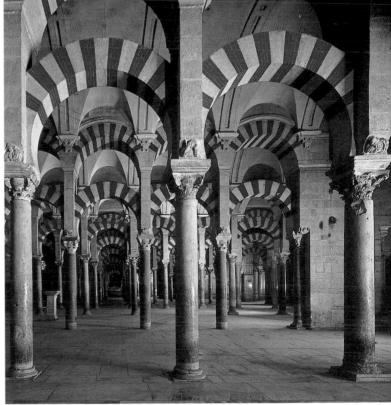

however, their role has been more complex and mysterious. For example, in some cultures images have been understood as a sort of conduit through which sacred power flows; in others they serve as a dwelling place for a deity, who is called upon through ritual to take up residence within.

Our next two images, one Buddhist and one Christian, were made at approximately the same time but some 4,000 miles apart, the Buddhist image in Tibet, the Christian one in Italy. The Buddhist painting portrays Rathnasambhava, one of the Five Transcendent Buddhas, seated in a pose of meditation on a stylized lotus throne (**3.6**). His right hand makes the gesture of bestowing vows; his left, the gesture of meditation. Unlike other buddhas, the Five Transcendent Buddhas are typically portrayed in the bejeweled garb of Indian princes. Arranged around Rathnasambhava are *bodhisattvas*, also in princely attire. Bodhisattvas are enlightened beings who have deferred their ultimate goal of *nirvana*—freedom from the cycle of birth, death, and re-birth—in order to help others attain that goal. All wear halos signifying their holiness. The buddha, being the most important of the personages depicted, dominates the painting as the largest figure. He faces straight front, in a pose of tranquility, while the others around him stand or sit in relaxed postures.

The second example, painted by the 13th-century Italian master Cimabue, depicts Mary, mother of Christ, with her son (**3.7**). Mary sits tranquilly on her throne, her hand in a classic gesture indicating the Christ child, who is the hope of earth's salvation. On both sides of her are figures of angels, heavenly beings who assist humankind in its quest for Paradise. Again, all these wear halos symbolizing their holiness. Yet again, the Virgin, being the most important figure in this painting, dominates the composition, is the largest, and holds the most serenely frontal posture.

3.6 (left) *Rathnasambhava, the Transcendent Buddha of the South.* Tibet, 13th century C.E. Opaque watercolor on cloth, height 36½". Los Angeles County Museum of Art.

3.7 (right) Cimabue. *Madonna Enthroned.* c. 1280–90. Tempera on wood, 12'7½" × 7'4". Galleria degli Uffizi, Florence.

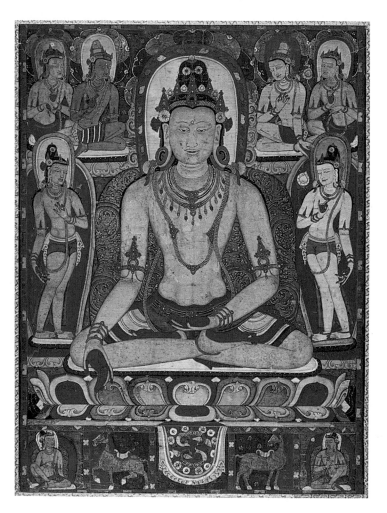

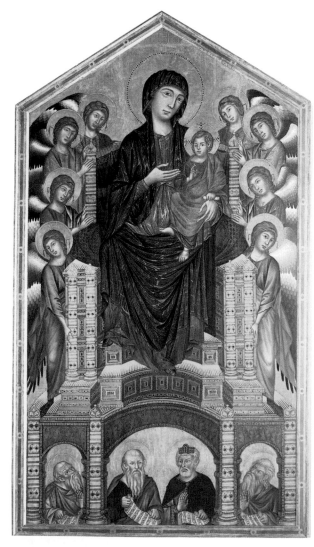

ICONOCLASM

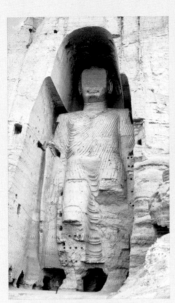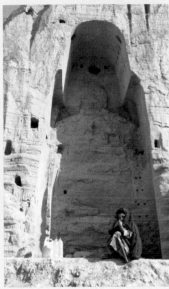

ON FEBRUARY 26, 2001, the Islamic fundamentalist rulers of Afghanistan, the Taliban, issued an edict that stunned the world: All statues in the country must be destroyed, for they were being worshiped and venerated by unbelievers. The order targeted statues large and small, those housed in museums and those on view in public places. But the statues that caught the public's attention were a pair of monumental Buddhas. Carved into the living rock of a cliff face sometime between the 3rd and 7th centuries, they were originally cared for by Buddhist monks and visited by pilgrims during religious festivals. The monks and pilgrims left centuries ago, but the statues had survived. It seemed scarcely credible that they were about to be blown up, but that is exactly what happened. In early March, despite international diplomatic efforts, the statues were destroyed.

Why would statues be destroyed in the name of religion? Like many other religions, Islam has at its core a set of texts that invite interpretation. One of these, the Traditions of the Prophet, contains two objections to representational images. The first objection is that making images usurps the creative power of God; the second is that images can lead to idolatry, the worship of the images themselves. Historically, the warnings have led Muslims generally to avoid rep-

resentational images in religious contexts such as mosques or manuscripts of the Qur'an, their holy book. Interpreted more radically, they have sometimes been used to forbid all representational images, no matter what their context. Our word for the destruction of images does not come from Islam, however, but from Christianity, which also has a history of destroying images in the name of spiritual purity. The word is iconoclasm.

Iconoclasm is derived from the Greek for "image breaking." It was coined to described one side of a debate that raged for over a century in the Christian empire of Byzantium (see page 381). Byzantine churches, monasteries, books, and homes were decorated with depictions of Christ, of the saints, and of Biblical stories and personages. Yet during the 8th century a movement arose against such depictions, and a series of emperors ordered the destruction of images throughout the realm. Again the objection was idolatry. Christianity too has at its core a set of texts. The most important of these is the Bible, which contains a very clear warning against making images. The warning comes directly from God as the second of the Ten Commandments.

Centuries after the Byzantine episode, iconoclasm arose in Western Europe when newly forming Protestant movements of the 16th century accused Catholics of idolatry. Protestant mobs ransacked churches, smashing stained glass, destroying paintings, breaking statues, whitewashing over frescoes, and melting down metal shrines and vessels. To this day, Protestant churches are comparatively bare.

Images have played an important role in almost every religion in the world. Many religions embrace them wholeheartedly. In Buddhism, for example, making religious images is viewed as a form of prayer. In Hinduism they may provide a dwelling place for a deity. The modern Western invention of "art" has seen many of these images moved to museums, and in the end this may have been part of the Taliban's point. We may not worship images for the deities they represent, but do we worship art?

(left) Large Buddha, Bamiyan, Afghanistan. 5th–7th century C.E. Stone, height 175'. (right) The empty niche after the statue was destroyed. March 2001.

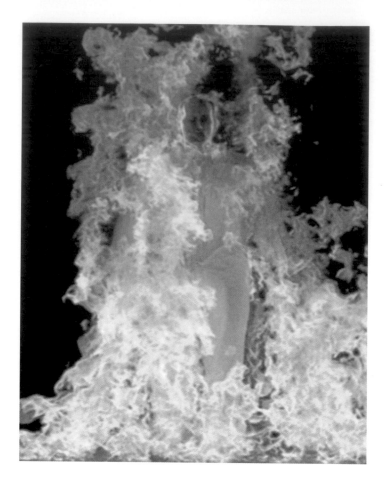
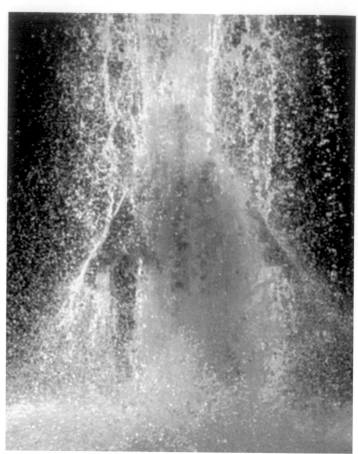

3.8 Bill Viola. *The Crossing.* 1996. Video/sound installation.

We should not conclude from the remarkable formal similarity of these works that any communication or influence took place between Italy and Central Asia. A safer assumption is that two artists of different faiths independently found a format that satisfied their pictorial needs. Both the Buddha and the Virgin are important, serene holy figures. Bodhisattvas and angels, who are always more active, attend them. Therefore, the artists, from their separate points of view, devised similar compositions.

The four works we have examined in this section were all created within the context of a particular religion, whether Islam, Christianity, or Buddhism. But art does not necessarily have to be linked to a specific faith in order for us to interpret it in light of spiritual concerns. Indeed, as we saw in Chapter 2, art has sometimes been thought to be inherently spiritual, and the 20th-century Western tradition of nonrepresentational art is rooted in this idea.

In video works such as *The Crossing*, contemporary artist Bill Viola creates imagery that conveys spiritual experience more generally (**3.8**). Viewers enter a darkened room containing a large, double-sided projection screen. On one side of the screen, they can watch the distant figure of a man approaching through a darkened space. When he is so close that his body almost fills the screen, he stops and stares directly ahead. A small votive candle appears at his feet. Suddenly, flames shoot upward from it, leaping higher and higher. Soon his entire body is engulfed and a roaring sound fills the room. When the flames die down, the man has disappeared. The screen darkens; then the cycle starts again. On the other side of the screen, another video is projected. Again a man approaches from the distance and stops. This time, however, it is water that annihilates him, falling first in droplets, then raging into a roaring deluge. The two videos are in perfect synchronization, with the appearance of the man, his drawing near, and the crescendos of fire and water happening at the same time.

"The two traditional natural elements of fire and water appear here not only in their destructive aspects, but manifest their cathartic, purifying, transformative, and regenerative capacities as well," the artist has written. "In this way self-annihilation becomes a necessary means to transcendence and liberation."[2] Transcendence is the idea, common to almost all religions, that there is a world beyond the world we can perceive with our senses, and that at certain rare moments we have access to it. Whether this is true or not, many of us long for such moments, and art such as *The Crossing* can embody our longing.

POLITICS AND THE SOCIAL ORDER

Of the many things we create as human beings, the most basic and important may be societies. How can a stable, just, and productive society best be organized? Who will rule, and how? What freedoms will rulers have? What freedoms will citizens have? How is wealth to be distributed? How is authority to be maintained? Many answers to these questions have been posed throughout history, and throughout history the resulting order has been reflected in art.

In many early societies, earthly order and cosmic order were viewed as interrelated and mutually dependent. Such was the case in ancient Egypt, where the pharaoh (king) was viewed as a link between the divine and earthly realms. The pharaoh was considered a "junior god," a personification of the god Horus and the son of the sun god, Ra. As a ruler his role was to maintain the divinely established order of the universe, which included the social order of Egypt. He communed with the gods in temples only he could enter, and he wielded theoretically unlimited power over a country that literally belonged to him.

When a pharaoh died, it was believed that he rejoined the gods and became fully divine. Preparations for this journey began even during his lifetime, as vast tombs were constructed and outfitted with everything he would need to maintain his royal lifestyle in eternity. The most famous of these monuments are the three pyramids at Giza (**3.9**), which served as the tombs of the pharaohs Menkaure, Khafre, and Khufu. Thousands of years later, the scale of these structures is still awe-inspiring. The largest pyramid, that of Khufu, originally reached a height of about 480 feet, roughly the height of a fifty-story skyscraper. Its base covers over 13 acres. Over two million blocks of stone, each weighing over 2 tons, went into building it. Each block had to be quarried with hand tools, transported to the site, and set in place without mortar. Tens of thousands of workers labored for years to build such a tomb and fill its chambers with treasures.

3.9 The Great Pyramids, Giza, Egypt. Pyramid of Menkaure (left), c. 2500 B.C.E.; Pyramid of Khafre (center), c. 2530 B.C.E.; Pyramid of Khufu (right), c. 2570 B.C.E.

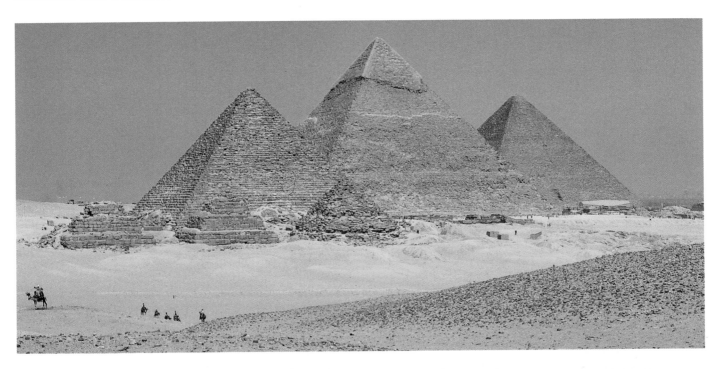

The pyramids reflect the immense power of the pharaohs who could command such forces, but they also reflect the beliefs underlying the social order that granted its rulers such power in the first place. In the Egyptian view, the well-being of Egypt depended on the goodwill of the gods, whose representative on earth was the pharaoh. His safe passage to the afterlife and his worship thereafter as a god himself were essential for the prosperity of the country and the continuity of the universe. No amount of labor or spending seemed too great to achieve these ends.

Visitors to the pyramids at Giza originally arrived by water, descending first at one of the temples that sat on the riverbank (each pyramid had its own). From there, they would have walked along a long, raised causeway to a second temple at the base of the pyramid, which itself could not be entered. The temples contained numerous shrines to the dead pharaoh, each with its own life-size statue of him. Statues lined the causeways as well, while still more were inside the pyramid itself. Before our modern mass media, it was art that served to project the presence and authority of rulers to the people throughout their lands. During the days of the Roman Empire, in the first centuries of our era, an official likeness of a new emperor was circulated throughout the realm so that local sculptors could get busy making statues for public places and civic buildings. As a practical, cost-cutting measure, the sculptors sometimes simply recarved a portrait of the former emperor with new features!

One of the finest of these ancient Roman works to come down to us is a bronze statue of the emperor Marcus Aurelius (**3.10**). Seated on his mount, he extends his arm in an oratorical gesture, as if delivering a speech. His calm in victory contrasts with the spirited motions of his horse, which was originally shown raising its hoof over a fallen enemy, now lost. The Roman fashion for

3.10 Equestrian statue of Marcus Aurelius (before restoration). 164–166 C.E. Bronze, height 11'6". Piazza del Campidoglio, Rome.

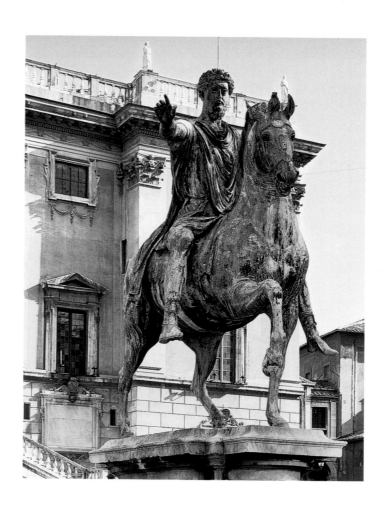

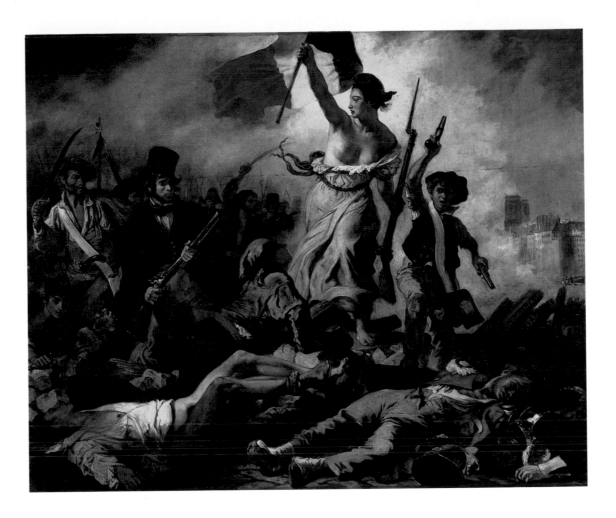

beards came and went, like all fashions. But the emperor's beard in the statue is significant, and part of the way he wanted to be portrayed. Beards were associated with Greek philosophers, and Marcus Aurelius' beard signals his desire to be seen as a philosopher-king, an ideal he genuinely tried to live up to.

During the often violent transition into our modern era, art remained deeply involved with politics and the social order. The perspective of the artist changed profoundly, however. Instead of exclusively serving those in power, the artist was now a citizen among other citizens and free to make art that took sides in the debates of the day. Eugène Delacroix's *Liberty Leading the People* leaves no doubt about the artist's support for the Revolution of 1830, a popular uprising in Paris that toppled one government and installed another (**3.11**). Delacroix completed the painting in the very same year, and it retains the passion of his idealized view of the insurrection and the hopes he had for the future it would bring. At the center is Liberty herself, personified as a Greek statue come to life. Holding the French flag high, she rallies the citizens of Paris, who surge toward us brandishing pistols and sabers as though about to burst out of the painting. Before them lie the bodies of slain government troops.

When the painting was displayed to the public in 1831, it was bought by none other than Louis-Philippe, the "citizen-king" that the revolution had put in power. But perhaps the image was a little *too* revolutionary, for the new king returned the painting to Delacroix after a few months. In fact, *Liberty Leading the People* did not go on permanent public display until 1863, after a vast urban renewal program had minimized the possibility of angry citizens again taking control of the streets.

Where Delacroix glorifies violence in the service of democracy in *Liberty Leading the People*, Picasso condemns the violence that fascism unleashed

3.11 Eugène Delacroix. *Liberty Leading the People, 1830*. 1830. Oil on canvas, 8'6" × 10'10". Musée du Louvre, Paris.

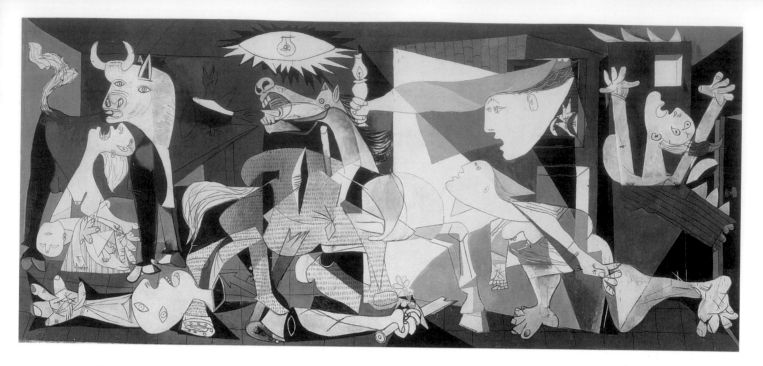

3.12 Pablo Picasso. *Guernica.* 1937. Oil on canvas, 11'5½" × 25'5¾".
Museo Nacional Centro de Arte Reina Sofia, Madrid.

against ordinary citizens in *Guernica*, one of the most famous paintings of the 20th century (**3.12**). *Guernica* depicts an event that took place during the Spanish Civil War, when a coalition of conservative, traditional, and fascist forces led by General Francisco Franco were trying to topple the liberal government of the fledgling Spanish Republic. In Germany and Italy, the fascist governments of Hitler and Mussolini were already in power. Franco willingly accepted their aid, and in exchange he allowed the Nazis to test their developing air power. On April 28, 1937, the Germans bombed the town of Guernica, the old Basque capital in northern Spain. There was no real military reason for the raid; it was simply an experiment to see whether aerial bombing could wipe out a whole city. Being totally defenseless, Guernica was devastated and its civilian population massacred.

At the time Picasso, himself a Spaniard, was working in Paris and had been commissioned by his government to paint a mural for the Spanish Pavilion of the Paris World's Fair of 1937. For some time he had procrastinated about fulfilling the commission; then, within days after news of the bombing reached Paris, he started *Guernica* and completed it in little over a month. The finished mural shocked those who saw it; it remains today a chillingly dramatic protest against the brutality of war.

At first encounter with *Guernica* the viewer is overwhelmed by its presence. The painting is huge—more than 25 feet long and nearly 12 feet high—and its stark, powerful imagery seems to reach out and engulf the observer. Picasso used no colors; the whole painting is done in white and black and shades of gray, possibly to create a "newsprint" quality in reporting the event. Although the artist's symbolism is very personal (and he declined to explain it in detail), we cannot misunderstand the scenes of extreme pain and anguish throughout the canvas. At far left a shrieking mother holds her dead child, and at far right another woman, in a burning house, screams in agony. The gaping mouths and clenched hands speak of disbelief at such mindless cruelty.

Like *Liberty Leading the People*, *Guernica* also has had an interesting political afterlife. Franco's forces were triumphant. Picasso refused to allow Guernica to reside in Spain while Franco was in power, and so for years it was displayed at the Museum of Modern Art in New York. When Franco died in 1975, the painting was returned to Spain, but there another debate ensued: Where in Spain should it stay? The town of Guernica wanted it. So did the town where Picasso was born. Madrid, the Spanish capital, won out in the end. The Basque Nationalist Movement, which would like to see the Basque territories secede from Spain, considers that Madrid kidnapped their rightful cultural property. Guernica is now displayed under bulletproof glass.

It was photography, of course, that made *Guernica* famous. When the painting was unveiled at the 1937 World's Fair, photographs of it circulated immediately in newspapers around the world. A photograph of the painting is what you see in this book. For anyone longing to reach a mass audience with images that urged a political or social message, photography—including films, newsreels, television, and photomechanically reproduced posters—emerged during the 20th century as the most effective means. Many artists involved in the traditional fine art fields of painting and sculpture—especially those pioneering nonrepresentational approaches—came to believe that art should have nothing to do with politics. Many felt that representation itself had become debased through the constant barrage of images in the mass media. Other artists continued to believe that making political and social statements was important, in part because of their personal beliefs, but also because the cultural prestige of art gave these statements a different weight.

During the 1980s, many artists began to work with photographic images, often from a critical standpoint. An important artist to emerge during this decade was Barbara Kruger, who juxtaposed found or created images with terse statements such as *We Will No Longer Be Seen and Not Heard* (**3.13**). Kruger's art was nourished by a strong feminist viewpoint. She had been an art director for leading women's magazines, and she knew well how such publications use images to manipulate their readers. Here she turns the tables, using the visual language of advertising to talk back to authority. Each word in the statement is juxtaposed with a photograph of its equivalent in sign language, suggesting that even if women are denied a voice within the current social order, they will find a way to make themselves understood.

3.13 Barbara Kruger. *Untitled (We Will No Longer Be Seen and Not Heard).* 1985. Nine color lithographs with photo-lino and silkscreen, each 20½ × 20½". Tate Gallery, London.

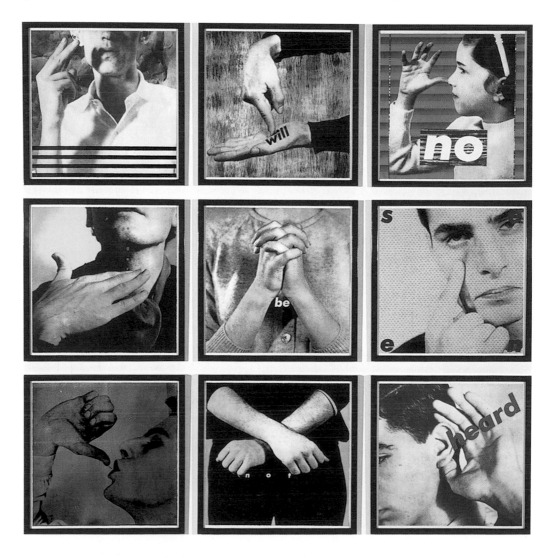

STORIES AND HISTORIES

Deeds of heroes, lives of saints, folktales passed down through generations, episodes of television shows that everyone knows by heart—shared stories are one of the ways we create a sense of community. Artists have often turned to stories for subject matter, especially stories whose roots reach deep into their culture's collective memory.

In Christian Europe of the early 15th century, stories of the lives of the saints were a common reference point. One of the best-loved saints was Francis of Assisi, who had lived only about two centuries earlier. The son of a wealthy merchant in the Italian town of Assisi, Francis as a young man renounced his inheritance for a life of extreme poverty in the service of God. He preached to all who would listen (including birds and animals) and cared for the poor and the sick. With the disciples who gathered around him he founded a religious community that was eventually formalized as the Franciscan Order of monks.

The painting here by the 15th-century Italian artist Sassetta illustrates two episodes from Saint Francis' life (**3.14**). To the left, Francis, still a wealthy young man, gives his cloak to a poor man. To the right, Sassetta cleverly uses the house—its front wall made invisible so we can see inside—to create a separate space, a sort of "painting within a painting," for the next part of the story.

3.14 Sassetta. *St. Francis Giving His Mantle to a Poor Man and the Vision of the Heavenly City.* c. 1437–44. Oil on panel, 34¼ × 20¾".
The National Gallery, London.

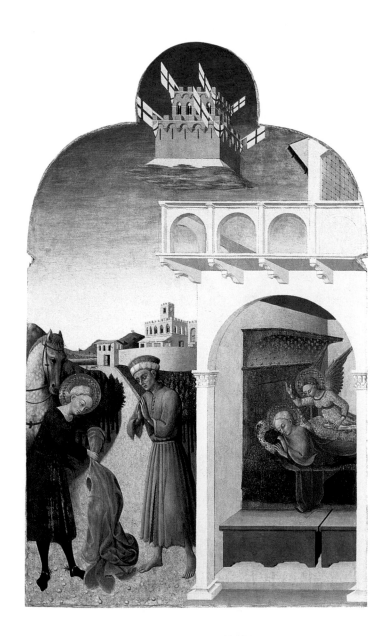

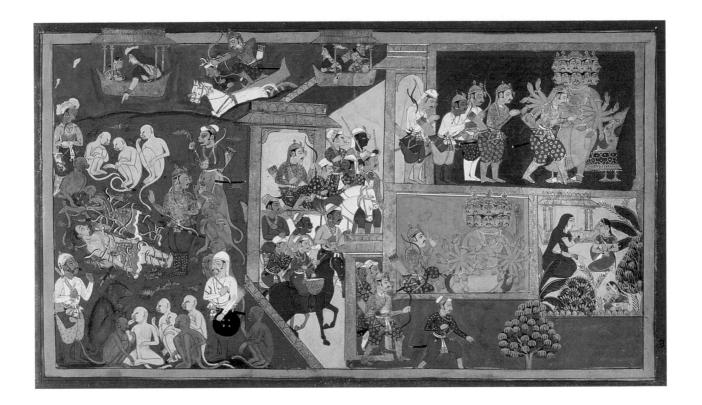

Here, an angel appears while Francis is sleeping and grants him a dream vision of the Heavenly City of God. The angel's upraised hand leads our eyes to the vision, which is portrayed at the top of the panel.

These "painting within a painting" areas are called space cells, and artists in many cultures have used them for narration. The Indian painter Sahibdin made ingenious use of space cells to relate a complicated episode from the epic poem *Ramayana*, or Story of Rama (**3.15**). One of the two great founding Indian epics, the *Ramayana* is attributed to the legendary poet Valmiki, and portions of it date as far back as 500 B.C.E. Rama, the hero of the epic, is a prince and an incarnation of the Hindu god Vishnu. He is heir to the throne of an important Indian kingdom, but due to jealous intrigue he is sent into exile before he can be crowned. Soon afterward, his wife, Sita, is carried off by the demon Ravana. The epic chronicles Rama's search for Sita and his long journey back to his rightful position as a ruler.

In the episode depicted here, Rama suffers a setback as he battles Ravana for Sita's release. The story begins in the small, rose-colored space cell to the right, where Ravana, portrayed with twenty heads and a whirlwind of arms, confers with his son Indrajit on a plan to defeat Rama, who is about to attack the palace. Below, the plan finalized, Indrajit is shown leaving the palace with his warriors. The action now shifts to the left side of the page, where Indrajit, aloft in an airborne chariot, shoots arrows down at Rama and his companion, Lakshmana. The arrows turn into snakes, binding the two heroes. The story continues on the ground, where Indrajit assures the monkey-king Sugriva that Rama and Lakshmana are not dead, but successfully captured. In the yellow cell at the center of the painting, Indrajit stages a triumphal procession back into the palace, where, in the upper right corner, he is joyfully received by Ravana. Meanwhile, Sita, imprisoned in the garden depicted in the yellow space cell immediately below, receives a visit from the demoness Trijata, who takes her in a flying chariot ride (upper left) to witness Rama's defeat. Sahibdin's illustration was made for an audience who knew the epic tale almost by heart and would have delighted in puzzling out the painting's ingenious construction.

3.15 Sahibdin and workshop. *Rama and Lakshmana Bound by Arrow-snakes*, from the *Ramayana*. Mewar, c. 1650–52. Opaque watercolor on paper, c. 9 × 15⅜". The British Library, London.

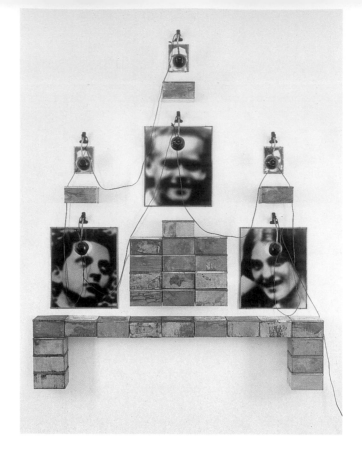

3.16 Christian Boltanski. *Altar to the Chases High School.* 1987. Photographs, tin frames, metal lamps.
Museum of Contemporary Art, Los Angeles.

History has furnished artists with many stories, for history itself is nothing more than a story we tell ourselves about the past, a story we write and rewrite. In *Altar to the Chases High School* (**3.16**) Christian Boltanski draws on our memory of the historical episode known as the Holocaust, the mass murder of European Jews and other populations by the Nazis during World War II. Chases was a private Jewish high school in Vienna. Boltanski began with a photograph that he found of the graduating class of 1931. Eighteen years old in the photograph, the students would have been twenty-seven when Austria was annexed by Germany at the start of the war. Most probably perished in the death camps. Boltanski rephotographed each face, then enlarged the results into a series of blurry portraits. The effect is as though someone long gone were calling out to us; we try to recognize them, but cannot quite. Our task is made even more difficult by the lights blocking their faces, lights that serve as halos on the one hand, but also remind us of interrogation lamps. We wonder, too, what the stacked tin boxes might hold. Ashes? Possessions? Documents? They have no labels, just as the blurred faces have almost no identities.

LOOKING OUTWARD: THE HERE AND NOW

The social order, the world of the sacred, history and the great stories of the past—all these are very grand and important themes. But art does not always have to reach so high. Sometimes it is enough just to look around ourselves and notice what our life is like here, now, in this place, at this time.

Among the earliest images of daily life to have come down to us are those that survived in the tombs of ancient Egypt. Egyptians imagined the afterlife as resembling earthly life in every detail, except that it continued through eternity. To ensure the prosperity of the deceased in the afterlife, scenes of the pleasures and bounty of life in Egypt were painted or carved on the tomb walls. Sometimes models were substituted for paintings (**3.17**).

This model was one of many found in the tomb of an Egyptian official named Meketre, who died around 1990 B.C.E. Meketre himself is depicted at the center, seated on a chair in the shade of a pavilion. Seated on the floor to his left is his son; to his right are several scribes (professional writers) with their writing materials ready. Overseers of Meketre's estate stand by as herders drive his cattle before the reviewing stand so that the scribes can count them. The herders' gestures are animated as they coax the cattle along with their sticks, and the cattle themselves are beautifully observed in their diverse markings.

Another model from Meketre's tomb depicts women at work spinning and weaving cloth. They would probably have been producing linen, which Egyptians excelled at. In China, the favored material since ancient times has been silk. *Court Ladies Preparing Newly Woven Silk* (**3.18**) is a scene from a long handscroll depicting women weaving, ironing, and folding lengths of silk. The painting is a copy made during the 12th century of a famous 8th-century work, now lost. In this scene, four ladies in their elegant robes stretch a length of silk. The woman facing us irons it with a flat-bottomed pan full of hot coals taken from the brazier visible at the right. A little girl too small to share in the task clowns around for our benefit. If this is a scene from everyday life, it is a very rarefied life indeed. These are ladies of the imperial court, and the painting is just as much an exercise in portraying beautiful women as it is in showing their virtuous sense of domestic duty.

3.17 (below, top) Model depicting the counting of livestock, from the tomb of Meketre, Deir el-Bahri. Dynasty 11, 2134–1991 B.C.E. Painted wood, length 5'8". Egyptian Museum, Cairo.

3.18 (below) *Court Ladies Preparing Newly Woven Silk*, detail. Attributed to Hui-zong (1082–1135) but probably by a court painter. Handscroll; ink, colors, and gold on silk; height 14½". Courtesy Museum of Fine Arts, Boston.

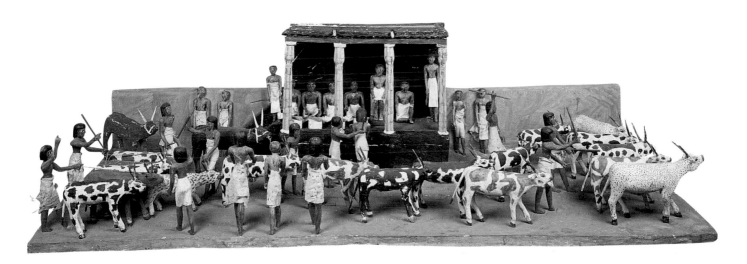

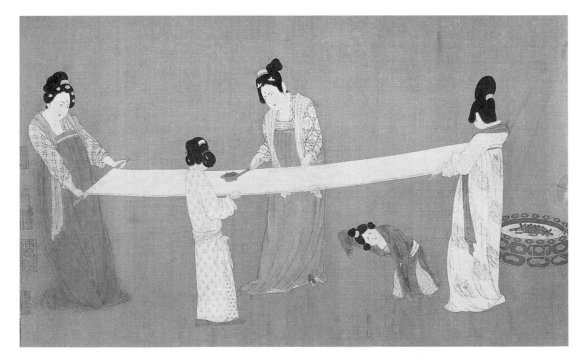

A day off from work altogether is the subject of Georges Seurat's painting *Bathers at Asnières* (**3.19**). Far from the refined atmosphere of the Chinese court, we find ourselves on an unremarkable stretch of river outside Paris, some 1,000 years later and half a world away. In place of the court ladies' sense of community through a shared task, we find a group of young men and boys who seem isolated from each other, alone in their thoughts. They sit at the river's edge or stand in its shallows, their white skin clearly not used to the sun. In the background, a long, low bridge spans the river. Behind it lies a factory with its many tall smokestacks. Industrialization was transforming the countryside during the late 19th century. An issue for artists of the day was how much of this new reality to accept into painting. Even today, many of us seeing such a scene would instinctively aim our cameras elsewhere, trying to preserve the illusion that the river was unspoiled. For Seurat, however, painting the here and now meant finding beauty even in a factory, and dignity in ordinary workers.

Living in New York in the 1960s, Robert Rauschenberg found that the visual impact of daily life had outgrown the ability of any single image to convey it (**3.20**). Instead, in order to communicate the energy and vitality of his time and place, Rauschenberg treated his canvas like a gigantic page in a scrapbook. The result is a kind of controlled chaos in which photographic images drawn from many sources are linked by a poetic process of free association. *Windward*, for example, includes images of the Statue of Liberty, a bald eagle against a rainbow, the Sistine Chapel with Michelangelo's famous frescoes (upper left), Sunkist oranges, Manhattan rooftops and their distinctive water towers (in red), building facades (in blue), and construction workers in plaid shirts and hard hats (in blue, lower right). Part of our pleasure as viewers lies in teasing out their visual and conceptual connections.

The Statue of Liberty and the eagle are symbols of the United States, and the statue is more specifically a tourist attraction of New York. Sunkist oranges are an American product, but Rauschenberg likes their name as well: sunkissed, kissed by the sun. In a repeat of the image directly below, he paints white all of the oranges but one. The single orange becomes a sun, and the rest are clouds. "Sun-kissed" also applies to the rainbow, which is moist air kissed by the

3.19 Georges Seurat. *Bathers at Asnières*. 1883–84. Oil on canvas, 6'10¾" × 9'10⅛".
The National Gallery, London.

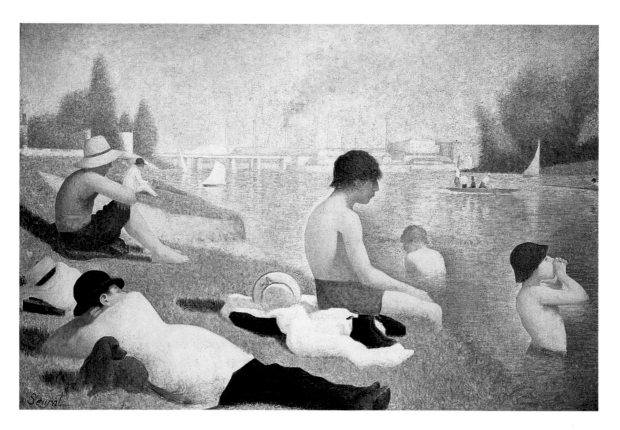

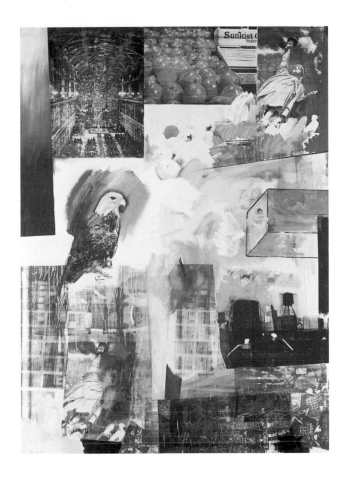

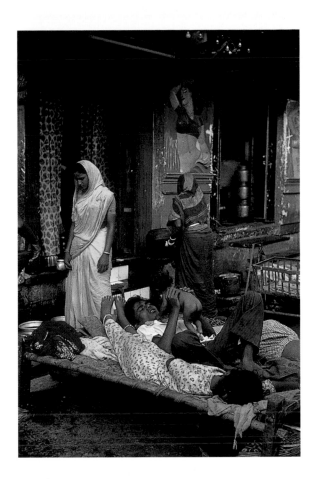

sun. It applies more generally to a clear day in New York, and in the company of the eagle and the statue it evokes the sentiments expressed in one of our most popular patriotic songs, which begins "O beautiful for spacious skies." Again and again we find the optimistic gesture of raising up: Liberty raises her torch high, the rooftops hold aloft their water towers, the Sistine Chapel holds up its great vaulted ceiling, the construction workers build a skyscraper.

Rauschenberg used photographic images to construct *Windward*, but he worked with them as a traditional fine artist would, slowly, over time, in his studio, until the composition that we see before us emerged. Photographers themselves, however, do not have the luxury of time. They must recognize and react instantly to moments when life seems to reveal itself with special clarity. *A Family, Kamathipura, Mumbai, Maharastra* (**3.21**) is one of the hundreds of photographs that the Indian photographer Raghubir Singh made on his journeys across the vast and varied subcontinent of his country. Formerly known as Bombay, Mumbai is a major metropolis that attracts a constant stream of immigrants from small towns and rural regions. They come to the city looking for work, and many, like this family, end up living on the street. Singh's photograph does not document their condition so much as capture a moment of unexpected beauty and mystery that passed through them. Repeating reds link the scene before us to the poster on the wall. The sensuous woman depicted there seems to have some relationship—though we cannot say precisely what it is—with the gentle woman in yellow who lowers her gaze.

When Singh began his career as a photographer, it was widely assumed that "serious" photography had to be in black and white. Color photography was vulgar, color was for painting—Singh's artistic heroes, the great Western photographers of the mid-20th century, had said and believed these things. Even as a young man, however, Singh sensed that India could only be captured in color. "Indians know color through intuition, while the West tries to know it through the mind," he wrote. "Indeed, India is a river of color."[3]

3.20 (left) Robert Rauschenberg. *Windward.* 1963. Oil and silkscreened ink on canvas, 8' × 5'10".
Fondation Beyeler, Riehen/Basel.

3.21 (right) Raghubir Singh. *A Family, Kamathipura, Mumbai, Maharastra.* 1977.
Courtesy the artist's estate.

ROBERT RAUSCHENBERG

b. 1925

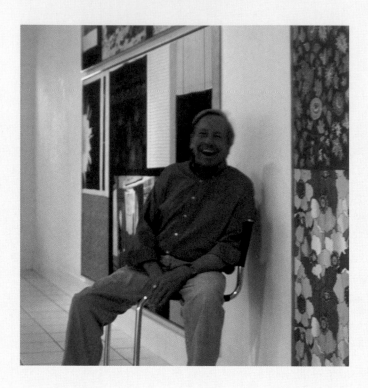

Bᴏʀɴ ɪɴ Pᴏʀᴛ Arthur, Texas, Milton Rauschenberg—who later became known as Bob and then Robert—had no exposure to art as such until he was seventeen. His original intention to become a pharmacist faded when he was expelled from the University of Texas within six months, for failure (he claims) to dissect a frog. After three years in the Navy during World War II, Rauschenberg spent a year at the Kansas City Art Institute; then he traveled to Paris for further study. At the Académie Julian in Paris he met the artist Susan Weil, whom he later married.

Upon his return to the United States in 1948, Rauschenberg enrolled in the now-famous art program headed by the painter Josef Albers at Black Mountain College in North Carolina. Many of his long-term attachments and interests developed during this period, including his close working relationship with the avant-garde choreographer Merce Cunningham. In 1950 Rauschenberg moved to New York, where he supported himself partly by doing window

displays for the fashionable Fifth Avenue stores Bonwit Teller and Tiffany's.

Rauschenberg's work began to attract critical attention soon after his first one-man exhibition at the Betty Parsons Gallery in New York. The artist reports that, between the time Parsons selected the works to be exhibited and the opening of the show, he had completely reworked everything, and that "Betty was surprised." More surprises were soon to come from this steadily unpredictable artist.

The range of Rauschenberg's work makes him difficult to categorize. In addition to paintings, prints, and combination pieces, he has done extensive set and costume design for dances by Cunningham and others, as well as graphic design for magazines and books. "Happenings" and performance art played a role in his work from the very beginning. In 1952, at Black Mountain College, he participated in *Theater Piece #1*, by the composer John Cage, which included improvised dance, recitations, piano music, the playing of old records, and projected slides of Rauschenberg's paintings. Even the works usually classified as paintings are anything but conventional. One has an actual stuffed bird attached to the front of the canvas. Another consists of a bed, with a quilt on it, hung upright on the wall and splashed with paint. Works that might be called sculptures are primarily assemblage; for example, *Sor Aqua* (1973) is composed of a bathtub (with water) above which a large chunk of metal seems to be flying.

In recent years the artist devoted much of his time to ROCI (pronounced "Rocky"), his Rauschenberg Overseas Culture Interchange, which had as its goal promoting international friendship, understanding, and peace. Through ROCI he brought his work to Mexico, Chile, China, Tibet, Germany, Venezuela, Japan, Cuba, and the former Soviet Union.

We get from Rauschenberg a sense of boundaries being dissolved—boundaries between media, between art and nonart, between art and life. He has said: "The strongest thing about my work . . . is the fact that I chose to ennoble the ordinary."[4]

Robert Rauschenberg at home in Captiva, June 1992. Photograph by Richard Schulman.

LOOKING INWARD:
THE HUMAN EXPERIENCE

An Egyptian official, a lady of the imperial Chinese court, and a worker in the suburbs of Paris would all have had very different lives. They would have known different stories, worshiped different gods, seen different sights, and had different understandings of the world and their place in it. Yet they also would have shared certain experiences, just by virtue of being human. We are all of us born, we pass through childhood, we mature into sexual beings, we search for love, we grow old, we die. We experience doubt and wonder, happiness and sorrow, loneliness and despair.

Surely one of the most common of human wishes is to talk, if only we could, if only for a moment, with someone who is no longer here. Many religions embrace the idea that the dead form a vast spirit community capable of helping us. Many rituals have been devised to honor ancestors and appease their spirits. But all of the rituals in the world do not compensate for the ache we sometimes feel when we wish we could speak to those who came before—to tell them what we have become, to ask for guidance, to compare experiences, to explain, to listen.

Meta Warrick Fuller's poignant sculpture *Talking Skull* depicts this wish being granted (**3.22**). Kneeling before the skull, naked and vulnerable, the boy seems to hear an answer to his pleading. On one level, *Talking Skull* embodies a universal message about the desire for communion beyond the boundaries of our brief lifetime. But it is also a specifically African-American work that addresses the traumatic rupture with ancestral culture that slavery had produced. Meta Warrick Fuller was a pioneering African-American artist. Born in 1877, she pursued her artistic training in both the United States and Europe, mastering the conservative, academic style that brought mainstream recognition to artists in her day. Like many of her generation she sought out themes that would help American blacks reconnect with and take pride in their African heritage.

What is our heritage? What role does it play in who we are? No one else can know how it feels to be us, yet we are often no better than others when it comes to understanding the strands of our own selves. *Hood's Red Rider #2* is

3.22 Meta Warrick Fuller. *Talking Skull.* 1937. Bronze, 28 × 40 × 15".
Museum of Afro American History, Boston.

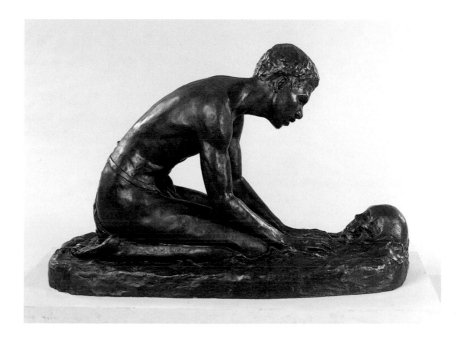

one of many works in which Shahzia Sikander attempts to express her own complex experience (**3.23**). Sikander grew up in Pakistan in a Muslim family, though she is just as intrigued by Hindu art and belief, the other great spiritual tradition of the South Asian subcontinent. As an art student she followed the unusual course of learning the techniques of traditional "miniature" Islamic painting, with its book-page-size images and wealth of detail (see 1.8, 18.7). Continuing her studies in the United States, where she now lives, she found that the miniature tradition provided an ideal form in which to create a sort of theater of her inner life.

A personage who appears again and again in Sikander's paintings is the many-armed floating figure seen here at the upper right. Clearly female, she wears a veil, as would a conservative Islamic woman. At the same time, her multiple arms bristling with weapons evoke the Hindu goddess Devi, the avenger of cosmic disorder. Instead of feet, ropelike forms connect the legs in a circuit, as though the figure drew its nourishment from itself. The figure is a stand-in for the artist, who has described her interest in being self-contained, floating between cultures, not rooted in any one context. "Are you Muslim, Pakistani, artist, painter, Asian, Asian-American, or what?" she says she is asked. "But it is not my agenda to say that I belong to any of these categories."[5]

One of the most reticent yet complete evocations of our existence and its fundamental questions is the Dutch painter Johannes Vermeer's quiet masterpiece *Woman Holding a Balance* (**3.24**). Stillness pervades the picture. A gentle half-light filtered through the curtained window reveals a woman contemplating an empty jeweler's balance. She holds the balance and its two glinting trays

3.23 Shahzia Sikander. *Hood's Red Rider #2*. 1997. Vegetable color, dry pigment, watercolor, tea on hand-prepared paper; 19⅛ × 7⅛".
Private collection.

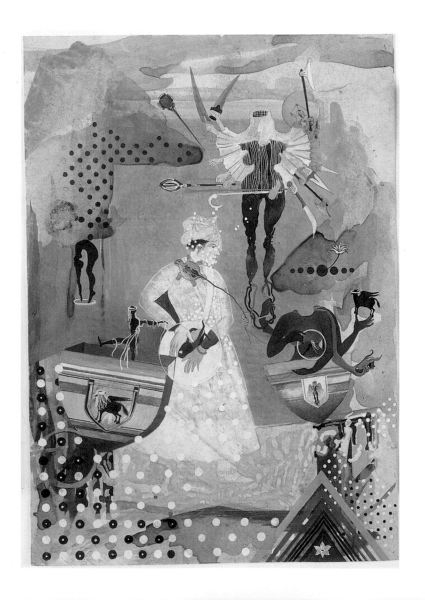

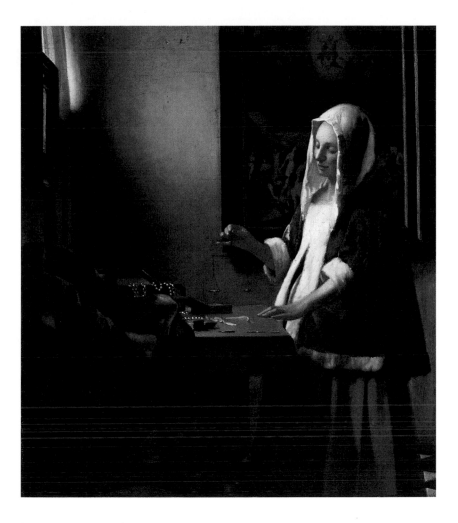

3.24 Johannes Vermeer. *Woman Holding a Balance.* c. 1664. Oil on canvas, 15⅞ × 14".
National Gallery of Art, Washington, D.C.

delicately with her right hand, which falls in the exact center of the composition. The frame of the painting on the wall behind catches the light, drawing our attention. The painting is a depiction of the Last Judgment, when according to Christian belief Christ shall come again to judge, to weigh souls. On the table, the light picks out strands of pearls. Jewels and jewelry often serve as symbols of vanity and the temptations of earthly treasure. Light is reflected too in the surface of the mirror, next to the window. The mirror suggests self-knowledge, and indeed if the woman were to look up, she would be facing directly into it. Scholars have debated whether the woman is pregnant or whether the fashion of the day simply makes her appear so. Either way, we can say that her form evokes pregnancy, the miracle of birth, and the renewal of life.

Birth, death, the decisions we must weigh on our journey through life, the temptations of vanity, the problem of self-knowledge, the question of life after death—all of these issues are gently touched on in this most understated of paintings.

INVENTION AND FANTASY

Renaissance theorists likened painting to poetry. With words, a poet could conjure an imaginary world and fill it with people and events. Painting was even better, for it could bring an imaginary world to life before your eyes. Poetry had long been considered an art, and the idea that painting was comparable to it is one of the factors that led to painting's being considered an art as well.

One of the most bizarrely inventive artists ever to wield a brush was the Netherlandish painter Hieronymus Bosch. When we first encounter his *The*

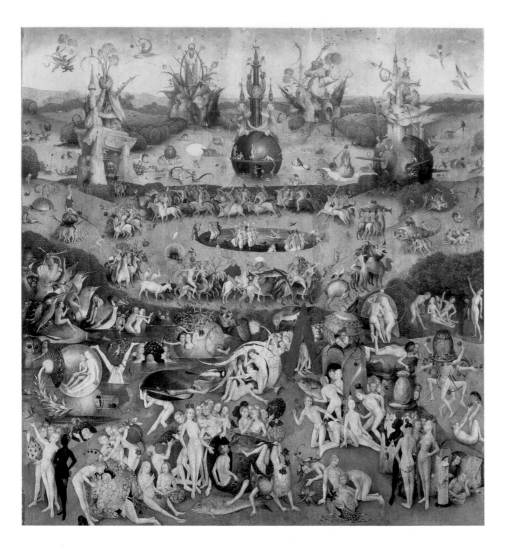

3.25 Hieronymus Bosch. *The Garden of Earthly Delights,* center section. c. 1505–10. Oil on panel, 7'2⅝" × 6'4¾".
Museo del Prado, Madrid.

Garden of Earthly Delights (**3.25**), we might think we have wandered into a fun house of a particularly macabre kind. Bosch's large **triptych** (a three-section panel, of which we show only the middle portion) is like a peep into Hell—but this is an X-rated earthly Hell. Hundreds of nude human figures cavort in a fantasy landscape peopled also by giant plants, animals both known and unknown, and strange creatures that are part human, part vegetation. Humans ride upon, emerge from, are devoured by, or become part of the plant and animal forms. Bosch drew upon many sources for his creations, including folklore, literature, astrology, and religious writings, but only his own inventiveness could have constructed such an amazing fantasy land.

A far more benign imagination was that of Henri Rousseau. Rousseau worked in France during the late 19th and early 20th centuries. He was acquainted with all the up-and-coming artists of the Parisian scene, and sometimes he exhibited with them. The naiveté of his expression came not so much from ignorance of formal art tradition as from indifference to that tradition. His last work, *The Dream* (**3.26**), combines typical elements: a monumental nude perched on a sofa that has no seat; improbable wild animals and birds that never coexist in nature; lush foliage no botanist ever identified; and a dark-skinned "native" (of where?) playing a musical instrument. Rousseau loved to copy plants and animals from books, to fill in from his imagination, to mix and match in a picture as the inspiration took him. He labored over the meticulous rendering of every leaf and stem, yet the rendering is not lifelike at all, for the landscape does not exist; it is a fantasy land. Rousseau's world—which was apparently very real for him—is the paint on canvas that makes a rich, complex design for the viewer's pleasure.

Rousseau's reclining woman strikes a classic pinup pose, one that was handed down through the history of Western art before passing into popular culture. We find it in an ancient Greek painting of shirtless young men at a party, and again in Michelangelo's famous envisioning of the creation of Adam (see 16.12), which may in part have inspired Rousseau's work. (Could this be Eve in Paradise?) Most especially, we find it from the Renaissance onward in numerous paintings of nude or scantily clad women, often representing mythical goddesses while at the same time answering to male fantasies. In *Empty Dream*, Japanese artist Mariko Mori inserts herself into this tradition even as she pokes fun at it (**3.27**). She sets her fantasy scene on a beach, where bodies are routinely on display, and casts herself as a mermaid—three mermaids, actually, all in rather hokey bathing beauty poses. "That's right," Mori's mermaid seems to say, "I'm a goddess." Ordinary mortals stare and point their video cameras. Mori pieced the image together on a computer from digitized photographic fragments, a process we can think of as similar to the way our brain draws on fragments of memory to create dreams.

3.26 (below, top) Henri Rousseau. *The Dream*. 1910. Oil on canvas, 6'8½" × 9'9½". The Museum of Modern Art, New York.

3.27 (below) Mariko Mori. *Empty Dream*. 1995. Cibachrome print, aluminum frame; 9' × 24' × 3". Courtesy Deitch Projects, New York.

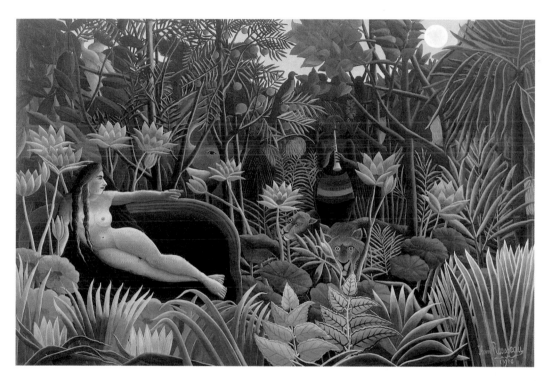

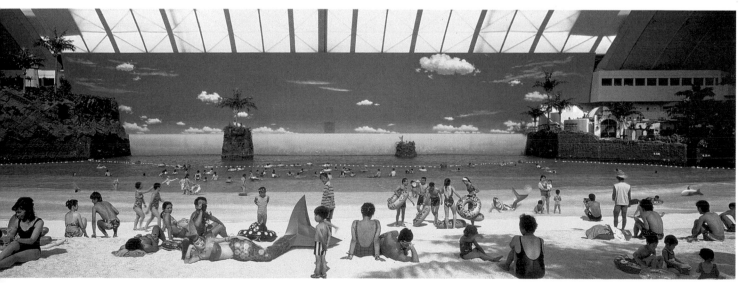

ART AND NATURE

As humans we make our own environment. From the first tools of the earliest hominids to today's towering skyscrapers, we have shaped the world around us to our needs. This manufactured environment, though, has its setting in quite a different environment, that of the natural world. Nature and our relationship to it are themes that have often been addressed through art.

During the 19th century, many painters set out to record the American landscape. For Thomas Cole, who as a young man had emigrated to America from England, the land itself was the new country's greatest heritage, the equal of the ancient architectural wonders of Europe. In *The Oxbow* Cole depicted a curiosity of the New England countryside, the great loop of the Connecticut River as it passes through Northampton, Massachusetts (**3.28**). To the left, a violent thunderstorm passes over a mountaintop where gnarled and damaged trees bear witness to the raw power of nature. To the right, emerging into the sunlight after the storm, there extends a broad settled valley. Fields have been cleared for grazing and for crops. Minute plumes of smoke mark scattered farmhouses, and a few boats dot the river. Cole even gives us a role to play: We have accompanied him on his painting expedition and climbed up a little higher for an even better view. On a promontory below us to the right, we see the artist's umbrella and knapsack. A little to the left and down from the umbrella, Thomas Cole himself, seated in front of a painting in progress, looks up at us over his shoulder.

Cole's canvas faithfully records a view he observed. In contrast, Wang Jian's *White Clouds over Xiao and Xiang* (**3.29**), while it is named for an actual place, portrays an imagined landscape, a construct of the mind. Landscape is

3.28 Thomas Cole. *The Oxbow (View from Mount Holyoke, Northampton, Massachusetts, After a Thunderstorm)*. 1836. Oil on canvas, 4'3½" × 6'4". The Metropolitan Museum of Art, New York.

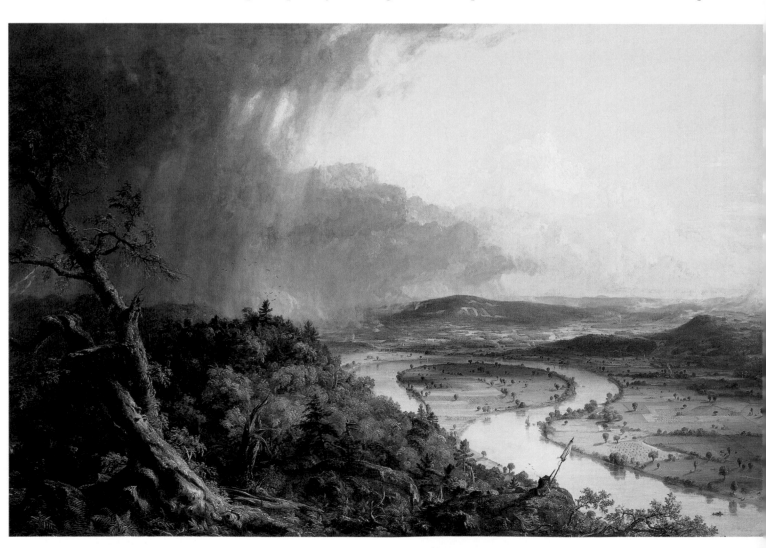

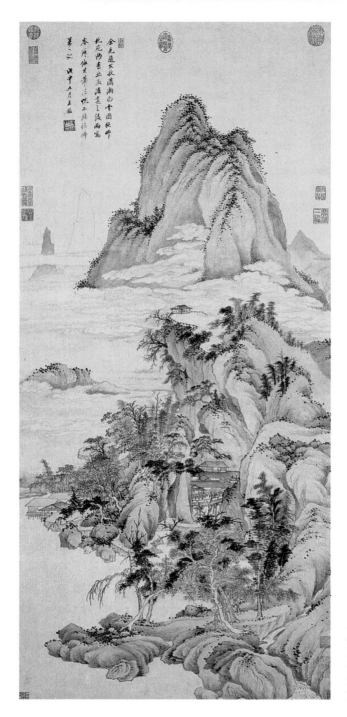

3.29 Wang Jian. *White Clouds over Xiao and Xiang.* 1668. Hanging scroll, ink and color on paper; height 53¼".
Freer Gallery of Art, Smithsonian Institution, Washington, D.C.

the most important and honored subject in the Chinese painting tradition, but its purpose was never to record the details of a particular site or view. Rather, painters learned to paint mountains, rocks, trees, and water so that they could construct imaginary landscapes for viewers to wander through in the mind's eye. Here, we might stroll along the narrow footpath by the water's edge to the pavilions that sit out over the lake, visit the rambling house nestled in the hillside, or stand in the pavilion on the overlook higher up, taking in the scenery. While Cole's painting places us on the mountain and depicts what can be seen from a fixed position, Wang Jian's suspends us in midair and depicts a view that we could see only if we were mobile, like a bird.

Nature has been more than a subject for art; it has also served as a material for art. The desire to portray landscapes has been matched by the desire to create them for the pleasure of our eyes. A work such as the famed stone and gravel garden of the Buddhist temple of Ryoan-ji in Kyoto, Japan, seems to occupy a position halfway between sculpture and landscape gardening

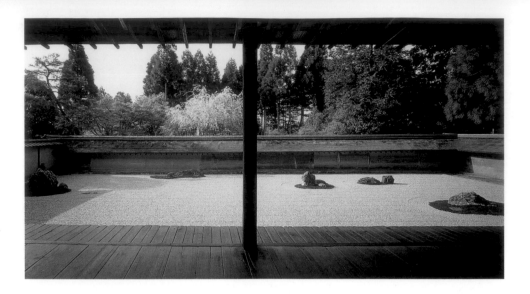

3.30 Stone and gravel garden, Ryoan-ji Temple, Kyoto. Muromachi period, c. 1480.

(**3.30**). Created toward the end of the 15th century and maintained continuously since then, the garden consists solely of five groupings of rocks set in a rectangular expanse of raked white gravel and surrounded by an earthen wall. A simple wooden viewing platform runs along one side. Over time, moss has grown up around the rock groupings, and oil in the clay walls has seeped to the surface, forming patterns that call to mind traditional Japanese ink paintings of landscape. The garden is a place of meditation, and viewers are invited to find their own meanings in it.

The simplicity of Ryoan-ji finds an echo in *Spiral Jetty,* an earthwork built by American artist Robert Smithson in 1970 in the Great Salt Lake, Utah (**3.31**). Smithson had become fascinated with the ecology of salt lakes, especially with the microbacteria that tinge their water shades of red. After viewing the Great Salt Lake in Utah, he leased a parcel of land on its shore and began work on this large coil of rock and earth. Smithson was drawn to the idea that an artist could participate in the shaping of landscape almost as a geological force. Like the garden at Ryoan-ji, *Spiral Jetty* continued to change according to natural processes after it was finished. Salt crystals accumulated and sparkled on its edges. Depths of water in and around it showed themselves in different tints of transparent violet, pink, and red.

Spiral Jetty was submerged by the rising waters of the lake soon after it was created. Recently it resurfaced, transformed by a coating of salt crystals. But most people know it (and will continue to know it) through photographs. The photograph here was taken by Smithson himself. Interestingly, like Brancusi, whose photograph of his own sculpture opened this book, Smithson chose to portray his work interacting with sunlight, thus emphasizing the shifts in mood and character that reflected its place as part of the natural world.

ART AND ART

When asked why he made art, the American painter Barnett Newman is said to have replied, "To have something to look at." There is more than a little truth in his comment. Art is an activity we have come to pursue for its own sake. As such, art can be its own theme, with no other purpose than to give visual pleasure or to pose another answer to the ongoing question, "What is art?"

Jeff Wall is an artist who often sets up a dialogue with earlier art in his work. *A Sudden Gust of Wind (after Hokusai)* (**3.33**) shows him thinking about Hokusai's *Ejira in Suruga Province* (**3.32**). Wall takes seriously the idea, touched on in Chapter 2, that photography has taken over from painting the project of depicting modern life. But he does not practice photography in a straightforward way, going into the world to take pictures of objects he sees or events he witnesses. Instead, he uses the technology of photography to construct an image, much as a painter organizes a painting or a film director goes about making the artificial reality of a film. He builds a set or scouts a location, he sets up the lighting or waits for the right weather, and he costumes and poses his models. Often, as here, he uses digital technology to combine many separately photographed elements into a single image. Wall displays the finished works as large-format transparencies lit from behind. *A Sudden Gust of Wind* is almost the size of a billboard, a glowing billboard.

Typically, what Wall wants us to see only comes into focus once we have the "art behind the art" in mind. Hokusai's *Ejira in Suruga Province* is from *Thirty-Six Views of Mt. Fuji,* a series of views of daily life in Japan linked by the presence of the serene mountain in the distance. Like Hokusai, Wall sets his scene in a nondescript place, a flat land that is nowhere in particular. He re-creates the two trees, the travelers, and the wind-scattered papers. But there is no sublime mountain in the background, nothing to give the scene a larger meaning or sense of purpose. Without knowing Hokusai's print, we would not realize that the most powerful presence in Wall's photograph is an absence, the mountain that is not there.

3.31 (left) Robert Smithson. *Spiral Jetty.* 1970. Rock, salt crystals, earth, algae, coil length 1500'. Great Salt Lake, Utah. Photograph by Robert Smithson, courtesy James Cohan Gallery, New York.

3.32 (right) Hokusai. *Ejira in Suruga Province,* from *Thirty-six Views of Mt. Fuji.* c. 1831. Polychrome woodblock print, 9⅜ × 14⅞". Honolulu Academy of Arts.

3.33 (below) Jeff Wall. *A Sudden Gust of Wind (after Hokusai).* 1993. Transparency in lightbox, 7'6⅞" × 12'4⁵⁄₁₆". Courtesy Marian Goodman Gallery.

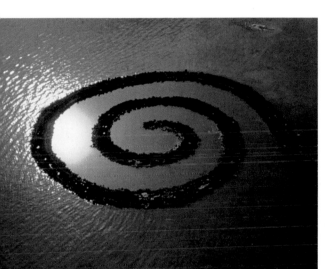

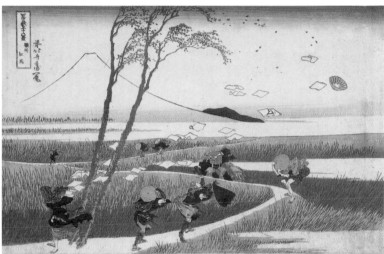

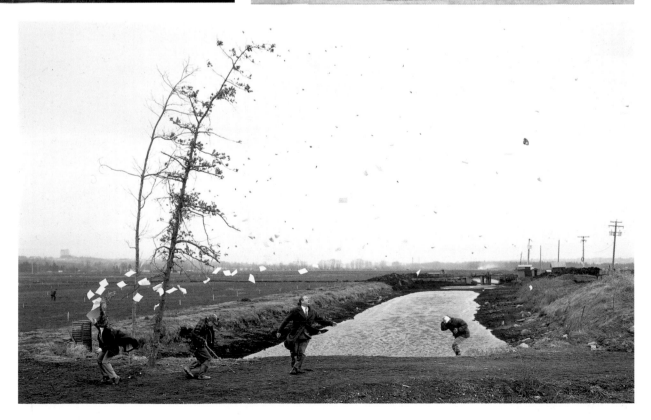

KATSUSHIKA HOKUSAI

1760–1849

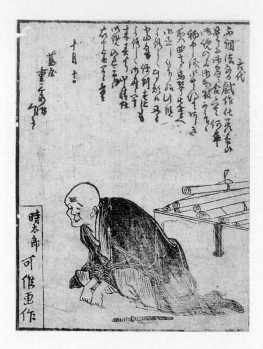

ONE OF THE most delightfully eccentric figures in the history of art is the Japanese painter and woodcut designer who has come to be known as Hokusai. During his eighty-nine years Hokusai lived in at least ninety different houses and used some fifty names. The name that stuck for posterity—Hokusai—means "Star of the Northern Constellation."

Hokusai was born in the city of Edo (now Tokyo), the son of a metal engraver. At the age of eighteen he was sent as an apprentice to the print designer Katsukawa Shunsho. So impressed was the master with his pupil's work that he allowed the young man to adopt part of his own name, and for several years Hokusai called himself "Shunro." Later the two quarreled, and Hokusai changed his name.

Even in his early years Hokusai always worked very quickly, producing huge quantities of drawings. As he finished a drawing, he would toss it on the floor, until there were papers scattered all over the studio, making cleaning impossible. When the house got too filthy and disorderly, he would simply move to another, followed by his long-suffering wife.

Hokusai's first book of sketches was published in 1800 and showed various scenes in and around Edo.

That same year the artist produced a novel, which he sent off to a publisher accompanied by the self-portrait shown here. (Hokusai's head is shaved in the manner of Japanese artists and writers of that time.) Both books achieved a popular success, but characteristically, Hokusai never bothered to open the packets of money sent by his publisher. If a creditor stopped by, he would hand over a packet or two without counting it. Throughout his life he remained indifferent to money and despite his great accomplishments was usually at the brink of starvation.

As Hokusai's fame spread he was often invited to give public drawing demonstrations. Legends of his virtuosity abound. On one occasion, the story goes, he stood before the assembled crowd outside a temple and drew an immense image of the Buddha, using a brush as big as a broom. Another time he drew birds in flight on a single grain of rice. Hokusai's sense of humor, never far below the surface, came bubbling out when he was asked to perform for the Shogun (the military governor). As onlookers gathered at the palace, Hokusai spread a large piece of paper on the floor, painted blue watercolor waves across it, then took a live rooster, dipped its feet in red paint, and allowed it to run across the painting. Bowing respectfully, he announced to the Shogun that his creation was a picture of red maple leaves floating down the river.[6]

Though well aware of his own skill, Hokusai often amused himself by pretending modesty. In the preface to one of his books he wrote: "From the age of six I had a mania for drawing. At seventy-three I had learned a little . . . in consequence when I am eighty I shall have made still more progress, and when I am a hundred and ten, everything I do . . . will be alive." But the artist did not make it quite that far. As he lay on his deathbed, he cried out: "If Heaven would grant me ten more years!" And then: "If Heaven would grant me *five* more years, I would become a real painter."[7] His grave is marked by a slab on which is carved the last of his names: Gwakio Rojin—Old Man Mad About Drawing.

Katsushika Hokusai. *Kamado Shogun Kanryaku no Maki (Self-Portrait),* from *The Tactics of General Oven.* 1800. Woodcut, 8⅞ × 5⅞". The Art Institute of Chicago.

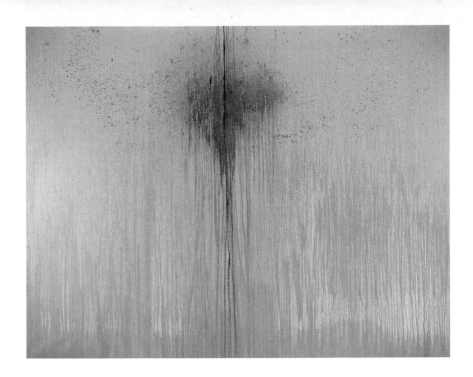

3.34 Pat Steir. *Summer Moon.* 2005. Oil on canvas, 9'1½" × 11'5". Courtesy Cheim and Read Gallery, New York.

Wall's photographs are an example of the intellectual side of art's involvement with art. The recent paintings of Pat Steir, in contrast, explore varieties of visual delight, the natural, instinctive pleasure we can take in the everyday experience of looking (**3.34**). At slightly over 9 feet in height and 11 feet wide, *Summer Moon* looms before us as an enveloping presence. Our attention gravitates initially to the dark shape at the center. Made of thinned paint that was thrown and spattered and allowed to trickle down the canvas, it embodies the energy of its formation. Seen against the calmer background, it evokes suddenness and surprise followed by echoes and fadings. It could be the record of an explosion, like a firework and its embers—an event in the night sky as the moon is an event. It could be a sound, like pebbles thrown into a night pond.

The rest of the painting appears as a lush, shimmering stillness, a landscape of pale green and gold formed by layers of thinned paint allowed to run in rivulets down the surface, like rain down a windowpane. Intermingled are rivulets of some clear liquid that stripped the paint away or diluted it to transparency. The building up and stripping away often seem to have occurred simultaneously, everywhere and all at once. From a purely technical point of view, the painting is a marvel. How was it done?

If we like, we can easily find ways of anchoring *Summer Moon* in the world of art that has preceded it. But the greater pleasure lies in the beauty of the paint itself, the wonder of its application, the shuttling back and forth between the words "summer moon" and what we see before us. That pleasure is available to anyone, no matter what they may or may not know about the concept of "art."

RELATED RESOURCES ONLINE

For more information, definitions, interactive activities, Web links, and videos related to the "Living with Art" material covered in this part, please go to **www.mhhe.com/lwa8.**

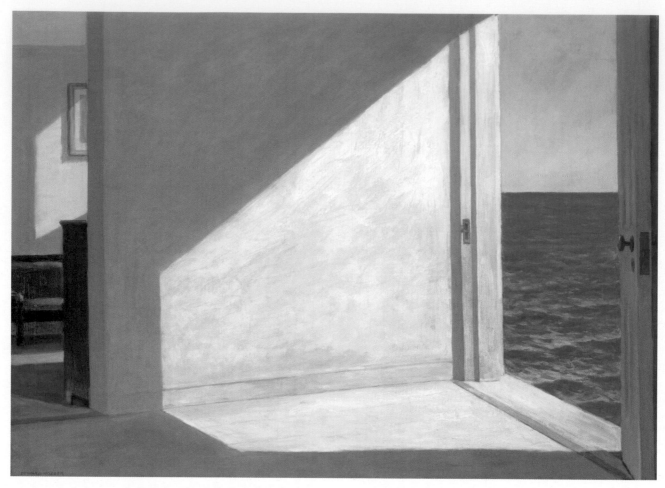

4.1 Edward Hopper. *Rooms by the Sea*. 1951. Oil on canvas, 29 × 40".
Yale University Art Gallery, New Haven

PART TWO
The Vocabulary of Art

CHAPTER FOUR

THE VISUAL ELEMENTS

I f somebody asked you what you see in our first illustration (**4.1**), you might say something like "a bright patch of sunlight and a doorway that opens onto an ocean view." This is a form of shorthand that we use all the time when looking at images, for we know of course that it is not a doorway and a patch of sunlight at all, but a painting of a doorway and sunlight, a painting by Edward Hopper. In learning to appreciate art, we want to become as aware of the painting as we are of what it depicts, and to do this we need a vocabulary for talking about what we see.

Earlier chapters have presented some terms that allow us to describe the painting's appearance in general: It is *representational and naturalistic,* yet it is also attentive to *abstract* values such as the rectangle of the sky and the trapezoids of the ocean, the light on the white wall, and the light on the yellow floor. *Stylistic* clues suggest that it is a Western work of the 20th century. Viewers who know many of Hopper's paintings might guess that this work is from his hand, but then again they might hesitate, since most of Hopper's interiors include people.

This chapter continues by introducing the elements from which the painting is constructed. Hopper focuses on the sharply defined *shapes* that the *light* creates as it enters the house. He depicts them through abrupt shifts in *value*—dark yellow to pale yellow, dark green to light green, grey to white. Subtler shifts in value also indicate the choppy *texture* of the ocean surface and the masses of the wall and the door. Hopper uses very few *colors* in the painting, primarily red, yellow, and blue. With the sole and small exception of the door handle, there are no curves. Instead, straight *lines* dominate, such as the vertical lines of the doorjamb, the horizontal line of the horizon, and the diagonal lines of the entering sunlight. The size of the sofa and the framed picture in the next room help us gauge the depth of the interior *space* the painting depicts. To the right, however, the space collapses, for there are no clues to help us sense how far away the ocean or the horizon is.

These eight things that Hopper used to construct his picture—line, shape, mass, light, value, color, texture, and space—are the ingredients an artist has available in making any work of art. Called the visual elements, they are the elements that we perceive and respond to when we look at a work's form. During the 20th century, time and motion came increasingly to be used as components of art, and we study them in this chapter as well.

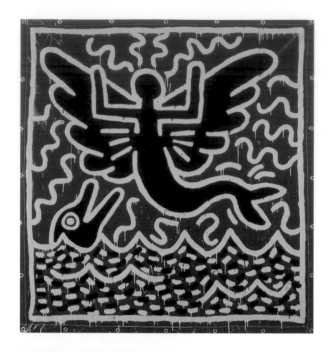

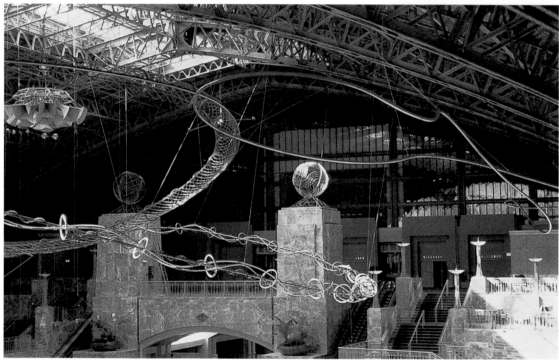

LINE

Strictly defined, a line is a path traced by a moving point. You poise your pencil on a sheet of paper and *move* its point along the surface to make a line.
When you sit down to write a letter or take out your date book to jot down a
note to yourself, you are making lines, lines that are symbols of sounds.

Artists, too, use lines as symbols. Keith Haring used thickly brushed
green lines to portray a winged merman appearing miraculously before an appreciative dolphin (**4.2**). The wavy lines that indicate spiritual energy radiating from the apparition's head are clearly symbolic. But in fact *all* of the lines
in the drawing are symbolic. The merman, for example, is drawn with a green

line, but in reality there is no line separating a body from the air around it. Rather, such lines are symbols of perception. Our mind detaches a figure from everything around it by perceiving a boundary between one region (a body) and another (the air). In drawing, we indicate that boundary with a line.

Lines can be expressive in themselves. Judy Pfaff's ebullient installation *Cirque, Cirque* (**4.3**) is made almost entirely of steel and aluminum tubes that "draw" great looping lines in the air. Pfaff intended the installation to evoke both the thrill of a circus, with its trapeze artists tumbling overhead, and the wonder of the night sky, with its shooting stars and orbiting planets. Following the plainest loop with our eyes, we go on a sort of roller-coaster ride, gliding along the gentle arcs, then speeding up around the tight curves. Following the golden orbit next to it, we spin around and around in a chain of somersaults. Pfaff's installation energizes the vast interior space of the convention center, and suddenly we begin to see lines everywhere—in the girders overhead, in the railings and windowpanes, along the edges of the massive towers.

The ways that Haring and Pfaff use line—to record the borders of form and to convey direction and motion—are the primary functions of line in art. We look more closely at them below.

Contour and Outline

Strictly speaking, an outline defines a two-dimensional shape. For example, drawing with chalk on a blackboard, you might outline the shape of your home state. On a dress pattern, dotted lines outline the shapes of the various pieces. But if you were to make the dress and then draw someone wearing it, you would be drawing the dress's *contours*. Contours are the boundaries we perceive of three-dimensional forms, and **contour lines** are the lines we draw to record those boundaries. Jennifer Pastor used pencil to make a contour drawing of a cowboy riding a bull at a rodeo, one of a series of drawings that record the entire ride from beginning to end (**4.4**). Her confident, even lines capture the contours so skillfully that they suggest fully rounded forms.

4.4 Jennifer Pastor. Sequence 6 from *Flow Chart for "The Perfect Ride" Animation*. 2000. Pencil on paper, 13½ × 17".
Courtesy Regen Projects, Los Angeles.

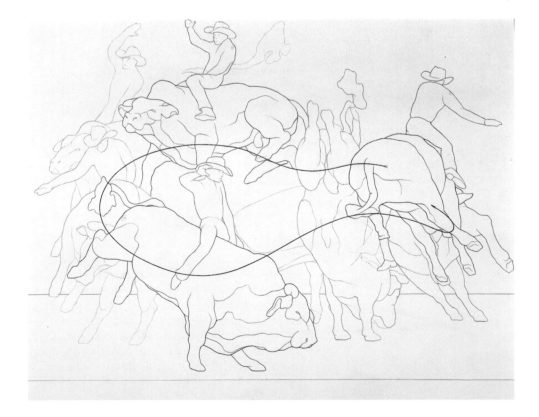

Direction and Movement

In following the looping lines of Judy Pfaff's *Cirque, Cirque,* we were doing what comes naturally. Our eyes tend to follow lines to see where they are going, like a train following a track. Artists can use this tendency to direct our eyes around an image and to suggest movement.

Directional lines play an important role in Henri Cartier-Bresson's photograph of a small Italian town (**4.5**). For Cartier-Bresson, the success of a photograph hinged on what he called the "decisive moment." Here, for example, what probably drew his attention was the woman climbing the stairs and balancing a tray of breads on her head. The small loaves resemble the paving stones so closely that it looks as though a piece of the street were suddenly in motion. Visual coincidences like this delighted Cartier-Bresson, but the decisive moment for the photograph occurred just as the woman was framed by the lines of the iron archway, creating a picture within a picture. Our eyes slide down the line of the steeply pitched railing right to her. Other railing lines carry our eyes into the background, where a cluster of town dwellers stand in the open square. Without the lines of the iron railings, our eyes would not move so efficiently through the picture, and we might miss what Cartier-Bresson wants us to notice.

You may have remarked that the lines our eyes followed most readily were diagonal lines. Most of us have instinctive reactions to the direction of line, which are related to our experience of gravity. Flat, horizontal lines seem

4.5 Henri Cartier-Bresson. *Aquila, Abruzzi, Italy, 1951.* Photograph.

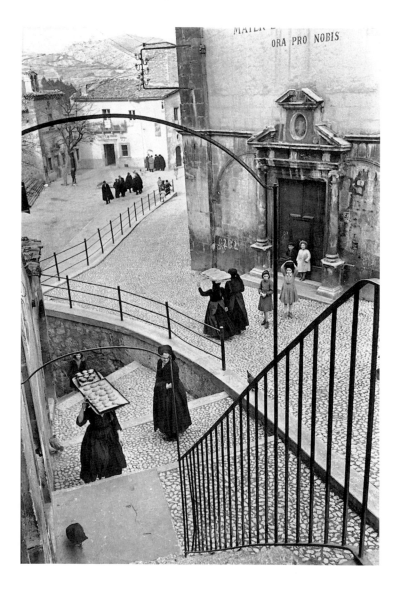

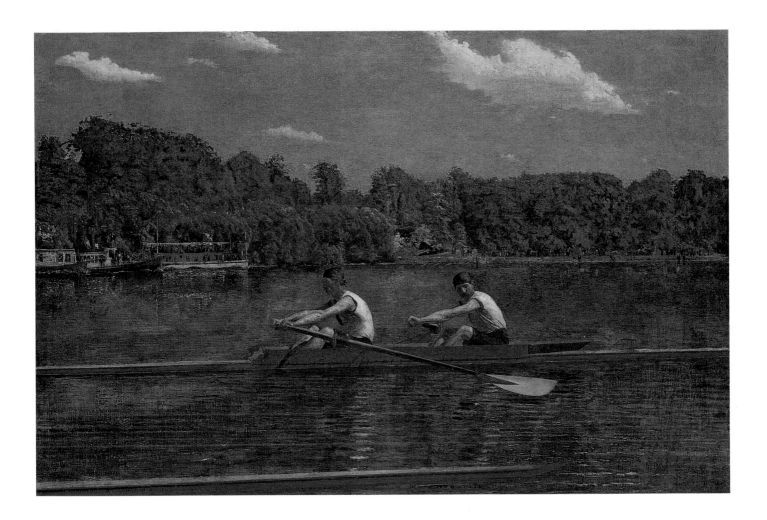

placid, like the horizon line or a body in repose. Vertical lines, like those of an upright body or a skyscraper jutting up from the ground, may have an assertive quality; they defy gravity in their upward thrust. But the most dynamic lines are the diagonals, which almost always imply action. Think of a runner hurtling down the track or a skier down the slope. The body leans forward, so that only the forward motion keeps it from toppling over. Diagonal lines in art have the same effect. We sense motion because the lines seem unstable; we half expect them to topple over.

Thomas Eakins' *The Biglin Brothers Racing* (**4.6**) is stabilized by the long, calm horizontal of the distant shore and its boathouse. The two boats in the foreground are set on the gentlest of diagonals—only a hint, but it is enough to convey their motion. More pronounced diagonals are found in the men's arms and oars. In rowing, arms and oars literally provide the power that sets the boat in motion. In Eakins' painting their diagonals provide the visual power. If you place a ruler over the near oar and then slide it slowly upward, you will see that the treetops to the left and the clouds in the sky repeat this exact diagonal (**4.7**). It is as if the swing of the oar set the entire painting in motion. The subdued diagonals of Eakins' painting perfectly capture the streamlined quality of sculling, in which slender boats knife smoothly and rapidly through the calm water of a river or lake.

Eakins' painting demonstrates that we experience more than literal drawn lines as lines. In fact, we react to any linear form as a line. For example, we can talk about the line of the men's arms or the line of an oar. Oars and arms are not lines, but they are linear. We also react to lines formed by edges. For example, the white contours of the men's backs contrast strongly with the dark behind them, and we perceive the edges of the backs as lines.

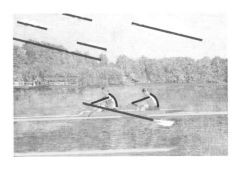

4.6 (above, top) Thomas Eakins. *The Biglin Brothers Racing.* 1873–74. Oil on canvas, 24⅛ × 36⅛".
National Gallery of Art, Washington, D.C.

4.7 (above) Linear analysis of *The Biglin Brothers Racing.*

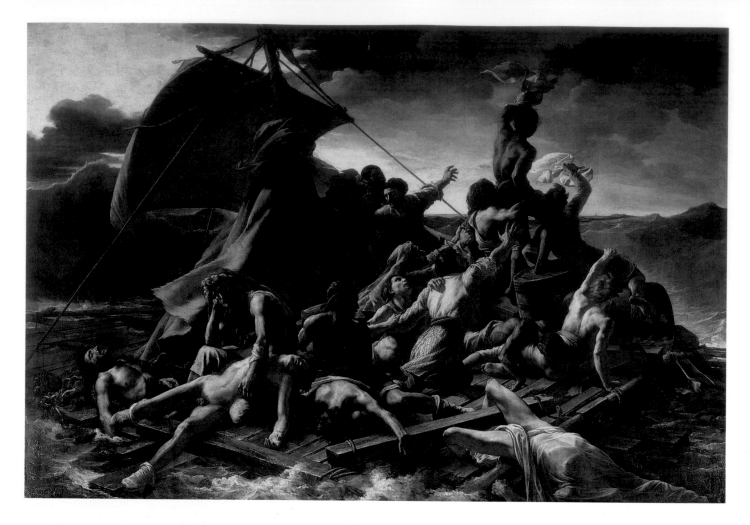

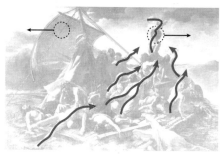

4.8 (above, top) Théodore Géricault. *The Raft of the Medusa.* 1818–19. Oil on canvas, 16'1⅜" × 23'9".

Musée du Louvre, Paris.

4.9 (above) Linear analysis of *The Raft of the Medusa.*

There is a great contrast in linear movement, and thus in emotional effect, between Eakins' work and the next illustration, Théodore Géricault's *The Raft of the Medusa* (**4.8**). Géricault's work is based on an actual event, the wreck of the French government ship *Medusa* off North Africa in 1816. Only a few of those on board survived, some by clinging to a raft. Géricault chose to depict the moment when those on the raft sighted a rescue ship. Virtually all the lines in the composition are diagonal. Géricault uses them to create two conflicting centers of interest, thus increasing the tension of the scene (**4.9**). Picked out by the light, the writhing limbs of the survivors carry our eyes upward to the right, where a dark figure silhouetted dramatically against the sky waves his shirt to attract the rescuers' attention. A lone rope, also silhouetted, carries our eyes leftward to the dark form of the sail, where we realize that the wind is not taking the survivors toward their salvation, but away from it.

Implied Lines

In addition to actual lines, linear forms, and lines formed by edges, our eyes also pick up on lines that are only implied. A common example from everyday life is the dotted line, where a series of dots are spaced closely enough that our mind connects them. The 18th-century French painter Jean-Antoine Watteau created a sort of dotted line of amorous couples in *The Embarkation for Cythera* (**4.10**). Starting with the seated couple at the right, our eyes trace a line that curves in a gentle S and leaves us evaporating into the gauzy air with the infant cupids (**4.11**). Cythera is the mythological island of love. Watteau specialized in elegant scenes in which aristocratic men and women gather in a leafy setting to play at love. Often, as here, the scenes are tinged with a gentle melancholy.

In representational art, the same directional cues we follow in life can create implied lines. When a person stops on a street corner and gazes upward, other passersby will also stop and look up, following the "line" of sight. When someone points a finger, we automatically follow the direction of the point. Watteau uses these implied lines here as well. Looking at the painting, we are drawn eventually to the statue of Venus at the far right. We could be "stuck" there if it were not for her extended arm, which directs our attention down to the first couple below, where the winding procession begins. In addition, most of the couples look at each other, but the most prominent gazes are directed to the right, especially that of the woman who turns at the crest of the hill to look at the couple behind her. The graceful procession toward the shore is undercut by the constant tug of backward glances, and in following them we too are gently pulled back. It is this that gives the painting its slight air of melancholy, prompting many scholars to wonder whether the couples are heading toward the island of love, or whether they are leaving it.

SHAPE AND MASS

A **shape** is a two-dimensional form. It occupies an *area* with identifiable boundaries. Boundaries may be created by line (a square outlined in pencil on white paper), a shift in texture (a square of unmowed lawn in the middle of mowed lawn), or a shift in color (blue polka dots on a red shirt). A **mass** is a three-dimensional form that occupies a *volume* of space. We speak of a mass of clay, the mass of a mountain, the masses of a work of architecture.

4.10 (bottom) Jean-Antoine Watteau. *The Embarkation for Cythera.* 1718–19(?). 50¹³⁄₁₆ × 76⅜". Schloss Charlottenburg, Staatliche Schlösser und Gärten Berlin.

4.11 (below) Linear analysis of *The Embarkation for Cythera.*

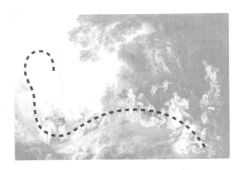

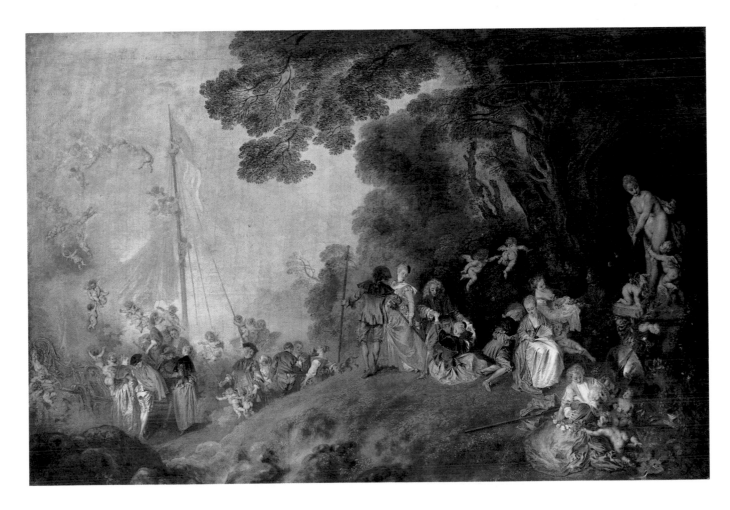

The volume of space displaced by the masses of Bill Reid's monumental sculpture *The Raven and the First Men* (**4.12**) is considerable! Carved from blocks of laminated cedar, the work depicts the birth of humankind as told in the creation stories of the Haida, a people of the Pacific Northwest Coast. The giant bird is a spirit hero called Raven. It was he who discovered the first humans hiding in a clam shell and coaxed them out into the world. The photograph of Reid's sculpture shows how light and shadow reveal the three-dimensional form of a mass to us, letting us sense where it bulges outward or recedes, where it is concave and where convex. But we cannot fully understand mass from a single two-dimensional representation. We would have to walk around the sculpture in person, or have it slowly circled with a video camera, to get a complete idea of its form.

Unlike the masses of *The Raven and the First Men*, the subtle, shadowy shapes of Emmi Whitehorse's *Chanter* are fully available to us on the page (**4.13**). A Navajo artist, Whitehorse is inspired in part by the signs and symbols carved centuries ago into the cliffs of her native region. The shapes in *Chanter* seem to appear and disappear into the background. Some are defined by line, others by a shift in color or value. Still other shapes are only implied—partially indicated in a way that encourages our mind to complete them.

Shapes and masses can be divided into two broad categories, geometric and organic. Geometric shapes and masses approximate the regular, named shapes and volumes of geometry such as square, triangle, circle, cube, pyramid, and sphere. Organic shapes and masses are irregular and evoke the living forms of nature. The masses of Reid's sculpture are organic, whereas Whitehorse used both geometric and organic shapes in her painting. The abstract blue bird at the

4.12 (left) Bill Reid. *The Raven and the First Men.* Completed 1983. Laminated yellow cedar, height 6'2¼".
Museum of Anthropology, University of British Columbia, Vancouver.

4.13 (right) Emmi Whitehorse. *Chanter.* 1991. Oil on paper, mounted on canvas, 39⅛ × 28".
The Saint Louis Art Museum.

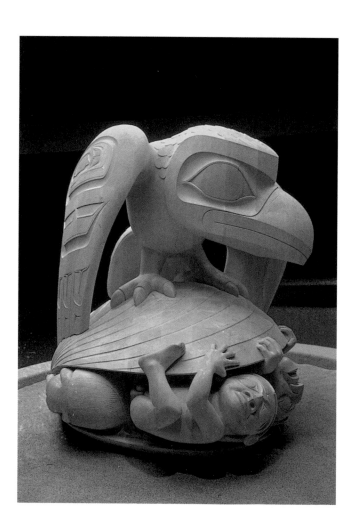

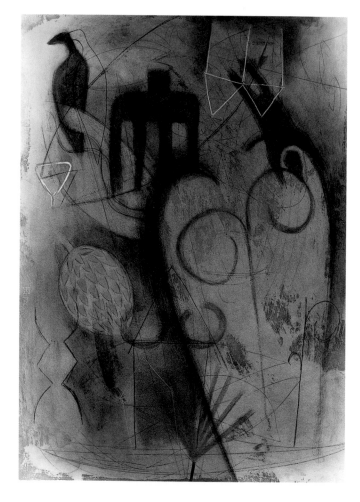

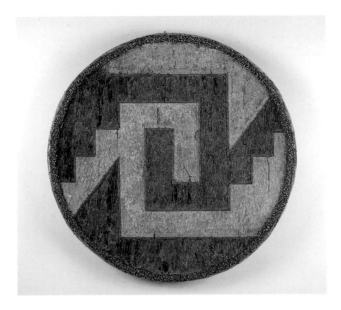

upper left is organic, for example, while the upside-down houselike shapes outlined in white at the top right, rectangle on triangle, are geometric.

We perceive shapes by mentally detaching them from their surroundings and recognizing them as distinct and coherent. We refer to this relationship as figure and ground. A **figure** is the shape we detach and focus on; the **ground** is the surrounding visual information the figure stands out from, the background. In the photograph of *The Raven and the First Men*, we easily recognize the sculpture as the principal figure and the rest of the image as the ground. In *Chanter*, on the other hand, things are not always so clear. For example, the dark blue figure of the bird at the upper left detaches clearly from the pale ground, but just below it this pale ground turns into a figure as well. Figure and ground shift and interpenetrate across the painting, creating a fluid sense of space and a dreamlike atmosphere.

The Aztec feathered shield illustrated next presents us with a further visual puzzle (**4.14**). Made for a military officer as a sign of rank, it can be understood equally well as a light figure on a dark ground or a dark figure on a light ground. If you place a piece of tracing paper over the image and trace the outlines of the light figure, you will find that you have automatically drawn the dark figure as well. In fact, any shape created on a limited, two-dimensional surface creates a second, complementary shape. This is because the surface is already a shape itself—the shield is a circle, *Chanter* and the photograph of *The Raven and the First Men* are rectangles. Any two-dimensional image is thus also a system of interlocking shapes. The shapes we perceive as figures we call **positive shapes;** the shapes of the ground are **negative shapes.** In the photograph of Reid's sculpture, for example, negative shapes appear between the bird's wings and its body. Artists learn to pay equal attention to positive and negative shapes in their work, and we will be better viewers for cultivating this habit as well.

Implied Shapes

Figure **4.15** shows three black circles, each with a wedge taken out, but the very first thing that most of us see is a floating white triangle. Our mind instantly perceived the visual information as a whole—even though that whole doesn't exist! Through optical puzzles such as this, psychology provided a scientific explanation for something that artists had been doing intuitively for centuries, using implied shapes to unify their compositions. In *The Madonna*

4.14 (above) Circular shield with stepped fret design. Aztec, before 1521. Feathers, diameter 27⅝". Württembergisches Landesmuseum, Stuttgart.

4.15 (below) The triangle that isn't there.

of the Meadows (**4.16**), Raphael has grouped the figures of Mary, the young John the Baptist (left), and the young Jesus (right) so that we perceive them as a single, triangular whole. Mary's head defines the apex, and John the Baptist the lower left corner. Defining the lower right corner is Mary's exposed foot, which draws our eye because of the way the pale flesh contrasts with the darker tones around it. If you place a finger over the foot, the implied triangle becomes much less definite, despite the fact that it is reinforced by Mary's red and blue robes.

Just as artists use implied lines to help direct our eyes around a composition, they have used implied shapes to create a sense of order, so that we perceive a work of art as a unified and harmonious whole.

LIGHT

To our distant ancestors light seemed so miraculous that the sun was often considered to be a god and the moon a goddess. Today we know that light is a type of radiant energy, and we have learned how to generate it ourselves through electricity, yet our day-to-day experience of the varying qualities and effects of light is no less marvelous.

4.16 Raphael. *The Madonna of the Meadows.* 1505. Oil on panel, 44½ × 34¼".
Kunsthistorisches Museum, Vienna.

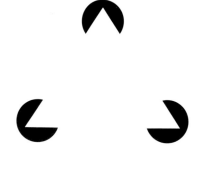

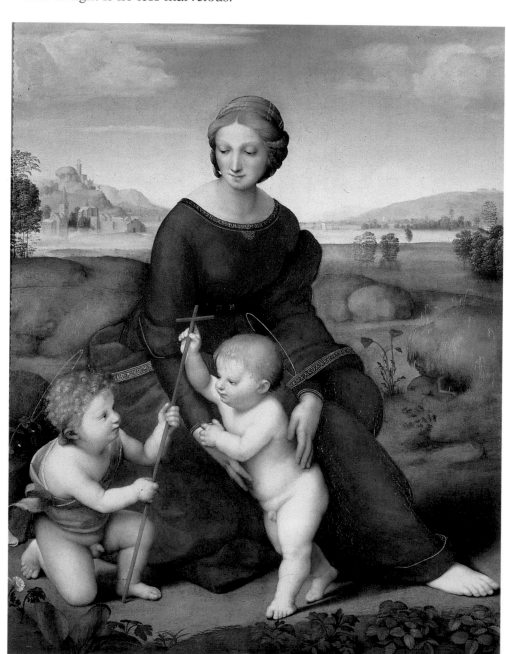

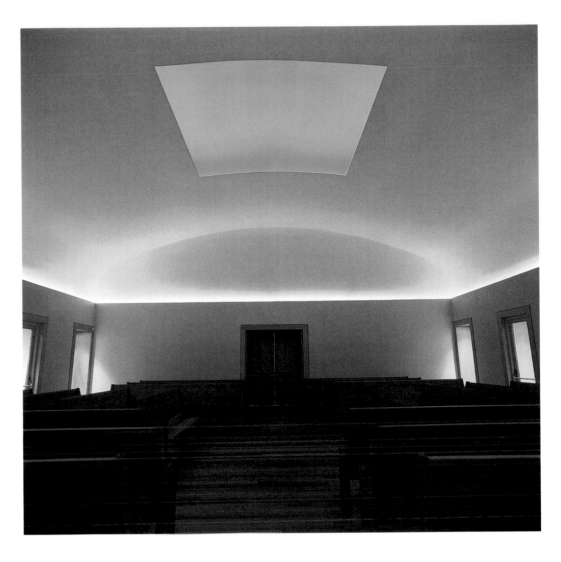

4.17 James Turrell. Live Oak Friends Meeting House, Houston. 2001.

James Turrell is a contemporary artist whose work increases our awareness of light as a presence in the world. Among his creations are ceiling openings he calls "skyspaces"—carefully calculated apertures that frame an unobstructed view of the sky. Turrell has created several skyspaces over the years, including this one in a meetinghouse he designed with architect Leslie K. Elkins for a Quaker community in Houston, Texas (**4.17**). Furnished simply with oak benches set facing each other, the plain white room serves as a neutral space where light can be experienced as a metaphor for spiritual awareness, which Quakers call "the light within." The skyspace here is a 12-foot-square opening set at the center of a curving white ceiling. At Turrell's instruction, overhanging trees that could be seen through the opening from inside were cut down. With no such visual information to serve as a figure, the sky no longer serves as a ground, and thus it no longer appears distant. Instead, a square of luminous color seems to hover close by, sometimes *inside* the room, an optical effect Turrell refers to as "bringing the sky down." Artificial lighting hidden along the base of the ceiling contributes to the impression by causing the ceiling to seem to detach itself from the walls, as though it too were floating.

Implied Light: Modeling Mass in Two Dimensions

Turrell's art is disorienting because it undercuts the most fundamental purpose that light serves for us, which is to reveal the material world to our eyes in a way that helps us understand forms and spatial relationships. In Manuel

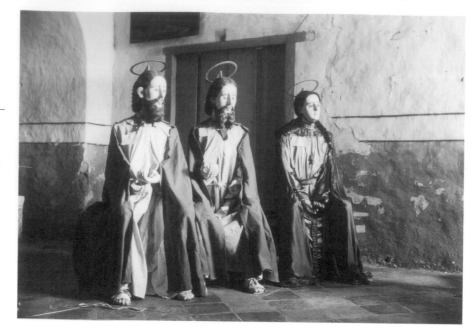

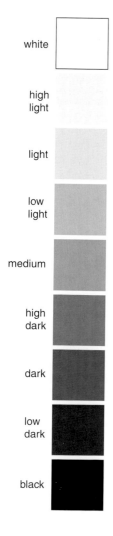

white

high light

light

low light

medium

high dark

dark

low dark

black

Alvarez Bravo's photograph *The Visit* (**4.18**), we understand something of the texture of the back wall and the masses of the robed sculptures because of the way light and shadow **model** them, or give them a three-dimensional appearance. We cannot see the source of light in the photograph, but we understand from the way the shadows fall that it is off to the right, and that the statues are facing almost directly into it.

Black-and-white film has transposed the colors of the original scene into their relative **values,** shades of light and dark. For example, we understand that the statues' cloaks are of a darker color than their robes, even though we don't know what the two colors are. Value exists in a seamless continuum from white (the highest value) to black (the darkest value). For convenience, we often simplify this continuum into a scale, a sequence of equal perceptual steps (**4.19**). The value scale here goes from black to white in nine steps (including both end points). Our eyes are more sensitive than film and can distinguish a greater and more subtle range of values. Nevertheless, thanks to black-and-white photography we can readily understand the idea that the world we see in full color can also be expressed in shades of light and dark, and that every color can also be spoken of in terms of its value.

Photography easily demonstrates how value models mass for our eyes. But photography was invented only in the mid-19th century. Long before then, European painters had become interested in modeling mass in two dimensions through value. Discovered and perfected by Italian painters during the Renaissance, the technique is called **chiaroscuro,** Italian for light/dark. With chiaroscuro, artists employ values—lights and darks—to record contrasts of light and shadow in the natural world, contrasts that model mass for our eyes. One of the great masters of chiaroscuro was Leonardo da Vinci. His unfinished drawing of *The Virgin and Saint Anne with the Christ Child and John the Baptist* (**4.20**) shows the miraculous effects he could achieve. Working on a middle-value brown paper, Leonardo applied charcoal for a range of darks and white chalk for lighter values. The figures seem to be breathed onto the paper, bathed in a soft, allover light that comes from everywhere and nowhere. The roundness that Leonardo's mastery conveys is immediately evident if we look between the heads of the two children at the raised hand of Saint Anne. Drawn with a contour line but not modeled, it looks jarringly flat, as though it does not yet belong to the rest of the image.

Leonardo used continuous tones in his drawing, values that grade evenly into one other. But value can also be indicated with surprising richness by line alone. In the etching shown here, Charles White relied solely on line to model the head of a woman seen in profile (**4.21**). Taking the pale gray of the paper as the highest value, White indicated the next step down in value with **hatching,** areas of closely spaced parallel lines, as on the front of the forehead or the side of the nose. Darker values were achieved through additional sets of parallel lines laid across the first, a technique called **cross-hatching.** Seen from up close the effect seems coarse, but at a certain distance the dark hatch marks seem to average out with the lighter paper into nuanced areas of gray, an effect of perception called optical mixing. Another technique for suggesting value is stippling, in which areas of dots average out through optical mixing into values (**4.22**). As with hatching, the depth of the value depends on density: the more dots in a given area, the darker it appears.

COLOR

It is probably safe to say that none of the visual elements gives us so much pleasure as color. Many people have a favorite color that they are drawn to. They will buy a shirt in that color just for the pleasure of clothing themselves in it, or paint the walls of their room that color for the pleasure of being surrounded by it. Various studies have demonstrated that color affects a wide range of psychological and physiological responses. Restaurants often are

4.20 (left) Leonardo da Vinci. *The Virgin and Saint Anne with the Christ Child and John the Baptist.* Charcoal, black and white chalk on brown paper, 54⅞ × 39⅞".
The National Gallery, London.

4.21 (right, top) Charles White. *Untitled.* 1979. Etching, 4 × 5½".
The Charles White Archives.

4.22 (below) Techniques for modeling mass with lines: hatching, cross-hatching, and stippling.

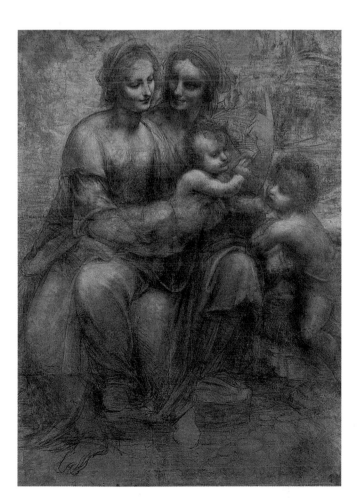

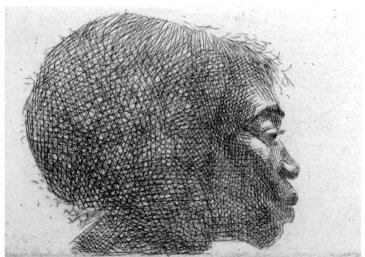

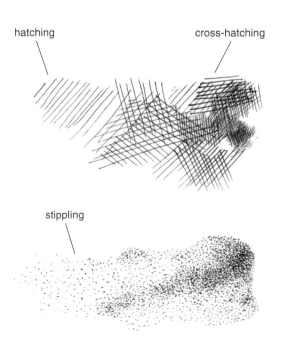

hatching

cross-hatching

stippling

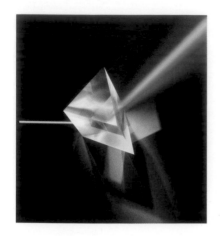

a.

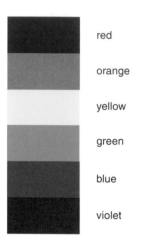

red

orange

yellow

green

blue

violet

b.

decorated in red, which is believed to increase appetite and therefore food consumption. Blue surroundings will significantly lower a person's blood pressure, pulse, and respiration rate. In one experiment subjects were asked to identify, by taste, ordinary mashed potatoes colored bright green. Because of the disorienting color cues, they could not say what they were eating. And in one California detention center violent children are routinely placed in an 8-by-4-foot cell painted bubble-gum pink. The children relax, become calmer, and often fall asleep within ten minutes. This color has been dubbed "passive pink." The mechanism involved in these color responses is still unclear, but there can be no doubt that color "works" on the human brain and body in powerful ways.

Color is a function of light. Without light there can be no color. The principles of color theory explain why this effect occurs.

Color Theory

Much of our present-day color theory can be traced back to experiments made by Sir Isaac Newton, who is better known for his work with the laws of gravity. In 1666 Newton passed a ray of sunlight through a prism, a transparent glass form with nonparallel sides. He observed that the ray of sunlight broke up or **refracted** into different colors, which were arranged in the order of the colors of the rainbow (**4.23**). By setting up a second prism Newton found he could recombine the rainbow colors into white light, like the original sunlight. These experiments proved that colors are actually components of light.

In fact, all colors are dependent on light, and no object possesses color intrinsically. You may own a red shirt and a blue pen and a purple chair, but these items have no color in and of themselves. What we perceive as color is

4.23 (above) **a.** White light separated into spectral colors by a prism. **b.** The colors of the visible spectrum.

4.24 (right) Color wheel.

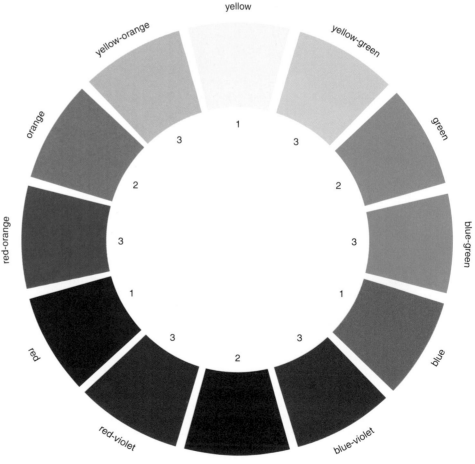

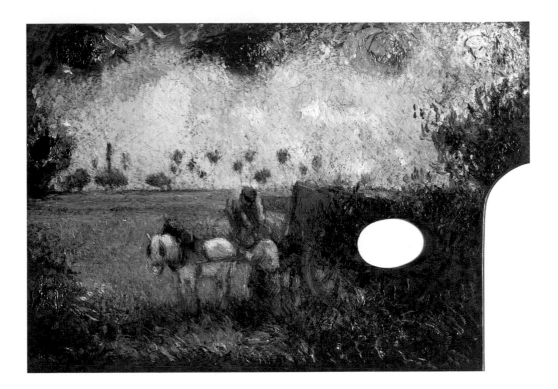

reflected light rays. When light strikes the red shirt, for example, the shirt absorbs all the color rays *except* the red ones, which are reflected, so your eye perceives red. The purple chair reflects the purple rays and absorbs all the others, and so on. Both the physiological activity of the human eye and the science of electromagnetic wavelengths take part in this process.

If we take the colors separated out by Newton's prism—red, orange, yellow, green, blue, and violet—add the transitional color red-violet (which does not exist in the rainbow), and arrange these colors in a circle, we have a **color wheel** (**4.24**). Different theorists have constructed different color wheels, but the one shown here is fairly standard.

Primary colors—red, yellow, and blue—are labeled with the numeral 1 on the color wheel. They are called primary because (theoretically at least) they cannot be made by any mixture of other colors.

Secondary colors—orange, green, and violet—are labeled with the numeral 2. Each is made by combining two primary colors.

Tertiary colors, labeled number 3, are the product of a primary color and an adjacent secondary color. For instance, mixing yellow with green yields yellow-green.

We speak of the colors on the red-orange side of the wheel as **warm colors,** perhaps because of their association with sunlight and firelight. The colors on the blue-green side are **cool colors,** again probably because of their association with sky, water, shade, and so on.

During the 19th century many scientific color theories were published, and painters were quick to try to take advantage of their findings. Some painters, for example, stopped using black altogether on the grounds that it was not a color found in the natural spectrum. Impressionist painter Camille Pissarro left us a witty demonstration of what could be accomplished using what he called a spectral palette (**4.25**). "Palette" refers to the wooden board on which artists traditionally set out their pigments, but it also refers to the range of pigments they select, either for a particular painting or characteristically. Pissarro here gives us both meanings, creating a painting on his wooden palette and leaving the colors he set out to make it around the edge. From the upper right, they are white, yellow, red, violet, blue, and green. Using only these colors and their mixtures, Pissarro painted a delightful landscape of a farmer and his wife with their hay wagon.

4.25 Camille Pissarro. *Palette with a Landscape.* c. 1878. Oil on wooden palette, 9½ × 13⅝". Sterling and Francine Clark Institute, Williamstown, Massachusetts.

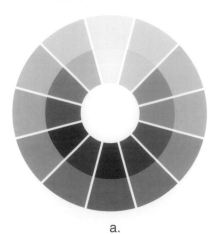

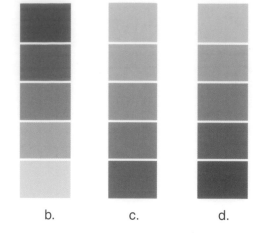

a.   b.   c.   d.

4.26 (above) Color value and intensity.
a. The spectral colors and their corresponding gray-scale values.
b. Blue in a range of values.
c. Yellow-orange progressively dulled with gray.
d. Yellow-orange progressively dulled with blue-violet.

4.27 (below) **a.** Light primaries and their additive mixtures. **b.** Pigment primaries and their subtractive mixtures.

Color Properties

Any color has three properties. They are called hue, value, and intensity.

Hue is the name of the color according to the categories of the color wheel—green or red or blue-violet.

Value, again, refers to relative lightness or darkness. Most colors are recognizable in a full range of values; for instance, we identify as "red" everything from palest pink to darkest maroon. In addition, all hues have what is known as a normal value—the value at which we expect to find that hue. We think of yellow as a "light" color and violet as a "dark" color, for example, even though each has a full range of values. Figure **4.26** shows the hues of the color wheel in relation to a gray value scale (**a**) and the hue blue taken through a range of values (**b**).

A color lighter than the hue's normal value is known as a **tint;** for example, pink is a tint of red. A color darker than the hue's normal value is called a **shade;** maroon is a shade of red.

Intensity—also called **chroma** or **saturation**—refers to the relative purity of a color. Colors may be pure and saturated, as they appear on the color wheel, or they may be dulled and softened to some degree. The purest colors are said to have high intensity; duller colors, lower intensity. To lower the intensity of a color when mixing paints or dyes, the artist may add a combination of black and white (gray) or may add a little of the color's complement, the hue directly opposite to it on the color wheel. Figure **4.26** shows a saturated yellow-orange lowered first with gray (**c**) and then with blue-violet (**d**).

Light and Pigment

Colors behave differently depending on whether an artist is working with light or pigment. In light, as Newton's experiments showed, white is the sum of all colors. People who work directly with light—such as lighting designers who illuminate settings for film, theater, or video productions—learn to mix color by an *additive* process, in which colors of light mix to produce still lighter colors. For example, red and green light mix to produce yellow light. Add blue light to the mix and the result is white. Thus red, green, and blue form the lighting designer's primary triad (**4.27a**).

Pigments, like any other object in the world, have to our eyes the color that they reflect. A red pigment, for example, absorbs all the colors in the spectrum except red. When pigments of different hues are mixed, the resulting color is darker and duller, because together they absorb still more colors from the spectrum. Mixing pigments is thus known as a *subtractive* process (**4.27b**). The closer two pigments are to being complementary colors on the color wheel, the duller their mixture will appear, for the more they will subtract each other from the mix. For example, while red and green light mix to produce yellow light, red and green pigment mix to produce a grayish brown or brownish gray pigment.

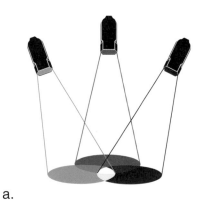

a.

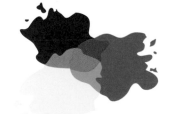

b.

Color Harmonies

A color harmony, sometimes called a color scheme, is the selective use of two or more colors in a single composition. We tend to think of this especially in relation to interior design; you may say, for instance, "The color scheme in my kitchen is blue and green with touches of brown." But color harmonies also apply to the pictorial arts, although they may be more difficult to spot because of differences in value and intensity.

Monochromatic harmonies are composed of variations on the same hue, often with differences of value and intensity. A painting all in reds, pinks, and maroons would be considered to have a monochromatic harmony. In *Nocturne in Blue and Gold* (see 4.34) James Whistler sets a nighttime scene before us entirely in tints and shades of blue. Flecks of yellow contribute animating sparks of light to this fundamentally monochromatic work.

Complementary harmonies involve colors directly opposite one another on the color wheel. The most obvious pairings are red and green, violet and yellow, blue and orange. Complementaries "react" with each other more vividly than other colors. Areas of complementary color placed next to or even near each other make both hues appear more intense. The Tibetan painting illustrated here of an arhat, a type of Buddha, makes good use of a complementary color scheme (**4.28**). The red and orange of the saint's robes are intensified by the complementary blue and green of the landscape, and the resulting radiance in color evokes the spiritual radiance of a holy man.

Analogous harmonies combine colors adjacent to one another on the color wheel, such as red, red-orange, and orange. In *Madrugada 2*, Stephen Mueller employed an analogous color scheme that moves from blue through green to yellow (**4.29**). *Madrugada* means "early morning" in Spanish, especially the time between the first pale light and sunrise. Mueller's color scheme evokes the shifts in light over these hours.

4.28 (left) *Arhat: possibly Chudapanthaka.* Tibet, mid- to late 15th century. Pigments and gold on cloth, 39 × 22½". Rubin Museum of Art, New York.

4.29 (right) Stephen Mueller. *Madrugada 2.* 2001. Acrylic on canvas, 70 × 80". Courtesy Rebecca Ibel Gallery, Columbus, Ohio.

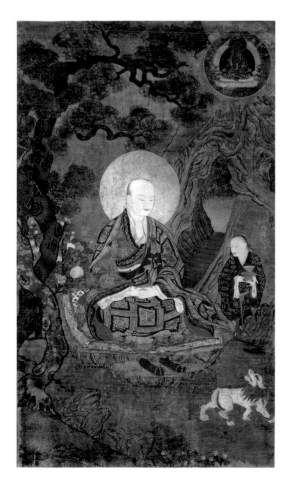

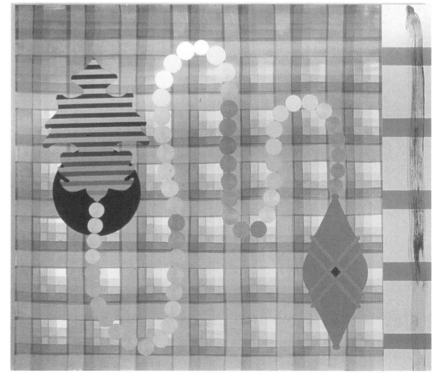

4.30 Demonstration of complementary color afterimage. Stare for a time at the black dot in the middle of the colored square. Then, with your eyes unfocused, stare at the white square above it. The colors will appear in ghostly reverse, with a blue-green inner square and a red outer square.

Triadic harmonies are composed of any three colors equidistant from each other on the color wheel. Hopper's *Rooms by the Sea,* the image that opened this chapter, uses the basic triadic harmony of red, yellow, and blue—the primary colors (see 4.1). Gaugin's *Te Aa No Areois* (see 21.9) owes a great deal to the triadic harmony of blue-green, red-violet, and yellow-orange, as well as to the complementary opposition of blue-green and red-orange.

Numerous other color harmonies have been identified and named. Artists themselves, however, are more likely to speak generally of working with a **restricted palette** or an **open palette.** Working with a restricted palette, artists limit themselves to a few pigments and their mixtures, tints, and shades. For an example of a painting created with a restricted palette, look at Copley's *Paul Revere,* in Chapter 17 (see 17.20). For an example of a painting created with an open palette, look again at Manohar's *Jahangir Receives a Cup from Khusrau,* in Chapter 1 (see 1.8).

Optical Effects of Color

Certain uses and combinations of colors can "play tricks" on our eyes or, more accurately, on the way we perceive colors registered by our eyes. One effect we have already touched on several times is **simultaneous contrast,** where complementary colors appear more intense when placed side by side. Simultaneous contrast is related to another fascinating optical effect, **afterimage.** Prolonged staring at any saturated color fatigues the receptors in our eyes, which compensate when allowed to rest by producing the color's complementary as a ghostly afterimage in the mind. You can experience this effect by following the instructions in the caption to Figure **4.30.**

Formulated and popularized during the 19th century, the principle of simultaneous contrast and the optical effect of afterimage were taken into account by artists of the time, especially by the Impressionist painters. Monet, for example, based many of his paintings on complementary pairings, including *Fisherman's Cottage on the Cliffs at Varengeville,* which we looked at in Chapter 2 (see 2.5). More subtly, Impressionist painters tinted the shadows in

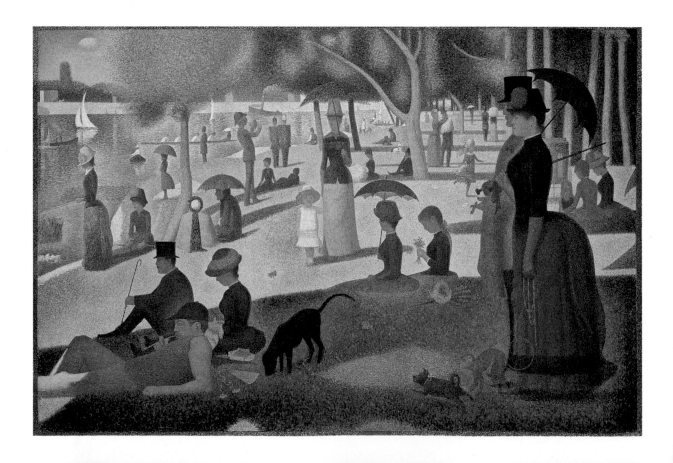

their paintings with the complementary color of a nearby highlight, thus recording the way the eye, resting by looking at a shadow, colors that shadow by producing an afterimage. In Monet's *Haystack at Sunset*, illustrated later in this chapter, the side of the haystack is tinted orange-red and the shadow next to it blue-green (see 4.52).

Some colors seem to "advance," others to "recede." Interior designers know that if you place a bright red chair in a room, it will seem larger and farther forward than the same chair upholstered in beige or pale blue. Thus, color can dramatically influence our perceptions of space and size. In general, colors that create the illusion of large size and advancing are those with the warmer hues (red, orange, yellow), high intensity, and dark value; small size and receding are suggested by colors with cooler hues (blue, green), low intensity, and light value.

Colors can be mixed in light or pigment, but they can also be mixed by the eyes. When small patches of different colors are close together, the eye may blend them to produce a new color. This is called **optical color mixture,** and it is an important feature in the painting of Georges Seurat.

Seurat was fascinated by the scientific color theories of his day, and he worked out his canvases with great precision. Most artists blend their colors, either on a palette or on the canvas itself, to produce gradations of hue, but Seurat did not. Instead, he laid down his paints by placing many thousands of tiny dots—or points—of pure color next to each other, a process that came to be called **pointillism.** From a distance of a few inches the dots are quite distinct. But as the viewer moves back, they merge to form a rich texture of subtly varied tones. The painting illustrated here is Seurat's masterpiece, *A Sunday on La Grande Jatte* (**4.31, 4.32**). Like most of this artist's works, it does not reproduce well in a book, where colors are reduced to ink on paper. Its many verticals of people and trees can make the painting seem static. Seen "in person," however, on the museum wall in Chicago, *La Grande Jatte* sparkles and vibrates with color, comes to life through its myriad little points of light.

The contemporary painter Chuck Close has taken optical mixing to new extremes, exploring the limits of perception. His chosen subject is the human

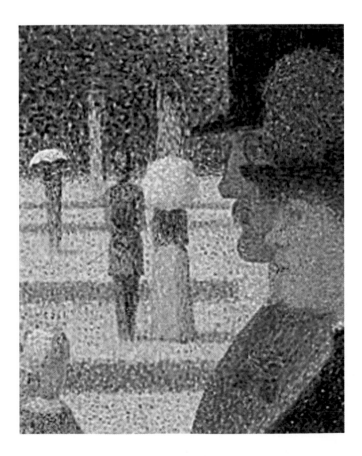

4.31 (opposite page) Georges Seurat. *A Sunday on La Grande Jatte.* 1884–86. Oil on canvas, 6'9¾" × 10'1⅜". The Art Institute of Chicago.

4.32 (left) *A Sunday on La Grande Jatte,* detail.

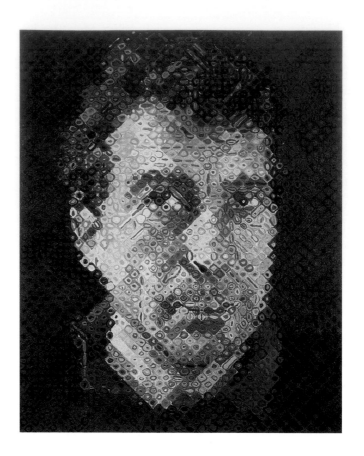

4.33 Chuck Close. *Bill.* 1990. Oil on canvas, 6 × 5'.
Courtesy Pace Wildenstein Gallery, New York.

head, or, rather, a photograph of a human head, generally the face of someone he knows (**4.33**). His working method is to draw a grid over the photograph, then a grid with the same number of squares over a much larger canvas. He copies or interprets each square of the photograph, one at a time, ignoring the larger image and focusing solely on the information in the square. The image results as a by-product of this activity. Over the years, Close has used progressively larger squares in his grids, and he has experimented with different kinds of marks to fill the squares. In *Bill,* the grid is set diagonally, and each square is filled with loosely brushed lines, circles, dots, and squares in pure colors.

Seen up close, *Bill* makes even less sense than *A Sunday on La Grande Jatte,* for the markings are much larger, and each square of the grid is virtually a composition in its own right. Up close, in fact, *Bill* looks like nothing so much as a vast honeycomb of hundreds of small nonrepresentational paintings. As viewers step back, the colors begin to mix, and a three-dimensional image seems to emerge from the flat surface.

Emotional Effects of Color

Color affects us on such a basic level that few would argue that we have a direct emotional response to it. The problem comes when we try to find universal principles, for we quickly discover that emotional responses to color are both culturally conditioned and intensely personal. For most people brought up in America, red and green have strong cultural associations with Christmas. Van Gogh, however, once made a painting of a café interior that juxtaposed red and green in order to suggest an environment so tense that men might go mad or be driven to commit a crime. Most colors could elicit a similar variety of response. For the German painter Franz Marc, blue was the color of male spirituality. As the color of the sky and the ocean, blue is often associated with freedom. It is a "cool" color and has been shown to have a calming effect. In the English language, blue is linked with sadness. In India, blue is the color of the god Vishnu, the god of order and stability, but it is also associated with the dark and disturbing power of the goddess Kali.

James Abbott McNeill Whistler certainly had calm in mind when he chose blue for the overall color of his *Nocturne in Blue and Gold* (**4.34**). Except for a distant spangle of fireworks and the reflection of a few lights in the water, the painting is entirely monochromatic, brushed in shades of grayish blue. Blue contributes significantly to the subdued emotional mood of the painting, although it does not create it all alone. The strong, stable vertical lines of the pier, the reassuring horizontals of the bridge and the horizon, the evident tranquility of the scene with its lone boatman silhouetted on the prow of his craft—these elements also play a role in the emotional "temperature" of the work.

Edvard Munch's harrowing painting *The Scream* also depicts a bridge, but the effect is much different (**4.35**). Concerning this work, the Norwegian artist wrote in his diary "I sensed a shriek passing through nature. . . . I painted this picture, painted the clouds as actual blood."[1] Munch uses red to indicate horror, blood, and anguish. But how, outside of his diary, are we to know that Munch did not intend simply to depict a splendid sunset? As in Whistler's nocturne, color does not carry the entire expressive burden by itself. While Whistler's painting is characterized by reassuring vertical and horizontal lines, here unstable diagonals and swirling lines dominate. The horizontal of the horizon is almost obliterated. The figure in the foreground clasps his hands over his ears to block the piercing sound. His head has become a death's head, his body wavers unsteadily. In contrast, the two pedestrians in the background remain unaffected. Evidently they hear nothing out of the ordinary. The scream is a silent one, the interior cry of a soul projected onto nature.

4.34 (left) James Abbott McNeill Whistler. *Nocturne in Blue and Gold (Old Battersea Bridge).* c. 1872–75. Oil on canvas, 23¾ × 18⅜".
Tate Gallery, London.

4.35 (right) Edvard Munch. *The Scream.* 1893. Tempera and casein on cardboard, 36 × 29".
Munch-Museet, Nasjonalgalleriet, Oslo.

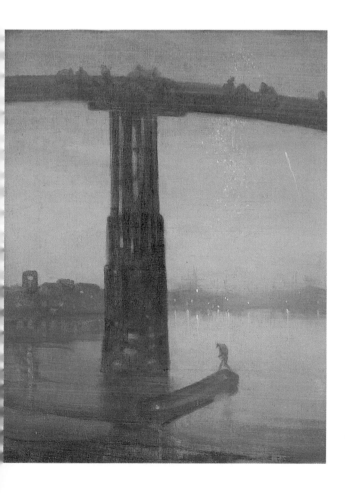

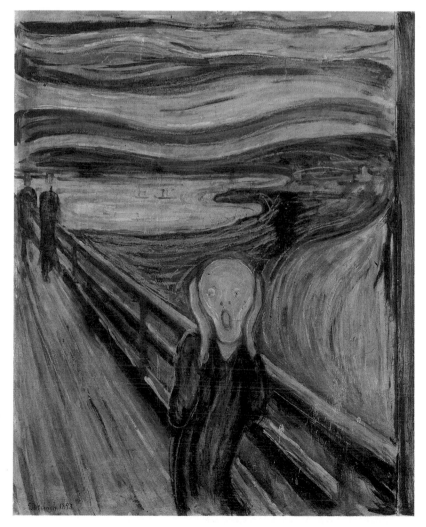

JAPANESE PRINTS

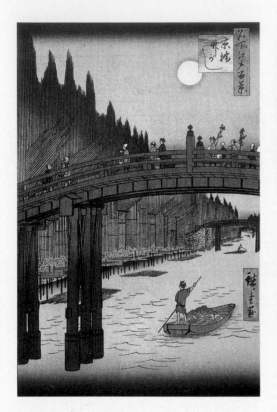

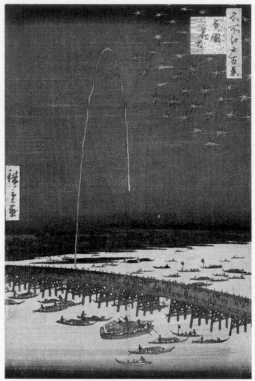

Whistler had fallen under the spell of Japanese prints during his stay in Paris in the late 1850s. He was hardly the only one. Almost all of the Impressionist painters in France collected Japanese prints, and many of the painters of the next generation were influenced by them as well. Why prints, and why then? In 1854, Japan, after being virtually closed to foreigners for over 200 years, had opened itself up to the outside world again. Europe, England, and America were suddenly fascinated by all things Japanese, but it was principally in Paris that artists seriously studied prints, which were the first examples of Japanese art to be imported in quantity. Elsewhere in this book, their influence can be seen in Mary Cassatt's *The Boating Party* (21.12), Toulouse-Lautrec's *Moulin Rouge: La Goulue* (10.11), and Edgar Degas' *Women at a Café, Evening* (21.7).

PAINTINGS SUCH as *Nocturne in Blue and Gold (Old Battersea Bridge)* (see 4.34) so enraged the English critic John Ruskin that he accused the artist, James Whistler, of flinging a pot of paint in the public's face. The articulate and flamboyant Whistler promptly took Ruskin to court. What angered Ruskin was that the painting didn't really resemble Battersea Bridge at all. "I do not intend it to be a 'correct' portrait of the bridge," Whistler replied. The painting was a moonlit scene, he continued, a reverie, and people could see something in it or not, as they liked.[2]

It is difficult to say whether Whistler would have helped or hurt his case by drawing the judge's attention to his collection of Japanese prints, which included the two works by Hiroshige illustrated here. With its dramatically cropped bridge, lone boatman, and moonlit river, Hiroshige's *Riverside Bamboo Market, Kyobashi* served as the principal model for Whistler's composition, though he imported the idea of fireworks from the Japanese master's *Fireworks at Ryogoku.*

Interestingly, one of the factors that allowed Western artists to borrow compositional ideas from Japanese prints so easily was that influence had already flowed in the other direction. The Western system of linear perspective had long been known to Japanese artists. During the 18th century, printmakers even created a special type of print called *uki-e*, "perspective pictures." By Hiroshige's time, printmakers had fully absorbed Western perspective into their own styles, especially in landscape, as the two examples here show so well.

Ando Hiroshige. *Riverside Bamboo Market, Kyobashi* (left) and *Fireworks at Ryogoku* (right), from *One Hundred Famous Views of Edo.* 1857. Honolulu Academy of Arts.

TEXTURE AND PATTERN

Texture refers to surface quality—a perception of smooth or rough, flat or bumpy, fine or coarse. Our world would be bland and uninteresting without contrasts of texture. Most of us, when we encounter a dog or cat, are moved to pet the animal, partly because the animal likes it, but also because we enjoy the feel of the fur's texture against our hands. In planning our clothes we instinctively take texture into account. We might put on a thick, nubby sweater over a smooth cotton shirt and enjoy the contrast. We look for this textural interest in all facets of our environment. Few people can resist running their hands over a smooth chunk of marble or a glossy length of silk or a drape of velvet. This is the outstanding feature of texture: It makes us want to touch it.

Actual Texture

Actual texture is literally *tactile,* a quality we could experience through touch. Anyone touching Mona Hatoum's *Prayer Mat,* however, would certainly want to go about it carefully (**4.36**). The "mat" is actually a dense field of brass pins glued onto a canvas backing. Hatoum's work refers to the small, portable rugs used for individual prayer by Muslims, who are required to pray five times daily in the direction of Mecca, one of the holy cities of Islam. Like the inexpensive prayer rugs available in many corner shops, *Prayer Mat* even has a compass embedded in it so that worshipers can orient themselves correctly, no matter where in the world they are. What would it be to kneel on such a rug? Is inflicting pain on ourselves a sacrifice that God receives with gratitude? Or is religion itself a torment that we have inflicted on ourselves, and one that we would perhaps be better off without? Like much art, Hatoum's *Prayer Mat* poses more questions than it answers.

4.36 Mona Hatoum. *Prayer Mat.* 1995. Nickel-plated brass pins, brass compass, canvas, glue; 26⅛ × 44⅛ × ⅝".
Courtesy Jay Jopling/White Cube, London.

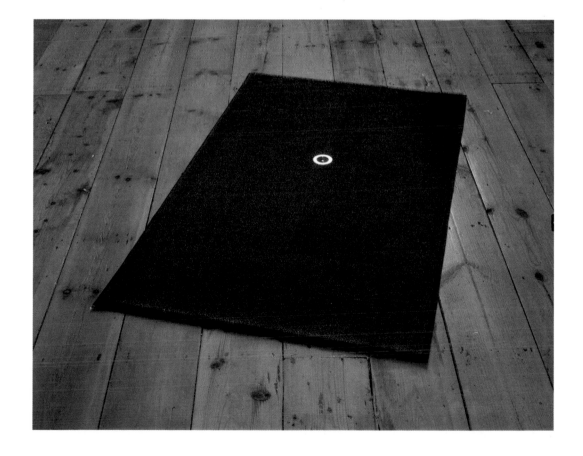

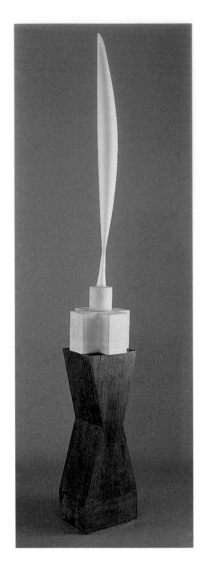

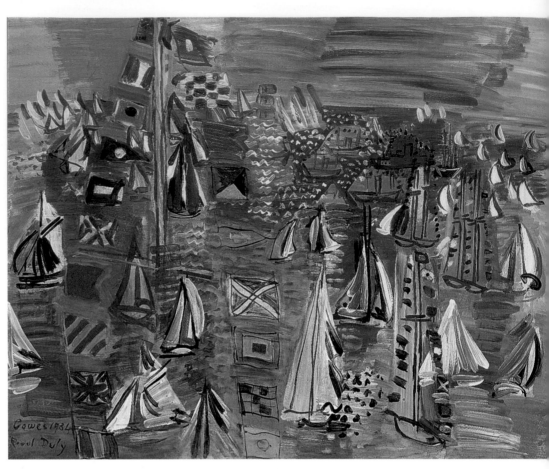

Like any other visual element, texture can contribute to our understanding and interpretation of a work. In the version here of Brancusi's *Bird in Space* (**4.37**), a roughly carved wooden pedestal supports a smoother limestone element, which in turn serves as a base for the bird. The bird is made of marble, a fine-grained stone that can be polished to a very smooth finish. The progression of textures contributes to our sense of the sculpture's movement. The wooden base exerts a powerful upward thrust, the limestone element acts as a kind of compression zone for gathering energy, then the marble figure makes a final leap into flight. At each step, the texture becomes more refined, less coarse, as though the weight of the material world were falling away.

Visual Texture

That we can appreciate the textures of Hatoum's *Prayer Mat* or Brancusi's *Bird in Flight* in a photograph shows that texture has a visual component as well as a tactile one. In fact, even before touching a surface we have formed an idea of its texture by observing the way it reflects light and associating what we see with a sense memory of touch. Brancusi's use of texture can thus be significant for us even though we would certainly not be permitted to touch the sculpture in a museum, and Hatoum's use of texture can give us a deeply unsettling visual experience even if we do not run our hands over her *Prayer Mat*. Naturalistic painting can suggest the texture of objects in the world in the same way that photography does, by faithfully recording their appearances. The surface of a painting has its own actual texture as well, whether smooth as glass or rough with many layers of thickly applied paint.

4.37 (left) Constantin Brancusi. *Bird in Space.* 1925. White marble, height 5'11⅜", on a base of wood and limestone.
National Gallery of Art, Washington, D.C.

4.38 (right) Raoul Dufy. *Regatta at Cowes.* 1934. Oil on linen, 32⅛ × 39½".
National Gallery of Art, Washington, D.C.

By visual texture, however, we mean something less literal. We may speak of visual texture in a painting or drawing when markings our eyes associate with texture are there, whether they actually depict texture or not. For example, the many dots and dashes of Seurat's *A Sunday on La Grande Jatte* (see 4.31) seem to weave a tapestry of many colors. Our eyes interpret this woven effect as a sort of allover texture, even though it does not describe any particular object depicted in the painting. Another example is Raoul Dufy's *Regatta at Cowes* (**4.38**). If you were to run your hands over the surface of the painting, you would find it to be smooth. As your eyes run over it, however, they encounter "rough patches" created by the closely spaced forms and small brush strokes, especially in the waves of the sea. The visual texture does not try to depict the texture of the water itself. Rather, it conveys a parallel idea of roughness or choppiness.

Pattern

Pattern is any decorative, repetitive motif or design. Pattern can create visual texture, although visual texture may not always be seen as a pattern. An interesting aspect of pattern is that it tends to flatten our perception of mass and space. The self-portrait here by African photographer Samuel Fosso illustrates the visual "buzz" and spatial ambiguity that patterns can produce (**4.39**). Everything clamors for our attention at once. Elements that should stay calmly in the background or firmly underfoot seem to come forward to meet us. In the middle of it all sits the artist, dressed as an outrageous parody of a traditional ruler. (For an example of the sort of royal display that Fosso is mocking, see 18.12.)

4.39 Samuel Fosso. *The Chief: He Who Sold Africa to the Colonists,* from *Self-Portraits I–V.* 1997. C-print photograph, 39¾ × 39¾". Centre Georges Pompidou, Musée National d'Art Moderne, Paris.

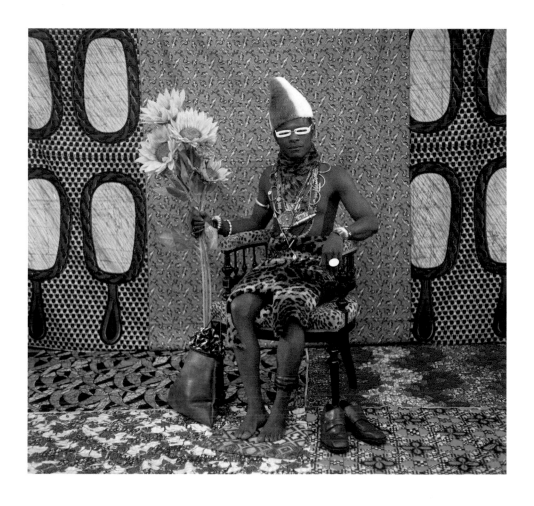

SPACE

The word "space," especially in our technological world, sometimes conveys the idea of nothingness. We think of outer space as a huge void, hostile to human life. A person who is "spaced out" is blank, unfocused, not really "there." But the space in and around a work of art is not a void, and it is very much there. It is a dynamic visual element that interacts with the lines and shapes and colors and textures of a work of art to give them definition. Consider space in this way: How could there be a line if there were not the spaces on either side of it to mark its edges? How could there be a shape without the space around it to set it off?

Three-Dimensional Space

Sculpture, architecture, and all other forms with mass exist in three-dimensional space—that is, the actual space in which our bodies also stand. These works of art take their character from the ways in which they carve out volumes of space within and around them.

The sculptor Alberto Giacometti was fascinated by how we perceive objects in space. He was intent on finding ways to suggest in his work the space he sensed between himself and his model, and also to situate his own sculptures in space for viewers. In *The Nose* (**4.40**) he went so far as to frame a cubic volume of space around his disturbing sculpture of a head. The image was prompted by a visit Giacometti paid to a friend in the hospital. As Giacometti looked down at his friend's face, gaunt and wasted with illness, it seemed to him that the eyes and cheeks were sinking farther down and that the bony nose was growing longer. He captured that momentary vision of death in this sculpture, which he then suspended in space like a hanged man, or like a shrunken head in an ethnographic museum.

Architecture in particular can be thought of as a means of shaping space. Without the walls and roof of a building, the space would be limitless; with them, space has boundaries, and therefore has volume. While from the outside we appreciate a work of architecture for its sculptural masses, from the inside we appreciate it as a shaped space or a sequence of shaped spaces. Our experience of architectural space is direct and physical, for we do not look *at* it but rather walk *through* it. When a ceiling is raised or lowered, when walls grow closer together or farther apart, we sense that we have made a transition from one kind of space to another. The photograph here of an exhibition hall from Frank O. Gehry's Guggenheim Museum Bilbao shows the architect's gift for creating fluid and dramatic interior spaces (**4.41**). We can only imagine the effect on someone walking toward us as the intimate area at the far end opens suddenly upward into a light-filled space crossed and recrossed by graceful white forms. (The undulating dark metal surface to the right is part of a sculpture by the artist Richard Serra.)

Implied Space: Suggesting Depth in Two Dimensions

Architecture, sculpture, and other art forms that exist in three dimensions work with actual space. When we view the work, we inhabit the same space it does, and we need to walk around it or through it to experience it completely. With painting, drawing, and other two-dimensional art forms, the actual space is the flat surface of the work itself, which we tend to see all at once. Yet on this literal surface, called the **picture plane,** other quantities and dimensions of space can be implied. For example, if you take an ordinary notebook page and draw a tiny dog in the center, the page has suddenly become a large

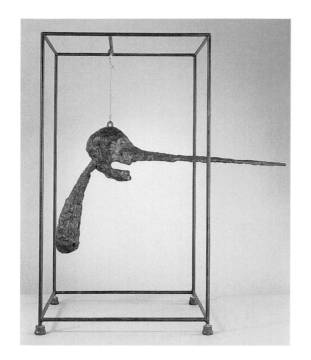

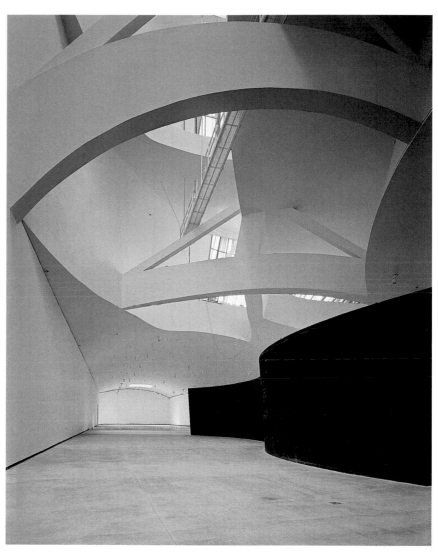

space, a field for the dog to roam about in. If you draw a dog that takes up the entire page, the page has become a much smaller space, just big enough for the dog.

Suppose now that you draw two dogs and perhaps a tree, and you want to show where they are in relation to each other. One dog is behind the tree, say, and the other is running toward it from the distance. These relationships take place in the third dimension, depth. There are many visual cues that we use to perceive spatial relationships in depth. One of the simplest is overlap: We understand that when two forms overlap, the one we perceive as complete is in front of the one we perceive as partial. A second visual cue is position: Seated at a desk, for example, we look *down* to see the objects closest to us and raise our head *up* to see objects that are farther away.

4.40 (left) Alberto Giacometti. *The Nose.* 1947. Bronze, iron, twine, and steel wire, 32 × 28½ × 15⅜".
Hirshhorn Museum and Sculpture Garden, Smithsonian Institution, Washington, D.C.

4.41 (right) Frank O. Gehry. Interior of the Guggenheim Museum Bilbao, Bilbao, Spain. 1997.

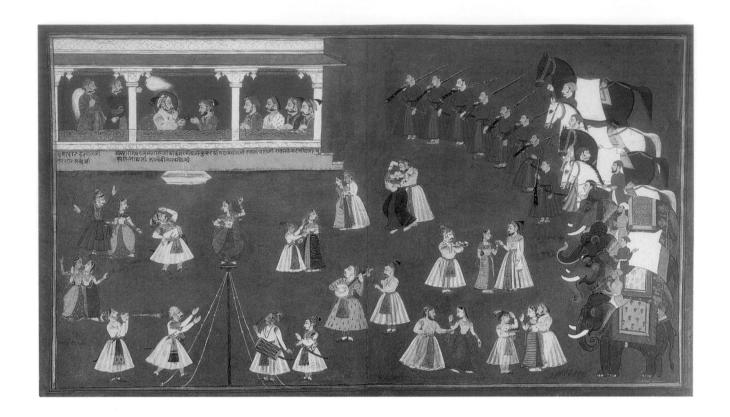

4.42 *Maharana Amar Singh II, Prince Sangram Singh, and Courtiers Watch the Performance of an Acrobat and Musicians.* Rajasthan, Mewar, c. 1705–08. Ink, opaque watercolor, and gold on paper; 20½ × 35¾". The Metropolitan Museum of Art, New York.

Many artistic cultures have relied entirely on these two basic cues to imply depth in two dimensions (**4.42**). In this lively scene of acrobats and musicians performing before an Indian prince, we understand that the performers toward the bottom of the page are nearer to us than ones higher up, and that the overlapping elephants and horses are standing next to each other in a row that recedes away from us. The most important person in the scene is the prince, and the painting makes this clear. Framed by the architectural setting, he sits amid his courtiers and attendants, all of whom are looking at him. The prince, too, is depicted in profile and does not seem to be watching the performance. Yet this seeming inattention is not to be taken literally. The prince would certainly have watched such a wonderful event. Indian artists favored profile views, for they give the least information about depth, and so lend themselves well to the overall flatness of Indian painting.

LINEAR PERSPECTIVE   The sense of space in the Indian painting is *conceptually* convincing, but not *optically* convincing. For example, we *understand* perfectly well that the prince's pavilion is on the distant side of the acrobats, but there is actually no evidence to tell our eyes that it is not hovering in the air directly over them. Similarly, we understand that the elephants and horses represent rounded forms even though they appear to our eyes as flat shapes fanned out like a deck of cards on the picture plane. Together, the flatness of Indian painting, the preference for profiles, the use of saturated colors, and the conceptual construction of space make up a coherent system for depicting the world. They work together to give Indian artists tremendous flexibility in assembling complex, vivid, and visually delightful scenes such as this one while preserving narrative clarity.

The chiaroscuro technique developed by Italian artists of the 15th century also forms part of a larger system for depicting the world. Just as Renaissance artists took note of the optical evidence of light and shadow to model rounded forms, they also developed a technique for constructing an optically convincing space to set these forms in. This technique, called linear perspective, is based in the systematic application of two observations:

- Forms seem to diminish in size as they recede from us.

- Parallel lines receding into the distance seem to converge, until they meet at a point on the horizon line where they disappear. This point is known as the vanishing point.

You can visualize this second idea if you remember gazing down a straight highway. As the highway recedes farther from you, the two edges seem to draw closer together, until they disappear at the horizon line (**4.43**).

The development of linear perspective profoundly changed how artists viewed the picture plane. For medieval European artists, as for Indian artists, a painting was primarily a flat surface covered with shapes and colors. For Renaissance artists it became a window onto a scene. The picture plane was reconceived as a sort of windowpane, and the painted view was imagined as receding from it into the distance.

Renaissance artists took up linear perspective with as much delight as a child takes up a new toy. Many paintings were created for no other reason than to show off the possibilities of this new technique (**4.44**). Here, the lines of the stone pavement lay bare the mechanics of linear perspective. We can actually observe the receding lines growing closer, and we can easily continue them in our imagination until they converge at a central point on the horizon, where the sea meets the sky. The rooflines of the various buildings converge at the same point, as do the lines that divide the ceiling of the covered portico in the immediate foreground.

4.43 Basic principles of linear perspective.

4.44 (below) Francesco di Giorgio Martini (attr.). *Architectural Perspective.* Late 15th century. Furniture decoration on poplar wood, 4'3⅝" × 7'7⅝". Staatliche Museen zu Berlin, Preussischer Kulturbesitz, Gemäldegalerie.

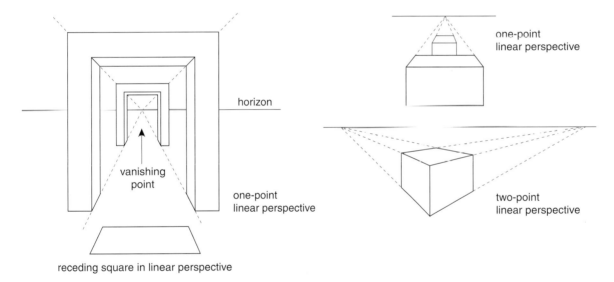

horizon

vanishing point

one-point linear perspective

receding square in linear perspective

one-point linear perspective

two-point linear perspective

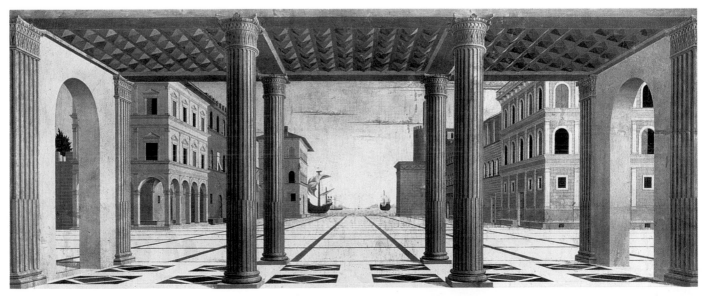

Leonardo da Vinci used linear perspective to construct a very similar space for his portrayal of *The Last Supper* (**4.45**). It was above all the measurable quality of the space created through linear perspective that intrigued Renaissance artists. Here, regular divisions of the ceiling measure out the recession just as the regular divisions of the pavement did in the example above.

Painted on a monastery wall in Milan, *The Last Supper* depicts the final gathering of Jesus Christ with his disciples, the Passover meal they shared before Jesus was brought to trial and crucified. Leonardo captures a particular moment in the story, as related in the Gospel book of Matthew in the Bible. Jesus, shown at the center of the composition, has just said to his followers: "One of you shall betray me." The disciples, Matthew tells us, "were exceeding sorrowful, and began every one of them to say unto him, Lord, is it I?"

In Leonardo's portrayal, each of the disciples reacts differently to the terrible prediction. Some are shocked, some dismayed, some puzzled—but only one, only Judas, knows that indeed, it is he. Falling back from Jesus' words, the traitor Judas, seated fourth from the left with his elbow on the table, clutches a bag containing thirty pieces of silver, his price for handing over his leader to the authorities.

To show this fateful moment, Leonardo places the group in a large banquet hall, its architectural space constructed in careful perspective. Cloth hangings on the side walls and panels in the ceiling are drawn so as to recede into space. Their lines converge at a vanishing point behind Jesus' head, at the exact center of the picture. Thus, our attention is directed forcefully toward the most important part of the composition, the face of Jesus. The central opening in the back wall, a rectangular window, also helps to focus our attention on Jesus and creates a "halo" effect around his head.

In the hands of the greatest artists, perspective became a vehicle for meaning, just as any other visual element. Here, for example, it is correct to say that the space is constructed so that the lines converge at a vanishing point in the distance behind Christ's head. But if we view the painting as a flat surface, we see that these lines can also be interpreted as radiating from Christ's head, as all of creation radiates from the mind of God. Leonardo has purposefully minimized Christ's shoulders so that his arms, too, take part in the system of radiating lines. Spreading his hands, then, God opens space to this moment, which He had foreseen since the beginning of time.

4.45 Leonardo da Vinci. *The Last Supper* (after restoration). c. 1495–97. Fresco, 15'1⅛" × 28'10½".
Refectory, Santa Maria delle Grazie, Milan.

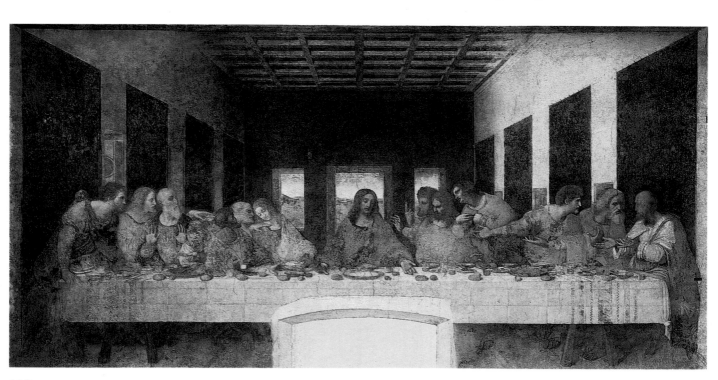

RESTORATION

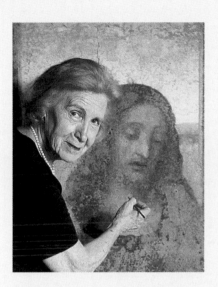

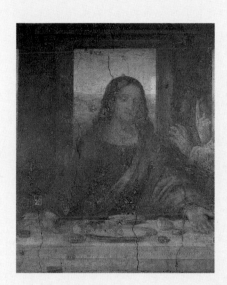

UNWISE RESTORATIONS HAVE been the plague of many a great work of art, and there can be no better example than Leonardo da Vinci's *Last Supper* (4.45). Leonardo worked on this masterpiece during the years 1495–97. Always a great one for innovation, he bypassed the established wall painting technique and devised an experimental method for this project. For once Leonardo's genius let him down. What may have been his greatest work soon became a ruin. Within ten years the painting was said to be flaking badly; within about fifty years the biographer Giorgio Vasari wrote that "Nothing is visible but a dazzling mass of blots."

The first major restoration was undertaken in 1726, and five others followed. Each of these restorers did more harm than good. One used a harsh solvent that dissolved Leonardo's colors. Another applied a strong glue that attracted dirt. Yet another restorer managed to give one of the Apostles six fingers on one hand.

To make matters worse, the physical environment of *The Last Supper* could scarcely be more precarious. Sharp variations in heat and humidity all but force the paint off the wall, bringing deep cracks in the surface. Sometime during the 18th century well-meaning friars in the monastery installed a curtain across the mural—which had the effect of trapping moisture on the wall and scraping off yet more paint each time the curtain was drawn back. French sol-diers of Napoleon who occupied the monastery in 1796 took turns throwing rocks at the mural and climbing ladders to scratch out the Apostles' eyes. A bomb fell on the monastery during World War II, missing the wall by a yard. It's a miracle that anything is left at all, and little is left.

Finally, nearly five hundred years after Leonardo put down his brushes, sensible measures were taken to save the mural. A Milanese restorer, Dr. Pinan Brambilla Barcilon, began a major restoration in 1977; the project would last more than twenty years. Dr. Brambilla had assets earlier restorers lacked—modern microscopes, chemicals, and measuring devices. Through sensitive probing she could determine what was Leonardo's work and what was somebody else's—and remove the latter. In areas where nothing is left of Leonardo's paint, she did not attempt to reconstruct the imagery, but simply painted in a neutral color.

It has not been easy. Dr. Brambilla's eyesight is permanently altered, and she suffers chronic pain in her shoulders and back. She says, "I often have to clean the same piece a second time, or even a third or fourth. The top section of the painting is impregnated with glue. The middle is filled with wax. There are six different kinds of plaster and several varnishes, lacquers, and gums. What worked on the top section doesn't work in the middle. And what worked in the middle won't work on the bottom. It's enough to make a person want to shoot herself."

Inevitably, Dr. Brambilla will have to cope with people who want to shoot *her.* Every art historian in the world will have an opinion about her restoration, and many of those opinions will be negative, even outraged. Still, she remains philosophical about her project. "I am at peace with what I have done here," she says.[3]

---

left: Dr. Pinan Brambilla Barcilon before a restored portion of Leonardo's *Last Supper*.

right: A portion of the mural before restoration.

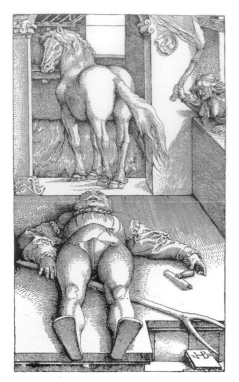

FORESHORTENING

In order for pictorial space to be consistent, the logic of linear perspective must apply to every form that recedes into the distance, including objects and human and animal forms. This effect is called foreshortening. You can understand the challenge presented by foreshortening by closing one eye and pointing upward with your index finger in front of your open eye. Gradually shift your hand until your index finger is pointing away from you and you are staring directly down its length and into the distance. You know that your finger has not changed in length, and yet it appears much shorter than it did when it was upright. It appears foreshortened.

Hans Baldung Grien portrays two foreshortened figures in *The Groom and the Witch* (**4.46**). The groom, lying perpendicular to the picture plane, is foreshortened. If we were to shift him so that he lay parallel to the picture plane with his head to the left and his feet to the right, we would have to stretch him back out. The horse, standing at a 45-degree angle to the picture plane, is also foreshortened, with the distance between his rump and his forequarters compressed by the odd angle at which we see him.

Foreshortening presented great difficulties to artists, for the complex, organic masses of a horse or a man do not offer the simple receding lines of architecture. Hans Baldung Grien's teacher, Albrecht Dürer, left us this wonderful image of an artist wrestling logically with a problem of extreme foreshortening (**4.47**). From our point of view, the woman lies parallel to the picture plane. From the point of view of the artist, however, she is directly perpendicular to it. Her knees are closest to him, her head farthest away. He has actually constructed a picture plane in the form of a gridded window through which he looks at his model. On the table before him lies a sheet of paper, gridded to match. Standing on the table within the embrace of his arms is an obelisk whose tip just reaches his eye. The obelisk serves to focus his glance, making sure that every time he returns his gaze to the model, it is at the exact same height.

Our artist will work slowly back and forth. Looking across the tip of the obelisk with one eye open, he will observe his model through the grid. Looking down, he will open both eyes and quickly draw from memory what he saw, using the grid lines as reference points. Looking up again, he will refocus one eye on his model over the obelisk and memorize another small bit. Glance by glance, he will complete the drawing.

Dürer's image illustrates well the strengths and drawbacks of linear perspective. It is a scientifically accurate system for rendering space and relationships within space as we perceive them standing in one fixed place, with one eye open, staring at fixed points along one eye level. But in life we have two eyes, not one, and they are always in motion. Nevertheless, the principles

4.46 (above) Hans Baldung Grien. *The Groom and the Witch.* c. 1540. Woodcut, image 13¹⁵⁄₁₆ × 7⅞".
Staatliche Museen zu Berlin, Preussischer Kulturbesitz, Kupferstichkabinet.

4.47 (below) Albrecht Dürer. *Draftsman Drawing a Reclining Nude,* from *The Art of Measurement.* c. 1527. Woodcut, 3 × 8½".

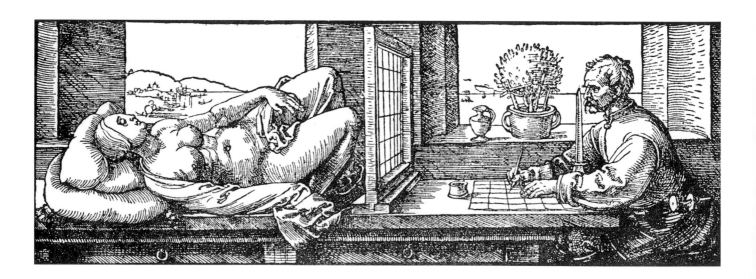

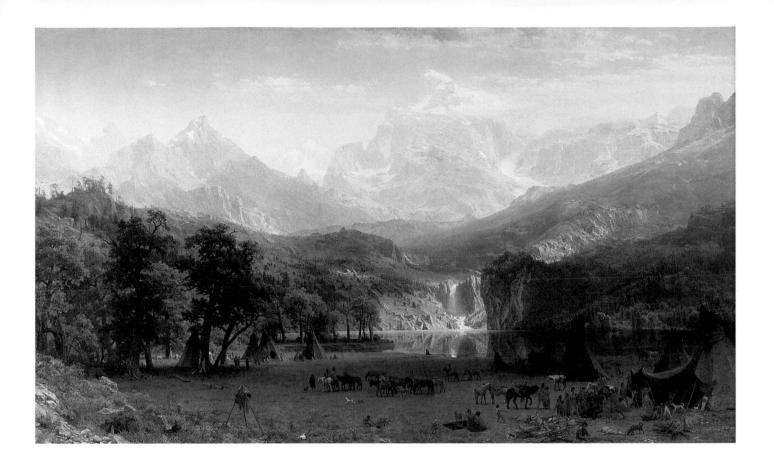

of linear perspective dominated Western views of space for almost 500 years, and they continue to influence us through images generated by the camera, which also shows the view seen by one eye (the lens) staring at a point on a fixed level (the center focus).

ATMOSPHERIC PERSPECTIVE   Staring off into a series of hills, you may notice that each succeeding range appears paler, bluer, and less distinct. This is an optical effect caused by the atmosphere that interposes itself between us and the objects we perceive. Particles of moisture and dust suspended in the atmosphere scatter light. Of all the colors of the spectrum, blue scatters the most; hence the sky itself appears to be blue, and things take on a bluish tinge as their distance from us increases. The first European artist to apply this observation systematically was Leonardo da Vinci, who called the effect "aerial perspective." A more common term today is atmospheric perspective.

Atmospheric perspective is the third and final element of the optically based system for representing the world that was developed during the Renaissance. For as long as naturalism remained a goal of Western art, these three techniques—modeling form through value, constructing space with linear perspective, and suggesting receding landscape through atmospheric perspective—remained central to painting.

During the 1850s, the German-born American painter Albert Bierstadt accompanied a corps of U.S. Army engineers on their expedition to map an overland route from St. Louis to the Pacific Ocean. The sketches he made on the journey later formed the basis for a series of spectacular paintings that gave Americans back East a look at the Western portions of the land, and at the Indian peoples who called them home (**4.48**). In this typically majestic view, Bierstadt uses dramatic lighting and atmospheric perspective to draw our eyes through the Indian encampment on the near shore to a waterfall in the middle distance and then upward to the towering mountain peaks in the far distance.

4.48 Albert Bierstadt. *The Rocky Mountains, Lander's Peak.* 1863. Oil on canvas, 6'1¼" × 10'¾".
The Metropolitan Museum of Art, New York.

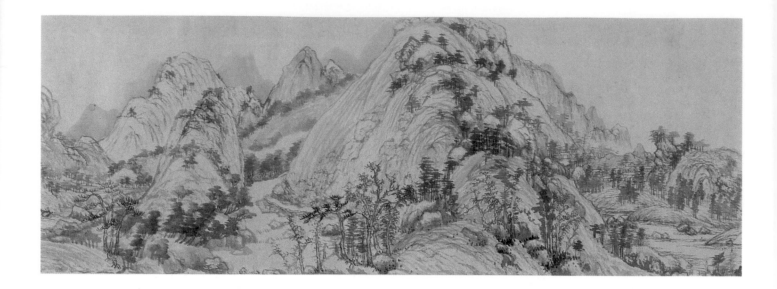

Chinese and Japanese painters also relied on atmospheric perspective to suggest broad vistas of receding landscape. One of the masterpieces of Chinese landscape painting is *Dwelling in the Fuchun Mountains*, by the 14th-century artist Huang Gongwang (**4.49**). Working in brush and black ink on paper, Huang built up the masses of his mountains with layers of contour strokes. Trees dot the slopes, and houses nestle cozily in the hills. Trees diminish in size and grow fainter as they recede into the distance, and the farthest mountains are rendered as washes of pale gray ink.

Dwelling in the Fuchun Mountains is an example of a handscroll, an intimate format of painting developed in China. Small enough to be held in the hands, as the name indicates, a handscroll was commonly only a foot or so in height, but many feet long. *Dwelling in the Fuchun Mountains,* for example, is about 13 inches in height and over 20 feet long. We illustrate only a small section of it. Handscrolls were not displayed completely unrolled, as today we might see them in museums. Rather, they were kept rolled up and taken out for viewing only occasionally. Viewers would savor the painting slowly, setting it on a table and unrolling a foot or two at a time. Working their way from one end of the scroll to the other, they journeyed through a landscape that commonly alternated stretches of open water and lowlands with hills and mountains. All is painted from a mobile, bird's-eye view, so that as the landscape rolls by us, we can be everywhere and see everything.

4.49 (above) Huang Gongwang. *Dwelling in the Fuchun Mountains*, detail. c. 1350. Handscroll, ink on paper; 1'⅞" × 20'11".
National Palace Museum, Taipei.

4.50 (below) Basic principles of isometric perspective.

ISOMETRIC PERSPECTIVE
As we have seen, the converging lines of linear perspective are based on the fixed viewpoint of an earthbound viewer. The viewpoint in Chinese painting, however, is typically mobile and airborne, and so converging lines have no place in their system of representation. Is-

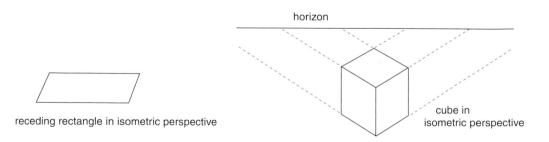

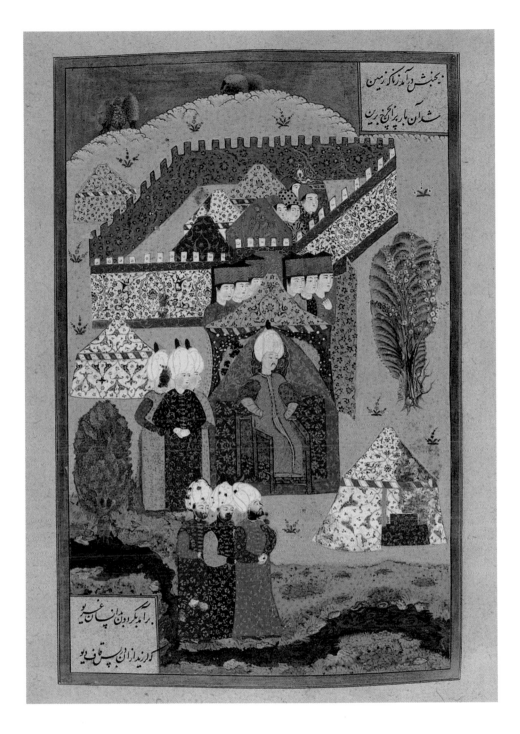

lamic painting often employs an aerial viewpoint as well, so that scenes are depicted in their totality as God might see and understand them. To suggest regular forms such as a building receding from the picture plane, Chinese and Muslim painters use diagonal lines, but without allowing parallels to converge. This system is known as isometric perspective (**4.50**). In the exquisite page illustrated here from a manuscript of the *Sulaymannama* ("History of Sulayman"), the blue-and-white fortress in the background is portrayed using isometric perspective (**4.51**). The side walls recede to the right in parallel diagonal lines; the rear wall is as wide as the wall nearest us. Sulayman was a famous Ottoman sultan of the 16th century. Toward the end of his reign, his official history was written by the poet Arifi, transcribed by a famous calligrapher, and lavishly illustrated by court artists.

4.51 *The Siege of Belgrade*, from a manuscript of *Sulaymannama.* Istanbul, 1558. Ink and opaque colors on paper.
Topkapi Palace Library, Istanbul.

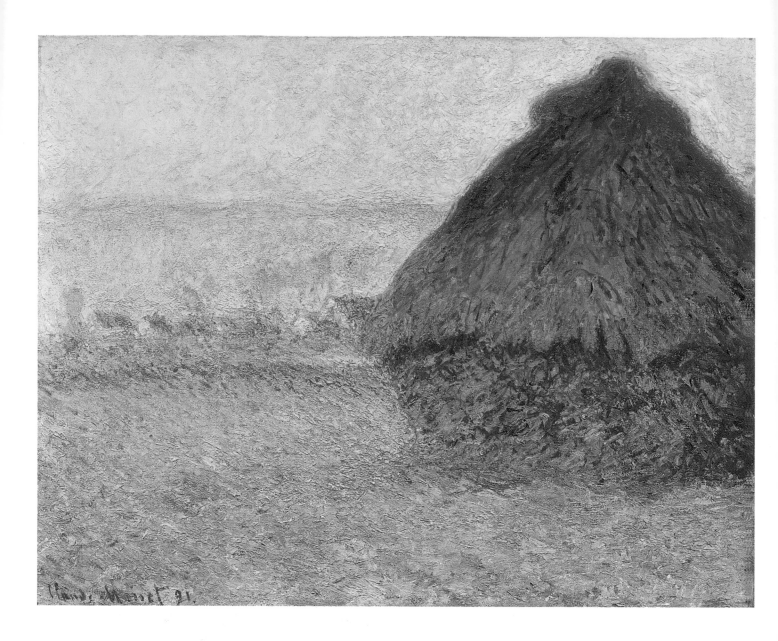

4.52 Claude Monet. *Haystack at Sunset.* 1891. Oil on canvas, 28⅞ × 36½".
Courtesy Museum of Fine Arts, Boston.

TIME AND MOTION

Time and motion have always been linked to art, if only because time is the element in which we live and motion is the very sign of life. It was only during the 20th century, however, that time and motion truly took their places as elements of Western art, and this for the simple reason that due to advances in science and technology, daily life itself became far more dynamic, and the nature of time and its relationship to space and the universe more a matter for thought.

Time became a conscious element of painting with work of the Impressionist painter Claude Monet, whose career began in the 19th century and continued into the first decades of the 20th. Monet's preoccupation with the effects of light led him to realize that each shift in light created a different subject, as though there were no continuing reality but only a collection of moments. He began to paint in series, with each painting catching the subject at a specific moment of time, as defined by light (**4.52**). Here, the simple yet monumental form of a haystack seems to have absorbed the glow of the setting sun. Monet would paint it again at dawn, at noon, in the snow, in the mist. Is there such a thing as a haystack, or are there only glimpses of a haystack in time?

During the first decade of the 20th century, inventions such as the racing automobile and the airplane convinced many artists that the world had changed and that art needed to change with it. Among these were a group of Italian artists who launched an art movement called **Futurism.** The Futurists called for an art that would celebrate motion, speed, energy, and daring. "The gesture which we would reproduce on canvas shall no longer be a fixed *moment* in universal dynamism. It shall simply be the dynamic sensation itself (made eternal)," they wrote in their manifesto of 1910. "A profile is never motionless before our eyes, but it constantly appears and disappears . . . moving objects constantly multiply themselves; their form changes like rapid vibrations . . . a running horse has not four legs, but twenty, and their movements are triangular."[4]

One of the painters who signed this manifesto was Giacomo Balla. His best-loved painting does not show a running horse, however, but a scurrying little dog (**4.53**). Paws a blur, tail wagging, ears flapping, leash vibrating—everything is dynamic. Today the visual symbols that Balla uses to indicate motion are familiar to us from cartoons, but in Balla's day they were new and radical, for they dissolved moving form into a blur of possibilities.

During the 1930s, the American artist Alexander Calder set sculpture in motion with works that came to be called mobiles. Constructed from abstract forms suspended on slender lengths of wire, they respond by their own weight to the lightest currents of air. Calder also created works he called stabiles—sculptures that did not move, but sat still on the ground like everyone else's. Often, he combined the two ideas, as here in his monumental *Southern Cross*

4.53 Giacomo Balla. *Dynamism of a Dog on a Leash*. 1912. Oil on canvas, 35⅜ × 43¼". Albright-Knox Art Gallery, Buffalo, N.Y.

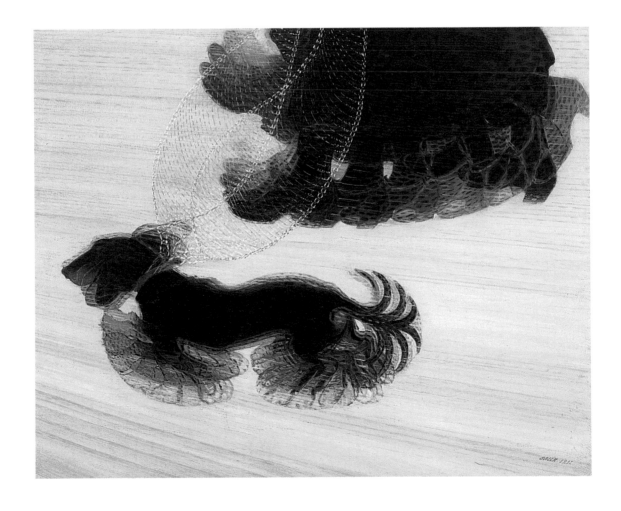

(**4.54**), where an orange stabile holds aloft a black mobile. *Southern Cross* is the popular name for a constellation called Crux, visible in the southern hemisphere. Sailors on the southern seas used to steer by it. Calder's mobile constellation seems to be made of pieces of night, and his stabile looks suspiciously capable of movement, as though it might skitter away on its pointy legs.

Art that moves is called **kinetic** art, from the Greek word *kinetos*, moving. Calder is considered to be one of its founders. But motion in the experience of art is not confined to the artworks themselves. As viewers, we also move, walking around and under Calder's *Southern Cross*, for example, to experience what it looks like from different distances and angles. We walk through architecture to explore its spaces, we draw near to and away from paintings to notice details or allow them to blur back into the whole. As we saw in Chapter 2, artists of the 20th century became increasingly conscious of the viewer's motion over time, especially in the context of gallery and museum spaces. Indeed, it would be difficult to understand how a work such as Eva Hesse's *Repetition Nineteen III* can be understood as art without imagining yourself in the same room with it, moving (**4.55**).

The nineteen units of *Repetition Nineteen III* sit on the floor. They are vessels of some kind, or receptacles. Irregular and organic, they seem oddly capable of movement, although they don't move. The translucent fiberglass is disturbingly reminiscent of skin. Their openings might be mouths. As we walk around them and crane to see into their depths, we become intensely self-conscious, painfully aware of our height, our awkwardness, our bodies. This uncomfortable self-awareness is part of the effect the artist intended.

The Greek word *kinetos* also gave us the word *cinema*, certainly the most significant new art form of the 20th century. Film and, later, video provided artists with new ways to work with time and motion. As these technologies become increasingly affordable and available, artists experimented with them more and more, to the point where video became an important medium for contemporary art.

In her video *89 Seconds at Alcázar*, Eve Sussman uses time and motion to meditate on the mysteries of one of the world's most famous paintings, *Las Meninas*, by the 17th-century Spanish painter Velázquez (**4.56**; for *Las Meninas*, see 17.11). Velázquez's painting has intrigued viewers for centuries, because while it claims to be a portrait of the Spanish princess and her handmaidens *(meninas)*, it also includes a self-portrait of Velázquez himself at work on a large canvas, as well as a portrait of the king and queen of Spain, who are reflected in the mirror on the far wall and who therefore must be standing next to us as we look. The implied space of the painting thus extends outward into our own world, confusing past and present, image and reality. In the background, a man stands in a doorway that opens onto a still deeper

4.54 Alexander Calder. *Southern Cross*. 1963. Sheet metal, rod, bolts, and paint; height 20'3". Courtesy Storm King Art Center, Mountainville, New York.

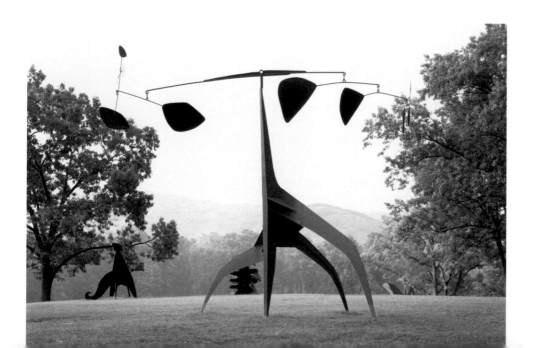

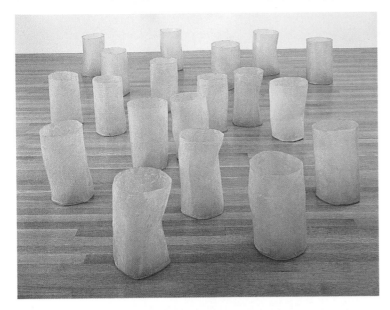

4.55 (above) Eva Hesse. *Repetition Nineteen III.* 1968. Nineteen tubular fiberglass units, height of each unit 19–20¼". The Museum of Modern Art, New York.

4.56 (below) Eve Sussman. *89 Seconds at Alcázar.* 2004. Single channel video. Courtesy Eve Sussman and The Rufus Corporation.

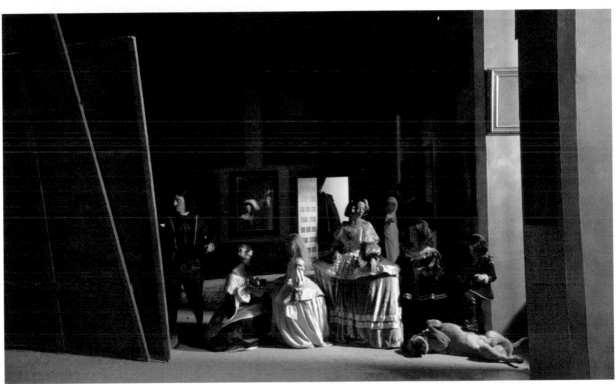

space. Finally, the princess and her retinue are depicted in mid-gesture, not sitting still as though for a portrait. Something is happening, but what, exactly? Is Velázquez working on a portrait of the king and queen who stand before him, and the princess has come in to greet them? Has he been working on a portrait of the princess, who is taking a break from her pose? The more we look, the more ingenious and mysterious the painting seems.

Sussman's video subtly explores these mysteries. Actors costumed as the people in the painting, including the king and queen, move about slowly and with great dignity. But they do not speak. The camera, too, moves fluidly into and around the space of the painting, another participant in motion. But we never do see what Velázquez is working on. The painting's mysteries are explored but not resolved or revealed, for we cannot know the answers. Like Brancusi's photograph of his own sculpture (see 1.2), Sussman's video shows how art lives in an attentive viewer's imagination, suggesting ways for us to make it live in our own as well.

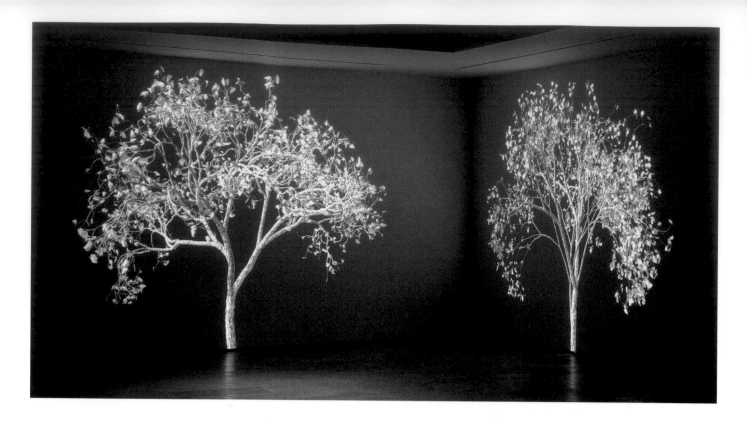

4.57 Jennifer Steinkamp. *Dervish*, detail. 2004. Video installation at Lehmann Maupin Gallery, New York, January 10–February 14, 2004; each tree 12 × 16' (size variable).

More recently, digital animation technology has allowed artists to create videos that do not necessarily rely on camera images. A beautiful example is Jennifer Steinkamp's installation *Dervish* (**4.57**). The installation was named for the order of Sufi mystics known in English as whirling dervishes, who enter into a state of spiritual ecstasy by means of a spinning dance. *Dervish* consisted of four digitally animated images of trees, each called *Dervish*, projected onto the walls of a darkened room. (The photograph here shows two of the trees.) Each individual branch, leaf, and blossom seemed alive as the trees twirled slowly, first one way and then the other, their virtual roots holding firm in the virtual ground, their trunks twisting like wrung laundry. Even more magically, each tree cycled through the seasons as it swayed, with spring blossoms giving way to summer foliage, then autumn colors, then bare branches.

To create her trees, Steinkamp began with an image of a maple. She modified each element digitally until she had created a tree that resembled no known tree at all, a completely artificial and virtual tree. Her only rule in her art, she says, is that everything must be simulated. Each *Dervish* can be programmed to display whatever season the viewer is in the mood for, or to change seasons on cue (the sound of a slamming door, for example, could cause spring to turn into summer). With strategies such as these, many digital artists surrender ultimate control over their creations.

Line, shape, mass, light, value, color, texture, pattern, space, time, and motion—these are the raw materials, the elements, of a work of art. In order to introduce them, we have had to look at each one individually, examining its role in various works of art. But in fact we do not perceive the elements one at a time but together, and almost any given work of art is not an example of one element but of many. In the next chapter, we examine how artists organize these elements into art, how this organization structures our experience of looking, and how an understanding of the visual elements and their organization can help us to see more fully.

CHAPTER FIVE

PRINCIPLES OF DESIGN

When an artist sets about making any work, he or she is faced with infinite choices. How big or small? What kinds of lines and where should the lines go? What kinds of shapes? How much space between the shapes? How many colors and how much of each one? What amounts of light and dark values? Somehow, the elements discussed in Chapter 4—line, shape, mass, light, value, color, texture, space, and possibly time and motion—must be organized in such a way as to satisfy the artist's expressive intent. In two-dimensional art this organization is often called **composition,** but the more inclusive term, applicable to all kinds of art, is **design.** The task of making the decisions involved in designing a work of art would be paralyzing were it not for certain guidelines that, once understood, become almost instinctive. These guidelines are usually known as the *principles of design.*

All of us have some built-in sense of what looks right or wrong, what "works" or doesn't. Some—including most artists—have a stronger sense of what "works" than others. If two families each decorate a living room, and one room is attractive, welcoming, and pulled together while the other seems drab and uninviting, we might say that the first family has better "taste." Taste is a common term that, in this context, describes how some people make visual selections. What we really mean by "good taste," oftentimes, is that some people have a better grasp of the principles of design and how to apply them in everyday situations.

The principles of design are a natural part of perception. Most of us are not conscious of them in everyday life, but artists usually are very aware of them, because they have trained themselves to be aware. These principles codify, or explain systematically, our sense of "rightness" and help to show why certain designs work better than others. For the artist they offer guidelines for making the most effective choices; for the observer an understanding of the principles of design gives greater insight into works of art.

The principles of design most often identified are unity and variety, balance, emphasis and subordination, proportion and scale, and rhythm. This chapter illustrates some thirty-four works of art that show these principles very clearly. But *any* work of art, regardless of its form or the culture in which it was made, could be discussed in terms of the principles of design, for they are integral to all art.

UNITY AND VARIETY

Unity is a sense of oneness, of things belonging together and making up a coherent whole. Variety is difference, which provides interest. We discuss them together because the two generally coexist in a work of art. A solid wall painted white certainly has unity, but it is not likely to hold your interest for long. Take that same blank wall and ask fifty people each to make a mark on it and you will get plenty of variety, but there probably will be no unity whatever. In fact, there will be so *much* variety that no one can form a meaningful visual impression. Unity and variety exist on a spectrum, with total blandness at one end, total disorder at the other. For most works of art the artist strives to find just the right point on that spectrum—the point at which there is sufficient visual unity enlivened by sufficient variety.

The first thing that strikes us when we look at Matisse's *Memory of Oceania* (**5.1**) is the exhilarating variety of the colors and shapes. On longer acquaintance, however, we can begin to see how the composition is unified around a few simple principles. The colors are in fact limited to six plus black and white, and all of them but the pale yellow in the upper left corner repeat, creating visual connections across the picture plane. The shapes, while highly varied, fall into three "families"—rectangles (mostly concentrated in the upper right quadrant), simple curves (mostly concentrated at the lower right), and waves (blue and white, alternating in positive and negative shapes at the far left and far right). Only the pale yellow shape is without an echo. After a lifetime spent painting in his native France, Matisse had voyaged to Tahiti, in the South Pacific, hoping to refresh his eyes in a different kind of light. *Memories of Oceania* is a distillation of what he found there.

5.1 Henri Matisse. *Memory of Oceania*. 1953. Gouache on paper, cut and pasted, and charcoal on white paper; 9'4" × 9'4⅞". The Museum of Modern Art, New York.

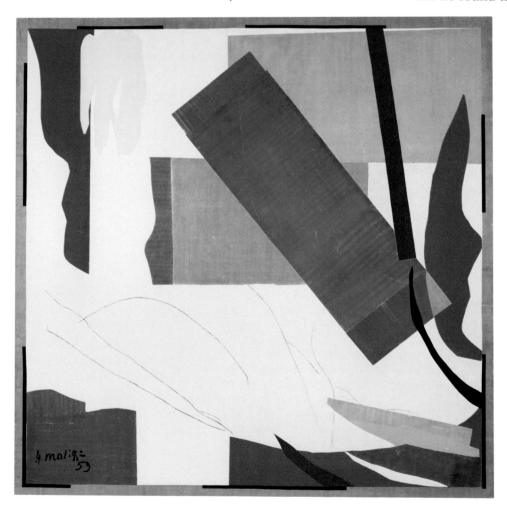

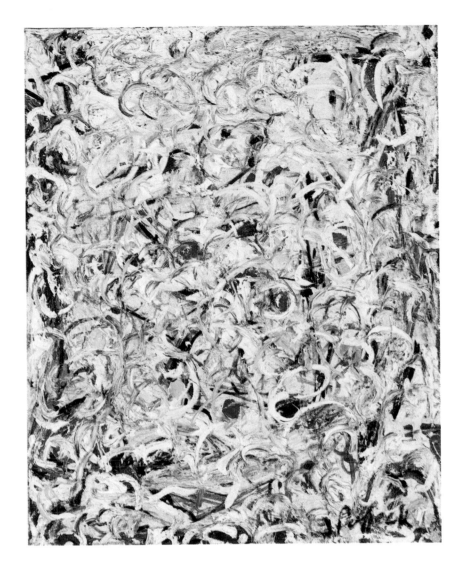

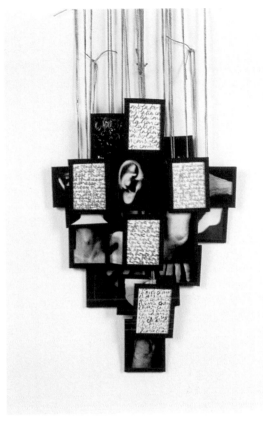

Jackson Pollock's *Shimmering Substances* (**5.2**) presents us with a different approach to balancing unity and variety. On the one hand, small patches and dashes of color appear in a bewildering variety that seems to have no logic or unity at all. On the other hand, short, lashing brush strokes thick with paint weave the entire surface together into a unifying visual texture that has very little variety. By taking both unity and variety to extremes, Pollock achieved his artistic breakthrough. Not long after painting *Shimmering Substances*, he made the first of the "drip" paintings that brought him lasting fame (see 22.1). Created by flinging and drizzling paint into a large canvas laid out on the floor, they too are based in the strategy of pushing unity and variety to such extremes that they seem to merge, allowing us to see them as nothing but unity, or nothing but variety.

The two works we have just considered demonstrate *visual* unity—unity based in the elements of shape, line, color, and so on. Art can also be unified *conceptually*, that is, through a unity of ideas. Annette Messager relies largely on conceptual unity in her assemblage called *Mes Voeux* (French for "my wishes," **5.3**). If we think about what the photographs have in common, we realize that they all portray isolated body parts—knee, throat, mouth, ear, hand. The framed texts ask not only to be looked at but to be read. Two repeat the word *tenderness* over and over again; another, the word *shame*. Understanding the grouping as a kind of body itself places *consolation* at the head, *tenderness* at the arms, *shame* at the sex, and *luck* at the legs. Repeating shapes and restricted color give visual unity to the work, but it is conceptual unity that asks for our interpretation.

5.2 (left) Jackson Pollock. *Shimmering Substance (Sounds in the Grass series)*. 1946. Oil on canvas, 30⅛ × 24¼".
The Museum of Modern Art, New York.

5.3 (right) Annette Messager. *Mes Voeux*. 1989. Framed photographs and handwritten texts, suspended with twine; 59 × 15¾".
Courtesy Marian Goodman Gallery, Paris.

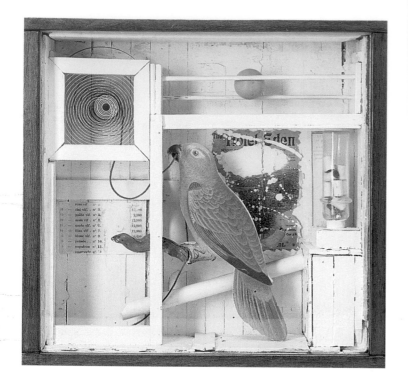

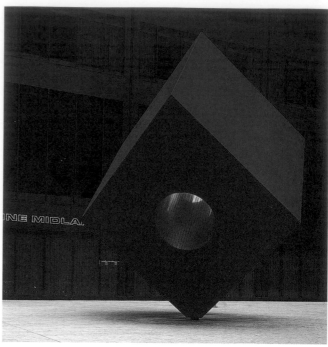

5.4 (left) Joseph Cornell. *The Hotel Eden.* 1945. Assemblage with music box, 15⅛ × 15⅛ × 4¾".
National Gallery of Canada, Ottawa.

5.5 (right) Isamu Noguchi. *Red Cube.* 1968. Steel painted red.
Photo courtesy The Isamu Noguchi Foundation, Inc.

Conceptual unity predominates as well in the works of Joseph Cornell, such as *The Hotel Eden* (**5.4**). Cornell devoted most of his career to making boxlike structures that enclosed many dissimilar but related objects. Contained within the boxes, these objects build their own private worlds. Cornell collected things, odds and ends, wherever he went. His studio held crates of stuff filed according to a personal system. There were even crates labeled "flotsam" and "jetsam." When making his box sculptures, Cornell would select and arrange these objects to create a conceptual unity that was meaningful to him, based on his dreams, nostalgia, and fantasies. By placing such disparate objects and images together in a boxed enclosure with still smaller boxlike divisions within, Cornell imposed a visual unity that asks us to accept them as a coherent whole and to spend some time puzzling out their connections.

BALANCE

Isamu Noguchi's delightful sculpture *Red Cube* (**5.5**) balances impossibly on one point. Noguchi wittily took the industrial materials and rectangular forms of mid-20th-century architecture and stood them on end, as though the buildings all around were pedestrians and his sculpture a dancer in their midst.

Noguchi's sculpture balances because its weight is distributed evenly around a central axis. The photograph of the sculpture is balanced as well, balanced *visually*. The simple red form set starkly against a dark background draws our attention strongly to the right. The white letters pull our eyes more gently to the left, as do the dark windows and the open hollow of the sculpture itself. Sculpture, hollow, letters, windows—all have a certain visual weight, and together they balance the photograph so that our gaze is never "stuck" in one place but moves freely around the image.

Visual weight refers to the apparent "heaviness" or "lightness" of the forms arranged in a composition, as gauged by how insistently they draw our eyes. When visual weight is equally distributed to either side of a felt or implied center of gravity, we feel that the composition is balanced.

Symmetrical Balance

With symmetrical balance, the implied center of gravity is the vertical axis, an imaginary line drawn down the center of the composition. Forms on either side of the axis correspond to one another in size, shape, and placement. Sometimes the symmetry is so perfect that the two sides of a composition are mirror images of one another. More often the correspondence is very close but not exact—a situation sometimes called relieved symmetry.

Georgia O'Keeffe used symmetrical balance in *Deer's Skull with Pedernal* (**5.6**). The skull itself is perfectly symmetrical, and O'Keeffe sets it directly on the vertical axis. She then softens the symmetry with subtle shifts in balance. Toward the top of the image, the dead tree branches off to the right, its branches rhyming with the skull's horns. To the bottom of the image, the trunk swerves off to the right as well, but a pale upward-thrusting branch, a lone cloud, and the distinctive silhouette of Pedernal mountain all add visual weight to the left.

5.6 Georgia O'Keeffe. *Deer's Skull with Pedernal.* 1936. Oil on canvas, 36 × 30".
Courtesy Museum of Fine Arts, Boston.

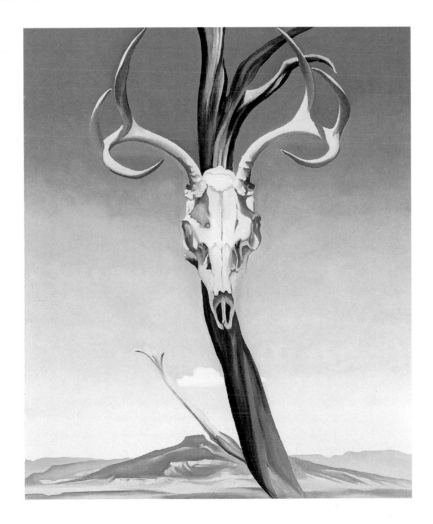

GEORGIA O'KEEFFE

1887–1986

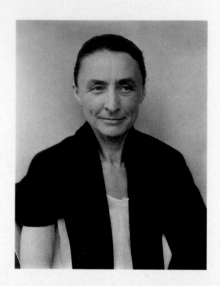

"**A**T LAST! A woman on paper!" According to legend, this was the reaction of the famed photographer and art dealer Alfred Stieglitz, in 1916, when he first saw the work of Georgia O'Keeffe. Whether accurate or not, the quote sums up Stieglitz' view of O'Keeffe as the first great artist to bring to her work the true essence and experience of womanhood. Ultimately, much of the critical art world came to share Stieglitz' opinion.

O'Keeffe was born on a farm in Wisconsin. She received a thorough, if conventional, art training at the School of the Art Institute of Chicago and the Art Students League in New York. During the early years she supported herself by teaching art in schools and colleges. By 1912 she was teaching in Amarillo, Texas—the beginning of a lifelong infatuation with the terrain of the Southwest.

In the winter of 1915–16 O'Keeffe sent a number of drawings to a friend in New York, asking her not to show the drawings to anyone. The friend violated this trust—and no doubt helped to set the path for O'Keeffe's entire life and career. She took the drawings to Stieglitz.

By 1916 Stieglitz had gained considerable fame, not only as a photographer but, through his "291" Gallery, as an exhibitor of the most innovative European and American painters. He was stunned by O'Keeffe's work. Later that year he included her in a group show at "291," and in 1917 he gave her a solo exhibition. This was the beginning of an extraordinary artistic and personal collaboration that would last until Stieglitz' death in 1946.

O'Keeffe moved to New York. Stieglitz left his wife and lived with her. O'Keeffe painted; Stieglitz exhibited her work and made hundreds of photographs of her. The couple married in 1924, but their union was always an unconventional one. For more than a quarter-century their paths crossed and separated. Stieglitz was most at home in New York City and at his family's summer place at Lake George. O'Keeffe was drawn increasingly to the stark landscapes of Texas and New Mexico. O'Keeffe treasured her husband's presence but could paint at her best only in the Southwest. Stieglitz longed for her company but also wanted her paintings for his gallery.

O'Keeffe gained critical acclaim with her first exhibition, and it never entirely left her. Although major showings of her work were rare after Stieglitz died, no one forgot Georgia O'Keeffe. She was part of no "school" or style. Her work took an exceptionally personal path, as did her life. She dressed almost exclusively in black. She came and went as she pleased and accepted into her world only those people whom she found talented and interesting. More than most, O'Keeffe marched to her own drummer.

After 1949 O'Keeffe lived permanently in New Mexico, the area with which she is most closely associated. In 1972, when she was eighty-four years old, a potter in his twenties, Juan Hamilton, came into her life, and they became close companions. Rumors that they married are probably unfounded, but Hamilton remained with the increasingly feeble, almost-blind artist until her death.

Early on, in her thirties, O'Keeffe had expressed her impatience with other people's standards for life and art: "I decided I was a very stupid fool not to at least paint as I wanted to and say what I wanted to when I painted as that seemed to be the only thing I could do that didn't concern anybody but myself— that was nobody's business but my own."[1]

Alfred Stieglitz. *Georgia O'Keeffe*. Gelatin silver print, 9⅓ × 7⅜". The Metropolitan Museum of Art, New York.

The central placement of the symmetrical deer skull gives O'Keeffe's painting a forceful, formal presence, as though it were a coat of arms or a symbol on a banner. Indeed, symmetrical balance is often used to express order, harmony, and authority, whether earthly and social or cosmic and spiritual. Cosmic order is the subject of one of the most distinctive of world art forms, the mandala (**5.7**). A mandala is a diagram of a cosmic realm. The most famous mandalas are connected with Buddhism, though there are Hindu mandalas as well. The mandala here is a Tibetan Buddhist one, and it depicts the cosmic realm emanating from the female buddha Jnanadakini, the Sky-goer of Transcendental Insight, who is shown seated in its centermost square. Everything radiates outward from her, including four more female buddhas, deities of the cardinal points (north, south, east, west), and other celestial beings.

The word *mandala* means "circle" in Sanskrit, the ritual language of early South Asia, where both Buddhism and Hinduism first took form. For practitioners, a mandala serves to focus meditation in the goal of achieving enlightenment. The basic message of its clear geometry and symmetry is this: We are living in a universe that makes sense, even if its logic and order are hidden from us during our brief lifetimes. Much religious art uses symmetrical balance to convey the same message.

5.7 Newar artists at Densatil Monastery, Central Tibet. *Thirteen-Deity Jnanadakini Mandala.* 1417–47. Opaque watercolor on cotton cloth, 33¼ × 28⅞" Metropolitan Museum of Art, New York.

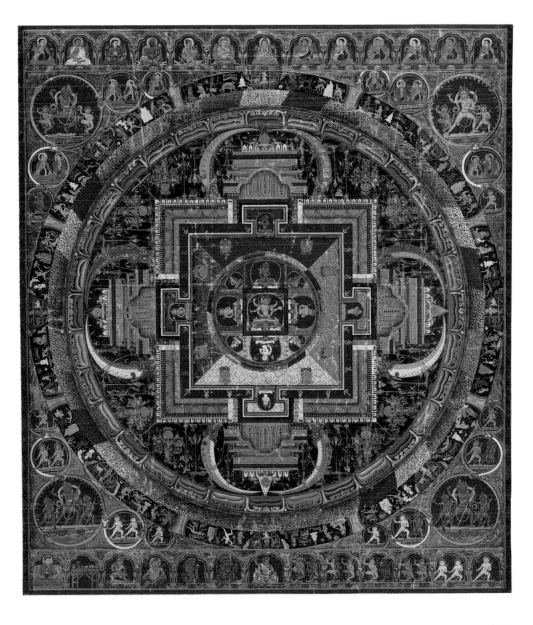

The Luo Brothers may have something similar in mind with the symmetrical design of their *Welcome the World Famous Brand Name* (**5.8**). The three brothers live in China, a country that is going through profound changes as it claims a place in the globalizing economy. *Welcome the World Famous Brand Name* depicts an extravagant patriotic pageant, with cheering spectators, banks of flowers, and representatives of the armed forces on parade. Stylized sunbeams radiate from behind a central building. Chinese viewers would recognize it instantly as the Temple of Heaven in Beijing, the Chinese capital. During the imperial era, the emperor himself came here to offer a yearly sacrifice to Heaven (as the supreme Chinese deity was known) so that the country might prosper.

Overhead, we see a second pageant, a heavenly one. Celestial infants riding immortal cranes bear aloft famous products—hamburgers, French fries, soft drinks, chewing gum, cookies, and more—all with their brand names on view. Along the spectator stands, banners of corporate sponsors proclaim the names again. (At the very center are the Chinese words for "Coca-Cola.") In case there's any doubt about what we're supposed to be feeling, two of the celestial infants hold up round signs with the Chinese word for "happiness" written on them. "Heaven and earth are in harmony!" the Luo brothers seem to say. "The cosmic order and the corporate order are one and the same!" Do they really mean it? You decide.

Symmetrical balance served the artist Frida Kahlo with exceptional force in *The Two Fridas* (**5.9**). Kahlo was born in Mexico in 1907, the child of a Hungarian/Jewish father and an Indian/Spanish mother. These two influences—the European and the Mexican—coexisted uneasily in her psyche and her art as long as she lived. *The Two Fridas* shows this graphically. At left is the "European Frida," dressed in an elegant white gown; at right, the "Mexican Frida" wears a costume suited to that country's natives. Both have their hearts exposed in gory anatomical detail, with veins connecting them. The Mexican Frida holds a tiny portrait of the artist Diego Rivera, to whom Kahlo was married. The European Frida uses a surgical clamp to hold a severed vein that drips blood onto her skirt. This picture's symmetrical format gives a chilling

5.8 The Luo Brothers. *Welcome the World Famous Brand Name.* Collage and lacquer on wood, 8⅞" × 4'1½" × 1³⁄₁₆" Courtesy the Luo Brothers and Ray Hughes Gallery, Sydney.

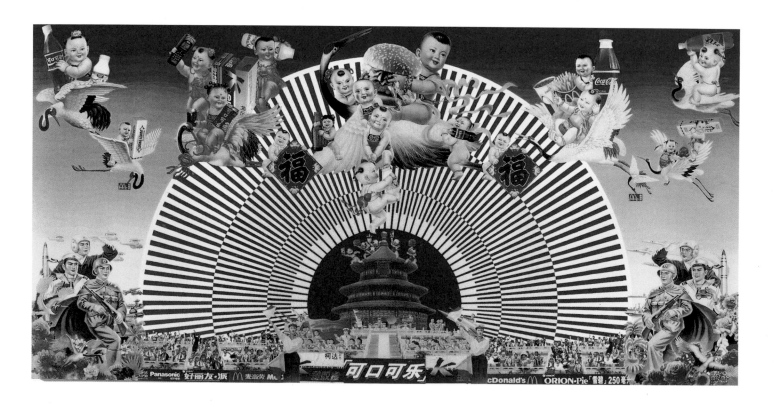

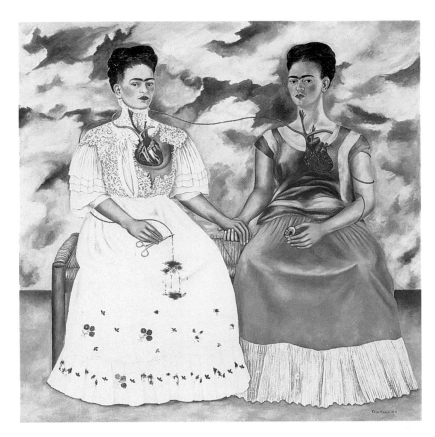

5.9 (left) Frida Kahlo. *The Two Fridas.* 1939. Oil on canvas, 5'8½" square.
Museo Nacionale de Arte Moderno, Instituto Nacional de Bellas Artes, Mexico City.

5.10 (below) Some principles of visual balance.

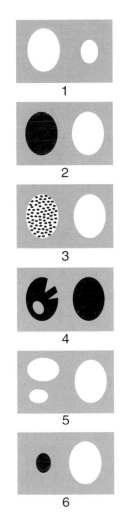

interpretation to the double identity of its maker, for it is a symmetry that is breaking down: The shapes are symmetrical, but the colors are not. There is a conflict, and something that should be whole is divided.

Asymmetrical Balance

When you stand with your feet flat on the floor and your arms at your sides, you are in symmetrical balance. But if you thrust an arm out in one direction and a leg out in the other, your balance is asymmetrical (not symmetrical). Similarly, an asymmetrical composition has two sides that do not match. If it seems to be balanced, that is because the visual weights in the two halves are very similar. What looks "heavy" and what looks "light"? The only possible answer is, that depends. We do not perceive absolutes but relationships. The heaviness or lightness of any form varies depending on its size in relation to other sizes around it, its color in relation to other colors around it, and its placement in the composition in relation to the placement of other forms there. The drawing (**5.10**) illustrates some very general precepts about asymmetrical or informal balance:

1. A large form is visually heavier than a smaller form.
2. A dark-value form is visually heavier than a light-value form of the same size.
3. A textured form is visually heavier than a smooth form of the same size.
4. A complex form is visually heavier than a simple form of the same size.
5. Two or more small forms can balance a larger one.
6. A smaller dark form can balance a larger light one.

5.11 (below) Gustav Klimt. *Death and Life*. Before 1911, finished 1915. Oil on canvas, 5'10" × 6'6". Museum Leopold, Vienna.

5.12 (right) Tawaraya (Nonomura) Sotatsu. *The Zen Priest Choka*. Edo period, late 16th–early 17th century. Hanging scroll, ink on paper; 37¾ × 14¼". The Cleveland Museum of Art.

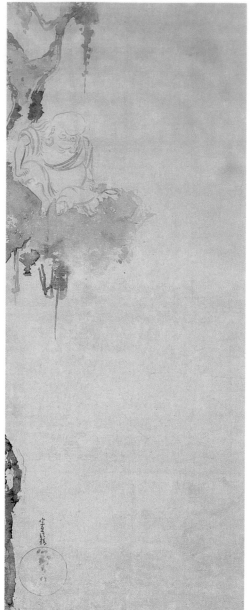

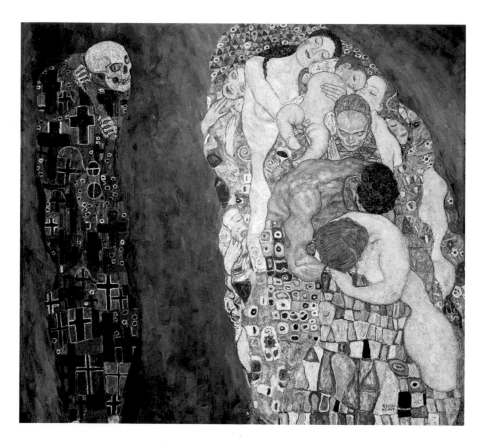

These are only a few of the possibilities. Keeping them in mind, you may still wonder, but how does an artist actually go about balancing a composition? The answer is unsatisfactory but true: The composition is balanced when it looks balanced. An understanding of visual weights can help the artist achieve balance or see what is wrong when balance is off, but it is no exact science.

In Gustav Klimt's *Death and Life* (**5.11**), asymmetrical balance dramatizes the opposition between life, envisioned to the right as a billowing form of light-hued patterns and slumbering human figures, and death, a dark skeletal presence at the far left, robed in a chilling pattern of grave markers. The two halves of the painting are linked by the gaze that passes between death and the woman he has come to claim. Klimt has placed her face exactly on the vertical axis of the painting, which here serves as a sort of symbolic border between life and death. The only waking person in the dreaming cloud of life, she smiles awkwardly and gestures as if to say, "Me?" Death leers back, "Yes, you." The intensity of their gaze exerts a strong pull on our attention to the upper left, and Klimt balances this with an equal pull of visual weight to the right and down.

It would be difficult to imagine a more daring asymmetrical composition than Tawaraya Sotatsu's ink painting of *The Zen Priest Choka* (**5.12**). The forms are placed so far to the left as to be barely on the page! Sotatsu relies on an implied line of vision both to balance the composition and to reveal its meaning. We naturally raise our eyes to look at the form of the priest sitting in the tree— that's all there is to look at. We then follow the direction of his gaze down to . . . nothing. Meditation on emptiness is one of the exercises prescribed by Zen Buddhism, and this ingenious painting makes it clear. Our eyes repeatedly seek out the priest, who repeatedly sends us back to focus on nothingness.

For a masterful example of asymmetrical balance as it is more typically found in Western painting, we turn to *The Burning of the Houses of Parliament* by the English painter J. M. Turner (**5.13**). Turner was an eyewitness to the catastrophe, which he watched from a boat on the Thames River in London. In his painting, he places the viewer on the opposite bank of the river. Our eyes are immediately drawn to the spectacular conflagration in the distance at the left. Turner balances this leftward attraction with the large white form of the bridge to the right, which brings us to the foreground of the painting where a crowd has gathered. A single white street lamp—the lightest value in the painting—draws our eyes to the left, and from there we circle back to the flames, this time allowing the directional lines of the rose and dark smoke to carry our eyes off into the night sky, where a few stars shine.

5.13 Joseph Mallord Turner. *The Burning of the Houses of Parliament.* c. 1835. Oil on canvas, 36¼ × 48½". Philadelphia Museum of Art.

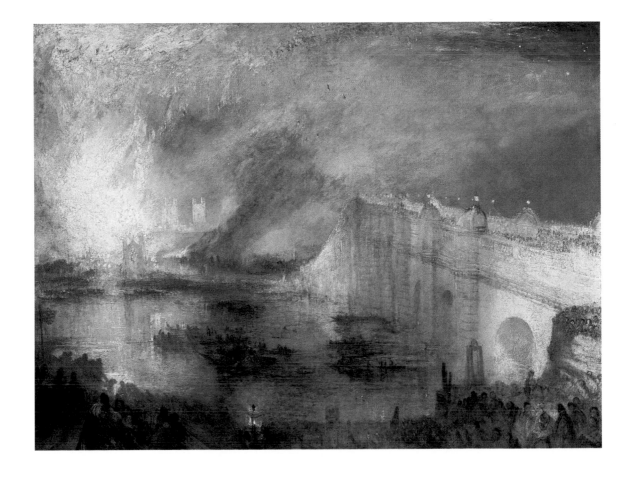

Turner's composition leads our eyes on a journey around the implied depth of the painting. Depth, or the lack of it, is a fascinating issue in Manet's *A Bar at the Folies-Bergère* (**5.14**). The barmaid seems to stand before a large interior that recedes far back into the distance. Actually she is wedged into a narrow space between the marble bar and a large mirror, which reflects all that she can see but cannot participate in. Her own reflection is displaced to the right, where we see that she is waiting on a man who must be standing where we are standing as we view the painting. Around the central, symmetrical form of the barmaid Manet scatters a dazzling display of visual weights and counterweights. The large dark form of the barmaid's reflection, the bowl of oranges next to the green bottle on the bar, the bottles to either side and their reflections in the mirror, the massive chandeliers and the moonlike white globes in the background, the woman in white who props her elbows on the balcony, even the green-clad feet of the trapeze artist visible at the upper left corner—all have a role to play. Place your finger over any element and you can see the life go out of that part of the painting and the overall balance become destabilized.

Balance, then, encourages our active participation in looking. By using balance to lead our eyes around a work, artists structure our experience of it. As an important aspect of form, balance also helps communicate a mood or meaning. The promise of an unchanging, eternal paradise is embodied in the stable, symmetrical balance of the *Jnanadakini Mandala* (see 5.7), just as the dramatic confrontation of life and death is embodied in the dynamic asymmetrical balance of Klimt's *Death and Life* (see 5.11).

5.14 Edouard Manet. *A Bar at the Folies-Bergère.* 1881–82. Oil on canvas, 37¾ × 51¼".
The Samuel Courtauld Trust, Courtauld Institute of Art Gallery, London.

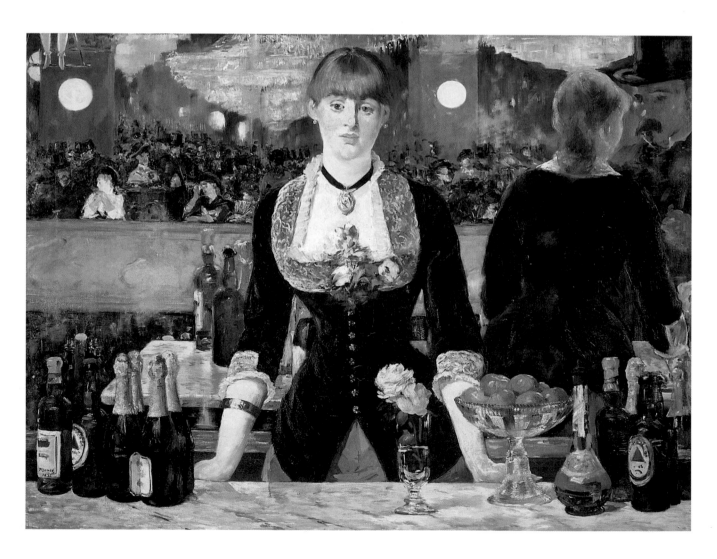

POINTS OF VIEW

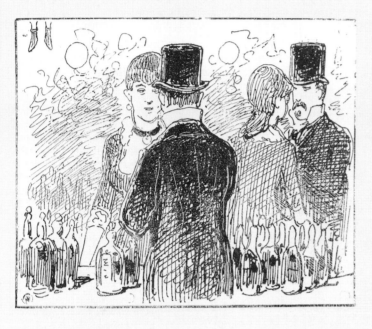

Art historians have developed many points of view, each with its own set of intellectual tools for seeing and making sense. One approach is called formalism. Formalism focuses on the formal elements of a work, especially its style. Viewed formally, Manet's *Bar* marks a milestone in the development of modern art, for the changes he made while creating it tended to eliminate any clear story it was telling and to flatten the space it was depicting—two prominent characteristics of modernism. Another approach is iconography, which focuses on subject matter and its meanings. Viewers taking an iconographic point of view have noticed that the painting contains the traditional elements of a *vanitas* image, with the reflected man taking the place of Death (see 5.32). A biographical point of view explores links between an artist's life and work. Scholars have noted that Manet was gravely ill when he painted the *Bar*. He could no longer go to such places as the Folies-Bergère, which had formerly delighted him.

Psychoanalysis provides another set of tools for looking at the relationship between creators and their creations. Scholars following this approach have talked about what one psychoanalyst calls the mirror stage of human development, when an infant first forms a sense of self, forever sundering the unity it felt while gazing into its mother's eyes. Another approach sets art in the social context of its time. Marxism has provided scholars with useful tools for looking at the economic basis of society and the dynamics of class within it. The barmaid, for example, is a member of the working class. Her job is to be pretty for the customers, and perhaps to be available in other ways as well. Feminism provides still other insights based in the observation that making and viewing art are gendered activities, which is to say that a culture's ideas about maleness and femaleness are in play. Feminist scholars have examined the complicated dynamic of gendered gazes in and around the painting—Manet's, the barmaid's, her customer's, those of the spectators in the background, and the viewer's.[2]

WHEN MANET's *Bar at the Folies-Bergère* was exhibited for the first time, the cartoonist Stop contributed this drawing of it to a Paris newspaper. Thanks to Stop, we can see that what strikes us as strange about the painting struck its first viewers as strange too: Why doesn't the reflection in the mirror match the scene before it, and where is the man whose reflection we see at the right? In a caption to his drawing, Stop joked that he felt it was his duty to correct these problems, which were no doubt due to the painter's momentary distraction.

Critics in Manet's day had a point of view, which was that a painting, before it was anything else, should at least be an accurate and believable representation. Today, with the benefit of hindsight, we begin with the assumption that what we see is what Manet intended. X-ray photographs of the painting in fact reveal that Manet twice shifted the barmaid's reflection further to the right. When he began, the composition was far more naturalistic. The barmaid's pose changed as well: She was not so still and symmetrical at first. We see the result of a long creative process. But how are we to interpret it? What is our point of view?

Stop. *Edouard Manet, Une Marchande de Consolation aux Folies-Bergère.* Wood engraving from *Le Journal Amusant*, May 27, 1882.

EMPHASIS AND SUBORDINATION

Emphasis and subordination are complementary concepts. Emphasis means that our attention is drawn more to certain parts of a composition than to others. If the emphasis is on a relatively small, clearly defined area, we call this a focal point. Subordination means that certain areas of the composition are purposefully made less visually interesting, so that the areas of emphasis stand out.

There are many ways to create emphasis. In *The Banjo Lesson* (**5.15**), Henry Ossawa Tanner used size and placement to emphasize the figures of the old man and young boy. Tanner set the pair in the foreground, and he posed them so that their visual weights combine to form a single mass, the largest form in the painting. Strongly contrasting values of dark skin against a pale background add further emphasis. Within this emphasized area, Tanner uses

5.15 Henry Ossawa Tanner. *The Banjo Lesson*. 1893. Oil on canvas, 49 × 35½".
Hampton University Museum, Hampton, Virginia.

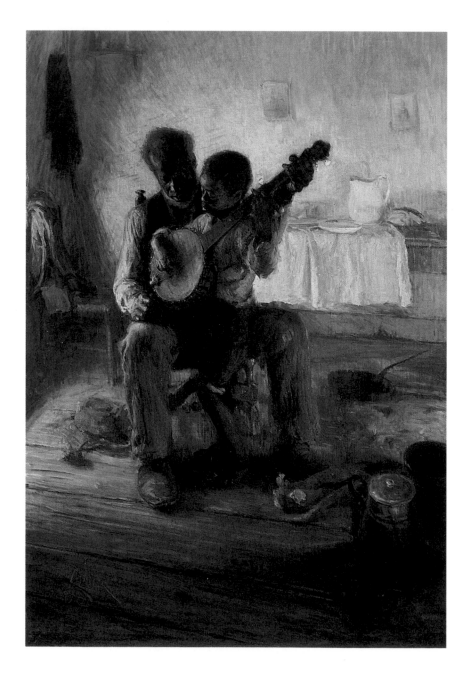

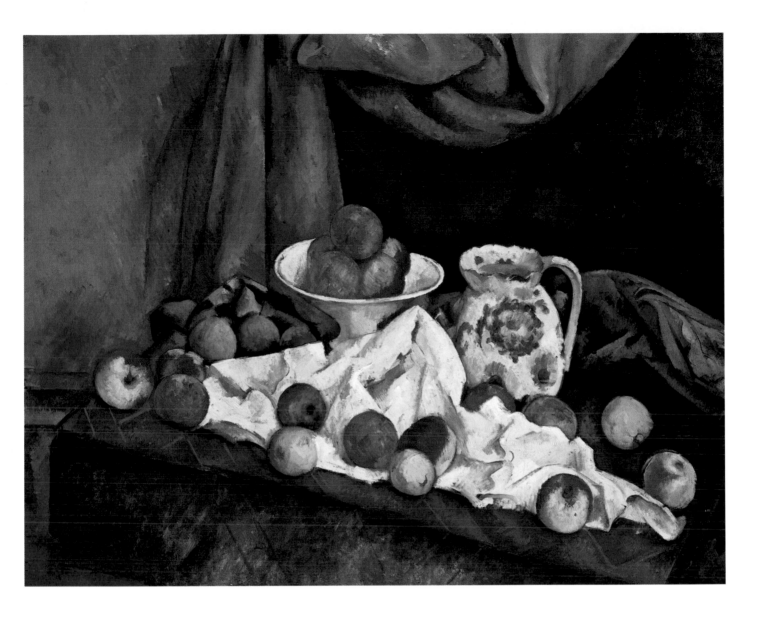

5.16 Paul Cézanne. *Still Life with Compotier, Pitcher, and Fruit.* 1892–94. Oil on canvas, 28¼ × 36¼".
The Barnes Foundation, Merion, Pennsylvania.

directional lines of sight to create a focal point on the circular body of the banjo and the boy's hand on it. Again contrast plays a role, for the light form of the banjo is set amid darker values, and the boy's hand contrasts dark against light. Tanner has subordinated the background so that it does not interfere, blurring the detail and working in a narrow range of light values. Imagine, for example, if one of the pictures depicted hanging on the far wall were painted in bright colors and minute detail. It would "jump out" of the painting and steal the focus away from what Tanner wants us to notice.

In his autumnal *Still Life with Compotier, Pitcher, and Fruit* (**5.16**), Paul Cézanne arranged a white napkin to create a central focal area and subordinated the rest of the image through a closely harmonized palette of earth tones. Drawn up into a peak at the center, the napkin looks like a domestic version of Mont Sainte-Victoire, the mountain that Cézanne painted so often (see 21.10). A white fruit dish (compotier) and a white pitcher flank the peak, lending additional visual weight to the center of the composition. Over this base of dark and light values, Cézanne scattered red, orange, yellow, and green fruits, patches of intense color. Each a brilliant focal point in its own right, the fruits are gathered into the larger order of the composition by the white cloth, and they culminate in the pyramid of oranges and apples raised high by the bowl.

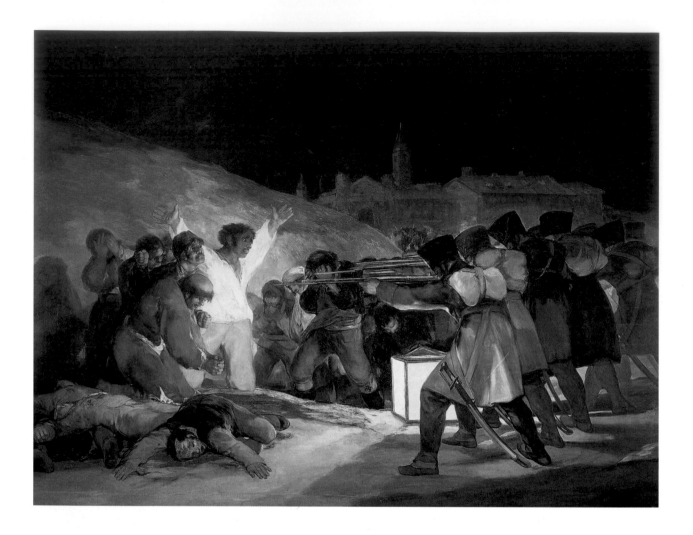

5.17 Francisco de Goya. *Executions of the Third of May, 1808.* 1814–15. Oil on canvas, 8'9" × 13'4". Museo del Prado, Madrid.

Francisco de Goya used almost the same color scheme to much different effect in *Executions of the Third of May, 1808* (**5.17**). Once again, white, yellow, and red demand our attention by creating a dramatic focal area against a background of earth tones and black. This time, however, the subject is not a napkin and fruit but a man about to die, the blood of those who have preceded him, and a lantern that casts a light as harsh as the sound of a scream. The scene is set as minimally as possible so that nothing distracts our attention from the terrible slaughter. A barren hillside. Madrid. Darkness. The event Goya depicted occurred during the invasion of Spain by Napoleon, when a popular uprising in Madrid was brutally suppressed by occupying French soldiers. In addition to dramatic contrasts in value, Goya uses psychological forces to direct not only our attention but also our sympathy. Faces serve as natural focal points. The victims of the firing squad have faces, and we can read their expressions; the soldiers are faceless, as though they were not even human. They lunge forward as we look at them, creating directional forces that send us back again to the incipient martyr, his hands flung outward in a gesture of crucifixion.

SCALE AND PROPORTION

Proportion and scale both have to do with size. **Scale** means size in relation to a standard or "normal" size. Normal size is the size we expect something to be. For example, a model airplane is smaller in scale than a real airplane; a 10-

pound prize-winning tomato at the county fair is a tomato on a large scale. The artist Claes Oldenburg delights in the effects that a radical shift in scale can produce. In *Plantoir*, created with Coosje van Bruggen, he presents a humble gardening tool on a heroic scale (**5.18**). Perhaps it is a monument, but to what? Part of the delight in coming across a sculpture by Oldenburg and Van Bruggen is the shock of having our own scale overthrown as the measure of all things. Many fairy tales and adventure stories tell of humans who find themselves in a land of giants. In the sculptures of Oldenburg and Van Bruggen, the giants seem to have left an item or two behind.

The Belgian painter René Magritte used many pictorial strategies to suggest that the world around us might not be as rational and ordered as we like to think. One of his favorites was a shift in scale. In *Delusions of Grandeur II* (**5.19**), he invented a sort of telescoping woman, with each section rising out of the one before and continuing on a smaller scale. Transforming one element into another was also a favorite ploy, as when the sky, which looks perfectly normal at the horizon, is revealed farther up to be made of solid blue blocks.

Proportion refers to size relationships between parts of a whole, or between two or more items perceived as a unit. For example, the proportions of each section of the body in the painting by Magritte are naturalistic. The breasts in the top section are in the correct proportion to the size of the neck and arm openings; the navel in the middle section is in the correct proportion to the overall size of the belly.

5.18 (left) Claes Oldenburg and Coosje van Bruggen. *Plantoir.* 2001. Stainless steel, aluminum, fiber-reinforced plastic, painted with polyurethane enamel; height 23'11".
Collection Fundação de Serralves, Porto.

5.19 (right) René Magritte. *Delusions of Grandeur II.* 1948. Oil on canvas, 39⅛ × 32⅛". Hirshhorn Museum and Sculpture Garden, Smithsonian Institution, Washington, D.C.

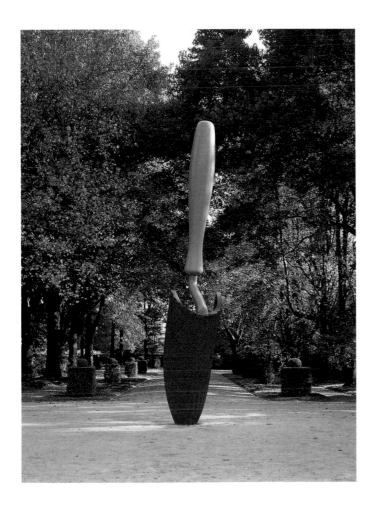

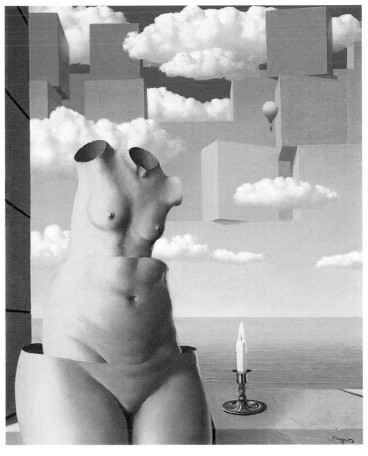

Many artistic cultures have developed a fixed set of proportions for depicting a "correct" or "perfect" human form. Ancient Egyptian artists, for example, relied on a squared grid to govern the proportions of their figures (**5.20**). Unfinished fragments such as this give us a rare insight into their working methods, for in finished works the grid is no longer evident. Egyptian artists took the palm of the hand as the basic unit of measurement. Looking at the illustration, you can see that each palm (or back) of a hand occupies one square of the grid. A standing figure measures 18 units from the soles of the feet to the hairline, with the knee falling at horizontal 6, the elbow at horizontal 12, the nipple at 14, and so on. The shoulders of a standing male were 6 units wide; the waist about 2½ units.

Artists have often varied human proportions for symbolic or aesthetic purposes, as in this royal altar from the African kingdom of Benin (**5.21**). Cast in brass, the altar is dedicated to the king's hand, a symbol of physical prowess. Hands are depicted around its base, where they alternate with rams' heads. The king is shown seated atop the altar, flanked by attendants in a symmetrical composition. The composition expresses a social hierarchy. As the most important person, the king is at the center. He is also portrayed on a larger scale than his attendants. The use of scale to indicate relative importance is called **hierarchical scale.** Proportionally, the king's head takes up a full third of his total height. "Great Head" is one of the terms used in praise of the king, who is felt to rule his subjects as the head, the seat of wisdom and judgment, rules the body. Representations of the king make these ideas manifest through proportion.

The painter El Greco, in contrast, elongated his figures and made their heads proportionally smaller (**5.22**). The twisting, sinuous contours and dramatic, flickering lighting create an effect so extreme and so original that for many generations it was assumed that the painter had some sort of eye trouble that caused him actually to see people this way. In fact, El Greco's treatment of the figure was influenced by contemporary theories that praised a candle flame as ideally beautiful because of its elongated, twisting contours. Here, the spiritual energy released by Christ's triumph over death is imagined as a sort of explosion, and the flamelike figures seem to burn with the intensity of the moment.

Among the many ideas from ancient Greece and Rome that were revived during the Renaissance was the notion that numerical relationships held the

5.20 (left) Stela of the sculptor Userwer, detail. Egypt, Dynasty 12, 1991–1783 B.C.E.
The British Museum, London.

5.21 (right) A royal altar to the hand *(ikegobo).* Benin, 18th century. Brass, height 18".
The British Museum, London.

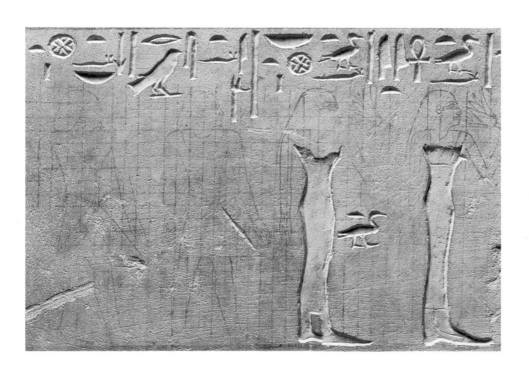
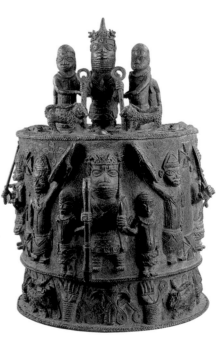

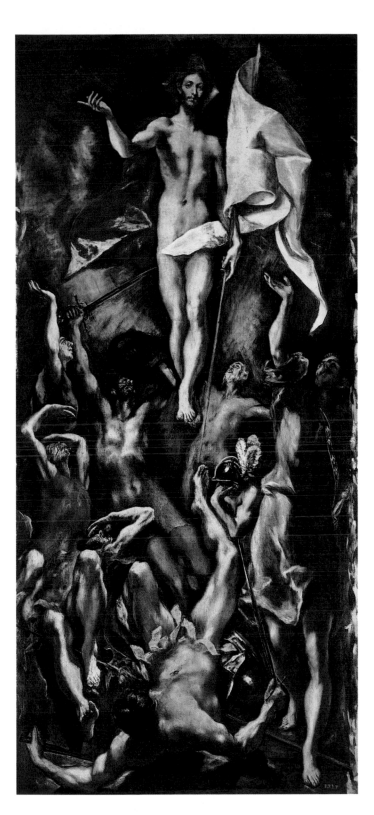

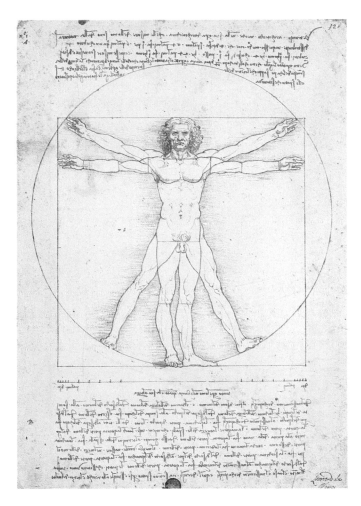

5.22 (left) El Greco. *Resurrection.* c. 1600–05. Oil on canvas, 9'¼" × 4'2".
Museo del Prado, Madrid.

5.23 (right) Leonardo da Vinci. *Study of Human Proportions according to Vitruvius.* c. 1485–90. Pen and ink, 13½ × 9¾".
Gallerie dell'Accademia, Venice.

key to beauty, and that perfect human proportions reflected a divine order. Leonardo da Vinci was only one of many artists to become fascinated with the ideas of Vitruvius, a Roman architect of the first century B.C.E. whose treatise on architecture, widely read during the Renaissance, related the perfected male form to the perfect geometry of the square and the circle (**5.23**). Leonardo's figure stands inside a square defined by his height and the span of his arms, and a circle centered at his navel.

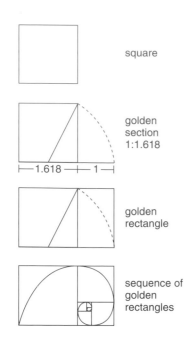

square

golden
section
1:1.618

├─ 1.618 ─┼─ 1 ─┤

golden
rectangle

sequence of
golden
rectangles

proportions of
the Parthenon

A proportion that has fascinated many artists and architects since its discovery by the ancient Greeks is the ratio known as the golden section. A golden section divides a length into two unequal segments in such a way that the smaller segment has the same ratio to the larger segment as the larger segment has to the whole. The ratio of the two segments works out to approximately 1 to 1.618. The golden section is more easily constructed than it is explained; Figure **5.24** takes you through the steps.

A rectangle constructed using the proportions of the golden section is called a golden rectangle. One of the most interesting characteristics of the golden rectangle, as Figure 5.24 shows, is that when a square is cut off from one end, the remaining shape is also a golden rectangle—a sequence that can be repeated endlessly and relates to such natural phenomena as the spiraling outward growth of a shell. For the Greeks, the intellectual and mathematical interest of the golden rectangle made it beautiful as well, an expression of the mathematical ordering of the universe, and they used it in the design of such structures as the Parthenon (see 14.26), an important and influential building that we will examine later in this book.

Artists and architects have often turned to the golden section when they sought a rational yet subtle organizing principle for their work. During the 20th century, the French architect Le Corbusier related the golden section to human proportions in a tool he called the Modulor (**5.25**). The Modulor is based on two overlapping golden sections. The first extends from the feet to the top of the head, with the section division falling at the navel; the second

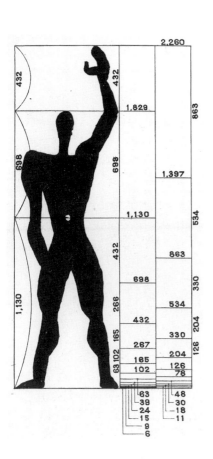

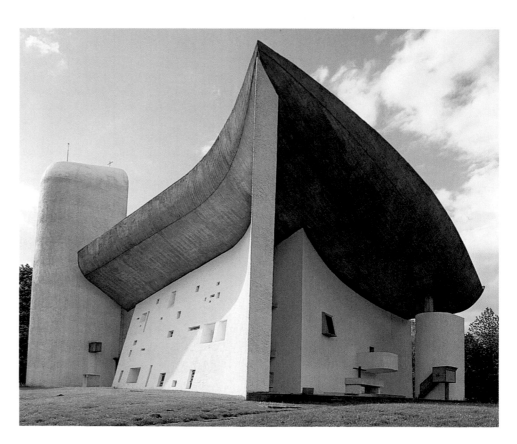

5.24 (top) Proportions of the golden section and golden rectangle.

5.25 (left) Le Corbusier. *The Modulor*. 1945.
Courtesy Fondation Le Corbusier.

5.26 (above right) Le Corbusier. Notre-Dame-du-Haut, Ronchamp, France. Exterior view from southeast. 1950–55.

extends from the navel to the tip of an upraised hand, with the section division falling at the top of the head. Using the height of an average adult, Le Corbusier derived several series of measurements based in the golden section. Le Corbusier offered the Modulor to architects as a tool that could help them arrive at proportions that were both poetic and practical. He used the Modulor himself in many of his own buildings, including the hilltop chapel of Notre-Dame-du-Haut (**5.26**), of which he wrote, "Hand-written over the facade is: Modulor throughout." Corbusier's Modulor acknowledges that there are no absolutes, only relationships, and that we experience the world in proportion to ourselves.

RHYTHM

Rhythm is based in repetition, and it is a basic part of the world we find ourselves in. We speak of the rhythm of the seasons, which recur in the same pattern every year, the rhythm of the cycles of the moon, the rhythm of waves upon the shore. These natural rhythms measure out the passing of time, organizing our experience of it. To the extent that our arts take place in time, they too structure experience through rhythm. Music and dance are the most obvious examples. Poetry, which is recited or read over time, also uses rhythm for structure and expression. Looking at art takes time as well, and rhythm is one of the means that artists use to structure our experience.

Through repetition, any of the visual elements can take on a rhythm within a work. In Lorna Simpson's *Easy to Remember* (**5.27**), shape provides the main rhythm—the repeated shape of lips, each pair a little different. "Easy to Remember" is the title of a well-known standard tune by the American song-writers Rogers and Hart. Simpson invited people individually to hum along to a jazz version recorded by the saxophonist John Coltrane, which she played over a headset to them so that only they could hear it. She recorded each person's humming, and filmed the face as he or she hummed. She then isolated each pair of lips and arranged them in a grid, blurring details of race, of age, of gender—of all that separates us. For the sound, she combined all of the humming, but she did not include the Coltrane version that coordinates it.

5.27 Lorna Simpson. Still from *Easy to Remember*. 2001. 16mm film transferred to DVD, sound. 2:35 minutes looped.
Courtesy Sean Kelly Gallery, New York.

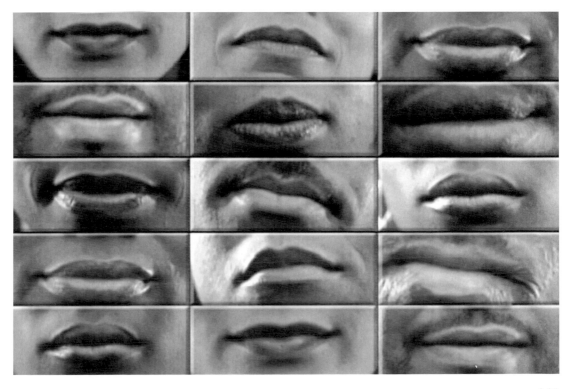

At first listening, the effect is of a calming, comforting drone that is somehow both public and private. We hum to ourselves, though others can hear. Listening repeatedly, differences begin to emerge. Each person takes little liberties, adds unique expressive details—or even gets momentarily lost. Coltrane's version of "Easy to Remember" is not easy to hum along to. In the end, Simpson's work presents a vision of a harmonious society as compelling as Seurat's *A Sunday on La Grande Jatte* (see 4.31). We are humming the same tune without realizing it, connected to a community that is bigger than we know. We are different and yet together, even if it isn't always easy.

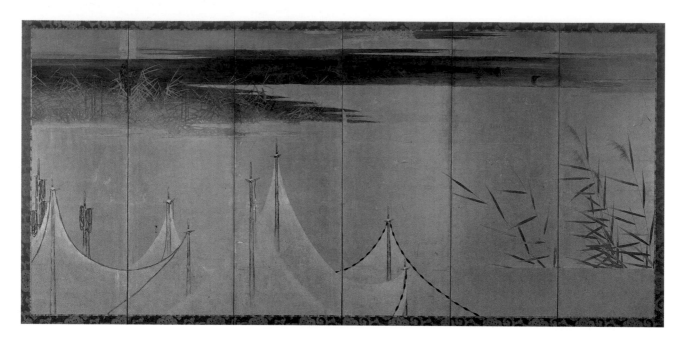

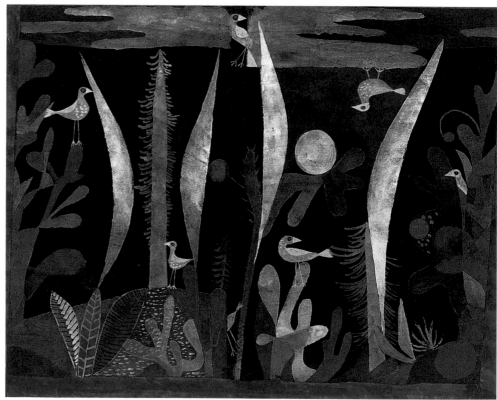

5.28 (above) Kaiho Yusho. *Fish Nets Drying in the Sun.* 17th century. One of a pair of six-panel screens; color and gold on paper, 5'3" × 11'6".
The Museum of the Imperial Collections, Sannomaru Shozokan.

5.29 (right) Paul Klee. *Landscape with Yellow Birds.* 1923. Watercolor and gouache on paper, 13⅞ × 17¼".
Private collection.

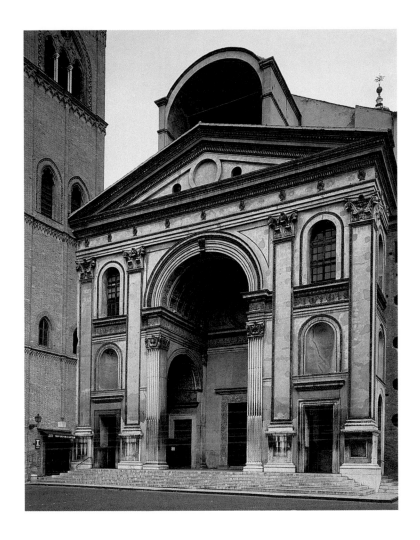

5.30 Leon Battista Alberti.
Facade of Sant'Andrea, Mantua.
Designed 1470.

In *Fish Nets Drying in the Sun* (**5.28**), Kaiho Yusho used line to create two starkly contrasting rhythms—the long, swooping lines of the drying nets at the left, and the short, straight lines of the leaves on the reeds to the right. If we imagined the lines as music, we might hear a beautiful, arching melody played by the cellos, interrupted suddenly by chirping and twittering from the flutes. If we imagined the lines as birds, we might picture the graceful glide of seagulls next to a flock of sparrows flitting in the undergrowth. And if they were fish . . . dolphins and minnows?

Paul Klee organized his strange little *Landscape with Yellow Birds* around several rhythms (**5.29**). First, there is the rhythm of the bulging, tapered silvery forms, which sway this way and that as they repeat across the image. Then there is the constellation of alert little yellow birds, which hold the composition together by forming an implied oval as our eyes follow them around the landscape. Perhaps they are circling the full moon, which forms part of an implied arc of circular rhythms (the rest of the circles are in red).

Earlier, we discussed how architects use proportion to create harmonious masses and spatial volumes—the positive and negative elements of a building. Through rhythm, they can articulate these proportions. When we articulate our speech, we take care to pronounce consonants and vowels clearly so that each syllable is distinct. Our goal is to be understood. Similarly, architects use rhythm to divide a building into distinct visual units so that we can grasp its logic. Renaissance architect Leon Battista Alberti used rhythms to articulate the monumental facade (exterior face) of the church of Sant' Andrea (**5.30**). A repeating vertical rhythm of pilasters (flat, ornamental columns) marks off one-quarter intervals across the facade, like an even beat. (There would be a fifth

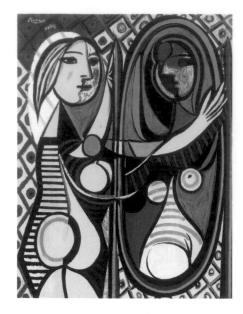

pilaster in the exact center if the large entryway did not intervene.) The arch of the large entryway is repeated in smaller arches between the pilasters. Similarly, the large rectangle of the principal doorway in this arched entryway repeats in the smaller side doors on the facade. (To see how the rhythms announced on the facade are carried through inside the church, see 16.4.)

ELEMENTS AND PRINCIPLES: A SUMMARY

In the second chapter of this book we examined two paintings by Henri Matisse in order to explore how form could suggest meaning (see 2.24, 2.25). This chapter and the preceding one have introduced the vocabulary of formal analysis, the terms that help us see and describe what we see. In the process, we have examined many artworks, each from a particular formal point of view—as an example of line, value, balance, rhythm, and so on. Before leaving this section, we should analyze one work more fully in order to show how these points of view combine into a more complete way of seeing, and to suggest again how form invites interpretation. The work we will look at is Picasso's *Girl Before a Mirror* (**5.31**).

5.31 (above) Pablo Picasso. *Girl Before a Mirror.* 1932. Oil on canvas, 5'4" × 4'3¼".
The Museum of Modern Art, New York.

5.32 (right) Hans Baldung Grien. *The Three Ages of Woman, and Death.* 1510. Oil on limewood, 18⅞ × 12¾".
Kunsthistorisches Museum, Vienna.

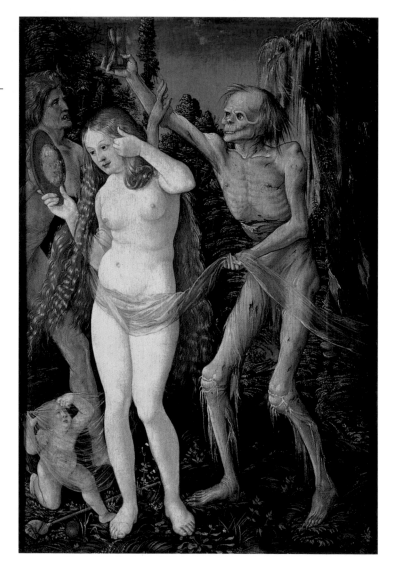

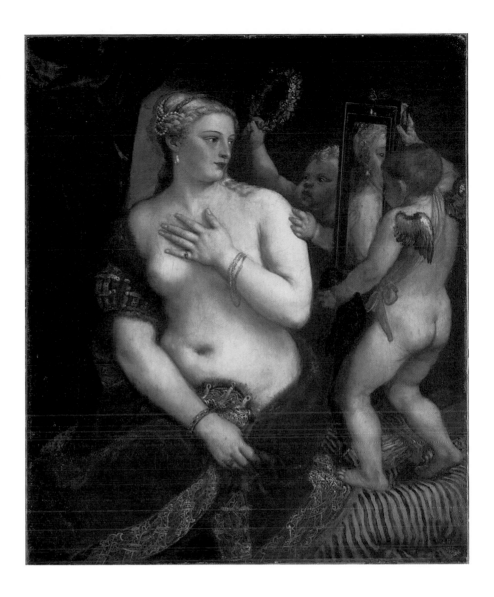

Painted in 1932, *Girl Before a Mirror* was probably inspired by Marie-Thérèse Walter, Picasso's lover at the time. In Western art, the motif of a woman before a mirror often calls to mind the *vanitas* tradition. Sometimes in such paintings, a woman stares into a mirror only to find a death's head staring back. In Chapter 1 we looked at a modern *vanitas* by Audrey Flack in which a framed photograph of a young girl is juxtaposed with a framed reflection of a skull (see 1.14). An older example is Hans Baldung Grien's *The Three Ages of Woman, and Death* (**5.32**). Here, the beautiful woman admiring herself in the mirror could see as well the reflection of Death, who stands behind her holding an hourglass over her head. Her child self plays at her feet; her aged self tries, futilely, to ward Death off. Another tradition that comes to mind is that of female beauty itself, and of men taking delight in painting a beautiful woman admiring herself. Of this there exists no more voluptuous example than Titian's *Venus with a Mirror* (**5.33**). Attended by cherubs, the goddess of love contemplates her eternal, unchanging beauty. We, through Titian, gaze at her. Finally, living in Paris, Picasso would have known that the French name for the type of mirror he painted was *psyché*, after the Greek goddess Psyche. Viewed as the personification of the human soul, she was loved by Eros, the god of love, who forbade her to look on him. This is some of the cultural context that Picasso could have expected viewers to bring to the painting. Now, what do we see?

5.33 Titian. *Venus with a Mirror.* c. 1555. Oil on canvas, 49 × 41½". National Gallery of Art, Washington, D.C.

Oriented vertically, *Girl Before a Mirror* is over 5 feet in height (**5.34**). The woman and her reflection occupy almost the entire canvas. Thus she is not miniaturized, as in the illustration here, but portrayed larger than life-size. The scale of the painting and of the woman represented within it makes a powerful impression when seen in person. We confront the work on an equal footing as a presence that rises up before us.

The design is based in symmetrical balance, with the woman on the left and her mirror image on the right. The left post of the mirror falls near the vertical axis, dividing the composition in two. As in Frida Kahlo's double self-portrait (see 5.9), the fundamental symmetry draws our attention to the ways in which the two sides are *not* alike, for it sets them in opposition. Indeed, the reflection of the girl's face in the mirror does not double her exactly. Warm colors are reflected as cool colors, and firm shapes become fluid. This is not the death's head of a traditional *vanitas*, but it is a transformation nevertheless, and it evokes a mysterious, shadowy realm of uncertainty—perhaps the girl's thoughts, perhaps her unconscious, perhaps her soul, perhaps her mortality.

A composition divided so cleanly in two could easily break apart, and Picasso uses several means to tie the two halves together. The most important is the girl's gesture as she reaches out to the far edge of the mirror, almost in an embrace. The gesture links the girl and her reflection, and it is so important to the composition that Picasso reinforces it with a red-striped shape that begins on the girl's chest and extends to her fingertips. Together, gesture and shape set up a pendulum motion, and as we look at the painting, our eyes swing rhythmically back and forth from one side to the other.

Overall, the unity of the composition rests on the rhythmical curves and repeating circles of the girl and her reflection, culminating in the great oval of

5.34 Pablo Picasso. *Girl Before a Mirror.* 1932. Oil on canvas, 5'4" × 4'3¼".
The Museum of Modern Art, New York.

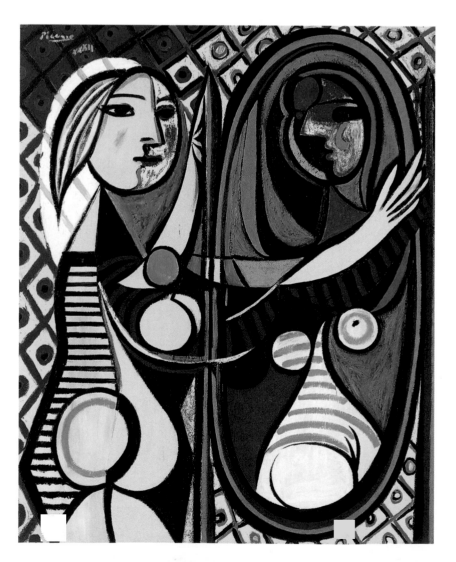

the mirror itself. A second unifying device is the lushly painted wallpaper, which extends across the entire canvas. Its diagonal geometric grid acts as a foil for the sweeping organic curves of the girl, and it is almost as important a presence in the painting as she is. Color unifies the composition as well, for while the colors are brilliantly varied, they fall generally in the same range of intensities and values, with the important exception of the girl herself.

And what of the girl? Picasso directs our attention first of all to her face, a natural focal point. He emphasizes it by painting one half bright yellow and by surrounding her head with an oval of white and green that isolates it from the busy pattern of the background and provides enough visual weight to balance the form of the mirror. He also modifies its proportions so that her facial features occupy the entire space of her head. With her yellow hair, circular half-yellow face, and white aura, she is like the sun of the painting, its source of light.

The pale violet portion of her face is depicted in profile, gazing at the mirror. With the addition of the yellow portion she turns her head to look at us—or at Picasso. Cool, pale colors set off by black shapes and lines draw our attention to her body, which is also divided vertically. The left portion is clothed in a striped garment, perhaps a bathing suit; the right portion is nude. The swell of the belly evokes childbearing and the renewal of life. In a remarkable X-ray view, Picasso even paints through her skin to the womb inside, envisioned as another circle. Her biological destiny is emphasized in the mirror image as well, for this part of her body is reflected confidently. Picasso draws our attention to it through an abrupt shift in value—in the dark world of the mirror, the breasts and belly are white.

What is the painting about? It does not have a single meaning, but many layers of meanings and associations. It is about a girl contemplating herself in a mirror, quiet before her own inner mysteries, aware of her life-affirming sexuality and procreative powers. It is about Picasso meditating on women as sensuous symbols of beauty, abundance, and fertility. It is also about Picasso looking with a lover's possessive gaze at Marie-Thérèse Walter, seeing through her clothing to the flesh underneath. Hovering behind the image are the tradition of the *vanitas* and its theme of mortality, and the story of Psyche, a girl who is aware of being loved and being gazed upon, and who turns fatefully to look at her lover.

Picasso did not have a checklist as he worked, dutifully adding the visual elements in the correct proportions of unity, variety, balance, scale, proportion, and rhythm. His student days were far behind him, and such thinking was by now second nature. But as the numerous reworkings evident in the finished painting show, he changed his mind often and made constant adjustments as he worked. Why? Any number of reasons, probably—because the balance was off, because his eye was not traveling freely over the canvas, because there was too much focus here and not enough there, because the mood of the colors was not right. The painting is the end result of all his decisions, a project he stopped at the moment when, as the picture's first viewer, he was content with what he saw. As later viewers, we articulate the elements and principles to make ourselves aware of the dynamic of seeing. With experience, this becomes second nature to us as well.

RELATED RESOURCES ONLINE

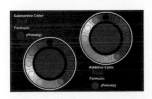

For more information, definitions, interactive activities, Web links, and videos related to the "Living with Art" material covered in this part, please go to **www.mhhe.com/lwa8.**

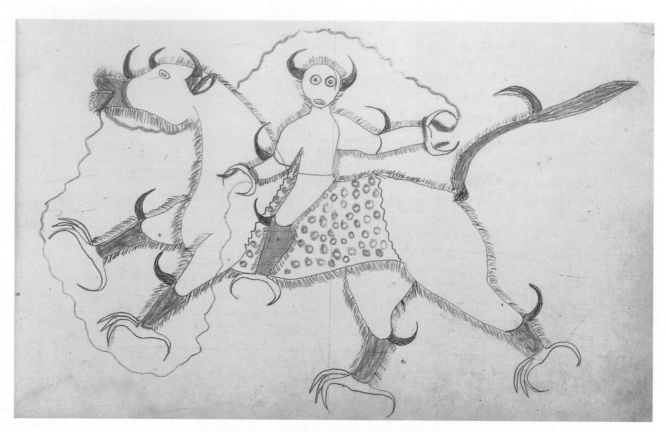

6.1 Black Hawk. *Spirit Vision*. 1880.
Pencil, colored pencil, and ink on paper, 9½ × 15½".
Eugene and Clara Thaw Collection, Fenimore Art Museum,
New York State Historical Association, Cooperstown.

PART THREE
Two-Dimensional Media

CHAPTER SIX

DRAWING

Everybody draws. There can scarcely be a person above the age of two who has never made a drawing. Many people take photographs, some paint, a few make sculpture, and a very few may even design a building. But everybody draws. You see a patch of wet sand at the beach, a dusty tabletop, or a blank notepad while you are sitting in class or at a business meeting—and your natural impulse is to draw something.

Children begin to draw long before they begin to write, sometimes before they can talk intelligibly. In drawing far more than in speech, children reveal their fantasies and their fears. Whatever the content, nearly all children draw, which shows how truly universal is this method of expression.

Two qualities often associated with drawing are familiarity and intimacy. Drawing is familiar in that it often uses materials we all are accustomed to— a pencil, a pen, a stick of chalk. There are no mysterious or exotic ingredients. The drawing illustrated on the facing page was done with pencil and colored pencil on the lined paper of an account book (**6.1**), yet these ordinary materials capture an extraordinary event. Drawn by a Lakota Indian named Black Hawk, the image records a vision he had in which he was transformed into a Thunder Being. Black Hawk was an *iyeska*, "one who moves between two worlds"—a shaman, in other words. His drawings form a priceless record of the Lakota worldview. For the Lakota, the dramatic storms that sweep across the Great Plains were the manifestations of Thunder Beings and their messenger horses. In Black Hawk's vision, the horse's hooves and the Being's hands are transformed into eagle claws, while buffalo horns spring from other parts of their bodies. Jagged lines of energy pass between the rider and his horse, a spiritual connection that renders reins unnecessary. The horse's blanket is patterned in hailstones. Lightning was said to spring from the Thunder Being's eyes, shown here wide open. In his vision, Black Hawk saw himself as the awesome, destructive power of a storm thundering across the plain. He died in 1890, at the Battle of Wounded Knee.

Drawing seems intimate because it is frequently the artist's private note-taking. Many drawings are not intended for exhibition and therefore are not shown publicly during the artist's lifetime. They may be preliminary sketches for some other work of art or just the artist's refined doodling. We think of such drawings as direct expression—from brain to hand—and they can offer fascinating glimpses into the creative process. Picasso, mindful of his own legacy, began early on to date and save all of his sketches. Thanks to this habit we have almost a complete visual record of his mind at work. Illustrated here

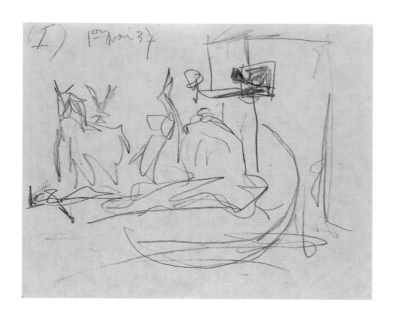

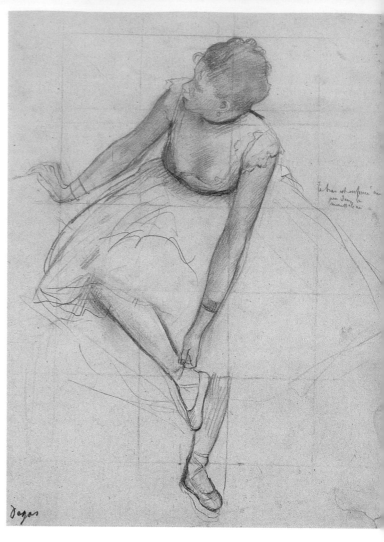

6.2 (left) Pablo Picasso. First composition study for *Guernica*. May 1, 1937. Pencil on blue paper, 8¼ × 10⅝".
Museo Nacional Centro de Arte Reina Sofia, Madrid.

6.3 (right) Edgar Degas. *Dancer Adjusting Her Slipper*. 1873. Graphite and charcoal heightened with white chalk on now-faded pink paper, 12⅞ × 9⅝".
The Metropolitan Museum of Art, New York.

is his first sketch for his great antifascist mural *Guernica* (**6.2;** for the completed mural see 3.12). Much changed between this first rapidly sketched idea and the final painting, but one essential gesture is already in place: The horror will be revealed to us by the light of a lamp held by a figure leaning out of an upper story window.

Other factors may contribute to drawing's sense of intimacy. Most drawings are relatively small (compared with paintings), and many are executed quickly. Drawings are often made in great quantities; some artists do hundreds of drawings for every "finished" work. There are exceptions to this generalization, drawings that are large and/or are executed with painstaking attention to detail, including several examples in this chapter. But part of the charm of drawing as a medium must surely be the fact that, even when a work is intended for exhibition, it still retains an air of intimacy.

In drawings such as *Dancer Adjusting Her Slipper* (**6.3**), we have the impression of being present at an intimate transaction between artist and model. We can easily imagine Degas adjusting the position of the arm, modifying the contour of the foot, his eyes shifting back and forth between his evolving drawing and the model standing a few feet away. Sketches like this served Degas as a sort of inventory of poses and people—raw materials from which larger compositions could be constructed. The drawing is "squared for transfer," that is, Degas drew a grid over it to make it easier to copy accurately. He used this pose in two finished works, both of dancers in rehearsal.

Artists may draw for no other reason than to understand the world around them, to investigate its forms. There is no better exercise in seeing

LEONARDO

1452–1519

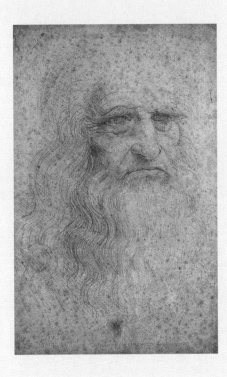

NO CLUES ARE offered by the scant knowledge about Leonardo's origins to explain what spawned perhaps the most complex imagination of all time. Leonardo was the illegitimate son of a peasant woman known only as Caterina and a fairly well-to-do notary, Piero da Vinci. He was raised in his father's house at Vinci and, when he was about fifteen, apprenticed to the Florentine artist Andrea del Verrocchio, in whose workshop he remained for ten years. It is said the pupil's talent so impressed his master that Verrocchio gave up painting forever.

In 1482 Leonardo left Florence for Milan, where he became official artist to Lodovico Sforza, duke of that city. There the artist undertook many projects, foremost among them his famous painting of the *Last Supper*. Leonardo remained with Sforza until the latter's fall from power in 1499, after which he returned to Florence.

Sketches and written records indicate that Leonardo worked as a sculptor, but no examples remain. Only about a dozen paintings can be definitely attributed to him, and several of these are unfinished. There are, however, hundreds of drawings, and the thousands of pages from his detailed notebook testify to the man's extraordinary genius. If Leonardo completed relatively few artistic works, this can only be ascribed to the enormous breadth of his interests, which caused him repeatedly to turn from one subject to another. He was a skilled architect and engineer, engrossed in the problems of city planning, sanitary disposal, military engineering, and even the design of weapons. He made sketches for a crude submarine, a helicopter, and an airplane—with characteristic thoroughness also designing a parachute in case the airplane should fail. He made innovative studies in astronomy, anatomy, botany, geology, optics, and above all mathematics. His contemporaries reported his great talent as a musician—he played and improvised on the lute—as well as his love of inventive practical jokes.

In 1507 Leonardo was appointed court painter to the King of France, Louis XII, who happened to be in Milan at the time. Nine years later the aging artist was named court painter to Louis' successor, Francis I. Francis seems to have revered him for his towering reputation as an artist and his crisp intellect, but to have expected little artistic production from the old man. The king provided comfortable lodgings in the city of Amboise, where Leonardo died.

Solitary all his life, Leonardo did not marry, and he formed very few close attachments. His obsession seems to have been with getting it all down, recording the fertile outpourings of his brain and hand. In his *Treatise on Painting*, assembled from his notebook pages and published after his death, he advised painters to follow his method: "You should often amuse yourself when you take a walk for recreation, in watching and taking note of the attitudes and actions of men as they talk and dispute, or laugh or come to blows with one another . . . noting these down with rapid strokes, in a little pocket-book which you ought always to carry with you . . . for there is such an infinite number of forms and actions of things that the memory is incapable of preserving them."[1]

Leonardo da Vinci. *Self-Portrait*. c. 1512.
Red chalk on paper, 13 × 8¼".
Biblioteca Reale, Turin.

than to take a small part of the natural world and try to draw it in all its detail. Leonardo had the curiosity and the powers of observation of a natural scientist. Some of his sketches served as studies that might find their way into larger compositions, but he also filled notebook after notebook with investigative drawings for their own sake. The drawing here (**6.4**) reflects his interest in parallels between the behavior of currents of water and the motions of waving grasses.

The drawings we have been looking at are all on paper, a material we associate closely with drawing. Historically, however, many other surfaces have been used to draw on. Among the oldest representational images that we know of are the cave drawings in southern France and in Spain (see 1.3). While these images are often referred to as paintings, many have a strong linear quality that would more accurately categorize them as drawings. The artists worked directly on the cave walls, possibly using mats of hair or charred sticks to draw the contours of the many animals they portrayed.

With the development of pottery during the Neolithic era, fired clay became a surface for drawing in many cultures. The durability of fired clay has meant that many examples have survived when works in more perishable materials have not. For example, we know of ancient Greek painting only from literary sources, for not a single example has come down to us. Thanks to the Greek custom of drawing on pottery, however, we have some understanding of what these paintings might have looked like (see 14.23). The Greeks also drew and wrote on papyrus, a paperlike material developed in ancient Egypt that was made from pressed plant stems. Rivaling papyrus was a later invention, parchment. Made from treated animal skins, it was widely used throughout

6.4 Leonardo da Vinci. *Star of Bethlehem and Other Plants.* c. 1506–08. Red chalk and pen, 7⅞ × 6⅜".
The Royal Collection, Windsor Castle, Windsor, England.

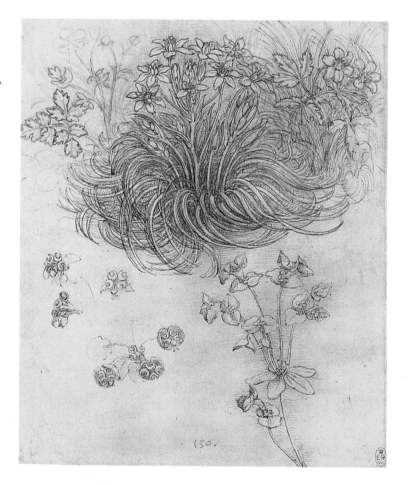

PAPER

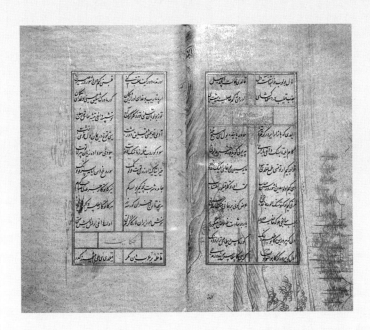

OUR WORD *paper* is derived from the Latin word *papyrus*, which the ancient Romans used to designate both a plant that grew along the banks of the Nile river and the writing material that the ancient Egyptians made from it. Yet the link to papyrus is misleading, for while paper may have reminded later Europeans of papyrus, it is made quite differently, and it was invented not in Egypt but in China. Traditional Chinese histories date the invention to 105 C.E. and attribute it to Cai Lun, a eunuch who served in the imperial court. Archaeologists have discovered fragments of paper in China that are far older, however, and scholars now agree that the process was known by the 2nd century B.C.E., well before Cai's time.

Paper is made from plant fibers, beaten to a pulp, mixed with water, then spread in a thin layer over a fine mesh surface and left to dry. To produce uniform sheets by hand (all paper was handmade until the 19th century), a mold is used—imagine a rectangle of wire or bamboo mesh attached to a wooden frame to form a shallow tray. The mold is dipped into a vat of thinned pulp, then lifted out, carrying with it a very fine layer of fibers. Before it can receive painting or writing with ink, paper must be *sized*, treated with a substance such as starch or glue to make it less

absorbent (otherwise it acts as a blotter). Techniques for sizing had certainly been perfected by Cai Lun's time, for paper was already in use then for writing with brush and ink in the Chinese way.

The secret of paper spread from China to neighboring peoples through Buddhism: Monks preaching their faith brought along brushes, ink, and papermaking know-how so that religious texts could be copied and circulated. Knowledge of papermaking was transmitted in this way to Korea, Japan, and Vietnam. As Islam extended into Central Asia during the 8th century, Muslims, too, came into contact with China and Buddhism. Legend has it that the secret of paper passed into Islamic culture when Muslim soldiers captured a group of Chinese papermakers during a famous battle in 751 C.E. The truth is probably less dramatic, a tale of cultural contact and exchange.

Over the ensuing centuries, Asian and Muslim papermakers made enormous strides, learning to make paper of ever greater variety and refinement. Their long centuries of contact can be seen in the pages reproduced here. Tinted blue, sprinkled with gold, and painted with a gold landscape, the paper was made in China. It was probably sent by a 15th-century Chinese emperor as a gift to the ruler of Iran, who in turn presented it to the famous calligrapher Sultan-Ali Qaini, who used it for a manuscript of Persian poems.

The transfer of paper and papermaking from Islamic lands to Christian Europe was a gradual and scattered affair. Christians under Muslim rule (as in Spain) or in close contact with Islamic culture (as in Sicily) bought paper from Muslim papermakers for well over a century before gradually starting to make it themselves. In northern Italy, paper manufacturing first flowered during the 13th century, using techniques that were probably learned from contacts made during the Crusades. It was not until the 14th century that a paper mill was founded north of the Alps, however, and that the word *paper* finally entered the English language—some 1,500 years after the material was first invented.

Blue Chinese paper with decoration in gold, inscribed by Sultan-Ali Qaini with a poem by Haydar. Tabriz, 1478. New York Public Library.

the Roman Empire and continued as the surface of choice in medieval Europe. The ancient Chinese drew on silk, their special material, and many Chinese artists still do. It is the Chinese, too, who are credited with the invention of paper.

Today, artists have a wide array of drawing surfaces and materials to choose from. Some materials have their origins in the distant past, while others depend on space-age technology. In this chapter we examine some of the traditional materials that have been used for drawing and the effects they can produce. Then we look briefly at some recent directions in this oldest of arts.

MATERIALS FOR DRAWING

All drawing media are based on **pigment**—powdered coloring material— mixed with a substance that enables it to adhere to the drawing surface. Drawing materials generally are divided into two categories—dry media and liquid

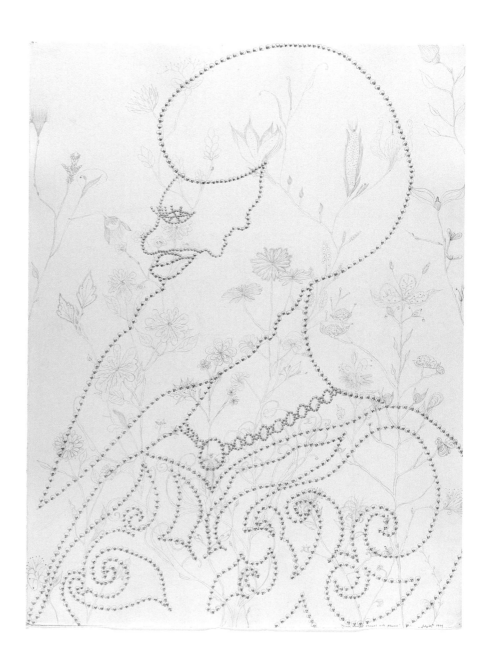

6.5 Chris Ofili. *Prince among Thieves with Flowers.* 1999. Pencil on paper, 29¾ × 22¼".
The Museum of Modern Art, New York.

media. The dry media tend to be abrasive. They "scratch" across a paper or some other surface, depositing particles wherever they come in contact with the surface. Liquid media, in contrast, have particles of pigment suspended in fluid, so they flow onto the surface much more freely.

Dry Media

PENCIL   The graphite pencil, sometimes called a "lead" pencil, probably has made more drawings than any other medium. Pencils are cheap, readily available, and easy to work with. Mistakes can be erased. If the drawing turns out badly, it can be thrown away at no great expense.

Despite the pencil's humble status, however, some of the most elegant drawings we know have been done with graphite pencil. Pencils made especially for artists are available in varying degrees of hardness and softness. The softer the graphite, the darker and richer the line it produces. The harder the graphite, the more pale and silvery the line. In his drawing *Prince among Thieves with Flowers* (**6.5**), Chris Ofili used a comparatively soft pencil for the image of the bearded man and a harder pencil for the pale but still precise flowers in the background. From a standard viewing distance, the lines that define the figure seem to be made of dots. But as viewers draw closer, the dots reveal themselves to be tiny heads, each sporting an afro, a black hairstyle popular during the 1970s (**6.6**). A young British artist of African ancestry, Ofili often uses imagery associated with the sense of black identity that emerged during the 1960s and 1970s, treating it with a complicated mixture of nostalgia, irony, affection, and respect.

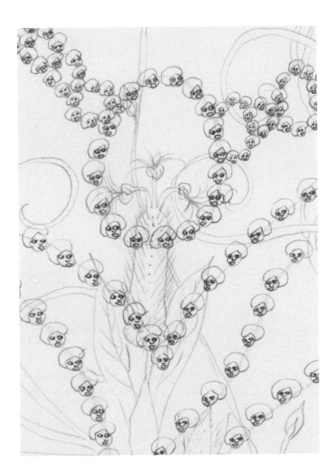

6.6 Chris Ofili. *Prince among Thieves with Flowers,* detail at actual size.

METALPOINT Metalpoint, the ancestor of the graphite pencil, is an old technique that was especially popular during the Renaissance. Few artists use it now, because it is not very forgiving of mistakes or indecision. Once put down, the lines cannot easily be changed or erased. The drawing medium is a thin wire of metal, often of pure silver (in which case the medium is called **silverpoint**), mounted in some kind of holding device, such as a wooden shaft or a modern mechanical pencil. The drawing surface must be specially coated with poster paint or a similar ground—historically, the coating was bone dust and glue. Silver tarnishes quickly, and while the drawing can be protected to prevent this from happening, the gray tonalities of tarnish are generally desired.

Metalpoint drawings are characterized by a fine, delicate line of uniform width. Making thrifty use of a single sheet of paper, Filippino Lippi drew two figure studies in metalpoint on a pale pink ground, building up the areas of shadow with fine hatching and cross-hatching, then delicately painting in highlights in white (**6.7**). The models were probably workshop apprentices.

6.7 Filippino Lippi. *Figure Studies: Standing Nude and Seated Man Reading.* c. 1480. Metalpoint, heightened with white gouache, on pale pink prepared paper, 9 11/16 × 8½".
The Metropolitan Museum of Art, New York.

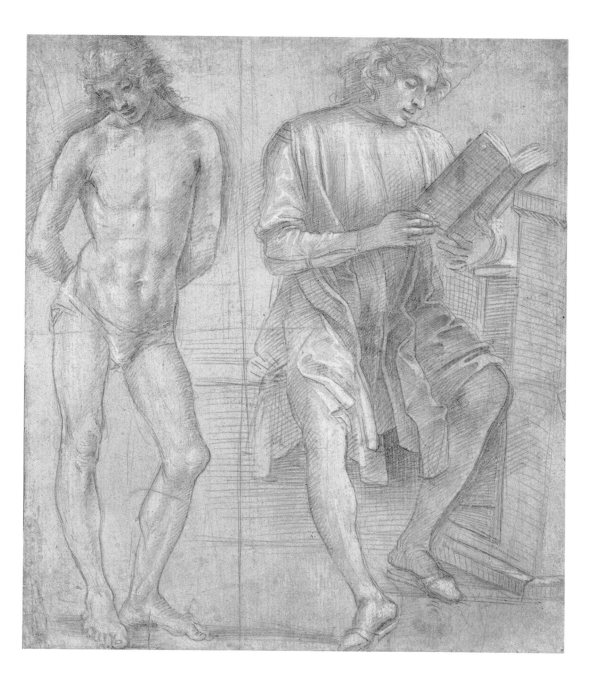

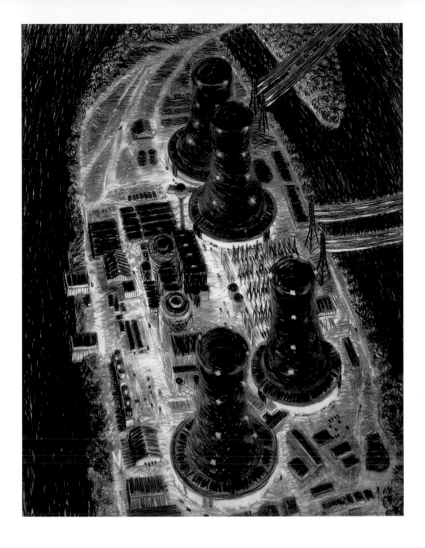

6.8 Yvonne Jacquette. *Three Mile Island, Night I.* 1982. Charcoal on laminated tracing paper, 48¹³⁄₁₆ × 38".
Hirshhorn Museum and Sculpture Garden, Washington, D.C.

Renaissance apprentices often posed for each other and for the master, and thus found their way into innumerable paintings. The figure on the left, for example, may well have been incorporated into a painting as Saint Sebastian, who was typically depicted with his arms bound and wearing only a loincloth.

CHARCOAL Charcoal's effects are almost the exact opposite of those offered by metalpoint. Where metalpoint produces a thin, delicate line, charcoal's line is dark, sometimes very soft, occasionally harsh. Charcoal is actually burned sticks of wood—the best-quality charcoal coming from special vine wood heated in a kiln until only carbon remains. Charcoal lines can be thin or thick, faint or dark. Yvonne Jacquette's *Three Mile Island, Night I* illustrates well the tonal range of charcoal, deepening from sketchy, pale gray to thick, velvety black (**6.8**). Jacquette has made a specialty out of depicting landscape as seen from an airplane. With the popularization of air travel during the second half of the 20th century, this view became common. Yet while we might consider it fundamental to our modern experience of the world, it has rarely been treated in art.

CHALK AND CRAYON A wide range of chalks and crayons are available to the artist, and nearly all of them offer color effects. Generally speaking, the main difference between chalks and crayons is the **binder**—the substance that holds particles of pigment together. Chalks have nonfat binders, whereas crayons have a fatty or greasy binder, so there is considerable variation in the way these materials react to contact with paper. If you imagine blackboard chalk and ordinary children's crayons, this difference in effect should be clear.

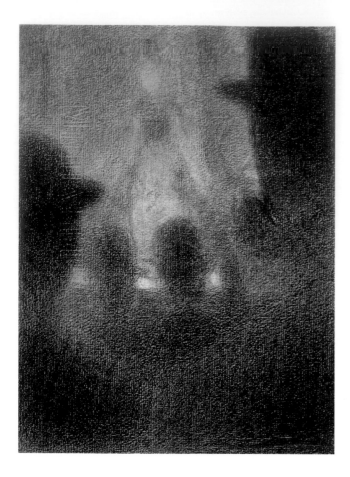

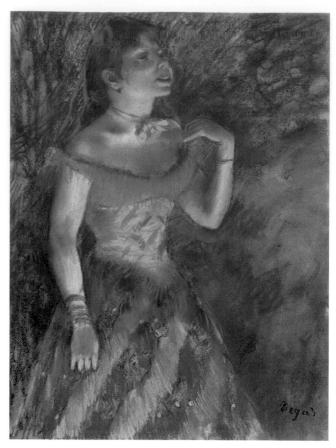

6.9 (left) Georges Seurat. *Café-concert.* c. 1887. Conté crayon heightened with white chalk on paper, 12⅜ × 9⅝".
The Cleveland Museum of Art.

6.10 (right) Edgar Degas. *The Singer in Green.* c. 1884. Pastel on light blue laid paper, 23¾ × 18¼".
The Metropolitan Museum of Art, New York.

Chalks, being drier and more crumbly, generally blend well and can be overlaid (two or more colors on top of one another) to produce shaded effects. They respond best to a paper with some tooth, are relatively fragile unless covered by a fixative, and offer a limited range of colors. The greasier crayons adhere well to paper and are more permanent, but they are difficult to blend with one another for subtle tones and gradations. (However, the newer oil-based crayons can be finger-blended almost as easily as oil paints blend.) Crayons usually offer a wider choice of colors than do chalks, and they come in varying degrees of hardness to permit sharp lines or tonal areas.

Crayon can mean anything from the wax crayons used by children through the lithographic crayon meant for drawing on stone in printmaking (Chapter 8). But the commonest drawing material is conté crayon—a fine-textured stick medium available in shades of red, brown, and black.

One artist who comes readily to mind in discussing conté crayon drawings is Georges Seurat. In Chapter 4 we looked at Seurat's painting technique, called pointillism, in which tiny dots of color are massed together to build form. Seurat also did many drawings. By working in conté on rough-textured paper he could approximate the effect of color dots in paint. *Café-concert* is one of several drawings Seurat made of an entertainment that was all the rage in his day (**6.9**). The cafés and their performers were condescended to by serious (and snobbish) cultural commentators, but ordinary people flocked to them. Artists went as well, attracted by the effects of the lighting, the colorful personalities of the performers, and the fascinating social mix of the crowd. By simplifying his forms and downplaying any sense of motion, Seurat tends to bring out the eerie side of almost any situation. Here, the distant, brightly lit female performer is watched rather spookily by an impassive audience of bowler-hatted men.

Another artist attracted to the café-concerts was Edgar Degas. While Seurat's drawing was made from the back of the hall, Degas' *The Singer in Green* (**6.10**) puts us right on stage next to the performer, who touches her shoulder in a gesture that Degas borrowed from one of his favorite café singers. Degas created his drawing in **pastel,** the most well-known chalk medium. Available in a full range of colors and several degrees of hardness, pastel is often considered a borderline medium, somewhere between painting and drawing. Artists favor soft pastels for most work, reserving the harder ones for special effects or details. Thanks to their fine texture, pastels can be easily blended by blurring one color into another, obliterating the individual strokes and creating smoothly graduated tones. Here, Degas has blended the tones that model the girl's face and upper torso as she is lit from below by the footlights. Her dress is treated more freely, with the individual strokes still apparent. The background is suggested through blended earth tones and roughly applied blue-greens that show the texture of the paper.

Liquid Media

PEN AND INK Ink flowing onto paper gives a smooth, uninterrupted line. As with other relatively permanent media, there is little possibility for correction once the lines have been inscribed. A major variable in the ink drawing, however, is the relative thickness or thinness of lines, which depends on the pen point used. The lines can be all one width, ranging from fine to heavy, or they can vary. A single line may change, perhaps starting as a fine thread, broadening into thickness, and then tapering down again. Such thick-and-thin lines are referred to as *calligraphic* or *gestural*.

While today most pen nibs are made of metal, this is a comparatively recent innovation, dating only from the second half of the 19th century. Prior to then, artists generally used either reed pens—pens cut from the hollow stems of certain plants—or quill pens—pens cut from the hollow shafts of the wing feathers of large birds. Both reed and quill pens respond sensitively to shifts in pressure, lending themselves naturally to the sort of calligraphic lines we see in Rembrandt's *Cottage among Trees* (**6.11**). One of the greatest draftsmen who ever lived, Rembrandt made thousands of drawings over the course of his lifetime. Many record ideas for paintings or prints, but many more are simply drawings done for the pleasure of drawing.

6.11 Rembrandt. *Cottage among Trees*. 1648–50. Pen and brown ink, brush and brown wash, on paper washed with brown; 6¾ × 10⅞".
The Metropolitan Museum of Art, New York.

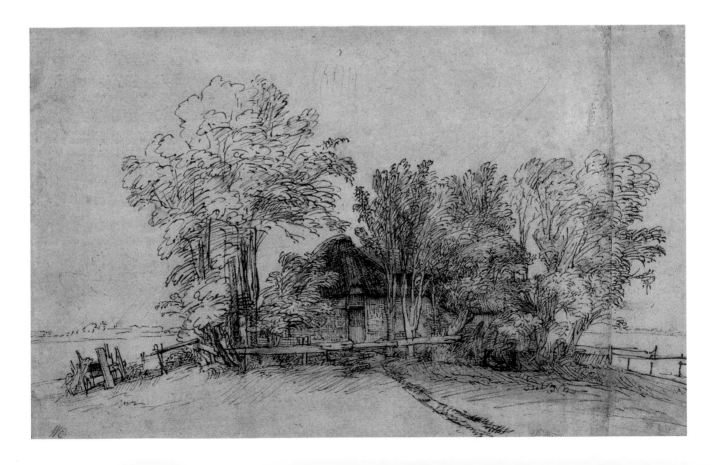

The wind-tossed foliage of the trees shows Rembrandt's virtuosity at its most rapid and effortless, while the solid volumes of the cottage were more slowly and methodically built up. Here and there Rembrandt used a **wash,** ink diluted with water and applied with a brush, to give greater solidity to the cottage and to soften the shadows beneath the trees. Before beginning his drawing, he prepared the paper by applying an all-over wash of pale brown. By tinting the paper, Rembrandt lowered the contrast between the dark ink and the ground, creating a more atmospheric, harmonious, and unified image.

A more recently developed type of ink pen is the rapidograph, a metal-tipped instrument that makes a fine, even, unvarying line. Compared with the line traced by a reed or quill pen, a line drawn with a rapidograph can seem mechanical and impersonal. In fact, the rapidograph was invented as a tool for technical drawing, such as the drawings that illustrate architectural systems in Chapter 13 of this book (see pages 315–316). Before the advent of the computer, architects often used the rapidograph to draw precise images of buildings they were planning.

Julie Mehretu purposefully evokes the association of the rapidograph with architecture in drawings such as the untitled example here (**6.12**). Fragments of urban plans along with details of buildings and infrastructure seem caught up in an explosive whirlwind. Mehretu's drawings thrive on the contrast between their seemingly apocalyptic subject matter and their cool, detached style, a style in which the even line of the rapidograph plays an important role. Mehretu makes her drawings on translucent Mylar, a polyester film used in architectural drafting. Often, as in the drawing here, she works on multiple, superimposed sheets of Mylar, so that elements placed on an underlayer appear as though seen through a fog.

6.12 Julie Mehretu. *Untitled.* 2001. Ink, colored pencil, and cut paper on Mylar; 21½ × 27⅜". Seattle Art Museum. Courtesy the artist and The Project, New York.

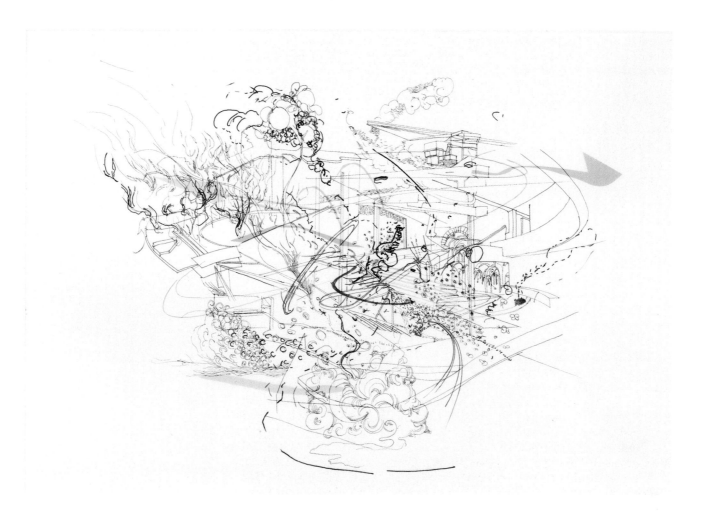

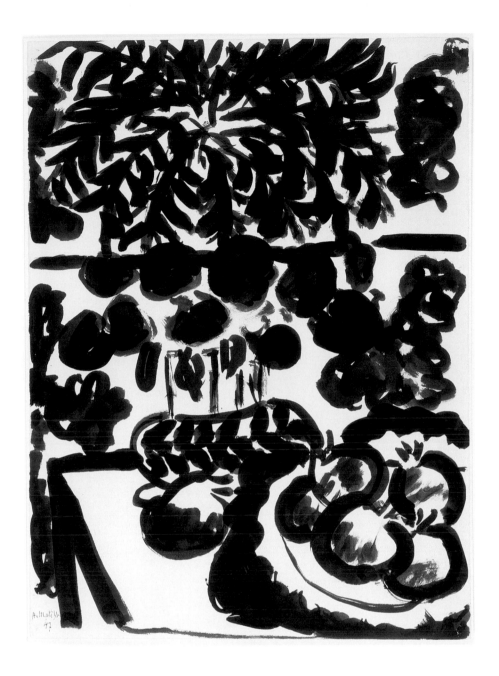

BRUSH AND INK The soft and supple brushes used for watercolor can also be used with ink. Brushes can be wielded boldly and brutally or with great delicacy and refinement, producing a broad range of effects. The concept of using a brush for drawing shows how difficult it can be to define exactly where drawing leaves off and painting begins. Is Matisse's vigorously brushed *Dahlias, Pomegranates, and Palm* a drawing or a painting (**6.13**)? We tend to classify it as a drawing because it was created on paper, is in black and white, and is largely linear in character—that is, Matisse used the brush mostly to make lines. Taken together, these characteristics are more closely associated with the Western tradition of drawing than painting. But if we shift our focus to China or Japan, we find a long tradition of works made with brush and black ink on paper, often linear in character, which by custom we call paintings. Look ahead, for example, to Ni Zan's *Rongxi Sudio* (see 19.21) or Toba Sojo's *Monkeys Worshiping a Frog* (see 19.28). Both were created with brush and ink on paper, and both are primarily linear. Yet within the cultural traditions of East Asia, both are clearly associated with the practice of painting.

6.13 Henri Matisse. *Dahlias, Pomegranates, and Palm.* 1947. Brush and ink on paper, 30 × 22¼".
Musée National d'Art Moderne, Centre Georges Pompidou, Paris.

Realizing that categories such as "drawing" and "painting" are cultural and somewhat fluid can be a freeing experience for both artists and viewers. A drawing does not have to be made of certain materials, be of a certain size, or look a certain way. In the next section, we examine how some contemporary artists are taking advantage of this freedom by pushing drawing beyond traditional limits.

RECENT DIRECTIONS: REACHING FOR THE WALL

Young artists looking for fresh territory to explore often turn received wisdom on its head, just to free up some space for themselves. Drawings, for example, are traditionally thought of as small and intimate—in part, because historically artists have used them to work out ideas for paintings or to gather visual

6.14 Paul Noble. *Nobspital.* 1997–98. Pencil on paper, 8'2½" × 59".
Collection Mark Hubbard.

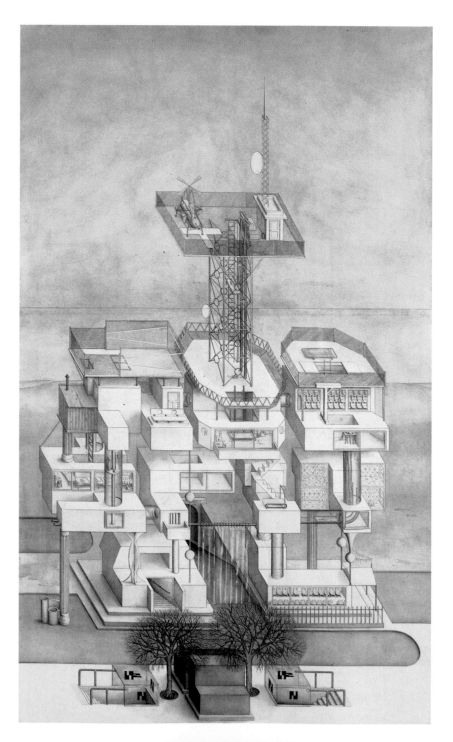

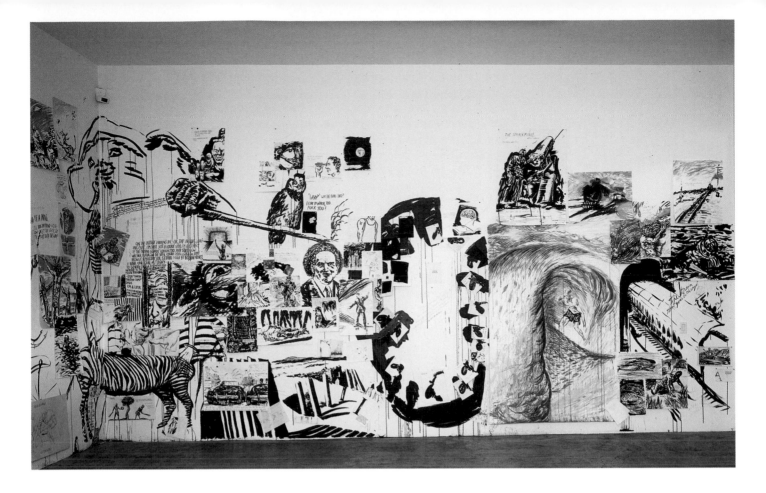

material more generally. However, this conception is due in part to another reason you might not think of: the size of paper. For centuries, artist-quality paper was made in single sheets in standard sizes. Today, however, quality paper is available in larger and larger sizes, including rolls 10 feet wide—taller than an average wall.

Paul Noble uses wall-size paper to make wall-size drawings. At just over 8 feet in height but only about 5 feet in width, *Nobspital* (**6.14**) is far from his largest effort. Drawn from an aerial "bird's eye" perspective and packed with minute detail, Noble's drawings document an imaginary town called Nobson Newtown. Nobspital is the town's hospital. Like all of the architecture in the town, it is formed from large block letters that spell out its name: NOB-SPIT-AL. The town motto of Nobson Newtown is "No style, only technique. No accidents, only mistakes." The town's name refers to the suburban "new towns" that optimistic city planners created in England during the 20th century. Nobson Newtown never seems to have a human presence, and much of it is polluted and crumbling away. Has the town been abandoned? Or are we perhaps flying over an abandoned dream, a dream about how modern architecture would create perfect communities?

The large scale of Noble's drawings gives them a strong physical presence that we traditionally associate with paintings, and that is part of Noble's point. The prestige of painting within the Western tradition has often relegated drawings to a sort of second-class status as finished artworks. However, like many artists today, Noble makes drawings as primary artistic statements, and one of the ways he makes these clear is through scale.

Another artist whose reputation rests almost entirely on drawings is Raymond Pettibon. While Pettibon's drawings are traditional in scale, he rarely exhibits them individually. Instead, he uses them as elements in larger installations, pinning them to the wall in large groupings, often with additional text and images drawn directly on the wall itself (**6.15**). The effect is of stepping into a picture book whose pages have scattered themselves around a room.

6.15 Raymond Pettibon. Installation at Regen Projects, Los Angeles, September 8–October 14, 2000 (detail). Ink on paper, ink on wall.
Courtesy the artist and Regen Projects, Los Angeles.

Pettibon himself has compared his installations to videos, for the groupings often imply a beginning, and some kind of story, and perhaps a future.

Pettibon is as interested in literature as he is in art, and his drawings typically combine both words and images. But the words in a Pettibon drawing are often slightly at odds with the image, setting up a kind of friction. Baseball is one recurrent theme, especially a moment at bat (**6.16**). Most of Pettibon's batters strike out. The batter here at least hits a single and brings in two runs, though he breaks his bat in the process. In the background, we can read the voice of the announcer, "What makes it a competition? Yes, the fans." But the caption beneath the batter is unexpected. "All things are magical when a mother's watching," it reads, "(Dad will come around.)" The words undercut our understanding of the drawing, which suddenly seems to be about something else—about trying to do something or to become your true adult self, perhaps. About wanting approval, wanting to please, family conflicts, hoping

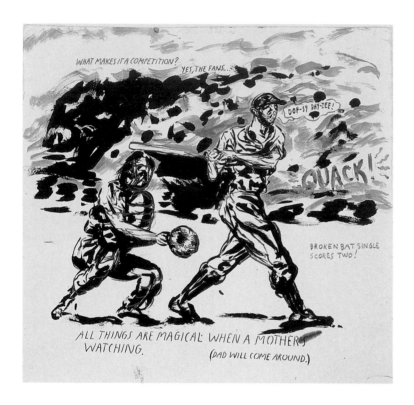

6.16 (above) Raymond Pettibon. *No title (What makes it).* 2003. Ink on paper, 21½ × 22".
Courtesy the artist and Regen Projects, Los Angeles.

6.17 (right) Sol LeWitt. *Wall Drawing #912.* 1999. White crayon and black pencil grid on gray walls. First drawn by Sachiko Cho and Emily Ripley, June 1999.
Collection Barbara Gladstone, Sag Harbor, New York.

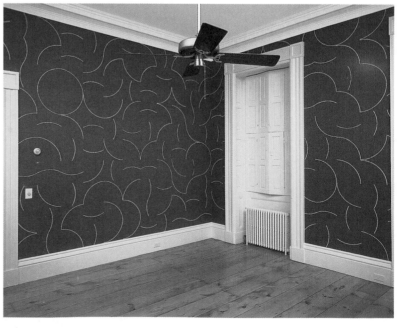

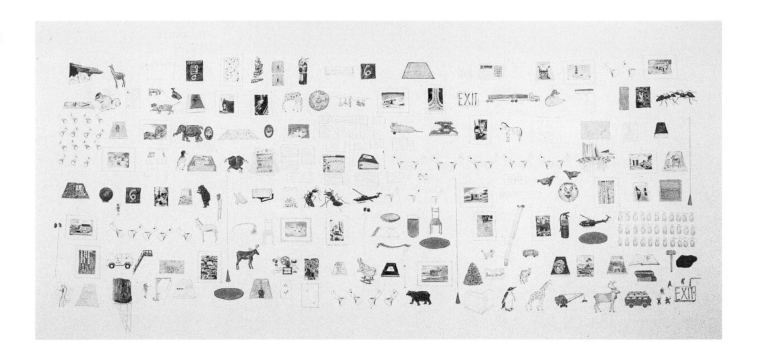

to be a hero, sensing that life is stacked against you. And why, now that we think of it, does the announcer say "competition" instead of "game"?

Other artists have taken drawing even further back to its roots, creating not just wall-size drawings but drawing on the wall itself. The large scale of wall drawings broadens our ideas of what a drawing can be, yet for all their impressive size, these drawings are in a sense even more vulnerable than traditional works on paper, for not only are they displayed in the open, without any protective covering, but they are rarely intended to be permanent. Instead they are drawn for a particular exhibition, then painted over when the exhibition ends. Some may later reappear in a varied form in other exhibitions, sort of migratory works that never show themselves in the same place twice. Others exist only once, and then are gone.

One of the first contemporary artists to create wall drawings was Sol LeWitt. LeWitt does not execute his drawings himself. Rather, he creates the instructions for making the drawing and entrusts their execution to others. The subject of the drawing is the set of instructions for its creation, and LeWitt insists that they be posted nearby. For example, the instructions for a work called *Wall Drawing #912* are: A 12-inch (30.5-cm) grid covering the walls. Within each 12-inch (30.5-cm) square, one arc from the corner or the midpoint of one side. (The direction of the arcs and their placement are determined by the draftsman.)

The instructions seem dry and uncompromising, as though the artist were reining in creativity rather than unleashing it. Yet as realized here in a private home (**6.17**), the resulting drawing is open, restrained, and elegant, with repeating arcs generating a rhythm like seagulls' wings or rolling waves. The instructions could produce a vast number of other drawings that would look quite different, yet they would all be related because they spring from the same idea. The idea, or concept, is the governing principle and, because of this, the work of LeWitt and other like-minded artists is known as **Conceptual Art.**

In contrast to the drawings of Sol LeWitt, Elise Engler's *Everything They Let Me Draw* (**6.18**) existed only once. Engler was asked by a gallery in New York to participate in an exhibit by drawing the exhibit itself on the wall. Working in colored pencil, Engler drew not only the art but everything in the exhibition space that could be looked at, including lighting fixtures, sockets,

6.18 Elise Engler. *Everything They Let Me Draw.* Pencil and colored pencil on wall, 9 × 5'. Art in General, New York, January 29–April 4, 1998.

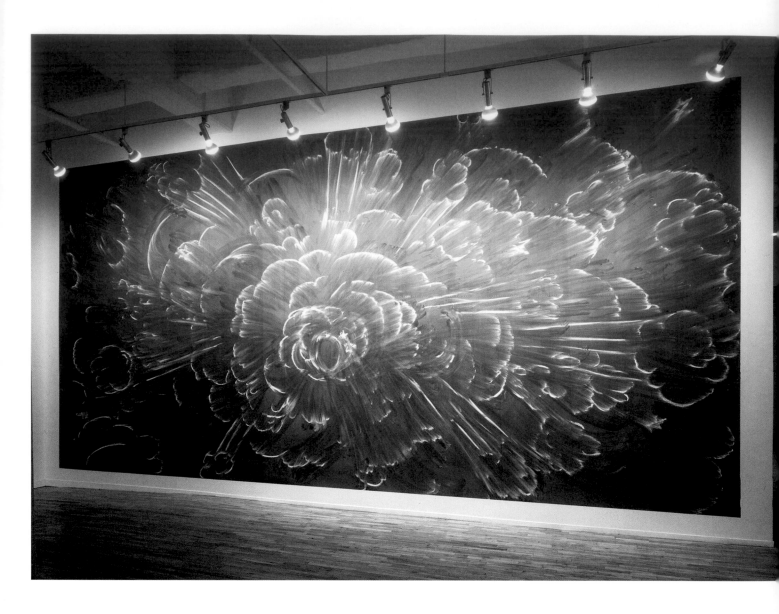

6.19 Gary Simmons. *boom*. 1996. Chalk and slate paint on wall, dimensions variable.
Installation at Metro Pictures Gallery, New York, 1996.

water pipes, elevator buttons, wall labels, window shades, and a fire extinguisher. She also broke each work of art down into its components and drew those separately, as though each were a thing worthy of attention in its own right. Everything is drawn roughly the same size, resulting in delightful and disorienting shifts in scale. By refusing to recognize any differences between the many objects that could be seen in the gallery, Engler's witty inventory raised interesting questions about art in a sly and playful way.

This chapter ends with a bang, or at least a drawing of one (**6.19**). Gary Simmons takes his inspiration from a drawing medium that accompanies most of us all through childhood and adolescence: chalk on blackboard. Simmons has created numerous drawings on actual blackboards. In gallery and museum settings, he often coats walls with slate paint to create blackboard-like mural surfaces, as here in *boom*. The immediate, instinctive association we make with school and schoolwork lets us imagine, for example, that some poor student's brain just couldn't hold one more piece of information. Boom! Or that a chemistry professor had just finished writing out an equation for an explosive compound. Boom!

But as always, good art holds many layers of meaning. As we allow our imagination to float free of the schoolroom, we may notice that the explosion also looks like a blossom, perhaps a peony or a rose. The drawing associates two opposites, it seems, a symbol of violence and destruction and a symbol of life and beauty. Looking at the drawing through the lens of art history, we may notice that the straight lines symbolizing rays of energy have often been used to symbolize rays of light, especially during the Baroque era. (See, for example, the *Cornaro Chapel* by Bernini, 17.1, 17.2). Seen in this way, the explosion resembles a stylized cloud with beams of light streaming from behind it, an image which in Baroque art was often used to signify the radiant glory of heaven. Does *boom* depict an episode of violent destruction or a burst of heavenly glory arriving in the world? Does it perhaps depict the Big Bang with which science tells us our universe began? Perhaps we should try to understand it as somehow all of these things at once.

The wall drawings of LeWitt, Engler, and Simmons bring us back full circle to the early art of the caves. In bypassing conventional surfaces such as paper, these artists show us that drawing need accept no limits, no restrictive sizes or shapes. Drawing is so much a natural impulse that it can be around us in the most natural way.

CHAPTER SEVEN

PAINTING

In the Western tradition, painting is the queen of the arts. Ask ten people to form a quick mental image of "art," and nine of them are likely to visualize a painting. There are several reasons for the prominence of painting. For one thing, paintings usually are full of color, which is a potent visual stimulus. For another, paintings usually are framed, some quite elaborately, so that one has the impression of a precious object set off from the rest of the world. Even without a frame, a painting may seem a thing apart—a focus of energy and life, a universe unto itself. Whatever the painting shows, it establishes its own visual scope, sets its own rules.

If we consider some of the earliest cave images, especially the more elaborate and colorful ones, to be paintings, then the art has been practiced for at least thirty thousand years. During that long history the styles of painting have changed considerably, as have the media in which paintings are done—the physical substances the painter uses. In the latter case it might be more accurate to say broadened, rather than changed, for few media have been completely abandoned, while many new options have been added to the painter's repertoire.

To begin this discussion of painting, we should define some terms that allow us to understand how, physically, such a work of art is put together. Paint is made of **pigment,** powdered color, compounded with a **medium** or **vehicle,** a liquid that holds the particles of pigment together without dissolving them. The vehicle generally acts as or includes a **binder,** an ingredient that ensures that the paint, even when diluted and spread thinly, will adhere to the surface. Without a binder, pigments would simply powder off as the paint dried.

Artists' paints are generally made to a pastelike consistency and need to be diluted in order to be brushed freely. Aqueous media can be diluted with water. Watercolors are an example of an aqueous medium. Nonaqueous media require some other diluent. Oil paints are an example of a nonaqueous medium; these can be diluted with turpentine or mineral spirits. Paints are applied to a **support,** which is the canvas, paper, wood panel, wall, or other surface on which the artist works. The support may be prepared to receive paint with a **ground** or **primer,** a preliminary coating.

It is impossible to tell which painting medium is the oldest, but we know that ancient peoples mixed their pigments with such things as fat and honey. Two techniques perfected in the ancient world that are still in use today are encaustic and fresco, and we begin our discussion with them.

ENCAUSTIC

Encaustic paints consist of pigment mixed with wax and resin. When the colors are heated, the wax melts and the paint can be brushed easily. When the wax cools, the paint hardens. After the painting is completed, there may be a final "burning in" as a heat source is passed close to the surface of the painting to fuse the colors.

Literary sources tell us that encaustic was an important technique in ancient Greece (the word *encaustic* comes from the Greek for "burning in"). The earliest encaustic paintings to have survived, however, are funeral portraits created during the first centuries of our era in Egypt, which was then under Roman rule (**7.1**). Portraits such as this were set into the casings of mummified bodies to identify and memorialize the dead (see 14.33). The colors of this painting, almost as fresh as the day they were set down, testify to the permanence of encaustic.

The technique of encaustic was forgotten within a few centuries after the fall of the Roman Empire, but it was redeveloped during the 19th century, partly in response to the discovery of the Roman-Egyptian portraits. One of the foremost contemporary artists to experiment with encaustic is Jasper Johns (**7.2**). *Numbers in Color* is painted in encaustic over a collage of paper on canvas. Encaustic allowed Johns to build up a richly textured paint surface (think of candle drippings and you will get the idea). Moreover, wax will not harm the paper over time as oil paint would.

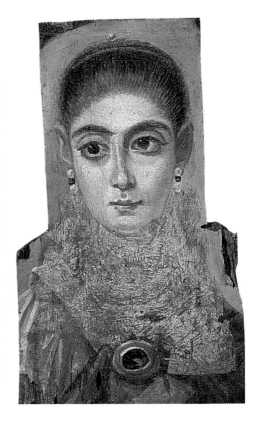

FRESCO

With fresco, pigments are mixed with water and applied to a plaster support, usually a wall or a ceiling coated in plaster. The plaster may be dry, in which case the technique is known as **fresco secco,** Italian for "dry fresco." But most often when speaking about fresco, we mean **buon fresco,** "true fresco," in which paint made simply of pigment and water is applied to wet lime plaster. As the plaster dries, the lime undergoes a chemical transformation and acts as a binder, fusing the pigment with the plaster surface.

Fresco is above all a wall-painting technique, and it has been used for large-scale murals since ancient times. Probably no other painting medium requires such careful planning and such hard physical labor. The plaster can be painted only when it has the proper degree of dampness; therefore, the artist must plan each day's work and spread plaster only in the area that can be painted in one session. (Michelangelo could cover about 1 square yard of wall or ceiling in a day.) Work may be guided by a full-size drawing of the entire project called a **cartoon.** Once the cartoon is finalized, its contour lines are perforated with pinprick-size holes. The drawing is transferred to the prepared surface by placing a portion of the cartoon over the damp plaster and rubbing pigment through the holes. The cartoon is then removed, leaving dotted lines on the plaster surface. With a brush dipped in paint the artist "connects the dots" to re-create the drawing; then the work of painting begins.

There is nothing tentative about fresco. Whereas in some media the artist can experiment, try out forms, and then paint over them to make corrections, every touch of the brush in fresco is a commitment. The only way an artist can correct mistakes or change the forms is to let the plaster dry, chip it away, and start all over again.

Frescoes have survived to the present day from the civilizations of the ancient Mediterranean (see 14.31), from China and India (see 19.6), and from the early civilizations of Mexico. Among the works we consider the greatest of all in Western art are the magnificent frescoes of the Italian Renaissance.

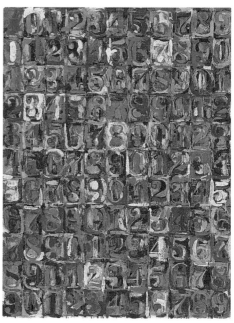

7.1 (above, top) *Young Woman with a Gold Pectoral,* from Fayum. 100–150 C.E. Encaustic on wood, height 12⅜".
Musée du Louvre, Paris.

7.2 (above) Jasper Johns. *Numbers in Color.* 1958–59. Encaustic and collage on canvas, 5'6½" × 4'1½".
Albright-Knox Gallery, Buffalo, New York.

While Michelangelo was at work on the frescoes of the Sistine Chapel ceiling (see 16.11, 16.12), Pope Julius II asked Raphael to decorate the walls of several rooms in the Vatican Palace. Raphael's fresco for the end wall of the Stanza della Segnatura, a room that may have been the Pope's library, is considered by many to be the summation of Renaissance art. It is called *The School of Athens* (**7.3**) and depicts the Greek philosophers Plato and Aristotle, centered in the composition and framed by the arch, along with their followers and students. The "school" in question means the two schools of philosophy represented by the two Classical thinkers—Plato's the more abstract and metaphysical, Aristotle's the more earthly and physical.

Everything about Raphael's composition celebrates the Renaissance ideals of perfection, beauty, naturalistic representation, and noble principles. The towering architectural setting is drawn in linear perspective with the vanishing point falling between the two central figures. The figures, perhaps influenced by Michelangelo's figures on the Sistine ceiling, are idealized—more perfect than life, full-bodied and dynamic. *The School of Athens* reflects Raphael's vision of one Golden Age—the Renaissance—and connects it with the Golden Age of Greece two thousand years earlier.

The most celebrated frescoes of the 20th century were created in Mexico, where the revolutionary government that came into power in 1921 after a decade of civil war commissioned artists to create murals about Mexico itself—the glories of its ancient civilizations, its political struggles, its people, and its hopes for the future. *Mixtec Culture* (**7.4**) is one of a series of frescoes painted by Diego Rivera in the National Palace in Mexico City. Mixtec people still live in Mexico, as do descendants of all the early civilizations of the region. The Mixtec kingdoms were known for their arts, and Rivera has portrayed a peaceful community of artists at work. To the left, two men, probably nobles, are being fitted with the elaborate ritual headdresses, masks, and

7.3 Raphael. *The School of Athens*. 1510–11. Fresco, 26 × 18'.
Stanza della Segnatura, Vatican, Rome.

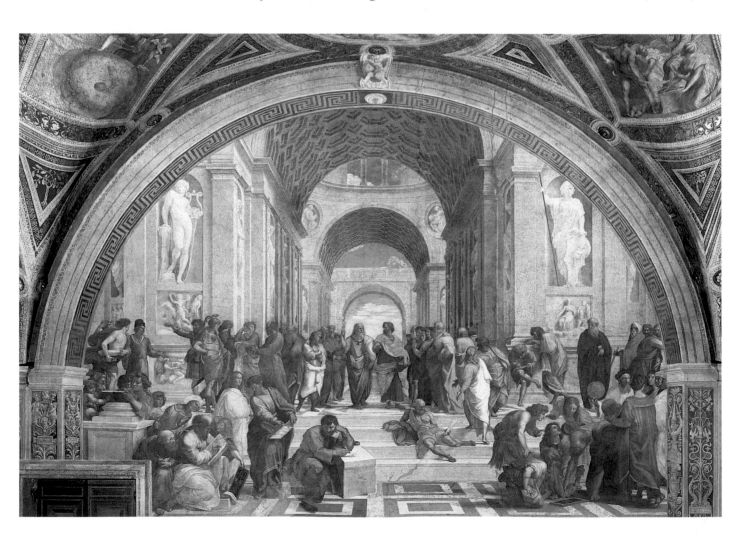

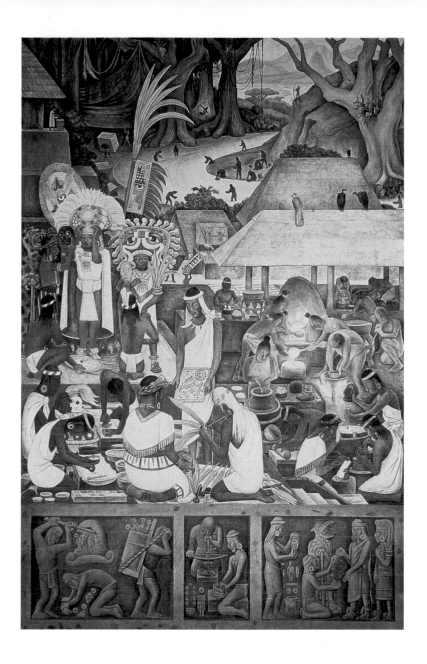

capes that were a prominent part of many ancient Mexican cultures (see 20.10, 20.12). To the right, smiths are melting and casting gold. In the foreground are potters, sculptors, feather workers, mask makers, and scribes. In the background, people pan for gold in the stream.

7.4 Diego Rivera. *Mixtec Culture.* 1942. Fresco, 16'1⅝" × 10'5⅝".
Palacio Nacional, Mexico City.

TEMPERA

Tempera shares qualities with both watercolor and oil paint. Like watercolor, tempera is an aqueous medium. Like oil paint, it dries to a tough, insoluble film. Yet while oil paint tends to yellow and darken with age, tempera colors retain their brilliance and clarity for centuries. Technically, tempera is paint in which the vehicle is an emulsion, which is a stable mixture of an aqueous liquid with an oil, fat, wax, or resin. A familiar example of an emulsion is milk, which consists of minute droplets of fat suspended in liquid. A derivative of milk called casein is one of the many vehicles that can be used to make tempera colors. The most famous tempera vehicle, however, is another naturally occuring emulsion, egg yolk. Tempera dries very quickly, and so colors cannot be blended easily once they are set down. While tempera can be

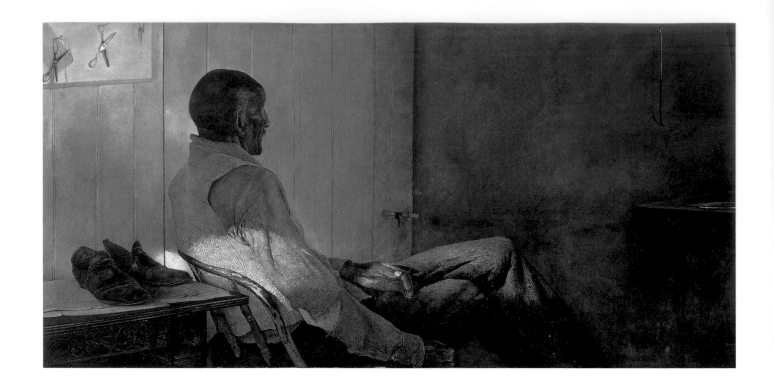

7.5 Andrew Wyeth. *That Gentleman.* 1960. Tempera on panel, 23½ × 47¾".
Dallas Museum of Art.

diluted with water and applied in a broad wash, painters who use it most commonly build up forms gradually with fine hatching and cross-hatching strokes, much like a drawing. Traditionally, tempera was used on a wood panel support prepared with a ground of **gesso,** a mixture of white pigment and glue that sealed the wood and could be sanded and rubbed to a smooth, ivorylike finish.

A 20th-century painter who has cultivated a classic tempera technique—although not on panel—is Andrew Wyeth. His painting *That Gentleman* shows the luminous qualities of the medium at their best (**7.5**). Executed in a restricted palette of earth tones, *That Gentleman* is one of a series of paintings that Wyeth made of friends and neighbors around the farm where he lived in Pennsylvania. Wyeth's patient technique seems particularly suited to evoking the dignified presence of an old man staring into the shadows, remembering. The painter's favorite detail was the battered pair of slippers, and he painted a separate study of them alone. He thought they said all anyone needed to know about the man, and that the rest of the painting was almost superfluous.

A different approach to tempera can be seen in the work of Jacob Lawrence. Lawrence said he was drawn to the "raw, sharp, rough" effect of vibrant tempera colors. *Cabinet Maker* (**7.6**) is a wonderful image of a carpenter, the curves of his powerful organic form about to burst out of the geometric shapes that constrain him. He holds the symbol of his profession, the carpenter's square, which guarantees that his work will be true. Before him lie more tools and a squared length of wood. At the outer edge of the carpenter's square and elsewhere, Lawrence allows his own ruled lines to be seen, emphasizing that he too used a straightedge in his work, and that his painting too is a well-made thing whose parts fit precisely together.

OIL

Oil paints consist of pigment compounded with oil, usually linseed oil. The oil acts as a binder, creating as it dries a transparent film in which the pigment is suspended. A popular legend claims that oil painting was invented early in the 15th century by the great Netherlandish artist Jan van Eyck, who experimented with it for this portrait (**7.7**). While we know now that Van Eyck did not actually invent the medium, we still point to him as the first important artist to understand and exploit its possibilities. From that time and for about five hundred years the word "painting" was virtually synonymous with "oil painting." Only since the 1950s, with the introduction of acrylics (discussed later in this chapter), has the supremacy of oil been challenged.

When oil paints were first introduced, most artists, including Jan van Eyck, continued working on wood panels. Gradually, however, artists adopted the more flexible canvas, which offered two great advantages. For one thing, the changing styles favored larger and larger paintings. Whereas wood panels were heavy and liable to crack, the lighter linen canvas could be stretched to almost unlimited size. Second, as artists came to serve distant patrons, their canvases could be rolled up for easy and safe shipment. Canvas was prepared by stretching it over a wooden frame, sizing it with glue to seal the fibers and protect them from the corrosive action of oil paint, and then coating it with a white, oil-base ground. Some painters then applied a thin, transparent layer of color over the ground, most often a warm brown or a cool, pale gray.

The outstanding characteristic of oil paint is that it dries very slowly. This creates both advantages and disadvantages for the artist. On the plus side, it means that colors can be blended subtly, layers of paint can be applied on top of other layers with little danger of separating or cracking, and the artist can rework sections of the painting almost indefinitely. This same asset becomes a liability when the artist is pressed for time—perhaps when an exhibition has been scheduled. Oil paint dries so *very* slowly that it may be weeks or months before the painting has truly "set."

7.6 (left) Jacob Lawrence. *Cabinet Maker.* 1957. Casein tempera on paper, 30½ × 22½". Hirshhorn Museum and Sculpture Garden, Smithsonian Institution, Washington, D.C.

7.7 (right) Jan van Eyck. *Man in a Red Turban (Self-Portrait?).* 1433. Tempera and oil on panel, 13⅛ × 10⅛". The National Gallery, London.

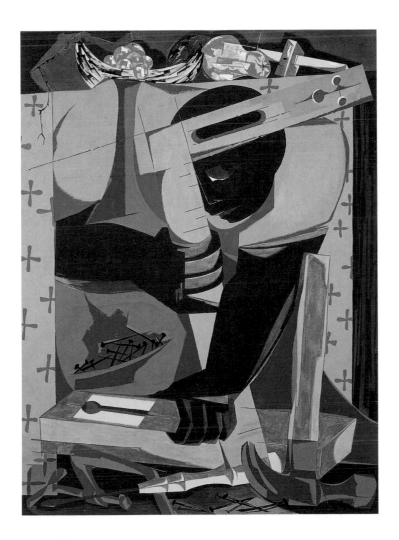

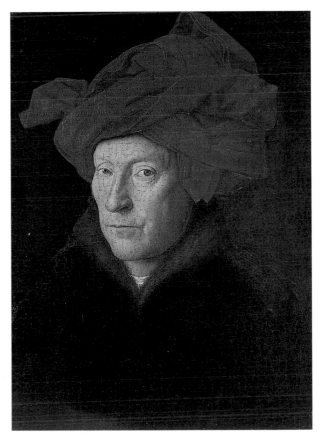

JACOB LAWRENCE

1917–2000

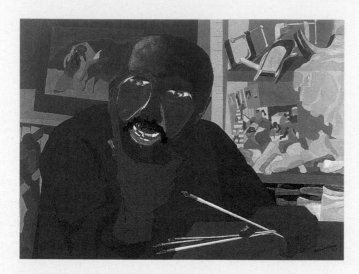

T HE NAME "HARLEM" is associated in many people's minds with hardship and poverty. Poverty Harlem has always known, but during the 1920s it experienced a tremendous cultural upsurge that has come to be called the Harlem Renaissance. So many of the greatest names in black culture—musicians, writers, artists, poets, scientists—lived or worked in Harlem at the time, or simply took their inspiration from its intellectual energy. To Harlem, in about 1930, came a young teenager named Jacob Lawrence, relocating from Philadelphia with his mother, brother, and sister. The flowering of the Harlem Renaissance had passed, but there remained enough momentum to help turn the child of a poor family into one of the most distinguished American artists of his generation.

Young Lawrence's home life was not happy, but he had several islands of refuge: the public library, the Harlem Art Workshop, and the Metropolitan Museum of Art. He studied at the Harlem Art Workshop from 1932 to 1934 and received much encouragement from two noted black artists, Charles Alston and Augusta Savage. By the age of twenty Lawrence had begun to exhibit his work. A year later he, like so many others, was being supported by the W.P.A. Art Project, a government-sponsored program to help artists get through the economic void of the Great Depression.

Even this early in his career, Lawrence had established the themes that would dominate his work. The subject matter comes from his own experience, from black experience: the hardships of poor people in the ghettos, the violence that greeted blacks moving from the South to the urban North, the upheaval of the civil rights movement during the 1960s. Nearly always his art has a narrative content or "story," and often the titles are lengthy. Although Lawrence did paint individual pictures, the bulk of his production was in series, such as *The Migration Series* and *Theater,* some of them having as many as sixty images.

The year 1941 was significant for Lawrence's life and career. He married the painter Gwendolyn Knight, and he acquired his first dealer when Edith Halpert of the Downtown Gallery in New York featured him in a major exhibition. The show was successful, and it resulted in the purchase of Lawrence's *Migration* series by two important museums.

From that point Lawrence's career prospered. His paintings were always in demand, and he was sought after as an illustrator of magazine covers, posters, and books. His influence continued through his teaching—first at Black Mountain College in North Carolina, later at Pratt Institute, the Art Students League, and the University of Washington. In 1978 he was elected to the National Council on the Arts.

Many people would call Lawrence's paintings instruments of social protest, but his images, however stark, have more the character of reporting than of protest. It is as though he is telling us, "this is what happened, this is the way it is." What happened, of course, happened to black Americans, and Lawrence the world-famous painter did not seem to lose sight of Lawrence the poor youth in Harlem. As he said, "My belief is that it is most important for an artist to develop an approach and philosophy about life—if he has developed this philosophy he does not put paint on canvas, he puts himself on canvas."[1]

Jacob Lawrence. *Self-Portrait.* 1977.
Gouache on paper, 23 × 31".
National Academy of Design, New York.

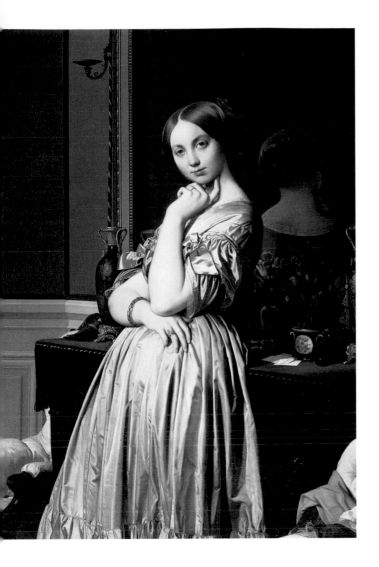

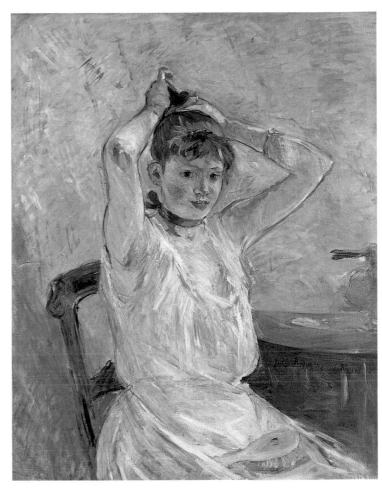

Another great advantage of oil is that it can be worked in an almost infinite range of consistencies, from very thick to very thin. Van Eyck, for example, did much of his painting in **glazes**—thin, translucent veils of color applied over a thicker layer of underpainting. Though less often used today, glazing remained an important technique in oil painting through the 19th century. Jean-Auguste-Dominique Ingres' exquisite portrait of the Countess of Haussonville shows the smooth, flawless finish and glowing color that glazes can produce (**7.8**).

Painting as practiced by artists such as Van Eyck and Ingres is a slow and time-consuming affair. The composition is generally worked out in advance down to the least detail, then built up methodically, layer after layer. A classic procedure is to complete the entire painting first in black and white, a technique called **grisaille** (gree-ZYE), from the French for "gray." Colored glazes are then floated over the monochrome image, whose lights and darks show through as modeling.

Artists who favor a more spontaneous approach may work directly in opaque colors on the white ground, a technique sometimes called **alla prima** (AHL-lah PREE-mah), Italian for "all in one go." We can see the difference in effect by comparing Ingres' portrait with a painting executed some forty years later, Berthe Morisot's *Girl Arranging Her Hair*, also known as *The Bath* (**7.9**). While Ingres' brush strokes are nowhere to be seen, Morisot's bold, slashing brush strokes are an important part of her style. In places the paint is layered quite thickly, a technique called **impasto**, from the Italian for "paste." At its

7.8 (left) Jean-Auguste-Dominique Ingres. *La Comtesse d'Haussonville*. 1845. Oil on canvas, 51⅞ × 36³⁄₁₆".
The Frick Collection, New York.

7.9 (right) Berthe Morisot. *Girl Arranging Her Hair ("The Bath")*. 1885–86. Oil on canvas, 35¾ × 28½".
The Sterling and Francine Clark Art Institute, Williamstown, Massachusetts.

most extreme, impasto can look as though the paint has been applied like frosting on a cake—and in fact miniature spatulas and trowels are available for just this purpose.

Morisot, like most of her Impressionist colleagues, favored **broken color.** The white of the girl's slip, for example, is made up of individual strokes of many different whites and tinted whites, as opposed to the single, uniform hue of Ingres' glaze. Like Seurat's technique of pointillism (see 4.32), broken color produces a lively, vibrant surface and mixes partially in the viewer's eye.

The thick, loaded brushwork that oil paint made possible added a new expressive element to painting, and painters were quick to take advantage of it. During the 20th century, this sort of brushwork came to be appreciated for its own sake. The energetic brushwork of Joan Mitchell's *La Grande Vallée XVII, Carl* (**7.10**) is reminiscent of the background in Morisot's painting, but here it no longer portrays anything but itself. The title asks us to view the painting as a kind of landscape or interpretation of a landscape. Reflections in a lake, blue shadows of morning, wild flowers, rain, a view through a window—all of these associations may come to mind, though the painting will never limit us to any one of them.

Oil paint is a sensuous medium—it has a distinctive feel and a distinctive smell—and working with it can be a pleasure in itself. The sheer joy of handling paint is part of the message of Joan Mitchell's *La Grande Vallée XVII, Carl,* and we find it again in Elizabeth Murray's *The Lowdown* (**7.11**). Murray makes art from ordinary, everyday moments—listening to a record, looking

7.10 Joan Mitchell. *La Grande Vallée XVII, Carl.* 1984. Oil on canvas, 9'2¼" × 8'6⅝".
FRAC Provence-Alpes-Côte d'Azur.

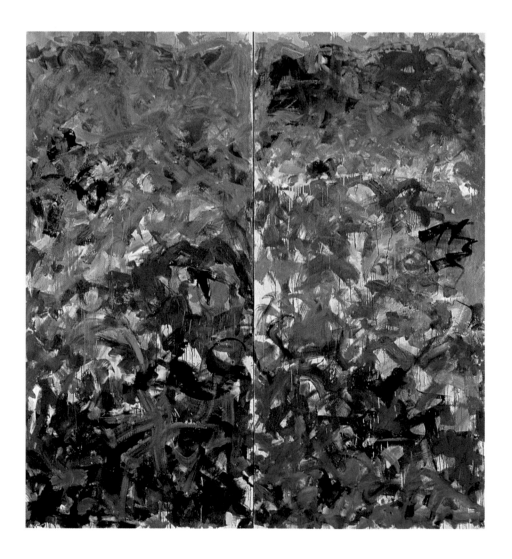

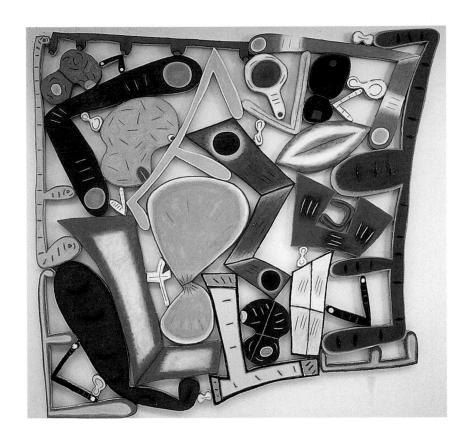

7.11 Elizabeth Murray. *The Lowdown.* 2001. Oil on canvas on wood, 7'4" × 8'2".
Courtesy PaceWildenstein Gallery, New York.

for your sneakers, running to answer the telephone. She takes her memories of moments like these and abstracts them into lively, bulging, cartoon shapes. She cuts the shapes from wood, covers them in canvas, and paints each one so that it has a character all its own.

Looking at *The Lowdown,* we can spot a head with a watchful eye, a raised arm, circular forms on a path, and small, scattering white forms. Are we . . . bowling? Possibly. And perhaps there are other games going on as well. The elements of Murray's giddy compositions are like a toddler's oversize puzzle pieces, except that they don't interlock. Instead, Murray herds them into a tottering unity, like a juggler keeping an impossible number of objects in the air. The paintings suggest a life that is a bit chaotic, but also a lot of fun.

WATERCOLOR

Watercolor consists of pigment in a vehicle of water and gum arabic, a sticky plant substance that acts as the binder. As with drawing, the most common support for watercolor is paper. Also like drawing, watercolor is commonly thought of as an intimate art, small in scale and free in execution. Eclipsed for several centuries by the prestige of oil paints, watercolors were in fact often used for small and intimate works. Easy to carry and requiring only a glass of water for use, they could readily be taken on sketching expeditions outdoors and were a favorite medium for amateur artists. Yet watercolors can be large and/or painstakingly executed as well, and we should bear in mind that the entire painting tradition of East Asia, with its monumental landscapes and lengthy scrolls, was created with water-based colors.

The leading characteristic of watercolors is their transparency. They are not applied thickly, like oil paints, but thinly in translucent washes. While opaque white watercolor is available, this is reserved for special uses. More usually, the white of the paper serves for white, and dark areas are built up through several layers of transparent washes, which take on depth without ever becoming completely opaque. John Singer Sargent's *Mountain Stream* (**7.12**) is a perfect example of what we might think of as "classic" watercolor technique. Controlled and yet spontaneous in feeling, it gives the impression of having been dashed off in a single sitting. The white of the paper serves for the foam of the rushing stream, and even the shadows on the opposite shore retain a translucent quality.

Elizabeth Peyton makes even greater use of white paper in this watercolor of her friend Tony, asleep in a hotel bed (**7.13**). White sheets and white pajamas are indicated by their contours and shadows in a dance of pale, slurpy brush strokes. Peyton allows, and perhaps encourages, the color to run down in drips, like rain running down a window—a good day to sleep in.

GOUACHE

Gouache is watercolor with inert white pigment added. Inert pigment is pigment that becomes colorless or virtually colorless in paint. In gouache, it serves to make the colors opaque, which means that when used at full strength, they can completely hide any ground or other color they are painted over. The poster paints given to children are basically gouache, although not of artist's quality. Like watercolor, gouache can be applied in a translucent wash, although that is not its primary use. It dries quickly and uniformly and is especially well suited to large areas of flat, saturated color. For example, Indian paintings such as 3.15 and 4.42 are done in opaque watercolor, although of a formula slightly different than gouache. The Cuban painter Wifredo Lam exploits both the transparent and opaque possibilities of gouache in *The Jungle* (**7.14**). Human and animal forms mingle in this fascinating work, which contains references to *Santería*, a Caribbean religion that combines West African and Roman Catholic beliefs.

7.12 John Singer Sargent. *Mountain Stream.* c. 1912–14. Watercolor and graphite on paper, 13¾ × 21". The Metropolitan Museum, New York.

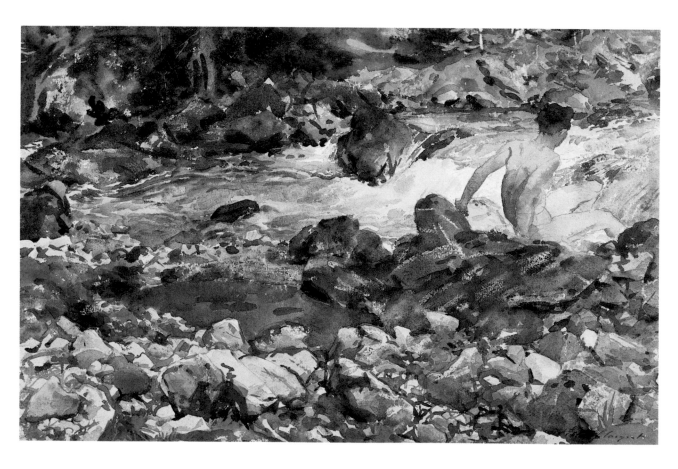

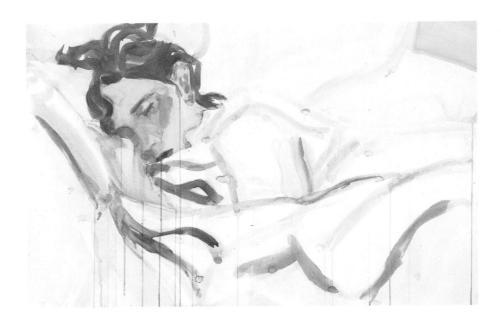

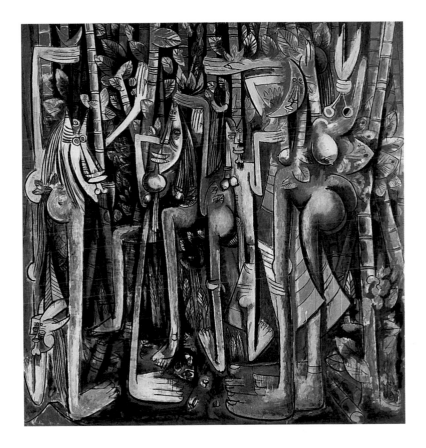

ACRYLIC

The enormous developments in chemistry during the early 20th century had an impact in artists' studios. By the 1930s, chemists had learned to make strong, weatherproof, industrial paints using a vehicle of synthetic plastic resins. Artists began to experiment with these paints almost immediately. By the 1950s, chemists had made many advances in the new technology and had also adapted it to artists' requirements for permanence. For the first time since it was developed, oil paint had a challenger as the principal medium for Western painting.

These new synthetic artists' colors are broadly known as acrylics, although a more exact name for them is polymer paints. The vehicle consists of acrylic resin, polymerized (its simple molecules linked into long chains) through emulsion in water. As acrylic paint dries, the resin particles coalesce to form a tough, flexible, and waterproof film.

Depending on how they are used, acrylics can mimic the effects of oil paint, watercolor, gouache, and even tempera. They can be used on both prepared or raw canvas, and also on paper and fabric. They can be layered into a heavy impasto like oils or diluted with water and spread in translucent washes like watercolor. Like tempera, they dry quickly and permanently. (Artists using acrylics usually rest their brushes in water while working, for if the paint dries on the brush, it is extremely difficult to remove.)

David Hockney's *Mount Fuji* illustrates two very distinct ways of working with acrylics (**7.15**). The tranquil blue background with its view of the famous mountain was created by diluting the paint to the consistency of a dye or stain and pouring it onto unprimed white cotton canvas, which partially absorbed the color. The vase of flowers and the ledge in the foreground were painted with brushes in a fairly heavy impasto.

Hockney presents us with an enchanted tourist's view of Japan, focusing on a traditional picturesque sight. From Japan itself, however, comes quite a different sort of image, Takashi Murakami's *The Castle of Tin Tin* (**7.16**). Murakami uses yet another technique that acrylic paints facilitate: airbrushing, in which diluted paint is sprayed onto a surface. Here, an airbrush was used to create the flat silver background, but the technique can also produce fine, detailed images. Murakami's style and subject matter are indebted to the wildly popular Japanese animated cartoons and feature-length films known as anime. In Murakami's hands, however, the large eyes of anime characters stare out at us from strangely colorful mushrooms and mutating organic forms. Murakami also links his work to what he views as the traditional Japanese

7.15 David Hockney. *Mount Fuji.* 1972. Acrylic on canvas, 60 × 48". The Metropolitan Museum of Art, New York.

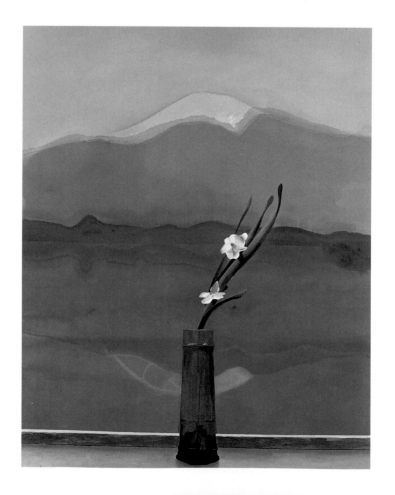

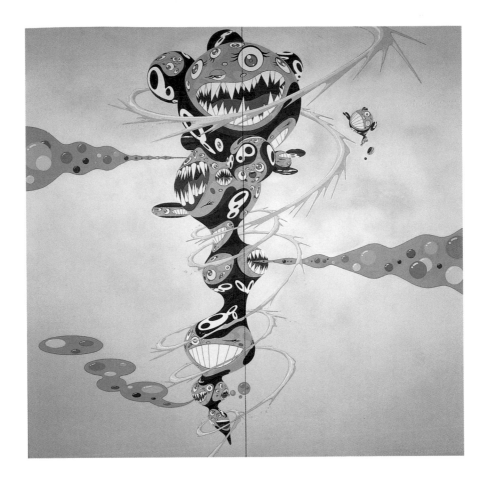

preference for flatness, as opposed to the longtime Western obsession with modeling and depth. To see what he means, compare *The Castle of Tin Tin* with Toshusai Sharaku's portrait of the famous actor Otani Oniji (8.4).

7.16 Takashi Murakami. *The Castle of Tin Tin.* 1998. Acrylic on canvas on board, 10 × 10'. Courtesy Blum & Poe, Los Angeles, and Takashi Murakami/Kaikai Kiki.

BLURRING THE BOUNDARIES

Like other traditional media, painting has been pushed in new directions by younger artists eager to stake out fresh territory to explore. This chapter ends by looking at two ways in which the practice of painting has been transformed by artists questioning its boundaries, both the boundary between painting and life, and the boundaries between painting and other media.

Collage

In representational painting, objects from the real world are transposed into art by the hand of a painter, who creates a likeness. This seems so basic that we rarely even consider it. Yet at the beginning of the 20th century this assumption received a shock from which it never recovered, a jolt that opened up an entirely new relationship between art and life. In the hands of two extraordinary artists, objects from the real world passed directly into art without any transformation at all. The artists were Pablo Picasso and Georges Braque, and the technique they pioneered is known as collage.

Collage is a French word that means "pasting" or "gluing." In art, it refers to the practice of attaching actual objects such as paper or cloth to the surface of a canvas or other support, as well as to the resultant artwork. It was Pablo Picasso, in the spring of 1912, who first used the technique, pasting a piece of patterned oilcloth onto a painting of a still life. But the idea lay fallow until

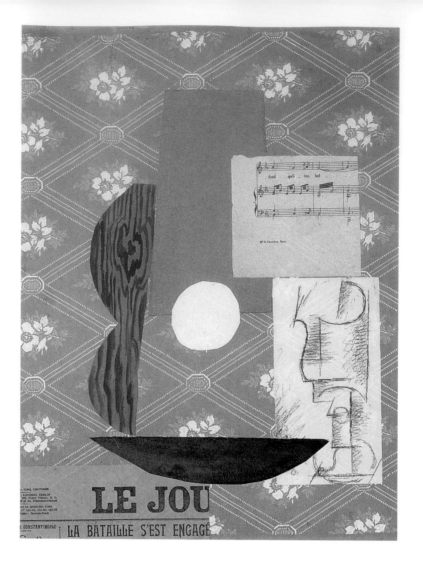

7.17 Pablo Picasso. *Guitar and Wine Glass.* 1912. Collage and charcoal on board, 18⅞ × 14¾". Collection The McNay Art Museum, San Antonio, Texas.

the fall, when Georges Braque began including shapes cut from wallpaper and newsprint in his drawings. Picasso saw what his friend was up to, took the idea, and ran with it.

Guitar and Wine Glass (**7.17**) is one of Picasso's earliest collages. In the lower left corner he has pasted a bit of the daily newspaper (in French, *Le Journal*), with the partial headline *"La Bataille s'est engagé"* (the battle has begun). As printed, the headline referred to the current Balkan wars, but what did Picasso mean? Did he go to battle to enrich the possibilities of art by the then-shocking practice of gluing objects to canvas? Or was his battle that of upstaging his ambitious colleague? Probably some of both. Elsewhere Picasso includes a corner torn from sheet music (both artists were absorbed by musical themes), a wood-grain fragment suggesting a guitar, and a sketch of a wine glass. All are pasted onto a patterned paper resembling wallpaper.

After Picasso and Braque, many artists adopted this method of composing a picture by gathering bits and pieces from various sources. An artist who made very personal use of collage was Romare Bearden. Pieced together from bits of photographic magazine illustrations, *Mysteries* (**7.18**) is one of a series of works that evoke the texture of everyday life as Bearden had known it growing up as an African-American in rural North Carolina. In Bearden's hands, the technique of collage alludes both to the African-American folk tradition of quilting, which also pieces together a whole from many fragments (see 12.15), and to the rhythms and improvisatory nature of jazz, another art form with African roots. The face on the far left includes a portion of an African sculpture (the mouth and nose). In the background appears a photograph of a train. A recurring symbol in Bearden's work, trains stand for the outside world, especially the white world. "A train was always something that could take you away and could also bring you to where you were," the artist explained. "And in the little towns it's the black people who live near the trains."[2]

More recently Fred Tomaselli has been breathing new and strange life into collage with works such as *Head* (**7.19**). On a black ground, Tomaselli has assembled photographic images of flowers, birds, insects, and body parts to form a human head seen in profile. Images of noses cluster around the nose region; images of mouths swarm toward where a mouth would be. A thick layer of clear resin seals the pasted images and provides a surface for painted additions such as the colored planets in the background and the branching

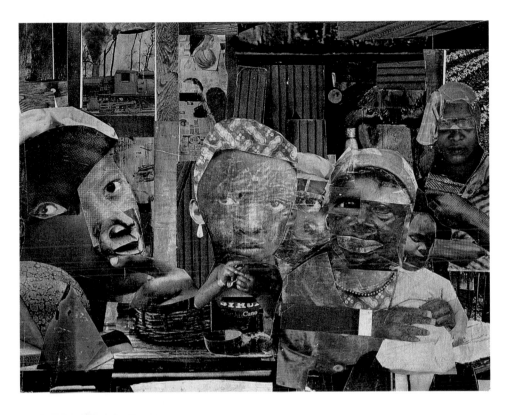

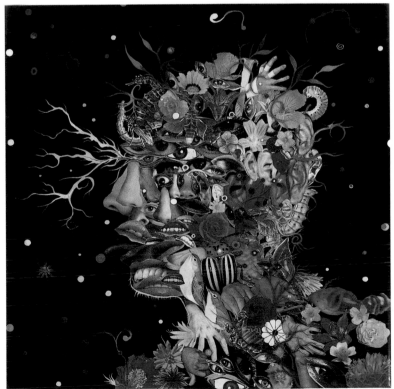

7.18 (above) Romare Bearden. *Mysteries*. 1964. Collage, polymer paint, and pencil on board, 11¼ × 14¼".
Courtesy Museum of Fine Arts, Boston.

7.19 (left) Fred Tomaselli. *Head*. 2002. Photocollage, gouache, acrylic paint, and resin on wood panel, 11 × 11".
Courtesy James Cohan Gallery, New York.

form that grows outward from the eye, like a root system reaching hungrily into the universe for nourishment. Like most of Tomaselli's work, *Head* evokes both mystical visions and drug-induced hallucinations. In both, the altered mind sees beyond everyday appearances.

Off the Wall!

However adventurous the collages of Picasso, Bearden, and Tomaselli may be, they leave certain traditional aspects of Western painting unchallenged. All three are flat, rectangular surfaces, for example. And all three are portable objects designed to be hanged on a wall for viewing. Contemporary artists have pushed at these formal boundaries as well, making paintings that break out of the traditional rectangular frame or even leave the wall altogether. We looked at the work of one such artist earlier in this chapter, Elizabeth Murray, whose paintings consist of clusters of shaped canvases (see 7.11).

Like Elizabeth Murray, Polly Apfelbaum also paints on individual elements that she then arranges in clusters. The support she favors is not canvas or paper, however, but white synthetic velvet; the paint she uses is not oil or watercolor, but fabric dye; and she arranges the elements not on the wall, but on the floor (**7.20**). *Big Bubbles* is a radiating, circular composition that consists of a single shape repeated again and again. Looking to anchor *Big Bubbles* in the world of art, we might compare it to the mosaics that often blanket

7.20 Polly Apfelbaum. *Big Bubbles*. 2001. Synthetic velvet, fabric dye; diameter approximately 18'; 1,040 separate pieces.
Courtesy D'Amelio Terras Gallery, New York.

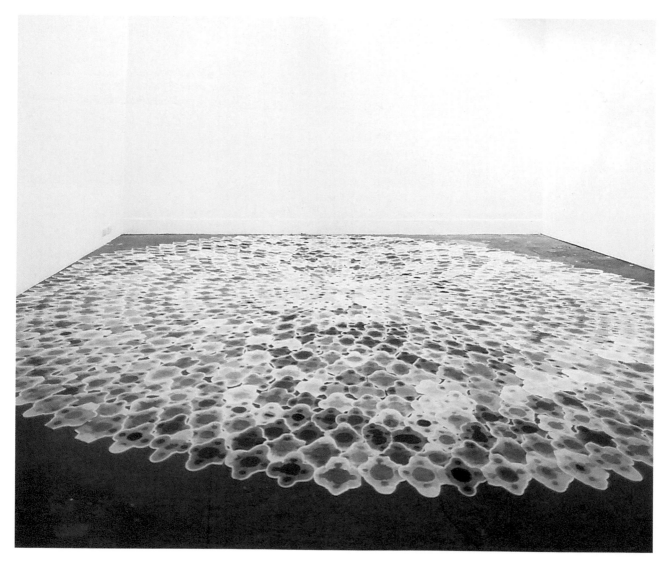

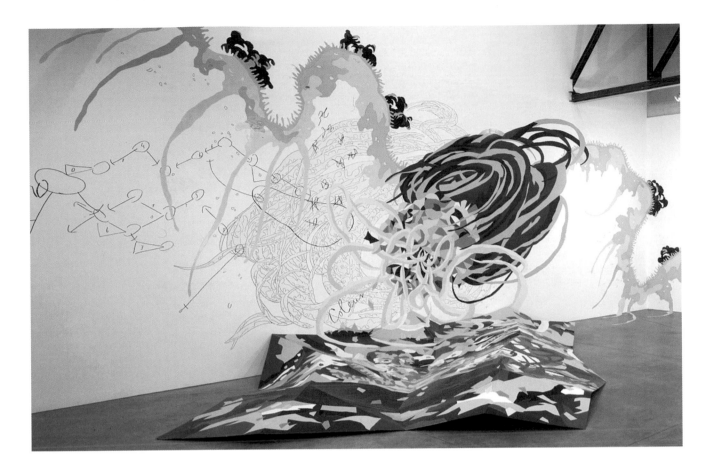

7.21 Matthew Ritchie. *Parents and Children,* 2000. Acrylic marker on wall, enamel on sintra; dimensions vary with installation.

the walls and ceilings of a mosque (see 3.3), or to the circular stained glass windows of medieval cathedrals (see 15.23), or to a mandala, a circular diagram of a cosmic realm (see 5.7). All of these forms suggest ways of imagining infinity.

Apfelbaum would probably not object to our thinking about *Big Bubbles* in these terms—she has said that she tries to keep the content of her work indirect, so that viewers can bring their own experiences to it. Her titles, however, often hint at what she herself had in mind. Bubbles turns out to be the name of one of the Powerpuff Girls, an animated cartoon series about a trio of adorable kindergarteners who happen also to be superheroines. Armed with this information, we could see Apfelbaum's radiant form as gigantic puff. We could also imagine it as a flower or a firework in celebration of strong female role models, including perhaps the many women artists who have recently claimed a place within the art establishment. Go, Powerpuff Girls!

Polly Apfelbaum began her artistic career as a sculptor. Perhaps because of this, critics sometimes refer to works such as *Big Blossom* as floor sculpture, even though they are most clearly linked to the 20th-century tradition of nonrepresentational painting. We might think of her as a sculptor who has colonized territory that once belonged exclusively to painting. Our next artist, Matthew Ritchie, has taken the opposite journey, beginning as a painter and then reaching out to annex the third dimension, which once belonged exclusively to sculpture. Ritchie's works may begin on the wall, but they are likely to sprawl across the surface, invade both the floor and the ceiling, and even spawn independent three-dimensional components, as here in *Parents and Children* (**7.21**)

Ritchie's chosen ground is sintra, a thin, lightweight, easily cut plastic material. Sintra is easily bent and molded, allowing Ritchie's works to cascade down the wall, curve onto the floor, and continue out into the room. As here, he often supplements painted elements by drawing or writing directly on the wall. Ritchie's works are visual epics inspired by science, including the far frontiers of contemporary research and theory. His compositions seem to generate themselves according to their own laws, growing like crystals over the centuries or evolving like organisms across generations. Here, sinuous elements coil like dragons or swamp vegetation outward from a raging vortex, firing off diagrams of molecular structures and mysterious equations. On the floor sits what looks like a topographical fragment, its colors interlocking as precisely as camouflage or countries on a map. Is this the "child" of the cosmic "parent"? Ritchie was once asked what message he hoped that viewers might take away from his work. His response? "Life is as complicated as it appears."[3]

This brief survey should have demonstrated that the various painting media and the artists who use them yield endless possibilities. It would be difficult to say which comes first—that artist's imagery or the material. Did the first cave artist have the impulse to paint something and search about for a material with which to do it? Or did the cave artist find some pigmented material and then speculate about what would happen if the substance were applied to a wall? The answer is not important, but the two aspects—idea and medium—feed upon each other. No visual image could be realized without the medium in which to make it concrete. And no medium would be of any consequence without the artist's idea—and the compelling urge to paint.

CHAPTER EIGHT

PRINTS

I f you have ever accidentally tracked mud into the house in your sneakers, then you understand the basic principle of making a print. When you stepped in the mud, some of it stuck to the raised surfaces of the sole of your sneakers. When you stepped on the floor afterward, the pressure of your weight transferred the mud from the raised surfaces of your sneaker to the floor, leaving an image. If you took a second step, the print you made was probably fainter, because there wasn't as much mud left on the sneaker. You would have to step in the mud again in order to produce a second print as good as the first one. With a little practice, you could probably make a row of sneaker prints that were almost exactly identical.

In the vocabulary of printmaking, the sole of your sneaker served as a **matrix,** a surface on which a design is prepared before being transferred through pressure to a receiving surface such as paper. The printed image it left is called an *impression.* You probably didn't make your own sneaker, but an artist makes a matrix in order to create prints from it. A single matrix can be used to create many impressions, all of them almost identical, and each of them considered to be an original work of art. For this reason, printing is called an art of multiples.

With the development of industrial printing technologies during the modern era, we have come to recognize a difference in value between original artists' prints and mass-produced reproductions such as the images in this book or a poster bought in a museum shop. Two broadly agreed upon principles have been adopted to distinguish original artists' prints from commercial reproductions.

The first is that the artist performs or oversees the printing process and examines each impression for quality. The artist signs each impression he or she approves; rejected impressions must be destroyed. The second is that there may be a declared limit to the number of impressions that will be made. This number, called an **edition,** is also written by the artist on each approved impression, along with the number of the impression within that edition. For example, a print numbered 10/100 is the tenth impression of a limited edition of 100. Once the entire edition has been printed, approved, signed, and numbered, the printing surface is canceled (by scratching cross marks on it) or destroyed so that no further prints can be made from it.

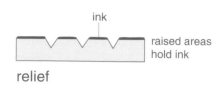

relief — raised areas hold ink

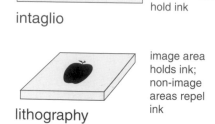

intaglio — incised areas hold ink

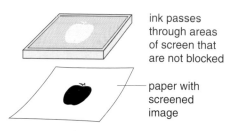

lithography — image area holds ink; non-image areas repel ink

ink passes through areas of screen that are not blocked

paper with screened image

screenprinting

Prints, however, were made for hundreds of years before these standards were in place. From the beginning, they have served to disseminate visual information and to bring the pleasure of owning art within reach of a broad public.

There are four basic methods for making an art print (**8.1**)—relief, intaglio, lithography, and screenprinting. This chapter takes up each one in turn.

RELIEF

The term *relief* describes any printing method in which the image to be printed is *raised* from a background (see 8.1). Think of a rubber stamp. When you look at the stamp itself, you may see the words "First Class" or "Special Delivery" standing out from the background in reverse. You press the stamp to an ink pad, then to paper, and the words print right side out—a mirror image of the stamp. All relief processes work according to this general principle.

Any surface from which the background areas can be carved away is suitable for relief printing, but the material most commonly associated with relief printing is wood.

Woodcut

To make a woodcut the artist first draws the desired image on a block of wood. Then all the areas that are not meant to print are cut and gouged out of the wood so that the image stands out in relief. When the block is inked, only the raised areas take the ink. Finally, the block is pressed on paper, or paper is placed on the block and rubbed to transfer the ink and make the print.

The earliest surviving woodcut image was made in China (**8.2**). Dated 868 C.E., this portrayal of the Buddha preaching appears at the beginning of the world's earliest known printed book, a copy of the Diamond Sutra, an important Buddhist text. The image probably reproduces an original drawing in brush and ink executed in the slender, even-width lines that Chinese writers likened to iron wire. Although only one copy survives, the edition of the sutra must have been quite large, for a postscript at the end of the

8.1 (above) The four basic print methods.

8.2 (right) Preface to the Diamond Sutra. 868. Woodblock handscroll.
The British Library, London.

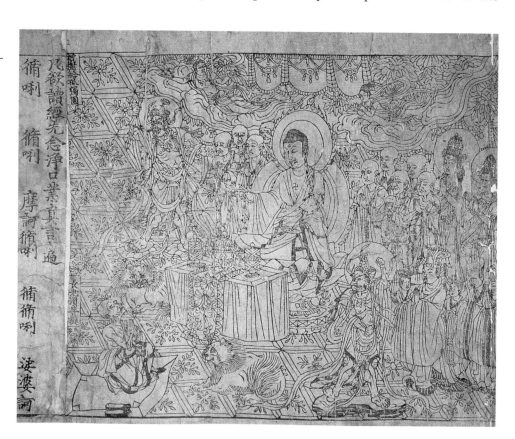

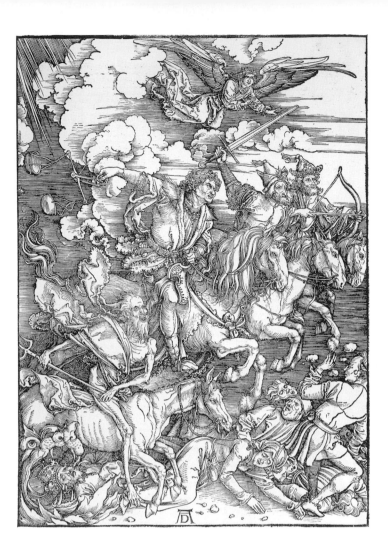

8.3 Albrecht Dürer. *Four Horsemen of the Apocalypse*, from the *Apocalypse* series. c. 1497–98. Woodcut, approx. 15⅜ × 11". The British Museum, London.

18-foot-long scroll tells us that the project was undertaken at the expense of one Wang Jie, "for universal free distribution." Two great Chinese inventions, paper and printing, are here united.

In Europe, woodblocks had been used to print patterns on textiles since as early as the 6th century C.E., but it was not until the introduction of paper that printing anything else became practical. Soon after, in the mid-15th century, the invention of the printing press and movable type launched Europe's first great "information revolution." For the first time in the West, information could be widely disseminated.

The printing press, of course, also made it easier to print images in quantity, often as illustrations for books. Albrecht Dürer created this harrowing image of the *Four Horsemen of the Apocalypse* (**8.3**) not long after the printing press was invented. The print was one of fourteen full-page illustrations for Dürer's edition of the biblical Book of Revelation, also known as the Apocalypse. Dürer at the time was a young artist struggling at the start of his career. He had turned to prints in an attempt to increase his income by reaching a larger audience, and indeed prints eventually made both his name and his fortune.

Like the Chinese illustration of the Diamond Sutra, Dürer's woodcut faithfully reproduces a drawing, probably one done in pen and ink. Even the minute hatching and cross-hatching lines used to model mass and suggest tonality have been painstakingly reproduced in wood. As was common practice in his day, Dürer probably did not carve the block himself, but rather employed a skilled carver to carry out his design. And what a design! Spurred on by an angel, the four horsemen ride in a dynamic diagonal, trampling a terrified humanity underfoot. In the lead is Victory with his crown, followed by War with his sword, then Famine with his scales for rationing food, and finally Death by Plague. In the lower left corner yawns the open mouth of the beast of Hell.

ALBRECHT DÜRER

1471–1528

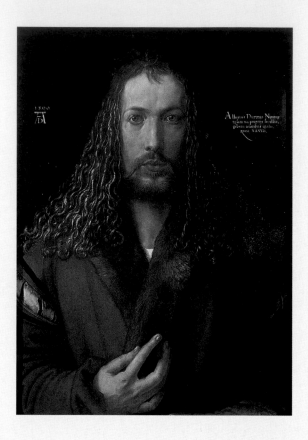

ALBRECHT DÜRER is the first of the northern European artists who seems to us "modern" in his outlook. Unlike most of his colleagues, he had a strong sense of being an *artist*, not a craftsman, and he sought—and received—acceptance in the higher ranks of society. Moreover, Dürer appears to have understood his role in the history of art—sensed that his work would exert great influence on his contemporaries and on artists of the future. This awareness led him to date his works and sign them with the distinctive "AD" (visible in the left background of his self-portrait)—a fairly unusual practice at the time.

Born in the southern German city of Nuremberg, Dürer was the son of a goldsmith, to whom he was apprenticed as a boy. At the age of fifteen young Albrecht was sent to study in the workshop of Michael Wolgemut, then considered a leading painter in Nuremberg. He stayed with Wolgemut for four years, after which he began a four-year period of wandering through northern Europe. In 1494 Dürer's father called him back to Nuremberg for an arranged marriage. (The marriage seems not to have been a happy one and produced no children.) Soon afterward Dürer established himself as a master and opened his own studio.

Dürer made a great many paintings and drawings, but it is his output in prints (engravings, woodcuts, and etchings) that is truly extraordinary. Many people would argue that he was the greatest printmaker who ever lived. His genius derived partly from an ability to unite the best tendencies in northern and southern European art of that period, for Dürer was a well-traveled man. In 1494 he visited Italy, and he returned in 1505, staying two years in Venice, where he operated a studio. This second trip was a huge success, both artistically and socially. The artist received many commissions and enjoyed the high regard of the Venetian painters as well as of important patrons in the city. Upon his return to Germany Dürer took his place among the leading writers and intellectuals of Nuremberg, who seem to have valued him for his knowledge and wit, as well as for his art. In 1515 he was appointed court painter to the Holy Roman Emperor Maximilian I.

The last years of Dürer's life were devoted largely to work on his books and treatises, through which he hoped to teach a scientific approach to painting and drawing. As a Renaissance artist, he was fascinated by perfection and by an ideal of beauty. He wrote: "What beauty is, I know not, though it adheres to many things. When we wish to bring it into our work we find it very hard. We must gather it together from far and wide, and especially in the case of the human figure throughout all its limbs from before and behind. One may often search through two or three hundred men without finding amongst them more than one or two points of beauty which can be made use of. You, therefore, if you desire to compose a fine figure, must take the head from some, the chest, arm, leg, hand, and foot from others; and likewise, search through all members of every kind. For from many beautiful things something good may be gathered, even as honey is gathered from many flowers."[1]

Albrecht Dürer. *Self-Portrait at Age 28.* 1500.
Oil on wood. 26⁵⁄₁₆ × 19⁵⁄₁₆".
Alte Pinakothek, Munich.

By the 14th century, China had advanced to the next step in woodcut by using multiple blocks to print images in full color. A few centuries later, this technique was transmitted to Japan, where during the 18th century it was brought to a level of perfection that has made Japanese prints famous the world over. One of the most intriguing Japanese printmakers from this time is Toshusai Sharaku, whose entire known output of some 150 prints was created in a single burst of activity that lasted for only ten months. Toshusai specialized in portraits of actors as they appeared in their most famous roles. Toshusai was an actor himself, and his experience on stage with his colleagues gave him a unique appreciation of their extravagant and highly stylized performances. His portrait of Otani Oniji III in the role of Edohei shows us an actor exaggerated to the point of caricature and bursting with life (**8.4**). Surely even the spectators in the very last row would have no trouble understanding his expression!

Production of such woodcuts in Japan was a true team effort. The artist was usually engaged by the publisher of the prints, who would eventually sell the edition. It was often the publisher who suggested the subject. The artist executed the design in brush and ink on paper, outlining the forms with slender "iron wire" lines. After his design was approved, it was passed along to the wood carver, who carved a block, called the key block, that reproduced the drawing. A print from the key block was sent to the artist, who approved it and made annotations about color. Guided by the key block, the carver proceeded to carve a series of color blocks, one for each color. For example, one block was carved to print only the light blue areas, another for dark blue. An entire block might need to be carved just to print a small detail in a new color. Elaborate prints often required as many as twenty blocks. The carver was also responsible for the **registration** of the blocks, that is, verifying that they lined up perfectly when printed, with no gaps or overlapping in the colors.

The completed set of blocks was then sent to a third specialist, the printer. Printers received general indications about coloring, but it seems that they

8.4 Toshusai Sharaku. *Otani Oniji III as Edohei*. 1794. Polychrome woodblock print, height 14¾".
The Art Institute of Chicago.

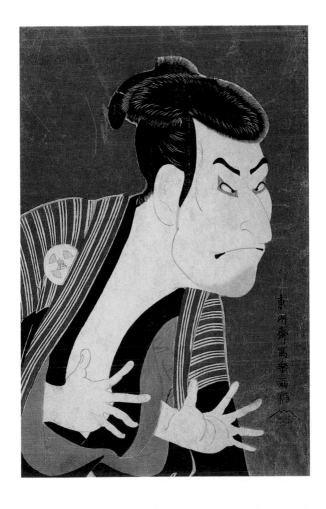

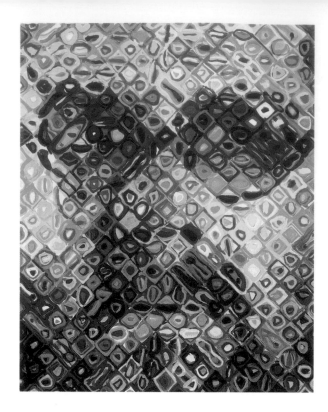

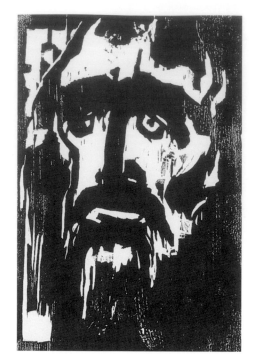

8.5 (left) Chuck Close. *Self-Portrait*. 2002. Polychrome woodblock print, image size 22½ × 17¾".
Courtesy the artist and Pace Editions, Inc.

8.6 (right) Emil Nolde. *The Prophet*. 1912. Woodcut, 12½ × 8¹³⁄₁₆".
National Gallery of Art, Washington, D.C.

had a great deal of leeway in adjusting the color harmonies to their own satisfaction. They might sometimes consult about color with the publisher, though, it seems, not with the artist. The key block was printed first, then each color block in turn, following a standard, fixed order. The completed prints were turned over for sale to the publisher, who had been advertising them in the meantime. As in the West, woodcuts in Japan made art available to people who would not have been able to afford unique works such as paintings.

During the latter part of the 19th century, Japanese woodcuts were exported in great quantities to Europe, where many artists fell under the spell of their innovative designs. Today, the virtuosity and expertise of Japanese woodblock carvers attract artists from many corners of the world. Master Japanese printmaker Yasuyuki Shibata has translated paintings into prints for numerous American artists, including Chuck Close (**8.5**). In a process quite similar to the production of traditional Japanese prints, Shibata was engaged by the publisher of the Close print, Pace Editions. Shibata worked with the artist to analyze the original painting, breaking it down into forty-three component colors and devising a strategy for printing them in sequence. He carved enough blocks to print each color individually, and printed the blocks by hand using inks he prepared himself. Close approved, signed, and numbered each print in the edition of sixty, and Pace Editions placed them on sale.

A radically different approach was pioneered during the early 20th century by German Expressionist artists who found in woodcut a medium uniquely compatible with their style. A splendid example is Emil Nolde's *The Prophet* (**8.6**). Expressionist imagery is stark, sometimes rough, and occasionally shocking. Woodcut readily lends itself to this style by allowing harsh contrasts of black and white as well as broad—even crude—drawing and cutting. Expressionism is just what its name implies—expressive, and also brooding, emotional, uncompromising. Of all the print methods, woodcut offers the greatest possibilities for that expression.

Influenced by the power and sincerity of the German Expressionist style, artists in many parts of the world took up the medium of woodcut, often using it for social and political purposes. One place where Expressionist woodcuts were admired was China, where woodcut began. In his woodcut *To the Front!* (**8.7**), Hu Yichuan, then twenty-two years old, employed the crude carving and dramatic immediacy of Expressionism in an attempt to rally the people of

China against Japanese invaders. Pressed up against the picture plane in diagonal slashes of black and white, the shouting figure in the foreground conveys a true sense of anguish and emergency.

Wood Engraving

Created during the same decade as *To the Front!* American artist Rockwell Kent's *Workers of the World, Unite!* also features a dramatic composition with a strong political theme (**8.8**). But while Hu Yichuan's print gives the impression of having been carved quickly with bold, gashing stokes, Rockwell Kent's image seems to have been created more patiently from innumerable fine white lines on a black ground. These white lines are characteristic of the medium Kent chose, wood engraving.

Wood engraving differs in several aspects from woodcut. For one thing, it is done on the end grain of the wood. If you imagine a board, say a 2-by-4, the long, smooth plank sides would be used for woodcut, but the grainy cut end would be used for wood engraving. Unlike the plank sides, the end grain can be cut in any direction without chipping or splintering. The tool used for cutting makes fine, narrow grooves in the wood, and these grooves, which do not take the ink, result in white lines when the inked woodblock is pressed to paper.

The 1930s in America were marked by the Great Depression. During this difficult decade, many artists' sympathies lay with industrial workers and their efforts to unionize in order to have a collective voice in their own future. In Kent's image, a lone, heroic worker wields a shovel against the threat of oncoming bayonets. The fire provides a sense of disaster, while in the background can be seen a factory, the source of the worker's livelihood. With its combination of dramatic nighttime lighting, a common worker, and anonymous bayonets, the composition calls to mind Goya's martyred Spaniards (see 5.17), now fighting back and refusing to die. Rockwell Kent was at the time the most well-known and successful graphic artist in the United States, and this print was commissioned from him by the American College Society of Print Collectors.

8.7 (left) Hu Yichuan. *To the Front!* 1932. Woodcut, 9⅛ × 12".
Lu Xun Memorial, Shanghai.

8.8 (right) Rockwell Kent. *Workers of the World, Unite!* 1937. Wood engraving, 8 × 6".
The Library of Congress, Washington, D.C.

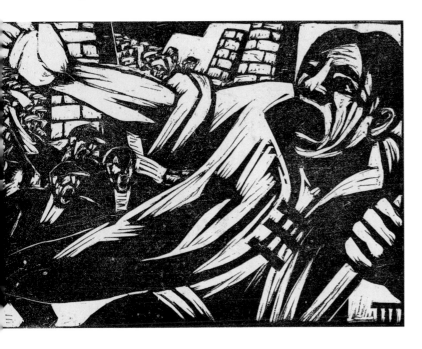

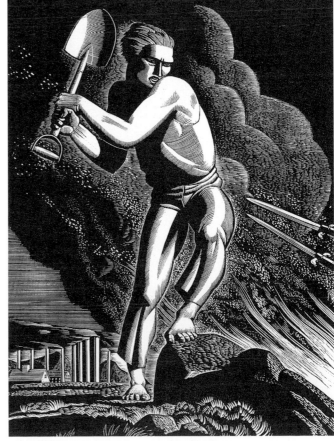

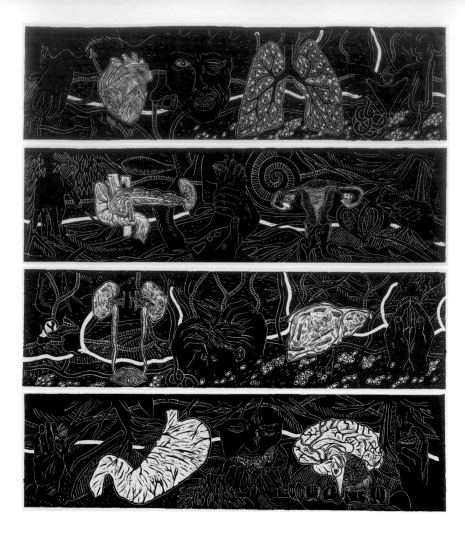

8.9 Kiki Smith. *How I Know I'm Here*. 1985–2000. Linocut; four sheets, each 11⅝ × 43⅛". Whitney Museum of American Art, New York.

Linocut

A linoleum cut, or linocut, is very similar to a woodcut. Linoleum, however, is much softer than wood. The relative softness makes linoleum easier to cut, but it also limits the number of crisp impressions that can be produced, since the block wears down more quickly during printing. Linoleum has no grain, so it is possible to make cuts in any direction with equal ease. Paradoxically, the ease with which linoleum could be carved initially caused artists to shun it, for it was generally felt that an important component of art lay in demonstrating control over a difficult and resistant medium. Schoolchildren, after all, could carve linoleum. This prejudice and others like it have since fallen away. Kiki Smith's *How I Know I'm Here* shows the almost liquid ease with which linoleum can be cut (**8.9**). The images appear as if drawn in white on a black ground, an effect that relief techniques lend themselves to quite naturally. *How I Know I'm Here* is an inventory of the artist's own body, both inside and out, with special references to the senses. It was inspired by photographs taken of her by David Wojnarowicz (see 22.27), a friend and fellow artist who died of AIDS, a disease that during the 1980s and 1990s prompted many artists to explore the theme of the body.

INTAGLIO

The second major category of printmaking techniques is intaglio (from an Italian word meaning "to cut"), which includes several related methods. Intaglio is exactly the reverse of relief, in that the areas meant to print are *below* the surface of the printing plate. The artist uses a sharp tool or acid to make depressions—lines or grooves—in a metal plate. When the plate is inked, the ink sinks into the depressions. Then the surface of the plate is wiped clean. When dampened paper is brought into contact with the plate under pressure, the paper is pushed into the depressions to pick up the image.

There are five basic types of intaglio printing: engraving, drypoint, mezzotint, etching, and aquatint.

Engraving

The oldest of the intaglio techniques, engraving developed from the medieval practice of incising (cutting) linear designs in armor and other metal surfaces. The armorer's art had achieved a high level of expertise, and it was just a short step to realizing that the engraved lines could be filled with ink and the design transferred to paper.

The basic tool of engraving is the burin, a sharp, V-shaped instrument used to cut lines into the metal plate (**8.10**). Shallow cuts produce a light, thin line, while deeper gouges in the metal result in a thicker and darker line. Engraving is closely related to drawing in pen and ink in both technique and the visual effect of the work. Looking at a reproduction it is hard to tell an engraving from a fine pen drawing. In both media, modeling and shading effects usually are achieved by hatching, cross-hatching, or stippling.

Until the invention of lithography and photography in the 19th century, engravings were the principal way in which works of art were reproduced and disseminated. Professional engravers were extraordinary draftsmen, capable of making extremely accurate copies of drawings, paintings, statues, and architecture. During the Renaissance, the awakening interest in ancient Roman art was fed by engravings, for no sooner was a newly discovered statue unearthed than it was recorded in a drawing, which was then engraved and distributed across Europe.

One of the first artists to create an original composition especially for engraving was Raphael, whose drawing of *The Judgment of Paris* (**8.11**) was entrusted to the engraver Marcantonio Raimondi. The print illustrates a famous episode from Greek mythology in which Paris, son of King Priam of Troy, settled a dispute among three goddesses. He is portrayed here at the left, awarding the golden apple to Aphrodite, the goddess of love. Other gods and goddesses swarm about. In return for a judgment in her favor, Aphrodite had promised Paris the most beautiful woman in the world. She gave him Helen,

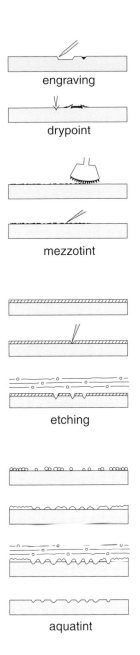

engraving

drypoint

mezzotint

etching

aquatint

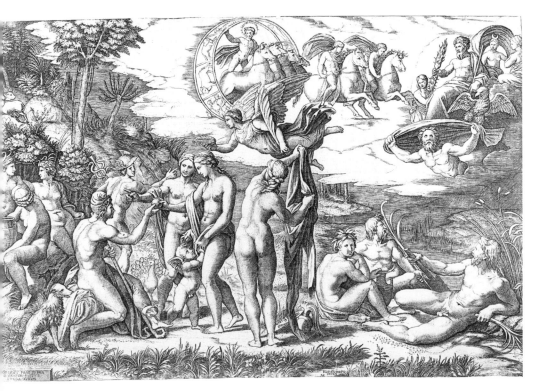

8.10 (above) Platemaking methods for intaglio printing.

8.11 (left) Marcantonio Raimondi, after Raphael. *The Judgment of Paris.* c. 1514–18. Engraving, sheet 11½ × 17". Bibliothèque Nationale, Paris.

the wife of a Greek king. Paris abducted Helen to Troy, thus touching off the Trojan War, the prolonged and disastrous conflict that inspired the two Greek epics, the *Iliad* and the *Odyssey*.

Engraved by Raimondi, Raphael's composition achieved immediate fame and was widely imitated. Its influence lasted well into the 19th century, when the three figures in the lower right corner turned up somewhat transformed in a painting that created a scandal (see 21.4). *The Judgment of Paris* shows the clean, sharp line characteristic of engraving, as well as the full range of tonal effects that can be created with fine hatching, cross-hatching, and stippling.

Drypoint

Drypoint is similar to engraving, except that the cutting instrument used is a drypoint needle. The artist draws on the plate, usually a copper plate, almost as freely as one can draw on paper with a pencil. As the needle scratches across the plate, it raises a burr, or thin ridge of metal (see 8.10). This burr holds the ink, making a line that is softer and less sharply detailed than an engraved line. If engraving is like fine pen drawing, sharp and distinct, then drypoint is more like drawing in soft pencil or crayon, with slightly blurred edges. In *Hard Climb* (**8.12**), Louise Bourgeois used the fragile line of drypoint to record her feelings about her youngest brother Pierre, who walks with difficulty because one of his legs is deformed. Pierre is at the left, struggling to climb a hill. The artist follows behind, trying to help and protect him. As might happen in a dream, she is symbolized by her cascading hair, which also extends as a sheltering canopy over them both.

Mezzotint

Almost all of the major printmaking techniques developed anonymously. We do not know who was the first person to make a woodcut, or who first realized that the lines incised into metal for decoration could also hold ink and be pressured into printing. With mezzotint, however, we know precisely who invented it, and when: It was devised by a 17th-century amateur artist named Ludwig von Siegen, who lived in Utrecht, in the Netherlands. In 1642, Von Siegen sent a print created with his new technique to the king of the Netherlands, together with a letter boasting that "there is not a single engraver, a single artist of any kind, who can account for, or guess how this work is done."[2] Mezzotint was indeed something new in printing, a method for producing finely graded tonal areas—areas of gray shading into one another—without using line.

Mezzotint is a reverse process, in which the artist works from dark to light. To prepare a mezzotint plate, the artist first roughens the entire plate with a sharp tool called a rocker. If the plate were inked and printed after this stage, it would print a sheet of paper entirely black, because each roughened spot would catch and hold the ink. Lighter tones can be created only by smoothing or rubbing out these rough spots so as not to trap the ink. To do this, the artist goes over portions of the plate with a burnisher (a smoothing tool) and/or a scraper to wear down the roughened burrs (see 8.10). Where the burrs are partially removed, the plate will print intermediate values. The lightest values print in areas where the burrs are smoothed away entirely.

Mezzotint found immediate favor as a method for reproducing famous paintings in black and white, thus making them available to a broad audience. While less often used today for original prints than other techniques, it is still the first choice for artists who want a seamless range of values at their disposal, especially if they work on a small scale. Vija Celmins's *Untitled (Sequoia and Moon)* takes full advantage of the tonal possibilities of mezzotint (**8.13**). No other intaglio technique would have been capable of producing the smooth gray scale needed for the chiaroscuro rendering of the sphere at the right.

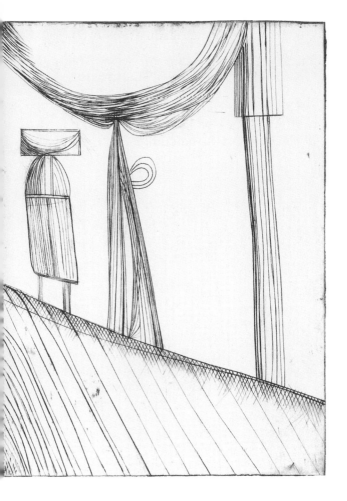

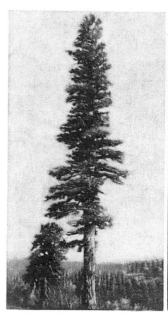

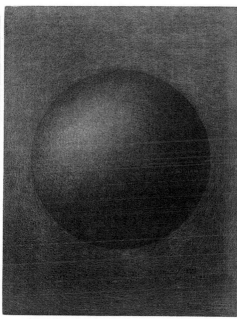

Etching

Etching is done with acids, which "eat" lines and depressions into a metal plate much as sharp tools cut those depressions in the other methods. To make an etching the artist first coats the entire printing plate with an acid-resistant substance called a **ground,** made from beeswax, asphalt, and other materials. Next, the artist draws on the coated plate with an etching needle. The needle removes the ground, exposing the bare metal in areas meant to print (see 8.10). Then the entire plate is dipped in acid. Only the portions of the plate exposed by the needle are eaten into by the acid, leaving the rest of the plate intact. Finally, the ground is removed, and the plate is inked and printed. Etched lines are not as sharp and precise as those made by the engraver's burin, because the biting action of the acid is slightly irregular.

Rembrandt, who was a prolific printmaker, made hundreds of etchings. Unfortunately, many of his plates were not canceled or destroyed. Long after his death, and long after the plates had worn down badly, people greedy to produce yet more "Rembrandts" struck impressions from the plates. These later impressions lack detail and give us little idea of what the artist intended. To get a true sense of Rembrandt's genius as an etcher, we must look at prints that are known to be early impressions, such as this impression of *Christ*

8.12 (left) Louise Bourgeois. *Hard Climb (Montée Difficile)*. 1946–47. Burin and drypoint. Bibliothèque Nationale, Paris.

8.13 (right) Vija Celmins. *Untitled (Sequoia and Moon)*, from *The View*. 1985. Mezzotint, image size 7⁵⁄₁₆ × 3¹³⁄₁₆" (left) and 7½ × 5⅝" (right). Whitney Museum of American Art, New York. Courtesy the artist.

Preaching (**8.14**). Using only line, Rembrandt gives us a world made of light and shade. He has set his scene in a humble quarter of town, possibly modeled on the Jewish section of the Amsterdam he knew well. Barefoot and bathed in sunlight, Christ preaches to the small but curious crowd that has gathered. His attention falls for a moment on the little boy in the foreground, who, too young to understand the importance of what he is hearing, has turned away to doodle with his finger in the dust. Rembrandt's greatness lay in part in his ability to imagine and portray such profoundly human moments.

Aquatint

A variation on the etching process, aquatint is a way of achieving flat areas of tone—gray values or intermediate values of color. To prepare the plate, the artist first dusts it with finely powdered resin. Several methods are available to control where and how thickly the resin is distributed on the plate. Then the plate is heated, so the resin sticks to it. When the plate is dipped in acid, the acid bites wherever there is no resin, all around the particles (see 8.10). For instance, if the particles are thinly dusted and far apart, the acid will be able to bite into larger areas of the plate, but if the particles are close together, the acid will have limited space to penetrate. Different tones, from light to dark, can be produced depending on the density of the particles, the length of time the plate is held in the acid, or the strength of the acid bath.

Because aquatint prints not lines but only areas of tone, it is nearly always combined with one or more of the other intaglio techniques—drypoint, etching, or engraving. Spanish artist Francisco de Goya combined aquatint with etching in *Hasta la Muerte* (*Until Death,* **8.15**). The black lines of the contours, hair, and facial features were etched, while the grays were produced with aquatint. The grainy quality of the tonal areas is typical of aquatint. *Hasta la Muerte* is from a

8.14 Rembrandt. *Christ Preaching.* c. 1652. Etching, 6½ × 8½".
The Pierpont Morgan Library, New York.

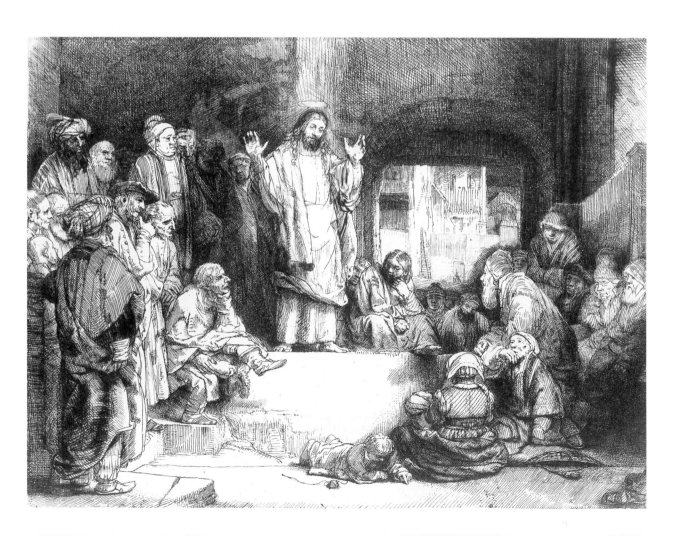

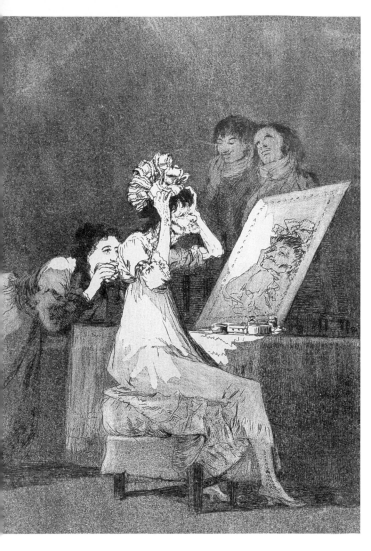

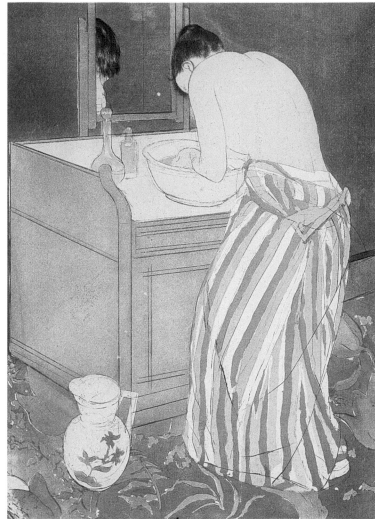

series of satirical prints called *Los Caprichos,* meaning caprices, whims, eccentricities, freakishness. We see a grotesque old woman, reflected even more horribly by her mirror, primping absurdly for her seventy-fifth birthday party. The look of satisfaction on her face suggests that *she* does not see the ugliness that we and the mocking onlookers see. Goya is poking none-too-gentle fun at her vanity, her girlish costume, her attempt at painting a very faded lily. The message of this print might be: "We do not see ourselves as others see us."

Mary Cassatt employed the more delicate line of drypoint for the contours of her exquisite *Woman Bathing* (**8.16**). The colors were printed in aquatint. Aquatint lends itself beautifully to areas of unmodulated, translucent color, and it allowed Cassatt to transpose the effects of the Japanese woodcuts she admired so much to a European medium.

By combining techniques the intaglio artist can get almost any result he or she wishes. Because the artist can achieve effects ranging from the most precisely drawn lines to the most subtle areas of tone, the possibilities for imagery are much greater than in the relief methods. We turn now, however, to a branch of printmaking that is even more flexible in its effects.

8.15 (left) Francisco de Goya. *Hasta la Muerte (Until Death),* from *Los Caprichos.* 1797–98. Etching and aquatint, 7½ × 5¼". Galerie P. Proute, Paris.

8.16 (right) Mary Cassatt. *Woman Bathing.* 1891. Drypoint and aquatint, 14⅜" × 10½". National Gallery of Art, Washington, D.C.

LITHOGRAPHY

Like mezzotint, lithography owes its existence to a single inventor, in this case a young German actor and playwright named Alois Senefelder. While living in Munich during the 1790s, Senefelder began to experiment with etching processes in an effort to find an inexpensive way to print music, which had traditionally been engraved. Too poor to invest much money in copper plates, he tried working on the smooth Bavarian limestones that lined the streets of Munich, which he excavated from the street and brought to his studio. One day, when he was experimenting with ingredients for drawing on the stone, his laundress appeared unexpectedly, and Senefelder hastily wrote out his laundry list on the stone, using his new combination of materials—wax, soap, and lampblack. Later, he decided to try immersing the stone in acid. To his delight he found that his laundry list appeared in slight relief on the stone. This event paved the way for his development of the lithographic process. While the relief aspect eventually ceased to play a role, the groundwork for lithography had been laid.

Lithography is a **planographic** process, which means that the printing surface is flat—not raised as in relief or depressed as in intaglio. It depends, instead, on the principle that oil and water do not mix. To make a lithographic print the artist first draws the image on the stone with a greasy material—usually a grease-based lithographic crayon or a greasy ink known by its German name, *tusche*. The stone is then subjected to a series of procedures, including treatment with an acid solution, that fix the drawing (bind it to the stone so that it will not smudge) and prepare it to be printed. To print the image, the printer dampens the stone with water, which soaks into the areas *not* coated with grease. When the stone is inked, the greasy ink sticks to the greasy image areas and is repelled by the water-soaked background areas. While limestone is still the preferred surface for art prints, lithographs can also be made using zinc or aluminum plates.

For artists, lithography is the most direct and effortless of the print media, for they can draw with a lithographic crayon on stone as freely as with a regular crayon on paper. Preparing the stone for printing and the printing itself are highly specialized skills, however, and artists usually work on their lithographs at a printer's workshop, often directly under the printer's guidance.

Käthe Kollwitz' *Death and the Mother* (**8.17**) illustrates well the direct quality of lithography. If you did not know it was a print, you could easily mistake it for a drawing with crayon or charcoal on paper. *Death and the Mother* depicts three figures locked together in a ghastly embrace. We see only one

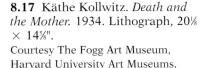

8.17 Käthe Kollwitz. *Death and the Mother*. 1934. Lithograph, 20⅛ × 14⅝".
Courtesy The Fogg Art Museum, Harvard University Art Museums, Cambridge, Massachusetts.

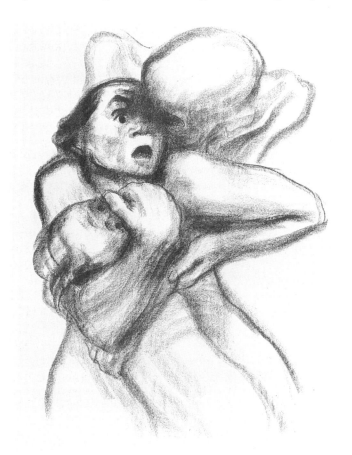

KÄTHE KOLLWITZ

1867–1945

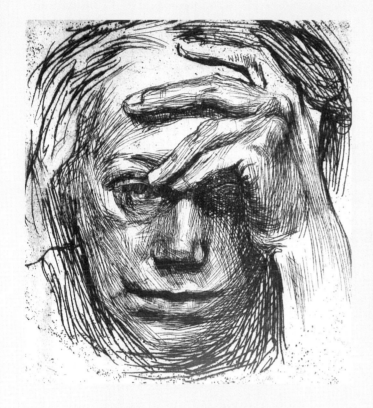

I N A TIME when the word "artist" usually meant a painter or a sculptor, Kollwitz did the bulk of her work in prints and drawings. In a time when vivid, sometimes startling color was preoccupying the art world, Kollwitz concentrated on black and white. And in a time when nearly all artists were men, Kollwitz was—triumphantly—a woman, a woman whose life and art focused on the special concerns of women. Taken together, these factors might have doomed a lesser artist to obscurity, but not one of Kollwitz' great gifts and powerful personality.

Käthe Schmidt was born in Königsberg (then in Prussia, now part of Russia), the second child in an intellectually active middle-class family. Her parents were remarkably enlightened in encouraging all their children to take an active part in political and social causes and to develop their talents—in Käthe's case a talent for drawing. Käthe received the best art training then available for a woman, in Berlin and Munich. In 1891, after a seven-year engagement, she married Karl Kollwitz, a physician who seems to have been equally supportive of his wife's career. The couple established themselves in Berlin, where they kept a joint doctor's office and artist's studio for fifty years.

During her student days Kollwitz had gradually focused on line and had come to realize that draftsmanship was her genius. Her conventional artistic training must have intensified the shock when she "suddenly saw that I was not a painter at all."[3] She concentrated then on drawings and prints—etchings and woodcuts early on, lithographs when her eyesight grew weaker.

Five major themes dominate Kollwitz' art: the artist herself, in a great many self-portraits and images for which she served as model; the ties between mothers and their children; the hardships of the working classes, usually interpreted through women's plight; the unspeakable cruelties of war; and death as a force unto itself. As a socialist Kollwitz identified passionately with the sufferings of working people; as a mother she identified with the struggle of women to keep their children safe.

Kollwitz bore two sons—Hans in 1892 and Peter in 1896. The first of many tragedies that marked her later life came in 1914, with the death of Peter in World War I. She lived long enough to see her beloved grandson, also named Peter, killed in World War II. During the almost thirty years between those losses, she continued to work prolifically, but her obsession with death never left her.

Few artists have so touchingly described their attempts to achieve a certain goal, and their continual frustration at falling short. In Kollwitz' case, the artistic goals were generally realized, but the emotional and political goals—never: "While I drew, and wept along with the terrified children I was drawing, I really felt the burden I am bearing. I felt that I have no right to withdraw from the responsibility of being an advocate. It is my duty to voice the sufferings of men, the never-ending sufferings heaped mountain-high. This is my task, but it is not an easy one to fulfill. Work is supposed to relieve you. . . . Did I feel relieved when I made the prints on war and knew that the war would go on raging? Certainly not."[4]

Käthe Kollwitz. *Self-Portrait with Hand on Her Forehead.* 1910. Etching, 6 × 5⅜".
Kupferstich-Kabinett, Staatliche Kunstsammlungen, Dresden.

face—the terrified face of the woman, who clutches her child against her breast as the featureless form of Death claims her from behind. We know the woman already belongs to Death and cannot escape; their union is shockingly intimate. Kollwitz' drawing seems simple, yet its expression is universal: the instinct of all mothers to protect their children and the dread felt by all creatures facing their own mortality.

By using multiple stones, lithography can reproduce images in full color, and during the 19th century it quickly became the preferred method for reproducing art. This book, for example, was printed using a lithographic process. Painters often take naturally to lithography, for it allows them to work in color and to draw freely with brush and ink. *Solomon* (**8.18**) shows how easily Marc Chagall adapted his painting style to the requirements of lithography. One of a series of lithographs illustrating stories from the Old Testament, *Solomon* relies on amorphous, floating areas of complementary color overlaid with a brush drawing in black that brings the image into focus. Many of Chagall's paintings from this period in his career use a similar approach, with color floating free of form.

Lithography is a remarkably flexible medium and capable of a broad range of effects. We can see this readily by comparing the charcoal-like lines of Kollwitz and the brushed and spattered style of Toulouse-Lautrec with the flat colors and precise contours of Elizabeth Catlett's *Singing Their Songs* (**8.19**). *Singing Their Songs* is one of a series of prints that Catlett made based on lines from Margaret Walker's remarkable poem "For My People."

8.18 Marc Chagall. *Solomon,* from *The Bible.* 1956. Lithograph, 13⅞ × 10¼".
Musée National Message Biblique Marc Chagall, Nice, France.

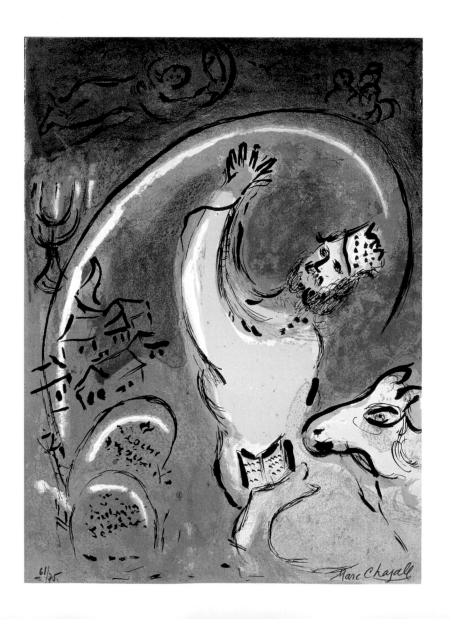

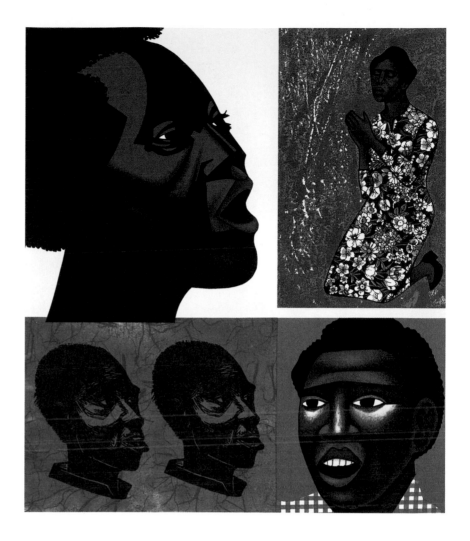

A touchstone of African-American literature, "For My People" builds its considerable power through repetition, with each stanza lifting its voice again in dedication. Catlett echoes this device, dividing her composition into four spaces the way a poem is divided into stanzas, and using each space to celebrate a new group—the people singing their songs, the people saying their prayers, the wise elders looking on, the young with their eyes on the future.

8.19 Elizabeth Catlett. *Singing Their Songs.* 1992. Color lithograph, 23 × 19".

SCREENPRINTING

To understand the basic principle of screenprinting, you need only picture the lettering stencils used by schoolchildren. The stencil is a piece of cardboard from which the forms of the alphabet letters have been cut out. To trace the letters onto paper, you simply place the stencil over the paper and fill in the holes with pencil or ink.

Today's art screenprinting works much the same way. The screen is a fine mesh of silk or synthetic fiber mounted in a frame, rather like a window screen. (Silk is the traditional material, so the process has often been called **silkscreen** or **serigraphy**—"silk writing.") Working from drawings, the printmaker stops out (blocks) screen areas that are *not* meant to print by plugging up the holes, usually with some kind of glue, so that no ink can pass through. Then the screen is placed over paper, and the ink is forced through the mesh with a tool called a squeegee. Only the areas not stopped out allow the ink to pass through and print on paper (see 8.1).

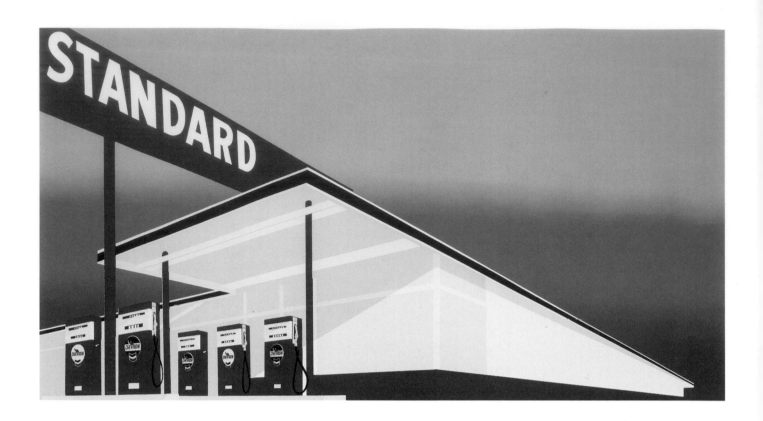

8.20 Ed Ruscha. *Standard Station.*
1966. Screenprint, image size
10½ × 36¹⁵⁄₁₆".
The Museum of Modern Art, New
York.

To make a color screenprint, the artist prepares one screen for each color. On the "blue" screen, for example, all areas not meant to print in blue are stopped out, and so on for each of the other colors. The preparation of multiple color screens is relatively easy and inexpensive. For this reason it is not unusual to see serigraphs printed in ten, twenty, or more colors.

Edward Ruscha's screenprint *Standard Station* (**8.20**) takes advantage of the medium's ability to produce broad areas of flat, uniform color. Popularly used for such humble purposes as printing T-shirts and posters, screenprinting is well suited to the banal, everyday subject matter of a roadside gasoline station. The two-toned background was created using a technique called split fountain, in which two colors are placed on a single screen, and their zone of contact is carefully controlled.

Edward Ruscha has lived in Los Angeles since his student days, and one way to understand his work is to think of the giant white letters of the famous HOLLYWOOD sign that can be seen there against the hills. The dramatic diagonal of Ruscha's gasoline station projects the word STANDARD across the page as boldly as a beam of light projecting a film title onto a screen. Indeed, the sign itself resembles a movie theater marquis. Standard Oil was the name of the first and most famous of all oil companies. But Ruscha leaves out the word "oil" so that "standard" can take on its other meanings as well: a norm, a benchmark, a banner, a flag. His image of a standard station slyly links two fundamental elements of American life, our love affair with the movies, and our love affair with the automobile.

MONOTYPE

There is one major exception to the rule, stated at the beginning of this chapter, that prints are an art of multiples. That exception is the monotype. Monotypes are made by an indirect process, like any other print, but, as the prefix "mono" implies, only one print results. To make a monotype, the artist draws on a metal plate or some other smooth surface, often with diluted oil paints. Then the plate is run through a press to transfer the image to paper. Or the artist may simply place a sheet of paper on the plate and hand-rub it to transfer the image. Either way, the original is destroyed or so altered that there can be no duplicate impressions. If a series of prints is planned, the artist must do more work on the plate.

Monotype offers several technical advantages. The range of colors is unlimited, as is the potential for lines or tones. No problems arise with cutting against a grain or into resistant metal. The artist can work as freely as in a direct process like painting or drawing. Yet the medium is not as simple and straightforward as it seems, for the artist cannot be quite sure how the print will look when it comes through the press. Transferred by pressure from a non-absorbent surface such as metal to the absorbent surface of paper, colors may blend and spread and contours may soften. The textures of brush strokes on the plate disappear into flatness on the paper. Differences between plate and print may be minute or dramatic, and the artist may try to control them as much as possible or play with the element of chance that they bring to the creative process.

Enrique Chagoya used monotype in an ingenious way in *Life Is a Dream, Then You Wake Up* (**8.21**). To create this image of time passing, Chagoya layered multiple monotypes one on top of the other. That is, he painted an image on the plate and printed it. Then he wiped the plate clean, painted another image, and printed it on top of the first one. Chagoya repeated this process several times to create the finished work, carefully controlling the transparency of each new print so that ghostly underlayers continued to show through. The layers of images are like the layers of the years that accumulate within us as we age. For Chagoya personally, they may also evoke cultural and professional layers, for he grew up in Mexico City before moving to California, and he was trained as an economist before turning to art.

8.21 Enrique Chagoya. *Life Is a Dream, Then You Wake Up.* 1995. Monotype, 42⅝ × 46⅝". Smithsonian American Art Museum, Washington, D.C.

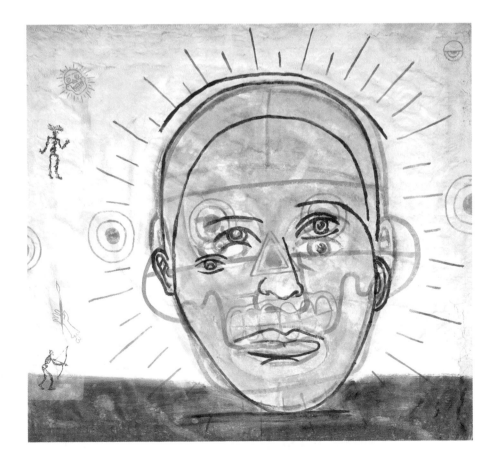

RECENT DIRECTIONS: THE COMPUTER AND PRINTMAKING

As noted earlier in this chapter, the technologies of printmaking and printing enabled Europe's first information revolution. Prior to the invention of the printing press, books circulated in handwritten copies, each one unique, and each potentially marred by errors introduced by tired or inattentive copyists. Prior to the development of printmaking, all images were likewise unique and created by hand. The only way to reproduce a painting, for example, was to paint a copy of it.

Printmaking and printing changed all that. Woodcuts appeared as illustrations in printed books, for a wooden block could be placed on the same form as type, and all could be inked and pulled through the printing press together. During the excitement of the Renaissance, when the Classical culture of ancient Rome was literally being excavated, engravings allowed visual information to spread quickly and accurately across Europe.

Small wonder, then, that printmaking should find itself a natural ally of two later revolutions in information technology, the camera and the computer. During the 20th century, techniques were developed to print photographic images by means of etching, lithography, and silkscreen, and many artists began including photographic images in their prints. The computer inserted itself easily into this process, allowing artists to digitize images, manipulate them as part of a design, and then print the result using traditional printmaking techniques. This was the procedure followed by Victor Burgin in creating the series of prints called *Fiction Film* (**8.22**). In the untitled print illustrated here, an overturned car has burst into flames, and through the smoke appears the face of a beautiful woman. The image pretends to be taken from a film version of a famous French novel called *Nadja*, but in fact such a film never existed. Burgin asks us to imagine that a film of *Nadja* was made and then lost. Only

8.22 Victor Burgin. *Untitled,* from *Fiction Film,* 1991. Computer-manipulated image printed as a photoscreenprint, varnished, on white paper; sheet 30⅞ × 37½".
Courtesy the artist.

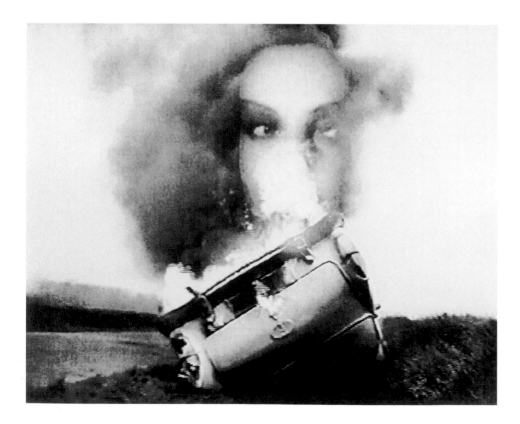

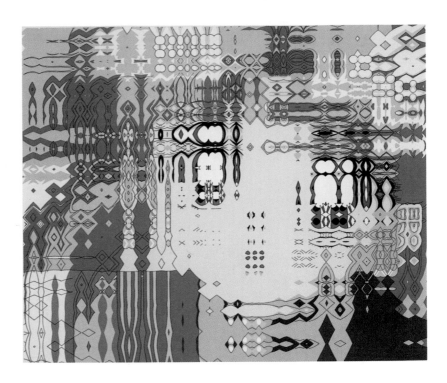

8.23 Carl Fudge. *Rhapsody Spray 2*. 2000. Screenprint, 52 × 62".
Courtesy Ronald Feldman Fine Arts, New York.

these few still pictures survive. Burgin created the prints using actual stills from old French movies and video footage he himself took in France. He fed the images into a computer, where he could combine and manipulate them freely. He then printed the results as a series of two-tone screenprints, which he varnished to give them the glossy finish of photographs. Burgin here plays games with illusion and reality, creating photographs that aren't photographs of a film that was never a film.

Like Victor Burgin, Carl Fudge feeds camera images into a computer and manipulates them digitally, though to far different effect. *Rhapsody Spray 2* (**8.23**) is one of a series of prints that began with an image of a Japanese anime character named Sailor Chibi Moon. Fudge scanned the image and reworked it digitally into a composition dominated by vertical and horizontal rhythms and pulsating lozenge shapes. He used the manipulated image as the model for a series of traditionally executed silkscreen prints in four different color harmonies. Chibi Moon is a magical character capable of shifting her shape and transforming herself. Fudge's work pays tribute to her abilities by transforming her in still more daring and abstract ways.

According to the traditional definition, a print is made from a matrix. For a woodcut or wood engraving, for example, the matrix is a piece of wood; for a lithograph, the matrix is a slab of stone. Within the past few years, however, this definition has been blurred by a computer-driven printing technology that has won acceptance as a fine art medium. Known as an Iris print or *giclée* print (zhee-CLAY), it does not use a matrix at all.

Giclée, French for "sprayed" or "squirted," refers to an advanced version of the common inkjet printer that many people have connected to their home or office computer. Iris is the name of a widely used *giclée* printer. Like all inkjet printers, a *giclée* printer forms an image by directing a fine spray of ink at a piece of paper. But whereas home or office printers can feed page after page in rapid succession through the spray, a *giclée* printer accepts a single sheet of paper only. The paper is attached to a drum, which rotates rapidly as nozzles spray it with millions of tiny droplets of colored inks. An electric charge allows some ink droplets to reach the paper, while others are deflected away. Over the course of an hour or so, the image gradually takes shape.

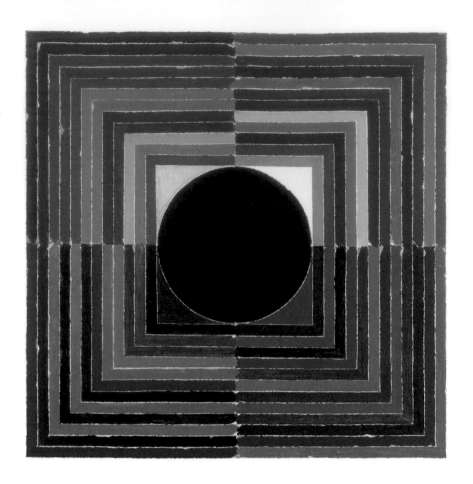

8.24 Sayed-Haider Raza. *Manavadhikar.* 2003. Iris print, image size 17½ × 17½". Courtesy Pace Editions, Inc.

An Iris print resembles a color woodcut or a watercolor, as Sayed-Haider Raza's *Manavadhikar* shows (**8.24**). *Manavadhikar* means "human rights" in Hindi. The circle-in-a-square design brings to mind the classic South Asian form of the mandala. But, whereas a mandala depicts the ordering of a cosmic realm, this image seems to evoke in non-representational terms an ideal ordering of our earthly realm according to the principles of social justice.

If you had any doubt at the beginning of this chapter that printmaking is a lively art, chances are you have changed your mind by now. In some ways it is an art ideally suited to today's lifestyles. The painter, the sculptor, the architect—all these make *one* work of art at a time, that will reside in one place. People who want to see the original must journey to do so. But the print made in an edition of a hundred will reside in a hundred different places and be enjoyed by thousands of people. Truly, the print allows nearly anyone to corner a small piece of the world of art.

CHAPTER NINE

CAMERA AND COMPUTER ARTS

In the world of art, the camera and the computer were born yesterday. Although the earliest known drawn and painted images date back to the Stone Ages, and the earliest surviving print was made well over one thousand years ago, images recorded by a camera or created on a computer belong entirely to our own modern era.

The camera relies on a natural phenomenon known since antiquity: that light reflected from an object can, under controlled circumstances, project an image of that object onto a surface. It was not until the 19th century, however, that a way was found to capture and preserve such a projected image. With that discovery, photography was born, and after photography, film and video, which recorded the projected image in motion over time.

The computer, too, is rooted in discoveries of earlier times. The first true computer, an electronic machine that could be programmed to process information in the form of data, was built around 1938. Early computers were so large that a single machine occupied an entire room! Over the following decades, technological advances chipped away at the size even as they made computers faster, more powerful, more affordable, and easier to use. Beginning around 1980, the pace of change accelerated so dramatically that we have come to speak of a digital revolution. The personal computer, the compact disc, the scanner, the World Wide Web, the digital video disk, and the digital camera appeared in rapid succession, together making it possible to capture, store, manipulate, and circulate text, images, and sound as digital data. With the digital revolution, the camera and the computer became intertwined.

Camera and computer technologies are essential to business, advertising, education, government, mass media, and entertainment. They have commercial applications and personal applications, and they are widely available to both professional organizations and individual consumers. Among these individuals are artists, who have carved out a space for human expression within the vast flow of information and images that the camera and the computer have enabled. This chapter explores the camera arts—photography, film, and video—from their beginnings through the digital revolution. Then it looks at how artists have begun to work with the possibilities offered by the global reach of the Internet.

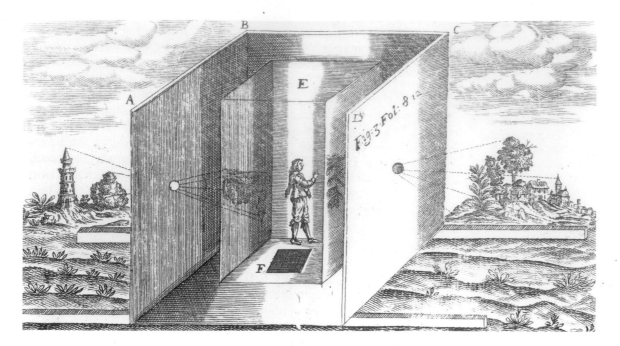

9.1 (above) *Camera Obscura*, in cutaway view. 1646. Engraving. International Museum of Photography at George Eastman House, Rochester, N.Y.

9.2 (below) The basic parts of a camera.

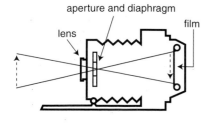

aperture and diaphragm
lens
film

PHOTOGRAPHY

The earliest written record that has come down to us of the principle behind photography is from a Chinese philosopher named Mo Ti, who lived during the fifth century B.C.E. Mo Ti noticed that light passing through a pinhole opening into a darkened chamber would form an exact view of the world outside, but upside down. A century or so later, the ancient Greek philosopher Aristotle observed similar phenomena, and he wondered what caused them. Early in the 11th century C.E., the Arab mathematician and physicist Abu Ali Hasan Ibn al-Haitham, known in the West as Alhazen, set up an experiment in a dark room in which light from several candles passed through a pinhole in a partition, projecting images of the candle flames onto a surface on the other side. From his observations, Alhazen deduced (correctly) that light travels in straight lines, and he theorized (also correctly) that the human eye worked along this same principle: Light reflected from objects passes through the narrow opening of the iris, projecting an image of the outside world onto a surface in the dark interior. Alhazen's works circulated in translation in Europe, where early scientists continued his investigations into the behavior of light, but it was not until the Renaissance that a practical device was developed to harness these principles. It was known as the *camera obscura*, Latin for "dark room."

You can make a camera obscura yourself. Find a light-tight room, even a closet or a very large cardboard box. Pierce a small hole, no bigger than the diameter of a pencil, in one wall of the room to admit light. Inside, hold a sheet of white paper a few inches from the hole. You will see an image of the scene outside the room projected on the paper—upside-down and rather blurry, but recognizable. That is the principle of the camera obscura, which simply means "dark room."

With the development of lenses during the 16th century, the camera obscura could be made to focus the image it projected. Artists of the time, concerned with making optically convincing representations through perspective and chiaroscuro, welcomed this improved camera obscura as a drawing tool. The illustration here (**9.1**) appeared in a book called *The Great Art of Light and Shadow*, published in 1646. It depicts an elaborate version of a portable camera obscura (note the poles on the ground for carrying it). The roof and fourth wall have been left out of the illustration to allow us to peer inside. Each of the four outer walls had a lens at its center (two lenses are shown here, at left and right). Entering through a trap door in the floor (marked F), the artist stood in an inner chamber made of four translucent paper screens. (The man here is drawn in miniature—the chamber was not really quite so large!) Each lens projected its view onto the paper chamber, and the artist traced the projections from the other side (thus not getting in the way of the light). It was none other than Leonardo da Vinci who first suggested this arrangement.

The Still Camera and Its Beginnings

Despite the sophistication of modern photographic equipment, the basic mechanism of the camera is simple, and it is no different in theory from that of the camera obscura. A camera is a light-tight box (**9.2**) with an opening at one end to admit light, a lens to focus and refract the light, and a light-sensitive surface (today it is usually film) to receive the light-image and hold it. The last of these—the holding of the image—was the major drawback of the camera obscura. It could capture an image—but there was no way to preserve the image, much less walk away with it in your hand. It was to this end that a number of people in the 19th century directed their attention.

One of these investigators was Joseph Nicéphore Niépce, a French inventor. Working with a specially coated pewter plate in the camera obscura, Niépce managed, in 1826, to record a fuzzy version of the view from his window after an exposure of eight hours. Although we may now consider Niépce's "heliograph" (or sun-writing), as he called it, to be the first permanent photograph, the method was not really practical.

Niépce was corresponding with another Frenchman, Louis Jacques Mandé Daguerre, who was also experimenting with methods to fix the photographic image. The two men worked separately and communicated in code to keep their progress from prying eyes. When Niépce died in 1833, his son Isidore continued the experiments. It was Daguerre, however, who in 1837 made the breakthrough, recording an image in his studio that was clear and sharp, by methods that others could duplicate easily. Daguerre's light-sensitive surface was a copper plate coated with silver iodide, and he named his invention the **daguerreotype.**

Daguerre made the image illustrated here in 1839, the year the French government announced his discovery to the world (**9.3**). In the entrancing detail characteristic of daguerreotypes, it records a seemingly deserted boulevard in Paris. In fact, the boulevard was a bustling thoroughfare. In order to

9.3 Louis Jacques Mandé Daguerre. *Le Boulevard du Temple.* 1839. Daguerreotype. Bayerisches Nationalmuseum, Munich.

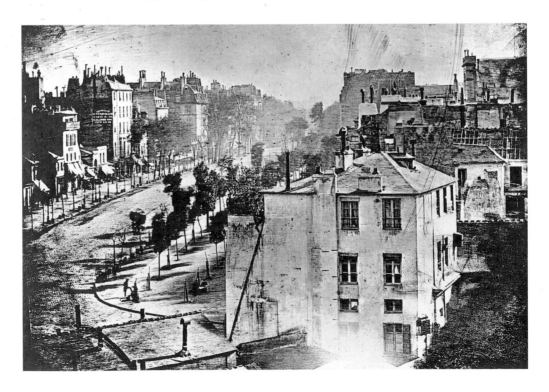

record an image, Daguerre's plate needed to be exposed to sunlight for ten or even twenty minutes! The only person to stand still long enough to be recorded was a man who had stopped to have his shoes shined. Visible at the lower left, he is one of the first people ever to appear in a photograph, and certainly the first to have his image taken without knowing it.

Within two years after Daguerre's discovery was made public, dramatic improvements were made. From England came a better method for fixing the final image so that it didn't continue to change in the light, and also a more light-sensitive coating for the plate that reduced exposure time. From Vienna came an improved lens that gathered sixteen times as much light as previous lenses, further reducing exposure time to around thirty seconds. Although still a far cry from the split-second exposures that later technology would make possible, the daguerreotype was now poised to become the first commercially viable method for making permanent images from reflected light.

Daguerre's invention caused great excitement throughout Europe and North America. Entrepreneurs and the general public alike were quick to see the potential of photography, especially for portraits. It is hard to realize now, but until photography came along only the rich could afford to have their likenesses made, by sitting for a portrait painter. Within three years after Daguerre made his first plate, a "daguerreotype gallery for portraits" had opened in New York, and such galleries soon proliferated.

Yet for all its early success, the daguerreotype was ultimately a blind alley for photography. The process produces a *positive* image, an image in which light and dark values appear correctly. This image is unique and cannot be reproduced. The plate is the photograph. The future of photography instead lay with technology that produced a *negative* image, one in which light and dark values were reversed. This negative could be used again and again to create multiple positive images on light-sensitive paper. Instead of a single precious and delicate object, photography found its essence as an art of potentially unlimited, low-cost multiples. An early version of the negative/positive print process was the calotype, which used a paper negative. Toward the middle of the 19th century, the vastly superior collodion process was developed, which produced a negative on glass.

The possibility of unlimited multiples touched off a craze for *cartes de visite*, French for "visiting card"—a photograph of yourself, roughly the size of a playing card, that you could hand out as a sort of introduction or souvenir. In 1860, a presidential hopeful named Abraham Lincoln dropped by the New York City studio of Mathew Brady to pose for a *carte de visite* (**9.4**). Lincoln was in town to make a speech at a college called Cooper Union. Brady was then the most renowned and successful portrait photographer in the United States. In 1844, at the age of twenty-one, he had opened a daguerreotype studio in New York. In 1858 he expanded his operations by opening Brady's Photographic Art Gallery in Washington D.C. From these bases he set out to photograph all the illustrious people of the time, and he very nearly succeeded. He employed many assistant photographers, called "operators," including Timothy O'Sullivan, whose work we shall see later in the chapter (see 9.6). In many cases it is impossible to tell which pictures Brady himself took, because his name appears on all products of his studios.

The photograph shown here, however, almost certainly came from Brady's own camera. Brady shows us Lincoln as a rising political star, a forceful and eloquent speaker whose views had already attracted national attention. His suit is obviously new, bought for the occasion, with the shirt cuff hanging down awkwardly from the jacket sleeve. Lincoln's facial expression is stern and dignified, but we also sense a bit of apprehension—perhaps caused by the leap into national politics, perhaps caused by the novel experience of having his portrait done.

Lincoln's Cooper Union speech was a success. Brady's photograph was in great demand, and thousands of copies were sold. After the election, Lincoln said, "Brady and the Cooper Union speech made me President."

Another famous portraitist of the 19th century, and an equally fascinating personality, was Julia Margaret Cameron, who, without benefit of multiple assistants, was fully as prolific as Brady. Cameron worked in England in the 1860s and 1870s. She had a wide circle of prominent friends and, by virtue of her strong personality, was able to cajole (or bully) most of them into posing for her. Cameron's photographs have given us likenesses of the great English poet Alfred, Lord Tennyson; the American poet Henry Wadsworth Longfellow; naturalist Charles Darwin, who developed the theory of evolution; and a great many others. The portrait of Darwin (**9.5**) illustrates many elements of Cameron's unique style: a strong contrast of dark and light, emphasis on the head and face, a soft—faintly blurred—focus, and fondness for the profile view. Over and over Cameron searched out the deepest character of her sitters, and then held that character at a slight distance from us through the soft focus of her lens. Cameron's studies show real people transformed into a photographic ideal.

Like cooperative portrait subjects, landscapes and cityscapes could also be relied on to hold still long enough to have their image recorded, and both were popular with early photographers. Some early photographers, like the

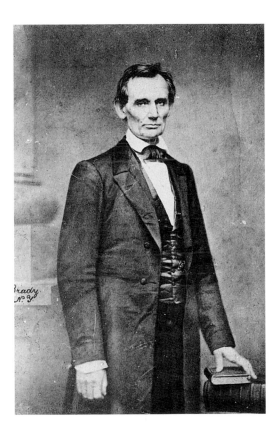

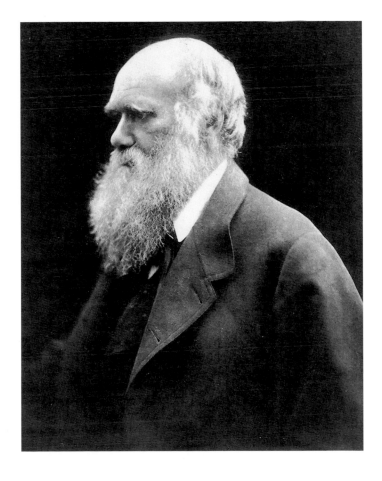

9.4 (left) Mathew Brady. *Lincoln "Cooper Union" Portrait*. 1860. Photograph.
Library of Congress, Washington, D.C.

9.5 (right) Julia Margaret Cameron. *Charles Darwin*. 1868. Carbon print, 10½ × 8¼".
The Museum of Modern Art, New York.

JULIA MARGARET CAMERON

1815–1879

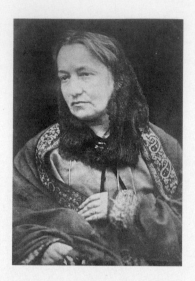

IN A LARGE family of colorful individuals, Julia Margaret Cameron was the standout. Her great-niece, the writer Virginia Woolf (no stranger herself to unconventional conduct), wrote with a kind of fond awe that Julia Cameron "had a gift of ardent speech and picturesque behaviour." Woolf continues: "There was no eccentricity that she would not have dared. . . ."[1]

Child of a Scottish father and a French mother, Julia Margaret Pattle was born in India, then educated in France and England. Of the seven Pattle sisters, only Julia was plain; the rest were exceptionally attractive. Julia Margaret, however, was not one to allow a lack of physical beauty to cramp her style. Possessed of an exuberant spirit and a zest for life, she set out to *make* beauty wherever she could. At twenty-three she married Charles Hay Cameron, a well-to-do scholar and legal reformer. Their marriage was to be a happy one. The couple settled in England, where they raised eleven children—six of their own and five adopted—while conducting an astonishingly active social life.

Stories abound of Mrs. Cameron's generosity, enthusiasm, energy, and strong will. She maintained a vast correspondence, averaging three hundred letters a month. She collected interesting and talented friends by the score, charming them with her wit and creative escapades, overwhelming them with gifts and favors. Her circle included poets, novelists, scientists, actors, politicians, diplomats—the cream of Britain's intellectual and artistic crop.

In 1863, when Julia Cameron was forty-eight, her daughter bought her a special present: a large wooden box camera and darkroom equipment. From that moment Cameron's life changed, for her energies were channeled into a new passion. A chicken coop on the Camerons' property was converted into a "glass house," or photographic studio. Servants, friends, and relatives were recruited as models, and her demands on them became the talk of the countryside.

Cameron favored long exposure times, so a sitter might be forced to maintain some horribly uncomfortable pose, without moving, for up to ten minutes. If that picture didn't turn out well, there must be another and another, hours of posing without rest, until the model staggered exhausted out of Cameron's "glass house." Virginia Woolf tells us that "boatmen were turned into King Arthur; village girls into Queen Guenevere. Tennyson was wrapped in rugs; Sir Henry Taylor was crowned with tinsel. . . . She cared nothing for the miseries of her sitters nor for their rank."[2]

Cameron's images mounted to the hundreds, eventually thousands, but she continued to think of herself as an amateur photographer. Although she exhibited her work and had several one-artist shows, she did not sell her photographs. Instead, she gave them away in great bunches to friends, or to whoever took her fancy. Only near the end of her life did Cameron offer for sale a series of photographs, beautifully bound and copyrighted in her name.

In 1865 the Camerons left England and settled in Ceylon (now Sri Lanka), the island nation off the coast of India, where Julia continued to pursue her art in her customary manner. One visitor, a Miss North, complained that "she made me stand with spiky coconut branches running into my head . . . and told me to look perfectly natural."[3] At the age of sixty-three Julia Cameron caught a bad chill and died. She left behind an unfinished memoir entitled "Annals of My Glass House," in which she wrote: "From the first moment I handled my lens with a tender ardour, and it has become to be as a living thing, with voice and memory and creative vigour."[4]

Henry Herschel Hay Cameron. *Julia Margaret Cameron.*
1870. Silver print, 9¾ × 8½".
Gernsheim Collection, Harry Ranson Humanities Research Center,
The University of Texas at Austin.

American Timothy O'Sullivan, went to great extremes to capture nature's forms. Hauling what was then very cumbersome photographic equipment through mountains and desert presented a real challenge, but the results were well worth the effort.

In 1867 O'Sullivan signed on as official photographer to an expedition commissioned by the federal government to explore the territories of Nevada and Colorado. One of his most dramatic photos from this trip (**9.6**) shows the mule-drawn ambulance O'Sullivan had hired to carry water for his traveling darkroom. Tiny and stark against the vast shifting dunes, the vehicle looks like a toy. We can easily imagine that all traces of its passing were erased by the wind soon after.

The long exposure time and bulky equipment of early photography meant that a photograph was still a special occasion, an occasion for standing still. By the 1880s, however, technical advances had reduced exposure time to a fraction of a second, allowing cameras to capture life as it happened, without asking it to pose. Then, in 1888, an American named George Eastman developed a camera called the Kodak that changed photography forever. Unlike earlier cameras, the Kodak was lightweight and handheld, which meant it could be taken anywhere. Sold with the slogan "You press the button, we do the rest," the camera came loaded with film for one hundred photographs. Users simply took the pictures (which quickly became known as "snapshots") and sent the camera back to the company. Their developed and printed photographs were returned to them along with their camera, reloaded with film.

The Kodak and cameras like it opened photography up to amateurs, and it quickly became a popular hobby. While serious photographers continued (and still continue) to oversee the development and printing of their own work, they, too, benefited from the portable, lightweight technology. Almost anywhere a person could go, a camera could now go; almost anything a person could see, a camera could record. Daily life, the life any one of us lives, became photography's newest and perhaps most profound subject.

9.6 Timothy O'Sullivan. *Sand Springs, Nevada.* 1867. Photograph.
Library of Congress, Washington, D.C.

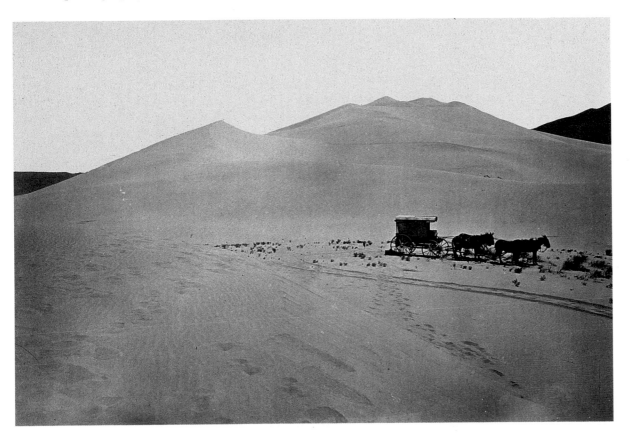

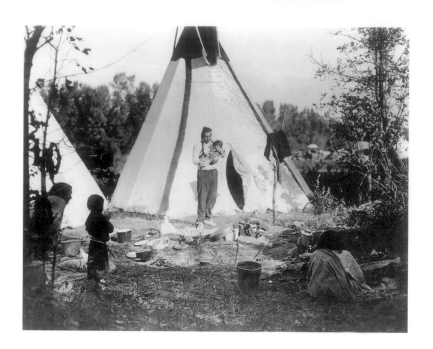

9.7 Richard Throssel. *Crow Camp, 1910.*
Modern print from a negative in the Lorenzo Creel Collection, Special Collections, University of Nevada, Reno Library.

Taken in 1910, *Crow Camp* (**9.7**) records a moment in the life of a Crow Indian family. A man stands in front of a dwelling, a tipi. In his arms he gently cradles a child. His wife and family look on from the foreground. The photograph may record a naming ceremony, a Crow tradition that continues to this day. Many fascinating photographs of American Indians have been preserved from the early decades of photography, most taken by European Americans determined to document what they saw as an exotic, sometimes noble, sometimes savage, but certainly vanishing way of life. What is remarkable about this photograph, however, is precisely that it is unremarkable, an ordinary human moment of family affection and intimacy. Not incidently, the photographer, Richard Throssel, was an American Indian himself, born a Cree and later adopted by the Crow people. The view is a view from inside, not "this is how we see you" but "this is how we see *ourselves,* this is what is important to us."

Bearing Witness and Documenting

One way in which photography changed the world was in the sheer quantity of images that could be created and put into circulation. Whereas a painter might take weeks or even months to compose and execute a scene of daily life, a photographer could produce dozens of such scenes in a single day. But what purpose could this facility be put to? What was the advantage of quantity and speed? One early answer was that photography could record what was seen as history unfolded, or preserve a visual record of what existed for a time. We could call these purposes bearing witness and documenting, and they continue to play important roles today.

Photographs bearing witness to events appear in newspapers and magazines the world over. It wasn't always this way. Newspapers during the 19th century were illustrated with wood engravings or lithographs. Artists were sent as reporters to major news events or drew images after the fact based on eye witness accounts. The first important conflict to be documented in photography was the American Civil War. Long exposure times, however, limited the photographs to posed portraits and images of the dead. Any "action" images that appeared with newspaper articles still had to be drawn, and even suitable photographs had to be recopied as engravings or lithographs, for the technology did not yet exist to print photographs commercially on ordinary paper. Then, around 1900, the first process for photomechanical reproduction—high-speed printing of photographs along with type—came into being, and with it a new concept, photojournalism.

Photojournalism quickly became concerned about more than just getting a photograph to illustrate an article. Although a single photograph may be all the general public sees at the time, photojournalists often create a significant body of work around an event, place, or culture. A historical episode that brought out the best in many of the finest photographers of the day was the Great Depression in the United States. The Great Depression, which began in 1929 and lasted until the onset of World War II, caused hardships for photographers as well as for the population as a whole. To ease the first problem and document the second, the Farm Security Administration (FSA) of the U.S. Department of Agriculture subsidized photographers and sent them out to record conditions across the nation. One of these photographers was Dorothea Lange.

Dorothea Lange's travels for the FSA took her to nearly every part of the country. In one summer alone she logged 17,000 miles in her car. Lange devoted her attention to the migrants who had been uprooted from their farms by the combined effects of Depression and drought. Lange's best-known image from this time is the haunting *Migrant Mother* (**9.8**). From this worried mother and her tattered clothing, from the two children who huddle against her, hiding their faces from the stranger with the camera, Lange created a photograph that touched the hearts of the world. "I do not remember how I explained my presence or my camera to her but I do remember she asked me no questions," the photographer recalled years later. "I made five exposures, working closer and closer from the same direction. I did not ask her name or her history . . ."[5] FSA photos like this one were offered free to newspapers and magazines.

9.8 Dorothea Lange. *Migrant Mother*. 1936.
Library of Congress, Washington, D.C.

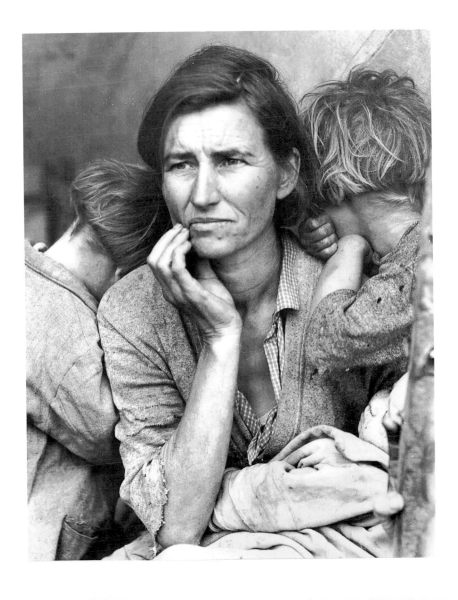

A photograph, of course, shows us the present moment, a split-second of today. But the present is always slipping into the past, and what exists today may well not exist tomorrow. This basic realization inspires photographers who use their artistic skills to document. Many documentation projects have earned a place in the history of photography. A recent example is a project called *The Chinese*, by the photographer Liu Zheng (**9.9**). Beginning in 1994 and continuing for eight years, Liu traveled the length and breadth of his rapidly modernizing country. Avoiding the elite worlds of politics, business, and intellectual life, he photographed ordinary people—beggars and monks, students and soldiers, coal miners and performers. Along with the living, he photographed the dead, and also museum exhibits of moments in Chinese history restaged with trompe l'oeil waxwork statues. In Liu's black-and-white photographs, the waxwork exhibits cannot always be distinguished from real life, and so past and present, individual vision and official memory, all merge.

One of the themes that runs through *The Chinese* is the persistence of traditional faiths in a society where most citizens no longer have any religious beliefs. In the photograph here, *A Young Monk in Front of an Ancient Mural*, Liu shows us a Buddhist monk standing before a vision of paradise painted centuries ago and now much damaged by time and vandalism. At his feet are broken bricks and roof tiles from the buildings of his monastery. How do we live in the present when the past has come down to us in tatters? The young monk's serenity seems to radiate his personal answer to that question: faith. Liu emphasizes the young man's dignity through a symmetrical composition. He clearly admires the monk's faith, even if he cannot share it. Liu's project shows us the changing face of China today. Future generations will look at it and see the vanished China of yesterday.

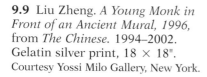

9.9 Liu Zheng. *A Young Monk in Front of an Ancient Mural, 1996,* from *The Chinese*. 1994–2002. Gelatin silver print, 18 × 18". Courtesy Yossi Milo Gallery, New York.

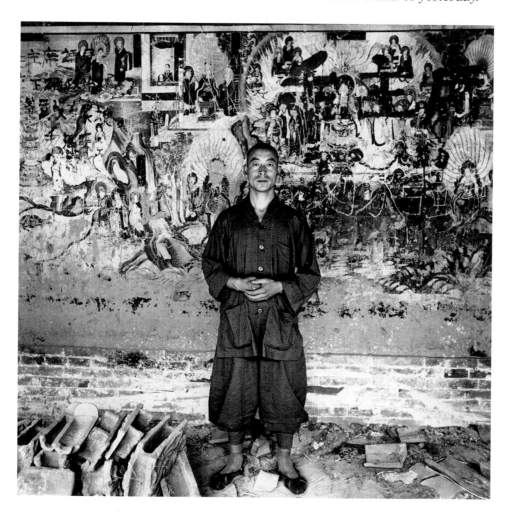

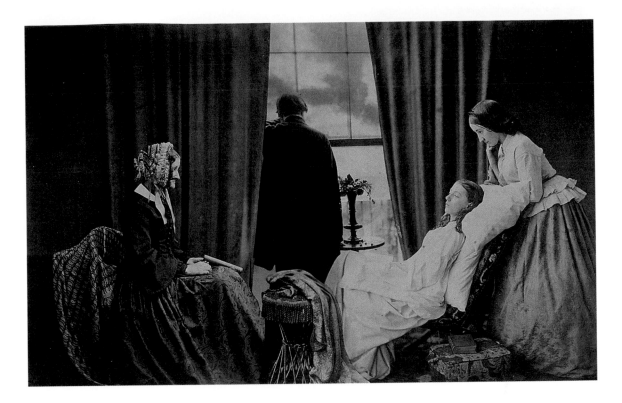

Photography and Art

The development of photography has been seen as freeing painting and sculpture from practical tasks such as recording appearances and events, and it is certainly true that Western artists began to explore the potential of abstraction and nonrepresentation only after photography was well established. Ironically, to many people's way of thinking, these older forms took the definition of "art" with them, leaving photography to assume many of the traditional functions of art with none of the rewards.

Yet from the beginning there were photographers and critics who insisted that photography could also be practiced as an art. Today, over 150 years later, photography is fully integrated into the art world of museums and galleries, and many artists who are not primarily photographers work with photographic images. This brief section looks at how photography found its way both as an art and *into* art.

The existing art that photography resembled most was painting. In practicing photography as an art, many early photographers naturally turned to painting as a model. A wonderful example is Henry Peach Robinson's *Fading Away* (**9.10**). The English public of the day reveled in paintings that told a story, preferably a sentimental one. Robinson created his photograph with this audience in mind. We see a young woman on her deathbed. Despite her being about to expire, she looks remarkably beautiful and remarkably healthy. Her grieving relatives hover at the bedside (one turns toward the window in despair), as our heroine prepares to expel her last shuddering breath. But this scene is not real. It was posed; in fact, it was made as a composite image from five separate negatives. The people are actors, and they were carefully arranged in this stagy episode.

One aspect of photography that some felt stood in the way of making art was its detailed objectivity, which seemed more suited to science. In a movement called pictorialism, photographers used a variety of techniques to undercut the objectivity of the camera, producing gauzy, atmospheric images that seemed more painterly, and thus more like art. An important American pictorialist was the photographer Alfred Stieglitz. Stieglitz, however, grew dissatisfied with pictorialism. He came to the conclusion that for photography to be an art, it must be true to its own nature; it should not try to be painting.

9.10 Henry Peach Robinson. *Fading Away.* 1858. Albumen composite print, 9⅜ × 15⅜". National Museum of Photography, Film & Television, Bradford, West Yorkshire.

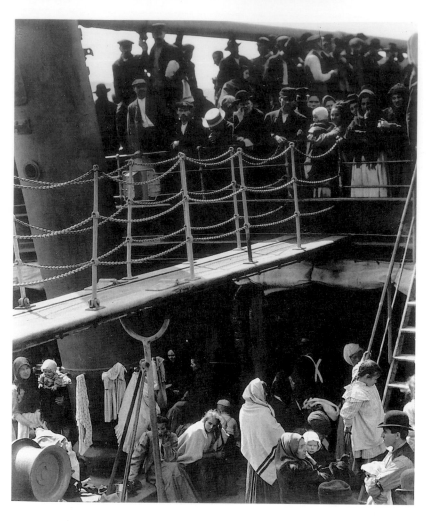

9.11 Alfred Stieglitz. *The Steerage.* 1907. Chloride print, 13⅛ × 10⁷⁄₁₆".
The Art Institute of Chicago.

The photograph that has become most closely associated with Stieglitz' revolutionary idea is *The Steerage* (**9.11**). The story of how *The Steerage* was made illustrates our point about photographers moving through the world with an invisible frame behind their eyes. In 1907 Stieglitz was aboard ship on his way to Europe, traveling first class. One day as he was walking the deck, he happened to look down into the lowest-class section, called steerage. Before him he saw a perfectly composed photograph—the smokestack leaning to the left at one end, the iron stairway leaning to the right at the other, the chained drawbridge cutting across, even such details as the round straw hat on the man looking down and the grouping of women and children below. Stieglitz knew he had only one unexposed plate left (the equivalent of one exposure at the end of a roll of film). He raced to his cabin to get his camera. When he returned, the scene was exactly the same; no one had moved. That one plate became *The Steerage.*

The type of photography that Stieglitz championed came to be known as "pure" or "straight" photography. Practitioners of "pure" photography consider it a point of honor not to crop or manipulate their photographs in any way. The composition is entirely visualized in advance, framed with the viewfinder, then photographed and printed. With its emphasis on formal values and faithfulness to the essence of the medium, the aesthetic of pure photography was enormously influential for much of the 20th century. One of its most famous adherents was Ansel Adams, who spent his life photographing the landscape of the American West, especially the unspoiled beauties of our national parks.

Autumn Tree against Cathedral Rocks, Yosemite illustrates both Adams' reverent regard for nature and the technical mastery that allowed him to express it (**9.12**). The rock formation rears majestically upward, reaching almost to the upper edge of the image, while before it a tree joyously offers up its sprays of pale foliage. We could almost imagine them in secret communion, mountain and tree, like the cypress and stars that seem to speak to each other in Van Gogh's *Starry Night* (see 1.10). The symmetrical composition emphasizes the dignity of the scene and gives us the impression that something important, perhaps even sacred, is happening. The absence of a ground line—Adams purposefully focused above it—contributes to the sensation of upward motion, as do the powerful diagonals of the rock cliff.

Adams believed that a good photographer had to be able to visualize the finished composition in advance, including how the myriad colors, details, and textures of nature would be transposed into values on a gray scale. A great technician of the camera, he developed a system for calibrating all aspects of the photographic process—exposure, development, and printing—to ensure that the final image would embody this initial vision. With this approach, Adams emphasized that photography was a product of science, and that only by understanding the science of it could photographers produce art.

Adams practiced photography as an art. Other artists have made photography itself part of the subject of their art, examining its role in society, the particular vision of the world it promotes, and the assumptions we make about it. One of the first artists to look critically at photography was Hannah Höch. Born in 1889, Höch came of age during the decades when photomechanical reproduction first allowed photographic images to appear in newspapers, periodicals, posters, and advertising. Everyday life was suddenly flooded with images, and a constant flow of secondhand reality began to compete with direct experience.

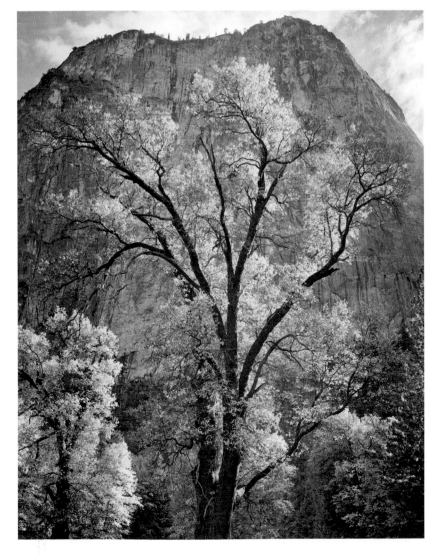

9.12 Ansel Adams, *Autumn Tree against Cathedral Rocks, Yosemite.* c. 1944. Gelatin silver print, 9⁷⁄₁₆ × 7⅜".
The Museum of Modern Art, New York.

Höch's response was to use these "found" images as a new kind of raw material. In works such as *Cut with the Kitchen Knife* (**9.13**) she combined images and letters she had clipped from printed sources to portray the overwhelming experience of a modern city with its masses of people and machines. The word *dada* that appears in several places refers to the art movement that Höch belonged to. **Dada** was formed in 1916 as a reaction to the unprecedented slaughter of World War I, which was then being fought. The word *dada* itself has no meaning, for, faced with the horror of mechanized killing and the corruption of the societies that allowed it, Dada refused to make sense in traditional ways. A Dada manifesto written in 1918, the year the war ended, called for an art "which has been visibly shattered by the explosions of the last week, which is forever trying to collect its limbs after yesterday's crash. The best and most extraordinary artists will be those who every hour snatch the tatters of their bodies out of the frenzied cataract of life."[6] Höch, for her part, spent her life snatching bits and pieces from the frenzied cataract of images.

Another artist formed by the ideas of Dada was Emmanuel Radnitzky, better known as Man Ray. Trained as a painter, Man Ray initially learned photography in order to document his paintings. When a year or two later he turned his attention to the art of photography itself, he reacted with characteristic Dada abandon: He threw away the camera. Instead of placing himself before the world armed with a camera and film, Man Ray retired to the dark room and began to experiment with the light-sensitive paper that photographs are printed on. He discovered that an object placed on the paper would leave its own shadow in white when the paper darkened upon exposure to light. Working with this simple idea, he invented a technique he called the rayograph (also known as the rayogram, **9.14**). Through such simple strategies as shifting the objects over time, suspending them at various heights over the paper, removing some and adding others, or shifting the light source, Man Ray

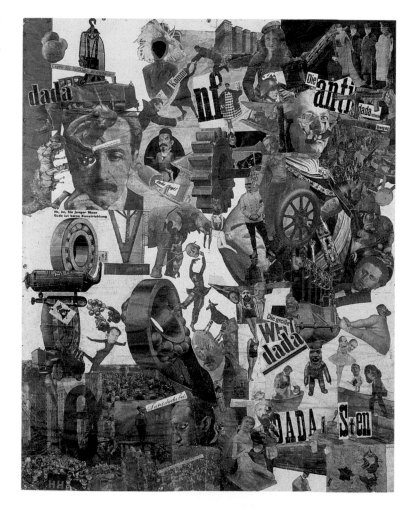

9.13 Hannah Höch. *Cut with the Kitchen Knife Dada through Germany's Last Weimar Beer Belly Cultural Epoch.* 1919. Collage, 44⅞ × 35⅜".
Staatliche Museen zu Berlin, Preussischer Kulturbesitz, Nationalgalerie.

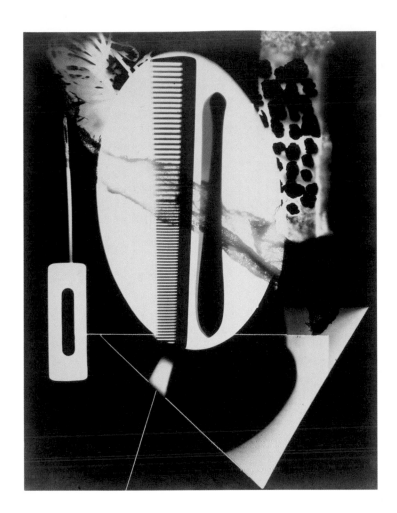

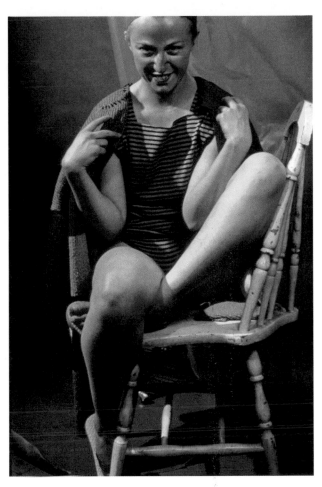

created mysterious images that looked like ordinary photographs, but which did not correspond to preconceived ideas of what a photograph was. Rayographs are far removed from the ideal of straight photography championed by Steiglitz and his followers. Yet, if we think of photography as a tool for making images instead of as a tool for recording the world, then there are no right or wrong ways to use it—only choices, discoveries, and experiments.

One complaint that had been lodged against photography from the very beginning was that it recorded the world in black and white instead of in full color. Early techniques for color were in place by around 1910, but it was not until the 1930s that color began to be widely used, and then only in advertising. Serious photographers continued for decades to prefer black and white, feeling that color lacked dignity and was suitable only for vulgar commercial photography. Such prejudices began to crumble during the 1960s and 1970s. Today, many artists have adopted color photography as a primary means of making images.

One such artist is Cindy Sherman. Sherman uses photography to create images of herself as someone else, often a woman she has invented or a woman who appears in a famous work of art. The characters that Sherman invents seem to represent types rather than individuals—the abandoned girlfriend, the vengeful hussy, the pert secretary, the society drunk, the party girl, the androgynous youth, and many others. Yet as we look, we realize that these are categories that we ourselves bring to the images, for the photographs are all called simply *Untitled*. Here, for example, is *Untitled #123* (**9.15**). As you invent a story for the woman Sherman portrays, you will find that you have made assumptions about what kind of person she is, assumptions based in part on the stereotypes you have absorbed through the films, television shows, and advertising images that surround us.

9.14 (left) Man Ray. *Champs délicieux, second rayogram.* 1922. Rayogram, silver salt print, 8¾ × 7½".
Musée National d'Art Moderne, Centre Georges Pompidou, Paris.

9.15 (right) Cindy Sherman. *Untitled #123.* 1983. Chromogenic color print, 35 × 24½".
Courtesy the artist and Metro Pictures Gallery, New York.

CENSORSHIP: ROBERT MAPPLETHORPE

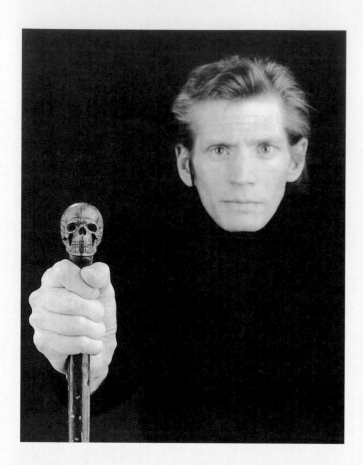

E ACH OF THE arts has had its lightning rods—works that, because of their form or content, attract the storm of attention and passion and controversy. These same works often raise the issue of censorship. In literature it was D. H. Lawrence's *Lady Chatterley's Lover,* which, because of its explicit sex scenes, was banned from publication in the United States for more than thirty years. In theater it was the musical *Hair,* which in 1968 confronted Broadway audiences with a shockingly new sight: the entire cast stark naked. And in photography it was the "X Portfolio" of Robert Mapplethorpe.

Starting in 1976, with his first solo exhibition, Mapplethorpe gained considerable fame, but the fame acquired a troublesome edge when the public at large became aware of his "X Portfolio," for that series of photographs contains images of sadomasochism and homoeroticism, images so frank as to be profoundly disturbing to many (even most) viewers.

Mapplethorpe died of AIDS in the spring of 1989. Soon after, an exhibition of his work was organized, including several examples from the "X Portfolio." The show was planned to tour the United States. Here the saga begins, and it probably will be discussed and debated in art circles for many years to come.

The Mapplethorpe show was scheduled to open at Washington's Corcoran Gallery of Art, a public museum, in the summer of 1989. Before the opening, however, it came to the attention of Senator Jesse Helms, Republican of North Carolina, who denounced the photographs as obscene. Senator Helms' chief objection was that part of the funding for the exhibition had come from the National Endowment for the Arts—in other words, from American taxpayers. His attempt to persuade Congress to prohibit funding for work he considered obscene caused a furor, with intense argument on both sides. In the heat of this controversy, the Corcoran canceled, but the show later opened, to general acclaim, at Washington's Project for the Arts.

After Washington, the Mapplethorpe show moved to Hartford, Connecticut, and Berkeley, California; in both places it ran without major incident or protest. Next on the itinerary, however, was a city well known for its strict opposition to pornography: Cincinnati. And in Cincinnati the controversy became an uproar. No longer was the issue merely public funding. Now it became: Should these photographs be shown at all?

On opening day in Cincinnati, police closed the Contemporary Arts Center while they videotaped the exhibition for evidence. Then the exhibition was reopened, and it played to huge crowds for the duration of its stay. But a grand jury indicted both the gallery and its director on obscenity charges. If convicted, the gallery's director could serve up to a year in jail.

Before discussing the outcome of the trial, it might be well to pause and consider some of the issues involved. Is the Mapplethorpe case really a matter of censorship, and what, in fact, is censorship?

For our purposes here, we will define censorship as the supervision by one individual or group over the artistic expression of another individual or group. This definition assumes that person or group A has the power to control the expression of person or group B. Usually, the power is exerted for political, religious, or moral reasons. In other words, A can prevent B from making or showing work that conflicts with A's political, religious, or moral point of view.

We expect to find censorship in totalitarian societies, and we are seldom disappointed. Absolute rule survives only *because* it is absolute, so it cannot tolerate other points of view. But in the United States today censorship for political reasons is far less an issue than is censorship concerning religious or moral standards.

We have a pluralistic society, representing many religions, many moral points of view. People of goodwill and thoughtful convictions disagree about what is "right" or "wrong," what should be allowed or not allowed. One of the most explosive areas of disagreement concerns the issue of free expression, specifically as it pertains to the arts. Should artists, writers, and performers be allowed to express whatever they wish? Or should there be limits on that expression to control material that large segments of society consider morally wrong?

Proponents of free expression cite the First Amendment to the Constitution, which states in part: "Congress shall make no law . . . abridging the freedom of speech." Yet that amendment does not give you the right to say anything you please. You cannot, for example, deliberately tell a lie about another person, either verbally (slander) or in print (libel). Such lies are prohibited, and the other person could sue you.

In a classic example from the early part of this century, Supreme Court Justice Oliver Wendell Holmes, Jr., said, "No one has a right falsely to shout 'fire' in a crowded theatre." So freedom of speech is *not* absolute; it has limits. Moreover, the Supreme Court historically has held that it is permissible to ban obscene speech, obscene writing, obscene imagery. The problem lies in deciding just *what* is obscene.

As of this writing the Supreme Court standard for obscenity comes from a 1973 case called *Miller v. California*, which held that something is obscene if the "average person applying contemporary community standards" would find it so, and if "the work taken as a whole lacks serious literary, artistic, political or scientific value." Obviously, this judgment raises more questions than it answers. Who is the average person? Which community? Who decides whether the artistic value is serious?

Further complicating the problem is the issue of public funding for the arts. Many people feel that taxpayers' money should not be used to support the arts at all. Others think the government should finance the arts, but not "obscene" art—whatever that is. Those who oppose limits on spending fear that such limits would lead to a situation like the one that has existed in totalitarian societies, where government controls the arts rigidly.

In our system we pay our taxes and allow our elected representatives to decide how the money should be spent. And in 1965 Congress passed the National Foundation on the Arts and Humanities Act, whose declaration of purpose includes this statement: "It is necessary and appropriate for the Federal Government to help create and sustain not only a climate encouraging freedom of thought, imagination and inquiry, but also the material conditions facilitating the release of this creative talent."

In 1996, under pressure from conservative organizations, Congress slashed funding for the National Endowment for the Arts by some 40 percent and eliminated grants to individual visual artists altogether. As of this writing, funding is still well below earlier levels, and individual grants are available only for literature, jazz, and traditional or folk arts. The question of funding for "obscene" art—and the method of determining what is "obscene"—remains vague. Of course, there will *never* be absolute answers to any of these questions, answers acceptable to everyone. Readers of this book must make up their own minds, as the courts continue to grapple with these complex issues. That brings us back to the Mapplethorpe case.

Six months after the Cincinnati gallery and its director were indicted on obscenity charges, a jury of local citizens found them not guilty. The jurors were not art experts; most of them had never been in an art museum, knew nothing about art, and cared little about it. Yet they were willing to be guided by opinions of people who were presented to them as experts, art professionals brought in by the defense. As one juror said afterward, "We had to go with what we were told. It's like Picasso. Picasso from what everybody tells me was an artist. It's not my cup of tea. I don't understand it. But if people say it's art, then I have to go along with it."

The Mapplethorpe jurors were "average persons" who, even when applying the standards of a rather conservative "community," found that the works in question *did* have "serious artistic value." That was the resolution of one case, but there will be many cases, and the question of censorship can never have a definite answer.

Robert Mapplethorpe. *Self-Portrait*. 1988. Photograph.

9.16 Sally Mann. *Untitled* #6, *Antietam*. 2001. Gelatin silver print, 38 × 48".
Courtesy Gagosian Gallery, New York.

Cindy Sherman's photographs rely on our experience of the contemporary world of mass media for their effect. A recent project by Sally Mann, on the other hand, reaches back into history, both our national history and the history of photography itself. Mann conceived her project after witnessing a strange and unsettling incident, the suicide of an escaped prisoner, who shot himself rather than surrender to the police who were chasing him. The incident took place on Mann's land, not far from her house. After the authorities had left, taking the body with them, she went to look at the spot where it had happened. She watched as the earth began to soak up a small pool of blood. The man had been about her son's age, barely more than a boy in her eyes.

Would a stranger coming upon this land a century from now sense that a death had occurred just there? For Mann, this question touched off a time of meditation on history and landscape, bloodshed and memory. She began to photograph her own land. Then she moved on to other landscapes that had been consecrated with the blood of young men, the famous battlefields of the Civil War: Appomattox, Manassas, Fredericksburg, Antietam (**9.16**). The Civil War (1861–1865) was one of the first conflicts to be documented by photography. To create her photographs of the battlefields today, Mann returned to the method used by the original Civil War photographers. Called wet-plate collodion, it produces a black-and-white negative on a piece of glass bathed in chemical solutions and exposed while still wet. Mann's battlefield photographs are dark, brooding, and imperfect. They demand that we look hard at them, that we take the time to decipher what we are seeing. They seem to reach out to us from the distant past, although they were made only a few years ago.

The computer has been welcomed by many artists who work with photography as a natural extension of the medium. Recently developed digital cameras use no film at all, but instead store photographs as data on disk. A printing process has also been developed to print images directly from a computer onto standard photography paper. For photojournalists, digital cameras allow images to be transmitted back to a newspaper over telephone lines, like e-mail. For artists, the new technology allows them to gather photographic images, feed them into a computer, work with them, and print the end product as a photograph.

To create photographs such as *Shanghai* (**9.17**), Andreas Gursky scans two or more large color negatives into the computer. He merges them into a single image, which he modifies until he is satisfied with every detail. The result is then generated as a new color negative and printed as a photograph— a very large photograph. At almost 10 feet in height, *Shanghai* has the kind of forceful presence we usually associate with paintings or billboards. In fact, like color and digital manipulation, large sizes were first pioneered in advertising. Gursky's success as an artist makes it possible for him to absorb the costs associated with creating photographs on this scale. It also enables him to travel to such places as Shanghai, where he found this cavernous hotel. A pure product of globalization, the anonymous interior could just as easily be in Atlanta, Sydney, Berlin, or any number of other cities.

Thomas Ruff takes the use of the computer a step further in series of works he calls *Substrata*, meaning underlayers (**9.18**). Rather than scan his own photographs into the computer, Ruff downloads images he finds on the Internet. For the *Substrata* series, Ruff used images taken from Japanese manga (comic books) and anime (animated films, see 9.30). Ruff layers the images one on top of the other, making them difficult to decipher individually. He manipulates the resulting image, blurring the contours until all traces of recognizable representation have disappeared, then prints the result. Like Gursky, Ruff works on a very large scale. *Substratum 12 III*, illustrated here, is over 8 feet in height.

In the tradition of Man Ray, Ruff has produced photographs without the aid of a camera at all. The raw material he uses, anime and manga images, depict stories about fantasy worlds. When Ruff finds them, they are doubly disconnected from reality: once by their imaginary subject matter, and a second time through their virtual existence on the Internet. Layering and blurring them, Ruff further dissolves their stories until they have no memory of their former life, existing only as a glowing, pulsating, jewel-toned field of light on a monitor. Then he gives them material form as a photograph.

9.17 (left) Andreas Gursky. *Shanghai*. 2000. C-print, 9'11" × 6'9".
Courtesy Matthew Marks Gallery, New York.

9.18 (right) Thomas Ruff. *Substratum 12 III*. 2003. C-print and Diasec, image size 8'4" × 5'5½".
Courtesy the artist and VG Bild-Kunst.

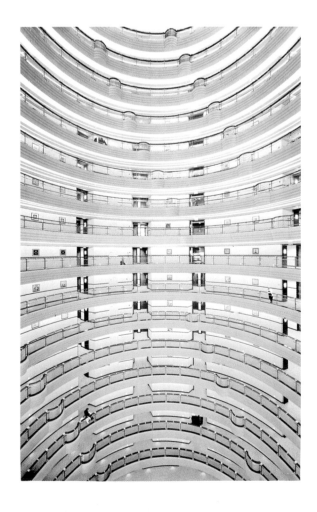

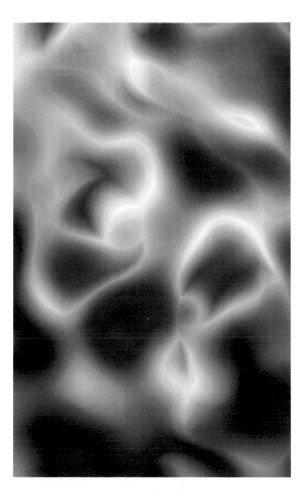

FILM

Throughout history artists have tried to create the illusion of motion in a still image. Painters have drawn galloping horses, running people, action of all kinds—never being sure that their depictions of the movement were "correct" and lifelike. To draw a running horse with absolute realism, for instance, the artist would have to freeze the horse in one moment of the run, but because the motion is too quick for the eye to follow, the artist had no assurance a running horse ever does take a particular pose. In 1878 a man named Eadweard Muybridge addressed this problem, and the story behind his solution is a classic in the history of photography.

Leland Stanford, a former governor of California, had bet a friend twenty-five thousand dollars that a horse at full gallop sometimes has all four feet off the ground. Since observation by the naked eye could not settle the bet one way or the other, Stanford hired Muybridge, known as a photographer of landscapes, to photograph one of the governor's racehorses. Muybridge devised an ingenious method to take the pictures. He set up twenty-four cameras, each connected to a black thread stretched across the racecourse. As Stanford's mare ran down the track, she snapped the threads that triggered the cameras' shutters—and proved conclusively that a running horse does gather all four feet off the ground at certain times (**9.19**). Stanford won the bet, and Muybridge went on to more ambitious studies of motion. In 1887, he published *Animal Locomotion*, his most important work. With 781 plates of people and animals in sequential motion, *Animal Locomotion* allowed the world to see for the first time what positions living creatures really assume when they move.

9.19 Eadweard Muybridge. *Horse Galloping.* 1878. Collotype, 9³⁄₁₆ × 12".
Courtesy George Eastman House, Rochester, New York.

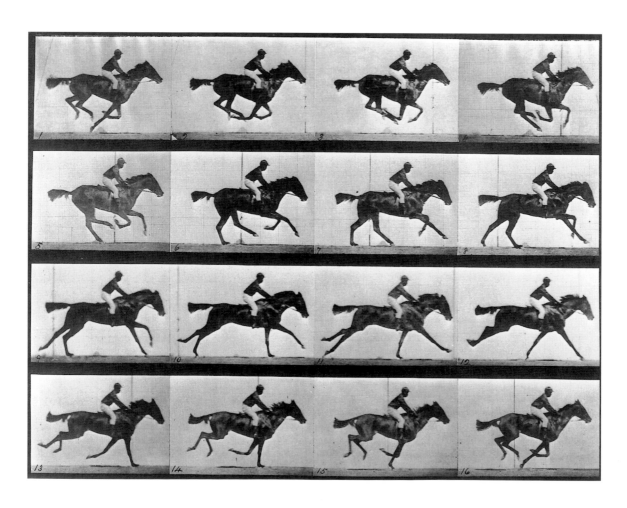

Eadweard Muybridge's experiments in the 1880s had two direct descendants. One was stop-motion photography, which became possible as both films and cameras became faster and faster. The other was *continuous*-motion photography. Undoubtedly, Muybridge had whetted the public's appetite to see *real* motion captured on film. The little room with a view had glimpsed a different world, a world that does not stand still but spins and moves and dances, and the public wanted more of this. The public did not have long to wait.

On the night of December 28, 1895, a small audience gathered in the basement of a Paris café, which was to become the first commercial movie theater in history. The audience viewed several very short films, including one of a baby being fed its dinner, another of a gardener being doused by a hose. One film in particular caused a strong reaction. *L'Arrivée d'un train en gare (The Arrival of a Train at the Station)* set the audience to screaming, ducking for cover, and jumping from their seats, because it featured a train hurtling directly toward the viewers. Never before, except in real life, had people seen anything of the kind, and they responded automatically. From the beginning, motion pictures could make an image on a screen seem real indeed.

The Origins of Motion Pictures

Film depends on a phenomenon called persistence of vision. The human brain retains a visual image for a fraction of a second longer than the eye actually records it. If this were not true, your visual perception of the world would be continually interrupted by blinks of your eyes. Instead, your brain "carries over" the visual image during the split second while the eyes are closed. Similarly, the brain carries over when still images are flashed before the eyes with only the briefest space between them. Motion-picture film is not real motion but a series of still images projected at a speed of twenty-four frames per second, which makes the action seem continuous.

Interest in moving pictures really predates the development of the still camera. As early as 1832 a toy was patented in Europe in which a series of drawn images, each slightly different from the next, was made to spin in a revolving wheel so that the image appeared to move. Eadweard Muybridge later applied this principle to his multiple photographic images, spinning them in a wheel he called the zoopraxiscope.

Commercial applications of the motion picture, however, awaited three major developments. In 1888 the American George Eastman introduced celluloid film, which made it possible to string images together. Another big step was taken by Thomas Edison, the famous American inventor. It was in Edison's laboratory, in 1894, that technicians created what was apparently the first genuine motion picture. Lasting only a few seconds, the film was made on celluloid. Its "star" was one of Edison's mechanics, a man who could sneeze amusingly on command. Its title: *Fred Ott's Sneeze.*

One major problem remained. There was no satisfactory method for projecting the films to an audience. Here the challenge was taken up by two Frenchmen, brothers appropriately named Lumière (*lumière* means "light"), who in 1895 succeeded in building a workable film projector. The films shown in that Paris café were made by the brothers Lumière. From that point the motion-picture industry was off and running.

Exploring the Possibilities

From the beginning of motion pictures there was no doubt about what the new technology would do best: At last visual art could tell stories. Paintings had always been able to allude to stories, or imply stories, or depict episodes from stories. Photography could do these things as well. But with film, stories could unfold over time and in motion, as they did in life or on stage in the theater.

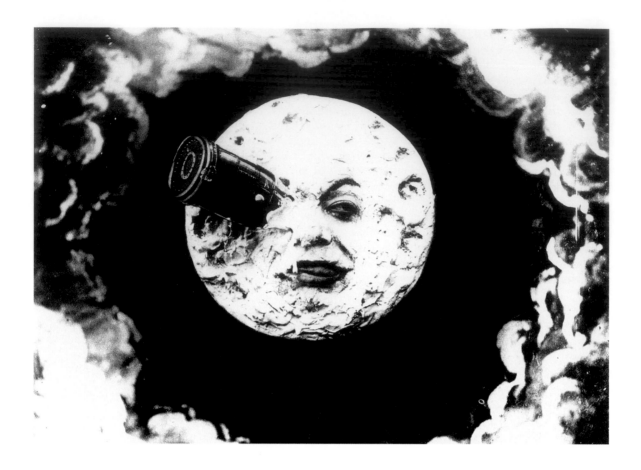

9.20 The space capsule lands, frame from *A Trip to the Moon*, directed by Georges Méliès. 1902.

The little film that the Lumière brothers showed told a brief, real-life story about a train pulling into a station. It was a documentary of something that had happened. Of course, not all stories we tell are set in the present time or the real world, at least not in the parts of it where a camera can travel. They may be set in an imaginary future, or in the historical past, or at the bottom of the sea, or at the center of the earth. Early filmmakers, already familiar with the tricks that photography could play, quickly set out to explore the new medium's ability to tell imaginary tales. A wonderful early example is *A Trip to the Moon*, by the French filmmaker Georges Méliès (**9.20**). Méliès made his film in 1902, when space travel was far in the future. Even the airplane hadn't yet been invented yet! (The Wright brothers' historic flight took place the next year, 1903.) One of the first science-fiction films ever made, *A Trip to the Moon* tells the story of a group of scientists who travel to the moon. How do they get there? They invent a "space-gun," which looks a lot like a cannon, and shoot themselves into space in a capsule that looks like a giant bullet. After landing smack in the moon's eye (ouch!), the adventurers do battle with a race of underground moon beings. The moon people win, taking the invaders prisoner. But the scientists manage to escape and return to earth, where they are greeted by a cheering crowd.

Méliès created his fourteen-minute film in a studio using painted scenery, just like that for a theatrical production. By the simple means of stop-motion photography, he also created sophisticated special effects. For example, on the moon, an opened umbrella belonging to one of the scientists suddenly turns into a giant mushroom. Méliès filmed the umbrella, then stopped the camera, replaced the umbrella with the mushroom, and began filming again. When the film was shown, the transformation seemed to happen by magic.

Méliès made his films using human actors. Other early filmmakers quickly discovered that stories could be "acted" by objects or drawings that seemed to come to life by themselves, a magical effect called animation, meaning "bringing to life." Animation takes advantage of the fact that, while a film camera can shoot continuously as motion unfolds, it can also shoot a single frame of film at a time. If you place, say, a spoon on a table, then shoot a single frame of it, then shift the spoon slightly and shoot another frame, then shift it again and shoot a third frame, when the film is projected, the spoon will appear to move by itself. Animating objects in this way is called pixilation, and early filmmakers were quite inventive with it. A French film made in 1907 included a sequence in which a knife buttered a piece of breakfast toast all by itself.

Hand-drawn animation works on the same frame-by-frame principle, except that in this case it is a drawing or cartoon that is photographed, not an object. To imagine the work involved, look back at Muybridge's sequential photographs of a horse galloping (see 9.19). If you drew each of these images and photographed them in sequence, you would produce a very short animated film. Animation is a time-consuming and laborious way of making a movie, for between 12 and 24 drawings are required per *second* of running time in order to create the illusion of smooth motion. An animated cartoon only three minutes in length may thus require up to 4,320 individual drawings!

One of the pioneers of animation in the United States was Winsor Mc-Cay. Before turning to animation, McCay was already famous for his innovative comic strip *Captain Nemo,* which he began drawing for the *New York Daily Herald* in 1905. He was also a successful stage performer, where he appeared as a chalk-talk artist—someone who told stories and illustrated them at the same time on a chalk board. McCay made several short animated features, but his most famous creation was *Gertie the Trained Dinosaur* (**9.21**). McCay created Gertie for his stage act. He had her projected onto a large sketchpad set on an easel. The effect was as though one of his own drawings had suddenly come to life. McCay interacted with the cartoon as it played, scolding Gertie, for example, who reacted by acting contrite. Gertie was not the first animal character invented for animated features, but she was the first to have a

9.21 Winsor McCay *Gertie the Trained Dinosaur.* 1914.

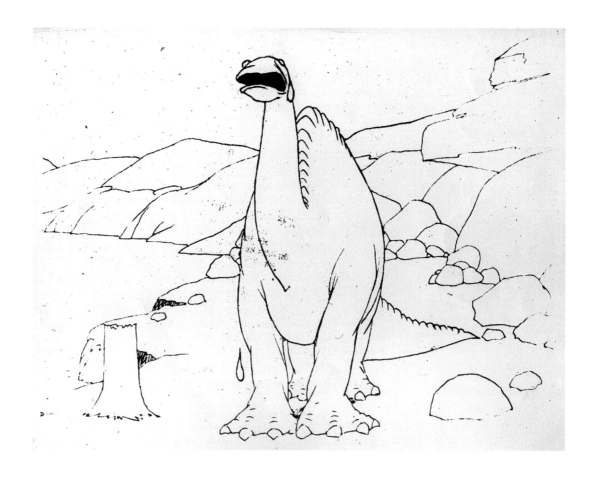

distinct personality, and as such she is the ancestor of Mickey Mouse, Donald Duck, Bugs Bunny, and other famous animated animal characters.

When it came to filming a story, early filmmakers looked naturally to theater as a model. At their most basic, they set up a camera in front of a staged performance and let it record the view, as though the camera were an audience member who stared straight ahead and never blinked. In fact, however, as audience members we don't quite sit and stare at the entire stage. We focus here and there, we follow the action. We concentrate sometimes on the setting, sometimes on a face, sometimes on a gesture. Filmmakers soon realized that the camera could do these things as well, entering the story and making it more vivid for spectators. Little by little, as filmmakers built on each other's experiments and discoveries, a repertoire of techniques for cinematic storytelling began to take shape. In America, one of its first great masters was D. W. Griffith.

D. W. Griffith began his movie career in 1908 as a director of very short (ten-minute) silent films cranked out at the rate of two a week. This apprenticeship taught him much about the mechanics of filmmaking, so that by the time Griffith had attained greater creative independence, he was ready for it. In 1914 the producer-director shot his first feature-length picture, and even its title proclaims an epic: *The Birth of a Nation* (**9.22**). Griffith took his story from a contemporary novel. *The Birth of a Nation* is set in the American South before, during, and after the Civil War. In a now-familiar device, it interweaves the histories of two families—one northern, one southern—whose paths cross and whose members fall in love with one another. The plot allowed for many battle scenes and a particularly effective staging of President Lincoln's assassination. We must remember that this was a *silent* film. All action, all plot, all emotions had to be conveyed by visual images only, without dialogue or sound effects. (There was usually live musical accompaniment in the early movie theaters.)

Most viewers today would find it difficult to sit through *The Birth of a Nation,* for when it is not exaggerated in style it is offensive in its racial prejudice and simplistic morality. Even in its day some audiences reacted strenuously to these aspects of the movie. Reviewing the film on March 4, 1915, *The New York Times* complained about "melodramatic and inflammatory material." The *Times,* however, went on to evaluate "the film as a film" and deemed it "an impressive new illustration of the scope of the motion picture camera."[7]

Each unbroken sequence of movie frames, with the camera rolling, is called a shot. In the first days of film, the standard shot had been the full shot, showing actors from head to toe. Griffith preferred to experiment with a range of shots for dramatic effect: the medium shot (from the waist up), the close-up (head and shoulders), the extreme close-up (part of a face), and the long shot (seen from the distance). Dissatisfied with the camera as immobile observer of a scene, Griffith used the pan shot (camera moving from side to side) and the traveling shot (camera moving from back to front on a track). He also perfected the technique of cross-cutting, in which two or more scenes are alternated to advance the action of the film. For example, he might film scenes of a heroine in distress and her hero rushing to save her, then cut back and forth rapidly between the two in order to build suspense.

Cross-cutting shows Griffith's mastery of film editing, or assembling the film creatively after all scenes have been photographed. In *The Birth of a Nation* Griffith also made effective use of the iris shot (see 9.22), in which the edges of the film are blacked out to create a circle of interest. *The Birth of a Nation* even has flashbacks, or cuts to episodes that are supposed to have taken place before the main action of the film.

Griffith later claimed to have invented many of these storytelling techniques himself, and until recently historians generally took his boast at face value. Today, after considerable research, we know that techniques such as pan shots, close-ups, and intercutting had been developed by many filmmakers in many places during those early years of cinema. Griffith, however, used them with great virtuosity and in daring new ways, producing touchstone works whose high artistic ambitions inspired future filmmakers.

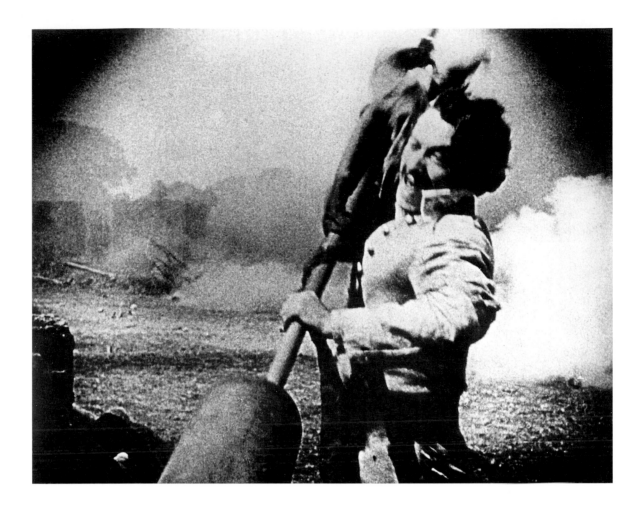

Studio Systems

The very first filmmakers were entrepreneurs. They worked alone or started up small businesses, much as photographers had done before them. But as the passion for making films spread around the world, as the technologies involved developed and grew more specialized, and as the public's appetite for movies continued to increase, organizations began to take shape that could produce movies efficiently on a much larger scale. These organizations were called studios, and the system they developed for making films is called the studio system. Studios began to take shape during the 1910s. Europe, however, was soon plunged into World War I, a four-year conflict that left its film industry severely crippled. Thus it was that the studio system reached its most influential and powerful form in the United States, in Hollywood.

The great Hollywood studios—names such as Paramount, Warner Brothers, and Metro Goldwyn Mayer (MGM)—integrated all aspects of the film industry under one roof. Studios not only made films but also distributed them and showed them in their own exclusive chain of theaters. Studios had writers to generate ideas and scripts, actors and directors under long-term contracts, and vast staffs of professionals such as camera operators, costume and set designers, scenery painters, lighting experts, make-up artists, and film editors. When sound came to motion pictures in the late 1920s, the studios added sound engineers to their staffs. Composers were hired to write film scores, and orchestras were formed to record them. Publicity departments kept the public informed not only about upcoming films but also about the lives of movie stars, for movie stars were expected to have glamorous lives, lived at least partially in public.

Making a film now involved coordinating the efforts of hundreds of people. In this atmosphere, the person who was in charge of the entire project, the

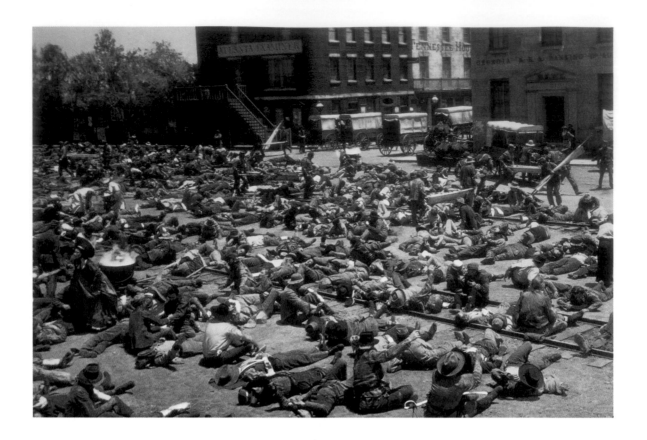

9.23 Vivien Leigh as Scarlet O'Hara in a scene from *Gone with the Wind,* produced by David O. Selznick. 1939.

producer, became increasingly important and powerful. One of the most famous producers of the Hollywood studio era was David O. Selznick. Selznick became so well known that he left his studio position at MGM to become an independent producer, and it was as an independent producer that he made one of the most famous Hollywood films of all time, *Gone with the Wind,* based on Margaret Mitchell's best-selling novel about the Civil War (**9.23**). Selznick's control over the project was legendary. He hired and fired a succession of writers as the script was being developed, and he continued to write and rewrite portions of it himself during the filming. After conducting a long and highly publicized search for the ideal cast, he began filming, only to fire the director a few weeks later. All in all, five directors worked on the film.

Gone with the Wind was filmed in color, which had been introduced earlier in the 1930s. Selznick and his production team took full advantage of the possibilities that color opened up. The scene illustrated here is one of the most memorable moments in the film. Scarlett O'Hara, the spoiled heroine, searches for Dr. Meade among the Confederate wounded from the Battle of Atlanta. The shot begins with a close-up of her, then the camera slowly draws backward and upward (it was mounted on a construction crane) to take in ever more of the scene. The wounded extend as far as the eye can see, and Scarlett is reduced to a small red shape running frantically among them. We become aware of the enormity of the war at the same time she does and through her experience. The expressive possibilities unique to film are here displayed at their most powerful.

Selznick's control of *Gone with the Wind* was considerable, but it may seem modest compared with the creative involvement by the next filmmaker we shall study. In 1941 R.K.O. released a film created almost single-handed by a twenty-six-year-old "boy genius" who played the starring role, produced and directed the film, co-authored the screenplay, supervised the editing and set design, and, it is said, even sewed some of the costumes himself. The film was not a success with contemporary audiences or critics. Today, however, when movie people compile lists of the "ten best" filmmakers and films, we are sure to find the names of Orson Welles and his masterpiece, *Citizen Kane* (**9.24**).

Welles based his story, loosely, on the life of the newspaper publisher William Randolph Hearst, here renamed Charles Foster Kane (played by Welles). What could have been a simple biography of a powerful man was turned by Welles into a startling cinematic achievement. *Citizen Kane* was innovative on a number of levels. Its structure, at first glance an ordinary flashback, begins with Kane's death, then traces his life from childhood and youth up through old age and back to his death again. But the actual telling of the story is far more complex than that. Kane's life on film is divided into five sections—the first played out in blaring newsreel films, the other four narrated in turn from the points of view of four people involved with Kane. Welles begins with a superficial outside view of the brash, successful young Kane, then gradually probes deeper and deeper into Kane's psychic center, as that center slowly disintegrates into lonely, bitter old age.

Cinematically, the movie opens the filmmaker's grab bag of tricks—all meant to highlight Kane's personality. There are low-angle shots (to show a towering Kane), dramatic long shots, and many traveling shots intended to convey physical and emotional separation. For instance, as Kane's relationship with his first wife becomes cooler, the camera shows the couple farther and farther apart at the ends of an ever-lengthening dinner table. Welles calculated every shot to convey the mood, the emotional symbols, the portrait of a character he intended. *Citizen Kane* could not be a stage play. It is too dependent on film techniques for its impact. More than any filmmaker before him, Welles had shown what the camera, used imaginatively, could do.

Artists and Film

The expense of making a film, together with the specialized equipment and technical knowledge involved, generally kept visual artists from experimenting with the new medium. It would not be until the invention of video, discussed

9.24 Orson Welles as Charles Foster Kane in a scene from *Citizen Kane*, directed by Orson Welles. 1941.

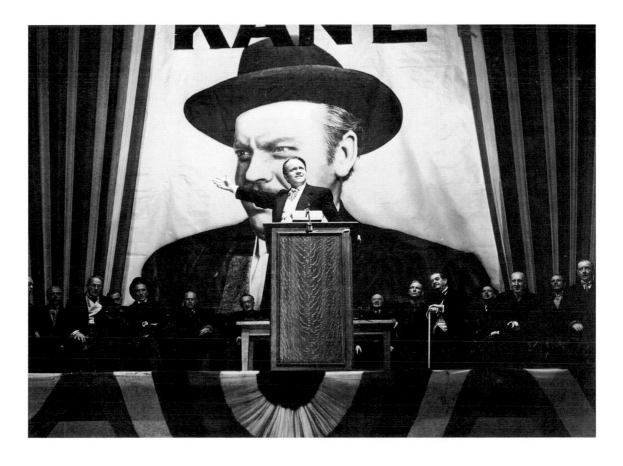

later in this chapter, that visual artists were able to work with recorded time and motion on a large scale. Nevertheless, alongside the rich, international history of the film industry before video runs a slender history of films by artists.

During the first decades of the 20th century, several important artistic movements found an echo in film. One example is Surrealism, the movement formed in Paris during the 1920s around a fascination with the workings of the unconscious and the imagery of dreams. Surrealism influenced all of the arts—not just painting and sculpture, but also poetry, fiction, film, photography, and theater. One of the most famous Surrealist painters was the Spaniard Salvador Dalí (see 21.26). A flamboyant character even as a young man, Dalí was kicked out of art school in Madrid just before he was set to graduate, having outraged his professors by claiming that they weren't qualified to judge him. He made his way to Paris, where he hooked up with his friend Luis Buñuel, a fellow Spaniard who had come to Paris earlier in order to study at the Film Academy there. The two friends decided to collaborate on a film. Over the course of three intense days they developed a screenplay based on their dreams and fantasies. They named it *An Andalusian Dog* (**9.25**). Assisted by Dalí, Buñuel shot the film in two weeks.

In typical Surrealist fashion, *An Andalusian Dog* has nothing to do with a dog at all. The plot involves a lovers' quarrel, but told as though it had furnished the material for a dream. In the scene illustrated here, ants swarm out of a hole in a hand that has appeared in a door set ajar. Elsewhere, a woman seems to have her eye slit with a razor, a man drags a piano filled with dead donkeys and two priests across the floor, two arms shaking a cocktail suddenly appear through a wall. Only sixteen minutes long, *An Andalusian Dog* is a classic of Surrealist film. Dalí and Buñuel collaborated on only one more project before going their separate ways, Buñuel as a filmmaker, Dalí as a painter.

The 1960s witnessed the birth of the movement known as Pop art and the rise to fame of one of its most famous practitioners, Andy Warhol (see 22.9). "Pop" is short for popular, and nothing was more popular by that time than the movies. Affordable film cameras had become widely available to the general public, leading to a thriving scene in underground or experimental filmmaking. Warhol had rented a large loft space in downtown New York. He called it The Factory, for it was a place where his art was to be manufactured—by himself, his assistants, his friends, hangers-on, visiting celebrities, and all manner of people. In this setting, Warhol began making films. Warhol's

9.25 Luis Buñuel and Salvador Dalí. *An Andalusian Dog.* 1928.

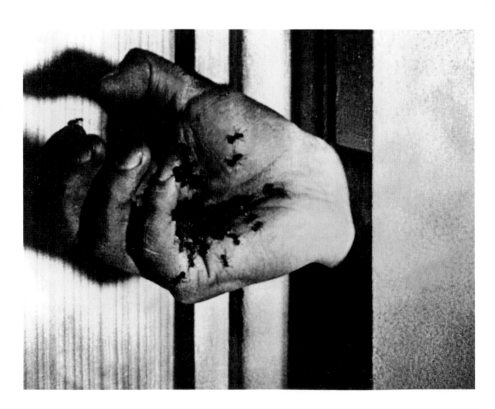

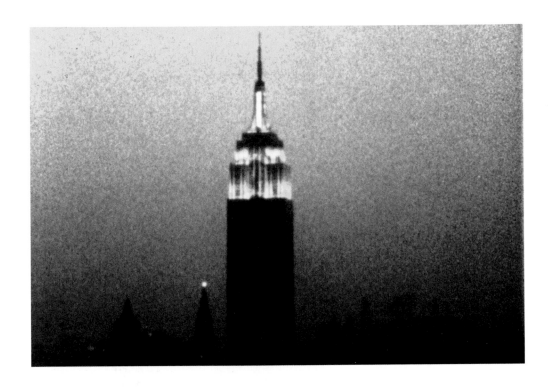

9.26 Andy Warhol. *Empire*. 1964. 16mm film, black and white, silent, 8 hours 5 minutes at 16 frames per second. Andy Warhol Museum, Pittsburgh.

early films were all silent and filmed in black-and-white. They resemble his paintings of the time in that they challenge our idea that something will "happen." For example, Warhol's 1963 film *Kiss* consisted of close-ups of couple after couple, kissing for three minutes, much like his paintings of soup cans consisted of can after can of soup, sometimes all the same flavor, sometimes different flavors. An even more radical film, *Empire,* followed the next year (**9.26**). Warhol and some friends set up a rented camera on the 44th floor of a building with a view of the Empire State Building. They filmed the Empire State Building for eight hours straight, from dusk until almost dawn. During all this time the camera did not move. The composition shown in the illustration here did not change. The reels of film were spliced end to end so that eight hours of filming produced an eight-hour film. What was the film about? *Empire,* Warhol said, was a way of watching time pass.

Independent Visions

From the beginning of film, there were people who claimed that, like photography, it could be practiced as an art. During the 1920s, the expression "art cinema" came into use, usually to indicate an independent movie that did not conform to popular storytelling techniques or aim to please a mass audience. Often these films were shown by small, specialized theaters, by cinema societies, or even by art museums—a network of venues that existed apart from the major commercial theatres. But in such a collaborative medium as film, who was the artist? The actors? The writers? The editor who put it together? All of them were artists in a way. Yet the most satisfying films, most viewers agreed, were those that seemed to be guided by a single vision. Many felt that this person was the director. During the 1950s, a group of young French film critics articulated this view with special force: The director, they said, was a film's *auteur,* French for author.

An ***auteur*** is a director whose films are marked by a consistent, individual style, just as a traditional artist's paintings or sculptures are. This style is the result of the director's control over as many aspects of the film as possible. Usually, an *auteur* will be closely involved in conceiving the idea for the film's story and in writing the script. He or she will direct the film, work with the

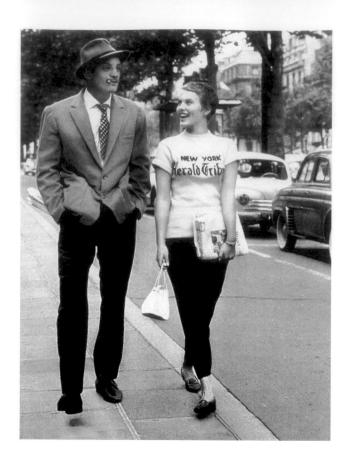

9.27 Jean-Paul Belmondo and Jean Seberg in a scene from *Breathless,* directed by Jean-Luc Godard. 1960.

camera operators to plan and frame each shot, then work closely with the editor when the final film is assembled.

The young critics behind the *auteur* concept were hoping to become filmmakers themselves, and their writings described the kind of films they admired and wanted to make. And make them they did, in the process launching a vibrant movement known as the New Wave. One of the first New Wave films to appear was Jean-Luc Godard's *Breathless* (**9.27**). The story of *Breathless* is fairly simple. A handsome petty criminal (Michel, played by Jean-Paul Belmondo) steals a car and heads north to Paris. On the way, he shoots a policeman who had pulled him over for speeding. In Paris, he meets up with a pretty American student journalist he knows (Patricia, played by Jean Seberg). They continue their affair, talk, go to the movies, steal cars, and plan to escape to Italy. But Patricia does not want to be in love, and to prove to herself that she isn't, she calls the police and turns Michel in.

The revolutionary nature of *Breathless* does not lie in the story, however, but in the way it is told. The rhythms of the editing are fast and nervous, giving the film a spontaneous, youthful energy (a more accurate translation of the French title would be "out of breath"). Jump cuts—cuts where either the figures or the background change abruptly, interrupting the smooth visual flow—abound. The camera is sometimes unsteady, as though it were being held by someone walking. The dialogue is part gangster film, part philosophy, and includes quotes from famous works of literature. Finally, the film contains allusions to famous films of the past, and the actors play characters who have been formed as much by the movies as by anything else. With the New Wave, the movies became self-conscious, just as painting had almost century earlier (see the discussion of Manet's *Déjeuner sur l'herbe,* page 509).

The early films of the French New Wave have since inspired numerous young filmmakers in search of a personal approach to their medium. A recent entry in the long line of films that pay tribute to the New Wave is *What Time Is It There?,* directed by the Taiwanese filmmaker Tsai Ming-liang (**9.28**). Set in Taipei and Paris, *What Time Is It There?* is a meditation on loss, loneliness,

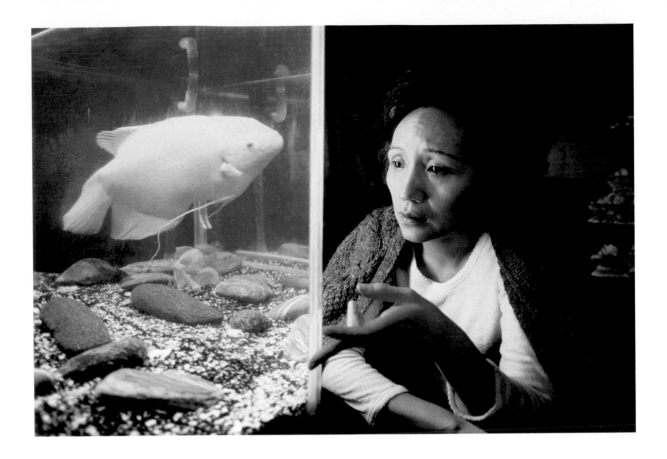

9.28 Lu Yi-Chang as Shiang-chyi Chan in *What Time Is It There?*, directed by Tsai Ming-liang. 2002.

and human isolation. At the beginning of the film, an old man dies, leaving behind his wife and teenage son. They mourn their loss, but alone and unable to connect with each other. The son makes a living selling watches on the street. His own watch tells dual time, one time for here, and one time for "there," wherever there is. He associates it with his father, who is no longer here, but "there." A young woman about to travel to Paris convinces him to sell it to her so that she can keep track of the time back home on her trip. After she leaves, he becomes obsessed with resetting all of the clocks in the city to Paris time. He also spends time alone in his room, watching the same film over and over again. Film lovers recognize it immediately as *The 400 Blows*, by François Truffaut. One of the most famous films of the early New Wave, *The 400 Blows* tells the story of a troubled adolescent in Paris. Truffaut drew on his own difficult childhood in creating it.

Meanwhile, in Paris, the young woman is having an equally lonely time, for she knows no one and does not speak the language. She has several odd encounters, including one with an older man on a park bench. He is played by Jean-Pierre Léaud, the actor who played the adolescent boy in *The 400 Blows* some forty-two years earlier.

With little dialogue and no music, *What Time Is It There?* relies almost entirely on images for its impact. Tsai likes to place his camera before a carefully framed view and let it record, neutral and motionless, as a scene unfolds. The camera often lingers after the action is over, still staring, though the characters have moved on. This sequence of lengthy, static shots gives *What Time Is It There?* a slow, hypnotic rhythm—the very opposite of Godard's nervous energy in *Breathless*. Bearing out the theme of the film, Tsai often framed the shots to include a "here" and a more mysterious "there." In the image shown here, for example, the edge of the aquarium divides the screen in two—the world of "here" to the right, where the widow mourns her dead husband, and the world of "there" to the left, where a large white fish looms like some ghostly apparition. Only in the last shot is the screen made whole, with the symmetrical image of a ferris wheel at the center. In true *auteur* fashion, Tsai

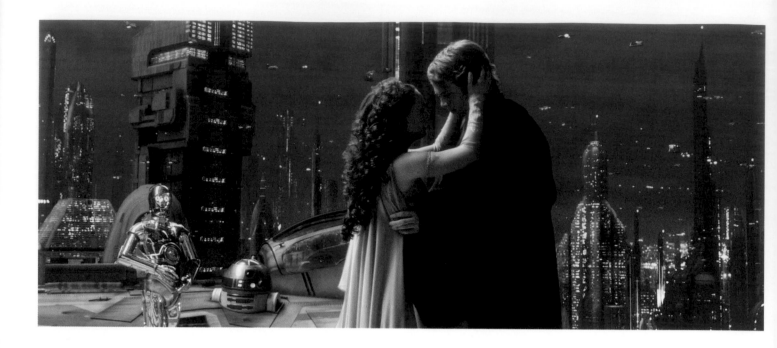

9.29 Natalie Portman and Hayden Christensen in a scene from *Star Wars, Episode III: Revenge of the Sith*, directed by George Lucas. 2005.

co-wrote the screenplay, and the story draws on his feelings and experiences after the death of his own father.

Digital Revolutions

During the late 1980s, digital technology came to film just as it did to photography. One of the most practical applications of digital technology has been in the realm of editing. Traditionally, editing involved physically cutting lengths of film from all of the footage that had been shot, and then taping these lengths together piece by piece. With digital editing, footage is either shot in digital format or digitized at the end of each day's work and stored as computer files. When it comes time to cut and assemble the final film, editing on the computer is faster and more flexible than editing manually. What is done can more easily be undone, and since the footage is not physically harmed when lengths are taken out of it (since on the computer they are copied out, and not actually removed) it is simpler to try various alternatives and even to compare them side by side.

For moviegoers, however, the most evident role of digital technology has been in the two areas we explored first in this brief discussion of film: special effects and animation. One of the leaders in developing computer-generated imagery has been Industrial Light & Magic, a company founded by director George Lucas in 1975. Lucas was then preparing the first of his Star Wars films, now known as *Star Wars IV: A New Hope*, and the mission of his company was to push the boundaries of what was possible in special effects. Indeed, one of the ways to gauge the progress of digital technology in film is to consider the six Star Wars films that have appeared over the ensuing years.

Released in 1977, the first film was praised for its astonishing effects, but only one brief sequence used imagery generated by computer. The majority of the effects were created using scale models filmed with an innovative new camera technology. By the time the fourth film was made—*Star Wars I: The Phantom Menace*, released in 1999—technology had advanced to the point where some 90 percent of the special effects were generated by computer. *The Phantom Menace* also introduced one of the first computer-animated characters to appear in a film, and it was the first film to be released in digital form to theaters. The next film in the series, *Star Wars II: Attack of the Clones*, released in 2002, was the first major motion picture to bypass traditional celluloid film entirely. It was filmed, edited, and distributed in digital form. One of the principal characters, the diminutive Yoda, played by a puppet in earlier Star Wars films, became a computer animation. The most recent and final film in the series, *Star Wars III: Revenge of the Sith,* takes computer-generated imagery to new heights (**9.29**). More than half of the film was created digitally, some 21,000 shots worked on by hundreds and hundreds of artists, who layered in digitally rendered sets, computer animated characters, and computer-generated effects over footage of human actors or scale models.

Computers have also found a role as a tool in traditional hand-drawn animated films. One of the most vibrant animation cultures in the world today flourishes in Japan, where animated films are known as anime. Perhaps the greatest contemporary master of anime is Hayao Miyazaki, whose full-length animated features such as *Spirited Away* have found admirers around the world (**9.30**). *Spirited Away* tells the story of a ten-year-old girl name Chihiro. Like all of the characters in Miyazaki's films, she is based on someone he knows, in this case the daughter of a friend. Miyazaki found himself wondering what sort of world this little girl would have to face as she grew up, and whether her youthful high spirits and happiness would last. *Spirited Away* is the result of his wonderings.

We first meet Chihiro in the film in the family car with her parents. They are driving to a new home, in a new town; and Chihiro is not happy at all about the move. In truth, she is whining and sulking and acting perhaps a little spoiled. Her adventures begin when her father loses the way, and the family stumbles on an odd tunnel in a hillside. Passing through it, they find a deserted, old-fashioned town. Tempting food is on display at an open counter, and Chihiro's parents can't resist. But once they begin eating, they can't seem to stop, and before Chihiro's eyes they turn into pigs. They are under a spell! As night falls, the enchanted town comes alive. Guests arrive, headed for the palatial bathhouse, the Japanese equivalent of a luxurious spa. They are all spirits, hundreds of spirits, and the last thing they want is a human in their midst. Chihiro must find a way to survive, to escape, and to rescue her parents. Will she? Yes, but it takes both courage and kindness—two key virtues she finds within herself. At the end of the film, she is wiser but just as plucky. Her character has been deepened but not broken.

9.30 Frame from *Spirited Away,* directed by Hayao Miyazaki. 2001.

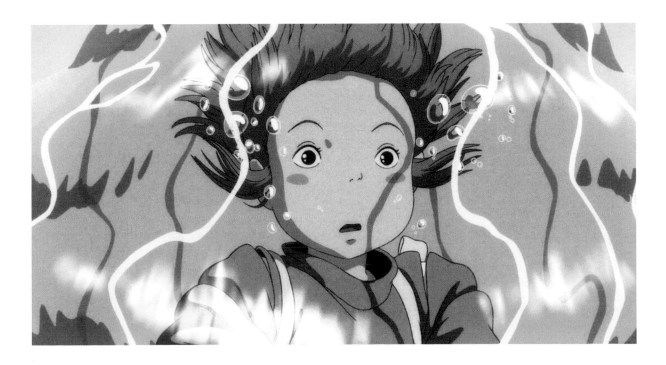

The earliest animators such as Winsor McCay worked virtually alone. The process of drawing an entire motion picture frame by frame is so time consuming, however, that it quickly became standard to divide the work between numerous artists, and various labor-saving techniques were developed. To realize his films, Miyazaki founded Studio Ghibli, where he employs a core team of artists. After he has written the script and produced sketches of the key characters and scenes, he meets with his artists to discuss the project and divide up the drawing assignments. The artists at Studio Ghibli work in the most traditional possible manner, in pencil on paper. When their work is complete, Miyazaki reaches outside the studio to employ still more people to complete the film, including digital animators. Miyazaki uses digital technology sparingly, for he wants his films to retain a hand-drawn look. The computer is used largely to add color to drawings, to create some of the backgrounds, and to add in elements that are too visually complex to animate by hand.

The possibilities for visual expression in film have expanded tremendously since the brothers Lumière set up their little projector barely a hundred years ago. But another medium, also based on the camera, has come farther and faster in half the time. The video arts—of which television is most prominent—probably touch more people more significantly than all the other media discussed in this book put together.

VIDEO

9.31 Nam June Paik. *TV Buddha.* 1974. Closed-circuit video installation with bronze sculpture, monitor, and video camera; dimensions vary with installation.
Stedelijk Museum, Amsterdam.

All art is about communication, but the video arts in particular are about *mass* communication. No other medium even approaches television in its potential for presenting to millions of people the same visual experience at the same moment. A national or international event—such as a grand wedding in the British royal family or the Olympic Games—is telecast simultaneously into homes around the globe, complete with the graphics and other visual trappings devised by the networks to capture our attention. The first official television broadcast in the United States took place in 1939, in connection with

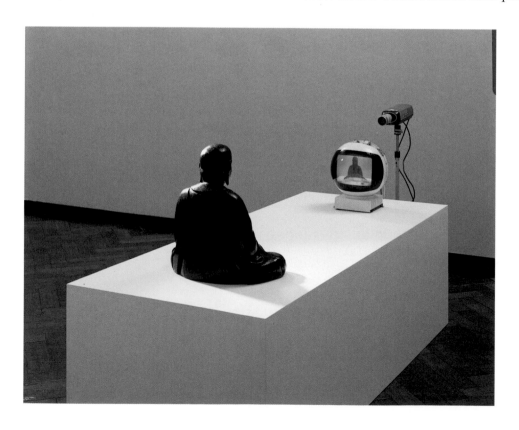

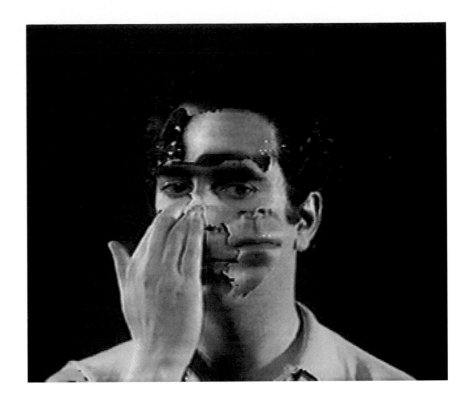

9.32 Peter Campus. *Three Transitions*. 1973. Video. Electronic Arts Intermix, New York.

the opening of the New York World's Fair. Few people noticed, however, because there were practically no television receivers to accept the transmission. Not until about 1950 did the television set become an expected fixture in American homes. Now, of course, more homes around the globe have television than have indoor plumbing.

Video cameras translate images into electronic signals. A television receives the signals, decodes them, and reconstitutes the image. While televisions themselves were from the first destined for the public, the cameras were initially made only for professionals such as the major network studios. It was not until the 1960s that a portable video camera was marketed to the general public, together with magnetic tape for recording video feed. This development brought video technology within the reach of individual artists, who began to experiment with it almost immediately.

One of the first artists to work with video was Nam June Paik. Paik was as fascinated by television sets themselves—their evolving styles and designs—as by the moving video image. One of his best-known early works is *TV Buddha* (**9.31**), an installation in which a sculpture of the Buddha contemplates its own image on a futuristic-style television that resembles an astronaut's helmet. Or is it the video camera that contemplates the Buddha? The camera and its hookup to the television are in full view, for Paik wants us to be aware of the entire mechanism of the relationship. Past and future confront each other here, as do religion and secular entertainment, alternate forms of representation, and stillness and movement. Viewers appear briefly on the screen as they stand behind the statue, their fleeting presence contrasting with the eternal existence of the Buddha and the unblinking stare of the camera.

Another type of video art is related to filmmaking in the sense that it creates a visual continuum, perhaps even a story. What sets it apart from film is the possibility for electronic manipulation of the imagery, the greater freedom to "play" offered by the video camera. Peter Campus' *Three Transitions* (**9.32**), a classic work in video art, is a very brief (less than five-minute) exercise in electronic displacement of the artist's own face and body. In the first "transition," Campus seems to stab himself in the back, climb out through the wound, then emerge intact on the other side. In the second he wipes away his face with his hand, revealing another same face underneath. And in the last Campus appears to burn his living face as though it were a photograph. These operations are made visually possible—even believable—through sophisticated video technology.

Peter Campus' *Three Transitions* was made to be shown on a television monitor, and it could be broadcast just like a commercial television program to reach people around the world. Campus also created video environments—rooms in which video was projected onto walls or other surfaces. The idea of involving the viewer more actively in the experience of video has appealed to many artists. Tony Oursler's video creations carry on long monologues, a device that catches many viewers off guard. Who expects art to talk? In *Coo*, a bulbous fiberglass form standing on the floor serves as a screen for a projected video of two eyes and a mouth (**9.33**). A strange knee-high creature, *Coo* does nothing but try out "o" sounds over and over, as though it were just discovering speech or making goo-goo talk to a baby. *Coo's* eyes, mouth, and voice belong to Tracy Leipold, a performer that Oursler has worked with for many years. Together Leipold and Oursler invent a character and decide what kinds of things it will say, from ranting about being stared at in a gallery ("Hey you. Get out of here. What are you looking at?" begins one monologue) to whining about not being able to get to sleep. Oursler makes a video of Leipold's face as she recites the text, then projects it onto a sculptural fiberglass form. The projectors, cables, and tape player are always in full view, and yet Oursler's creatures still seem strangely alive—amusing, endearing, vulnerable, unsettling, and annoying by turns.

Iranian-born Shirin Neshat has used simultaneous projections to involve viewers more actively in her work. In *Rapture* (**9.34**), two videos are projected simultaneously onto opposite walls, placing viewers literally in the middle, forced to turn from one to the other in trying to experience the whole of the story. In one video, a group of men enter a fortified hilltop castle. In the other, a group of women approach the castle from a vast distance across a windy desert. The men take little notice of the women, but instead engage in ritualized activities that seem important to them, though trivial to us. The women observe, shut out. Suddenly, they shriek in unison. The men stop, and both groups look at each other. The women turn their backs and continue across

9.33 Tony Oursler. *Coo.* 2003. DVD projection on fiberglass sculpture, height 43".
Courtesy the artist and Metro Pictures Gallery, New York.

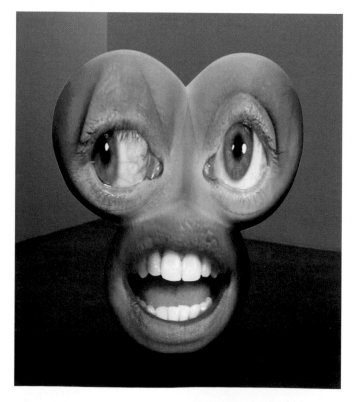

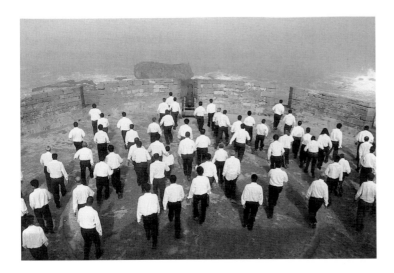

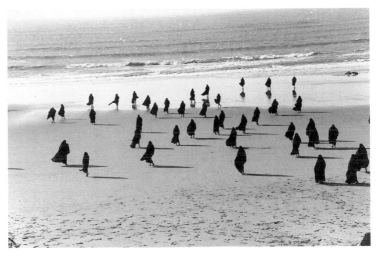

the barren landscape toward the sea, laboriously dragging a heavy boat through the sand. The men return to their important activities. At the water's edge, six of the women climb into the boat and set out to sea with neither oars nor sails, trusting to the current, yet free. The men, who have gathered on the ramparts of the castle—or is it now a prison?—wave.

Neshat's immediate subject is the situation of women in contemporary Islamic societies, yet her work goes beyond the specifics of Islam to address men and women in general, gender and society, outcasts and power, freedom and bondage, and perhaps as well two ways of being in the world. It is a fable that seems timeless and universal, where every action is symbolic, but where no fixed interpretation is offered.

9.34 Shirin Neshat. *Rapture.* 1999. Production stills. Courtesy Gladstone Gallery.

THE INTERNET

Thus far in this book we have discussed the computer as a tool that expands the possibilities of older art forms such as printmaking, photography, film, and video. Yet, in addition to being a tool, the computer is also a place. Images can be created, stored, and looked at on a computer without being given a traditional material form at all. With the development of the Internet, the World Wide Web, and browser applications capable of finding and displaying Web pages, a computer became a gateway to a new kind of public space, one that was global in scope and potentially accessible to everyone. Not only could

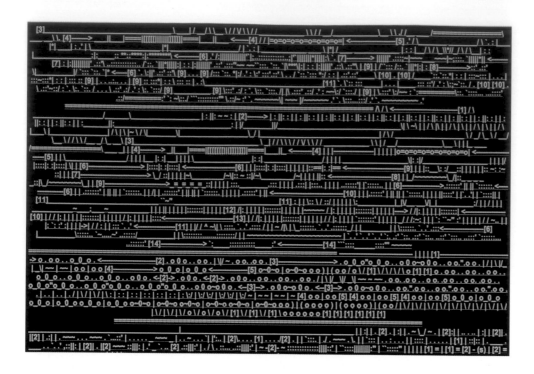

9.35 Jodi (Joan Heemskerk and Dirk Paesmans). *wwwwwwwww.jodi.org.* 1995. Web page.

anyone find information on the Internet, but anyone could claim a presence on the Internet by creating a site on the World Wide Web, a Web site.

Among the first artists to create Web sites as an art form were Joan Heemskerk and Dirk Paesmans, who collaborate under the name Jodi. Figure **9.35** illustrates the home page of one of their first sites. As in much of their work, jodi.org here uses elements of computer code, the language of the Internet, for purely visual effect. The symbols and numbers that repeat across the page can be seen as the computing equivalent of an abstract painting or poem. To see what the page is abstracted *from*, visitors can view the source code, which is arranged to suggest traditional diagrams and images—that is, representationally. Links embedded in the page take visitors on a journey through page after page of what looks like information, but which never makes any sense—maps, images, graphs, diagrams, all visually stimulating but incomprehensible. Sites such as this build on the Conceptualist practice called intervention, in which something unexpected is slipped into an everyday environment. The photograph by Felix Gonzalez-Torres that we discussed in Chapter 2 is another example of an intervention (see 2.41). Like jodi.org's site, it slips a moment of poetry and playfulness into a context dedicated largely to information and commerce.

The Internet is the latest in a long line of communications technologies that have changed our experience of time and place. It was film that first allowed people to witness events that had happened in a distant place and at an earlier time. Yet viewing a film was still a special occasion, and it involved going to a special place, a theater. Television, in contrast, came into private homes and became part of daily life. During live broadcasts, what happened in one part of the world could be seen simultaneously in another. Crossing over time zones and continents, views from around the globe poured into daily life, even as daily life itself continued. With the Internet, this experience has become even more pervasive and more personal, in part thanks to Web cameras, or Webcams—real-time cameras whose output can be viewed over the World Wide Web. Thousands of Webcams have been set up around the world, transmitting panoramic views of cities and landscapes as well as nearer views of public places, office buildings, and private homes. Webcams attached to personal computers transmit even more personal images for online conversations. Webcams respond to our seemingly endless curiosity and longing to *see*. Yet they also raise questions about voyeurism, surveillance, and privacy.

One artist who works with this aspect of the Internet is Wolfgang Staehle. For an exhibition called *2001*, Staehle had video cameras installed facing three sites: the Television Tower in Berlin (**9.36**), the skyline of lower Manhattan, and a monastery in Germany. Images transmitted over the Internet from the cameras were projected onto the walls of a darkened gallery, where they suggested large, luminous paintings. One way to think of *2001* is as an update of Warhol's film *Empire*. Like *Empire*, *2001* was a way of watching time go by. But, whereas *Empire* recorded time passing in a single location, *2001* showed it flowing in widely separated places simultaneously. And, whereas *Empire* was filmed for viewing at a later time, *2001* unfolded almost in real time (the images were delayed by several seconds). Visitors to the gallery could watch the night sky around the tower in Berlin, then turn to the panoramic landscape of Manhattan, where the sun was just setting.

The subjects that Staehle chose for *2001* were not expected to move or change. Apart from incidental details (a passing cloud, a boat on the river) they were expected to remain as motionless as a photograph or a painting, just as the Empire State Building had for Warhol. The exhibit opened in a New York gallery on September 6th. Five days later, terrorists crashed two hijacked passenger planes into the World Trade Towers. The attack and all that followed were projected onto the gallery walls. After much discussion, the artist and his gallerist decided to let the exhibit continue. The meaning of the work, however, had shifted radically. It was no longer about landscape, but about history.

9.36 Wolfgang Staehle. *TV Tower, Berlin*, from *2001*.
Video installation at Postmasters Gallery, New York, September 6–October 6, 2001.

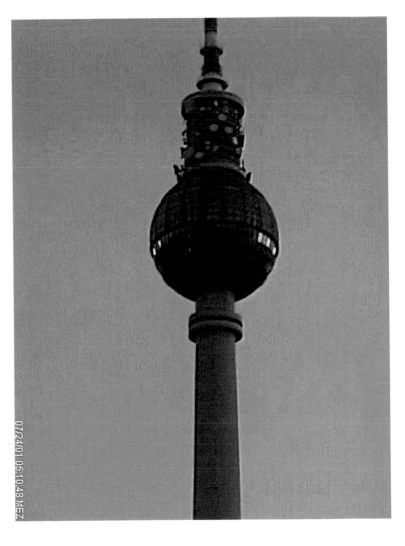

Staehle's work grows from the connections to the world that the Internet makes possible. Ben Fry's *Anemone*, on the other hand, visualizes connections made within the Internet itself as users explore its sites (**9.37**). Fry's *Anemone* is an example of organic information design, which is the process of creating software visualizations of large, dynamic data sources. The traffic on a Web site is an example of such a source: at any given moment, there may be hundreds of users, each following his or her own path through the site. *Anemone* responds to all of this information as it happens, creating a constantly evolving image of how the site is being used. Each node on *Anemone* represents a specific Web page. (Viewers can click on a node to learn the name of the page it represents.) The more frequently a page is visited, the larger its node grows. When a user moves to a different page, *Anemone* grows a branch with a node for that page. If more and more users visit the page, its branch and node thicken in response. If, after a while, the page receives no further visits, the node withers and disappears. *Anemone* is aptly named, for as users come and go, the map blossoms into flowerlike formations that quiver and shift. Although we discuss it here as an example of Internet art, *Anemone* has practical applications, and we could just as easily introduce it in the next chapter, Graphic Design, which is about the visual presentation of information. Much Internet art, especially art that takes the Internet itself for its subject, explores this same territory.

The Internet has also become a place to view software art, which is art produced by a program written by an artist. A program is a set of step-by-step instructions that can be executed by a computer. A variety of languages have been developed for instructing computers, and each language has its own code, or way of expressing instructions. Just like spoken languages, computer languages have grammatical rules, but they also allow for individual styles to emerge. Like all programmers, artists take pride in the code they write, much as a poet would take pride in a poem. Most viewers never see the code that lies

9.37 Ben Fry. *Anemone.* 1999.

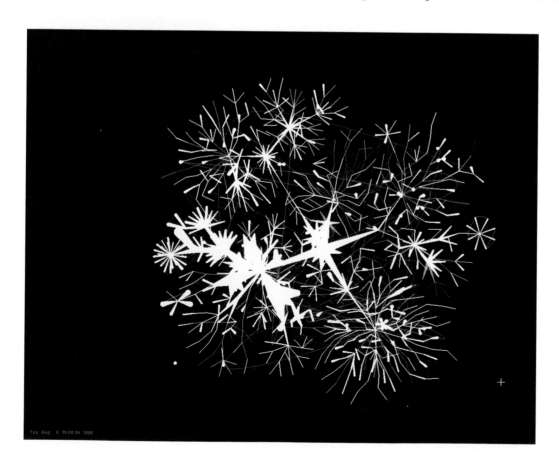

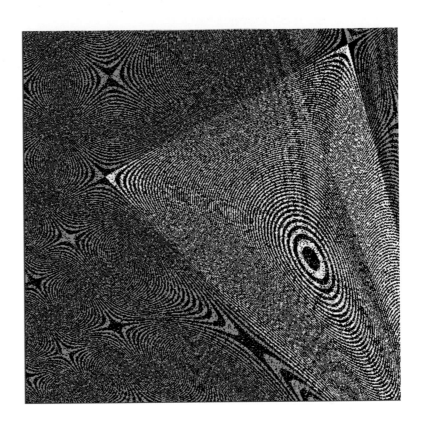

9.38 Martin Wattenberg. *Connection Study, project for CODeDOC*. 2002. Whitney Artport, Whitney Museum of American Art, New York.

behind the images of software art, although in some ways the code *is* the art, or at least half of it. No other medium has such a dual nature.

In an effort to explore individual styles of coding and to examine code itself as an artistic product, the Whitney Museum of American Art commissioned for its Web site an exhibition called *CODeDOC*. Participating artists were asked to respond to the same assignment, to move and connect three points in space. Martin Wattenberg's submission was called *Connection Study* (**9.38**). *Connection Study* opens with a white field. Minute black dots begin to speckle onto it, slowly revealing a white triangle on a black and grey patterned ground. The work is interactive: Viewers can click and drag the corners of the triangle, which affects the developing patterns of the ground in increasingly complex ways.

Before getting to the visual portion of *Connection Study*, however, visitors to the site were first sent to a page that displayed the code that would produce it. Written in the language called Java, it contains passages such as this:

```
synchronized void updatePicture() {
    for (int i=0; i<5000; i++) {
        int x=(int) (w*Math.random());
        int y=(int) (h*Math.random());
        long a1=f(p[0],p[2],x,y),
             a2=f(p[1],p[2],x,y),
             a3=f(p[2],p[0],x,y);
```

Artists were also asked to comment on each other's code, and these comments were posted as well. *CODeDOC* gave viewers an opportunity to see the dual nature of software art, as well learn what the artists appreciate about each other's coding.

Communications technologies of the modern age, the camera and the computer have transformed our world. They were not developed with art in mind; yet, because artists chose to work with them, they have yielded new art forms for our era.

CHAPTER TEN

GRAPHIC DESIGN

Earlier chapters have emphasized that art is open to interpretation, and that a work of art can hold many meanings. This chapter explores the issue of meaning from another point of view, for a graphic designer's task is to try to limit interpretation and to control meaning as much as possible. Graphic design has as its goal the communication of some *specific* message to a group of people, and the success of a design is measured by how well that message is conveyed. The message might be "This is a good product to buy," or "This way to the elevators (or rest rooms or library)," or any of countless others. If it can be demonstrated that the public received the intended message—because the product sold well or the traveler found the right services—then the design has worked.

Not all graphic design has to do with selling, but much of it does, and so for a long time it was known as "commercial art." The term "graphic design" is more inclusive and describes more accurately what artists in this field really do: They attend to the visual presentation of information as it is embodied in words and/or images. Books, book jackets, newspapers, magazines, advertisements, packaging, Web sites, CD covers, television and film credits, road signs, and corporate logos are among the many items that must be designed before they can be printed or produced.

Graphic design is as old as civilization itself. The development of written languages, for example, entailed a lengthy process of graphic design, as scribes gradually agreed that certain symbols would represent specific words or sounds. Over the centuries, these symbols were refined, clarified, simplified, and standardized—generation after generation of anonymous design work. The field as we know it today, however, has its roots in two more recent developments: the invention of the printing press in the 15th century and the Industrial Revolution of the 18th and 19th centuries.

Anyone can write up a notice to be posted on a door. The printing press made it possible to devise a notice that could be reproduced hundreds of times and distributed widely. Someone, however, had to decide exactly how the notice would look; they had to design it. How would the words be placed on the page? Which words should be in large type, which small? Should there be a border around them? An image to accompany them?

The Industrial Revolution, for its part, dramatically increased the commercial applications of graphic design. Before the Industrial Revolution, most products were grown or produced locally to serve a local population. A person who wanted a new pair of shoes, say, could walk down the road to the village cobbler, or perhaps wait for the monthly fair at which several cobblers from neighboring towns might appear. With the advent of machines, huge quantities of goods were produced in centralized factories for wide distribution. For manufacturers to succeed in this newly competitive and anonymous environment, they had to market both themselves and their wares through advertising, distinctive packaging, and other graphic means. At the same time, the invention of faster presses, automated typesetting, lithography, and photography expanded designers' capabilities, and the growth of newspapers and magazines expanded their reach.

Today, international commerce, communications, and travel continue to feed the need for graphic design; and technological developments, most notably the computer, continue to broaden its possibilities.

SIGNS AND SYMBOLS

On the most basic level, we communicate through symbols. The sound of the syllable *dog*, for example, has no direct relation to the animal it stands for. In Spanish, after all, the syllables *perro* indicate the same animal. Each word is part of a larger symbolic system, a language. Visual communication is also symbolic. Letters are symbols that represent sounds; the lines that we use to draw representational images are symbols for perception.

Symbols convey information or embody ideas. Some are so common that we find it difficult to believe they didn't always exist. Who, for example, first used arrows to indicate directions? → ↑ ↓ ↖ ↗ ↙ ↘. We follow them instinctively now, but at some point they were new and had to be explained. Other symbols embody more complex ideas and associations. Two well-known and ancient symbols are the yin-yang symbol and the swastika (**10.1**).

The yin yang symbol, also known as the *taiji* (or *tai chi*) diagram, embodies the worldview expressed in ancient Chinese philosophy. It gives elegant visual form to ideas about the dynamic balance of opposites that are believed to make up the universe and explain existence: male (yang) and female (yin), being and nonbeing, light and dark, action and inaction, and so on. The symbol makes it clear that these opposites are mutually interdependent, that as one increases the other decreases, that a portion of each is in the other, that they are defined by each other, that both are necessary to make the whole, and many other ideas. It is a model of successful graphic design.

The swastika has an important lesson to teach about symbols, which is that they have no meaning in themselves but are given a meaning by a society or culture. The swastika was first used as a symbol in India and Central Asia, possibly as early as 3000 B.C.E. It takes its name from the Sanskrit word *svastika*, meaning "good luck" or "good fortune." (Sanskrit was the most important language of ancient India.) In Asia, the swastika is still widely used as an auspicious symbol, even on commercial products. Until the 1930s, the

10.1 Yin-yang symbol (left) and swastika (right).

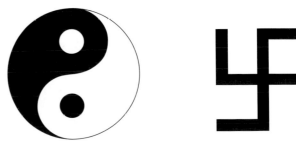

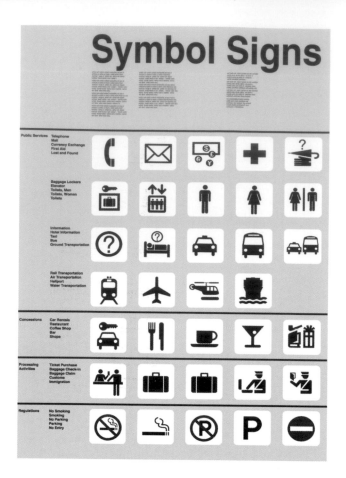

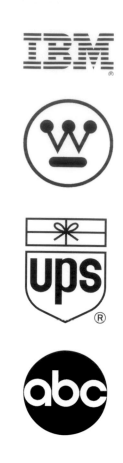

10.2 (left) Roger Cook and Don Shanosky. Poster introducing the signage symbol system developed for the U.S. Department of Transportation. 1974.

10.3 (right) Paul Rand. Logos for IBM (1956), Westinghouse (1960), UPS (1961), and ABC (1962).

swastika was a popular good-luck symbol in the West as well. Today, however, it is so thoroughly associated with the Nazis, who adopted it as their emblem, that it has become for us a symbol of fascism, racial hatred, and the unspeakable atrocities of the concentration camps. Our instinctive recoil from the swastika underscores not only the power of symbols to serve as repositories for ideas and associations, but also the ability of those ideas and associations to change, sometimes radically.

Graphic designers are often asked to create visual symbols. In 1974, the U.S. Department of Transportation commissioned the American Institute of Graphic Arts to develop a set of symbols that could communicate essential information across language barriers to international travelers (**10.2**). Designers selected by the institute researched symbols then in use in transportation centers around the world, evaluating them for clarity and effectiveness. Their findings informed the design of the symbols illustrated here, which were drawn by the firm of Cook and Shanosky Associates. Today, the symbols are a familiar part of signs in airports and train stations, where they help direct travelers to bus and taxi stands, telephones, hotel information, rest rooms, and other key facilities.

Among the most pervasive symbols in our visual environment today are logos and trademarks, which are symbols of an organization or product. An impressive number of these are the work of Paul Rand, one of the most influential of all American graphic designers (**10.3**). Simple, clear, distinctive, and memorable, each of these corporate logos has become familiar to millions of people around the world, instantly calling to mind the company and its products or services. As with any symbol, a logo means nothing in itself. It is up to an organization to make its logo familiar and to convince people through sound business practices to associate it with such virtues as service, quality, and dependability. Because symbols serve as focal points for associations of ideas and emotions, one of the most effective ways for a company to change its image is to redo its logo.

By the 1980s, corporate logos had become such a familiar part of the visual landscape that one of the most powerful symbols of the decade consciously appropriated their authority (**10.4**). Designed by an artists' collective called the Silence=Death Project, the Silence=Death logo was developed to operate just as a corporate logo does: It would appear everywhere, on everything, gradually penetrating the public consciousness, in this case with a message about AIDS—that the disease existed, that people were dying, that they weren't going to go quietly, and that something needed to be done. Like the swastika, the pink triangle had been used by the Nazis, in this case to distinguish homosexual prisoners from others they considered undesirable such as Jews and Gypsies. Gay activists had taken over the symbol during the 1970s, turning it into a badge of courage. The Silence=Death logo vividly rekindled the link with death, in this case from a disease that was viewed initially by many segments of the public as specifically targeting gay people.

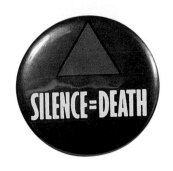

More recently, corporate logos have been used by artists concerned with issues raised by globalization. One of the most instantly recognizable logos ever designed is the casual, cursive checkmark that serves as the logo for Nike (**10.5**). Known as the swoosh, it was created in 1971 by a graphic arts student named Carolyn Davidson. The illustration here shows the swoosh translated into three dimensions as a large outdoor sculpture and set down in the Karlsplatz, one of the most beloved public squares in Vienna, Austria. While the swoosh makes a perfectly believable sculpture, this image was actually part of an elaborate hoax, a performance staged by artists who collaborate under the name of 0100101110101101.org.

0100101110101101.org called their project *Nike Ground*. Their idea was to pretend that Nike had decided to purchase, transform, and rename public spaces in major cities around the world, beginning with Vienna. The artists set up a two-story, translucent "information container" in the Karlsplatz. On the outside, large letters announced "Nikeplatz (formerly Karlsplatz)." Inside the container, performers pretending to be Nike representatives explained the benefits of the program to passersby. More information, including plans for the Nike monument shown here, could be found on the project's Web site, nikeground.com. Citizens of Vienna were scandalized by Nike's supposed plans. Also angered was Nike itself, which briefly pursued the artists on legal grounds. All of the reactions were considered part of the performance by the artists, whose purpose was to provoke.

10.4 (above) *Silence=Death* button. Logo designed by the Silence=Death Project, New York. 1986.

10.5 (below) 0100101110101101. org (Eva and Franco Mattes). Project for the fake Nike Monument in Karlsplatz, from *Nike Ground*. Computer print on canvas, 37¾ × 60".
Courtesy Postmasters Gallery, New York.

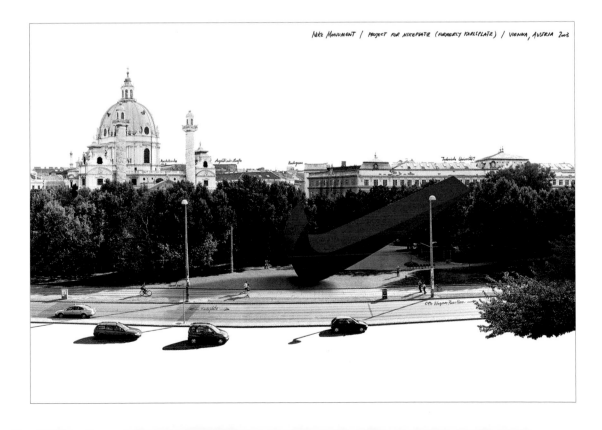

TYPOGRAPHY AND LAYOUT

Part of the power of the Silence=Death logo is in its **typography,** the arrangement and appearance of the letters. The stark, no-nonsense letterforms convey a mood of seriousness and urgency. The carnival mood of *silence=death,* for example, would have had a completely different and inappropriate visual impact.

Cultures throughout history have appreciated the visual aspects of their written language. In China, Japan, and Islamic cultures, calligraphy is considered an art. Although personal writing in the West has never been granted that status, letters for public architectural inscriptions have been carefully designed since the time of the ancient Romans, whose alphabet we have inherited. With the invention of movable type around 1450, the alphabet again drew the attention of designers. Someone had to decide on the exact form of each letter, creating a visually unified alphabet that could be mass-produced as a **typeface,** a style of type. No less an artist than Albrecht Dürer turned his attention to the design of well-balanced letterforms (**10.6**). Constructing each letter within a square, Dürer paid special attention to the balance of thick and thin lines and to the visual weight of the serifs, the short cross-lines that finish the principal strokes (at the base of the As, for example).

The letters Dürer designed would have been laboriously carved in wood or cast in metal, and they would have been set (placed in position) by hand prior to printing. Today, type is created and set by computer and photographic methods. The design of typefaces continues to be an important and often highly specialized field, and graphic designers have literally thousands of styles to choose from. The text of this book, for example, is set in New Aster, which is popular for books since it is easy to read, legible in fairly small sizes, and not tiring to the eyes. The chapter titles, in contrast, are set in a sans-serif face, a face without finishing lines on the strokes, called Optima.

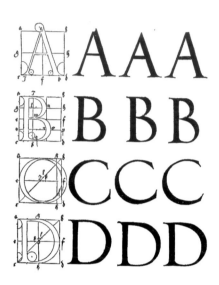

10.6 (above) Albrecht Dürer. Letters, from *Treatise on Measurement*. 1525.

10.7 (right) Erik Spiekermann and Christian Schwartz, United Designers Network. *FF Unit Typeface*. 2003.

"FF Unit is Meta's more responsible sister. Puppy fat is off, some curves are gone and the shapes are tighter. While FF Meta has always been a little out-of-line, FF Unit is less outspoken and more disciplined. It is – like all of this designer's faces – very suitable for use in small sizes and critical conditions. FF Unit is not cold or uptight, just cool: no redundant ornamentation, but a lot of character. The tighter shapes make it suitable for big headlines, while smaller sizes benefit from contrast between vertical and horizontal strokes and open spacing. There are alternate shapes for **aaggiijjlIIIJJMMUU.** They add variety and make very tight headlines."

SMALL CAPS have old style figures. *The quote above is set in FF Unit Light.*

abcdeffighijklmnopqrstuvwxyzß
H£$1234567890H€1234567890
TaglineTaglineaaggiijjlIIIJJMMUU

FF Unit Thin | Thin Alt | THIN CAPS		FF Unit Thin | Thin Alt | THIN CAPS
FF Unit Light | Light Alt | LIGHT CAPS		FF Unit Light | Light Alt | LIGHT CAPS
FF Unit Regular | Regular Alt | REGULAR CAPS		FF Unit Regular | Regular Alt | REGULAR CAPS
FF Unit Medium | Medium Alt | MEDIUM CAPS		FF Unit Medium | Medium Alt | MEDIUM CAPS
FF Unit Bold | Bold Alt | BOLD CAPS		FF Unit Bold | Bold Alt | BOLD CAPS
FF Unit Black | Black Alt | BLACK CAPS		FF Unit Black | Black Alt | BLACK CAPS
FF Unit Ultra | Ultra Alt | ULTRA CAPS		FF Unit Ultra | Ultra Alt | ULTRA CAPS

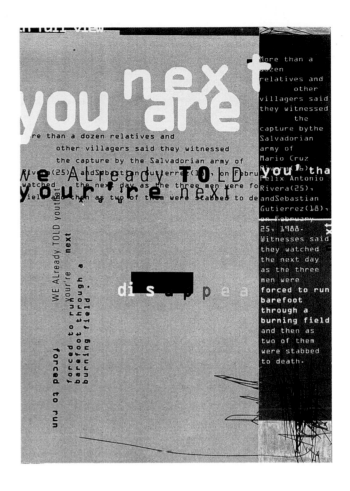

A typeface generally becomes available as a family of fonts. The letterforms of each font in the family share the same proportions and construction—that is what marks them as a family—but they differ in weight (heavy bold versus slender light, for example) and orientation (vertical roman versus diagonal italic). Because the fonts all belong to the same family, they can be used together and still produce a harmonious effect. The poster (**10.7**) introduces a typeface called *FF Unit,* designed by Erik Spiekermann and Christian Schwartz of United Designers Network in 2003. The text in the upper portion of the poster explains the characteristics of the typeface, including the mood it conveys and special virtues such as legibility at small sizes. At the bottom of the poster are listed some of the fonts that the typeface is available in such as FF Unit Fine and FF Unit Ultra. Italic fonts have since been designed, and FF Unit is now available in some seventy fonts.

Joan Dobkin combined commercial typefaces and handmade letterforms in her informational leaflet for Amnesty International, an organization that monitors human rights around the world (**10.8**). Menacing phrases jump out at us from a disorienting tangle of words: *You are next* and *Already told you.* The word *disappear* itself disappears. Dobkin took the texts from first-person accounts of political terror in El Salvador. By fragmenting and layering their words, she communicates the helplessness and terror felt by the victims in order to provoke a direct, emotional response from the pamphlet's target audience: potential supporters of Amnesty International.

However evocative the cover portion of Dobkin's design may be, inside the leaflet a certain amount of information would need to be presented, and presented clearly. One of the most important tasks of a graphic designer is to devise visual presentations that make potentially confusing information easier to grasp. The effect that design can have on our ability to get the information we

10.8 Joan Dobkin. Informational leaflet for Amnesty International. 1991.

NEW YORK TO NEW HAVEN

MONDAY TO FRIDAY, EXCEPT HOLIDAYS

Leave	Arrive	Leave	Arrive	Leave	Arrive
New York	New Haven	New York	New Haven	New York	New Haven
AM	AM	PM	PM	PM	PM
12:35	2:18	2:05	3:45	T 6:25	8:19
5:40	7:44	3:05	4:45	T 7:05	8:56
7:05	8:45	T 4:01	5:45	T 8:05	9:45
8:05	9:45	T 4:41	6:25	T 9:05	10:50
9:05	10:45	T 4:59	6:53	10:05	11:45
10:05	11:45	XT 5:02E	6:33	11:20	1:05
11:05	12:45	XT 5:20	7:08	12:35	2:18
12:05	1:45	X 5:42	7:26	....	....
1:05	2:45	XT 6:07E	7:46	....	....
PM	PM	PM	PM	PM	PM

SATURDAY, SUNDAY & HOLIDAYS

AM	AM	PM	PM	PM	PM
12:35	2:18	2:05	3:45	7:05	8:45
5:40	7:37	S 3:05	S 4:45	H 8:05	H 9:45
8:05	9:45	4:05	5:45	9:05	10:45
10:05	11:47	5:05	6:48	11:20	1:00
12:05	1:45	6:05	7:48	12:35	2:18
PM	PM	PM	PM	AM	AM

The service shown herein is operated by Metro-North Commuter R.R.

REFERENCE NOTES
Economy **off-peak** tickets are **not** valid on trains in shaded areas.
Check displays in G.C.T. for departure tracks.
E -Express
X-Does not stop at 125th Street.
S-Saturdays and Washington's Birthday only.
H-Sundays and Holidays only.
T-Snack and Beverage Service.
HOLIDAYS-New Year's Day, Washington's Birthday, Memorial Day, Independence Day, Labor Day, Thanksgiving and Christmas.

NEW YORK → NEW HAVEN
Grand Central Station

Monday to Friday, except holidays		Saturday, Sunday, and holidays	
Leaves New York	Arrives New Haven	Leaves New York	Arrives New Haven
12.35 am	2.18	12.35 am	2.18
5.40 am	7.44 am	5.40 am	7.37 am
7.05	8.45		
8.05	9.45	8.05	9.45
9.05	10.45		
10.05	11.45	10.05	11.47
11.05	12.45 pm		
12.05 pm	1.45	12.05 pm	1.45 pm
1.05	2.45		
2.05	3.45	2.05	3.45
3.05	4.45	3.05 Saturdays only	4.45
4.01	5.45	4.05	5.45
4.41	6.25		
4.59	6.53		
x 5.02 •	6.33	5.05	6.48
5.20 •	7.08		
5.42	7.26		
x 6.07 •	7.46	6.05	7.48
6.25	8.19		
7.05	8.56	7.05	8.45
8.05	9.45	8.05 Sundays only	9.45
9.05	10.50	9.05	10.45
10.05	11.45		
11.20	1.05 am	11.20	1.00 am
12.35 am	2.18	12.35 am	2.18

(Economy off-peak tickets are not valid on trains in boxed areas.)

X Express
• Does not stop at 125th Street
Holidays: New Year's Day, Washington's Birthday, Memorial Day, Independence Day, Labor Day, Thanksgiving and Christmas.

10.9 (left) Metro North Railroad. Schedule for the New York–New Haven line, c. 1989. (right) The same schedule as redesigned by Ani Stern and Edward Tufte, 1990.

need quickly and easily is well illustrated by the two train schedules (**10.9**). To the left is the schedule that the railroad company distributed for many years. To the right is the same schedule as redesigned by student Ani Stern and her instructor, noted graphic design expert Edward Tufte. The redesign acts as a criticism of the original, and comparing the two can teach us something about what distinguishes a successful design from a less successful one.

On the schedule to the left, only a small portion of the page is devoted to the actual departure and arrival times, which thus appear cramped and crowded. And yet this is the most important information the schedule has to convey! Train times across the day are split into three pairs of columns, so that the eye needs to follow a tricky serpentine path through them. Rush hour times are distinguished with a tinted ground, making them more difficult to read. Mysterious symbols crowd the schedule still further, and much space is wasted below in explaining them. Numerous ruled compartments give the impression of organization, but in fact they do little useful work. Weekend train times are set so far from the arrival and departure headings that it is not immediately clear how they are organized.

The redesign clears up all of these problems and more. The train times are presented in two pairs of columns, clearly separated: weekdays to the left, weekends and holidays to the right. Unnecessary ruled lines are eliminated, and many of the annotations are taken up into the schedule itself. The colon in time listings has been replaced with a visually simpler period.

A **layout** is a designer's blueprint for an extended work in print such as a book or a magazine. It includes such specifications as the dimensions of the page, the width of the margins, the sizes and styles of type for text and headings, the style and placement of running heads or feet (lines at the top or bottom of the page that commonly give the chapter or part title and page number), and many other elements. The layout of this book, for example, places a single column of text asymmetrically on the page, leaving a slender outer column (for captions) and a narrow inner margin. Each spread (two facing pages) is thus fundamentally symmetrical, with left and right pages in mirror image. Illustrations are placed to relieve and even disguise this symmetry, and the page makeup artists took pains to arrange each spread in a pleasing asymmetrical composition.

Beginning in the 1980s, a number of designers began to experiment with more radical approaches that sacrificed easy legibility for visual appeal. Among the most controversial of these designers is David Carson. In magazines such as *Beach Culture* and *Ray Gun,* Carson rarely used a consistent layout, preferring to create each spread as a new composition. Text might be scattered, run upside down or on an angle, printed over itself, or made to disappear into a photograph. One spread often continued over the page turn into the next, creating a free-flowing, cinematic feel.

The spread illustrated here opened a 1994 *Ray Gun* article on musician Morrissey (**10.10**), and it shows how David Carson turned traditional graphic design principles on their heads. The title of the article would normally be considered the most important typographic element, but Carson splits it up and sets it in small type, part vertically (mor- rissey) and part on a subtle diagonal (the loneliest monk). A quote from the musician, also fragmented and scattered, serves as the principal typographic focus. The photograph of the star, conventionally as important as the title, is cropped to hide half of his face and seems to be fading into invisibility. To detractors who claim that his work is chaotic and illegible, Carson points out that legibility and communication are not the same thing. Communication begins by attracting and engaging the viewer's attention. Readers attracted to the mood of the design will be willing to make an effort to decipher its message.

10.10 David Carson, art director, and Chris Cuffaro, photographer. "Morrissey the Loneliest Monk," *Ray Gun,* 1994.

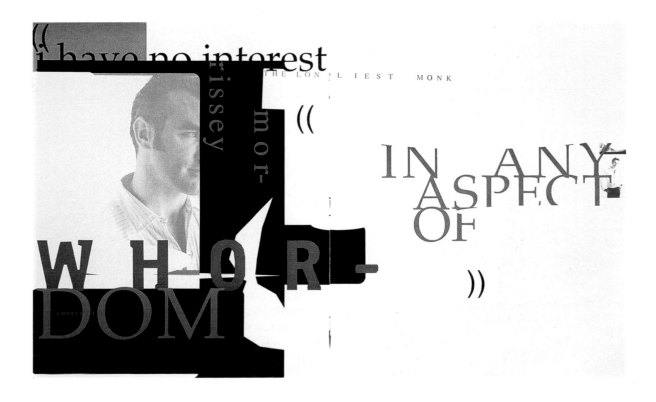

WORD AND IMAGE

Among the services offered by early printers in the 15th century was the design and printing of single sheets called broadsides. Handed out to town dwellers and posted in public spaces, broadsides argued political or religious causes, told of recent events, advertised upcoming festivals and fairs, or circulated woodcut portraits of civic and religious leaders. They were the direct ancestors not only of advertising and posters but also of leaflets, brochures, newspapers, and magazines.

With the development of color lithography in the 19th century, posters came into their own as the most eye-catching form of advertising, for color printing was not yet practical in magazines or newspapers, and television was still a hundred years away. Among the most famous of all 19th-century posters are those created by Toulouse-Lautrec for the cabarets and dance halls of Paris (10.11). In this poster for a famous dance hall called the Moulin Rouge, the star performer, La Goulue, is shown dancing the cancan, while in the foreground rises the wispy silhouette of another star attraction, Valentin, known as "the boneless one." The flattened, simplified forms and the dramatically cropped composition show the influence of Japanese prints, then so popular in Europe. Lautrec's posters were immediately recognized as collectors' items, and instructions circulated secretly for detaching them from the kiosks on which they were pasted.

An extraordinary flowering of graphic design occurred during the decade following the Russian Revolution of 1917, when an art movement called **Constructivism** called on artists to be actively involved in creating the new society for which all had such high hopes. Constructivists believed that instead of making paintings and sculpture for an elite audience, artists should apply their skills to designing posters, magazines, theatrical productions, industrial products, and other useful objects. Naturally, they believed that a new and

10.11 (left) Henri de Toulouse-Lautrec. *La Goulue at the Moulin Rouge.* 1891. Poster, lithograph printed in four colors; 6'2⅖" × 3'9¹³⁄₁₆".
The Metropolitan Museum of Art, New York.

10.12 (right) Vladimir and Georgii Stenberg. Poster for *Nepobedimye (The Unvanquished).* 1928. Offset lithography, 39⅜ × 28⅜".
The Museum of Modern Art, New York.

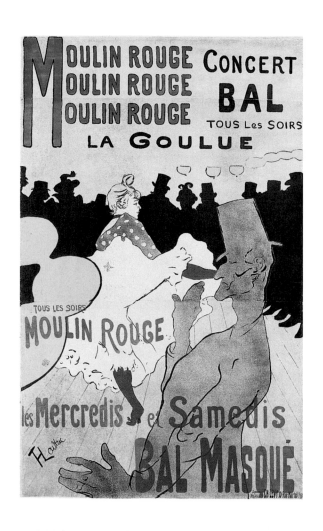

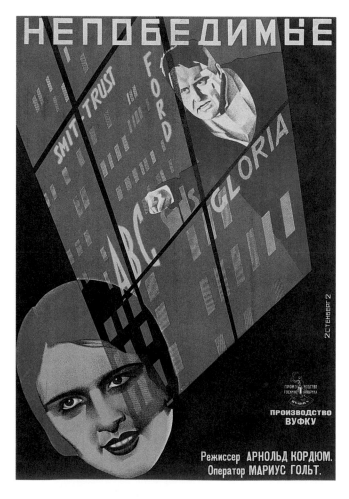

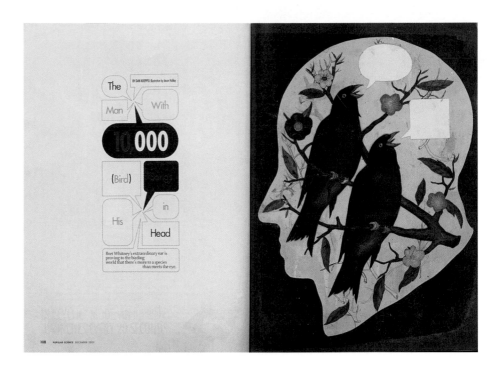

10.13 Jason Holley, illustrator, and Dirk Barnett, designer. Opening spread of "The Man with 10,000 Bird Songs in His Head," *Popular Science,* December 2003.

advanced society could only be brought about by the newest and most advanced art, and so the radical art trends of the day were suddenly applied to everyday concerns, as in this bold film poster designed by the brothers Vladimir and Georgii Stenberg, who had originally been trained as sculptors (**10.12**). Such artistic freedom and optimism were not to last, however. During the 1930s, the Soviet government came to view advanced art with distrust. Independent artists' groups were abolished, and the government decreed that all artists must now work in a clear, easy-to-understand, realistic style. Those suspected of resisting risked imprisonment and death.

In a poster, word and image are inseparable. Toulouse-Lautrec and the Stenberg brothers integrated letter forms into their designs as expressive elements, just as David Carson and Joan Dobkin did earlier. An illustration, in contrast, is an image created separately to accompany words. It may help readers imagine what the words are describing, or it may simply provide visual interest and appeal. Many of the works of art included in this book were created as illustrations. Examples include Sahibdin's intricate imagining of an episode from the Hindu epic the *Ramayana* (3.15) and the Limbourg brothers' exquisite winter scene from *Les Très Riches Heures* (16.20). As we saw in Chapter 8, the earliest extant printed book, a 9th-century copy of the Diamond Sutra, opens with a woodblock illustration (8.2), and Albrecht Dürer issued his *Apocalypse* prints as illustrations to the biblical text (8.3).

Jason Holley's illustration for an article in the magazine *Popular Science* shows how illustrator and designer can work together even as their creations remain distinct (**10.13**). Holley was commissioned to illustrate an article about a man who could identify birds by their song—not just the species of bird, but the actual individual bird itself, an extraordinary accomplishment. The article was titled "The Man with 10,000 Bird Songs in His Head." Holley responded with a silhouette of a man's head that opens onto the sky. In it, we see what he hears. Two identical birds are perched on a flowering branch. Speech balloons, familiar from comic strips, symbolize their song. But instead of resorting to words or notes or some other indication of sounds, Holley used a purely visual means, shape, to indicate that the birds' songs are different from one another: one bird warbles a square, the other sings an oval. On the facing page, designer Dirk Barnett picked up on Holley's idea by setting the title of the story in a series of speech balloons.

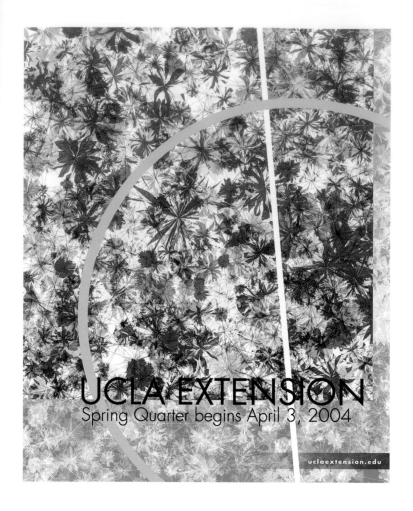

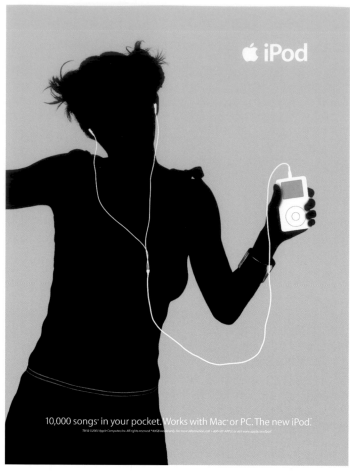

10.14 (left) John Maeda. Cover for UCLA Extension Spring Quarter Catalog. 2004. Courtesy John Maeda, MAEDASTUDIO.

10.15 (right) TBWA\Chiat\Day. iPod silhouette advertisement campaign. 2004.

Holley created his illustration using a traditional medium, paint on wood. It was photographed for reproduction, just as any other traditional work of art would be. John Maeda's cover design for a University of California course catalog, in contrast, was created on the computer (**10.14**). Many if not almost all designers today work on the computer. Maeda distinguishes himself, however, in that he relies very little on commercial software. Instead, he writes his own code. To rely on off-the-shelf software, he has said, is to accept the limits of someone else's imagination, and he has urged all designers and artists to learn programming skills.

For all their technological sophistication, Maeda's designs are known for their clarity and simplicity. Here, a kaleidoscopic jumble of colorful translucent shapes suggests flowers without actually depicting them. Set over it are a straight line and an arc. Elementary symbols of geometry, they are also the basic materials of the sans-serif font that Maeda selected for the title. We might interpret the contrasting elements of the cover as evoking the principal divisions of knowledge: mathematics and science on the one hand, and the arts and humanities on the other. Less grandly, we could see them as symbols of nature and human ordering, or simply of spring and studies.

In addition to his work as a graphic designer and artist, Maeda teaches at the Massachusetts Institute of Technology, where he is currently co-director of an experimental research program called SIMPLICITY. The goal of the program is develop ways for powerful technologies to be elegant in design and easy to use. In Maeda's vision, technology should be pleasurable, not intimidating. As an example of elegance and ease combined with power, the SIMPLICITY program points to iPod, the portable digital music player from Apple. The iPod was launched in 2001, but for the first two years it sold only moderately well. It was not until an advertising campaign known as iPod Silhouette appeared that sales skyrocketed (**10.15**). The black silhouettes of young people dancing against neon-colored backgrounds to music they heard over a handheld white iPod were graphically bold, clear, and simple. The minimal text and Apple logo were also set in white, linking them clearly with the product. Realized as posters, billboards, and television commercials, the advertisements stood out easily in cluttered visual environments, and they conveyed an image of unselfconscious enjoyment that appealed to a broad public.

MOTION AND INTERACTIVITY

With the development of film and television, graphic design was set in motion. Words and images worked together in film titles, television program titles, and advertisements, all of which needed to be designed. With the digital revolution, a new element was added for designers to work with, interactivity—the possibility of give and take between users and technology by means of an interface.

When episodes of *The Day Today*, a popular British television comedy from the 1990s, were released on digital video disk (DVD), an interactive opening menu sequence was needed so that viewers could choose which episode they wanted to watch (**10.16**). *The Day Today* was a satirical show that spoofed television programs devoted to current affairs. With a wickedly accurate ear and a keen eye for detail, *The Day Today* mocked everything about news programs, including the high-speed, high-tech, overly dramatic graphics that they used. In creating the opening menu, designer Adam Parry at Framestore Design picked up on this aspect of the show. Upon loading the disk, viewers are treated to a sort of bar graph run amok. A single yellow bar zigs and zags at high speed through a gridded, three-dimensional space that is constantly shifting its orientation. Each time the bar pauses at an absurdly labeled graph, an episode choice is displayed. When the bar reaches the end of its over-excited path, eight colored bars spring up to form a three-dimensional graph pointing to the words *Episode 6*, the final episode on the disk.

As we have seen, graphic design can reveal information by organizing facts or data in a visually coherent way. The train schedules discussed earlier are examples of this (see 10.9). Both take the facts of arrival and departure times and arrange them so that we can more easily retrieve the information

10.16 Adam Parry, Framestore Design. Opening menu sequence for disk 1 of the DVD release of *The Day Today*. Interactive digital video animation.

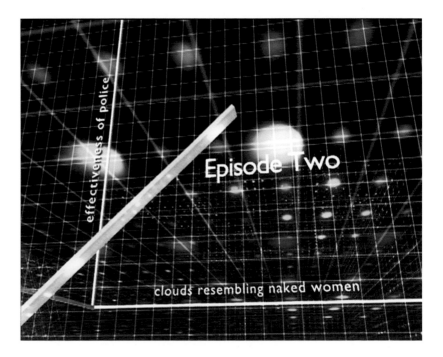

we need. The redesigned schedule reveals even more information than the original schedule does, for it shows the relationship between weekday and weekend train times. The original schedule is not arranged in a way that makes this information visible. We can see these same principles at work in an interactive setting on a Web site called *Graffiti Archaeology* (**10.17**). Like the train schedules, *Graffiti Archaeology* takes isolated facts—in this case individual photographs—and sets them in a structure that reveals the information they contain.

Designed by Cassidy Curtis, *Graffiti Archaeology* makes visible the evolution of graffiti sites over time as graffiti writers paint on top of each other's work. To the left is a list of sites, grouped by general area. When a site is selected, all of the available images for it are loaded onto the screen, with the most recent layer displayed on top. A graphic display at the bottom of the screen shows how many layers of photographs are available and situates them on a time line. Moving backward in time, we can peel back layer after layer of imagery to see what is hidden underneath. At the lower left, zoom controls and a navigator allow us to examine images in greater detail.

One special challenge for interaction designers is how to create visual clarity from the vast quantities of data that computers are capable of processing. W. Bradford Paley takes up this challenge in TextArc, a program that displays the entire text of a book on a single screen and allows users to explore relationships between its words (**10.18**). Paley conceived TextArc as a tool that would allow a user to quickly gain some understanding of the contents of an unknown text—a business report, for example. In the illustration here, TextArc has displayed the text to *Alice's Adventures in Wonderland.* The entire text appears twice, in two concentric spirals. The outer spiral reproduces the book line-for-line (the font is a single pixel in height). The inner spiral consists of each word in the book at readable size. Words that appear more than once in the text are set in the inner oval-shaped field. Their exact position there is determined by where in the text they occur. Frequently used words are displayed brighter than less frequently used words, so that merely by loading

10.17 Cassidy Curtis. *Graffiti Archaeology.* 2004–present. Interactive Web site. Web page illustrated is layer 17 of the graffiti site eastZ, featuring works by ZEROS, AWAKE, and anonymous artists.

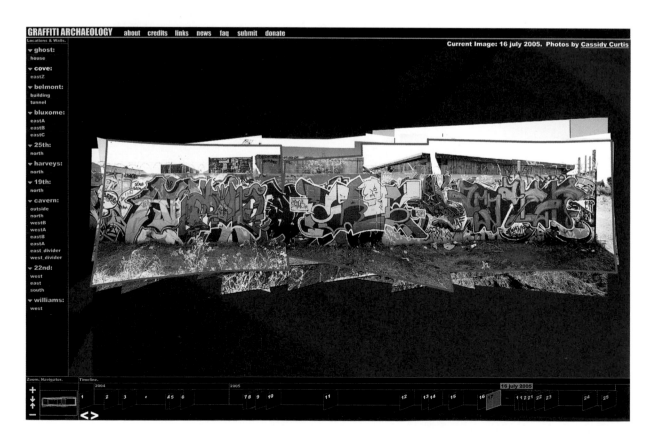

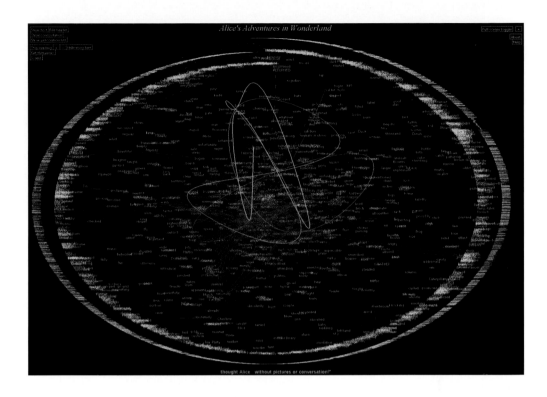
Alice's Adventures in Wonderland

10.18 W. Bradford Paley. *A TextArc of 'Alice's Adventures in Wonderland.'* TextArc tool created by W. Bradford Paley, 2003.

Alice's Adventures in Wonderland into TextArc we would know that Alice, Hatter, Queen, Gryphon, Rabbit, and Duchess are important personages in the story. By selecting individual words or sentences and by working with a series of menus, we can envision the many verbal relationships of the novel. For example, selecting a word from the field causes orange lines to radiate from it to each place in the inner spiral of words where it belongs, while each line that it appears in turns green in the outer spiral. TextArc can also simply "read" the text from beginning to end, a slow but visually fascinating process that illuminates key words, associations, locations, and relationships as they pass by.

Although they are working with the most advanced technology of the day, designers such as Curtis and Paley are actually quite conservative, for their work embraces the principles of visual elegance and communicative clarity that have been at the core of graphic design since anonymous scribes first developed writing.

RELATED RESOURCES ONLINE

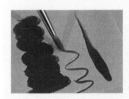

For more information, definitions, interactive activities, Web links, and videos related to the "Two-Dimensional Media" material covered in this part, please go to **www.mhhe.com/lwa8.**

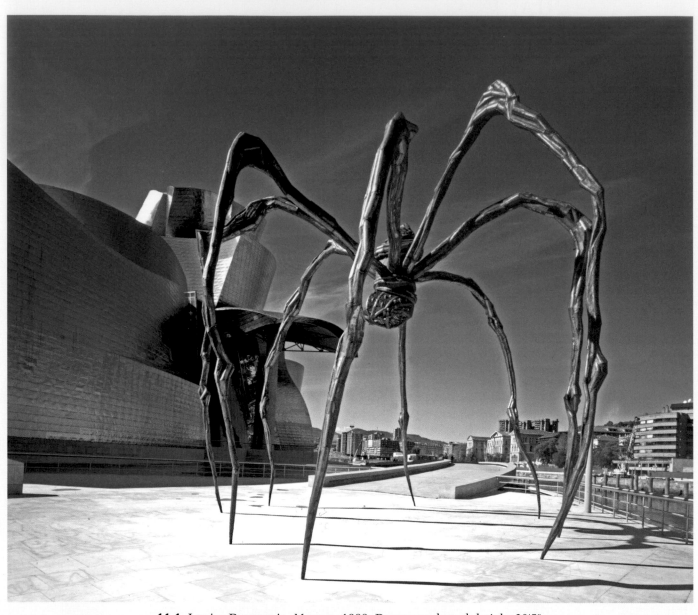

11.1 Louise Bourgeois. *Maman*. 1999. Bronze and steel, height 30'5".
Guggenheim Museum Bilbao, Bilbao, Spain.

PART FOUR
THREE-DIMENSIONAL MEDIA

CHAPTER ELEVEN

SCULPTURE AND INSTALLATION

Visitors arriving at the Guggenheim Museum Bilbao find it guarded by a very strange and unsettling presence: a 30-foot-tall bronze sculpture of a spider (**11.1**). Even less expected is the spider's name: *Maman*, French for "mom." For the artist Louise Bourgeois, *Maman* is a metaphor for her own mother as seen through a child's eyes—awesomely tall, protective, patient, and skilled. Perhaps the association of mother and spider was born from the strange logic of dreams. Bourgeois' mother wove and repaired tapestries for a living; a female spider spins a web to provide for herself and a cocoon to protect her young. Viewers make their own associations and explore their own feelings as they circle the bronze figures, or wander into the open cage of *Maman's* cascading legs, or gaze upward at the compact body with its clutch of eggs suspended high overhead.

Circling, wandering into, gazing up—sculpture confronts us with the third dimension, with the concept of *depth*. This seems like an easy and obvious point, but there is more to it than you might imagine. Our everyday lives are so flooded with images from the media that we have grown used to adjusting our perceptions of depth to compensate. We see images of people on the movie screen or on television, photographs of people in newspapers and magazines. Even though these are, in reality, two-dimensional images, we understand the people to be full-bodied and three-dimensional. This correction for depth becomes automatic, and we don't have to think about it.

As we approach sculpture, however, we might suspend this visual habit and train ourselves to be more *actively* aware of depth, for a heightened perception of the third dimension is essential to our full appreciation of sculpture. The experience of looking at a flat painting on a wall—or a photograph in an art book—is quite unlike the experience of walking up to a freestanding sculpture, circling it, observing it from various viewpoints. As an exercise, you might pick up a nearby object. It almost doesn't matter what it is—a desk lamp, stapler, telephone, notebook—all will do. Rotate it slowly in a complete 360-degree turn, watching the forms shift. From some angles it probably looks quite foreign. From others, it looks more characteristic. But notice that only when you integrate many visual perceptions can you begin to understand the form as a whole.

Sculpture has one of the longest histories of any art, and yet it is especially exciting today. One reason for the vitality of contemporary sculpture is the use of materials and techniques that were unaccepted or even unheard of a century ago. In this chapter, for example, we will encounter works not only in metal, wood, and stone but also in fiberglass, fabric, fluorescent light, and even flowers. Another reason is sculpture's recent offshoot, installation, which embraces an entire space as a work of art.

METHODS AND MATERIALS OF SCULPTURE

There are four basic methods for making a sculpture: modeling, casting, carving, and assembling. **Modeling** and **assembling** are considered additive processes. The sculptor begins with a simple framework or core or nothing at all and *adds* material until the sculpture is finished. **Carving** is a subtractive process in which one starts with a mass of material larger than the planned sculpture and *subtracts,* or takes away, material until only the desired form remains. **Casting** involves a mold of some kind, into which liquid or semiliquid material is poured and allowed to harden.

Let us consider each of these methods in more detail and look as well at some of the materials they are used with.

Modeling

Modeling is familiar to most of us from childhood. As children we experimented with play dough or clay to construct lopsided figures of people and animals. For sculpture, the most common modeling material is clay, an earth substance found in most parts of the world. Wet clay is wonderfully pliable; few can resist the temptation to squeeze and shape it. As long as clay remains wet, the sculptor can do almost anything with it—add on more and more clay to build up the form, gouge away sections, pinch it outward, scratch into it with a sharp tool, smooth it with the hands. But when a clay form has dried and been fired (heated to a very high temperature), it becomes hard. Fired clay, sometimes called by the Italian name *terra cotta,* is surprisingly durable. Much of the ancient art that has survived was formed from this material.

Gesturing exquisitely with one hand, the other hand posed on her knee, this graceful female figure was modeled of clay over a thousand years ago by an artist of the Mayan civilization in Mesoamerica (**11.2**). The figure was built up by hand, then sensitively worked with tools of stone and wood (the Maya did not know metal). Gentle, rounded forms predominate, from the masses of the head and body to the heavy ornaments and elaborate hairdo. Like much ancient art, this sculpture survived as part of a group of objects buried in a tomb.

In some ways modeling is the most direct of sculpture methods. The workable material responds to every touch, light or heavy, of the sculptor's fingers. Sculptors often use clay modeling in the same way that painters traditionally have used drawing, to test ideas before committing themselves to the finished work. As long as the clay is kept damp, it can be worked and reworked almost indefinitely.

Casting

In contrast to modeling, casting seems like a very *indirect* method of creating a sculpture. Sometimes the sculptor never touches the final piece at all. Metal, and specifically bronze, is the material we think of most readily in relation to casting. Bronze can be superheated until it flows, will pour freely into the tini-

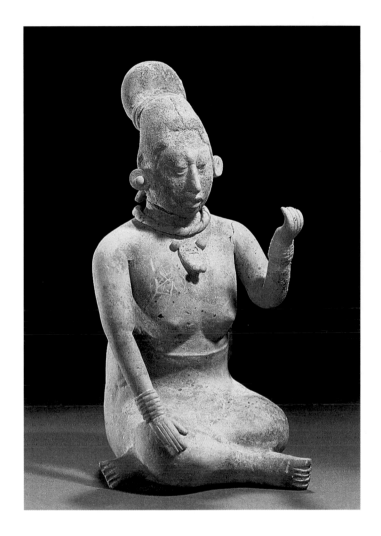

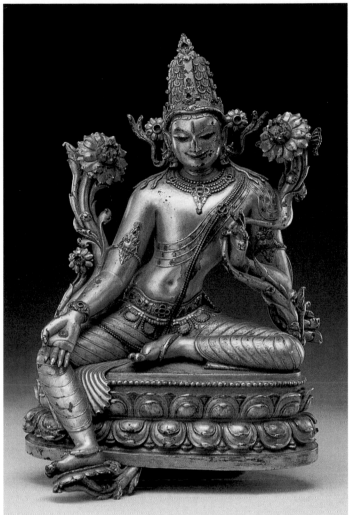

est crevices and forms, and then hardens to extreme durability. Even for a thin little projection, like a finger, there is no fear of it breaking off. Also through casting, the sculptor can achieve smooth rounded shapes and a glowing, reflective surface, such as we see in this Indian sculpture of the bodhisattva Avalokiteshvara (**11.3**). Cast in bronze and then gilded (covered with a thin layer of gold), the smooth, gleaming surfaces of the body contrast with the minutely detailed jewelry, hairstyle, and flowers, demonstrating the ability of metal to capture a full range of effects. In Buddhism, bodhisattvas are those spiritually advanced beings who have chosen to delay their own buddhahood in order to help others. Avalokiteshvara is the most popular and beloved of these saintly presences. He is depicted here in princely garb, his hair piled high, seated in a relaxed and sinuous pose on a stylized lotus throne. Lotus blossoms, symbols of purity, twine upward beside him.

The most common method for casting metal is called the **lost-wax** process, sometimes known by its French name, *cire perdue*. Dating back to the third millennium B.C.E., the basic concept is simple and ingenious. We describe it here as it was practiced by the African sculptors of ancient Ife to create heads such as the one illustrated in Chapter 2 (see 2.16).

11.2 (left) *Figurine of a Voluptuous Lady.* Maya, Late Classic period, 700–900 C.E. Ceramic with traces of pigment, height 8¾".
The Art Museum, Princeton University.

11.3 (right) *The Bodhisattva Avalokiteshvara,* from Kurkihar, Bihar, Central India. Pala Dynasty, 12th century. Gilt bronze, height 10".
Patna Museum, Patna.

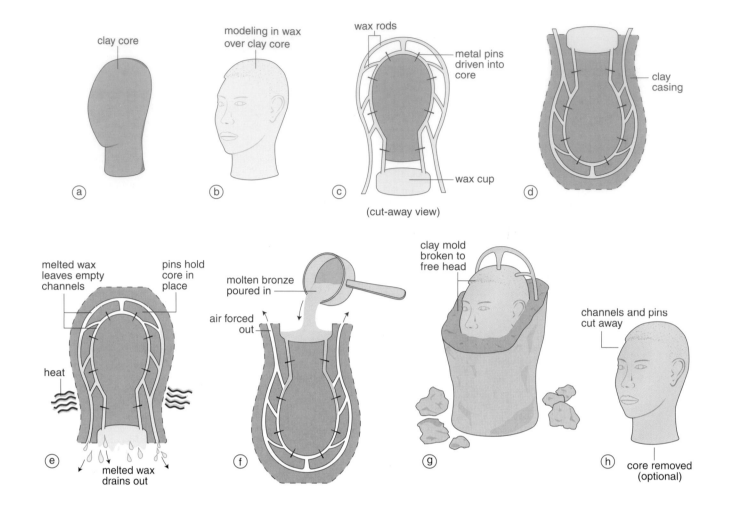

11.4 The lost-wax casting process.

First, a core is built up of specially prepared clay (**11.4**, a). Over this core, the sculptor models the finished head in a layer of wax (b). When the sculpture is complete, wax rods and a wax cup are attached to it to form a sort of "arterial system," and metal pins are driven through the wax sculpture to the core inside (c). The whole is encased in specially prepared clay (d). When the clay has dried, it is heated so that the wax melts and runs out (hence "lost wax") and the clay hardens (e). The lost wax leaves a head-shaped void inside the block. Where the wax rods and block were, channels and a depression called a pouring cup remain. The pins hold the core in place, preserving the space where the wax was. Next, the **mold** is righted, and molten metal is poured into the pouring cup. The metal enters the mold through the channels, driving the air before it (f). When the metal bubbles up through the air channels, it is a sign that the mold is probably filled. Metal, therefore, has *replaced* the wax, which is why casting is known as a replacement method. When the metal has cooled, the mold is broken apart, freeing the head (g). The channels, now cast in metal as well, are cut away, the clay core is removed (if desired), holes or other flaws are patched or repaired, and the head is ready for smoothing and polishing (h).

A sculpture cast in this way is unique, for the wax original is destroyed in the process. Standard practice today is a variation called indirect or investment casting, which allows multiples to be made. In this method, the artist finishes the sculpture completely in clay, plaster, or other material. A mold is formed around the solid sculpture (today's foundries use synthetic rubber for this mold). The mold is removed from the sculpture in sections, then reassembled. Melted wax is painted or "slushed" inside the mold to build up an inner layer about ³⁄₁₆″ thick. After it has hardened, this wax casting is removed from the mold and checked against the original sculpture for accuracy: It should be an exact duplicate, but hollow. The wax casting is fitted with wax rods, pierced with pins, then encased in solid plaster, which both fills and surrounds it, just as in 11.4d. This plaster is called the *investment*. From this point on, the process is the same: The investment is heated so that the wax melts and runs out, metal is poured into the resulting void, and the investment is broken away to free the casting. The key difference is that the mold that makes the wax casting is reusable, thus multiple wax versions of an original can be prepared and multiple bronzes of a sculpture cast. All but the simplest sculptures are cast in sections, which are then welded together. (Imagine two halves of an eggshell being cast separately in metal, then welded together to form a hollow metal egg.) As with prints (see Chapter 8), each casting is considered an original work of art, and a limited edition may be declared and controlled.

Although metal has historically been the most common material used for casting art objects, any material that can be poured and then hardened will do. For example, we cast small sculptures every time we make a tray of ice cubes, pouring water into a mold, freezing the water until it is solid, then unmolding the forms. Plastic resins and other synthetic materials developed by modern chemistry have opened up new possibilities for sculptors. Luis Jiménez cast *Vaquero* in fiberglass (**11.5**). Widely employed commercially for such products as surfboards, boat hulls, and automobiles, fiberglass is strong and yet lightweight. Jiménez believes in using contemporary materials for contemporary art. He even paints his sculptures using acrylic urethane enamels, the industrial "wet-look" paints used for cars.

Vaquero was cast in sections and then assembled around a steel armature, which supports and strengthens the sculpture from inside. Without such an armature, the daredevil composition wouldn't be possible—the statue wouldn't be stable enough to stand on its own. Set on a pedestal in front of the Smithsonian American Art Museum in Washington, D.C., *Vaquero* pays tribute to the American West in its wildest days, while also reminding us that cowboy culture originated in Mexico. Our vocabulary reflects these origins clearly: *Corral, lariat,* and *lasso* are Spanish words that were adopted into English.

11.5 Luis Jiménez. *Vaquero.* Modeled 1980, cast 1990. Acrylic urethane, fiberglass, steel armature, height 16'7". Smithsonian American Art Museum, Washington, D.C.

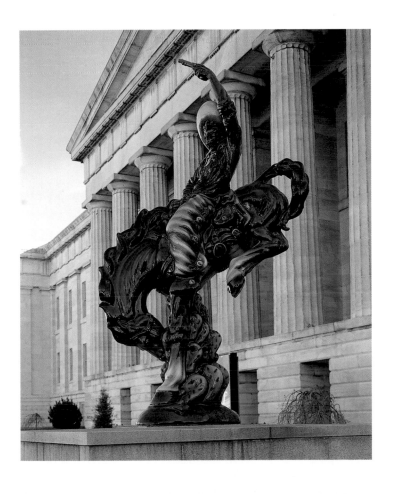

Carving

Carving is more aggressive than modeling, more direct than casting. In this process the sculptor begins with a block of material and cuts, chips, and gouges away until the form of the sculpture emerges. Wood and stone are the principal materials for carving, and both tend to resist the sculptor's tools. When approaching the block to be carved, the sculptor must study the grain of the material—its fibrous or crystalline structure—so as to work *with* that material. Any attempt to violate the grain could result in a failed sculpture.

A poem sung in West Africa about the Yoruba sculptor Olowe of Ise praises him for carving the hardest wood as though it were as soft as melon, and looking at the spectacular bowl illustrated here, we can sense the justice of the compliment (**11.6**). The lid of the bowl, crowned by four dancing women with towering crested hairstyles, is carved from a single piece of wood. Even more astonishing, the base—including the bowl, the tall kneeling woman presenting it, and the numerous shorter supporting figures—is also carved from a single piece. As though that were not impressive enough, Olowe permitted himself a further bravura touch by carving a freely rolling head *inside* the cage formed by the supporting figures beneath the bowl.

Types of wood and stone vary considerably in their suitability for carving. Jade, for example, is too hard to be carved at all and can be shaped only through abrasion—patient rubbing with an even harder stone such as quartzite or diamond. Artists throughout history have learned to work with the natural properties of available materials and to master the capabilities of available tools. The ancient Olmec sculptors of Mesoamerica understood well the properties of the local basalt that they favored for monumental works (**11.7**). A volcanic stone, fine-grained but exceedingly hard, basalt does not lend itself to highly detailed work. Olmec sculptors instead devised a broad style of plain surfaces and subtle modeling. Using stone tools—probably quartz blades—they carved numerous colossal heads such as this one. Among the most famous works of Mesoamerican art, the heads are thought to be portraits of rulers.

11.6 (left) Olowe of Ise. *Bowl with Figures.* Early 20th century. Wood, pigment; height 25". National Museum of African Art. Smithsonian Institution, Washington, D.C.

11.7 (right) *Colossal Head.* Olmec, 1500–300 B.C.E. Basalt, height c. 8'. Museo de Antropología, Veracruz.

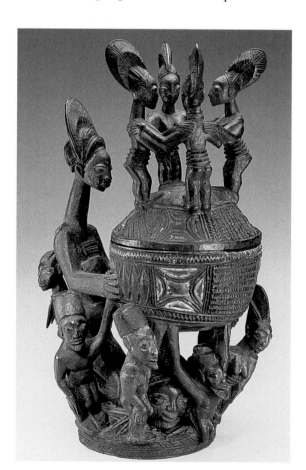

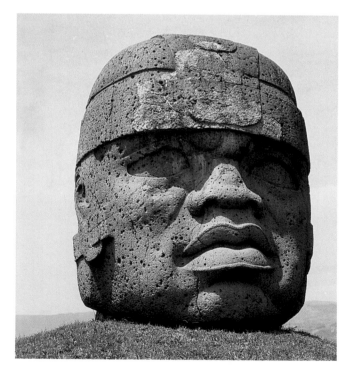

OLOWE OF ISE

18??–1938

OLOWE OF ISE was born in the Nigerian town of Efon Alaye, less than fifty miles from Ife, the holy city of the Yoruba. We do not know the date of Olowe's birth; since he was a respected elder at his death in 1938, he was probably born between 1850 and 1880. We also know little about his training as an artist, although we assume that he apprenticed to an older sculptor before establishing himself as a master.

By the end of the 19th century, Olowe had moved to the royal city of Ise, where he became an emissary to the king. As an artist who was given commissions by kings and religious groups throughout the easternmost Yoruba lands, Olowe was well qualified for the position. Olowe also acted as court sculptor for the king of Ise, and he supervised a workshop in the palace that employed a dozen assistants.

During his lifetime, Olowe of Ise's work was known in England as well as in Nigeria. One of his elaborate wooden bowls with figures (similar to Figure 11.6) was brought back to England by a British visitor around 1900. In 1924, a pair of doors sculpted by Olowe and belonging to the king of Ikere were displayed at the British Empire Exhibition in London. They depicted the king receiving the British colonial officer who was helping to impose British rule over the formerly independent Yoruba kingdoms. The king was persuaded to donate the doors to the British Museum, receiving in exchange an elaborate English chair he could use as a throne. He commissioned a new pair of doors from Olowe to replace them. Strange as it seems today, no one at the museum asked the king for the name of the artist who had carved the doors, and for the next twenty years they were attributed to an "unknown"

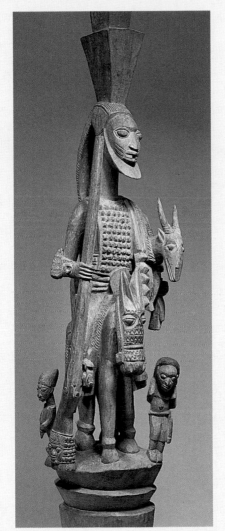

Yoruba artist. Many European collectors of African art even assumed that Yoruba artists worked in complete anonymity. Such notions were not challenged until Olowe of Ise was interviewed by a British researcher shortly before his death.

Like many prosperous Yoruba men of his generation, Olowe of Ise married several wives and had many children. His fourth wife, Oloju-ifun Olowe, was interviewed more than fifty years after his death. She was able to recite a praise poem, or *oriki*, in his honor. It includes the following lines:

> Olowe, my excellent husband . . .
> One who carves the hard wood
> of the *iroko* tree as though it
> were soft as a calabash.
> One who achieves fame with the
> proceeds of his carving . . .
> My lord, I bow down to you.
> Leader of all carvers . . .

There are no surviving photographs of Olowe of Ise, and no painted or sculpted artworks capture his physical likeness. Instead, the carved roof support illustrated here can be seen as revealing the basic character of this artist. Although it was once owned by a king, it is a metaphorical self-portrait of the artist as well as the patron, the visual and tactile equivalent of these descriptive lines from the *oriki* of Olowe of Ise:

> Outstanding leader in war.
> Emissary of the king.
> One with a mighty sword.
> Handsome among his peers.

Olowe of Ise. *Veranda Post with Mounted Hunter*. Before 1938. Wood, pigment; height 7'. Staatliches Museum für Völkerkunde, Munich.

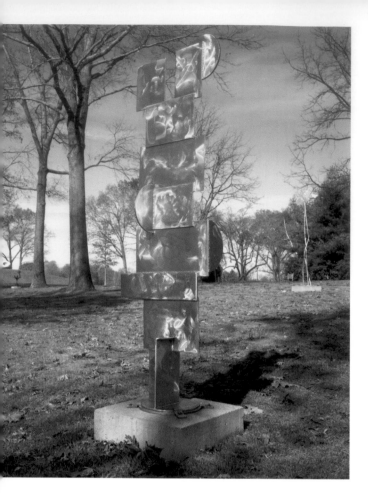

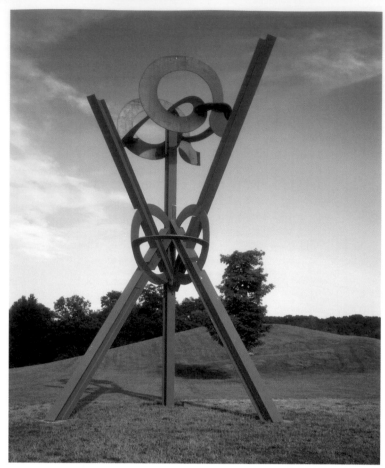

11.8 (left) David Smith. *XI Books and III Apples*. 1959. Stainless steel, height 7'10".
Storm King Art Center, Mountainville, New York.

11.9 (right) Mark di Suvero. *Origins*. 2001–2004. Painted steel, height 36'4".
Courtesy the artist, Spacetime C.C., and Paula Cooper Gallery, New York.

Assembling

Assembling is a process by which individual pieces or segments or objects are brought together to form a sculpture. Some writers make a distinction between assembling, in which parts of the sculpture are simply placed on or near each other, and constructing, in which the parts are actually joined together through welding, nailing, or a similar procedure. This book uses the term *assemblage* for both types of work.

The 20th-century American sculptor David Smith came to assemblage in an unusual way. While trying to establish himself as an artist, Smith worked as a welder. Later, when he began to concentrate on sculpture, he adapted his welding skills to a different purpose. His mature works broke new ground in both materials and forms (**11.8**). Smith's *XI Books and III Apples* is made of steel, a material closely identified with our modern era. Steel had been produced in small quantities since ancient times for such purposes as swords and armor, but only during the second half of the 19th century were technologies developed for mass producing the metal, making steel widely and cheaply available for the first time. The architecture of the 20th century would not have been possible without it. Assembled from basic geometric shapes welded together, *XI Books and III Apples* rises up before us like an odd but friendly being with no arms. Smith wanted his sculptures to be displayed out of doors, and he polished their surfaces so that they would blaze in the sunlight. The wild scribbling of the polishing markings contrasts with the calm geometry of the forms that Smith favored.

Steel is also the preferred material of contemporary sculptor Mark di Suvero (**11.9**). Di Suvero makes sculptures from steel I-beams, the same kind of girders that are used in construction, and he assembles them by bolting the elements together, just as construction workers bolt together the steel skeleton of a building. Di Suvero explores ideas for his sculptures in loose, gestural drawings, and his finished works retain something of these drawings' improvisatory quality. The black element at the top of *Origins* resembles nothing so much as a giant doodle in steel, and the supporting I-beams seem as casually gathered together as a few sticks tied with twine. The effect is as though someone had come upon an abandoned construction site, picked up some of the materials that were lying about, worked them into a happy arrangement, and then continued on his way.

Numerous African cultures have long used assemblage in order to create meaningful objects. An example is this *Leopard Society Emblem* (**11.10**), from the Ejagham culture of southeastern Nigeria. The leopard is an animal admired for its speed, stealth, and lethal power. The Leopard Society is a secret, all-male organization that, according to Ejagham belief, draws its power from the leopard spirit. Each Ejagham community includes a Leopard Society lodge, where secret meetings are held and secret objects such as this emblem are displayed. The elements assembled in the emblem are symbolic, and they relate to various activities and roles of the society. The skulls and bones, for example, are the remains of animals eaten during the society's rituals. The slender palm-fiber brooms crossed over the center are like those used ceremonially to sweep away hostile magical substances. There are probably many more meanings to be discovered in the emblem, but the Ejagham have kept them secret.

Like the *Leopard Society Emblem*, Petah Coyne's *Untitled #1111 (Little Ed's Daughter Margaret)* is assembled from materials that we don't normally associate with sculpture (**11.11**). As in the African work, its individual components have meanings that contribute to a larger whole. Some of the meanings we may find by exploring associations that we bring to our experience of looking, while others probably remain private for the artist. Attached to the wall behind it by a hidden support, *Untitled #1111 (Little Ed's Daughter Margaret)* hovers before us like a presence, a human presence. Branches and silk flowers dipped in midnight blue wax droop downward, as do the heavy tassles on the headlike form near the top. Silk and satin ribbons, feathers, stuffed pheasants, empty bird skins, the remains of a gown, and a braid of hair slowly reveal

11.10 (left) *Leopard Society Emblem.* Ejagham culture. Late 19th–early 20th c. Animal bones, wood cane, raffia, vegetable fibers; 47⅛ × 41¾".
Princeton University Art Museum, Princeton, New Jersey.

11.11 (right) Petah Coyne. *Untitled #1111 (Little Ed's Daughter Margaret).* 2003–2004. Wax, fiberglass cast statuary, velvet, satin, ribbon, thread, PVC pipe and fittings, steel understructure, branches, fabricated branches, silk flowers, wire, hat pins, tassels, feathers, pumps, irrigation tubing, water, hair, black paint; height 11'.
Courtesy Galerie Lelong, New York.

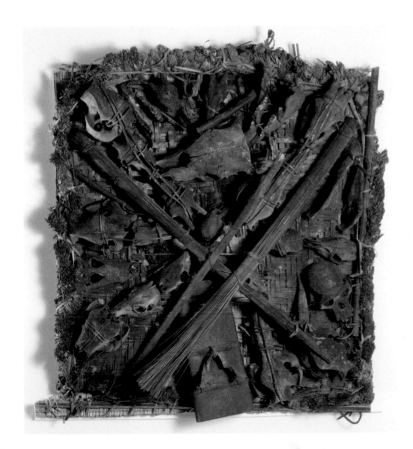

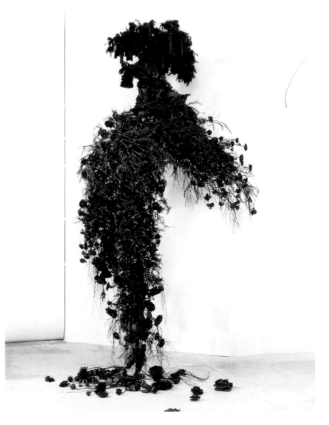

themselves to patient observers, who may also see droplets of water drip down the work: Hidden inside it is a fiberglass cast of a statue that "weeps" from time to time, as water pumped through tubing connected to its eyes overflows. *Untitled #1111 (Little Ed's Daughter Margaret)* is mournful and tragic, but perhaps also a little over-the-top; it is creepy and funny, sad and silly all at the same time.

SCULPTURE AND THE THIRD DIMENSION

Most of the sculptures we have looked at are in the round, or freestanding and completely finished on all sides. However, another category of sculpture, called **relief** sculpture, is meant to be viewed from one side only. Relief sculptures have three-dimensional depth, but they do not occupy space as independently as sculptures in the round. Often they are used to decorate architecture or functional objects.

If you have a nickel in your pocket, take it out and look at it. On the face you'll see a profile of Thomas Jefferson. The image is in **low relief,** sometimes called by the French name **bas-relief.** The subject projects very slightly from its background. Many kinds of flat surfaces serve as fields for low-relief sculpture—coins, tombstones, walls, decorative plates, book covers. The illustration here (**11.12**) depicts the lid of the sarcophagus of Pacal, a Mayan ruler who died in 683 C.E. Carved in low relief on a slab of limestone, the scene portrays the exact moment of the ruler's death as it was understood in Mayan belief. We easily recognize Pacal himself near the center. Knees drawn up, head tilted back, he is falling from life to death. The rest of the motifs, which at first glance seem merely decorative, are actually highly stylized representations of deities and cosmic symbols. They make it clear that Pacal is dying as a god and will rise as one after his death.

When a sculpture projects more boldly from the background, we call it **high relief.** To fit this category, the sculptured elements should project by at least half their depth, and parts of the figures may be in the round, unattached to the background as in this 7th-century monumental relief panel from a tem-

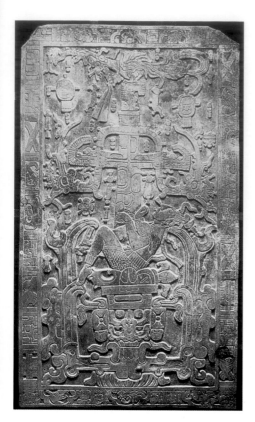

11.12 (above) Sarcophagus lid, from the Temple of Inscriptions, Palenque, Chiapas, Mexico. Maya, late Classic period, 684 C.E. Limestone, 12'2⅜" × 7'1⅜".

11.13 (right) *Durga Fighting the Buffalo Demons,* Mahishamardini Cave, Mamallapuram, Tamil Nadu, India.

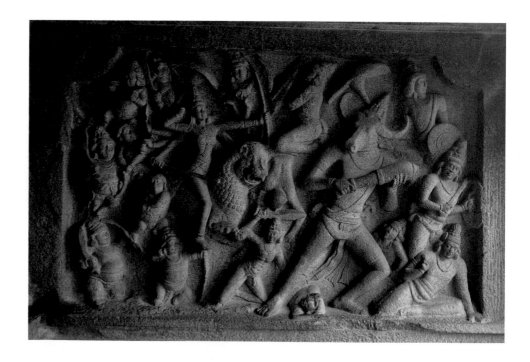

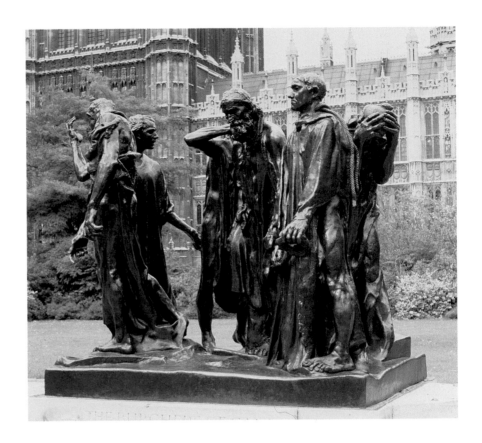

11.14 Auguste Rodin. *The Burghers of Calais*. 1884–85. Bronze, 6'10½" × 7'11" × 6'6". Palace of Westminster, London.

ple in Mamallapuram, India (**11.13**). The panel depicts a battle between the goddess Durga and the buffalo demon. To the left, eight-armed Durga, mounted on a lion, rushes forward with her victorious army. To the right, the buffalo demon and his supporters flee in defeat. The figures in this dynamic composition are all carved well away from the background, some considerably more than half-round. The panel belongs to an extraordinary Indian tradition in which entire temples were cut directly into cliffsides or carved from gigantic boulders. Interior and exterior—columns, doorways, arched ceilings, statues, and reliefs—were hewn from living rock, making of the temple itself a gigantic piece of walk-in sculpture.

Although we have already looked at several examples of sculpture in the round, it will be useful here to consider one work primarily from the standpoint of its complex interaction with space. Sculpture in the round exists wholly in our world. We can walk around it and see it from every angle. This is a terrific challenge to the sculptor's compositional ability, since every viewpoint must be under control. Even when there is a definite front and back, as there usually is in figurative sculpture, all viewpoints should be interesting. And the fact that the work looks different from every angle makes the observer's experience much richer.

An excellent example of sculpture in the round is Rodin's *The Burghers of Calais* (**11.14**). Rodin made this sculpture for public display in the city of Calais, in France, and it depicts an episode from the town's medieval history. Six men have offered to give their lives to ransom their city from the English, who hold it captive. Each of them faces certain death, but they confront their sacrifice in different ways. One is angry, one sorrowful, one merely resigned, and so on—but each is unique, facing a personal tragedy amid shared crisis. We can read the men's emotions from their various postures, facial expressions, and gestures. The six hostages march in an irregular circle, some determinedly erect, others drooping in despair. And the viewer must also walk in a circle, because there is no angle from which all faces are visible. Rodin's message is complex, so he expressed it in the complex form of sculpture in the round.

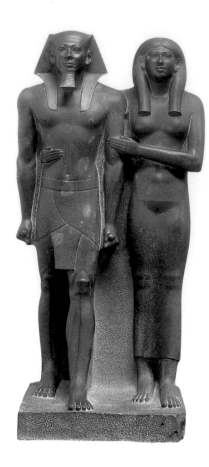

11.15 *Menkaure and Khamerernebty.* Egypt, c. 2490–2472 B.C.E. Greywacke, height 4'6½".
Courtesy Museum of Fine Arts, Boston.

THE HUMAN FIGURE IN SCULPTURE

A basic subject for sculpture, one that cuts across time and cultures, is the human figure. If you look back through this chapter, you will notice that almost all the representational works portray people. One reason, certainly, must be the relative permanence of the common materials of sculpture. Our life is short, and the desire to leave some trace of ourselves for future generations is great. Metal, terra cotta, stone—these are materials for the ages, materials mined from the earth itself. Even wood may endure long after we are gone.

From earliest times, rulers powerful enough to maintain a workshop of artists have left images of themselves and their deeds. The royal tombs of ancient Egypt, for example, included statues such as the one illustrated here of the pharaoh Menkaure and Khamerernebty, his Great Royal Wife (**11.15**). Portrayed with idealized, youthful bodies and similar facial features, the couple stand proudly erect, facing straight ahead. Although each has the left foot planted slightly forward, there is no suggestion of walking, for their shoulders and hips are level. Menkaure's arms are frozen at his sides, while his wife touches him in a formalized gesture of "belonging together." This formal pose is meant to convey not only the power of the rulers but also their serene, eternal existence. The pharaoh, after all, ruled as a "junior god" on earth and, at death, would rejoin the gods in immortality. Egyptian rulers must have been pleased with this pose, for their artists repeated it again and again over the next two thousand years.

A second reason for the many human forms portrayed in sculpture is a little more mysterious. We might call it "presence." Sculpture, as pointed out earlier in this chapter, exists wholly in our world, in three dimensions. To portray a being in sculpture is to bring it into the world, to give it a presence that is close to life itself. In the ancient world, statues were often believed to have an ambiguous, porous relationship to life. In Egypt, for example, the Opening of the Mouth ceremony that was believed to help a dead person reawaken in the afterlife was performed not only on his or her mummified body but also on his or her statue. In China, the tomb of the first emperor was "protected" by a vast army of terra-cotta soldiers, buried standing in formation (see 19.14). A famous Greek myth tells of the sculptor Pygmalion, who fell so in love with a statue that it came to life.

Among the human images that artists are most often asked to make present in the world through sculpture are those connected with religion and the spirit realm. A lovely example is this figure of the *Virgin and Child on the Crescent Moon* (**11.16**), carved of lime wood by Tilman Riemenschneider, one of the foremost German sculptors of the late Middle Ages. Mary stands in a gentle, informal S-curve, as though she might move at any moment. The infant Jesus is even more animated, and his body twists in a spiral motion. Like many artists of his time, Riemenschneider depicted Jesus unclothed and in motion in order to emphasize the completeness of his incarnation as a man. Just as the formal pose of the Egyptian rulers emphasizes their godly status, the informal pose of Mary and Jesus emphasizes their connection to humanity.

A similar contrast between the meanings of formal and informal poses can be seen in the art of Buddhism. As a perfected being, Buddha has liberated himself from the repeating cycle of life and time and exists in an eternal, unchanging realm. The formal symmetry of his typical seated pose reflects this idea well (see 2.28). Bodhisattvas, on the other hand, are more directly available to the human world and are commonly shown in a relaxed, informal pose (see 11.3). Buddhist priests, saints, and other role models of the past are also often brought into the world through statues. A touching example is this wooden statue of *Kuya Preaching* (**11.17**), by the Japanese sculptor Kosho. Kuya was a Buddhist monk who lived during the 10th century. He devoted his life to roaming the countryside and teaching people to chant the simple phrase

Namu Amida Butsu (Hail to Amida Buddha). Kosho beautifully captures the monk's endearing humility, but his stroke of artistic genius lies in the six small buddhas that issue from Kuya's mouth, one for each voiced syllable of the chant he taught to help people enter paradise: *na-mu-a-mi-da-bu-(tsu)*.

The human figure is also the most common subject of traditional African sculpture, yet in fact the sculptures rarely represent humans. Instead, they generally represent spirits of various kinds. This masterful carving by a Baule sculptor of a seated woman carrying a child on her back depicts a spirit spouse (**11.18**). Once again, a formal pose and an impassive face are used to express the dignity of an otherworldly being. Baule belief holds that each person has, in addition to an earthly spouse, a spirit spouse in the Other World. If this spirit spouse is happy, all is well. But an unhappy or jealous spirit spouse may cause trouble in one's life. A remedy is to give the spirit spouse a presence in this world by commissioning a statue (called a "person of wood"). The statue is made as beautiful as possible in order to encourage the spirit to take up residence within it, and it is placed in a household shrine and tended to with gifts and small offerings.

Portrayals of rulers, heroes and heroines, and religious or spirit figures unite the many sculptural traditions of the world. Western culture, however, is marked as well by a tradition of sculpting the human figure for its own sake and of finding the body to be a worthy subject for art. This we owe ultimately to the ancient Greeks. Cultivating the body through gymnastics and sport was an important part of Greek culture, and they admired their athletes greatly. (The Olympics, after all, were a Greek invention.) Not surprisingly, perhaps, they came to believe that the body itself was beautiful. From the many athletic bodies on view, sculptors derived an ideally beautiful body type, governed by harmonious proportions. They gave these idealized, perfected bodies to images of gods and mythological heroes, who were usually depicted nude, and

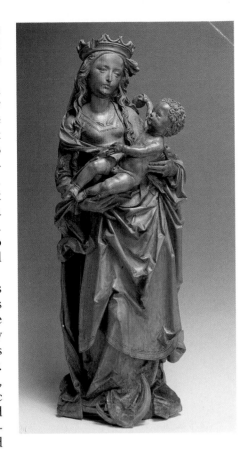

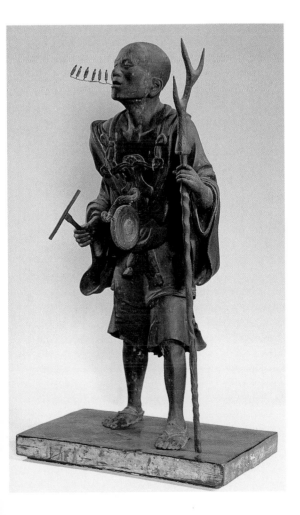

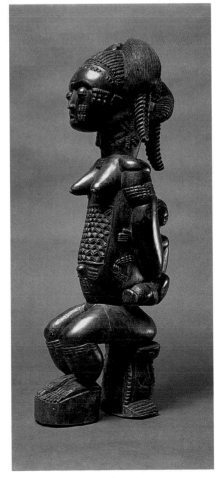

11.16 (above) Tilman Riemenschneider. *Virgin and Child on the Crescent Moon.* c. 1495. Lime wood, height 34⅛". Museum für Angewandte Kunst, Cologne.

11.17 (far left) Kosho. *Kuya Preaching.* Kamakura period, before 1207. Wood, with paint and inlaid eyes; height 46½". Rokuhara Mitsu-ji Temple, Kyoto.

11.18 (left) *Spirit Spouse*, from Ivory Coast. Baule, early 20th century. Wood, height 17⅛". University of Pennsylvania Museum, Philadelphia.

PRIMITIVISM

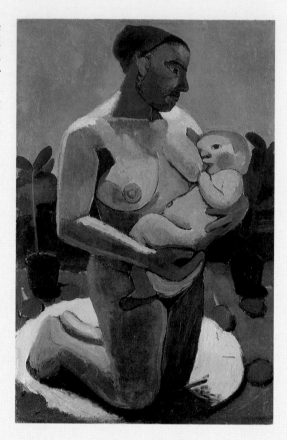

Looking back years later, the artists themselves disagreed on who was the first. Historians may never fully sort the matter out, but all agree that around 1906, in Paris, advanced young artists began to take an interest in African carvings. One of the first was the Fauve painter André Derain. Matisse and Picasso quickly followed suit, along with Brancusi and many others. The artists purchased their first examples of African sculpture in flea markets and antique shops. European colonial rule over Africa, consolidated at the turn of the 20th century, resulted in hundreds of carvings being imported as "curiosities." When the artists wanted to see more, they went to the museum. Not an art museum, for African carvings were not then considered to be art, but to a museum of ethnography, where sculptures, masks, utensils, weapons, ornaments, and other artifacts were jumbled together in dusty display cases. And yet, the young artists insisted, these carvings were art, and art of a very high order.

The "discovery" of African art was the culmination of several decades of interest in cultures outside of the European mainstream, beginning with the Impressionists' fascination with Japanese prints in the 1860s. (See Crossing Cultures: Japanese Prints, page 102.) More recently, exhibitions had been held in Paris of Islamic art (1904) and ancient Iberian art (1906)—art from the region of present-day Spain from the 5th and 6th centuries B.C.E. The decorative patterns of Islamic art had a lasting influence on Matisse, while Picasso went through a brief "Iberian" phase. African art was the next step, the latest and most radical reach outside of the West.

For artists seeking ways to break free of the tradition of European naturalism, African sculpture offered a seemingly limitless supply of ingenious solutions for abstracting the human face and form. Fascination with the beauty and power of African art quickly extended beyond Paris into advanced artistic circles across Europe, and it lasted for most of the first half of the 20th century. The interest in African art was more than formal, however. It was part of a larger, more complex, and more troubling phenomenon called primitivism. The word *primitive* refers to something that is less complex, less sophisticated, or less advanced than what it is being compared to—an earlier stage of it. Designating a culture as "primitive" excused European domination of it. Yet artists, at odds with the larger culture, admired all things primitive. Hoping to renew art by taking it back to its infancy, they looked to the "primitive" arts of Africa and Oceania, which they believed to be instinctive, unchanging, and primordial.

In *Kneeling Mother and Child*, Paula Modersohn-Becker portrays woman in her aspect of life-giver and nurturer, a basic force of nature itself. African sculptures often emphasize these female roles. The woman's monumentalized naked form has an earthbound, sculptural presence. The face especially is "primitivized"—painted in a purposefully unsophisticated, unbeautiful way.

The legacy of primitivism is complicated. Artists were instrumental in drawing serious attention to African and Oceanic art, yet they were completely wrong in thinking of it as primitive. A century later, we are still struggling to see African art on its own terms.

Paula Modersohn-Becker. *Kneeling Mother with a Child at Her Breast.* 1907. Oil on canvas, 44½ × 29⅛". Staatliche Museen zu Berlin, Preussischer Kulturbesitz, Nationalgalerie.

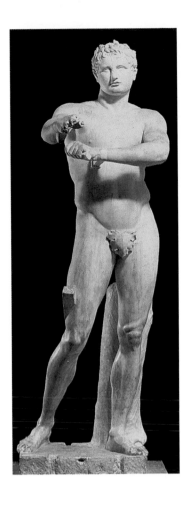

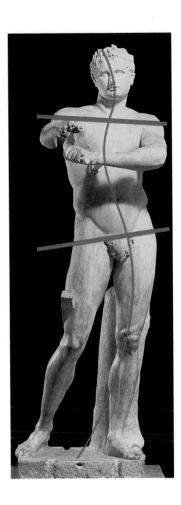

11.19 (far left) *Apoxyomenos (Scraper).* Roman copy of a bronze original by Lysippos, c. 320 B.C.E. Marble, height 6'8¾".
Musei Vaticani, Museo Pio Clementino, Rome.

11.20 (left) The dynamics of contrapposto.

11.21 (below) Michelangelo. *The Dying Slave.* 1513–16. Marble, height 7'6".
Musée du Louvre, Paris.

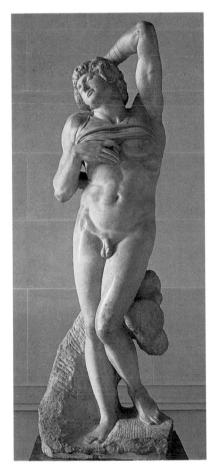

also to images of male athletes, who actually did train and compete unclothed. Finally, Greek artists developed a distinctive stance for their standing figures. Called **contrapposto,** it can be seen here in this statue of an athlete scraping himself off after a workout (**11.19**).

Contrapposto, meaning "counterpoise" or "counterbalance," sets the body in a gentle S-shaped curve through a play of opposites (**11.20**). Here, the athlete's weight rests on his left foot, so that his left hip is raised and his right leg is bent and relaxed. To counterbalance this, his right shoulder is raised. By portraying the dynamic interplay of a standing body at rest, contrapposto implies the potential for motion inherent in a living being. We can easily imagine that a moment earlier the athlete's weight was arranged differently, and that it will shift again a moment from now.

During the Renaissance, the study of Greek and Roman achievement brought the expressive, idealized body and the contrapposto stance back into Western art. We can see this clearly in such works as Michelangelo's *The Dying Slave* (**11.21**). The sculpture is one of a series of works that Michelangelo planned for the tomb of Pope Julius II, a project he never completed. We do not know what the figure represents: *The Dying Slave* is simply a name that has become attached to it over the centuries. A companion work depicting a muscular nude struggling against his bonds is known as *The Rebellious Slave*. The two statues may represent the arts in bondage after the death of Pope Julius, one of their great patrons. Less literally, they may also represent two reactions to the bondage of the soul, which longs for release from its earthly prison, the body. What is clear is that the figures are not meant to represent a specific person such as a saint or a martyr, but rather to express an idea or emotion through the body.

Since the Renaissance, the body has continued to serve as a subject through which sculptors express feelings and ideas about the human experience. One 20th-century sculptor who devoted most of his career to the human form was Henry Moore (**11.22**). Moore's particular fascination lay in abstracting the body to explore its visual harmonies with landscape, especially with the sea-smoothed rock formations of his native English coast. The reclining female figure here seems to be sheathed in some kind of close-fitting, elastic covering that she has "sculpted" from within by movements of her limbs. Her alert, vertical torso and head express the idea of consciousness rising out of the natural forms of the earth.

In contrast to Moore's soothing vision of our harmony with natural creation, the works of Polish sculptor Magdalena Abakanowicz suggest a more troubling view of humanity. Many of Abakanowicz' sculptures consist of body parts, repeated over and over, acquiring power and intensity—even menace—by their very repetition. A well-known piece from the late 1970s consisted of eighty headless human torsos, seated and viewed from behind, called *Backs*. A more recent work, *Puellae (Girls, **11.23**)*, presents a gathering of headless figures. They are young girls, the title tells us. They face the same direction, as though they had assembled for some purpose, though where they have come from and what they are here for is not clear. Are they victims of violence? Of disaster? Have they come back to accuse us? To bear witness? Faced with their silence, we invent explanations. The artist has spoken of her own anxieties about crowds. "People in an airport, people on a metro or on a tram, can seem threatening, horrible, a brainless entity," she has said. "I create these crowds of figures as a warning: they're saying we are so many."[1]

For Kiki Smith, who came of age artistically during the decade around 1990, the body is a subject that connects the universal and the personal in a unique way. "I think I chose the body as a subject, not consciously, but because it is the one form that we all share," she has said. "It's something that everybody has their own authentic experience with."[2] *Honeywax* (**11.24**) depicts a

11.22 Henry Moore. *Reclining Figure: Hand*. 1979. Bronze, length 7'3".
The Henry Moore Foundation, Perry Green, England.

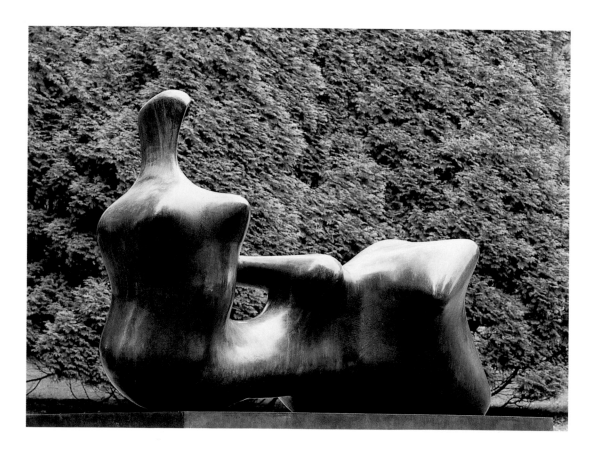

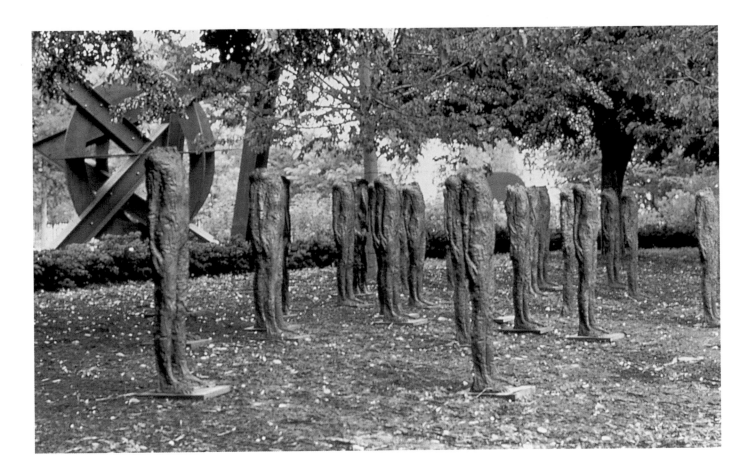

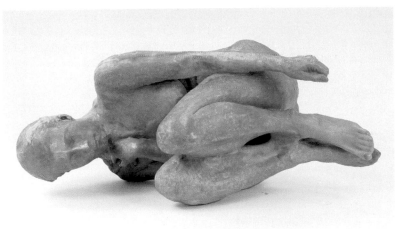

woman, her knees and right hand drawn up to her chest, her left arm relaxed at her side, her eyes closed. It is hard to say whether she is retreating from the world or about to be born into it. Though Smith set the work on the floor, the figure's pose is that of a person suspended—in air, in fluid, in a dream. Translucent and easily injured, the wax surface suggests human skin, vulnerability, and impermanence. Within the history of sculpture, wax is the material of lost-wax casting, the material that will be discarded to make way for something else, something durable. "I feel I'm making physical manifestations of psychic and spiritual dilemmas," Smith has said. "Spiritual dilemmas are being played out physically."[3] Her words might just as easily have been spoken by Michelangelo about his *Dying Slave* (11.21), and they demonstrate the continuing vitality of the human body as a vehicle for expressing the human experience.

11.23 (above, top) Magdalena Abakanowicz. *Puellae (Girls)*. 1992. Bronze, average height 39¾".
National Gallery of Art, Washington, D.C.

11.24 (above) Kiki Smith. *Honeywax*. 1995. Beeswax, 15½ × 36 × 20".
Milwaukee Art Museum.

WORKING WITH TIME AND PLACE

We live in an environment sculpted by the forces of nature. Millions of years ago drifting continents collided, the shock sending up towering mountain ranges. Glaciers advanced and retreated, gouging out lakes and valleys, creating hills and waterfalls, grinding down rock faces and distributing boulders. Rivers carved channels and canyons. Still today mountains are slowly being pushed upward, the ocean constantly rearranges the shoreline, and wind shifts the desert sands. Some shapings happen quickly, others take millions of years. Some last for centuries, others for only a moment.

People, too, have worked to sculpt the landscape. Often the shaping is purely practical, like digging a canal to enable boats to penetrate inland, or terracing a hillside so that crops can grow. But just as often we have shaped places for religious purposes or for aesthetic contemplation and enjoyment. When the Western category of art was first formulated, landscape gardening was often mentioned along with painting and sculpture. In Chapter 3 we looked at one of the most famous gardens in the world, the stone and gravel garden at Ryoan-ji Temple (see 3.30). We also looked at Robert Smithson's *Spiral Jetty*, a coil of rock and earth extending into the Great Salt Lake in Utah (see 3.31).

Spiral Jetty is an **earthwork,** a work of art made for a specific place using natural materials found there, especially the earth itself. Earthworks were one of the ways in which artists of Smithson's generation tried to move away from inherited ideas about art as an object that could be bought and sold. As with many developments of those years, earthworks built bridges of understanding to other world traditions. One of the most famous earthworks in the United States is the Serpent Mound, near Locust Grove, Ohio (**11.25**). For almost 5,000 years, numerous Eastern American peoples built large-scale earthworks as burial sites and ceremonial centers. Serpent Mound was long thought to have been formed by the Hopewell people during the early centuries of our era. Recently, however, scientific methods have suggested a date of around 1070 C.E., long after the decline of Hopewell culture. Serpent Mound contains no burials, and one archaeologist has suggested that the mound may have been created in response to a celestial event, the sighting of Halley's comet, which flamed through the skies in 1066.[4]

11.25 Serpent Mound, near Locust Grove, Ohio. c. 1070 C.E. Overall length (uncoiled) c. 1300'.

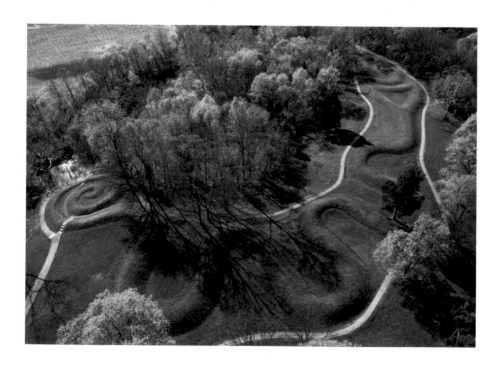

PUBLIC ART

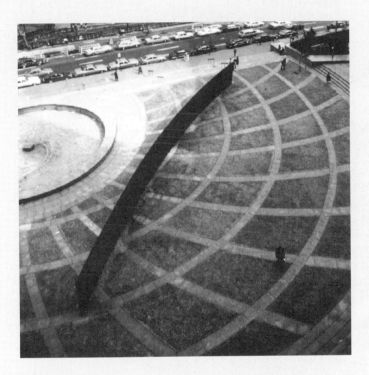

RARELY HAS THE question "What is art?" caused such a public uproar as in a controversy that erupted in New York City in the early 1980s. At the center of the drama was a monumental sculpture by Richard Serra, entitled *Tilted Arc,* a 12-foot-high, 120-foot-long steel wall installed in a plaza fronting a government building in lower Manhattan.

Commissioned by the Art-in-Architecture division of the General Services Administration, *Tilted Arc* was part of a program that allocates 0.5 percent of the cost of federal buildings to the purchase and installation of public art. Soon after the sculpture's installation, however, the public for whom it was intended spoke out, and their message was a resounding *"That's not art!"* More than 7,000 workers in surrounding buildings signed petitions demanding the sculpture's removal. Opponents of the work had numerous com-

plaints. *Tilted Arc,* they maintained, was ugly, rusty, and a target for graffiti. It blocked the view. It disrupted pedestrian traffic, since one had to walk all the way around it rather than straight across the plaza. It ruined the plaza for concerts and outdoor ceremonies. At a public hearing, one man summed up the opposition view: "I am here today to recommend its relocation to a better site—a metal salvage yard."[5]

Artists, dealers, and critics rushed to the sculpture's defense. The sculptor himself argued vehemently against any attempt to move *Tilted Arc,* maintaining that it had been commissioned specifically for that site and any new location would destroy its artistic integrity.

The battle raged for many months, and, while there were dissenting voices from all sides, it shaped up principally as a struggle between the art establishment (pro) and the general public (con). At last, in an unusual editorial, *The New York Times*—a newspaper that heavily supports the arts—took a stand. "One cannot choose to see or ignore 'Tilted Arc,' as if it were in a museum or a less conspicuous public place. To the complaining workers in Federal Plaza, it is, quite simply, unavoidable. . . . The public has to live with 'Tilted Arc'; therefore the public has a right to say no, not here."[6]

This time the public won, and the question "What is art?" was answered by a kind of popular referendum, a majority decision. *Tilted Arc* was dismantled and removed in March of 1989.

Does this outcome mean that *Tilted Arc* is not art, or that it isn't good art? No, it does not mean either of those things. It means simply that, in this particular circumstance, the people for whom the art was intended chose to reject the art. And similar circumstances have, very likely, occurred since the earliest artists of prehistory began painting on the walls of their caves.

Richard Serra. *Tilted Arc.* 1981. Cor-Ten steel, 12' × 120' × 2½". Installed at Federal Plaza, New York; Collection General Services Administration (destroyed 1989).

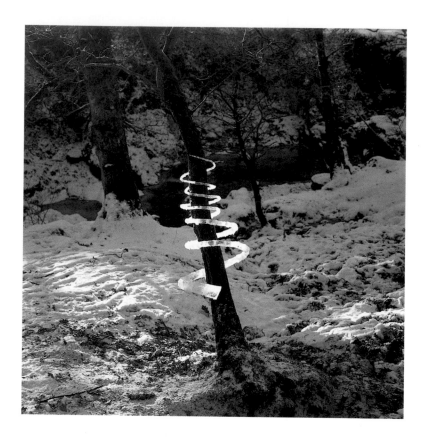

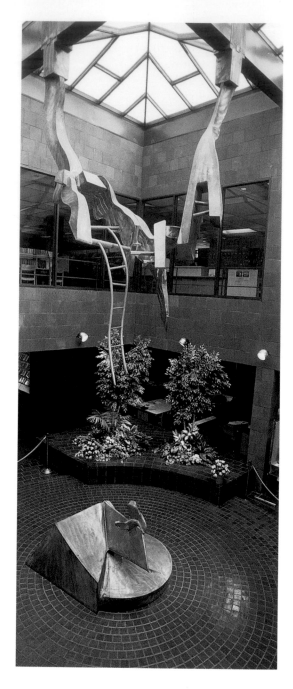

11.26 (left) Andy Goldsworthy. *Reconstructed Icicles, Dumfriesshire, 1995.* 1995. Icicles, reconstructed and refrozen.

11.27 (right) Richard Hunt. *Jacob's Ladder.* 1977. Bronze, overall height of space 18'. Installed at the Carter G. Woodson Regional Library, Chicago.

Earthworks such as Serpent Mound and *Spiral Jetty* enter into the natural world and participate in its changes—the rain and snow that fall, the vegetation that grows and blossoms, even eventual decay. For artists such as Smithson, participating in natural processes was part of the art. He assumed that his work would change slowly over time, and he embraced those changes as part of the ongoing life of his sculpture. In the earthworks of Andy Goldsworthy, the element of time moves to center stage (**11.26**). Goldsworthy makes earthworks that are ephemeral, often from such fleeting materials as ice, leaves, or branches. Many of his works last no more than a few hours before the wind scatters them, or the tide sweeps them away, or, in the case of *Reconstructed Icicles, Dumfriesshire, 1995*, the sun melts them. Goldsworthy tries to go into nature every day and make something from whatever he finds. He documents his work in photographs, including photographs that record the work's disappearance over time, as nature "erases" it. "Time and change are connected to place," he has written. "Real change is best understood by staying in one place."[7]

Earthworks are one way in which artists have expanded the idea of sculpture to embrace time and place. Another is installation, which was introduced in Chapter 2 (see 2.40). The word *installation* covers a range of approaches, but it always implies a link between art and place. An example is Richard Hunt's *Jacob's Ladder* (**11.27**), which was designed both physically and iconographically for the place it resides in, Chicago's Carter G. Woodson Regional Library. The sculpture relates, in abstract terms, the story of the biblical patriarch Jacob. While traveling in the desert, Jacob fell asleep one night and dreamed of a ladder reaching from the earth to Heaven. Angels were moving up and down the ladder, and God appeared at the top, speaking to Jacob. "Jacob's ladder" thus becomes a metaphor for the gateway to Heaven.

In Hunt's interpretation, two giant bronze arms reach down from the skylight (symbolically Heaven), and one holds a curving ladder. On the floor below is a bronze sculpture representing an altar in the desert, with Jacob just waking from his sleep. This metaphor, however, has another layer of meaning. The Carter Woodson Library is located in a predominantly black section of Chicago and is staffed and used mostly by blacks. Richard Hunt, who himself is black, intends his "Jacob's ladder" to represent learning, knowledge, literacy—all of which can be acquired in the library—as the gateway to the "heaven" of equality.

Jacob's Ladder is a permanent installation, for it will remain where it is for as long as the library stands. It is also referred to as a **site-specific** installation, for it was created for a particular site and can only be fully understood in the context of that site. Perhaps because new art is primarily shown in galleries or special museum exhibits, many installations created today are temporary. Like the wall drawings we looked at in Chapter 6, they exist for the duration of an exhibition, after which they are dismantled and destroyed or dispersed. An engaging example was created recently by a group of African artists (**11.28**). The occasion was a 1999 exhibit of photographs by the Malian photographer Malick Sidibé. Taken during the 1950s and 1960s, the decades in which much of Africa gained its freedom from colonial rule, the photographs capture the vibrant club scene that flourished in the city of Bamako, in Mali, where young people danced every weekend to a mix of European, American, and African hits.

For this exhibit, Coulibaly Siaka Paul, a sculptor from Ivory Coast, was commissioned to carve life-size figures of some of the dancers from the

11.28 Coulibaly Siaka Paul, Emile Guebehi, and Koffi Kouakou, sculptors, with photographs by Malick Sidibé. *The Clubs of Bamako*. Installation at Deitch Projects, New York, 1999.

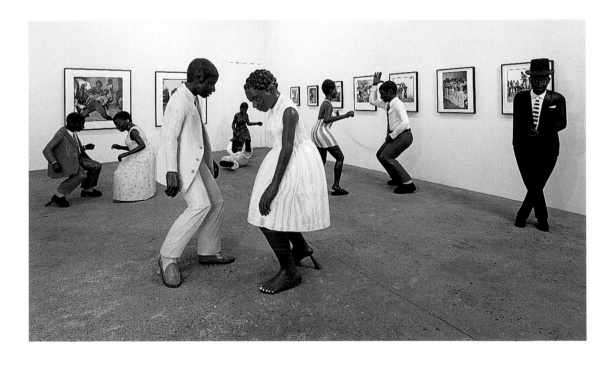

photographs. He in turn invited three colleagues to help him meet the tight deadline. Carved from wood in the naturalistic style favored by many contemporary African sculptors, the wonderfully gyrating figures are painted with glossy enamel paint in flesh tones, shades and tints of gray, and pale yellow, situating them somewhere between the black-and-white world of the photographs and the full spectrum of life itself. Dance music from the period filled the gallery, and few viewers could suppress a smile when they found themselves wandering amid the joyful sights and sounds of Bamako in the 1960s.

The idea of a room remains at the heart of many installations. A room is a space set apart from the rest of the world. It may be a place of refuge, of discovery, of secrets, or even of imprisonment. In *Fireflies on the Water*, Yayoi Kusama created a room that is a paradox: a small and intimate space that seems to open up to infinity (**11.29**). *Fireflies on the Water* consists of a room 12 feet square and just shy of 10 feet in height. The walls are entirely lined with mirrors, and a reflecting pool is sunk into the center of the floor. One hundred fifty small white lights suspended from the ceiling provide the only illumination—tiny points of brightness reflected in the water and multiplied into infinity by the mirrors. Following the wishes of the artist, only one person is allowed into the room at a time. The door shuts, and the viewer is alone. Visitors can certainly share their experiences of the work later, but the experience itself is solitary.

In *Fireflies on the Water*, Kusama created a room that viewers enter in order to shut out the world. We enter it as we might enter our own imagination, where no one else can follow. In her installation *Red Room (Child)*, Louise Bourgeois turns this idea inside out, creating a place that viewers want to enter but cannot (**11.30, 11.31**). *Red Room (Child)* is a chamber created by setting old wooden doors in a ring, each one hinged to the next. A window in one of the doors allows us to peer inside (11.30). The act feels somehow both shameful and fascinating, like secretly reading someone else's diary. Inside are

11.29 Yayoi Kusama. *Fireflies on the Water*. 2002. Mirror, Plexiglas, 150 lights, and water; 9'7" × 12' × 12'.
Whitney Museum of American Art, New York. © Yayoi Kusama. Courtesy Robert Miller Gallery.

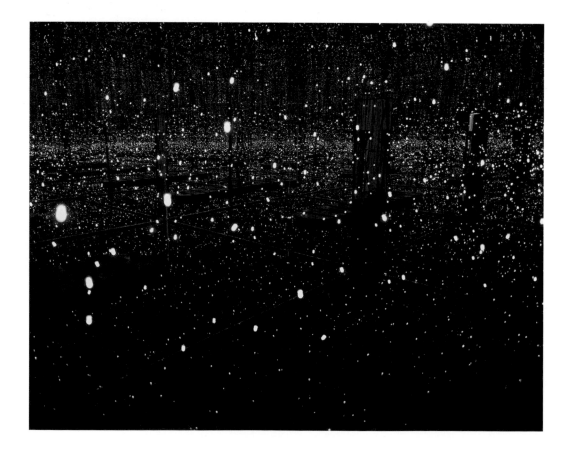

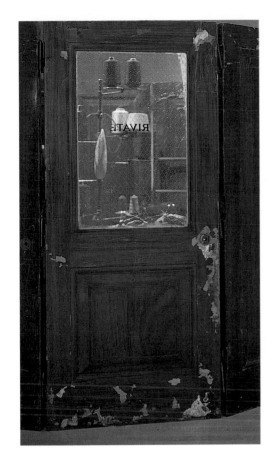

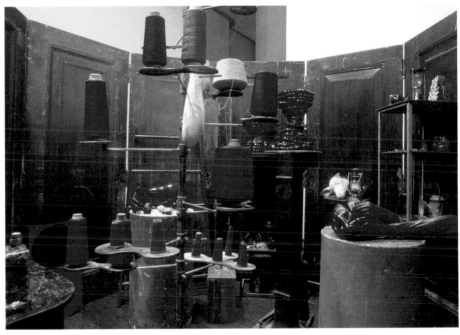

many stands set with spools of red thread. Shelves and pedestals hold other red objects such as large and small forearms and hands (11.31). On one pedestal, a large hand seems to protect the small ones. On another, small hands imitate the large hands—learning how to do something, perhaps, something to do with the thread. *Red Room (Child)* was originally shown with a companion piece, a red room for the parents. Also defined by a ring of doors, this was clearly a marital bedroom, and so neat as to be almost sterile. Bourgeois' subject, as so often, is the psychological scarring of her own childhood, which was spent with a mother she adored and a father she hated for his infidelity to her mother. As viewers we may be led to contemplate more generally the intense psychological bonds between parents and children.

Previous chapters have explored how light can be used to create a sense of place, as with the colored light that suffuses the Sainte-Chapelle in Paris (see 3.4) or James Turrell's skyspace in the Live Oak Friends Meeting House in Houston (see 4.17). Another artist who devoted his career to exploring the effects of light on our perception of space was Dan Flavin. His means were simple, and they never varied: Flavin made constructions from standard, commercially available fluorescent light tubes and fixtures. At first he focused

11.30 (left) Louise Bourgeois. *Red Room (Child)*, exterior detail. 1994. Installation: wood, metal, thread, glass.
Musée d'Art Contemporain, Montréal.

11.31 (right) Louise Bourgeois. *Red Room (Child)*, interior.

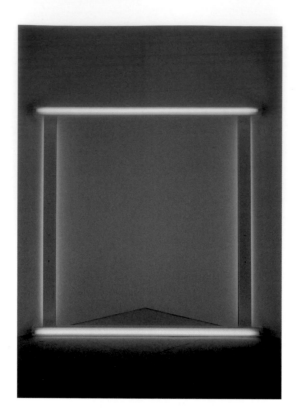

11.32 Dan Flavin. *Untitled (to Karin and Walther),* from the *European Couples* series. 1966–71. Fluorescent light fixtures with blue tubes, 8 × 8'. Dia Art Foundation.

his attention on the lights themselves as sculptural objects, but he quickly came to realize, as he put it, that "the actual space of the room could be disrupted and played with" through light.[8] *Untitled (to Karin and Walther)* (**11.32**) consists of four blue fluorescent lights arranged in a square and stood on the floor in a corner. Two lights face inward, two outward. From these simple means a whole range of blues arises as light reflects off the white walls and radiates into the room.

Flavin was associated with an art movement of the 1960s called **Minimalism.** Like other movements of those years, Minimalism was part of an ongoing argument about the appropriate purpose, materials, and look of art in the modern era. Minimalist artists believed that art should offer a pure and honest aesthetic experience instead of trying to influence people through images or transmit the ego of the artist through self-expression. They favored materials associated more with industry or construction than with art, and they let those materials speak for themselves.

Several of the works we have examined in this section no longer exist, not because they were lost or destroyed, but because they were not meant to last in the first place. The idea of impermanent sculpture may surprise us at first, but in fact most of us not only are familiar with it but have made it. An outdoor figure modeled in snow on a cold winter afternoon is destined to melt before spring, but we take pleasure in sculpting it anyway. Castles and mermaids modeled in wet sand by the shore will be washed away when the tide comes in, but we still put great energy and inventiveness into creating them. For festivals and carnivals the world over, weeks and even months are spent creating elaborate figures and floats, all for the sake of a single day's event.

Since the 1960s, many artists have been intrigued by these kinds of events and activities—by the way they bring people together, focus their energy, and intensify life for a moment before disappearing. In their different ways, festivals and sandcastles suggested answers to such questions as how to bring art closer to daily life, and how to make art without making an object that could be sold and owned.

Among the most famous artists to work with these ideas are the husband and wife team of Christo and Jeanne-Claude. For over three decades they have planned and carried out vast art projects involving the cooperation of hundreds of people. Their most recent work was *The Gates* (**11.33**), a project for New York City's Central Park. Hundreds of paid workers arrived from all over the country to help Christo and Jeanne-Claude set up 7,503 saffron-colored, rectangular gateways along the 23 miles of the park's footpaths. Rolled up and secured against the high horizontal beam of each gate was a saffron-colored banner of nylon fabric. On the opening day of the project, the workers went from gate to gate freeing the banners, which unfurled and began to billow in the wind as the pale winter sunlight played over and through them. *The Gates* remained in place for sixteen days, attracting four million visitors from all over the world. The American composer Aaron Copland once wrote an orchestral piece called *Fanfare for the Common Man*. In a similar spirit, *The Gates* were like a majestic ceremonial walkway for everyone. After sixteen days, the project was removed. The materials it was made of—steel, vinyl, and nylon fabric—were all recycled, and the park was left as pristine as it had been before.

Christo and Jeanne-Claude accept no funding from outside sources for such projects, preferring instead to raise the money themselves by selling drawings and collages generated during the planning stages, as well as early artworks. They are careful to emphasize that their art is not just the end result, but the entire process from planning through dismantling, including the way it energizes people and creates relationships.

11.33 Christo and Jeanne-Claude. *The Gates*. 1979–2005. Installation in Central Park, New York City, February 12–27, 2005.

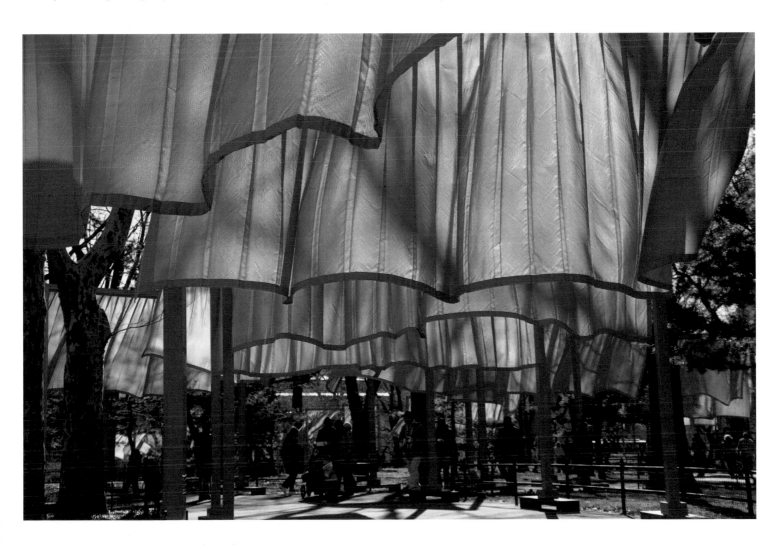

CHRISTO AND JEANNE-CLAUDE

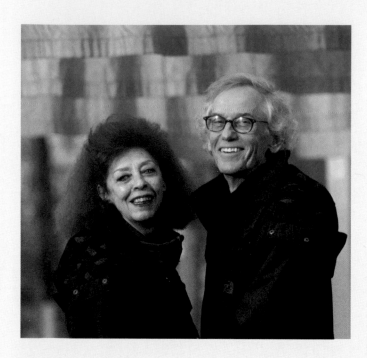

Many artists over time have worked on a grand scale, but none have done so as consistently and as spectacularly as Christo and Jeanne-Claude. Their body of work consists of "projects," most of which have been colossal. Often they wrap things—*large* things—like giant gift packages. They have wrapped a whole section of the Australian coast, cliffs and all, in woven erosion-control fabric. They have wrapped a historic bridge in Paris with 10 acres of silky champagne-colored fabric. In 1995 they wrapped the Reichstag, the German Parliament building in Berlin, with more than a million square feet of shiny aluminum-hued cloth. No passerby could possibly miss these "projects" or ignore them.

Christo and Jeanne-Claude's art is very public, but the artists themselves remain something of a mystery. According to the brief and rather formal biography they release, Christo Javacheff was born in 1935 in Bulgaria, in eastern Europe. He studied at the Fine Arts Academy in Sofia, then traveled by way of Prague and Vienna to Paris. It was in Paris, in 1958, that Christo began wrapping, at first on a modest scale. As he tells it, he began with small objects, such as chairs and tables and bottles. In Paris, too, Christo met Jeanne-

Claude de Guillebon, born in Casablanca, Morocco, of a French military family, who became his partner.

The first of the large-scale wrapped projects was made in Cologne, Germany, in 1961, when Christo and Jeanne-Claude allowed their own art exhibition to spill outside a gallery beside the Rhine harbor onto the docks. A stack of barrels and other paraphernalia, plus rolls of industrial paper, became the *Dockside Packages.* Other ambitious wrappings followed, but the two artists had yet grander plans. The project that established their international reputation was not a wrapping but a *draping.* In 1972 Christo and Jeanne-Claude strung a 4-ton orange nylon curtain between two mountains in Colorado, an arrangement that held intact only long enough to be photographed. They called it *Valley Curtain.*

Two projects in particular transformed Christo and Jeanne-Claude into media celebrities. The first was *Running Fence,* in the mid-1970s, which set up a white nylon barrier 24½ miles long over the hills of northern California. The other was *Surrounded Islands,* in the early 1980s, for which eleven little islands in Florida's Biscayne Bay were circled with pink, floating, polypropylene cloth. Earlier projects had been remarkable, daring, extravagant—but these two were lovely. Even people who had objected to such manipulations of the landscape came to admire them. People had to admire quickly, though, for Christo and Jeanne-Claude's structures are meant to stand physically for only a few days or weeks. After a predetermined period, workers remove them, leaving no trace, and the materials are recycled. The projects live on afterward in preparatory sketches, photographs, books, and films.

Some observers have criticized the artists for the transitory nature of their works, but Christo has a ready reply: "I am an artist, and I have to have courage. . . . Do you know that I don't have any artworks that exist? They all go away when they're finished. Only the sketches are left, giving my works an almost legendary character. I think it takes much greater courage to create things to be gone than to create things that will remain."[9]

Christo and Jeanne-Claude at *The Gates.* 2005. Photo by Wolfgang Volz.

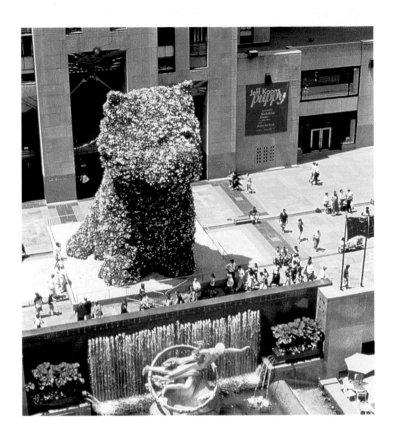

11.34 Jeff Koons. *Puppy*. 1992. Installation at Rockefeller Center, New York, Summer 2000. Live flowering plants, earth, geotextile, and internal irrigation system; 39'4" × 16'5" × 21'4".
Courtesy the artist.

The Gates existed only once. In contrast, Jeff Koons' *Puppy* (**11.34**) made several appearances around the world before settling down in Spain. One of the most talked-about sculptures of the 1990s, *Puppy* is a 43-foot-tall West Highland terrier made of marigolds, begonias, impatiens, and other flowering plants set into a steel framework. Koons created *Puppy* for an exhibit in Germany in 1992. In the years that followed, it appeared in Sydney, Australia, at Rockefeller Center in New York City, and at the Guggenheim Museum Bilbao in Spain, where it is now part of the permanent collection. *Puppy* is strictly a warm-weather sculpture. Over the months, his trim green silhouette grows shaggy as he blossoms more and more profusely (an interior irrigation system keeps *Puppy* watered).

Like much of Koons' work, *Puppy* explores issues of taste. It takes its inspiration from objects that people who learn to admire "high art" are traditionally taught to look down on—sentimental paintings of big-eyed dogs on velvet, or little porcelain figurines of adorable animals in pastel colors. Koons enlarges the idea to monumental proportions, covers it in flowers, and dares us not to like it. But it's impossible not to like *Puppy*, a joyful work that wants nothing but to make us happy and to gain our affection.

Apart from its sheer charm, *Puppy* makes an important point about the nature of sculpture. Classical civilizations made sculptures to survive for all eternity, but they will not. Wood sculptures may burn; stone sculptures are eaten away by acid rain and industrial pollution; metal sculptures have sometimes been melted down. What is important is the sculptor's expression and the experience of the viewer—even if it lasts only for a moment.

CHAPTER TWELVE

CRAFTS

T HE WORKS of art considered in this chapter have certain things in common with one another, but they also share traits with other media, such as sculpture. Most of them have roots in the traditional trades of the European Middle Ages—potter, glassblower, blacksmith, woodworker, weaver. It is from this background that the word "craft" derives, referring to expert work done by hand. We still describe as "well crafted" anything finely made, including a chair, an automobile, a house, even sometimes a painting or sculpture. The specific connotation of craft, however, is an object made by hand, not by machine, and this is true of all the works shown in this chapter.

As we discussed in Chapter 2, "craft" and "art" originally shared the same meaning. It was only during the Renaissance that painting, sculpture, and architecture began to be seen as different kinds of activities from carving a chair or forging a wrought iron gate. Indeed, as you read the chapters in the next part of this book, which examine art in a historical context, you will find that art history prior to the Renaissance includes many objects that we might consider crafts, such as Greek vases or medieval European stained glass.

Exploring artistic traditions beyond the West often challenges our categories of art and craft. Many cultures, for example, attribute the kind of meanings that we associate with art to objects we think of as crafts, such as textiles or basketry (see, for example, the Pomo basket, 3.1). Others may value painting as highly as we do, but give equal status to media that we do not, such as ceramics. One common assumption that people make is that craft objects are functional, while art objects are not. Yet in many cultures art objects are quite functional (see, for example, the Baule spirit spouse sculpture, 11.18, which was carved to help solve its owner's personal problems, and which functioned as a dwelling for a spirit).

What, then, separates the craft object from the art object? There is no definite line, nor should there be one. Labels are a convenience for talking about art, but they should not force artworks into cubbyholes. What *may* help to distinguish the crafts from the other arts is their emphasis on particular materials. The traditional materials of the crafts are clay, glass, metal, wood, and fiber. To these we might add jade and lacquer, two materials with important traditions outside the West. Most craft artists concentrate on one material only and have learned to realize its potential for many different kinds of expression. Each of these materials has its own capabilities and limitations, and each lends itself to certain kinds of structural and decorative possibilities. We begin by considering each of these materials in turn.

CLAY

The craft of **ceramics** involves making objects from clay, a naturally occurring earth substance. When dry, clay has a powdery consistency; mixed with water it becomes **plastic**—that is, moldable and cohesive. In this form it can be modeled, pinched, rolled, or shaped between the hands. Once a clay form has been built and permitted to dry, it will hold its shape, but it is very fragile. To ensure permanence the form must be fired in a kiln, at temperatures ranging between about 1,200 and 2,700 degrees Fahrenheit, or higher. Firing changes the chemical composition of the clay so that it can never again be made plastic.

Nearly every culture we know of has practiced the craft of ceramics, and civilizations in the Middle East understood the basic techniques by as early as 5000 B.C.E. A major requirement for most ceramic objects is that they be hollow, that they have thin walls around a hollow core. There are two reasons for this. First, many ceramic wares are meant to contain things—food or liquids, for instance. Second, a solid clay piece is difficult to fire and may very well explode in the kiln. To meet this need for hollowness, ceramists over the ages have developed specialized forming techniques.

One such technique is called slab construction. The ceramist rolls out the clay into a sheet, very much as a baker would roll out a pie crust, and then allows the sheet to dry slightly. The sheet, or slab, can then be handled in many ways. It can be curled into a cylinder, draped over a mold to make a bowl, shaped into free-form sculptural configurations, or cut into flamboyantly shaped pieces, as in this colorful vase by Betty Woodman (**12.1**). Woodman attached each of the shapes to a tall central cylinder made of three pots stacked one on top of the other. She painted the ensemble in an abstract composition that suggests fragments of a larger, imaginary painting—perhaps a painting of a still life with a vase. The color scheme shifts as the viewer circles the work, modulating from blue and green accents on one side (left) to pink and black stripes on the other (right).

12.1 Betty Woodman. *Aztec Vase Number 5*, two views. 2006. Glazed earthenware, epoxy resin, lacquer, and paint; height 37". Courtesy Max Protetch Gallery, New York.

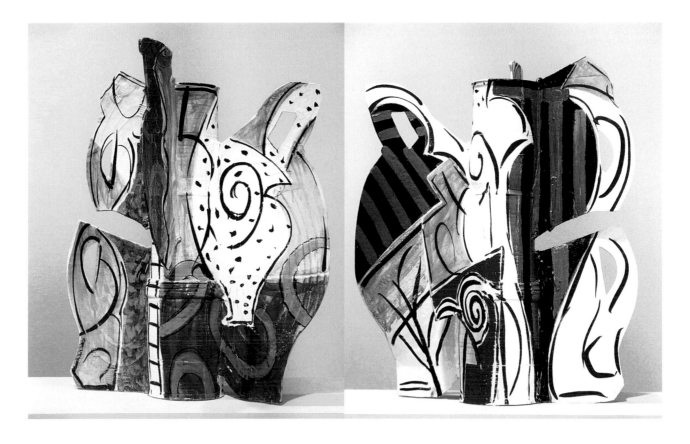

The brilliant colors of Woodman's vases were produced through a process called glazing. Ceramic glazes consist of powdered mineral ingredients mixed with water. They are applied like paint to the surface of an already fired piece. The piece is then fired a second time, melting the minerals and fusing them into a glasslike, nonporous coating that bonds with the clay body. The heat also sets off chemical reactions that produce color (most glazes are an unpromising grayish color when painted on).

Coiling is another technique for making a thin, hollow form. The ceramist rolls out ropelike strands of clay, then coils them upon one another and joins them together. A vessel made from coils attached one atop the other will have a ridged surface, but the coils can be smoothed completely to produce a uniform, flat wall. The native peoples of the southwestern United States made extraordinarily large, finely shaped pots by coiling. In this century their craft has been revived by a few supremely talented individuals, including the famous Pueblo potter María Martínez (**12.2**).

The black-on-black designs of Martínez' pots were not produced by glazing but rather through the firing process itself. After building, smoothing, and air-drying her pots, Martínez laboriously burnished them to a sheen with a smooth stone. Next, a design was painted on with slip (liquid clay). The pot was then fired. Partway through the firing, the flames were smothered with dried manure, and the pot blackened in the resulting smoke. Areas painted with slip remained matte (dull), while burnished areas took on a high gloss.

African-born ceramist Magdalene Odundo also builds her pots by hand, burnishes them, and sometimes blackens them through firing (**12.3**). The elegant, organic forms of Odundo's ceramics are inspired by the human body. Comparisons between ceramic vessels and our physical selves are common to many cultures. Even the words we use to talk about ceramics reflect them. We speak, for example, of the mouth of a vessel, the neck and shoulders of a vase, and the body of a pot. The flaring top of the vessel illustrated here resembles the headdress traditionally worn by women of the Mangbetu people of central Africa. We can see the rest of the vessel as an abstracted head and body.

12.2 (left) María and Julian Martínez. Jar. c. 1939. Blackware, height 11⅛".
National Museum of Women in the Arts, Washington, D.C.

12.3 (right) Magdalene Odundo. Vessel. 2000. Burnished terra cotta, height 19⅝".
The British Museum, London.

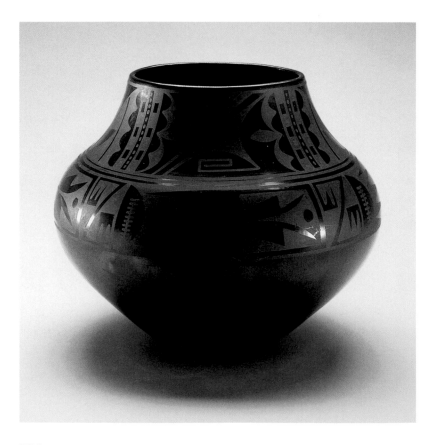

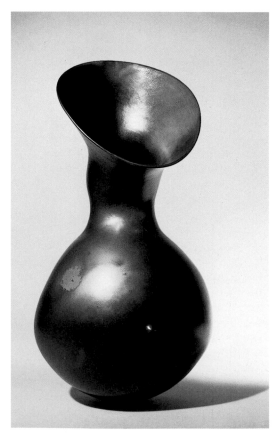

MARÍA MARTÍNEZ

1881(?)–1980

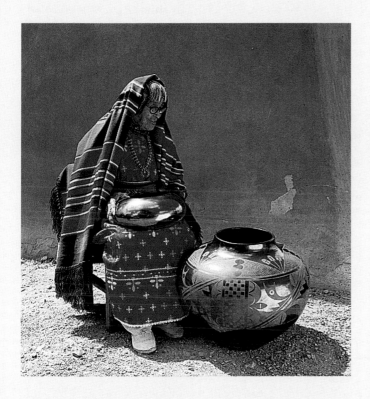

IT IS A long way in miles and in time between the tiny pueblo of San Ildefonso in New Mexico and the White House in Washington, D.C. But the extraordinary ceramic artist María Martínez made that journey, and many others, in a long lifetime devoted to the craft of pottery making. María—as she signed herself and is known professionally—began her career as a folk potter and ended it six decades later as a first-ranked potter of international reputation.

A daughter of Pueblo people, María most likely was born in 1881, but there are no records. As a child she learned to make pottery, using the coil method, by watching her aunt and other women in the community. Part of her youth was spent at St. Catherine's Indian School in Santa Fe, where María became friends with Julián Martínez. The couple married in 1904.

Although the husband worked at other jobs, the two Martínezes early formed a partnership for making pottery—she doing the building, he the decorating. Between 1907 and 1910 he was employed as a laborer on an archaeological site near the pueblo, under the direction of Dr. Edgar L. Hewett. The amazing career of María Martínez was launched in a simple way; Dr. Hewett gave her a broken piece of pottery from the site and asked her to reconstruct a whole pot in that style using the traditional blackware techniques.

About 1919 the Martínezes developed the special black-on-black pottery that was to make them and the pueblo of San Ildefonso famous. The shiny blackware—created from red clay by a process of smothering the bonfire used for firing—was decorated with matte-black designs. This black-on-black ware was commercially quite successful. María Martínez and her husband became wealthy by the standards of the pueblo and, as was customary, shared that wealth with the entire community.

María bore four sons who survived. Eventually they and their wives and children and grandchildren became partners in her enterprise. One shadow on her domestic life was her husband's serious alcoholism, which began early in their marriage and contributed to his death in 1943. After he was gone, María's daughter-in-law Santana took over much of the decorating of pots, later to be followed by María's son Popovi Da.

As María's fame spread, she traveled widely, giving demonstrations at many world's fairs. Among the awards she received were an honorary doctorate from the University of Colorado and the American Ceramic Society's highest honor for a lifetime of devotion to clay. Her visit to Washington during the 1930s was a highlight. President Franklin D. Roosevelt was not at home, but Mrs. Eleanor Roosevelt was, and she told María, "You are one of the important ones. We have a piece of your pottery here in the White House, and we treasure it and show it to visitors from overseas."

Undoubtedly, María's greatest achievement was in reviving and popularizing the traditions of fine pottery making among the Pueblo people. Not long before her death, according to her great-granddaughter, she said: "When I am gone, essentially other people have my pots. But to you I leave my greatest achievement, which is the ability to do it."[1]

Photograph of María Martínez.

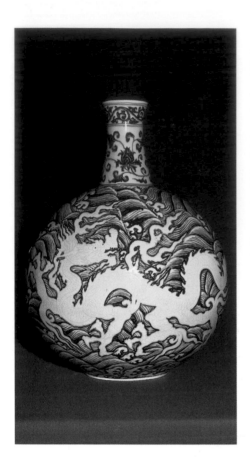

12.4 Flask. China, c. 1425–35. Porcelain with blue underglaze decoration, height 18". Palace Museum, Beijing.

By far the fastest method of creating a hollow, rounded form is by means of the potter's wheel. Egyptian potters were using the wheel by about 4000 B.C.E. Despite some modern improvements and the addition of electricity, the basic principle of wheel construction remains the same as it was in ancient times. The wheel is a flat disk mounted on a vertical shaft, which can be made to turn rapidly either by electricity or by foot power. The ceramist centers a mound of clay on the wheel and, as the wheel turns, uses the hands to "open," lift, and shape the clay form—a procedure known as throwing. Throwing on the wheel always produces a rounded or cylindrical form, although the thrown pieces can later be reshaped, cut apart, or otherwise altered. Thrown on a wheel, the Chinese vase illustrated here is made of a special clay mixture called **porcelain** (**12.4**). When fired at very high temperatures, porcelain produces a translucent, white, glasslike ceramic that is much stronger than it looks. The secret of porcelain was discovered and perfected in China, and for hundreds of years potters elsewhere tried without success to duplicate it. European potters finally stumbled onto the secret in 1710, but even today our word for the finest pottery is the same as the name of the country that invented it, china.

Porcelain is made of a mixture of a fine white clay called kaolin and a feldspar quartz called petuntse. Other types and mixtures of clay result in other types of ceramic, each with its own characteristics. Stoneware clays, which fire at medium temperatures, are generally brown or grayish. Much commercial dinnerware is made of stoneware, and these clays have been popular among artist-potters. Earthenware clays, generally red or brown, fire at lower temperatures. Fired earthenware is often called by its Italian name, terra cotta. Flowerpots are a good example of terra cotta in everday use.

GLASS

If clay is one of the most versatile of the craft materials, glass is perhaps the most fascinating. Few people, when presented with a beautiful glass form, can resist holding it up to the light, watching how light changes its appearance from different angles.

Although there are thousands of formulas for glass, its principal ingredient is usually silica, or sand. The addition of other materials can affect color, melting point, strength, and so on. When heated, glass becomes molten, and in that state it can be shaped by several different methods. Unlike clay, glass never changes chemically as it moves from a soft, workable state to a hard, rigid one. As glass cools it hardens, but it can then be reheated and rendered molten again for further working.

Glass as a material holds many risks, both during the creative process and afterward. The shaping of a glass object demands split-second timing— quick decisions and quick handwork—while the glass remains hot. In addition a finished glass piece is the most fragile of all craft wares. One swift blow can shatter it irreparably. There is something almost heroic about an artist who would spend days, weeks, even months making an object that is so vulnerable.

A special branch of glass craft, **stained glass** is a technique used for windows, lampshades, and similar structures that permit light to pass through. Stained glass is made by cutting sheets of glass in various colors into small pieces, then fitting the pieces together to form a pattern. Often the segments are joined by strips of lead, hence the term *leaded* stained glass. The 12th and 13th centuries in Europe were a golden age for stained glass. In the religious philosophy that guided the building of the great cathedrals of that time, light was viewed as a spiritually transforming substance. The soaring interiors of the new cathedrals were illuminated by hundreds of jewel-like windows such as the one illustrated here from the Cathedral of Notre Dame at Chartres, France (**12.5**). The central motif is a branching tree that portrays the royal lineage of Mary, mother of Jesus. The tree springs from the loins of the biblical patriarch Jesse, depicted asleep at the base of the window. Growing upward, it enthrones in turn four kings of Judaea, then Mary, then Jesus himself.

Glass is commonly shaped by blowing, a technique that dates from Roman times. To blow glass, the artist dips up a portion of molten glass at the end of a long pipe. By blowing through the opposite end of the pipe he or she produces a glass bubble that can be shaped or cut by various methods while it is still hot. Dale Chihuly assembled dozens of delicate, blown, leaflike forms to create his *Persian Chandelier* (**12.6**), shown here displayed inside a greenhouse at England's famed Royal Botanic Gardens. Chihuly had been invited to create a series of works for display both in the greenhouses and on the extensive grounds of the gardens. The organic forms and tropical colors he favors harmonized elegantly with the garden's magnificent collection of plants from around the world.

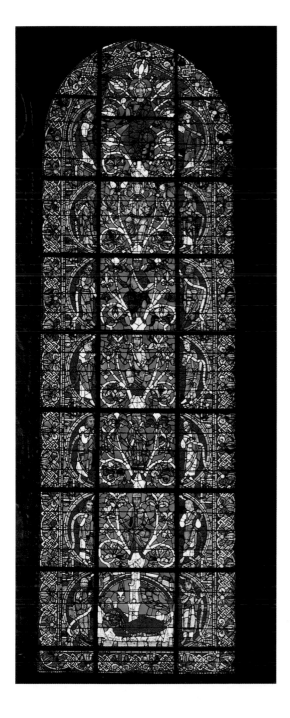

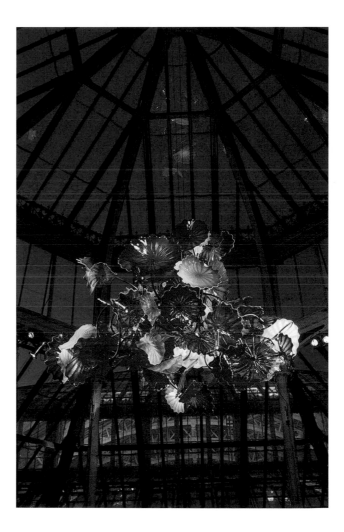

12.5 (left) *Tree of Jesse,* west facade, Chartres Cathedral, France. c. 1150–70. Stained glass.

12.6 (right) Dale Chihuly. *Persian Chandelier.* 2005. 7'10" × 9'10" × 9'4". Installation at the Royal Botanic Gardens, Kew, Surrey, United Kingdom, May 28, 2005–January 15, 2006.

METAL

From the most fragile craft material we turn to the most indestructible. Metals rust and corrode under some circumstances, but they do not shatter, chip, or rot away. Ever since humans learned to work metals, they have made splendid art, as well as functional tools, from this versatile family of materials. One distinctive aspect of metal is that it is equally at home in the mundane and the sublime—the bridge that spans a river or the precious ring on a finger; the plow that turns up the earth or the crown on a princess's head. Whatever the application, the basic composition of the material is the same, and the methods of working it are similar.

As discussed in Chapter 11, metal can be shaped by heating it to a liquid state and pouring it into a mold, a process known as casting (see 11.4). Another ancient technique is **forging**—the art of the blacksmith. Forging involves heating a chunk of metal over a fire until it is red-hot, then beating and shaping it with hammers. This is how horseshoes traditionally were made, and it is also the method of making wrought iron, as for balconies and railings.

In Europe, forging reached unsurpassed heights of virtuosity in the hands of the great armor makers of the Renaissance. Among the most renowned of these was Filippo Negroli, who together with his brother Francesco created this burgonet, a type of helmet (**12.7**). Forged from a single plate of steel, it was part of a complete suit of armor made for the Holy Roman Emperor Charles V to wear on ceremonial occasions.

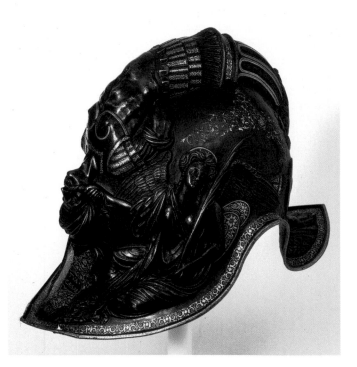

12.7 (left) Filippo and Francesco Negroli. *Burgonet of Charles V.* 1545. Steel and gold. Real Armeria, Palacio Real, Patrimonio Nacional, Madrid.

12.8 (below) Basin made for Sultan al-Nasir Muhammad ibn Qala'un. Cairo or Damascus, c. 1320–41. Brass, gold, silver; height 9"; diameter 21¼". The British Museum, London.

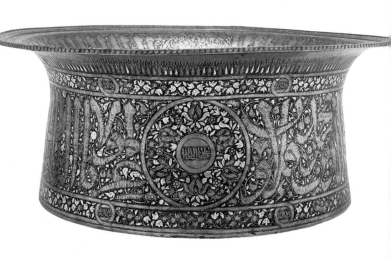

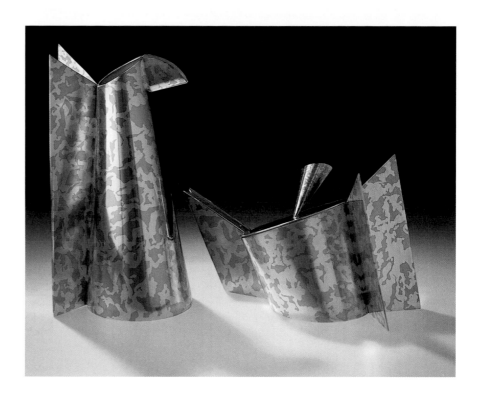

12.9 Susan Ewing. Winged pitcher and sugar container. 1991. Sterling silver, 24K vermeil, height of pitcher 7¼". Collection Jean-Marie Clemes, Luxembourg.

The helmet is decorated with figures in relief. Along its crest arcs the body of a Turkish warrior. His hands are behind his back, presumably bound, while his long moustache is held like a leash to either side by two winged deities dressed in Classical draperies. One is Victory, visible in the illustration here, and the other is Fame. The Ottoman Empire of the Turks was the most formidable foreign power of the day, and the helmet suggests that Charles V has earned renown through his victory over them (though in fact he ultimately settled for a truce). The figures were raised into relief by hammering the red-hot metal from behind (that is, from inside the helmet), a technique called **embossing.** Once they were as finely formed as this technique would allow, the metal was allowed to cool, then details and outlines were added from the front using special chisels and punches, a process called **chasing.** All of this work was done by Filippo, who then turned the piece over to Francesco to be **demascened,** inlaid with an intricate design in gold.

Renaissance metalworkers had learned the technique of damascene from their Islamic colleagues, whose works they admired. They named the technique after the Islamic city of Damascus, where this basin may have been made (**12.8**). Fashioned of hammered brass and richly decorated in gold and silver damascene, it was created during the 14th century for a sultan of the Mamluk dynasty, which ruled over an extensive empire from its capital in Cairo, in Egypt. The principal decoration is a flowing calligraphic inscription in praise of the sultan himself. The roundels (circular areas) are filled with a design of lotus flowers and were probably inspired by imported Chinese textiles.

Contemporary metalsmith Susan Ewing pays tribute to the silver-and-gold color combination of classical Islamic metalwork in this small milk pitcher and sugar container (**12.9**). Ewing works out ideas for her creations using cardboard or heavy paper, which she cuts, folds, bends, and glues—processes she then applies to sheets of silver to create the finished work. (Metal can be "glued" with solder, molten metal used like drops of glue, pronounced SAH-der.) The camouflage-like pattern was created by plating a microscopically thin layer of 24-karat gold to the finished silver forms, a technique known as vermeil (vair-MAY).

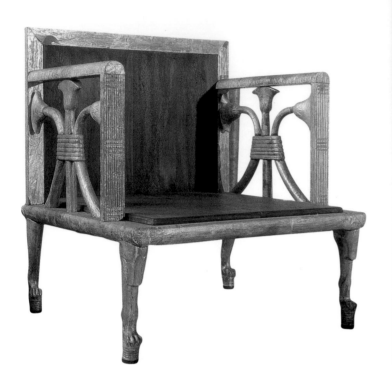

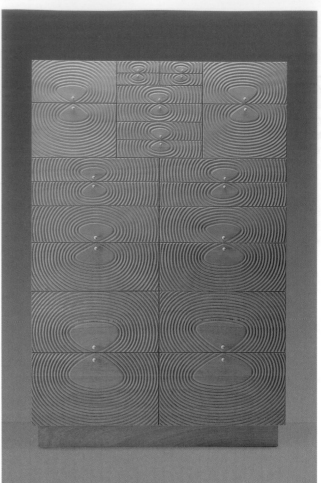

12.10 (left) Chair of Hetepheres. Egypt, Dynasty 4, reign of Sneferu, 2575–2551 B.C.E. Wood and gold leaf.
Egyptian Museum, Cairo.

12.11 (right) Judy Kensley McKie. *Shell Chest*. Obeche. Constructed and carved, 64 × 42 × 16".
Courtesy Pritam & Eames.

WOOD

There are two reasons for the great popularity of wood as a craft material. One is that it is relatively easy to work. The simplest tools will shape it, and there is no need for extreme heat, as with clay, glass, or metal. The second reason is that wood is so widely available. In most inhabited areas of the globe, wood is abundant and easy to obtain. These two qualities would make wood the ideal material were it not for certain drawbacks. Because of its organic nature, wood is not very durable. Cold and heat distort it, water rots it, and insects can eat it away. We must assume that only a tiny fraction of the wood objects made over the centuries have survived.

The most common product of the woodworker's art is furniture. The basic forms of furniture are surprisingly ancient. The chair, for example, seems to have been developed in Egypt around 2600 B.C.E. Massive thrones for rulers and humble stools for ordinary people had existed earlier, but the idea of a portable seat with a back and armrests was an innovation (**12.10**). Miraculously preserved by the dry desert climate of Egypt, this chair, one of the oldest known, shows that artistic attention was lavished on furniture from the very beginning. The chair's legs are carved as the legs and paws of a lion, an emblem of royal power. Within the open frames of the armrests are carved bouquets of papyrus flowers, a symbol of Lower (northern) Egypt.

Furniture makers in the royal workshops of ancient Egypt generally covered their work with precious materials such as gold. Elsewhere, wood has been appreciated for its own inherent beauty. Wood occurs in an extraordinary natural palette that ranges from lustrous black through pale tints of earth tones. Contemporary sculptor and furniture maker Judy Kensley McKie created the chest of drawers illustrated here from obeche, an African tree that yields a pale, fine-grained, yellow-tinted wood (**12.11**). In McKie's simple and elegant design, carved channels repeat around the small knob of each drawer like ripples radiating outward from a pebble cast in a lake. We could also see the knobs as pearls in an opened shell, an image that suggested McKie's name for her design.

FIBER

The design possibilities for works of fiber are enormous. By fiber we mean a narrow strand of vegetable or animal material (cotton, linen, wool, silk) or the modern-day synthetic equivalents. Like wood, fiber is widely available and quite perishable, but the construction methods used for fiber are unique to this pliable medium.

For centuries the most common method of working with fiber has been weaving. Weaving involves placing two sets of parallel fibers at right angles to one another and interlacing one set through the other in an up-and-down movement, generally on a loom or frame. One set of fibers is held taut; this is called the warp. The other set, known as the weft or woof, is interwoven through the warp to make a textile. Nearly all textiles, including those used for our clothing, are made by some variation of this process.

The ancient Incas, whose civilization flourished in the mountains of Peru during the 15th century, held textiles in such high regard that they draped gold and silver statues of their deities with fine cloth offerings. Textiles were also accepted as payment for taxes, for they were considered a form of wealth. Standardized patterns and colors on Incan tunics instantly signaled the wearer's ethnicity and social status. Woven around 1500, the fascinating royal tunic illustrated here (**12.12**) is a virtual catalogue of such patterns, although scholars have not yet succeeded in identifying them all. The black-and-white checkerboard pattern, for example, represents the Inca military uniform in miniature. By wearing this tunic, the king visually declared his dominance over all of Incan society.

12.12 Tunic, from Peru. *Inca,* c. 1500. Wool and cotton, 35⅞" × 30".
Dumbarton Oaks Research Library and Collections, Washington, D.C.

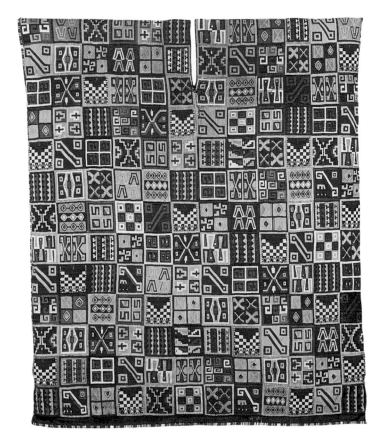

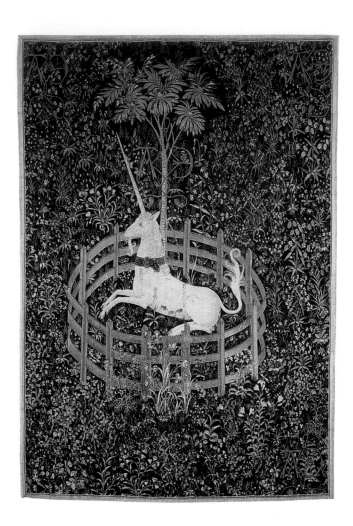

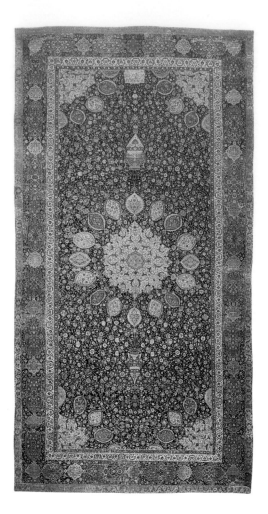

12.13 (left) *The Unicorn in Captivity* from *The Hunt of the Unicorn*. Southern Netherlandish, 1475–1500. Wool, silk, and metallic threads; 12' × 8'3". The Metropolitan Museum of Art, New York.

12.14 (right) Ardabil carpet. Persia (Tabriz?). 1539–40. Wool pile on undyed silk warps, length 34'5¾". Victoria and Albert Museum, London.

Tapestry is a special type of weaving in which the weft yarns are manipulated freely to form a pattern or design on the front of the fabric. Often the weft yarns are of several colors, and the weaver can use the different-colored yarns almost as flexibly as a painter uses pigment on canvas. Tapestry weaving experienced a golden age in Europe from the late 14th through the 17th centuries. For those who could afford it, tapestry was the art of choice. In place of the paintings we would expect to see now, the castles and great houses of Europe were hung with finely woven cloths, often with elaborate pictorial images.

Among the best-known and most admired of these works is *The Hunt of the Unicorn,* a series of seven panels depicting a popular medieval story. According to legend, the unicorn, a wild and fleet one-horned beast, could be tamed only by a virgin. Early panels in the series show the unicorn being hunted by a band of men. When it lays its head in a virgin's lap, it is captured and killed, then brought back to the castle. The final tapestry shows *The Unicorn in Captivity* (**12.13**), mysteriously alive and seemingly content in its wooden pen. Medieval European art and storytelling often mix mythological and religious themes, and *The Hunt of the Unicorn* provides an excellent example. The unicorn legend is intended as a parallel to the Passion of Christ, who assumed a human nature through being born of the Virgin Mary, was killed, and then was resurrected. Yet another layer of meaning shows in the last panel, for the abundant foliage surrounding the captive unicorn was associated with love and fertility, suggesting that these tapestries were woven to celebrate a marriage. The unicorn thus also represents a lover held happily captive by devotion and desire.

Islamic cultures, in contrast, do not have a history of tapestries, but instead have focused a great deal of aesthetic attention on carpets and rugs. Among the most famous Islamic textiles is the pair of immense rugs known as the Ardabil carpets, of which we illustrate the one in the collection of London's Victoria and Albert Museum (**12.14**). Like most Islamic carpets, they were created by knotting individual tufts of wool onto a woven ground. The labor was minute and time-consuming: The London Ardabil carpet has over 300 knots per square inch, or over twelve million knots in all!

The design features a central sunburst medallion with sixteen radiating pendants. Two mosque lamps, one larger than the other, extend from the medallion as well. Quarter segments of the medallion design appear in the corners of the rug. These elements seem to float over a deep blue ground densely patterned with flowers, making the carpet a sort of stylized garden. (In a similar figure of speech, we talk of a field in springtime as being "carpeted in flowers.") Paradise in Islam is imagined as a garden, and such flower-strewn carpets represent a luxurious, domesticated reminder of this ideal world to come.

In the United States, one of the most popular textile arts is quilting. Quilting has a strong social component, for it has often furnished a regular occasion for women to spend an evening together, sewing, telling stories, sharing their lives. Quilting also has a special relationship to the African-American community, for examples survive made by slaves and former slaves during the 19th century. One of the most famous of these is the *Bible Quilt* by Harriet Powers (**12.15**). Unlike many quilts, this was not a group effort but represents Powers' own unique artistic vision. Using a technique called appliqué, in which pieces of colored fabric are cut and sewn to a fabric ground to create a design, she illustrated a series of scenes drawn from the Bible as well as moments from local lore that were believed to show God's working in the world.

12.15 Harriet Powers. *Bible Quilt*. c. 1898. Pieced, appliquéd, and printed cotton embroidered with plain and metallic yarns. 5'8⅞" × 8'9⅛". Courtesy Museum of Fine Arts, Boston.

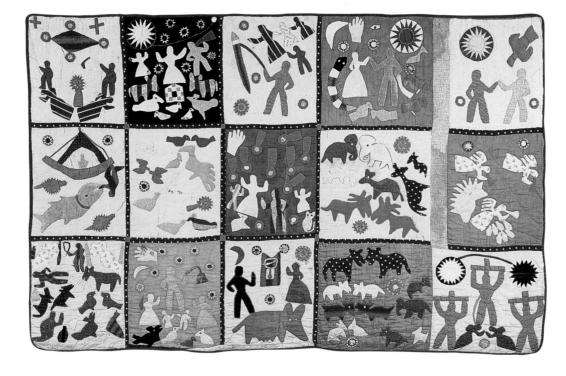

The scene at the very center, for example, depicts a meteor show that was witnessed over Georgia in November 1833. It was interpreted as a sign that the world was coming to an end, Powers later explained, until God's hand stayed the falling stars. Two squares to the left is a depiction of Jonah being swallowed by a great fish, as related in the Bible.

JADE AND LACQUER

Jade and lacquer have long histories as craft media, although not in the West. Jade is a common name for two minerals, nephrite and jadeite. Ranging in color from white through shades of brown and green, the two stones are found principally in East and Central Asia and Central America. Although their underlying structures differ, both share the extreme hardness, the ice-cold touch, and the mesmerizing, translucent beauty that have caused jade to be treasured in cultures lucky enough to have access to it.

The ancient Olmecs, whose jade figure of a shaman we looked at in Chapter 2 (see 2.37), prized green jade. They associated its color with plant life—especially with corn, their most important crop—and its translucence with rainwater, on which agricultural bounty depended. In China, jade of all colors has been prized and carved for some 6,000 years. In early Chinese belief, the stone was credited with magical properties.

One of the oldest of Chinese jade forms is the *bi*, a flat, round disk with a hole at the center (**12.16**). Examples have been recovered from Neolithic burial sites dating as far back as the third millennium B.C.E. The shape clearly had a precise ritual significance for Neolithic peoples, but by the time this *bi* was carved thousands of years later, the original meaning had long been forgotten. Instead, the shape served to remind discerning collectors of the great age and continuity of Chinese culture. Whereas Neolithic *bi* were plain and unadorned, the *bi* here swarms with dragons. These, too, are carved in an antique style evoking China's distant past.

12.16 *Bi* disk with dragons. China, c. 1550–1644. Jade, height 7¾".
Los Angeles County Museum of Art.

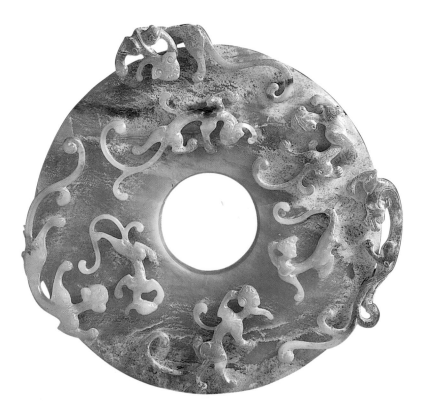

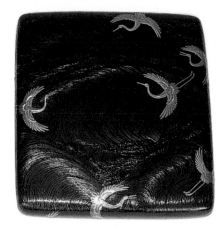

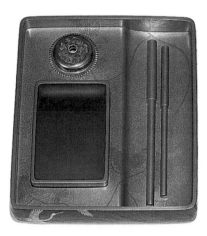

Lacquer is a material specific to East Asia, for it is made of the sap of a tree that originally grew only in China. Harvested, purified, colored with dyes, and brushed in thin coats over wood, the sap hardens into a smooth, glasslike coating. The technique demands great patience, for up to thirty coats of lacquer are needed to build up a substantial layer, and each must dry thoroughly before the next can be applied. Ancient Chinese artisans used lacquer to create trays, bowls, storage jars, and other wares that were lightweight and delicate-looking yet water-resistant and airtight. Exported along with other luxury goods over the long overland trade route known as the Silk Road, Chinese lacquerware was admired as far away as the Roman Empire.

The technique of lacquer spread early from China to Korea and Japan, as did cultivation of the sap-producing tree. A 20th-century example of lacquerware is this box for writing materials by the Japanese lacquer artist Jitoku Akazuka (**12.17**). Built up over a thin wooden core, the black lacquer surface is subtly textured to suggest flowing water. Cranes created with mother-of-pearl inlay and sprinkled gold powder wheel gracefully over the lacquer waves. An auspicious symbol of longevity, cranes are a popular decorative motif in East Asia.

12.17 Jitoku Akazuka. Writing box entitled *Dancing Cranes*. 1921. Lacquer, gold, and mother-of-pearl on wood, 8¾ × 10 × 2⅛". The National Museum of Modern Art, Kyoto.

BLURRING THE BOUNDARIES: ARTISTS AND CRAFTS

Most people are surprised to learn that Leonardo da Vinci, in addition to painting, designed costumes and scenery for elaborate theatrical productions. Another Renaissance artist, Raphael, drew designs for tapestries. During the 20th century, Picasso designed and decorated pottery, the sculptor Alexander Calder made jewelry, and Matisse designed stained glass windows and rugs.

Artists have often reached out to apply their talents for visual expression and organization to crafts. Beginning in the 1960s, however, some artists also began bringing the materials and techniques of crafts into art. Perhaps it should not surprise us that the trend was initiated by potters. Clay, after all, had long led a double life, used at once for sculpture and for ceramics. Peter

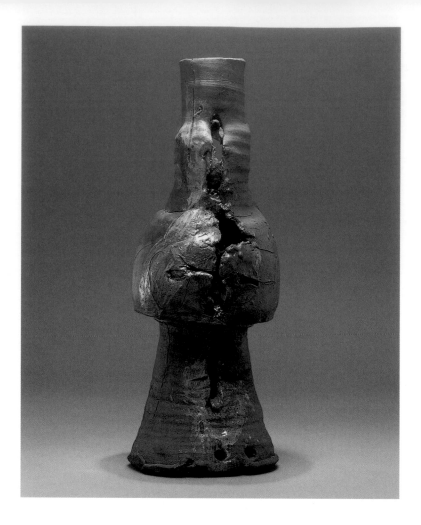

12.18 Peter Voulkos. *Untitled Stack Pot.* 1964. Stoneware, partially glazed, height 30". The Detroit Institute of Arts.

Voulkos explored the border territory between art and craft in such works as *Untitled Stack Pot* (**12.18**). *Untitled Stack Pot* clearly takes its basic form from a traditional wheel-thrown pot, a craft product. Yet the open gash in its side dispenses immediately with the idea that this object is practical. Instead, Voulkos asks us to look at it as a carrier of meaning, as art. The sense that some physical or psychic violence has been done might lead us to compare *Untitled Stack Pot* to the headless figures of Magdalena Abakanowicz (see 11.23). Our understanding of the pot as a metaphor for the human body might also call to mind the sculptures of Henry Moore, who abstracted the human figure to bring it into harmony with natural rock formations (11.22). In other words, we find that we can easily talk about the pot in ways in which we talk about art.

The first wave of feminism during the 1970s prompted a still broader and more profound reconsideration of the categories of art and craft. Angered by a gallery and museum system that overwhelmingly favored male artists and by a standard account of art history in which women artists played virtually no role, early feminist artists sought to create art that was specifically female, art rooted in the biological, psychological, social, and historical experience of women.

Judy Chicago's *The Dinner Party* (**12.19**) is perhaps the most important and influential work from this time. A collaborative work, *The Dinner Party* was executed with the help of hundreds of women and several men. Arranged around a triangular table are thirty-nine place settings, each one created in honor of an influential woman such as the Egyptian ruler Hatshepsut and the novelist Virginia Woolf. The names of an additional 999 important women are written on the tile floor. By using such craft techniques as ceramics, weaving, needlepoint, and embroidery, Chicago demanded artistic equality for occupations that had long been considered "women's work." Confined to the domestic sphere, the vast majority of women throughout history had been limited to these expressive outlets—including the expressive outlet of setting and decorating a table—and *The Dinner Party* honors them. The thirteen places on each side of the triangle intentionally evoke the seating arrangement of Leonardo's *Last Supper* (see 4.45), a central work in the history of Western art, and one that depicts an all-male gathering.

Another artist who draws on the historical role of crafts in women's lives is Faith Ringgold, whose *Tar Beach* (**12.20**) is painted on canvas and surrounded with a border of pieced and quilted fabric. The title is city slang for a flat, asphalt-covered roof that serves apartment dwellers as an all-purpose yard—for parties and picnics, for hanging out laundry to dry, for catching some sun, or for sleeping outdoors in the summer. Text written in the border recounts a childhood memory of magically flying over the rooftops at night. "All

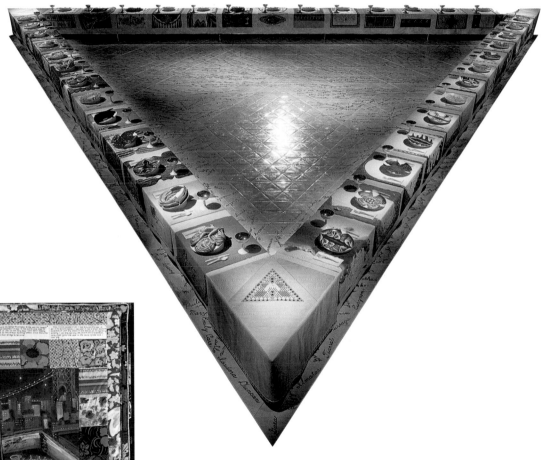

12.19 (above, top) Judy Chicago. *The Dinner Party*. 1979. Mixed media, each side 48'.
The Brooklyn Museum of Art.

12.20 (left) Faith Ringgold. *Tar Beach*. 1988. Acrylic on canvas, tie-dyed and pieced fabric, 6'2" × 5'9".
Solomon R. Guggenheim Museum, New York.

you need is somewhere to go that you can't get to any other way," it reads. "The next thing you know you're flying among the stars." Ringgold draws on the tradition of such textile works as Harriet Powers' *Bible Quilt* (see 12.15) in order to link her own inner-city childhood to the larger African-American experience.

Textiles are again the inspiration for El Anatsui's *Sasa,* a large sculpture in metal (**12.21**). Shown here draped over shrubbery outdoors, *Sasa* has also been displayed in museum spaces suspended from the ceiling and cascading lavishly onto the floor. In both the material and the construction of *Sasa,* Ghana-born El Anatsui challenges our traditional understanding of both sculpture *and* textiles. A sculpture that can be draped? Textiles made of metal? *Sasa* is made of bottle caps and small food tins such as sardine cans, flattened and then stitched together with copper wire. It recycles materials imported into Africa, goods that flow from wealthier places into a poor continent. In its visual splendor, *Sasa* draws on the tradition of African royal textiles such as *kente* (see 1.7). *Kente,* too, was an art of recycling, for it was originally made of silk fabric imported from China. African weavers patiently separated the silk fabric into threads, which they then reweave in patterns that expressed their own culture. With *Sasa,* El Anatsui works even greater magic, for he transforms trash into something opulent, and uses the materials of poverty to evoke riches.

Another humble material is used with dignity in Oliver Herring's *Castle,* from the series *A Flower for Ethyl Eichelberger* (**12.22**). Ethyl Eichelberger was the stage name of a performance artist who committed suicide while dying of

12.21 El Anatsui. *Sasa.* 2004. Aluminum and copper wire, 21' × 27'6¾".
Musée National d'Art Moderne, Centre Georges Pompidou, Paris. Courtesy October Gallery, London.

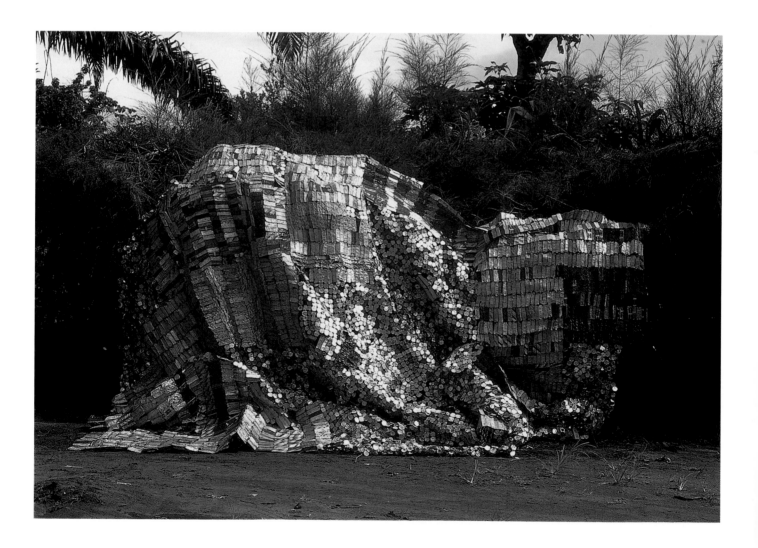

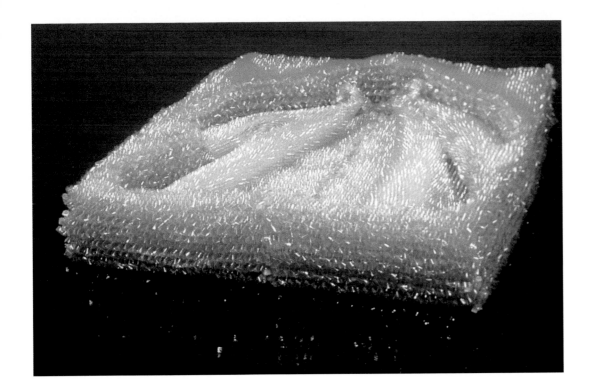

AIDS. Shortly afterward, in 1991, Herring began an extended memorial project, knitting a series of garments in Mylar, a flimsy, shiny plastic material with no "art pedigree." Knitting is a traditionally feminine craft, and Herring chose it deliberately as a tribute to Eichelberger's gender-bending stage persona. Monotonous and repetitive, knitting is also a way of marking time. Looking at the light-filled, almost ghostlike coat, we sense time's slow passing as stitch by stitch, row by row, the minutes, hours, and weeks of grief pass by for the survivor. Both the open coat and the bed it lies on point to the person who is absent, whose body will no longer fill the coat, no longer rest in the bed.

Herring could have carved his tribute in marble or cast it in bronze, but the ordinary, everyday materials and techniques of craft add a layer of poignancy that these more majestic and durable materials could not offer. Like *Castle*, much recent art formed of craft materials speaks of intimate or deeply personal concerns, reminding us that while spectacular craft objects may often have been made for the rich and powerful, the roots of craft are in our daily lives.

12.22 Oliver Herring. *Castle, from A Flower for Ethyl Eichelberger.* 1994. Knitted transparent Mylar, 9 × 47 × 65". Courtesy Max Protech Gallery, New York.

CHAPTER THIRTEEN

ARCHITECTURE

Architecture satisfies a basic, universal human need for a roof over one's head. More than walls, more than a chair to sit on or a soft bed to lie on, a roof is the classic symbol of protection and security. We've all heard the expression "I have a roof over my head," but it would be unusual to hear someone say, "I'm all right because I have walls around me." Of course, in purely practical terms a roof does keep out the worst of the elements, snow and rain, and in warm climates a roof may be sufficient to keep people dry and comfortable. The roof seems to be symbolic of the nature of architecture.

More than any of the other arts, architecture demands structural stability. Every one of us daily moves in and out of buildings—houses, schools, offices, stores, churches, bus stations, banks, and movie theaters—and we take for granted, usually without thinking about it, that they will not collapse on top of us. That they do not is a tribute to their engineering; if a building is physically stable, it adheres faithfully to the principles of the particular *structural system* on which its architecture is based.

STRUCTURAL SYSTEMS
IN ARCHITECTURE

Any building is a defiance of gravity. Since earliest times architects have tackled the challenge of erecting a roof over empty space, setting walls upright, and having the whole stand secure. Their solutions have depended upon the materials they had available, for, as we shall see, certain materials are better suited than others to a particular structural system. There are two basic families of structural systems: the shell system and the skeleton-and-skin system.

In the shell system one building material provides both structural support and sheathing (outside covering). Buildings made of brick or stone or adobe fall into this category, and so do older (pre-19th-century) wood buildings constructed of heavy timbers, the most obvious example being the log cabin. The structural material comprises the walls and roof, marks the boundary between inside and outside, and is visible as the exterior surface. Shell construction prevailed until the 19th century, when it began to fall out of favor. Today, however, the development of strong cast materials, including many plastics, has brought renewed interest in shell structures.

The skeleton-and-skin system might be compared to the human body, which has a rigid bony skeleton to support its basic frame and a more fragile skin for sheathing. We find it in modern skyscrapers, with their steel frames (skeletons) supporting the structure and a sheathing (skin) of glass or some other light material. Also, most houses today—at least in the United States—are built with a skeleton of wood beams nailed together, topped with a sheathing of light wood boards, shingles, aluminum siding, or the like. Skeleton-and-skin construction is largely a product of the Industrial Revolution; not until the mid-19th century could steel for beams or metal nails be manufactured in practical quantities.

Two factors that must be considered in any structural system are weight and tensile strength. Walls must support the weight of the roof, and lower stories must support the weight of upper stories. In other words, all the weight of the building must somehow be carried safely to the ground. You can get a sense of this if you imagine your own body as a structural member. Suppose you are lying flat on your back, your body held rigid. You are going to be lifted high in the air, to become a "roof." First you are lifted by four people: One supports you under the shoulders, one under the buttocks, one holds your arms extended above your head, another holds your feet. Because your weight is therefore channeled down through four vertical people to the ground, you can hold yourself horizontally with some ease. Next you are lifted by two people, one holding your shoulders, another your feet. A lot of your weight is concentrated in the center of your body, which is unsupported, so eventually you sag in the middle and fall to the floor. Then you are lifted by one person, who holds you at the center of your back. The weight at both ends of your body has nowhere to go, nothing to carry it to the ground, and you sag at both ends.

Tensile strength, as applied to architecture, is the ability of a material to span horizontal distances with minimum support from underneath. Returning to the analogy of the body, imagine you are made not of flesh and blood but of strong plastic or metal. Regardless of how you are held up in the air, you can stay rigid and horizontal, because you have great tensile strength.

If you keep these images in mind, you may find it easier to understand the various structural systems we shall consider below. They are introduced here in roughly the chronological order in which they were developed. As was mentioned earlier, all will be of the shell type until the 19th century.

Load-Bearing Construction

Another term for load-bearing construction is "stacking and piling." This is the simplest method of making a building, and it is suitable for brick, stone, adobe, ice blocks, and certain modern materials. Essentially, the builder constructs the walls by piling layer upon layer, starting thick at the bottom, getting thinner as the structure rises, and usually tapering inward near the highest point. The whole may then be topped by a lightweight roof, perhaps of thatch or wood. This construction is stable, because its greatest weight is concentrated at the bottom and weight diminishes gradually as the walls grow higher.

Load-bearing structures tend to have few and small openings (if any) in the walls, because the method does not readily allow for support of material above a void, such as a window opening. Yet it would be a mistake to think that such basic methods must produce basic results. The Great Friday Mosque

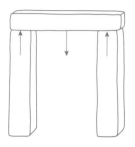

post-and-lintel

13.1 (below) Great Friday Mosque, Djenne, Mali. Rebuilt 1907 in the style of a 13th-century original.

13.2 (opposite page, top) View of the hypostyle from the courtyard temple of Amon-Mut-Khonsu, Luxor. Begun c. 1390 B.C.E. Height of columns 30'.
Photo by Wim Swaan. Library, Getty Research Institute, Los Angeles, Wim Swaan Photograph Collection, 96.P.21.

at Djenne, in Mali, is a spectacular example of monumental architecture created from simple techniques and materials (**13.1**). Constructed of **adobe** (sun-dried brick) and coated with mud plaster, the imposing walls of this mosque have a plastic, sculptural quality. The photograph shows well the gentle tapering of the walls imposed by the construction technique as well as the small size of the windows that illuminate the covered prayer hall inside. The protruding wooden poles serve to anchor the scaffolding that is erected every few years so that workers can restore the mosque's smooth coating of mud plaster.

Post-and-Lintel

After stacking and piling, post-and-lintel construction is the most elementary structural method, based on two uprights (the posts) supporting a horizontal crosspiece (the lintel, or beam). This configuration can be continued indefinitely, so that there may be one very long horizontal supported at critical points along the way by vertical posts to carry its weight to the ground. The most common materials for post-and-lintel construction are stone and wood. Since neither has great tensile strength, these materials will yield and cave in when forced to span long distances, so the architect must provide supporting posts at close intervals.

Post-and-lintel construction has been, for at least four thousand years, a favorite method of architects for raising a roof and providing for open space underneath. The ruins of a portion of the ancient Egyptian temple of Amon-Mut-Khonsu illustrate the majesty and also the limits of post-and-lintel construction in stone (**13.2**). Carved as bundles of stems capped by stylized papyrus-flower buds, the stone columns support rows of heavy stone lintels, with each lintel spanning two columns. The lintels would in turn have supported wooden roof beams and roofing. Because stone does not have great ten-

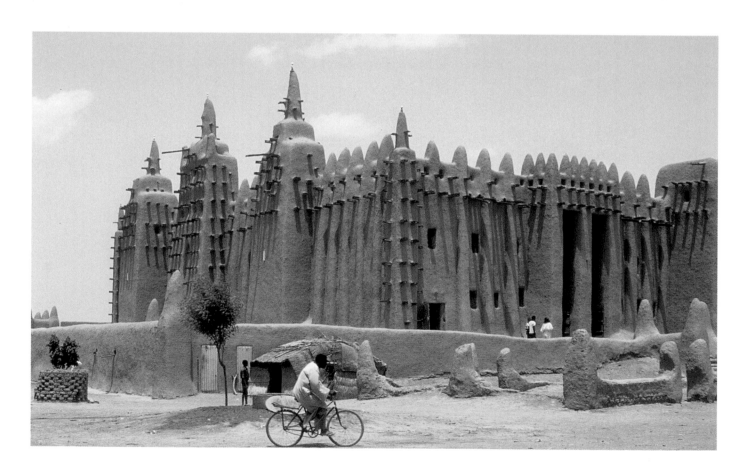

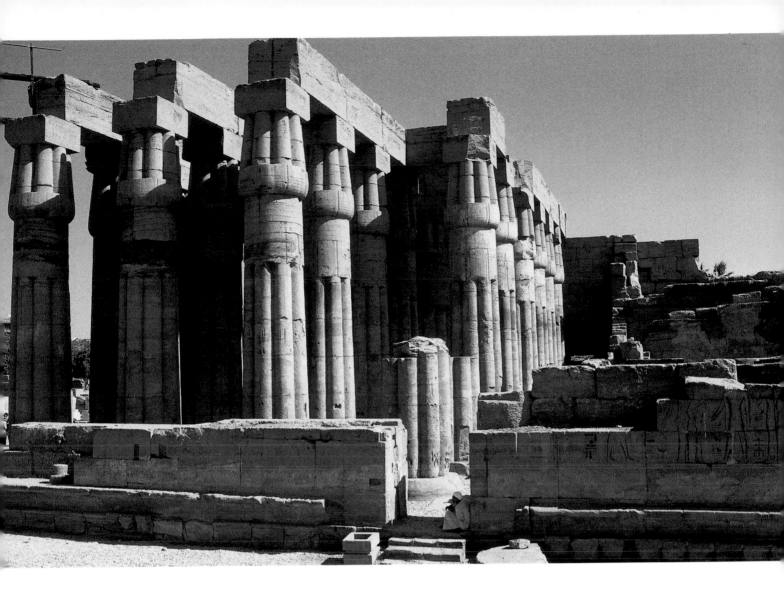

sile strength, the supporting columns must be closely spaced. A large hall erected in post-and-lintel construction was thus a virtual forest of columns inside. We call such spaces **hypostyle** halls, from the Greek for "beneath columns." Ancient Egyptians associated hypostyle halls with the primal swamp of creation, where, according to Egyptian belief, the first mound of dry land arose at the dawn of the world. To make this connection clear, they designed their columns as stylized versions of plants that grew in the marshes of the Nile. Surrounded by load-bearing walls pierced high up by small windows, the hypostyle halls of Egyptian temples were dark and mysterious places.

In ancient Greece, the design of post-and-lintel buildings, especially temples, became standardized in certain features. Greek architects developed and codified three major architectural styles, roughly in sequence. We know them as the Greek **orders.** The most distinctive feature of each was the design of the column (**13.3**). By the 7th century B.C.E. the **Doric** style had been introduced. A Doric column has no base, nothing separating it from the floor below; its **capital,** the topmost part between the shaft of the column and the roof or lintel, is a plain stone slab above a rounded stone. The **Ionic** style was developed in the 6th century B.C.E. and gradually replaced the Doric. An Ionic column has a stepped base and a carved capital in the form of two graceful spirals known as volutes. The **Corinthian** style, which appeared in the 4th century B.C.E., is yet more elaborate, having a more detailed base and a capital carved as a stylized bouquet of acanthus leaves.

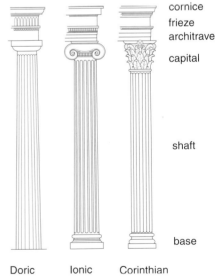

13.3 Column styles of the Greek orders.

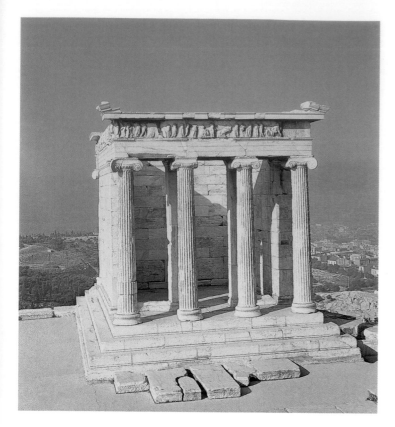

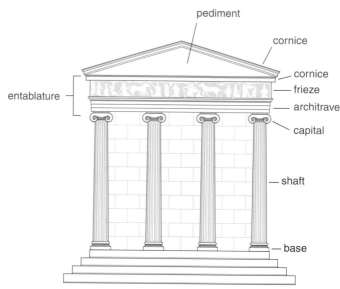

13.4 (left) Kallikrates. Temple of Athena Nike, from the east, Acropolis, Athens. 427–424 B.C.E. Pentelic marble.

13.5 (right) Elevation, Temple of Athena Nike.

The most famous and influential work of Greek architecture is certainly the Parthenon, a Doric temple that we will examine in Chapter 14 (see 14.26). Here we look at the smaller Temple of Athena Nike (**13.4**), which stands nearby on the hilltop site in Athens known as the Acropolis. With their stepped bases and volute capitals, the columns indicate that this is an Ionic temple. The columns support a structure whose remains, reconstructed here in a line drawing (**13.5**), display other important elements of Greek architecture. The plain, horizontal stone lintels of Egypt are here elaborated into a compound structure called an **entablature.** The entablature consists of three basic elements. The simple, unadorned band of lintels immediately over the columns is the **architrave.** The area above the architrave is the **frieze,** here ornamented with sculpture in relief. The frieze is capped by a shelflike projection called a **cornice.** The entablature in turn supports a triangular element called a **pediment,** which is itself crowned by its own cornice. Like the frieze, the pediment would have been ornamented with sculpture in relief. If these elements look familiar to you, it is because they have passed into the vocabulary of Western architecture and form part of the basis of the style we refer to broadly as classical. For centuries, banks, museums, universities, government buildings, and churches have been built using the elements first codified and named by the Greeks, then adapted and modified by the Romans.

Many of the great architectural traditions of the world are based in post-and-lintel construction. The architectural style developed in China provides a good contrast to that of Greece, for while its principles were developed around the same time, the standard material is not stone, but wood. We know from terra-cotta models found in tombs that the basic elements of Chinese architecture were in place by the second century B.C.E. During the 6th century C.E., this architectural vocabulary was adopted by Japan along with other elements of Chinese culture. We illustrate it here with a Japanese building, the incomparable Byodo-in (**13.6**).

Built as a palace, Byodo-in was converted to a Buddhist shrine after the death of the original owner in 1052 C.E. Among the works of art it houses is Jocho's sculpture of Amida Buddha, discussed in Chapter 2 (see 2.28). Our first impression is of a weighty and elaborate superstructure of gracefully curved roofs resting—lightly, somehow—on slender wooden columns. The effect is miraculous, for the building seems to float; but how can all of that weight rest on such slender supports? The answer lies in the cluster of interlocking wooden brackets and arms that crowns each column (13.7). Called bracket sets, they distribute the weight of the roof and its large, overhanging eaves evenly onto the wooden columns, allowing each column to bear up to five times the weight it could support directly. Chinese and Japanese architects developed many variations on the bracket set over the centuries, making them larger or smaller, more elaborate or simpler, more prominent or more subtle.

The distinctive curving profile of East Asian roofs is made possible by a stepped truss system (13.8). (Western roofs, in contrast, are usually supported by a rigid triangular truss, as in the Greek pediment.) By varying the height of each level of the truss, builders could control the pitch and curve of the roof. Taste in roof styles varied over time and from region to region. Some roofs are steeply pitched and fall in a fancifully exaggerated curve, almost like a ski jump; while others are gentler, with a subtle, barely noticeable curve.

The post-and-lintel system, then, offers potential for both structural soundness and grandeur. When applied to wood or stone, however, it leaves one problem unsolved, and that is the spanning of relatively large open spaces. The first attempt at solving this problem was the invention of the round arch.

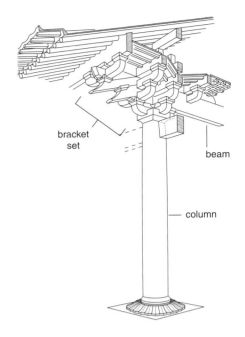

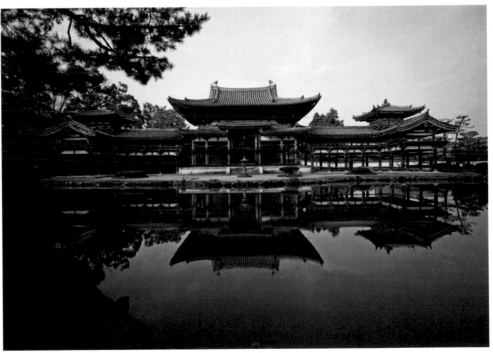

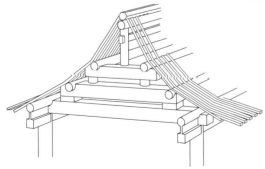

13.6 (center) Hoodo (Phoenix Hall), Byodo-in Temple, Uji, Kyoto Prefecture, Japan. Heian period, c. 1053.

13.7 (above, right) Bracket system.

13.8 (left) Stepped truss roof structure.

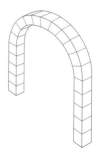

round arch

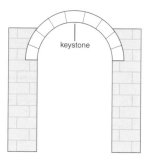

round arch with outward
thrust contained

13.9 Pont du Gard, Nîmes,
France. Early 1st century C.E.
Length 902'.

Round Arch and Vault

Although the round arch was used by the ancient peoples of Mesopotamia several centuries before our common era (see 14.9), it was most fully developed by the Romans, who perfected the form in the 2nd century B.C.E. To get a sense of how the arch works, we might go back to the analogy of the body. Imagine that, instead of lying flat on your back, you are bent over forward into a curve, and again you will be lifted into the air. One person will support your hands, another your feet. As long as your body follows the proper arc—that is, your two supporters stand the correct distance apart—you can maintain the pose for some time. If they stand too close together, you start to topple first one way and then the other; if they move too far apart, you have insufficient support in the middle and plunge to the floor. An arch incorporates more complex forces of tension (pulling apart) and compression (pushing together), but the general idea is the same.

The arch has many virtues. In addition to being an attractive form, it enables the architect to open up fairly large spaces in a wall without risking the building's structural soundness. These spaces admit light, reduce the weight of the walls, and decrease the amount of material needed. As utilized by the Romans, the arch is a perfect semicircle, although it may seem elongated if it rests on columns. It is constructed from wedge-shaped pieces of stone that meet at an angle always perpendicular to the curve of the arch. Because of tensions and compressions inherent in the form, the arch is stable only when it is complete, when the topmost stone, the **keystone,** has been set in place. For this reason an arch under construction must be supported from below, usually by a wooden framework. In addition, an arch exerts an outward thrust at its base that must be contained (see diagram).

Among the most elegant and enduring of Roman structures based on the arch is the Pont du Gard at Nîmes, France (**13.9**), built about 15 C.E. when the empire was nearing its farthest expansion (see map, p. 372). At this time Roman industry, commerce, and agriculture were at their peak. Engineering was applied to an ambitious system of public-works projects, not just in Italy but in the outlying areas as well. The Pont du Gard functioned as an aqueduct, a structure meant to transport water, and its lower level served as a footbridge across the river. That it stands today virtually intact after nearly two thousand years (and is crossed by cyclists on the route of the famous Tour de France bicycle race) testifies to the Romans' brilliant engineering skills. Visually, the

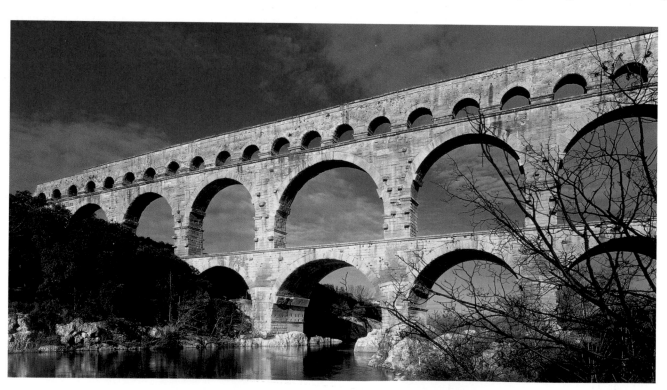

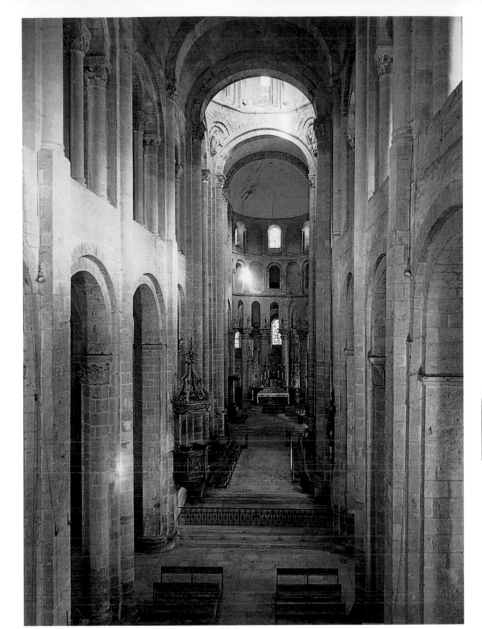

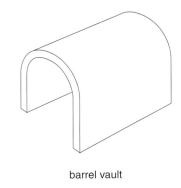

barrel vault

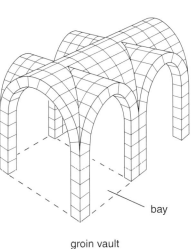

bay

groin vault

Pont du Gard exemplifies the best qualities of arch construction. Solid and heavy, obviously durable, it is shot through with open spaces that make it seem light and its weight-bearing capabilities effortless.

When the arch is extended in depth—when it is, in reality, many arches placed flush one behind the other—the result is called a **barrel vault.** This vault construction makes it possible to create large interior spaces. The Romans made great use of the barrel vault, but for its finest expression we look many hundreds of years later, to the churches of the Middle Ages.

The church of Sainte-Foy (**13.10**), in the French city of Conques, is an example of the style prevalent throughout Western Europe from about 1050 to 1200—a style known as **Romanesque.** Earlier churches had used the Roman round arch to span the spaces between interior columns that ultimately held up the roof. There were no ceilings, however. Rather, worshipers looked up into a system of wooden trusses and the underside of a pitched roof (see 15.2, 15.3). Imagine looking directly up into the attic of a house and you will get the idea. With the Romanesque style, builders set a stone barrel vault as a ceiling over the **nave** (the long central area), hiding the roof structure from view. The barrel vault unified the interior visually, providing a soaring, majestic climax to the rhythms announced by the arches below.

13.10 Interior, Sainte-Foy, Conques, France. c. 1050–1120.

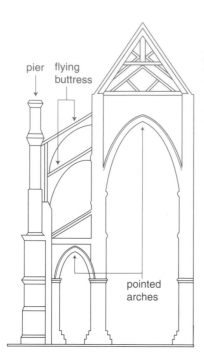

pier flying
buttress

pointed
arches

Elements of Gothic architecture

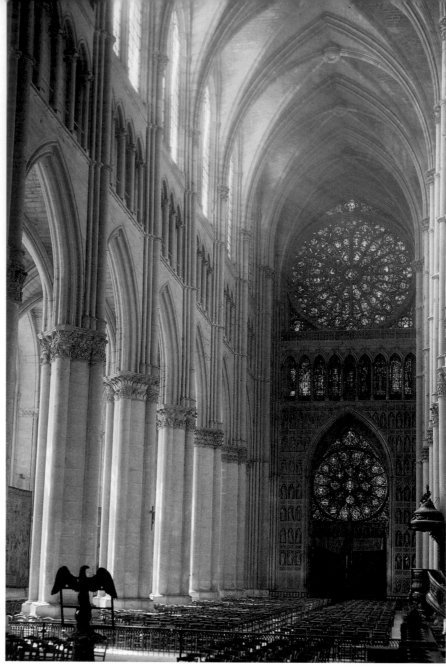

13.11 Nave, Reims Cathedral, France. 1211–c. 1290. Height 125'.

On the side aisles of Sainte-Foy (not visible in the photograph) the builders employed a series of **groin vaults.** A groin vault results when two barrel vaults are crossed at right angles to each other, thus directing the weights and stresses down into the four corners. By dividing up a space into square segments known as **bays,** each of which contains one groin vault, the architects could cover a long span safely and economically. The repetition of bays also creates a satisfying rhythmic pattern.

Pointed Arch and Vault

While the round arch and vault of the Romanesque era solved many problems and made many things possible, they nevertheless had certain drawbacks. For one thing, a round arch, to be stable, must be a semicircle; therefore, the height of the arch is limited by its width. Two other difficulties were weight and darkness. Barrel vaults are both literally and visually heavy, calling for huge masses of stone to maintain their structural stability. They exert an outward thrust all along their base, which builders countered by setting them in massive walls that they dared not weaken with light-admitting openings. The **Gothic** period in Europe, which followed the Romanesque, solved these problems with the pointed arch.

The pointed arch, while seemingly not very different from the round one, offers many advantages. Because the sides arc up to a point, weight is channeled down to the ground at a steeper angle, and therefore the arch can be taller. The vault constructed from such an arch also can be much taller than a barrel vault. Architects of the Gothic period found they did not need heavy masses of material throughout the curve of the vault, as long as the major points of intersection were reinforced. These reinforcements, called ribs, are visible in the nave ceiling of Reims Cathedral (**13.11**).

The light captured streaming into the nave of Reims Cathedral in the photograph vividly illustrates another important feature of Gothic church architecture: windows. Whereas Romanesque cathedrals tended to be dark inside, with few and small window openings, Gothic builders strove to open up their walls for large stained glass windows such as the two radiant round windows, called rose windows, visible in the photograph. (Most of the stained glass windows in Reims Cathedral have suffered damage and been replaced with clear glass, which is why the light is so evident in the photograph.) Fearing that the numerous window openings could disastrously weaken walls that were already under pressure from the outward thrust of arches, Gothic builders reinforced their walls from the outside with **buttresses, piers,** and a new invention, **flying buttresses.** The principles are easy to understand if you imagine yourself using your own weight to prop up a wall. If you stand next to a wall and press the entire length of your body against it, you are a buttress. If you stand away from the wall and press against it with outstretched arms, your body is a pier, and your arms are flying buttresses. The illustration here (**13.12**) of the exterior of the Cathedral of Le Mans, in France, shows the Gothic system of buttresses, piers, and flying buttresses, as well as the numerous windows that made them necessary.

13.12 Exterior of the Cathedral of Le Mans, France, showing buttresses, piers, and flying buttresses. 1217–54.

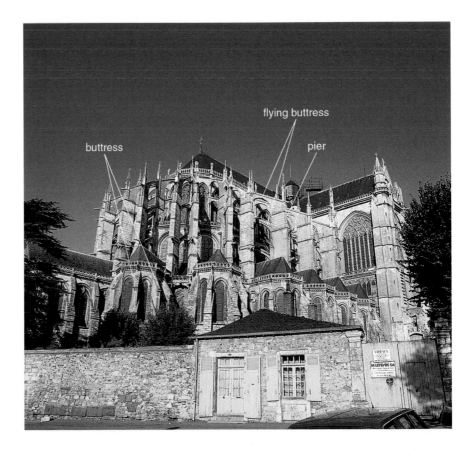

Dome

A dome is an architectural structure generally in the shape of a hemisphere, or half globe. One customary definition of the dome is an arch rotated 360 degrees on its axis, and this is really more accurate, because, for example, the dome based on a pointed arch will be pointed at the top, not perfectly hemispherical. The stresses in a dome are much like those of an arch, except that they are spread in a circle around the dome's perimeter. Unless the dome is buttressed—supported from the outside—from all sides, there is a tendency for it to "explode," for the stones to pop outward in all directions, causing the dome to collapse.

Like so many other architectural structures, the dome was perfected under the incomparable engineering genius of the Romans, and one of the finest domed buildings ever erected dates from the early 2nd century. It is called the Pantheon (**13.13, 13.14**), which means a temple dedicated to "all the gods"—or, at least, all the gods who were venerated in ancient Rome. We reproduce here an 18th-century painting of the interior (**13.15**) because the circular building is so vast that it is impossible to find a camera angle to convey adequately its shape and scale.

As seen from the inside, the Pantheon has a perfect hemispherical dome soaring 142 feet above the floor, resting upon a cylinder almost exactly the same in diameter—140 feet. The ceiling is **coffered**—ornamented with recessed rectangles, coffers, which lessen its weight. At the very top of the dome is an opening 29 feet in diameter called an **oculus,** or eye, thought to be symbolic of the "eye of Heaven." This opening provides the sole (and plentiful) illumination for the building. In its conception, then, the Pantheon is amazingly simple, equal in height and width, symmetrical in its structure, round form set upon round form. Yet because of its scale and its satisfying proportions, the effect is overwhelming.

13.13 (left) Pantheon, Rome. 118–125 C.E.

13.14 (right) Section drawing of the Pantheon.

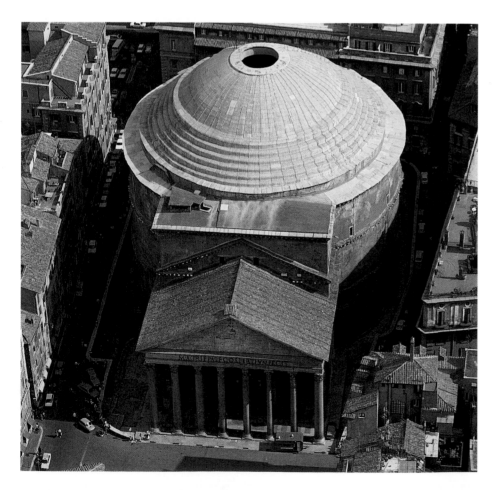

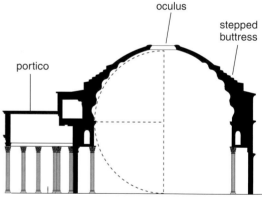

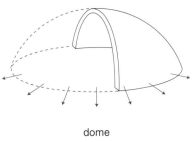

dome

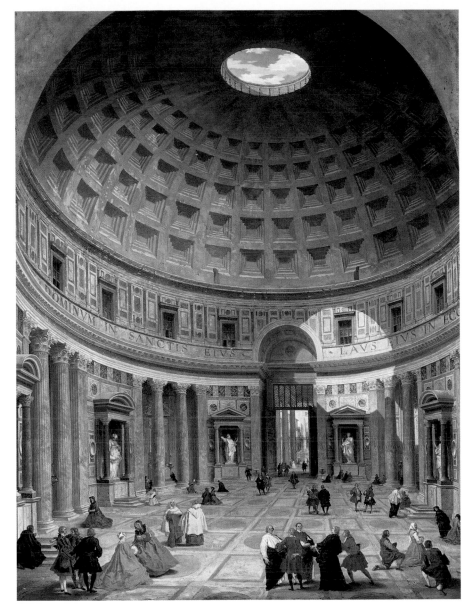

The combined structural possibilities of the dome and the vault enabled the Romans to open up huge spaces such as the Pantheon without interior supports. Another important factor that allowed them to build on such a scale was their use of concrete. While Greek and Egyptian buildings had been made of solid stone, monumental Roman buildings were made of concrete, poured into hollow walls of concrete brick as though into a mold, then faced with stone veneer to look as though they were made of solid stone. An important technological breakthrough, the use of concrete cut costs, sped construction, and enabled building on a grand scale.

Visitors enter the Pantheon through the rectangular **portico,** or porch, that is joined somewhat incongruously to it. Here we recognize the characteristic form of the Greek temple as inherited by the Romans: post-and-lintel construction, Corinthian order, entablature, and pediment. Faced in plain brick, the outside of the domed chamber is drab and uninteresting by comparison. In fact, visitors were not supposed to be too aware of it. In Roman times, an approach to the building was constructed to lead to the portico while obscuring the rest of the temple. Thinking that they were entering a standard post-and-lintel temple, visitors must have been stunned to see the enormous round space open up before their eyes. Tourists today experience the same theatrical surprise.

13.15 Giovanni Paolo Panini. *Interior of the Pantheon.* c. 1740. Oil on canvas, 4'2½" × 3'3". National Gallery of Art, Washington, D.C.

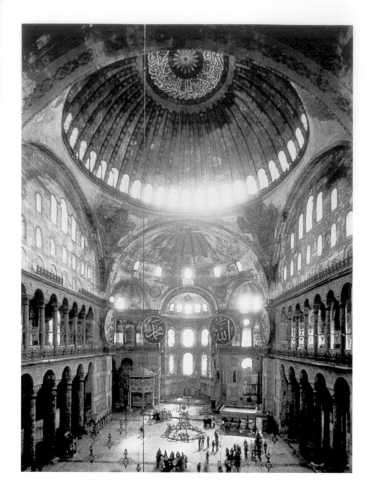

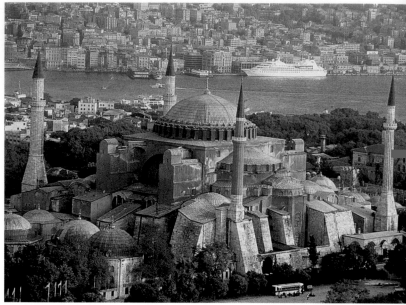

13.16 (left) Interior, Hagia Sophia, Istanbul. 532–37. Height of dome 183'.

13.17 (right) Hagia Sophia, Istanbul. 532–37.

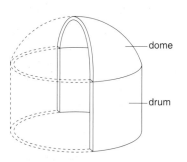

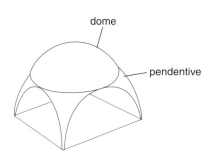

The Pantheon is a **rotunda,** a round building, and its dome sits naturally on the circular **drum** of the base. Often, however, architects wish to set a dome over a square building. In this case, a transitional element is required between the circle (at the dome's base) and the square (of the building's top). An elegant solution can be found in Hagia Sophia (the Church of the Holy Wisdom) in Istanbul (**13.16, 13.17**). Designed by two mathematicians, Anthemius of Tralles and Isidorus of Miletus, Hagia Sophia was built as a church during the 6th century, when Istanbul, then called Constantinople, was the capital of the Byzantine Empire. When the Turks conquered the city in the 15th century, Hagia Sophia was converted for use as a mosque. It was at this time that the four slender towers, **minarets,** were added. The building is now preserved as a museum. In sheer size and perfection of form it was the architectural triumph of its time and has seldom been matched since then.

The dome of Hagia Sophia rises 183 feet above the floor, with its weight carried to the ground by heavy stone piers—in this case, squared columns—at the four corners of the immense nave. Around the base of the dome is a row of closely spaced arched windows, which make the heavy dome seem to "float" upward. (The exterior view makes it clear that these windows are situated between buttresses that ring the base of the dome, containing its outward thrust and compensating for any structural weakening caused by the window openings.) Each of the four sides of the building consists of a monumental round arch, and between the arches and the dome are curved triangular sections known as **pendentives.** It is the function of the pendentives to make a smooth transition between rectangle and dome.

The domes of the Pantheon and the Hagia Sophia serve primarily to open up vast interior spaces. Seen from the outside, their hemispherical form is obscured by the buttressing needed to contain their powerful outward thrust. Yet the dome is such an inherently pleasing form that architects often used it for purely decorative purposes, as an exterior ornament to crown a building. In this case, it is often set high on a drum, a circular base, so that it can be seen from the ground. A famous example of a building crowned by an ornamental dome is the Taj Mahal, in Agra, India (**13.18**).

The Taj Mahal was built in the mid-17th century by the Muslim emperor of India, Shah Jahan, as a tomb for his beloved wife, Arjummand Banu. Although the Taj is nearly as large as Hagia Sophia and possessed of a dome rising some 30 feet higher, it seems comparatively fragile and weightless. Nearly all its exterior lines reach upward, from the graceful pointed arches, to the pointed dome, to the four slender minarets poised at the outside corners. The Taj Mahal, constructed entirely of pure white marble, appears almost as a shimmering mirage that has come to rest for a moment beside the peaceful reflecting pool.

The section drawing (**13.19**) clarifies how the dome is constructed. Over the underground burial chambers of Shah Jahan and his wife, the large central room of the tomb rises to a domed ceiling. Over this, on the roof of the building, sits a tall drum crowned by a pointed dome. A small entryway gives access to the inside for maintenance purposes, but it is not meant to be visited. The exterior is shaped in a graceful, bulging S-curve silhouette that obscures the actual drum-and-dome structure evident in the cutaway view.

13.18 (below, top) Taj Mahal, Agra, India. 1632–53.

13.19 (below) Section, Taj Mahal.

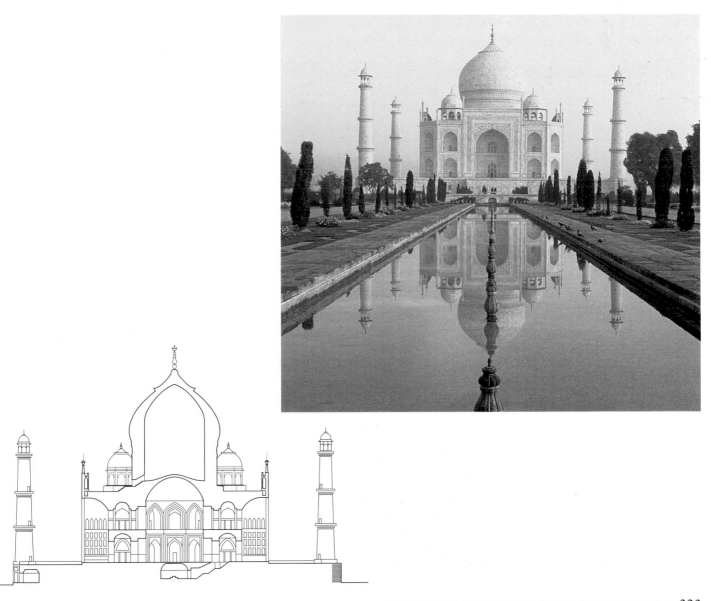

Corbelled Arch and Dome

Islamic architects knew the use of the arch and the dome because Islam came of age in a part of the world that had belonged first to the Roman and then to the Byzantine empires. When Islamic rulers settled in India, their architects brought these construction techniques with them, resulting in such buildings as the Taj Mahal. Indigenous Indian architecture, in contrast, does not make use of the arch or dome, but is based on post-and-lintel construction. To create arch- and dome-like forms, Indian architects used a technique called corbelling. In a corbelled arch, each course (row) of stones extends slightly beyond the one below, until eventually the opening is bridged.

Just as a round Roman arch can be rotated 360 degrees to create a dome, corbelling can also be used to create a dome form, as in this temple interior (**13.20**). Ornamented by band upon band of ornate carving and set with figures of the sixteen celestial nymphs, the corbelled dome rests on an octagon of lintels supported by eight columns. Pairs of stone brackets between each column provide additional support. The elaborate, filigreed carving that decorates every available surface testifies to the virtuosity of Indian stoneworkers, in whose skillful hands stone was made to seem as light as lace.

Although to the naked eye a corbelled arch may be indistinguishable from the round arch described above, it does not function structurally as a round arch does, channeling weight outward and downward, and so does not enable the construction of large, unobstructed interior spaces.

13.20 Interior of the Jain temple of Dilwara, Vimala temple, Mount Abu, South Rajasthan, India. Completed 1032.

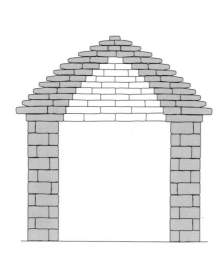

corbelled dome

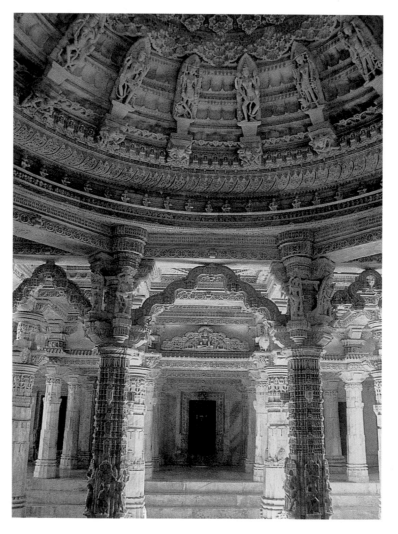

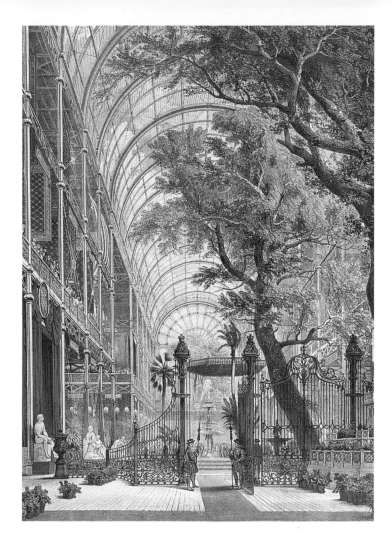

Cast-Iron Construction

With the perfection of the post-and-lintel, the arch, and the dome, construction in wood, stone, and brick had gone just about as far as it could go. Not until the introduction of a new building material did the next major breakthrough in structural systems take place. Iron had been known for thousands of years and had been used for tools and objects of all kinds, but only in the 19th century did architects realize that its great strength offered promise for structural support. This principle was demonstrated brilliantly in a project that few contemporary observers took seriously.

In 1851 the city of London was planning a great exhibition, under the sponsorship of Prince Albert, husband of Queen Victoria. The challenge was to house under one roof the "Works of Industry of All Nations," and the commission for erecting a suitable structure fell to Joseph Paxton, a designer of greenhouses. Paxton raised in Hyde Park a wondrous building framed in cast iron and sheathed in glass—probably the first modern skeleton-and-skin construction ever designed (**13.21**). The Crystal Palace, as Paxton's creation came to be known, covered more than 17 acres and reached a height of 108 feet. Because of an ingenious system of prefabrication, the whole structure was erected in just sixteen weeks.

Visitors to the exhibition considered the Crystal Palace a curiosity—a marvelous one, to be sure, but still an oddity outside the realm of architecture. They could not have foreseen that Paxton's design, solid iron framework clothed in a glass skin, would pave the way for 20th-century architecture. In fact, Paxton had taken a giant step in demonstrating that as long as a building's skeleton held firm, its skin could be light and non-load-bearing. Several intermediary steps would be required before this principle could be translated into today's architecture.

13.21 Joseph Paxton. Crystal Palace, Hyde Park, London. 1851, destroyed by fire 1936.
Contemporary lithograph by Joseph Nash. Guildhall Library, London.

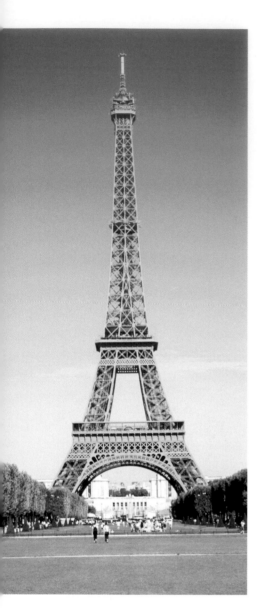

13.22 Alexandre Gustave Eiffel. Eiffel Tower, Paris. 1889. Iron, height 934'.

Another bold experiment in iron construction came a few decades later just across the English Channel, in France, and involved a plan that many considered to be foolhardy, if not downright insane. Gustave Eiffel, a French engineer, proposed to build in the center of Paris a skeleton iron tower, nearly a thousand feet tall, to act as a centerpiece for the Paris World's Fair of 1889. Nothing of the sort had ever been suggested, much less built. In spite of loud protests, the Eiffel Tower (**13.22**) was constructed, at a cost of about a million dollars—an unheard-of sum for those times. It rises on four arched columns, which curve inward until they meet in a single tower thrusting up boldly above the cityscape of Paris. (The writer Guy de Maupassant claimed that he lunched in a restaurant on the tower as often as possible, because "it's the only place in Paris where I don't have to see it."[1])

The importance of this singular, remarkable structure for the future of architecture rests on the fact that it *was* a skeleton that proudly showed itself without benefit of any cosmetic embellishment. No marble, no glass, no tiles, no skin of any kind—just the clean lines drawn in an industrial-age product. Two concepts emerged from this daring construction. First, metal in and of itself can make beautiful architecture. Second, metal can provide a solid framework for a very large structure, self-sustaining and permanent. Today the Eiffel Tower is the ultimate symbol of Paris, and no tourist would pass up a visit. From folly to landmark in a century—such is the course of innovative architecture.

Iron for structural members was not the only breakthrough of the mid-19th century. The Industrial Revolution also introduced a new construction material that was much humbler but equally significant in its implications for architecture: the nail. And for want of that simple little nail, most of the houses we live in today could not have been built.

Balloon-Frame Construction

So far in this chapter the illustrations have concentrated on grand and public buildings—churches, temples, monuments. These are the glories of architecture, the buildings we admire and travel great distances to see. We should not forget, however, that the overwhelming majority of structures in the world have been houses for people to live in, or domestic architecture.

Until the mid-19th century houses were of shell construction. They were made of brick or stone (and, in warmer climates, of such materials as reeds and bamboo) with load-bearing construction, or else they were post-and-lintel structures in which heavy timbers were assembled by complicated notching and joinery, sometimes with wooden pegs. Nails, if any, had to be fabricated by hand and were very expensive.

About 1833, in Chicago, the technique of balloon-frame construction was introduced. Balloon-frame construction is a true skeleton-and-skin method. It developed from two innovations: improved methods for milling lumber and mass-produced nails. In this system, the builder first erects a framework or skeleton by nailing together sturdy but lightweight boards (the familiar 2-by-4 "stud"), then adds a roof and sheathes the walls in clapboard, shingles, stucco, or whatever the homeowner wishes. Glass for windows can be used lavishly, as long as it does not interrupt the underlying wood structure, since the sheathing plays little part in holding the building together.

When houses of this type were introduced, the term "balloon framing" was meant to be sarcastic. Skeptics thought the buildings would soon fall down, or burst just like balloons. But some of the earliest balloon-frame houses stand firm today, and this method is still the most popular for new house construction in Western countries.

The balloon frame, of course, has its limitations. Wood beams 2 by 4 inches thick cannot support a skyscraper ten or fifty stories high, and that was the very sort of building architects had begun to dream of late in the 19th century. For such soaring ambitions, a new material was needed, and it was found. The material was steel.

Steel-Frame Construction

Although multistory buildings have been with us since the Roman Empire, the development of the skyscraper, as we know it, required two late-19th-century innovations: the elevator and steel-frame construction. Steel-frame construction, like balloon framing, is a true skeleton-and-skin arrangement. Rather than piling floor upon floor, with each of the lower stories supporting those above it, the builders first erect a steel "cage" that is capable of sustaining the entire weight of the building; then they apply a skin of some other material. But people could hardly be expected to walk all the way to the top of a ten-story building, to say nothing of a skyscraper. Hence another invention made its appearance, the elevator.

What many consider to be the first genuinely modern building was designed by Louis Sullivan and built between 1890 and 1891 in St. Louis. Known as the Wainwright Building (**13.23**), it employed a steel framework sheathed in masonry. Other architects had experimented with steel support but had carefully covered their structures in heavy stone so as to reflect traditional architectural forms and make the construction seem reliably sturdy. Centuries of precedent had prepared the public to expect bigness to go hand in hand with heaviness. Sullivan broke new ground by making his sheathing light, letting the skin of his building echo, even celebrate, the steel framing underneath. Regular bays of windows on the seven office floors are separated by

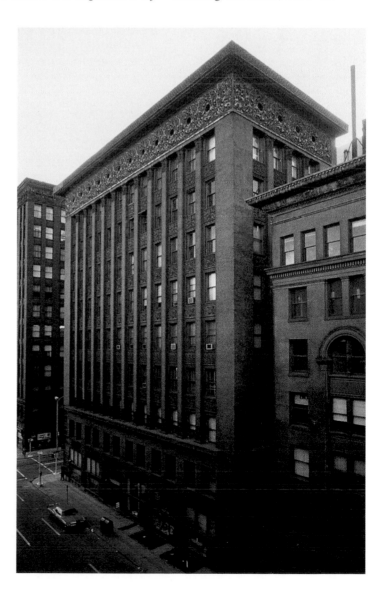

13.23 Louis Sullivan. Wainwright Building, St. Louis, 1890–91.

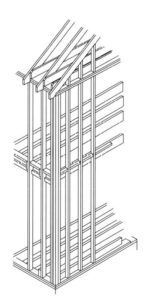

balloon-frame construction

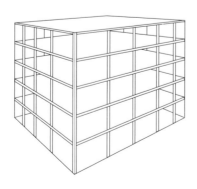

steel-frame construction

strong vertical lines, and the four corners of the building are emphasized by vertical piers. The Wainwright Building's message is subtle, but we cannot mistake it: The nation had stopped growing outward and started growing *up*.

Sullivan's design looks forward to the 20th century, but it nevertheless clings to certain architectural details rooted in classical history, most notably the heavy cornice (the projecting roof ornament) that terminates upward movement at the top of the building. In a very few decades even these backward glances into the architectural past would become rare.

Toward the middle of the 20th century skyscrapers began to take over the downtown areas of major cities, and city planners had to grapple with unprecedented problems. How high is too high? How much air space should a building consume? What provision, if any, should be made to prevent tall buildings from completely blocking out the sunlight from the streets below? In New York and certain other cities ordinances were passed that resulted in a number of look-alike and architecturally undistinguished buildings. The laws required that if a building filled the ground space of a city block right up to the sidewalk, it could rise for only a certain number of feet or stories before being "stepped back," or narrowed; then it could rise for only a specified number of additional feet before being stepped back again. The resultant structures came to be known as "wedding-cake" buildings. A few architects, however, found more creative ways of meeting the air space requirement. Those working in the **International** style designed some of the most admired American skyscrapers during the 1950s and 1960s. International style architecture emphasized clean lines, geometric (usually rectilinear) form, and an avoidance of superficial decoration. The "bones" of a building were supposed to show and to be the only ornament necessary. A classic example of this pure style is Lever House.

13.24 Gordon Bunshaft of Skidmore, Owings, and Merrill. Lever House, New York. 1952.

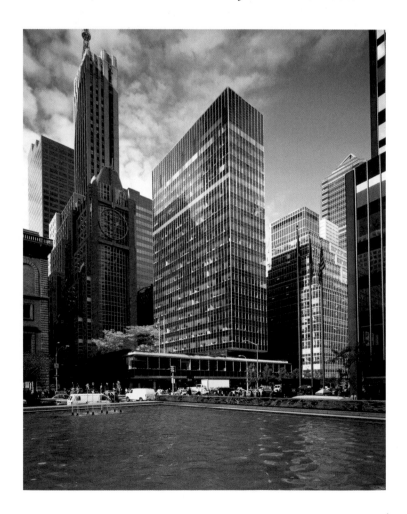

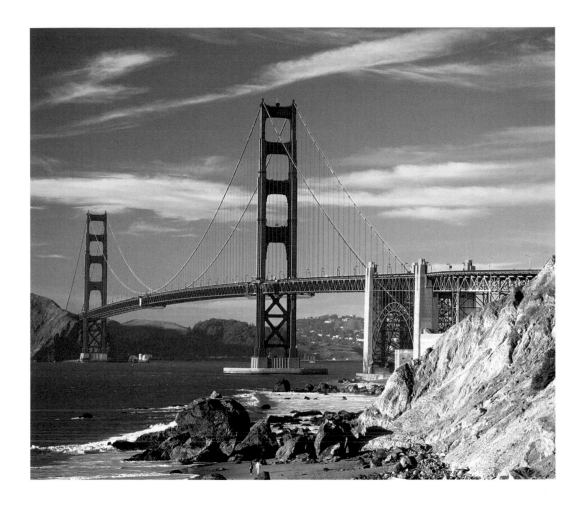

13.25 Golden Gate Bridge, San Francisco. 1937. Joseph B. Strauss, chief engineer; O. H. Ammann, Charles Derleth, Jr., and Leon S. Moisseiff, consulting engineers; Irving F. Morrow, consulting architect.

Lever House in New York (**13.24**), designed by the architectural firm of Skidmore, Owings, and Merrill and built in 1952, was heralded as a breath of fresh air in the smog of look-alike structures. Its sleek understated form was widely copied but never equaled. Lever House might be compared to two shimmering glass dominoes, one resting horizontally on freestanding supports, the other balanced upright and off-center on the first. At a time when most architects of office buildings strove to fill every square inch of air space to which they were entitled—both vertically and horizontally—the elegant Lever House drew back and raised its slender rectangle aloof from its neighbors, surrounded by free space. Even its base does not rest on the ground but rides on thin supports to allow for open plazas and passageways beneath the building. Practically no other system of construction except steel frame could have made possible this graceful form.

Suspension

Also made feasible by steel, suspension is the structural method we associate primarily with bridges, although it has been employed for some buildings as well. The concept of suspension was developed for bridges late in the 19th century. In essence, the weight of the structure is suspended from steel cables supported on vertical pylons, driven into the ground. A long bridge, such as the Golden Gate Bridge in San Francisco (**13.25**), may have only two sets of pylons planted in the riverbed, but the steel cables suspended under tension from their towers are strong enough to support a span between them almost four-fifths of a mile long. With their long sweeping curves and slender lines, suspension structures are among the most graceful in architecture.

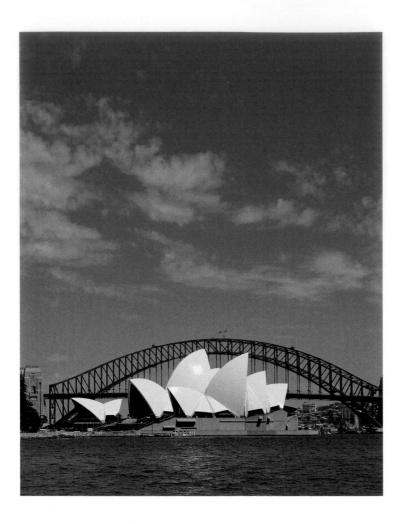

13.26 Joern Utzon. Sydney Opera House, Australia. 1959–72. Reinforced concrete, height of highest shell 200'.

Reinforced Concrete

Concrete is an old material that was known and used by the Romans. A mixture of cement, gravel, and water, concrete can be poured, will assume the shape of any mold, and then will set to hardness. Its major problem is that it tends to be brittle and has low tensile strength. This problem is often observed in the thin concrete slabs used for sidewalks and patios, which may crack and split apart as a result of weight and weather. Late in the 19th century, however, a method was developed for reinforcing concrete forms by imbedding iron rods inside the concrete before it hardened. The iron contributes tensile strength, while the concrete provides shape and surface. In the 20th century reinforced concrete, also known as **ferroconcrete,** has been used in a wide variety of structures, often in those with free-form, organic shapes. Although it may seem at first to be a skeleton-and-skin construction, ferroconcrete actually works more like a shell, because the iron rods (or sometimes a steel mesh) and concrete are bonded permanently and can form structures that are self-sustaining, even when very thin.

A special kind of ferroconcrete construction—precast reinforced sections—was used to create the soaring shell-like forms of the Sydney Opera House in Australia (**13.26**). The Opera House, which is really an all-around entertainment complex, is almost as famous for its construction difficulties as it is for its extraordinary design. So daring was its concept that the necessary technology virtually had to be invented as the project went along. Planned as a symbol of the great port city in whose harbor it stands, the Opera House gives the impression of a wonderful clipper ship at full sail. Three sets of pointed shells, oriented in different directions, turn the building into a giant sculpture in which walls and roof are one. Reinforced concrete is the sort of material that allows the builder to experiment and try new techniques, that allows the architect to dream impossible dreams.

Geodesic Domes

Of all the structural systems, probably the only one that can be attributed to a single individual is the geodesic dome, which was developed by the American architectural engineer R. Buckminster Fuller. Fuller's dome is essentially a bubble, formed by a network of metal rods arranged in triangles and further organized into tetrahedrons. (A tetrahedron is a three-dimensional geometric figure having four faces.) This metal framework can be sheathed in any of several lightweight materials, including wood, glass, and plastic.

The geodesic dome offers a combination of advantages never before available in architecture. Although very light in weight in relation to size, it is amazingly strong, because its structure rests on a mathematically sophisticated use of the triangle. Because it requires no interior support, all the space encompassed by the dome can be used with total freedom. A geodesic dome can be built in any size. In theory, at least, a structurally sound geodesic dome 2 miles across could be built, although nothing of this scope has ever been attempted. Perhaps most important for modern building techniques, Fuller's dome is based on a modular system of construction. Individual segments—modules—can be prefabricated to allow for extremely quick assembly of even a large dome. And finally, because of the flexibility in choice of sheathing materials, there are virtually endless options for climate and light control.

Fuller patented the geodesic dome in 1947, but it was not until twenty years later, when his design served as the U.S. Pavilion at the Montreal World's Fair, that the public's attention was awakened to its possibilities. The dome at Expo 67 (**13.27**) astonished the architectural world and fair-goers alike. It was 250 feet in diameter (about the size of a football field rounded off) and, being sheathed in translucent material, lighted up the sky at night like a giant spaceship set down on earth.

13.27 R. Buckminster Fuller. U.S. Pavilion, Expo 67, Montreal. 1967. Geodesic dome, diameter 250'.

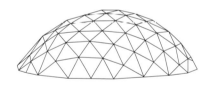

geodesic dome

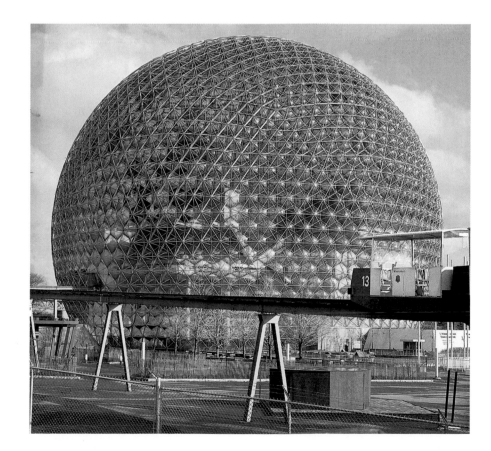

After Expo 67 some people predicted that before long all houses and public buildings would be geodesic domes. This dream has faded considerably, but Fuller's dome has proved exceptionally well suited for government and scientific operations in arctic climates. To build a habitable structure in the freezing wastes of Antarctica, for example, requires a lightweight material that can be shipped and assembled easily, great strength to withstand below-freezing temperatures and high winds, and control of the interior environment. The geodesic dome meets all these requirements.

In this brief survey of the major structural systems we have seen that the form of architecture and its method of construction are largely determined by the materials available. Wood readily lends itself to post-and-lintel construction and balloon-frame construction; stone works for post-and-lintel also, as well as for the arch and dome; metal allows for steel-frame construction, suspension, or reinforced concrete; and so on. But there is another factor—often a more important one—that affects the shape of architecture, and that is the purpose a building will serve.

PURPOSES OF ARCHITECTURE

Architecture is seldom miscellaneous. Nearly every structure is designed to serve a specific function, and we evaluate a structure according to the way in which it fulfills its purpose. Although architecture through the ages has been enormously diverse, almost every structure fits into one of just a few major categories: government buildings; other public buildings, such as libraries or museums; commercial buildings, including offices, banks, and shops; buildings for transportation—airline terminals, train stations, and the like; religious buildings; and, of course, residences.

Beyond function, every structure has a particular character or style. It creates a certain environment within its walls and projects a certain image to the broader environment outside. A bank, for instance, may seem grand and imposing, or small-town and friendly, or modern and high-tech. By choosing a style of architecture, the bankers tell us about their self-image and about the customers they hope to attract. Similar effects are evident with other types of structures.

This section looks briefly at function and style in architecture. We begin by comparing individual buildings that serve the same function, examining in turn examples of museums, office buildings, and dwellings.

Three Museums

Museums make an interesting study in architectural design, because they are works of art meant to display other works of art or history. How they go about fulfilling this purpose tells us much about the nature of architecture.

The National Gallery of Art in Washington, D.C., houses one of the finest collections of Western art in the world (**13.28, 13.29**). Built between 1937 and 1941, the museum was a gift to the nation from the banker and industrialist Andrew Mellon, who not only engaged the architect and funded construction but also donated his own personal art collection to the museum and encouraged his friends to do likewise. The architect Mellon selected was John Russell Pope, a master of the Neoclassical ("new classical") style, which is a style based on the vocabulary of ancient Greek and Roman architecture. Pope had already designed two important buildings in the capital, Constitution Hall and the National Archives, as well as the Baltimore Museum of Art and numerous private residences.

The focal point at the center of Pope's symmetrical building is a temple facade leading to a domed rotunda, a combination clearly derived from the

Pantheon in Rome (see 13.13, 13.15). To either side of the rotunda, great barrel-vaulted corridors provide access to suites of skylit galleries. For Pope, the Pantheon was not merely a great building from the distant past but also one with distinctly American overtones. In founding the United States as a republic, the framers of the Constitution had looked to the example of the Republic of Rome. Thomas Jefferson, seeking to link the young country to the heritage of Greece and Rome, had designed a domed rotunda for his home, Monticello, and another as part of the campus of the University of Virginia. In fact, Pope paid a final tribute to Jefferson with still another rotunda, the Jefferson Memorial, also in Washington, which he created at the same time as the National Gallery.

Sadly, neither Pope nor Mellon lived to see the museum dedicated by President Franklin D. Roosevelt in 1941. Although it was an instant hit with the public, the building was not well received by critics and younger architects, who found its conservative design both bombastic and boring. Defenders have since pointed out that the building is very well suited to the art it was meant to house, which is art from the heart of the Western tradition as it defined itself from the Renaissance through the 19th century. Today, the initial controversy having long ago died away, Pope's building looks timeless and confident, and its generous spaces provide a deeply pleasurable environment for looking at art.

Pope's National Gallery quietly assumed its place in the Neoclassical fabric of Washington D.C. The White House, the Capitol, the Supreme Court, and other important structures employ the same architectural vocabulary. For his museum in Bilbao, in the Basque region of northern Spain, Frank O. Gehry

13.28 (right) John Russell Pope. The National Gallery (now known as the West Building), Washington, D.C. Completed 1941.

13.29 (left) Schematic plan of the National Gallery.

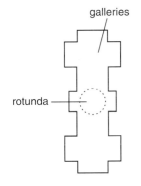

galleries

rotunda

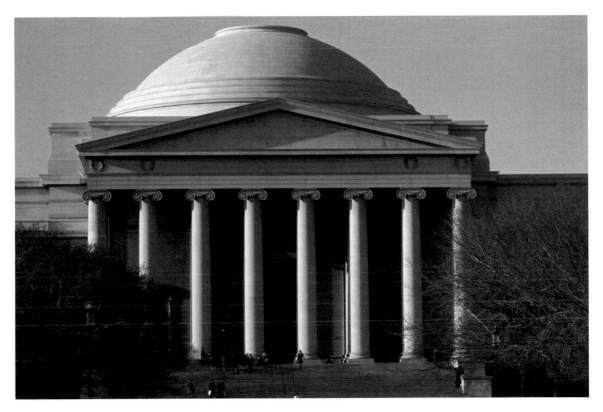

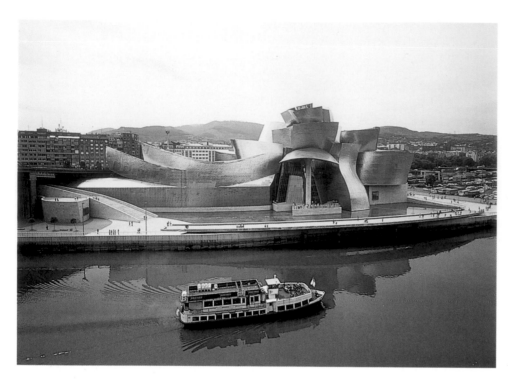

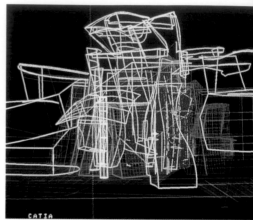

13.30 (left) Frank O. Gehry. Guggenheim Museum Bilbao, Bilbao, Spain. 1997.

13.31 (right) Catia rendering of the Guggenheim Museum Bilbao.

decided on the opposite strategy. Instead of trying to fit in with the existing architecture, he aimed for the greatest possible contrast with it (**13.30**). Gehry had originally been asked to evaluate the possibility of converting a huge abandoned warehouse in Bilbao into a museum, preserving the industrial exterior and redesigning the interior. However, it quickly became clear to all concerned that the warehouse was not workable (Gehry suggested that it might be better converted into a hotel with places to shop), and that a much more exciting site could be found by the river that flowed through the town, an area that the city was trying to revitalize. Instead of preserving an old building, Gehry would create a new one.

In Chapter 4 we saw a view of the museum's dramatic interior spaces (see 4.41). Here we have a view of the museum as a whole, set in its water garden by the river. In Gehry's words, its titanium-clad forms unfold like a great "metal flower." Others have seen in their fluid curves the forms of boats or fish.

The organic forms of Gehry's building have an intuitive, almost improvisational quality, as though they might be assembled differently tomorrow or grow and shift on their own as the "flower" unfolds. This is an illusion, of course, for in order to be constructed the forms had to be drawn and measured with great precision. This overwhelming task was helped enormously by a computer program called Catia. Originally developed for the French aerospace industry, Catia generated renderings of the museum (**13.31**) by digitally mapping a working model constructed of wood and paper. The program enabled Gehry's team to work within the construction budget by allowing them to follow every design decision through to its practical consequences in terms of construction methods and exact quantities of materials. In essence, the program built and rebuilt a virtual museum many times before the actual museum was begun.

The Guggenheim Museum Bilbao's expansive, undulating forms are well suited to the spacious waterfront site that Gehry had to work with. In contrast, the tight corner lot available to Iraqi-born British architect Zaha Hadid for her new Lois & Richard Rosenthal Center for Contemporary Art in Cincinnati required a different kind of building, one that would fit snugly into an urban context. Hadid responded to the corner site by creating a building with two quite different facades (**13.32, 13.33**). The narrow east facade is an asymmetrical composition of cubic forms projecting dynamically into space (13.32). The effect is as though the building were bursting out of its cramped quarters, as though it had more energy than it could contain. The transparent glass wall that defines the ground floor and continues in a channel up the north (right) end of facade creates a visual "breathing space" around the black-and-white forms, which appear as though they were floating. The south facade (to the left in 13.33) displays a much calmer sense of movement. If we think of the east facade as being in high relief, then the south facade is in low relief, dominated by slender horizontal elements that make the building seem more elongated than it actually is. The nighttime photograph shows clearly the bank of windows that Hadid provided for the museum offices. The windows not only provide employees with ample daylight, but they also make it clear to passersby that the building is an active one full of people.

Hadid wanted her museum to be a welcoming presence that would encourage visitors to enter. To achieve this, she created a design element she calls the "urban carpet," visible in 13.32. The concrete floor of the ground level extends outside the museum to form the surrounding sidewalk. The glass wall is the only barrier between interior and exterior. To the right, the floor curves gently upward and rises flush with the neighboring building. Truly, it is as though Hadid had draped a concrete carpet on the site and then set her museum gently down onto it.

13.32 (left) Zaha Hadid. East facade, Lois & Richard Rosenthal Center for Contemporary Art, Cincinnati. Inaugurated May 2003.

13.33 (right) Lois & Richard Rosenthal Center for Contemporary Art, view from the southeast.

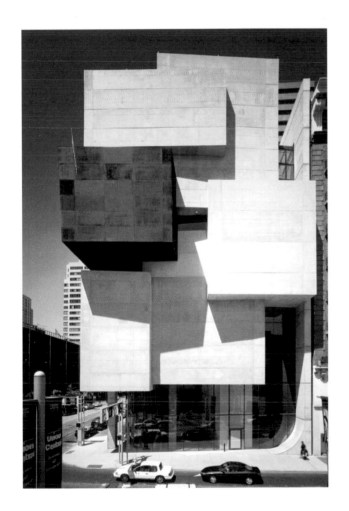

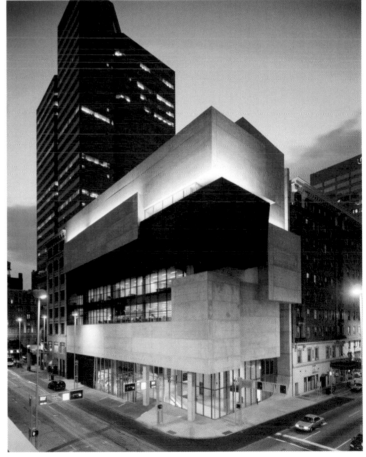

Three Office Buildings

The architecture of commerce, like that of government, often has strong symbolic value. Its primary purpose is to house offices, but a secondary one may be to make a statement about the firm that owns the building. When a company decides to erect a new office building, its leaders give serious thought to the images that will be projected by that building and lodged in the minds of the public. Unlike the government structure, however, the office building rarely seeks a model in traditional architecture, but rather attempts to convey the impression of dynamic modernism—of a company forging ahead to the future. Office buildings have therefore tended to be a creature of fashion, taking their design from the trend of the times. Three examples spanning sixty years will illustrate this.

The Chrysler Building in New York, indisputably the gem of early skyscrapers, was completed in 1930 and was the first office building to rise above 1,000 feet. Its slender, elegantly pointed spire (**13.34**) changed the skyline of New York dramatically and still remains distinctive, in spite of later, taller buildings around it. We might list three elements that contributed to this splendid building: the great success of the automobile industry, which enabled Walter Percy Chrysler to erect a monument to his name; the relative cheapness of fine building materials and labor; and the prevalence of the style known as **Art Deco.**

Art Deco, then at the height of fashion, was marked by geometric patterns and a rich display of surface decoration. (The term "deco" came from the Exposition des Arts Décoratifs, held in Paris in 1925, where the style first appeared as a significant force.) Art Deco was definitely a product of the machine age, for its favorite materials were chrome and steel and glass and aluminum—modern materials that glitter and sparkle, preferably in elaborate combinations to dazzle the eye. Its symbolism, unquestionably, is razzle-dazzle, and it celebrates the speed of the automobile and the airplane, people on the move. The top of the Chrysler Building is layered in an overlapping sunburst pattern pierced with triangular windows—a streamlined, geometric sculpture cutting through the sky.

The patterned forms of Art Deco gave way in the 1940s to the pared-down, austere design aesthetic of the International style. In a sense the roots of the International style might be traced back to Louis Sullivan (see 13.23), who insisted that "form follows function." In other words, the form of a building or any other object should be expressive of what it is supposed to do, not overlaid with arbitrary decoration. This theme was taken up by two European architects, Le Corbusier and Ludwig Mies van der Rohe, and translated into a style that dominated American architecture through the 1970s. Le Corbusier would eventually discard the geometric simplicity of the International style in favor of more organic expressions like the Ronchamp chapel (see 5.26), but Mies van der Rohe added another catchphrase to the history of art when he made his often-quoted statement: "Less is more." By this he meant that architects (and other designers) must strip their forms to the barest essentials, the parts necessary to the work's function, so as to achieve a more honest, satisfying design.

As mentioned earlier, the International style was introduced to the United States by such buildings as Lever House (see 13.24). Diagonally across the street from Lever House is a building many consider to be the quintessence of that style. The Seagram Building (**13.35**), designed by Mies van der Rohe and Philip Johnson, is almost the direct opposite of the Chrysler Building in its design aesthetic. A stark vertical slab resting on stilts, the Seagram Building rises abruptly from the base and terminates abruptly at the top, with no attempt at accent or decoration. Its form is the extended cube, and much of its visual appeal comes from the combination of bronze-colored steel and amber glass sheathing.

For more than twenty years after the Seagram Building was completed, through the 1970s, the International style held sway as the most luxurious and

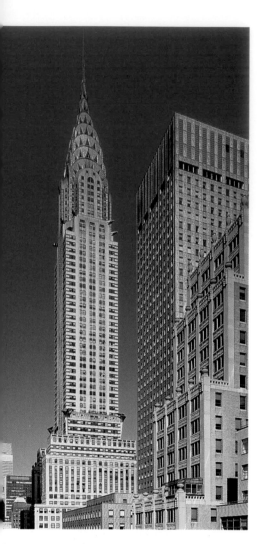

13.34 William Van Alen. Chrysler Building, New York. Completed 1930.

sophisticated style for skyscraper architecture. Across the United States towers of steel and glass vied with one another for height and simplicity of design. By about 1980 it became clear that some change was due, that the business firm of the 1980s and 1990s would be looking for an image quite different from "the old company that lived in a box." Architects too were ready for change, and so the Postmodern style came to corporate America. Not surprisingly, one of the companies that would most ardently embrace Postmodernism was the Disney organization.

The Team Disney Building near Orlando, Florida (**13.36**), captures the style at its most inventive, being complex, irregular, exuberant, and colorful. The building *does* have cubes, but they are not always vertical, not always parallel to one another, and certainly not a uniform, muted color. Disney's architect, Arata Isozaki, splashed a palette of pink and green and blue and red and yellow over the building's facade, and designed the side wings (which are much longer than this photo shows) to look rather like plaid. The huge central funnel introduces a curving form to play against the square shapes. It is actually a working sundial, the world's largest, inside which Isozaki constructed a Japanese garden of river-washed stones. Above the main entrance projects a stylized, elegant version of—yes—*mouse ears.* This may be an office building where serious business takes place, but it is, after all, an office building at Walt Disney World.

The commercial building, by its design, not only sends a message to the outside world about the image a given company wishes to project. It also sends a message to the people who work inside the building: This is who we want you to be. In the case of Team Disney, we must assume the company wants its employees to be creative, colorful—and a bit outside the traditional mold.

13.35 (left) Ludwig Mies van der Rohe and Philip Johnson. Seagram Building, New York. 1958.

13.36 (right) Arata Isozaki & Associates. Team Disney Building, Orlando, Florida. Completed 1991.

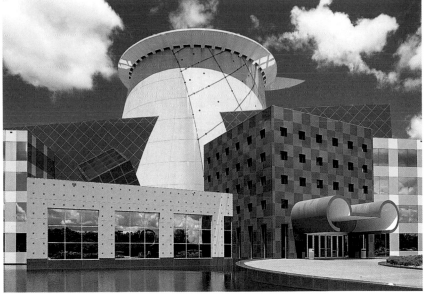

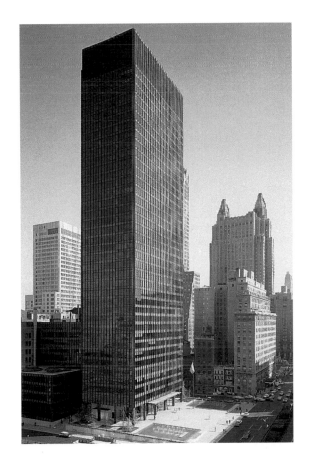

Three Dwellings

Ever since humans came down from the trees or out of their caves, most of the architecture built has been in the form of dwellings. Needless to say, dwellings from different times and places have displayed enormous variety. Each of the three examples considered here reflects a special point of view about what it means to dwell within a building—that is, what kind of roof one should have over one's head.

A type of dwelling that has been with us at least since the times of the ancient Romans is the apartment house, and as space on our planet gets tighter and tighter, such dwellings will no doubt become even more common. Except that their height was limited to five stories, Roman apartment houses resembled most apartment houses today—a more or less massive building, subdivided inside into individual "cookie-cutter" dwellings all more or less the same. In most modern apartment buildings, the most coveted apartments are those at the very top, the penthouses, which offer amenities most apartment dwellers must do without, including light and air on all sides and a private outdoor area.

One of the most famous experiments in apartment design attempted to bring these luxuries to everyone. Habitat in Montreal (**13.37**), designed by Moshe Safdie, was intended as an experiment in the housing of the future, in both form and construction. Like Fuller's dome (see 13.27), it was unveiled at Expo 67, the Montreal World's Fair. The complex consists of 354 prefabricated concrete boxes, stacked one on top of another to form 158 apartments, some on one level, others constructed as duplexes. Although the boxes are of uniform size, they were ingeniously designed for varied uses and floor plans. One box could be a living-dining area with kitchen, another two bedrooms and a bath; some boxes are self-contained units of living room, kitchen, bedroom, and bath. Through this modular system, almost any family size can be accommodated. Each apartment has a private entrance, windows on all sides, and a terrace—the flat roof of one dwelling providing the garden terrace for its neighbor above. In effect, every family lives in a penthouse.

When it first opened, Habitat was considered exciting as a concept but rather sterile as a living environment. But Habitat has aged quite well in the three decades since, as residents have impressed their human stamp on

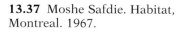

13.37 Moshe Safdie. Habitat, Montreal. 1967.

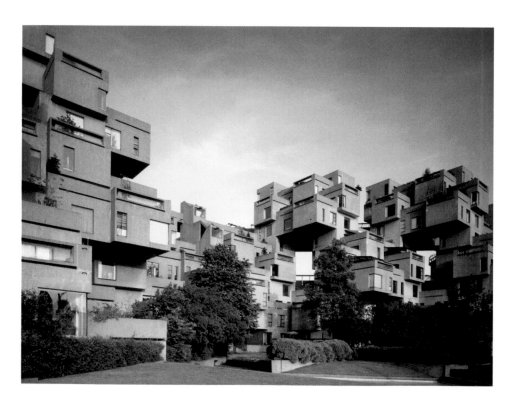

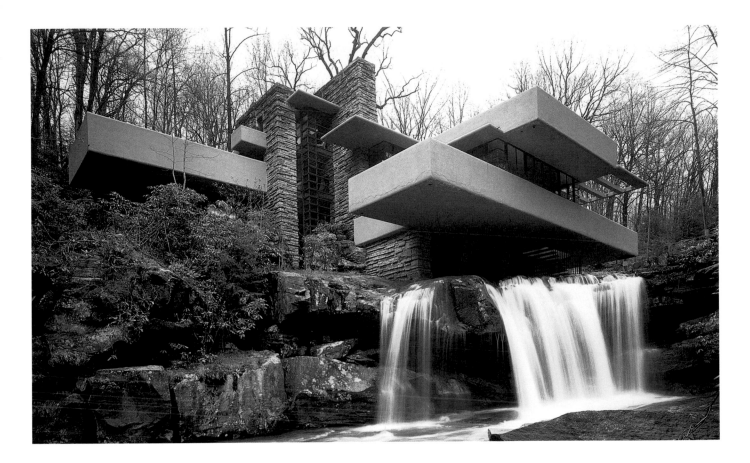

13.38 Frank Lloyd Wright. Fallingwater, Bear Run, Pennsylvania. 1936.

technology. Some families have added sun porches, some skylights; everywhere there are trees, plants, and flowers. All these touches have turned the apartment house of the future into a sought-after home for the present.

Architects usually make their reputations on the "big" commissions—the office buildings, museums, airport terminals, hotels—and only incidentally design private houses. But for the man often considered to have been America's greatest architect, the reverse is true. Although he did design important public buildings, Frank Lloyd Wright will always be remembered as a builder of houses.

Wright's approach to domestic architecture was characterized by two related principles: First, a house should blend with its environment; second, the interior and exterior of a house should be visually and physically integrated. Together, these principles comprised Wright's theory of "organic" architecture. The Kaufmann House in Bear Run, Pennsylvania, usually known as "Fallingwater," is considered to be his masterpiece (**13.38**).

Kaufmann house was designed for a wooded site beside a stream with a little waterfall. Much of the house is built of stone quarried from the immediate area, creating a conceptual as well as a visual relationship to the surroundings. Three terraces project outward from the house, two of them cantilevered over the waterfall. A **cantilever** is a horizontal form supported at one end and jutting out into space at the other. Reinforced concrete, with its high tensile strength, makes such a construction possible. Wright was among the first to use the cantilever for domestic architecture. Here, the cantilevered terraces echo the shape of the stone ledge at the head of the waterfall, further linking the house visually to the site.

The interior of "Fallingwater" consists mainly of one large room opening out to the terraces, providing an "organic" flow of spaces with no disruptive partitions. Wright believed that a hearth is the core of a home, so his plans included a massive stone fireplace, the chimney of which is visible in this photograph. As was his custom in private commissions, the architect also

FRANK LLOYD WRIGHT

1867–1959

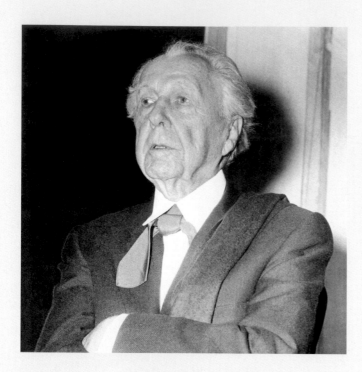

MANY CRITICS CONSIDER Frank Lloyd Wright to have been the greatest American architect of his time; certainly few would dispute the claim that he was the greatest designer of residential architecture. To see a Wright-designed building dating from the first decade of the 20th century is to be shocked by how remarkably modern it seems.

Wright had very little formal education. He attended high school in Madison, Wisconsin, but apparently did not graduate. Later, he completed the equivalent of about one year's course work in civil engineering at the University of Wisconsin, while holding down a job as a draftsman. In 1887 he moved to Chicago and eventually found work in the architectural firm headed by Louis Sullivan, the great designer of early office buildings. Before long Wright had assumed responsibility for fulfilling most of the residential commissions that came into the company, and in 1893 he opened a firm of his own.

During the next two decades Wright refined the principles of the "Prairie houses" that are his trademark. Most are in the Midwest, and they echo that flat expanse of the Great Plains—predominantly horizontal, stretching out over considerable ground area but usually in one story. All expressed Wright's special interest in textures and materials; he liked whenever possible to build with materials native to the immediate surroundings, so that the houses blend with their environments. Interiors were designed in an open plan, with rooms flowing into one another (an unusual practice for the time), and the inside and outside of the house were also well integrated. These ingredients added up to what Wright always referred to as "organic" architecture.

For most of his long life Wright's personal situation was far from tranquil. His parents seem to have had a bitterly unhappy marriage, and they divorced in 1885, when Wright was seventeen—an extraordinary event for that era. Wright himself had a troubled marital history. His first marriage ended when he eloped to Europe with Mamah Brothwick, the wife of a former client, leaving his own wife and six children behind. Five years later, back in Wisconsin, Brothwick was brutally murdered by a deranged servant while Wright was out of the house. This tragedy sent the architect off on a period of wandering through faraway parts of the world. A final marriage in the late 1920s lasted out his lifetime and appears to have given him his first real happiness.

Although he is best known for his domestic architecture, Wright also designed many large-scale commercial and public buildings, including the Solomon R. Guggenheim Museum in New York. His innovative design for the Imperial Hotel in Tokyo, planned to be stable in an area plagued by earthquakes, proved successful when the hotel survived without damage a devastating quake just a year after it was completed.

Wright was the author of several books on his theories of architecture, and always he focused on the organic nature of his work and on his own individuality. "Beautiful buildings are more than scientific. They are true organisms, spiritually conceived, works of art, using the best technology by inspiration rather than the idiosyncrasies of mere taste or any averaging by the committee mind."[2]

Photograph of Frank Lloyd Wright.

designed much of the furniture, building it into the structure so the owners could not tamper with his overall scheme.

The third dwelling we take up here makes a fundamental but often overlooked point: Architecture is for everybody. Everyone deserves a comfortable dwelling. This is the philosophy behind Rural Studio, a program for architecture students founded by architect Samuel Mockbee at Auburn University in Alabama. For the duration of the three-month-long course, the students live together in an old abandoned house in distant, rural Greensboro. There they design a project and then build it with their own hands, using whatever materials they can find and whatever money is available. Their clients are local county people, usually poor, who could never hire an architect on their own.

Rural Studio's first full-scale residential project was Bryant House (**13.39**). It was built for Shephard and Alberta Bryant, an aging couple who had made do for most of their lives with a leaky, patchwork shed. Reviving an ancient practice, the students constructed the walls from bales of hay, a material that is inexpensive, easy to work with, and a natural insulator. Stucco plastering inside and out gives the walls a smooth, weatherproof coating. Across the front of the house, in keeping with southern tradition, is a long and hospitable porch whose inexpensive acrylic sun-visor roof is poised on colorful yellow pillars. Inside the house, a hearth with a wood-burning stove provides heat in the winter, and cozy sleeping niches set in a wall await visiting grandchildren. The entire house, including plumbing and kitchen fixtures, cost only $16,500 to build, a sum covered by grants and gifts from local merchants.

After the house was completed, one student returned to build an outbuilding, a small smokehouse where Mr. Bryant, an avid fisherman, could cure his catch. Visible to the right in the photograph, it was constructed almost entirely of found materials. The walls, made of fragments of concrete curbstones, are inset with colored glass bottles that admit light. The gently twisting tin roof is supported by salvaged timbers. Inside, the ceiling is lined with old street signs. Total cost of materials, $40.

Rural Studio helps students bridge a gap between theory and practice, between learning about architecture and hands-on experience, while also benefiting the local community. It reminds us that architecture is fundamentally about how we live. Through architecture, we build our own human environment within the natural world.

13.39 Rural Studio. Bryant House, Mason's Bend, Alabama. 1994.

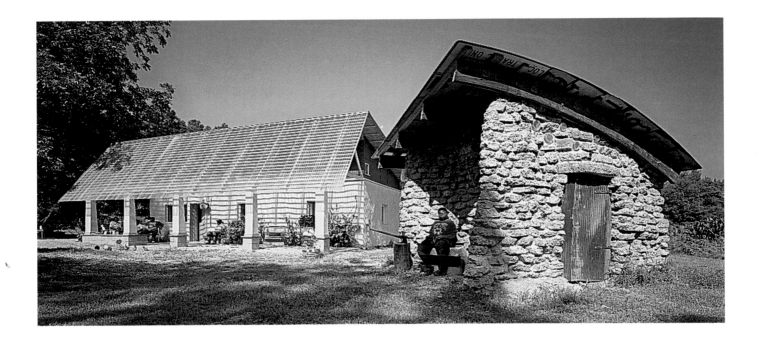

SAMUEL MOCKBEE

1944–2001

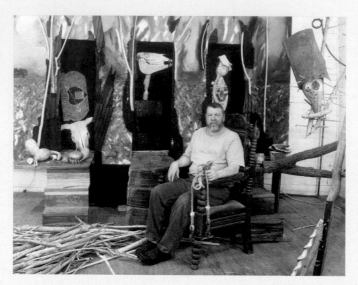

"THE PROFESSIONAL CHALLENGE," said architect Sam Mockbee, "is how to avoid becoming so stunned by the power of modern technology and economic affluence that I lose focus on the fact that people and place matter."[3]

Born on December 23, 1944, in Meridian, Mississippi, Mockbee never strayed far from his southern birthplace. He served as artillery officer in Fort Benning, Georgia, for two years before attending Auburn University's College of Architecture, Design and Construction, where he received his bachelor's degree in 1974. A decade of independent work led to his partnership with fellow architect Coleman Coker. The Mockbee-Coker firm garnered a great deal of success: In 1987 they won a Progressive Architecture Honor award; in 1990, they were selected by the Architectural League of New York to participate in the prestigious Emerging Voices series.

But Mockbee, fundamentally ill-at-ease with what he called the "gluttonous affluence" of the business of architecture, made a definitive break with private practice by joining the faculty of Auburn University's architecture department. There, in 1993, he and colleague D. K. Ruth founded what would become Mockbee's true legacy: Rural Studio. At a time when middle-income homes were mass-produced from a single blueprint, while homes for the very rich were overdesigned simply because clients had the money, Mockbee began a program that would provide the rural poor of Hale County, Alabama, with something few people in the country could obtain: one-of-a-kind architecture.

Rural Studio began as an experiment—an unlikely version of the junior-year-abroad program—that had Mockbee and twelve of his students knocking on Hale County doors, offering to replace dilapidated or makeshift structures with uniquely designed and constructed homes. Using donated materials and found objects such as license plates, discarded tires, and hay, members of Rural Studio worked long hours to create homes that were at once inexpensive and innovative. Their work paid off: Despite some initial trepidation, residents of Hale County came to embrace Rural Studio as part of their community, and what began as a one-year experiment is now the signature component of Auburn University's Architecture Department; it is also the only program of its kind in the country.

Mockbee's work with Rural Studio was unflinchingly hands-on. A typical week saw him living, Monday to Friday, with his students in the 1890s farmhouse that had become their base. He spent his days negotiating with local merchants, meeting with benefactors, coaching his students, and maintaining the Studio's relationship with Hale County. As he put it, "If you're going to do this you gotta pack your bags, kiss your wife goodbye, and go to war."[4] In 2000, his dedication was rewarded with a MacArthur Foundation "genius grant."

In what spare time he could muster, Mockbee liked to paint—large, brightly colored canvases, rich with rural mythology and suffused, as always, with social conscience. When asked to describe his commitment to both painting and architecture, he said, "This is my passion—to be responsible to the creative process."[5]

Samuel Mockbee died of complications from leukemia on December 30, 2001, in Jackson, Mississippi. Family, friends, and students remember him as a large, burly man whose gruff exterior belied a deeply compassionate nature. In the words of his colleague and longtime friend Dan Bennett, "The world is a better place because of Sambo Mockbee."[6]

Photograph of Samuel Mockbee seated in front of one of his paintings, *The Children of Eutaw Pose Before Their Ancient Cabins*. 1992.

RECENT DIRECTIONS: GREEN ARCHITECTURE

For some 250 years we have been living in the industrial age, which began when inventors discovered how to manufacture energy by harnessing the power of steam, which they created with heat generated by burning fossil fuels—coal and, later, oil. The steam engine was born, followed a century later by the internal combustion engine and the turbine.

During the 19th century industry produced iron and steel in such large quantities that they became available as building materials. The Crystal Palace (13.21) and the Eiffel Tower (13.22) were conceived as showpieces for the kind of structures this made possible. Processing coal also produced coal gas, which was piped through cities and into buildings as fuel for street lamps and houselights, lighting the night on a large scale for the first time. But night was truly conquered when inventors discovered how to convert the energy into electricity, and then how to convert electricity into light with the incandescent lamp.

During the first decades of the 20th century industrial methods for making sheet glass were developed, the advent of low-wattage fluorescent lamps made it practical to illuminate vast interior spaces artificially, and the triumph of air-conditioning allowed buildings to be sealed off from the natural environment around them. Lever House (13.24) and the Seagram Building (13.35) epitomize the aesthetic that developed around these new materials and technologies. Grids of concrete and steel sheathed in glass, their walls and ceilings hide pipes that invisibly deliver and remove hot and cold water, ducts that circulate air and regulate its temperature and humidity, and cables that make electricity available for lighting, appliances, and machines. Such buildings have since been erected all over the world.

Like other benefits of industrialization, these buildings come at a significant cost to the environment, and one that we cannot continue to pay indefinitely. The question of whether we can create a healthier and less wasteful human habitat is at the heart of green architecture. Maya Lin addressed many green concerns in the Langston Hughes Library (**13.40, 13.41**), which she created for the Children's Defense Fund. The modern library interior was slipped into the "skin" of a 19th-century barn. Preserving and updating existing structures is one of the basic practices of green architecture. It is not always necessary to build new. Into what were originally two cribs at ground level, Lin set a bookstore and the entrance to the library proper upstairs. In the library,

13.40 (left) Maya Lin. Langston Hughes Library, Haley Farm, Clinton, Tennessee. 1999.

13.41 (right) Langston Hughes Library, interior.

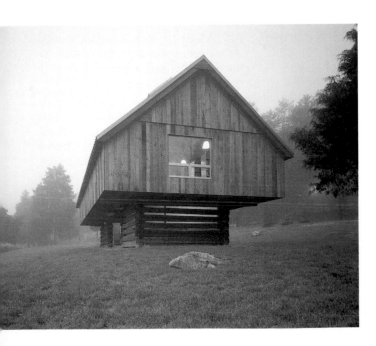

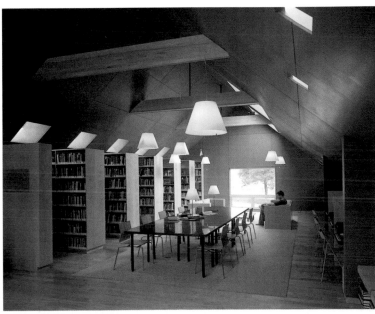

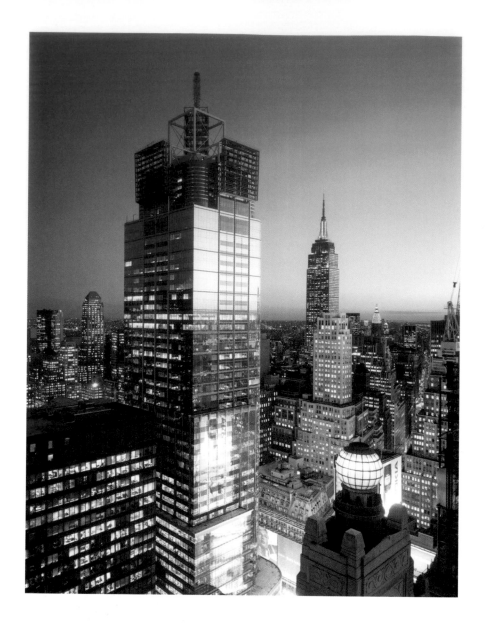

13.42 Fox & Fowle Architects. The Condé Nast Building at Four Times Square, New York. 1999.

skylights and a large picture window admit daylight into the stacks and the reading area, reducing the need for artificial lighting. Working in harmony with nature—using the sun for light and warmth, the wind for ventilation and cooling, trees and water for air quality—is another goal of green architecture. Lin's skylights are a straightforward example. More complex is her use of a nearby pond as a natural heat exchanger, which helps reduce the amount of energy needed to heat and cool the building.

The materials for the interior were also chosen with green concerns in mind, including the health of the library's staff and visitors. Many common building materials give off chemical vapors. Circulated by air-conditioning systems, these vapors contribute to the phenomenon known as Sick-Building syndrome, in which people who spend time in a particular building feel unwell, though no specific illness can be diagnosed. Particle board, for example, often contains formaldehyde, but the particle board that Lin chose for the walls and ceilings of the library does not. The floors are made of maple. Wood is a renewable resource; more can be grown. (Steel is an example of a nonrenewable resource, for we cannot make more iron ore.)

For an example of green thinking on a much larger scale we turn to Four Times Square (**13.42**), designed by the architecture firm of Fox & Fowle. Completed in 1999, Four Times Square is the largest building in the United States to establish standards for energy conservation, indoor air quality, recycling systems, and sustainable manufacturing processes. During construction, contractors were required to recycle waste whenever possible, and about 65 percent of the construction debris was reclaimed. The steel structure that crowns the building is a stabilizing and strengthening device that significantly reduced the amount of steel needed in the building overall. The exterior glass sheathing is made of an advanced type of glass that admits a maximum amount of daylight, blocks solar heat and harmful ultraviolet rays, and minimizes heat loss during the winter. Inside the building, the emphasis is on biodegradable, renewable, and nontoxic materials, including sustainably harvested wood. Energy-efficient lighting and low-use water systems were installed to conserve resources. Gray water—water from uses such as washing—is recycled. On the roof, systems powered by natural gas produce cold and hot water to chill and heat the building. Unlike standard cooling technology, they do not use chlorofluorocarbons, gases that are harmful to the ozone layer. Fresh air is taken into the building at high elevations, to avoid picking up street exhaust, and then filtered and circulated throughout.

Four Times Square produces much of its own energy. Voltaic panels, which convert sunlight into electricity, are incorporated into two of the facades. Additional power comes from two fuel cells set lower down on the exterior. Fuel cells use natural gas to generate power through a chemical reaction. The two cells here provide about 60 percent of the building's nighttime electricity needs. Though it is a nonrenewable fossil fuel, natural gas is far cleaner than either coal or oil, and fuel cells are the cleanest and most efficient means yet developed for producing electricity from it.

Renzo Piano's recently completed Jean-Marie Tjibaou Cultural Center (**13.43**) illustrates another central tenet of green architecture, which is that architects should respond to the local landscape, climate, culture, and building traditions instead of imposing a modern Western building where it may not be suitable. Why should architecture everywhere look the same? The Jean-Marie Tjibaou Cultural Center is in New Caledonia, an island in the South Pacific that is an overseas territory of France. Tjibaou was a leader of the Kanak people, the indigenous people of the island, and the center named in his memory is dedicated to preserving and transmitting Kanak culture.

13.43 Renzo Piano. Jean-Marie Tjibaou Cultural Center, Nouméa, New Caledonia. 1991–98.

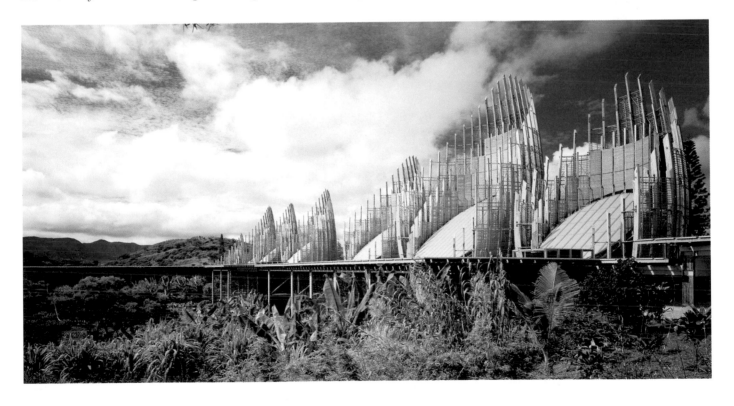

Working with a local anthropologist and Kanak advisors, Piano researched Kanak culture extensively. His goal was to blend contemporary building technology with Kanak traditions. The gently bulging, basketlike forms visible in the photographs are derived from Kanak dwellings (**13.44**). (Actual dwellings continue the vertical staves until they meet at the top and weave the horizontal elements in and out, as in basketry). The Center consists of ten of these pavilions linked by a covered walkway, an arrangement that recalls the plan of a Kanak village. Each "unfinished" open basket form embraces a large cylindrical room, also made of wood. The baskets serve as wind scoops, catching breezes and directing them downward to ventilate the inner rooms, which are lit largely by daylight. The wood and bamboo construction is endlessly renewable.

Major international exhibitions often serve as showplaces for new ideas in architecture. Moshe Safdie's Habitat (13.37) and Buckminster Fuller's U.S. Pavilion (13.27) were both created for Expo 67 in Montreal, and they have served as points of reference ever since. Expo 2000, held in Hanover, Germany, took the environment for its main theme. One of the most talked about structures there was Shigeru Ban's Japan Pavilion (**13.45, 13.46**), for it was constructed almost entirely from a material that is easily and inexpensively manufactured, available almost everywhere, and completely recyclable: paper.

Ban has been working with paper as a building material for some time, and the Japan Pavilion is his most advanced and ambitious structure to date. Ban's goal was to create a temporary structure that could be entirely recycled or reused. The inner framework is made from weatherproofed paper tubes lashed together with tape. The undulating form of the building adds to the framework's stability. The exterior paper membrane is stretched over an outer framework of lightweight wooden arches, allowing daylight to filter into the interior (think of a paper lantern). Between the paper bands, narrow strips of recyclable plastic sheeting admit still more light. Instead of concrete, the building rests on a foundation of steel-reinforced wooden boxes filled with sand.

One important use for Ban's paper architecture has been in constructing emergency housing for refugees of wars and natural disasters. After a major earthquake struck Japan in 1995, Ban and a crew of student volunteers erected houses made of paper "logs" (picture a log cabin with vertical logs). The roofs were made of tenting material. Beer crates loaded with sandbags served as a foundation, raising the houses off the ground. Other paper projects have included a private library, a gallery, a community center, and a festi-

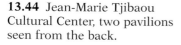

13.44 Jean-Marie Tjibaou Cultural Center, two pavilions seen from the back.

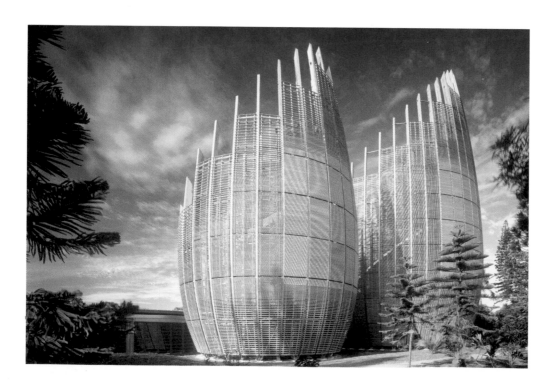

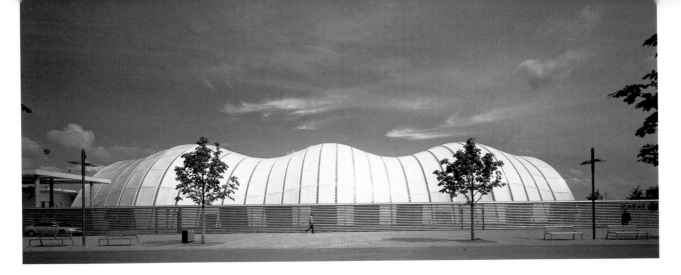

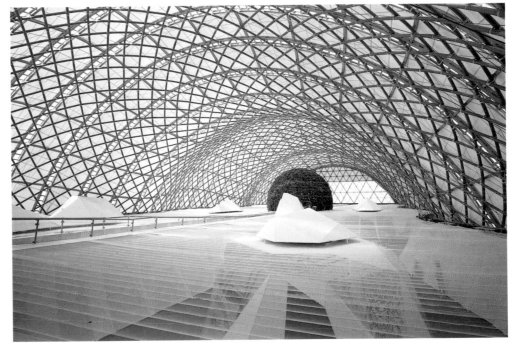

val hall. Many of Ban's paper projects are intended to be temporary. Yet he is careful to point out that, properly cared for, a paper building could last for one hundred years. How much longer do we really need many of our structures to stand?

Green architecture is an aspect of a larger concern called sustainable development, which has been defined as providing for the needs of the present without compromising the ability of future generations to provide for their own needs. Just as industrial progress inspired new architectural styles, so green architecture may eventually change the way buildings look and the way we live.

13.45 (above, top) Shigeru Ban. Japan Pavilion, Hanover Expo, Hanover, Germany. 2000.

13.46 (above) Japan Pavilion, interior.

RELATED RESOURCES ONLINE

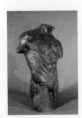

For more information, definitions, interactive activities, Web links, and videos related to the "Three-Dimensional Media" material covered in this part, please go to **www.mhhe.com/lwa8.**

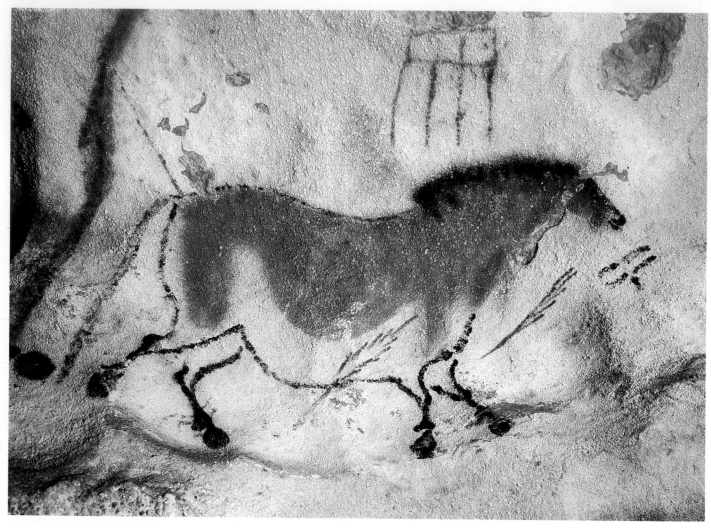

14.1 *Horse and Geometric Symbol.* Cave painting, Lascaux, France. c. 13,000 B.C.E.

PART FIVE
Arts in Time

CHAPTER FOURTEEN

ANCIENT MEDITERRANEAN WORLDS

An important factor in understanding and appreciating any work of art is some knowledge of its place in time. When and where was it made? What traditions was the artist building on or rebelling against? What did society at that time expect of its artists? What sort of tasks did it give them?

For this reason, the last part of this book is devoted to a brief survey of art as it has unfolded in time. As elsewhere, we focus mainly on the Western tradition, but we also examine the development of art in the cultures of Islam and Africa; of India, China, and Japan; and of Oceania, Australia, and the early Americas. Not only are these non-Western artistic traditions fascinating in their own right, but they also introduce us to other ways of thinking about art, other roles that art can play in society, and other formal directions that art can take. Many Western artists today draw as deeply on non-Western traditions as they do on Western ones, just as many contemporary artists beyond the West have been profoundly influenced by Western developments. More than at any other time in history, the entire range of humankind's artistic past nourishes its present.

THE OLDEST ART

The title of this chapter narrows our focus from the entire globe to the region around the Mediterranean Sea. It is here—in Africa, the Near East, and Europe—that the story of Western art begins. In these lands, beginning around 3000 B.C.E., numerous ancient civilizations arose, overlapped, and interacted; learned from each other and conquered each other; and finally faded into the world we know today.

These civilizations—the "worlds" of our title—were preceded by far older human societies about which we know very little. Scattered evidence of their existence reaches us over a vast distance of tens of thousands of years, fascinating, mysterious, and mute. In Chapter 1, we looked at a detail from the wall paintings in the Chauvet cave in present-day France (see 1.3). Dating from later in the Upper Paleolithic Period are the paintings of the caves at Lascaux, also in France (**14.1**). Until the discovery of the Chauvet cave in 1996, the

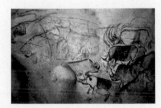

1.3 Lion panel, Chauvet cave

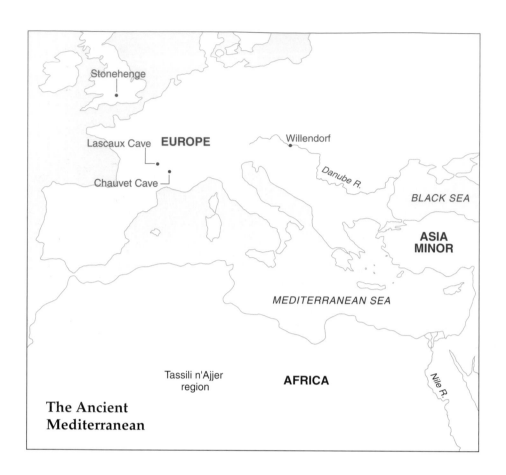

The Ancient
Mediterranean

RELATED WORKS

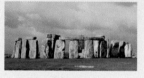

1.4 Stonehenge

images at Lascaux were the oldest known paintings in Europe. The horse illustrated here has fascinated scholars because of its seemingly pregnant condition, the feathery forms near its forelegs, and the mysterious geometric symbol depicted above it. The paintings at Chauvet are even more finely executed, and they must surely be the result of a long tradition whose origins go back even further in time.

As at Chauvet, the paintings at Lascaux are almost all of animals. Experts agree that the images are meaningful, although what their exact meaning is remains obscure. The once-popular theory that they were made as a form of magic to ensure success in the hunt no longer seems credible. Recent theories have focused on the arrangement of the animals by species or gender, or on their distribution through the various chambers of the caves. Perhaps certain animals are symbolic. Perhaps others represent mythical spirits or spirit "contacts" in the other world. Perhaps some images track migration patterns. Artifacts and traces of human footprints suggest that many painted chambers served as gathering places, perhaps for ritual occasions. Do the images relate to these gatherings? Perhaps.

The question of why a work of art was made arises also with ancient sculptures. Nearly as old as the Chauvet cave paintings is a little female statuette that often serves as an emblem of art history's beginnings. She is made of stone, was formed about 25,000 years ago, and was found near a town in present-day Austria. Most people call her the *Venus of Willendorf* (**14.2**).

The title "Venus" may seem strange, given our usual image of the goddess of love. The name, of course, was applied by modern scholars, possibly supposing that people many thousands of years ago considered this sort of figure a sexual ideal. It seems clear that the statuette was a fertility image, possibly meant to be carried around as an amulet, or good-luck charm (the *Venus* is less than 5 inches tall). Only the features associated with childbearing have been stressed—the belly, breasts, and pubic area. Venus' face is obscured. Her arms, crossed above the breasts, are barely defined, and her legs taper off to nothing. If we take this figure literally, she could not see or speak or walk or carry. What she could do was bear and nurture children.

How difficult it is for us living now to imagine what childbirth meant all those millennia ago. On the one hand it must have been a pressing necessity. Children were needed to help in the task of survival, and there may also have been an instinct to continue life through future generations. On the other hand, however, the process by which children are conceived and born was a mystery to these early peoples. No wonder elements of magic and ritual became associated with childbirth. Many scholars assume that fertility figures like the *Venus of Willendorf,* which are extremely common in early art, were meant to play a cause-and-effect role. The sculptor would form an image of a woman with exaggerated reproductive features, and this figure would *result* in a child being born. (It would be fascinating to know whether this figure was carved by a woman or a man.) Much prehistoric art seems to have been created for this purpose—to make sense out of the universe and to exert some control over the forces of nature.

Beginning around 9000 B.C.E. and continuing over the next 4,000 years, the Paleolithic Period, or Old Stone Age, gradually gave way to the Neolithic, or New Stone Age. The Neolithic is named for new types of stone tools that were developed, but these tools were only one aspect of what in fact was a completely new way of life. Instead of gathering wild crops as they could find them, Neolithic people learned to cultivate fruits and grains. Farming was born. Instead of following migrating herds to hunt, Neolithic people learned to domesticate animals. Dogs, cattle, goats, and other animals served variously for help, labor, meat, milk, leather, and so on. Dugout boats, the bow and arrow, and the technology of pottery—clay hardened by heat—vastly improved the standard of living. Settled communities grew up, and with them, architecture of stone and wood. The most famous work of Neolithic architecture in Europe is the monument known as Stonehenge, in England, which we discussed in Chapter 1 (see 1.4).

Tantalizing glimpses of daily life in the Neolithic Period survive in the rock paintings of the Tassili n'Ajjer region of Algeria, in northern Africa (**14.3**).

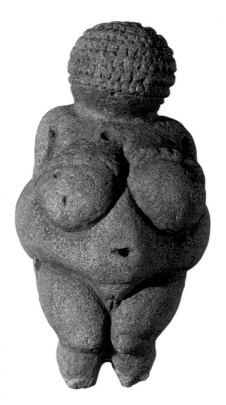

14.2 (above) *Female Figure ("Venus of Willendorf").* c. 23,000 B.C.E. Limestone, height 4⅜". Naturhistorisches Museum, Vienna.

14.3 (below) *Women and Cattle.* Rock painting at Tassili n'Ajjer, Algeria. Pastoralist style, after 5000 B.C.E.

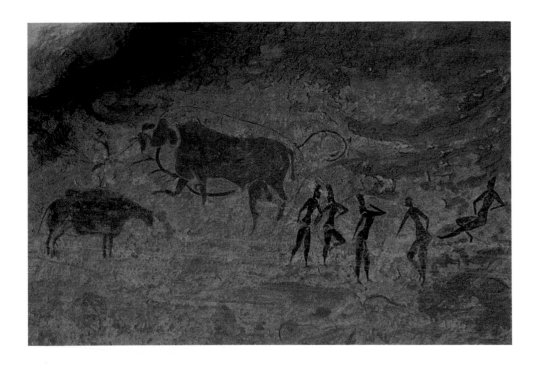

Today, Tassili n'Ajjer is part of the Sahara, the world's largest desert. But at the time these images were painted, roughly between 5000 and 2000 B.C.E., the desert had not yet emerged. Instead, the region was a vast grassland, home to animals, plants, and the people we see depicted here—five women, gathered near their cattle. Other images painted on the rock walls at Tassili n'Ajjer depict women harvesting grain or occupied with children, men herding cattle, and enclosures that may represent dwellings.

The art that has come down to us from the Stone Age is fragmentary and isolated. Ancient cave paintings. A small statue of a woman. A circular stone monument. Paintings on rock walls in the desert. Our examples are separated from one another by thousands of years and thousands of miles. Each one must have been part of a long local artistic tradition that stretched back into the past and continued for many millennia afterward. Yet for each one, we are faced with questions: "What came before, what came after, and where is it?"

In studying art of the past, it is important to keep in mind that the cultures we examine most fully are not necessarily those in which the *most* art was made or the *best* art was made. They are, rather, the cultures whose art *has been found or preserved.* Art has been produced at all times and in all places and by all peoples. But in order for it to be available to future generations for study, it must survive—possibly even after the culture that produced it has disappeared. Certain conditions foster the preservation of art, and the ancient cultures that we are able to study in depth across time fulfill most of them.

First, the artists worked in durable materials such as stone, metal, and fired clay. Second, the local environment is not destructive to artworks; for instance, the hot, dry climate of Egypt provides an excellent milieu for preservation. Third, the culture was highly organized, with stable population centers. Great cities normally house the richest troves of artwork in any culture, for they are where rulers dwell, wealth is accumulated, and artists congregate. Fourth, the culture had a tradition of caching its artworks in places of limited or no accessibility. A huge portion of the ancient art that has survived comes from tombs or underground caves.

The first cultures of the ancient Mediterranean world to meet most of these conditions arose in Mesopotamia—a region in the Near East—and in Egypt, in northeastern Africa. Here, for the first time, we find a coherent, reasonably intact artistic production about which we have come to know a good deal. It is no accident that the civilizations of both Mesopotamia and Egypt developed along the banks of mighty rivers—the Tigris and Euphrates in Mesopotamia and the Nile in Egypt. Rivers provided both a means of transportation and a source of water. Water enabled irrigation, which in turn allowed for vaster and more reliable farming, which in turn supported larger and denser populations. Cities developed, and with them social stratification (the division of society into classes such as rulers, priests, nobles, commoners, and slaves), the standardization of religions and rituals, the creation of monumental architecture, and the specialization that allowed some people to farm, some to be merchants, and others to make art.

Our study of ancient Mediterranean worlds properly begins here, in the lands along the great rivers.

MESOPOTAMIA

The region known to the ancient world as Mesopotamia occupied a large area roughly equivalent to the present-day nation of Iraq. Fertile soil watered by the Tigris and Euphrates rivers made Mesopotamia highly desirable, yet a lack of natural boundaries made it easy to invade and difficult to defend. Successive waves of people conquered the region in ancient times, yet each new ruling group built on the cultural achievements of its predecessors. Thus we can speak with some justice of a continuing Mesopotamian culture.

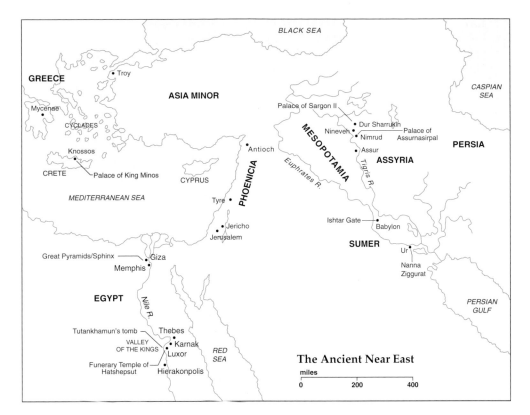

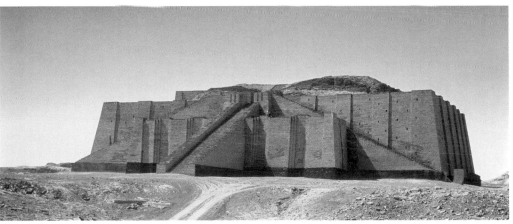

The first cities of Mesopotamia arose in the southernmost area, a region called Sumer. By about 3400 B.C.E. some dozen Sumerian city-states—cities that ruled over their surrounding territories—had emerged. The Sumerians were the first people to leave behind them not just artifacts but words: the wedge-shaped marks that they pressed into damp clay to keep track of inventories and accounts developed over time into a writing system capable of recording language. Called cuneiform (Latin for "wedge-shaped"), it served as the writing system of Mesopotamia for the next 3,000 years.

Lacking stone, the Sumerians built their cities of sun-dried brick. The largest structure of a Sumerian city was the **ziggurat,** a temple or shrine raised on a monumental stepped base (**14.4**). The example illustrated here, partially restored but still missing its temple, was dedicated to the moon god Nanna, the protective deity of the Sumerian city of Ur. In the flat land of Sumer, ziggurats were visible for miles around. They elevated the temple to a symbolic mountain top, a meeting place for heaven and earth, where priests and priestesses communicated with the gods.

14.4 Nanna Ziggurat, Ur (present-day Maqaiyir, Iraq). c. 2100–2050 B.C.E.

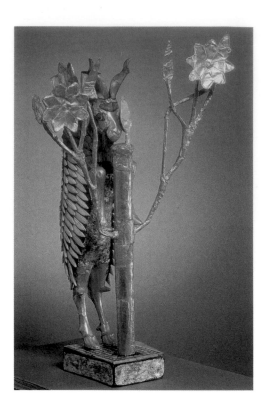

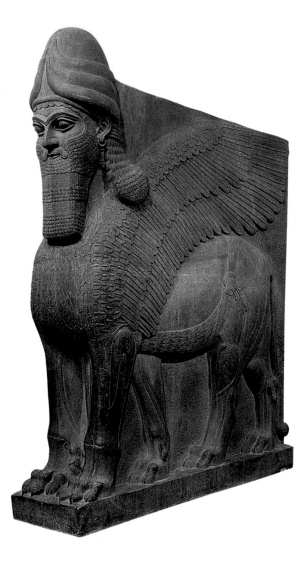

14.5 (left) *Ram in Thicket*, from Ur. c. 2600 B.C.E. Wood, gold foil, lapis lazuli; height 10".
The University of Pennsylvania Museum, Philadelphia.

14.6 (below left) Head of an Akkadian ruler (Sargon I?), from Nineveh, Iraq. c. 2250 B.C.E. Bronze, height 12".
Museum of Antiquities, Baghdad.

14.7 (right) *Human-Headed Winged Lion*. Assyrian, from Nimrud. 883–859 B.C.E. Limestone, height 10'2½".
The Metropolitan Museum of Art, New York.

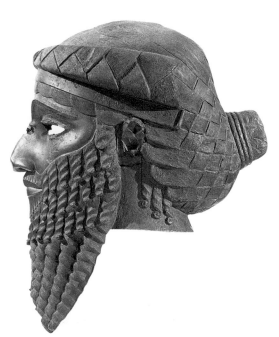

The refined and luxurious aspect of Sumerian art is evident in this small figure of a goat standing with its forelegs propped on a flowering tree (**14.5**). Crafted over a wooden core (now lost) of gold, silver, and a precious stone called lapis lazuli, the delicate figure probably served to support a small tray or tabletop.

By 2300 B.C.E., the Sumerian city-states had been conquered by their neighbors to the north, the Akkadians. Under their ruler Sargon I, the Akkadians established the region's first empire. Though it crumbled quickly, the empire seems to have extended all the way from the shores of the Mediterranean to the Persian Gulf. Sargon himself may be portrayed in the splendid Akkadian sculpture illustrated here (**14.6**). Certainly the expensive material and the fine workmanship suggest that it represents a ruler of some kind. The lifelike features—heavy-lidded eyes, strong nose, and sensitive mouth—argue that this is a naturalistic portrait of a real person and not a generic or idealized head. Such naturalism is extremely rare in early art.

A more stable and long-lived Mesopotamian empire was established by the Amorites, who consolidated their rule over the region by about 1830 B.C.E. and established a capital at Babylon. The most important legacy of the Babylonian empire is not artistic but legal: a set of edicts and laws compiled under the ruler Hammurabi (ruled c. 1792–1750 B.C.E.). Known as Hammurabi's Code, it is the only complete legal code to survive from the ancient world, and it has provided historians with valuable insights into the structure and concerns of Mesopotamian society.

Mesopotamia's history was marked by almost continual warfare and conquest, and a major goal of architecture was the erection of mighty citadels to ensure the safety of temples and palaces. Such a citadel was that of the Assyrian ruler Assurnasirpal II, built at Nimrud in the 9th century B.C.E. Based in northern Mesopotamia, the Assyrians had been gathering power and territory since before 1100 B.C.E. Their military strength increased greatly under Assurnasirpal II, and within a few centuries they would amass the largest empire the region had yet seen. Assurnasirpal's palace had gates fronted by monumental stone slabs carved into enormous human-headed winged beasts, a bull and a lion. The lion (**14.7**) wears a horned cap indicating divine status. Its body has five legs, so that from the front it appears motionless but from the side it is understood to be walking. Visitors to the citadel were meant to be impressed—and no doubt intimidated—by these majestic creatures.

The walls of the palace were lined with alabaster reliefs depicting Assyrian triumphs and royal power. A popular subject is the lion hunt (**14.8**), in which the king is depicted slaying the most powerful of beasts. The ceremonial hunt was probably carried out as it is pictured here, with armed guards releasing captive animals into an enclosure for the king to kill from his chariot. Slaying lions was viewed as a fitting demonstration of kingly power. The lions' anatomy is beautifully observed, and the many overlapping figures show the sculptor's confidence in suggesting three-dimensional space.

When the Babylonians again came to power in Mesopotamia, late in the 7th century B.C.E., they formed a kingdom now called Neo-Babylonian. These "new" Babylonians surely must be ranked among the great architects of the ancient world. They developed a true arch before the Romans did and were masters of decorative design for architecture. Moreover, like their forebears, they

14.8 *Lion Hunt*, from the palace complex of Assurnasirpal II, Kalhu (present-day Nimrud, Iraq). c. 850 B.C.E. Alabaster, height 39".
The British Museum, London.

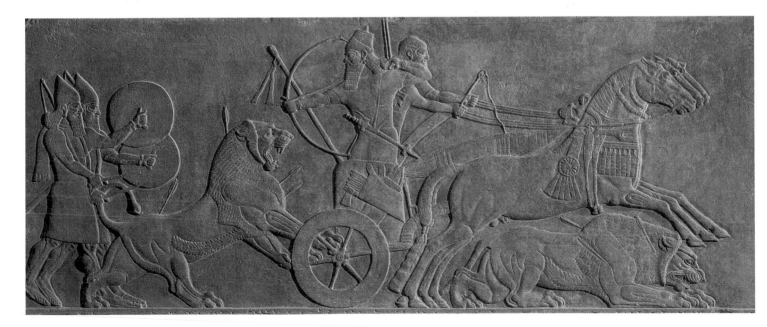

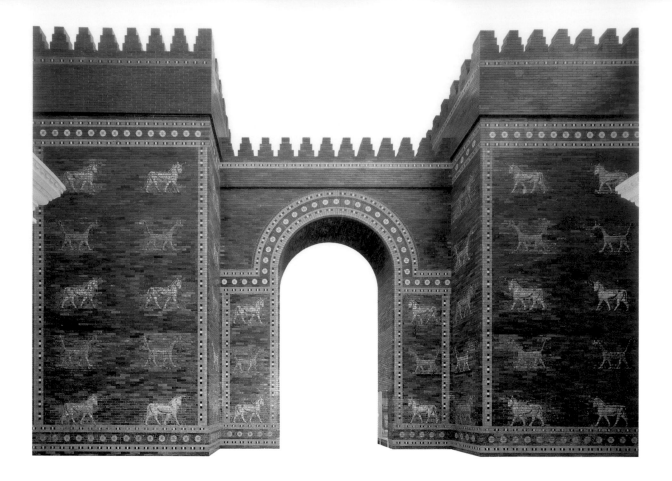

14.9 Ishtar Gate (restored), from Babylon. c. 575 B.C.E. Glazed brick, height 48'9".
Staatliche Museen zu Berlin, Preussischer Kulturbesitz, Vorderasiatisches Museum.

had a formidable leader in the person of Nebuchadnezzar, an enthusiastic patron of the arts who built a dazzling capital city at Babylon.

A genuine planned city, Babylon was constructed as a square, bisected by the Euphrates River, with streets and broad avenues crossing at right angles. Because stone is scarce in this region of Mesopotamia, the architects made liberal use of glazed ceramic bricks. Babylon must have been a city of brilliant color. Its main thoroughfare was the Processional Way, at one end of which stood the Ishtar Gate (**14.9**), built about 575 B.C.E. and now restored in a German museum. The gate consists of thousands of glazed mud bricks, with two massive towers flanking a central arch. On ceremonial occasions Nebuchadnezzar would sit under the arch in majesty to receive his subjects. The walls of the gate are embellished with more glazed ceramic animals, probably meant as spirit-guardians.

The history of Mesopotamia parallels in time that of its neighbor to the southwest, the kingdom of Egypt, with which it had regular contacts. In Egypt, however, we will find considerably less political turmoil. Protected to the south by a series of cataracts (rocky, unnavigable stretches of the Nile) and to the east and west by vast deserts, Egypt during much of its long history was spared the waves of immigration and invasion that continually transformed Mesopotamia.

EGYPT

The principal message of Egyptian art is continuity—a seamless span of time reaching back into history and forward into the future. The Greek philosopher Plato wrote that Egyptian art did not change for ten thousand years; although this is an exaggeration, there were many features that remained stable over long periods of time. The Sphinx (**14.10**), the symbol of this most important characteristic of Egyptian art, is the essence of stability, order, and endurance. Built about 2530 B.C.E. and towering to a height of 65 feet, it faces into the rising sun, seeming to cast its immobile gaze down the centuries for all eternity. The Sphinx has the body of a reclining lion and the head of a man, thought to be the pharaoh Khafre, whose pyramid tomb is nearby. Egyptian kings ruled absolutely and enjoyed a semidivine status, taking their authority from the sun-god, Ra, from whom they were assumed to be descended. Both power and continuity are embodied in this splendid monument.

An even earlier relic from Egyptian culture, the so-called *Palette of Narmer* (**14.11**), illustrates many characteristics of Egyptian art. The palette (so named because it takes the form of a slab for mixing cosmetics) portrays a victory by the forces of Upper (southern) Egypt, led by Narmer, over those of Lower (northern) Egypt. Narmer is the largest figure and is positioned near the center of the palette to indicate this high status. He holds a fallen enemy by the hair and is about to deliver the death blow. In the lowest sector of the tablet are two more defeated enemies. At upper right is a falcon representing Horus, the god of Upper Egypt. In its organization of images the palette is strikingly logical and balanced. The central section has Narmer's figure just to left of the middle, with his upraised arm and the form of a servant filling the space, while the falcon and the victim complete the right-hand side of the composition.

Narmer's pose is typical of Egyptian art. When depicting an important personage, the Egyptian artist strove to show each part of the body to best advantage, so it could be "read" clearly by the viewer. Thus, Narmer's lower body is seen in profile, his torso full front, his head in profile, but his eye front again. This same pose recurs throughout most two-dimensional art in Egypt. It is believed that the priests, who had much control over the art, established this figure type and decreed that it be maintained for the sake of continuity. Obviously, it is not a posture that suggests much motion, apart from a stylized gesture like that of Narmer's upraised arm. But action was not important to Egyptian art. Order and stability were its primary characteristics, as they were

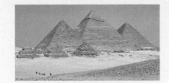

3.9 Pyramids at Giza

14.10 (left) *The Great Sphinx*, Giza. c. 2500 B.C.E. Limestone rock, height 66'.

14.11 (right) *Palette of Narmer*, from Hierakonpolis. c. 3100 B.C.E. Slate, height 25".
Egyptian Museum, Cairo.

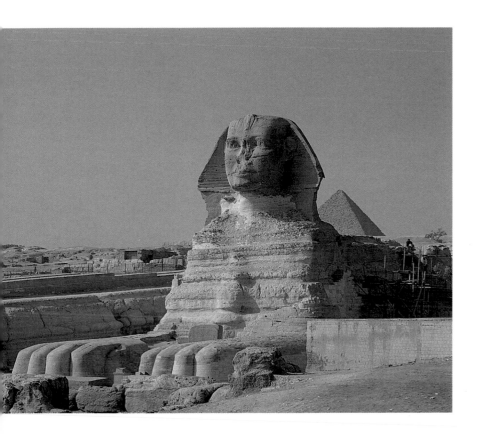

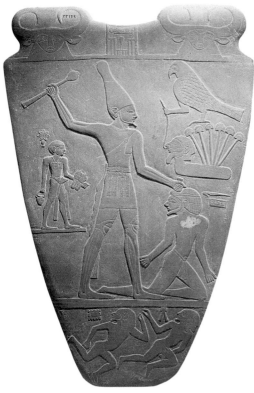

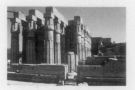

13.2 Temple of Amon-Mut-Khonsu

the goals of Egyptian society. We see this in official sculptures, such as the double portrait of Menkaure and Khamerernebty in Chapter 11 (see 11.15), and also in less formal works.

A common sculpture type from the same period as the Menkaure figure is the *Seated Scribe* (**14.12**), depicting a high court official whose position might be explained as "professional writer." In an era when literacy was rare, the scribe played a vital role in copying important documents and sacred texts, and his work commanded much respect. This sculpture, although somewhat more relaxed than standing pharaoh portraits, is still symmetrical and reserved. The scribe's face shows intelligence and dignity, and his body is depicted realistically as thickening and rather flabby, no doubt a sign of his age and sedentary occupation, perhaps also an indicator of wisdom.

The most famous architectural creation of Egypt is the pyramid (see 3.9), but Egyptian architects also built homes, palaces, temples, shrines, and other structures. A pyramid, in fact, was only one element of a royal funerary complex, which also included a temple for the worship of the deceased ruler, who had rejoined the gods in immortality. One of the best-preserved and most innovative funerary temples is that of Hatshepsut, one of the few female rulers in Egypt's history (**14.13**). Planned by the architect Senenmut, it rises in a series of three broad terraces and then continues *into* the steep cliffs behind it, from which an inner sanctuary was hollowed out. Over 200 statues of Hatshepsut once populated the vast complex, which contained shrines to several Egyptian deities as well as to Hatshepsut and her father, the ruler Tuthmose I.

Egyptian painting reveals the same clear visual design and illustrative skill as the works in stone. A wall painting from Thebes (**14.14**), depicting a hunting scene, poses the main figure very much like the figure of Narmer, although the two works are separated in time by some 1,650 years. Again the hunter's body is stylized: His head, eyes, torso, and legs are each shown from the most advantageous viewpoint. In keeping with the Egyptians' love of exact detail, this painter draws the birds and other creatures with almost biological

14.12 (left) *Seated Scribe*, from Saqqara. c. 2450 B.C.E. Painted limestone, with alabaster and rock crystal eyes, height 21". Musée du Louvre, Paris.

14.13 (right) Funerary temple of Hatshepsut, Deir el-Bahri. c. 1460 B.C.E.

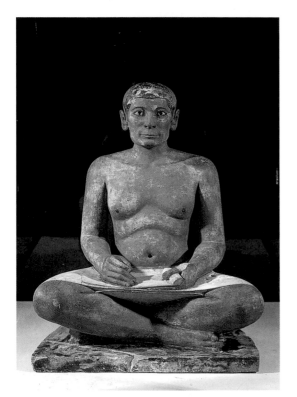

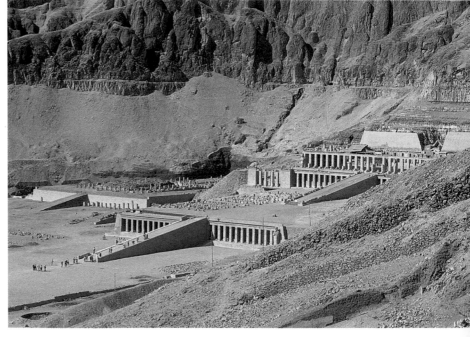

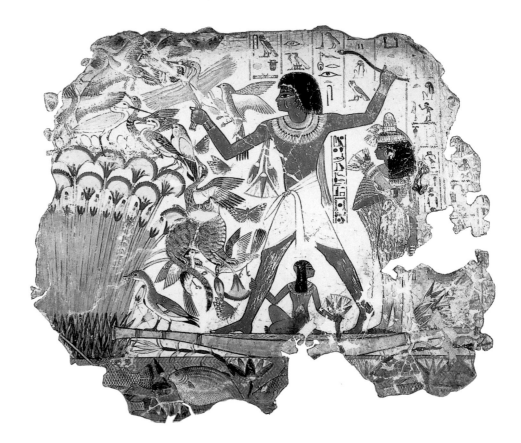

14.14 Fragment of a wall painting from the tomb of Nebamun, Thebes. c. 1450 B.C.E. Paint on plaster, height 32". The British Museum, London.

precision. If we recognize the species, we can identify them. Even the fish are rendered meticulously; we don't see them as we would through a blur of water, but rather as we *know* the fish to look.

We know other things as well. The use of hierarchical scale tells us that the hunter, probably a nobleman, is the most important figure in the composition, because he is the biggest. Apart from clues provided by clothing, we know that he is a man and the figure at right is a woman. By convention, regardless of race or complexion, the Egyptians painted men darker (reddish) and women lighter (yellowish).

Typical of Egyptian art, the image has many layers of meaning. The man is depicted young and in the prime of life, the form he hopes to have in eternity. His victorious pose proclaims his ability to triumph in the journey to the afterlife, which was thought to be fraught with peril. The marsh setting is also significant. It was in a marsh that the Egyptian goddess Isis prepared her husband Osiris for resurrection, and that life itself began at the time of creation. A marsh is thus a site where life renews itself, just as the man will renew himself by rising from death.

One brief period in the history of Egyptian culture stands apart from the rest and therefore has fascinated scholars and art lovers alike. This was the reign of pharaoh Amenhotep IV, who came to power about 1353 B.C.E. For a civilization that prized continuity above all else, Amenhotep was a true revolutionary. He changed his name to Akhenaten and attempted to establish monotheism (belief in one god) among a people who had traditionally worshiped many gods. He built a new capital at what is now called Tell el-Amarna, so historians refer to his reign as the Amarna period. Akhenaten was apparently quite active in creating a new style of art for his reign, and under his direction the age-old, rigid postures of Egyptian art gave way to more relaxed, naturalistic, and even intimate portrayals.

RELATED WORKS

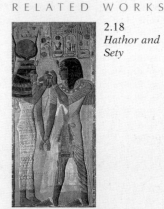

2.18
Hathor and Sety

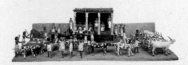

3.17 Model from the tomb of Meketre

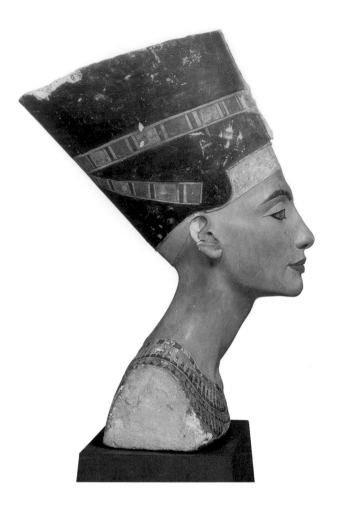

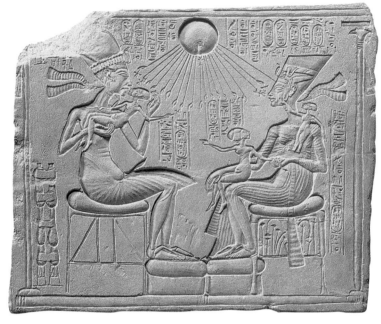

14.15 (left) *Queen Nefertiti.* c. 1345 B.C.E. Painted limestone, height 20".
Staatliche Museen zu Berlin, Preussischer Kulturbesitz, Ägyptisches Museum.

14.16 (right) *Akhenaten and His Family,* from Akhetaten (modern Tell el-Amarna). c. 1345 B.C.E. Painted limestone relief, 12¼ × 15¼".
Staatliche Museen zu Berlin, Preussischer Kulturbesitz, Ägyptisches Museum.

Nowhere is this new style more apparent than in the famous portrait bust of his queen, Nefertiti (**14.15**). While enchanted by Nefertiti's beauty, the modern viewer is perhaps even more taken by how contemporary she seems, how she appears to bridge the gap of more than three thousand years to our own world. With her regal headdress and elongated neck, Nefertiti presents a standard of elegance that is timeless.

Even more intimate is the charming domestic scene depicted in this limestone relief (**14.16**). Akhenaten and Nefertiti sit facing each other on cushioned thrones. Akhenaten tenderly holds one of their three daughters, who gestures toward her mother and sisters. Seated on Nefertiti's lap, the older daughter looks up at her mother as she points across to her father; the youngest daughter tries to get her mother's attention by caressing her cheek. Above, Akhenaten's god, Aten, the sun-disk, shines his life-giving rays upon them. The sculpture is an example of **sunken relief.** In this technique, the figures do not project upward from the surface. Instead, outlines are carved deep into the surface, and the figures are modeled within them, from the surface down.

Akhenaten's reforms did not last. After his death, temples to the old gods were restored and temples that had been built to Aten were dismantled. The city of el-Amarna was abandoned, and the traditional Egyptian styles of representation were reimposed. Thus it is that the immobile mask of eternity greets us again in the stunning gold burial mask of Akhenaten's son-in-law and successor, the young Tutankhamun (**14.17**).

From earliest times, Egyptians had buried their most lavish art in royal tombs. Rulers were sent into eternity outfitted with everything they would need to continue life in the sumptuous style they had known on earth—furniture, jewelry, chariots, clothing, and artifacts of all kinds. From earliest times as well, grave robbers have coveted that buried treasure—and not for its artistic merits. Most of the royal tombs that have been discovered in modern times have been empty, their fabulous contents looted long ago. It was not until 1922 that modern eyes could assess the full splendor of ancient Egypt. In that year, the English archaeologist Howard Carter discovered the tomb of Tutankhamun, its treasures virtually intact after 3,000 years.

Tutankhamun—quickly dubbed "King Tut" by the 1922 newspapers—was a relatively minor ruler. The tombs of the great would have been far more lavish. Yet even Tutankhamun's tomb was a virtual warehouse of priceless objects superbly crafted of alabaster, precious stones, and above all gold—gold in unimaginable quantities. Gold in Egyptian thought signified more than mere wealth. It was associated with the life-giving rays of the sun and with eternity itself. The flesh of the gods was believed to be gold, which would never decay. Tutankhamun's solid gold coffin, and the solid gold face mask (14.17) that rested on the head and shoulders of his mummified body inside, were meant to confer immortality. Projecting over the young king's forehead are the alert heads of a cobra and a vulture, symbols of the ancient protective goddesses of Lower and Upper Egypt.

When Tutankhamun died, around 1323 B.C.E., Egyptian civilization was already ancient—a continuous culture that looked back confidently on some 1,700 years of achievement and power. Egypt would continue for another 1,300 years into the future, yet its years of supremacy were waning. Other, younger cultures were gathering force elsewhere around the Mediterranean. Two of these upstarts, Greece and Rome, would eventually conquer Egypt. We turn our attention to Greece next, after a brief look at some of the cultures that preceded it on the islands of the Aegean Sea.

14.17 Burial mask of Tutankhamun. c. 1325 B.C.E. Gold, inlaid with blue glass and semiprecious stones; height 21¼". Egyptian Museum, Cairo.

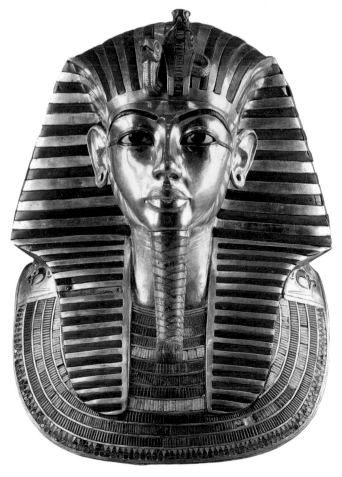

WHOSE GRAVE?

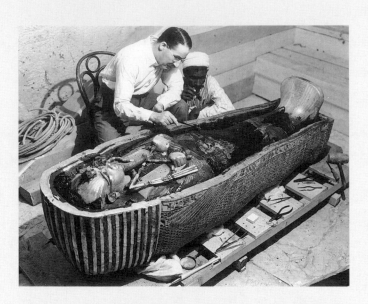

When HOWARD CARTER and his party opened the tomb of the Egyptian king Tutankhamun in 1922, there was rejoicing around the world. The tomb was largely intact, not seriously pillaged by ancient grave robbers—it still contained the wonderful artifacts that had been buried with the young king more than three millennia earlier. Over the next several years Carter and his team systematically photographed and catalogued the objects from the tomb, then transported them to the Cairo Museum.

There is a certain irony in this story that raises complex ethical questions. Why are Carter and his party not called grave robbers? Why are their actions in stripping the tomb acceptable—even praiseworthy—when similar behavior by common thieves would be deplored? No matter who opens a tomb and takes away its contents, that person is violating the intentions of those who sealed the tomb originally. No matter what the motivation, a human body that was meant to rest in peace for all time has been disturbed. Should this not make us feel uncomfortable?

At the time some people were uneasy about the propriety of unearthing Tutankhamun's remains. When Lord Carnarvon, Carter's sponsor, died suddenly from a mosquito bite, and several others connected with the project experienced tragedies, rumors arose about the "curse of King Tut." But Carter himself died peacefully many years later, and the talk subsided.

Perhaps it is the passage of time that transforms grave robbing into archaeology. Carter would no doubt have been outraged if, say, his grandmother's coffin had been dug up to strip the body of its jewelry. But after three thousand years Tutankhamun has no relatives still around to protest.

Perhaps it is a question of the words we use to describe such ancient finds. We speak of Tutankhamun's "mummy," and mummy is a clean, historical-sounding word. Parents bring their children to museums to see the mummies and mummy cases. We can almost forget that a mummy is the embalmed body of a dead human being pulled out of its coffin so that we can marvel at the coffin and sometimes the body itself.

Or, perhaps the difference between grave robbing and archaeology lies in the motives of the perpetrators. Common thieves are motivated by greed, by their quest for money to be made by selling stolen objects. Carter and his team did not sell the treasures from Tutankhamun's tomb but stored them safely in the Cairo Museum, where art lovers from around the world can see them. They were, in effect, making a glorious gift to the people of our century and centuries to come (while at the same time, of course, acquiring significant glory for themselves).

The basic issue is a clash of cultural values. To the Egyptians, it was normal and correct to bury their finest artworks with the exalted dead. To us, the idea of all that beauty being locked away in the dark forever seems an appalling waste. We want to bring it into the light, to have it as part of our precious artistic heritage. Almost no one, having seen these magnificent treasures, would seriously propose they be put back in the tomb and sealed up.

In the end, inevitably, our cultural values will prevail, simply because we are still here and the ancient Egyptians are not. After three thousand years, Tutankhamun's grave really isn't his anymore. Whether rightly or wrongly, it belongs to us.

Howard Carter and an assistant unwrapping the innermost of Tutankhamun's three nested coffins. The third coffin is solid gold and contained the king's mummified body.

THE AEGEAN

Between the Greek peninsula and the continent of Asia Minor (modern-day Turkey) is an arm of the Mediterranean Sea known as the Aegean (see map, p. 365). Greek culture arose on the lands bordering this small "sea within a sea," but the Greeks were preceded in the region by several fascinating cultures that thrived on the islands that are so plentiful there.

The artistic cultures of the Aegean parallel in time those of Egypt and Mesopotamia, for the earliest begins about 3000 B.C.E. There were three major Aegean cultures: the Cycladic, centered on a group of small islands in the Aegean; the Minoan, based on the island of Crete at the southern end of the Aegean; and the Mycenaean, on the mainland of Greece.

Cycladic art is a puzzle, because we know almost nothing about the people who made it. Nearly all consists of nude female figures like the one illustrated here (**14.18**)—simplified, abstract, composed of geometric lines and shapes and projections. The figures vary in size from the roughly 2-foot height of our example to approximately life-size, but they are much alike in style. Presumably they were meant as fertility images, although they are a far cry from the fleshier "Venuses" found earlier in the north. To modern eyes the Cycladic figurines seem astonishingly sophisticated in their sleek abstraction of the human figure. Indeed, 20th-century artists such as Alberto Giacometti (see 4.40) studied Cycladic art when they were forging their own abstract styles.

Centered around the great city of Knossos, Minoan culture can be traced to about 2000 B.C.E. We take the name from a legendary king called Minos, who supposedly ruled at Knossos and whose queen gave birth to the dreaded creature, half-human, half bull, known as the Minotaur. Numerous frescoes survive at Knossos—some fragmentary, some restored—and from these we have formed an impression of a lighthearted, cheerful people devoted to games and sport. Among the finest wall paintings is a work known as the *Toreador Fresco* (**14.19**), featuring the Minoans' special animal, the bull. This modern title suggests the Spanish sport of bullfighting (a *toreador* being a bullfighter), but we can see that the Minoans' game was unique to them. A young male acrobat vaults over the back of the racing bull; he will be caught in the waiting arms of the young woman at right. Another female player, at left, grasps the bull's horns; perhaps she is ready to take her turn somersaulting over the animal.

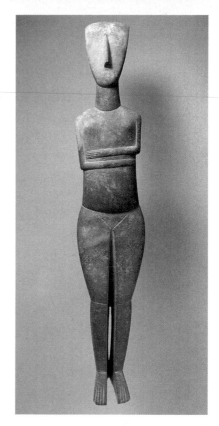

14.18 (above) *Statuette of a Woman.* Cycladic, c. 2600–2400 B.C.E. Marble, height 24¾". The Metropolitan Museum of Art, New York.

14.19 (below) *Toreador Fresco,* from the palace at Knossos. c. 1500 B.C.E. Fresco, height approx. 32". Archaeological Museum, Herakleion, Crete.

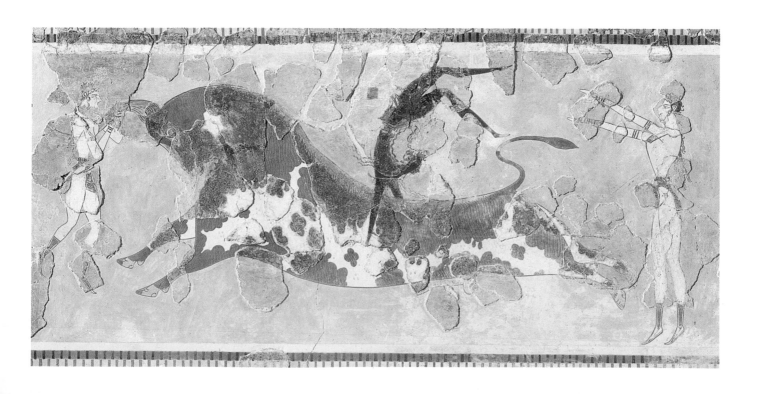

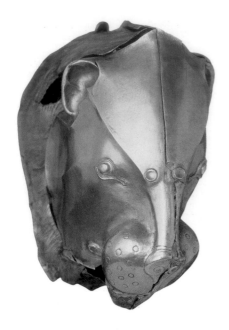

14.20 Rhyton in the shape of a lion's head, from Mycenae. c. 1550 B.C.E. Gold, height 8". National Museum, Athens.

Most striking here is the contrast between the hefty, charging bull and the lithe, playful flip of the acrobat. The composition is marvelously balanced, with the women at both sides serving as anchors, the tumbling male figure and the curving tail counterweighing the massive bull's head. Many graceful curves—of the bull's back, the bull's underbelly, the tumbler's arched body—reinforce our experience of motion, captured to the split second.

Mycenaean culture, so called because it formed around the city of Mycenae, flourished on the south coast of the Greek mainland from about 1600 to 1100 B.C.E. Like the Minoans, the Mycenaeans built palaces and temples, but they are also noted for their elaborate burial customs and tombs—a taste apparently acquired from the Egyptians, with whom they had contact. It seems probable that Egypt or Nubia was also the source of the Mycenaeans' great supplies of gold, for they alone among the Aegean cultures were master goldsmiths. Burial places in and around Mycenae have yielded large quantities of exquisite gold objects, such as the *rhyton*, or drinking cup, in the shape of a lion's head (**14.20**). The craftsmanship of this vessel is wonderful, contrasting smooth planar sections on the sides of the face with the more detailed snout and mane. The Mycenaeans also used gold for masks, jewelry, and weapons.

THE CLASSICAL WORLD: GREECE AND ROME

When we use the word "Classical" in connection with Western civilization, we are referring to the two cultures discussed next in this chapter—ancient Greece and ancient Rome. The term itself indicates an aesthetic bias, for anything "classic" is supposed to embody the highest possible standard of quality, to be the very best of its kind. If true, this would mean that Western art reached a pinnacle in the few hundred years surrounding the start of our common era and has not been equaled in the millennium and a half since then. This is a controversial idea that many would dispute vehemently. Few can deny, however, that the ancient Greeks and Romans *intended* to achieve the highest standards. Art and architecture were matters of public policy, and it was accepted that there could be an objective, shared standard for the best, the purest, the most beautiful.

Greece

No doubt a major reason we so respect the ancient Greeks is that they excelled in many different fields. Their political ideals serve as a model for contemporary democracy. Their poetry and drama and philosophy survive as living classics, familiar to every serious scholar. Greek philosophers, in fact, were the first to speculate on the nature and purpose of art, though they did not call it that. Sculpture, painting, and architecture were discussed as *techne*, roughly "things requiring a special body of knowledge and skill to make," a large category that included such products as shoes and swords. The idea survives in our words *technology* and *technique*.

Greek architecture and sculpture had an enormous influence on the later civilizations of Rome and, through Rome, Europe. We assume that Greek painting was equally brilliant, for ancient historians wrote vividly about it. Descriptions abound of such marvels as fruit painted so convincingly that even ravenous birds were fooled, and of rival artists striving to outdo each other in skill. But of the works themselves almost nothing has survived. Instead, we must content ourselves with images painted on terra-cotta vessels, which archaeologists have uncovered in large quantities.

An early example is the *krater* illustrated here (**14.21**). One of many standard Greek pottery shapes, a *krater* is a vessel used for wine. This *krater* dates

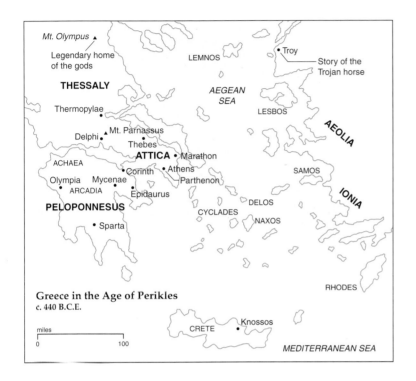

Greece in the Age of Perikles
c. 440 B.C.E.

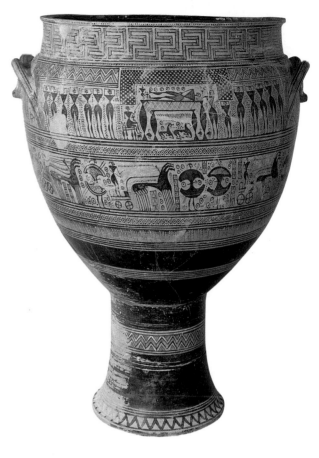

14.21 *Krater,* from the Dipylon Cemetery. Athens, 8th century B.C.E. Terra cotta, height 42⅜". The Metropolitan Museum of Art, New York.

from the 8th century B.C.E., when Greek culture first comes into focus. Stylistically it belongs to the Late Geometric period, when human figures begin to appear amid the geometric motifs that had decorated earlier Greek ceramics. In the upper register, a funeral ceremony is depicted. We see the deceased laid out on a four-legged couch. The checkerboard pattern above probably represents the textile that covered him. Wasp-waisted mourners stand to either side, slapping their heads and tearing their hair in grief. In the lower register a procession of foot soldiers and horse-drawn chariots passes by. The highly abstracted figures are only beginning to break free from their geometric world. Notice, for example, the triangular torsos of the mourners and the squares framed by their arms and shoulders.

The *krater* not only depicts a funeral but served as a grave marker itself. It was found in the Dipylon Cemetery, a burial ground near the entrance to ancient Athens. Other funerary vessels have been found with a hole punched through the base, suggesting that libations—offerings of wine and water— were poured into them to pass directly into the earth of the grave beneath. Compared to the lavish burials of Egyptian pharaohs, the burial customs of the Greeks were bleak. Tombs of the Egyptian elite were fitted out for a luxurious life in eternity, since that is what they expected. The Greeks were not so optimistic. Death was death. The next world was imagined as a gray and shadowy place of little interest.

The sculptural tradition of Greece begins with small bronze figures of horses and men in styles much like the figures on the *krater* we just examined. At some point, however, Greek sculptors seem to have begun looking closely at the work of their neighbors the Egyptians, with whom they were in contact.

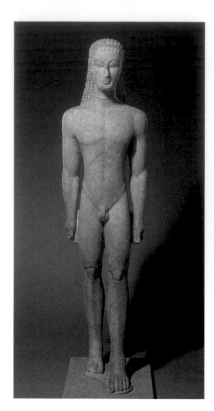

14.22 *Kouros.* c. 580 B.C.E.
Marble, height 6'4".
The Metropolitan Museum of Art,
New York.

Egyptian influence is clear in this life-size statue of a young man (**14.22**). Not only does the work reproduce the characteristic Egyptian pose—one leg forward, arms at the sides, hands clenched (see 11.15)—but it even follows the Egyptian grid system of proportions (see 5.20). Like Egyptian works, too, the block of original stone can still be sensed in the squared-off appearance of the finished sculpture.

In other respects, however, this figure is radically different from Egyptian works. Whereas Egyptian sculptors left their figures partially embedded in the granite block they were carved from, the Greek figure is released completely from the stone, with space between the legs and between the arms and the body. Whereas Egyptian men were depicted wearing loincloths, the Greek figure is nude. His neck ornament and elaborately braided hairstyle suggest that despite this nudity he is carefully groomed and appropriately dressed. His nudity, in other words, is a positive statement, not a temporary absence of clothing. Finally, whereas Egyptian statues depict specific individuals—rulers and other members of the elite—the Greek statue depicts an anonymous boy. Thousands of such figures were carved—perhaps as many as 20,000—all of them in the same pose, and all nude, broad-shouldered, slim-waisted, fit, and young. They were placed as offerings in sanctuaries to the gods and set as grave markers in cemeteries. Scholars refer to them generically by the Greek word for youths or boys, *kouroi* (singular *kouros*). Statues of maidens, *korai* (singular *kore*), were also carved, though these are fewer in number and always fully clothed.

Kouroi and *korai* were created largely during the 6th century B.C.E., the **Archaic** period of Greek art, so called because what would later be leading characteristics can be seen in their early form. In the *kouros* depicted here, the earliest known example, the treatment of the body and face are still fairly abstract. As the tradition evolved, sculptors aimed increasingly at giving their statues a lifelike, convincing presence. They observed human bodies more attentively and copied them more faithfully, leading eventually to a style we know as naturalism. One reason for this was that many statues depicted gods. The Greeks imagined their gods in thoroughly human form, many of them dazzlingly beautiful and eternally young. Every sanctuary contained a statue of the god or goddess it was dedicated to, and the more believable the statue was, the more present to believers the deity seemed.

Created only sixty years after the *kouros* we have been looking at, the amphora (storage vessel) illustrated next shows how rapidly Greek art evolved toward naturalistic representation (**14.23**). It also shows us something of the culture that made men's bodies available for direct observation. Created by the potter Andokides and a painter we recognize only as the "Andokides Painter," the vessel is one of the earliest examples of the red-figure style, which evolved toward the end of the Archaic period. In the red-figure style, the ground is painted black, while figures are left unpainted. The red that results is the natural color of fired earth. Earlier Archaic pottery had employed the reverse color scheme, with black figures painted on a red ground.

The amphora is decorated with a scene set in a gymnasium. From childhood on, exercise at the gymnasium was as much a part of Greek education as learning mathematics, music, and philosophy. Male citizens were in constant training, for they also formed their city's army. Greek athletes trained and competed in public in the nude. The scene on the amphora depicts two pairs of men wrestling. A trainer stands watching them, holding a flower up to his face. The flower, a symbol of beauty, indicates that the toned bodies of the athletes are to be as openly admired as their wrestling ability. Well-developed male bodies were on constant display, and their beauty was celebrated and depicted in art. There was an erotic component to this, but also a moral one, for beauty was felt to go hand in hand with nobility and goodness. Men in ancient Greece had public lives, and their bodies were public bodies. Women were largely confined to the domestic realm, and their bodies were not for public display, either in life or in art.

The Greek concern with lifelike representation flowered fully in statues such as this bronze warrior (**14.24**). Here is an idealized, virile male body, its anatomy distilled from observing hundreds of athletic physiques. The warrior stands in a relaxed yet vigilant contrapposto—the pose the Greeks invented to express the potential for motion inherent in a standing human. (To review the principles of contrapposto, see page 279.) Bronze was the favored material for freestanding sculpture in ancient Greece, yet very few examples survive. The metal was too valuable for other purposes—especially weapons—and most ancient sculptures were melted down centuries ago. If it were not for marble copies of bronze works commissioned by later Roman admirers, we would know far less than we do about Greek art. The statue here is one of two life-size warrior figures discovered off the coast of Riace, Italy, in 1972. They had escaped destruction only by being lost at sea.

The Riace warriors were created during the **Classical** period of Greek art, which dates from 480–323 B.C.E. Although all ancient Greek and Roman art is broadly known as Classical, the art produced during these decades was considered by later European scholars to be the finest of the finest. During this period, Greece consisted of several independent city-states, often at war among themselves. Chief among the city-states—from an artistic and cultural point of view, if not always a military one—was Athens.

Like many Greek cities, Athens had been built around a high hill, or acropolis. Ancient temples on the Acropolis had crumbled or been destroyed in the wars. About 449 B.C.E. Athens' great general Perikles came to power as head of state and set about rebuilding. He soon embarked on a massive construction program, meant not only to restore the past glory of Athens but to raise it to a previously undreamed-of splendor.

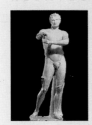
14.23 (left) Andokides and the "Andokides Painter." Amphora with gymnasium scene. c. 520 B.C.E. Terra cotta, height 22¹³⁄₁₆". Staatliche Museen zu Berlin, Preussischer Kulturbesitz, Antikensammlung.

14.24 (right) *"Warrior A,"* discovered in the sea near Riace, Italy. c. 450 B.C.E. Bronze, with bone and glass eyes, silver teeth, and copper lips and nipples, height 6'8". Museo Archaeològico Nazionale, Reggio Calabria, Italy.

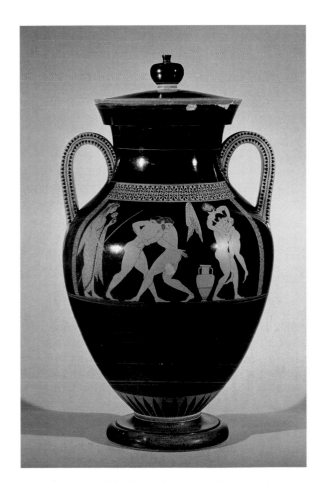

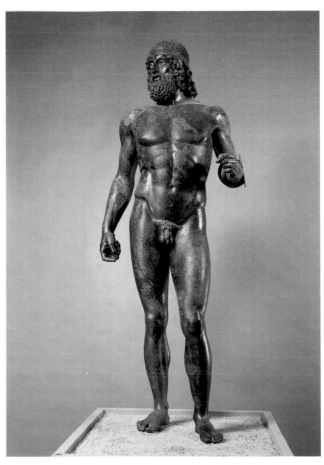

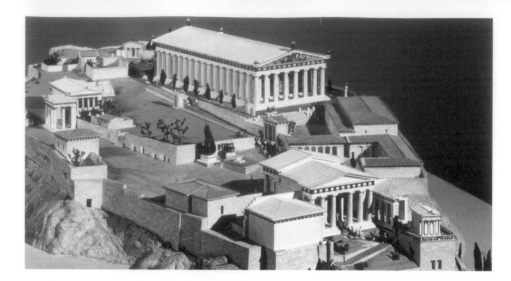

14.25 (above) Model reconstruction of the Acropolis, Athens, viewed from the northwest.
Courtesy Royal Ontario Museum, Toronto.

14.26 (below) Iktinos and Kallikrates. Parthenon, Athens. 447–432 B.C.E.

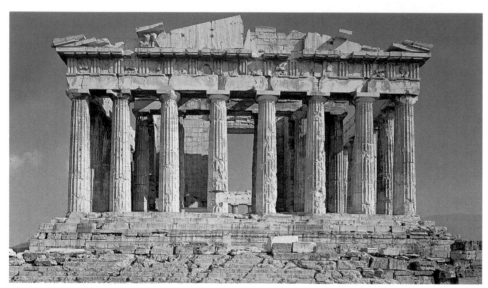

RELATED WORKS

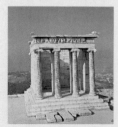

13.4 Kallikrates, Temple of Athena Nike

Perikles' friend, the sculptor Phidias, was given the job of overseeing all architectural and sculptural projects on the Acropolis. The work would continue for several decades, but it took an amazingly short time given the ambitious nature of the scheme. By the end of the century the Acropolis probably looked much like the reconstruction shown here (**14.25**). The large columned building at lower right in the photo is the Propylaea, the ceremonial gateway to the Acropolis through which processions winding up the hill would pass. At left in the photo, the building with columned porches is the Erechtheum, placed where Erechtheus, legendary founder of the city, supposedly lived.

But the crowning glory of the Acropolis was and is the Parthenon (**14.26**). Dedicated to the goddess Athena *parthenos*, or Athena the warrior maiden, the Parthenon is a Doric-style temple with columns all around the exterior and an inner row of columns on each of the short walls. The roof originally rose to a peak, leaving a pediment (visible in the reconstruction) at each end. The pediments were decorated with sculptures, as was the frieze. (To review the vocabulary of Classical architecture, see p. 314.) In the manner of Greek temples, the Parthenon was painted in vivid colors, principally red and blue. The architects Iktinos and Kallikrates, directed by Phidias, completed the structure in just fifteen years.

The Parthenon has been studied in greater detail than perhaps any other building in the Western tradition, for it served generations of European

THE MARBLES AND THE MUSEUMS

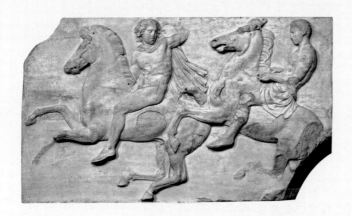

LIKE MOST MONUMENTAL buildings in antiquity, the Parthenon was originally ornamented with a rich program of sculpture. Only about half of the Parthenon sculptures survive today, and of these, half are in the British Museum. How they got there and whether they should be returned are the subjects of this essay.

To set the stage, we need to sketch in a quick history of Greece. The Parthenon was built in the city-state of Athens during the 5th century B.C.E. Three centuries later, Greece was subsumed into the growing empire of Rome. The western portion of the Roman empire disintegrated during the 5th century C.E.; the eastern portion continued for another thousand years as Byzantium, a Greek-speaking Christian empire ruled from Constantinople (present-day Istanbul). In 1453 Constantinople was conquered by Muslim forces, and Greece was absorbed into the Ottoman Empire where it remained until modern times.

In 1799 Thomas Bruce, 7th Earl of Elgin, was appointed ambassador of England to the Ottoman court. By this time, the Parthenon was in ruins. Early Christians had converted it to a church, in the process destroying many of its sculptures. During the 17th century, invading Venetian forces had fired on the Parthenon, which the Ottomans were then using to store gunpowder. The resulting explosion caused severe damage. Lord Elgin arrived with a plan to make plaster copies of the remaining Parthenon sculptures and send them back to England, but he quickly became convinced that the sculptures themselves needed to be removed in order to preserve them for posterity. As a diplomatic favor, the Ottoman court granted him a royal mandate to proceed. Detaching the sculptures from the building and shipping them to England took five years; Elgin paid for it out of his own personal fortune. Lord Elgin had intended to donate the marbles to the nation, but severe financial problems prompted him to ask for compensation. In the end, the British Museum, funded by Parliament, purchased the marbles for a fraction of what Elgin had spent to obtain them. The sculptures went on display to the public in 1817, and they have been on permanent display ever since, the object of scholarly research and conservation efforts.

Not long after Elgin shipped the Parthenon marbles off to England, Greece launched a war of independence against the Ottomans, which ended with a Greek victory in 1832. Almost immediately, Greek calls for the return of the marbles were heard. These calls have recurred regularly and with increasing frequency over the years. The British Museum has refused. The argument on both sides has taken many forms, but the trump card in the British response has always been this: How would you care for them? Indeed, sculptures left behind by Lord Elgin remained on the Parthenon until 1977, slowly decaying in the increasingly polluted air of modern Athens. Even now, all of them have not been removed, and most of the ones that have are stored out of the public view. Greek plans to build a museum for them repeatedly came to naught—until recently.

In 2002, work was begun on a new museum in Athens. As of this writing it is scheduled to open in 2007. Situated at the foot of the Acropolis, it includes a large gallery designed especially to receive the Parthenon marbles. The Greek government is now calling for the British Museum to send the marbles to Athens on extended loan. The British Museum responds that no official offer has been received, and that Greece must first acknowledge that the marbles are the legitimate property of the British Museum's trustees. Talks are ongoing. Should the marbles be returned?

Two Horsemen, from the west frieze of the Parthenon. c. 438–432 B.C.E. Marble, originally polychrome; height 39⅜".
The British Museum.

architects as a model of perfection. Research has discovered numerous painstaking refinements that contribute to the temple's pleasing effect. First, as mentioned in Chapter 5, the ratio of length to height of the facade reproduces the proportion known as the golden section (see 5.24), which the Greeks found intellectually and aesthetically pleasing. Legend claims there are no straight lines in the Parthenon, but this is probably a romantic exaggeration. Many of the lines we expect to be straight, however, are not. Instead, the builders adjusted the physical lines of the temple so they would appear to be straight. For example, tall columns that are absolutely straight may *appear* to bend inward at the center, like an hourglass, so the columns on the Parthenon have been given a slight bulge, known as **entasis,** to compensate for the visual effect. Also, a long horizontal, such as the Parthenon's porch steps, may appear to sag in the middle; to correct for this optical illusion, the level has been adjusted, rising about 2½ inches to form an arc higher at the center. A large building rising perpendicular to the ground may loom over the visitor and seem to be leaning forward; to avoid this impression, the architects of the Parthenon tilted the whole facade back slightly. Corner columns, seen against the sky, would have seemed thinner than inside columns, which have the building as a backdrop; therefore, the outside columns were made slightly heavier than all the others.

The inner chamber of the Parthenon once housed a monumental statue of the goddess Athena, made by Phidias himself of gold and ivory and standing 30 feet tall atop its pedestal. Contemporary sources tell us Phidias was an artist of unsurpassed genius, but we must take their word for it, since neither the Athena nor any of his other sculptures are known to survive. Other sculptures from the Parthenon have been preserved, however, and these were probably made by Phidias' students, under his supervision.

The Parthenon sculptures represent a high point in the long period of Greek experimentation with carving in marble. One existing sculpture group, now in the British Museum, depicts *Three Goddesses* (**14.27**). In Perikles' time this group stood near the far right side of the pediment; if you imagine the figures with their heads intact, you can see how they fit into the angle of the triangle. Carved from marble and now headless, these goddesses still seem to breathe and be capable of movement, so convincing is their roundness. The draperies flow and ripple naturally over the bodies, apparently responding to living flesh underneath.

The last phase of Greek art is known as **Hellenistic**—a term that refers to the spread of Greek culture eastward through Asia Minor, Egypt, and Mesopotamia—lands that had been conquered by the Macedonian Greek ruler Alexander the Great. The beginning of the Hellenistic era is usually dated to Alexander's death in 323 B.C.E.

14.27 *Three Goddesses*, from the east pediment of the Parthenon. c. 438–432 B.C.E. Marble, over life-size.
The British Museum, London.

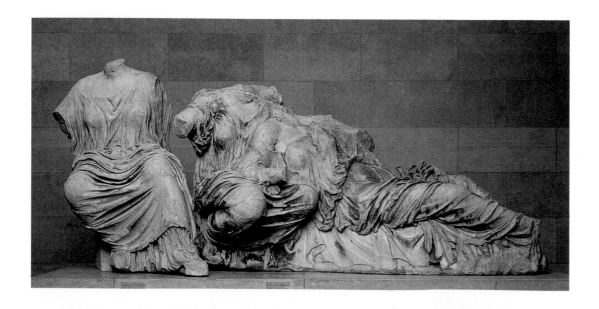

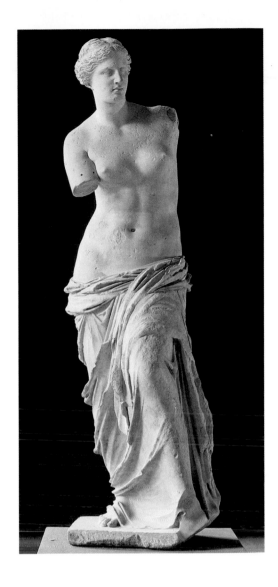

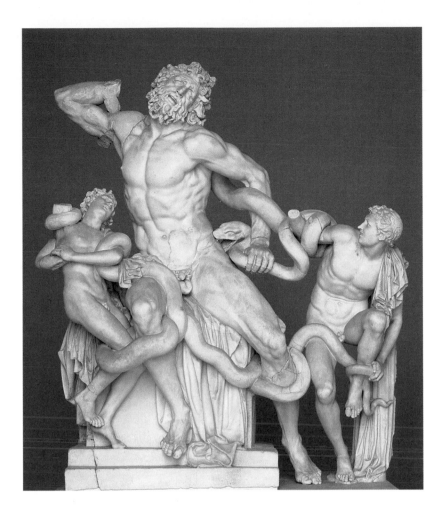

14.28 (left) *Aphrodite of Melos* (also called *Venus de Milo*). c. 150 B.C.E.
Marble, height 6'10".
Musée du Louvre, Paris.

14.29 (right) *Laocoön Group.* Roman copy, late 1st century B.C.E. early
1st century C.E., of a Greek bronze(?) original, possibly by Agesander,
Athenodorus, and Polydorus of Rhodes. Marble, height 8'.
Musei Vaticani, Rome.

Hellenistic sculpture developed in several stylistic directions. One was a
continuing Classical style that emphasized balance and restraint, as seen in
one of the most famous of extant Hellenistic works, the *Aphrodite of Melos*,
also known as the *Venus de Milo* (**14.28**). Venus was the Roman equivalent of
Aphrodite, the Greek goddess of love, beauty, and fertility. Sculptors of the late
Classical period had begun admitting female nudes into the public realm—
though only as goddesses or mythological characters. This statue exemplifies
the ideal of female beauty that resulted. Her twisting pose may be explained
by the theory that her missing arms once held a shield propped up on her
raised knee. She would have been admiring her own reflection in a mirror, her
draperies slipping provocatively as she contemplated her beauty.

A second Hellenistic style overthrew Classical values in favor of dynamic
poses and extreme emotions. One of the best-known examples of this style is
the *Laocoön Group* (**14.29**), which we know from what is probably a Roman
copy of a Greek bronze of the 2nd century B.C.E.

Laocoön was a priest of the sun-god, Apollo, and his story involves one
of the most famous events in Greek mythology. In the last year of the war between the Greeks and the Trojans, the Greeks devised a fabulous ruse to over-
run the city of Troy. They built a giant wooden horse, concealed inside it a

large number of Greek soldiers, and wheeled it up to the gates of Troy, claiming it was an offering for the goddess Athena. While the people of Troy were trying to decide whether to admit the horse, their priest, Laocoön, suspected a trick and urged the Trojans to keep the gates locked. This angered the sea-god, Poseidon, who held bitter feelings toward Troy, and he sent two dreadful serpents to strangle Laocoön and his sons. The sculpture depicts the priest and his children in their death throes, entwined by the deadly snakes.

Compared with statues from the Classical period, such as the Riace *Warrior*, the *Laocoön Group* seems theatrical. Its subject matter, filled with drama and tension, would have been unthinkable three centuries earlier. The Classical sculptor wanted to convey an outward serenity, and thus showed the hero in perfection but not in action, outside of time, not throwing the spear but merely holding it. Hellenistic sculptors were far more interested than their predecessors in how their subjects reacted to events. Laocoön's reaction is a violent, anguished one, and the outlines of the sculpture reflect this. The three figures writhe in agony, thrusting their bodies outward in different directions, pushing into space. Unlike earlier figures, with their dignified reserve, this sculpture projects a complicated and intense movement.

Rome

The year 510 B.C.E. is usually cited as the beginning of the Roman era, for it was then, according to ancient historians, that the Roman Republic was founded. There followed a long period of expansion and consolidation of ter-

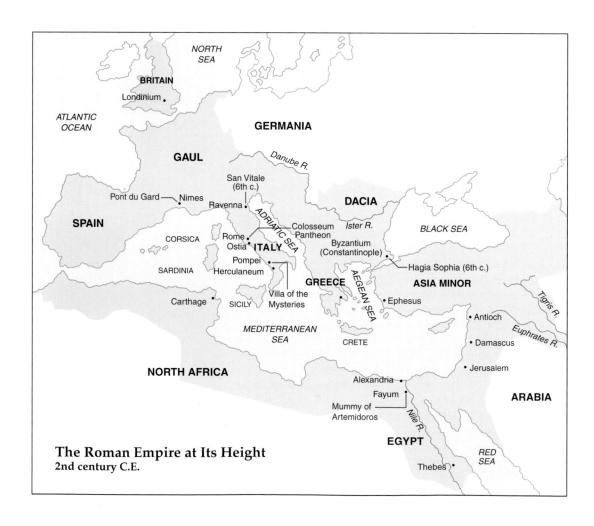

The Roman Empire at Its Height
2nd century C.E.

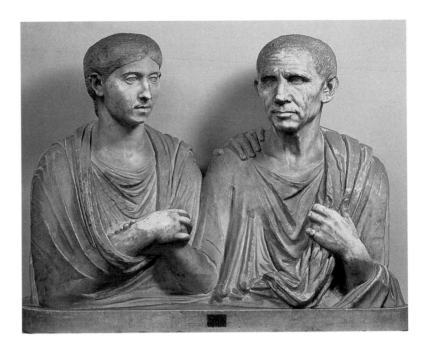

14.30 *Double Portrait of Gratidia M.L. Chrite and M. Gratidius Libanus.* Late 1st century B.C.E. White marble with traces of color, height 23¾".
Museo Pio Clementino, Musei Vaticani, Rome.

ritories brought under Roman rule. Roman legions swept eastward through Greece into Mesopotamia, west and north as far as Britain, across the sea to Egypt, throughout the rim of northern Africa. In 27 B.C.E., when Augustus took the title of "caesar," Rome officially became an empire.

Rome came of age during the Hellenistic period, when the prestige of Greek culture was at its height in the ancient Mediterranean world. The Romans were great admirers of Greek achievements in the arts. Many works were taken from Greece and brought to Rome. Statues and paintings were commissioned from Greek artists, and copies were made in marble of Greek bronze originals, such as the *Laocoön Group* (14.29) illustrated above.

One aspect of Hellenistic art was a tendency toward realistic portrayals of individuals, as opposed to idealized portrayals of *types* of people. No longer forever young and perfect, an athlete such as a boxer might be portrayed as the survivor of years of physically punishing bouts, his face lined, his body thickening with the onset of middle age. Roman sculptors excelled at this realism in their portrait busts of ordinary citizens.

One such example (**14.30**) is a portrait of a Roman husband and wife who are fully realized as individuals. Obviously, we cannot know what these people actually looked like, but it is safe to assume the sculptor made a good likeness, with a minimum of idealizing. The husband is old, the creases in his face are well defined, his expression is patient; we might read from his image a long experience in the trials of the world and gentle resignation to those trials. His wife seems stronger, less marked by pain, and her supportive clasp of the husband's hand is touching. Scholars have read into this pose the highly esteemed Roman virtues of *fides* (faith or fidelity) and *concordia* (harmony). Whereas the Greek sculptures and many of the Roman ones seem to exist in a world apart, these portrait busts are wonderfully accessible. They allow us to identify with people who have been dead for two thousand years.

One highly influential invention of Roman sculptors was the equestrian portrait—the portrayal of an admired leader on horseback. The sole Roman example that has survived into modern times is the bronze statue illustrated in Chapter 3 of the emperor Marcus Aurelius (see 3.10). The equestrian statues that ornament our cities—monuments to leaders of the American Revolution, the Civil War, and other conflicts—are the direct descendants of this fine Roman work, which has inspired imitations ever since it was rediscovered during the Renaissance.

RELATED WORKS

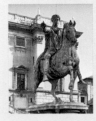

3.10
Marcus
Aurelius

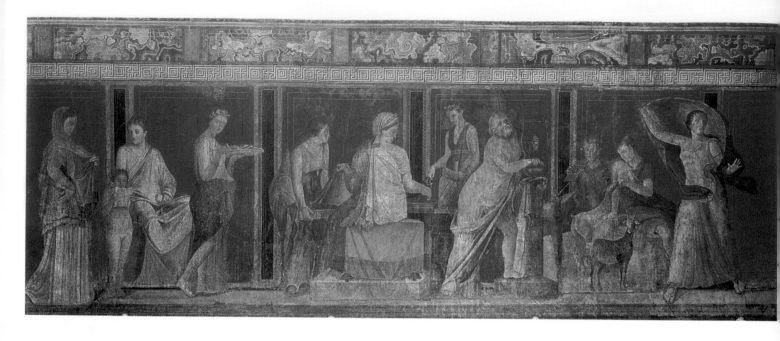

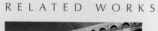

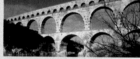

14.31 Wall painting, from Villa of the Mysteries, Pompeii. c. 50 B.C.E. Fresco.

The Romans were equally masterful at painting, but were it not for a tragedy that occurred in 79 C.E., we would know little more about Roman painting than we do about the Greek. In that year Mt. Vesuvius, an active volcano, erupted and buried the town of Pompeii, about a hundred miles south of Rome, along with the neighboring town of Herculaneum. The resulting lava and ashes spread a blanket over the region, and this blanket acted as a kind of time capsule. Pompeii lay undisturbed, immune to further ravages of nature, for more than sixteen centuries. Then in 1748 excavations were undertaken, and their findings were made public by the famous German archaeologist Joachim Winckelmann. Within the precincts of Pompeii the diggers found marvelous frescoes that were exceptionally well preserved. Pompeii was not an important city, so we cannot assume that the most talented artists of the period worked there. In fact, there is some evidence to suggest that the fresco painters were not Roman at all, but immigrant Greeks. Nevertheless, these wall paintings do give some indication of the styles of art practiced within the empire at the time.

One fresco, from a house known as the Villa of the Mysteries (**14.31**), shows a scene believed to represent secret cult rituals associated with the wine god Dionysus. The figures stand as though on a ledge, in shallow but convincing space, interacting only slightly with one another. Although the artist has segmented the mural into panels separated by black bands, the figures overlap these panels so freely that there is no strong sense of individual episodes or compartments. Rather, the artist has established two rhythms—one of the figures and another of the dividing bands—giving a strong design unity.

For all their production in sculpture and painting, the Romans are best known for their architecture and engineering. We saw two of their masterpieces, the Pont du Gard and the Pantheon, in Chapter 13 (see 13.9, 13.13, 13.15). But the most familiar monument—indeed, for many travelers the very symbol of Rome—is the Colosseum (**14.32**).

The Colosseum was planned under the Emperor Vespasian and dedicated in 80 C.E. as an amphitheater for gladiatorial games and public entertainments. A large oval covering 6 acres, the Colosseum could accommodate some fifty thousand spectators—about the same number as most major-league baseball stadiums today. Few of the games played inside, however, were as tame as baseball. Gladiators vied with one another and with wild animals in bloody and gruesome contests. On special occasions the whole structure could be filled with water for realistic naval battles.

Even in its ruined state this structure displays the genius of the Romans as builders. The Colosseum rises on three tiers of arches, each of the levels distinguished from the next by a different style of column between the arches—Doric on the lowest level, Ionic on the second, and Corinthian on the third. Around the base are eighty arched openings for entry and exit; it is said that the entire building could be emptied in a matter of minutes. Above all, the structure is logical and coherent. Roman architects tell us in visual detail exactly how the building is organized—which parts are separate from other parts, where to enter, where to go, and so on. The exterior view gives us a clear sense of the inside, the walkways, the scheme as a whole.

By the year 100 of our era, the Roman Empire ringed the entire Mediterranean Sea. It extended eastward through Asia Minor and into Mesopotamia, westward through Spain, northward into England, and south across North Africa and Egypt. Yet the many cultures that came under Roman rule did not cease to be themselves and suddenly become Roman. Instead, the empire extended its umbrella over a vast array of cultures, languages, and religions, all of which now mingled freely thanks to Roman rule and Roman roads.

Our last illustration gives us a glimpse of the multicultural world of late Rome (**14.33**). The illustration shows the mummy of a young man named Artemidoros, from Fayum, in Egypt. It dates from sometime in the 2nd century of our era. Egypt was then part of the Roman Empire, and Artemidoros was a Roman subject. Artemidoros, however, is a Greek name, and it is written in Greek letters on his mummy. Why a Greek in Egypt? Alexander the Great had conquered Egypt in 323 B.C.E. For the next 300 years, Egypt was ruled by a Greek dynasty, the Ptolomies. Greeks constituted an elite part of the population, but while they preserved their own language, they adopted the Egyptian religion, with its comforting belief in an eternal afterlife. Thus

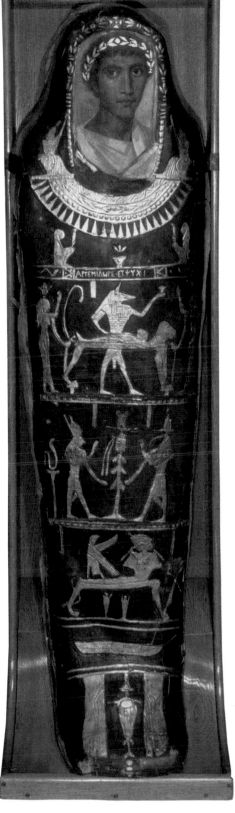

14.32 (left) Colosseum, Rome. 72–80 C.E.

14.33 (right) Mummy case of Artemidoros, from Fayum. 100–200 C.E. Stucco casing with portrait in encaustic on limewood with added gold leaf, height 67¼". The British Museum, London.

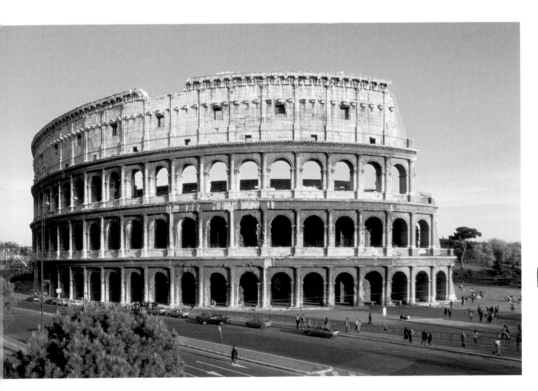

the body of Artemidoros, an Egyptian of Greek ancestry and identity, was mummified for burial, and on his mummy are depicted ancient Egyptian gods, including Anubis, the jackal-headed god of the dead, visible at the center just under Artemidoros' name.

Rome conquered Egypt from the last of the Ptolomies, the celebrated queen Cleopatra, in 31 B.C.E. Greek remained the principal administrative language of Egypt, even under Roman rule. Roman customs and fashions, however, were widely imitated by Egyptians who wanted to appear "up to date." One such custom was the funeral portrait, a commemorative painting of a recently deceased person. Thus Artemidoros' mummy includes a funeral portrait, painted in encaustic on wood in a Greek-Roman style. (To review the technique of encaustic, see page 169.) What are we to call Artemidoros? Roman-Greek-Egyptian? After thousands of years of history, cultural identities could have many layers in the ancient Mediterranean world.

Influence flowed from Rome's conquests to Rome as well. Like the Greeks before them, the Romans were fascinated by Egyptian culture, which was so much older than their own. They imported many Egyptian statues to Rome, and Roman artists worked to satisfy a craze for new sculptures in the Egyptian style. While Roman gods and goddesses remained the official deities of Rome, the worship of the Egyptian goddess Isis spread through the empire as far away as Spain and England. So did Mithraism, the worship of the sun-god of the Persians, some of whose ancient territories also fell under Roman rule.

In these heady if sometimes perplexing times, who could have foreseen that the future would belong to a completely new religion that had only recently arisen in the eastern part of the vast empire? Based in the teachings of an obscure Jewish preacher named Jesus, it was called Christianity.

CHAPTER FIFTEEN

CHRISTIANITY AND THE FORMATION OF EUROPE

According to tradition, Jesus, known as the Christ or "anointed one," was born in Bethlehem during the reign of Emperor Augustus. In time his followers would become so influential in world affairs that our common calendar takes as its starting point the presumed date of Jesus' birth, calling it "year 1." As a matter of fact, the 6th-century calendar makers who devised this plan were wrong in their calculations. Jesus probably was born between four and six years earlier than they had supposed, but the calendar has nevertheless become standard.

The faith preached by the followers of Jesus spread with remarkable speed through the Roman Empire, yet that empire itself was about to undergo a profound transformation. Overextended, internally weakened, and increasingly invaded, it would soon disintegrate. The western portion would eventually reemerge as western Europe—a collection of independent, often warring kingdoms united by a common religious culture of Christianity. The eastern portion would survive for a time as the Byzantine Empire, a Christianized continuation of a much-diminished Roman Empire. The Near East, Egypt, North Africa, and most of Spain, meanwhile, would become the heartlands of yet another new religious culture, Islam.

We will discuss the arts of Islam in Chapter 18. This chapter continues the story of the Western tradition with the rise of Christianity, the arts of Byzantium, and the formation of western Europe.

THE RISE OF CHRISTIANITY

Christianity was but one of numerous religions in the late Roman Empire, but it quickly became one of the most popular and well organized. Rome's attitude toward this new cultural force within its borders varied. Often, the faith was tolerated, especially since it came to attract an increasing number of wealthy and influential people. At other times, Christians were persecuted, sometimes officially and sometimes by mobs. One reason for the persecutions was that Christians refused to worship the gods and goddesses of the state religion, including the emperor himself, in addition to their own god. Clearly such people were a threat to the political stability and well-being of the empire.

Little art that is specifically Christian survives from these first centuries. Gathering places for the faithful were probably built in some of the major centers of the empire, but none survive. Most early worship took place in private homes, although only one such early house-church has been discovered. Some of the earliest Christian art has been preserved in underground burial chambers that were later forgotten. The portion of a mosaic illustrated here is from the vault of an underground necropolis (from the Greek for "city of the dead") in Rome (**15.1**). The mosaic was created around the same time as the mummy of Artemidoros discussed in Chapter 14 (see 14.33), and it offers a similarly fascinating mixture of imagery.

In depicting Christ in triumph, the artist has borrowed the iconography of the Greek and Roman god Apollo, who was often portrayed riding his chariot across the sky as the sun god. Rays of light emanating from the head of this Christ-Apollo are modified to suggest a cross. The grape leaves of the surrounding pattern were associated with the Greek god Dionysus, known to the Romans as Bacchus, the god of fertility and wine. Christians appropriated the grape leaf as a symbol, for Christ had spoken of himself as the true vine, whose branches (the faithful) would bear fruit (the kingdom of God on earth). The benefit for artists was that the grape-leaf patterns they had learned as apprentices could serve for Christian clients as well as pagan ones.

Christianity's situation changed abruptly in the year 313, when the Roman emperor Constantine issued an edict of tolerance for all religions. Not only were all faiths now free to practice openly, but Constantine himself patronized Christianity, for he attributed his success in a key battle to the Christian god. Under his imperial sponsorship, architects raised a series of large and opulent churches at key locations in the empire. One of these was Old St. Peter's, built on the spot in Rome where it was believed that Peter, Jesus' first apostle, had been buried. This structure was demolished in 1506 to erect the "new" St. Peter's now in Rome (see 16.13), but contemporary descriptions and drawings have enabled scholars to make informed guesses about its design

15.1 *Christ as the Sun*, detail of a mosaic under Saint Peter's necropolis, Rome. Mid-3rd century.

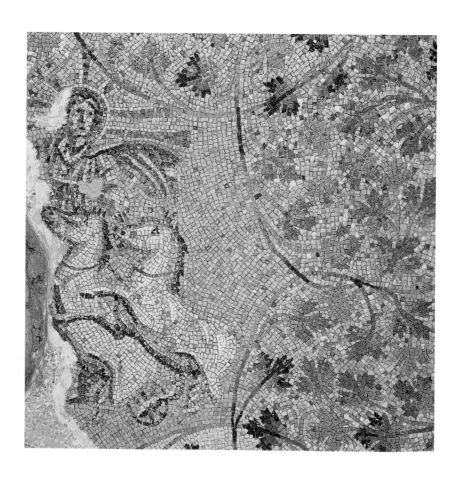

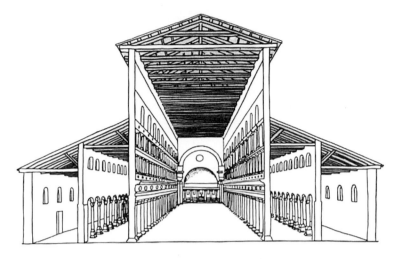

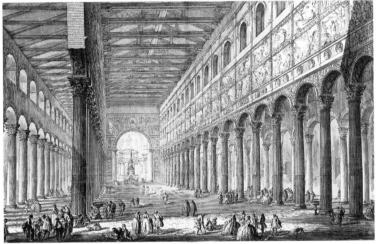

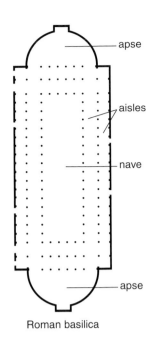

apse

aisles

nave

apse

Roman basilica

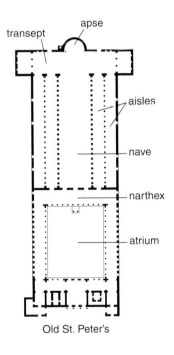

transept apse

aisles

nave

narthex

atrium

Old St. Peter's

(**15.2**). A similar church built some sixty years later, St. Paul's Outside the Walls, stood intact until the 19th century, and an artist's rendering gives testimony to its grandeur (**15.3**).

What should a church look like? Most Roman, Greek, and even Egyptian and Mesopotamian temples had essentially been conceived as dwelling places for the gods they were dedicated to. Priests might enter to perform rites of sacrifice and worship, but groups of ordinary people viewed these rites from outside, if they viewed them at all. Christianity from the beginning emphasized congregational worship, and so a fundamentally different kind of building was needed, one that could contain a lot of people. Roman architects already had such a structure in their repertoire of standard building types, a multipurpose meeting hall called a **basilica** (**15.4**, top).

As the plan shows, a basilica was basically a long rectangular hall. Entrances might be on the long or short sides (here, they are on the long sides). At one or both ends (both, in this example) might be a curved section called an **apse.** In order to admit light, the open center space, called the **nave,** extended up higher than the surrounding **aisles.** This upward extension was called the **clerestory,** and it was pierced with windows called clerestory windows. If you look back at the drawing of Old St. Peter's (15.2), you can now clearly see the central nave with its clerestory windows and the lower side aisles that buttress it. In the distance, at the far end of the nave, is an apse.

A plan of Old St. Peter's (**15.4,** bottom) makes this clear and also shows an additional element. The basilica form is designed with the entry on one of the short sides. Inside we find the wide central nave flanked by narrower aisles. At the far end is the apse. A natural focal point for anyone entering the

15.2 (above left, top) Reconstruction of Old St. Peter's, Rome. Begun c. 320.

15.3 (above left) St. Paul's Outside the Walls, Rome. Begun c. 385. Interior. Engraving by Piranesi.

15.4 Plan of a Roman basilica (above, top) and plan of Old St. Peter's (above).

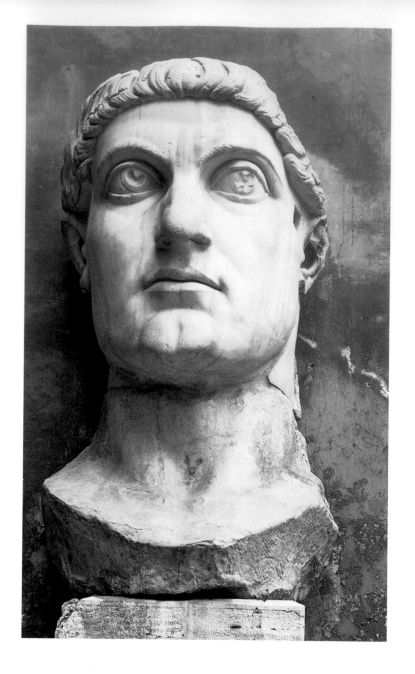

15.5 *Constantine the Great.*
325–26. C.E. Marble, height of
head 8'6".
Palazzo dei Conservatori, Rome.

church, the apse provides a setting for the altar, the focal point of Christian worship. In addition, this far wall is extended slightly to each side of the building. The extensions create a lengthwise section perpendicular to the nave called a **transept.** Together, nave and transept form a cross, a fundamental Christian symbol. Preceding the church was an atrium. An open courtyard surrounded by a covered walkway, the atrium was a standard element of Roman domestic architecture. The arm of the walkway directly in front of the church served as an entry porch called a **narthex.** The elements here—nave, aisles, clerestory, apse, transept, and narthex—formed the basic vocabulary of church architecture in the West for many centuries. We will use them often in this chapter.

In 324, Constantine made another decision with far-reaching consequences: Judging that the empire could be more securely ruled from the East, he ordered his architects and engineers to transform the ancient Greek colony of Byzantio, known in Latin as Byzantium, into a new capital city called Constantinople (present-day Istanbul, in Turkey). Six years later, he moved his administration there. As a symbol of his continuing presence in Rome, Constantine commissioned a 30-foot-tall statue of himself, portrayed seated in majesty, and had it installed in an apse added especially for that purpose to a prominent Roman basilica. Fragments of the statue have survived, including the massive head (**15.5**). The prominent nose and chin undoubtedly reproduce Constantine's distinctive features. But the overall style of the image is far from the idealized naturalism of Greece and the realism of earlier Rome. Instead, exaggerated, stylized eyes stare out from geometric, semicircular sockets under an abstracted representation of hair. The stage is set for the art of Byzantium.

BYZANTIUM

The actual territory ruled from Constantinople varied greatly over the centuries. At first, it was the entire Roman Empire. By the time the city was conquered by Islamic forces in 1453, it was a much-reduced area. But no matter the actual extent of their dominion, the title that Byzantine rulers inherited was "emperor of all the Romans." They viewed themselves as the legitimate continuation of the ancient Roman Empire, with one important difference: Byzantium was Christian. Whereas Constantine had extended his protection and patronage to Christianity, his successors went one step further: They made Christianity the official state religion. Church and state were intertwined in Byzantium, and its art marries the luxurious splendor of a powerful earthly kingdom—its gold and silver and jewels—with images that focus on an eternal, heavenly one.

The great masterpiece of early Byzantine architecture is the Hagia Sophia, which we examined in Chapter 13 (see 13.16, 13.17). A smaller gem of the early Byzantine style is San Vitale, built during the 6th century in Ravenna, Italy, which was then under Byzantine control (**15.6, 15.7**). San Vitale does not follow the cross plan that became standard for Western churches, but instead uses a central plan favored in the East. Central plan churches are most often square with a central dome, as is the Hagia Sophia. San Vitale, however, takes the unusual form of an octagon. Although an apse protrudes from one wall and a narthex is attached to two others, the fundamental focus of the building is at its center, over which rises a large dome. The major axis of a central-plan church is thus vertical, from floor to dome, or symbolically from earth to the vault of heaven.

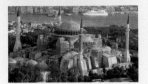
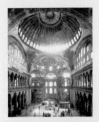
15.6 (left) San Vitale, Ravenna. c. 527–47.

15.7 (right) Plan of San Vitale.

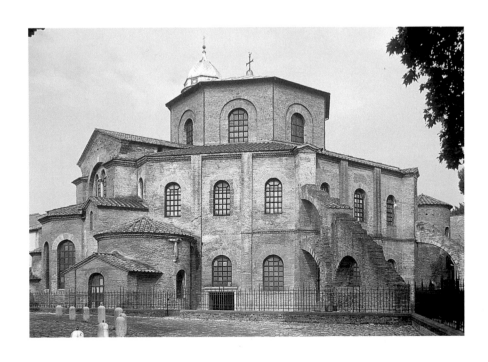

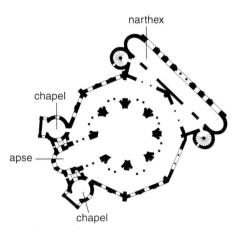

narthex

chapel

apse

chapel

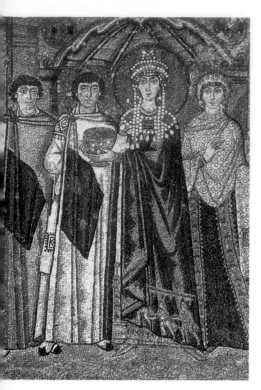

The interior of San Vitale is decorated in glittering mosaics, including portrayals of the emperor Justinian and the empress Theodora (**15.8**), under whose patronage the church was built. Like the statue of Constantine we examined earlier (15.5), the images conveyed the rulers' symbolic presence in this distant portion of their empire. Mosaic continued as a favored Byzantine technique, resulting in such masterpieces as the interior of the Santa Maria la Nuova, a 12th-century Byzantine church in Sicily (**15.9**). Set in the half-dome crowning the apse illustrated here is a large figure of Christ as *Pantokrator*, Greek for "Ruler of All." A standard element of later Byzantine iconography, the *Pantokrator* image emphasizes the divine, awe-inspiring, even terrifying majesty of Christ as opposed to his gentle, approachable, human incarnation as Jesus. Directly below Christ is Mary, the mother of Jesus, enthroned with the Christ child on her lap. She is flanked by angels and saints.

We can see here how Byzantine artists had moved away from the naturalism and realism of classical Greece and Rome toward a flattened, abstracted style. Like the artists of ancient Egypt, Byzantine artists strove to portray often complex religious doctrines and beliefs, not scenes from daily life. Their subject was not the impermanent earthly world of the flesh, but the eternal and sacred world of the spirit. By de-emphasizing the roundness, the weight, the "hereness" of human bodies in this world, they emphasize that what we are looking at is not in fact *here*, but *there*. The glittering gold background of the mosaics is typical, and it sets the figures in a Byzantine vision of heavenly splendor.

A characteristic Byzantine art form is the **icon,** a picture of a sacred subject painted on a wooden panel (**15.10**). The example here shows the crucified Christ flanked by his mother, Mary, and his disciple John. Above the arms of the cross, two angels representing all of heaven lament. Again the elongated, weightless figures stand not in an earthly landscape but in the gold realm of heaven, for this is a painting about ideas, not an attempt to envision the actual event. Mary's head is lowered in mourning and reflection. With her gesture she directs our attention to the pitiable sight of Jesus on the cross. John is there as a witness, but also because Christian scripture relates that Christ

15.8 (above) *Empress Theodora and Retinue,* detail. c. 547. Mosaic.
San Vitale, Ravenna.

15.9 (right) Mosaic depicting *Christ as Pantokrator,* Santa Maria la Nuova, Monreale, Sicily. Before 1183.

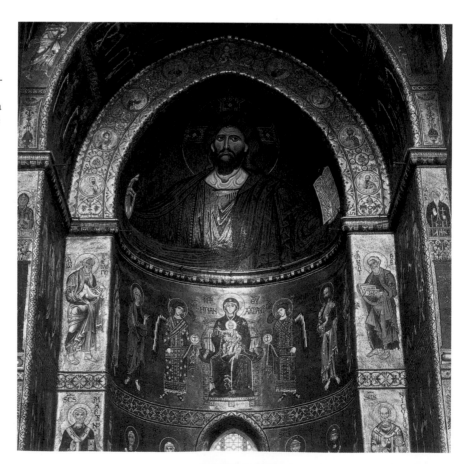

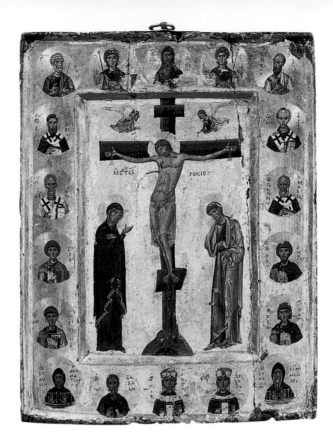

15.10 *Icon with the Crucifixion.*
Byzantine, c. 1100. Tempera on
wood, 11⅛ × 8½".
The Holy Monastery of Saint
Catherine, Sinai, Egypt.

during his final agonies offered John as a son to Mary, and Mary to John as a
mother. This gesture was interpreted symbolically as designating Mary as a
new Eve, mother of all the faithful. John thus stands for all Christians. The
artist has taken pains to depict Christ as dead and yet alive, a central miracle
of Christianity. Struggling for words to express this difficult concept, medieval
writers sometimes spoke of Christ as "asleep" on the cross, and that is the effect here. Framing this central grouping are painted medallions of saints,
angels, and important men and women of the early Church.

By the time this icon was painted, around 1100 C.E., vast changes had occurred in the territories that Constantinople was built to rule. Constantine's vision of a unified Roman Empire did not prevail: The territory was simply too
vast. His successors partitioned the empire into eastern and western halves,
each with its own emperor. Within 150 years, the western empire had fallen,
overwhelmed by a massive influx of Germanic peoples arriving from the north
and east. Constantinople again claimed authority over the entire empire, but
could not enforce it. The western Church, based in Rome, preserved its imperial organization and religious authority, but true political and military power
had passed to the local leaders of the newcomers, who settled throughout the
lands of western Europe. It is to these peoples and their art that we now turn
our attention.

THE MIDDLE AGES IN EUROPE

The Middle Ages is the name that historians long ago gave to the period in Europe between the defeat of the last western Roman emperor in 476 and the beginnings of the Renaissance in the 15th century. To these early historians, the
period was a dark one of ignorance and decline, an embarrassing "middle" time
between one impressive civilization and another. Today, we view the Middle
Ages as a complex and fascinating period worthy of study in its own right. During these centuries, Europe was formed, and a distinctive Christian culture
flowered within it. Far from ignorant, it was a time of immense achievement.

The Early Middle Ages

The kingdoms of the early Middle Ages in Europe were inhabited by descendants of migratory tribes that had traveled southward and westward on the continent during the 4th and 5th centuries. Ethnically Germanic, these peoples emerged, for the most part, from the north-central part of Europe, or what today we would call northern Germany and Scandinavia. The Romans referred to them as "barbarians" (meaning "foreigners") and considered them crude—with some justification, for, being nomadic, they had a considerably lower level of culture than did the settled citizens of the empire. Moreover, it was continual invasion by the "barbarians" that brought about the empire's ultimate collapse, near the end of the 5th century.

By the year 600 the migrations were essentially over, and kingdoms whose area roughly approximated the nations of modern Europe had taken form. Their inhabitants had steadily been converted to Christianity. For purposes of this discussion, we will focus initially on the people who settled in two areas—the Angles and Saxons in Britain, and the Franks in Gaul (modern France).

On the island of Britain north of London (then Londinium) was Sutton Hoo, where the grave of an unknown 7th-century East Anglian king has been found. Objects discovered at the burial site include a superb gold and enamel purse cover (**15.11**), with delicately made designs. The motifs are typical of the **animal style** prevalent in the art of northwestern Europe at that time—a legacy, very likely, from the migratory herdsmen who were these people's ancestors. Animal-style images were often accompanied by **interlace,** patterns formed by intricately interwoven ribbons and bands. We can see interlace clearly in the upper-center medallion of the Sutton Hoo purse cover, where it is combined with abstracted animals.

Among the most important artistic products of the early Middle Ages were copies of Christian scriptures. In these days before the printing press, each book had to be copied by hand. During the early Middle Ages, this copying was carried out in monasteries, for monks, educated by the Church, were the only literate segment of the population. Monks not only copied texts but also **illuminated** them—furnished them with illustrations and decorations. The full-page illumination here (**15.12**) was probably made by Irish monks working in Scotland. It announces the beginning of the Gospel of Mark—one of the four accounts in the Bible of the life and works of Jesus—and it shows how the monks adapted animal style and interlace to a Christian setting. At the center of the page is St. Mark's symbolic animal, the lion. Monks in Scotland could never have seen a lion, of course, and the fanciful creature they have come up with closely resembles the beasts on the cover of the Sutton Hoo purse. The borders of the illumination display the intricate interlace patterns that became a specialty of Irish illuminators.

15.11 Purse cover, from the Sutton Hoo ship burial. 625–33. Gold with garnets and enamels, length 7½".
The British Museum, London.

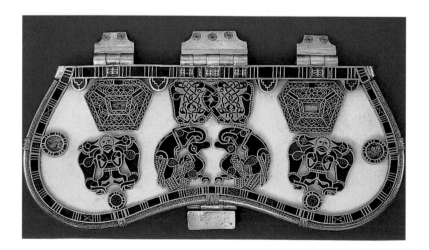

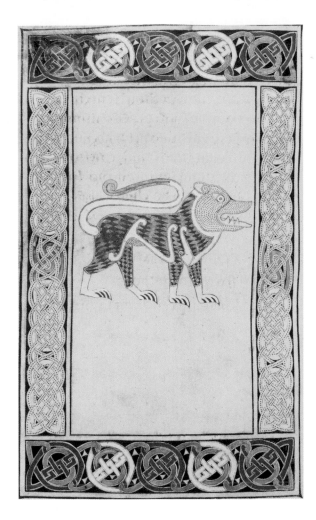

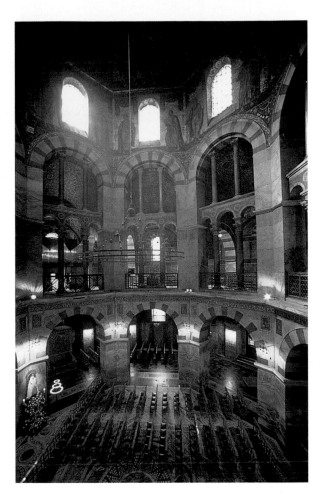

In France a different style of art was taking root, called **Carolingian** after the emperor Charlemagne. Charlemagne, or Charles the Great, was a powerful Frankish king whose military conquests eventually gave him control over most of western Europe. On Christmas Day of the year 800 the Pope crowned Charlemagne Holy Roman Emperor—making him the first of many rulers to bear that title. The title is significant because it united two major forces. Charlemagne was *Roman* in that he thought of himself as inheriting the legacy of the old Roman Empire. He was called *holy* for being a Christian king, the dominant Christian king.

Charlemagne seems to have been much aware of the past glories of the old Roman Empire, and he wished to imitate or surpass them in his own reign, his own empire. Following the example of Roman emperors before him, he took an active interest in artistic and cultural matters. At his capital, Aachen, Charlemagne ordered a splendid Palace Chapel built to be his personal place of worship (**15.13**). The architecture of the chapel gives several clues to his ambitions. Its basic design is modeled after San Vitale in Ravenna (see 15.6), which Charlemagne apparently had seen and admired. Very likely he wished to copy the perfection of that octagonal church, to match the architectural ideals of Byzantium. At the same time, however, the details of the Palace Chapel are much heavier, more massive, more *Roman*, especially the robust Roman arches. Charlemagne—the Frankish king from the north—intended to be a Roman emperor, even to the design of his holy place.

Some writers consider Charlemagne's coronation day to be the end of the early Middle Ages. The emperor was crowned not by his own people but rather by the Pope, the leader of the Christian religion, and he was crowned *Holy* Roman Emperor. For the first time a political ruler had the sanction of the Church of Rome, and this opened a new chapter in European history.

15.12 (left) Page with *Lion*, from the *Gospel Book of Durrow*. Scotland(?), c. 675. Ink and tempera on parchment, 9⅝ × 5¹¹⁄₁₆".
The Board of Trinity College, Dublin.

15.13 (right) Interior, Palace Chapel of Charlemagne, Aachen. 792–805.

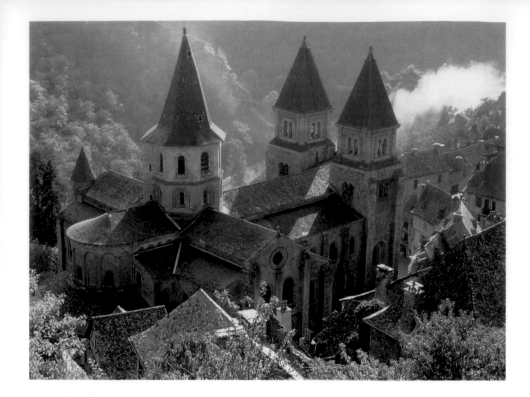

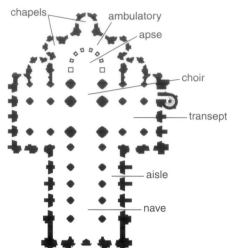

15.14 (left) Aerial view of Sainte-Foy, Conques, Auvergne, France. c. 1050–1120.

15.15 (right) Plan of Sainte-Foy.

RELATED WORKS

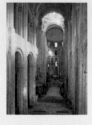

13.10
Interior,
Sainte-Foy

The High Middle Ages

The Middle Ages was a time of intense religious preoccupation in Europe. It was during this era that most of the great cathedrals were built. Also, a major portion of the art that has come down to us is associated with monasteries, churches, and cathedrals.

Historians generally divide the art and architecture of the high Middle Ages into two periods: the Romanesque, from about 1050 to 1200, based on southern styles from the old Roman Empire; and the Gothic, from about 1200 into the 15th century, which has more of a northern flavor. (The term "Gothic" derives from the Goths, who were among the many nomadic tribes sweeping through Europe during the 4th and 5th centuries. It was applied to this style by later critics in the Renaissance, who considered the art and architecture of their immediate predecessors to be vulgar and "barbarian.")

The Romanesque period was marked by a building boom. Contemporary commentators were thrilled at the beautiful churches that seemed to be springing up everywhere. Later art historians called the style of these buildings Romanesque, for despite their great variety they shared certain features reminiscent of ancient Roman architecture, including an overall massiveness, thick stone walls, round arches, and barrel-vaulted stone ceilings.

One reason for the sudden burst of building was the popularity of pilgrimages. In the newly prosperous and stable times of the 11th and 12th centuries, people could once again travel safely. Although some made the trip all the way to Jerusalem, in the Holy Land, most confined their pilgrimages to sites associated with Christian saints in Europe. Churches—and also lodgings and other services—arose along the most popular pilgrimage routes as way stations for these large groups of travelers.

The earliest Romanesque pilgrimage church still standing is the Abbey Church of Sainte-Foy, in France (**15.14, 15.15**). This aerial photograph makes clear the church's cross-form plan. Even from the exterior we can distinguish the nave, the slightly less tall aisles, and the transept. Two square towers flank the entry portal, and an octagonal tower marks the intersection of the transept and the nave. The round arches of the windows are continued in the interior, which has a barrel-vaulted nave and groin-vaulted aisles. The interior of Sainte-Foy is illustrated in Chapter 13 (see 13.10).

The plan (15.15) shows how Romanesque architects modified church design in order to accommodate large crowds of pilgrims. Aisles now line the transept as well as the nave and continue in a semicircle around the back of the apse, allowing visitors to circulate freely. The aisle around the apse is called an **ambulatory,** Latin for walkway. Small chapels radiate from the ambulatory. The apse itself is now preceded by an area called the choir. Together, apse and choir served as a small "church within a church," allowing monks to perform their rites even as pilgrims visited.

Pilgrims stopping at Sainte-Foy would have come to see the relics of Saint Foy herself, which were kept there in a statue made of gold hammered over a wooden core and set with gems (**15.16**). Saint Foy, known in English as Saint Faith, was supposed to have been put to death as a young girl, possibly in the 3rd century, for refusing to worship pagan gods.

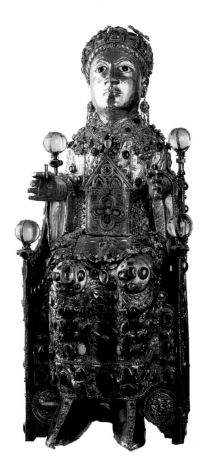

The reliquary statue of Saint Foy is a fine example of the treasures that were offered to and displayed in medieval churches. Another famous work of Romanesque art originally commissioned for display in a church is the *Bayeux Tapestry* (**15.17**)—misnamed, because it is actually a work of embroidery. (In the past, large-scale fabrics, especially those hung in buildings, often were loosely called "tapestries," regardless of the construction method.) **Embroidery** is a technique in which colored yarns are sewn to an existing woven background; frequently the sewing takes the form of decorative motifs or images, as here. The *Bayeux Tapestry* is like a long picture book—20 inches high and 231 feet long—telling the story of the conquest of England by William of Normandy in 1066. The scene illustrated, one of seventy-two separate episodes reading from left to right, shows a group of Anglo-Saxons, who fought on foot, making a stand on a hill against a Norman cavalry assault. Soldiers and horses tumble spectacularly, and casualties from both sides fill the lower border. Despite the charming naïveté of these images, however, scholars have learned more about the events surrounding the Norman Conquest from the *Bayeux Tapestry* than they have from any of the literature of the time.

We rarely know exactly where and how architectural styles started. Who "invented" the Romanesque style? Where did it first appear? With the Gothic style that followed it, however, we are in the unusual position of knowing where, when, and how it came about. A powerful French abbot named Suger wanted to enlarge and remodel his church, the Abbey Church of Saint-Denis, near Paris. Inspired by early Christian writings, he came to believe that an ideal church should have certain characteristics: It should appear to reach up to heaven, it should have harmonious proportions, and it should be filled with light. To fulfill these goals, his architects responded with pointed arches, ribbed vaulting, flying buttresses, and stained glass windows so large they seemed like translucent walls. (To review these architectural terms, see Chapter 13, pp. 318–319.) Finished in two stages in 1140 and 1144, the graceful,

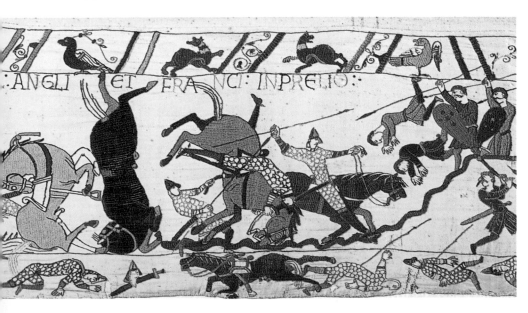

15.16 (above) Reliquary statue of Sainte Foy. Late 10th–early 11th century. Gold and gemstones over a wooden core, height 33½".
Cathedral Treasury, Conques, France.

15.17 (left) *English and French Fall in Battle*, detail of the *Bayeux Tapestry*. c. 1073–88. Wool embroidery on linen; height 20", overall length 231'. Town Hall, Bayeux.
Reproduced with special authorization of the City of Bayeux.

15.18 (bottom left) Chartres Cathedral, France. Begun 1134, completed c. 1260.

15.19 (bottom right) West facade, Chartres Cathedral.

15.20 (below) Plan of Chartres Cathedral.

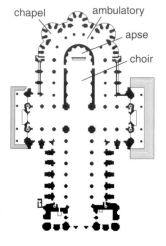

light-filled interior of Saint-Denis immediately attracted attention and imitation. Gothic style was born, the creation of a brilliant architect whose name the good abbot did not bother to record.

The cathedral at Chartres, in France, shows the soaring quality of Gothic architecture (**15.18**). Here, the unadorned, earthbound masses of the Romanesque have given way to ornate, linear, vertical elements that direct the eye upward. Clearly visible are the flying buttresses that line the nave and apse to contain the outward thrust of the walls. Because portions of Chartres were built at different times, the cathedral also allows us to see something of the evolution of Gothic style. For example, the first thing most people notice about the facade of the cathedral (**15.19**) is the mismatched corner towers and spires. The north (left) tower was built first, between 1134 and 1150. Its plain, unadorned surfaces and solid masses are still fundamentally Romanesque. The south (right) tower and its spire were completed next, between 1142 and 1160. Designed in the very earliest Gothic style, they are conceived so that each level grows out of the one before, and all the elements work together to lead the eye upward.

The towers, south spire, and facade had originally been built as additions to an older Romanesque church that stood on the site. When a fire in 1194 burned this church to the ground, it was rebuilt over the course of the next sixty years in the Gothic style we see today. The plan (**15.20**) shows the familiar cross form, but the choir and ambulatory have taken on much larger proportions compared with those at Sainte-Foy. The soaring, open spaces of the interior were created with ribbed vaulting and pointed arches much like those we saw in Chapter 13 in the cathedral at Reims, built around the same time (see 13.11). The final addition to Chartres was the north (left) spire of the facade. Built in the early 16th century, it illustrates the last phase of Gothic style—a slender, elongated, and highly ornamental style called Flamboyant, French for "flamelike."

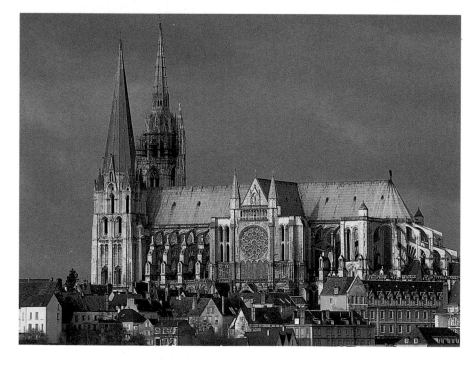

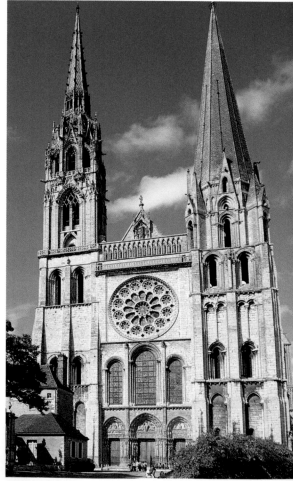

Sculpture in the Middle Ages was often created to embellish architecture. Over two thousand carved figures decorate the exterior of the Chartres Cathedral. Concentrated especially around principal entryways, they serve as a transition between the everyday world of the town and the sacred space within, forming a sort of "welcoming committee" for the faithful as they enter. Like the architecture itself, the sculptures were created at different times, and in them, too, we can appreciate the transition from Romanesque to Gothic.

Romanesque style can be seen in the elongated and flattened bodies of these 12th-century carvings from the principal entry of the cathedral (**15.21**). In fact, it is difficult to believe that there are actual bodies under the draperies at all. The linear folds of the draperies are not so much sculpted as incised—drawn into the stone with a chisel. We can think of them as a sculptural equivalent of the garments in the Byzantine mosaic we looked at earlier (see 15.9), created around the same time.

Carved a mere hundred years later, this second group of figures (**15.22**) displays the mature Gothic style. Whereas the bodies of the earlier statues took the form of the columns they adorned, the bodies here are more fully rounded and have begun to detach themselves from their architectural supports. The three saints on the right still seem to float somewhat, as though suspended in midair, but the figure of Saint Theodore at the far left truly stands, his weight on his feet. A sense of underlying musculature is evident in armor covering his arms, and his garment, although not yet fully naturalistic, is carved with an awareness of a body underneath. It will remain for another era to conceive of the body *first,* and then figure out how clothing would drape over it.

15.21 (left) Door jamb statues, west facade, Chartres Cathedral. c. 1145–70.

15.22 (right) *Saints Theodore, Stephen, Clement, and Lawrence,* door jamb, south transept, Chartres Cathedral. 13th century.

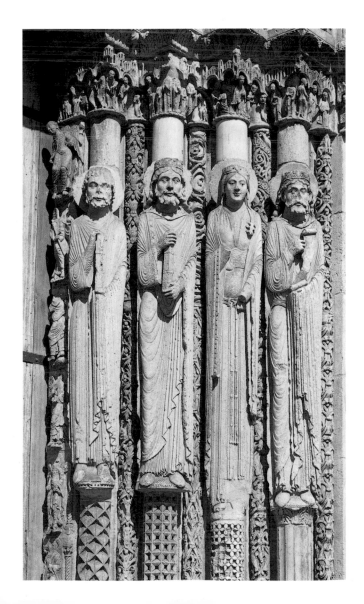

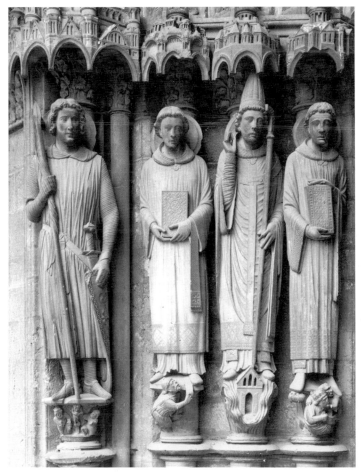

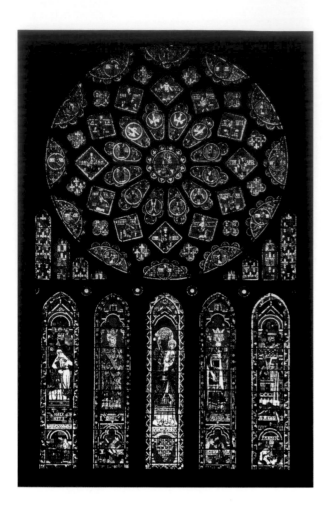

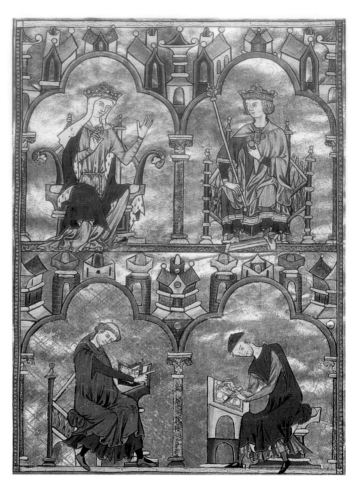

15.23 (left) Rose window and lancets, north transept, Chartres Cathedral. 13th century. Diameter of rose window, 42'.

15.24 (right) Page with *Louis IX and Queen Blanche of Castile*, Moralized Bible, from Paris. 1226–34. Ink, tempera, and gold leaf on vellum, 15 × 10½". The Pierpont Morgan Library, New York.

The glory of Gothic cathedrals is their magnificent stained glass. Chartres contains over 150 stained glass windows. Their motifs include stories from the Bible, lives of the saints, signs of the zodiac, and donors from every level of society, from knights and nobles to tradespeople such as butchers and bakers. Among the most resplendent medieval windows are the great, radiating, circular groupings called rose windows (**15.23**). This rose window, one of three at Chartres, is dedicated to Mary, the mother of Jesus. She is depicted at its center enthroned as the Queen of Heaven. Radiating from her are windows portraying doves and angels, Biblical kings, symbols of French royalty, and prophets. Like the gold of Byzantine mosaics, the gemlike colors of stained glass represent a medieval vision of heavenly splendor.

Gothic style became known in the rest of Europe as "French style," after the country where it originated. France was equally famous as a center for the production of luxuriously illuminated books. This page from a manuscript produced in Paris in the early 13th century shows the influence of stained glass on manuscript illumination (**15.24**). On a radiant ground of gold, subtly embossed, four figures sit in their individual compartments, set off like four medallions in a stained glass window. The upper two figures represent Louis IX, then king of France, and his mother, Blanche of Castile, who had ruled until he came of age. Still a young man here, Louis will later commission the Sainte-Chapelle, which we looked at in Chapter 3 (see 3.4). Beneath the royal pair sits a monk reading a text to a scribe, who dutifully writes it all down. The circles on the page the scribe is busy with define areas that will later be filled in with illuminations.

TOWARD THE RENAISSANCE

The Gothic style lasted in northern Europe into the early 16th century. By this time, however, it was overlapping with far different ideas about art that had their origins in the south, in Italy. Living in the heart of what was the ancient Roman Empire, Italians were surrounded with the ruins of the Classical world. More treasures lay buried in the earth, awaiting excavation. All that was needed was an intellectual climate that encouraged an interest in such things. This climate eventually arose, and we call it the Renaissance. But the Renaissance did not happen all at once. Many developments prepared the way, some in scholarship, some in political thought, others in art.

The last two artists in this chapter were influential in making the shift from art styles of the Middle Ages to the quite different styles of the Renaissance. Duccio was an artist of Siena, in Italy. His masterpiece was the *Maestà Altar*, a multisection panel meant to be displayed on the altar of a church, of which we illustrate the part showing *Christ Entering Jerusalem* (**15.25**). What is most interesting about this painting is Duccio's attempt to create believable space in a large outdoor scene—a concern that would absorb painters of the next century. Christ's entry into the city, celebrated now on Palm Sunday, was thought of as a triumphal procession, and Duccio has labored to convey the sense of movement and parade. A strong diagonal thrust beginning at the left with Christ and his disciples cuts across the picture to the middle right, then shifts abruptly to carry our attention to the upper left corner of the painting—a church tower that is Christ's presumed goal. The architecture plays an important role in defining space and directing movement. This was Duccio's novel, almost unprecedented, contribution to the art of the period, the use of architecture to demarcate space rather than to act as a simple backdrop.

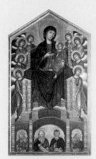
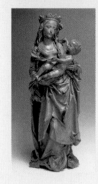
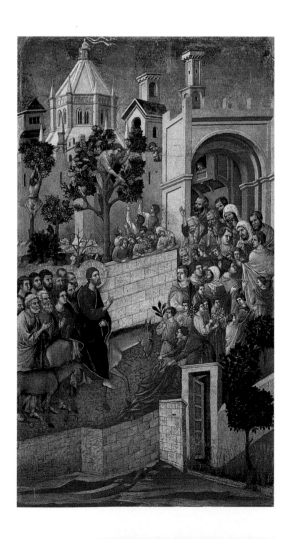

15.25 Duccio. *Christ Entering Jerusalem*, detail of *Maestà Altar.* 1308–11. Tempera on panel, 40 × 21".
Museo dell'Opera, Siena.

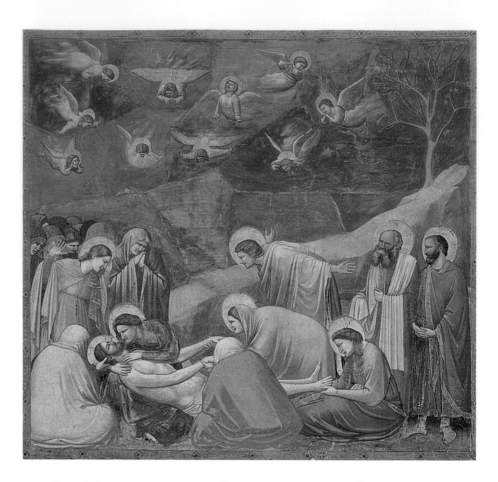

15.26 Giotto. *The Lamentation.* 1305–06. 7'7" × 7'9". Arena Chapel, Padua.

Duccio's contemporary, a Florentine artist named Giotto, made an even more remarkable break with art traditions of the Middle Ages. Most of Giotto's best work was in fresco, and the most notable examples are in a small church in Padua called the Arena Chapel. *The Lamentation* (**15.26**), a work depicting Mary, St. John, and others mourning the dead Christ, illustrates Giotto's highly original use of space in painting. The scene has been composed as though it were on a stage and we the viewers are an audience participating in the drama. In other words, space going back from the picture plane seems to be continuous with space in front of the picture plane, the space in which we stand. Accustomed as we are now to this "window" effect in painting, it is difficult to imagine how revolutionary it was to medieval eyes, used to predominantly flat, decorative space in painting. Moreover, Giotto seems to have developed this concept of space largely on his own, with little artistic precedent. The figures in *The Lamentation* are round and full-bodied, clustered low in the composition to enhance the effect of an event taking place just out of our reach.

Giotto's grouping of the figures is unusual and daring, with Christ's body half-hidden by a figure with its back turned. This arrangement seems casual and almost random, until we notice the slope of the hill directing attention to Christ's and the Virgin's heads, which are the focal point. Yet another innovation—perhaps Giotto's most important one—was his interest in depicting the psychological and emotional reactions of his subjects. The characters in *The Lamentation* interact in a natural, human way that gives this and the artist's other religious scenes a special warmth.

Neither Duccio nor Giotto had an especially long career. Each did his most significant work in the first decade of the 14th century. Yet in that short time the course of Western art history changed dramatically. Both artists had sought a new direction for painting—a more naturalistic, more human, more engaging representation of the physical world—and both had taken giant steps in that direction. Their experiments paved the way for a flowering of all the arts that would come in the next century.

CHAPTER SIXTEEN

THE
RENAISSANCE

Throughout the Middle Ages, painters were considered skilled crafts workers on a level with goldsmiths, carpenters, and other tradespeople. By the mid-16th century, in contrast, Michelangelo could claim that "in Italy great princes as such are not held in honor or renown; it is a painter that they call divine."[1] From anonymous crafts workers to divinely talented individuals more honored and renowned than princes—what had happened?

The simplest answer is that Michelangelo lived and worked during the time that we call the Renaissance. Covering the period roughly from 1400 to 1600, the Renaissance brought vast changes to the world of art. The way art looked, the subjects it treated, the way it was thought about, the position of the artist in society, the identities and influence of patrons, the cultures that served as points of reference—all of these things changed. We might even say that the Renaissance was the time when the concept of "art" arose, for it was during these centuries that painting, sculpture, and architecture began to earn their privileged positions in Western thought.

The word *renaissance* means "rebirth," and it refers to the revival of interest in ancient Greek and Roman culture that is one of the key characteristics of the period. Scholars of the day worked to recover and study as many Greek and Latin texts as possible. Referring to themselves as humanists, they believed that a sound education should include not only the teachings of the Church and the study of early Christian writers but also the study of the liberal arts—grammar, rhetoric, poetry, history, politics, and moral philosophy—about which the pre-Christian world had much to teach.

Renaissance humanists believed in the pursuit of knowledge for its own sake. Above all, they held that humankind was not worthless in the eyes of God, as the Church had taught during the Middle Ages. Rather, humankind was God's finest and most perfect creation. Reason and creativity were God's gifts, proof of humankind's inherent dignity. People's obligation to God was thus not to tremble and submit but rather to soar, striving to realize their full intellectual and creative potential.

The implications of these ideas for art were tremendous. Artists became newly interested in observing the natural world, and they worked to reproduce it as accurately as possible. Studying the effects of light, they developed the technique of chiaroscuro; noting that distant objects appeared smaller than near ones, they developed the system of linear perspective; seeing how detail and color blurred with distance, they developed the principles of atmospheric perspective.

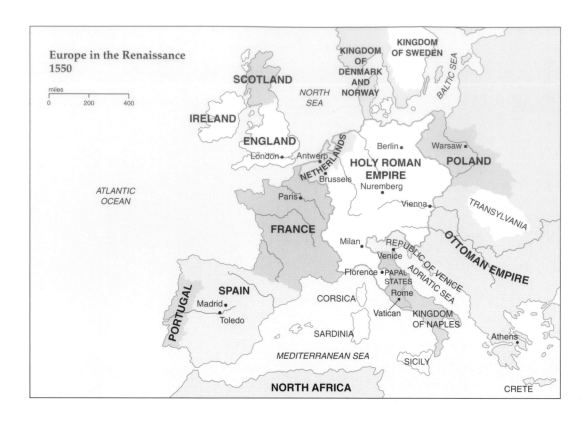

Europe in the Renaissance 1550

The nude reappeared in art, for the body was held to be the noblest of God's creations. "Who is so barbarous as not to understand that the foot of a man is nobler than his shoe," said Michelangelo, "and his skin nobler than that of the sheep with which he is clothed?"[2] To portray the body with understanding, artists studied anatomy, even going so far as to dissect cadavers.

Under the influence of the ancient Greek philosopher Plato, whose works were newly available, beauty became equated with moral goodness. Renaissance artists sought an idealized beauty, one they created by taking the most beautiful features of numerous examples and combining them. "Be on the watch to take the best parts of many individual faces," wrote Leonardo da Vinci.[3] And the German Renaissance painter Dürer advised the same: "You, therefore, if you desire to compose a fine figure, must take the head from some, the chest, arm, leg, hand, and foot from others. . . . For from many beautiful things something good may be gathered, even as honey is gathered from many flowers."[4]

The ten-volume treatise on architecture by the Roman writer Vitruvius was read avidly in an attempt to understand Classical thought and practice, including ideas about beauty and harmonious proportions. Greek and Roman ruins still standing were studied in detail—described, measured, analyzed, and drawn. Excavations revealed still more examples, along with astonishing statues such as the *Laocoön Group* (see 14.29), which served as an inspiration and ideal for Renaissance artists.

Perspective and chiaroscuro, close observation of nature, the study of anatomy, theories of beauty and proportion—these established painting, sculpture, and architecture as intellectual activities allied with mathematics, science, and poetry. Artists were no longer mere crafts workers, but learned persons whose creative powers were viewed as almost miraculous. The greatest artists were considered a breed apart, comprising a class of their own that transcended the social class determined by birth—not nobility, not bourgeoisie, not clergy, but a separate and elite category of people respected not because of who they were, but because of what they could do. They lived in the courts of the nobles and popes, they moved freely in good society, their company was sought after, their services in demand.

The character of art patronage reflected the changing times. Before the Renaissance only two groups of people could afford to be art patrons—the nobility and the clergy. Both continued to be active sponsors of art, but they were joined in the 15th century by a new class of merchant-rulers, very rich, socially ambitious, fully able to support extravagant spending on art. The climate could not have been more fertile for a flowering of art: The best artists were available, and virtually unlimited funds existed to support them. With this preamble, then, let us look at the artists of the Renaissance.

THE EARLY AND HIGH RENAISSANCE IN ITALY

Why did the Renaissance begin in Italy and not elsewhere? Scholars have offered many reasons. First, Italy had been among the first areas to recover economically from the chaos of the early Middle Ages. Powerful city-states engaged in extensive trade and banking had developed. Wealthy, independent, and fiercely competitive, the city-states would vie with each other to engage the finest artists, as would the merchant-princes whose fortunes sustained them. The Church, also an important patron of the arts, was centered in Italy as well. Humanism arose first in Italy, and it was in Italy that the first university position in Greek studies was established. Finally, Italians had long lived amid the ruins of ancient Rome, and they viewed themselves as the direct descendants of the citizens of the earlier civilization. If anyone could bring back its glories, surely it was they.

Among the first generation of Renaissance artists, the finest sculptor by far was Donatello. His statue of *Saint Mark* (**16.1**), an early work, shows the characteristics of this new era, especially if we compare it to the statue of Saint Theodore from Chartres Cathedral, carved during the High Middle Ages (see 15.22). Whereas Gothic sculptors carved what they observed from the surface—face, clothing, limbs—Donatello thought methodically in the new way: the body provides the framework on which the fabric drapes, and therefore it must be considered first. Renaissance sculptors often created a full-scale model of a nude figure in clay, then draped clay-soaked linen about it to create garments, arranging the folds before the fabric dried. This model was then copied in marble. Scholars believe that Donatello was one of the first sculptors to use this method.

The statue is placed in a niche, but unlike most architectural sculptures from the Middle Ages, it does not depend on this framework for support. Rather, the fully rounded figure stands independently in true contrapposto, the weight on the right leg, left leg bent. The shoulders compensate: right shoulder lower, left shoulder higher. The clothing responds to the form underneath. Where the left knee bends outward, the robe falls back; where the right arm is pressed to the body, the sleeve wrinkles. We sense that if St. Mark moved, the garments would move with him. The figure is as naturalistic as any ancient Greek statue, yet there is a stamp of individual personality in both face and body that may have come from Donatello's reading of Mark's Gospel.

Donatello's teacher was an artist named Lorenzo Ghiberti, who had established his reputation in 1401 by winning a competition to design a set of bronze relief sculptures for the doors of the baptistry of the Cathedral in his native town of Florence. In 1425, a second set of doors was commissioned from Ghiberti. In between these two dates, the system of linear perspective had been discovered, described, and published. Ghiberti took full advantage of the possibilities opened up by the new discovery, as we can see in *The Story*

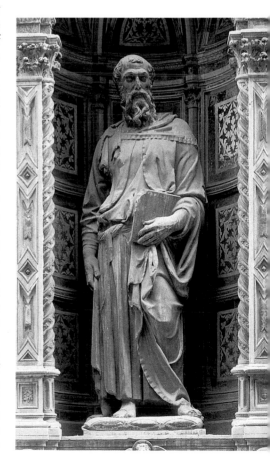

16.1 Donatello. *St. Mark.* 1411–13. Marble, height 7'9". Or San Michele, Florence.

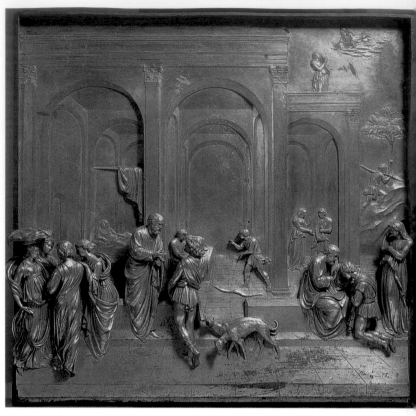

16.2 (right) Lorenzo Ghiberti. *The Story of Jacob and Esau, from The Gates of Paradise.* c. 1435. Gilt bronze, 31¼" square. Museo dell'Opera del Duomo, Florence.

16.3 (left) Masaccio. *Trinity with the Virgin, St. John the Evangelist, and Donors.* 1425. Fresco. 21'9" × 9'4". Santa Maria Novella, Florence.

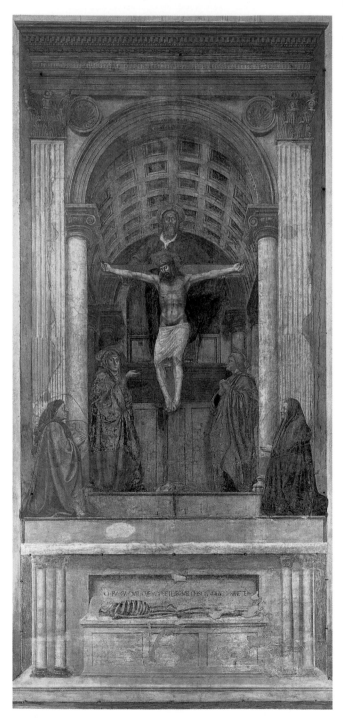

of Jacob and Esau (**16.2**), one of the ten panels he executed for this second set of doors. The graceful, rounded figures in the foreground stand on a pavement whose converging lines begin a recession in space that is carried systematically through the architectural setting sculpted in low relief in the background. Renaissance artists used this new, rationally conceived space to bring clarity and order to their compositions, two qualities that Greek philosophy associated with beauty.

Artists had long used architectural settings to structure their compositions. Ghiberti's great innovation was to conceive of the architecture and the figures on the same scale instead of relying on the miniaturized, symbolic architecture of earlier artists such as Duccio (see 15.25). Ghiberti quite rightly boasted of this in his *Commentaries.* "I executed this work with the most painstaking and loving care," he wrote, ". . . with the buildings drawn with the same proportions as they would appear to the eye and so true that, if you stand far off, they appear to be in relief. Actually they are in very low relief. The figures in the foreground look larger and those in the distance smaller, just as they do in reality."[5]

The youth of the great innovators of the Renaissance can sometimes astonish us. Donatello was twenty-five when he began work on *St. Mark;* Ghiberti was twenty-three when he won the competition for the baptistry doors. Our next artist, Masaccio, transformed the art of painting at age twenty-four with his fresco *Trinity with the Virgin, St. John the Evangelist, and Donors* (**16.3**) in the church of Santa Maria Novella in Florence. Masaccio does here for painting what Ghiberti did for sculpture in relief, using the new technique of linear perspective to construct a deep, convincing architectural space as a setting for his figures. Comparing this painting to the Byzantine icon we looked at in Chapter

15 (see 15.10), we can see both the continuity of the iconography (the two works depict the same subject) and the profound stylistic changes of the Renaissance.

Masaccio has arranged the figures in a stable triangle that extends from the head of God the Father, who stands over the dead Christ, through the two donors who kneel to either side of the holy grouping and outside their sacred space. Triangular (or pyramidal) organization would remain a favorite device of Italian Renaissance artists. Earlier in this book, we noticed it in Raphael's *The Madonna of the Meadows* (see 4.16). Masaccio's composition is organized by a vanishing point located directly under the cross, at the midpoint of the ledge on which the donors kneel. Five feet above the floor, it is at the eye level of an average viewer. To visitors to the church the painting thus is designed to present as convincing an illusion as possible that the sacred scene is really present before them.

Even the architectural setting that Masaccio has painted is in the new Renaissance style. We can see the sort of interior that inspired him in the church of Sant'Andrea in Mantua (**16.4, 16.5**), by the architect Leon Battista Alberti. In Chapter 5 we examined the rhythms of the facade of this church (see 5.30). The photograph here is taken looking up the nave toward the apse; the light in the middle distance is entering through the dome that rises over the intersection of the transept and the nave.

Sant'Andrea was Alberti's last work. Construction began in 1472, the year of his death, and was completed two decades later. Though marred by some changes carried out during the 18th century, the interior still allows us to see how Alberti developed the themes and elements announced by his facade. As in the facade, the square, arch, and circle dominate. The aisles of the standard basilica plan have given way to a procession of square, barrel-vaulted chapels along a majestic barrel-vaulted nave. This sequence of barrel-vaulted spaces placed at right angles to each other carries through the theme announced in the entryway while also preparing us for the grander right-angle crossing of the transept. The roundel (circular area) set in the pediment of the facade and again over its doors is repeated on the walls of the nave between the chapels and culminates with the great circular opening of the dome. The vast interior space composed of geometric volumes harks back to Roman examples such as the Pantheon (see 13.13).

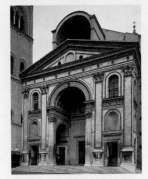

5.30 Alberti, Sant'Andrea

16.4 (left) Leon Battista Alberti. Interior of Sant'Andrea, Mantua. 1470–1493.

16.5 (right) Plan of Sant'Andrea.

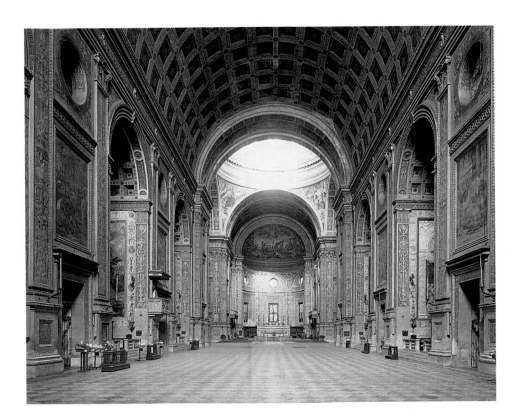

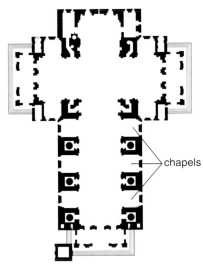

chapels

In addition to Christian themes, Renaissance artists also turned to stories of Greek and Roman gods and goddesses for subject matter, as did many Renaissance poets. An example is *The Birth of Venus* (**16.6**), by Sandro Botticelli. Born in 1445, Botticelli belonged to the third generation of Renaissance artists. Early in his career, he had the great fortune to enjoy the patronage of the Medici, the ruling merchant family of Florence, who probably commissioned this painting. The Medici sponsored an Academy—a sort of discussion group—where humanist scholars and artists met to discuss Classical culture and its relationship to Christianity. The reconciliation of these two systems of thought gave rise to a philosophy known as Neo-Platonism, after the Greek philosopher Plato.

Venus was the Roman goddess of love and beauty. According to legend, she was born from the sea, and so Botticelli depicts her on a floating shell. The wind god Zephyr and his wife blow her gently toward the shore, where a figure representing spring waits ready to clothe Venus in a flowing garment. Botticelli paints the goddess in the nude, with strategically placed hands and a tress of hair the only concessions to modesty. Such a large-scale depiction of the female nude in art had been virtually unknown since Classical times. Venus' pose is modeled after a Roman sculpture of the goddess, which Botticelli had studied in the Medici collection, but her lightness, her fragile quality, her delicate beauty and billowing hair—these are Botticelli's own.

Although Botticelli's unusual linear style and shallow modeling was an exception to Renaissance norms, it was highly appreciated by the Medici circle. Venus, for example, looks as though she might be modeled in high relief, but not fully rounded. The implied space is shallow, with the sea and receding shoreline serving almost as a flat backdrop, as in a theatrical production. Medici intimates would also have understood the subtle Neo-Platonic overtones of the scene. In Neo-Platonic thought, Venus was identified with both Eve and the Virgin Mary; her birth from the water was related to the baptism

16.6 Sandro Botticelli. *The Birth of Venus*. c. 1480. Tempera on canvas, 6'7" × 9'2". Galleria degli Uffizi, Florence.

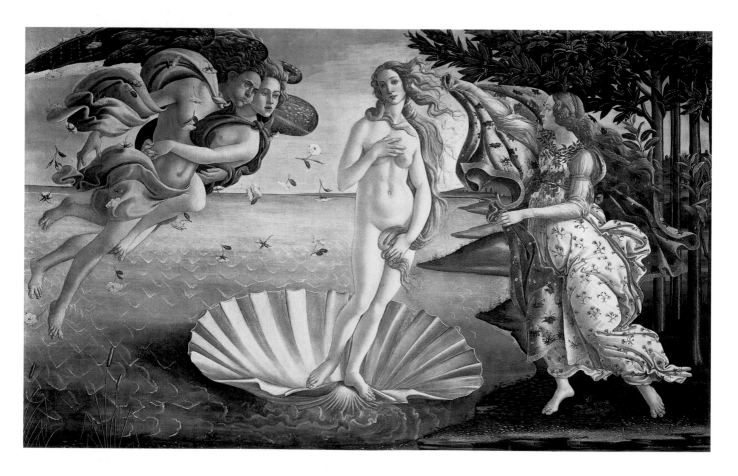

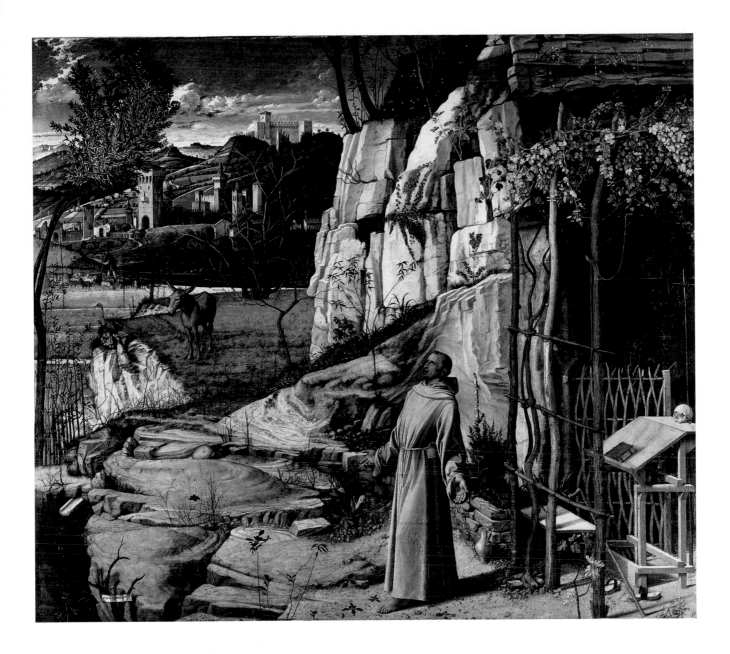

of Christ by John the Baptist. Botticelli's work displays the rarefied and learned side of Renaissance art. It was painted not for a large public, but for a cultivated audience of initiates.

Botticelli painted in tempera. The favorite medium of medieval and early Renaissance artists, tempera was about to be eclipsed by oil paint, which had recently been developed in northern Europe. An early master of the new medium was the Venetian painter Giovanni Bellini. Whereas the artists of Florence and Rome emphasized sound drawing above all other artistic virtues, the painters of Venice became known for their interest in color and light. Oil paint lent itself especially well to their concerns, as we can see in Bellini's *St. Francis in the Desert* (**16.7**).

Francis was a holy man, a monk and preacher, born in the Italian town of Assisi in the late 12th century. According to legend, he was able to converse with the birds and animals, in a language both man and creatures understood freely. Francis' goodness was so profound that God bestowed upon him the stigmata—marks or wounds upon his hands and feet like those Christ had suffered when he was nailed to the cross at his Crucifixion. The artist Bellini has chosen to capture the moment when Francis received the stigmata, a moment

16.7 Giovanni Bellini. *St. Francis in the Desert*. c. 1485. Oil on panel, 4'½" × 4'7". The Frick Collection, New York.

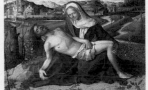

of intense pain and great joy. A brilliant golden light bathes the scene, presumably the light of God shining down on the holy man. Francis stands in awe of the light, his arms outstretched, his gaze cast upward, welcoming this sign of God's favor.

Bellini frames the saint in a protective craggy foreground landscape as solidly constructed as a work of architecture. The middle ground is defined by a grassy knoll on which a donkey stands. In the distance is a town at the foot of a hill; still farther is a hilltop fortress, and in the farthest blue-tinted distance a mountain. Unlike the setting for Botticelli's *Venus*, Bellini's magnificent landscape recedes convincingly into deep space. The recession is not smooth and continuous, however. Rather, it proceeds step by step by giving us something to look at in each new area. Our eyes follow a series of focal points into the distance, ignoring the gaps between them. (For example, there is no transition between the rocky foreground and the grassy knoll. One stops, then the other begins.) To create a continuous recession into deep space in a landscape is quite difficult. More progress would be made by the painters of the next generation, many of whom would be indebted to Bellini's explorations of color, light, and atmosphere.

We come now to a period known as the High Renaissance—a brief but glorious time in the history of art. In barely twenty-five years, from shortly before 1500 to about 1525, some of the most celebrated works of Western art were produced. Many artists participated in this brilliant creative endeavor, but the outstanding figures among them were unquestionably Leonardo da Vinci and Michelangelo.

The term "Renaissance man" is applied to someone who is very well informed about, or very good at doing, many different, often quite unrelated, things. It originated in the fact that several of the leading figures of the Renaissance were artistic jacks-of-all-trades. Michelangelo was a painter, sculptor, poet, architect—incomparably gifted at all. Leonardo was a painter, inventor, sculptor, architect, engineer, scientist, musician, and all-around intellectual. In our age of specialization these accomplishments seem staggering, but during the heady years of the Renaissance nothing was impossible.

Leonardo is the artist who most embodies the term "Renaissance man"; many people consider him to have been the greatest genius who ever lived. Leonardo was possessed of a brilliant and inquiring mind that accepted no limits. Throughout his long life he remained absorbed by the problem of how things work, and how they might work. A typical example of his investigations is the well-known *Study of Human Proportions* (see 5.23), in which the artist sought to establish ideal proportions for the human body by relating it to the square and the circle. Above and below the figure is Leonardo's eccentric mirror writing, which he used in his notes and journals.

Leonardo's interest in mathematics is also evident from his careful rendering of perspective. In Chapter 4 we examined his masterpiece *The Last Supper* (see 4.45), which uses one-point linear perspective to organize the many figures in the composition and set them into deep space. Yet another interest, experimental painting techniques, served the artist less well in *The Last Supper*. Rather than employing the established fresco method, Leonardo worked in a medium he devised for the *Last Supper* project, thus dooming his work to centuries of restoration (p. 111).

In spite of his vast accomplishments, Leonardo often had difficulty completing specific projects. Many of his most ambitious works were left unfinished, including this lovely painting of the *Madonna and Child with Saint Anne* (**16.8**). Leonardo has arranged his figures in a triangular grouping by having the Virgin Mary, a grown woman, sit rather improbably on the lap of her mother, Saint Anne. As so often with Leonardo, the composition is not meant to be realistic but rather to suggest theological meanings. The three figures form a single unit because they are a single lineage. Looking at the image, our gaze falls across the generations, from Saint Anne to her daughter Mary to Mary's son Jesus. Jesus attempts to climb onto a lamb, a symbol of his future

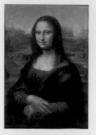

2.4 Leonardo, *Mona Lisa*

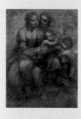

4.20 Leonardo, *Virgin and St. Anne*

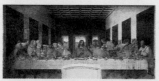

4.45 Leonardo, *Last Supper*

5.23 Leonardo, *Study of Human Proportions*

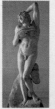

11.21 Michelangelo, *Dying Slave*

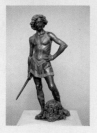

2.6 Verrocchio, *David*

sacrifice. (The lamb was a sacrificial animal, and Christ is thus referred to as the Lamb of God.) He exchanges a look with his mother, as though both know what his destiny holds. She tenderly holds him back, as if to say, "Yes, soon enough, but not yet." Leonardo destabilizes his triangular grouping by plunging the lower left corner into darkness, then restores the balance by placing a dark tree at the upper right, an allusion to the cross on which Jesus will die. In the background is an uninhabited, primal landscape of rocks and water, suggesting perhaps the creation of the world and the beginning of time. The entire scene is bathed in the gentle light of **sfumato** (derived from the Italian for "smoke"), Leonardo's specialty, in which layer upon layer of translucent glazes produce a hazy atmosphere, softened contours, and velvet shadows.

Leonardo was based in Florence at the time he painted *Madonna and Child with Saint Anne.* Living there as well was Michelangelo, a quarter-century younger yet already thought of as Leonardo's rival in greatness. Michelangelo had established his reputation as a sculptor by the age of twenty-five. A year later he received the commission for a colossal image of the biblical hero David (**16.9**), the young Hebrew shepherd who killed the giant Goliath with a single stone from his slingshot. The *David* statue reveals Michelangelo's debt to Classical sculptures. *David* is not, however, a simple restatement of Greek

16.8 (left) Leonardo da Vinci. *Madonna and Child with Saint Anne.* c. 1503–06. Oil on wood, 5'6⅛" × 3'8". Musée du Louvre, Paris.

16.9 (right) Michelangelo. *David.* 1501–04. Marble, height 18'. Galleria dell'Accademia, Florence.

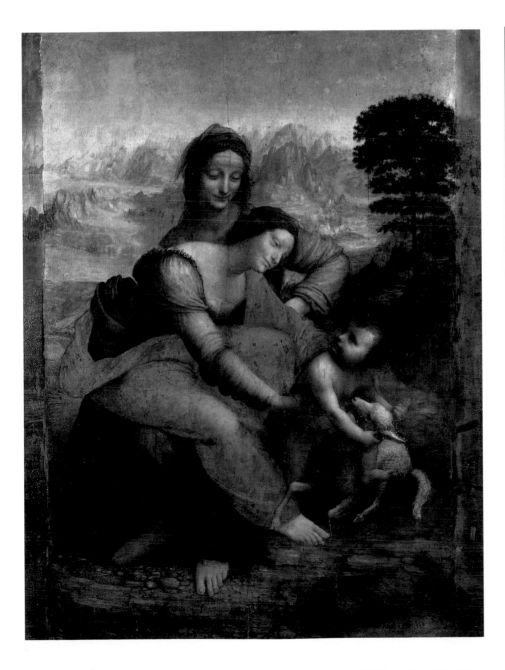

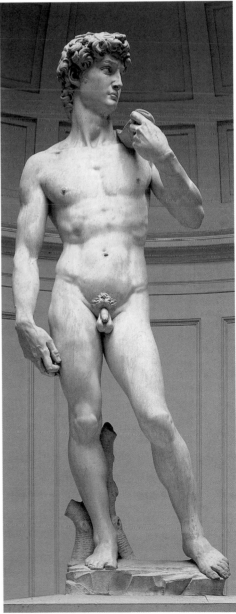

MICHELANGELO

1475–1564

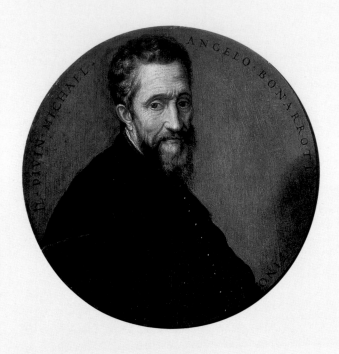

H<small>E IS BEYOND</small> legend. His name means "archangel Michael," and to his contemporaries and those who came after, his stature is scarcely less than that of a heavenly being. He began serious work as an artist at the age of thirteen and did not stop until death claimed him seventy-six years later. His equal may never be seen again, for only a particular time and place could have bred the genius of Michelangelo.

Michelangelo Buonarroti was born in the Tuscan town of Caprese. According to his devoted biographer and friend, Giorgio Vasari, the young Michelangelo often was scolded and beaten by his father for spending too much time drawing. Eventually, however, seeing his son's talent, the father relented and apprenticed him to the painter Domenico Ghirlandaio. At the age of fourteen Michelangelo was welcomed into the household of the wealthy banker Lorenzo de' Medici, who operated a private sculpture academy for promising young students. There he remained until Lorenzo's death, after which Michelangelo, just seventeen years old, struck out permanently on his own.

He traveled to Venice and Bologna, to Florence, then finally to Rome, where he attracted the first of what would become a long list of patrons among the clergy. A *Pietà* (Virgin mourning the dead Christ) made in 1500 and now in St. Peter's established his reputation as a sculptor. Within a dozen years after that he had completed the two works most closely associated with his name: the *David* statue and the ceiling frescoes in the Sistine Chapel.

From his teen years until his death Michelangelo never lacked for highly placed patrons. He served—and survived—six popes, and in between accepted commissions from two emperors, a king, and numerous members of the nobility. All his life he struggled to keep a balance between the work he wanted to do and the work demanded of him by his benefactors. His relationships with these powerful figures were often stormy, marked by squabbles about payment, insults given and forgiven, flight from the scene followed by penitent return.

Michelangelo served these masters, at various times, as painter and architect, but he considered himself above all to be a sculptor. Much of his time was spent supervising the quarrying of superior stones for sculptural projects. His greatest genius lay in depictions of the human figure, whether in marble or in paint. Vasari writes that "this extraordinary man chose always to refuse to paint anything save the human body in its most beautifully proportioned and perfect forms." To this end Michelangelo made extensive anatomical studies and dissected corpses to better understand the inner workings of the body.

Michelangelo formed a number of passionate attachments during his life. These inspired the artist, always a sensitive and gifted poet, to write numerous sonnets. One of his most poignant verses, however, was written as a commentary on his labors up on the scaffold under the Sistine Chapel ceiling. We might find it amusing if it were not so heartfelt:

> I've grown a goiter by dwelling in this den—
>   As cats from stagnant streams in Lombardy,
>   Or in what other land they hap to be—
>   Which drives the belly close beneath the chin;
> My beard turns up to heaven; my nape falls in,
>   Fixed on my spine; my breast-bone visibly
>   Grows like a harp: a rich embroidery
>   Bedews my face from brush-drops thick and
>   thin. . . .[6]

Workshop of Frans Floris. *Portrait of Michelangelo Buonarotti.* 16th century. Oil on wood, diameter 11¾". Kunsthistorisches Museum, Vienna.

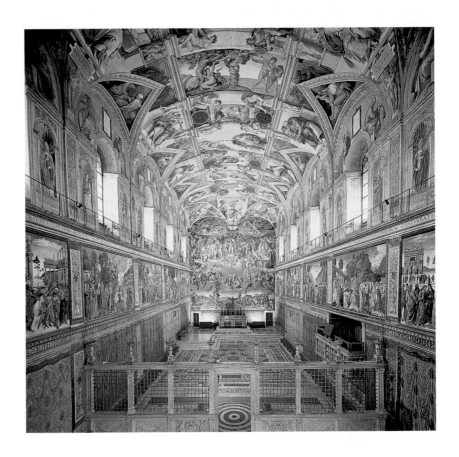

16.10 Interior, Sistine Chapel, Vatican, Rome. 1473–80.

art. The Greeks knew how bodies looked on the outside. Michelangelo knew how they looked on the inside, how they worked, because he had studied human anatomy and had dissected corpses. He translated this knowledge into a figure that seems made of muscle and flesh and bone, though all in marble.

There are other characteristics that make *David* a Renaissance sculpture, not a copy of a Greek one. For one thing, it has a tension and energy that are missing from Greek art. Hellenistic works such as the *Laocoön Group* (see 14.29) expressed these qualities through physical contortions, but to have this energy coiled within a figure standing quietly was new. David is not so much standing in repose as standing in readiness. Another Renaissance quality is the expression on David's face. Classical Greek statues tended to have calm and even vacant expressions. But David is young and vibrant—and angry, angry at the forces of evil represented by the giant Goliath. Contemporary Florentines found David a fitting emblem for their small but proud city, which had recently battled giants by expelling the ruling Medici family and then founding a republic. They placed the statue in the city square in front of the seat of the new government. (It has since been moved indoors.)

Not long after completing the *David*, Michelangelo embarked on the masterpiece that has become his best-known work, the ceiling frescoes of the Sistine Chapel in the Vatican, in Rome (**16.10**). He had been called to Rome by Pope Julius II, who wanted the artist to design his tomb, a large monument with numerous sculptures. Michelangelo set to work, but a year later Julius abandoned this project and proposed instead to use the artist's skills as a painter. Michelangelo, whose distaste for painting is well documented, resisted the plan, but in the end he was forced to capitulate. For the next four years, he would spend most of his waking hours on a scaffold 68 feet above the floor.

The Sistine Chapel, named after an earlier pope called Sixtus, has a high vaulted ceiling 128 feet long and 44 feet wide. Julius required that

Michelangelo cover this entire expanse, 700 square yards, with a painted decoration based on religious themes. Fresco was the only practical medium, and the difficulties of this technique are considerable (Chapter 7). Paint must be applied to fresh plaster just when it has the proper degree of dampness; only a small area can be covered at a time; and the painting must be done directly, with no allowance for correction of mistakes. For this project the artist had to work in a cramped position, with paint and plaster continually dripping in his face. So situated, he was only inches away from the working surface, yet the paintings had to be readable and compelling to a viewer standing on the floor, nearly 70 feet below.

Even more overwhelming than the physical constraints was the challenge of making a coherent composition in such a huge area. Michelangelo or-

16.11 Michelangelo. Ceiling, Sistine Chapel. 1508–12. Fresco, 44 × 128'. Vatican, Rome.

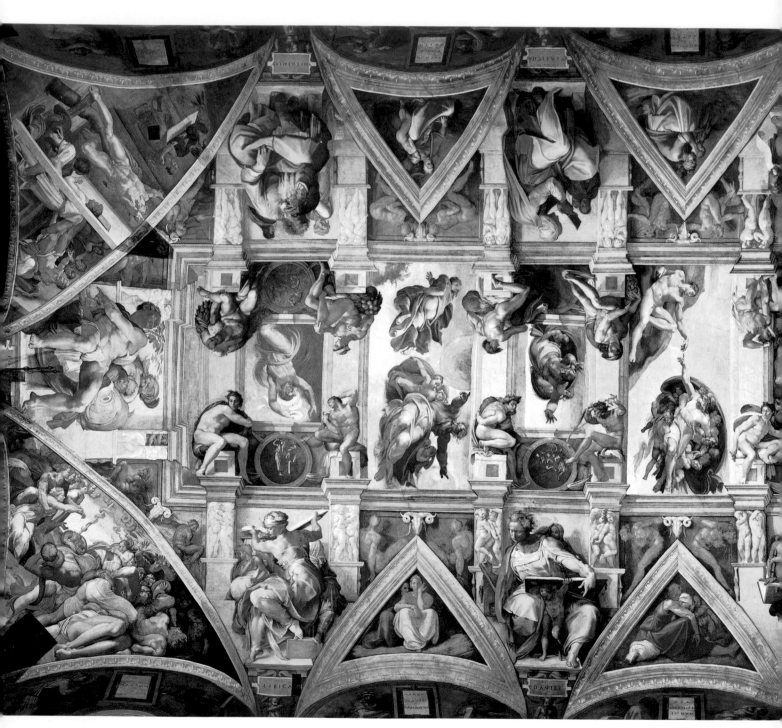

ganized the ceiling into a painted architectural framework of squares, rectangles, and triangles (**16.11**). These segments depict Old Testament stories of the creation of the world, the creation of Adam and Eve, the Fall of Man, and other biblical events. Some figures on the ceiling are from Greek and Roman mythology, for Michelangelo meant to connect the older Classical cultures with Christian theology of his own time.

Each of the segments is self-contained, yet the panels flow gracefully from one to the next, thanks to the artist's placement of overlapping *ignudi* (nude youths) in the spaces between them. The iconography of the *ignudi* is unknown. Some historians have suggested they may represent angels. Throughout the composition Michelangelo's painted figures have the same anatomical fullness and muscular energy as his sculptures.

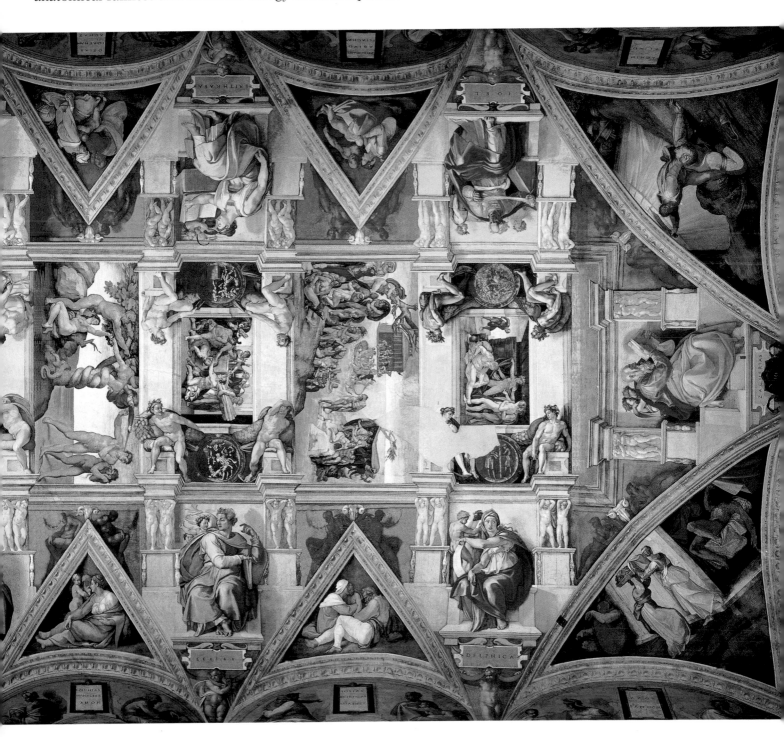

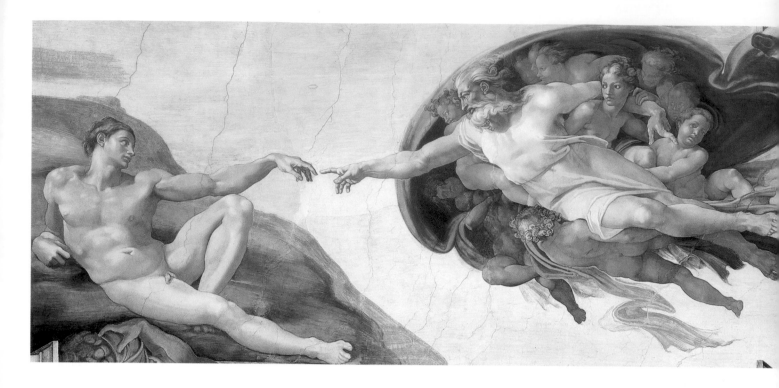

16.12 Michelangelo. *Creation of Adam*, detail of Sistine Chapel ceiling. 1511.

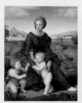
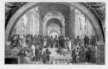
The *Creation of Adam* (**16.12**) is the most familiar of the ceiling images. Based on the biblical book of Genesis, this scene shows Adam, the first man, reclining on a rock. He is well-formed but listless; the spirit of life—the soul— has not yet been breathed into him. At right the dynamic figure of God sweeps toward Adam, wrapped in a symbolic cloak of Heaven. God's left arm embraces a woman thought to represent Eve, the first woman, who at this point in the story is still an idea in God's mind. His left forefinger points to a child, probably meant to be the Christ child, who will come much later to redeem the world. The focal point of this composition is the two hands, stretching toward one another. In a split second they will meet, and the long history of humankind will begin. Michelangelo's genius is nowhere clearer. He does not show us the consummation. He shows us, rather, the thrilling potential.

The ceiling frescoes were an immediate success, and Michelangelo continued as a papal favorite, although his commissions were not always in his preferred line. Just as Pope Julius had urged the sculptor to work as a painter, one of Julius' successors, Pope Paul III, encouraged the sculptor to work as an architect. In 1546 Paul named Michelangelo the official architect of the new St. Peter's, the ceremonial cathedral that is the "headquarters" of the Roman Catholic Church. This structure would be erected on the site of *old* St. Peter's (see 15.2), dating from the Early Christian era in the 4th century. By the time he began work on the project, Michelangelo was an old man, well into his seventies and physically tired, but his creative vigor was undiminished.

Construction on the new church had already begun, based on a plan by an architect named Bramante, who had died in 1514. Michelangelo revised Bramante's plan, gathering its elaborate fussiness into a bold and harmonious design (**16.13, 16.14**). Central and cross plans here merge in a new idea that relates the powerfully symbolic cross to the geometric forms that Renaissance artists loved, the square and the circle. Michelangelo did not live to see his church finished. The magnificent central dome was completed after his death by another architect, who modified its silhouette. During the 17th century, the nave was lengthened and the facade remodeled. The photograph illustrated here, however, was taken from the rear of the church and shows the building that Michelangelo conceived. An organic whole with pulsating contours and a powerful upward thrust, it is the architectural equivalent of his muscular nudes.

The concentration of artistic energy in Rome during the Renaissance was such that while Michelangelo was working on the Sistine ceiling, his slightly younger rival Raphael was only a few steps away, painting his fresco *The School of Athens* (see 7.3) in the private library of the same pope, Julius II. In 1513, Julius was succeeded as pope by Giovanni de' Medici, whose family was now back in power in Florence. Raphael was increasingly in demand as a portraitist, and Giovanni de' Medici, now Pope Leo X, commissioned a likeness from him (**16.15**). Leo X was a passionate collector of books and manuscripts, and he eventually amassed a fine library. Raphael portrays him seated before one of his prized illuminated manuscripts, a magnifying glass in his left hand. Standing beside him are two nephews he had elevated to the office of cardinal (church officials next in rank to the pope). The rich fabrics, sumptuously painted, tell of the worldly splendor of the Church in Rome, while the keenly observed faces convey without flattery the aura of power and ambition that drove Leo X and his family.

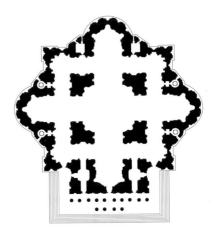

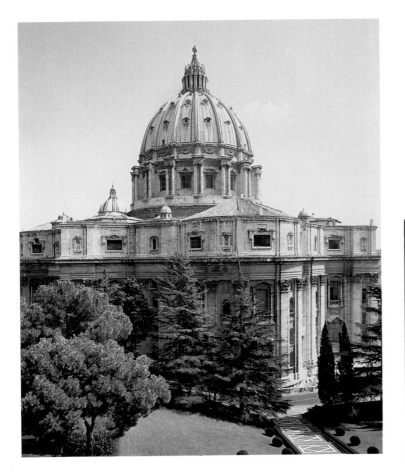

16.13 (right) Michelangelo. Saint Peter's Basilica, Vatican. c. 1546–64 (dome completed 1590 by Giacomo della Porta).

16.14 (above) Plan of St. Peter's.

16.15 (below) Raphael. *Pope Leo X with Two Cardinals.* c. 1518. Oil on wood, 5'⅜" × 3'8⅞". Galleria degli Ufizzi, Florence.

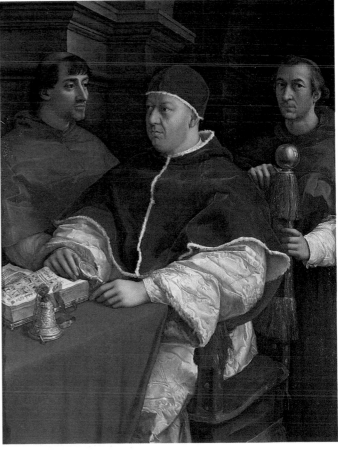

After Rome and Florence, the third great artistic center of Italy was Venice, where Giovanni Bellini worked and taught (see 16.7). Bellini's two finest students, Giorgione and Titian, went on to become the greatest Venetian painters of the High Renaissance.

The iconography of Giorgione's painting *The Tempest* (**16.16**) is unknown. Even the artist's contemporaries seem not to have known what story he was depicting or to have been able to identify the nude woman nursing a child at right and the soldier (or shepherd) at left. Regardless of the meaning of its subject, *The Tempest* makes an important contribution to Renaissance art in the way it is composed. Artists of earlier generations would compose a scene by concentrating on the figures and painting the landscape as a kind of backdrop. Giorgione, however, has started by constructing a landscape and then placing his figures in it. This approach paved the way for the great landscape paintings of the centuries to follow.

In *The Tempest*, as the title implies, the subject is really the approaching storm, which closes in dramatically over the city while the two foreground figures are still bathed in sunlight. The artist's debt to his teacher, Bellini, will be obvious if you compare this work with the older master's *St. Francis in the Desert* (see 16.7), which also shows a highlighted foreground figure and a dis-

16.16 Giorgione. *The Tempest*. c. 1505. Oil on canvas, 32¼ × 28¾". Gallerie dell'Accademia, Venice.

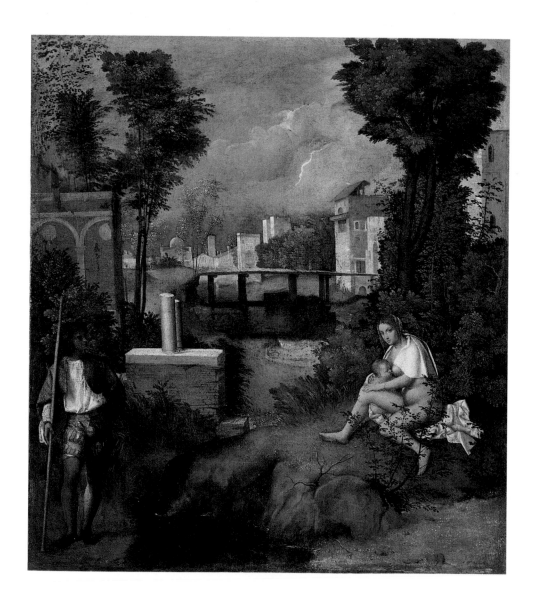

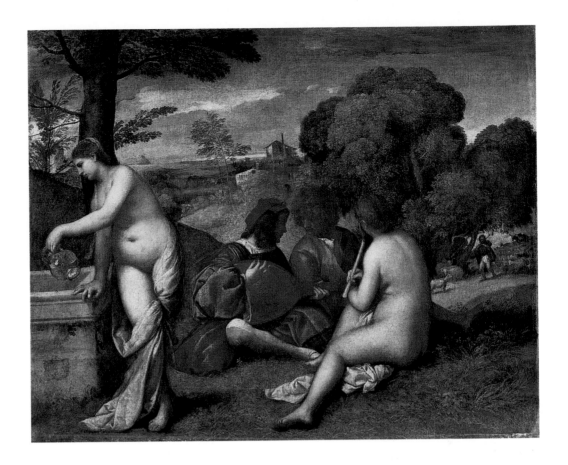

16.17 Titian. *Fête Champêtre.*
1511. Oil on canvas, 43⁵⁄₁₆ × 51⅛".
Musée du Louvre, Paris.

tant landscape. Giorgione, however, is less concerned with the human experience. His principal interest seems to have been the contrast of bucolic foreground against the city rendered in careful perspective, with the two drawn together by the violent effects of nature. The storm and the lush vegetation create a world in which nature dominates, not people, and the painting evokes a powerful, compelling mood of apprehension and anticipation.

Giorgione died in his early thirties; thus we will never know what other wonders he might have accomplished. Titian, however, lived a long and productive life, and his career, like that of Michelangelo, allows us to witness the full arc of a great artist from youth through maturity to old age. Like many other Venetian painters, Titian absorbed the lessons of Giorgione's poetic style. In fact, an early work of Titian's known as *Fête Champêtre* (**16.17,** also known as *Pastoral Concert* or *Pastoral Scene*) was attributed to Giorgione until quite recently. Like *The Tempest*, it places figures in a landscape that evokes a mood. It is a poetic reverie, not a depiction of an actual event or a mythological scene.

Fête Champêtre stands near the beginning of a long tradition of painting that looks back to the Classical Roman writer Virgil, whose poems called eclogues celebrated the pleasures of the country as appreciated by sophisticated urban dwellers. The group here are evidently from the town depicted in the background. The young men may be poets and the unclad women their muses. The well-dressed, aristocratic youth recites his verses to the accompaniment of a lute, a courtly instrument. In contrast, an untutored shepherd in the distance plays the rustic bagpipes.

Titian became the most sought after portraitist of his day. Scholars, philosophers, and friends sat for him, as did popes, emperors, and Venetian rulers, but he never painted a more engaging portrait than the one here

RELATED WORKS

2.33 Titian,
Assumption

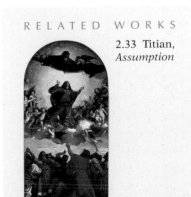

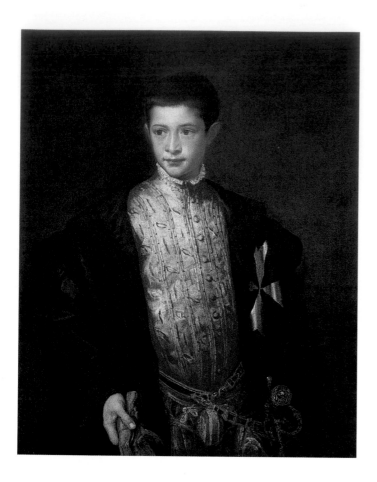

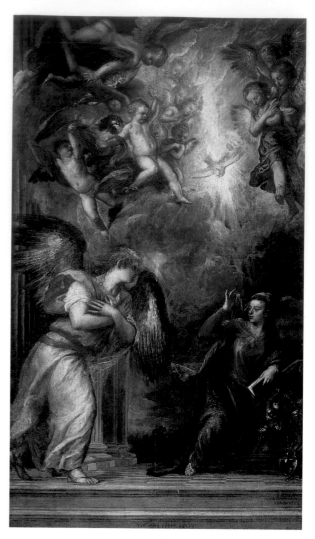

16.18 (left) Titian. *Portrait of Ranuccio Farnese.* 1542. Oil on canvas, 35¼ × 29".
National Gallery of Art, Washington, D.C.

16.19 (right) Titian. *The Annunciation.* c. 1560. Oil on canvas, 13'2⅝" × 7'8½".
Chiesa di San Salvador, Venice.

of a twelve-year-old boy named Ranuccio Farnese (**16.18**). The grandson of Pope Paul III, Ranuccio Farnese was pursuing his studies in nearby Padua at the time that Titian painted him. The painting shows well the sympathetic insight that Titian could bring to his portraits. It shows us, too, something of what it meant to grow up within a powerful Renaissance family. Ranuccio's endearing, shy expression undercuts the worldly confidence his silk clothing tries to project, and the sword and cloak of the military-religious order of the Knights of Malta, recently conferred upon him, weigh heavily—perhaps too heavily—on his young frame. He would be made a cardinal at the age of fifteen.

As Titian aged, his brushwork became freer and his colors grew more subdued and burnished. Contemporaries marveled that his paintings, seen up close, seemed nothing but a senseless frenzy of brush strokes. Yet as the viewer stepped back, there came into focus an image of unparalleled richness. An example is *The Annunciation* (**16.19**), painted when the artist was seventy-five. The subject is the moment when an angel appears to Mary to tell her that she has been chosen to bear the Son of God. In Titian's imagining of the event, Mary turns quietly from her prayers and lifts her veil to look at her visitor. The angel arrives as though in a hurry, his cheeks still flush with the excitement of the news he brings. Mary does not see that behind her the air itself has opened with the force of an explosion, and from the golden light formed of endless cherubim descends the dove of the Holy Spirit. In this work, Titian produced a vision of heavenly glory as rhapsodic as the gold realm of Byzantium or the stained glass of the Middle Ages.

THE RENAISSANCE IN THE NORTH

In the northern countries of western Europe—Switzerland, Germany, northern France, and the Netherlands—the Renaissance did not happen with the sudden drama that it did in Italy, nor were its concerns quite the same. Northern artists did not live among the ruins of Rome, nor did they share the Italians' sense of a personal link to the creators of the Classical past. Instead of the exciting series of discoveries that make the Italian Renaissance such a good story, the Northern Renaissance style evolved gradually out of the late Middle Ages, as artists became increasingly entranced with the myriad details of the visible world and better and better at capturing them.

We can see this fondness for detail in one of the most famous works of the late Middle Ages, the illuminated prayer book known as *Les Très Riches Heures* ("the very rich hours"). The book was created at the beginning of the 15th century by three artist brothers, the Limbourgs, for the duke of Berry, brother to the king of France.

Meant for daily religious devotion, the *Très Riches Heures* contains a calendar, with each month's painting featuring a typical seasonal activity of either the peasantry or the nobility. Our illustration shows the *February* page (**16.20**). At top in the lunette (half-moon shape) the chariot of the Sun is shown making its progress through the months and signs of the zodiac. Below, the Limbourgs depict their notion of lower-class life in the year's coldest month.

This view of everyday life focuses on a small peasant hut with its occupants clustered around the fire, their garments pulled back to get maximum benefit from the warmth. With a touch of artistic license, the Limbourgs have

16.20 Limbourg Brothers. February, from *Les Très Riches Heures du Duc de Berry*. 1416. Illumination, 8⅞ × 5⅜". Musée Condé, Chantilly.

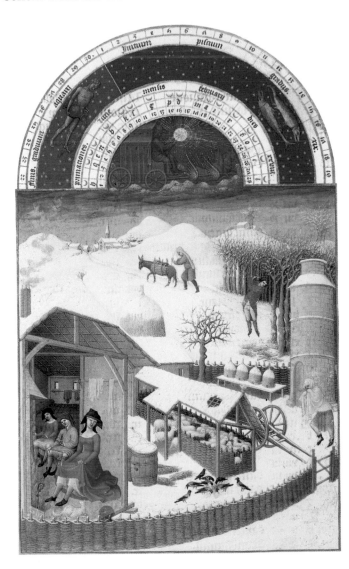

removed the front wall of the hut so we can look in. Outside the cozy hut we see what may be the earliest snow-covered landscape in Western art. Sheep cluster in their enclosure, a peasant comes rushing across the barnyard pulling his cloak about his face to keep in the warm breath. From there the movement progresses diagonally up the slope to a man chopping firewood, another urging a donkey uphill, and finally the church at the top.

To appreciate the richness of details, we should bear in mind this is a miniature, only 9 inches high. So acute is the Limbourgs' observation, on so tiny a scale, that we understand the condition of each player—the exertion of the woodcutter, the chill of the running figure, the nonchalant poses of the couple in the hut, and the demure modesty of the lady in blue.

The Limbourgs' manuscript marks a high point in a medieval tradition dating back hundreds of years (see 15.12). Within a few decades, however, the printing press would be invented, and the practice of copying and illustrating books by hand would gradually die out. In the meantime, an increasing number of Northern artists were turning to painting on panel with the newly developed medium of oil paint. An early master of the medium was Robert Campin, a prominent artist in the Flemish city of Tournai, in present-day Belgium. The subject of his *Mérode Altarpiece* (**16.21**) is the Annunciation, the same event we saw depicted by Titian earlier in this chapter (see 16.19). Campin painted this work in 1426, right around the time that the principles of linear perspective were discovered in Italy. The Italian system would not make its way north for another seventy-five years. Campin relies instead on intuitive perspective, in which receding parallel lines converge unsystematically. He uses it here with charming inconsistency, tilting the tabletops toward us, for example, so we can get a look at everything that sits on them.

The Annunciation setting is replete with symbols, most of them referring to Mary's purity: the lilies on the table, the just-extinguished candle, the white linen, among others. At upper left, between two round windows, the tiny figure of a child carrying a cross flies down a light ray toward Mary's ear, signifying that the infant Jesus will enter Mary's womb through God's will, not through human impregnation. The right wing of the altarpiece shows Joseph, who will become Mary's husband, at work in his carpenter shop. By tradition, Joseph is making a mousetrap, symbolic of the soon-to-come Jesus' "trapping" the Devil, bringing good to banish evil. In the left wing the donors, who commissioned the painting, kneel to witness the holy scene.

16.21 Robert Campin. *Mérode Altarpiece.* c. 1426. Oil on panel, 25⁵⁄₁₆ × 24⁷⁄₈" (center), 25⅜ × 10¾" (each wing).
The Metropolitan Museum of Art, New York.

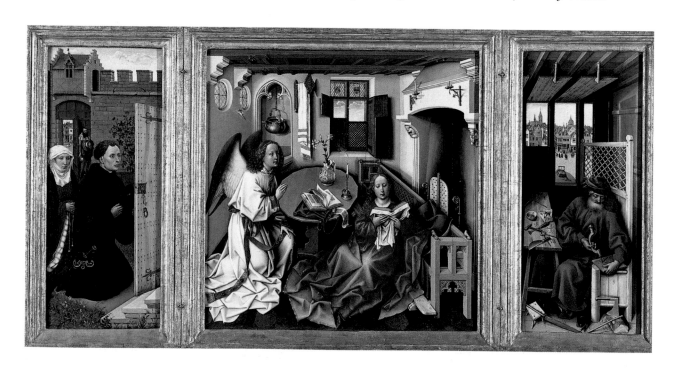

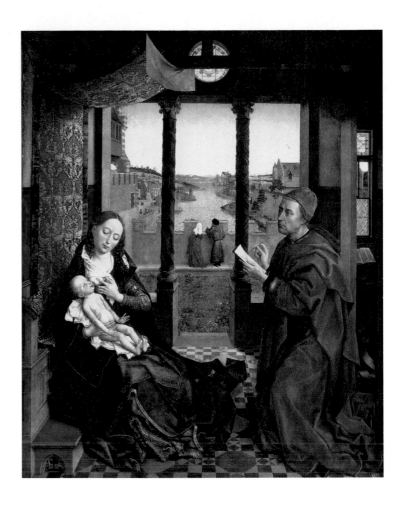

No recitation of this picture's details should overshadow its sheer beauty. Mary's face, modest above her crimson gown, is among the loveliest in all Renaissance art. The angel, with his luminous face and brilliant gold wings, displays an unearthly radiance. Both central figures wear robes that flow into rivers of sculptural folds. The *Mérode Altarpiece* is only about 2 feet in height. Its exquisitely rendered details, its clear colors, and the artist's skillful placement of light and shadow combine to give it a jewel-like quality.

Northern artists' preoccupation with decoration and surface and *things* derives naturally from their heritage. The North had a long tradition of painted miniatures, manuscript illuminations, stained glass, and tapestries—all decorative arts with a great deal of surface detail. Whereas the Italian masters were obsessed with structure—accurate perspective and the underlying musculature of the body—Northern artists perfected their skill at rendering the precise outer appearance of their subjects. They were unsurpassed at capturing in paint the textures of satin or velvet, the sheen of silver and gold, the quality of skin to its last pore and wrinkle.

In a fundamental way, Northern paintings are about looking. An apt example is Rogier van der Weyden's *St. Luke Drawing the Virgin* (**16.22**). At left is the Virgin Mary nursing the infant Jesus. At right is St. Luke, author of one of the four Gospels in the Bible and patron saint of artists, drawing the mother and child in silverpoint. The two larger figures are carefully balanced in an architectural setting, behind which, through a window, we glimpse a landscape in depth. Typical Northern touches include Rogier's minute attention to detail in the room—woodwork, tiles, canopy, window panes; wonderfully lavish drapery in the garments; rich colors; and faces so finely modeled and human we can think of them as portraits. There is great emotional warmth in this picture. The Virgin and Child exchange tender glances, while St. Luke, in his

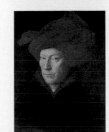
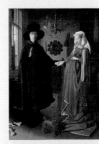

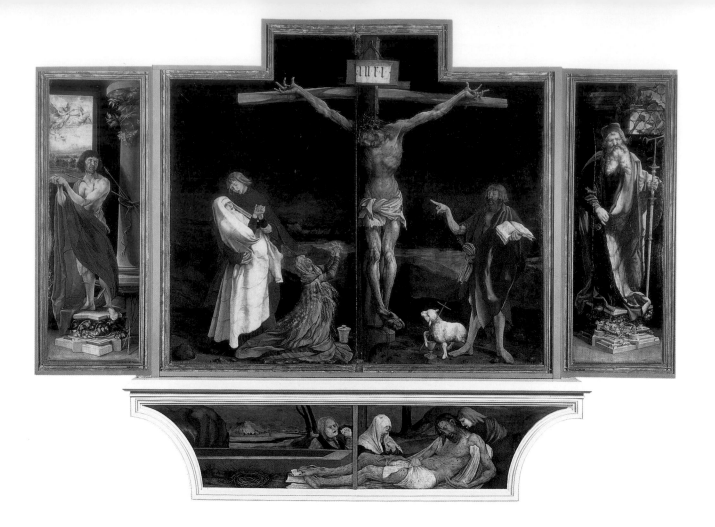

16.23 Matthias Grünewald. *Isenheim Altarpiece* (exterior). 1515. Panel, 8'10" × 10'1". Musée d'Unterlinden, Colmar.

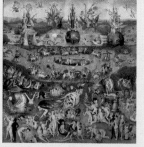
effort to capture their likeness, seems almost overcome with reverence and love. Everyone in the painting is caught up in looking, including the distant couple gazing out at the horizon.

While Rogier's painting is gentle, religious art of the Northern Renaissance could also be harsh in its emotionalism—far harsher than that of Italy. Northern art abounds in truly grim Crucifixions, gory martyrdoms of saints, and inventive punishments for sinners. Italian artists did sometimes undertake these subjects, but they never dwelt so fondly on the particulars.

Matthias Grünewald, a German artist active in the early 16th century, painted the Crucifixion of Christ as the center of his great masterpiece, the *Isenheim Altarpiece* (**16.23**). Originally, the altarpiece reposed in the chapel of a hospital devoted to the treatment of illnesses afflicting the skin, including syphilis. This setting helps to explain the horrible appearance of Christ's body on the cross—pockmarked, bleeding from numberless wounds, tortured beyond endurance. Without question the patients in the hospital could identify with Christ's sufferings and thus increase their faith.

In Grünewald's version of the Crucifixion, the twists and lacerations of the body speak of unendurable pain, but the real anguish is conveyed by the feet and hands. Christ's fingers splay out, clutching at the air but helpless to relieve the pain. His feet bend inward in a futile attempt to alleviate the pressure of his hanging body. To the left of the Cross the Virgin Mary falls in a faint, supported by St. John, and Mary Magdalene weeps in an agony that mirrors Christ's own. To the right John the Baptist offers the only sign of hope. He points calmly at the dying Savior in a gesture that foreshadows Christ's Resurrection. Grünewald's interpretation of the Crucifixion is in keeping with a stark Northern tradition in which depictions of extreme physical agony were commonplace.

It was Albrecht Dürer (see 4.47) who more than any other artist attempted to fuse Italian ideas and discoveries with the Northern love of meticulous observation. Dürer had visited Italy as a young artist in 1494 and returned for a longer stay in 1505. He came to share the Italian preoccupation with problems of perspective, ideal beauty, and harmony. In Dürer's view, Northern art had relied too heavily on instinct and lacked a firm grounding in theory and science. Toward the end of his life he summarized his philosophy of art by writing and illustrating two important works, *Treatise on Measurement* and *Four Books on Human Proportions*.

An artist who matured in the climate of thought that Dürer had created was the German painter Hans Holbein. Although not as intellectual as Dürer, Holbein recognized the need to grapple with the issues that Dürer had introduced. He mastered perspective and studied Italian paintings. Under their influence his modeling softened and his compositions grew more monumental. He did not lose the great Northern gift for detail, however, as his masterpiece known as *The Ambassadors* makes clear (**16.24**).

Holbein painted *The Ambassadors* in England, where his skills as a portraitist earned him the position of court painter to King Henry VIII. The painting was commissioned by the man on the left, Jean de Dinteville, the French ambassador to England. To the right is his friend Georges de Selve, a French bishop who also served as an ambassador. They look out at us from either side of a table richly laden with objects symbolizing the four humanist sciences—music, arithmetic, geometry, and astronomy. The imported Islamic rug speaks of contacts with the wider world, and the globe placed on the lower shelf reminds us that the Renaissance was also the age of European exploration and discovery. Close inspection reveals that the lute resting on the lower shelf has a broken string and that the book before it is open to a hymn by Martin Luther. The broken string symbolizes discord: Europe was no longer in harmony because of the difficult issues raised by Martin Luther's recent accusations against the Church in Rome. The movement Luther started, known as the Reformation, would very soon see Europe permanently divided

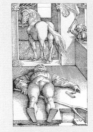

4.46 Grien,
Groom

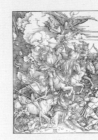

8.3 Dürer,
*Four
Horsemen*

16.24 Hans Holbein the Younger.
The Ambassadors. 1533. Oil on
panel, 6'9½" × 6'10½".
The National Gallery, London.

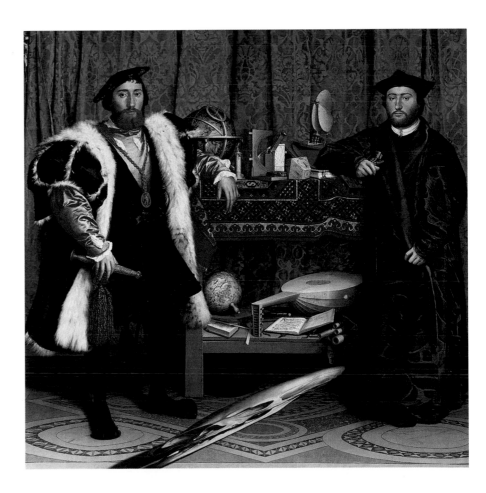

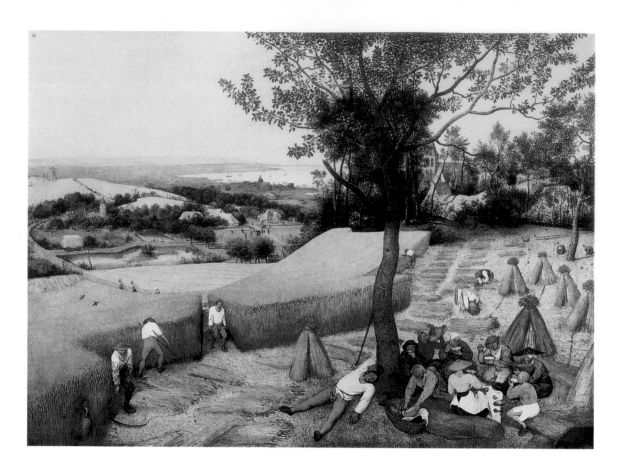

16.25 Pieter Bruegel the Elder. *The Harvesters.* 1565. Oil on panel, 46½ × 63¼". The Metropolitan Museum of Art, New York.

into Protestant countries and Catholic countries. The religious unity that had characterized the Middle Ages would be gone forever.

The strangest element in the painting is the amorphous diagonal shape that seems to float in the foreground. Dinteville's personal motto was *memento mori*, Latin for "remember you must die." Holbein acknowledged this with a human skull, stretched as though made of rubber. The skull is painted to come into focus when the painting is viewed up close and at an angle. Death thus cuts across life and shows itself by surprise. Holbein's painting celebrates worldly splendor and human achievement even as it reminds us that death will eventually triumph. It stands as a portrait of two men, a portrait of a friendship, and a portrait of an era.

Protestant reforms of the 16th century included an attitude toward religious images that ranged from wariness to outright hostility. Images of saints and other figures, reformers felt, had all too often been thought to possess sacred powers themselves. In their view the Church in Rome had encouraged these beliefs, which amounted to idol worship. The walls of Protestant churches were bare: "The kingdom of God is a kingdom of hearing, not of seeing," said Martin Luther.[7] One result was that Northern artists turned increasingly to the everyday world around them for subject matter, and one of the most fruitful subjects they began to explore was landscape.

We opened this brief survey of Northern Renaissance art with a manuscript page by the Limbourg brothers depicting a peasant household with a winter landscape in the background (see 16.20). *The Harvesters* (**16.25**), by the 16th-century Netherlandish painter Pieter Bruegel the Elder, advances the season to late summer and shows us how far painting has come in 150 years. Like the February page from the *Très Riches Heures, The Harvesters* formed part of a cycle depicting the months of the year. In the foreground, a group of peasants have paused for their midday meal in the shade of a slender tree. No doubt they have been working in the fields since dawn. The little group sits, chatting and eating. One man has loosened his breeches and stretched out for a nap. In the middle ground, the still unmowed portion of the field stretches out like a golden carpet. Some people are still at work, the men mowing with their scythes, the women stooping to gather the wheat into sheaves. Beyond there opens a vast panorama, a peaceful, domesticated landscape stretching as far as the eye can see. Landscape, which served the Limbourg brothers as a backdrop, has here become the principal theme, a grand setting in which humans take their appointed place, the rhythm of their work and lives falling in with the rhythm of the seasons and of creation.

THE LATE RENAISSANCE IN ITALY

Scholars generally date the end of the High Renaissance in Italy to the death of Raphael in 1520. The next generation of artists came of age in the shadow of this great period and with two of its most intimidating artists, Titian and Michelangelo, still going strong. Of the various artistic trends that emerged, the one that has interested art historians most is known as Mannerism.

The word Mannerism comes from the Italian *maniera*, meaning "style" or "stylishness," and it was originally used to suggest that these painters practiced an art of grace and sophistication. Later critics characterized Mannerism as a decadent reaction against the order and balance of the High Renaissance. Today, however, most scholars agree that Mannerism actually grew out of possibilities suggested by the work of High Renaissance artists, especially Michelangelo, whose influence on the next generation was enormous.

Agnolo Bronzino's bizarre *Allegory* (**16.26**) illustrates some of the fascinating and unsettling characteristics of Mannerism. In an allegory, all of the

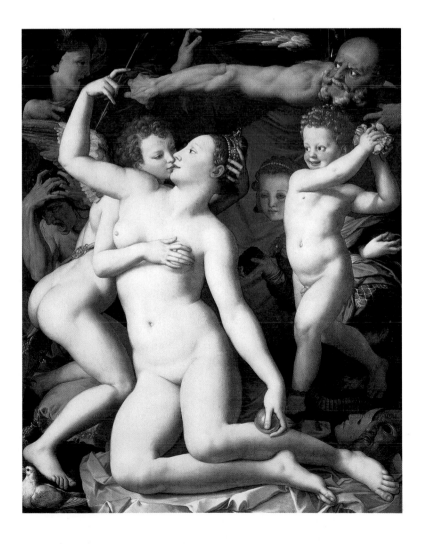

16.26 Agnolo Bronzino. *Allegory ("Venus, Cupid, Folly, and Time")*. c. 1545. Oil on wood, 5'1" × 4'8¾".
The National Gallery, London.

figures and objects also stand for ideas or concepts, and we should be able to "decode" their interaction, perhaps to draw a moral lesson. But the allegory here is so obscure that scholars have yet to reconstruct it. This fondness for elaborate or obscure subject matter is typical of Mannerist artists and the highly cultivated audience they painted for. Also typical is the "forbidden" erotic undercurrent. We recognize Venus and Cupid in the foreground. They are mother and son, but their interaction hints at a different sort of relationship, and both are clearly arranged for our erotic appraisal as well. The elongated figures and twisting S-shaped poses are part of the Mannerist repertoire, as is the illogical picture space—a shallow, compressed zone filled with an impossible number of people.

Bronzino's painting is an extreme example of the highly artificial and self-conscious aspects of Mannerist art. But Mannerist elements can also be seen in less exotic works such as Sofonisba Anguissola's lovely *Portrait of Amilcare, Minerva, and Asdrubale Anguissola* (**16.27**). The first woman artist known to have achieved celebrity among her contemporaries, Anguissola was born about 1535 in Cremona, the eldest of six sisters and one brother. She was well educated and was trained in painting; by about age twenty-two she had attracted the admiring attention of Michelangelo.

The *Portrait of Amilcare, Minerva, and Asdrubale Anguissola*—the artist's father, sister, and brother—dates from around 1557. Sofonisba Anguissola here brought something new to the art of Renaissance portraiture, a feeling

16.27 Sofonisba Anguissola. *Portrait of Amilcare, Minerva, and Asdrubale Anguissola.* c. 1558. Oil on canvas 61¾ × 48". Nivaagaards Malerisamling, Niva.

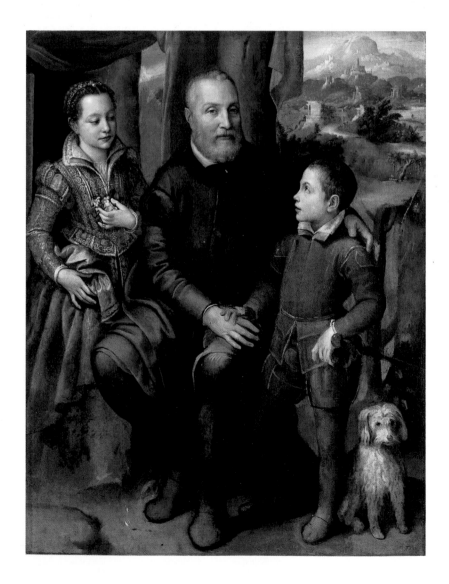

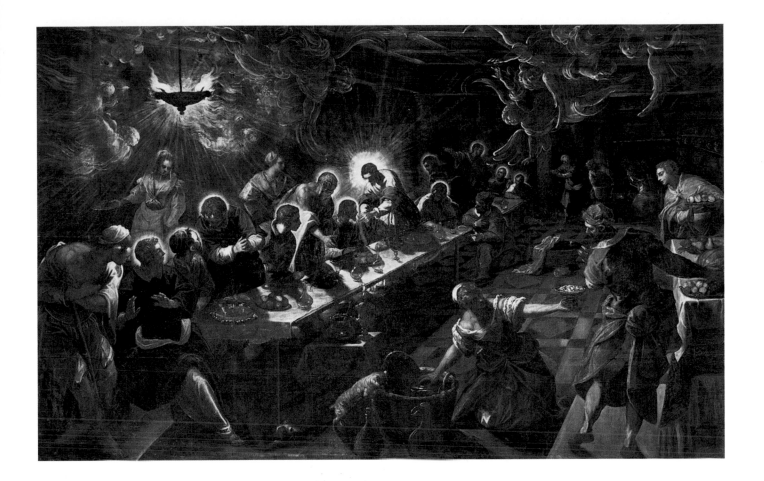

for family interaction, tenderness, and affection. Fate did not allow her to develop this gift, however. Her career took her to the court of Spain, where she had obtained a position as portrait painter and drawing instructor. Her departure, in fact, may have been what caused her to abandon work on this portrait, which remains unfinished. The Spanish court favored a far more stiff and formal style, and Anguissola, like all Renaissance artists, needed to please her patrons.

The Protestant Reformation in northern Europe drew large numbers of people away from the Roman Catholic Church. Deeply wounded, the Church of Rome regrouped itself and struck back. The Catholic Counter-Reformation, begun in the second half of the 16th century and continuing into the 17th, aimed at preserving what strength the Church still had in the southern countries and perhaps recovering some lost ground in the North. The concerns of the reformers extended to art, which they recognized as one of their strongest weapons. They insisted that all representations of sacred subjects conform strictly to the teachings of the Church and that artists arrange their compositions to make these teachings evident. They also understood and encouraged art's ability to appeal to the emotions, to engage the hearts of the faithful as well as their intellects.

The Last Supper (**16.28**) by the Venetian painter Tintoretto is an excellent example of the art encouraged by the Counter-Reformation. The greatest painter of the generation after Titian, Tintoretto developed his style from the virtuosic brushwork and dramatic lighting effects of Titian's late works (see 16.19). Tintoretto has chosen to portray the central theological moment of the Last Supper, when Christ breaks bread and gives it to his disciples to eat—the basis for the Christian sacrament of communion. The dramatic diagonal of the table sweeps our eyes into the picture and toward the figure of Christ, who stands near the very center of the canvas. His potentially obscure position in

16.28 Tintoretto. *The Last Supper.* 1592–94. Oil on canvas, 12' × 18'8".
San Giorgio Maggiore, Venice.

RELATED WORKS

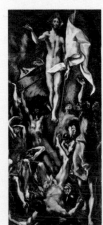

5.22
El Greco,
Resurrection

the distance is compensated for by the light that radiates from his head. Lesser glows of saintliness shine from the heads of his apostles, who sense the importance of the moment. Only Judas, who will soon betray Christ, does not emit the light of understanding. He is seated close to Jesus, but alone on the opposite side of the table, a symbolic placement that is both obvious and effective. Witnesses from heaven crowd into the scene from above, swirling in excitement. Though unseen by the servants, who go about their business, they are visible to us, who are left in no doubt that a miracle is taking place.

Comparing Tintoretto's version of *The Last Supper* to Leonardo's High Renaissance fresco (see 4.45), we can see that what was internalized, subtle, and intellectual has here become externalized, exaggerated, and emotional. Tintoretto's work prepares us well for the next era in art, for key elements of his *Last Supper*—the dramatic use of light, the theatricality, the heightened emotionalism, and even the diagonal composition—will play prominent roles in a style soon to be taken up across all of Europe during the Baroque.

CHAPTER SEVENTEEN

THE 17TH AND 18TH CENTURIES

T he period encompassing the 17th and 18th centuries in Europe has often been called "The Age of Kings." Some of the most powerful rulers
in history occupied the thrones of various countries during this time:
Frederick the Great of Prussia, Maria Theresa of Austria, Peter the
Great and Catherine the Great of Russia, and a succession of grand kings
named Louis in France, to name but a few. These monarchs governed as virtual dictators, and their influence dominated social and cultural affairs of the
time as well as political matters.

This same period could equally be called "The Age of Colonial Settlement." By the early 17th century the Dutch, the English, and the French had
established permanent settlements in North America. (Spain and Portugal had
earlier laid claim to much of Central and South America.) The first successful
English colony was at Jamestown, in Virginia, where a party led by John
Smith arrived in 1607. Thirteen years later the plucky little ship *Mayflower*
made landing in what is now Massachusetts. The settlers endured many hardships as they struggled through their first winters in the New World. At
Jamestown the colonists went through a period still known as the "starving
time." Ironically, the "starving time" in North America coincided exactly
with a European style so opulent that its name is now synonymous with
extravagance: the Baroque.

THE BAROQUE ERA

Baroque art differs from that of the Renaissance in several important respects.
Whereas Renaissance art stressed the calm of reason, Baroque art is full of
emotion, energy, and movement. Colors are more vivid in Baroque art than in
Renaissance, with greater contrast between colors and between light and
dark. In architecture and sculpture, where the Renaissance sought a classic
simplicity, the Baroque favored ornamentation, as rich and complex as possible. Baroque art has been called dynamic, sometimes even theatrical. This theatricality is clearly evident in the work of the Baroque's leading interpreter, the
artist Gianlorenzo Bernini.

Bernini would have been a fascinating character in any age, but if ever
an artist and a style were perfectly suited for one another, this was true of
Bernini and the Baroque. Largely for his own pleasure, he was a painter,

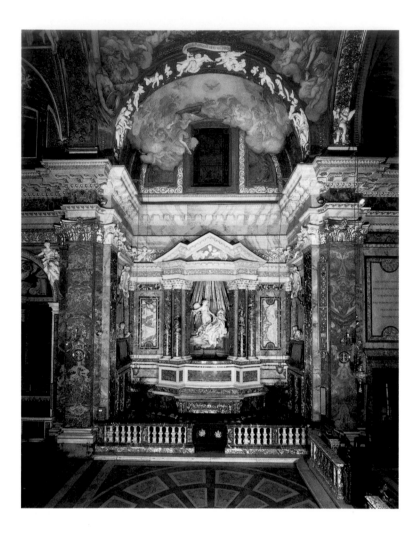

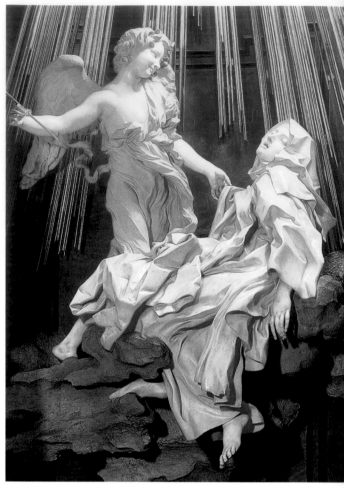

17.1 (left) Gianlorenzo Bernini. Cornaro Chapel, Santa Maria della Vittoria, Rome. 1642–52.

17.2 (right) Gianlorenzo Bernini. *St. Teresa in Ecstasy,* from the Cornaro Chapel. 1645–52. Marble and gilt bronze, lifesize.

dramatist, and composer. In architecture and sculpture, however, his gifts rose to the level of genius. Bernini's talents are on full display in the Cornaro Chapel in the church of Santa Maria della Vittoria in Rome (**17.1**). In this small alcove, the funeral chapel of Cardinal Federigo Cornaro, Bernini integrated architecture, painting, sculpture, and lighting into a brilliant ensemble. On the ceiling is painted a vision of heaven, with angels and billowing clouds. At either side of the chapel sit sculptured figures of the Cornaro family, donors of the chapel, in animated conversation, watching the drama before them as though from opera boxes. The whole arrangement is lighted dramatically by sunlight streaming through a yellow-glass window.

The centerpiece of the chapel is Bernini's sculptured group known as *St. Teresa in Ecstasy* (**17.2**). Teresa was a Spanish mystic, founder of a strict order of nuns, and an important figure in the Counter-Reformation. She claimed to be subject for many years to religious trances, in which she saw visions of Heaven and Hell and was visited by angels. It is in the throes of such a vision that Bernini has portrayed her. Teresa wrote:

Beside me, on the left hand, appeared an angel in bodily form, such as I am not in the habit of seeing except very rarely. . . . He was not tall but short, and very beautiful; and his face was so aflame that he appeared to be one of the highest rank of angels, who seem to be all on fire. . . . In his hands I saw a great golden spear, and at the iron tip there appeared to be a point of fire. This he plunged into my heart several times so that it penetrated to my entrails. When he pulled it out, I felt that he took them with it, and left me utterly consumed by the great love of God. The pain was so severe that it made me utter several moans. The sweetness caused by this intense pain is so extreme that one cannot possibly wish it to cease. . . . This is not a physical, but a spiritual pain, though the body has some share in it—even a considerable share.

Just as Bernini transformed the chapel itself into a sort of theater complete with sculpted spectators, he has set the drama of Saint Teresa as if on a stage. We can imagine that the curtains have just parted, revealing Teresa in a swoon, ready for another thrust of the angel's spear. She falls backward, yet is lifted up on a cloud, the extreme turbulence of her garments revealing her emotional frenzy. The angel, wielding his spear, has an expression on his face of tenderness and love; in other contexts he might be mistaken for a Cupid. Master of illusions, Bernini has anchored the massive blocks of marble into the wall with iron bars so that the scene appears to float. The gilt bronze rods depicting heavenly rays of light are themselves lit from above by a hidden window: This little stage set has its own lighting. The deeply cut folds of the swirling garments create abrupt contrasts of light and shadow, dissolving solid forms into flamelike flickerings. Standing before the chapel, our experience is also theatrical, for we can both watch the ecstasy and watch people watching the ecstasy; we are both caught up in the performance and aware of it *as* a performance.

One of the great projects of Baroque Rome was the completion of St. Peter's, which had been designed by Michelangelo (see 16.13, 16.14). During the early 17th century, an architect named Carlo Maderno lengthened the nave and created a new facade. Upon Maderno's death, Bernini continued the redecoration of the interior and designed a spectacular colonnade (row of columns) to enclose the vast square in front of the church. Interestingly, Bernini's architecture was more conservative than his sculpture. To fully appreciate the innovative daring of Italian Baroque architecture we should turn to his principal rival, Carlo Maderno's nephew Francesco Borromini.

Like the architects of the Renaissance, Borromini worked his designs out logically so that every least detail reflected a guiding idea. But instead of basing his work in the square and the circle, he favored more subtle and dynamic forms such as the oval. Borromini's most influential building is a small church called San Carlo alle Quattro Fontane ("Saint Charles at the Four Fountains"). The domed interior, designed first, takes the form of an oval gently indented to suggest a cross (**17.3**). The resulting walls alternate between convex and concave curves, creating a softly undulating motion and an organic, almost pulsating space. The church became instantly famous, and requests for the plans flooded in from all over Catholic Europe.

The facade (**17.4**), designed twenty-five years later and completed after Borromini's death, carries the logic through to the exterior. Alternating convex and concave elements dominate, their curves describing sections of ovals. The interplay of surfaces is complex. Notice, for example, how the central portion of the facade is convex at the street level but becomes a concave setting for convex elements above, culminating in a framed oval held aloft by two angels that seem to hover in front of the building. The protrusion of the facade forward into the viewer's space is typical of Baroque architecture, as is the buildup of interest in the central portion and the overall sense of plasticity—the sense that a building can be modeled and sculpted almost like clay.

Unlike architecture or sculpture, a painting cannot literally project its figures into the viewer's space. Baroque artists, however, learned to create a similar effect by lighting their figures dramatically and plunging the backgrounds into shadow. Artemisia Gentileschi used this technique effectively in

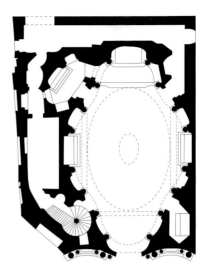

17.3 (above) Plan of San Carlo alle Quattro Fontane.

17.4 (below) Francesco Borromini. Facade of San Carlo alle Quattro Fontane, Rome. 1665–67.

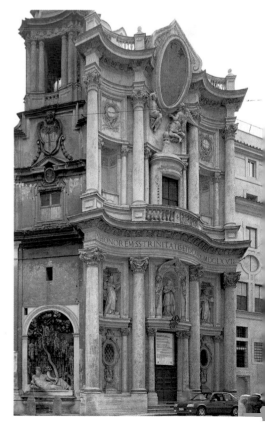

Judith and Maidservant with the Head of Holofernes (**17.5**). The artist took her subject from the biblical story of Judith. According to the scripture, Judith, a pious and beautiful Israelite widow, volunteered to rescue her people from the invading armies of the Assyrian general Holofernes. Judith charmed the general, accepted his invitation to a banquet, waited until he drank himself into a stupor, then calmly beheaded him, wrapped up his head in a sack, and escaped.

Other of Gentileschi's paintings show the decapitation in progress. Here she focuses on the moments after the gory deed is done. She poses Judith tensely, caught in the wavering light from a single candle, one hand still clutching the bloody sword, the other poised in a gesture of silence. These Baroque devices heighten the sense of danger, the urgency of deeds committed in the dark of night.

Gentileschi's dramatic way with light and dark was the influential invention of a painter named Caravaggio. His magnificent *Entombment of Christ* (**17.6**) is an example of the kind of painting that inspired Gentileschi and many other artists. The *Entombment* depicts the crucified Christ being lowered into an open grave. The body is held by two of Christ's followers—his disciple St. John and the Jewish ruler Nicodemus, to whom Christ had counseled that a man must be "born again" to enter Heaven. The group also includes the three Marys—Christ's mother, the Virgin Mary, at left; Mary Magdalene, center; and Mary Cleophas, at right—who look on in despair. Caravaggio's structure is a strong diagonal leading from the upraised hand at top right down through the cluster of figures to Christ's face. The light source seems to be coming from somewhere outside the top left edge of the picture. Light falls on the participants in different ways, but always enhances the sense of drama.

17.5 (left) Artemisia Gentileschi. *Judith and Maidservant with the Head of Holofernes.* c. 1625. Oil on canvas, 6'1½" × 4'7¾". The Detroit Institute of the Arts.

17.6 (right) Caravaggio. *Entombment of Christ.* 1604. Oil on canvas, 9'9⅛" × 6'7¾". Musei Vaticani, Pinacoteca, Rome.

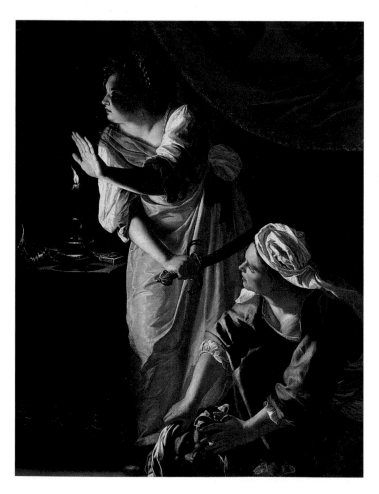

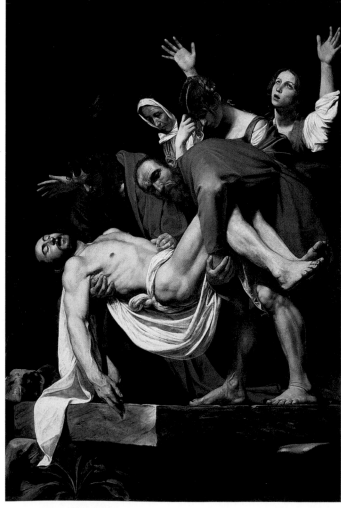

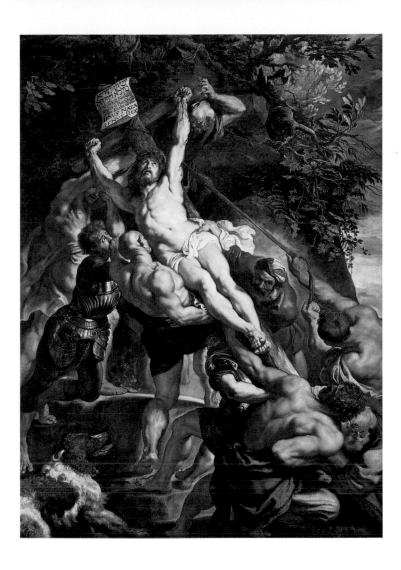

17.7 Peter Paul Rubens. *The Raising of the Cross*. 1609–10. Oil on canvas, 15'2" × 11'2". Antwerp Cathedral.

Mary Magdalene's face, for example, is almost totally in shadow, but a bright light illuminates her shoulder to create a contrast with the bowed head. Light also catches the pathetic outstretched hand of the Virgin. Christ's body is the only figure lit in its entirety; the others stand in partial darkness.

The perspective of the painting places the viewer's eye level at the slab the grouping stands on. Set on a diagonal, the slab seems to project forward from the picture plane and into our space, involving us in the action. We may imagine ourselves standing in the grave that is about to receive Christ: Perhaps this is why Nicodemus looks at us. Caravaggio painted this work to hang over an altar, and the head of a priest standing at the altar would have been at the ideal viewing level, the level of the slab. During the most solemn moment of the mass, the priest holds the communion bread aloft and repeats the words Christ spoke at the Last Supper, "This is my body." The raised bread would have been visibly juxtaposed with the body in the painting, restoring to the words an intense emotional impact.

We might compare Caravaggio's *Entombment* with a work painted just a few years later, *The Raising of the Cross* (**17.7**) by the Flemish artist Peter Paul Rubens. Although he spent most of his life in Antwerp (in modern Belgium), Rubens had traveled to Italy and studied the works of Italian masters, including Caravaggio. There are similarities between these two paintings—in the sharply diagonal composition and dramatic lighting—but we also find several differences in the two masters' styles. Caravaggio's figures seem almost frozen in a moment of anguish, but Rubens' painting teems with movement and energy, each of the participants balanced precariously and straining at his task. While the Caravaggio group projects from the picture plane, its action is

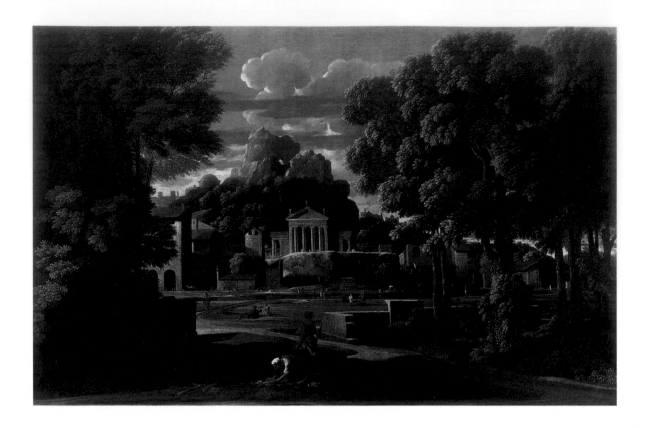

17.8 Nicholas Poussin. *The Ashes of Phokion.* 1648. Oil on canvas, 3'9¾" × 5'9¼".
Walker Art Gallery, National Museums Liverpool.

contained on four sides within the frame of the canvas. But Rubens' figures burst outside the picture in several directions, suggesting that the action continues beyond the painting. Rubens' heroic treatment of musculature recalls Michelangelo's paintings on the Sistine Chapel ceiling (see 16.11), but the writhing S-curve of Christ's body is typically Baroque.

While Baroque artistic principles were taken up across Europe, each country developed them in its own way. France, for example, favored a more restrained, "classical" version of Baroque style in which the order and balance of the Renaissance were retained, though infused with a new theatricality and grandeur.

Foremost among French painters of the 17th century was Nicolas Poussin, who actually spent most of his career in Rome. Steeped in the philosophy and history of the Classical past, he came to believe that art's highest purpose was to represent noble and serious human actions. An example is his painting *The Ashes of Phokion* (**17.8**). Phokion was a famous Athenian general of the 4th century B.C.E. In his old age, he was unjustly accused of treason, tried, and sentenced to death. The cremation or burial of his remains was outlawed. His friends and supporters dared not defy the court to accord him an honorable funeral. Only his widow did not desert him, arranging for cremation and performing the rites herself. She is shown here gathering up her husband's ashes outside of the city walls. Her virtuous act was much admired by the ancient Roman Stoic philosophers, who taught that virtue was the only good, vice the only evil, and that the triumphs and sufferings of life were to be accepted calmly and without passion.

Poussin's visual response to this story and its Stoic setting inspired a composition that is far removed from the emotionalism of Caravaggio or the energy of Rubens. In place of their active diagonals, calm verticals and horizontals dominate. Only the manipulation of light marks the painting as Baroque. Zones of light and shadow alternate across the canvas, and the white of the widow's clothing is lit as if with a spotlight, drawing our attention to the principal actor on this vast stage. In the foreground, wind-tossed trees watch over Phokion's widow and her anxious servant. The trees are linked by visual rhymes to the mountain and clouds in the distance, emphasizing that her courageous act answers to a higher law than that of the city: the natural law of instinct.

To grasp fully the flavor of the Baroque in France, we should look at a king who for all time exemplifies the term "absolute monarch"—Louis XIV. Louis ascended the throne of France in 1643, at the age of four. He assumed total control of the government in 1661 and reigned, in all, for seventy-two years. During that time he made France the artistic and literary center of Europe, as well as a political force to be reckoned with. Showing the unerring instincts of a master actor, he created an aura around his own person that bolstered the impression of divinity. Each day, for example, two ceremonies took place. In the morning half the court would file into Louis' chambers, in full pageantry, to participate in the king's *lever*—the king's "getting up." At night the same cast of characters arrived to play ritual roles in the king's *coucher*—his "going to bed."

A life in which the simple act of climbing in and out of bed required elaborate ceremony surely also needed an appropriate setting, and Louis did not neglect this matter. He summoned Bernini from Rome to Paris to work on completion of the Louvre palace (although the final design of the building was the work of others). But Louis' real love was the Palace of Versailles, in a suburb of the capital, which he substantially rebuilt and to which he moved his court in 1682. It was from this remarkable structure that the power of kingship flowed forth.

In all, Versailles occupies an area of about 200 acres, including the extensive formal gardens and several grand châteaux. The palace itself, redesigned and enlarged during Louis' reign, is an immense structure, more than a quarter of a mile wide (**17.9**). The illustration here shows the central portion of the west façade, which overlooks the gardens and houses the royal apartments. Baroque style is evident in the way the façade occasionally breaks forward and in the way interest gathers toward its center, but these effects are realized in a very understated way.

17.9 Louis Le Vau and Jules Hardouin Mansart. Central portion of the garden (west) facade, Palace of Versailles. 1669–85.

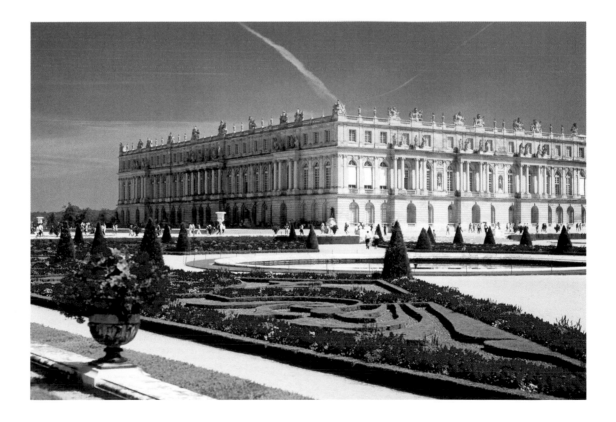

If the exterior of the palace reflects the continuing classical tendencies of France, the interior revels in full Baroque splendor. As in Bernini's Cornaro Chapel, though on a much grander scale, architecture, sculpture, and painting are united, creating a series of lavish settings for the pageantry of Louis XIV and his court. Of the countless rooms inside, the most famous is the Hall of Mirrors (**17.10**), 240 feet long and lined with large reflective glasses. In Louis' time the Hall of Mirrors was used for the most elaborate state occasions, and even in our own century it has served as the backdrop for momentous events. The treaty ending World War I was signed in the Hall of Mirrors.

The French court clearly was a model of pomp and pageantry, and the Spanish court to the south was eager to emulate that model. King Philip IV of Spain reigned for a shorter time than his French counterpart and could not begin to match Louis in either power or ability. Philip had one asset, however, that Louis never quite managed to acquire—a court painter of the first rank. That painter was one of the geniuses of Spanish art—Diego Velázquez.

In his capacity as court painter Velázquez created his masterpiece, *Las Meninas (The Maids of Honor)* (**17.11**). At left we see the artist, working on a very large canvas, but we can only guess at the subject he is painting. Perhaps it is the young princess, the *infanta*, who stands regally at center surrounded by her attendants *(meninas)*, one of whom is a dwarf. Or perhaps Velázquez is actually painting the king and queen, whom we see reflected in a mirror on the far wall. Their participation is clear, but where are they standing? Possibly they are outside the picture, standing next to us, the observers. This ambiguity is part of the picture's fascination, as is the dual nature of the scene. Although it shows a formal occasion, the painting of an official portrait, Velázquez has given the scene a warm, "everyday" quality.

17.10 Jules Hardouin Mansart and Charles Le Brun. Hall of Mirrors, Palace of Versailles. c. 1680.

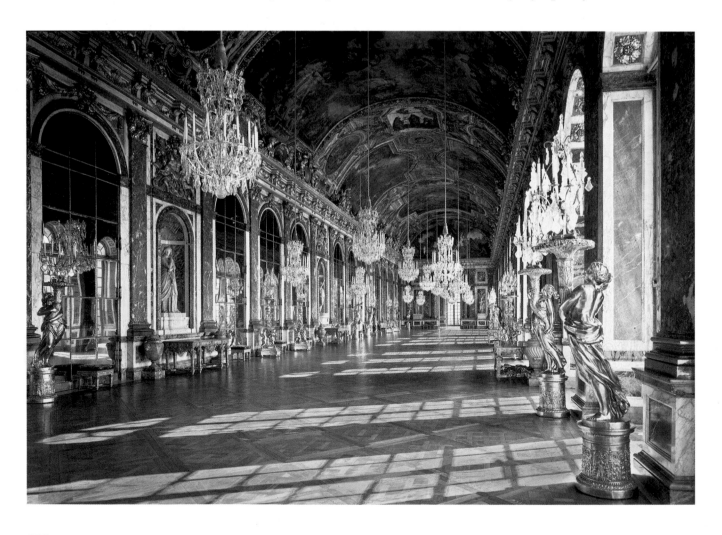

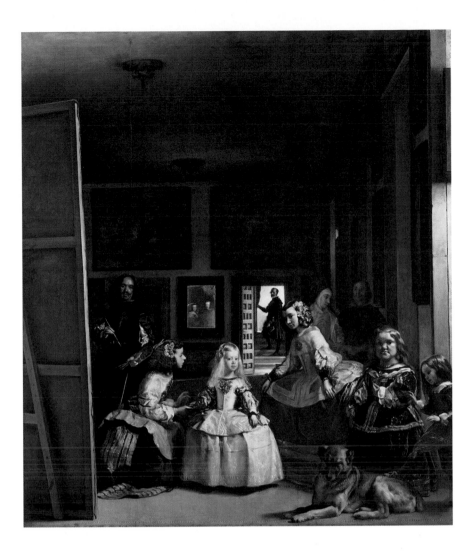

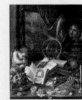

Like Caravaggio, Velázquez uses light to create drama and emphasis, but light also serves here to organize and unify a complex space. The major light source comes from outside the top right corner of the painting, falling most brilliantly on the *infanta,* leaving the others in various degrees of shadow. Another light source illuminates the mysterious figure in the open doorway at back. Velázquez may have put him there to direct attention to the reflected images of the king and queen. Light also strikes the artist's face and the mirror reflection. What could have been a very disorderly scene has been pulled together by the device of spotlighting, much as a designer of stage lighting would control what the audience sees. The theatricality of the Baroque is more subtle in Velázquez than in Bernini, but it is no less skillful.

To end this discussion of 17th-century art, we move north, to the Netherlands. The Dutch Baroque, sometimes called the "bourgeois Baroque," is quite different from Baroque movements in France, Spain, and Italy. In the North, Protestantism was the dominant religion, and the outward symbols of faith— imagery, ornate churches, and clerical pageantry—were far less important. Dutch society, and particularly the wealthy merchant class, centered not on the church but instead on the home and family, business and social organizations, the community. We see this focus in the work of two Dutch artists with very different styles—Rembrandt and Judith Leyster.

Rembrandt's principal teacher, a painter named Lastman, had traveled in his youth to Italy, where he had come under the influence of Caravaggio. Returning to the Netherlands to establish his career, he brought with him the new kind of dramatic lighting that Caravaggio had invented. We can see how

17.11 Diego Velázquez. *Las Meninas (The Maids of Honor).* 1656. Oil on canvas, 10'5¼" × 9'¾".
Museo del Prado, Madrid.

RELATED WORKS

1.13 Valdés, *Vanitas*

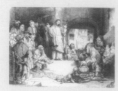
Rembrandt incorporated this lighting into his own personal style in the famous group portrait *Sortie of Captain Banning Cocq's Company of the Civic Guard* (**17.12**).

The painting portrays a kind of private elite militia. Such groups had played a prominent role in defending the city during the recent wars against Spanish domination, and although by Rembrandt's time their function was largely ceremonial, they were still widely respected, and all the most important men of the town belonged to one. Dutch civic organizations often commissioned group portraits, and painters usually responded by portraying the members seated around a table or lined up for the 17th-century equivalent of a class photograph. Rembrandt's innovation was to paint individual portraits within the context of a larger activity, a call to arms. He groups the figures naturally, in deep space, with Captain Cocq, resplendent in a red sash, at the center. The composition builds on a series of broad V-shapes, pointing upward and outward. The nested V-shapes make the picture seem to burst out from its core—and may have made its subjects feel they were charging off heroically in all directions, into battle. Lest this geometric structure seem rigid, Rembrandt has "sculpted" it into greater naturalness through his dramatic lighting of the scene. Light picks out certain individuals: Captain Cocq himself; the drummer at far right; the lieutenant at Cocq's side, awaiting orders; and especially the little girl in a golden dress, whose identity and role in the picture remain a mystery.

For many years Rembrandt's painting was known as *The Night Watch*, and it is still informally called by that name. The reason has nothing to do with the artist's intent. A heavy layer of varnish on top of the oil paint

17.12 Rembrandt. *Sortie of Captain Banning Cocq's Company of the Civic Guard (The Night Watch).* 1642. Oil on canvas, 12'2" × 17'7". Rijksmuseum, Amsterdam.

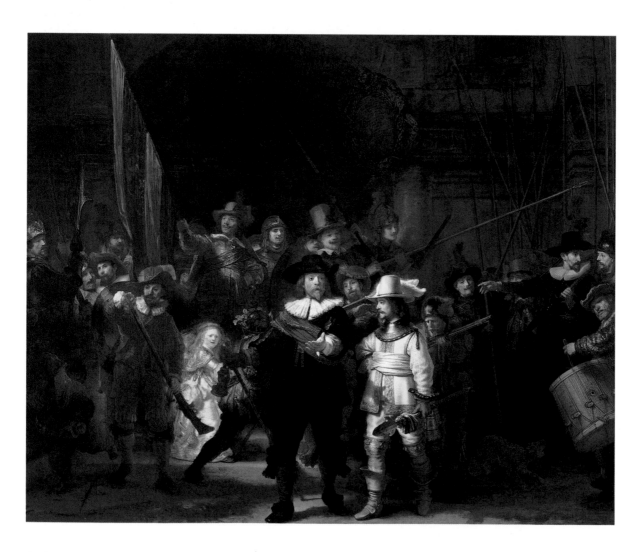

REMBRANDT

1606–1669

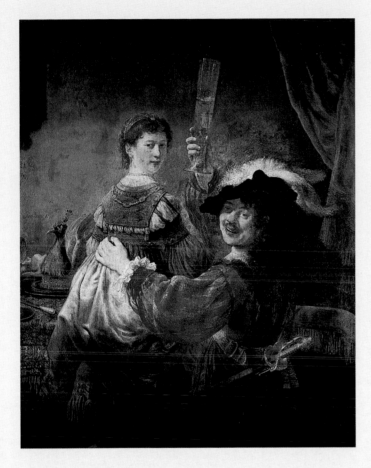

OF THE FEW artists classified as "greatest of the great," Rembrandt seems the most accessible to us. His life encompassed happiness, success, heartbreak, and failure—all on a scale larger than most of us are likely to know. Through his many self-portraits and his portraits of those he loved, we can witness it all.

Born in the Dutch city of Leiden, Rembrandt Harmensz. van Rijn was the son of a miller. At fourteen he began art lessons in Leiden and later studied with a master in Amsterdam. By the age of twenty-two he had pupils of his own. About 1631 he settled permanently in Amsterdam, having by then attracted considerable fame as a portrait painter. Thus began for Rembrandt a decade of professional success and personal happiness—a high point that would never come again in his life.

In 1634 Rembrandt married Saskia van Uijlenburgh, an heiress of good family, thus improving his own social status. The pair must have been rather a dashing couple-about-Amsterdam. The artist's portraits were in demand, his style was fashionable, and he had money enough to indulge himself in material possessions, especially to collect art. One blight on this happy period was the arrival of four children, none of whom survived. But in 1641 Rembrandt's beloved son Titus was born.

Rembrandt's range as an artist was enormous. He was master not only of painting but of drawing and of the demanding technique of etching for prints. (It is said that Rembrandt went out sketching with an etcher's needle as other artists might carry a pencil.) Besides the many portraits, the artist displayed unparalleled genius in other themes, including landscapes and religious scenes.

In 1642 Rembrandt's fortunes again changed, but this time for the worse. Saskia died not long after giving birth to Titus. The artist's financial affairs were in great disarray, no doubt partly because of his self-indulgence in buying art and precious objects. Although he continued to work and to earn money, Rembrandt showed little talent for money management. Ultimately he was forced into bankruptcy and had to sell not only his art collection but even Saskia's burial plot. About 1649 Hendrickje Stoffels came to live with Rembrandt, and she is thought of as his second wife, although they did not marry legally. She joined forces with Titus to form an art dealership in an attempt to protect the artist from his creditors. Capping the long series of tragedies that marked Rembrandt's later life, Hendrickje died in 1663 and Titus in 1668, a year before his father.

Rembrandt's legacy is almost totally a visual one. He does not seem to have written much. Ironically, one of the few recorded comments comes in a letter to a patron, begging for payment—payment for paintings that are now considered priceless and hang in one of the world's great museums. "I pray you my kind lord that my warrant might now be prepared at once so that I may now at last receive my well-earned 1244 guilders and I shall always seek to recompense your lordship for this with reverential service and proof of friendship."[1]

Rembrandt. *Self-Portrait with Saskia in the Parable of the Prodigal Son*. c. 1635–39.
Oil on canvas, 5'3½" × 4'3½".
Gemäldegalerie Alte Meister, Staatliche Kunstsammlungen, Dresden.

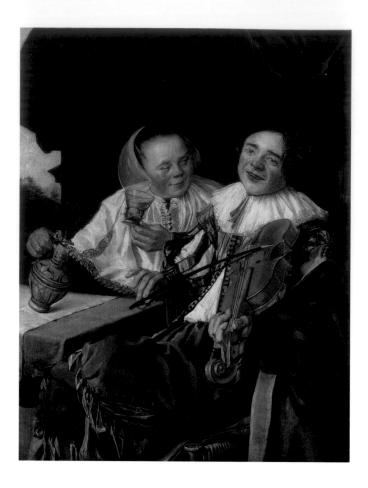

17.13 Judith Leyster. *Carousing Couple.* 1630. Oil on panel, 26¾ × 22⅝".
Musée du Louvre, Paris.

RELATED WORKS

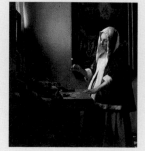

3.24 Vermeer,
*Woman Holding a
Balance*

combined with smoke from a nearby fireplace had gradually darkened the picture's surface until it seemed to portray a nighttime scene. No one alive could remember it any differently. It was only when the work was cleaned in the mid-20th century that the light-filled painting we know today reemerged. Even now, though, some members of the group can be seen more clearly than others, and viewers have often wondered how this could have been acceptable to the militia. Documents have revealed that each member contributed to the commission according to how prominently he would appear in the finished painting, and history records no complaints about the results.

The 17th century was the great age of Dutch **genre** painting—painting that focused on scenes of everyday life—and during her lifetime Judith Leyster was highly regarded as a genre painter. After her death, however, she was virtually forgotten. Paintings from her hand made their way into important collections, but many seem to have been attributed to another (in our time, far better known) Dutch painter, Frans Hals. Leyster had studied with Hals; thus the confusion is not altogether surprising. Still, her disappearance from art history prevailed for some two centuries. Then, in 1893, a Dutch art historian who had just sold a "Hals" to the Louvre museum in Paris discovered Leyster's distinctive monogram on the canvas. Since then, other works by "Hals" have been reattributed to Leyster.

Carousing Couple (**17.13**) is Leyster's version of a standard genre subject, the "merry company" scene. Looking more than a little tipsy, a man grins blurrily at us as he plays a viol—probably none too steadily. His companion holds up a glass and lifts a tankard of wine, suggesting just one more. Merry company scenes look like great good fun, and they can leave us with the idea that 17th-century Holland was a rollicking place. But the scene would have carried a warning for its original audience. The young man is being led astray, and we are supposed to fear that he may give himself over to a life of pleasure instead of pursuing a life of good, productive work. It is difficult to say how seriously artists and their audience took such stern moralizing, however. The woman here whose wiles are presumably to be condemned is in all likelihood a self-portrait of the artist!

The 17th century was also a great period for landscape painting in the Netherlands. Typical of Dutch landscape painting was the work of Jacob van Ruisdael. Van Ruisdael's *Extensive Landscape with a View of the Town of Ootmarsum* (**17.14**) shows not only the famed flatness of the Dutch landscape, but also the artist's reaction to that flatness as an expression of the immense, limitless grandeur of nature. The artist makes a contrast between the land—where human order has been established in the form of buildings and cultivation—and the sky, with its billowing clouds, yielding to the wind, which mere people can never tame. The horizon line is set quite low, and, significantly, only the church steeple rises up in silhouette against the sky, perhaps symbolizing that humankind's one connection with the majesty of nature is through the church.

Despite this emphasis on the church building, Van Ruisdael's art is essentially secular, as is that of Leyster and Rembrandt. Although religious subjects continued to appear in art—and do so even now—never again would religious art dominate as it did in the Renaissance and Italian Baroque periods. No doubt this is largely because of the change in sponsorship; popes and cardinals became less important as patrons, while kings, wealthy merchants, and the bourgeoisie became more so. We can follow this increasing secularization of art as we move out of the 17th century into the 18th.

THE 18TH CENTURY

The first half to three-quarters of the 18th century is often thought of as the age of **Rococo**—a development and extension of the Baroque style. The term "rococo" was a play on the word "baroque," but it also refers to the French words for "rocks" and "shells," forms that appeared as decorative motifs in architecture, furniture, and occasionally in painting. Like the Baroque, Rococo

17.14 Jacob van Ruisdael. *View of Ootmarsum.* 1628/29–82. Oil on canvas, 23¼ × 28⅞".
Alte Pinakothek, Munich.

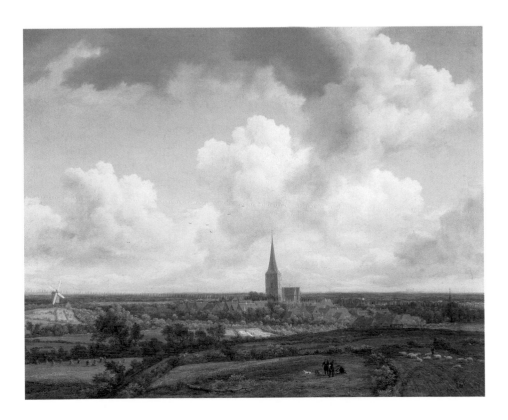

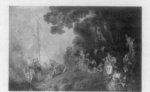

4.10 Watteau, *Embarkation for Cythera*

is an extravagant, ornate style, but there are several points of contrast. Baroque, especially in the South, was an art of cathedrals and palaces; Rococo is more intimate, suitable for the aristocratic home and the drawing room. Baroque colors are intense; Rococo leans more toward the gentle pastels. Baroque is large in scale, massive, dramatic; Rococo has a smaller scale and a lighthearted, playful quality.

The Rococo style of architecture originated in France but was soon exported. We find some of the most developed examples in Germany, especially in Bavaria. The Mirror Room of the Amalienburg, a little house in Nymphenburg Park near Munich (**17.15**), demonstrates amply why the word "rococo" has come to mean "elaborate and profuse." Designed by a Frenchman, François Cuvilliès the Elder, the Mirror Room is a perfect riot of sinuous, twisting, almost visibly *growing* decorative forms. The line between walls and ceiling has been obscured deliberately to create the illusion of "sky" above the room. Large arched mirrors multiply the effect of playful design everywhere the eye might focus. Rococo was above all a sophisticated style, and the Amalienburg shows us the height of that sophistication.

Sophistication was paramount in painting as well. In Chapter 4 we looked at *Embarkation for Cythera* by Jean-Antoine Watteau (see 4.10). Painted in 1718, it stands at the very beginning of the Rococo style. The dreamlike world Watteau invented must have appealed to French aristocrats weary of the formal grandeur of Versailles and the ceremonial character of daily life there.

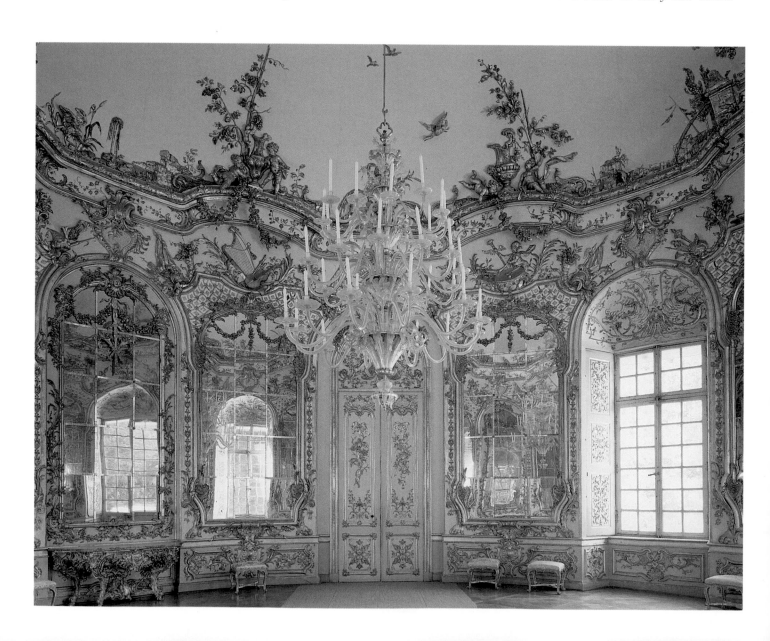

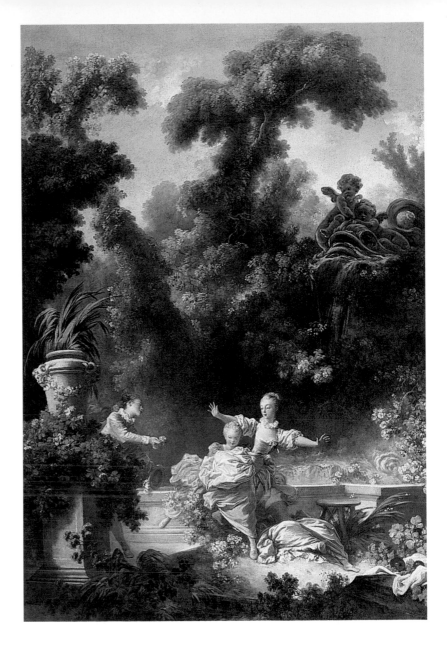

17.15 (opposite page) François Cuvillies the Elder. Mirror Room, Amalienburg. 1734–39. Nymphenburg Park, Munich.

17.16 (right) Jean-Honoré Fragonard. *The Pursuit*, from *The Progress of Love*. 1771–73, 1790–91. Oil on canvas, height approx. 10'5". The Frick Collection, New York.

Even the new king, Louis XV, seems to have found his role exhausting, for he created within the palace a modest apartment that he could escape to and live, if only for a few hours, like a simple (if rather well off) gentleman.

Just over half a century later, the aging king's mistress, the Countess du Barry, commissioned one of the last masterpieces of Rococo art, a set of four large paintings by Jean-Honoré Fragonard called *The Progress of Love*, of which we illustrate *The Pursuit* (**17.16**). Through a lushly overgrown garden on the grounds of some imaginary estate, an ardent youth chases after the girl who has captured his heart. He holds out to her a single flower, plucked from the abundance that surrounds them. She, surprised while sitting with her friends, flees, but so prettily that we know it is all a game. She will surely not run *too* fast. Above, a statue of two cupids seems to participate, watching over this latest demonstration of their powers to see how it will all turn out.

Madame du Barry had commissioned the paintings to decorate a new pavilion she had just had built on her estate. Although Fragonard never painted a lovelier set of works, his patron rejected them. She considered them too old fashioned and sentimental. Rococo taste had run its course. Seriousness was now in vogue, together with an artistic style called Neoclassicism ("new classicism"). Since 1748, excavations at the Roman sites of Pompeii

ACADEMIES

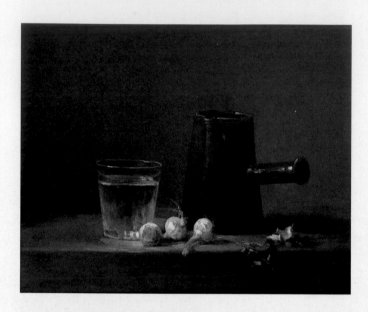

THE PAINTING DEPICTED here is a still life by the 18th-century French artist Jean-Siméon Chardin. Chardin's career followed a typical path for his time and place. After completing his artistic training, he presented a group of his works for consideration by the Royal Academy of Painters and Sculptors, a powerful organization sponsored by the king. A committee judged his paintings worthy, and he was accepted into the Academy as a "painter of animals and fruits." As a member of the Academy, Chardin was entitled to show his paintings in a biennial exhibition called the Salon, thus gaining attention and attracting commissions. He became an officer of the Academy, and then its treasurer. Eventually the king granted him a small yearly stipend along with a place to live in the Louvre Palace. Later in life he was even placed in charge of hanging the Salon show, a delicate task that required the skills of a diplomat.

Academies were one of the many ways in which Renaissance humanists had attempted to revive Classical culture. Their model was the celebrated Academy of the ancient Greek philosopher Plato, which earned its name from the park in Athens where the brilliant thinker met with his students, the Akademeia. Early Renaissance academies were private, informal gatherings that brought small groups of scholars and artists together to discuss ideas. In 1561, however, the artist Giorgio Vasari persuaded Cosimo de' Medici, a wealthy art patron, to sponsor a formal academy devoted to art, the Academy of Design, in Florence. By founding the first public academy, Vasari sought to underscore the prestige of art as an intellectual endeavor and to solidify the social status that artists had achieved during the Renaissance. Over the course of the next two centuries, art academies were founded across Europe. By the close of the 18th century they were at the center of artistic life.

Academies were inherently conservative. Their aim was to maintain official standards of skill and taste by perpetuating models of greatness from the past, especially the Classical past. Although women artists could often be accepted as members, only men could enroll as students, for academic training revolved around mastering the human figure, and it was deemed improper for young girls to gaze upon naked models. Students began by copying drawings, then advanced to drawing fragments of Classical statues—isolated heads, feet, torsos. They learned to draw gestures, poses, and facial expressions that expressed all variety of dramatic situations and emotions. They studied anatomy. Eventually they progressed to drawing from live models. They came to know the human form so thoroughly that they could draw it from memory, creating complex compositions without recourse to models at all.

This emphasis on mastering the human form was linked to the belief that the greatest subject for art was history, including biblical and mythological scenes, historical events, and episodes from famous literary works. After history, portraiture had the most prestige. Then, in descending order, came genre, still life, and landscape. These beliefs had direct consequences for painters: Upon his retirement, Chardin asked for a pension, pointing to his 20 years of service as treasurer. He was turned down. The new director of the Academy was an ambitious history painter who thought that Chardin had been far too amply rewarded already. After all, he was only a painter of animals and fruits.

Jean-Siméon Chardin. *Glass of Water and Coffeepot.* c. 1760. Oil on canvas, 12⅜ × 16¼". Carnegie Museum of Art, Pittsburgh.

and Herculaneum in Italy had been uncovering wonders such as the wall paintings we looked at in Chapter 14 (see 14.31). Patrons and artists across Europe were newly fascinated by the Classical past, and their interest was encouraged by rulers and social thinkers hoping to foster civic virtues such as patriotism, stoicism, self-sacrifice, and frugality—virtues they associated with the Roman Republic.

Among the many young artists who flocked to Italy to absorb the influence at first hand was a young painter named Jacques-Louis David. Upon his return to France, David quickly established himself as an artist of great potential, and it was none other than the new king, Louis XVI, who commissioned his first resounding critical success, *The Oath of the Horatii* (**17.17**).

The painting depicts the stirring moment when three Roman brothers, the Horatii of the painting's title, swear before their father to fight to the death three brothers from the enemy camp, the Curiatii, thus sacrificing themselves to spare their fellow citizens an all-out war. The subject combines great patriotism with great pathos, for as David's audience would have known, one of the Horatii was married to a sister of the Curiatii, and one of the Curiatii was engaged to a sister of the Horatii. David paints these two women at the right. They are overcome with emotion, knowing that tragedy is the only possible outcome. In fact, of the six brothers, only one, one of the Horatii, will survive the bloody combat. Arriving home, he finds his sister in mourning for her slain fiancé. Outraged at her sorrow, he kills her.

17.17 Jacques-Louis David. *The Oath of the Horatii.* 1784–5. Oil on canvas, approx. 11 × 14'. Musée du Louvre, Paris.

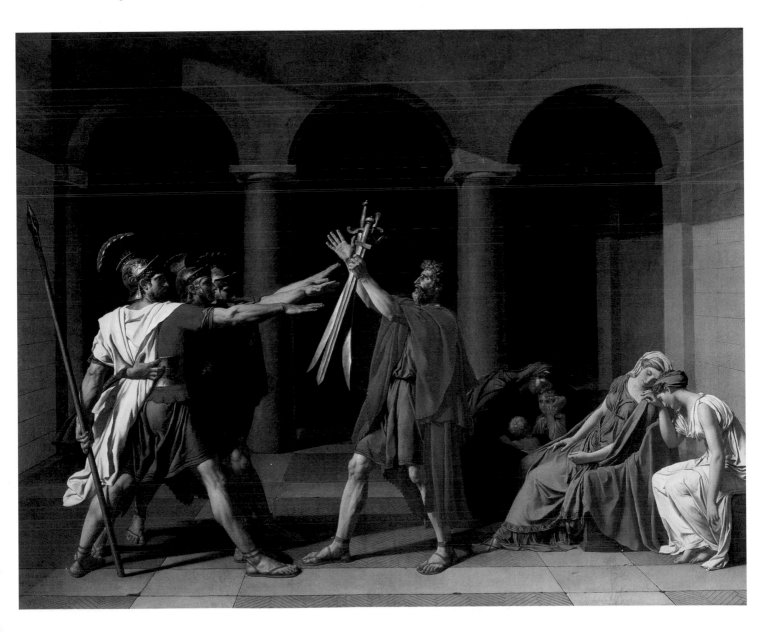

Gone are the lush gardens and pastel colors of the Rococo. In their place, David has conceived an austere architectural setting beyond which there is merely darkness. Spread across the shallow foreground space, the dramatically lit figures are portrayed in profile as though carved in relief. The creamy brush strokes and hazy atmosphere of Fragonard have given way to a smooth finish and a cool, clear light. Colors are muted except for the father's tunic, which flows like a river of blood next to the three gleaming swords.

Along with the stern "Roman family values" promoted by Neoclassicism, the late 18th century was under the spell of a new taste for simplicity and naturalness. One of the people most taken by the new informality was Louis XVI's queen, Marie-Antoinette. Another advocate of all that was unaffected was the queen's favorite portrait painter, Elisabeth Vigée-Lebrun. Inspired in part by the spareness of classical costume (note the women in David's painting) and in part by an ideal of the "innocent country girl," Vigée-Lebrun coaxed her highborn models into posing in airy white muslin dresses, their hair falling loosely about their shoulders, a straw bonnet tied with a satin ribbon on their head, and a flower or two in their hands.

The image confirmed the public's worst suspicions: Their queen was frivolous and flirtatious. In an attempt to repair the queen's reputation, Vigée-Lebrun was asked to paint a different sort of portrait, *Marie-Antoinette and Her Children* (**17.18**). Here, Marie-Antoinette is portrayed as a devoted and beloved mother. She is a woman who knows that her place is in the home, not meddling in politics or advertising her charms. In a gesture meant to tug at viewers' heartstrings, her elder son, the heir to the throne, draws our attention to an empty cradle; his youngest sibling had recently died in infancy. The queen's formal velvet gown and the glimpse of the fabled Hall of Mirrors in the background are meant to convey that she is aware of the seriousness of her position and fully capable of the quiet dignity needed to fulfill it.

It was too late. Far too much damage had already been done for a single painting to repair. The nation was teetering on the brink of financial disaster. Popular opinion blamed the deficit on the queen's extravagant ways and sus-

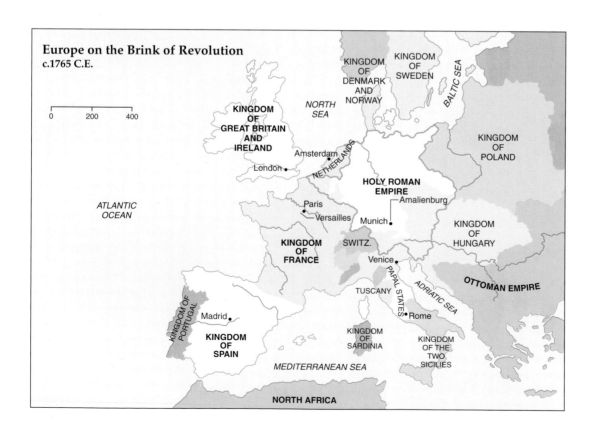

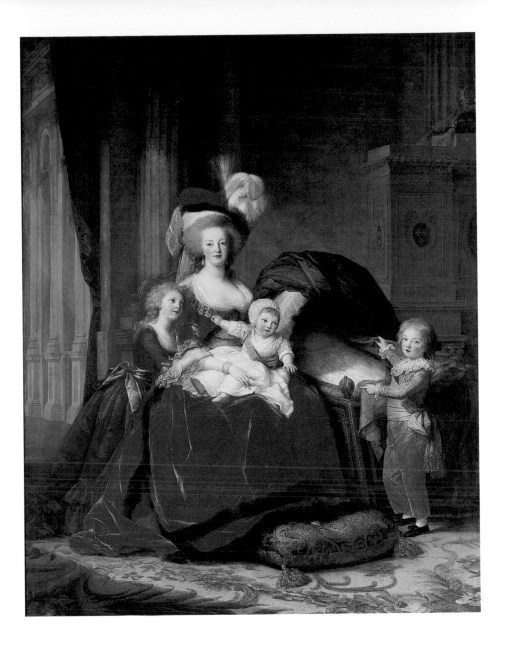

pected her as well of shocking personal vices. Vigée-Lebrun herself tells us that when the large canvas was carried into the palace, she heard angry voices crying, "There is the deficit."

Although Vigée-Lebrun later made several copies of her own portraits of the queen, she never again painted Marie-Antoinette from life. Within two years revolution had swept the country, ultimately destroying the monarchy and the aristocracy. The artist fled and took refuge outside France. The queen died by the guillotine.

17.18 Elisabeth Vigée-Lebrun. *Marie-Antoinette and Her Children.* 1787. Oil on canvas, 8'8" × 6'10". Palace of Versailles, France.

REVOLUTION

The leaders of the French Revolution continued to evoke the example of Rome and to admire Roman civic virtues. Neoclassicism became the official style of the Revolution and Jacques-Louis David its official artist. David served the Revolution as propaganda minister and director of festivals. As a deputy to the Convention of 1792 he was among those who voted to send his former patron Louis XVI to the guillotine. One of the events orchestrated by David was the funeral of the revolutionary leader Jean-Paul Marat. David staged the

ELISABETH VIGÉE-LEBRUN

1755–1842

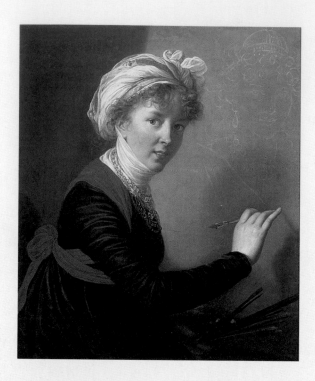

FROM HER SELF-PORTRAIT she gazes directly at us, her viewers—calm, self-possessed, sure of her talent, sure of her place in the world. Her chalk is poised over the canvas; we have momentarily interrupted her work on a portrait. She will not be interrupted for long. Throughout her remarkable life, Elisabeth Vigée-Lebrun knew where she was going and remained steadfast on that path.

Born in Paris, the daughter of a portrait painter, Elisabeth Vigée was convent-educated and encouraged from an early age to draw and paint. At eleven she began serious art studies. After her father's untimely death, Elisabeth resolved to work as a painter, and by age fifteen she was her family's chief financial support. Patrons flocked to her studio, eager to have their portraits done by the young artist, and her fees multiplied.

One dark spot was her mother's remarriage, to a man who seems mainly to have coveted his stepdaughter's income. Because of this unpleasant circumstance, Elisabeth made the one real mistake of her life. Although she "felt no manner of inclination for matrimony," she succumbed to her mother's urgings and accepted the proposal of Jean-Baptiste-Pierre Lebrun, hoping "to escape from the torture of living with my stepfather." Alas for the twenty-year-old artist, she had merely "exchanged present troubles for others." Lebrun was "quite an agreeable person," but, his wife soon discovered, "his furious passion for gambling was at the bottom of the ruin of his fortune and my own." The happiest result of the union was Vigée-Lebrun's only child, her daughter Julie.

Neither marriage nor motherhood interfered with the artist's burgeoning career and social life. By all evidence she was lovely, witty, charming, and perfectly at home in any company. Quite independent of her husband, she entertained a growing circle of aristocratic friends, many of whom commissioned portraits. In 1779 a summons came from the Palace of Versailles. Marie-Antoinette sought her services, and Vigée-Lebrun made the first of some twenty portraits of the queen. The two women became friends—a splendid advantage for the artist initially, but a dangerous liability as resentment of the monarchy grew. When revolution came in 1789, Vigée-Lebrun fled the country, taking Julie with her. Lebrun was left behind forever.

Then commenced Vigée-Lebrun's twelve years of "exile" from France. And what an exile it was! She traveled first to Rome and Vienna, then to St. Petersburg and Moscow, spending six years altogether in czarist Russia. Wherever she went she was treated like visiting royalty, entertained lavishly, invited to join the local painters' Academy. Wherever she went she was overwhelmed with portrait commissions. Kings and queens, princesses, counts, duchesses—she painted them all, in between the elaborate dinners and balls to which they invited her. In her memoirs she tells us she missed painting Catherine the Great because the empress died just before the first scheduled sitting.

In 1801, the furies of the revolution having abated, Vigée-Lebrun returned to Paris. She had not, however, quite satisfied her urge to travel. Only after a three-year stay in London and two visits to Switzerland did she finally settle down to write her memoirs and paint the survivors of the French nobility. She died in her eighty-seventh year, having painted more than 660 portraits. Her memoirs conclude with these words: "I hope to end peacefully a wandering and even a laborious but honest life."[2] And she did.

Elisabeth Vigée-Lebrun. *Self-Portrait.* 1800. Oil on canvas, 31 × 26¾". State Hermitage Museum, St. Petersburg, Russia.

exhibition of Marat's embalmed cadaver to the public, and he memorialized the leader's death in what has become his most famous painting, *The Death of Marat* (**17.19**).

A major figure in the Revolution, Jean-Paul Marat pursued the goal of wiping out France's greedy and corrupt aristocracy. He was responsible for the execution by guillotine of hundreds of people. Because of a painful skin ailment Marat spent his days in the bathtub, which was fitted out with a writing desk so he could work, and there he received callers. A woman named Charlotte Corday, incensed by Marat's excesses with the guillotine, gained entry to his apartment and stabbed him to death.

In lesser hands Marat's demise could have been laughable—a naked man murdered in his tub by a furious woman caller. But David has invested the event with all the pathos and dignity of Christ being lowered into his tomb. (Compare Caravaggio's *Entombment*, 17.6.) Marat is shown, in effect, as a kind of secular Christ martyred for the Revolution. All the forms are concentrated in the lower half of the composition, and light bathes the fallen leader in an unearthly glow, both of these devices contributing to the sense of tragedy. Marat's face and body could be those of a fallen Greek warrior, sculpted in marble by an ancient master. David's purpose in this work was to transform a man whom many considered Satan himself into a sainted hero. He projected the image the leaders of the Revolution wished to have of themselves, just as Vigée-Lebrun's art had projected the image desired by the French monarchs.

Two other revolutions occurred at more or less the same time as that in France. One was the American Revolution, preceding the French by thirteen years. During the relatively brief period covered by this chapter, the American

17.19 Jacques-Louis David. *The Death of Marat*. 1793. Oil on canvas, 5'5" × 4'2½". Musée Royaux des Beaux-Arts de Belgique, Brussels.

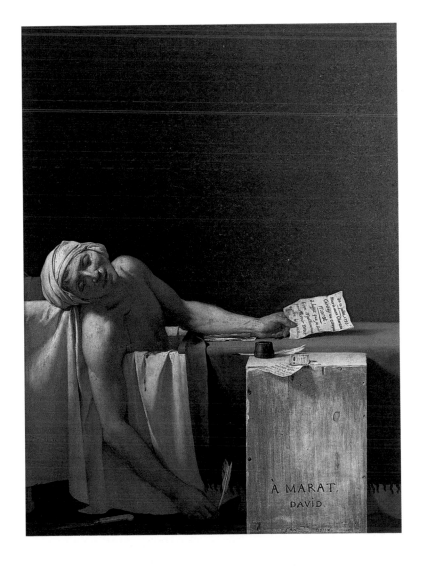

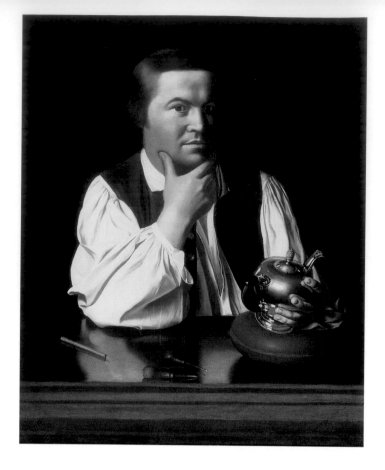

17.20 John Singleton Copley. *Paul Revere.* 1768–70. Oil on canvas, 35 × 28½".
Courtesy Museum of Fine Arts, Boston.

colonists had progressed from the "starving time" of Jamestown to a nation of people capable of independence and self-government. During that time also the area that was to become the United States had developed its own artistic styles. And by the eve of the Revolution the colonies had their own master artist, born on home soil—John Singleton Copley.

Born in Boston, Copley would paint many people who later became heroes of the Revolution, including *Paul Revere* (**17.20**). Legend and poetry have preserved the image of Paul Revere taking his "midnight ride" on horseback, from Boston to Concord, to warn his fellow colonists that "the British are coming!" In his day, however, Revere was better known as a silversmith. The artist poses him with a silver teapot in one hand, the tools of his trade scattered elegantly on the table.

Copley's portrait is in much the same Neoclassical style as David's tribute to Marat. The subject sits quietly behind his table, gazing straight toward us. We as viewers might be seated just opposite him. Although he is dressed informally, Revere shows great dignity and an obvious pride in his work. Copley has rendered his subject's features, the garments, and the polished tabletop with wonderful fidelity. We sense fullness, a three-dimensional volume, in the body and especially in the hand clasping the teapot.

The third revolution of this time was not a political uprising but an economic and social upheaval. Many would argue that the Industrial Revolution, which began slowly in the last half of the 18th century, is still going on.

It is difficult to overestimate the impact—social, economic, and ultimately political—of the change from labor done by hand to labor done by machine. Within the space of a few decades the machine drastically altered a way of life that had prevailed for millennia. People who had formerly worked in their homes or on farms suddenly were herded together in factories, creating a new social class—the industrial worker. Fortunes were made virtually overnight by members of another new class—the manufacturers. Naturally, all this upheaval was reflected in art. At the beginning of the 19th century, then, Western civilization faced a totally new world.

CHAPTER EIGHTEEN

ARTS OF ISLAM AND OF AFRICA

The ancient civilizations discussed in Chapter 14 culminated with the growth of the Roman Empire, which by 100 C.E. encompassed the entire Mediterranean region. Chapter 15 saw the empire divided into eastern and western halves after the death of the emperor Constantine. The eastern portion continued for a time as Byzantium. The western portion, after an unstable period, emerged as Europe, which we left in the last chapter on the brink of our own modern age. But what of the Roman lands along the southern shores of the Mediterranean, the lands of North Africa, Egypt, the Near East, and Mesopotamia? The answer is the religious culture of Islam, and thus it is with Islam that our brief exploration of artistic traditions beyond the West begins. (The story of Western art resumes with Chapter 21.)

ARTS OF ISLAM

Islam arose during the early 7th century C.E. on the Arabian Peninsula. There, according to Islamic belief, God—who had spoken through such prophets as Abraham, Moses, and Jesus—spoke directly to humanity for the last time. Through the angel Gabriel, He revealed His word to the Prophet Muhammad. Stunned by the revelations, Muhammad began to preach. At the heart of his message was *islam*, Arabic for "submission," meaning submission to God. Those who accepted Muhammad's teachings were called Muslims, "those who submit." Collected and set in order after his death, the revelations Muhammad recited make up the Qur'an ("recitation"), the holy book of Islam.

In 622, Muhammad emigrated from the city of Mecca northward to the city of Medina. Known as the *hijra*, this move marks the year 1 in the Islamic calendar, the beginning of a new era. Muhammad became a political leader in Medina as well as a spiritual one, and much of the Arabian Peninsula was brought into the Islamic community. After Muhammad's death in 632, his successors led Arab armies to victory after victory, and by the middle of the 8th century, Islamic rule extended from Spain and Morocco in the west to the borders of India in the east.

Islam transformed the Arab peoples from a collection of warring tribes with a largely oral culture to a people united by faith, anchored by the written word, and sovereign over vast territories. These new conditions nurtured the growth of a new artistic culture. The need for places to worship and palaces for rulers inspired works of monumental architecture; the establishment of princely courts supported the production of luxury arts such as fine textiles

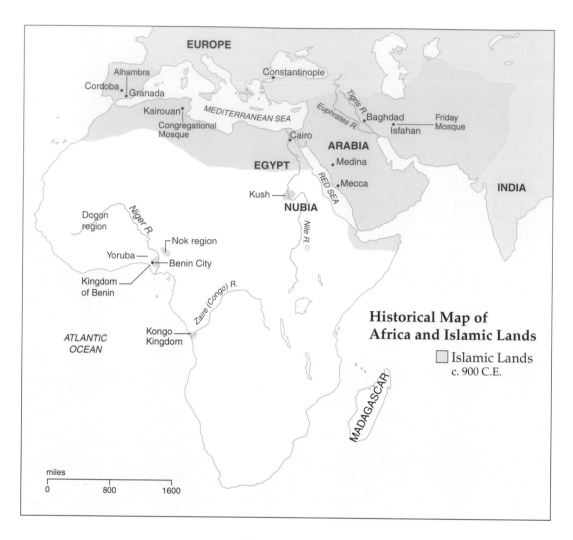

Historical Map of Africa and Islamic Lands

☐ Islamic Lands
c. 900 C.E.

and ceramics; and the centrality of the Qur'an led to a flowering of book arts, including calligraphy and illustration. Wherever Islam extended its influence, local artistic traditions were transformed by Islamic patronage. At the same time, converts from many lands transformed Islam itself into a true world religion. From its beginnings as an Arab faith, Islam became a spiritual and intellectual environment in which many cultures have thrived.

Architecture: Mosques and Palaces

One of the first requirements of Islamic rulers in new lands was a suitable place for congregational prayer, a mosque (from the Arabic *masjid,* "place for bowing down"). Early Islamic architects drew their inspiration from descriptions of the Prophet's house in Medina. Like most houses in Arabia, Muhammad's residence was built of sun-dried brick around a central courtyard. An open porch made of palm trunks supporting a roof of palm fronds ran along one wall, providing shade and shelter. There the Prophet had preached to the gathered faithful.

The Congregational Mosque at Kairouan, in Tunisia, shows how these elements were translated into monumental form (**18.1**). The shaded porch of Muhammad's house became a large prayer hall (the covered structure to the left). Just as the roof of Muhammad's porch was supported by rows of palm trunks, the roof of the hall is supported inside by rows of columns. The courtyard before the prayer hall is lined with covered arcades (rows of arches). Over the entry to the courtyard rises a large, square tower called a minaret. From its height a crier calls the faithful to prayer five times a day.

Two domes visible on the roof mark the prayer hall's center aisle. A worshiper entering from the courtyard and walking up this aisle would be walking toward the *mihrab*, an empty niche set into the far wall. This is the *qibla* wall, which indicates the direction of Mecca. Muhammad told his followers to face Mecca during prayer, and all mosques, no matter where in the world, are oriented toward that city. Inside every mosque, a *mihrab* marks the *qibla* wall, the wall Muslims face during prayer.

The minaret of the Kairouan Mosque was modeled on a Roman lighthouse, and the mosque's vocabulary of column, arch, and dome is based in Roman and Byzantine architecture. Cultural exchange between Islam and Byzantium can be seen again in the Great Mosque at Córdoba, in Spain. We looked at the interior of the prayer hall of this mosque in Chapter 3 (see 3.5). The illustration here shows the dome before the *mihrab* (**18.2**). Eight intersecting arches rising from an octagonal base lift a fluted, melon-shaped dome

18.1 (below, top) Congregational Mosque, Kairouan. 836 and later.

18.2 (below) Dome in front of the *mihrab*, Great Mosque, Córdoba. c. 965. Mosaic.

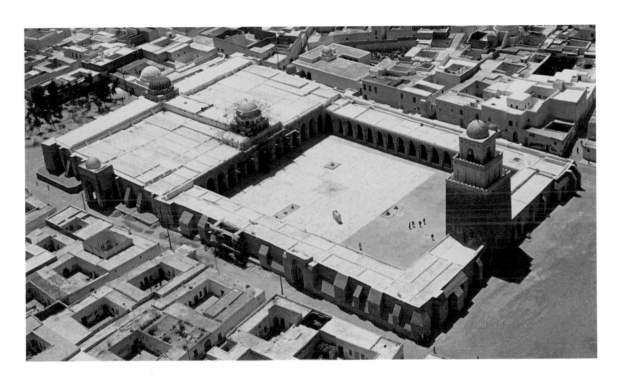

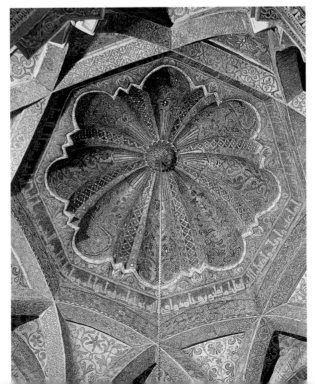

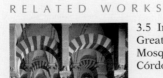

RELATED WORKS

3.5 Interior, Great Mosque, Córdoba

over the hall below. Light entering through windows opened up by the arches plays over the glittering gold mosaics that cover the interior. Gold mosaics may remind you of Byzantine churches (see 15.9). In fact, the 10th-century ruler who commissioned the mosaics sent an ambassador to the Byzantine emperor requesting a master artisan to oversee the work. The emperor reportedly sent him not only the artisan but also a gift of 35,000 pounds of mosaic cubes.

Whereas the mosaics in a Byzantine church might depict Jesus, Mary, and saints, the mosaics here do not portray any people, much less God himself. The Qur'an contains a stern warning against the worship of idols, and in time this led to a doctrine forbidding images of animate beings in religious contexts. As a result, artists working for Islamic patrons poured their genius into decorative geometric patterns and stylized plant forms—curving tendrils, stems, foliage, and flowers. Arabic script, too, became an important element of decoration. A passage from the Qur'an appears here in an octagonal band over the arches.

To the east, Islamic civilization was colored by the culture of Persia (present-day Iran), which had been Byzantium's great rival before its empire fell to Arab armies. During the 12th century, Persian architecture inspired a new form of mosque, illustrated here by one of the earliest and most influential examples, the Friday Mosque at Isfahan, in Iran (**18.3**). The photograph shows the view from the entrance to the courtyard. Directly ahead is a large vaulted chamber whose pointed-arch opening is set in a rectangular frame. This is an *iwan*, a form that served to mark the entry to a royal reception hall in Persian palaces.

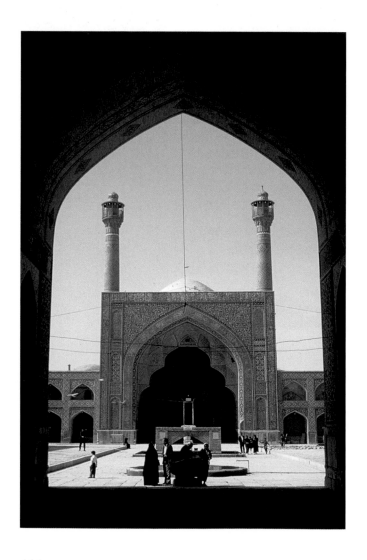

18.3 *Qibla iwan*, Friday Mosque, Isfahan. Rebuilt after 1121–22 (with later work).

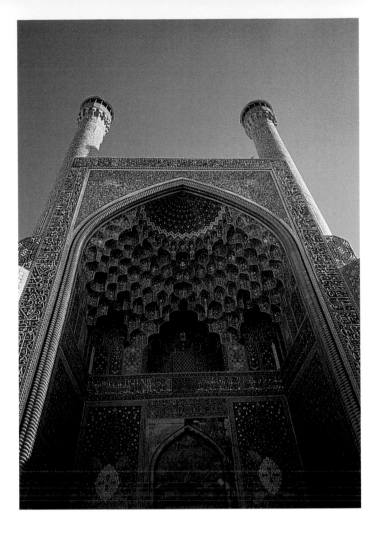

18.4 Entry portal, Shah Mosque, Isfahan. 1611–66.

Each side of the mosque's courtyard is set with an *iwan*. This four-*iwan* plan became standard in Persia, and its influence extended west to Egypt and east into Central Asia and India. The Taj Mahal in India, for example, is based in Persian architectural forms, and each of its four facades is set with an *iwan* (see 13.18). The photograph of the Friday Mosque at Isfahan was taken from the shade of the entry *iwan*, whose great pointed arch frames the view. Across the courtyard is the *qibla iwan*, oriented toward Mecca. Two slender minarets rise over its corners. The *qibla iwan* serves as a prayer hall, while the other three *iwans* are used as places for study, rest, or schooling. In back of the *qibla iwan* is a large domed chamber. Constructed for the private prayers of the ruler and his court, the domed chamber contains the *mihrab*.

The interior of the *qibla iwan* seems to be formed of triangular scoops as though it had been hollowed out by a giant spoon. Added during the 14th century, these niche-like scoops, *muqarnas*, are one of the most characteristic of Islamic architectural ornaments. They appear in more typical form in the stunning entryway to the 17th-century Shah Mosque, also in Isfahan (**18.4**). Cascading downward from a sunburst motif at the top of the pointed arch, the tiers of clustered *muqarnas* seem to multiply into infinity, like honeycomb or stalactites.

The blue glazed tile mosaic that blankets every surface of the entryway was a specialty of Persian artists. Glazed tile had been used to decorate buildings in the region since the ancient civilizations of Mesopotamia (see 14.9). An inscription flows around the perimeter of the frame, brilliant white on a deep blue ground, another band of calligraphy appears beneath the *muqarnas*. The rest is patterned in stylized flowering plants. Like the *muqarnas*, the patterns seem to multiply into infinity, as though a garden with blossoms as numerous as the stars had spread itself like a carpet over the building.

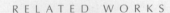

RELATED WORKS

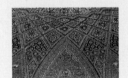

3.3 Nasr al-Mulk mosque

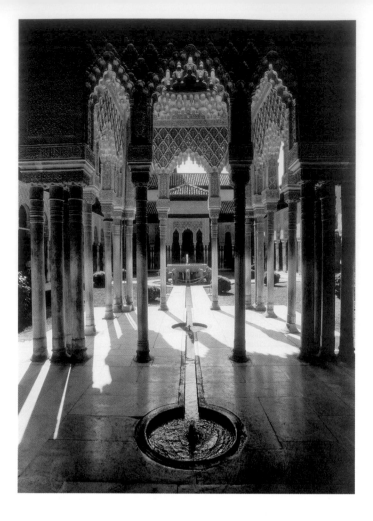

18.5 Court of the Lions, Alhambra Palace, Granada. Mid-14th century.

After roughly a century of unity under Arab leadership, Islamic lands were ruled by regional dynasties, and Arab dynasties took their place alongside dynasties founded by African, Persian, Turkish, and Central Asian groups. Little survives of the sumptuous palaces built for these rulers, for palaces were commonly destroyed or abandoned when a dynasty fell from power. A rare exception is the Alhambra, in Granada, Spain. Constructed largely during the 14th century under the Nasrid dynasty, the Alhambra was a royal city of gardens, palaces, mosques, baths, and quarters for artisans, all built within the protective walls of an older hilltop fortress. From the outside, the Alhambra looks every inch the forbidding fortress it began as. Once inside, however, visitors find themselves in a sheltered world of surpassing delicacy and refinement (**18.5**).

The Court of the Lions, shown here, takes its name from the stone lions supporting the fountain at its center. Water brought from a distant hill flows through the Alhambra in hidden channels, surfacing in fountains and pools. Indoor and outdoor spaces also flow into each other through open entryways, porches, and pavilions. Here, stucco screens carved in lacy openwork patterns and "fringed" with *muqarnas* are poised on slender columns, allowing light and air to filter through. The Nasrids were to be the last Islamic dynasty in Spain. Christian kings had already reclaimed most of the peninsula, and in 1492 Granada fell to Christian armies as well, ending almost 800 years of Islamic presence in western Europe.

Book Arts

Writing out the Qur'an—which Islamic scholars commonly memorize—is viewed as an act of prayer. Calligraphy thus became the most highly regarded art in Islamic lands, and great calligraphers achieved the renown Europeans accorded to painters and sculptors. As a religious text, the Qur'an was never illustrated with images of animate beings. Instead, artists ornamented manuscripts with geometric patterns and stylized plant forms, just as they did mosques. An example is this page from a Qur'an copied in 1307 by a famous calligrapher named Ahmad al-Suhrawardi (**18.6**). The top and bottom bands of the painted frame are ornamented in gold with interlacing plant forms and a line of text in an archaic style of Arabic script called Kufic. Ahmad's own bold and graceful calligraphy fills the framed area. One of the most gifted students of an even more famous calligrapher named Yaquat al-Mustasimi, Ahmad lived and worked in Baghdad, which was a major center for book production and scholarship.

Although the Qur'an could not be illustrated with images, other books could. Books were the major artistic outlet for painters in Islamic culture. Working with the finest pigments and brushes that tapered to a single hair, artists created scenes of entrancing detail such as *Bahram Gur and the Princess in the Black Pavilion* (**18.7**). Bahram Gur was a pre-Islamic Persian king whose legendary exploits were often recounted in poetry. *Haft Manzar* ("seven portraits"), by the 16th-century Persian poet Hatifi, tells of Bahram Gur's infatuation with the portraits of seven princesses. He eventually wins them all and builds for each a pavilion decorated in a different color. The Russian princess is housed in a red pavilion, the Greek princess in a white one. Here, Bahram Gur visits the Indian princess in her black pavilion.

The complex, flattened architectural setting and strong colors mark the style of the artist Shaykhazada, whose work this probably is. Floor coverings piled pattern on pattern are tilted toward the picture plane, while the brass vessels set on them are seen in perspective. The king and his princess sit demurely on their individual carpets before a wall ornamented with glazed tile. The setting above resembles the square frame and arched opening of an *iwan*, the pervasive Persian architectural form that might well have graced a pavilion built for an Indian princess.

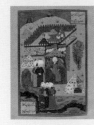
18.6 (left) Ahmad al-Suhrawardi, calligrapher. Page from a copy of the Qur'an. Baghdad, 1307. Ink, colors, and gold on paper, 20⅜ × 14½".
The Metropolitan Museum of Art, New York.

18.7 (right) *Bahram Gur and the Princess in the Black Pavilion*, from a manuscript of Hatifi's *Haft Manzar*. Bukhara, 1538.
Freer Gallery of Art, Washington, D.C.

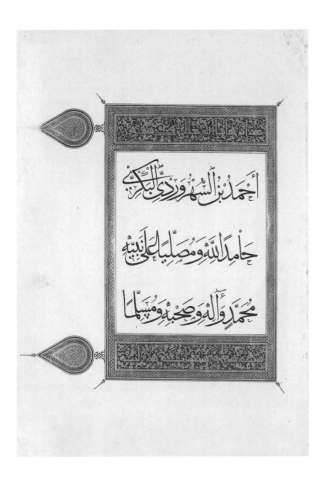

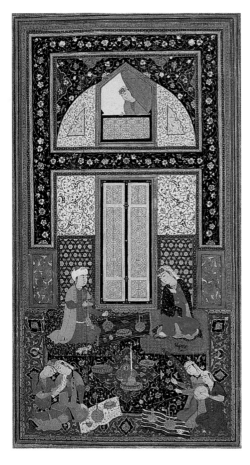

Arts of Daily Life

Western thinking about art has tended to relegate decorative art such as rugs and ceramics to "minor" status. Islamic cultures, while holding book arts in especially high esteem, have generally considered all objects produced with skill and taste to be equally deserving of praise and attention. Carpets and other textiles, for example, are an important facet of Islamic art. We saw one of the most famous of all Persian textiles in Chapter 12, the Ardabil carpet (see 12.14). Metalwork was highly prized in such works as the brass basin made in Cairo for Sultan al-Nasir Muyammad ibn Qalawun (see 12.8).

We end this look at Islamic arts with an example of ceramic art, a mosque lamp made during the 16th century in the Ottoman Empire (**18.8**). Based in Turkey, the Ottoman dynasty came to power in 1281. In 1453, Ottoman armies took Constantinople, putting an end to the Byzantine Empire. Constantinople, later called Istanbul, served as the Ottoman capital until the creation of the present-day nation of Turkey in the 20th century. The lamp was found in the Dome of the Rock, a 7th-century building in Jerusalem that is often called the first work of Islamic architecture. Ottoman rulers sponsored a renovation of that monument, and this lamp may have been made for it. Modeled after similar hanging lamps of glass, it probably served a symbolic function, for it would not have shed any light. The palette of blue, turquoise, and white, familiar from mosques at Isfahan (see 18.3, 18.4), points to the presence of Persian potters at the Ottoman court. The mixture of decorative motifs includes elements derived from Chinese ceramics, which were collected and admired in eastern Islamic lands. Finally, we see again the proud verticals and swirling ribbons of the Arabic script, writing made beautiful enough to carry God's word.

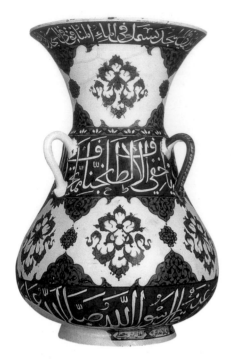

18.8 Underglaze-painted mosque lamp from the Dome of the Rock in Jerusalem. Isnik, 1549. Height 15⅛".
The British Museum, London.

ARTS OF AFRICA

When Arab armies invaded Africa in the 7th century c.e., their first conquest was the Byzantine province of Egypt, the site of Africa's best-known early civilization. Chapter 14 introduced ancient Egypt in the context of the Mediterranean world, for its interactions with Mesopotamia, Greece, and Rome are an important part of Western art history. But it is useful to remember that Egyptian culture arose in Africa and was the creation of African peoples.

The Nile that nourished Egypt also supported kingdoms farther to the south, in a region called Nubia. Nubia was linked by trade networks to African lands south of the Sahara, and it was through Nubia that the rich resources of Africa—ebony, ivory, gold, incense, and leopard skins—flowed into Egypt. The most famous Nubian kingdom was Kush, which rose to prominence during the 10th century b.c.e. and lasted for over 1,400 years. The gold ornament illustrated here comes from a Kushan royal tomb, the pyramid of Queen Amanishakheto (**18.9**). A sensitively modeled ram's head protrudes from the center of the ornament, a symbol in Kush, as in Egypt, of the solar deity Amun. Over the ram's head, the disk of the sun rises before a faithful representation of an entryway to a Kushan temple.

Carrying their conquests farther west across the Mediterranean coast of Africa, Arab armies quickly routed Byzantine forces from the Roman coastal cities. Far more difficult to subdue were the African people known as Berbers. Berber kingdoms were well known to the ancient Mediterranean world. In the days of the Roman Empire, Berbers mingled with the Roman population in Africa and occasionally rose to high rank in the Roman army. One Berber general became a Roman emperor. After the Islamic conquests, Berbers gradually converted to Islam, and Islamic Berber dynasties held sway in Morocco, Algeria, and Spain. Berber groups were also involved in the long-distance trade across the Sahara that linked the Mediterranean coast with the rest of the con-

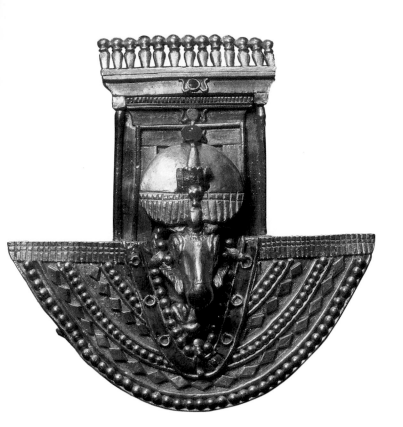

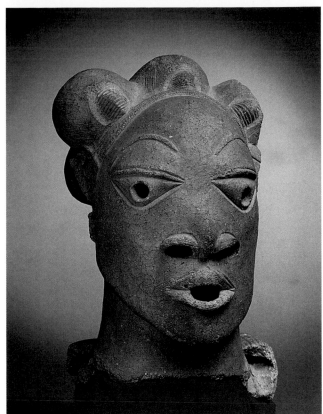

tinent to the south. Along these ancient trade routes, Islam spread peacefully through much of West Africa, eventually resulting in such African Islamic art as the mosque at Djenne, in Mali (see 13.1).

The Africa that Islamic travelers found south of the Sahara was and is home to literally hundreds of cultures, each with its own distinctive art forms. More than any other artistic tradition, the arts of Africa challenge us to expand our ideas about what art is, what forms it can take, what impulses it springs from, and what purposes it serves. Much of the history of these arts is lost to us, in part for the simple reason that most art in Africa has been made of perishable materials such as wood. Nevertheless, excavations during the 20th century have revealed many fascinating works in stone, metal, and terra cotta, including sculptures such as this terra-cotta head (**18.10**).

The smooth surfaces and *D*-shaped eyes are characteristic of works from the culture known as Nok, named after the town in Nigeria where the first examples of its art were found. Scientific testing suggests that most Nok works were made between 500 B.C.E. and 200 C.E., or around the time of ancient Greece and Rome. Broken off at the neck, the life-size head here probably formed part of a complete figure. Judging by the few complete figures that have been recovered, its elaborate, sculptural hairstyle would have been complemented by lavish quantities of jewelry and other ornaments.

It seems likely that Nok culture influenced later cultures in the region, although we cannot say for sure. What is certain is that two of the most sustained art-producing cultures of Africa arose some centuries later not far from the Nok region. One is the kingdom of Benin, which began to take shape during the 13th century. Located in a region of Nigeria south of the Nok sites, Benin continues to the present day under a dynasty of rulers that dates back to the first century of its existence.

Like the rulers of ancient Egypt, the kings of Benin are viewed as sacred beings. Sacred kingship is common to many African societies, and art is often used to dramatize and support it. In Chapter 5, we looked at a brass altar to the Benin king's hand (see 5.21). The altar conveyed the king's centrality

18.9 (left) Ornament from the tomb of Queen Amanishakheto. Kush, Meroitic period, 50–1 B.C.E. Gold with glass inlay, height 2½". Ägyptisches Museum, Staatliche Museen zu Berlin.

18.10 (right) Head, fragment of a larger figure. Nok culture, 500 B.C.E.–200 C.E. Terra cotta, height 14 3/16".
The National Commission for Museums and Monuments, Lagos.

RELATED WORKS

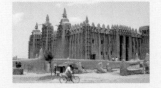

13.1 Great Mosque, Djenne

RELATED WORKS

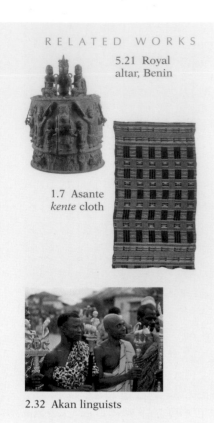

5.21 Royal altar, Benin

1.7 Asante *kente* cloth

2.32 Akan linguists

18.11 The palace altar to King Ovonramwen (r. 1888–97), Benin, Nigeria.

through symmetrical composition, his importance through hierarchical scale (he is larger than his attendants), and the symbolic role of his head through proportion (the head takes up one-third of his total height).

These elements can be seen again in the royal altars of the palace compound (**18.11**). Traditionally, each king upon assuming office commissioned and dedicated an altar to his father. The altar illustrated here is dedicated to Ovonramwen, who ruled toward the close of the 19th century. At the center of the altar is a brass statue depicting a standing king flanked by two attendants. As in the small altar to the hand, hierarchical proportion underscores the king's importance. This symmetrical composition stands at the center of a still larger symmetrical composition, the assemblage of the altar itself. Around the perimeter of the platform, ceremonial brass bells are displayed, three to the left, three to the right. Four large brass sculptures depicting heads of rulers are also set out symmetrically, each capped by an elephant tusk carved in relief with dozens of royal motifs.

In 1897, British forces attacked the Benin palace and took much of the art it contained—works in brass, ivory, terra cotta, and wood produced over a period of about 400 years. As a result, objects like the ones shown in the photograph here can be found in museums around the world. Examining a brass head or a carved tusk from Benin is a rewarding experience, yet these objects were not meant to be seen in isolation, much less in a museum. Rather, they were intended to take their place as elements in a larger, composite work of art—the assemblage of a sacred altar.

According to oral tradition, the current dynasty of Benin rulers was founded by a prince from the Yoruba city of Ife to the northwest. Yoruba rulers, too, were considered sacred, and artists sculpted portrait heads in their honor. We saw two of these sculptures in Chapter 2: a naturalistic work from the 13th century representing the ruler's outer, physical head and an abstract work representing his inner, spiritual head (see 2.16, 2.17). Although Yoruba artists no longer make such works, Yoruba kings are still regarded as sacred, and art still serves to dramatize their exceptional nature.

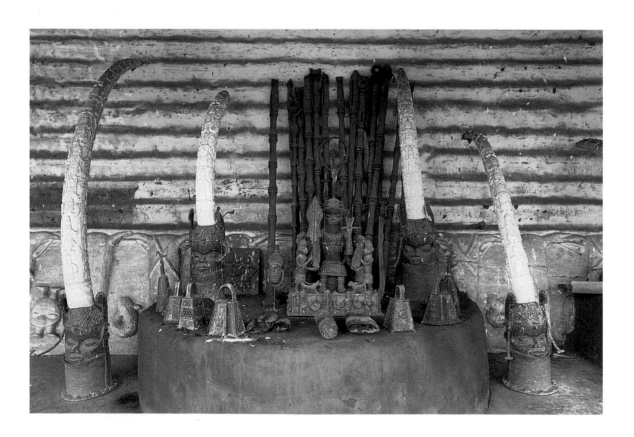

AFRICA LOOKS BACK

Africa Masquerades range from sacred and secret performances before a small group of initiates to public spectacles that verge on secular entertainment, though no masquerade is ever entirely secular. The largest masquerades may be performed in stages over many days and feature dozens of masks. Spirits of nature and natural forces; spirits of ancestors and of the recent dead; spirits of human types or social roles such as young maidens, blacksmiths, and farmers; spirits of abstract ideas such as beauty or fertility or wisdom—all may put in an appearance. Our knowledge of this rich and varied art form comes largely from Western researchers such as anthropologists and art historians, who over the past century have spent time "in the field"—that is, in various African communities, where they observe, photograph, and document the performances. Yet the nature of masquerades is such that often the observers have found themselves to be the observed.

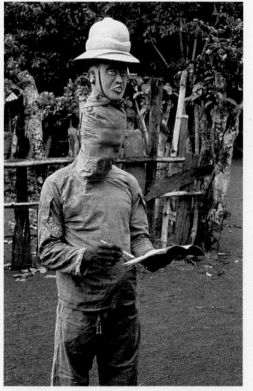

The masker illustrated here was photographed during a masquerade performed in an Igbo community. He is *onyeocha,* "white man." With his pith helmet, notepad, and pen, he may be a scholar who has come to do important research on these interesting Africans. While the other maskers in his troupe danced, he did not. Instead, he haughtily observed the goings on and took notes. Europeans, it is well known, are obsessed with writing everything down. But what can they hope to understand that way?

White-man masks depicting European government officers began to appear during the early 20th century, when colonial rule was imposed over the continent. Today, when tourism helps support many public masquerades, masks depicting tourists often appear. Armed with a carved wooden "camera," they elbow their way through the crowd, angling for a good view. One European couple portrayed in a Yoruba masquerade actually danced, but what a dance! They began with a waltz, then switched to a disco number that got them so overheated they ended up writhing on the ground making love! To the Yoruba, the public displays of affection that Europeans commonly indulge in are shocking. Indeed, the European couple was followed in the performance by maskers portraying a dignified, well-behaved Yoruba couple for contrast. In a masquerade performed by the Dogon people, a white-man mask sat at a table and asked silly questions. He was an anthropologist, of course!

Europeans are not the only outsiders to have been incorporated into masquerades. Masks of Muslim scholars have appeared, as have masks portraying irksome neighboring peoples. Most outside characters are portrayed satirically, often providing comic relief in a masquerade where genuinely powerful and sacred masks will also dance. The new masks demonstrate the vitality of this living art form, which easily absorbs new powers and presences into its view of the world. Yet the masks also bring us up short by questioning the limits of our ability to "study" another culture while it "holds still." "You do not stand in one place to watch a masquerade" goes an Igbo saying. Indeed, all cultures are always in motion, affecting each other through contact, both the observer and the observed.

Onyeocha ("white man") at an Igbo masquerade, Amagu Izzi, Nigeria, 1983.

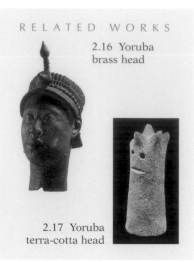

2.16 Yoruba
brass head

2.17 Yoruba
terra-cotta head

Taken in 1977, the photograph here shows the Yoruba ruler Ariwajoye I seated in his regal robes (**18.12**). His right hand grasps a beaded staff, and on his head is a cone-shaped beaded crown. Abstracted faces of the king's ancestors stare out from the crown; their dark, white-rimmed eyes are easily discernible. At the pinnacle of the crown is a beaded bird, and numerous bird heads protrude from the cone. The birds refer to the female ancestors whose powers the king must draw on. Known as Our Mothers, they are believed able to transform themselves into night birds. A beaded veil obscures the ruler's face, for his subjects are not allowed to gaze directly on a sacred being. The crown gives form to the idea that the living king is one with his godly ancestors, for in wearing it his head merges with theirs, and their many eyes look out.

Similar ideas are conveyed by a spectacular beaded display piece commissioned by a Yoruba king in the early 20th century (**18.13**). The base of the piece resembles the conical royal crown. As on the crown, faces of ancestors stare out from the front and back (visible in profile here). Over this base rises the figure of a royal wife with a magnificent crested hairstyle and a child on her back. It is as though the bird at the pinnacle of Ariwajoye's crown had turned back into one of the female ancestors who guarantees his power. The woman carries an offering bowl with a small bird on its lid. Female attendants flock around her body, while four protective male figures with guns ring the crown at the base. Male power is here seen as based in strength, while female power, greater and more mysterious, generates ritual (the offering) and new life (the child).

Complementary gender roles are also the subject of this elegant sculpture by an artist of the Dogon people, who live in present-day Mali (**18.14**). The sculpture portrays a couple seated side by side, rendered in a highly conventionalized, abstract manner. The stool they share links them physically and symbolically, as does the man's arm placed around the woman's shoulder. With their tilted heads, tubular torsos, angular limbs, horseshoe-shaped hips, and

18.12 Ariwajoye I, ruler of Orangun-Ila, seated in state, 1977.

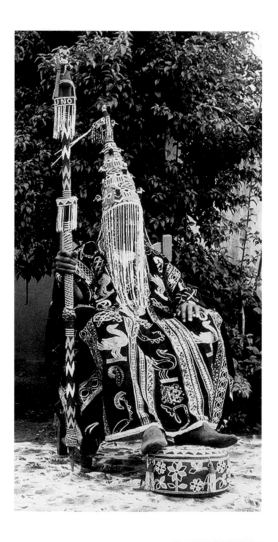

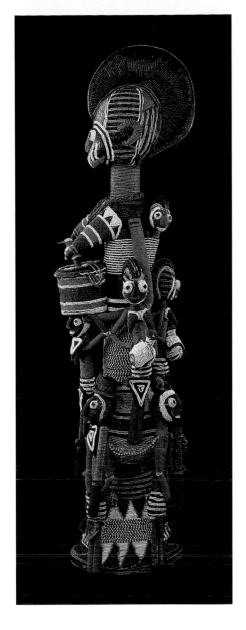

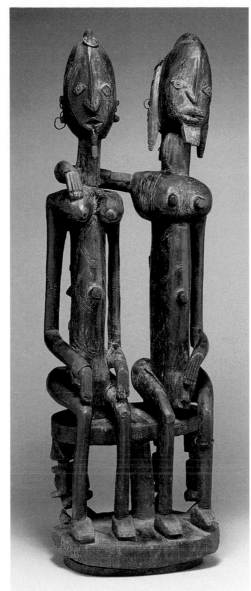

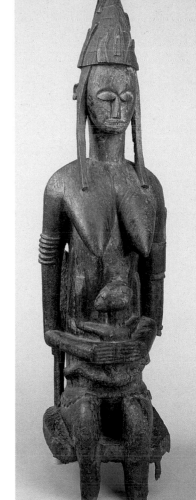

evenly spaced legs, the two bodies are almost mirror images of each other. Yet within this fundamental unity, differences appear. The man, slightly larger, speaks for the couple through his gestures, while the woman is quiet. His right hand touches her breast, suggesting her role as a nurturer. His left hand rests above his own genitals, signaling the idea of procreation. On her back, not visible here, she carries a child; on his back he carries a quiver. As often in African sculpture, abstraction is a clue here that the work does not represent specific people but spirits or ideas. He is the begetter, hunter, warrior, and protector; she is the life-bearer, mother, and nurturer. Together with their child they form a family, the basic unit of a Dogon community. The four small figures beneath the stool may refer to the support they receive from ancestors or other spirits. The carving probably would have been kept in a shrine, where it served as a kind of altar—a site for communication between this world and the world of spirits, including spirits of ancestors.

In many African cultures, men's and women's organizations play important roles. Such associations may be in charge of initiations, preparing young boys and girls for their adult roles. Others help govern their communities or provide spiritual services and counseling. The dignified figure here belonged to a Gwan or Jo society (**18.15**). Formed among the Bamana, who live in Mali to the southwest of the Dogon, these associations help women generally,

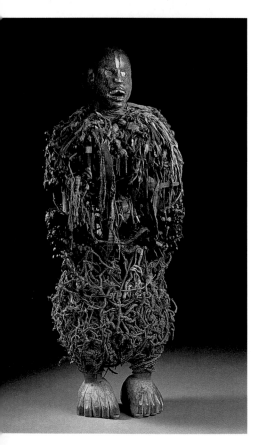

11.18 Baule spirit-spouse

11.10 Ejagham Leopard Society emblem

18.16 *Nkondi* figure. Lower Congo. Before 1878. Royal Museum for Central Africa, Tervuren.

especially those who have had trouble conceiving, bearing, or rearing children. With her regal bearing and downcast eyes, the seated figure seems to summon up strength from within herself. On her head is a cap hung with amulets. The cap marks her as an exceptional woman, for such caps are usually worn only by powerful male hunters or sorcerers. On her lap she holds a baby, carved so that it melts into her form; perhaps it is being formed *from* her. Above the child's upraised arms, full breasts promise nourishing milk. Displayed in annual festivals, the statue embodies the central wish of those who come to Gwan or Jo for help.

Art in Africa often serves as an agent in order to bring about some desired state of affairs, usually through contact with spirit powers. Among the most well known and visually compelling works of spiritual agency are the power figures, *minkisi* (singular *nkisi*, "medicine"), of the Kongo and neighboring peoples of central Africa (**18.16**). *Minkisi* are containers. They hold materials that allow a ritual specialist to harness the powers of the dead in the service of the living. Almost any container can be a *nkisi*, but the most famous *minkisi* outside of Africa are statues of ferocious hunters such as the one here. Called *minkondi* (singular *nkondi*), they hunt down and punish witches and wrongdoers.

A *nkondi* begins its life as a plain carved figure, commissioned from a sculptor like any other. To empower it, the ritual specialist adds packets of materials to its surface, materials linked to the dead and to the dire punishments the *nkondi* will be asked to inflict. Other materials may be added as well. Hunting nets tangled around the legs of the *nkondi* here remind him of his purpose, while mirrors in his eyes enable him to see approaching witches. Working on behalf of a client who has sought his help, or even a whole community, the specialist invokes and enrages the *nkondi* into action, particularly by driving iron nails or blades violently into it. Over the years, nails and other materials accumulate, offering visual testimony to the *nkondi*'s fearsome prowess.

The great African art of spiritual agency, and perhaps the greatest of African arts, is the masquerade. Involving sculpture, costume, music, and movement, a masquerade does not merely contact spirit powers to effect change; it brings the spirits themselves into the community. In Western museums, African masks are commonly exhibited and admired as sculpture. But in Africa a mask is never displayed in public as an isolated, inert object. It appears only in motion, only as the head or face of a spirit being that has appeared in the human community.

The mask photographed here is *nowo* (**18.17**), the guiding spirit of a Temne women's organization called Bondo, which regulates female affairs. Bondo prepares young girls for initiation into adult status and afterward presents them to the community as fully mature women. As in many African societies, young people deemed ready for initiation are taken from their families. Isolated together away from the community, they learn the secrets of adulthood and undergo physical ordeals. During this time, they are considered to be in a vulnerable "in between" condition, neither children nor adults. They need the protection, guidance, and sponsorship of spirits to make the transition successfully from one stage of life to the next.

Nowo appears here accompanied by several attendants as part of a Bondo ceremony. The lustrous black mask represents a Temne ideal of feminine beauty and modesty. The rings around the base are compared to the chrysalis of a moth: Just as the caterpillar emerges from its chrysalis transformed, so girls emerge from Bondo as women. The rings are also seen as ripples of water, for *nowo* is said to have risen out of the depths of a pool or river, where female spirits dwell. The white scarf tied to *nowo*'s elaborate hairstyle indicates her empathy for the initiates under her care, whose bodies are painted white during their isolation as a sign of their "in between" state.

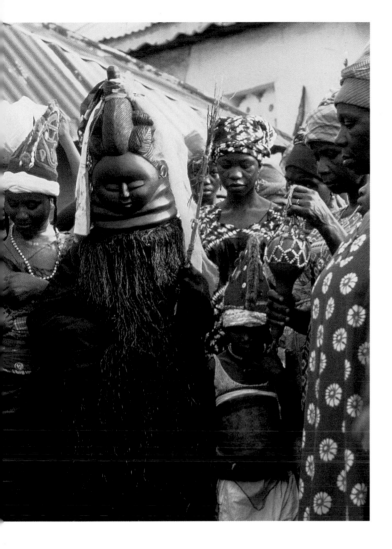

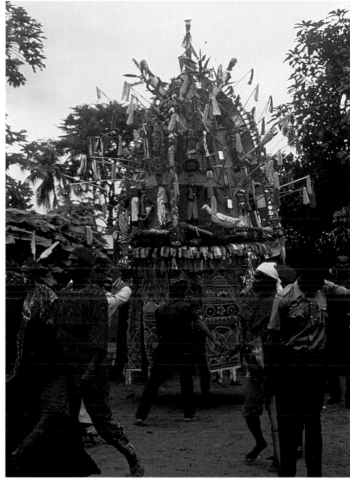

18.17 (left) Temne *nowo* masquerade with attendants, Sierra Leone, 1976.

18.18 (right) *Ijele* masquerade at an Igbo second burial ceremony, Achalla, Nigeria, 1983.

Even our preconceived ideas of what a mask *is* must be discarded when faced with the extraordinary spectacle of *ijele* (**18.18**). The most honored mask of the Igbo people of Nigeria, *ijele* appears at the funeral of an especially important man, welcoming his spirit to the other world and easing his transition from one stage of being to the next. The meanings of *ijele* are fluid and layered. In its towering aspect, *ijele* resembles an anthill—structures that in Africa may reach a height of 8 feet and which the Igbo regard as porches to the spirit world. *Ijele* is also a venerable tree, the symbol of life beneath whose branches wise elders meet to discuss weighty matters. Amid the tassels, mirrors, and flowers on *ijele*'s "branches" are numerous sculpted figures of people, animals, and other masks—a virtual catalogue of the Igbo and their world. Multiple large eyes suggest the watchfulness of the ever-present (though usually invisible) community of spirits. Majestic in appearance, *ijele* nevertheless moves with great energy, dipping, whirling, shaking, and turning. It is the great tree of meaning—of life itself—appearing briefly in the human community.

RELATED WORKS

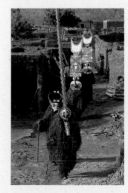

2.39 Bwa
masqueraders

CHAPTER NINETEEN

ARTS OF EAST ASIA: INDIA, CHINA, AND JAPAN

The previous chapter took us from the Mediterranean world into Asia with the spread of Islam to the east. This chapter continues our eastward journey with a brief look at three of the most influential civilizations of East Asia: India, China, and Japan.

In truth, these civilizations have already appeared "behind the scenes" many times in this story of art. Chapter 14, for example, pointed out that the regions of Mesopotamia and Egypt were in contact with each other from early on. But Mesopotamia was also in contact with India to the east, where an impressive civilization had arisen in the Indus River Valley. Akkadian writings from around 2300 B.C.E. mention the presence of Indus merchants and ships in Mesopotamia, along with their valuable goods of copper, gold, ivory, and pearls. Later, during the days of the Roman Empire, a long network of trade routes called the Silk Road allowed the citizens of Rome to enjoy the lacquerware and silk textiles of China. Rome had only the vaguest idea about where these exquisite products came from. China, more curious, avidly collected information about Rome and other Western lands. Still later, during the Renaissance, European explorers stumbled on the island nation of Japan. Japanese artists of the time delighted in recording the appearance of these exotic visitors from the West, whose customs were so strange.

Closer and more influential, however, were the contacts between these three Asian cultures themselves. China's greatest exports were writing, urban planning, administration, and philosophy, all of which it transmitted to Japan, together with styles of painting and architecture. India's greatest export was the religion of Buddhism, which travelers and missionaries brought over the Silk Road to China, and which then passed from China to Japan. With these paths of contact in mind, we begin our look at the arts of East Asia.

ARTS OF INDIA

The area of India's historical territories is so large and distinct that it is often referred to as a subcontinent. Another name for it is South Asia. Jutting out in a great triangle from the Asian landmass, South Asia is bordered along most of its northern frontier by the Himalaya Mountains, the tallest mountain range in the world. To the northwest, the mountain range known as the Hindu Kush gradually descends to the fertile valley of the Indus River, in present-day Pakistan.

Indus Valley Civilization

Like the Tigris and Euphrates in Mesopotamia and the Nile in Egypt, the Indus River provided water for irrigation and a central artery for transportation and travel. Cities arose along its length around 2600 B.C.E., or roughly the same time as Sumerian civilization developed in Mesopotamia. The engineering skills of the Indus architects were quite advanced. The most famous Indus city, Mohenjo-Daro, was built on stone foundations, with straight, stone-paved streets laid out in a grid pattern. Houses constructed of fired brick were connected to a citywide drainage system.

The Indus people did not bury their dead with troves of precious objects, and thus we do not have an extensive record of their art. One of the most intriguing sculptures to have been found is this small sandstone torso (**19.1**). The softly modeled, rounded forms contrast dramatically with the armor-like musculature of ancient Mediterranean sculpture, reflecting a different way of thinking about the body. Later Indian sculpture will continue in this same vein. Scholars have interpreted the relaxed abdomen as a sign that the Indus people practiced the breathing exercises we know from later Indian culture as a component of yoga, the system of physical self-mastery that can be used to lead to spiritual insights.

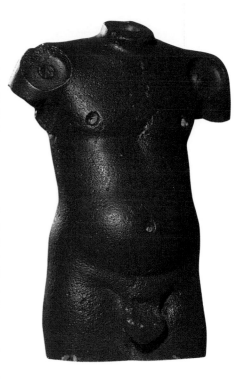

19.1 Torso, from Harappa. Indus Valley civilization, c. 2000 B.C.E. Red sandstone, height 3¾". National Museum, New Delhi.

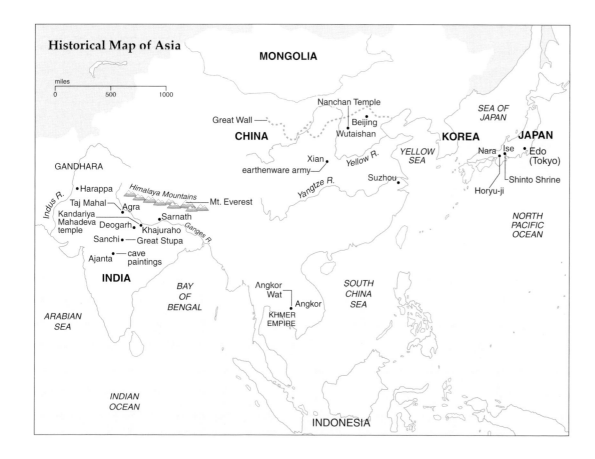

Historical Map of Asia

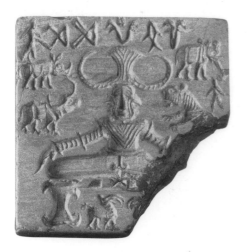

A meditating yogi certainly seems to be the subject of this small, slightly damaged seal (**19.2**). Thousands of such seals have been found. Carved of steatite stone, they served to stamp an impression in wax or clay. At the top of the seal is an inscription. Scholars have not been able to decipher the Indus writing system, and anything it has to tell us about Indus culture must remain a mystery. His knees outspread, his feet tucked back and crossed, the yogi sits in the classic Indian pose of meditation familiar from later images of the Buddha. Other aspects of the image—the headdress with its curved horns and the small animals in the background—suggest the later Hindu god Shiva. We saw Shiva in his guise as Nataraja in Chapter 1 (see 1.9), but in another guise he is known as Lord of Beasts.

Indus culture began to disintegrate around 1900 B.C.E. Until recently, scholars believed that the cities were conquered by invaders entering the subcontinent from the northwest, a nomadic people who called themselves Aryas, "noble ones." New findings have overturned the idea of conquest, suggesting instead that Mohenjo-Daro was abandoned after the Indus River changed its course and that other cities were ruined when a parallel river ran dry. During these same centuries, the Aryas began to arrive.

Buddhism and Its Art

Beginning around 800 B.C.E., urban centers again arose in northern India, and by the 6th century B.C.E. numerous principalities had taken shape. During this time, Aryan religious practice became increasingly complex. The priestly class of Aryan society, brahmins, grew powerful, for only they understood the complicated sacrificial rituals that were now required. Brahmins also began to impose rigid ideas about social order derived from the Vedas, their sacred texts. Disturbed by these developments, many sages and philosophers of the day sought a different path, preaching social equality and a more direct and personal access to the spiritual realm. Of these numerous leaders, the one who has had the most lasting impact on the world was Siddhartha Gautama, later known as the Buddha.

Gautama was born a prince of the Shaka clan in northern India, near present-day Nepal. His dates are traditionally given as 563–483 B.C.E., although recent research suggests that he lived slightly later, dying around 400 B.C.E. According to tradition, his life was transformed when a series of chance encounters brought him face to face with suffering, sickness, and mortality.

19.2 (above) "Yogi" seal, from Mohenjodaro. Indus Valley civilization, 2300–1750 B.C.E. Steatite.
National Museum, New Delhi.

19.3 (below) Great Stupa, Sanchi, India. Sunga and early Andhra periods, 3rd century B.C.E.–1st century C.E.

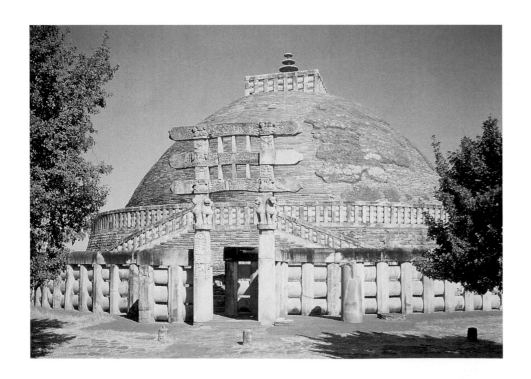

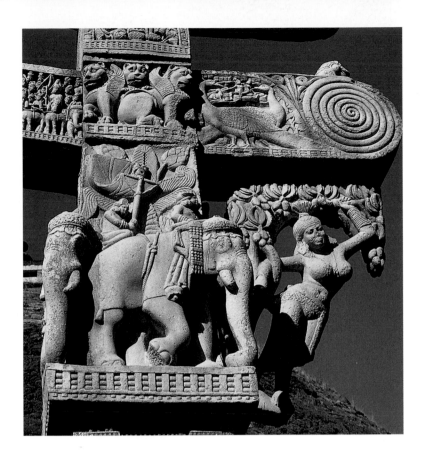

19.4 Detail of east gate with *yakshi*. Great Stupa, Sanchi. Early Andhra period, 1st century B.C.E. Sandstone, height of figure 5'.

These, he realized, were our common fate. What is to be done? Renouncing his princely comforts, he studied with the spiritual masters of the day and tried every accepted path to understanding, but to no avail. He withdrew into meditation until one day, finally, everything became clear. He was *buddha,* "awakened."

Buddha accepted the belief, current in the India of his day, that time is cyclical and that all beings, even gods and demons, are condemned to suffer an endless series of lives unless they can gain release from the cycle. His insight was that we are kept chained to the world by desire. His solution was to extinguish desire by cultivating nonattachment, and to this end he proposed an eightfold path of moral and ethical behavior. By following this path we too may awake, see through the veil of illusion to the true nature of the world, and free ourselves from the cycle of life, death, and rebirth.

Buddha attracted followers from all walks of life, from beggars to kings, both men and women. After his death, his cremated remains were distributed among eight memorial mounds called stupas. During the 3rd century B.C.E., a Buddhist king named Ashoka called for these remains to be redistributed among a much larger number of stupas, including this one at Sanchi (**19.3**). A stupa is a solid earthen mound faced with stone. Over it rises a stylized parasol that symbolically shelters and honors the relics buried inside. Pilgrims come to be near the energy that is believed to emanate from the Buddha's remains. They visit the stupa by ritually walking around it. The two stone fences evident in the photograph, one at ground level and one higher up, enclose paths for circling the stupa.

Four gateways erected late in the 1st century B.C.E. punctuate the outer enclosure at Sanchi. Their crossbars are carved in relief with stories from the Buddha's life. Numerous figures ornament the gateways, including this voluptuous female (**19.4**). This is probably a *yakshi,* a nature spirit embodying ideas of fertility and abundance. The *yakshi* is not part of the Buddhist faith but belongs to older and more widespread Indian beliefs. The female form was considered auspicious in Indian thought. It was even held that women were able

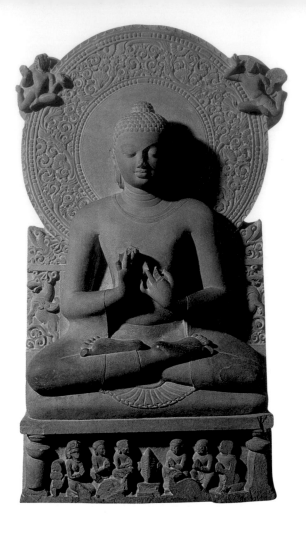

19.5 *Buddha Preaching the First Sermon*, from Sarnath. c. 465–85 C.E. Sandstone, height 5'3". Archaeological Museum, Sarnath.

to cause trees to blossom or bear fruit. The *yakshi* here enlaces her arms in a mango tree, which has blossomed at the sound of her laughter. Together with her numerous companions on the other gateways, she showers blessings of abundance on the site and all who enter it.

Interestingly, the reliefs at Sanchi that narrate the story of the Buddha do so without showing the Buddha himself. Early Buddhist art avoided depicting the Buddha directly. Instead, sculptors indicated his presence through symbols. A pair of footprints, for example, indicated the ground where he walked; a parasol indicated space he occupied. Nevertheless, the Buddhist community must eventually have felt the need for an image to focus their thoughts, for toward the end of the 1st century C.E. such images began to appear.

Several artistic centers in India were famous for images of the Buddha, and their styles are distinct. The statue here was carved in the 5th century C.E. in the workshops at Sarnath, in northern India (**19.5**). Typical of Sarnath style, the robe the Buddha wears molds itself discretely to the smooth, perfected surfaces of his body. The neckline and the hanging sleeves are almost the only signs that he is wearing a robe at all. Seated in the pose of meditation, the Buddha forms the *mudras* (hand gesture) that indicates preaching. He is understood to be preaching his first sermon, known as the Sermon at Deer Park (note the two deer carved in relief to either side of him).

The workshops at Sarnath were patronized by the Gupta dynasty. Based in central India, these rulers had brought many of the regional kingdoms of the subcontinent into an empire. The Gupta period, which lasted from around 320 to 647 C.E., is regarded as a high point in Indian culture. During this time, Buddhism attained its greatest influence and often benefited from royal patronage, which enabled larger and more expensive projects to be undertaken. One of the most extraordinary projects was realized at Ajanta, in central

THE EARLY BUDDHA IMAGE

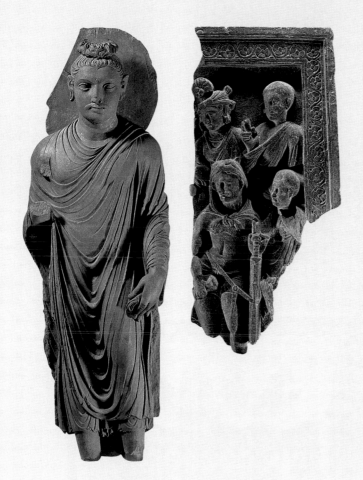

THE EARLY ART of Buddhism did not include an image of its founder. Instead, in such works as the relief carvings at Sanchi (see 19.3, 19.4), the Buddha was represented by symbolic traces of his presence. Thus, an empty chair represented his seated presence, and a pathway represented him walking. That artists should have avoided depicting the Buddha directly is not so surprising. After all, the entire point of his teaching was that he was in his last earthly life. Henceforth, he would have no bodily form. Besides, the Buddha had lived 550 lives before his final one. Clearly he had passed through many bodily forms.

So we may well wonder why images of the Buddha began to appear when and where they did, in northern India during the 1st century C.E. One of the reasons has to do with changes in Buddhism itself. By this time, the Buddha was no longer thought of as an exemplary man but as a god, and his followers now wanted an image to help them focus their devotion. Another reason was the artistic heritage of Greece.

What does Greece have to do with India? During the 4th century B.C.E., the Macedonian Greek conqueror Alexander the Great led his armies not only through Egypt and the Persian Empire, but all the way to the Indus River in South Asia. For centuries afterward, regions bordering on India were part of the extensive Hellenistic world. Hellenistic culture was particularly vital in a region called Bactria, which bordered the mountains of the Hindu Kush. During the 1st century B.C.E., Bactria was conquered by a people of Chinese origin called the Kushans, who eventually established an empire that reached across northern India, where they encountered and embraced Buddhism. Having no monumental art of their own, the Kushans also embraced the Hellenistic culture of Bactria.

The Greeks had long envisioned their gods in sculpture as perfected humans. Under Kushan rulers, this Hellenistic heritage and the desire for an image of the Buddha merged in fascinating figures such as the one shown here. Modeled on statues of the Greek god Apollo, who was typically portrayed as a handsome youth, the Buddha stands in gentle contrapposto, the great contribution of the Greeks to art. His robe, reminiscent of a Roman toga, hangs in heavy folds over a naturalistically muscled body. The fragment of the relief illustrated to the right offers something even more surprising: a guardian of the Buddha dressed in a lion skin like the Greek hero Hercules and holding a thunderbolt like the Greek god Zeus! This fascinating Hellenistic-Indian hybrid style disappeared with the end of the Kushan Empire in the 3rd century C.E., but its effects were lasting. Contrapposto spread throughout India, where it is a prominent feature of later Hindu art. And the Buddha image was started on its long history.

(left) *Standing Buddha,* from Takht-i-Bahi, Gandhara. Kushan period, c. 100 C.E. Schist, height 35⅞". The British Museum, London. (right) *Vajrapani, Guardian of the Buddha, as Hercules.* Fragment of a relief from Gandhara. 1st century C.E. Stone, height 21¼". The British Museum, London.

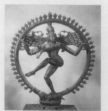

1.9 Shiva

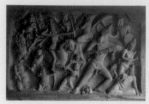

11.13 Durga

India, where a series of halls, shrines, and residences for monks were hollowed out from an exposed cliff face. Murals ornamenting the walls of these sculpted caves are among the earliest examples of Indian painting to have come down to us. The detail illustrated here depicts the bodhisattva Padmapani, an image so lovely that it has become known as *The "Beautiful Bodhisattva"* (**19.6**). Bodhisattvas are saintly beings who have delayed their own release in order to help others attain enlightenment. Padmapani is a special form of Avalokiteshvara, whom we met in Chapter 11 (see 11.3). Known as the Lotus-Giver, he is shown here holding a lotus blossom in his right hand and a begging bowl in his left. His hair is piled high, and he wears the jewels of a prince. His smooth, languorous body resembles that of the Buddha image from Sarnath (19.5), and it illustrates well the refined Gupta style in painting. The artist has given unforgettable form to the compassion a perfected being feels for the rest of humanity, still trapped in the world's illusions.

Hinduism and Its Art

The Gupta rulers who patronized Buddhist art so lavishly were Hindu, as was the local dynasty that sponsored the creation of the magnificent Ajanta caves. Hinduism would become the dominant religion of India over the coming centuries, and Buddhism, having already spread to China and Southeast Asia, would virtually disappear from the land of its birth.

Hinduism developed as the older Vedic religion, with its brahmins and its emphasis on ritual sacrifice, evolved in its thinking and mingled with local Indian beliefs, probably including those hinted at in ancient Indus art. Like Buddhism, Hinduism has at its core a belief in the cyclical nature of time, including the cosmic cycles of the creation, destruction, and rebirth of the world and the briefer cycles of our own repeating lives within it. The ultimate goal is liberation from these cycles into a permanent state of pure consciousness.

19.6 (left) *The "Beautiful Bodhisattva,"* from Cave 1, Ajanta. c. 462–500 C.E. Fresco, detail.

19.7 (right) *Vishnu Dreaming the Universe,* relief panel, temple of Vishnu, Deogarh, Uttar Pradesh. Early 6th century C.E.

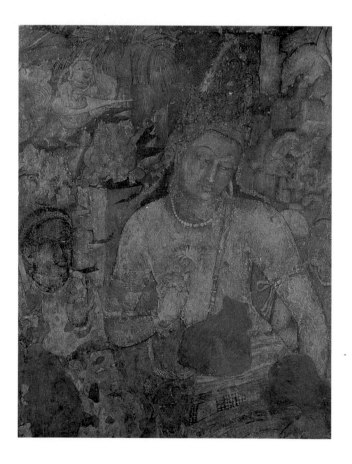

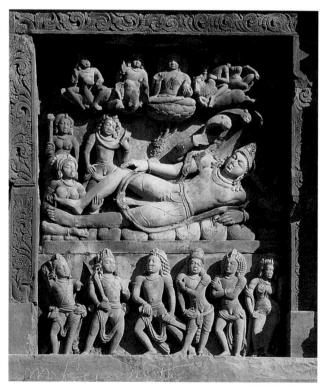

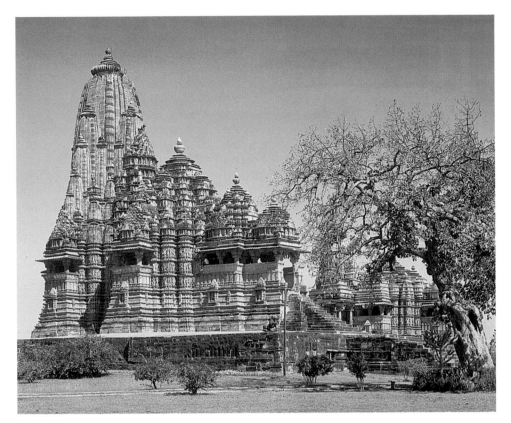

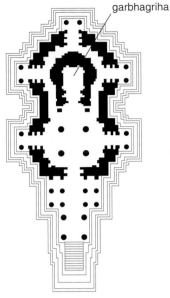

garbhagriha

This liberation will be granted to us by a god in return for our devotion. Strictly speaking, Hinduism is not one religion but many related faiths, each one taking its own deity as supreme. We have met two of the three principal deities of Hinduism in earlier chapters of this book, the god Shiva (see 1.9) and the goddess Devi or Shakti ("power"), whom we saw in her manifestation as Durga (see 11.13). The third principal deity is Vishnu.

Carved in stone, the relief illustrated here depicts Vishnu dreaming the world into existence (**19.7**). Wearing his characteristic cylindrical crown, he slumbers on the coiled serpent of infinity, Ananta. The goddess Lakshmi holds his foot. She represents the female side of his energy. Moved by her, Vishnu dreams the god Brahma into existence. Brahma appears at the center of the uppermost row of figures, sitting in a meditative pose on a lotus blossom that is understood to grow from Vishnu's navel. Brahma in turn will create the world of space and time by thinking, "May I become Many." In the smooth surfaces of Vishnu's body, delicately set with jewelry, we see the Gupta style in a Hindu setting.

This relief appears on the exterior of one of the earliest surviving Hindu stone temples, a small structure dating from around 500 C.E. Temple architecture evolved rapidly over the ensuing centuries, and by 1000 C.E. monumental forms had been perfected. A masterpiece of the monumental temple as it developed in northern India is the Kandariya Mahadeva (**19.8, 19.9**). Dedicated to Shiva, the temple rests on a stone platform that serves to mark out a sacred area and separate it from the everyday world. Visitors climb the stairs, visible to the right, and proceed through a series of three halls, each of which is distinguished on the exterior by a pyramidal roof. These roofs grow progressively taller, culminating in a majestic curving tower called a *shikhara*. Conceived as a cosmic mountain ringed around with lesser peaks, the *shikhara* rises over the heart of the temple, a small, dark, cavelike chamber called a *garbhagriha* ("womb-house"). The *garbhagriha* houses a statue of the deity, a statue in which the god is believed to be truly present.

19.8 (left) Kandariya Mahadeva temple, Khajuraho, Madhya Pradesh, India. c. 1000 C.E.

19.9 (right) Plan of the Kandariya Mahadeva temple.

RELATED WORKS

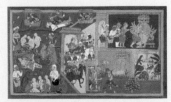

3.15 *Ramayana* illustration

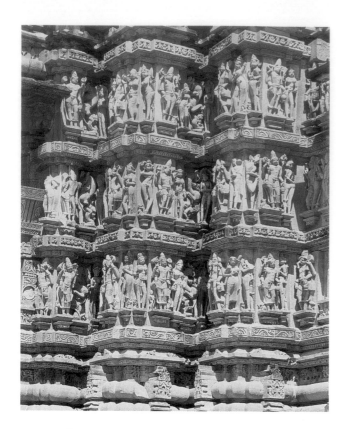

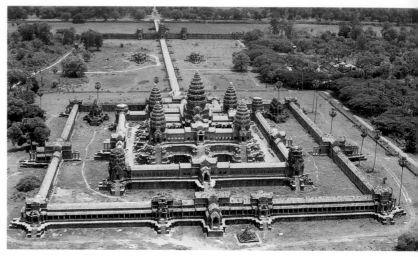

19.10 (left) Exterior detail of the Kandariya Mahadeva temple.

19.11 (right) Central temple complex at Angkor Wat, Cambodia. c. 1113–50. C.E.

Indian architects worked with post-and-lintel construction techniques, and thus the interior spaces of Hindu temples are not large. They do not need to be, for Hindu religious practice is not based in congregational worship. Instead, devotees approach the deity individually with such gifts as flowers, food, and incense. These are offered as sacrifices by a brahmin, who receives them at the entrance to the *garbhagriha*.

Like the form of the temple itself, the sculptures on its exterior represent the energies of the god radiating outward into the world. The myriad Hindu gods and goddesses in their many guises are favorite subjects. On northern temples such as the Kandariya Mahadeva, voluptuous women and sensuous loving couples are depicted as well (**19.10**). The presence of women is mandated in the texts that guided northern architects, and it demonstrates how belief in such auspicious presences as *yakshi* (see 19.4) found a place in Hinduism.

From as early as the 2nd century B.C.E., India exerted an influence on developing cultures in Southeast Asia. Kingdoms of Southeast Asia adopted both Buddhism and Hinduism, and they created their own styles of the art forms that came with them. Among the greatest architectural treasures of Southeast Asia is Angkor, the capital of the Khmer kingdom. The Khmer kingdom dominated the region of present-day Cambodia and much of the surrounding area between the 9th and 15th centuries. Taking the title *devaraja*, "god-king," Khmer rulers identified themselves with a deity such as Vishnu, Shiva, or the bodhisattva Lokeshvara. A temple erected to the deity was also thus a temple erected to the king, who was viewed as one of the deity's earthly manifestations. The finest and largest example is the beautiful temple complex known as Angkor Wat (**19.11**).

SAVING ANGKOR WAT

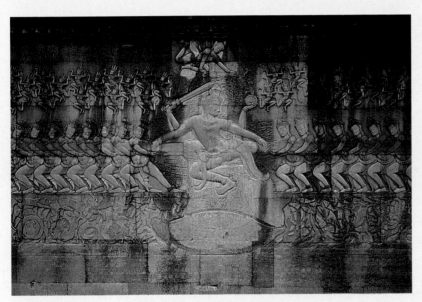

H ERE IS THE challenge: An ancient temple, magical in its beauty and thick with magnificent sculptures, is located deep inside a jungle. The climate is tropical—hot, humid, subject to monsoon rains. Algae and fungi grow unchecked, loving the moist atmosphere. Plants of all kinds flourish, boring their roots under and around temple stones, climbing the walls, penetrating every crevice. Bats proliferate, and their acidic droppings eat away the rock. Colonies of insects build their nests in the ground, in the cracks, in the delicate features of stone reliefs. When the rains come, water seeps through any opening, causing further erosion of the stone.

To make matters worse, the temple attracts other sorts of predators, predators encouraged not by the climate but by the treasures to be found inside. Because the temple complex is very large and difficult to guard, thieves regularly plunder the site for whatever artworks they can cut and carry away to sell to eager collectors. If a whole sculpture cannot be removed conveniently, looters simply slice off a portion. There are many headless statues in this temple.

Is that all? No, not quite. This temple happens to be located in Cambodia, in an area that has endured warfare variously involving government troops, the communist Khmer Rouge, the Vietnamese, and even the Americans. Bullet holes and mortar wounds give testimony to the fact that Angkor Wat stands in a battle zone.

The Khmer people abandoned their old capital at Angkor in the 15th century. Apparently, the site was more or less forgotten until 1861, when the French, who had colonized the region, rediscovered Angkor and literally hacked it out of the jungle. French researchers worked on the vast site for a century, slowly restoring monument after monument even as they carted artistic treasures back to France for display in museums, standard practice for the time. During the 1970s, as Khmer Rouge insurgents grew increasingly murderous, the French researchers fled the country. A few years later, the Vietnamese invaded, ousting the Khmer Rouge from power and occupying Cambodia for ten years. The Communist government they installed invited "friendly" countries to continue work on Angkor, with the jewel of the city, Angkor Wat, being awarded to India.

The world first got a look at the results in 1989, when the Vietnamese ended their occupation and negotiations sponsored by the United Nations began to envision a stable and peaceful future for Cambodia. Many experts were angered by what they saw. Indian teams had cleaned the structures too aggressively, they said, scrubbing off exquisite artistic details along with vegetation. Cracks had been repaired with cement.

In 1993 the United Nations Educational, Scientific, and Cultural Organization (UNESCO) added Angkor to its list of World Heritage sites. Since then, the former capital of the Khmer empire has been the focus of international efforts. A dozen nations currently contribute funding and conservation teams, including France, Japan, Indonesia, Germany, China, Switzerland, and the United States. Tourists are newly welcome at the site, bringing in much-needed revenue. And as of this writing, India has again been invited to participate.

Bas-relief sculpture at Angkor Wat, depicting the god Vishnu in the story called "Churning the Sea of Milk." The relief has been partially cleaned.

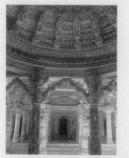

13.20 Interior, Jain temple

Built in the early 12th century under the patronage of the god-king Suryavarman II and dedicated to Vishnu, Angkor Wat consists of five shrines on a raised, pyramidal stone "mountain." Each shrine houses a *garbhagriha*, the womblike dwelling place of the deity. Colonnaded galleries connect and enclose the five shrines, their walls carved with reliefs depicting dancing figures, celestial beings, and the many guises and adventures of Vishnu. Visitors approach the complex by a long walkway that originally crossed over a surrounding moat. Like Hindu temples in India, the plan of Angkor Wat is based in a mandala, a diagram of a cosmic realm, and thus the entire site reflects the meaning and order of the spiritual universe.

Jain Art

The Jain religion traces its beginnings to a sage named Mahavira, who lived during the 6th century B.C.E. Like the Buddha, Mahavira left the comforts of home in his youth to pursue spiritual wisdom. Upon achieving enlightenment, he became known as the Jina, or "victor." In the religion developed by his followers, Mahavira is considered to have been the last in a line of twenty-four Jinas. Unlike Buddhism, the Jain religion did not become a world faith, yet within India it has remained an important presence.

In Chapter 13, we looked at the interior of a Jain temple (see 13.20). The hundreds of Jain temples constructed between the 11th and 16th centuries testify to the wealth of the merchants and traders who were the primary adherents of the Jain faith. Jains also commissioned thousands of illuminated manuscripts for donation to temple libraries (**19.12**). The scene reproduced here is from a manuscript of the *Kalpa Sutra*, a work that narrates the lives of the Jain saints. The restricted palette dominated by saturated red and blue is typical of Jain manuscripts. As in later Indian painting, position and overlap are the primary clues to spatial depth. The decorative flatness of the style alternates easily with passages of text, so readers pass from reading words to reading images with little sense of a shift in visual "gears." Wiry, linear drawing and oddly protruding eyes give the figures a sense of great alertness and spiritual energy.

19.12 (left) Detail of a leaf with *The Birth of Mahavira*, from the *Kalpa Sutra*. Gujarat, c. 1400 C.E. Opaque watercolor on paper, 3⅜ × 3".
Prince of Wales Museum, Bombay.

19.13 (right) Ritual wine vessel, *jia*. Late Shang period. Bronze, height 13½".
Nelson-Atkins Museum of Art, Kansas City, Missouri.

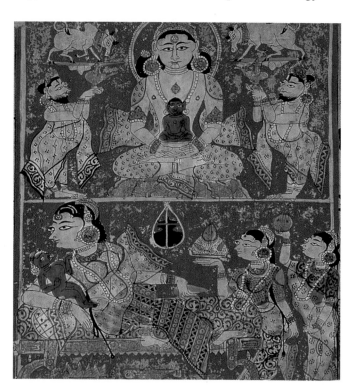

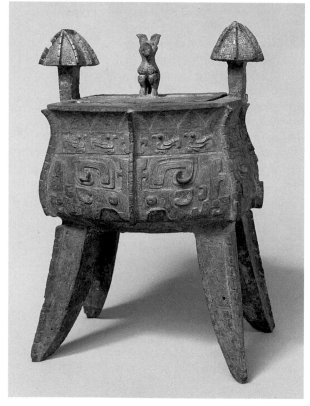

Mughal Art and Influence

A new culture developed in India with the arrival of the Mughals, an Islamic people from Central Asia who established an empire on the subcontinent beginning in the 16th century. Like most Islamic groups from Central Asia, the Mughals were influenced by Persian culture. In India, Persian forms mingled with Indian elements to create a uniquely Indian form of Islamic art. The most beloved work of Mughal architecture is the Taj Mahal (see 13.18). In Chapters 13 and 18, we pointed out the Persian aspects of the monument: its *iwan* entryways, its central domed interior, and its crowning ornamental onion-shaped dome. (To review the form of an *iwan*, see 18.3.) Looking at the building again, you can see that it rests on a stone platform in the manner of Hindu temples. The open, domed pavilions that sit on the roof and cap the four minarets are *chattri*, a traditional embellishment of Indian palaces.

Illustrated books were a second great Persian artistic tradition. The Mughal painting atelier was directed by Persian painters, who introduced new techniques, styles, subjects, and materials to the subcontinent. The influence of such Mughal masterpieces as the *Hamzanama* (see 2.7) was felt in Indian courts, where painters absorbed the Mughal love of detail and jewel-toned palette while retaining the decorative flatness and saturated color of earlier Indian manuscript painting (see 19.12). An example of the new style that resulted is *Maharana Amar Singh II, Prince Sangram Singh, and Courtiers Watch the Performance of an Acrobat and Musicians* (4.42).

1.8 Manohar, *Jahangir and Khusrau*

2.7 *Hamzanama* illustration

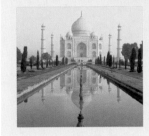

13.18 Taj Mahal

ARTS OF CHINA

Unlike India, China is not protected to the north by intimidating mountains. The vast and vulnerable northern frontier is one of the themes of Chinese history, for it resulted in a constant stream of influence and interaction. Peaceful contacts produced fruitful exchanges between China, India, Central Asia, and Persia. But repeated invasion and conquest from the north also shaped Chinese thinking and Chinese art.

Fundamental features of the Chinese landscape are the three great rivers that water its heartland, the Yellow in the north and the Yangtze and the Xi in the south. The Yellow River is traditionally spoken of as the "cradle of Chinese civilization." Advanced Neolithic cultures built settlements along the Yellow River from around 5000 B.C.E., yet recent archaeological research has found Neolithic sites together with artifacts in jade and ceramic over a much broader area, giving us a more complicated and still incomplete picture of the early stages of Chinese culture. All we can say now is that over time these many distinct Neolithic cultures seem to have merged.

The Formative Period: Shang to Qin

The history of China begins firmly with the Shang dynasty (c. 1500–c. 1050 B.C.E.), whose kings ruled from a series of capitals in the Yellow River Valley. Archaeologists have discovered foundations of their palaces and walled cities, and excavations of royal tombs have yielded thousands of works in jade, lacquer, ivory, precious metals, and bronze. The illustration here shows a bronze *jia*, a vessel for wine (**19.13**). Valued and valuable possessions of elite families, bronze vessels were used at banquets for ritual offerings of food to ancestors. Visible on each side of the *jia* is the most famous and mysterious of Shang decorative motifs, the stylized animal or monster face known as *taotie*. Its two horns curling away from the raised center axis are clearly distinguishable, as are the staring eyes just beneath them. The *taotie* may relate to shamanism,

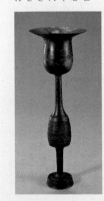

1.5 Stemmed vessel

the practice of communicating with the spirit world through animal go-betweens. Birds appear in a band above the *taotie*, the legs of the vessel are decorated with stylized dragons, and an animal of some kind sits on the lid. Whether directly associated with shamanism or not, animals both fantastic and real are a haunting presence in Shang art.

Around 1050 B.C.E. the Shang were conquered by their neighbors to the northwest, the Zhou, who ruled for the next 800 years. The first 300 years of this longest dynasty were peaceful. During later centuries, however, the states over which the Zhou presided grew increasingly independent and treacherous, finally descending into open warfare. The deteriorating situation inspired much thought about how a stable society could be organized. One of the philosophers of the day was Confucius, who lived around the turn of the 5th century B.C.E. His ideas about human conduct and just rule would later be placed at the very center of Chinese culture.

In 221 B.C.E., the state of Qin (pronounced "chin") claimed victory over the other states, uniting all of China into an empire for the first time. The first emperor, Shihuangdi, was obsessed with attaining immortality. Work on his underground burial site began even before he united China and continued until his death. The mound covering the burial itself has always been visible, but the accidental discovery in 1974 of a buried terra-cotta army guarding it was one of the most electrifying moments in 20th-century archaeology (**19.14**). Row upon row the lifesize figures stand in their thousands—soldiers, archers, cavalrymen, and charioteers—facing east, the direction from which danger was expected to come. Time has bleached them to a ghostly gray, but when they were new, they were painted in lifelike colors, for only by being as realistic as possible could they effectively protect the emperor's tomb behind them, about half a mile to the west.

19.14 View of Pit no. 1, part of the "terra-cotta army" surrounding the tomb-mound of the First Emperor of Qin (d. 210 B.C.E.).

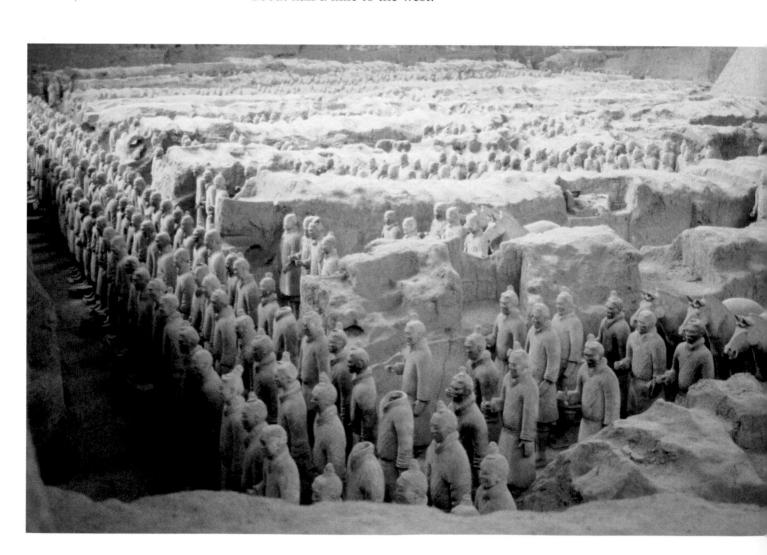

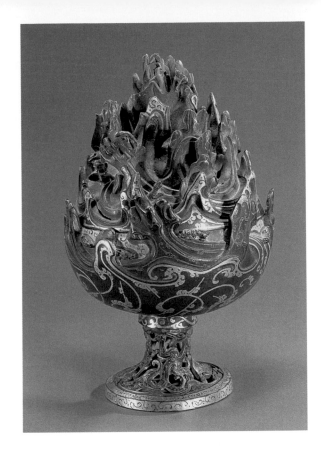

19.15 Incense burner from the tomb of Prince Liu Sheng, Mancheng, Hebei. Han dynasty, 113 B.C.E. Bronze with gold inlay, height 10¼".
Hebei Provincial Museum, Shijiazhuang.

Confucianism and Daoism: Han and Six Dynasties

Our name for China comes from the first dynasty, Qin. Chinese historians, however, reviled the Qin for their brutal rule. Ethnic Chinese instead refer to themselves as Han people, after the dynasty that overthrew the Qin. Han rule endured, with one brief interruption, from 206 B.C.E. to 220 C.E. During these centuries many features of Chinese culture came into focus, including the central roles played by two systems of thought, Confucianism and Daoism.

The philosophy of Confucius is pragmatic; its principal concern is the creation of a peaceful society. Correct and respectful relations among people are the key, beginning within the family, then extending outward and upward all the way to the emperor. Han rulers adopted Confucianism as the offical state philosophy, in the process elaborating it into a sort of religion in which social order was linked to cosmic order.

Confucius urged people to honor ancestors and Heaven, as the Zhou deity was called. Apart from that, he had little to say about spiritual matters. For answers to questions about what lies beyond the physical world, the Chinese turned to Daoism. Daoism is concerned with bringing human life into harmony with nature. A *dao* is a "way" or "path." The Dao is the Way of the Universe, a current that flows through all creation. The goal of Daoism is to understand the Way and be carried along by it, and not to fight it by striving. The first Daoist text, the famous *Dao De Jing* ("the Way and its power") dates to around 500 B.C.E.; the materials it draws together are much older.

Among scholars, Daoism continued as a philosophy, but on a popular level it also became a religion; and in doing so it absorbed many folk beliefs, deities, and mystical concerns, including the search for immortality. The incense burner shown here, found in the tomb of a Han prince, portrays the Daoist paradise, the Isle of the Immortals in the Eastern Sea (**19.15**). A close look amid the crags of the mountainous island gradually reveals myriad small people, animals, and birds. They are the happy beings who have discovered

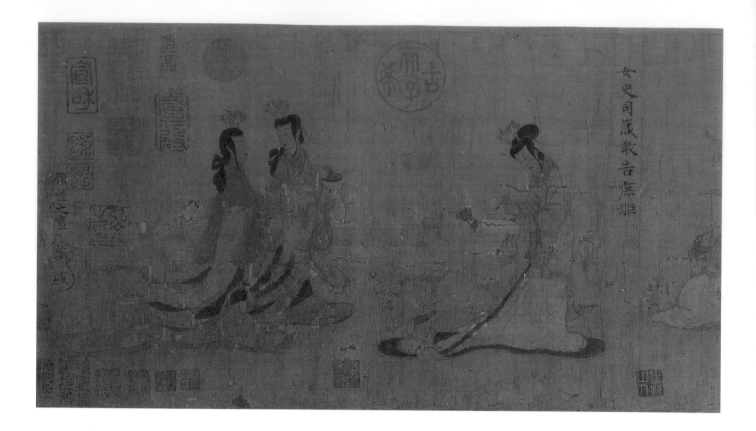

19.16 Attributed to Gu Kaizhi. *Admonitions of the Instructress to the Ladies of the Palace*, detail. Handscroll, ink and color on silk; height 9¾". Tang (?) copy after a 4th-century original.
The British Museum, London.

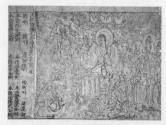
the secret of immortality. Stylized waves inlaid in gold swirl around the base. Smoke from burning incense would have wreathed the island in clouds of fog, adding to its otherworldly appearance.

Not long after the end of the Han dynasty, invaders from inner Asia conquered the northern part of China. The imperial court fled to the south. For the next 250 years, China was divided. Numerous kingdoms—many under non-Chinese rulers—rose and fell in the north, while six weak dynasties succeeded each other in the south. For the educated elite, philosophical Daoism provided an escape route. To converse brilliantly, to wander the landscape, to drink and write poetry—these were suitable occupations for those who were alienated by debased times. Nevertheless, Confucianism, with its stern emphasis on duty to society, remained the official ideal, and Confucian themes continued to appear in art.

A famous example is the handscroll known as *Admonitions of the Instructress to the Ladies of the Palace*, attributed to the 4th-century painter Gu Kaizhi (**19.16**; to review the handscroll format see page 114). *Admonitions* illustrates a series of Confucian lessons in correct behavior for court ladies. In the very last scene, shown here, the instructress is portrayed writing down her words of wisdom. To the left, two court ladies glide in to witness the event, their robes fluttering gracefully behind them. With its thin, even lines and sparing use of color, the style of the painting is typical of the 4th century. There is no hint of a setting, and only the sensitive placement of the figures suggests depth.

The Age of Buddhism: Tang

Buddhism had begun to filter into China during the Han dynasty, when missionaries from India arrived over the Silk Road. During the Six Dynasties period, it spread increasingly through the divided north and south. When China was reunited under the Sui dynasty (581–618 C.E.), the new emperor was a devout Buddhist; and during the first century of the Tang dynasty (618–906 C.E.), virtually the entire country adopted the Buddhist religion, and vast quantities of art were created for the thousands of monasteries, temples, and shrines that were founded.

The most popular form of Buddhism in China was the sect called Pure Land, named for the Western Paradise where the buddha Amitabha dwells. The fragment of a hanging scroll illustrated here (**19.17**) portrays a bodhisattva leading the soul of a fashionably plump, well-dressed little Tang lady to her eternal reward in the Western Paradise, imagined in the upper left corner as a Chinese palace. The magnificently attired bodhisattva is a Chinese fantasy of an Indian prince. In his right hand he holds an incense burner. His left hand holds a lotus flower and a white temple banner. Flowers fall about the couple, symbols of holiness and grace.

Much Buddhist art of the Tang dynasty was destroyed during the 9th century, when Buddhism was briefly persecuted as a "foreign" religion. One building that somehow escaped destruction is the Nanchan Temple (**19.18**). Little Chinese architecture has survived from before 1400, and thus the Nanchan Temple, though small, takes on added importance. Like all important buildings in China, the Nanchan Temple is raised above ground level by a stone platform. Wooden columns capped by bracket sets bear the weight of the tiled roof with its broad overhanging eaves. (To review the structural system of Chinese architecture, see page 315.) The gentle curve of the roof draws our eyes upward to the ridge, where two ornaments based on upsweeping fishtails serve symbolically to protect the building from fire.

The same basic principles and forms served Chinese architects for temples, palaces, and residences. Multiplied a hundredfold, this pleasing, sturdy temple lets us imagine the grandeur of the multistoried palaces of the Tang just as the painted bodhisattva, multiplied into a cast of hundreds, lets us imagine the vanished murals that were the glory of Tang Buddhist art.

19.17 (left) *Bodhisattva Guide of Souls.* Tang dynasty, late 9th century C.E. Ink and colors on silk, height 31⅜".
The British Museum, London.

19.18 (right) Nanchan Temple, Wutaishan, Shanxi. Tang dynasty, 782 C.E.

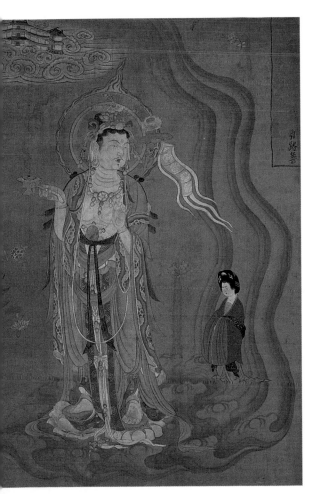

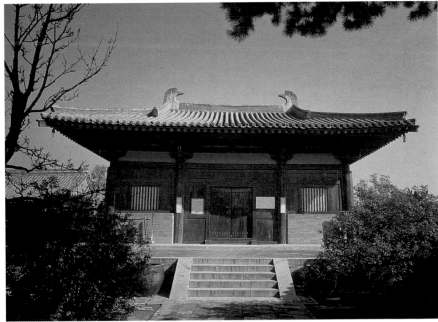

The Rise of Landscaping Painting: Song

China again splintered after the fall of the Tang but was quickly reunited under the rulers of the Song dynasty (960–1279 C.E.). Artists during the Song continued to create works for Buddhist and Daoist temples and shrines. Sculpture played an important role in these contexts. The altar of a Buddhist shrine consists of figures from the Buddhist pantheon set on a platform and protected by a railing. A visitor to a large temple might find inside the entire assembly of heaven—buddhas, bodhisattvas, lesser deities, guardians, and other celestial beings—carved as life-size figures and arranged to reflect the hierarchy of paradise.

The bodhisattva Guanyin, known in India as Avalokiteshvara (see 11.3), became the object of special affection in China. As Guanyin of the Southern Seas, he was believed to reside high on a mountain and offer his special protection to all who traveled the sea. Carved from wood and richly painted and gilded, the sculpture here depicts Guanyin atop his sacred mountain (**19.19**). Left leg dangling down, right leg drawn up, he sits in a position known as the pose of royal ease, as befits his princely nature. He would have been surrounded on his altar by attendants, making his high status even clearer. Cascading swags of drapery animate this serene figure, whose benevolent gaze is like the calm center within the storm, saving us from shipwreck, both at sea and in life.

19.19 (left) *Guanyin.* Song dynasty, c. 1100. Painted wood, height 7'11".
The Nelson-Atkins Museum of Art, Kansas City, Missouri.

19.20 (right) Li Cheng (attrib.). *A Solitary Temple amid Clearing Peaks.* Northern Song dynasty, c. 960. Hanging scroll, ink and slight color on silk, height 44".
The Nelson-Atkins Museum of Art, Kansas City, Missouri.

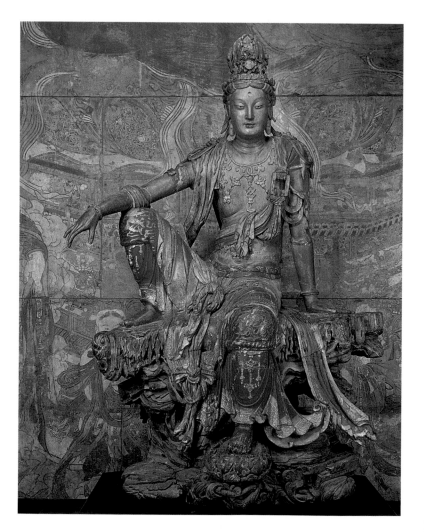

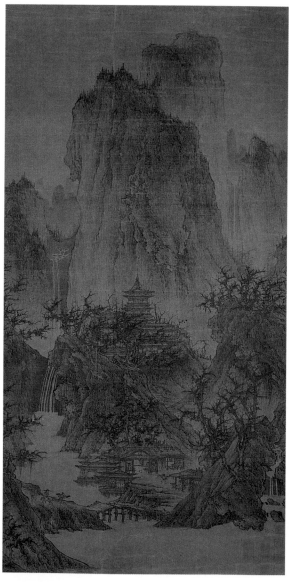

We do not know who carved Guanyin with such virtuosity. Chinese thinking about art did not concern itself with sculpture and architecture but valued above all the "arts of the brush," calligraphy and painting. Often, paintings were preserved for future generations through the practice of copying. Many famous works of the Tang are known to us only through Song copies, such as Zhang Xuan's *Ladies Preparing Newly Woven Silk* (see 3.18). The Tang dynasty was viewed by later writers as the great age of figure painting, and Song copies help us see why. Song painters, in turn, cast their own long shadow over the future with landscape.

The Song style of monumental landscape was largely the creation of Li Cheng, whose *A Solitary Temple amid Clearing Peaks* is illustrated here (**19.20**). Li built on the work of his predecessors of the early 10th century, when landscape first became an independent subject for painting. In his hands, the elements they had explored—mobile midair perspective, monochrome ink, vertical format, flowing water, shrouding mists, and a buildup of forms culminating in towering mountains—were gathered into a newly harmonious and spacious whole. Typically, paths are offered for us to walk in and people for us to identify with. Entering the painting with the traveler on the donkey at the lower left, we can cross the rustic bridge to a small village where people are talking and working. A glimpse of a stepped path farther up gives us access to the temple in the middle distance. But, also typically, there is a limit to how high we can climb. Mists separate the middle distance from the towering presences that rise up suddenly in the background. At this point, we must leave the painting and draw back, and when we do, we see a totality that is hidden from us in daily life: the whole of nature and our small place in it. Yet in this view of nature we seem to distinguish an ordering principle, and our place, though small, is in harmony with it: The temple raises its tower upward, and the mountains continue the gesture.

Li Cheng's vision of nature ordered by some higher force and human life in harmony with it clearly echoes the ideas of Daoism. In fact, some art historians believe that such paintings may originally have been understood to portray the Daoist Isle of the Immortals (see 19.15). Yet we can also view the painting in a Confucian perspective as a mirror of the order of China itself, with the emperor towering above, surrounded by his officials, as well as through a Buddhist lens as the great example of the Buddha flanked by bodhisattvas.

Scholars and Others: Yuan and Ming

During the Song dynasty, a new social class began to make itself felt in Chinese cultural life, scholars. Scholars were the product of an examination system designed to recruit the finest minds for government service. Candidates spent many years studying for the grueling test, which became the gateway to political power, social prestige, and wealth. Scholars did not study anything so practical as administration, however. Their education was in the classic texts of philosophy, literature, and history; and its purpose was to produce the Confucian ideal of a cultivated person, right-thinking and right-acting in all situations. Among their other accomplishments, scholars were expected to write poetry and practice calligraphy. During the Song dynasty, they also took an interest in painting.

The ideals of scholar painting were formed within the refined and cultivated Song court. During the ensuing Yuan dynasty, however, a split developed between scholars and the government. The Yuan (1279–1368 C.E.) was a foreign dynasty founded by the Mongols, a Central Asian people who had conquered China. The Mongol court continued to sponsor art, as had all of China's past rulers, but scholars regarded everything connected with the court as illegitimate. They viewed themselves as the true inheritors of China's past.

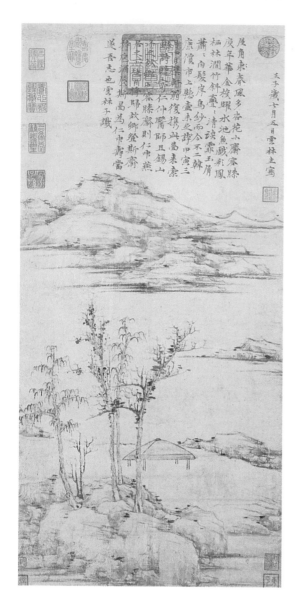

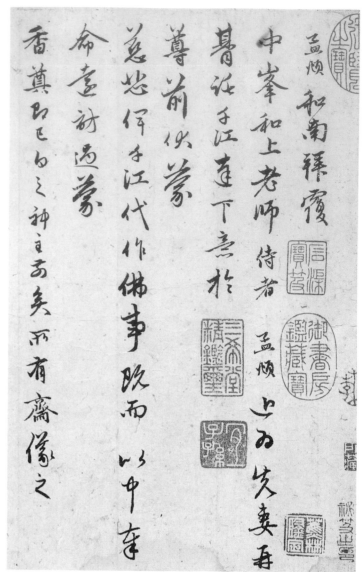

19.21 (left) Ni Zan. *The Rongxi Studio.* Yuan dynasty, 1372. Hanging scroll, ink on paper; height 29⅜".
National Palace Museum, Taipei.

19.22 (right) Zhao Mengfu. *Letter to Zhongfeng Mingben,* detail. 1321. Ink on paper, mounted as a handscroll, height 11⅜".
The Art Museum, Princeton University, Princeton, New Jersey.

Four scholar-painters of this time have come to be known as the Four Great Masters of Yuan. One is Huang Gongwang, whose *Dwelling in the Fuchun Mountains* is illustrated in Chapter 4 (see 4.49). Another was Ni Zan, whose best-known work is the beautiful, lonely *Rongxi Studio* (**19.21**). Typical of scholar paintings, the *Rongxi Studio* is painted in monochrome ink on paper. Vivid color and silk were both considered too pretentious, too professional. The brushwork is spare and delicate. Compared to the carefully drawn temple in Li Cheng's *A Solitary Temple amid Clearing Peaks* (see 19.20), Ni Zan's little studio is almost childlike. Like most scholar-painters, Ni Zan claimed that he painted merely to amuse himself, and that making a convincing likeness was the farthest thing from his mind. Also important is the inscription in Ni's own hand telling when, how, and for whom the picture was painted. Scholar-painters were not supposed to sell their work but to give it freely to each other as a token of friendship or in thanks for a favor. Their paintings almost always included an inscription and sometimes a poem as well. In their view, calligraphy and painting were closely related, for both consisted of brush strokes that revealed character.

Calligraphy, in fact, was the art that scholars admired above all others. The example here is a part of a letter written by the scholar Zhao Mengfu

(**19.22**). The content of such letters is viewed as unimportant (this one thanks a monk for ceremonies conducted in memory of Zhao's deceased wife). Rather, it was the visual style of the writing itself that was admired. The red elements are seals, personal stamps. Zhao Mengfu stamped his own seal after his signature, according to custom. The seals visible here are those of the many collectors who have owned this precious example of a great man's calligraphy over the centuries.

The Ming dynasty (1368–1644) returned Chinese rulers to the imperial throne. The scholar-painter ideal retained enormous prestige during this and the ensuing Qing dynasty (1644–1911), and Chinese writing about art focused on it almost exclusively. The writers, of course, were themselves scholars. In truth, scholar-painting was only one of many types of art that were being made.

One lively sphere of artistic activity revolved around the large cities that had grown up during the late Song dynasty, especially in the south, and the wealthy middle-class patrons who lived in them. Thanks to these new markets for their work, numerous professional painters had thriving careers outside the imperial court. The most admired professional painter of the Ming dynasty, Qiu Ying, lived and worked in the southern city of Suzhou. Even scholars respected this gifted painter, who was born into a poor family and died young: His knowledge of art history equaled theirs, he could imitate any number of ancient styles, his taste was impeccable, and his abilities were beyond question. No scholar would have tackled such an exacting composition as *Golden Valley Garden* (**19.23**). The subject, probably drawn from literary sources, is a host receiving his guest, and the painting itself would have been displayed in the

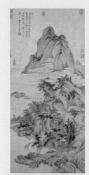
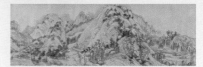
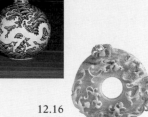
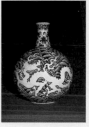
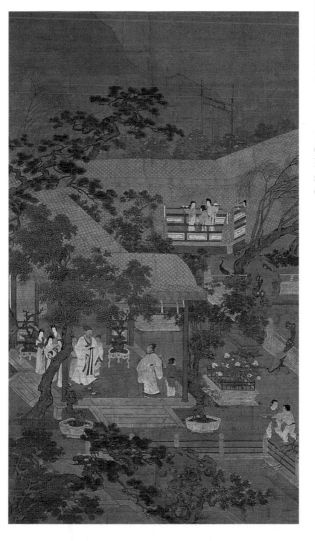

19.23 Qiu Ying. *Golden Valley Garden*. First half 16th century. Hanging scroll, ink and color on silk, height 7¹³⁄₄". Chion-in Temple, Kyoto.

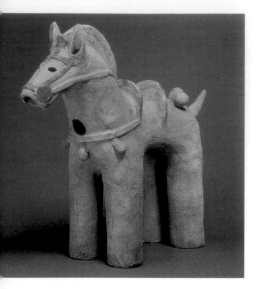

reception hall of a well-to-do household. At the entrance to a pavilion set in a garden of rocks, trees, peonies, and peacocks, two men with a retinue of servants and musicians greet each other with utmost dignity. Undoubtedly they know the words of Confucius, who said, "If you study culture widely and sum it up in an orderly way of life, you may therefore avoid being uncivilized."[1]

ARTS OF JAPAN

Separated from the Asian landmass by the Sea of Japan, the islands of Japan form an arc curving northward from the tip of the Korean Peninsula. Neolithic cultures were established on the islands by 10,000 B.C.E. The ceramics they produced are not only the oldest known pottery in the world but some of the most fanciful as well, shaped with a seemingly playful streak that resurfaces regularly in Japanese art.

Japanese culture comes into clearer focus during the first centuries of our era. Large burial mounds from that time have yielded terra-cotta figures such as the horse illustrated here (**19.24**). Called *haniwa*, they embody a taste for simple forms and natural materials that is one of the themes of Japanese art. We can see these characteristics again in the shrine at Ise (**19.25**). Erected during the first century C.E., the shrine has been ritually rebuilt on a regular basis since then, an unusual custom that allows this very early style to appear before our eyes in all its original freshness. The simple cylindrical shapes of the *haniwa* horse are echoed here in the wooden piles that raise the structure off the ground and the horizontal logs that hold the precisely trimmed thatch roof in place. The shrine is left unpainted, just as *haniwa* were left unglazed.

Housed in the shrine, which can be entered only by members of the imperial family and certain priests, are a sword, a mirror, and a jewel—the three

19.24 (above) *Haniwa* figure of a horse. Japan, 3rd–6th century C.E. Earthenware with traces of pigment, height 23".
The Cleveland Museum of Art.

19.25 (below) Inner shrine, Ise, Mie Prefecture. Early 1st century C.E.; rebuilt every 20 years; most recent rebuilding, 1993.

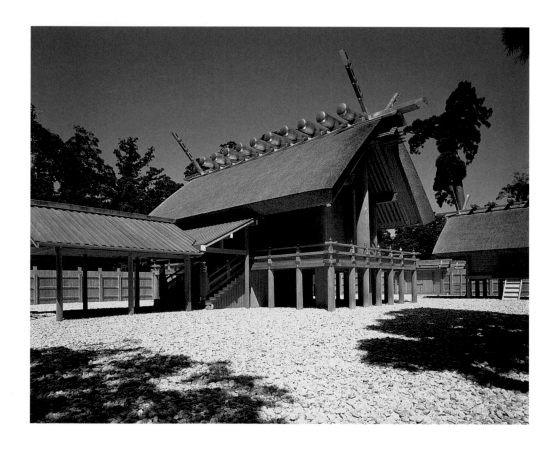

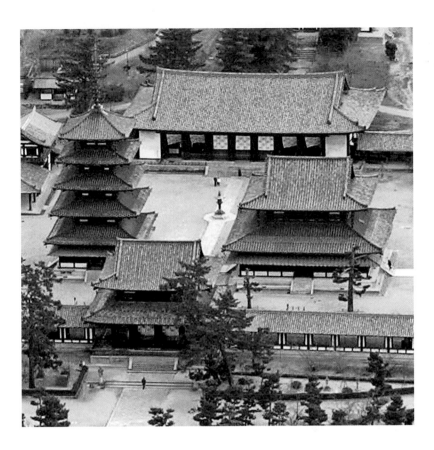

sacred symbols of Shinto. Shinto is often described as the native religion of Japan, but religion is perhaps too formal a word. Shinto involves a belief in numerous nature deities that are felt to be present in such picturesque sites as gnarled trees, imposing mountains, and waterfalls. A simple, unpainted wooden gate may be erected to mark a particularly sacred site. The chief deity of Shinto is female, the sun goddess. Purification through water plays an important role, as does the communion with and appeasement of spirits, including spirits of the newly dead. The constant presence of nature in Japanese art, together with the respect for natural materials simply used, reflects the continuing influence of these ancient beliefs.

New Ideas and Influences: Asuka

Japan was profoundly transformed during the Asuka period (552–646 C.E.), when elements of Chinese culture reached the islands through the intermediary of Korea. One profound and lasting acquisition was the religion of Buddhism, accompanied by the art and architecture that China had developed to go with it. A perfected example of early Japanese Buddhist architecture is the temple compound Horyu-ji (**19.26**). Dating from the 7th century, Horyu-ji contains the oldest surviving wooden buildings in the world. The architecture reflects the elegant style of the Six Dynasties period in China. We could imagine that Gu Kaizhi's ethereal palace ladies (see 19.16) would feel at home here.

Inside the gateway and to the left stands a pagoda, a slender tower with multiple roof lines. The equivalent of an Indian stupa (see 19.3), a pagoda serves as a shrine for the relics of a buddha or saintly person. Its ancestors are the tall, multistoried watchtowers of Han dynasty China. When Buddhism entered China, Chinese architects adapted the watchtower form to this new sacred purpose. To the right of the pagoda is the *kondo* ("golden hall"). Used for worship, the *kondo* houses devotional sculpture also based in Chinese models.

Buddhism did not eclipse Shinto, which continued to exist alongside it. Similarly, the earlier architectural ideas that produced the shrine at Ise were continued along with the newer Chinese-inspired forms. This ability to absorb and transform new ideas while keeping older traditions vital is one of the enduring strengths of Japanese culture.

Refinements of the Court: Heian

At the beginning of the Asuka period, Japan was ruled by powerful aristocratic clans, each of which controlled its own region. Inspired by the highly developed bureaucracy of China, the country moved toward unification under a centralized government. In 646 C.E., the first imperial capital was established at Nara. During the 8th century, the capital was moved to Kyoto, marking the beginning of the Heian period (794–1185 C.E.).

A highly refined and sophisticated culture developed around the court at Kyoto. Taste was paramount, and both men and women were expected to be accomplished in several arts. Perhaps the most important art was poetry. Through the miniature thirty-one-syllable form known as *tanka*, men and women communicated their feelings for each other, but always indirectly. The emphasis on literary accomplishment resulted in what many consider to be the greatest work of Japanese literature, *The Tale of Genji*, by Murasaki Shikibu. A lady of the court, Murasaki Shikibu wove aristocratic manners into a long narrative of love and loss that is often called the world's first novel.

Some of the earliest examples of secular painting in Japan survive in a copy of *The Tale of Genji* made during the 12th century (**19.27**). Written out and illustrated as a series of handscrolls (another imported Chinese idea), the monumental project brought together the specialized talents of a team of artists. The illustration here depicts a group of court ladies and their servants. As in all of the *Genji* paintings, we are given a bird's-eye view of an interior with the roof conveniently removed so we can see inside. The textile in the

19.27 Illustration I from the "Azamaya" chapter of *The Tale of Genji*. Heian period, first half of 12th century. Handscroll (now preserved in sections), ink and color on paper; height 8½". Tokugawa Art Museum, Nagoya.

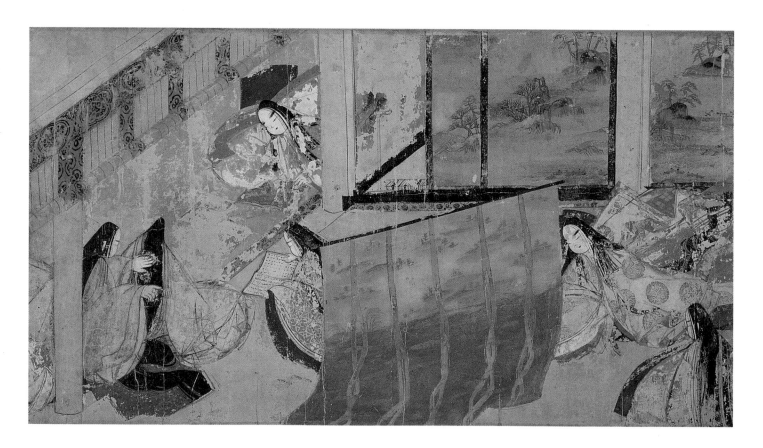

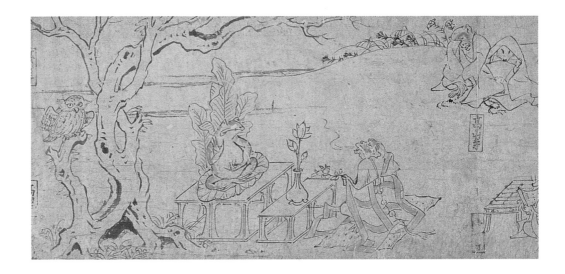

foreground, for example, is understood to be hanging from near the ceiling. Behind it, paper-covered sliding doors painted with a landscape lead to another room. To the left, a woman seated with her back to us is having her hair combed. Facing her across the alcove, in robes of green and orange, is Ukifune, the heroine of the last portion of *Genji*. She looks at a picture scroll while a nearby servant reads aloud.

Emerging from stylized renderings of starched and pleated robes, the women's white-powdered, masklike faces seem tranquil and composed. Yet in fact the scene has great underlying tension, for only hours before, Ukifune was the victim of a seduction attempt bordering on rape. Emotion is never betrayed by expressions or gestures in the *Genji* paintings. Just as Heian aristocrats conveyed their feelings indirectly through poems, the artists of the *Genji* scrolls conveyed emotions by other means, especially by the construction of space. Here, the characters are as hemmed in by their architectural setting as they are by their flawless manners. The room is closing in on them.

Buddhism remained central to Japanese life during the Heian period. Heian aristocrats at first favored esoteric Buddhism, an intellectually challenging faith that involved a hierarchy of deities as complicated as the hierarchy of the court itself. Later, as troubles grew, the simpler and more comforting message of Pure Land Buddhism became popular, as it had in China. In earlier chapters we looked at two of the loveliest masterpieces of Heian Pure Land Buddhist art, the temple Byodo-in (see 13.6) and the statue it houses, Jocho's *Amida Nyorai* (see 2.28). Amida is the Japanese name for Amitabha, the Buddha of the Western Paradise. One of the most delightful products of Heian art is also connected with Buddhism, Toba Sojo's *Frolicking Animals* (**19.28**). In the section of the handscroll illustrated here, a frog assumes the pose of a buddha while a monkey dressed in priests' robes ostentatiously prays aloud to it. Given the irreverent humor on display, it may come as a surprise to learn that the artist was an abbot of a Buddhist temple. Toba Sojo did not limit himself to religion but used his animals to poke fun at all levels of Heian society. The precise lines of his brush are as sharp as his wit. Not a stroke is wasted.

19.28 Attrib. Toba Sojo. *Monkeys Worshipping a Frog*, from *Frolicking Animals (Choju Jimbutsu Giga)*. Heian period, late 12th century. Handscroll, ink on paper; height 12½". Kozan-ji Temple, Kyoto.

RELATED WORKS

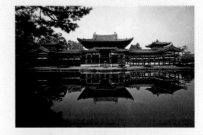

13.6 Phoenix Hall, Byodo-in

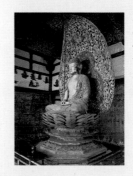

2.28 Jocho, *Amida Nyorai*

Samuri Culture: Kamakura and Muromachi

The last decades of the Heian period were increasingly troubled by the rise of regional warriors, samurai. During the 12th century, civil war broke out as powerful regional clans, each with its army of samurai, battled for control of the country. With the triumph of the Minamoto clan in 1185, a military

RELATED WORKS

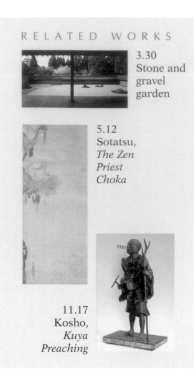

3.30
Stone and
gravel
garden

5.12
Sotatsu,
*The Zen
Priest
Choka*

11.17
Kosho,
*Kuya
Preaching*

government was installed. The office of emperor was retained, but true power resided with the commander-in-chief, the shogun. A military capital was established at Kamakura, far from the distractions of the Heian court.

One of the great works of the Kamakura period (1185–1392) is the *Heiji Monogatari Emaki* ("the illustrated story of the Heiji era"), a set of handscrolls that tell of the wars between the Minamoto and their great rivals, the Taira. *The Burning of Sanjo Palace* (**19.29**) portrays a dramatic episode of 1159 when Taira forces abducted the emperor in a surprise nighttime attack. Never have the cinematic possibilities of the handscroll format been employed more effectively! Scene after scene scrolls by like an epic film with a cast of thousands: marshaling forces, surprise attack, spectacular conflagration, wild-eyed horses, streaming warriors, bloody hand-to-hand combat, and the emperor and his retinue fleeing in terror and disarray. In the detail shown here, mounted samurai archers surge toward a gate, the palace in flames behind them. The event is captured in minute and realistic detail, though the anonymous artists could only have known it through stories.

Just as dramatic in its own way is this Buddhist painting of a subject called *raigo* (**19.30**). Instead of samurai streaming through a gate in the light of a burning palace we see a buddha and his attendants streaming down from heaven in the light of their own glory. They flow toward a small house where an old man lies dying. Literally "welcoming approach," *raigo* depicts the buddha Amida arriving to escort a believer's soul to the Western Paradise. The gold on this *raigo* has dimmed with age, but when the painting was new, the heavenly procession shimmered into view over flowering mountains painted blue and green. Amida is preceded by numerous bodhisattvas; behind him celestial musicians play. Tiny saints hover like lanterns around the old man's cottage, while in the upper right is a distant view of the Western Paradise itself. *Raigo* were taken to the homes of the dying in the hopes that the vision they depicted might come true.

19.29 *The Burning of Sanjo Palace,* detail from *Heiji Monogatari Emaki.* Kamakura period, late 13th century. Handscroll, ink and color on paper; height 16¼", overall length 22'9". Courtesy Museum of Fine Arts, Boston.

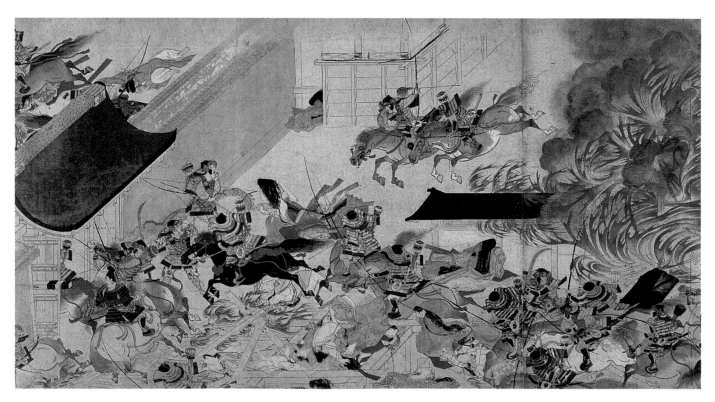

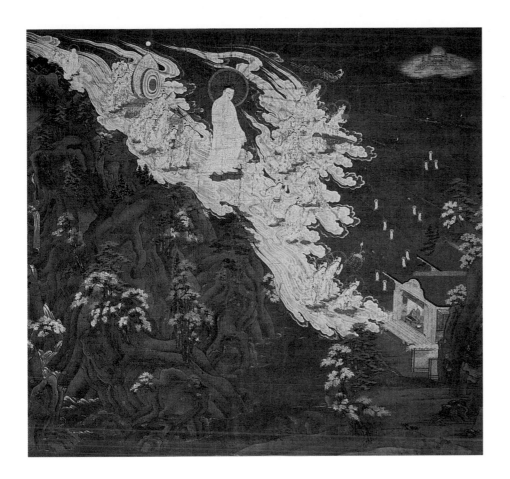

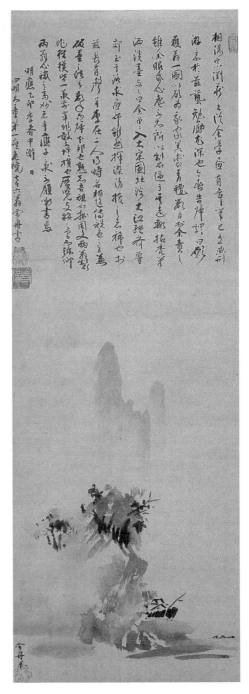

Pure Land Buddhism continued to win the hearts of ordinary people during the Kamakura period. The faith was spread through the countryside by wandering monks who taught a simple chant guaranteed to bring salvation. We saw a statue of one of these monks in Chapter 11, Kosho's affecting *Kuya Preaching* (see 11.17), carved in the new naturalistic style of the time.

Toward the end of the 14th century, the Ashikaga family gained control of the shogunate, and the military capital was moved to the Muromachi district of Kyoto. During the Muromachi period (1392–1568), a new type of Buddhism, Zen, became the leading cultural force in Japan. Zen reached Japan from China, where it was already highly developed. Following the example of the historical Buddha, it stressed personal enlightenment through meditation. Centuries of accumulated writings and scripture were cast aside in favor of direct, one-on-one teaching, master to student. The best known Zen teaching tools are *koan*, irrational questions designed to "short-circuit" logical thought patterns. "What is the sound of one hand clapping?" is a well-known *koan*. Zen training was (and is) spartan and rigorous, qualities that appealed to the highly disciplined samurai.

Enlightenment in Zen is above all *sudden*. Zen priest-painters embodied this sudden appearance of meaning out of chaos in a painting technique called *haboku*, "splashed ink." Sesshu Toyo's *Landscape* (**19.31**) is a masterpiece of this difficult technique—difficult because most attempts end in a mess. Sesshu drew together his "splashes" with a few expertly placed dark strokes, giving us all the clues we need to see a forested hillside by the water. A small house nestles at the foot of the hill, and on the water floats a lone boat. Although Sesshu Toyo was primarily a painter, he had trained as a Zen monk. He painted this work as a farewell gift for one of his pupils, and in the long inscription above he speaks of his own artistic path.

19.30 (left) *The Descent of Amida and the Twenty-five Bosatsu (Bodhisattvas).* Gold and color on silk, height 57". Kamakura period, early 13th century.
Chion-in Temple, Kyoto.

19.31 (right) Sesshu Toyo. *Landscape* (in the *haboku* technique). 1495. Hanging scroll, ink on paper, width 12⅞".
Tokyo National Museum.

Splendor and Silence: Momoyama

The shogun's control over regional lords and their samurai weakened during the Muromachi period, and devastating civil wars broke out. After the Ashikaga family fell from power in 1568, three strong leaders controlled the shogunate in succession. The decades of their rule are known as the Momoyama period (1568–1603).

For all its turbulence, the Momoyama period was a time of splendor for the arts. Fortified castles and great residences were built by powerful regional lords, and their interiors were decorated by the finest painters. One of the most influential artists of this time was Kano Eitoku, who developed a bold and highly colored decorative style that was much imitated in later Japanese art (**19.32**). *Cypress Trees* was originally painted to decorate the paper-covered sliding doors of a large interior. It was later remounted as a folding screen—a portable partition that serves to mark off space within a larger room. A venerable cypress, gnarled and twisted with age, reaches from its roots at the right across the entire width of the screen. Stylized clouds of gold leaf float behind it over a blue and green landscape.

Golden screens, as they are known, represent only one side of Momoyama taste. The other side is almost the exact opposite: a hushed and understated monochrome such as we see in Hasegawa Tohaku's *Pine Wood* (**19.33**). *Pine Wood* consists of a pair of six-panel folding screens, of which we show one. Painted with great simplicity in ink on paper, the ghostly trees ap-

19.32 (below, top) Attrib. Kano Eitoku. *Cypress Trees*. Momoyama period, late 16th century. Eight-panel screen; color, gold leaf, and ink on paper, 5'7" × 15'1½". Tokyo National Museum.

19.33 (below) Hasegawa Tohaku. *Pine Wood*. Momoyama period, late 16th century. One of a pair of six-panel screens, ink on paper, height 5'1". Tokyo National Museum.

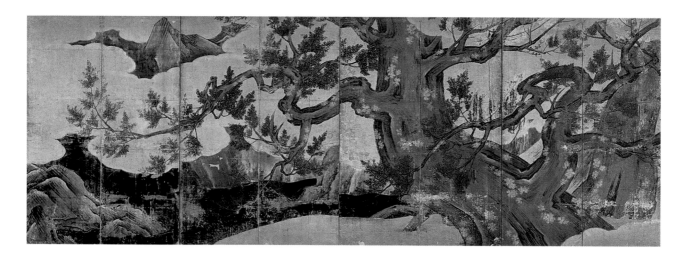

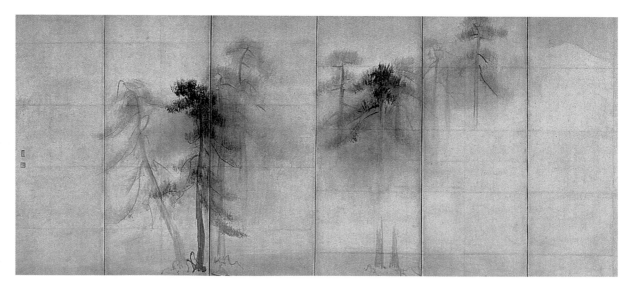

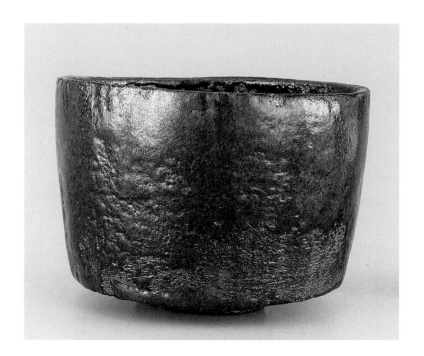

19.34 Hon'ami Koetsu. Teabowl. Momoyama–Edo period, late 16th–early 17th century. Raku ware, height 3⅜". Freer Gallery of Art, Smithsonian Institution, Washington, D.C.

pear through veils of mist. The paper itself, though technically blank, seems full of presences—trees we cannot see at the moment, or perhaps the edge of a lake. Tohaku's genius was to fashion monumental, decorative works from a fundamentally intimate style.

Art for Everyone: Edo

Still another shift in the control of the shogunate signaled the beginning of the Edo period (1603–1868), named as before for the new capital city (present-day Tokyo). The many types of art that had been set in motion over the centuries continued during the Edo period. Decorative styles were carried on by such artists as Kaiho Yusho, whose golden screen painting is illustrated in Chapter 5 (see 5.28). The tradition of ink painting and the continuing influence of Zen produced such playful wonders as Nonomura Sotatsu's *The Zen Priest Choka* (see 5.12). But the great artistic event of the Edo period was the popularity of woodblock prints, a new form that made art available to everyone. Through the imagination of such masters as Hiroshige (see Crossing Cultures, page 102) and Hokusai (see 3.32), prints transcended their initial destiny as throwaway souvenirs to become lasting treasures of world art.

We end this look at Japanese art with a quiet and unassuming work, a teabowl by the calligrapher and tea-master Hon'ami Koetsu (**19.34**). The appreciation of tea in Japan grew up within the climate of Zen thought, and the rituals associated with it share Zen's appreciation for what is natural, spontaneous, and austere. Tea was prepared with a few intimates in a small room whose rustic simplicity was the product of sophisticated aesthetic choices. The objective was to clear the mind, to focus aesthetic attention on humble everyday objects, and to converse. Each utensil was regarded with the kind of rapt attention we might bring to an exceptionally well-shaped piece of driftwood or a small, finely formed stone. When all is said and done, it isn't easy to make things as perfect and effortless as these. The uneven surfaces of Koetsu's bowl are designed to please both eye and hand, and the subtle glaze is drawn from nature's palette. We have come a long way in time from the *haniwa* figures and the shrine at Ise. In spirit, however, there is almost no distance at all.

RELATED WORKS

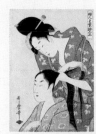

2.21
Utamaro,
Hairdressing

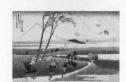

3.32
Hokusai, *Ejira in Suruga Province*

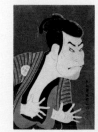

8.4
Sharaku,
Otani Oniji

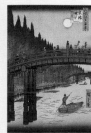

p. 102
Hiroshige,
Riverside Bamboo Market

CHAPTER TWENTY

ARTS OF THE PACIFIC AND OF THE AMERICAS

Continuing eastward around the world, we come to two regions that together cover almost half the globe: the vast ocean of the Pacific and the double continent of the Americas. We began the previous chapter by stressing the contacts that had linked India and China to the evolving Mediterranean world since ancient times. Here, we might do the opposite. From the end of the last Ice Age around 10,000 years ago, when rising waters submerged the land bridge that once linked Asia and Alaska, contact between Europe, Africa, and Asia on the one hand and the Americas and the Pacific Islands on the other was largely cut off.

In Chapter 16, there is a sign of the moment when one-half of the world rediscovered the other. If you look again at Holbein's *The Ambassadors* (see 16.24), painted in 1533, you will notice a globe on the lower shelf. Globes were all the rage in the early 16th century, spurred by Columbus' accidental discovery in 1492 of lands across the Atlantic Ocean and Vasco da Gama's discovery in 1498 that it was indeed possible to sail all the way around Africa and arrive in India. Holbein's globe is placed so that Europe is facing us. If you were to turn it around, you would see an emerging idea of the rest of the world. In this chapter, we fill in Holbein's map with a look at art as it had been developing in the cultures of the Pacific and the Americas.

PACIFIC CULTURES

The lands of the Pacific include the continent of Australia and the thousands of islands grouped together as Oceania, "lands of the ocean." Australia was settled by the ancestors of the peoples today known as Aborigines, who arrived by sea from Southeast Asia as early as 50,000 years ago. The neighboring island of New Guinea was settled around the same time. The peopling of the rest of the Pacific Islands was the result of centuries of maritime courage, as seafaring settlers set out across uncharted waters in search of land they could not have known existed. Among the first islands to be settled, beginning around 1500 B.C.E., were those to the east of New Guinea. These are grouped together with New Guinea as the cultural region of Melanesia. The last islands to be settled were the widely scattered islands of Polynesia, the easternmost cultural region of Oceania that includes Hawaii (settled around 500 C.E.) and New Zealand (settled between 800 and 1200 C.E.).

The oldest examples of Pacific art are the earliest rock engravings of the Aborigines, some of which may date to 30,000 B.C.E. The meanings of these images are not known, but more recent Aboriginal art is intimately connected with the religious beliefs known as Dreamtime or the Dreaming. Dreamtime includes the distant past, when ancestral beings emerged from the earth. Their actions shaped the landscape and gave rise to all forms of life within it, including humans. Dreamtime also exists in the present, and each individual is connected to it. With age a person draws closer to the realm of ancestors, and at death the spirit is reabsorbed into the Dreaming.

Ritual help for a spirit on its journey back to the Dreaming is the subject of Lipundja's *Djalambu* (**20.1**). Born in 1912, Lipundja was a member of the Yolngu, an Aboriginal people who live in Eastern Arnhem Land, in northern Australia. The Yolngu have many ways of talking about the journey back to the Dreaming. Often the soul is said to be carried by a current of water, in which case it may be thought of as a catfish that must avoid being eaten by diver birds. Catfish and diver birds are painted on Yolngu hollow-log coffins. During funerary rites, bullroarers (noisemakers) are whirled in the air to suggest diver birds in flight, while dancers painted as catfish scatter in fear. The central form of *Djalambu* is a log coffin, which is also understood to represent a catfish in the river. A diver bird and a long-neck tortoise appear near the base of the coffin-catfish, and seven bullroarers accompany it. The linear patterns of hatching and cross-hatching are characteristic of much Aboriginal art.

The most haunting elements of *Djalambu* are the two circular eyes of the coffin, the alert and otherworldly gaze of an ancestor looking into this world from the Dreamtime. Eyes from another realm meet our own again in this

20.1 Lipundja. *Djalambu*. 1964. Earth pigments on bark, 53 × 29¼".
National Gallery of Victoria, Melbourne.

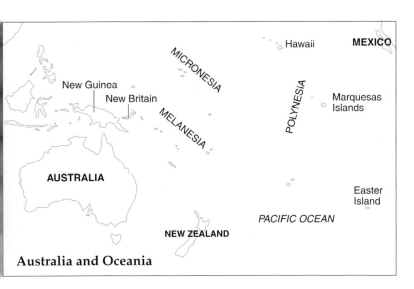

Australia and Oceania

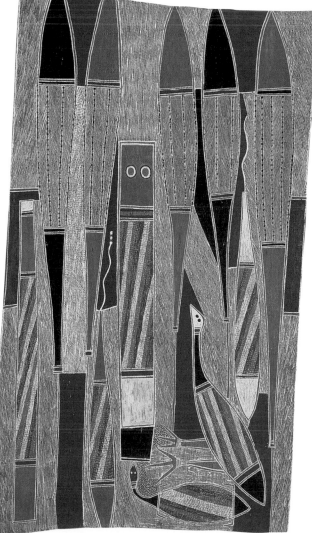

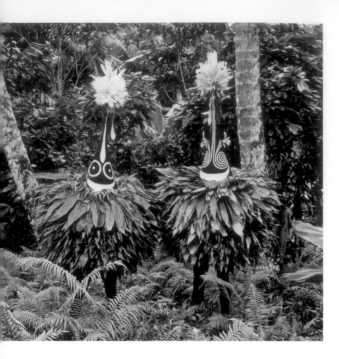

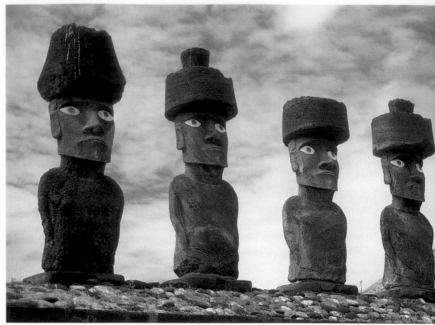

20.2 (left) *Duk duk* maskers, East New Britain, Papua New Guinea. Photograph 1994.

20.3 (right) Stone figures on Ahu Naunau, Anakena, Easter Island (Rapanui), Chile.

mask from the Tolai people of New Britain, one of the islands of Melanesia (**20.2**). Masks and masquerades play important roles in many Melanesian cultures. As in Africa (see Chapter 18), masks are used to materialize spirit beings. These masks are *tubuan*, the female spirits of a society called *duk duk*. *Duk duk* are male spirits, also danced by maskers, that punish lawbreakers at the bidding of the community's leaders. The male spirits are reborn each year from the *tubuan*, who are immortal. With their costume of leaves, *tubuan* represent nature and the natural order of things, and they lend their support to the authority of the human community's leaders. Yet all is not so simple, for the powers of the *tubuan* are volatile and potentially a force for chaos, and a true leader must show that he can control them.

Among the most well-known works of the Pacific are the monumental stone figures of Easter Island, the most remote and isolated island of Polynesia (**20.3**). Almost 1,000 of the monolithic statues have been found. Scholars believe they were carved as memorials to dead rulers or other important ancestors. Whatever purpose the statues served, the islanders must have believed it to be vital to their community, for they went to heroic efforts to erect them. The stones were quarried and partially carved in the island's volcanic mountains. The average height of the figures is about 36 feet, and each one weighs tens of tons, yet somehow they were dragged for miles across the island and set upright on elevated stone platforms that probably served as altars.

Easter Islanders seem to have begun erecting the figures around 900 C.E. Six centuries later, conflicts apparently broke out on the island, and a period of warfare ensued. Most of the figures were knocked down and destroyed. The statues photographed here were restored in 1978, their heads crowned again with red stone topknots and their faces set with white coral eyes. Stones that had slumbered for centuries suddenly awoke. Lined up once more along the shoreline, they stare hypnotically out to sea in an eternal vigil whose purpose we may never fully understand.

Polynesian peoples believed that certain materials were sacred to the gods. Among these materials were feathers. Rulers and other high-ranking members of society traced their descent from the gods, and they adorned themselves with feathered garments as a sign of their status. With their bold geometric designs and brilliant colors, the feather cloaks of Hawaii are the most spectacular products of this unique art form (**20.4**). Although both men and women of the Hawaiian elite wore many types of feathered garments, majestic cloaks such as this, reaching from the shoulders to the ground, belonged exclusively to the highest-ranking men. The creation of such a cloak was itself a ritual activity limited to high-ranking men. As the makers wove and knotted the cloak's plant-fiber foundation, they chanted the names of the ancestors of the man who would eventually wear it. The names were thus captured in the cloak, imbuing it with protective spiritual power. Feathers were tied onto the completed fiber netting in overlapping rows. Feathers were collected by commoners, who offered them as part of their yearly tribute to their rulers.

The feather cloaks of Hawaii embody ideas about the order of society, the respective roles of men and women, the continuing presence of ancestors, and the protective power of the gods. Similar concerns are given architectural form in the men's meeting houses of the Maori people of New Zealand, the southernmost of the Polynesian islands (**20.5**). The house is understood as the body of the sky father, the supreme deity of the Maori. The ridgepole is his spine, and the rafters are his ribs. His face is carved on the exterior, where other elements symbolize his embracing arms. Meetings thus take place within the god, which is to say within his protection, sanction, and authority.

The freestanding figures that support the ridgepole from inside portray ancestors. Their knees are bent in the aggressive posture of the war dance, reminding the living of their courage and great deeds. More stylized portrayals of snarling, powerful ancestors are carved in the series of reliefs that line the walls. Each relief panel meets a rafter whose lower portion is carved with still more ancestors. Everywhere, iridescent shell eyes gleam and glimmer as they catch the light. Ancestors were believed to participate in the discussions held

20.4 (below, top) Feather cloak. Hawaii. Feathers, fiber; height 5'9".
The British Museum, London.

20.5 (below) Interior of a Maori meeting house, Waitangi, North Island, New Zealand. Photograph 1999.

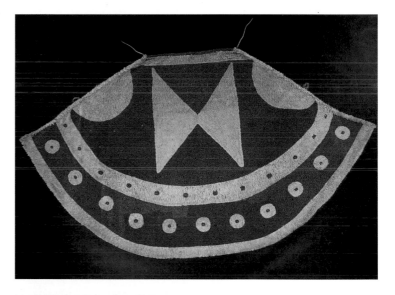

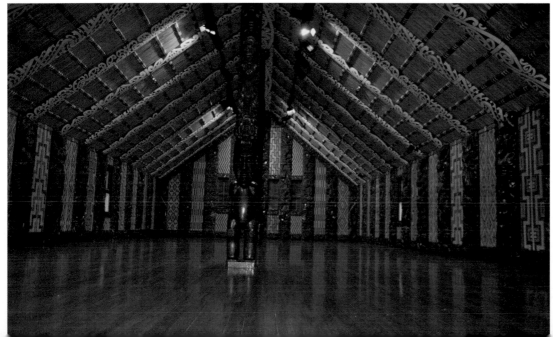

in the house, and these sculptures make their watchful presence felt. The reliefs along the walls alternate with panels of lattice woven in symbolic patterns that relate to stories about Maori deities and heroes. The panels were woven by women. Women, however, are not permitted to enter the meeting house, and so they wove the panels from the back, standing outside.

The patterns that swirl over the surfaces of the rafter and carved poles of the meeting house echo the tattoo patterns that ornament the bodies of Maori men and women. All Polynesian peoples practiced tattoo, but nowhere was the art cultivated with greater virtuosity than among the inhabitants of the Marquesas Islands in the South Pacific (**20.6**). The illustration here shows two Marquesan men in different stages of the lifelong tattooing process. The mature man at the left is completely tattooed from head to foot, while the younger man at the right is only partially ornamented. If life granted him enough time, prestige, and wealth, he gradually had the remaining blank areas of his skin decorated.

Like all other arts, the act of tattooing was considered sacred by the Marquesans. It was performed ritually by a specialist, *tukuka*, who invoked the protective presence of specific deities. The designs were created using a bone tool that resembled a small comb with sharp, fine teeth. The specialist dipped the teeth in black pigment made of soot or ground charcoal, set them against his client's skin, then gave the tool a sharp rap with a stick to puncture the skin and insert the pigment. Because tattooing was expensive and painful, only a small area of the body was usually decorated during each session. Nearly all adult Marquesans both male and female wore tattoos, although only the wealthiest and most highly regarded chiefs and warriors reached the all-over patterning of the man to the left in our illustration.

20.6 *Inhabitants of the Island of Nuku Hiva.* 1813. Hand-colored copperplate engraving after original drawings by Wilhelm Gottlieb Tilesius von Tilenau. Archiv für Kunst und Geschichte, Berlin.

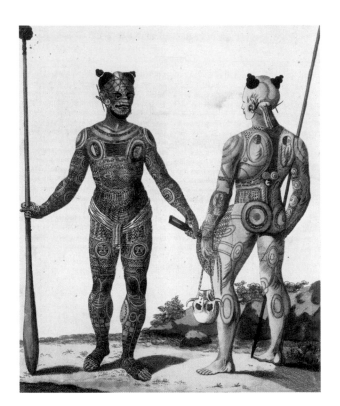

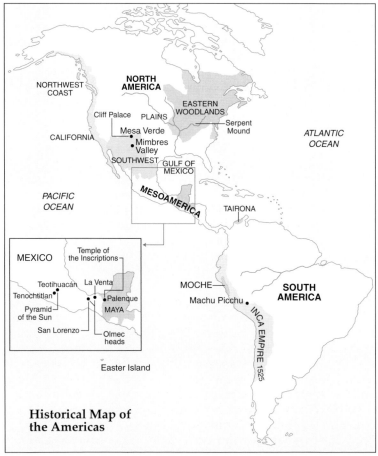

Historical Map of the Americas

THE AMERICAS

No one knows for sure when humans first occupied the double continent of the Americas or where those people came from. The most widely accepted theory is that sometime before 12,000 years ago—and possibly as early as 30,000 years ago—migrating peoples crossed over a now-submerged land bridge linking Siberia with Alaska, then gradually pushed southward, seeking hospitable places in which to dwell. Firm evidence of human presence at the tip of South America has recently been dated to about 12,500 years ago, indicating that by then both continents were populated, if only sparsely.

By 3000 B.C.E. we can identify developed cultures in three important centers: the Northwest Coast of North America, the fertile plateaus and coastal lowlands of Mesoamerica, and the Pacific Coast of South America. During the ensuing centuries, peoples in these and other territories created rich and sophisticated artistic expressions. Their early art has sometimes been called "pre-Columbian," meaning that it was created before Columbus' voyages to the Americas. The term acknowledges that the arrival of Europeans changed everything, and that the civilizations of the Americas were interrupted as decisively as if they had been hit by a meteor. Yet it is best to approach them on their own terms and not to think of them as "before" something else. After all, they did not think of themselves as coming "before" anything, but rather *after* their many predecessors, whose achievements they knew and admired.

Mesoamerica

"Mesoamerica" describes a region that extends from north of the Valley of Mexico (the location of present-day Mexico City) through the western portion of modern Honduras. Mesoamerica is a cultural and historical designation as well as a geographical one, for the civilizations that arose in this region shared many features, including the cultivation of corn, the building of pyramids, a 260-day ritual calendar, similar deities, an important ritual ball game, and a belief in the role of human blood in sustaining the gods and the universe. Mesoamerican peoples themselves were conscious of their common cultural background. Thus the Aztecs, who were the most powerful culture in the region at the time of the Spanish conquests of the early 16th century, collected and admired jade sculptures by the Olmec, whose civilization had flourished over 2,000 years earlier.

Olmec civilization, which flourished between about 1500 and 300 B.C.E., is often called the "mother culture" of Mesoamerica, for it seems to have institutionalized the features that mark later civilizations of the region. The principal Olmec centers were concentrated in a small region on the Gulf Coast of Mexico, but the influence of Olmec culture extended over a much broader area. Chapter 11 illustrated one of the colossal stone heads carved by Olmec sculptors (see 11.7). Chapter 2 included a finely worked Olmec jade depicting a shaman (see 2.37). Olmec leaders may have derived their power by claiming ability as shamans. Rulers in later Mesoamerican societies were also expected to have privileged access to the sacred realm.

A few centuries after the decline of the Olmecs, the city of Teotihuacán, located to the northeast of present-day Mexico City, began its rise to prominence. At its height, between 350 and 650 C.E., Teotihuacán was one of the largest cities in the world. Laid out in a grid pattern with streets at right angles, the city covered 9 square miles and had a population of around 200,000. Teotihuacán exerted great influence over the rest of Mesoamerica, though whether this was through trade or conquest we do not know.

The heart of the city was its ceremonial center, a complex of pyramids and temples lining a 3-mile-long thoroughfare known as the Avenue of the Dead. To the Aztecs, who arrived in the region long after Teotihuacán had been abandoned, it seemed hardly possible that humans were capable of such

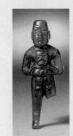

2.37
Olmec jade figure

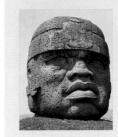

11.7
Olmec colossal head

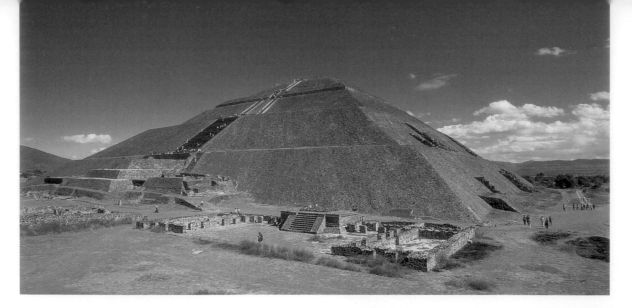

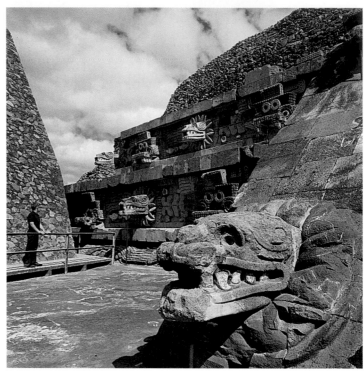

20.7 (above) Pyramid of the Sun, Teotichuacán, Mexico, 50–200 C.E.

20.8 (right) Temple of the Feathered Serpent, the Ciudadela, Teotihuacán, Mexico. 2nd century C.E.

wonders. They viewed the city as a sacred site where the gods had created the universe, and it was they who named its largest structure the Pyramid of the Sun (**20.7**). Made of stone and brick, the Pyramid of the Sun rises to a height of over 210 feet. A temple originally stood at its summit. Like the ziggurats of ancient Mesopotamia, Mesoamerican pyramids were symbolically understood as mountains. Excavations have discovered a tunnel leading to a natural cave containing a spring directly beneath the center of the Pyramid of the Sun. Perhaps it was this womblike source of water and life that was considered sacred by the city's original inhabitants.

Farther north along the Avenue of the Dead is a large sunken plaza surrounded by temple platforms. The focal point of this complex, the Temple of the Feathered Serpent, gives us our first look at a deity shared by many of the Mesoamerican civilizations (**20.8**). The Olmec pantheon included a feathered serpent, although its exact meaning is unclear. To the Aztecs, the feathered serpent was Quetzalcoatl, the god of windstorms that bring rain. Here, representations of the deity—its aggressive head emerging from a collar of feathers—alternate with the more abstract figure of the god of rain, distinguished by his goggle eyes. Rain, water, and the wind that brought them were essential to the agricultural societies of Mesoamerica.

One of the most fascinating of all Mesoamerican civilizations was that of the Maya, which arose in the southeastern portion of Mesoamerica, primarily in the Yucatán Peninsula and present-day Guatemala. Mayan culture began to form around 1000 B.C.E., probably under the influence of the Olmecs. The Maya themselves come into focus just after the final decline of Olmec civilization around 300 B.C.E. Mayan civilization flourished most spectacularly between 250 and 900 C.E. It was still in existence when the Spanish arrived in the early 16th century, however, and speakers of Mayan languages live in the region today.

Among their other accomplishments (including astronomy, biology, and the mathematical concept of zero), the Maya developed the most sophisticated version of the Mesoamerican calendar and the most advanced of the region's many writing systems. Scholars began to crack the code of Mayan writing in the 1960s, and since then the steady deciphering of inscriptions has provided new insights into Mayan civilization, in the process overturning much of what earlier scholars assumed.

The Maya were not a single state but a culture with many centers, each ruled by a hereditary lord and an elite class of nobles. Warfare between the centers was common, and its purpose was not conquest but capture: Prisoners of war were needed for the human sacrifices that were thought necessary to sustain the gods and maintain the universe. The official and ceremonial architecture of the Maya was meant to impress, and it does (**20.9**). The photograph illustrated here shows the structures known as the Palace and the Temple of the Inscriptions at Palenque, in the Chiapas region of Mexico. The royal dynasty of Palenque was founded in 431 C.E. and rose to prominence under Lord Pacal, who died in 683 C.E. Pacal was buried in a small chamber deep beneath the Temple of the Inscriptions. The carved lid of his sarcophagus is illustrated in Chapter 11 (see 11.12).

The Palace probably served as an administrative and ceremonial center. Set on a raised terrace, it is constructed on two levels around three courtyards. Like the Temple of the Inscriptions atop the pyramid, the buildings of the Palace take the form of long, many-chambered galleries. The square pillars of their open porches support massive stone ceilings with corbelled vaulting. (To review corbelling, see page 324.)

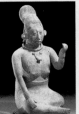

11.2
Maya figurine

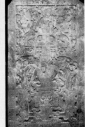

11.12
Sarcophagus
of Lord Pacal

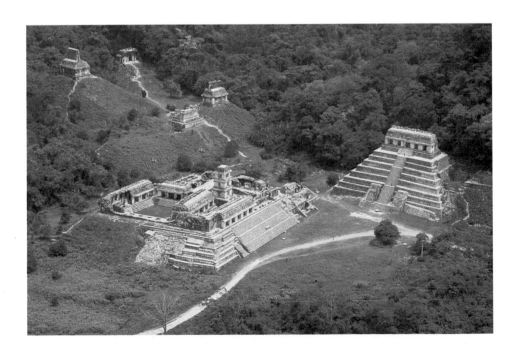

20.9 Palace and Temple of the Inscriptions, Palenque, Mexico. Maya, 7th century C.E.

A series of murals discovered at Bonampak, in Mexico, help us imagine the kinds of ceremonies that took place in Mayan palaces (**20.10**). Painted in 800 C.E., the original murals are today badly faded and crumbling, and we appreciate them best in this careful copy that restores their original colors. The murals depict events surrounding the presentation of an heir to the throne. In the upper band, nobles and lords gather. We can see four of the lords clearly in this view, with their white capes and feather-crowned headdresses. Vertical panels of writing next to them record their names. The assembly continues around the wall to the right and culminates with a view of the young heir himself (not visible here). In the lowest band, a colorful and evidently noisy procession winds around the walls against a vivid blue background. The jaguar pelts, finely woven textiles, abundant jewelry, and feathered ornaments of the Maya have not survived, but this mural and others like it allow us to restore a sense of color and pageantry to the deserted ruins we study today.

The first scholars to study the Maya believed that their art was primarily sacred and depicted cosmic events such as stories of the gods. Thanks to our understanding of Mayan writing, we now realize that Mayan art is almost entirely concerned with history. Like the murals at Bonampak, it memorializes rulers and portrays important moments of their reigns. Preeminent among Mayan arts are narrative stone relief carvings such as this lintel from a building in Yaxchilan, in Mexico (**20.11**). The scene is the second in a sequence of three compositions that portray a royal bloodletting ceremony. Bloodletting was a central Mayan practice, and almost every ritually important occasion was marked by it. Lady Xoc, the principal wife of Lord Shield Jaguar, is seated at the lower right. The previous panel showed her pulling a thorn-lined rope through her tongue in the presence of Shield Jaguar himself. Here, she experiences the hallucinatory vision that was the ceremony's purpose. From the bowl of blood and ritual implements on the floor before her there rises the Vision Serpent. A warrior, possibly one of Shield Jaguar's ancestors, issues from its gaping jaws. Dated with the Mayan equivalent of October 23, 681 C.E., the ceremony probably marked the accession of Shield Jaguar as ruler. Bloodletting and the visions it produced seem to have been the Mayan rulers' way of communicating with the spirits and gods. This communication was their privilege, their duty, and the source of their power.

20.10 East wall, Room 1, Bonampak, Mexico. Maya, 800 C.E. Polychromed stucco. Copy by Felipe Dávalos and Kees Grotenberg.
Florida State Museum, Gainesville.

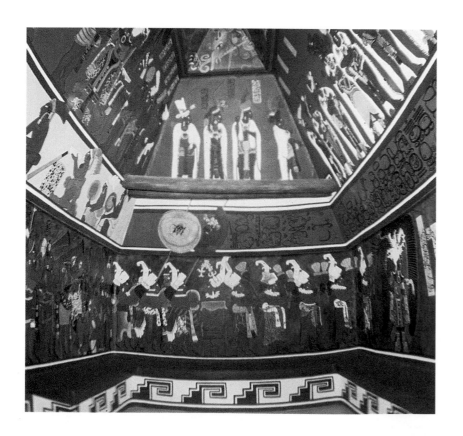

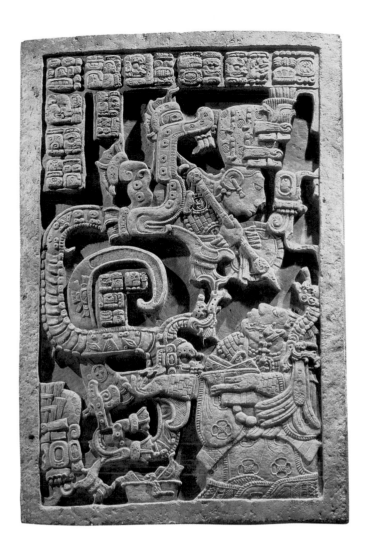

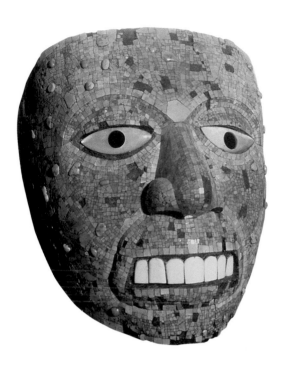

20.11 (left) Lintel 25 (*The Vision of Lady Xoc*), Yaxchilan, Chiapas, Mexico. Maya, 725 C.E. Limestone, 5¹³⁄₁₆" × 34" × 4". The British Museum, London.

20.12 (right) Ritual mask. Aztec, early 16th century C.E. Turquoise, pearl shell. The British Museum, London.

The last Mesoamerican empire to arise before the arrival of European conquerors was built by the Aztecs. According to their own legends, the Aztecs migrated into the Valley of Mexico during the 13th century C.E. from their previous home near the mythical Lake Aztlan (hence Aztec). They settled finally on an island in Lake Tezcoco, and there they began to construct their capital, Tenochtitlán. Tenochtitlán grew to be a magnificent city, built on a cluster of islands connected by canals and linked by long causeways to cities on the surrounding shores. Massive pyramids and temple platforms towered over the ritual precincts, and in the market squares goods from all over Mesoamerica changed hands. By 1500 Aztec power reached its height, and much of central Mexico paid them tribute.

Almost nothing remains of Tenochtitlán. Spanish conquerors razed its pyramids, and Mexico City has since been built on the same site. Aztec books were consigned to the fire, and their arts in precious metals were melted down for gold and silver. Yet the Spaniards were deeply impressed by the arts they found, and many objects were sent back to Europe. The mask illustrated here (20.12) was probably made by Mixtec artists living in Tenochtitlán. Mixtec artists also made gold and silver objects for the Aztecs, who greatly admired their work. (For Diego Rivera's re-creation of a Mixtec artistic community, see 7.4.) Mosaic of turquoise painstakingly applied in minute squares follows every curve of the face. Pearl shell serves for teeth and eyes. Such a mask would have been worn in one of the numerous ceremonies of song and dance that were central to Aztec life. Masks had a long history in Mesoamerica. The Aztecs collected jade masks carved by the Olmecs and in Teotihuacán. Maya artists also carved ritual masks of jade.

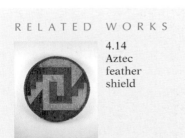

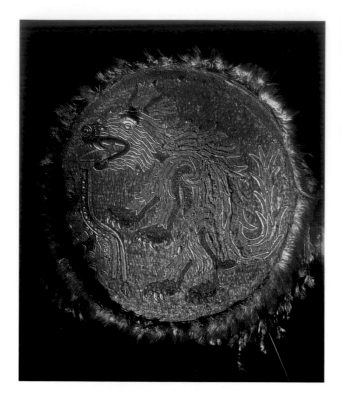

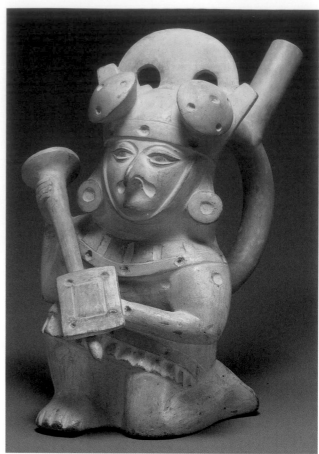

20.13 (left) Ceremonial shield. Aztec, early 16th century. Feather mosaic and gold on wicker base, diameter 27½".
Museum für Völkerkunde, Vienna.

20.14 (right) Stirrup vessel. Moche, 200–500 C.E. Earthenware with cream slip, height 9⅛".
The Metropolitan Museum of Art, New York.

Featherwork was greatly prized in Mesoamerica, and a specialized group of weavers in Tenochtitlán produced featherwork headdresses, cloaks, and other garments exclusively for nobles and high officials. The ceremonial shield here (**20.13**) shows their vivid sense of design and color. The heraldic coyote depicted in blue feathers edged in gold is the Aztec god of war. From his mouth issues the symbol for "water burning," an Aztec term for war. Rich in metaphors, Aztec speech also referred to warfare as "the song of the shields" and "flowers of the heart upon the plain." Feather shields such as this were part of the lavish dance costumes worn by warriors in ritual re-creations of the warfare of the gods.

South and Central America

Like Mesoamerica to the north, the region of the central Andes on the Pacific Coast of South America provided a setting in which numerous cultures developed. Pyramids, temple platforms, and other monuments have been found dating to the third millennium B.C.E., making them the oldest works of architecture in the Americas, contemporary with the pyramids of Egypt. Textiles of astonishing intricacy have also been found from this time.

Among the first South American peoples to leave a substantial record of art are the Moche, who dominated a large coastal area at the northern end of the central Andes during the first six centuries C.E. The Moche were exceptional potters and goldsmiths. Tens of thousands of Moche ceramics have been found, for one of their great innovations was the use of molds for mass production.

Kneeling warriors are a standard subject of Moche ceramic art (**20.14**). The large ear ornaments and elaborate headdress capped with a crescent-shaped element are typical of the costume on these figures. The warrior carries a shield and a war club; the heads of two more war clubs protrude from his headdress. His beaked nose probably links him to the barn owl, which was regarded as a warrior animal for its fierce and accurate nocturnal hunting abilities. Much of the finest Moche pottery takes the form of stirrup vessels, so called after the *U*-shaped spout (here attached to the warrior's back). The innovative spout pours well, can be carried easily, and minimizes evaporation. Yet such elaborate vessels cannot have been primarily practical.

One of the most spectacular archaeological sites in the world is the Inca city of Machu Picchu, in Peru (**20.15**). Beginning around 1430 and moving with amazing swiftness, the Incas created the largest empire of its time in the world. By 1500, Inca rule extended for some 3,400 miles along the Pacific Coast. Incan textiles are some of the finest in the long tradition of South American fiber work (see 12.12). Incan artists also excelled in sculptures and other objects of silver and gold. But the most original Incan genius expressed itself in stonework. Over 20,000 miles of stone-paved roads were built to speed communication and travel across the far-flung empire. Massive masonry walls of Incan buildings were constructed of large blocks of granite patiently shaped through abrasion until they fit together perfectly with no mortar.

Machu Picchu is set high in the Andes Mountains overlooking a hairpin turn in the Urubamba River thousands of feet below. Builders leveled off the site to create a small plateau and constructed terraces for houses and agriculture. Also visible at Machu Picchu is the wholly distinctive Incan sensitivity to the natural landscape. At the northern end of Machu Picchu, for example, a free-standing boulder was carved to resemble the silhouette of a peak that can be seen beyond it in the distance. Elsewhere a rounded building known as the Observatory accommodates a huge boulder into its walls and interior. Part of the boulder is subtly sculpted to create a staircase and chamber. The Inca believed stones and people to be equally alive and capable of changing into one another. This attitude seems to have resulted in their unique approach of relating architecture to its setting.

RELATED WORKS

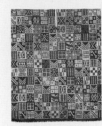

12.12
Inca tunic

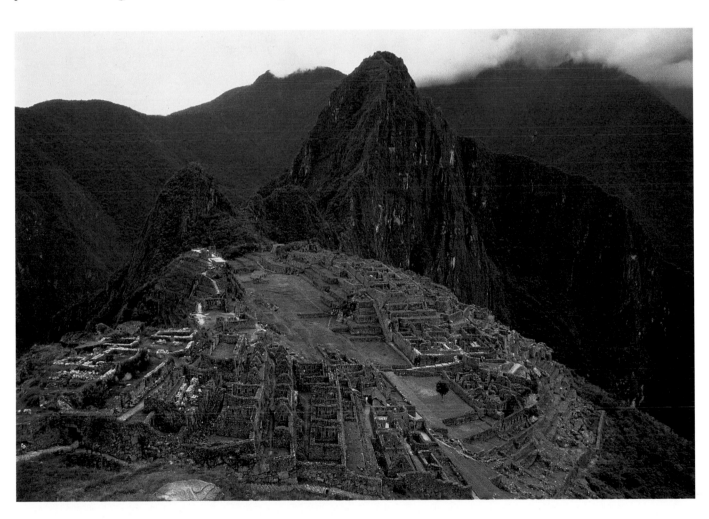

20.15 Machu Picchu, Peru. Inca, 15th–16th centuries.

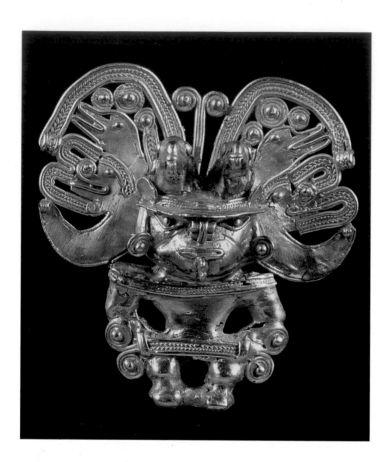

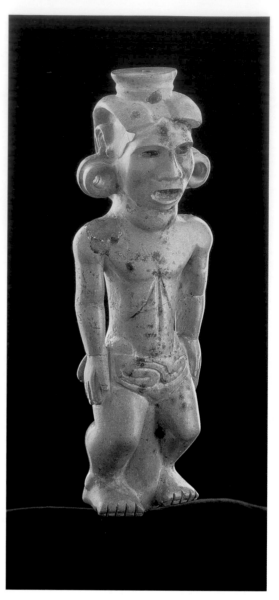

20.16 (left) Pendant depicting a ruler. Tairona culture, 1000–1300 C.E. Copper and gold alloy, height 2¾".
Museu Barbier-Mueller d'Art Precolombí, Barcelona.

20.17 (right) Effigy pipe. Adena culture, 500–200 B.C.E. Stone, height 8".
Ohio Historical Society, Columbus.

We end this section with an object made of the material that proved to be the Americas' undoing, gold (**20.16**). Fashioned of a gold and copper alloy called *tumbaga*, this pendant figure was made by artists of the Tairona culture, which flourished in northern Colombia after about 1000 C.E. The Tairona belong to the cultural region of Central America, which extends from the southern part of present-day Honduras into northwestern Colombia, where a mountain range called the Cordillera Oriental forms a natural boundary. The knowledge of extracting and working gold was first developed to the south, in Peru. Over generations it spread northward, with the goldsmith's art becoming increasingly refined and technically advanced.

Cast using the lost-wax technique, the pendant here portrays a ruler. He is probably also a shaman, and the birds that unfold like wings from either side of his head are the spirit alter egos that give him access to the other world. Tairona smiths added copper to the gold to lower its melting point and create a harder, more durable object. After casting, the pendant was bathed in acids that removed the outermost layer of copper particles, leaving the impression of solid gold. The taste for ornaments in precious metals spread from Central

America northward into Mesoamerica. There the finest artists in precious metals were the Mixtec, who supplied the Aztecs with their legendary and now lost works. Earlier cultures such as the Olmecs and the Maya had preferred jade.

North America

It might be expected that those of us who live in North America would have a clear picture of the history of art on our own continent, since we are, after all, right here where it happened. Unfortunately, we do not. In general, the ancient arts of North America are much less available to us than those of many other parts of the world—partly because the early inhabitants seem to have made their artifacts from perishable materials such as wood and fiber. Partly it is due to the absence of large urban centers. Patterns of life developed differently in the North.

Many arts of later North American peoples—Indians, as we have come to call them—are arts of daily life: portable objects such as baskets, clothing, and tools imbued with meanings that go far beyond their practical functions. In Chapter 3, we used as an example of such arts a basket from the Pomo of California (see 3.1). Pomo thought links the basket to the story of the sun's journey across the sky, and a flaw woven purposefully into the basket provides a way for spirits to enter and leave. The basket is thus connected to the sacred realm and to ritual. And yet it is also a basket.

The first clearly identifiable culture group of North America populated an area known as the Eastern Woodlands—in parts of what are now Ohio, Indiana, Kentucky, Pennsylvania, and West Virginia—starting about 700 B.C.E. Several Eastern Woodlands cultures are known collectively as the "mound builders," because they created earthworks, some of them burial mounds, in geometric forms or in the shapes of animals. The Serpent Mound in Ohio, illustrated in Chapter 11, is the most famous of the mounds still visible (see 11.25). Among the arts of daily life that have come down to us from early Eastern Woodlands cultures are pipes carved of stone (20.17). The pipe illustrated here was excavated in 1901 from an Adena burial mound. Like the Moche warrior earlier (see 20.14), the figure wears a crescent-shaped head ornament and large ornaments called ear spools. The gently rounded musculature and slightly bent knees convey a sense of movement and life.

Tobacco was considered a sacred substance by many North American peoples. First domesticated in the Andes around 3000 B.C.E., it made its way north by way of Mexico some 2,000 years later. In North America, smoking tobacco became viewed as a form of prayer. The rising smoke faded into the other world, bidding its spirits to come witness or sanction human events. Interestingly, whereas knowledge of tobacco arrived from the South, the stone pipe itself is a North American invention.

Europeans arriving in America introduced such new materials as glass beads, and Indian beadwork became justifiably famous. An older Indian art, however, is quillwork (20.18). Quills from porcupine or birds were softened by soaking, then dyed to produce a palette of colors and worked into a surface of deerskin or birch bark. The quillwork on the tabbed deerskin bag illustrated here portrays a thunderbird, a sky deity recognized by many Indian peoples. The thunderbird rises over a horizontal band that signifies earth. Below, two reptiles abstracted to diagonal lines are denizens of a symbolic underworld. The three levels of existence—sky, earth, and underworld—are summarized with great economy of means.

Whereas Eastern Woodlands culture was based in a settled way of life, the Plains culture that formed to the west was nomadic, organized around the herds of buffalo that roamed the Great Plains. European explorers' greatest although accidental contribution to Plains culture was undoubtedly the horse, which was brought to America by Spanish colonists and spread throughout Indian cultures over the course of the 18th century.

RELATED WORKS

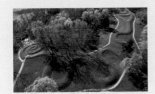

11.25
Serpent
Mound

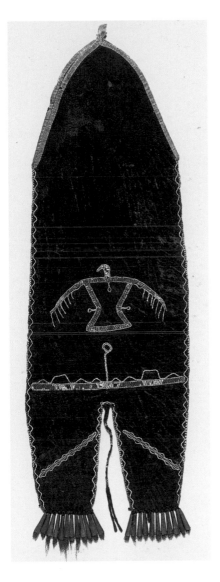

20.18 Tabbed skin bag. Ottowa(?) culture. Eastern Great Lakes, c. 1790. Black-dyed deerskin, porcupine quills, silk binding, hair tassels, tin cones; length 20½".
New York State Historical Association, Fenimore House Museum, Cooperstown.

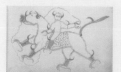
Buffalo hides provided not only clothing but also shelter in the form of covering for tents, tipis (also spelled "tepees"). Hides provided a surface on which Plains men recorded their exploits as warriors (**20.19**). Drawn by Lakota warriors, the images here record a battle between the Lakota and the Crow, depicted with the vivid recall of participants. Such a hide would have been worn around the shoulders as a robe. Other garments such as shirts and leggings were also painted. Clearly visible are the feathered headdresses that were a distinctive feature of Plains costume. Headdresses were made from the tail feathers of eagles, which were identified with the thunderbird. Some offered protective spiritual power; others were merely finery. Only a proven warrior was permitted to wear one in battle, however.

Urban life was not entirely absent from North America. The Anasazi people, who lived in the southwestern part of the continent, created ambitious communal dwelling sites. One such dwelling at Mesa Verde, in Colorado, has become known as Cliff Palace (**20.20**). The Anasazi had been present in the region from the first several centuries B.C.E. Around the 12th century C.E. they began clustering their buildings in protected sites on the undersides of cliffs. A complex system of handholds and footholds made access difficult. (Modern tourists have been provided an easier way in.) This arrangement allowed the Anasazi to ward off invaders and maintain a peaceful community life.

Cliff Palace, dated to about 1200 C.E., has more than 200 rooms organized in apartment-house style, most of them living quarters but some at the back meant for storage. In addition, there are twenty-three *kivas*—large, round chambers, mostly underground and originally roofed, used for religious or other ceremonial purposes. The structures are of stone or adobe with timber, and so harmonious is the overall plan that many scholars believe a single architect must have been in charge. Cliff Palace was occupied for about a hundred years before being mysteriously abandoned in the early 14th century.

20.19 Hide painted with scenes of warfare. Western Lakota culture, North or South Dakota, c. 1880. Horsehide and pigments, branded; 8'2" × 7'9".
New York State Historical Association, Fenimore House Museum, Cooperstown.

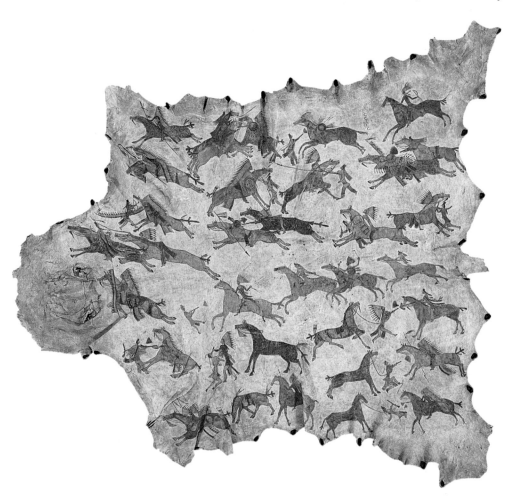

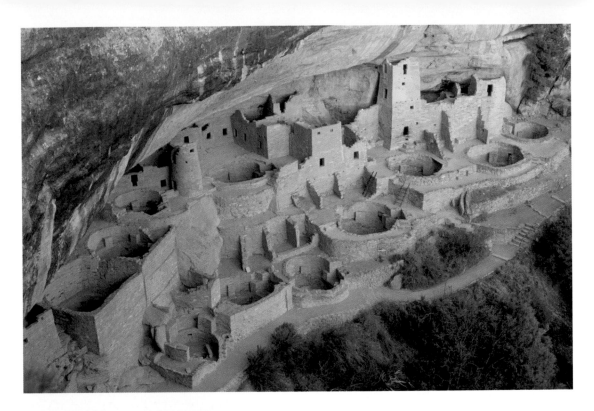

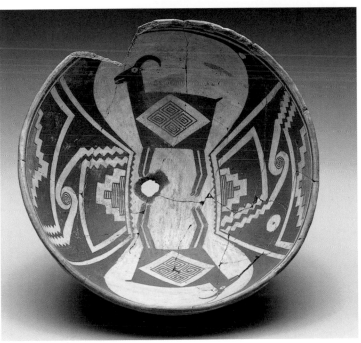

20.20 (above) Cliff Palace, Mesa Verde, Colo. Anasazi culture, c. 1200 C.E.

20.21 (left) *Bowl with Mountain Sheep.* Mimbres culture, c. 1100 C.E. Painted pottery, diameter 10½".
Frederick R. Weisman Art Museum, University of Minnesota, Minneapolis.

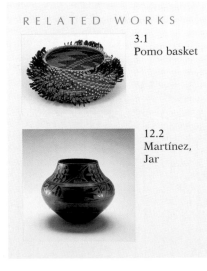

RELATED WORKS

3.1
Pomo basket

12.2
Martínez, Jar

The Anasazi's neighbors in the Southwest were a people we know only as the Mogollon culture, which flourished in the Mimbres Valley of what is now New Mexico between the 3rd and 12th centuries C.E. Today the word *Mimbres* is associated with a type of ceramic vessel developed about 1000 C.E. Mimbres jars and bowls were decorated with geometric designs or with stylized figures of animals or humans. Often these motifs appeared as paired figures (**20.21**). Although Mimbres ceramics were probably used in households in some way, most examples that have come down to us have been recovered from burials. As grave goods the vessels often seem to have been ritually "killed," either by shattering or, as here, by being pierced with a hole. The act draws a parallel with the human body, which is a vessel for a soul. In death, the vessel is broken and the soul released.

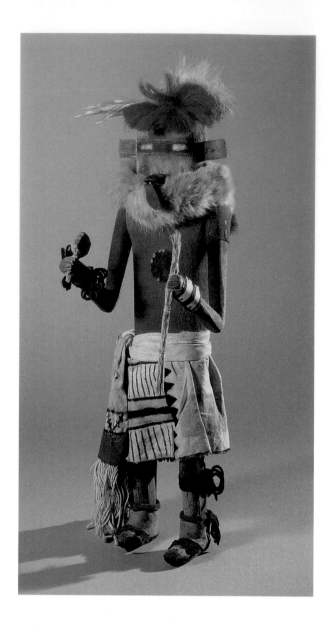

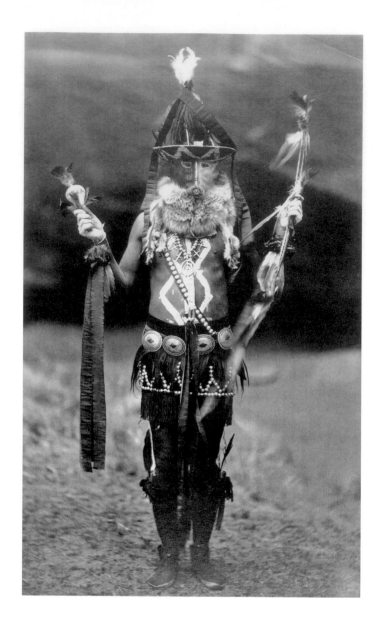

20.22 (left) Kachina doll. Zuni culture, before 1903. Wood, pigments, hair, fur hide, cotton, wool, yucca, height 19". The Brooklyn Museum, New York.

20.23 (right) Edward S. Curtis. *Navajo Zahadolzha Masker,* from Volume 1 of *The North American Indian.* Photograph. 1907.

Masks and masking played important roles in some Indian cultures. The Pueblo cultures of the Southwest acknowledge numerous supernatural beings called kachina (from the Hopi *katsina*). Danced by maskers, kachina enter into the community at important times to bring blessings. They may appear, for example, early in the year as auspicious presences so that rain will follow for the new crops. Later, after a successful growing season, they dance at harvest ceremonies. Over 200 kachina have been identified, each with its own name, mask, character, dance movements, and powers.

Hopi and Zuni Indians make doll-size versions of kachina as educational playthings so that children may learn to identify and understand the numerous spirits (**20.22**). The kachina themselves often presented the dolls to the young members of the community during their appearances. The doll here portrays a kachina named *tamtam kushokta*. The spirit wears a white Hopi blanket around its waist and a coyote mask. A spectator who witnessed kachina maskers dancing in 1907 wrote, "In their right hands they carried a tortoise-shell rattle, which they shook with vigor when they danced, and in the left hand, a bundle of prayer sticks, tied up in corn husk, with a kind of handle attached by which it was held."[1] These handheld objects are faithfully represented on the doll. Kachina dolls were believed to contain some of the power of the spirit they represented. Early in the 20th century, admirers managed to purchase or commission kachina dolls, but this move caused great unease among the Zuni, who believed that letting the dolls out of the community would result in crop failures or other disasters. Selling the dolls to outsiders was a crime subject to severe punishment, although it seems that some were indeed sold.

Contact often led to cultural borrowing among Indian groups, as indeed it has with peoples all over the world throughout history. The Navajo people arrived in the Southwest between 1200 and 1500 c.e., after a long migration from their original lands in Alaska. Although they never quite adopted the settled life of their new Pueblo neighbors, they did adapt aspects of Pueblo arts and religious beliefs to their own use, including the practice of making spirit beings manifest through masks (**20.23**). As the photograph here shows, Navajo spirit masks resemble Kachina, and indeed scholars believe that the two sets of deities may be distantly linked. The Navajo, however, call their spirits *Yei*, Holy People. Spirit masks such as this one might have appeared at the climax of a particularly elaborate healing ceremony, during which their powers had been invoked through a sand painting such as the one we looked at in Chapter 2 (see 2.36).

Masks are also danced by many peoples of the Pacific Northwest, including the Kwakiutl, who live along the southern coast of British Columbia. The flamboyant Kwakiutl mask illustrated here is Crooked Beak, one of the four mythical Cannibal Birds who live at the north end of the world and eat human flesh (**20.24**). During the winter, the four monsters ritually invade the human community. They kidnap young men of noble families and turn them into cannibals. This kidnapping and transformation take place within the larger ceremony of potlatch, in which a host generously feeds guests from numerous villages over the course of many days. On the final day, the elders of the gathering ritually cure the young man of his cannibalism. The four Cannibal Bird masks dance as part of this ritual, after which they are banished for another year.

The long beak is hinged, and a skillful dancer can make it open and snap menacingly shut. Cannibal Bird masks are carved to this day, both for use and to be sold to collectors. Their tremendous formal variety shows how much room for creativity and individual expression an artist actually has within forms that are too often thought of as unchanging and "traditional."

20.24 Johnnie Davis. *Crooked Beak*. 19th century. Wood, red cedar bark, cord, leather, and paint; length 35¼".
Royal British Columbia Museum, Victoria.

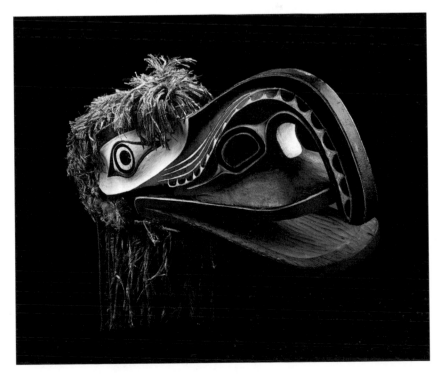

SACRED AND SECULAR

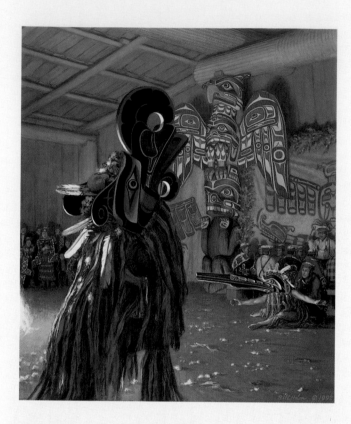

Bill Holm's painting *Hamsamala* depicts a ceremonial dance of the Kwakiutl peoples of the Pacific Northwest. The large mask in foreground is none other than Crooked Beak, the spirit portrayed in the mask we looked at by Johnnie Davis (fig. 20.23).

Holm is a respected scholar of Northwest Coastal Indian cultures, and his painting combines an artist's imaginative flair with a scholar's concern for accuracy. The masks being danced are faithful depictions of works by Willie Seaweed, perhaps the most renowned Kwakiutl carver of the 20th century. The setting is the Raven House of chief John Scow. The carved posts from this house are today in the Seattle Art Museum. The cloth curtain in the background can be seen in an early photograph of the house. Today, it is in the Denver Museum of Natural History. Holm's painting evokes a time when these dispersed elements were at the center of a vibrant community.

American Indian art can be an uneasy presence in museums. While the objects that Holm paints were purchased and donated legally, this has not always

been the case. In the past, artworks were often taken from conquered Indian peoples without permission, as were the contents of their graves, including ritual objects and human remains. During the 1970s, the Zuni people of the American Southwest began asking museums to return part of their cultural heritage. Specifically, they requested return of the sacred carvings known as War Gods, *Ahayu:da*.

A witness later recalled the moving plea of a Zuni spokesperson to the Denver Museum of Art, which owned two such carvings. "The War Gods were given to the Zuni Nation directly from our Creator," the spokesperson said. "The Creator entrusted us with the sacred objects to protect, guide, and direct our people. The War Gods came to us with a language. They came to us with specific prayers, specific songs, and specific instructions directly from God. The War Gods are sad and lonely. No one in America, no people walking by them in museums know their songs, their names, and their prayers . . . No one cleanses them or prays for them."[2] The theft of the War Gods a century earlier, the spokesperson continued, had left the Zuni unable to speak to Nature. The result was disorder, both in the Zuni nation and in the wider world. The Denver Museum acquiesced to the Zuni's request, the first of many institutions to do so.

Through their quiet, reasoned persistence, the Zuni inaugurated a new era of cooperation between Indian peoples and the museums that preserve their art. When Congress created the National Museum of the American Indian as a branch of the Smithsonian Institution in 1989, it also required the Smithsonian to develop a repatriation policy for Indian remains and grave goods. In 1990 the Native American Graves Protection and Repatriation Act was passed. And in 1996 the Smithsonian legislation was amended to include provisions for repatriating funerary objects in general, sacred objects, and objects of cultural patrimony (objects central to a people's sense of their collective identity). By making a distinction between sacred and secular, the Zuni lead us again to think about the borders of the word "art," and to examine our assumptions about the role of museums, the practice of collecting, and the concept of ownership.

Bill Holm. *Hamsamala.* 1992. Acrylic on canvas, 30 × 24". Courtesy the artist.

CHAPTER TWENTY-ONE

THE MODERN WORLD: 1800–1945

For 19th-century artists and writers, walking through the teeming city streets was the equivalent of today's channel surfing—one sensation followed quickly on another, offering fleeting glimpses of thousands of lives. They found it overwhelming—sometimes thrilling, sometimes disturbing—but they recognized it as new and they called it "modern." Modernity reflected the emergence of a new kind of society in the wake of the three revolutions discussed at the end of Chapter 17: the French Revolution, the American Revolution, and the Industrial Revolution. Driven by technological progress and characterized by rapid change, the 19th century gave birth to our industrialized middle-class culture of mass production, mass advertising, and mass consumption, including the mass consumption of leisure activities such as shopping, going to entertainments, or visiting art museums.

Art museums themselves were a development of the 19th century, and they made art available to the public (including artists) in a way we now take for granted. The first national museum was the Louvre in Paris. Opened in 1793 during the fervor of the French Revolution, it placed the art that had been the private property of the kings of France on public view in what used to be the royal residence. Like everything else that used to belong to aristocrats, art was now for everybody, but what kind of art did everybody want? What kind of art was suited to a society no longer dominated by the Church or by the nobility, but by the middle class and its leaders of finance and industry? Debates about art and modernity began during the 19th century and continued into the 20th, resulting in the ever-increasing number of "isms" that appear in art history from this point on: Realism, Impressionism, Pointillism, Fauvism, Cubism, Futurism, Surrealism—each one staking out a different viewpoint about what art can be, what subjects it can treat, and how it can look. During this time as well, photography revolutionized the making of images. From the Chauvet cave paintings of 30,000 B.C.E. until the first successful daguerreotype in 1837, images had been made by hand. Suddenly, there was another way, and it posed profound questions about the nature and purpose of art even as it opened up new possibilities.

The changes of modernity occurred everywhere in Europe, but the debates they provoked in the visual arts played out most dramatically in France, especially in Paris, and this brief survey largely focuses there.

RELATED WORKS

7.8
Ingres, *La
Comtesse
d'Haussonville*

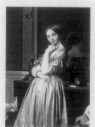

NEOCLASSICISM
AND ROMANTICISM

As we saw in Chapter 17, France's foremost Neoclassical painter, Jacques-Louis David, was an ardent supporter of the Revolution and portrayed several of its heroes (see 17.19). David went on to become the official painter to Napoleon, a position that gave him great influence over the artistic life of France. When Napoleon fell from power in 1815, David went into exile, but Neoclassical style was carried forward into the new century by his students, the foremost of whom was Jean-Auguste-Dominique Ingres.

In Chapter 7, we looked at Ingres' portrait of the Countess of Haussonville (see 7.8). Here, we illustrate an earlier work, *Jupiter and Thetis* (**21.1**). The subject is drawn from Homer's *Iliad*, the Greek epic of the Trojan War. The nymph Thetis is shown pleading with Jupiter, ruler of the gods, to intervene in the war on behalf of her son, the warrior Achilles. To the left, hidden in the clouds, Jupiter's jealous wife, Juno, spies on the encounter. With its clear contours, clean colors, and precise draftsmanship, the painting clearly shows Ingres' debt to his teacher.

Although today Ingres' portraits and nudes are among his most admired works, Ingres himself staked his reputation on paintings such as *Jupiter and Thetis*. He had inherited the view that great art can only be made from great

21.1 Jean-Auguste-Dominique Ingres. *Jupiter and Thetis*. 1811. Oil on canvas, 10'8⅝" × 8'6⁵⁄₁₆". Musée Granet, Aix-en-Provence.

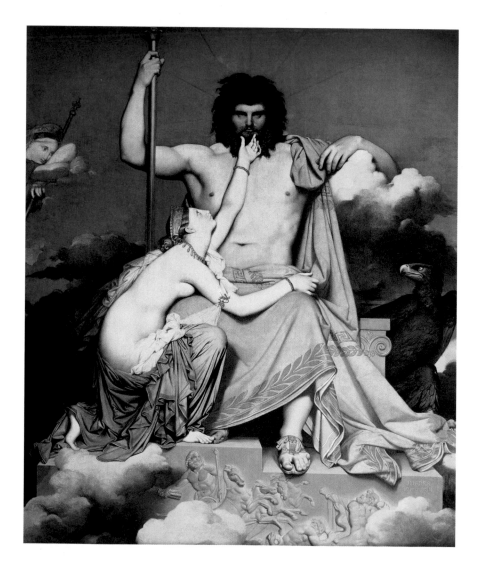

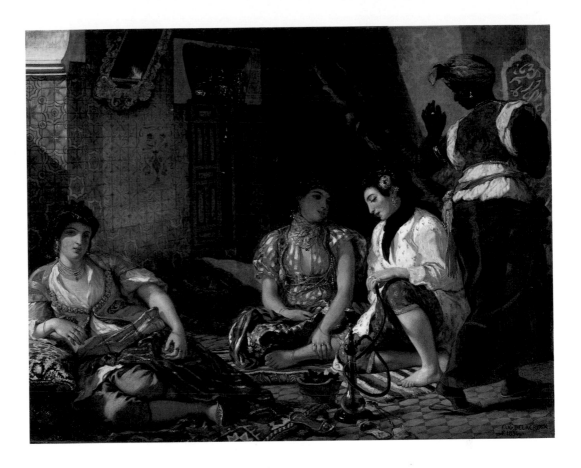

21.2 Eugène Delacroix. *The Women of Algiers*. 1834. Oil on canvas, 5'10⅞" × 7'6⅛". Musée du Louvre, Paris.

subject matter, and that the greatest subject matter of all was history—a category that included Classical mythology and biblical scenes. This viewpoint and the highly polished style that went with it became enshrined as academic art, the art that was encouraged by the official art schools and institutions of the 19th century.

The second dominant trend of the time, Romanticism, also had its roots in the preceding century. Romanticism was not a style so much as a set of attitudes and characteristic subjects. The 18th century is sometimes known as the Age of Reason, for its leading thinkers placed their faith in rationality, skeptical questioning, and scientific inquiry. Rebelling against these, Romanticism urged the claims of emotion, intuition, individual experience, and, above all, the imagination. Romantic artists gloried in such subjects as mysterious or awe-inspiring landscapes (see 4.48), picturesque ruins, extreme or tumultuous human events (see 4.8), the struggle for liberty (see 3.11 and 5.17), and scenes of exotic cultures.

Geographically, the closest "exotic" cultures to Europe were the Islamic lands of North Africa. To European thinking, these were part of "the Orient"—a realm imagined as sensuous and seductive, full of barbaric splendor and cruelty. Eugène Delacroix, the leading painter of the Romantic movement in France, spent several months in North Africa in 1832. Fascinated by all he saw, he filled sketchbook after sketchbook with drawings, watercolors, and observations. Later, he drew upon this material to create numerous paintings, including *The Women of Algiers* (**21.2**), which portrays three women and their servant in a harem, the women's apartment of an Islamic palace. Delacroix had apparently been allowed to visit an actual harem, a rare privilege for a man, not to mention a European. Compared with the cool perfection of Ingres' careful drawing and glazed colors, Delacroix's technique is freer and more painterly. Forms are built up with fully loaded brush strokes, contours are blurred, and colors are broken.

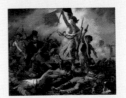
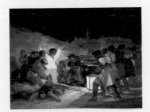

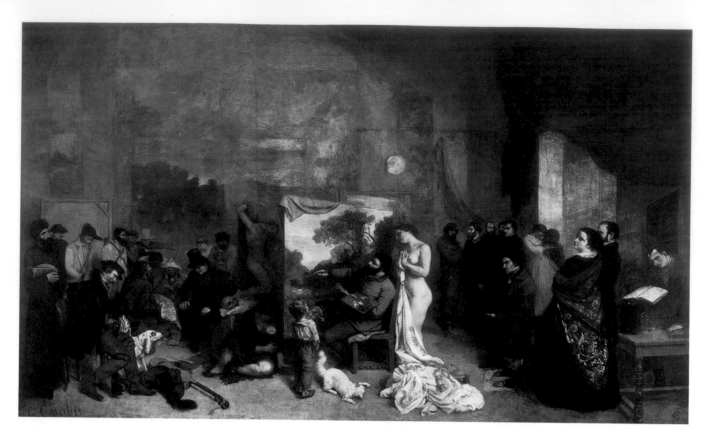

21.3 Gustave Courbet. *The Artist's Studio: A Real Allegory Summing Up Seven Years of My Life as an Artist.* 1855. Oil on canvas, 11'9¾" × 19'6⅝". Musée d'Orsay, Paris.

REALISM

The first art movement to be born in the 19th century was **Realism,** which arose as a reaction against both Neoclassicism and Romanticism. Realist artists sought to depict the everyday and the ordinary, rather than the historic, the heroic, or the exotic. Their concerns were very much rooted in the present. One of the leaders of the Realist movement was Gustave Courbet, who in 1855 exhibited a huge painting, *The Artist's Studio* (**21.3**), subtitled *A Real Allegory Summing Up Seven Years of My Life as an Artist.*

At the center of the canvas sits Courbet himself, at work on a landscape painting. Although a great many people crowd into the studio, the artist seems aloof from them, as though his aesthetic concerns are all-consuming. A little boy (usually identified as Innocence) gawks up at the work in progress. Behind the artist stands a nude model, whom some consider to be his Muse, or inspiration, others the personification of Truth (that is, the "naked truth"). All the figures to the left of the composition are common people; they are "types," not individuals, derived from Courbet's origins in a rural village. At right are the artist's "intellectual" friends, many of them identifiable figures—his patrons, other artists, writers, and so on. Perhaps Courbet is saying the artist represents a special elite, fed by his origins and by his comrades, but apart from them, alone with Innocence and Truth. We know from Courbet's work as a whole that here the artist was trying to make a particular point—that everyday activities, such as an artist working at his easel or peasants toiling in the fields, were fit subject matter for grand-scale art. In an age when only paintings of religious or historical or mythological scenes were considered "great art," this was a revolutionary idea.

Two of the paintings we have considered so far include a nude or semi-nude woman. In each case, their nudity served a specific, accepted purpose. Thetis, for example, is a character from Classical mythology. Her nudity was underwritten by the art of ancient Greece and Rome, which cultivated viewers had been taught to admire. But eight years after Courbet exhibited *The Artist's Studio,* a painting was placed on display in Paris that portrayed female nudity without any apparent justification at all. It caused a terrific scandal—the first of many artistic scandals that would shock the art world in the decades to come. The artist responsible for setting off this earthquake was a mild, conventional, well-to-do gentleman: Edouard Manet.

MANET AND IMPRESSIONISM

In 19th-century France the mark of an artist's success was acceptance at the annual Salon, a state-sponsored exhibition of paintings. Artists submitted their work for consideration by an official jury, whose members varied from year to year but tended to be conservative, if not downright stodgy. In 1863 the Salon jury rejected almost 3,000 of the submitted works, which caused such an uproar among the spurned artists and their supporters that a second official exhibition was mounted—the "Salon des Refusés" (showing of those who had been refused). Among the works in the "refused" show—and very soon the most notorious among them—was Edouard Manet's painting *Le Déjeuner sur l'herbe* (**21.4**).

Luncheon on the Grass, as it is usually translated, shows a kind of outdoor picnic. Two men, dressed in the fashions of the day, relax and chat in a woodland setting. Their companion is a woman who has, for no apparent reason, taken off all her clothes. In the background another woman, wearing only a filmy garment, bathes in a stream.

Manet seems to have wanted to accomplish two goals with this work. The first was to join Courbet and other artists in painting modern life. But the other was to prove that modern life could produce eternal subjects worthy of the great masters of the museums. His solution was to "update" two famous Renaissance images, Titian's *Fête Champêtre* (see 16.17) and Raphael's *The Judgment of Paris* (see 8.11, lower right). The public saw what Manet was doing: the Titian, after all, was in the Louvre Museum close by, and the Raphael was routinely copied by art students. They saw what he was doing, and they didn't like it. Surely Manet was making fun of them. In place of Titian's idealized and dignified nudes, he had painted a common woman of loose morals:

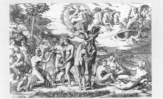

8.11 Raimondi/Raphael,
The Judgment of Paris

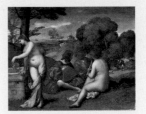

16.17 Titian, *Fête Champêtre*

21.4 Edouard Manet. *Le Déjeuner sur l'herbe.* 1863. Oil on canvas, 7' × 8'10".
Musée d'Orsay, Paris.

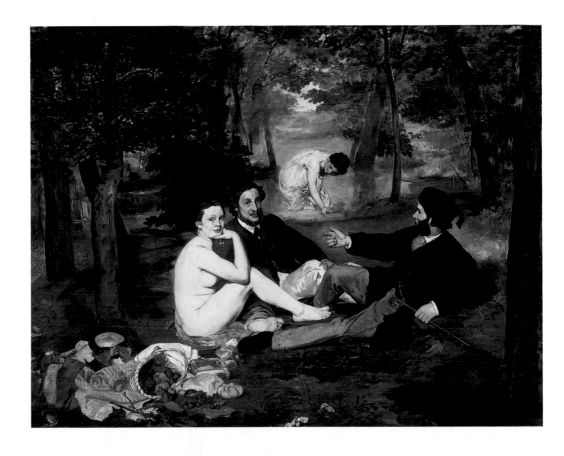

who else would sit there with no clothes on, meeting our gaze so frankly? The men in the painting, too, were completely undistinguished—not noble poets as in Titian, but ordinary students on holiday. One critic lamented that Manet was trying to achieve celebrity the easy way, by shocking his public. Others found the technique inept. Perhaps if Manet would learn something about perspective and drawing, they said, his taste might improve as well.

Manet's painting *is* odd, and art historians still debate just what he meant by it. In modeling his figures, Manet focused on the highest and lowest values, all but eliminating the middle, transitional tones. As a result, the forms appear flattened, as though illuminated by a sudden flash of light. The perspective is off: Contemporary viewers were quite right. The bather is as far away as the rowboat, but if you imagine her standing in it, you see that she is a giantess. It was evidently more important to Manet to have her form the apex of his triangle of figures than to place her correctly in perspective. This, too, flattens the painting, for the bather seems to move forward to join the rest of the figures, compressing the space between foreground and background. The spatial tension plays out in the landscape itself: On the left side of the painting, the ground recedes convincingly into the distance, but on the right side there is no recession—just flat bright green. Nor do we believe for a minute that these people are really sitting outdoors. Clearly they are posing in a studio. The landscape is painted around them like a stage set or a photographer's backdrop. Finally, the borrowed composition *feels* borrowed, as though it were in quotation marks.

All of these qualities—the public scandal, the flatness, the artificiality, the ambiguity, and the self-conscious relation to art history—have made the painting a touchstone of modern art. Painting in the modern era could no longer be a simple, transparent window on the world. It would also be increasingly conscious of itself *as* a painting.

During the years following Manet's sensation in the Salon des Refusés, young French artists increasingly sought alternatives to the Salon. One group in particular looked to Manet as their philosophical leader, although he never consented to exhibit with them. They thought of themselves as Realists, for like Manet and Courbet they believed that modern life itself was the most suitable subject for modern art. In 1874 they organized their first exhibition as The Anonymous Society of Artists, Painters, Sculptors, Printmakers, etc. A painting in the exhibit by Claude Monet called *Impression: Sunrise,* however, earned the special scorn of one critic, who dubbed the whole endeavor Impressionism. The name stuck in the public imagination, and the artists largely accepted it: Scenes glimpsed for a moment, sketched rapidly in paint as impressions of light and color on the eye—these were indeed some of their concerns.

With Impressionism, art moved outdoors—not the artificial outdoors of Manet, but the true outdoors. Painting up until then had been a studio product, in part because of the cumbersome materials it involved. Thanks to the new availability of portable oil colors in tubes (as they are still manufactured today), many of the Impressionists took their canvases, brushes, and paints outside to be part of the shifting light they wanted to depict. A lovely example of the new "open air" painting is Berthe Morisot's *The Harbor at Lorient* (**21.5**). The diagonal of a parapet leads our eyes into the composition to the demure figure of Morisot's sister Edma, who has been out for a stroll. Lost in a daydream, she does not return our gaze, which is now free to roam over the harbor with its milling people and accurately observed ships. The expanses of pale blue sky and water convey the feeling of a wide open space filled with light. Manet admired the painting so extravagantly that Morisot gave it to him.

The light in Renoir's enchanting *Le Moulin de la Galette* (**21.6**) is a light we have not seen before in painting, the dappled, shifting light that filters through leaves stirred by a breeze. Traditional chiaroscuro required a steady and even source of light for modeling form. But light in nature wasn't always like that. It moved, it shifted, it danced. And the forms it revealed weren't always clear. A house in the distance might just seem like a patch of yellow. A

RELATED WORKS

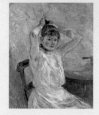

5.14
Manet,
*A Bar at
the Folies-
Bergère*

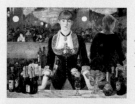

4.25
Pissarro,
*Palette with
a Landscape*

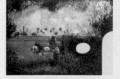

7.9
Morisot, *Girl
Arranging
Her Hair*

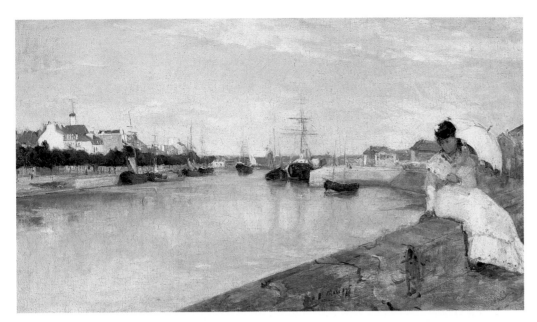

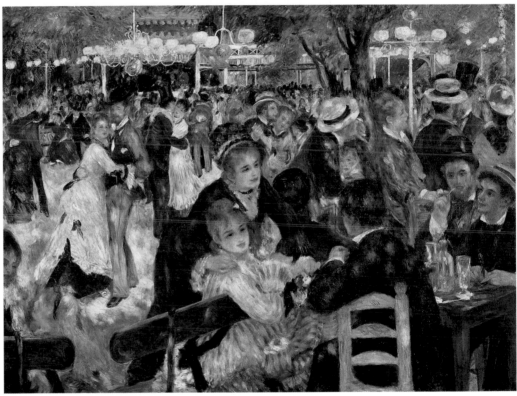

waltzing couple might be a blur. The desire to capture such optical sensations of perception required a new kind of painting technique. Instead of building a painting up from preliminary layers of drawing and modeling, Renoir began directly with paint, weaving individual brush strokes into an allover tapestry of colors that resolve into forms. The Impressionists surrendered the smooth surface of academic painting, with its layers of glazes and other studio refinements, for a straightforward painting technique devoted to capturing the fleeting sensations of perception. The resulting sketchiness disturbed Impressionism's critics; to them, the paintings looked unfinished and the forms not solid. Renoir would later adjust his style to create more solid figures and largely abandon modern life for "timeless" subjects, but here he is in his full Impressionist glory, capturing a moment's pleasure with flickering strokes of paint that record sensations of light, color, and movement.

21.5 (above) Berthe Morisot. *The Harbor at Lorient.* 1869. Oil on canvas, 17⅛ × 28¾".
National Gallery of Art, Washington, D.C.

21.6 (below) Pierre-Auguste Renoir. *Le Moulin de la Galette.* 1876. Oil on canvas, 4'3½" × 5'9".
Musée d'Orsay, Paris.

Le Moulin de la Galette was an establishment on the outskirts of Paris where working people gathered on their day off to relax and enjoy themselves. Renoir paints a group of his own more elegant friends there, dancing and talking, drinking and flirting. The leisure activities of the emerging middle class were a favorite subject of the Impressionists, and we may be forgiven if because of them we picture 19th-century France as a land where there is always time to stroll in the country, where a waltz is always playing under the trees.

Another member of the Impressionist group was Edgar Degas. Degas' concerns were somewhat different from the rest of the Impressionists. He was not interested in painting outdoors, or in recording sensations of perception, or in landscape. A superb draftsman, his great interest was the human figure, and he was endlessly ingenious at finding subjects in contemporary life that allowed him to depict it (see 6.3, 6.10). Degas was a Parisian to the core and a keen observer of Parisian life. He was reported to be an excellent mimic, and he delighted in capturing the characteristic gestures of people he watched. We can be sure that the gesture of the woman biting the tip of her thumb in *Women at a Café, Evening* (**21.7**) was one he saw and filed away for use later. Typical of Degas, the composition seems as spontaneous as a snapshot, though it is actually carefully calculated. From Japanese prints, then widely collected in Paris, Degas borrowed the device of having an element such as a lamppost or pillar interrupt the composition and block our view. Such interruptions also reflect Degas' interest in photography, which lent itself naturally to intriguingly cropped views.

Degas drew the scene in black paint as a monotype, then worked over the print with pastels. Perhaps he felt such an improvised technique was better suited to the unstable nature of contemporary life than oil paint with its history of masterpieces and museums. Above all, the scene reflects Degas' fascination with the social levels of Paris, which were mingling in new ways during his lifetime. The women are prostitutes, gathered at a café to swap stories or wait for clients. The clues are lost on us today, but Degas' contemporaries had no trouble recognizing them, and they took the artist to task for depicting the women with what one critic called "terrifying realism."

21.7 Edgar Degas. *Women at a Café, Evening.* 1877. Pastel on monotype, 16⅛ × 23⅝". Musée d'Orsay, Paris.

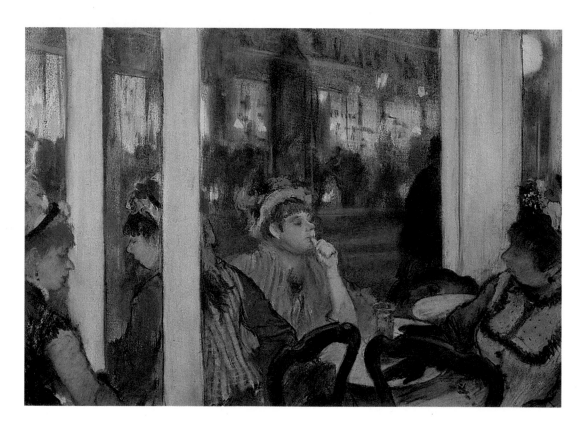

PRESENTING THE PAST

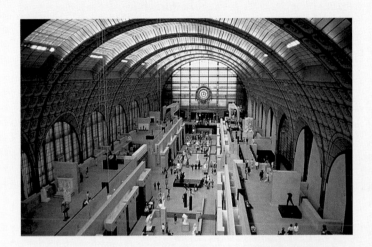

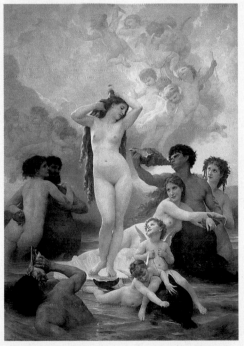

Gᴇɴᴇʀᴀᴛɪᴏɴs ᴏꜰ ᴀʀᴛ lovers have enjoyed the story of the triumph of Impressionism. So familiar have many of these paintings become, so central to our idea of "great art," that we find it hard to believe that critics and the public initially disliked them. Who could be so blind? Impressionism's important role in the history of modern art even earned the movement its very own museum in Paris, the intimate Jeu de Paume.

Many were horrified, then, when the French government announced in 1978 that it was going to move the Jeu de Paume's collection to the nearby Gare d'Orsay, a cavernous railway station that was to be renovated as a museum. There, the paintings would be united with works drawn from museums all over France and representing all the arts and artistic trends of the 19th century—not just progressive styles but conservative ones as well, not just painting and sculpture, but architecture, photography, popular arts and illustration, decorative arts such as furniture and porcelain, and exhibits about the political and social history of the time. Folded back into the larger con-

text of the era, the Impressionists would hang alongside the academic painters and forgotten favorites of the Salon. "Just the people they'd been trying to get away from all their lives," grumbled one Parisian painter.[1]

One of these people was the arch-academic William-Adolphe Bouguereau, whose *The Birth of Venus* is illustrated here. Bouguereau began his career painting tormented Romantic themes, yet he quickly discovered that what the public wanted was Venuses and Cupids, and that is what he gave them—slick, sentimental, and mildly titillating—until his death in 1905. It made him rich. Looking at this painting, with its clear contours and flawless finish, we can better understand the artistic debates of the day. No wonder Impressionist works looked sketchy and even vulgar! Suddenly our own position becomes less clear: What would we have preferred ourselves? Venus, or some uncouth students at a picnic? Stylish escape, or raw modern life? Which, honestly, do we prefer now?

In 1986, after a widely publicized battle of powerful public officials, critics, patrons, and artists, the Gare d'Orsay reopened as the Musée d'Orsay, now one of the most popular and visited showplaces of art in Europe. By blurring distinctions between high and low, academic and avant-garde, its inclusive collection has challenged some of our most accepted understandings of art history, while its user-friendly design has democratized and made accessible the stuffy and exclusive space of the fine arts museum. For these reasons, it is perhaps the first exhibition hall of our own Postmodern era.

(top) Interior of the Musée d'Orsay.
(center) William Bouguereau. *The Birth of Venus*. 1879. Oil on canvas, 9'10⅛" × 7'1⅜". Musée d'Orsay, Paris.

The painter who best exemplifies the ideas of Impressionism, and who remained most faithful to them throughout his long life, was Claude Monet. Monet's great subject was landscape. While still in his teens he had taken up the new practice of painting outdoors. As a mature artist Monet roamed the countryside, painting the views near wherever he happened to be living. He often spent the summer months painting along the French seacoast, and he made several painting trips to London and Venice as well. Monet eventually settled in Giverny, a town along the Seine river north of Paris. There he created a garden that became the favorite subject of his later years (**21.8**). Here is a miracle of Impressionist sensibility, a painting woven entirely of broken greens, the flicked brush strokes suggesting now masses of foliage, now their reflection in the smooth surface of a pond. Water lilies float between the open parentheses of an arching bridge and its shadow. Everything shimmers in the light.

21.8 (left) Claude Monet. *A Bridge Over a Pool of Water Lilies.* 1899. Oil on canvas, 36½ × 29". The Metropolitan Museum of Art, New York.

21.9 (right) Paul Gauguin. *Te Aa No Areois (The Seed of Areoi).* 1892. Oil on burlap, 36¼ × 28⅜". The Museum of Modern Art, New York.

POST-IMPRESSIONISM

The next generation of artists admired many aspects of Impressionism, especially its brightened palette and direct painting technique. But they reacted in various ways to what they perceived as its shortcomings. Their styles are so highly personal that we commonly group them together under the neutral term *Post-Impressionists,* meaning simply the artists that came after Impressionism. They include Georges Seurat, Vincent van Gogh, Paul Gauguin, and Paul Cézanne.

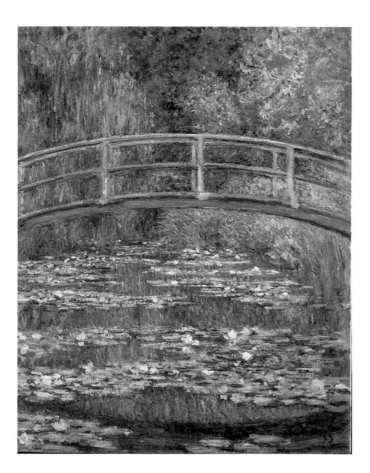

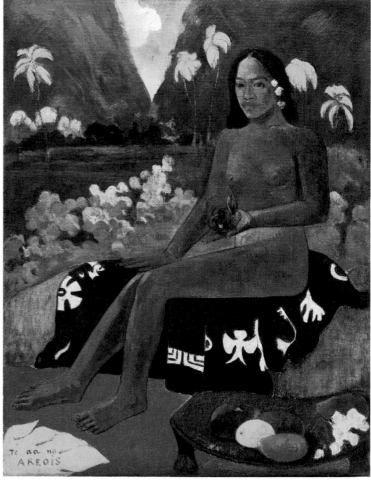

Seurat wanted to place Impressionism's intuitive recording of optical sensations on a more scientific footing. His reading of color theories led him to develop the technique of Pointillism, in which discrete dots and dashes of pure color were supposed to blend in the viewer's eye. Of all the Post-Impressionists, Seurat was the most faithful to the idea of painting modern life. In *A Sunday on La Grande Jatte* (see 4.31), he portrayed ordinary people enjoying their day off with ceremony and dignity, and *Bathers at Asnières* (see 3.19), set in the working-class outskirts of Paris, frankly acknowledged the factories that were now a part of the landscape.

For other Post-Impressionists, the industrialized modern world was not something that needed to be confronted but something that needed to be escaped. Vincent van Gogh arrived in Paris from Antwerp in 1886, but he stayed for only two years—just long enough to catch up with the latest developments in art. Van Gogh settled instead in Arles, a small, rural town in the south of France, where he painted the landscape, people, and things closest to him. The high-key colors, agitated brushwork, and emotional intensity of such works as *The Starry Night* (see 1.10) and *Wheat Field and Cypress Trees* (see 2.1) would have an enormous influence on the next generation of artists.

Paul Gauguin worked in an Impressionist style early in his career, but he soon became dissatisfied. He felt the need for more substance, more solidity of form than could be found in optical perceptions of light. Beyond this, Gauguin was interested in expressing a spiritual meaning in his art. All these he sought on the sun-drenched islands of the South Pacific, where he journeyed to escape what he called "the disease of civilization." The brilliant high-keyed colors of Gauguin's Tahitian paintings reveal his debt to Impressionism. To this lightened palette he added his own innovations: flattened forms and broad color areas, a strong outline, tertiary color harmonies, a taste for the exotic, an aura of mystery, and a quest for the "primitive."

Te Aa No Areois (The Seed of the Areoi) (**21.9**) was painted about a year into Gauguin's first long stay in Tahiti, and it shows all of these characteristics. Whereas Monet's painting is woven together out of distinct brush strokes like a piece of fabric, Gauguin's seems pieced, like a puzzle or a quilt. We can almost imagine assembling it by cutting the shapes from sheets of colored paper. The white motifs on the blue cloth dance free of their ground, as do the yellow palm trees in the background. In the midst of all this whirling brilliance, a golden brown woman sits in quiet dignity, holding a sprouting seed in the palm of her hand. Her pose—legs shown in profile, shoulders depicted frontally—is derived from Egyptian art. Gauguin believed that European art had been in thrall for too long to the legacy of Greece and Rome, and he looked to the art of Egypt, Islam, and Asia to renew it. The woman's gesture is mysterious, yet we sense that there is some profound meaning to it, if only we could understand what she is offering us. Though he painted a paradise, Gauguin in fact was bitterly disappointed in Tahiti. He felt that European missionaries and colonists had already ruined it. In the end, he painted what he dreamed of finding, because what he found was that there was no escape.

In contrast to Gauguin's need for travel and exotic subjects, Paul Cézanne found everything he needed within walking distance of his home in the south of France. Cézanne admired the Impressionists' practice of working directly from nature, and he approved of their bright palette and their individual strokes of color. He was dissatisfied, though, with their casual compositions and their emphasis on what is transitory, such as the dappled sunlight on Renoir's spinning dancers. He felt that what had made painting great in the past was structure and order. He admired, for example, Poussin's majestic structuring of nature in such paintings as *The Ashes of Phokion* (see 17.8). Could the brush strokes that the Impressionists used to register optical sensations be used to build something more solid and durable? Could an artist paint directly from nature and find in it the order and clarity of Poussin? These were the goals that Cézanne set for himself.

RELATED WORKS

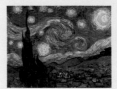

1.10
Van Gogh,
*Starry
Night*

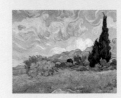

2.1
Van Gogh,
*Wheat
Fields and
Cypress
Trees*

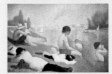

3.19
Seurat,
*Bathers at
Asnières*

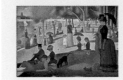

4.31
Seurat, *A
Sunday on
La Grande
Jatte*

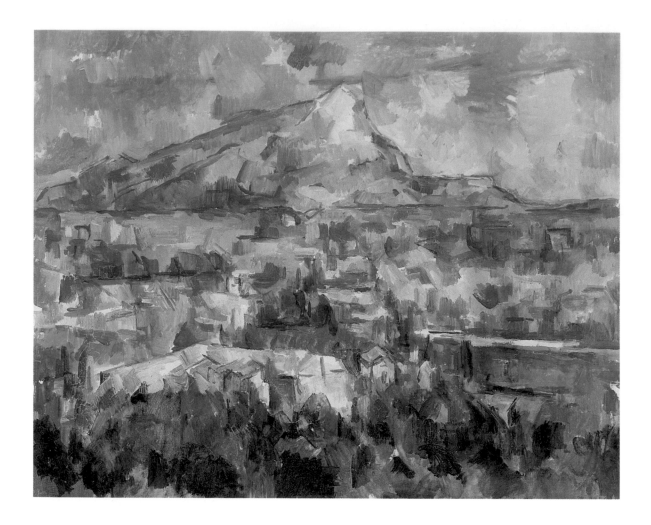

21.10 Paul Cézanne. *Mont Sainte-Victoire*. 1902–04. Oil on canvas, 27½ × 35¼". Philadelphia Museum of Art.

RELATED WORKS

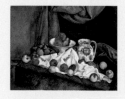

5.16 Cézanne, *Still Life*

A favorite subject of Cézanne's last years was Mont Sainte-Victoire, a mountain near his home (**21.10**). Altogether he made seventy-five painted or drawn versions of the scene. The broad outlines of the composition are simple and noble: a rectangular band of landscape surmounted by the irregular pyramid of the mountain. This underlying geometry emerges clearly from hundreds of small, vivid patches of color. Each patch is composed of the terse, precise, parallel strokes that Cézanne used to register what he called his "little sensations before nature"—the impressions that colors shimmering in the hot southern sun made on his eyes. Near the foreground, the red tile roofs of farmhouses are like ready-made color patches. The roof of the isolated house near the center reproduces exactly the silhouette of the mountain. To the left, the upward diagonal of the ocher area around the group of three farmhouses is exactly parallel to the upward slope of the mountain. These echoes are a key to Cézanne's way of thinking: Major structural lines are echoed everywhere. The line of the horizon, for example, is broken into segments, none of them quite horizontal. Segments of almost-horizontal lines appear throughout the painting, even in the sky, which is also painted in patches of color.

With paintings such as *Mont Sainte-Victoire*, Cézanne's treatment of nature grew increasingly abstract. Repetitions and echoes of key contour lines help unify the composition, but they have also begun to take on their own independent logic apart from the subject. Similarly, the terse strokes and color patches help unify the painting's surface, but they tend to fracture the image into facets. The next generation of painters would study these devices and build on them.

BRIDGING THE ATLANTIC: AMERICA IN THE 19TH CENTURY

Europe remained America's artistic touchstone during the 19th century, for America viewed itself then as a continuation of European culture. American artists often went to Europe for part of their training, not only to study with European teachers but also to see the collections of the great museums. In Europe, they could absorb more easily the history of their art at first hand. There was no American substitute, for example, for wandering through the ruins of ancient Rome or visiting a Gothic cathedral. Some American artists remained in Europe and spent their careers there. Similarly, some European artists emigrated to America, where opportunity seemed greater. Neoclassicism, Romanticism, Realism, and Impressionism were broad trends in America as they were in Europe, though without the intense battles they provoked in Paris.

Romanticism was a many-sided movement, and in America it expressed itself most clearly through an attitude toward landscape, an almost mystical reverence for the natural beauty of the unspoiled land itself. The broad vista and threatening storm of Thomas Cole's *The Oxbow* (see 3.28) display one aspect of American Romanticism. Cole was born in England, and his family emigrated to America when he was seventeen. His artistic training was in the United States, although he later spent two years looking at art in Europe.

In contrast to Cole, American-born George Caleb Bingham was largely self-taught. Bingham was the first major painter to live and work west of the Mississippi River. His *Fur Traders Descending the Missouri* (**21.11**), painted around 1845, portrays a French trapper and his son gliding down the Missouri River in a dugout canoe. The air is heavy with the golden light of dawn about to break. The son leans on their cargo, casually cradling a rifle. A duck he has recently shot lies in front of him. Father and son both look our way. The son's gaze is open; his father's more guarded. But the strangest and most haunting gaze in the painting is one we can't decipher at all: that of a bear cub chained to the prow of the canoe. Stock still, doubled by its lengthening reflection in the river, the bear has an eerie presence, reminding us of how mysterious and unknowable nature truly is.

21.11 George Caleb Bingham. *Fur Traders Descending the Missouri.* c. 1845. Oil on canvas, 29 × 36½".
The Metropolitan Museum of Art, New York.

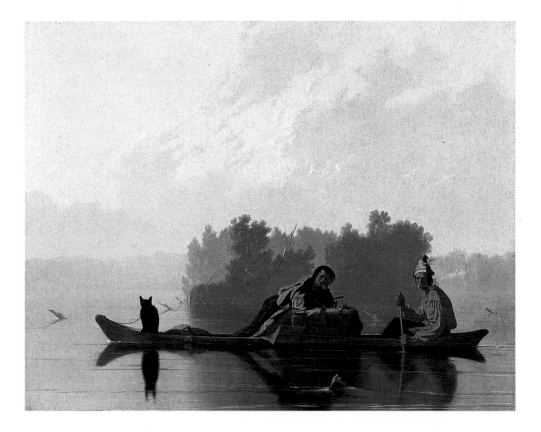

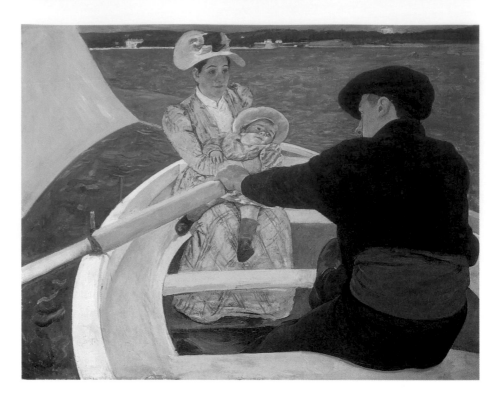

21.12 Mary Cassatt. *The Boating Party*. 1893–94. Oil on canvas, 35½ × 46⅛".
National Gallery of Art, Washington, D.C.

RELATED WORKS

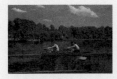

4.6
Eakins,
*The Biglin
Brothers
Racing*

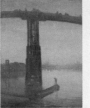

4.34
Whistler,
Nocturne

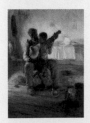

5.15
Tanner,
*Banjo
Lesson*

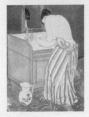

8.16
Cassatt,
*Woman
Bathing*

Realism found its finest American practitioner in Thomas Eakins, whose *The Biglin Brothers Racing* is illustrated in Chapter 4 (see 4.6). Eakins had studied in Paris and toured the museums of Europe, but he returned to Philadelphia to paint American lives. Eakins had a distinguished career as a teacher. Among his students was Henry Ossawa Tanner, whose *Banjo Lesson* is illustrated in Chapter 5 (see 5.15). One of the first important African-American artists, Tanner moved to Paris in 1894, where he turned increasingly to religious subjects and exhibited regularly in the Salon.

Another American artist who traveled to Paris and remained there was Mary Cassatt. While her artistic training in America had been conservative and academic, her natural inclination drew her toward scenes from daily life, especially intimate domestic scenes of mothers and children—a world men rarely depicted in art. Degas was impressed by the paintings she exhibited at the Salon during the 1870s, and he invited her to show with the Impressionists instead. "Finally I could work with absolute independence without concern for the eventual opinion of a jury," Cassatt later wrote. "I admired Manet, Courbet, and Degas. I detested conventional art. I began to live."[2]

Painted in 1893, Cassatt's *The Boating Party* shows the joyous results of her artistic liberation (**21.12**). A well-to-do woman has hired a boatman to take her and her child on a pleasurable outing. The child, sprawled contentedly across her mother's lap, stares at the boatman with undisguised curiosity. The mother looks at him as well, pleasantly, but from a more polite distance. The bold, simplified forms and the broad areas of color reflect the influence of Japanese prints, which had been the subject of a major exhibition in Paris three years earlier. The straightforward color harmony of blue, yellow, and red is set singing by the boatman's deep blue clothing and the boat's brilliant white gunwale.

INTO THE 20TH CENTURY: THE AVANT-GARDE

When you hear people talking about the newest, latest, most advanced art, you may hear them use the French term *avant-garde*. Avant-garde was originally a military term, referring to the detachment of soldiers that went first into battle. By the 1880s, younger artists began to refer to themselves as the avant-garde. They were the boldest artists, going first into uncharted territory and waiting for others to catch up. Their "battle" was to advance the progress of art against the resistance of conservative forces. Newness and change became artistic ideals. Each generation, even each group, believed it was their duty to go further than the one before. As the 20th century began, the idea of the avant-garde was firmly in place, and two of art's basic building blocks, form and color, were the focus of great innovation.

Freeing Color: Fauvism and Expressionism

Though it no longer wielded the power it once did, the annual Salon of Paris was still a conservative force in artistic life, and movements regularly arose against it. In 1903, a group of young artists founded the Salon d'Automne, the "autumn salon," as a progressive alternative. From the exhibits they organized, it was clear who their heroes were. In 1904, the artists of the Salon d'Automne organized a large exhibition of Cézanne. In 1906, they mounted a major retrospective of Gauguin. But the most notorious exhibit of the Salon d'Automne was the one they organized for themselves in 1905. It was then that a critic dubbed them *fauves*, "wild beasts."

One of the paintings that earned the wild beasts their name was André Derain's *View of Collioure* (**21.13**). Collioure is a small port on the Mediterranean coast of France. Derain and his friend Henri Matisse had spent the summer painting there. Like many young artists, they had been experimenting with the Pointillism of Seurat, which seemed to embody the most advanced thinking of the day. But they found it too theoretical and constraining. The more instinctive works of Van Gogh and Gauguin offered a way out. Derain's debt to Van Gogh is clear in the whirlwinds of short brush strokes, but Van Gogh would never have considered a painting this bare to be finished, nor would he have used pure, unmixed pigments, applied sometimes straight from the tube. The foreground, which Van Gogh would have labored over until it lay firmly underfoot, is nothing but swarms of brush strokes that register a kind of visual excitement. Most important, color is freed from its role in describing objects. Surely the distant hills and the near grasses were not orange! Derain painted them that way because orange, vibrating strongly near its complementary blue, seemed to convey the emotions he felt in the warmth, the sun, the sea air, the breeze.

21.13 André Derain. *View of Collioure.* 1905. Oil on canvas, 26 × 32⅜".
Museum Folkwang, Essen, Germany.

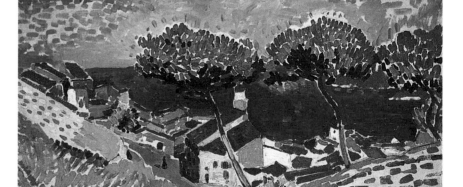

Derain's fellow Fauve Henri Matisse took the liberation of color even further in a major work of the following year, *The Joy of Life* (**21.14**). Pink sky, yellow earth, orange foliage, blue tree trunks—in Matisse's hands, color itself became a world, a place to be. The discrete dots of color that were a legacy of Seurat are gone, as are the frantic brush strokes of Van Gogh. In their place is a radiant sense of well-being, a calm that Gauguin had often sought in his pictures of Tahiti.

Fauvism did not last long, a mere three years or so. *The Joy of Life* is already in some ways beyond it. Though brief, Fauvism was crucial for the development of modern art. Never again would artists feel they must confine themselves to replicating the "real" colors of the natural world. Freed from its descriptive role, color could be used as an independent expressive element.

Fauvism was part of a larger trend in Europe called expressionism, which arose as artists came to believe that the fundamental purpose of art was to express their intense feelings toward the world. Broadly speaking, **expressionism** describes any style where the artist's subjective feelings take precedence over objective observation. Spelled with a capital E, it refers especially to an art movement that developed in Germany in the early 20th century, where the expressive ideal had its greatest influence. Like the Fauves, Expressionist artists looked to Gauguin and Van Gogh as their predecessors. They admired as well the stark works of the Norwegian artist Edvard Munch, who was then living in Berlin (see 4.35).

One important Expressionist group was Die Brücke ("The Bridge"), founded in Dresden 1905, the same year as the Fauve exhibit in Paris. The bridge the artists had in mind was one they would build through their art to a

21.14 Henri Matisse. *The Joy of Life*. 1905–06. Oil on canvas, 5'8½" × 7'9¾".
The Barnes Foundation, Merion, Pennsylvania.

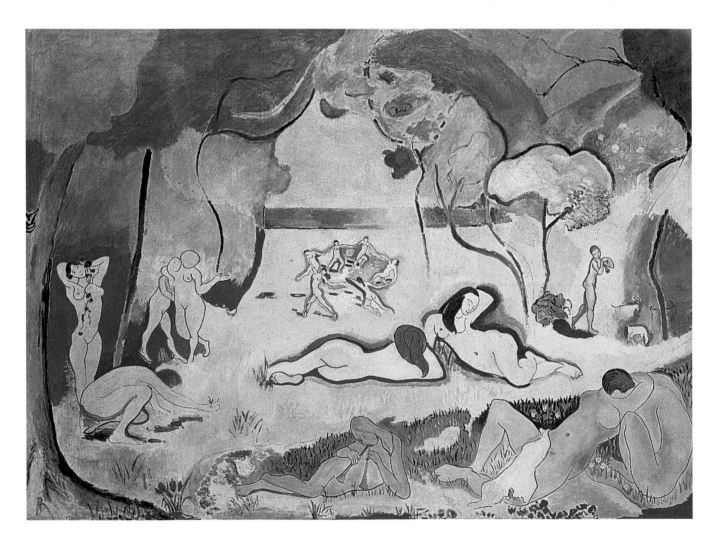

HENRI MATISSE

1869–1954

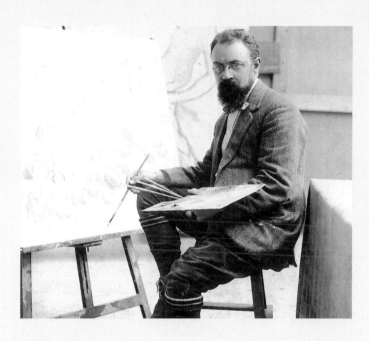

HOW IRONIC IT is that Matisse, of all people, should have provoked a critic to call him a "wild beast," for, while his art may indeed have seemed a bit wild at first, the artist himself could scarcely have been less so. Cautious, reserved, cheerful, hardworking, dedicated to his family, frugal, painstaking—these are the qualities that describe Matisse. His longtime friend and rival Picasso captured more of the headlines, but the steadfast Matisse created art no less innovative and enduring.

Matisse's father intended him to be a lawyer, but a severe bout of appendicitis at the age of twenty-one changed his life—and changed the course of all modern art. Henri's mother bought him a box of paints as a diversion, and, for once, Matisse reacted strongly. Much later he said of this experience, "It was as if I had been called. Henceforth I did not lead my life. It led me."

Matisse enrolled at the Ecole des Beaux-Arts in Paris and studied with the painter Gustave Moreau, a brilliant teacher who is said to have told his young pupil, "You were born to simplify painting." After a period of experimentation in various styles, Matisse exploded onto the Parisian art scene at the Salon d'Automne (autumn salon) in 1905, when he exhibited, along with several younger colleagues, works of such pure, intense, and arbitrary color that a critic labeled the artists *fauves*—wild beasts. In these early years Matisse did not fare much better with the general public. However, he had the good fortune to attract the attention of certain wealthy Americans who have achieved fame as inspired collectors, including the Stein family (Gertrude and her brothers) and the eccentric Cone sisters of Baltimore.

Considering the period in which he lived encompassing two world wars, Matisse kept himself remarkably outside the fray. His art did not touch upon politics or social issues. Throughout his life, his favorite subjects remained the human body (usually a beautiful female body) and the pleasant domestic interior. The joys of home life, of family, of cherished objects dominate his expression. In 1898 Matisse married Amélie Parayre, with whom he maintained a contented relationship for many years. Mme. Matisse was lovely, a willing model, charming and lively, and devoted to her husband's career. Their three children all chose art-related lives, Pierre becoming a prominent art dealer in New York.

We think of Matisse as a painter, but he worked in many fields—sculpture, book illustration, architectural design (of a small, jewel-like chapel near his home), and finally in *découpage*. By the early 1930s Matisse had begun to use cut-up paper as a means of planning his canvases, and a decade later the cut paper had become an end in itself. When he was very old and could no longer stand at his easel, Matisse sat in his wheelchair or in his bed, cutting segments of prepainted paper and arranging them into compositions, some of mural size.

Perhaps it was at the end that he came nearest to his goal: "What I dream of is an art of balance, of purity and serenity, devoid of troubling or depressing subject matter, an art which might be for every mental worker, be he businessman or writer, like an appeasing influence, like a mental soother, something like a good armchair in which to rest from physical fatigue."[3]

Matisse in his studio, 1909 or 1912. Photograph by Henri Monet(?). Pierre Matisse Gallery Archives, The Pierpont Morgan Library, New York.

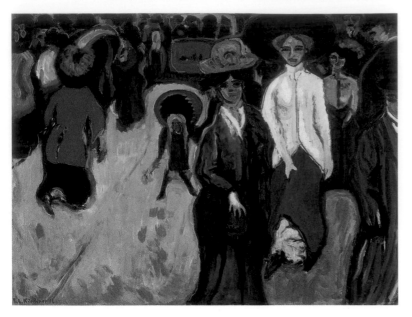

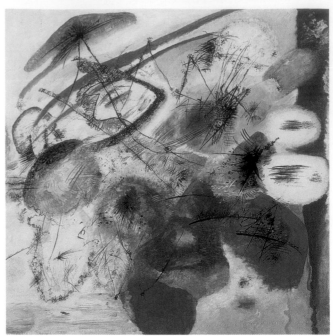

21.15 (left) Ernst Ludwig Kirchner. *Street, Dresden.* 1907. Oil on canvas, 4'11¼" × 6'6⅞". The Museum of Modern Art, New York.

21.16 (right) Vasili Kandinsky. *Black Lines No. 189.* 1913. Oil on canvas, 51 × 51⅝". Solomon R. Guggenheim Museum, New York.

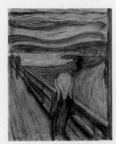
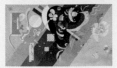
better, more enlightened future. One of the founders was Ernst Ludwig Kirchner, whose *Street, Dresden* we see here (**21.15**). The intense, arbitrary colors show Expressionism's link with Fauvism, and the wavering contours suggest the influence of Munch. To the right, a crowd moves toward us. Everyone seems to have a purpose—shopping, going to work, all of the usual reasons that keep city streets teeming with people. To the left, a crowd walks in the other direction. In the center is the small figure of a child. She stands isolated from the crowds, her feet planted apart, resisting the flow. Perhaps she is a stand-in for the artist, who also questions all this coming and going, what purpose it serves, and why everyone is alone.

Another Expressionist group was Der Blaue Reiter ("The Blue Rider"), organized in 1911 by the Russian painter Vasili Kandinsky. Kandinsky had been teaching law in Moscow when an exhibit of Impressionist painting so moved him that he abandoned his career and moved to Germany to study art. Kandinsky's early paintings were intensely colored, Fauve-like works on Russian mystical themes. He never abandoned his idea that spirituality and art were linked, but he became increasingly convinced that art's spiritual and communicative power lay in its own language of line, form, and color, and it was he who took the decisive step of eliminating representation altogether in such works as *Black Lines* (**21.16**). In his own telling, Kandinsky discovered the power of nonrepresentational art when he was struck by the beauty of a painting he didn't recognize in his studio. It turned out to be one of his own works, set the wrong way up. He realized then that subject matter was only incidental to art's impact. About color, Kandinsky wrote, "Generally speaking, color influences the soul. Color is the keyboard, the eyes are the hammers, the soul is the piano with many strings. The artist is the hand that plays, touching one key or another purposively, to cause vibrations in the soul."[4]

Shattering Form: Cubism

While artists associated with Europe's many expressionist tendencies were exploring the possibilities of color, two artists in Paris were reducing the role of color to a minimum in order to concentrate on the problem of representing form in space. One of these artists was a young Spanish painter, Pablo Picasso. In 1907, at age twenty-six, Picasso had already painted what is widely regarded as a pivotal work in the development of 20th-century art, *Les Demoiselles d'Avignon* (**21.17**).

Les Demoiselles d'Avignon was not Picasso's title but was given to the painting years later by a friend of his. It translates as "the young women of Avignon" and refers to the prostitutes of Avignon Street, a notorious district of Barcelona, Picasso's hometown. In early sketches for the painting Picasso included a sailor entering at left to purchase the prostitute's services, but as the composition evolved, the sailor was eliminated. Instead, the prostitutes display themselves to us.

If these are prostitutes, then how extraordinary they are! They are far from enticing. Picasso has chopped them up into planes—flat, angular segments that still hint at three-dimensionality but have no conventional modeling. Almost as an affront to traditional pictures of curvaceous nude bathers, the artist has defined his nudes in sharp geometric shapes. Figure and ground lose their importance as separate entities; the "background"—that is, whatever is not the five figures—is treated in much the same way as the women's bodies. As a result, the entire picture appears flattened; we have no sense of looking "through" the painting into a world beyond, as with Delacroix or even Manet.

To many people who see *Les Demoiselles* for the first time, the faces cause discomfort. The three at left seem like reasonable enough, if abstract, depictions of faces, except for the fact that the figure at far left, whose face is in profile, has an eye staring straight ahead, much as in an Egyptian painting. But the two faces at right are clearly masks—images borrowed from "primitive" art—and they create a disturbing effect when set atop the nude bodies of European females.

In *Les Demoiselles* Picasso was experimenting with several ideas that he would explore in his art for years to come. First, there is the inclusion of nontraditional elements. Picasso had recently seen sculptures from ancient Iberia (Spain before the Roman Empire), as well as art from Africa. In breaking with Western art conventions that reached back to ancient Greece and Rome, Picasso looked for inspiration from other, equally ancient, traditions. Second, there is the merging of figure and ground, reflecting the assumption that all

21.17 Pablo Picasso. *Les Demoiselles d'Avignon.* 1907. Oil on canvas, 8' × 7'8".
The Museum of Modern Art, New York.

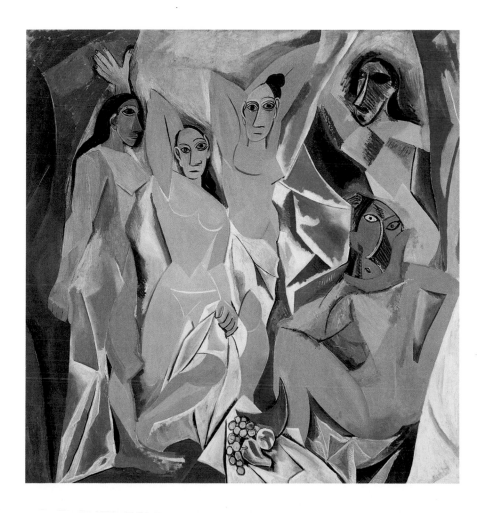

portions of the work participate in its expression. And third, there is fragmenting of the figures and other elements into flat planes, especially evident in the breasts of the figure at upper right and the mask just below. This last factor proved especially significant for an artistic journey on which Picasso was soon to embark—the movement known as **Cubism.**

Picasso's partner in this venture was the artist Georges Braque. Braque was older than Picasso in years but younger as an artist. Picasso, after all, had been an artist since his early teens (see 2.12). He was one of the most naturally gifted artists in history, and his hand could produce any kind of style he asked it to. Braque was less precocious, but because of that more disciplined and determined. He developed an intense personal identification with Cézanne, who also progressed from awkward beginnings to mastery. Picasso grew to share this interest, and for a time he renounced his natural gifts to pursue together with Braque this new line of investigation. Both artists emerged stronger for it.

Picasso and Braque began working together in 1909, and by 1910 their experiments were so closely intertwined that their styles became virtually identical. For a time, they even ceased signing their works. "We were prepared to efface our personalities in order to find originality,"[5] Braque later recalled. Illustrated here are two paintings by Braque that demonstrate how Cézanne's methods led to something new, *The Castle at La Roche-Guyon* (**21.18**) and *Le Portugais (The Emigrant)* (**21.19**).

The Castle at La Roche-Guyon depicts a hillside town of houses surmounted by a castle. Following Cézanne's advice, Braque has reduced the architecture to its simplest geometric forms: cube, cylinder, cone. (It was a painting of similar hillside houses that prompted a visiting friend to remark, "Look, little cubes," thus accidentally and misleadingly naming the style.) We recognize Cézanne's parallel brush strokes and color patches, which seem to break the surface into facets (see 21.10). Also learned from Cézanne is the way the principal linear motifs of the composition echo outward to influence

21.18 (left) Georges *Braque. The Castle at La Roche-Guyon.* 1909. Oil on canvas, 28¾ × 23¾". Musée d'Art Moderne de Lille, Villeneuve-d'Ascq.

21.19 (right) Georges Braque. *Le Portugais (The Emigrant).* 1911–12. Oil on canvas, 46 × 32". Kunstmuseum Basel.

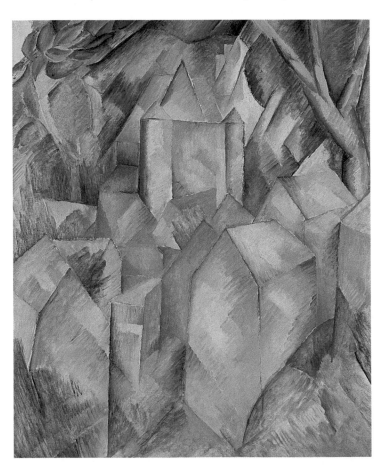

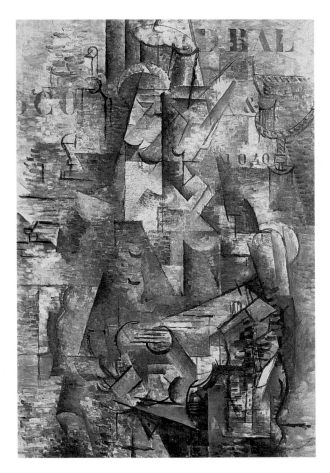

PABLO PICASSO

1881–1973

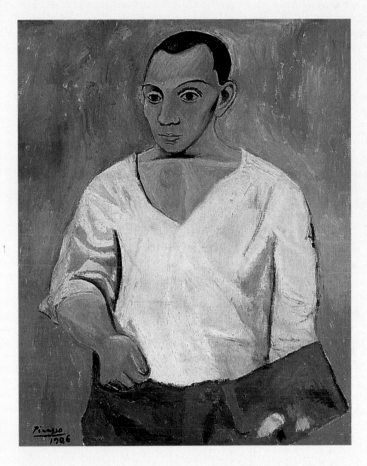

Pablo Picasso. *Self-Portrait with Palette.* 1906.
Oil on canvas, 36¼ × 28¾".
Philadelphia Museum of Art.

T HE LIFE OF Picasso defies summary in a one-page biography. Few artists have lived so long; none have produced such an immense volume of work in so diverse a range of styles and media; and only a rare few can match him in richness and variety of personal history.

Pablo Ruiz y Picasso was born in the Spanish city of Málaga. He attended art schools in Barcelona and Madrid but became impatient with their rigid, academic approach and soon abandoned formal study. After two trips to Paris—where he saw the work of Van Gogh, Gauguin, and Lautrec—he settled permanently in that city in 1904 and never again lived outside France.

Although Picasso worked in many different styles throughout his life, much of his art is classifiable into the well-known "periods": the "Blue" period, when his paintings concentrated on images of poverty and emotional depression; the "Rose" period, whose paintings included depictions of harlequins and acrobats; the Cubist period, when he worked with the painter Georges Braque; and the "Neoclassical" period, in which the figures took on qualities resembling ancient Greek sculptures.

Success came early to Picasso. Except for brief periods when he was short of funds (usually because of some romantic entanglement), he lived well and comfortably and enjoyed a large circle of friends. His work was always in demand, whether in painting, sculpture, prints (of which he made thousands), theatrical design, murals, or ceramics (he took up ceramic art in 1947 and decorated some two thousand pieces in a single year).

It would be impossible to discuss Picasso's life without reference to the women who shared it, because they are a constant presence in his art. Picasso married only twice, but he maintained long, occasionally overlapping, liaisons with several other women. His attachments included Fernande Olivier; Eva Gouel; Olga Koklova, his first wife and the mother of his son Paulo; Marie-Thérèse Walter, mother of his daughter Maïa; Dora Maar; Françoise Gilot, who bore him Claude and Paloma, then later wrote a scandalous memoir of her years with the artist; and finally Jacqueline Roque, whom he married in 1961, in his eightieth year.

Despite his international celebrity, Picasso gave almost no interviews. One of the few took place in 1935 and included this insight into the nature of art: "Everyone wants to understand art. Why not try to understand the song of a bird? Why does one love the night, flowers, everything around one, without trying to understand them? But in the case of a painting people have to understand. If only they would realize above all that an artist works of necessity, that he himself is only a trifling bit of the world, and that no more importance should be attached to him than to plenty of other things which please us in the world, though we can't explain them. People who try to explain pictures are usually barking up the wrong tree."[6]

RELATED WORKS

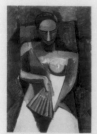

2.13
Picasso,
*Seated
Woman*

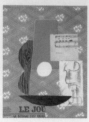

7.17
Picasso,
*Guitar and
Wine Glass*

everything around them. Here, the earth around the castle and the surrounding green of nature all partake of the angles and facets of the houses. Braque has reined in Cézanne's bright Impressionist palette to a restricted range of gray, ocher, and green, allowing the forms to interpenetrate more easily. Some of the forms seem solid, but others shade off into transparency.

In *The Emigrant*, a fully Cubist work, these discoveries are taken to their logical conclusion. The figure of a seated man playing his guitar is broken into facets based in simple geometric shapes—triangle, circle, line. Because the forms are so basic, they easily echo throughout, unifying the composition. Color is reduced to gray warmed with ocher, allowing the shards of the foreground and background to interpenetrate at will. The principal lines of the composition suggest a classic Renaissance pyramid such as Leonardo used for *Mona Lisa* (see 2.4). Visual cues help viewers orient themselves: the open hole and strings of the guitar, the player's mustache, the rope to the right that sets the scene on a dock. The addition of stenciled letters, an intrusion from the "real world," was Braque's innovation. As Cubism progressed, the two artists experimented with incorporating other elements such as newspaper, wallpaper, and fabric. The psychological tension of merging the "real" with the "not real" (the illusory world of paint on canvas) would have important applications for later 20th-century art. Picasso and Braque also realized that the geometric rhythms of an object could be assembled from multiple views. For example, if you look at a pitcher from the front, the side, the top, the bottom, you will see a number of versions, but your true understanding of a pitcher is the sum of all of these. With Cubism, this sum of viewpoints could be painted. Cubism thus followed up on another discovery implicit in much of Cézanne's work: The eye is always moving, and motion is how we assimilate the world.

The great beauty of Cubism was that, like linear perspective, anyone could do it. Cubism offered the most original and powerful system for re-thinking the representation of form and space since the Renaissance. Over the ensuing decade and more, many young artists in Europe passed through a Cubist phase in order to break free of the past.

Fantasy and Futurism

Cubism poured all its energy into formal concerns. The subjects that Braque and Picasso treated while working out their discoveries were so traditional as to be neutral—a still life on a table top, a seated figure with a musical instrument, a landscape with some houses. Any of these subjects could have been painted in the 17th century. Other innovators, however, believed that art would move forward only through exploring new subjects. One of the most original and influential of these artists was the Italian painter Giorgio de Chirico. "It is most important that we should rid art of all that it has contained of *recognizable material* to date, all familiar subject matter, all traditional ideas, all popular symbols must be banished forthwith," he wrote. "To become truly immortal a work of art must escape all human limits: logic and common sense will only interfere. But once these barriers are broken it will enter the regions of childhood vision and dream."[7]

Dreams are what come to mind in front of *The Disquieting Muses* (**21.20**). The hot afternoon sun casts long shadows across an open plaza. There are no trees, no people. Nothing of nature at all. In the background, banners snap in the wind over an early Renaissance fortress. Next to the fortress is a factory. In the shade, a statue in classical garments stares (though her face is featureless) at the two presences in the foreground, the disquieting muses themselves: a pockmarked classical column, a sculpture with a hat-maker's dummy for a head, a tailor's dummy seated nearby. The painting is composed of fragments of Italy's own past and present—ancient Rome, the Renaissance, the Industrial Revolution. How can we make any sense out of what history has left to us, it seems to ask? What do we do now?

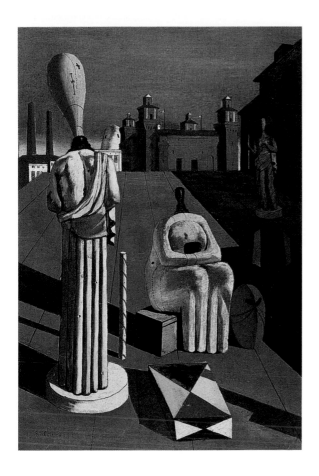

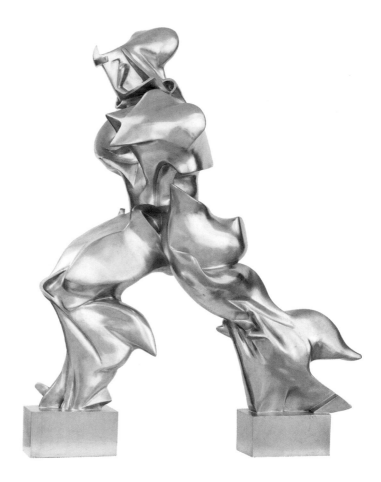

In contrast to De Chirico's motionless dream world, a group of Italian artists calling themselves the Futurists decided that motion itself was the glory of the new 20th century, especially the motion of marvelous new machines. The view from an airplane, the feeling of racing through the countryside in an automobile—how could these new sensations not be reflected in art? In Chapter 4 we looked at a Futurist painting by Giacomo Balla (see 4.53). Here we see a work by the movement's foremost sculptor, Umberto Boccioni (**21.21**). *Unique Forms of Continuity in Space* represents a striding human figure as the Futurist imagined it to be in the light of contemporary science: a field of energy interacting with everything around it. "Sculpture," wrote Boccioni, "must give life to objects by making their extension in space palpable, systematic, and plastic, since no one can any longer believe that an object ends where another begins and that our body is surrounded by anything . . . that does not cut through it and section it in an arabesque of directional curves."[8]

21.20 (left) Giorgio de Chirico. *The Disquieting Muses.* 1916. Oil on canvas, 38¼ × 26". Private collection.

21.21 (right) Umberto Boccioni. *Unique Forms of Continuity in Space.* 1913. Bronze, height 43⅞". The Museum of Modern Art, New York.

WORLD WAR I AND AFTER: DADA AND SURREALISM

In 1914, conflict broke out in the Balkan Peninsula. Soon, as the result of treaties and alliances, every major power in Europe was drawn into war. Soldiers with their heads full of gallant ideas about battle rushed headlong into the most horrible deaths imaginable. Trench warfare, poison gas, bombardment by air, machine guns, tanks, submarines—science and technology, in which the 19th century had put its faith, revealed their dark side. The ideal of progress was shown to be utterly hollow, and ten million people lost their lives in one of the bloodiest wars in history.

RELATED WORKS

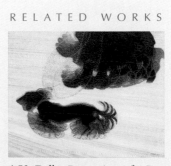

4.53 Balla, *Dynamism of a Dog*

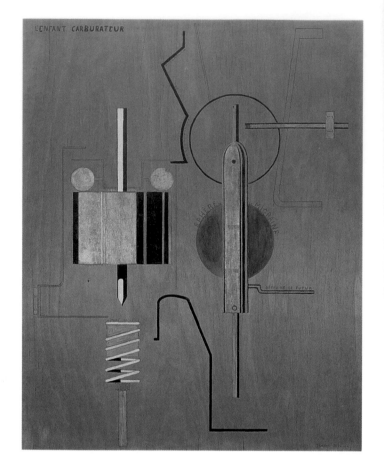

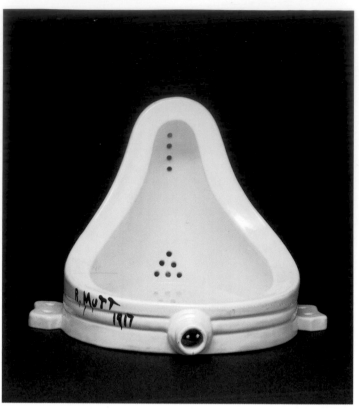

21.22 (left) Francis Picabia. *The Child Carburetor (L'Enfant Carburateur.)* 1919. Oil, enamel, metallic paint, gold leaf, pencil and crayon on stained plywood, 49¾ × 39⅞". Solomon R. Guggenheim Museum, New York.

21.23 (right) Marcel Duchamp. *Fountain.* 1917/1964 Edition Schwartz, Milan. Ceramic compound, height 14". Indiana University Art Museum, Bloomington.

RELATED WORKS

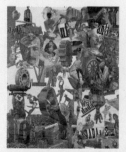

9.13 Höch, *Cut with the Kitchen Knife*

In 1916, a group of artists waiting out the war in Zurich, in neutral Switzerland, banded together as a protest art movement called Dada. What did Dada protest? Everything. Dada was anti. Anti art, anti middle-class society, anti politicians, anti good manners, anti business-as-usual, anti all that had brought about the war. In that sense, Dada was a big *no*. But Dada was also a big *yes*. Yes to creativity, to life, to silliness, to spontaneity. Dada was provocative and absurd. Above all, it refused to make sense or to be pinned down.

More an attitude than a coherent movement, Dada embraced as many different kinds of art as there were artists. In Germany, Dada developed a biting political edge in the work of Hannah Höch and others (see 9.13). In France, its absurd and philosophical aspects came to the fore. Picabia, a French artist who joined the Dada movement, delighted in the similarities between humans and machines, and he created paintings that looked like diagrams. *L'Enfant Carburateur (The Child Carburetor)* (**21.22**) would seem to offer a perfectly reasonable plan for constructing a child if the child you have in mind is part of an internal combustion engine. A carburetor is designed to produce an explosive mixture of fuel and air, and perhaps Picabia thought that children weren't so different. Labels point out such key areas as "Sphere of the Migraine" and "Destroy the Future." The materials include gold leaf, which gives the work a strangely precious and perhaps even sacred aura.

The Dadaist with the most lasting impact on American art in the 20th century was Marcel Duchamp, whose "ready-mades" probed the border between art and life in a way that later generations have returned to again and again. A ready-made is a work of art that the artist has not *made* but *designated*. Undoubtedly the most notorious of Duchamp's ready-mades was

Fountain, a work of 1917 shown here in a signed replica of 1964 (**21.23**). *Fountain* was an ordinary porcelain urinal set on its back. Duchamp entered it into a New York art exhibition under a pseudonym, R. Mutt, which he slopped on in black paint as a signature. Here we see a replica because Duchamp never intended for his ready-mades to be permanent. His project was to find an object—he insisted that it be an object with no aesthetic interest whatsoever—and exhibit it as art. After the exhibition, the object was to be returned to life.

Fountain was pure provocation. The exhibition organizers had stated that all entries would be accepted, and Duchamp wanted to see whether they really meant it. Yet as Duchamp well knew, *Fountain* also raised interesting philosophical questions: Does art have to be made by an artist? Is art a form of attention? If we have spent our lives perfecting this form of attention on various acknowledged masterpieces, can we then bestow it on absolutely anything? If so, how is an art object different from any other kind of object? Does art depend on context, on being shown in an "art place" such as a museum or gallery? Can something be art in one place and not another? Is *Fountain* still art today, or was it only art for the time that Duchamp said it was? Duchamp thought that art and life could regularly trade places, and he suggested helpfully that one could use a Rembrandt as an ironing board.

A movement that grew out of Dada was Surrealism, which was formulated in Paris in the 1920s. Like Dada, Surrealism was not a style but a way of life. Fascinated by the theories of Sigmund Freud, who was then setting out his revolutionary ideas in Vienna, the Surrealists appreciated the logic of dreams, the mystery of the unconscious, and the lure of the bizarre, the irrational, the incongruous, and the marvelous. A central Surrealist practice, at least theoretically, was automatism—writing or drawing that flowed straight from the subconscious, unchecked by reason or inhibitions. The combination of automatism and dream imagery resulted in paintings such as André Masson's *The Blood of the Birds* (**21.24**). Onto a surface of sand, Masson glued feathers collected during random walks. He then dripped and spattered paint across the surface in a series of "automatic" gestures. The American artist Jackson Pollock would later draw on these ideas to make his famous drip paintings, which also grew out of a Surrealist belief in the creative superiority of the unconscious (see 22.1).

21.24 André Masson. *The Blood of the Birds.* 1925/26. Tempera, sand, and feathers on canvas; 29½ × 29½".
Musée National d'Art Moderne, Centre Georges Pompidou, Paris.

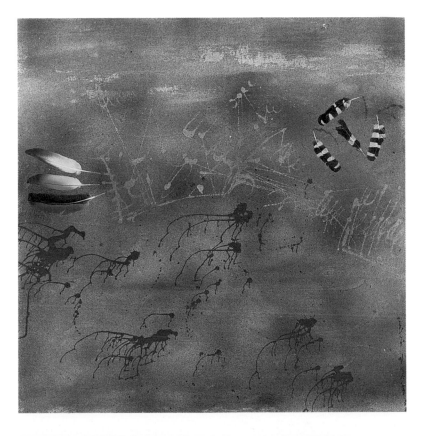

RELATED WORKS

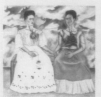

5.9
Kahlo,
*The Two
Fridas*

5.19
Magritte,
*Delusions of
Grandeur II*

A distinctive contribution of Surrealism to art was the poetic object—not a sculpture as it had traditionally been understood but a *thing*. Surrealist objects often juxtapose incongruous elements in order to provoke a shiver of strangeness or disorientation. One of the most famous and unsettling Surrealist objects is Meret Oppenheim's *Object (Luncheon in Fur)* (**21.25**). Perhaps Oppenheim witnessed two ladies taking tea together in their best fur coats and melted them into a dreamlike object? Perhaps we really are supposed to imagine bringing the furry cup to our lips for lunch. Freud's theories famously claimed a large role for unconscious sexual desire, and Surrealist works often have erotic overtones.

Possibly the most famous of all Surrealist works is Salvador Dali's *The Persistence of Memory* (**21.26**), a small painting that many people call simply "the melted watches." Dali's art, especially here, offers a fascinating paradox: His rendering of forms is precise and meticulous—we might say *super*realistic—yet the forms could not possibly be real. *The Persistence of Memory* shows a bleak, arid, decayed landscape populated by an odd, fetal-type creature (some think representative of the artist) and several limp watches—time not only stopped but melting away. Perhaps in this work Dali's fantasy, his dream, is to triumph once and for all over time.

Joan Miró's *Carnival of the Harlequin* (**21.27**) offers a Surrealist view of one of the most famous of all Spanish paintings, *Las Meninas*, by Velázquez (see 17.11). Miró's fantasy world is aswarm with odd little creatures—animals and fish and insects and perhaps a snake or two—as well as nameless abstract forms that participate in the artist's madcap party. Much of Miró's imagery suggests a cheerful sexuality, as though the whole space of the universe were occupied with lighthearted erotic play and reproduction. In contrast to the utter stillness of Dali's *The Persistence of Memory*, Miró's *Carnival* is all movement. There are even a few musical notes at the top to accompany the dance. As interpreted by Miró, Surrealism's dreams are lively ones.

21.25 (right) Meret Oppenheim. *Object (Luncheon in Fur)*. 1936. Fur-covered cup, saucer and spoon; overall height 2⅞".
The Museum of Modern Art, New York.

21.26 (below) Salvador Dali. *The Persistence of Memory*. 1931. Oil on canvas, 9½ × 13".
The Museum of Modern Art, New York.

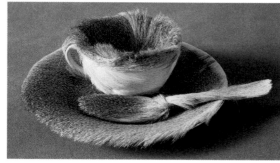

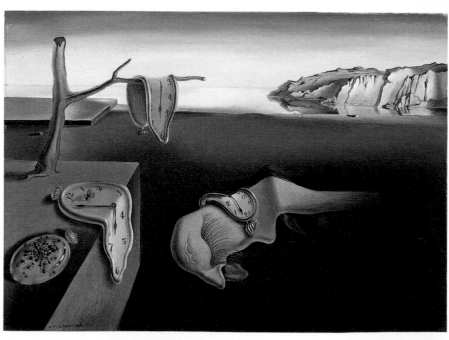

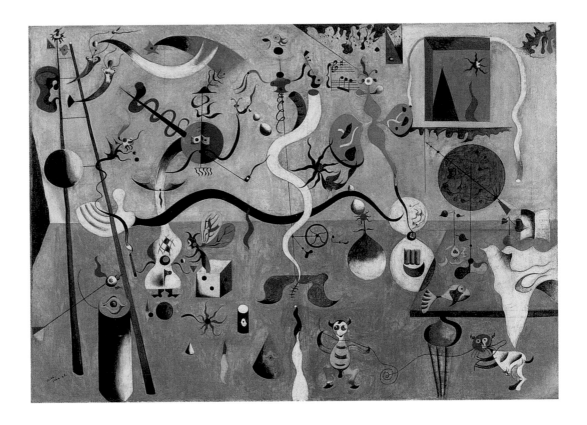

BETWEEN THE WARS: BUILDING NEW SOCIETIES

Surrealism offered a personal solution to life during the years following the trauma of World War I. But in the view of many artists, society, and possibly even human nature itself, had to be transformed so that such a horror would not happen again. That art could play a central role in bringing about a better society was a 19th-century idea, yet it found renewed application after World War I in a collective approach. It was not through the personal insights of individual artists that the world would change, but through the cooperative endeavors of artists, designers, and architects. Together, they could create a new environment for living, one that was completely modern, purged of associations with the past, and comfortable with the new spirit of the machine age.

Even more radical opportunities presented themselves in Russia and Mexico, where successful revolutions had toppled older governments. In these countries, new societies were being formed that embraced lofty ideals of social and economic equality for all and a concern for ordinary workers. In Chapter 7, we looked at a fresco commissioned from Diego Rivera by the revolutionary Mexican government (see 7.4). Prior to the Mexican Revolution, Rivera had been living in Paris and painting in an advanced Cubist style. On his return to Mexico, he developed a more accessible style for his murals, and he stayed with it for the rest of his career. His great desire was to communicate with everyone, to leave no one out. The demands of the European avant-garde must have seemed far away.

The Soviet government of Russia would eventually demand that its artists similarly turn their backs on modern tendencies, but during the first few years after the Russian Revolution of 1917, many artists believed that only the most revolutionary art could bring about a new world. One important movement was Constructivism, which had been founded by Vladimir Tatlin in 1913. Tatlin believed that advanced ideas about art should be put to practical

RELATED WORKS

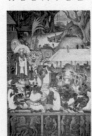

7.4
Rivera,
Mixtec Culture

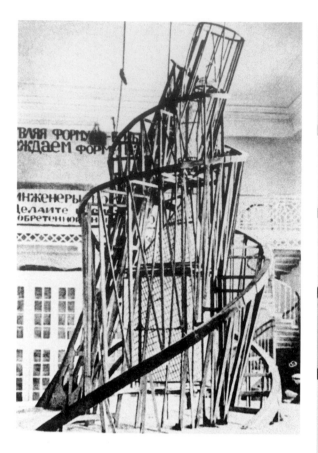

21.28 (left) Vladimir Tatlin. Model for the Monument to the Third International. 1919–1920. Wood, iron, and glass. Destroyed.

21.29 (right) Piet Mondrian. *Trafalgar Square.* 1939–43. Oil on canvas, 57¼ × 47¼". The Museum of Modern Art, New York. © 2007 Mondrian/Holtzman Trust c/o HCR International, Warrenton, Virginia, U.S.A.

use, and that artists should apply their talents to architecture, graphic design, theatrical productions, textiles, monuments, festivals, and all other visual forms. Tatlin's own design for the Monument to the Third International demonstrates what he thought could be done (**21.28**). Designed to house the Russian congress, the monument was never built, but what a work of architecture it would have been! An open steel framework would support the building from the outside, its spiral combining the industrial look of the Eiffel Tower (see 13.22) with a Futurist sense of motion. Suspended inside would be four chambers in pure geometric forms: a cube, a pyramid, a cone, and a sphere. The various branches of the government would meet in these rooms, which would rotate at speeds varying from one revolution per year (the large cube at the bottom) to one revolution per hour (the small sphere at the top).

When Constructivism was condemned by the Soviet regime in 1922, many of its artists left the Soviet Union to spread its ideals elsewhere. One of the European movements touched by Constructivist ideas was De Stijl, in the Netherlands. The most famous artist associated with De Stijl was Piet Mondrian. Beginning as a painter of flowers and landscapes, Mondrian distilled his art to what he considered to be the most universal signs of human order: vertical and horizontal lines, and the primary colors of red, yellow, and blue (**21.29**). To Mondrian, these formal elements radiated a kind of intellectual beauty that was humanity's greatest achievement. Nature, with its irrationality and irregularity, encouraged humankind's primitive, animal instincts, resulting in such disasters as war. In Mondrian's vision of the world, people would be surrounded by rational beauty, and thus become balanced themselves.

Mondrian thought of his canvases as places where we could turn to stabilize ourselves and restore our calm. He also believed that they would not be necessary—no art would be necessary—in a future where people lived in environments such as Gerrit Rietveld's Schroeder House (**21.30**). Rietveld was the foremost architect of De Stijl, and Schroeder House looks very much like a Mondrian painting projected into three dimensions. Schroeder House is like an inhabitable sculpture—a construction in space of intersecting vertical and horizontal planes, color-coded inside and out in primary colors. As in Mondrian's painting, symmetrical elements are placed in subtle asymmetrical balance. No art hangs inside. Instead, the floor of one room is painted red, the wall of another is painted blue, and so on. Movable partitions allow the interior space to be reconfigured, and spaces flow into each other rather than being clearly separated.

Construction by intersecting planes in space is also the principle behind Marcel Breuer's famous armchair, designed in 1928 (**21.31**). Breuer was a teacher and a former student at the Bauhaus, a school of design founded in Germany in 1919 by the architect Walter Gropius. The Bauhaus was yet another incarnation of the ideal of collective artistic endeavor in the years following World War I. Students studied a variety of disciplines, and their education was designed to eliminate traditional divisions between painters, sculptors, architects, craft artists, graphic designers, and industrial designers. The word *Bauhaus* translates roughly as "building house," and its leaders sought to "build" new guiding principles of design compatible with 20th-century technology. Structures, rooms, furniture, and everyday household objects were stripped of superficial embellishment and pared down to clean lines. Breuer's armchair, made of canvas panels and steel tubing, was supposed to be economical to manufacture, making good design available to everyone. After the Nazis closed the Bauhaus in 1933, several of its key members emigrated to the United States, and the school's influence continued to be felt in all design disciplines for decades.

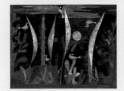
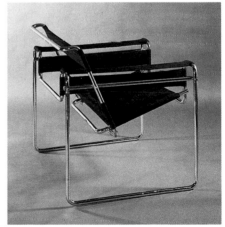

21.30 (left) Gerrit Rietveld. Schroeder House, Utrecht, The Netherlands. 1923–24.

21.31 (right) Marcel Breuer. Armchair. c. 1928. Chrome-plated tubular steel with canvas slings. The Museum of Modern Art, New York.

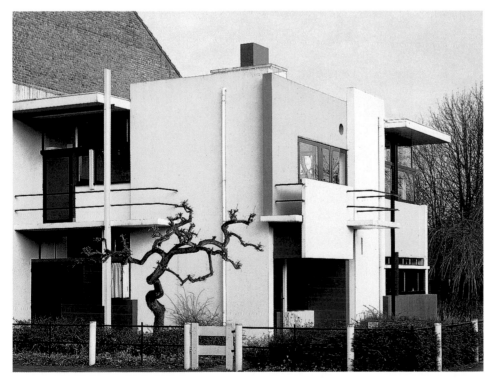

The Bauhaus and De Stijl both sought to create harmony between individual lives and modern industry and technology. A man who painted visions of what this might be like was Fernand Léger (**21.32**). *Woman and Child* is a grand, symphonic composition like those of the 19th century, but this is a *modern* symphony, with straight lines, right angles, clear shapes, and forthright colors. Léger forged a painting style that has the honest surfaces of industrial production—even the bodies seem to be made of manufactured parts. Yet the effect is not alienating at all. The woman and child are content in their calm, ordered, well-lit world. In a lecture entitled "The Machine Aesthetic," Léger praised the beauty of industrial products and the dedication of those who made them. "A worker would never dare deliver a product other than clear-cut, polished, burnished," he later said. "The painter must aim at making a clear-cut picture, clean, with *finish*."[9] Léger had painted in a radical Cubist style before the war. After the war, he was not the only artist to step back from the avant-garde in what one French critic called "the return to order."

In the United States, the period following World War I also saw the flowering of art dedicated to building a better society. One of the most vibrant movements of the time arose in the New York neighborhood called Harlem. Harlem is the northeast section of Manhattan Island. It was and is home to many black Americans, of all economic classes. During the decade of the 1920s Harlem served as a magnet for some of the greatest talents of that generation—artists, musicians, composers, actors, writers, poets, scientists, and educators. Louis Armstrong came to Harlem, and so did Duke Ellington. The writer Langston Hughes and the poet Countee Cullen were in residence. Creative energy was in the air, and for a time it seemed as though almost every

21.32 Fernand Léger. *Woman and Child.* 1922. Oil on canvas, 5'7¼" × 7'11". Öffentliche Kunstsammlung, Kunstmuseum, Basel.

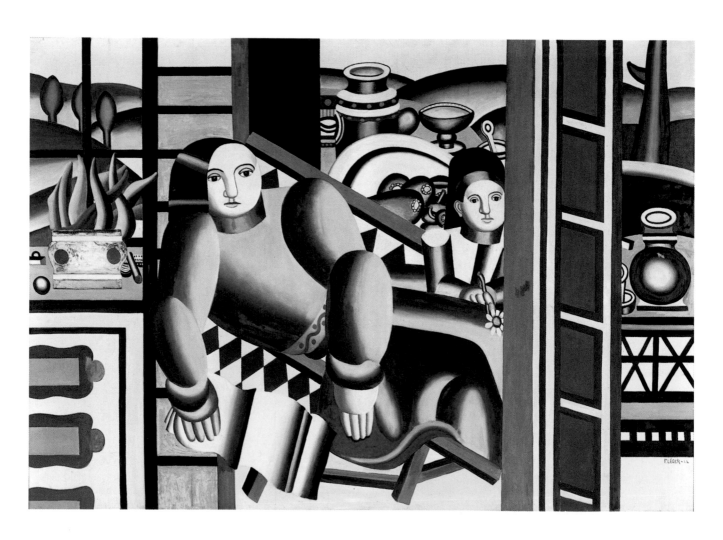

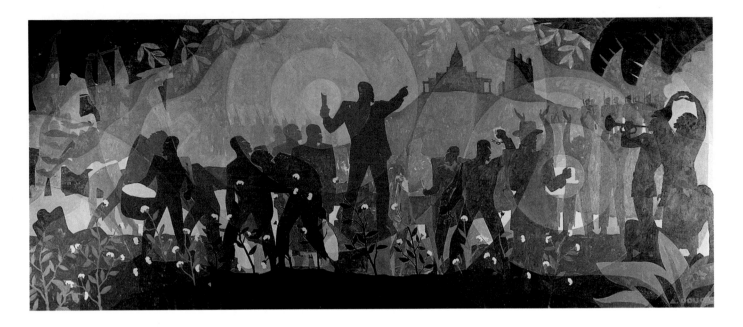

Harlemite was doing something wonderful—a book, a play, a Broadway show, a sculpture series, a jazz opera, a public mural. This phenomenon came to be called the Harlem Renaissance.

Much of the spirit embodied in the Harlem Renaissance had to do with merging three experiences: the rich heritage of Africa, the ugly legacy of slavery in America (ended barely more than fifty years earlier), and the realities of modern urban life. There is no single style associated with artists of the Harlem Renaissance, but the work of the painter and illustrator Aaron Douglas is representative of the spirit and aspirations of the group. Douglas, who was born in Kansas, moved to Harlem in 1924. During the Harlem Renaissance years he gradually developed a style he called "geometric symbolism." He worked prolifically through the twenties but is perhaps most noted for a series of murals done a few years later, for the 135th Street branch of the New York Public Library. The series is called *Aspects of Negro Life*. Our illustration shows the segment that Douglas called *From Slavery Through Reconstruction* (**21.33**).

Several of Douglas' influences are evident in the mural. Douglas' simplification and stylization of forms surely derived from his studies of West African sculpture. Space is flattened, as in the paintings of modern masters like Gauguin (see 21.9), and the palette of colors is limited, as in Cubism (see 21.18, 21.19). This section of the mural shows a progression from left to right and (as the title implies) from slavery to freedom. At left, the silhouette figures seem bowed down and fearful. One plays a drum, symbolic of African heritage. At right, the figures are upright and proud and joyful. One plays a trumpet, symbolic of the Jazz Age and of black musical brilliance. The dominant center figure synthesizes these polarities. He points upward, toward freedom.

The Harlem Renaissance, as a movement, lasted only a decade. Its momentum was stopped by the stock market crash of 1929 and the ensuing Great Depression of the 1930s. Aaron Douglas' vision of a better society was actually painted during the early years of the Depression, as the dream of the Harlem Renaissance faded. It is nevertheless a vision of hope. Other artists continued to believe that art had a social mission during these difficult times. Dorothea Lange documented the dignity of ordinary people faced with extraordinary adversity in photographs such as *Migrant Mother* (see 9.8). Rockwell Kent produced a stirring call to action in *Workers of the World, Unite!* (see 8.8). The Depression was in fact worldwide. In Europe, severe hardship fueled nationalist resentments against the unjust settlement of World War I. Anger swept the fascist regimes of Hitler and Mussolini into power in Germany and Italy. In 1939, the world was plunged again into war.

21.33 Aaron Douglas. *Aspects of Negro Life: From Slavery Through Reconstruction*. 1934. Oil on canvas, 5' × 11'7".
Schomburg Center for Research in Black Culture, The New York Public Library.

RELATED WORKS

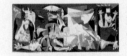
3.12
Picasso,
Guernica

7.6
Lawrence,
Cabinet Maker

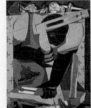
8.7
Hu Yichuan,
To the Front!

8.8
Kent, *Workers of the World, Unite!*

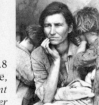
9.8
Lange,
Migrant Mother

CHAPTER TWENTY-TWO

ART SINCE 1945

The art made in Europe and North America since the end of World War II is dizzying in its variety and complexity. Nevertheless, we as viewers have one great advantage in approaching this art. We live now. All the artworks considered in this chapter were made during the lifetimes of people still alive today. Although we can have only limited success in getting "inside" the minds of Michelangelo or Rembrandt, we inhabit the same world as contemporary artists. We have walked the same streets, watched the same movies and television programs, experienced the same world events. We share a culture with contemporary artists, and so this is *our* art. If we take the trouble to look and study, we may find it is the art with which we feel most connected.

The year 1945 is considered a turning point in the history of Western art. For long years most of the world had been preoccupied with killing and death and hardship—the horrors of World War II. When hostilities ended in late summer of 1945, there was a natural yearning to start afresh, to redirect energies toward creating rather than destroying. But another factor in this turning point was the shift in focus from the old world to the new. Since the time of the ancient Greeks the great centers of Western art had been in Europe—Athens, Rome, Florence, Paris, London. Now, suddenly, the art capital had crossed an ocean and settled in North America. Its hub was New York City.

THE NEW YORK SCHOOL

In the aftermath of World War II most of western Europe was completely devastated. The United States, while exhausted, was not. No bombs had fallen or battles been fought in New York, as they had in London and Paris and Amsterdam and most of the cities in Germany. When the time came to resume the normal activities of life, New York became the center of a vibrant art revival. Many of the most progressive European artists had immigrated to the United States, and they served as teachers and inspiration for a new generation of artists—most of them American—who gravitated to New York. In fact, painters associated with the first major postwar art movement are referred to as the New York School.

Not a school in the sense of an institution or of instruction, the New York School was a convenient label under which to lump together a group of painters also known as the **Abstract Expressionists.** Primary among them were Jackson Pollock and Willem de Kooning. Abstract Expressionism had many sources, but the most direct influence was Surrealism, with its emphasis on the creative powers of the unconscious and its technique of automatism as a way to tap into them. The painters of the New York School developed highly individual and recognizable styles, but one element their paintings had in common was scale: Abstract Expressionist paintings are generally quite large, and this is important to their effect. Viewers are meant to be engulfed, to be swept into the world of the painting the way we may be swept into a film by sitting so close that the screen fills our entire field of vision.

The quintessential Abstract Expressionist was Jackson Pollock, who by the late 1940s had perfected his "drip technique." To create such works as *Number 1, 1949* (**22.1**), Pollock placed the unstretched canvas on the floor and painted on it indirectly, from above, by casting paint from a brush in controlled gestures or by dripping paint from a stir-stick. Layer after layer, color after color, the painting grew into an allover tangle of graceful arcs, dribbled lines, spatters, and pools of color. There is no focal point, no "composition." Instead we find ourselves in front of a field of energy like the spray of a crashing wave. A critic of the time coined the term **action painting** to describe the work of Pollock and others, for their paintings are not images in the traditional sense but traces of an act, the painter's dance of creation. Pollock said that his method of working allowed him to be "in" the painting, to forget himself in the act of painting, and that is also the best way to look at his works, to lose ourselves in them.

Strictly speaking, Pollock's painting is not abstract but nonrepresentational. As always, the terminology of art evolved haphazardly and inconsistently as people grasped for terms to speak about what was new. Critics and artists of the day used *abstract* and *nonrepresentational* interchangeably, and in casual speech and writing *abstract* is still the more common term.

RELATED WORKS

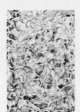
5.2
Pollock,
*Shimmering
Substance*

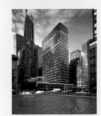
13.24
Bunshaft,
Lever
House

22.1 Jackson Pollock. *Number 1, 1949.* Enamel and metallic paint on canvas, 5'3" × 8'6". Museum of Contemporary Art, Los Angeles.

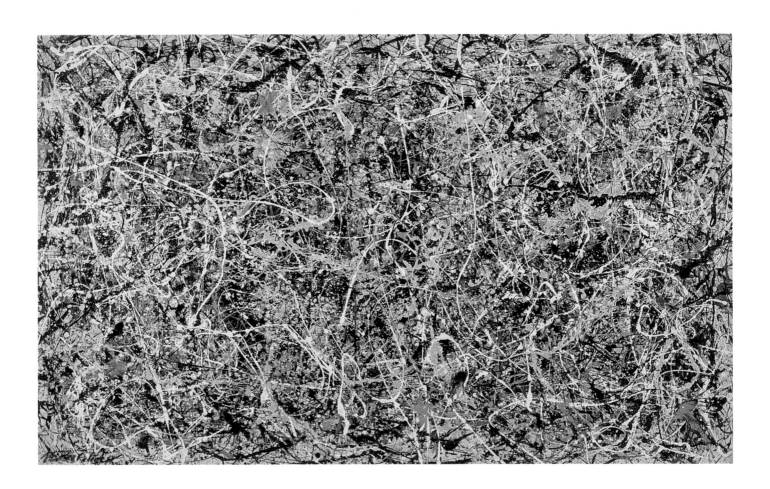

JACKSON POLLOCK

1912–1956

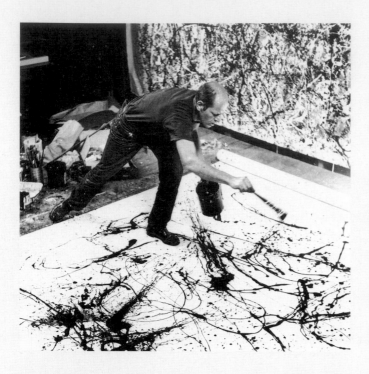

JACKSON POLLOCK was born on a sheep ranch in Cody, Wyoming, the youngest son in a family of five boys. During his youth the family moved around a good deal and led a fairly unstable existence. By the age of fifteen Jackson had begun to show signs of the alcoholism that would plague him all of his life.

In 1930 Pollock went to New York to study at the Art Students League. His principal teacher there was Thomas Hart Benton, a realistic painter of regional Americana, best known for his murals. Later, Pollock would say he was glad to have had the experience with Benton, because he then had to struggle all the harder to make art so very different from that of his mentor.

Money was a critical problem throughout the early years in New York. By 1935 Pollock was employed on the Federal Art Project of the Works Progress Administration—a Depression-era program meant to provide employment for artists. He was required to turn out, every four to eight weeks, one painting suitable for installation in public buildings, for which he was paid a stipend of about $100 a month. Frequent alcoholic binges often interfered with this work, and in 1937 Pollock began psychotherapy in an attempt to overcome his addiction.

Pollock's work was first exhibited in 1942, as part of a group show that also included the work of painter Lee Krasner. Krasner and Pollock soon formed a close relationship, and they were married in 1945. Gradually, Pollock's work began to change, to be freer and more spontaneous, to contain fewer and fewer figural elements. During the late 1940s he began exhibiting works in his mature style.

Some critics praised Pollock as the greatest of all American artists, but the general public was very slow to accept his revolutionary art. *Time* magazine epitomized the bewilderment of the popular press, dubbing him "Jack the Dripper." Nevertheless, some collectors were willing to invest, so finances became less pressing.

The years 1948 to 1952 were the artist's prime, when he was at the height of his creative powers. After that, he seemed less sure where to go with his art, and even the sympathetic critics were not so responsive to the work. Pollock began to paint less and drink more. On the night of August 11, 1956, Pollock—along with two young women friends—was driving his convertible near his home when he lost control of the car and rammed into a clump of trees at high speed. Pollock and one of the women were killed instantly. The artist was only forty-four years old.

Pollock drunk could be violent and brutish; Pollock sober was shy, introverted, and uncommunicative. Few ever succeeded in getting him to talk about his art, but there is one quote, reprinted many times, that gives voice to his truly remarkable vision: "On the floor I am more at ease. I feel nearer, more a part of the painting, since this way I can walk around it, work from the four sides and literally be *in* the painting. . . . When I am *in* my painting, I am not aware of what I'm doing. It is only after a sort of 'get acquainted' period that I see what I have been about. I have no fears about making changes, destroying the image, etc., because the painting has a life of its own. I try to let it come through. It is only when I lose contact with the painting that the result is a mess. Otherwise there is pure harmony, an easy give and take, and the painting comes out well."[1]

Jackson Pollock in his studio at East Hampton, N.Y. 1950, photographed by Hans Namuth. Center for Creative Photography, University of Arizona, Tucson.

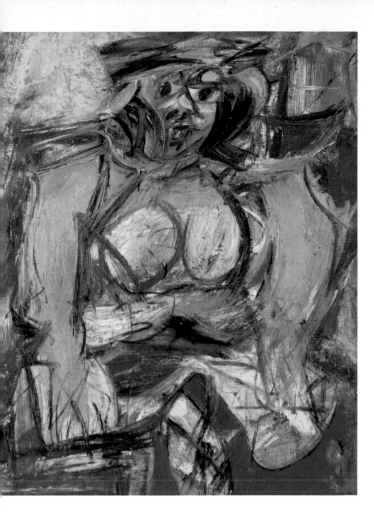

De Kooning's *Woman IV* (**22.2**) is abstract in our strict sense. Like Pollock, de Kooning had developed a nonrepresentational, gestural style during the 1940s. During the next decade, however, he returned to the human figure, most notoriously in the *Women* series.

Even today the *Women* paintings retain their power to disturb. De Kooning admitted that he began each painting from a magazine photograph of a beautiful woman, yet as he worked, they mutated into grimacing monsters. The artist was dismayed, for this wasn't his goal at all. We can see the paintings as reflecting de Kooning's conscious and unconscious feelings toward women. Yet they also record a struggle between two ways of thinking about art. Forceful gestures keep trying to establish a painting about the act of painting, but against this effort the image keeps reasserting itself, demanding to be recognized. Hovering in the background are the spirits of such great painters of human flesh as Rembrandt and Titian, who also used paint in an intensely physical way.

Another form of abstraction that came into prominence in the postwar period is known as **Color Field** painting. As the name implies, imagery is reduced to a large "field" or area of color, in some cases one pure color filling the entire canvas. In contrast to the dynamic emotionalism of Abstract Expressionism, Color Field paintings have a meditative tranquility that draws the viewer in and invites contemplation. The work of Mark Rothko in the late forties through the sixties (**22.3**) usually features one or more soft-edged color rectangles floating in the larger color rectangle of the canvas. The inner rectangle has sides parallel to the canvas edges, and its boundaries are blurred and gently blended, causing the inner sections to float. Where Kline and De Kooning emphasized the physical presence of paint, Rothko did the opposite, thinning his paints so much that the pigment powder barely holds to the canvas. He wanted to communicate a sensation of pure dematerialized color.

22.2 (left) Willem de Kooning. *Woman IV*. 1952–53. Oil, enamel, and charcoal on canvas, 58½" × 45⅞".
The Nelson-Atkins Museum of Art, Kansas City, Missouri.

22.3 (right) Mark Rothko. *Orange and Yellow*. 1956. Oil on canvas, 7'7" × 5'11".
Albright-Knox Art Gallery, Buffalo, N.Y.

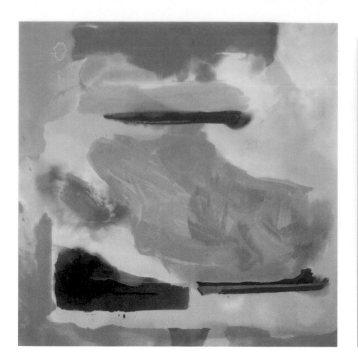

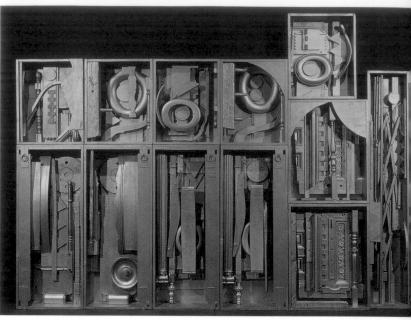

22.4 (left) Helen Frankenthaler. *Spring Bank*. 1974. Acrylic on canvas, 8'10" × 9'.
Musée National d'Art Contemporain, Centre Georges Pompidou, Paris.

22.5 (right) Louise Nevelson. *Royal Tide II*. 1961–63. Painted wood, 7'10½" × 10'6½" × 8".
Whitney Museum of American Art, New York.

Many of the next generation of artists continued to explore the directions opened up by Abstract Expressionism and Color Field painting. Helen Frankenthaler, for example, pioneered a staining technique, pouring thinned paint onto canvas and controlling its flow in various ways (**22.4**). Joan Mitchell took up the energetic brushwork of Abstract Expressionism and combined it with an interest in landscape filtered through the late paintings of Monet (see 7.10).

Sculptors transposed the ideas of Abstract Expressionism and Color Field painting into three dimensions. In works such as *Royal Tide II* (**22.5**), Louise Nevelson arranged wooden crates, dowels, balusterrs, and other odds and ends into large, standing, wall-like compositions. By painting her works in a single color she emphasized the formal values of her materials—their lines, curves, and angles—as opposed to their real-world origins.

INTO THE SIXTIES: ASSEMBLAGE AND HAPPENINGS

By the middle of the 1950s, Abstract Expressionism had been the "new" style for fifteen years. Many artists felt it was time to move on. One of the most influential voices of the time was the composer John Cage, whose writings and speeches suggested a different path for art to follow. Music and art, Cage said, should be "an affirmation of life—not an attempt to bring order out of chaos nor to suggest improvements in creation, but simply a way of waking up to the very life we're living."[2] Like the Dadaists of forty years earlier, young artists began mixing art back up with life as they found it, sometimes literally and often humorously. Critics called the trend Neo-Dada ("new Dada").

An example of Neo-Dada is Robert Rauschenberg's witty *Factum II* (**22.6**). In the tradition of Dada artists such as Hannah Höch (see 9.13), Rauschenberg culled images from mass-printed sources such as magazines. The images relate to the idea of doubleness—a photograph of two trees, side-by-side photographs of a burning building, and even a **T** for "two." Rauschenberg pasted the images onto canvas and tied them together visually with paint applied in the gestures that Abstract Expressionism found so meaningful. Here, however, the gestures are not meant to express anything at all. Rauschenberg "found" them in Abstract Expressionist art just the way he found the images in magazines. Both were part of his life: Why not throw them together? Rauschenberg carried his idea through to its logical conclusion by making the painting twice: There is a *Factum I* that looks just like this. In action painting, gestural brush strokes and drips were the spontaneous and authentic signs of a unique moment of creative frenzy. With sly humor, *Factum II* shows that they can be reproduced like any other image.

Rauschenberg referred to his works as combine paintings, but a more general term is **assemblage.** Another artist who made assemblages was Rauschenberg's friend Jasper Johns. Johns chose as his subjects some of the most familiar images one could imagine: the American flag, a map of the United States, numerals, letters of the alphabet, and targets (**22.7**). He said that by choosing these motifs the work of composition had already been done for him, and he could concentrate on "other things." What other things? Paradoxes, for one. Painted in encaustic over newsprint, the target is textured, sensuous, and unique. Yet the idea of a target exists potentially in endless multiples. Above the target are portions of four faces. Johns took the casts from the same person, making a series of anonymous mechanical multiples from a unique individual. Like all of Johns' favorite motifs, a target is not only familiar but two-dimensional, abstract, and symbolic. Is the painting a representation of a target or a target? What is the difference? It also teases us into thinking about aesthetics and emotional distance. For example, if we appreciate the painting as an abstract composition of concentric circles, does that spare us from thinking about it as a target and the blindfolded victims of a firing squad?

Cage had also suggested that visual art look to the lively art of theater for renewal. The composer's friend Allan Kaprow followed through on this suggestion by eliminating the art object altogether and staging events he called

22.6 (left) Robert Rauschenberg. *Factum II.* 1957. Combine painting: oil, ink, pencil, crayon, paper, fabric, newspaper, printed reproductions, and printed paper on canvas, 61⅜ × 35½". The Museum of Modern Art, New York.

22.7 (right) Jasper Johns. *Target with Four Faces.* 1955. Assemblage: encaustic on newspaper and collage on canvas with objects, 26" square, surmounted by four tinted plaster faces in wood box with hinged front; overall dimensions with box open 33⅝ × 26 × 3". The Museum of Modern Art, New York.

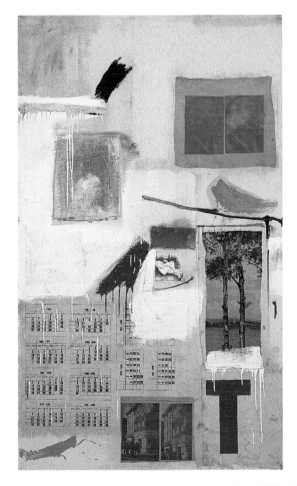

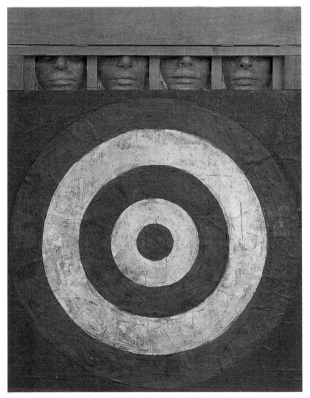

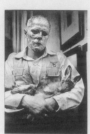
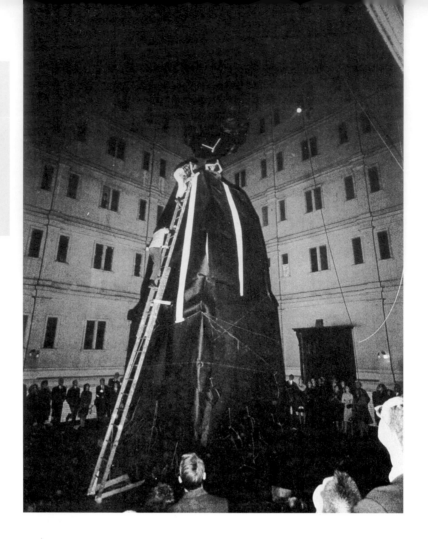

22.8 Allan Kaprow. *The
Courtyard.* 1962. Happening at
the Mills Hotel, New York.
Courtesy of the Library, Getty
Research Institute, Los Angeles.

happenings. Kaprow's *The Courtyard* (**22.8**) happened in the courtyard of a
seedy hotel. Kaprow and his assistants erected a five-story "mountain" of scaffolding covered with black paper. On a platform atop it they set an "altar" of
mattresses. Over the mattresses was suspended a large dome, also covered in
black paper. After audience members helped sweep the space clean, black paper scraps were showered down from above. A woman in white danced
around the base of the mountain and then climbed up to the mattresses. She
was followed by photographers who took pictures of her as she continued to
dance. Accompanied by shrieks, sirens, and thunder effects, the dome was
lowered over them.

Among the spectators at *The Courtyard* was Hans Richter, one of the original members of Dada. None other than Marcel Duchamp, then living in New
York, had drawn his attention to it. The Dadaists, too, had staged provocative
events. "A Ritual!" Richter wrote. "It was a composition using space, color and
movement, and the setting in which the Happening took place gave it a nightmarish, obsessive quality. . . ."[3] The Dadaists recognized their successors
clearly. Just as Dada had created both art and anti-art as "shock therapy"
for the complacent, conformist society that had produced World War I, this
later generation was producing art and anti-art to jolt into awareness the
complacent, conformist society of prosperous, postwar America.

ART OF THE SIXTIES AND SEVENTIES

Does art exist in its own aesthetic realm apart from life? Is it important for us
to have art as an alternative to our social experience, a refuge from everyday
concerns that keeps us in touch with spiritual or abstract matters? Or is art

deeply involved with life? Is it important for us to see the lives we live, the issues that concern us, our sense of what it is like to be in the world here and now given form through art? These questions have animated the history of art since the beginning of the modern era. As viewers, we have the luxury of appreciating all types of art, but artists have to choose one path or the other. During the sixties and seventies, the directions that had been set out in the previous decade were continued, questioned, and complicated by new trends.

Pop Art

Even the name is breezy: "pop," for popular. The artists of Pop found a gold mine of visual material in the mundane, mass-produced objects and images of America's popular culture—comic books, advertising, billboards, and packaging; the ever-expanding world of home appliances and other commodities; and photographic images from cinema, television, and newspapers. Like Neo-Dada, Pop drew art closer to life, but life as it had already been transformed into images by advertising and the media.

The most enigmatic of Pop artists was Andy Warhol, who frustrated critics by refusing to explain what he meant by such painting as *100 Cans* (**22.9**). Was this a criticism of consumer culture? A celebration of it? Was Warhol saying "how awful" or "how wonderful"? Was he saying anything at all? Warhol even adopted the methods of mass production. He called his studio the Factory, and there he and his assistants manufactured his art. The use of photographic silkscreen gave the images a mechanical look removed from the personal touch of the artist's own hand. In a few years, Warhol's subjects grew to form a sort of portrait of America of the early sixties—products such as Campbell soup cans, Coca-Cola bottles, and Brillo boxes; people such as

RELATED WORKS

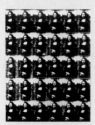

2.3
Warhol,
Thirty Are Better than One

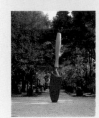

5.18
Oldenburg &
Van Bruggen,
Plantoir

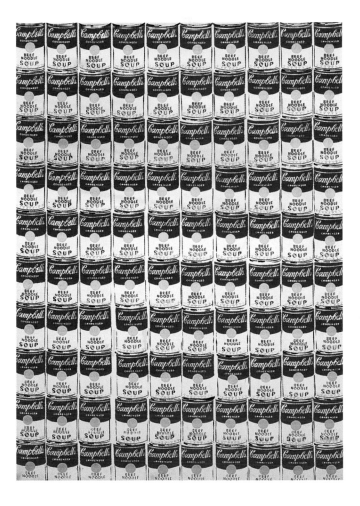

22.9 Andy Warhol. *100 Cans.* 1962. Oil on canvas, 6' × 4'4". Albright-Knox Art Gallery, Buffalo, N.Y.

ANDY WARHOL

1928–1987

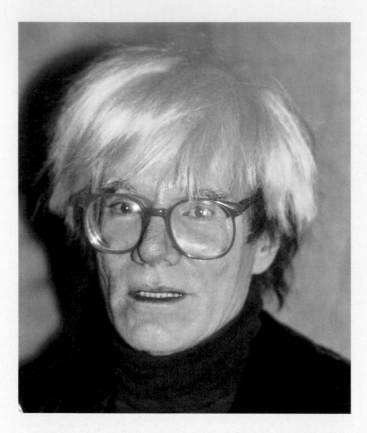

WHEN FRIENDS RECALL the most visible and colorful of the Pop artists, they often remark that he was two people. There was Andy Warhol—media celebrity, high priest of commercial and show-business imagery, wearer of bizarre white wigs, leader to an entourage of quirky New York types, maker of sexually explicit cult films. Then there was Andrew Warhola—child of struggling Czech immigrants, devout Roman Catholic, prolific worker, introvert often paralyzed by shyness, adoring son who, as an adult, brought his mother to live with him for twenty years.

Warhol, born Warhola, grew up in Pittsburgh and attended Carnegie Institute of Technology. After graduation in 1949 he moved to New York, where he launched what would become a highly successful career as a commercial artist. Over the next ten years his employers included most of the chic fashion magazines and elegant Fifth Avenue stores, for which he designed advertisements, promotional pieces, and window displays. He was also—ironically, in view of his later adventures—one of the illustrators for the first edition of *Amy Vanderbilt's Complete Book of Etiquette.*

By 1960 the artist and his style had found each other. Warhol, the gifted commercial artist, slipped into Pop, the "fine art" style of commercial images, without missing a beat. For a decade Pop would remain a dominant art wave in the United States, and Warhol sailed on the crest of that wave. The themes with which he is most closely associated appeared repeatedly in prints and paintings: Marilyn Monroe, Elizabeth Taylor, Jackie Kennedy, and, of course, the famous Coke bottles and Campbell's soup cans.

A turning point in Warhol's career occurred in 1963, when the artist moved into a new studio in New York. A friend decorated the entire space in silver paint and aluminum foil, a large group of acquaintances and admirers and hangers-on converged, and thus was born—the Factory. At the Factory Warhol continued his enormous output of prints, paintings, and sculptures. At the Factory he directed the production of many avant-garde (some would say outlandish) films, featuring actors with names like Viva, Ultra Violet, and International Velvet. And at the Factory, in 1968, a woman who announced herself as the founder of SCUM (Society for Cutting Up Men) shot Warhol and nearly killed him.

Many observers felt that Warhol ran out of steam after the shooting, that his art no longer showed the edge and excitement it once had. Nevertheless, he worked steadily, developing his familiar themes and some new ones, until his death at age fifty-eight, of complications following gall bladder surgery.

Warhol often liked to say he was a "machine." He claimed to be devoid of emotion or feeling, just a machine that produced a product, called art, in a place called a Factory. One of his much-quoted statements sums this up. "If you want to know all about Andy Warhol, just look at the surface: of my paintings and films and me, and there I am. There's nothing behind it."[4]

Photograph of Andy Warhol, 1983.

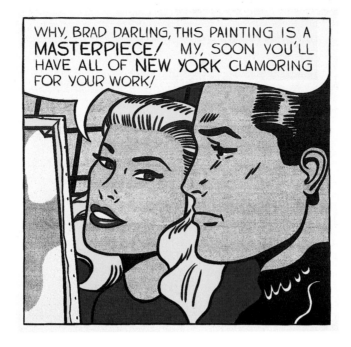

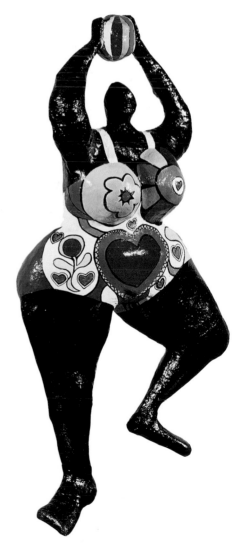

22.10 (above) Roy Lichtenstein. *Masterpiece*. 1962. Oil on canvas, 4'6" square.

22.11 (below) Niki de Saint-Phalle. *Black Venus*. 1965–67. Painted polyester, 9'2" × 2'11" × 2'.
Whitney Museum of American Art, New York.

Marilyn Monroe, Jackie Kennedy, and Elvis Presley; symbols such as dollar bills and the Statue of Liberty; newspaper photos of car crashes, race riots, and an electric chair. All were repeated again and again across the surface of the canvas. Warhol's style was cool and detached. He said that everything that mattered, everything that was interesting, was right on the surface where you could see it, and he acted mystified when people wanted there to be more.

Roy Lichtenstein often based his imagery on the comic book. Many of Lichtenstein's paintings (**22.10**) are large, meticulously rendered frames adapted from comic strips, accurate down to the dialogue in the speech balloons and the dot pattern of crude newspaper reproduction. The artist did not hesitate to introduce a touch of irony by poking fun at himself and the art world in proclaiming this work a "masterpiece." Pop Art attempted to show that a detached look at the overfamiliar objects of daily life could give them new meaning as visual emblems.

The energies of Pop and Neo-Dada mingle in the work of Niki de Saint-Phalle. Among her early works were events called *shootings*, in which people gathered to watch the artist take aim at her own sculptures and assemblages with a pistol. Pouches of paint were hidden in the works, and each successful shot produced an explosion of color. The combination of playfulness and violent aggression was intriguing, and the sight of a beautiful woman coolly firing a gun was part of the event. Beginning in 1965, Saint-Phalle affirmed the powers of women less ambiguously and more joyously in a series of Pop-inspired sculptures called *Nanas*, a French slang word for women. *Black Venus* (**22.11**), a painted polyester *Nana* more than 9 feet tall, exhibits a sexuality that is both powerful and buoyantly cheerful. The figure almost busts out of a sort of bathing suit gaily colored in hearts and flowers, clutching a beach ball. Her breasts and hips and thighs are enormous (remember the *Venus of Willendorf*, 14.2), but her pose is dynamic; she stands ready to run or jump or dance. Saint-Phalle's *Venus* is an earth mother, but an earth mother who wants to play.

Minimal Art and Earthworks

Coexisting with Pop in the 1960s was a trend called Minimalism, which continued to explore the nonrepresentational directions that art could take. Minimalism was primarily concerned with three-dimensional art, but it was

RELATED WORKS

11.32
Flavin,
Untitled

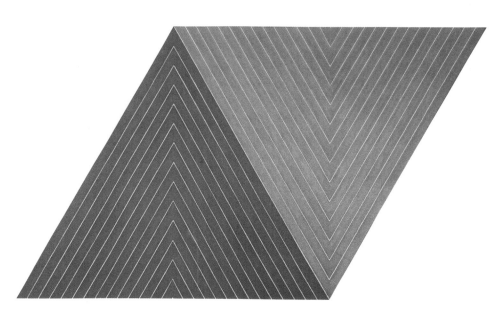

inspired by developments in painting such as Frank Stella's *Valparaiso Flesh and Green* (**22.12**). Abstract painting was certainly not new, but Stella's approach was fundamentally different in one important way: Unlike the Abstract Expressionists and their heirs, he did not conceive of his work as a visual field that the viewer would see *into* but as an object the viewer would look *at*. The shape of *Valparaiso Flesh and Green* immediately signals that this painting is not a window onto anything—not a deep Renaissance perspective, not a shallow Cubist space, not an Abstract Expressionist infinity of tangled lines or hovering color. This painting is a *thing*.

Stella used color to divide the parallelogram into two equilateral triangles. His composition consists in repeating two of the three outlines of each triangle again and again, producing a series of chevrons (**V**s) of diminishing size in bands of color (the white between the colored chevrons is bare canvas). The reflective, metallic paint has an industrial look, and it further emphasizes the surface of the work. "What you see is what you see," Stella said about his painting, meaning that he did not intend anything by it other than what was there: the beauty of the color, the logic of the composition, the satisfaction of repetition. That was all there was, and he found it to be enough.

Considered purely as an object *Valparaiso Flesh and Green* becomes a kind of shallow, colored sculpture attached to the wall. This point was not lost on artists who were more interested in three-dimensional work, and they began to explore the implications. Donald Judd's *Untitled* (**22.13**) embodies many of the characteristics associated with Minimalism. It is made of common industrial and construction materials. These materials are used literally;

22.12 (left) Frank Stella.
Valparaiso Flesh and Green. 1963.
Metallic paint on canvas, 6'6" ×
11'3¼" × 3".
Collection the artist.

22.13 (right) Donald Judd.
Untitled. 1969. Brass and red
fluorescent Plexiglas, ten units,
6⅛ × 24 × 7" each, with 6"
intervals.
Hirshhorn Museum and Sculpture
Garden, Smithsonian Institution,
Washington, D.C.

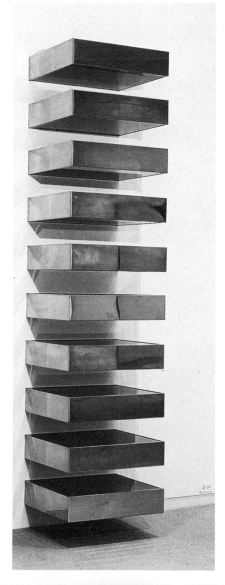

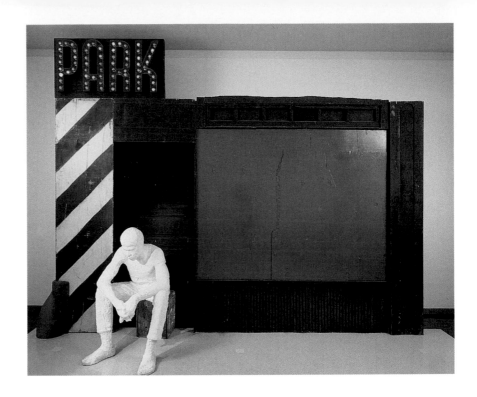

22.14 George Segal. *The Parking Garage.* 1968. Plaster, wood, metal, electrical parts, and lightbulbs, 9'9¾" × 12'8" × 4'. The Newark Museum, New Jersey.

they do not try to suggest or depict anything else. The composition is based in repeating units of simple geometric shapes. There is no trace of the artist's "hand" or "touch." Rather, the sculpture has the impersonal look of industrial fabrication. And yet it can be immensely satisfying to look at. The stacked boxes are like a lesson in seeing and perspective. The various shadows they cast, the even slices of space between them, the way the light filters through the red Plexiglas, the reflections of the polished brass—all give undeniable pleasure. The clear logic and straightforward repetition are strangely reassuring, like a nursery rhyme or a child counting its fingers, one to ten.

Minimalism was not a movement founded and defined by artists but a term invented by critics in an attempt to get a handle on the new art they were seeing. Many artists of the time were interested in simplified forms and honest materials, and the label Minimalism loosely includes a broad range of work. The organic fiberglass forms of Eva Hesse's *Repetition 19 III* (see 4.55) are an aspect of Minimalism. The sculptor Robert Smithson gradually abandoned industrial materials for natural ones and galleries for nature itself in earthworks such as *Spiral Jetty* (see 3.31). Like many earthworks of the 1970s, *Spiral Jetty* combines the aesthetics of Minimalism with the principles of Conceptualism (discussed below).

Real, Super Real

Still another trend that emerged around 1960, as the dominance of abstract art was increasingly challenged, was a revival of interest in the human figure. One of the most fruitful approaches to the figure was developed by George Segal. Segal began as an abstract painter during the late 1950s, but he grew to feel that too much of the world outside of the studio door had to be ignored. He experimented with constructing plaster figures, but the technique he quickly came to prefer was making casts of live people by covering them with strips of plaster-soaked cloth.

Segal typically placed his figures in realistic, three-dimensional settings, as in *The Parking Garage* (**22.14**). Built like stage sets and including actual objects as props, the settings usually evoke an urban environment. The result is like a moment of theater with plaster actors. Segal's works capture a particular kind of city experience: the hundreds of people we come into contact with every day but do not know. We see them only for a moment, in passing. Yet

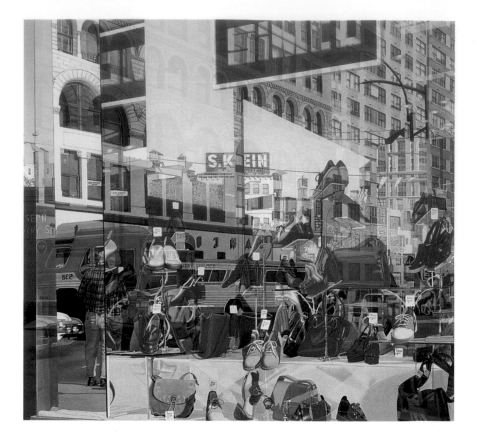

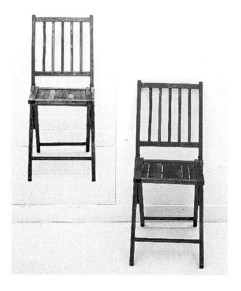

22.15 (left) Don Eddy. *New Shoes for H.* 1973–74. Acrylic on canvas, 3'8" × 4'.
The Cleveland Museum of Art.

22.16 (right) Joseph Kosuth. *One and Three Chairs.* 1965. Folding wooden chair, photograph, blown-up dictionary definition.

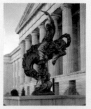

they often leave an impression—the girl on the subway, the man waiting for the light to change, the woman in the restaurant window, or the boy in front of the parking garage. In some ways, they are the ghosts of our day, and Segal portrays them that way. The rough, unpainted plaster surfaces encourage us to experience his figures as anonymous types, but we see that they were cast directly from life and are thus individuals.

Like Neo-Dada and Minimalism, Segal's realism has a strong literal component, relying on ordinary materials that are what they are. The diverse painting trends of the time also share this trait in various ways. Pop artists, for example, took their inspiration from two-dimensional images, and Minimalist painters such as Frank Stella created paintings meant to be experienced as objects. At first glance, Don Eddy's *New Shoes for H.* would seem to be an exception (**22.15**). But in fact this is not a painting of a store window but a painting of a *photograph* of a store window. During the 1970s many painters became intrigued by the view through the lens. One of the trends this produced was known as **Photorealism,** meaning the particular kind of realism that the camera produces. *New Shoes for H.* depicts a photograph that Eddy took himself. He was interested in the double layer of information that windows offer by being both transparent and reflective. Photography's ability to capture a dizzying amount of detail for later study is on full view here. The painting, however, is not an exact copy of the photograph. First, the photograph was in black and white. More important, Eddy has given his painting and allover sharp focus that photographs do not possess. The result is a sort of hallucinatory superrealism.

Conceptual Art

Conceptual Art is art in which ideas are paramount and the form that realizes these ideas is secondary—often lightweight, ephemeral, unpretentious, cheap, ordinary, unremarkable. Arising in the mid-1960s as yet another echo of Dada, Conceptual Art is especially indebted to Marcel Duchamp, whose ready-mades such as *Fountain* (see 21.23) can be considered as Conceptual works, though they made their appearance before the term was invented. In *Fountain*, the idea of placing a urinal in a gallery for consideration as a work of art was paramount. The form the urinal took—steel or porcelain, large or small, angular or curving—did not matter, nor did Duchamp actually make the urinal himself.

Conceptualism is not a style but a way of thinking about art, and artists have put it to many different uses. Joseph Kosuth's *One and Three Chairs* (**22.16**) places three alternative representations of a chair together for comparison: an actual chair, a photograph of that chair, and a dictionary definition of the word *chair*. The definition is merely a blown-up photograph of a dictionary entry, and the chair a simple folding wooden chair. Kosuth did not even take the photograph of the chair himself. What we see is not a work of art but one of many possible ways to document a concept Kosuth had for raising questions about representation, and thus about art.

Like many early Conceptualists, Kosuth's desire to get rid of the art object was motivated by his opposition to the burgeoning art market, which implicitly equated art with luxury commodities such as antique furniture or designer clothing. He shifted his art into ideas and documented them in ways that had little or no perceived material value. Other artists enjoy the aesthetic liberation of Conceptualism. For Sol LeWitt, whose wall drawings consist solely of instructions to be executed by others (see 6.18), Conceptualism allows the artist to surrender direct control, open art up to chance, and involve other people.

Feminism and Feminist Art

If you had been reading a book like this around 1968, the chapters of Part Five, "Arts in Time," would most likely not have introduced you to Sofonisba Anguissola (16.27), Artemisia Gentileschi (17.5), Judith Leyster (17.13), Elisabeth Vigée-Lebrun (17.18), Berthe Morisot (21.5), or Mary Cassatt (21.12). Art historians knew of works by these women. They just didn't make an effort to include them in their telling of the history of art. It was quite possible to come away from a course in art history or a visit to a museum believing that women had played little or no role in the art of the past. If you look forward in this book to the art of the eighties and nineties, you will find not only many more women but greater diversity in general. This diversity accurately reflects the makeup of the contemporary art world, and it is due in large measure to the impact of feminism and related social and political movements of the 1970s.

Feminist organizations had originally been formed around such issues as equal rights and equal pay. Because images are powerful and pervasive in contemporary society, visual culture quickly became a feminist concern, both in art and in the media. Women art professionals organized to recover women's art of the past, to push for more equitable representation in museums and galleries, and to nurture contemporary women artists. During this first phase of feminism, a project that intrigued many artists was the creation of a specifically female art. One of the most influential early feminist works was Judy Chicago's *Dinner Party* (see 12.19), which brought crafts media into art to honor the domestic realm, a feminine world through most of history.

RELATED WORKS

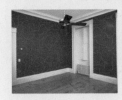
6.17
LeWitt,
Wall Drawing #912

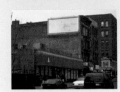
2.41
Gonzalez-Torres,
Untitled

RELATED WORKS

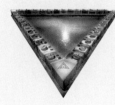
12.19
Chicago,
Dinner Party

Chicago's colleague Miriam Schapiro also evokes the domestic realm in *Heartfelt* (**22.17**). Shaped like a schematic house, *Heartfelt* is layered with mosaic and floral patterns, falling blossoms, and a big red heart. The crowded, unashamedly decorative surface and the popular, easily understood symbols of house and heart were intended as a female rebuke to the stripped-down industrial forms of Minimalism, which Schapiro considered typically male.

Feminist thought has since developed considerably, and most feminists today consider these early ideas about women's (and men's) essential natures to be too limiting. As for Minimalism, the organic work of Eva Hesse (see 4.55) has been at least as influential as any of the "male" versions. Nevertheless, the work of Chicago and Schapiro marked an important step in the full participation of women in contemporary artistic life. Early feminism also served to draw attention to many living women artists whose long careers had not received sufficient recognition. One of these was Alice Neel (**22.18**). Neel painted people. That was her interest. She was, it is now plain to see, one of the finest, most original, and most insightful painters of people of the 20th century. Unfortunately, her mature career overlapped almost exactly with the decades when abstract painting dominated the art world. She was far from the only artist to be pushed aside as irrelevant to the progress of art history as contemporary critics, curators, and gallery owners saw it. Later, when many younger artists began to explore figurative painting again, they discovered a master in their midst. Neel had been working all along.

22.17 (left) Miriam Schapiro. *Heartfelt*. 1979. Acrylic and fabric on canvas, 5'10" × 3'4". Collection the Norton Neuman Family.

22.18 (right) Alice Neel. *Hartley*. 1965. Oil on canvas, 50 × 36". National Gallery of Art, Washington, D.C.

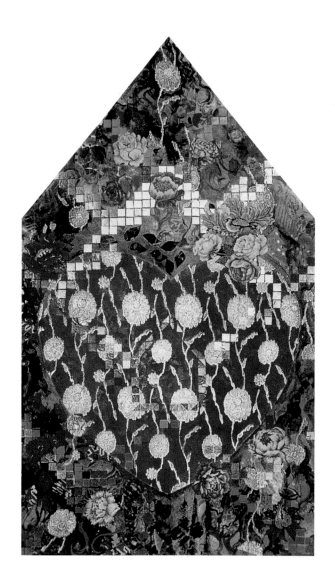

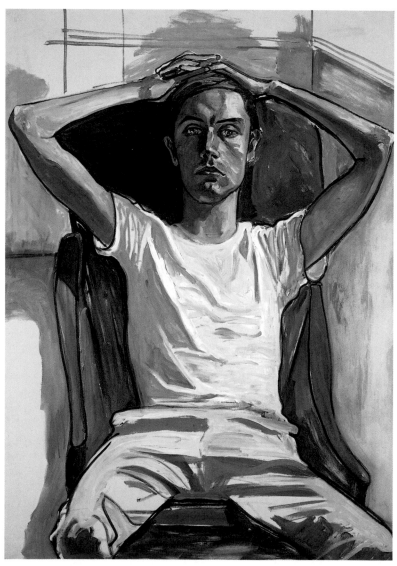

ALICE NEEL

1900–1984

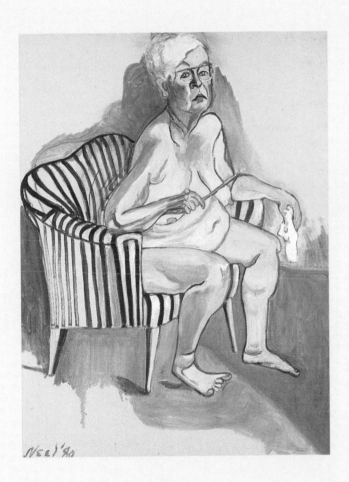

WHEN AN ACQUAINTANCE once remarked that Alice Neel painted "like a man," the artist retorted, "No, I don't paint like a man; but I don't paint like they expect a woman to paint." As a matter of fact, this extraordinary woman spent a long lifetime doing the unexpected, with cheerful disregard for the prevailing mores and fashions.

Alice Neel was born in Merion Square, Pennsylvania, the daughter of a proper middle-class family that she described as "anti-bohemian." She studied at what was then the Philadelphia School of Design for Women—"a school where rich girls went before they got married"—and received a thorough, if conventional, grounding in art techniques.

Her personal life, too, was conventional up to that point, but soon it changed drastically. Neel referred to the men who played important roles in her life by stereotype, rather than by name. Upon leaving art school she married "the Cuban." The couple moved to Havana, where Neel continued to paint and had her first exhibition in 1926. The Cuban marriage eventually broke up, after which Neel returned to New York and worked on the W.P.A. Art Project—the government-sponsored Depression program to help support artists. Along the way she took up with "the sailor," with whom she lived until he cut up and burned all her work. ("You know how men are, they get jealous, they're possessive.") There was also "the Puerto Rican singer." From these liaisons came four children, one of whom died in infancy. Later there would be several grandchildren, who became favorite subjects for Neel's art.

From the beginning Neel was a portraitist, although she preferred to call herself a "people painter," feeling that portraitists are looked down on. This assessment actually proved correct through most of her career. Just at the point when Neel should have been in her artistic prime—the 1940s and 1950s—abstraction had completely taken over the art world. The painter of figures was out of fashion and remained so for at least twenty years. Not until 1974, at the age of seventy-four, did Neel have her first important show—at the Whitney Museum in New York. The show included some fifteen pictures that had not previously been "off the shelf." Alice Neel waited a long time to hear an important critic name her as the best portrait painter of the 20th century, and then she herself did not contradict that statement. The pictures, however, have transcended portrait status in the sense of recording someone's looks. They are major paintings that happen to have people as their subjects.

Quite obviously, Alice Neel was an original, an exceptionally self-directed artist and human being. Neither her personal life nor her career was modeled after any example, nor did she follow anything but her own inclinations: "When they asked me if I had influences I said I never copy anybody. I never did, because I feel that the most important thing about art and in art—and I tell students this—is to find your own road."[5]

Alice Neel. *Self-Portrait*. 1980. Oil on canvas, 4'6" × 3'4". National Portrait Gallery, Smithsonian Institution, Washington, D.C.

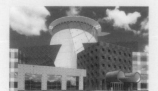

13.36 Isosaki, Team Disney
Building

ART SINCE THE EIGHTIES: POSTMODERN WORLD?

Over the course of the seventies, it became clear to many people that ideas about art that seemed to have been in place for much of the modern era were eroding and that something different was taking their place. This new climate of thought has come to be called Postmodernism. Whether Postmodernism is truly a new era or whether it is simply a new phase of Modernism is much debated. Future generations will no doubt decide; it is always difficult to understand and label one's own time.

The term *postmodern* was first used to describe architecture such as Renzo Piano and Richard Rodgers' Georges Pompidou National Center of Art and Culture (**22.19**). Designed in 1971 and completed six years later, the Pompidou Center created a sensation. Encased in scaffolding, pipes, tubes, and funnels—all color-coded according to function—it looks like a building turned inside out. The architects themselves likened it to "a Jules Verne spaceship that can't fly."[6] The Pompidou Center was one of many buildings of the time that turned away from the International style that had dominated Western architecture after World War II (see 13.24, 13.35). The International style had grown from the thinking of early-20th-century Modernist movements such as De Stijl and the Bauhaus (see pages 532–533). Its industrial materials, clean lines, and rectilinear forms sought not only to express the modern age but also to create a luminous, rational environment in which humanity itself would progress. By the mid-sixties, however, many began to find International style buildings oppressive and sterile. A new direction was called for, but instead of building on Modernist ideas and progressing *forward*, architects reached both *backward*—adapting ornaments and forms from traditions as distant as ancient

22.19 Renzo Piano and Richard Rodgers. Georges Pompidou National Center of Art and Culture, Paris. 1977.

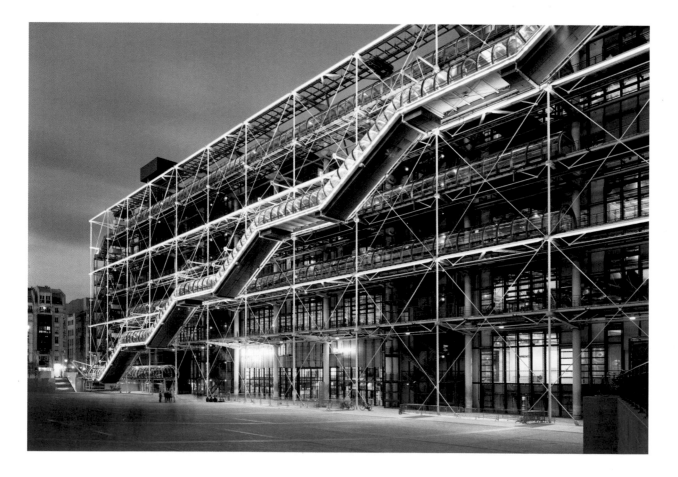

Egypt—and *outward*—looking seriously at common, everyday architecture. Instead of the rational order of International style, they often emphasized other, equally human qualities such as playfulness, curiosity, and eccentricity.

The notion that there may be no such thing as "progress" in art is part of the web of related ideas that make up Postmodernism. Another is a more complex view of history. Feminism had clearly shown that within art history as it was usually told lay other histories that were untold. Art history was not the straightforward progression of one style to another that it had been made to seem. Rather, each historical moment was full of multiple directions, contradictions, and debates. Perhaps a fairer way to study history would be to study everything that happened, not just the "winners" whose style seemed to be part of "progress." This way of thinking led to the creation of museums such as the Gare d'Orsay in Paris. (See "Art Issues: Presenting the Past," page 513.) Applying these ideas to the present moment logically leads to pluralism, the idea that art can take many directions at the same time, all of them equally valid. Historians of the future should no longer select one as "correct" and sweep the rest under the carpet. Pluralism in turn recognizes that there is no longer any single leading artistic center. Rather, the world of art consists of many centers and has many levels.

Sherrie Levine's 1991 *Fountain* may be the ultimate Postmodern statement (**22.20**). *Fountain* was the most notorious of Duchamp's ready-mades, an ordinary porcelain urinal that he contributed to an art exhibit in 1917 (see 21.23). Levine presents a gleaming bronze version. Her *Fountain* is a valuable, even sacred object, suggesting that the original *Fountain* and all it stands for are now firmly enshrined in the thinking of contemporary artists. At the same time, we notice that she has not called her work *Homage to Duchamp*, or *After Duchamp*, or acknowledged Duchamp in any way. She presents the work as her own, a Postmodern practice known as **appropriation.** Loosely, appropriation refers to the artistic recycling of existing images. In this sense, it acknowledges that images circulate in such vast quantities through our society that they have become a kind of public resource that anyone can draw on. More strictly, appropriation is linked to Duchamp himself, who presented the creations of others (a urinal) as his own and in doing so gave them a new meaning. In music, many of the same ideas lie behind the practice of sampling—taking bits of music from prerecorded songs and giving them new meaning by placing them in a new context. Both appropriation and sampling form part of larger theories that doubt whether any artist is the sole creator of his or her work or the final authority about what it means. All artists borrow ideas in one way or another, and the meaning of a work is unstable and varies from viewer to viewer. The creation of meaning, and thus of art, is a communal project.

These, then, are some of the ideas that make up Postmodernism. This chapter closes with a brief look at the art of what may be the Postmodern era.

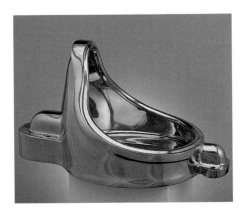

22.20 Sherrie Levine. *Fountain.* 1991. Bronze, 14½ × 14¼ × 25". Walker Art Center, Minneapolis.

The Painterly Image

For many observers, art history seemed to stop running forward in the mid-1970s, when one artist after another began to make paintings—not the minimal objects of Frank Stella (22.12) or the silkscreened ironies of Andy Warhol (22.9), but paintings where paint was freely manipulated as a sensuous material in order to make a recognizable, expressive image. That kind of painting was supposed to be over.

During the early 1980s some of these artists became known as Neo-Expressionists, for their work recalled the sincerity and emotional intensity of the Expressionist movement of early 20th-century Europe (see page 520). German artist Anselm Kiefer became one of the most talked about of this group, for his work often dealt directly with the great trauma of his country's past: the horrors of Nazi power under Adolf Hitler and the atrocities of World

War II. *Interior* (**22.21**) was copied from a photograph of Hitler's Chancellery (office of state), a building designed by the ambitious Nazi architect Albert Speer. In Kiefer's work the Chancellery, rendered in dramatic perspective, is abandoned and decaying. A fire burns in the center of the room; perhaps it will destroy the building and the regime it represents. Most critics have read Kiefer's work as a kind of exorcism—an attempt to drive out the evil spirits of Germany's past. And, to be sure, the artist's vast theatrical spaces, almost like stage sets, are empty. The actors are gone.

An American artist who was associated at first with Neo-Expressionism is Eric Fischl. Fischl's early paintings explored the strangeness that lay just under the surface of ordinary suburban life. *Barbeque* (**22.22**) presents a slice of all-American normality in the vertiginous perspective of a wide-angle

22.21 (right) Anselm Kiefer. *Interior.* 1981. Oil, paper, and straw on canvas; 9'5¼" × 10'2½". Collection Stedelijk Museum, Amsterdam.

22.22 (below) Eric Fischl. *Barbeque.* 1982. Oil on canvas. 5'5" × 8'4". Collection Steve Martin, Los Angeles. Courtesy the artist and Mary Boone Gallery, New York.

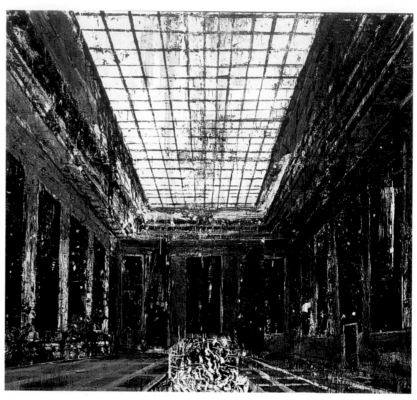

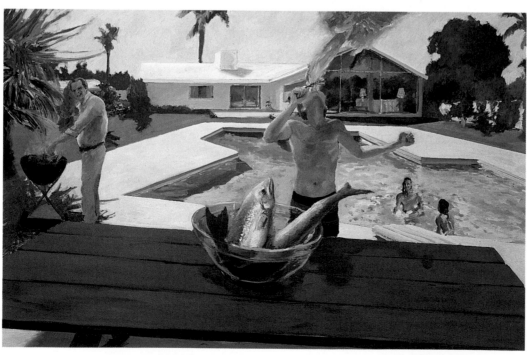

photograph. Objects in the foreground appear larger than they should, and the scene goes rushing into the distance as though it were being sucked down a wind tunnel. The father turns from his labors at the barbeque to smile approvingly at the hijinks of his son, who seems to be doing an amusing trick. But this is not a trick. The boy is breathing fire, smoldering in an adolescent rage that says GET ME OUT. He is an alien in their midst. In front of him, an arching fish seems to make a bid for freedom. It, too, is out of its element.

While Fischl mined the suburbs for material, many young New York artists drew their energy from street life, the punk scene, and the graffiti images that then were appearing on subways, storefronts, and almost every urban surface. One of these painters was Jean-Michel Basquiat, who began as a graffiti artist in the late 1970s. His work came to the attention of gallery owners when it was included in an exhibit of street art in 1980. Between his first gallery exhibit the following year and his death from a drug overdose at the age of twenty-eight, Basquiat blazed with amazing intensity, producing a large and compelling body of work. The subject of *Gold Griot* (**22.23**) is an African ceremonial storyteller, or *griot*. Painted on a gold background that indicates a sacred area and over a panel of wooden slats that evoke poor Caribbean dwellings, the *griot* shows Basquiat's purposefully "primitive" or "naive" style. In fact, Basquiat was anything but primitive. Growing up in a middle-class family in Brooklyn, son of a Haitian father and a Puerto Rican mother, Basquiat read widely and studied a broad range of art and artists. In his work he tried to encompass the many layers of the hybrid culture that he belonged to, the Afro–Caribbean–African–American–New York culture that admired opera *and* jazz, that spoke Spanish *and* English, that danced the salsa *and* hip-hop, went to museums *and* clubs. Basquiat's death ended an astonishing career that straddled many worlds.

A 1978 exhibition at the Whitney Museum of American Art entitled "New Image Painting" was one of the events that first drew the public's attention to the fact that painting had become newly interesting to young artists. One of the painters included was Susan Rothenberg, whose paintings of ghostly horses—their dark outlines emerging from a web of white brush strokes—

RELATED WORKS

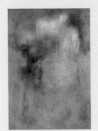
2.20
Purdum,
Chin Up

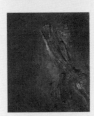
2.23
Rothenberg,
*Maggie's
Ponytail*

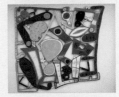
7.11
Murray,
The Lowdown

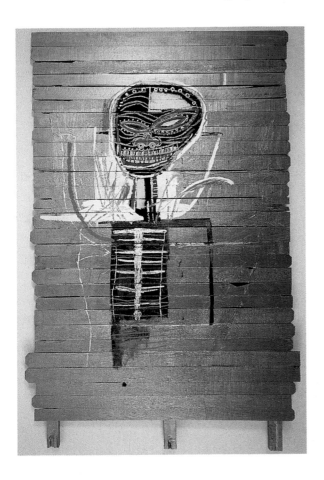

22.23 Jean-Michel Basquiat. *Gold Griot.* 1984. Oil and oil paintstick on wood, 9'9" × 6'1". The Broad Art Foundation.

22.24 (right) Susan Rothenberg. *A Golden Moment.* 1985. Oil on canvas, 54 × 48".
The Broad Art Foundation.

22.25 (below) Terry Winters. *Color and Information.* 1998. Oil and alkyd resin on canvas, 9 × 12'.
Courtesy the artist and Matthew Marks Gallery, New York.

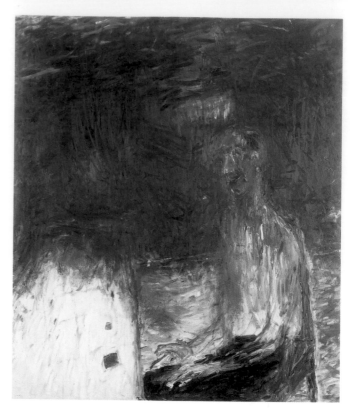

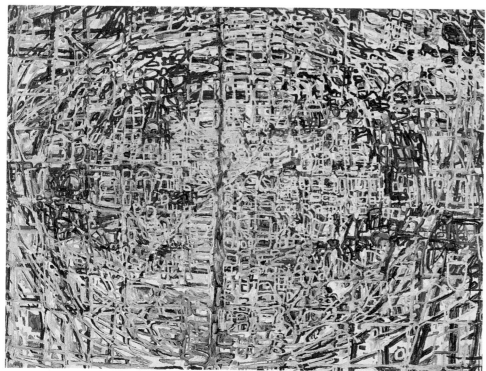

seemed to evoke the return of the image from abstraction itself. In *A Golden Moment* (**22.24**), a furious storm of brush strokes resolves into an image of a gaunt man seated before a table, his hands resting on his legs. It is the artist Mondrian. Before him lie the bare materials of his art: A white surface. A square of red. A square of blue. The "golden moment" of the title appears around him in the glow of yellow, the third primary hue. The title refers as well to the golden moment of modernism, when idealistic artists such as Mondrian believed that they could bring a better society into being through an art of pure color and form.

The recent paintings of Terry Winters attempt to find a visual equivalent for the invisible, unquantifiable, overwhelming, abstract entity that is also the central reality of our time: information. *Color and Information* (**22.25**) defies conventional categories of representation and abstraction. Winters has developed a linear visual language whose basic markings of **I** and **O** reflect the on/off, if/then binary logic of computers. Just as streams of these simple choices generate complicated programs, so Winters uses them to create dense, layered paintings that seem to allude at once to a satellite photograph of a city, the twin lobes of the human brain, the circuitry of a computer, the explosion of a galaxy being born, the intricate maze of the World Wide Web, pure energy expanding outward. "I believe it is the first Millennium picture I have seen," wrote one critic.[7] Painting, long written off as dead, suddenly seems uniquely suited to carry us into the future.

Words and Images, Issues and Identities

In works such as *Guitar, Sheet Music, and Glass* (7.17) and *The Emigrant* (21.19), Cubist artists at the beginning of the 20th century imported words into art. With the growth of advertising in the form of posters and newspapers, words had taken on a new visual presence in the environment, and Cubist paintings were the first to acknowledge this. During the 1960s, Conceptual Art often took the form of words or juxtaposed words and images in a critical spirit, as in Kosuth's *One and Three Chairs* (22.16). By the 1980s it had become clear to many that advertising was the prevalent visual reality of our time, and a number of artists adopted its techniques, most commonly to address political and social issues.

Jenny Holzer's *Protect Me from What I Want* (**22.26**) is one of a series of works in which the artist inserted words that closely resembled advertising slogans into public places. The photograph here shows the work installed at Caesar's Palace, a famous hotel and casino in Las Vegas. The photograph gives some idea of the dense advertising environment the sign was part of. Advertising, of course, is precisely about wanting, about creating desire. How many

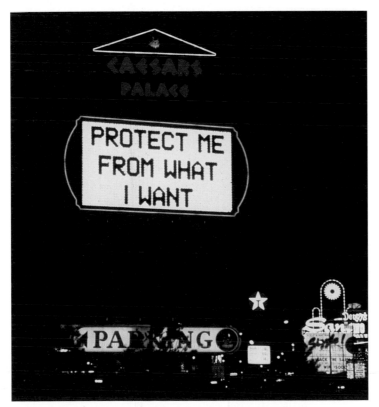

22.26 Jenny Holzer. *Survival.* 1983–85. Darktronics double-sided electronic sign, *Protect Me from What I Want.* Caesar's Palace.
Nevada Institute for Contemporary Art, Caesar's Palace, Las Vegas, Nevada, Sept. 2–6, 1986.

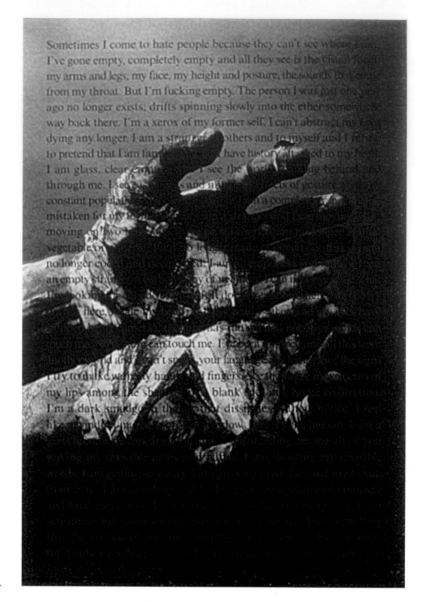

22.27 David Wojnarowicz. *Untitled (Sometimes I come to hate people).* 1992. Gelatin silver print and silk-screened text on museum board, 38 × 26". Courtesy the Estate of David Wojnarowicz and P.P.O.W., New York.

RELATED WORKS

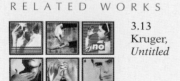

3.13 Kruger, *Untitled*

people noticed Holzer's prayerlike slogan shouting its warning amid the dazzling display of neon signs promoting hotels, casinos, restaurants, and other temptations? ("Win $5000 dollars!" reads a sign in the lower right.) We have no way of knowing, of course, but those who did may have paused for a moment.

One of the most highly charged issues of the 1980s was the AIDS epidemic, which forced deep-lying prejudices to the surface of public life. In one of his last works, David Wojnarowicz used the formal means of advertising to channel his emotions as the disease ravaged his body (**22.27**). Text set in deep red type lures viewers closer to an image they might normally shy away from, a pair of bandaged hands held out perhaps in pleading, perhaps as evidence. The text expresses the artist's rage, frustration, fatigue, and despair. But above all it embodies his refusal to go quietly. "I am vibrating in isolation among you," the text concludes. "I am screaming but it comes out like pieces of clear ice. I am signaling that the volume of all this is too high. I am waving. I am waving my hands. I am disappearing. I am disappearing but not fast enough."

Artists associated with the feminist movement of the 1970s and the gay activism of the 1980s were instrumental in opening the art world to works that addressed human difference, just as American culture in general became more aware of the many identities it embraced and, all too often, silenced. Jaune

THE GUERRILLA GIRLS

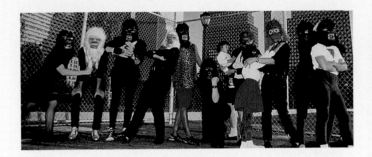

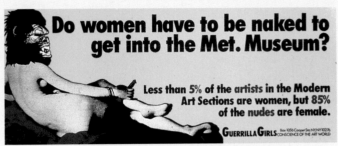

Who are they? That's a secret. How many of them are there? That's a secret too. How do you find them? You don't. You leave a message and, if they wish, they'll find you. If you are fostering sexism or racism in the art world, they'll find you whether you like it or not. They strike without warning, often by night, in the manner of guerrilla fighters, wearing the fierce, menacing head masks of gorillas. Each of them is a working artist, and together they have become a force to be reckoned with. They are the Guerrilla Girls.

The Guerrilla Girls came into being in 1985, shortly after the opening of a huge exhibition at New York's Museum of Modern Art. The show, entitled "International Survey of Contemporary Painting and Sculpture," included works by 169 artists, fewer than 10 percent of whom were women. One April morning residents of lower Manhattan, where many artists live and work, awakened to find copies of a distinctive poster plastered on outdoor walls. In bold type the poster inquired, "WHAT DO THESE ARTISTS HAVE IN COMMON?" Underneath were the names of 42 prominent artists—all male. The poster text continued, "They all allow their work to be shown in galleries that show no more than 10 percent women or none at all."

More posters followed. One asked, "DO WOMEN HAVE TO BE NAKED TO GET INTO THE MET. MUSEUM?" Another catalogued "THE ADVANTAGES OF BEING A WOMAN ARTIST," a sweetly sarcastic list that included such benefits as "Working without the pressure of success" and "Seeing your ideas live on in the work of others." Prime targets for the Guerrilla Girls' scorn were art critics, museums, and galleries that concentrate attention on white male artists, all but ignoring women and minority artists. The posters achieved almost instant chic, partly because of their excellent graphic design, partly because of the Guerrilla Girls' aura of mystery.

From posters, the Guerrilla Girls progressed to on-site appearances. Let a museum present a male-dominated exhibition, and the Guerrilla Girls were sure to turn up—wearing their gorilla masks (often with short skirts and lacy stockings), waving bananas, making street theater for an appreciative audience. Given such a cleverly designed campaign, media attention was inevitable. Scores of articles about the Guerrilla Girls have been published in newspapers and magazines. They have been interviewed on television and often speak at colleges. They maintain a Web site, www.guerillagirls.com, and have published several books, including *The Guerilla Girls' Art Museum Activity Book* (2004).

For ease of communication, each of the Guerrilla Girls has taken the name of a noted woman artist who is dead. (Material for this essay was supplied to the author by "Alice Neel.") It is believed that several members of the group are quite well-known artists, but this cannot be proved, because the women never appear in public as Guerrilla Girls without their masks.

The gorilla masks serve a double purpose. Of course, they protect the wearers' identities, but they also put everybody else at a disadvantage. We know these are women, so it is more than a little disconcerting to be confronted with a ferocious, toothy ape face. This effect is no doubt intended. Individually, women artists may lack clout, but the Guerrilla Girls, as a group, know a thing or two about power.

There is no way to determine how much influence the Guerrilla Girls have had in improving prospects for women and minority artists. Still, as every reformer knows, the first step toward making a change is getting attention, and that has been taken care of. The Guerrilla Girls have a great many secrets. Just possibly, one of them may be the secret of success.

Some Guerrilla Girls (left) and one of their posters (right).

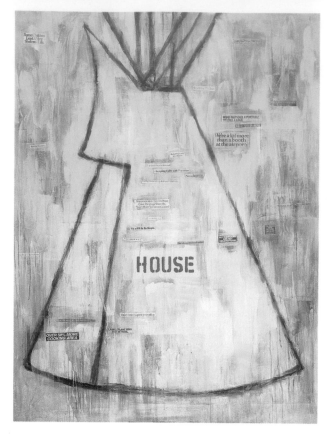

22.28 (right) Jaune Quick-to-See Smith. *House*. 1995. Acrylic and mixed media on canvas. 6'8" × 5'. Courtesy the artist and Bernice Steinbaum Gallery, Miami.

22.29 (below) Kerry James Marshall. *Past Times*. 1997. Acrylic and collage on canvas, 9'6" × 13'. Metropolitan Pier and Exhibition Authority, Chicago. Courtesy Jack Shainman Gallery.

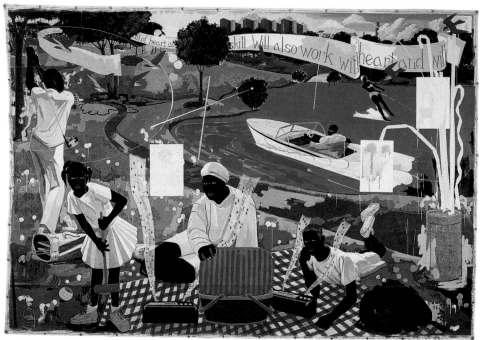

Quick-to-See Smith's *House* makes its point quietly but firmly (**22.28**). On a textured yellow field that could itself be an abstract work about the landscape of the Great Plains the artist has drawn a simple, schematic tipi and stenciled the word "house" on it. We might see these elements of *House* as gentle rebuke to Miriam Schapiro's *Heartfelt* (see 22.17): Not everyone has the same mental image of a house. Slogans culled from advertisements are pasted over the surface of the painting. Their juxtaposition with the image of a tipi produces delicate ironies. "Remember how easily a home came together when you didn't have to choose carpet?" reads one. "Keeping faith with function" claims another, a reference to the famous Modernist motto, "Form follows function."

In *Past Times* (**22.29**) Kerry James Marshall revisits Manet's *Déjeuner sur l'herbe* (see 21.4) and the Impressionist world of middle-class leisure. A family enjoys an outing by the lake with golf, croquet, music, boating, and waterskiing. Marshall has painted the skin tones flat black-brown, pointedly making his subjects as dark as possible. The composition alludes to Manet's famous work, but the most Manet-like element is the gaze of the three figures in the foreground. We see it time and again in Manet's paintings: the blank, mildly inquisitive gaze in our direction that makes us suddenly aware that we are staring. Like Manet's paintings, Marshall's painting looks back. When we move on, the three will return to their pleasures in the private space they have created temporarily in the public park.

In the background, the sun, a symbol of hope, rises next to a housing project. Blue birds of happiness twitter around a banner that proclaims bright sentiments for building the future. The golfer looks back at the city in much the same way that the central figure in Aaron Douglas' *From Slavery Through Reconstruction* (see 21.33) points upward to the "city on the hill" with its promise of freedom and justice. A housing project may not be paradise on earth, Marshall's painting suggests, but it can be a fine place, and good lives can be led there. With allusions to famous paintings, Marshall anchors his work firmly in the pastoral tradition that begins with Giorgione and Titian (see 16.16, 16.17) and passes through such visions of an ideal society as Seurat's *A Sunday on La Grande Jatte* (see 4.31). Along the way, he claims a place for black faces and everyday life in the history of painting, long the most esteemed Western art.

Toward Theater: Performance and Installation

"Where do we go from here?" the composer John Cage asked rhetorically in 1957. His answer: "Toward theater."[8] Cage believed that art's purpose was to heighten our awareness of being alive, and his suggestion for how this might be accomplished inspired the artists who created the happenings and events of the 1950s and 1960s. During the 1980s, this approach to art was developed considerably, and in a more sophisticated and self-aware form it became known as Performance Art.

One of the names most closely connected with Performance Art is Laurie Anderson. For *Stories from the Nerve Bible* (**22.30**), a full-length, multimedia performance work first presented in 1993, Anderson created an elaborate, computerized projection environment whose many screens and monitors fill

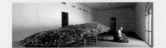
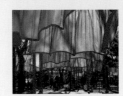
22.30 Laurie Anderson performing *Stories from the Nerve Bible*. 1993.
Courtesy Canal St. Communications.

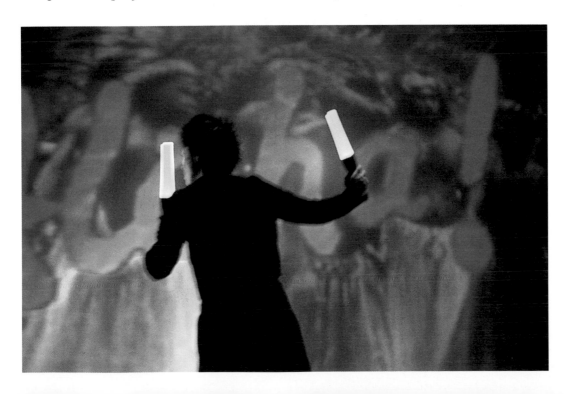

the stage with constantly shifting images and sounds. Standing before the screens, she tells stories and sings, sometimes in her own voice, sometimes through an electronic device that alters the sound. At times she plays an electronic keyboard or an electronic violin. The term *nerve bible*, Anderson has said, refers to the human body. The theme of *Stories from the Nerve Bible* is time, and especially the future, but all of Anderson's other preoccupations are reflected as well, including language, memory, art, culture, faith, politics, technology, power, men, and women. "The art I aspire to make," she has written, "helps people live this life as well as possible."[9]

Performance is one way in which contemporary artists have "raised the volume" of their work in order to reach a public accustomed to such enveloping experiences as film, television, dance clubs, and rock concerts. Another way has been through the form of installation. Like performances, installations can create an absorbing theatrical experience, though it is one in which the actors have gone and only the setting for the play remains.

Visitors to Cai Guo-Qiang's *Dream* (**23.31**) entered a magical space lit by red silk lanterns shaped variously like stars, refrigerators, laptops, skyscrapers, the McDonald's arches, missiles, tanks, airplanes, and a battleship. On the floor, a wall-to-wall length of red silk billowed gently in the breeze generated by industrial fans. Cai created the installation especially for an exhibition in his native China, and it refers to elements of Chinese culture that thoughtful visitors would have recognized. One of the most famous of all works of Chinese literature is an 18th-century novel called *Dream of the Red Chamber*, a sprawling work that paints a broad picture of Chinese society by relating the story of a wealthy and powerful family's decline. Cai's red chamber is a dream about Chinese society today. Red in Chinese culture is the color of happiness and wealth; it is also the color of communism. The lanterns present symbols of affluence, symbols of military power, and the stars of the Chinese flag. Like much contemporary art, *Dream* does not have a direct and simple message. Rather, it encourages viewers to make connections, to ask questions of themselves, and to reflect on their world.

22.31 Cai Guo-Qiang. *Dream.* Installation at the Shanghai Art Museum, 2002. Suspended red silk lanterns, red silk flags, electric light, industrial fans, dimensions variable.
Courtesy the artist.

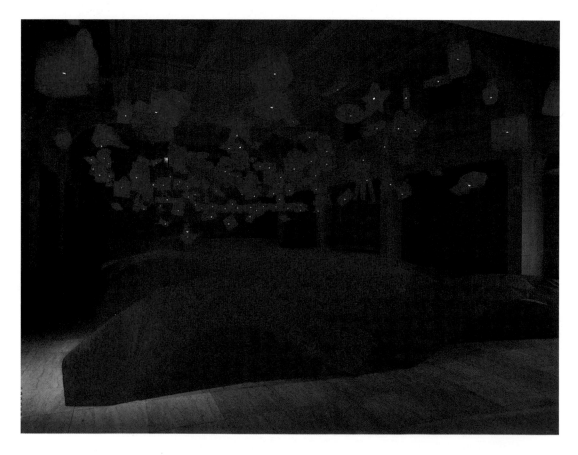

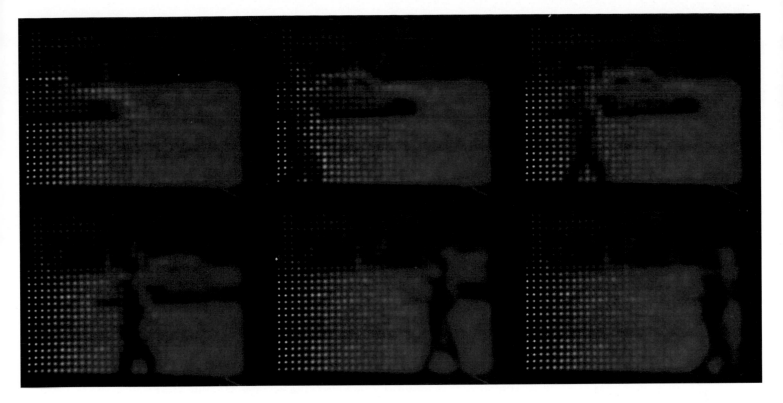

The Digital Realm

The development of digital technologies over the past twenty years has allowed images and sounds to be encoded and transmitted as patterns of numbers. Raw information—streams of numbers—flows rapidly around the world, decoded by machines into forms that have meaning for us—into text, into still and moving images, and into sounds. Increasingly, all of these functions are concentrated in personal computers, which in turn are linked in a vast network through the World Wide Web. Earlier chapters of this book have introduced several artists who work with digital technology, including Jennifer Steinkamp (4.57), Carl Fudge (8.23), Thomas Ruff (9.18), and Cassidy Curtis (10.17). Here, we look at two artists who use digital technologies to meditate on the nature of the digital realm itself.

Jim Campbell explores the relationship between information and meaning that digital technologies have made so much a part of our daily lives. In *Fifth Avenue Cutaway #1* (**22.32**), Campbell programmed a panel of 768 red LEDs (light-emitting diodes) to display slow-motion images, derived from a digital video feed, of pedestrians and traffic on a New York street. In front of the panel he set a piece of Plexiglas, treated to diffuse light. The Plexiglas is set at an angle. At the left, where the Plexiglas is closest to the panel, we see the individual LEDs dimming and brightening in seemingly random patterns. Toward the right, as the Plexiglas moves away from the panel, the lights start to blur, and an image forms. Further to the right, as the Plexiglas continues to pull away from the lights, the image destabilizes again, this time blurring into cloudiness. The illustration here shows six sequential still images taken from the work. Seen in person, the slow motion produces a haunting effect, and the only sound is the constant, soft hum of electricity. We watch as pedestrians entering from the left pass from the digital world of information into our analog world of perception, and pedestrians entering from the right pass from our world into the digital realm.

Since their earliest development, computers have called forth analogies with the human brain. Increasingly, the comparisons flow both ways, as

22.32 Jim Campbell. Six stills from *Fifth Avenue Cutaway #1*. 2001. LEDs, custom electronics, and treated Plexiglas. 22 × 30 × 12".
Courtesy Hosfelt Gallery, San Francisco.

RELATED WORKS

8.23 Fudge, *Rhapsody Spray 2*

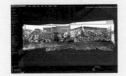
10.17 Curtis, *Graffiti Archaeology*

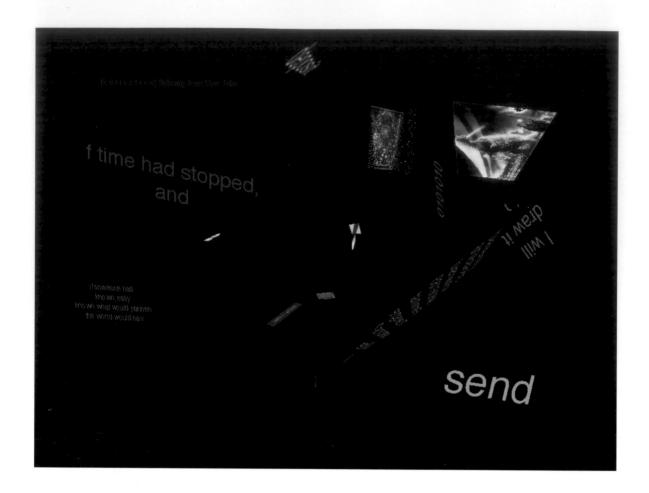

22.33 Mary Flanagan. *[collection]*. 2001. *www.maryflanagan.com/collection.htm.*

computer-based expressions such as "I can't process that information" find their way into popular speech. Meanwhile, researchers in artificial intelligence investigate the computer's ability to think. In *[collection]*, Mary Flanagan has created a work that gives visible form to another brainlike aspect of computers, the unconscious (**22.33**). *[collection]* is a program that can be downloaded from Flanagan's Web site (the address is provided in the caption). Once downloaded, the program scours the host computer for bits of data stored in memory—e-mails, images cached by a Web browser, documents, photographs, videos, sound files, and so on. It samples these and contributes the fragments to a vast Internet collection of similar data from thousands of other computers. From this immense pool of fragments it fashions a constantly shifting collage floating in a dark, cinematic space. At the beginning of the 20th century, the psychologist Carl Jung famously proposed the idea of the collective unconscious, a storehouse of symbols shared by all humans, built up over the millions of years of the human experience. Flanagan's *[collection]* creates a collective unconscious from the depths of computer memories.

Being Human: Life of the Body, Life of the Spirit

Our earthly life is the life of the body, a physical, animal existence in time. Contemporary artists have continued the long Western tradition of expressing the human experience through works that portray the body. Each generation has its own questions to ask about our physical nature, and each generation of artists expands the boundaries of art as they seek a formal language that lets them address new concerns. Chapter 8 illustrated Kiki Smith's linocut *How I Know I'm Here* (see 8.9), which catalogs the artist's body. Smith's focus on the inner, unseen, parts of the body began at a time when the blood-borne AIDS epidemic was raging. Just as the slogan "silence=death" insisted that socially imposed conversational taboos could now be fatal, Smith's work broke artistic silence about the body's full reality. Annette Messager's assemblage *Mes Voeux* (see 5.3) is concerned with the body as a location of desire, identity, and shame.

Like Smith and Messager, Louise Bourgeois refuses to maintain polite artistic silence about potentially upsetting topics. As she herself has advanced into old age, her art has confronted the physical experience of aging with unsparing honesty. *Untitled* (**22.34**) is one of a number of recent works in which the artist's own clothes from decades gone by are used to evoke the passing of time, the decay of the body, and the many versions of the self that we discard or outgrow as we journey through life. The hanging dress is spread out as though it had a life of its own. Other items of clothing are stuffed less flatteringly, as though in our fleshly existence we were all so much meat in a butcher shop. Bourgeois came to her first artistic maturity in the artistic environment of Surrealism, and her works today combine the Surrealists' fondness for disturbing dream images with a constantly evolving formal approach that has renewed her art for each generation of viewers.

We have no proof that the body is not all there is to us. Yet for as long as humans have been expressing themselves through art, an idea that recurs again and again is that there is something more, something we agree to call spirit, or soul, or essence. Art itself is deeply entwined with our faith that there is something that transcends our physical nature, for through art we communicate meanings that go beyond their materials. We believe that an image can carry some kind of meaning beyond the subject it literally depicts; that in dance, we can use our bodies in order to forget them, soaring for a moment beyond physical limits; that in music, pure sound with no material existence at all, we can communicate feelings that go beyond words.

RELATED WORKS

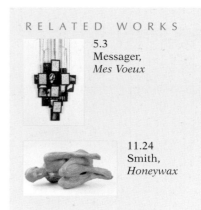

5.3
Messager,
Mes Voeux

11.24
Smith,
Honeywax

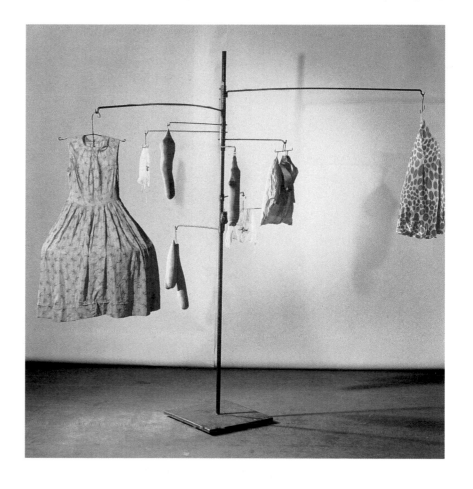

22.34 Louise Bourgeois. *Untitled.* 1996. Cloth, bone, rubber, and steel; height 9'3½". Courtesy Cheim and Read Gallery, New York.

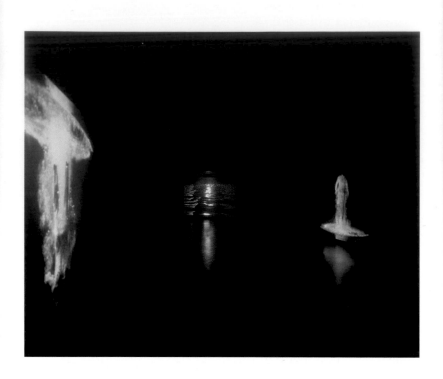

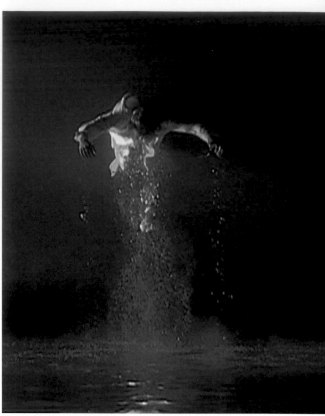

22.35 Bill Viola. (left) *Departing Angel, Fire Angel,* and *Birth Angel,* from *Five Angels for the Millennium.* (right) *Ascending Angel,* detail, from *Five Angels for the Millennium.* 2001. Video/sound installation. Courtesy the artist.

In *Five Angels for the Millennium,* video artist Bill Viola depicts the arrival of the spiritual messengers we call angels (**22.35**). *Five Angels for the Millennium* consists of five individual video and sound loops, each between 10 and 15 minutes long, projected continuously and simultaneously on the walls of a large, dark, empty room. Entering the room is disorienting, and it is intended to be. There may be other people there, but you cannot make them out until your eyes adjust to the darkness. Images play on all four walls, and it is not clear where you should look first, or whether this matters. The sound is a constant, low rumble of white noise. There is a feeling of immanence, of something about to happen. What happens is so strange that it may take many viewings to understand: Very slowly, in one image after another, a figure erupts into view, plunging—usually upward—through the darkness, trailing what seem to be bubbles of light. The sound grows louder and more chaotic. The figure slowly passes, the bubbles dissipate, the sound dies down, and the video begins again.

Viola's means are simple, even if the technology behind them is advanced. Using high-speed, high-definition video, he recorded a series of bodies falling or diving into water. The images and their accompanying sound were then radically slowed down. Most of the videos are projected upside-down, so that the figures plunge upward. The effect is extraordinary: One after another, presences crash through a barrier and into our world. Perhaps they are being born. Perhaps they are dying. Perhaps they bring a message. Perhaps all of these things.

Opening Up to the World

While theorists of postmodernity have embraced pluralism in art, suggesting that there will no longer be any single leading artistic center and that art will henceforth take many equally valid directions at once, globalization has been binding the nations of the world together both economically and culturally. As

RELATED WORKS

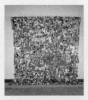

1.15 Hodges, *Every Touch*

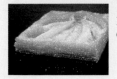

12.22 Herring, *Castle*

part of this process, Western ideas about art have been adopted far beyond their original borders, together with new media such as video and the Internet and recent practices such as installation, performance, and conceptual strategies. The Western institutional context for new art—schools, museums, galleries, large biennial exhibitions—has also spread, giving rise to an international network in which art from many points of origin circulates and becomes known. We close this chapter by looking at the work of six contemporary artists from the wider world.

At first glance, Yinka Shonibare's installation *Victorian Philanthropist's Parlour* looks as though it might be an exhibit in a museum of European culture (**22.36**). Here, the installation suggests, is the living room of a typical middle-class English family of the late-19th century. But just as that thought registers, we notice as well that the walls and furniture are covered with colorful African textiles. Why? We might remember that the Victorian era saw the dramatic expansion of the British empire, which came to include extensive colonies in Africa. Perhaps the textiles make plain what was hidden in Victorian life: that prosperity at home was sustained by unpleasant means abroad.

In fact, Shonibare's installation is more subtle than this. The textiles, while widely used in West Africa for clothing, are not actually African in origin. They were first produced around 1900 by the Dutch, who developed them in imitation of the batik textiles of Indonesia, which was then *their* colony. The British soon began producing similar textiles, and both countries marketed them to West Africa, where they became popular. Still today these "typically African" fabrics are made in England and the Netherlands. Shonibare's installation invites us to meditate on the complicated back-and-forth of these relationships, which destabilize simplistic ideas about cultural authenticity and purity. Shonibare is well positioned to explore such issues. Born in London to Nigerian parents, he moved to Nigeria with his family at the age of three. Growing up, he spoke Yoruba at home and English at school; the academic year was spent in Africa, but summers were spent in England. Shonibare considers himself to be both Nigerian and British. Such forms of hybrid, cosmopolitan identity will probably become more common in the globalizing world.

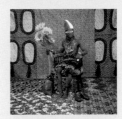
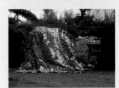
22.36 Yinka Shonibare. *Victorian Philanthropist's Parlour.* 1996–97. Installation; mixed media, dimensions variable.
Courtesy Stephen Friedman Gallery, London, and James Cohan Gallery, New York.

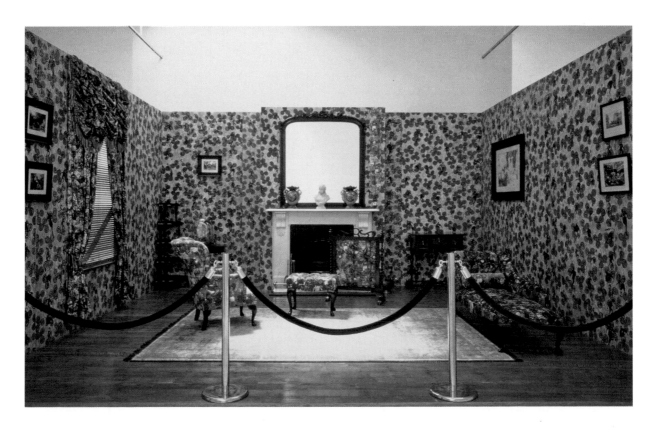

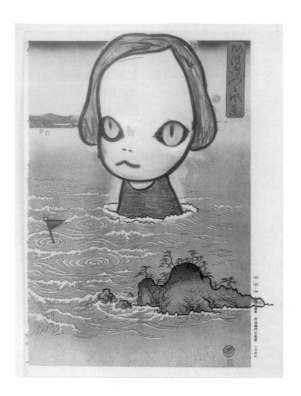

22.37 Yoshitomo Nara. *U-ki-yo-e.* 1999. Oil on book pages, one of 16 parts. 16⅝ × 13". Courtesy Blum & Poe, Los Angeles.

RELATED WORKS

7.16 Murakami, *The Castle of Tin Tin*

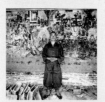

9.9 Liu, *A Young Monk*

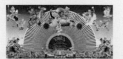

5.8 Luo Brothers, *Welcome the World Famous Brand Name*

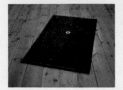

4.36 Hatoum, *Prayer Mat*

Cultural identity appears again as a theme in *U-ki-yo-e,* by Japanese artist Yoshitomo Nara (**22.37**). Nara is one of many Japanese artists to find inspiration in contemporary Japanese popular culture, including the comic books known as manga. The drawing illustrated here is one of a series that Nara executed on the pages of a book of reproductions of Japanese woodblock prints from the Edo era. Known as *ukiyo-e,* the prints were the popular art of their day—produced by the thousands and sold for roughly the price of a bowl of noodles. Over time, *ukiyo-e* have shifted in meaning, and today they are housed in museums as important works of art. For many people around the world, the prints have come to represent the essence of Japanese art and culture. Nara here reclaims an *ukiyo-e* for popular art and for the present day by drawing one of his own manga-inspired young girls over it. Nara's young girl looms out of the water like a monster, although she hardly seems monstrous. The little island looks like a bath toy next to her! Nara's drawing emphasizes both continuity and change, as the innocence of the contemporary young girl is set against a distant and idealized Japanese past.

To Nara's juxtaposition of past and present, Chinese artist Yang Fudong adds concern about the future in his video *Seven Intellectuals in a Bamboo Forest, Part I* (**22.38**). Yang's video, the first installment of what will eventually be a full-length film, follows a group of stylish young friends as they pay a visit to Huangshan (Yellow Mountain), a famously beautiful and historic site. There they gaze at the landscape, talk about their lives, wonder what the future holds, and perform ancient wish-making rituals while at the same time not quite believing in them.

The title of the video alludes to the Seven Sages of the Bamboo Grove, a group of Daoist scholars and writers who lived during another uncertain time in China's long history, the decades of political instability that followed the fall of the Han dynasty in 220 C.E. As scholars, they should have been serving as officials in the government. Instead, they retired to the countryside, meeting occasionally in a bamboo grove to drink wine, write poems, and enjoy each other's conversation. They were the free spirits of their day, brilliant and eccentric dropouts, and they have been admired and celebrated for it ever since. And Yang's seven friends? As China enters the global, market-driven economy, will they play the game and hope for success, or will they opt for quieter, humbler lives? They seem to have made their choice already, although the call of the seven sages may haunt them.

With Emily Jacir, we come to an artist who has been formed by several cultures in succession. Born in Bethlehem, in the West Bank, she grew up in Saudi Arabia, attended high school in Italy, then studied art in the United States. Jacir carries an American passport, which permits her a freedom of movement in her homeland that is denied to many Palestinians. She used this privilege in a project called *Where We Come From*, a detail of which is illustrated here (**22.39**). Jacir asked Palestinians living in the territories or in exile abroad a simple question: "If I could do anything for you, anywhere in Palestine, what would it be?" Over the next few years she fulfilled their requests, documenting her actions in photographs and text. Some requests were practical (Go to the Israeli post office in Jerusalem and pay my phone bill), many were nostalgic (Drink the water in my parents' village), but all were touching in their modesty. The illustration here documents the request of a young

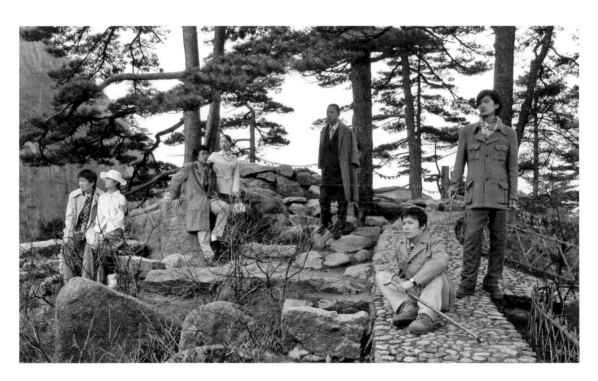

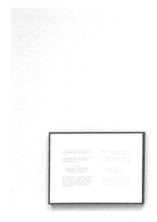

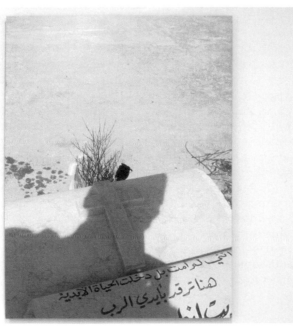

22.38 (above) Yang Fudong. *Seven Intellectuals in a Bamboo Forest, Part 1*. 2003. 35mm black-and-white film transferred to video, 30 minutes.
Courtesy Marian Goodman Gallery, Paris.

22.39 (left) Emily Jacir. *Where We Come From* (detail). 1997–2003. Photographs and framed texts, dimensions variable.
Courtesy Alexander and Bonin Gallery, New York.

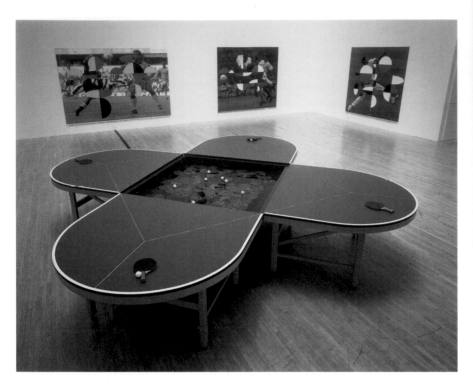

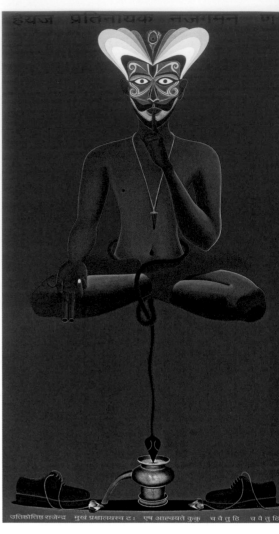

22.40 (left) Gabriel Orozco. *Ping Pond Table (Mesa de ping-pong con estanque).* 1998. Mixed media, 30 × 167¾ × 167¾".
The Museum of Contemporary Art, Los Angeles.

22.41 (right) Surendran Nair. *Mephistopheles . . . Otherwise, the Quaquaversal Prolix (Cuckoonebulopolis).* 2003. Oil on canvas. 210 × 120 cm.
Collection Usha Mirchandani, The Fine Art Resource, Bombay.

Palestinian man living in Bethlehem. "Go to my mother's grave in Jerusalem on her birthday," he asked, "and put flowers and pray." The accompanying text panel explains in English and Arabic that he himself requires special authorization to enter Jerusalem, and that in the past it has not been granted. The text also recounts Jacir's experience as she visited the grave on his behalf.

Jacir's project touches on the theme of space and how it is divided—ideas about land and landscape, frontiers and territories, and politics and their human consequences. Mexican artist Gabriel Orozco touches on similar ideas on a far more abstract level in his *Ping Pond Table* (**22.40**). Orozco is fascinated by games and how they reflect a culture's ideas about nature, landscape, and even the workings of the universe. He likes to invent games himself, and in his sculpture he sometimes takes games and gives them a new dimension, turning them into what he calls "philosophical games." What intrigued Orozco about the game of ping pong was the space defined by the net, which serves as a frontier—a neutral "non-space" in a game designed for two players. In opening the game up to four players, Orozco opened up the net's space as well, transforming it into a central pool of water. Water can also serve as a frontier, and many countries are separated by rivers or lakes. In the context of games, we are familiar with water hazards from golf, which also has close ties to landscape. But Orozco notes that his new game-space can also be seen as four petals opening up from a central spring, as in South Asian thought the universe is imagined to open like a flower from the source of life. Orozco has taken a game invented in one culture and re-imagined it from the worldview of another.

Indian painter Surendran Nair draws more directly on traditional South Asian religious imagery in *Mephistopheles . . . Otherwise, the Quaquaversal Prolix (Cuckoonebulopolis)* (**22.41**). The title, however, alludes to the cultural heritage of Europe and ancient Greece. This mixture is typical for Nair, whose work refers freely to world myths and legends, history and politics, literature and folklore, cultural rituals and personal experience. Mephistopheles is the name of the Devil in the medieval German legend of Faust. In the tale, Faust is an alchemist and magician who offers his soul to the Devil in exchange for the Devil's knowledge and services. Nair's Mephistopheles has cast off his shoes, assumed the cross-legged posture of a meditating yogi, and levitated. His face has become a stylized mask; his turban glows like a lamp. His hands make the kind of meaningful gestures we associate with depictions of buddhas (see 2.28, 3.6, and 19.5). The right hand forms the gesture of bestowing gifts, but two of the fingers have metamorphosed into a gun barrel. The left hand gestures for silence. What gifts does Mephistopheles offer, and what does he want in return? The alternate title Nair supplies does not offer much help. "Quaquaversal prolix" means roughly "an endless torrent of words flowing in all directions." Cuckoonebulopolis, also known as "Cloud Cuckooland," is taken from *The Birds,* a satirical play by the ancient Greek playwright Aristophanes. It names a utopian community created by birds for two refugees from war-torn Athens.

Surendran Nair's painting is propped up by the many words of its title, but these words are not equal to the mystery of the image, which holds more meanings than they can convey. Something in art will always escape our attempt to translate it into words. The image rises up as a presence before us, and bids us be silent.

RELATED RESOURCES ONLINE

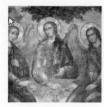

For more information, summaries, interactive activities, videos, Web links, and interactive timelines related to the "Arts in Time" material covered in this part, please go to **www.mhhe.com/lwa8.**

PRONUNCIATION GUIDE

This guide offers pronunciations for names and foreign terms appearing in the text. It uses the sounds available in standard North American English to approximate the original languages. The phonetic system includes the following conventions:

ah—spa, hurrah **dj**—jump, bridge **ow**—cow, how
air—pair, there **j**—mirage, barrage **uh**—bus, fuss
an—plan, tan **eh**—pet, get **ye**—pie, sky
aw—thaw, autumn **er**—her, fur
ay—play, say **oh**—toe, show

Aachen AHK-en

Abakanowicz, Magdalena mahg-dah-LAY-nuh ah-bah-kah-NOH-vich

Akan AH-kahn

Akhenaten AH-keh-NAH-ten

Alberti, Leon Battista LAY-on bah-TEES-tuh ahl-BAIR-tee

Alhambra ahl-AHM-bruh

Alvarez Bravo, Manuel mahn-WELL AHL-vah-rez BRAH-voh

Amida Nyorai ah-MEE-duh nyoh-RYE

Amitayus AH-mee-TYE-OOS

Anatsui, El el ah-nah-TSOO-ee

Andokides ahn-DOH-kee-dayz

Angkor Wat ANG-kohr WAHT; *also,* VAHT

Anguissola, Sofonisba soh-foh-NEEZ-bah ahn-gwee-SOH-lah

Antoni, Janine jah-NEEN an-TOH-nee

Aphrodite ah-froh-DYE-tee

Apoxyomenos ah-PAHK-see-oh-MEN-ohs

Arhat AR-huht

Ariwajoye ah-ree-wah-DJOH-yay

Arnolfini ahr-nohl-FEE-nee

Artemidoros ar-teh-mee-DOR-ohs

Asante ah-SAHN-tay

Athena Nike uh-THEE-nuh NYE-kee

Aurelius, Marcus aw-REE-lee-oos

auteur oh-TER

Avalokiteshvara ah-vah-loh-kih-TESH-vahr-uh

avant garde AH-vawn GARD

Badi'uzzaman bah-DEE-ooz-(ah)-MAHN

Balla, Giacomo DJAH-koh-moh BAH-lah

Ban, Shigeru shee-GEH-roo BAHN

Basquiat, Jean-Michel ZHAWN-mee-SHELL BAHS-kyah

bas-relief BAH ruh-LYEF

Baule BOW-lay

Bayeux bye-YE(r)

Bellini, Giovanni djoh-VAHN-ee bell-EE-nee

Benin beh-NEEN

Bernini, Gianlorenzo djahn-loh-REN-zoh bayr-NEE-nee

Beuys, Joseph YOH-sef BOYZ

Bierstadt, Albert BEER-shtaht

Bilbao bil-BAH-oh

Boccioni, Umberto oom-BAIR-toh boh-CHOH-nee

bodhisattva boh-dih-SAHT-vuh

Borromini, Francesco frahn-CHESS-koh boh-roh-MEE-nee

Bosch, Hieronymus heer-AHN-ih-mus BAHSH

Botticelli, Sandro SAN-droh bot-ee-CHEL-ee

Bourgeois, Louise boor-JWAH

Brancusi, Constantin KAHN-stan-teen BRAHN-koosh; *also,* brahn-KOO-zee

Braque, Georges jorj BRAHK

Breuer, Marcel mahr-SELL BROY-er

Bronzino, Agnolo AHN-yoh-loh brahn-ZEE-noh

Bruegel, Pieter PEE-tur BROO-g'l; *also,* BROY-g'l

Bruggen, Coosje van KOHSH-yuh fahn BRUHK-en

Buñuel, Luis loo-EES boon-WELL

buon fresco boo-OHN FRES-koh

Byodo-in BYOH-doh-een

Cai Guo-Qiang KYE gwoh-CHANG

camera obscura KAM-er-uh ob-SKOOR-uh

Campin, Robert KAHM-pin

Caravaggio kah-rah-VAH-djoh

Cartier-Bresson, Henri awn-ree KAR-tee-ay bress-AWN

Cellini, Benvenuto ben-veh-NOO-toh cheh-LEE-nee

Cézanne, Paul POHL say-ZAHN

Chagall, Marc shah-GAHL

Chagoya, Enrique en-REE-kay chah-GOY-ah

Chartres SHAR-tr'

Chauvet cave shoh-VAY

chiaroscuro kee-AH-roh-SKOOR-oh

Chudapanthaka choo-duh-PUHN-tuh-kuh

Cimabue chee-mah-BOO-ay

cire perdue seer payr-DOO

contrapposto kohn-trah-POH-stoh

Copley, John Singleton KAHP-lee

Córdoba KOR-doh-buh

Courbet, Gustave goos-TAHV koor-BAY

Coyne, Petah PEE-tuh KOYN

Cuvillies, François FRAWN-swah koo-vee-YEHS

Daguerre, Louis Jacques Mandé loo-ee JAHK mahn-DAY dah-GAIR

Dali, Salvador sal-vah-DOHR DAH-lee

Dasavanta duh-shuh-VUHN-tuh

David, Jacques Louis jahk loo-EE dah-VEED

De Chirico, Giorgio DJOR-djoh deh-KEER-ee-koh

Degas, Edgar ed-GAHR deh-GAH

de Kooning, Willem VILL-um duh KOON-ing

Delacroix, Eugène uh-ZHEN duh-lah-KWAH

Derain, André ahn-DRAY deh-RAN

diptych DIP-tik

dipylon DIH-puh-lon
Dogon doh-GAWN
Donatello dohn-ah-TELL-oh
Duccio DOO-choh
Duchamp, Marcel mahr-SELL doo-SHAWM
Dufy, Raoul rah-OOL doo-FEE
Dürer, Albrecht AHL-brekt DOOR-er
Eakins, Thomas AY-kins
facade fuh-SAHD
Fante FAHN-tay
Fauve fohv
Flavin, Dan FLAY-vin
Fragonard, Jean-Honoré jawn AW-nor-ay FRA-goh-nahr
Francescso di Giorgio Martini frahn-CHES-koh
    dee DJOR-djoh mahr-TEE-nee
Frankenthaler, Helen FRANK-en-thahl-er
fresco secco FRES-koh SEK-oh
Gauguin, Paul POHL goh-GAN
Genji Monogatari GEHN-jee mohn-oh-geh-TAHR-ee
Gentileschi, Artemisia ahr-tuh-MEE-jyuh djen-till-ESS-kee
Géricault, Théodore tay-oh-DOHR jay-ree-KOH
Ghiberti, Lorenzo loh-REN-zoh gee-BAIR-tee
Giacometti, Alberto ahl-BAIR-toh jah-koh-MET-ee
Giorgione djor-DJOH-nay
Giotto DJOH-toh
Godard, Jean-Luc jawn(n)-look goh-DAHR
Gonzales-Torres, Felix gawn-ZAH-layss TOH-rayss
gouache gwahsh
Goya, Francisco de frahn-SISS-koh day GOY-ah
Grien, Hans Baldung GREEN
grisaille gree-ZYE
Grünewald, Matthias mah-TEE-ess GROON-eh-vahlt
Gu Hongzhong GOO hong-JUNG
Gu Kaizhi goo kye-JR
Guanyin gwahn-YEEN
Guernica GWAIR-nih-kuh
Hadid, Zaha ZAH-hah hah-DEED
Hagia Sophia HYE-uh soh-FEE-uh
Hamzanama HAHM-zah-NAH-mah
Han Xizai HAHN shee-ZYE
Hasegawa Tohaku HA-suh-gah-wuh TOH-hah-koo
Heian hay-AHN
Heiji Monogatari HAY-djee mohn-oh-geh-TAHR-ee
Hesse, Eva AY-vuh HESS-uh
Hiroshige, Ando AHN-doh heer-oh-SHEE-gay
Hokusai, Katsushika kat-s'-SHEE-kah HOH-k'-sye
Holbein, Hans HAHNS HOHL-byne
Hon'ami Koetsu HOH-nah-mee ko-EH-tsoo
Horyu-ji hor-YOO-djee
Hu Yichuan HOO yee-CHWAHN
Huang Gongwang HWANG gung-WANG
Hui-zong hway-DZUNG
hypostyle HYE-poh-styel
Ife EE-fay
ijele ee-JAY-lay
Inca ING-keh
Iktinos IK-tin-ohs
Ingres, Jean-Auguste-Dominique jawn oh-GOOST
    dohm-een-EEK AN-gr'

intaglio in-TAHL-yoh
Iraj EE-raj
Ise EE-say
iwan EE-wahn
Jacir, Emily djah-SEER
Jacquette, Yvonne ee-VAHN dja-KET
Jahangir ja-HAHN-GEER
Jain DJAYN
Jiménez, Luis loo-EES hee-MAY-nez
Jnanadakini ee-NUH-nuh-DUH-kee-nee
Jocho DJOH-CHOH
Kaiho Yusho kah-ee-hoh yoo-shoh
Kairouan KAIR-wahn
Kallikrates kah-LIK-rah-teez
Kandariya Mahadeva kahn-DAHR-yuh mah-hah-DAY-vuh
Kandinsky, Vasili vah-SEE-lee kan-DIN-skee
Kangxi kang-SHEE
Kano Eitoku KAH-no ay-TOH-koo
kente KEN-tay
Khamerernebty kah-mair-air-NEB-tee
Khurd, Madhava MAH-duh-vuh KOORD-(uh)
Khusrau koos-ROW
Kiefer, Anselm AHN-zelm KEE-fur
Kirchner, Ernst Ludwig AYRNST LOOT-vik KEERSH-nur
Klee, Paul KLAY
Klimt, Gustav GOOS-tahv KLEEMT
Knossos NAW-sis
Kollwitz, Käthe KAY-tuh KOHL-vitz
Kruger, Barbara KROO-ger
Kusama, Yayoi yah-yoy k'-SAH-mah
Lakshmana LAHK-shmah-nah
Laocoön lay-AH-coh-un
Lascaux las-COH
Le Corbusier luh KOHR-boo-(zee)-AY
Léger, Fernand fayr-NAHN lay-JAY
Li Cheng lee CHENG
Lippi, Filippino fee-lee-PEE-noh LEEP-pcc
Leonardo da Vinci lay-oh-NAHR-doh dah VEEN-chee
Leyster, Judith YOO-dit LYE-stur
Limbourg lam-BOOR
Liu Zheng lyoo jeng
Louvre LOOV-r'
Lysippos lye-SIP-os
Machu Picchu MAH-choo PEEK-choo
Maeda, John MAY-duh
Magritte, René reh-NAY ma-GREET
Mahavira mah-hah-VEE-ruh
Malevich, Kasimir kah-ZEE-meer mah-LAY-vitch
Manet, Edouard ayd-WAHR mah-NAY
Manohar mah-NOH-hahr
Mapplethorpe, Robert MAY-p'l-thorp
Martínez, María & Julian mah-REE-uh & HOO-(lee)-ahn
    mahr-TEE-nez
Masaccio mah-ZAH-choh
Masombuka, Selina say-LEE-nuh mah-sohm-BOO-kuh
Masson, André ahn-DRAY mah-SAWN
Matisse, Henri ahn-REE mah-TEES
Mattes, Iva and Franco MAH-tayss
Maya MAH-yah

Mehretu, Julie   MAIR-eh-too
Menkaure   men-KOW-ray
Mesa Verde   MAY-suh VAIR-day
Messager, Annette   MESS-ah-JAY
mezzotint   MET-zoh-tint
Michelangelo   mye-kel-AN-jel-oh; *also,* mee-kel-AHN-jel-oh
Mies van der Rohe, Ludwig   LOOT-fik mees van der ROH-eh
mihrab   MI-hrahb
Mimbres   MIM-bres
Miró, Joan   HWAHN meer-OH
Miyazaki, Hayao   hah-yah-oh mee-yah-ZAH-kee
Moche   MOH-chay
Modersohn-Becker, Paula   MOH-der-zun BEK-er
Mondrian, Piet   PEET MOHN-dree-ahn
Monet, Claude   CLOHD moh-NAY
Morisot, Berthe   BAYR-t' mohr-ee-ZOH
mosque   mahsk
Mughal   MOO-gahl
Munch, Edvard   ED-vahrd MOONK
Murakami, Takashi   tah-KAH-shee moo-ruh-KAH-mee
Muromachi   MOOR-oh-MAH-chee
Muybridge, Eadweard   ED-werd MY-bridj
Mycenae   my-SEEN-ay, or my-SEEN-ee
Nair, Surendran   SOO-REN-drun nair
Nara, Yoshitomo   yoh-shee-toh-mo NAH-rah
Nefertiti   NEF-er-TEE-tee
Ni Zan   nee DZAHN
Nicephore Niepce   NEE-say-for n'YEPS
nkisi nkondi   en-KEE-see en-KOHN-dee
Noguchi, Isamu   EE-sah-moo noh-GOO-chee
Nolde, Emil   AY-meel NOHL-duh
Notre-Dame-du-Haut   NOH-tr' DAHM doo OH
Ofili, Chris   oh-FEE-lee
Oldenburg, Claes   klahs
Olmec   OHL-mek
Olowe of Ise   OH-loh-way of EE-say
Orozco, Gabriel   GAH-bree-el oh-ROHZ-ko
Paik, Nam June   nahm djoon PYEK
Palenque   pah-LENG-kay
Pantokrator   pan-TAW-kruh-ter
Pei, Ieoh Ming   ee-OH ming PAY
Perugino   PAIR-oo-DJEE-noh
Pettibon, Raymond   PEH-tee-bahn
Pfaff, Judy   FAFF
Piano, Renzo   PYAH-noh
Picabia, Francis   frahn-SEES pee-KAH-byuh
pointillism   PWAN-tee-ism; *also,* POYN-till-izm
Pollock, Jackson   PAHL-uck
Pompeii   pahm-PAY
Pont du Gard   pohn doo GAHR
Poussin, Nicolas   nee-coh-LAH poo-SAN
qibla   KIB-luh
Qiu Ying   chyoo YING
Qur'an   koor-'AHN
raigo   rye-GOH
Raimondi, Marcantonio   MAHRK-ahn-TOH-nee-oh rye-MOHN-dee
Rama   RAH-mah

Raphael   RAHF-yell; *also,* RAF-fye-ell
Rathnasambhava   ruht-nuh-SUHM-buh-vuh
Rauschenberg, Robert   ROW-shen-burg
Renoir, Pierre-Auguste   pyair oh-GOOST rehn-WAHR
repoussé   reh-poo-SAY
Rheims   RANS
rhyton   RYE-ton
Riemenschneider, Tilman   TEEL-mahn REE-men-shnye-der
Rietveld, Gerrit   GAY-rit REET-velt
Rivera, Diego   dee-AY-goh ree-VAIR-uh
Rococo   roh-coh-COH
Rodin, Auguste   oh-GOOST roh-DAN
Rogier van der Weyden   roh-JEER van dur VYE-den
Rongxi   rong-HSEE
Rousseau, Henri (le Douanier)   ahn-REE roo-SOH (luh dwahn-YAY)
Ruscha, Ed   roo-SHAY
Ryoan-ji   RYOH-ahn-djee
Saint-Phalle, Niki de   nee-kee duh san-FAHL
Sainte-Chapelle   sant shah-PELL
Sainte-Foy   sant FWAH
Sakai Hoitsu   SAH-kye HOY-ts'
San Vitale   san vee-TAHL-ay
Sassetta   sah-SEH-tuh
Sesshu   SESS-yoo
Seurat, Georges   jorj sur-RAH
sfumato   sfoo-MAH-toh
Sharaku, Toshusai   toh-shoo-SYE SHAH-rah-kooj
Shiva Nataraja   SHEE-vuh NAH-tah-rah-juh
Shonibare, Yinka   YING-kuh shoh-nee-BAHR-ay
Shravana   SHRUH-vuh-nuh
Sikander, Shahzia   SHAHZ-yuh sik-AN-dur
Singh, Raghubir   RAH-goo-beer SING
Sotatsu, Nonomura   noh-noh-MOOR-ah SOH-taht-s'
Spiekermann, Erik   SHPEE-ker-mahn
Staehle, Wolfgang   VOLF-gahng SHTEH-luh
Stieglitz, Alfred   STEEG-litz
stupa   STOO-puh
al-Suhrawardi, Ahmad   AHK-mahd ah-soo-rah-WAHR-dee
Suvero, Mark di   dih SOO-veh-roh
Taj Mahal   tahj meh-HAHL
tathagata   tah-tah-GAH-tah
Teotihuacán   tay-OH-tee-hwah-CAHN
Titian   TISH-an; *also,* TEE-shan
Tjibaou, Jean-Marie   jawn-mah-REE tjee-BOW
Todai-ji   toh-DYE-djee
Tori Busshi   toh-ree BOO-shee
Toulouse-Lautrec, Henri de   awn-REE duh too-LOOZ loh-TREK
trompe-l'oeil   tromp-LOY
Tsai Ming-liang   tsye ming-lyang
Tufte, Edward   TUHF-tee
Tutankhamun   toot-an-KAH-mun
Utamaro, Kitagawa   kee-TAH-gah-wuh oo-TAH-mah-roh
Utzon, Joern   yern OOT-suhn
Valdés Leal, Juan de   (hoo)-AHN day vahl-DAYS lay-AHL
Van Eyck, Jan   YAHN van IKE
Van Gogh, Vincent   van GOH; *also,* van GAWK
Van Ruisdael, Jacob   YAH-cub van ROYS-dahl

Vasari, Giorgio DJOHR-djoh va-ZAHR-ee

Velázquez, Diego DYAY-goh vay-LASS-kess

Vermeer, Johannes yoh-HAH-ness vair-MAYR; *also,* vair-MEER

Verrocchio, Andrea del ahn-DRAY-ah del veh-ROH-kyo

Versailles vair-SYE

Vigée-Lebrun, Elisabeth ay-leez-eh-BETT vee-JAY leh-BRUN

Vishnu VISH-noo

Wang Hui wang HWAY

Wang Jian wang JYAHN

Watteau, Antoine ahn-TWAHN wah-TOH; *also,* vah-TOH

Willendorf VILL-en-dohrf

Wojnarowicz, David voy-nyah-ROH-vitz

Xoc shawk

Yang Fudong yahng foo-dong

Yoruba YAW-roo-buh

Yosa Buson yoh-sah BOO-sohn

Yucatán yoo-cuh-TAN

Zahadolzha zah-ha-DOHL-jah

Zhao Mengfu jow meng-FOO

Zhou Dynasty JOH

ziggurat ZIG-oor-aht

SUGGESTED READINGS

GENERAL REFERENCE

Barnet, Sylvan. *A Short Guide to Writing about Art*, 8th ed. Upper Saddle River, NJ: Prentice Hall, 2005.

Brigstocke, Hugh, ed. *The Oxford Companion to Western Art*. Oxford: Oxford University Press, 2001.

Clarke, Michael. *The Concise Oxford Dictionary of Art Terms*. Oxford: Oxford University Press, 2001.

Cummings, Paul. *Artists in Their Own Words*. New York: St. Martin's, 1982.

Goldwater, Robert, and Marco Treves, eds. *Artists on Art: From the Fourteenth to the Twentieth Century*. New York: Pantheon, 1974.

Langmuir, Erika, and Norbert Lynton. *The Yale Dictionary of Art and Artists*. New Haven, CT: Yale University Press, 2000.

Nelson, Robert S., and Richard Shiff, eds. *Critical Terms for Art History*, 2nd ed. Chicago: The University of Chicago Press, 2003.

Tucker, Amy. *Visual Literacy: Writing About Art*. New York: McGraw-Hill, 2002.

Turner, Jane, ed. *The Dictionary of Art*. 34 volumes. New York: Groves Dictionaries, 1996.

PART 1
INTRODUCTION

Anderson, Richard L. *Calliope's Sisters: A Comparative Study of Philosophies of Art*, 2nd ed. Englewood Cliffs, NJ: Prentice Hall, 2004.

Arnheim, Rudolf. *Visual Thinking*. Berkeley: University of California Press, 1972.

Carroll, Noel, ed. *Theories of Art Today*. Madison: University of Wisconsin Press, 2000.

Dissanayake, Ellen. *Homo Aestheticus: Where Art Comes From and Why*. Seattle: University of Washington Press, 1995.

————. *Art and Intimacy: How the Arts Began*. Seattle: University of Washington Press, 2000.

Elkins, James. *Why Art Cannot Be Taught: A Handbook for Art Students.*

Urbana: University of Illinois Press, 2001.

Shiner, Larry. *The Invention of Art: A Cultural History*. Chicago: The University of Chicago Press, 2001.

Staniszewski, Mary Anne. *Believing Is Seeing: Creating the Culture of Art*. New York: Penguin Books, 1995.

PART 2
THE VOCABULARY OF ART

Albers, Josef. *Interaction of Color*, rev. ed. New Haven, CT: Yale University Press, 1975.

Arnheim, Rudolf. *The Power of the Center: A Study of Composition in the Visual Arts*. Berkeley: University of California Press, 1988.

Elam, Kimberly. *Geometry of Design: Studies in Proportion and Composition*. New York: Princeton Architectural Press, 2001.

Elkins, James. *The Poetics of Perspective*. Ithaca: Cornell University Press, 1994.

Feldman, Edmund Burke. *Varieties of Visual Experience*. New York: Abrams, 1987.

Gage, John. *Color and Culture: Practice and Meaning from Antiquity to Abstraction*. Boston: Little, Brown, 1993.

Gage, John. *Color and Meaning: Art, Science, and Symbolism*. Berkeley: University of California Press, 1999.

Goldstein, Nathan. *Design and Composition*. Englewood Cliffs, NJ: Prentice Hall, 1989.

Lauer, David. *Design Basics*, 3rd ed. Fort Worth, TX: Harcourt Brace, 1990.

Nelson, George. *How to See: A Guide to Reaching Our Manmade Environments*. Boston: Little, Brown, 1979.

O'Connor, Charles. *Perspective Drawing and Applications*, 3rd ed. Upper Saddle River, NJ: Prentice Hall, 2005.

Puttfarken, Thomas. *The Discovery of Pictorial Composition*. New Haven, CT: Yale University Press, 2000.

Stewart, Mary. *Launching the Imagination: A Comprehensive Guide to Basic Design*, 2nd ed. New York: McGraw-Hill, 2006.

Willats, John. *Art and Representation: New Principles in the Analysis of Pictures*. Princeton, NJ: Princeton University Press, 1997.

PART 3
TWO-DIMENSIONAL MEDIA

Albus, Anita. *The Art of Arts: Rediscovering Painting*. Michael Robertson, trans. Berkeley: University of California Press, 2001.

Bellatoni, Jeff, and Matt Woolman. *Type in Motion: Innovations in Digital Graphics*. New York: Rizzoli, 1999.

Betti, Claudia, and Teel Sale. *Drawing, a Contemporary Approach*, 3rd. ed. Fort Worth, TX: Harcourt Brace, 1983.

Bloom, Jonathan M. *Paper Before Print: The History and Impact of Paper in the Islamic World*. New Haven: Yale University Press, 2001.

Clarke, Graham. *The Photograph*. Oxford: Oxford University Press, 1997.

Edwards, Betty. *Drawing on the Right Side of the Brain*, rev. ed. Los Angeles: Tarcher, 1989.

Ellis, Jack C., and Virginia Wright Wexman. *A History of Film*, 5th ed. Boston: Allyn and Bacon, 2002.

Getlein, Frank, and Dorothy Getlein. *The Bite of the Print*. New York: C. N. Potter, 1963.

Goldstein, Nathan. *Painting: Visual and Technical Fundamentals*. Englewood Cliffs, NJ: Prentice Hall, 1979.

Greene, Rachel. *Internet Art*. London: Thames & Hudson, 2004.

Hirsch, Robert. *Seizing the Light: A History of Photography*. New York: McGraw-Hill, 2000.

Lambert, Susan. *Prints: Art and Techniques*. London: V & A Publications, 2001.

London, Barbara, with John Upton. *Photography*, 5th ed. New York: Longman, 1994.

Lupton, Ellen. *Mixing Messages: Graphic Design in Contemporary Culture*. New York: Princeton Architectural Press, 1996.

Mast, Gerald, and Bruce Kawin. *A Short History of the Movies*, 9th ed. New York: Longman, 2006.

Mayer, Ralph. *The Artist's Handbook of Materials and Techniques*, 5th ed. New York: Viking, 1991.

Meggs, Philip B. *A History of Graphic Design*, 3rd ed. New York: John Wiley and Sons, 1998.

Nowell-Smith, Geoffrey, ed. *The Oxford History of World Cinema*. Oxford: Oxford University Press, 1996.

Paul Rand: A Designer's Art. New Haven, CT: Yale University Press, 1985.

Platzker, David, and Elizabeth Wyckoff. *Hard Pressed: 600 Years of Prints and Process*. New York: Hudson Hill Press, 2000.

Ross, John, Clare Romano, and Timothy Ross. *The Complete Printmaker: Techniques, Traditions, Innovations*, rev. and exp. ed. New York: Free Press, 1990.

Rush, Michael. *New Media in Art*, 2nd ed. London: Thames & Hudson, 2005.

Stephenson, Jonathan. *The Materials and Techniques of Painting*. London: Thames and Hudson, 1989.

Thompson, Kristin and David Bordwell. *Film History: An Introduction*, 2nd ed. New York: McGraw-Hill, 2003.

Whale, George, and Naren Barfield. *Digital Printmaking*. New York: Watson-Guptill, 2003.

PART 4

THREE-DIMENSIONAL MEDIA

Andrews, Oliver. *Living Materials: A Sculptor's Handbook*. Berkeley: University of California Press, 1983.

Beardsley, John. *Earthworks and Beyond: Contemporary Art in the Landscape*, 3rd ed. New York: Abbeville Press, 1998.

Bourdon, David. *Designing the Earth: The Human Impulse to Shape Nature*. New York: Abrams, 1995.

Flynn, Tom. *The Body in Sculpture*. London: Weidenfeld and Nicholson, 1998.

Ginsburg, Madeleine, ed. *The Illustrated History of Textiles*. London: Studio Editions, 1991.

Gissen, David, ed. *Big & Green: Toward Sustainable Architecture in the 21st Century*. New York: Princeton Architectural Press; Washington, D.C.: National Building Museum, 2002.

Harris, Jennifer, ed. *5000 Years of Textiles*. London: British Museum Press, 1993.

Kaplan, Wendy. *The Arts and Crafts Movement in Europe and America: Design for the Modern World*. New York: Thames & Hudson in association with the Los Angeles County Museum of Art, 2004.

Kastner, Jeffrey, ed., and Brian Wallis. *Land and Environmental Art*. London: Phaidon, 1998.

Keverne, Roger, ed. *Jade*. London: Anness, 1991.

Kostof, Spiro. *A History of Architecture: Settings and Rituals*, rev. ed. Oxford: Oxford University Press, 1995.

Langland, Tuck. *Practical Sculpture*. Englewood Cliffs, NJ: Prentice Hall, 1988.

Lucie-Smith, Edward. *The Story of Craft: The Craftsman's Role in Society*. Ithaca, NY: Cornell University Press, 1981.

Mills, John W. *Encyclopedia of Sculpture Techniques*. London: B. T. Batsford, 1990.

Salvadori, Mario. *Building: The Fight against Gravity*. New York: Atheneum, 1979.

Shepheard, Paul. *What Is Architecture? An Essay on Landscapes, Buildings, and Machines*. Cambridge, MA: The MIT Press, 1994.

Speight, Charlotte. *Hands in Clay*, 5th ed. New York: McGraw-Hill, 2004.

Thomas, Michel, Christine Mainguy, and Sophie Pommier. *Textile Art*. New York: Rizzoli, 1985.

Trench, Lucy, ed. *Materials and Techniques in the Decorative Arts: An Illustrated Dictionary*. Chicago: University of Chicago Press, 2000.

Wines, James. *Green Architecture*. Cologne: Taschen, 2000.

PART 5

ARTS IN TIME

Adams, Laurie Schneider. *Art across Time*, 2nd ed. New York: McGraw-Hill, 2002.

Arnason, H. H., and Peter Kalb. *History of Modern Art*, 5th ed. Upper Saddle River, NJ: Prentice Hall, 2003.

Batchelor, David. *Minimalism*. Cambridge: Cambridge University Press, 1997.

Beard, Mary, and John Henderson. *Classical Art: From Greece to Rome*. Oxford: Oxford University Press, 2001.

Berlo, Janet. *Native North American Art*. Oxford: Oxford University Press, 1998.

Blier, Suzanne. *The Royal Arts of Africa: The Majesty of Form*. New York: Abrams, 1998.

Bloom, Jonathan, and Sheila Blair. *Islamic Arts*. London: Phaidon, 1997.

Brend, Barbara. *Islamic Art*. Cambridge, MA: Harvard University Press, 1991.

Camille, Michael. *Gothic Art: Glorious Visions*. New York: Abrams, 1996.

Chauvet, Jean-Marie, et al. *Dawn of Art: The Chauvet Cave*. New York: Abrams, 1996.

Chipp, Hershell B. *Theories of Modern Art: A Source Book by Artists and Critics*. Berkeley: University of California Press, 1968.

Clark, T. J. *The Painting of Modern Life: Paris in the Art of Manet and His Followers*, rev. ed. Princeton, NJ: Princeton University Press, 1999.

Clunas, Craig. *Art in China*. Oxford: Oxford University Press, 1997.

Coe, Michael D., et al. *The Olmec World: Ritual and Rulership*. Princeton, NJ: The Art Museum, Princeton University, 1995.

D'Alleva, Anne. *Art of the Pacific*. London: Weidenfeld and Nicolson, 1998.

Dawtrey, Liz, et al., eds. *Investigating Modern Art*. New Haven, CT: Yale University Press in association with the Open University, 1996.

Dehejia, Vidya. *Indian Art*. London: Phaidon, 1997.

Diepeveen, Leonard, and Timothy Van Laar. *Art with a Difference: Looking at Difficult and Unfamiliar Art*. Mountain View, CA: Mayfield, 2001.

Eisenmann, Stephen. *Nineteenth-Century Art: A Critical History*. London: Thames and Hudson, 1994.

Elsner, Jas. *Imperial Rome and Christian Triumph*. Oxford: Oxford University Press, 1998.

Fineberg, Jonathan. *Art Since 1940: Strategies of Being*, 2nd ed. Upper Saddle River, NJ: Prentice Hall, 2000.

Gale, Matthew. *Dada and Surrealism*. London: Phaidon, 1997.

Godfrey, Tony. *Conceptual Art*. London: Phaidon, 1998.

Green, Christopher. *Cubism and Its Enemies*. New Haven, CT: Yale University Press, 1991.

Harbison, Craig. *The Mirror of the Artist: Northern Renaissance Art in Its Historical Context*. New York: Abrams, 1995.

Hartt, Frederick. *History of Italian Renaissance Art*, 4th ed. Englewood Cliffs, NJ: Prentice Hall, 1994.

Hopkins, David. *After Modern Art, 1945–2000*. Oxford: Oxford University Press, 2000.

Hughes, Robert. *The Shock of the New*. New York: McGraw-Hill, 1991.

Lee, Sherman. *A History of Far Eastern Art*, 5th ed. New York: Abrams, 1994.

Lowden, John. *Early Christian & Byzantine Art*. London: Phaidon, 1997.

Malek, Jaromir. *Egyptian Art*. London: Phaidon, 1999.

Mason, Penelope. *History of Japanese Art*, 2nd ed. Upper Saddle River, NJ: Prentice Hall, 2005.

Miller, Mary Ellen. *Maya Art and Architecture*. London: Thames and Hudson, 1999.

Miller, Rebecca Stone. *Art of the Andes: From Chavin to Inca*. London: Thames and Hudson, 1995.

Minor, Vernon Hyde. *Baroque and Rococo: Art and Culture*. Englewood Cliffs, NJ: Prentice Hall, 2000.

Mitter, Partha. *Indian Art*. Oxford: Oxford University Press, 2001.

Morphy, Howard. *Aboriginal Art*. London: Phaidon, 1998.

Osborne, Robin. *Archaic and Classical Greek Art*. Oxford: Oxford University Press, 1998.

Paoletti, John, and Gary M. Radke. *Art in Renaissance Italy*, 3rd ed. Upper Saddle River, NJ: Prentice Hall, 2006.

Pasztory, Esther. *Aztec Art*. Norman, OK: University of Oklahoma Press, 1998.

Penny, David W. *Native American Art*. New York: Hugh Lauter Levin, 1994.

Perry, Gill, and Paul Wood, eds. *Themes in Contemporary Art*. London: Yale University Press in association with The Open University, 2004.

Rewald, John. *A History of Impressionism*, 4th ed. rev. New York: Museum of Modern Art, 1973.

Robins, Gay. *The Art of Ancient Egypt*. Cambridge, MA: Harvard University Press, 2000.

Rosenblum, Robert, and H. W. Janson, *19th-Century Art*, 2nd ed. Upper Saddle River, NJ: Prentice Hall, 2005.

Schele, Linda, and Mary Ellen Miller. *The Blood of Kings: Dynasty and Ritual in Maya Art*. New York: George Braziller, in association with the Kimbell Art Museum, Fort Worth, TX, 1986.

Seitz, William C. *Abstract Expressionist Painting in America*. Cambridge, MA: Harvard University Press, 1983.

Sekules, Veronica. *Medieval Art*. Oxford: Oxford University Press, 2001.

Smith, Paul. *Impressionism: Beneath the Surface*. New York: Abrams, 1995.

Spivey, Nigel. *Greek Art*. London: Phaidon, 1997.

Stokstad, Marilyn. *Medieval Art*. New York: Harper & Row, 1986.

Stokstad, Marilyn, with the collaboration of David Cateforis. *Art History*, 2nd ed. New York: Abrams, 2002.

Thompson, Robert Farris. *African Art in Motion*. Berkeley and Los Angeles: University of California Press, 1974.

Thorp, Robert L., and Richard Ellis Vinograd. *Chinese Art and Culture*. New York: Abrams, 2001.

Townsend, Richard F. *The Aztecs*. London: Thames and Hudson, 1992.

Visonà, Monica, et al. *A History of Art in Africa*. New York: Abrams, 2001.

White, Randall. *Prehistoric Art: The Symbolic Journey of Humankind*. New York: Abrams, 2003.

NOTES TO THE TEXT

CHAPTER 1

1. Quoted in Friedrich Teja Bach, "Brancusi: The Reality of Sculpture," *Brancusi* (Philadelphia Museum of Art, 1995), p. 24.
2. Quoted in Dawtrey et al., *Investigating Modern Art* (London: Yale University Press in association with The Open University, 1996), p. 139.
3. All quotes in this essay are from Maya Lin, *Boundaries* (New York: Simon & Schuster, 2000).
4. Quoted in Marilyn Stokstad, *Art History* (New York: H. N. Abrams Inc., 1995), p. 1037.
5. Mark Roskill, ed., *The Letters of Vincent van Gogh* (New York: Atheneum, 1977), p. 188.
6. Adapted from Sidney J. Parnes and Harold F. Harding, eds., *A Source Book for Creative Thinking* (New York: Scribner's, 1962); and Daniel M. Mendelowitz, *Children Are Artists*, 2nd ed. (Stanford, Calif.: Stanford University Press, 1963).

CHAPTER 2

1. Letter 489, c. 19 May 1888, from *The Complete Letters of Vincent van Gogh* (London: Thames and Hudson, 1958); quoted in A. M. and Renilde Hammacher, *Van Gogh* (New York: Thames and Hudson, 1982), p. 157.
2. Letter 557, 24 October 1888, ibid., p. 169.
3. Quoted in Dore Ashton, *Picasso on Art: A Selection of Views* (New York: Viking, 1972), p. 109.
4. Ibid.
5. Quotations in this essay are taken from the texts collected in Louise Bourgeois, *Death of the Father, Reconstruction of the Father: Writings and Interviews, 1923–1997* (London: Violette, 1998).
6. Quoted in Margarete Moorman, "Rebecca Purdum: In a Mysterious Light," ART-News, March 1988, p. 106.
7. For the first theory see Erwin Panofsky, *Early Netherlandish Painting, Its Origins and Character* (Cambridge: Harvard University Press, 1953); for the second, see Edwin Hall, *The Arnolfini Betrothal* (Berkeley: University of California Press, 1994).
8. Quoted in "Interview: Dennis Cooper in Conversation with Tom Friedman," *Tom Friedman* (London: Phaidon Press Limited, 2001), p. 39.

CHAPTER 3

1. Margaret Courtney-Clarke, *Ndebele* (New York: Thames & Hudson, 2002), p. 23.
2. *Bill Viola* (New York and Paris: Whitney Museum of American Art in association with Flammarion, 1997), p. 65.
3. Raghubir Singh, "River of Colour: An Indian View," *River of Colour: The India of Raghubir Singh* (London: Phaidon Press Limited, 1998), p. 9.
4. Robert Rauschenberg, *An Interview with Robert Rauschenberg by Barbara Rose* (New York: Elizabeth Avedon Editions, 1987), p. 59. Information in this biography is adapted from *Robert Rauschenberg* (Washington, D.C.: National Collection of Fine Arts, 1976).
5. "Chillava Klatch: Shahzia Sikander Interview by Homi Bhabha," *Shahzia Sikander* (Chicago: Renaissance Society, University of Chicago, 1999), p. 19.
6. Elizabeth Ripley, *Hokusai: A Biography* (Philadelphia: Lippincott, 1968), p. 24.
7. Ibid., pp. 62, 68.

CHAPTER 4

1. Quoted in Marilyn Stokstad, *Art History* (New York: H. N. Abrams, 1995), p. 1038.
2. John McCoubrey, ed., *American Art, 1700–1960: Sources and Documents* (Englewood Cliffs, NJ: Prentice Hall, 1965), p. 184.
3. Quoted in Ken Shulman, "Monumental Toil to Restore the Magnificent," *The New York Times* (July 2, 1995), pp. 31, 34.
4. F. T. Marinetti, "Futurist Painting: Technical Manifesto" in Hershell Chipp, *Theories of Modern Art* (Berkeley and Los Angeles: University of California Press, 1968), p. 289.

CHAPTER 5

1. Exhibition catalogue statement, Anderson Galleries, January 29, 1923; quoted in Laurie Lisle, *Portrait of an Artist: Georgia O'Keeffe* (New York: Seaview Books, 1980), p. 66.
2. For interpretations based in these and other points of view, see T. J. Clark, *The Painting of Modern Life,* rev. ed. (Princeton: Princeton University Press, 1999); Bradford Collins, ed., *12 Views of Manet's Bar* (Princeton: Princeton University Press, 1996); and Novelene Ross, *Manet's Bar at the Folies-Bergère and the Myths of Popular Illustration* (Ann Arbor: University of Michigan Press, 1982).

CHAPTER 6

1. Quoted in Robert Wallace and the Editors of Time-Life Books, eds., *The World of Leonardo* (New York: Time Incorporated, 1966), p. 17.

CHAPTER 7

1. Black Mountain College Records, 1946; quoted in Ellen Harkins Wheat, *Jacob Lawrence: American Painter* (Seattle: Seattle Art Museum, 1986), p. 73.
2. Quoted in Sharon F. Patton, *African-American Art* (Oxford: Oxford University Press, 1998), p. 188.
3. Owen Drolet, "Matthew Ritchie Interview," *Urban Desires*, March/April 1995 (www.desires.com/1.3).

CHAPTER 8

1. Robert Goldwater and Marco Treves, eds., *Artists on Art: From the Fourteenth to the Twentieth Century* (New York: Pantheon, 1972), p. 82.
2. Quoted in Carol Wax, *The Mezzotint: History and Technique* (New York: H. N. Abrams, 1990), p. 15.
3. Martha Kearns, *Käthe Kollwitz: Woman and Artist* (Old Westbury, N.Y.: Feminist Press, 1967), p. 48.
4. Ibid., p. 164.

CHAPTER 9

1. *Victorian Photographs of Famous Men and Fair Women by Julia Margaret Cameron* (Boston: Godine, 1973), p. 13.
2. Ibid., p. 18.
3. Ibid., p. 19.
4. Helmut Gernsheim, *Julia Margaret Cameron* (New York: Aperture, 1975), p. 180.
5. Cited in Graham Clarke, *The Photograph* (Oxford; New York: Oxford University Press, 1997), p. 151.
6. Richard Huelsenbeck's "Dadaist Manifesto" quoted in Matthew Gale, *Dada & Surrealism* (London: Phaidon Press Ltd, 1997), p. 121.
7. *The New York Times Film Reviews 1913–1970* (New York: Arno Press, 1971), p. 6.

CHAPTER 11

1. Quoted in Rita Reif, "The Jackboot Has Lifted. Now the Crowds Crush," *The New York Times*, June 3, 2001, Arts & Leisure, p. 34.
2. Quoted in Helaine Posner, *Kiki Smith/ Helaine Posner;* interview by David Frankel (Boston: Bulfinch, 1998), p. 12.
3. Ibid., p. 32.
4. The suggestion was made by Bradley Lepper. See David Hurst Thomas, *Exploring Ancient Native America: An Archaeological Guide* (New York: Macmillan, 1994), p. 133.
5. Douglas C. McGill, "Artists and Officials Argue over Removing Sculpture," *The New York Times* (March 7, 1985), p. B1.
6. "Intrusive Arc," *The New York Times* (May 31, 1985), p. A26.
7. Andy Goldsworthy, "Time, Change, Place," *Time* (New York: Harry N. Abrams, Inc., 2000), p. 7.
8. Cited in David Batchelor, *Minimalism* (Cambridge: Cambridge University Press, c1997 Tate Gallery), p. 55.
9. Steven R. Weisman, "Christo's Intercontinental Umbrella Project," *The New York Times* (November 13, 1990), p. C13.

CHAPTER 12

1. Susan Peterson, *The Living Tradition of María Martínez* (New York: Kodansha International, 1977), p. 191.

CHAPTER 13

1. Quoted in Stanley Meisler, "Long Live Paris, with Her Pleasures and Complexities," *Smithsonian* (August 1991), p. 44.
2. Frank Lloyd Wright, *A Testament* (New York: Horizon Press, 1957), p. 64.
3. Quoted in "The Hero of Hale County: Samuel Mockbee," interview by Andrea Oppenheimer Dean, *Architectural Record.* http://archrecord.construction.com/people/ interviews/archives/0102mockbee-1.asp
4. Quoted in Andrea Oppenheimer Dean and Tim Hursley, *Rural Studio: Samuel Mockbee and an Architecture of Decency* (New York: Princeton Architectural Press, 2002).
5. Quoted in "The Hero of Hale County."
6. Quoted in Mockbee's obituary in the *Mobile Register*, January 1, 2001.

CHAPTER 16

1. Quoted in R. Goldwater and M. Treves, eds., *Artists on Art: From the Fourteenth to the Twentieth Century* (New York: Pantheon, 1972), p. 69.
2. Ibid., p. 70.
3. Ibid., p. 52.
4. Ibid., p. 82.
5. Ibid., p. 30.
6. Ibid., p. 60–61.
7. Quoted in Hans Belting, *Likeness and Presence: A History of the Image before the Era of Art* (London and Chicago: The University of Chicago Press, 1994), p. 465.

CHAPTER 17

1. Joan Kinnier, *The Artist by Himself* (New York: St. Martin's, 1980), p. 101.
2. *Memoirs of Madame Vigée-Lebrun,* trans. Lionel Strachey (New York: Braziller, 1989), pp. 20, 21, 214.

CHAPTER 19

1. Quoted from Thomas Cleary, trans., *The Essential Confucius* (San Francisco: HarperSanFrancisco, c. 1992), p. 31.

CHAPTER 20

1. Quoted in Diana Fane, *Objects of Myth and Memory: American Indian Art at the Brooklyn Museum* (Brooklyn, N.Y.: The Museum in association with the University of Washington Press, 1991), p. 107.
2. Marilyn Youngbird, "The Web that Connects the Heart and Mind," *News & Notes (American Indian Ritual Object Repatriation Foundation),* vol. 9, no. 1, spring/ summer 2003.

CHAPTER 21

1. Simon Hantaï, in a conversation reported to the author.
2. Quoted in Ian Dunlop, *Degas* (New York: Galley Press, 1979), p. 168.
3. Robert Goldwater and Marco Treves, eds., *Artists on Art: From the Fourteenth to the Twentieth Century* (New York: Pantheon, 1972), p. 413.

4. Quoted in Hershel B. Chipp, *Theories of Modern Art: A Source Book by Artists and Critics* (Berkeley: University of California Press, 1968), pp. 154–155.
5. Quoted in William Rubin, *Picasso and Braque: Pioneering Cubism* (New York: The Museum of Modern Art, 1989), p. 19.
6. Robert Goldwater and Marco Treves, eds., *Artists on Art: From the Fourteenth to the Twentieth Century* (New York: Pantheon, 1972), p. 417.
7. Quoted in Chipp, pp. 401–402.
8. Ibid., p. 300.
9. Quoted in Christopher Green, *Cubism and Its Enemies* (New Haven and London: Yale University Press, 1987), p. 147.

CHAPTER 22

1. Quoted in Irving Sandler, *The Triumph of American Painting: A History of Abstract Expressionism* (New York: Harper & Row, 1976).
2. John Cage, "Experimental Music" (1957) in *Silences* (Middletown, Conn.: Wesleyan University Press, 1961), p. 12.
3. Hans Richter, *Dada: Art and Anti-Art* (New York, Toronto: McGraw-Hill Book Company, 1965), p. 213.
4. Gretchen Berg, "Andy: My True Story," *Los Angeles Free Press* (March 17, 1967), p. 3; quoted in Knaston McShine, ed., *Andy Warhol: A Retrospective* (New York: Museum of Modern Art, 1989), p. 460.
5. Barbaralee Diamonstein, *Inside New York's Art World* (New York: Rizzoli, 1979), pp. 261–262.
6. Quoted in Alan Riding, "Showcasing a Rise from Rebellion to Respectability," *The New York Times,* March 5, 2000.
7. Ronald Jones, "Notebook," in *Terry Winters: Graphic Primitives* (New York: Matthew Marks Gallery, 1999), p. 44.
8. Cage, "Experimental Music," p. 12.
9. Cited in Roselee Goldberg, *Laurie Anderson* (New York: Harry N. Abrams, Inc., 2000), p. 164.

GLOSSARY

Words in *italics* are also defined in the glossary. Numbers in **boldface** following the definitions refer to the numbers of figures in the text that illustrate the definitions.

abstract Descriptive of art in which the forms of the visual world are purposefully simplified, fragmented, or otherwise distorted. Compare *representational, naturalistic, stylized, nonrepresentational.* **(2.14)**

Abstract Expressionism An American art movement of the mid-20th century characterized by large ("heroic") *scale* and *nonrepresentational* imagery. An outgrowth of *surrealism,* Abstract Expressionism emphasized the artist's spontaneous expression as it flowed from the subconscious, which in turn was believed to draw on primal energies. See also *action painting.* **(22.1)**

acrylic A synthetic plastic resin used as a *binder* for artists' paints. Also used in the plural to refer to the paints themselves: acrylics. **(7.15)**

action painting *Nonrepresentational* painting in which the physical act of applying paint to a *support* in bold, spontaneous gestures supplies the expressive content. First used to describe the work of certain *Abstract Expressionist* painters. **(22.1)**

adobe Sun-dried (as opposed to furnace-baked) brick made of clay mixed with straw. **(13.1)**

aesthetics The branch of philosophy concerned with the feelings aroused in us by sensory experiences such as seeing and hearing. Aesthetics examines, among other things, the nature of art and the nature of beauty.

afterimage An image that persists after the visual stimulus that first produced it has ceased. The mechanics of vision cause an afterimage to appear in the *complementary* hue of the original stimulus. **(4.30)**

aisle Generally, a passageway flanking a central area. In a basilica or cathedral, aisles flank the *nave.* **(15.4)**

alla prima Italian for "all in one go." In oil painting, the technique of completing a painting in a single session, as opposed to building it up slowly over a period of time. *Alla prima* technique rules out such time-consuming procedures as *glazing* in favor of a more spontaneous approach that often features opaque *impasto* and visible brush strokes. **(7.9)**

ambulatory In church architecture, a vaulted passageway for walking (ambulating) around the *apse.* An ambulatory allows visitors to walk around the altar and choir areas without disturbing devotions in progress. **(15.15)**

analogous harmony The juxtaposition of hues that contain the same color in differing proportions, such as red-violet, pink, and yellow-orange, all of which contain red. **(4.29)**

animal style A style in European and western Asian art in ancient and medieval times based in linear, stylized animal forms. Animal style is often found in metalwork. **(15.11)**

appropriation A postmodern practice in which one artist reproduces an image created by another artist and claims it as his or her own. In postmodern thought, appropriation is felt to challenge traditional ideas about authenticity and individuality, the location of meaning within a work of art, and copyright issues involving intellectual property. **(22.20)**

apse The semicircular, protruding niche at one or both ends of the *nave* of a Roman *basilica.* In basilica-based church architecture, an apse houses the altar and may be elongated to include a choir. **(15.4)**

aquatint An *intaglio* printmaking method in which areas of tone are created by dusting resin particles on a plate and then allowing acid to bite around the particles. Also, a *print* made by this method. **(8.15)**

arch In architecture, a curved structure, usually made of wedge-shaped stones, that serves to span an opening. An arch may be semicircular or rise to a point at the top. **(13.9)**

Archaic In the history of ancient Greece, the period between 8th and 6th centuries B.C.E., when what would later be leading characteristics of Greek art can be seen in their earliest form. **(14.22)**

architrave In *Classical* architecture, the lowest band of the *entablature.* **(13.5)**

Art Deco An art style of the 1920s and 1930s based on modern materials (steel, chrome, glass) and repetitive geometric patterns. **(13.34)**

assembling The technique of creating a sculpture by grouping or piecing together distinct elements, as opposed to *casting, modeling,* or carving. An assembled sculpture may be called an **assemblage. (11.10)**

asymmetrical Not *symmetrical.* **(5.11)**

atmospheric perspective See *perspective.* **(4.48)**

auteur French for "author," the word describes a filmmaker, usually a director, who exercises extensive creative control over his or her films, imbuing them with a strong personal style. **(9.27)**

axis In three-dimensional art, an imaginary straight line that serves as an implied center of gravity and around which elements are grouped. In two-dimensional art, an imaginary straight line that divides a pictorial field into two equal parts either horizontally (a horizontal axis), vertically (a vertical axis), or diagonally from corner to corner (a diagonal axis).

Baroque The period of European history from the 17th through the early 18th centuries, and the styles of art that flourished during it. Originating in Rome and associated at first with the Counter Reformation of the Catholic Church, the dominant style of Baroque art was characterized by dramatic use of light, bold colors and *value* contrasts, emotionalism, a tendency to push into the viewer's space, and an overall theatricality. Pictorial composition often emphasized a diagonal *axis*, and sculpture, painting, and architecture were often combined to create ornate and impressive settings. **(17.1)**

barrel vault   See *vault.* **(13.10)**

basilica   In Roman architecture, a standard type of rectangular building with a large, open interior. Generally used for administrative and judicial purposes, the basilica was adapted for early church architecture. Principal elements of a basilica are *nave, clerestory, aisle,* and *apse.* **(15.4)**

bas-relief   See *relief.* **(11.12)**

Bauhaus   A school of art and architecture in Germany from 1919 to 1933 whose influence was felt across the 20th century. Bauhaus instructors broke down the barriers between art, craft, and design, and they believed that artists could improve society by bringing the principles of good design to industrial mass production. **(21.31)**

bay   In architecture, a modular unit of space, generally cubic and generally defined by four supporting *piers* or columns. **(13.10)**

binder   A substance in paints that causes particles of *pigment* to adhere to one another and to a *support.*

broken color   1. A color whose pure *hue* has been toned down ("broken") through the addition of a second color, often a *complementary.* 2. In painting, the practice, popularized by the *Impressionists,* of creating a color area from small strokes of individual colors, often closely related, that blend optically when seen at a certain distance. See *optical color mixture.* **(2.5)**

buttress, buttressing   In architecture, an exterior support that counteracts the outward thrust of an arch, dome, or wall. A **flying buttress** consists of a strut or arch segment running from a freestanding *pier* to an outer wall. **(13.12)**

calligraphy   From the Greek for "beautiful writing," handwriting considered as an art, especially as practiced in China, Japan, and Islamic cultures. **(19.22)**

cantilever   In architecture, a horizontal structural element supported at one end only, with the other end projecting into space. **(13.38)**

capital   In architecture, the decorative sculpted block surmounting a column. In *Classical* architecture, the form of the capital is the most distinctive element of the various *orders.* **(13.3)**

Carolingian   The period in medieval European history dominated by the Frankish rulers of the Carolingian dynasty, roughly 750–850 C.E. In art, the term refers especially to the artistic flowering sponsored by Charlemagne (ruled 800–840). **(15.13)**

cartoon   A full-scale preparatory drawing for a *fresco* or *mural.*

casting   The process of making a sculpture or other object by pouring a liquid into a *mold,* letting it harden, and then releasing it. Common materials used for casting include bronze, plaster, clay, and synthetic resins. **(11.4)**

ceramic   Made of baked ("fired") clay. See also *terra cotta.* **(12.1)**

chasing   In metalwork, the technique of incising a design into cold metal with chisels and punches. **(12.7)**

chiaroscuro   Italian for "light-dark." In two-dimensional, representational art, the technique of using *values* to record light and shadow, especially as they provide information about three-dimensional *form.* See *model.* **(4.20)**

chroma   See *intensity.* **(4.26)**

cire-perdue   See *lost-wax casting.* **(11.4)**

Classical   Most narrowly, the "middle" period of ancient Greek civilization, beginning around 480 B.C.E. and lasting until around 350 B.C.E. More broadly, the civilizations of ancient Greece and ancient Rome, and the centuries during which they flourished. Most generally, and with a lowercase *c,* any art that emphasizes rational order, balance, harmony, and restraint, especially if it looks to the art of ancient Greece and Rome for models. **(14.24, 13.28)**

clerestory   The topmost part of a wall, extending above flanking elements such as *aisles.* and set with windows to admit light. In a *basilica* or church, the clerestory is the topmost zone of the *nave.* **(15.2)**

coffer   A recessed, geometrical panel in a ceiling, often used in multiples as a decorative element. **(13.15)**

collage   From the French for "glue," the practice of pasting shapes cut from such real-world sources as magazines, newspapers, wallpaper, and fabric onto a surface. Also, a work of art made in this way. **(7.18)**

Color Field painting   A style of nonrepresentational painting featuring broad "fields" or areas of color. Arising in the 1950s after *Abstract Expressionism,* it shared that movement's fondness for large *scale* as well as its desire to transcend the visible world in favor of universal truths viewed as unconscious or spiritual. **(22.3)**

color wheel   A circular arrangement of hues used to illustrate a particular color theory or system. The most well-known color wheel uses the spectral *hues* of the rainbow plus the intermediary hue of red-violet. **(4.24)**

complementary colors   *Hues* that intensify each other when juxtaposed and dull each other when mixed (as pigment). On a *color wheel,* complementary hues are situated directly opposite one another. **(4.24, 4.28)**

composition   The organization of lines, shapes, colors, and other art elements in a work of art. More often applied to two-dimensional art; the broader term is design.

Conceptual Art   Art created according to the belief that the essence of art resides in a motivating idea, and that any physical realization or recording of this idea is secondary. Conceptual art arose during the 1960s as artists tried to move away from producing objects that could be bought and sold. Conceptual works are often realized physically in materials that have little or no inherent value, such as a series of photographs or texts that document an activity. They are often ephemeral. **(22.16)**

Constructivism   A Russian art movement of the early 20th century. Based in the principles of geometric abstraction, Constructivism was founded around 1913 by Vladimir Tatlin and condemned in 1922 by the Soviet government. **(21.28)**

content   What a work of art is about, its subject matter as interpreted by a viewer.

context   The personal and social circumstances surrounding the making, viewing, and interpreting of a work of art; the varied connections of a work of art to the larger world of its time and place.

contour   The perceived edges of a three-dimensional form such as the human body. Contour lines are lines used to indicate these perceived edges in two-dimensional art. **(4.4)**

contrapposto   A pose that suggests the potential for movement , and thus life, in a standing human figure. Developed by sculptors in ancient Greece, contrapposto places the figure's weight on one foot, setting off a series of adjustments to the hips and shoulders that produce a subtle S-curve. **(11.20)**

cool colors Colors ranged along the blue curve of the *color wheel*, from green through violet. **(4.24)**

Corinthian order See *order*. **(13.3)**

cornice In *Classical* architecture, the uppermost element of an *entablature;* a raking cornice frames the upper, slanting edges of a *pediment*. More generally, a horizontal, projecting element, usually molded and usually at the top of a wall. **(13.5)**

cross-cutting In film, the technique of alternating between two or more ongoing scenes so that all seem to move forward simultaneously.

cross-hatching See *hatching*.

Cubism A movement developed during the early 20th century by Pablo Picasso and Georges Braque. In its most severe "analytical" phase, Cubism abstracted the forms of the visible world into fragments or facets drawn from multiple points of view, then constructed an image from them which had its own internal logic. A severely restricted *palette* (black, white, brown) and a painting technique of short, distinct "touches" allowed shards of figure and ground to interpenetrate in a shallow, shifting space. **(21.19)**

Dada An international art movement that emerged during World War I (1914–1918). Believing that society itself had gone mad, Dada refused to make sense or to provide any sort of aesthetic refuge or comfort. Instead, it created "anti-art" that emphasized absurdity, irrationality, chance, whimsy, irony, and childishness. Deliberately shocking or provocative works, actions, and events were aimed at disrupting public complacency. **(21.23)**

daguerreotype The first practical photographic process. Invented by Jacques Louis Mandé Daguerre and made public in 1839, it produced a single permanent image directly on a prepared copper plate. **(9.3)**

damascening In metalwork, the technique of inlaying one metal with an intricate pattern in another (silver with gold, for example). **(12.8)**

design The organization of visual elements in a work of art. In two-dimensional art, often referred to as composition.

diptych A composition consisting of two panels side by side, often hinged to open and close like a book. **(7.10)**

dome In architecture, a convex, evenly curved roof; technically, an arch rotated 360 degrees on its vertical *axis*. Like an arch, a dome may be hemispherical or pointed. **(13.13)**

Doric order See *order*. **(13.3)**

drum In architecture, a cylindrical wall used as a base for a dome. **(13.18)**

drypoint An *intaglio* printmaking technique similar to *engraving* in which the design is scratched directly into a metal plate with a sharp, pointed, tool that is held like a pen. As it cuts through the metal, the tool raises a rough edge called a burr, which, if left in place, produces a soft, velvety line when printed. Also, a print made by this method. **(8.12)**

earthwork A work of art created at, for, and from a natural site, for example by reshaping the earth or rearranging natural elements found there. **(11.25)**

edition In printmaking, the total number of prints made from a given plate or block. According to contemporary practice, the size of an edition is written on each print, and the prints are individually numbered with it. The artist's signature indicates approval of the print and acts as a guarantee of the edition.

embossing In metalwork, raising a design in relief by hammering a sheet of heated metal from the back. **(12.7)**

embroidery A technique of needlework in which designs or figures are stitched into a textile ground with colored thread or yarn. **(15.17)**

encaustic Painting *medium* in which the *binder* is wax, which is heated to render the paints fluid. **(7.1)**

engraving An *intaglio* printmaking method in which lines are cut into a metal plate using a sharp tool called a burin, which creates a clean, v-shaped channel. Also, a print resulting from this technique. **(8.11)**

entablature In *Classical* architecture, the horizontal structure supported by capitals and supporting in turn the pediment or roof. An entablature consists of three horizontal bands: *architrave, frieze*, and *cornice*. **(13.5)**

entasis In *Classical* architecture, the slight swelling or bulge built into the center of a column to make the column seem straight visually. **(14.26)**

etching An *intaglio* printmaking method in which the design is bitten into the printing plate with acid. Also, the resultant print. To create an etching, a metal plate is covered with an acid-resistant *ground*. The design is drawn with a sharp, pen-like tool that scratches the ground to reveal the metal beneath. The plate is then submerged in acid, which bites into the exposed metal. The longer the plate remains in contact with the acid, the deeper the bite, and the darker the line it will print. **(8.14)**

Expressionism An art movement of the early 20th century, especially prevalent in Germany, which claimed the right to distort visual appearances in order to express psychological or emotional states, especially the artist's own personal feelings. More generally, and with a lower-case e, any art style that raises subjective feeling above objective observation, using distortion and exaggeration for emotional effect. **(21.15)**

Fauvism A short-lived but influential art movement in France in the early 20th century that emphasized bold, arbitrary, expressive color. **(21.13)**

ferroconcrete Concrete reinforced internally with iron rods or steel mesh. **(13.26)**

figure See *figure-ground relationship*.

figure-ground relationship In two-dimensional images, the relationship between a *shape* we perceive as dominant (the figure) and the background shape we perceive it against (the ground). Figure shapes are also known as **positive shapes,** while the shapes of the ground are **negative shapes.** Psychologists have identified a list of principles we use to decide which shapes are figure and which ground. When none of these conditions are met, figure and ground may seem to shift back and forth as our brain organizes the information first one way and then another, an effect known as figure-ground ambiguity. **(4.12, 4.13, 4.14)**

flashback In filmmaking, a cut from events occurring in the present to events that are understood to have occurred earlier.

flying buttress See *buttress*. **(13.12)**

foreshortening The visual phenomenon whereby an elongated object projecting toward or away from a viewer appears shorter than its actual length, as though compressed. In two-dimensional representational art, the portrayal of this effect. **(4.46)**

forging The technique of shaping metal, especially iron, by heating it until it softens and then beating or hammering it.

form 1. The physical appearance of a work of art—its materials, style, and *composition*. 2. Any identifiable shape or mass, as a "geometric form."

fresco A painting medium in which colors are applied to a plaster ground, usually a wall *(mural)* or ceiling. In *buon fresco,* also called **true fresco,** colors are applied before the plaster dries and thus bond with the surface. In *fresco secco* ("dry fresco") colors are applied to dry plaster. **(7.4)**

frieze Generally, any horizontal band of *relief* sculpture or painted decoration. In *Classical* architecture, the middle band of an *entablature*, between the *architrave* and *cornice*, often decorated with relief sculpture. **(13.5)**

Futurism Art movement founded in Italy in 1909 and lasting only a few years. Futurism concentrated on the dynamic quality of modern technological life, emphasizing speed and movement. **(4.53)**

genre The daily lives of ordinary people considered as subject matter for art. Also, **genre painting,** painting that takes daily life for its subject. **(17.13)**

geodesic dome An architectural structure invented by R. Buckminster Fuller, based on triangles arranged into tetrahedrons (four-faceted solids). **(13.27)**

gesso A brilliant white undercoating made of inert pigment such as chalk or plaster and used as *ground* for paint, especially for *tempera.*

giclée From the French for "sprayed" or "squirted," an advanced computer inkjet printing technology in which mists of ink are sprayed at a piece of paper attached to a rotating drum; also known as an Iris print. **(8.24)**

glaze In oil painting, a thin, translucent layer of color, generally applied over another color. (For example, blue glaze can be applied over yellow to create green.) In ceramics, a liquid that, upon firing, fuses into a vitreous (glasslike) coating, sealing the porous clay surface. Colored glazes are used to decorate ceramics. **(12.1)**

Gothic Style of art and architecture that flourished in Europe, especially northern Europe, from the mid-12th to the 16th centuries. Gothic architecture found its finest expression in cathedrals, which are characterized by soaring interiors and large stained glass windows, features made possible by the use of the pointed *arch* and *flying buttress.* **(15.18)**

grisaille A painting executed entirely in gray-scale values, often as a foundation for colored glazes.

groin vault See *vault.*

ground 1. A preparatory coating of paint, usually white but sometimes colored, applied to the *support* for a painting or drawing. 2. An acid-resistant coating applied to a metal plate to ready it for use in *etching.* 3. The information that is perceived as secondary in a two-dimensional image; the background. See *figure-ground relationship.*

happening An event staged or directed by artists and offered as art. Coined in 1959 and widely used during the 1960s, the term has generally been replaced today by *performance art.* Compared to contemporary performance art, happenings were more open to spontaneity and often encouraged audience participation. **(22.8)**

hatching Closely spaced parallel lines that mix optically to suggest *values.* Hatching is a linear technique for modeling *forms* according to the principles of *chiaroscuro.* To achieve darker values, layers of hatching may be superimposed, with each new layer set at an angle to the one(s) beneath. This technique is called **cross-hatching. (4.21)**

Hellenistic Literally "Greek-like" or "based in Greek culture." Descriptive of the art produced in Greece and in regions under Greek rule or cultural influence from 323 B.C.E. until the rise of the Roman Empire in the final decades of the 1st century B.C.E. Hellenistic art followed three broad trends: a continuing classicism; a new style characterized by dramatic emotion and turbulence; and a closely observed *realism.* **(14.28, 14.29)**

hierarchical scale The representation of more important figures as larger than less important figures, as when a king is portrayed on a larger scale than his attendants. **(5.21)**

high relief See *relief.* **(11.13)**

hue The "family name" of a color, independent of its particular *value* or *saturation.* **(4.24)**

hypostyle An interior space filled with rows of columns that serve to support the roof. **(3.5)**

icon In Byzantine and later Orthodox Christian art, an image of a holy person such as Jesus, the Virgin Mary, or a saint. Generally small in scale and painted in a highly stylized manner on a gold ground over a wooden support, icons are often themselves held to be sacred. **(15.10)**

iconography The identification, description, and interpretation of subject matter in art. **(2.28)**

illumination 1. The practice of adding hand-drawn illustrations and other embellishments to a manuscript. 2. An illustration or ornament thus added. **(15.24)**

impasto From the Italian for "paste," a thick application of paint. **(2.1)**

Impressionism A movement in painting originating in the 1860s in France. Impressionism arose in opposition to the academic art of the day. In subject matter, Impressionism followed *Realism* in portraying daily life, especially the leisure activities of the middle class. Landscape was also a favorite subject, encouraged by the new practice of painting outdoors. In technique, Impressionists painters favored *alla prima* painting and *broken color,* which were put into the service of recording fleeting effects of nature and the rapidly changing urban scene. **(21.8)**

installation An art form in which an entire room or similar space is treated as a work of art to be entered and experienced. More broadly, the placing of a work of art in a specific location, usually for a limited time. **(2.40)**

intaglio Printmaking techniques in which the lines or areas that will take the ink are incised into the printing plate, rather than raised above it (compare *relief*). *Aquatint, drypoint, etching,* and *mezzotint* are intaglio techniques. **(8.10)**

intensity The relative purity or brightness of a color. Also called *chroma* or *saturation.* **(4.26)**

interlace Decoration composed of intricately intertwined strips or ribbons. Interlace was especially popular in medieval Celtic and Scandinavian art. **(15.12)**

International style A style that prevailed after World War II as the aesthetic of earlier Modernist movements such as de Stijl and the Bauhaus spread throughout the West and beyond. International style buildings are generally characterized by clean lines, rectangular geometric shapes, minimal ornamentation, and steel-and-glass construction. **(13.24)**

Ionic order See *order.* **(13.3)**

Iris print See *giclée.* **(8.24)**

isometric perspective See *perspective.* **(4.50)**

keystone The wedge-shaped, central stone in an arch. Inserted last, the keystone locks the other stones in place. **(13.9)**

kinetic Having to do with motion. Kinetic art incorporates (rather than depicts) real or apparent movement. Broadly defined, kinetic art may include film, video, and performance art. However, the term is most often applied to sculpture that is set in motion by motors or air currents. **(4.54)**

kore Greek for "maiden" or "girl," used as a generic name for the many sculptures of young women produced during the *Archaic* period of Greek civilization.

kouros Greek for "youth" or "boy," used as a generic name for the numerous sculptures of nude youths produced during the *Archaic* period of Greek civilization. **(14.22)**

layout In graphic art, the disposition of text and images on a page, or the overall design of *typographic* elements on page, spread, or book. **(10.9)**

linear perspective See *perspective*. **(4.43)**

linocut A *relief* printmaking technique in which the printing surface is a thick layer of linoleum, often mounted on a wooden block for support. Areas that will not print are cut away, leaving raised areas to take the ink. **(8.9)**

lintel In architecture, a horizontal beam or stone that spans an opening. See *post-and-lintel*. **(13.2)**

lithography A *planographic* printmaking technique based on the fact that oil and water repel each other. The design to be printed is drawn in greasy crayon or ink on the printing surface—traditionally a block of fine-grained stone, but today more frequently a plate of zinc or aluminum. The printing surface is dampened, then inked. The oil-based ink adheres to the greasy areas and is repelled by the damp areas. **(8.17)**

lost-wax casting Also known by the French name *cire-perdue*, a technique for *casting* sculptures or other objects in metal. A model of the object to be cast is created in wax, fitted with wax rods, then encased in a heat-resistant material such as plaster or clay, leaving the rods protruding. The ensemble is heated so that the wax melts and runs out (is "lost"), creating a mold. Molten metal is poured into the mold through the channels created by the melted wax rods, filling the void where the wax original used to be. When the metal has cooled, the mold is broken open to release the casting. **(11.4)**

low relief See *relief*. **(11.12)**

mandala In Hinduism and especially Buddhism, a diagram of a cosmic realm, from the Sanskrit for "circle." **(5.7)**

Mannerism From the Italian for "style" or "stylishness," a trend in 16th-century Italian art. Mannerist artists cultivated a variety of elegant, refined, virtuosic, and highly artificial styles, often featuring elongated figures, sinuous contours, bizarre effects of scale and lighting, shallow pictorial space, and intense colors. **(16.26)**

mass Three-dimensional *form*, often implying bulk, density, and weight. **(4.12)**

matrix In printmaking, a surface (such as a block of wood) on which a design is prepared before being transferred through pressure to a receiving surface (such as a sheet of paper).

medium 1. The material from which a work of art is made. 2. A standard category of art such as painting or sculpture. 3. A liquid compounded with *pigment* to make paint, also called a *vehicle* and often acting as a *binder*.

megalith A very large stone. **(1.4)**

metalpoint A drawing technique in which the drawing medium is a fine metal wire. When the metal employed is silver, the technique is known as **silverpoint. (6.7)**

mezzotint An *itaglio* printmaking technique in which the printing plate is first roughened with a special tool called a rocker, which creates a fine pattern of burrs. Inked and printed at this point, the plate would print a velvety black. *Values* are created by smoothing away the burrs in varying degrees (smoothing the plate altogether creates a nonprinting area, or white). Also, the resultant print. **(8.13)**

minaret A tower forming part of a mosque and serving as a place from which the faithful are called to prayer. **(18.1)**

Minimalism A broad tendency during the 1960s and 70s toward simple, primary forms. Minimalist artists often favored industrial materials (sheet metal, bricks, plywood, fluorescent lights), and their sculptures (which they preferred to call objects) tended to be set on the floor or attached to the wall rather than placed on a pedestal. **(22.13)**

mixed media Descriptive of any work of art employing more than one *medium*—for example, a work that combines painting, *collage*, and *screenprinting*. **(7.19)**

modeling 1. In sculpture, manipulating a plastic material such as clay or wax to create a *form*. 2. In figurative drawing, painting, and printmaking, simulating the effects of light and shadow in order to portray optically convincing *masses*. **(11.2, 4.20)**

mold A casing containing a shaped void in which liquid metal, clay, or other material may be *cast*. **(11.4)**

monochromatic Having only one color. Descriptive of work in which one *hue*—perhaps with variations of *value* and *intensity*—predominates. **(4.34)**

monotype A *planographic* printmaking method resulting in a single impression. A typical technique is to paint the design in oil paint on a plate of glass or metal. While the paint is still wet, a piece of paper is laid over it, and pressure is applied to transfer the design from the plate to the paper. **(8.21)**

mosaic The technique of creating a design or image by arranging bits of colored ceramic, stone, glass, or other suitable materials and fixing them into a bed of cement or plaster. **(15.1)**

mural Any large-*scale* wall decoration in painting, *fresco*, *mosaic*, or other *medium*. **(20.10)**

narthex In early Christian architecture, the porch or vestibule serving as an entryway to a church. **(15.4)**

naturalistic Descriptive of an approach to portraying the visible world that emphasizes the objective observation and accurate imitation of appearances. Naturalistic art closely resembles the forms it portrays. Naturalism and *realism* are often used interchangeably, and both words have complicated histories. In this text, naturalism is construed as a broader approach, permitting a degree of idealization and embracing a stylistic range across cultures. *Realism* suggests a more focused, almost clinical attention to detail that refuses to prettify harsh or unflattering matters. **(2.12)**

nave In an ancient Roman *basilica*, the taller central space flanked by *aisles*. In a cruciform church, the long space flanked by *aisles* and leading from the entrance to the *transept*. **(15.4)**

negative shape See *figure-ground relationship*.

Neoclassicism Literally "new classicism," a Western movement in painting, sculpture, and architecture of the late-18th and early 19th centuries that looked to the civilizations of ancient Greece and Rome for inspiration. Neoclassical artists worked in a variety of individual styles, but in general, like any art labeled *classical*, Neoclassical art emphasized order, clarity, and restraint. **(17.17)**

neutral   Descriptive of colors that cannot be classified among the spectral hues and their intermediaries on the color wheel: black, white, gray, and the browns and brownish grays produced by mixing complementary colors.

nonobjective   Descriptive of art that does not represent or otherwise refer to the visible world outside of itself. Synonymous with *nonrepresentational*. Compare *abstract*, *stylized*. **(2.19)**

nonrepresentational   See *nonobjective*. **(2.19)**

oculus   A circular opening in a wall or at the top of a dome. **(13.13)**

open palette   See *palette*. **(1.8)**

optical color mixture   The tendency of the eyes to blend patches of individual colors placed near one another so as to perceive a different, combined color. Also, any art style that exploits this tendency, especially the *pointillism* of Georges Seurat. **(4.33)**

order   In *Classical* architecture, a system of standardized types. In ancient Greek architecture, three orders pertain: Doric, Ionic, and Corinthian. The orders are most easily distinguished by their columns. **Doric:** The shaft of the column may be smooth or fluted. It does not have a base. The capital is a rounded stone disk supporting a plain rectangular slab. **Ionic:** The shaft is fluted and rests on a stepped base. The capital is carved in graceful scrolling forms called volutes. **Corinthian:** The shaft is fluted and rests on a more detailed stepped base. The elaborate capital is carved with motifs based on stylized acanthus leaves. **(13.3)**

palette   1. A surface used for mixing paints. 2. The range of colors used by an artist or group of artists, either generally or in a specific work. An **open palette** is one in which all colors are permitted. A **restricted palette** is limited to a few colors and their mixtures, tints, and shades. **(4.25, 21.19)**

pastel   1. A drawing medium consisting of sticks of color made of powdered *pigment* and a relatively weak *binder*. 2. A light-*value* color, especially a *tint*. **(6.10)**

pediment   In *classical* architecture, the triangular element supported by the columns of a *portico*. More generally, any similar element over a door or window. **(13.5)**

pendentive   In architecture, a curving, triangular section that serves as a transition between a *dome* and the four walls of a rectangular building. **(13.16)**

performance art   An event or action carried out by an artist and offered as art. In widespread use since the 1970s, *performance art* is an umbrella term that embraces earlier practices such as the *happenings* of the 1960s and the events staged by *Dada* artists in 1920s. Performances may range from improvisatory to highly scripted, and from actions of daily life to elaborately staged spectacles. **(22.26)**

perspective   A system for portraying the visual impression of three-dimensional space and objects in it on a two-dimensional surface. **Linear perspective** is based on the observation that parallel lines appear to converge as they recede from the viewer, finally meeting at a vanishing point on the horizon. Linear perspective relies on a fixed viewpoint. **Atmospheric perspective** is based on the observation that distant objects appear less distinct, paler, and bluer than nearby objects due to the way moisture in the intervening atmosphere scatters light. **Isometric perspective** uses diagonal lines to convey recession, but parallel lines do not converge. It is principally used in East Asian art, which is not based in a fixed viewpoint. **(4.44)**

Photorealism   Also called *superrealism*, a movement in painting and sculpture of the 1960s and 70s that imitated the impersonal precision and wealth of minute detail associated with photography. Photorealist sculptors sometimes clothed their figures in real clothing, and painters sometimes took an actual photographs for their subject, faithfully depicting the effects of depth of field (sharp detail giving way to blurred areas), forced perspective, and other characteristics of the technology. **(22.15)**

picture plane   The literal surface of a painting imagined as window, so that objects depicted in depth are spoken of as behind or receding from the picture plane, and objects in the extreme foreground are spoken of as up against the picture plane. A favorite trick of *trompe-l'oeil* painters is to paint an object that seems to be projecting forward from the picture plane into the viewer's space.

pier   A vertical support, often square or rectangular, used to bear the heaviest loads in an arched or vaulted structure. A pier may be styled to resemble a bundle of columns. **(13.11)**

pigment   A coloring material made from various organic or chemical substances. When mixed with a *binder*, it creates a drawing or painting *medium*.

plane   A flat surface. See *picture plane*.

planography   Printmaking techniques in which the image areas are level with the surface of the printing plate. *Lithography* and *monotype* are planographic methods. **(8.1)**

plastic   1. Capable of being molded or shaped, as clay. 2. Any synthetic polymer substance, such as *acrylic*.

pointillism   A quasi-scientific painting technique of the late-19th century, developed and promulgated by Georges Seurat and his followers, in which pure colors were applied in regular, small touches (points) that blended through *optical color mixture* when viewed at a certain distance. The drive behind pointillism was a desire to produce more brilliant paintings by avoiding *broken colors*. **(4.31)**

Pop Art   An art style of the 1960s, deriving its imagery from the popular, mass-produced culture. Deliberately mundane, Pop Art focused on the overfamiliar objects of daily life to give them new meanings as visual emblems. **(22.9)**

porcelain   A *ceramic* ware, usually white, firing in the highest temperature ranges and often used for fine dinnerware, vases, and sculpture. **(12.4)**

portico   A projecting porch with a roof supported by columns, often marking the entrance to a building. **(13.13)**

positive shape   See *figure-ground relationship*.

post-and-lintel   In architecture, a structural system based on two or more uprights (posts) supporting a horizontal crosspiece (lintel or beam). **(13.6)**

Post-Impressionism   A term applied to the work of several artists—French or living in France—from about 1885 to 1905. Although all painted in highly personal styles, the Post-Impressionists were united in rejecting the relative absence of *form* characteristic of *Impression-*

ism. The group included Vincent van Gogh, Paul Cézanne, Paul Gauguin, and Georges Seurat. **(1.10)**

primary color A *hue* that, in theory, cannot be created by a mixture of other hues. Varying combinations of the primary hues can be used to create all the other hues of the spectrum. In pigment the primaries are red, yellow, and blue. **(4.24)**

primer A preliminary coating applied to a painting *support* to improve adhesion of paints or to create special effects. A traditional primer is gesso, consisting of a chalky substance mixed with glue and water. Also called a *ground.*

print An image created from a master wood block, stone, plate, or screen, usually on paper. Prints are referred to as multiples, because as a rule many identical or similar impressions are made from the same printing surface, the number of impressions being called an *edition.* See *relief, intaglio, lithography, screenprinting.* **(8.3)**

proportion Size relationships between parts of a whole, or between two or more items perceived as a unit; also, the size relationship between an object and its surroundings. Compare *scale.* **(5.20)**

Realism Broadly, any art in which the goal is to portray forms in the natural world in a highly faithful manner. Specifically, an art style of the mid-19th century, identified especially with Gustave Courbet, which fostered the idea that everyday people and events are fit subjects for important art. Compare *naturalism.* **(21.3)**

refraction The bending of a ray of light, for example, when it passes through a prism. **(4.23)**

registration In printmaking, the precise alignment of impressions made by two or more printing blocks or plates on the same sheet of paper, as when printing an image in several colors. **(8.5)**

relief Anything that projects from a background. 1. Sculpture in which figures are attached to a background and project from it to some degree. In **low relief,** also called **bas-relief,** the figures project minimally, as on a coin. In **high relief,** figures project substantially from the background, often by half their full depth or more. In **sunken relief,** outlines are carved *into* the surface and the figure is modeled within them, from the surface down. 2. In printmaking, techniques in which portions of a block meant to be printed are raised. See *woodcut, linocut, wood engraving.* **(16.2, 8.1)**

Renaissance The period in Europe from the 14th to the 16th century, characterized by a renewed interest in *Classical* art, architecture, literature, and philosophy. The Renaissance began in Italy and gradually spread to the rest of Europe. In art, it is most closely associated with Leonardo da Vinci, Michelangelo, and Raphael. **(16.9)**

representational Descriptive of a work of art that depicts *forms* in the natural world. **(2.6)**

restricted palette See *palette.* **(21.19)**

ribbed vault See *vault.* **(13.11)**

Rococo A style of art popular in Europe in the first three quarters of the 18th century. Rococo architecture and furnishings emphasized ornate but small-*scale* decoration, curvilinear *forms,* and *pastel* colors. Rococo painting, also tending toward the use of pastels, has a playful, light-hearted, romantic quality and often pictures the aristocracy at leisure. **(17.15)**

Romanesque A style of architecture and art dominant in Europe from the 9th to the 12th century. Romanesque architecture, based on ancient Roman precedents, emphasizes the round *arch* and *barrel vault.* **(13.10)**

Romanticism A movement in Western art of the 19th century, generally assumed to be in opposition to *Neoclassicism.* Romantic works are marked by intense colors, turbulent emotions, complex *composition,* soft outlines, and sometimes heroic or exotic subject matter. **(21.2)**

rotunda An open, cylindrical interior space, usually covered by a dome. **(13.15)**

saturation See *intensity.* **(4.26)**

scale Size in relation to some "normal" or constant size. Compare *proportion.* **(5.18)**

screenprinting A printmaking method in which the image is transferred to paper by forcing ink through a fine mesh in which the areas not meant to print have been blocked; a stencil technique. **(8.20)**

secondary color A *hue* created by combining two *primary colors,* as yellow and blue mixed together yield green. In pigment the secondary colors are orange, green, and violet. **(4.24)**

serigraphy See *screenprinting.* **(8.20)**

sfumato From the Italian word for "smoke," a technique of painting in thin *glazes* to achieve a hazy, cloudy atmosphere, often to represent objects or landscape meant to be perceived as distant from the *picture plane.* **(16.8)**

shade A color darker than a hue's normal value. Maroon is a shade of red. **(4.26)**

shape A two-dimensional area having identifiable boundaries, created by lines, color or *value* changes, or some combination of these. Broadly, *form.* **(4.14)**

silkscreen See *screenprinting.* **(8.20)**

silverpoint See *metalpoint.*

simultaneous contrast The perceptual phenomenon whereby *complementary* colors appear most brilliant when set side by side. **(4.28)**

site-specific Descriptive of art that was conceived for display in a particular place, and which generally can only be fully understood in the context of that place. **(11.27)**

stained glass The technique of creating images or decorations from precisely cut pieces of colored glass held together with strips of lead. **(12.5)**

still life A painting or other two-dimensional work in which the subject matter is an arrangement of objects—fruit, flowers, tableware, pottery, and so forth—brought together for their pleasing contrasts of shape, color, and texture. Also, the arrangement of objects itself. **(5.16)**

stippling A pattern of closely spaced dots or small marks used to create a sense of three-dimensionality on a flat surface, especially in drawing and printmaking. See also *cross-hatching, hatching.* **(4.22)**

stupa A shrine, usually dome-shaped, associated with Buddhism. **(19.3)**

style A characteristic, or a number of characteristics, that we can identify as constant, recurring, or coherent. In art, the sum of such characteristics associated with a particular artist, group, or culture, or with an artist's work at a specific time.

stylized Descriptive of *representational* art in which methods for depicting *forms* have become standardized, and can thus be repeated without further observation of the real-world model. Compare *abstract.* **(2.18)**

subject matter In *representational* or *abstract* art, the objects or events depicted. **(2.24, 2.25)**

sunken relief See *relief*. **(14.16)**

support The surface on which a work of two-dimensional art is made; for example, canvas, paper, or wood.

Surrealism A movement of the early 20th century that emphasized imagery from dreams and fantasies. **(21.25)**

suspension A structural system in architecture, most common in bridges, in which the weight of a horizontal member is suspended from steel cables supported by uprights called pylons. **(13.25)**

symbol An image or sign that represents something else, because of convention, association, or resemblance. **(10.1)**

symmetrical Descriptive of a design in which the two halves of a composition on either side of an imaginary central vertical *axis* correspond to one another in size, shape, and placement. **(5.8)**

tapestry An elaborate textile meant to be hung from a wall and featuring images and motifs produced by various weaving techniques. **(12.13)**

tempera Paint in which the pigment is compounded with an aqueous, emulsified *vehicle* such as egg yolk. **(7.5)**

tensile strength In architecture, the ability of a material to span horizontal distances with minimum support from underneath.

terra cotta Italian for "baked earth." A *ceramic* ware, usually reddish, fired in the low temperature ranges and somewhat porous and fragile; earthenware. **(12.3)**

tertiary colors Colors made by mixing a primary color and an adjacent secondary color (for example, red and violet). **(4.24)**

tint A color lighter than a hue's normal value. Pink is a tint of red. **(4.26)**

transept The arm of a cruciform church perpendicular to the *nave*. The transept often marks the beginning of the *apse*. **(15.15)**

triadic harmony A color scheme based in three *hues* equidistant from one another on the *color wheel*, such as yellow-orange, blue-green, and red-violet. **(21.9)**

triptych A composition consisting of three panels side by side, generally hinged in such a way that the outer two panels can close like shutters over the central one. **(16.21)**

trompe l'oeil French for "fool the eye," *representational* art that mimics optical experience so faithfully that it may be mistaken momentarily for reality. **(2.15)**

typeface In graphic design, a style of type. **(10.7)**

typography In graphic design, the arrangement and appearance of printed letter forms (type). **(10.8)**

value The relative lightness or darkness of a *hue*, or of a *neutral* varying from white to black. **(4.26)**

vanishing point In *linear perspective*, the point on the horizon where parallel lines appear to converge. **(4.44)**

vault An arched masonry structure or roof that spans an interior space. A **barrel vault** is a half-round arch extended in depth. A **groin vault** is formed by the intersection of two barrel vaults of equal size at right angles. A **ribbed vault** is a groin vault in which the lines marking the intersection of the vaults are reinforced with a raised rib. A **corbelled vault** is a vault made with the technique of **corbelling**, in which each course of stone projects slightly beyond the one below to create an arch form (but not a true, weight-bearing arch). **(13.10)**

vehicle Another term for *medium*, in the sense of a liquid compounded with pigment to make paint.

visual weight The apparent "heaviness" or "lightness" of the forms arranged in a composition, as gauged by how insistently they draw the viewer's eye. **(5.10)**

volume Similar to *mass*, a three-dimensional *form* implying bulk, density, and weight; but also a void or empty, enclosed space. **(4.41)**

volute In architecture, a spiral, scroll-like ornament such as the *capital* of a column in the *Ionic order*. **(13.4)**

warm colors Colors ranged along the orange curve of the *color wheel*, from red through yellow. **(4.24)**

wash Ink or *watercolor* paint thinned so as to flow freely onto a *support*. **(6.11)**

watercolor A painting *medium* in which the *binder* is gum Arabic. **(7.12)**

woodcut A *relief* printmaking method in which a block of wood is carved so as to leave the image areas raised from the background. Also, the resultant *print*. **(8.7)**

wood engraving Similar to *woodcut*, a *relief* printmaking process in which the image is cut on the end grain of a wood plank, resulting in a "white-line" impression. **(8.8)**

ziggurat In ancient Mesopotamian architecture, a monumental stepped structure symbolically understood as a mountain and serving as a platform for one or more temples. **(14.4)**

PHOTOGRAPHIC CREDITS

Abbreviations:
AR = Art Resource, NY
ARS, NY = Artists Rights Society (ARS), New York
B-G/AR = Bridgeman-Giraudon/Art Resource, NY
BPK/AR = Bildarchiv Preussischer Kulturbesitz/Art Resource, NY
L/AR = Erich Lessing/Art Resource, NY
RMN/AR = Réunion des Musées Nationaux/Art Resource, NY
S/AR = Scala/Art Resource, NY

Front cover: Eve Sussman and The Rufus Corporation, Dog Rolls, 2004. The Rufus Corporation in a Video Still from "89 Seconds at Alcázar" by Eve Sussman and The Rufus Corporation. Photo: Eve Sussman and The Rufus Corporation. © 2004 All rights reserved. Courtesy Eve Sussman and The Rufus Corporation.

Back cover: Diego Velázquez, *Las Meninas*, 1656. Oil on canvas; 10 ft. 7 in. x 9 ft. ½ in. (3.23 x 2.76m). Museo del Prado, Madrid. Erich Lessing/Art Resource, NY.

Chapter 1: 1.1 © Michel Denancé/Renzo Piano/Artedia. © 2008 ARS, NY/ADAGP, Paris; **1.2** CNAC/MNAM/Dist RMN/AR. © 2008 ARS, NY/ADAGP, Paris; **1.3** Courtesy of the French Ministry of Culture and Communication, Regional Direction for Cultural Affairs - Rhône-Alpes, Regional Department of Archaeology. Photo: Jean Clottes. Slide 26. (www.culture.gouv.fr/rhone-alpes/chauvet/anglais/lettre3/album.htm); **1.4** © Alvis Upitis/Getty Images; **1.5** By Courtesy of Institute of Archaeology and Cultural Relics of Shandong Province. © Cultural Relics Publishing House, Beijing; **1.6** © Catherine Karnow/Corbis; **1.7** The Newark Museum/Art Resource, NY; **1.8** HIP/Art Resource, NY; **1.9** Rijksmuseum, Amsterdam; **1.10** The Museum of Modern Art, New York. Acquired through the Lillie P. Bliss Bequest. Digital Image © The Museum of Modern Art/Licensed by SCALA/Art Resource, NY; **1.11** © Ernst Haas. Image via Hulton/Archive by Getty Images; **1.12** Courtesy of ACE Gallery and Andrea Nasher; **1.13** Wadsworth Atheneum, Hartford. The Ella Gallup Sumner and Mary Catlin Sumner Collection Fund, 1939.270; **1.14** Courtesy Louis K. Meisel Gallery, New York; **1.15** Philadelphia Museum of Art. Purchased with funds contributed by Mr. and Mrs. W. B. Dixon Stroud. Acc. # 1995-55-1 Courtesy of the artist and CRG Gallery.

p. 8 © Bettmann/Corbis
p. 11 S/AR
p. 17 Image © Board of Trustees, National Gallery of Art, Washington, Archives Collection

Chapter 2: 2.1 © The National Gallery, London; **2.2** Photograph courtesy Robert Watts Studio Archive, New York; **2.3** The Andy Warhol Foundation, Inc./Art Resource, NY. © 2008 Andy Warhol Foundation for the Visual Arts/ARS, NY; **2.4, 2.18** RMN/AR; **2.5** Museum of Fine Arts, Boston, Massachusetts, USA /Bridgeman Art Library; **2.6** © Quattrone - Firenze; **2.7** MAK - Austrian Museum of Applied Arts/Contemporary Art, Vienna. Photograph: © MAK/Georg Mayer; **2.8** Smithsonian American Art Museum, Washington, DC/Art Resource, NY; **2.9** Collection Center for Creative Photography, ©1981 Center for Creative Photography, Arizona Board of Regents; **2.10** Cameraphoto/Art

Resource, NY; **2.11** S/AR; **2.12** B-G/AR © 2008 Estate of Pablo Picasso/ARS, NY; **2.13** S/AR. © 2008 Estate of Pablo Picasso/ARS, NY; **2.14** Cheim and Reid Gallery. Courtesy Louise Bourgeois Studios. Photograph by Christopher Burke. Art © Louise Bourgeois/Licensed by VAGA, New York, NY; **2.15** Courtesy Mrs. Duane Hanson. Art © Estate of Duane Hanson/Licensed by VAGA, New York, NY; **2.16** Werner Forman/Art Resource, NY; **2.17** Ursula Held; **2.19** CNAC/MNAM/RMN/AR. © 2008 ARS, NY/ADAGP, Paris; **2.20** Courtesy of the artist and Jack Tilton Gallery, New York; **2.21** Art Gallery of South Australia, Adelaide; **2.22** The Metropolitan Museum of Art, H. O. Havemeyer Collection, Bequest of Mrs. H. O. Havemeyer, 1929 (29.100.35). Photograph © 1984 The Metropolitan Museum of Art; **2.23** Courtesy Sperone Westwater, New York. © 2008 Susan Rothenberg/ARS, NY; **2.24** The Museum of Modern Art, New York. Digital Image © The Museum of Modern Art/Licensed by SCALA/Art Resource, NY. © 2008 Succession H. Matisse, Paris/ARS, NY; **2.25** The Barnes Foundation, Merion, Pennsylvania, USA/Bridgeman Art Library. © 2008 Succession H. Matisse, Paris/ARS, NY; **2.26, 2.29** L/AR; **2.27 a-e** Courtesy of the artist and Luhring Augustine, New York; **2.28** © Sakamoto Photo Research Laboratory/Corbis; **2.30** © The National Gallery, London; **2.31** © abm – archives barbier-mueller – Photographer Pierre-Alain Ferrazzini; **2.32** Photo courtesy Professor Herbert M. Cole; **2.33** Cameraphoto/Art Resource, NY; **2.34** Courtesy Marian Goodman Gallery, New York; **2.35** Courtesy of the artist; **2.36** © Horace Bristol /Corbis; **2.37** The Collection of Robin B. Martin, The Guennol Collection, The Brooklyn Museum. Photograph Justin Kerr; **2.38** Photo: Walter Vögel. Courtesy Ronald Feldman Fine Arts, New York. © 2008 ARS, NY/VG Bild-Kunst, Bonn; **2.39** Carol Beckwith/Angela Fisher, Robert Estall Photo Library; **2.40** Courtesy: Sean Kelly Gallery, New York. Photo: Thibault Jeanson; **2.41** © The Felix Gonzalez-Torres Foundation. Courtesy of Andrea Rosen Gallery, NY. Photo: Paul Jeremias, The Solomon R. Guggenheim Foundation, New York.

p. 25 Private Collection. Photograph by Michael Gray, courtesy of GRACE (Grass Roots Art and Community Effort)
p. 31 Photo courtesy Cheim and Read. Art © Louise Bourgeois/Licensed by VAGA, New York, NY
p. 45 Victoria & Albert Museum, London/Art Resource, NY

Chapter 3: 3.1 Gift of Clark Field, 1948.39.37. © The Philbrook Museum of Art, Tulsa, Oklahoma; **3.2** © Margaret Courtney-Clarke; **3.3** © Gérard Degeorge; **3.4** Art Resource, NY; **3.5** A.F. Kersting, London; **3.6** Los Angeles County Museum of Art, from the Nasli and Alice Heeramaneck Collection, Museum Associates Purchase. Photograph © 2007 Museum Associates/LACMA; **3.7** Galleria degli Uffizi, Florence, Italy/Giraudon/Bridgeman Art Library; **3.8** Bill Viola, The Crossing, 1996, video/sound installation, consists of two pictures one of fire and one of water. Collection: Edition 1, Collection of the Solomon R. Guggenheim Museum, New York, gift of The Bohen Foundation. Edition 2, Collection of Pamela and Richard Kramlich, San Francisco. Edition 3, Dallas Museum of Art, Texas. Photo: Kira Perov; **3.9** Carolyn Clarke/Spectrum Color Library, London; **3.10,**

3.17, 3.25 S/AR; **3.11** RMN/AR; **3.12** Museo Nacional Centro de Arte Reina Sofia, Photographic Archive, Madrid, Spain. © 2008 Estate of Pablo Picasso/ARS, NY; **3.13** Tate Gallery, London/Art Resource, NY. Courtesy of the artist and Mary Boone Gallery, New York; **3.14** © The National Gallery, London; **3.15** By Permission of the British Library, London, MS. Add. 15297(1), fol. 34r; **3.16** The Museum of Contemporary Art, Los Angeles, Gift of Peter and Eileen Norton. Photo: Paula Goldman. © 2008 ARS, NY/ADAGP, Paris; **3.18** Special Chinese and Japanese Fund, 12.886. Museum of Fine Arts, Boston. Photograph © 2007 Museum of Fine Arts, Boston; **3.19** © The National Gallery, London; **3.20** Fondation Beyeler, Riehen/Basel. Art © Robert Rauschenberg /Licensed by VAGA, New York, NY; **3.21** Photo © Estate of Raghubir Singh; **3.22** Museum of Afro-American History, Boston; **3.23** Courtesy Brent Sikkema, NYC; **3.24** Image © Board of Trustees, National Gallery of Art, Washington, Widener Collection. 1942.9.97 (693)/PA; **3.26** The Museum of Modern Art, New York, Gift of Nelson A. Rockefeller. Digital Image © The Museum of Modern Art/Licensed by SCALA/Art Resource, NY; **3.27** Courtesy Deitch Projects and American Fine Arts, New York; **3.28** The Metropolitan Museum of Art, New York, Gift of Mrs. Russell Sage, 1908 (08.228). Photograph © 1995 The Metropolitan Museum of Art; **3.29** Freer Gallery of Art and Arthur M. Sackler Gallery, Smithsonian Institution, Washington DC. Purchase F1956.27; **3.30** Photo credit: Haruzo Ohashi, Saitama; **3.31** Estate of Robert Smithson, Courtesy James Cohan Gallery, New York. Collection: DIA Center for the Arts, New York. Photo by Gianfranco Gorgoni. Art © Estate of Robert Smithson/Licensed by VAGA, New York, NY; **3.32** Honolulu Academy of Arts, Gift of James A. Michener, 1991 (22,941). Permission of Honolulu Academy of Arts must be obtained before any re-use of this image; **3.33** Courtesy Marian Goodman Gallery, New York; **3.34** © 2005 Pat Steir. Courtesy Cheim & Read, New York.

p. 55 left © R. Edwards. Courtesy ACSAA Color Slide Project, University of Michigan, #2871
p. 55 right AP/Wide World Photos
p. 68 © Richard Schulman/Corbis
p. 78 The Art Institute of Chicago, Ryerson Collection. Photography © The Art Institute of Chicago.

Chapter 4: 4.1 Yale University Art Gallery, New Haven. Bequest of Stephen Carlton Clark, B. A. 1903. 1961.18.29; **4.2** Stiftung Sammlung Marx, Hamburger Bahnhof - Museum für Gegenwart, Berlin. © The Estate of Keith Haring. Photograph courtesy of Heiner Bastian Fine Art; **4.3** Courtesy of the artist; **4.4** Courtesy Regen Projects, Los Angeles; **4.5** © Henri Cartier-Bresson/Magnum Photos; **4.6** Image © Board of Trustees, National Gallery of Art, Washington,. Gift of Mr. and Mrs. Cornelius Vanderbilt Whitney. 1953.7.1. (PA); **4.7** Image © Board of Trustees, National Gallery of Art, Washington, Gift of Mr. and Mrs. Cornelius Vanderbilt Whitney. 1953.7.1. (PA); **4.8, 4.9** RMN/AR; **4.10, 4.11** Artothek; **4.12** Courtesy of the Collection of the Museum of Anthropology, University of British Columbia, Vancouver, Canada. Photo: Bill McLennan; **4.13** Saint Louis Art Museum. Museum Shop Fund. © Emmi Whitehorse; **4.14** Württembergisches Landesmuseum, Stuttgart; **4.16** Kunsthistorisches Museum,

589

Vienna, Austria; **4.17** © James Turrell, courtesy PaceWildenstein, New York. Photo Robert Baldridge; **4.18** Collection Center for Creative Photography. The University of Arizona, Tucson. © Manuel Alvarez Bravo; **4.20** © The National Gallery, London; **4.21** © 1979 The Charles White Archives. Photographer: Darryl Allan Smith; **4.23 a** © Clayton Price Photography/Corbis; **4.25** Sterling and Francine Clark Institute, Williamstown, Massachusetts. 1955.827; **4.28** Rubin Museum of Art, New York. C2003.50.3 (HAR 129); **4.29** Courtesy Rebecca Ibel Gallery in Ohio; **4.31, 4.32** The Art Institute of Chicago, Helen Birch Bartlett Memorial Collection, 1926.224. Photography © The Art Institute of Chicago; **4.33** © Chuck Close, courtesy PaceWildenstein, New York. Photograph by K. Schles; **4.34** Tate Gallery, London/Art Resource, NY; **4.35** Munch-Museet. Nasjonalgalleriet, Oslo, Norway. Photo: J. Lathion, Nasjonalgalleriet. © 2008 The Munch Museum/The Munch-Ellingsen Group/ARS, NY; **4.36** © Mona Hatoum. Photographer Edward Woodman. Courtesy Jay Jopling/White Cube (London); **4.37** Image © Board of Trustees, National Gallery of Art, Washington, Gift of Eugene and Agnes E. Meyer. 1967.13.3. © 2008 ARS, NY/ADAGP, Paris; **4.38** Image © Board of Trustees, National Gallery of Art, Washington, Ailsa Mellon Bruce Collection. 1970.17.30. © 2008 ARS, NY/ADAGP, Paris; **4.39** CNAC/MNAM/Dist. RMN/AR. Copyright Samuel Foss, courtesy D Shainman Gallery NY/JM. Patras, Paris; **4.40** Hirshhorn Museum and Sculpture Garden, Smithsonian Institution, Gift of Joseph H. Hirshhorn, 1972. Photo: Lee Stalsworth. © 2008 ARS, NY/ADAGP, Paris; **4.41** Photo: © Timothy Hursley; **4.42** The Metropolitan Museum of Art, New York, Gift of Mr. and Mrs. Carl Bimel Jr., 1996 (1996.357). Photograph © 1996 The Metropolitan Museum of Art; **4.44, 4.46** BPK/AR; **4.45** Canali Photobank, Milan, Italy; **4.47** Foto Marburg/Art Resource, NY; **4.48** The Metropolitan Museum of Art, New York, Rogers Fund, 1907 (07.123). Photograph © 1986 The Metropolitan Museum of Art; **4.49** National Palace Museum, Taipei, Taiwan, Republic of China; **4.51** Topkapi Palace Library, Istanbul. MS. H. 1517, folio 108v; **4.52** Juliana Cheney Edwards Collection, Bequest of Robert J. Edwards in memory of his mother (25.112). Museum of Fine Arts. Boston. Photograph © 2007 Museum of Fine Arts, Boston; **4.53** Albright-Knox Art Gallery, Buffalo, New York, Bequest of A. Conger Goodyear and Gift of George F. Goodyear, 1964. © 2008 ARS, NY/SIAE, Rome; **4.54** Photograph by Jerry L. Thompson, courtesy Storm King Art Center, Mountainville, NY. © 2008 Estate of Alexander Calder/ARS, NY; **4.55** The Museum of Modern Art, New York, Gift of Charles and Anita Blatt, 1969. Digital Image © The Museum of Modern Art/Licensed by SCALA/Art Resource, NY. © The Estate of Eva Hesse. Hauser & Wirth Zürich London; **4.56** Photo: Eve Sussman and The Rufus Corporation. © 2004 All rights reserved. Courtesy Eve Sussman and The Rufus Corporation; **4.57** Courtesy of the Artist and Lehmann Maupin Gallery, New York.

p. 102 left Honolulu Academy of Arts, Gift of James A. Michener, 1976, (16,822)
p. 102 right Honolulu Academy of Arts, Gift of James A. Michener, 1991 (22,792)
p. 111 left © Eric Vandeville
p. 111 right L/AR

Chapter 5: 5.1 The Museum of Modern Art, New York. Digital Image © The Museum of Modern Art/Licensed by SCALA/Art Resource, NY. © 2008 Succession H. Matisse, Paris/ARS, NY; **5.2** The Museum of Modern Art, New York. Digital Image © The Museum of Modern Art/Licensed by SCALA/Art Resource, NY. © 2008 Pollock-Krasner Foundation/ARS, NY; **5.3** © permission of the artist and courtesy of Marian Goodman Gallery. © 2008 ARS, NY/ADAGP, Paris; **5.4** National Gallery of Canada, Ottawa. Photo © National Gallery of Canada. Art © The Joseph and Robert Cornell Memorial Foundation/Licensed by VAGA, New York, NY; **5.5** Courtesy of the Isamu Noguchi Foundation, Inc. Photographed by Michio Noguchi. © 2008 The Isamu Noguchi Foundation and Garden Museum, New York/ARS, NY; **5.6** Gift of the William H. Lane Foundation, 1990.432. Museum of Fine Arts. Boston. Photograph © 2008 Museum of Fine Arts, Boston. © 2008 The Georgia O'Keeffe Museum/Artist Rights Society (ARS), New York; **5.7** The Metropolitan Museum of Art, Purchase, Lita Annenberg Hazen Charitable Trust Gift, 1987 (1987.16). Photograph © 1997 The Metropolitan Museum of Art; **5.8** Courtesy the Luo Brothers and Ray Hughes Gallery, Australia; **5.9** Bob Schalkwijk/Art Resource, NY/© 2007 Banco de Mexico Diego Rivera & Frida Kahuems Trust. Av. Cinco de Mayo No.2, Col. Centro, Del. Cauahtémoc 06059, Mexico, D. F./INBA; **5.11, 5.17, 5.32** L/AR; **5.12** © The Cleveland Museum of Art, 2007. Norman O. and Ella S. Stone Memorial Fund, 1958.289; **5.13** Philadelphia Museum of Art: The John H. McFadden Collection. 1928. Photo: Graydon Wood; **5.14** The Samuel Courtauld Trust, Courtauld Institute of Art Gallery, London; **5.15** Hampton University Museum, Hampton, Virginia; **5.16** © The Barnes Foundation, Merion, Pennsylvania, USA/Bridgeman Art Library; **5.18** © Claes Oldenburg and Coosje van Bruggen; **5.19** Hirshhorn Museum and Sculpture Garden, Smithsonian Institution, Washington, DC, Gift of Joseph H. Hirshhorn, 1966. Photo: Lee Stalsworth. © 2008 C. Herscovici, Brussels/ARS, NY. HMSG 66.3199; **5.20** © The Trustees of The British Museum; **5.21** HIP/Art Resource, NY; **5.22** B-G/AR; **5.23** S/AR; **5.25** © Fondation Le Corbusier/© 2008 ARS, NY/ADAGP, Paris/FLC; **5.26** Vanni/Art Resource, NY; **5.27** Courtesy: Sean Kelly Gallery, New York; **5.28** The Museum of the Imperial Collections, Sannomaru Shozokan; **5.29** Hans Hinz - Artothek. © 2008 ARS, NY/VG Bild-Kunst, Bonn; **5.30** Alinari/Art Resource, NY; **5.31** The Museum of Modern Art, New York Gift of Mrs. Simon Guggenheim. Digital Image © The Museum of Modern Art/Licensed by SCALA/Art Resource, NY. © 2008 Estate of Pablo Picasso/ARS, NY; **5.33** Image © Board of Trustees, National Gallery of Art, Washington, DC. , Andrew W. Mellon Collection. 1937.1.34; **5.34** The Museum of Modern Art, New York, Gift of Mrs. Simon Guggenheim. Digital Image © The Museum of Modern Art/Licensed by SCALA/Art Resource, NY. © 2008 Estate of Pablo Picasso/ARS, NY.

p. 126 The Metropolitan Museum of Art, New York, Gift of Georgia O'Keeffe through the generosity of The Georgia O'Keeffe Foundation and Jennifer and Joseph Duke, 1997 (1997.61.34). Photograph © 1996 The Metropolitan Museum of Art
p. 133 © Bibliothèque Nationale de France, Paris

Chapter 6: 6.1 Eugene and Clara Thaw Collection, Fenimore Art Museum, Cooperstown, NY. Photo: John Bigelow Taylor, NYC; **6.2** Museo Nacional Centro de Arte Reina Sofia, Photographic Archive, Madrid, Spain. © 2008 Estate of Pablo Picasso/ARS, NY; **6.3** The Metropolitan Museum of Art, New York, H. O. Havemeyer Collection, Bequest of Mrs. H. O. Havemeyer, 1929 (29.100.941). Photograph © 1987 The Metropolitan Museum of Art; **6.4** The Royal Collection © 2007, Her Majesty Queen Elizabeth II; **6.5** The Museum of Modern Art, New York. Gift of David Teiger and the Friends of Contemporary Drawing. (393.1999). Digital Image © The Museum of Modern Art/Licensed by SCALA/Art Resource, NY. Courtesy Chris Ofili - Afroco; **6.6** The Museum of Modern Art, New York. Gift of David Teiger and the Friends of Contemporary Drawing. (393.1999). Digital Image © The Museum of Modern Art/Licensed by SCALA/Art Resource, NY. Courtesy Chris Ofili - Afroco; **6.7** The Metropolitan Museum of Art, Harris Brisbane Dick Fund, 1936 (36.101.1). Photograph © 1997 The Metropolitan Museum of Art; **6.8** Hirshhorn Museum and Sculpture Garden, Washington, D.C. HMSG 83.153 Courtesy DC Moore Gallery, New York, NY; **6.9** © The Cleveland Museum of Art, 2007. Leonard C. Hanna Jr., Fund, 1958.344; **6.10** The Metropolitan Museum of Art, Bequest of Stephen C. Clark, 1960 (61.101.7). Photograph © 1987 The Metropolitan Museum of Art; **6.11** The Metropolitan Museum of Art, H. O. Havemeyer Collection, Bequest of Mrs. H. O. Havemeyer, 1929 (29.100.939). Photograph © 1995 The Metropolitan Museum of Art; **6.12** Seattle Art Museum, Gift of the ContemporaryArt Project, Seattle. acc. no. 2002.30. Courtesy of the artist and The Project, New York; **6.13** CNAC/MNAM/Dist. RMN/AR © 2008 Succession H. Matisse, Paris/ARS, NY; **6.14** Courtesy Maureen Paley, London; **6.15, 6.16** Courtesy the artist and Regen Projects, Los Angeles; **6.17** Collection of Barbara Gladstone, New York. © 2008 Sol LeWitt/ARS, NY; **6.18** Photo courtesy Elise Engler. Photo: James Whitaker; **6.19** Courtesy of the Artist and Metro Pictures Gallery.

p. 151 S/AR

p. 153 New York Public Library. Spencer Collection, Persian ms. 41, folios 21b, 22a. The New York Public Library/Art Resource, NY.

Chapter 7: 7.1 L/AR; **7.2** Albright-Knox Art Gallery, Buffalo, New York, Gift of Seymour H. Knox, Jr., 1959. Art © Jasper Johns/Licensed by VAGA, New York, NY; **7.3** S/AR; **7.4** Bob Schalkwijk/Art Resource, NY. © 2007 Banco de Mexico Diego Rivera & Frida Kahlo Museums Trust. Av. Cinco de Mayo No.2, Col. Centro, Del. Cauahtémoc 06059, Mexico, D. F./INBA; **7.5** Dallas Museum of Art. Dallas Art Association purchase, 1962.27. © Andrew Wyeth; **7.6** Hirshhorn Museum and Sculpture Garden, Smithsonian Institution, Washington, D.C. Gift of Joseph H. Hirshhorn, 1966. HMSG 66.2920. © 2008 The Jacob and Gwendolyn Lawrence Foundation, Seattle/ARS, NY; **7.7** © The National Gallery, London; **7.8** Copyright The Frick Collection, New York; **7.9** Sterling and Francine Clark Art Institute, Williamstown, Massachusetts. Inv. /Acc. no. 1955.926; **7.10** Collection Fonds régional d'art contemporain Provence-Alpes-Côtes d'Azur, France. Photo: Gérard Bonnet. © The Estate of Joan Mitchell; **7.11** IVAM Centre Julio González Collection, Valencia, Spain. © Elizabeth Murray. Courtesy PaceWildenstein Gallery, New York. Photograph by Ellen Page Wilson; **7.12** The Metropolitan Museum of Art, Purchase, Joseph Pulitzer Bequest, 1915 (15.142.2). Photograph © 1989 The Metropolitan Museum of Art; **7.13** Courtesy the artist and Gavin Brown's Enterprise (Modern); **7.14** The Museum of Modern Art, New York, Inter-American Fund. Digital Image © The Museum of Modern Art/Licensed by SCALA/Art Resource, NY. © 2008 ARS, NY/ADAGP, Paris; **7.15** The Metropolitan Museum of Art. Purchase, Mrs. Arthur Hays Sulzberger Girft, 1972 (1972.128). Photograph by Lynton Gardiner. Photograph © 1977 The Metropolitan Museum of Art. © David Hockney; **7.16** Courtesy Blum & Poe, Los Angeles, and Takashi Murakami/Kaikai Kiki. Photo: Yoshitaka Uchinda. Courtesy: Blum & Poe and Kaikai Kiki. Reproduced with permission. © 1998 Takashi Murakami. All rights reserved; **7.17** Collection of the McNay Art Museum, Bequest of Marion Koogler McNay. © 2008 Estate of Pablo Picasso/ARS, NY; **7.18** Ellen Kelleran Gardner Fund, 1971. 63 Museum of Fine Arts. Boston. Photograph © 2007 Museum of Fine Arts, Boston. Art © Romare Bearden Foundation/Licensed by VAGA, New York, NY; **7.19** Courtesy James Cohan Gallery, New York; **7.20** Image courtesy of the artist and D'Amelio Terras, New York; **7.21** Courtesy of Andrea Rosen Gallery, NY.

p. 174 National Academy of Design, New York. © 2008 The Jacob and Gwendolyn Lawrence Foundation, Seattle/ARS, NY

Chapter 8: 8.2 Art Resource, NY; **8.3** HIP/Art Resource, NY; **8.4** The Art Institute of Chicago. Clarence Buckingham Collection, 1934.207. Photography © The Art Institute of Chicago; **8.5** Courtesy Chuck Close and Published by Pace Editions, Inc; **8.6** Image © Board of Trustees, National Gallery of Art, Washington, Rosenwald Collection. 1943.3.6698. (PR) © Nolde-Stiftung Seebüll; **8.7** Lu Xun Memorial, Shanghai; **8.8** Library of Congress, Washington, DC; **8.9 a-d** Whitney Museum of American Art, New York; Purchase, with funds from the Print Committee 2000.229a-d. Photograph by Sheldan C. Collins. © Kiki Smith, courtesy PaceWildenstein, New York; **8.11, 8.15** B-G/AR; **8.12** © Bibliothèque Nationale de France, Paris. Art © Louise Bourgeois/Licensed by VAGA, New York, NY; **8.13** The Whitney Museum of American Art; Gift of Vija Celmins in honor of Flora Miller Biddle. 98.84.3. © Vija Celmins; **8.14** The Pierpont Morgan Library/Art Resource, NY; **8.16** Image © Board of Trustees, National Gallery of Art, Washington, Chester Dale Collection. 1963.10.253. (PR) 9B4; **8.17** © President and Fellows of Harvard College. Courtesy of the Fogg Art Museum, Harvard University Art Museums, Gray Collection of Engravings Fund. © 2008 ARS, NY/VG Bild-Kunst, Bonn; **8.18** RMN/AR © 2008 ARS, NY/ADAGP, Paris; **8.19** Art © Elizabeth Catlett/Licensed by VAGA, New York, NY; **8.20** The Museum of Modern Art, New York. Digital Image © The Museum of Modern Art/Licensed by SCALA/Art Resource, RY. Courtesy the artist and Leo Castelli Gallery, New York; **8.21** Smithsonian American Art Museum, Washington, D.C./Art Resource. Courtesy the artist and Gallery Paule Anglim; **8.22** Courtesy of the artist; **8.23** Courtesy Ronald Feldman Fine Arts, New York. Photo: Hermann Feldhaus; **8.24** Published by Pace Editions, Inc. Courtesy of the artist.

p. 190 B-G/AR
p. 201 Kupferstich-Kabinett, Staatliche Kunstsammlungen, Dresden, Germany. © 2008 ARS, NY/VG Bild-Kunst, Bonn

Chapter 9: 9.1 Courtesy George Eastman House, Rochester, NY; **9.3** © Bayerisches Nationalmuseum, Munich, Germany; **9.4, 9.6** Library of Congress, Washington, DC; **9.5** The Museum of Modern Art, New York. Gift of Edward Steichen. Digital Image © The Museum of Modern Art/Licensed by SCALA/Art Resource, NY; **9.7** Lorenzo D. Creel Collection, Special Collections, University of Nevada-Reno Library; **9.8** Library of Congress, Washington, DC. LC-USF34-T01-009058-C (b&w film dup. neg.); **9.9** © Liu Zheng. Courtesy Yossi Milo Gallery, New York. Courtesy of the artist and Yossi Milo Gallery, NYC; **9.10** National Museum of Photography, Film & Television; **9.11** The Art Institute of Chicago. Alfred Stieglitz Collection, 1949.705. Photography © The Art Institute of Chicago; **9.12** The Museum of Modern Art, New York, Gift of David H. McAlpin. (1731.1968). Digital Image © The Museum of Modern Art/Licensed by SCALA/Art Resource, NY. © Ansel Adams Publishing Rights Trust/Corbis; **9.13** BPK/AR. Photo: Jörg P. Anders © 2008 ARS, NY/VG Bild-Kunst, Bonn; **9.14** CNAC/MNAM/Dist. RMN/AR. © 2008 May Ray Trust/ARS, NY/ADAGP, Paris; **9.15** Courtesy of the Artist and Metro Pictures Gallery; **9.16**

© Sally Mann; Courtesy Gagosian Gallery, New York; **9.17** © Andreas Gursky, Courtesy Matthew Marks Gallery, New York. © 2008 Andreas Gursky/ARS, NY/VG Bild-Kunst, Bonn; **9.18** Courtesy VG-Bild Kunst and Artist Rights Society, NY. © 2008 George Eastman House, Rochester, NY; **9.19** Courtesy George Eastman House, Rochester, NY; **9.20, 9.21, 9.22, 9.23, 9.25, 9.29, 9.30** The Kobal Collection; **9.24** © Bettmann/Corbis; **9.26** © 2008 The Andy Warhol Museum, Pittsburgh, PA, a museum of Carnegie Institute. All rights reserved; **9.27** Courtesy Everett Collection; **9.28** Photo12.com - Collection cinéma; **9.31** Courtesy Nam June Paik and Stedelijk Museum, Amsterdam; **9.32** Courtesy of Electronic Arts Intermix, New York; **9.33** Courtesy of the Artist and Metro Pictures Gallery; **9.34** © 1999 Shirin Neshat. Courtesy Gladstone Gallery. Photo Larry Barns; **9.35** www.jodi.org; **9.36** Courtesy Postmasters Gallery, New York; **9.37** Courtesy Ben Fry. © 1999-2005. MIT Media Laboratory, Aesthetics + Computation Group © 1999-2005; **9.38** Courtesy Martin Wattenberg and Whitney Museum of American Art, New York.

p. 214 Gernsheim Collection, Harry Ransom Humanities Research Center, The University of Texas at Austin
p. 224 © Copyright The Robert Mapplethorpe Foundation. Courtesy Art + Commerce

Chapter 10: 10.2 Library of Congress, Washington, DC; **10.3 a-d** Logos for IBM (1956), Westinghouse (1960), UPS (1961), and ABC (1962). Courtesy Paul Rand Archives; **10.4** The New York Public Library/Art Resource, NY; **10.5** 0100101110101101.ORG. Eva and Franco Mattes. Courtesy Postmasters Gallery, New York; **10.6** The New York Public Library/Art Resource, NY; **10.7** Spiekermann at United Designers Network. Contact info on their site: http://www.uniteddesigncrs.com/main.php; **10.8** © Joan Dobkin; **10.9 a** Courtesy Metro North Railroad; **10.9 b** Edward R. Tufte, Envisioning Information (Cheshire, Connecticut: Graphics Press, 1990); **10.10** © David Carson; **10.11** The Metropolitan Museum of Art, New York, Harris Brisbane Dick Fund, 1932 (32.88.12). Photograph © 1996 The Metropolitan Museum of Art; **10.12** The Museum of Modern Art, New York. Gift of Susan Pack. Digital Image © The Museum of Modern Art/Licensed by SCALA/Art Resource, NY. Art © Estate of Vladimir and Gerogii Stenberg/RAO, Moscow/VAGA, New York, NY; **10.13** Courtesy Popular Science. Courtesy New York Public Library; **10.14** Courtesy John Maeda, MAEDASTUDIO; **10.15** © Apple Computer, Inc. Use with permission. All rights reserved. Apple® and the Apple logo are registered trademark of Apple Computer, Inc. Photo: Matthew Welch Photography, represented by Radical Media; **10.16** Courtesy Framestore Design; **10.17** Courtesy Cassidy Curtis. Photo © Cassidy Curtis; **10.18** Courtesy the artist. TextArc tool created by W. Bradford Paley, details available at TextArc.org.

Chapter 11: 11.1 © FMGH Guggenheim Bibao Museoa, 2007. All rights reserved. Partial or total reproduction prohibited. © TAMCB, Guggenheim Bilbao Museoa, 2007. Art © Louise Bourgeois/Licensed by VAGA, New York, NY; **11.2** © Justin Kerr; **11.3** Photograph © 1979 Dirk Bakker; **11.5** Smithsonian American Art Museum, Washington, D.C./Art Resource, NY. © 2008 Luis Jiminez/ARS, NY; **11.6** National Museum of African Art, Smithsonian Institution. Bequest of William A. McCarty-Cooper, 95-10-1. Photo: Franko Khoury; **11.7** Werner Forman/Art Resource, NY; **11.8** Photograph by Jerry L. Thompson, courtesy Storm King Art Center, Mountainville, NY. Art © Estate of David Smith/Licensed by VAGA, New York, NY; **11.9** © J. Price. Courtesy of Mark di Suvero, Space-

time C. C. and the Paula Cooper Gallery, New York; **11.10** Princeton University Art Museum, Gift of H. Kelley Rollings, Class of 1948, and Mrs. Rollings. y1995-408; **11.11** © Petah Coyne. Courtesy Galerie Lelong, New York; **11.12** Copyright Merle Greene Robertson, 1976; **11.13** © Trip/Eric Smith; **11.14** Pronin Anatoly/Art Resource, NY; **11.15** King Menkaure (Mycerinus) and Queen, Egyptian, Old Kingdom, Dynasty 4, reign of Menkaure, c. 2490-2472 BC. Found in Egypt, Giza, Menkaure Valley Temple. Greywacke, 56 × 22½ × 21¾". Harvard University–Museum of Fine Arts Expedition. 11.1738. Museum of Fine Arts. Boston. Photograph © 2007 Museum of Fine Arts, Boston; **11.16** Museum für Angewandte Kunst, Cologne. Sammlung Wilhelm Clemens. Rheinisches Bildarchiv Cologne; **11.17** Photo credit: Asanuma Photo Studio, Kyoto; **11.18** University of Pennsylvania Museum (neg. #T4-827c); **11.19, 11.20, 11.21** S/AR; **11.22** Collection of the Henry Moore Foundation. Credit: Michel Muller. The work illustrated has been reproduced by permission of the Henry Moore Foundation; **11.23** Image © Board of Trustees, National Gallery of Art, Washington, Gift of The Morris and Gwendolyn Cafritz Foundation. (1998.148.1/SC). © Magdalena Abakanowicz, courtesy, Marlborough Gallery, New York; **11.24** Milwaukee Art Museum, Gift of Contemporary Art Society. © Kiki Smith, courtesy PaceWildenstein, New York; **11.25** © Richard A. Cooke/Corbis; **11.26** © Andy Goldsworthy. Courtesy Galerie LeLong, New York; **11.27** © Richard Hunt. Photograph by Michael Melford; **11.28** Courtesy Deitch Projects, New York. Photo: Tom Powel; **11.29** Whitney Museum of American Art, New York; Purchase with funds from the Postwar Committee and the Contemporary Committee and partial gift of Betsy Wittenborn Miller. 2003.322 a-ttttttt. © Yayoi Kusama. Courtesy Robert Miller Gallery, New York; **11.30** Collection Musée d'art contemporain de Montréal. Photo Richard-Max Tremblay. A9514I1. Art © Louise Bourgeois/Licensed by VAGA, New York, NY; **11.31** Collection Musée d'art contemporain de Montréal. Photo Richard-Max Tremblay. A9514I1. Art © Louise Bourgeois/Licensed by VAGA, New York, NY; **11.32** Collection Dia Art Foundation. Photo Cathy Carver. © 2008 Stephen Flavin /ARS, NY; **11.33** © Christo 2005. Photo: Wolfgang Volz; **11.34** © Jeff Koons.

p. 271 Staatliches Museum für Völkerkunde, Munich
p. 278 BPK/AR
p. 283 Courtesy of the artist. © 2008 Richard Serra/ARS, NY
p. 290 © Christo and Jeanne-Claude/Photo: Wolfgang Volz

Chapter 12: 12.1 Courtesy of Max Protetch Gallery; **12.2** National Museum of Women in the Arts, Washington, D.C. Gift of Wallace and Wilhelmina Holladay; **12.3** © The Trustees of The British Museum © Magdelene Odundo; **12.4** © Cultural Relics Publishing House, Beijing; **12.5** Sonia Halliday Photographs; **12.6** Photo Terry Rishel. © Dale Chihuly. Courtesy of the artist; **12.7** Copyright © Patrimonio Nacional; **12.8** © The Trustees of The British Museum; **12.9** © Susan Ewing. Collection of Jean-Marie Clemes, Luxembourg. Photo by Rick Potteiger; **12.10** Werner Forman/Art Resource, NY; **12.11** Courtesy of PRITAM & EAMES; **12.12** © Justin Kerr; **12.13** The Metropolitan Museum of Art, New York, Gift of John D. Rockefeller, Jr., 1937 (37.80.6). Photograph © 1993 The Metropolitan Museum of Art; **12.14** Victoria & Albert Museum. London/Art Resource, NY; **12.15** Bequest of A Maxim Karolik. 64.619. Museum of Fine Arts. Boston. Photograph © 2007 Museum of Fine Arts, Boston; **12.16** Los Angeles County Museum of Art, Gift of Marcia Israel Collection. Photograph © 2007 Museum Associates/LACMA; **12.17** The National Museum of Modern Art, Kyoto; **12.18** The Detroit Institute of Arts. Founders Society Purchase, Miscellaneous Memorials Fund. Accession No. 1985.28. Photograph © 1986 The Detroit Institute of Arts. © Peter Voulkos; **12.19** © Judy Chicago, 1979. Collection of the Brooklyn Museum of Art, Gift of The Elizabeth A. Sackler Foundation. Photo: © Donald Woodman. © 2008 Judy Chicago /ARS, NY; **12.20** Solomon R. Guggenheim Museum, New York. Gift of Mr. and Mrs. Gus and Judith Lieber, 1988. (88.3620). © Faith Ringgold; **12.21** Musée National d'Art Moderne, Centre Pompidou, Paris. Courtesy October Gallery, London. Photograph by Martin Barlow, Oriel Mostyn Gallery, Llandvdno; **12.22** Courtesy the artist and Max Protetch Gallery, New York.

p. 295 © Jerry D. Jacka Photography

Chapter 13: 13.1 Photo courtesy Elizabeth Evanoff Etchepare; **13.2** Wim Swaan Photographic Collection Research Library, The Getty Research Institute, Los Angeles, California (96.P.21); **13.4, 13.10** S/AR; **13.6** © Archivo Iconografico, S.A./Corbis; **13.7** The MIT Press; **13.9** © Paul M.R. Maeyaert; **13.11** RMN/AR; **13.12** Spectrum Colour Library; **13.13** © Blaine Harrington III; **13.15** Image © Board of Trustees, National Gallery of Art, Washington, Samuel H. Kress Collection. 1939.1.24.(135)/PA; **13.16, 13.23** © Marvin Trachtenberg; **13.17** © Harvey Lloyd/Getty Images; **13.18, 13.20** akg-images/Jean-Louis Nou; **13.21** Guildhall Library, Corporation of London, UK/ Bridgeman Art Library; **13.22** © Stock Photos/Corbis; **13.24** © Angelo Hornak/Corbis; **13.25** © Charles O'Rear/Corbis; **13.26** © Alex Bartel /Esto. All rights reserved; **13.27** © Gardner/Halls/Architectural Association Photograph; **13.28** © Bettmann/Corbis; **13.30, 13.31** © FMGB Guggenheim Bilbao Museoa. Photograph by Erika Barahona Ede. All rights reserved; **13.32** Photograph courtesy of Paul Warchol Photography; **13.33** Roland Halbe; **13.34** © Peter Mauss/Esto. All rights reserved; **13.35** Ezra Stoller © Esto. All rights reserved; **13.36** © Richard Berenholtz Photography; **13.37, 13.39, 13.40, 13.41** Photo: © Timothy Hursley; **13.38** © Scott Frances/Esto. All rights reserved; **13.42** © Jeff Goldberg/Esto. All rights reserved; **13.43, 13.44** © Hans Schlupp/archenova; **13.45, 13.46** Photo © Hiroyuki Hirai. Courtesy Shigeru Ban Associates.

p. 340 © Bettmann/Corbis
p. 342 Photo: © Timothy Hursley

Chapter 14: 14.1 Colorphoto Hans Hinz; **14.2, 14.12, 14.28** L/AR; **14.3** F. Jack Jackson/Bruce Coleman, Inc; **14.4** Photograph: Erwin Böhm, Mainz; **14.5** University of Pennsylvania Museum (neg. #T4-1000c); **14.6, 14.17, 14.24, 14.26, 14.30, 14.31** S/AR; **14.7** The Metropolitan Museum of Art, New York, Gift of John D. Rockefeller, Jr., 1932 (32.143.2). Photograph © 1981 The Metropolitan Museum of Art; **14.8, 14.33** HIP/Art Resource, NY; **14.9, 14.15, 14.16, 14.23** BPK/AR; **14.10** Spectrum Colour Library; **14.11** B-G/AR; **14.13** Luise Villota/Bruce Coleman, Inc; **14.14** Werner Forman/Art Resource, NY; **14.18** The Metropolitan Museum of Art, New York, Gift of Christos G. Bastis, 1968 (68.148). Photograph © 1996 The Metropolitan Museum of Art; **14.19, 14.20, 14.29** Nimatallah/Art Resource, NY; **14.21** The Metropolitan Museum of Art, New York, Rogers Fund, 1914 (14.130.14). Photograph © 1996 The Metropolitan Museum of Art; **14.22** The Metropolitan Museum of Art, New York, Fletcher Fund, 1932 (32.11.1). Photograph © 1997 The Metropolitan Museum of Art; **14.25** With permission of the Royal Ontario Museum, © ROM; **14.27** © The Trustees of The British Museum; **14.32** © Robert Harding Picture Library.

p. 362 Photography by Egyptian Expedition, The Metropolitan Museum of Art. Image © The Metropolitan Museum of Art
p. 369 © The Trustees of The British Museum

Chapter 15: 15.1, 15.5, 15.8, 15.23, 15.25 S/AR; **15.3** The New York Public Library, Miriam and Ira D. Wallack Division of Art, Prints and Photographs; **15.6** akg-images/Heiner Heine; **15.9** B-G/AR; **15.10** Courtesy The Holy Monastery of St. Catherine, Sinai, Egypt and The Metropolitan Museum of Art. Photograph by Bruce White; **15.11** © The Trustees of The British Museum; **15.12** Library of Trinity College, Dublin, MS. 57, fol. 191v. The Board of Trinity College Dublin; **15.13** akg-images/Hilbich; **15.14** Erich Lessing/Art Resource, NY; **15.16** © Paul M.R. Maeyaert; **15.17** Tapisserie de Bayeux, Musee de l'Eveche, Bayeux, by special permission of the City of Bayeaux; **15.18** Adam Woolfitt/Woodfin Camp & Associates, Inc; **15.19** John Elk III/Bruce Coleman, Inc; **15.21** © Edouard Fiévet; **15.22** © James Austin; **15.24** The Pierpont Morgan Library/Art Resource, NY; **15.26** Alinari/ Art Resource, NY.

Chapter 16: 16.1, 16.2, 16.3, 16.4, 16.6, 16.9, 16.13, 16.16, 16.28 S/AR; **16.7** Copyright The Frick Collection, New York; **16.8, 16.17, 16.20** RMN/AR; **16.10** Monumenti Musei e Gallerie Pontificie, Vatican, Rome, Italy, Photo Vatican Museums: A. Bracchetti - P. Zigrossi, Mar. 2004; **16.11** Monumenti Musei e Gallerie Pontificie, Vatican, Rome, Italy, Photo Vatican Museums: A. Bracchetti - P. Zigrossi, Mar. 1992; **16.12** Photo Vatican Museums/A. Bracchetti - P. Zigrossi © 2000 24734 D; **16.15** Nicolo Orsi Battaglini/Art Resource, NY; **16.18** Image © Board of Trustees, National Gallery of Art, Washington, Samuel H. Kress Collection. 1952.2.11. (PA); **16.19, 16.27** L/AR; **16.21** The Metropolitan Museum of Art, New York, The Cloisters Collection, 1956 (56.70). Photograph © 1996 The Metropolitan Museum of Art; **16.22** Gift of Mr. and Mrs. Henry Lee Higginson, 93.153. Museum of Fine Arts. Boston. Photograph © 2007 Museum of Fine Arts, Boston; **16.23** B-G/AR; **16.24, 16.26** © The National Gallery, London; **16.25** The Metropolitan Museum of Art, New York, Rogers Fund, 1919 (19.164). Photograph © 1998 The Metropolitan Museum of Art.

p. 402 L/AR

Chapter 17: 17.1 akg-images/Pirozzi; **17.2, 17.4, 17.6** S/AR; **17.5** The Detroit Institute of Arts, Gift of Mr. Leslie H. Green. Photograph © 1984 The Detroit Institute of Arts. 52.253; **17.7** Onze Lieve Vrouwkerk, Antwerp Cathedral, Belgium/Peter Willi/Bridgeman Art Library; **17.8** Walker Art Gallery, National Museums Liverpool; **17.9** © Jose Fuste Raga/Corbis; **17.10, 17.13, 17.17, 17.18** RMN/AR; **17.11** Institut Amatller d'Art Hispanic, © Museo del Prado. All rights reserved; **17.12** Rijksmuseum, Amsterdam; **17.14** Artothek; **17.15** L/AR; **17.16** Copyright The Frick Collection, New York; **17.19** Musées Royaux des Beaux-Arts de Belgique, Museum of Modern Art, Bruxelles Inv. 3260 Ekta nr MD019 © MRBAB/KMSKB (Photo Cussac); **17.20** Gift of Joseph W. William B., and Edward H.R. Revere, 30.781. Museum of Fine Arts, Boston. Photograph © 2007 Museum of Fine Arts, Boston.

p. 431 L/AR
p. 436 Carnegie Museum of Art, Pittsburgh, Howard A. Noble Fund. 66.12. Photo: Tom Barr
p. 440 S/AR

Chapter 18: 18.1 © Roger Wood/Corbis; **18.2** Institut Amatller d'Art Hispanic, © Museo del Prado. All rights reserved; **18.3** © Barbara Brend; **18.4** Robert Harding Picture Library; **18.5** © Eddi Böhnke/zefa/Corbis; **18.6** The Metropolitan Museum of Art, Rogers Fund, 1955 (55.44). Photograph © 1992 The Metropolitan Museum of Art; **18.7** Freer Gallery of Art, Smithsonian Institution, Washington, DC: Purchase F1956.14 folio 22r; **18.8** HIP/Art Resource, NY; **18.9** BPK/AR; **18.10** Photograph © 1979 Dirk Bakker; **18.11** Photo: Eliot Elisofon, 1970. Image no. 7590. Eliot Elisofon Photographic Archives, National Museum of African Art, Smithsonian Institution, Washington, DC; **18.12** © John Pemberton III; **18.13** © The Trustees of The British Museum; **18.14** The Metropolitan Museum of Art, New York, Gift of Lester Wunderman, 1977 (1977.394.15). Photograph © 1993 The Metropolitan Museum of Art; **18.15** The Metropolitan Museum of Art, New York, The Michael C. Rockefeller Memorial Collection, Bequest of Nelson A. Rockefeller, 1979 (1979.206.121). Photograph © 1992 The Metropolitan Museum of Art; **18.16** © Royal Museum of Central Africa, Tervuren, Belgium. Photo Plusj; **18.17** Photograph by Frederick Lamp; **18.18** Photo courtesy Elizabeth Evanoff Etchepare.

p. 453 Photo courtesy of Professor Herbert M. Cole

Chapter 19: 19.1, 19.7, 19.8, 19.10 Borromeo /Art Resource, NY; **19.2** National Museum of India, New Delhi, India/Bridgeman Art Library; **19.3, 19.4** S/AR; **19.5, 19.6, 19.12** akg-images/Jean-Louis Nou; **19.11** Paul Miller/Black Star; **19.13** The Nelson-Atkins Museum of Art, Kansas City, Missouri (Purchase: Nelson Trust). 34-66; **19.14** Robert Harding Picture Library; **19.15** © Cultural Relics Publishing House, Beijing; **19.16** © The Trustees of The British Museum; **19.17** HIP/ Scala/Art Resource, NY; **19.18** © Cultural Relics Publishing House, Beijing; **19.19** The Nelson-Atkins Museum of Art, Kansas City, Missouri (Purchase: Nelson Trust). 34-10. Photo Credit: Robert Newcombe; **19.20** The Nelson-Atkins Museum of Art, Kansas City, Missouri (Purchase: Nelson Trust). 47-71 Photo Credit: Robert Newcombe; **19.21** National Palace Museum, Taipei, Taiwan, Republic of China CN 264; **19.22** Princeton University Art Museum. Bequest of John B. Elliot Class of 1951. accession no. 1998-54. Photo credit: Bruce M. White. © 2003 Photo: Trustees of Princeton University; **19.23** Chion-in Temple, Kyoto. Photograph courtesy of Kyoto National Museum; **19.24** © The Cleveland Museum of Art, 2007. Norweb Collection, 1957.27; **19.25, 19.26** Photo credit: Kyodo News, Tokyo; **19.27** Tokugawa Art Museum, Nagoya; **19.28** Kozan-ji Temple, Kyoto. Photo courtesy, Tokyo National Museum; **19.29** Fenollosa-Weld Collection, 11.4000. Museum of Fine Arts. Boston. Photograph © 2007 Museum of Fine Arts, Boston; **19.30** Chion-in Temple, Kyoto. Photo credit: Sakamoto Photo Laboratory, Tokyo; **19.31, 19.32, 19.33** Tokyo National Museum. TNM Image Archives Source:http//TNM Archives.jp/; **19.34** Freer Gallery of Art, Smithsonian Institution, Washington, DC: Gift of Charles Lang Freer, F1899.34.

p. 463 left & right HIP/AR
p. 467 © Michael Freeman

Chapter 20: 20.1 Lipundja, 1912-1968, Daygurrgurr clan, Gopapuyngu language, Milingimbi, central Arnhem Land. Djalambu, 1964. Earth pigments on bark. 134.5 x 74.5 cm. National Gallery of Victoria, Melbourne, Australia. Purchased through the Art Foundation of Victoria with the assistance of Esso Australia Ltd. Fellow 1989. © 2008

ARS, NY/VISCOPY, Australia; **20.2** © Chris Rainier/Corbis; **20.3** Georgia Lee, Rapa Nui Journal-Easter Island Foundation, CA; **20.4** HIP/Art Resource, NY; **20.5** © Earl and Nazima Kowall/Corbis; **20.6** akg-images; **20.7** Carl Frank/Photo Researchers, Inc; **20.8** SEF/Art Resource, NY; **20.9** J. G. Sidaner/Art Resource, NY; **20.10** Courtesy Florida Museum of Natural History, Gainesville, FL; **20.11** © Justin Kerr; **20.12** Werner Forman/Art Resource, NY; **20.13** L/AR; **20.14** The Metropolitan Museum of Art, Gift of Nathan Cummings, 1963 (63.226.8). Photograph © 1994 The Metropolitan Museum of Art; **20.15** Nick Saunders/Barbara Heller Photo Library, London/Art Resource, NY; **20.16** © abm – archives barbier-mueller – Photographer Pierre-Alain Ferrazzini inv. 531-3; **20.17** Ohio Historical Society, Columbus; **20.18** New York State Historical Association, Cooperstown, New York. Fenimore Art Museum, The Eugene and Clare Thaw Collection. Photo: John Bigelow Taylor, NYC; **20.19** New York State Historical Association, Cooperstown, New York. Fenimore Art Museum, The Eugene and Clare Thaw Collection. Photo: John Bigelow Taylor, NYC; **20.20** © Kevin Fleming/Corbis; **20.21** Collection of the Frederick R. Weisman Art Museum at the University of Minnesota, Minneapolis. Transfer, Department of Anthropology; **20.22** Brooklyn Museum of Art, Museum Collection Fund, 03.325.4653; **20.23** © Corbis; **20.24** Royal British Columbia Museum, Victoria, catalogue no.: 15828 A,B.

p. 504 Courtesy the artist, © Bill Holm

Chapter 21: 21.1, 21.3, 21.7 L/AR; **21.2, 21.4, 21.6** RMN/AR; **21.5** Image © Board of Trustees, National Gallery of Art, Washington, Ailsa Mellon Bruce Collection. 1970.17.48; **21.8** The Metropolitan Museum of Art, H. O. Havemeyer Collection, Bequest of Mrs. H. O. Havemeyer, 1929 (29.100.113). Photograph © 1996 The Metropolitan Museum of Art; **21.9** The Museum of Modern Art, New York. Digital Image © The Museum of Modern Art/Licensed by SCALA/Art Resource, NY; **21.10** Philadelphia Museum of Art: George W. Elkins Collection. Photo: Graydon Wood; **21.11** The Metropolitan Museum of Art, New York, Morris K. Jesup Fund, 1933 (33.61). Photograph © 1992 The Metropolitan Museum of Art; **21.12** Image © Board of Trustees, National Gallery of Art, Washington, Chester Dale Collection. 1963.10.94. (1758)/PA; **21.13** Artothek. © 2008 ARS, NY/ADAGP, Paris; **21.14** The Barnes Foundation, Merion, Pennsylvania, USA/Bridgeman Art Library. © 2008 Succession H. Matisse, Paris/ARS, NY; **21.15** The Museum of Modern Art, New York. Purchase. Digital Image © The Museum of Modern Art/Licensed by SCALA/Art Resource, NY. © (for works by E. L. Kirchner) by Dr. Wolfgang & Ingeborg Henze-Ketterer, Wichtrach/Bern; **21.16** Solomon R. Guggenheim Museum, New York. Gift, Solomon R. Guggenheim, 1937. Photo: David Heald © Solomon R. Guggenheim Foundation, New York. © 2008 ARS, NY/ADAGP, Paris; **21.17** The Museum of Modern Art, New York , Acquired through the Lillie P. Bliss Bequest. Digital Image © The Museum of Modern Art/Licensed by SCALA/Art Resource, NY. © 2008 Estate of Pablo Picasso/ARS, NY; **21.18** Musée d'art moderne de Lille Métrople, Villeneuve d'Ascq, Gift of Geneviève and Jean Masurel in 1979. © Muriel Anssens. © 2008 ARS, NY/ADAGP, Paris; **21.19** Hans Hinz - Artothek, © 2008 ARS, NY/ADAGP, Paris; **21.20** S/AR. © 2008 ARS, NY/SIAE, Rome; **21.21** The Museum of Modern Art, New York , Acquired through the Lillie P. Bliss Bequest. Digital Image © The Museum of Modern Art/Licensed by SCALA/Art Resource, NY; **21.22** Solomon R. Guggenheim Museum, New York. Photo Credit: David Heald. © 2008 ARS, NY/ADAGP, Paris; **21.23** Indiana University Art Museum, Partial gift of Mrs. William Conroy. IUAM#71.37.7 Photo credit: Michael Cavanagh and Kevin Montague © 2008 ARS, NY/ADAGP, Paris/Succession Marcel Duchamp; **21.24** CNAC/MNAM/Dist RMN/AR. © 2008 ARS, NY/ADAGP, Paris; **21.25** The Museum of Modern Art, New York. Purchase. Digital Image © The Museum of Modern Art/Licensed by SCALA/Art Resource, NY/© 2008 ARS, NY/ProLitteris, Zürich; **21.26** The Museum of Modern Art, New York. Given anonymously. Digital Image © The Museum of Modern Art/Licensed by SCALA/Art Resource, NY. © 2008 Salvador Dali, Gala-Salvador Dali Foundation/ARS, NY; **21.27** Albright-Knox Art Gallery, Buffalo, New York, Room of Contemporary Art Fund, 1940. © 2008 Successió Miró/ARS, NY/ADAGP, Paris; **21.28** Photo: Sovfoto /Eastfoto; **21.29** The Museum of Modern Art, New York. Gift of Mr. and Mrs. William A.M. Burden. (510.1964).Digital Image © The Museum of Modern Art/Licensed by SCALA/Art Resource, NY © 2007 Mondrian/Holtzman Trust c/o HCR International Warrenton VA USA; **21.30** Centraal Museum, Utrecht; **21.31** The Museum of Modern Art, New York. Gift of Herbert Bayer. Digital Image © The Museum of Modern Art/Licensed by SCALA/Art Resource, NY; **21.32** Hans Hinz/Artothek. © 2008 ARS, NY/ADAGP, Paris; **21.33** Schomburg Center, The New York Public Library/AR.

p. 513 left akg-images/Robert O'Dea
p. 513 center L/AR
p. 521 The Pierpont Morgan Library, New York/Art Resource, NY
p. 525 Philadelphia Museum of Art: A. E. Gallatin Collection. Photo: Graydon Wood. © 2008 Estate of Pablo Picasso/ARS, NY

Chapter 22: 22.1 The Museum of Contemporary Art, Los Angeles, The Rita and Taft Schreiber Collection. Photo: Fredrik Nilsen.© 2008 The Pollock-Krasner Foundation/Artist Rights Society (ARS), New York; **22.2** The Nelson-Atkins Museum of Art, Kansas City, Missouri. Gift of William Inge, 56-128. Photograph by Jamison Miller. © 2008 The Willem de Kooning Foundation/ARS, NY; **22.3** Albright-Knox Art Gallery, Buffalo, New York, Gift of Seymour H. Knox Jr. , 1956. © 1998 Kate Rothko Prizel & Christopher Rothko /ARS, NY; **22.4** CNAC/MNAM/Dist. RMN/AR; **22.5** Whitney Museum of American Art, New York. Gift of the artist 69.161a-n. Photograph © 1996: Whitney Museum of American Art, New York. Photo by Geoffrey Clements. © 2008 Estate of Louise Nevelson/ARS, NY; **22.6** The Museum of Modern Art, New York. Purchase and an anonymous gift and Louise Reinhardt Smith Bequest. Digital Image © The Museum of Modern Art/Licensed by SCALA/Art Resource, NY. Art © Robert Rauschenberg/Licensed by VAGA, New York, NY; **22.7** The Museum of Modern Art, New York. Gift of Mr. and Mrs. Robert C. Scull. Digital Image © The Museum of Modern Art/Licensed by SCALA/Art Resource, NY. Art © Jasper Johns/Licensed by VAGA, New York, NY; **22.8** Research Library, The Getty Research Institute, Los Angeles, California (980063). Photo: Lawrence Shustak; **22.9** Albright-Knox Art Gallery, Buffalo, New York, Gift of Seymour H. Knox, 1963. © 2008 Andy Warhol Foundation for the Visual Arts/ARS, NY/TM Licensed by Campbell's Soup Co. All rights reserved; **22.10** © Estate of Roy Lichtenstein. Photo: Robert McKeever; **22.11** Whitney Museum of American Art, New York. Gift of Howard and Jean Lipman Foundation, Inc. 68.73. Photograph © 2007: Whitney Museum of American Art. © 2008 ARS, NY/ADAGP, Paris; **22.12** © ARS, NY, Collection of the Artist. Art Resource, NY. © 2008 Frank Stella/ARS, NY; **22.13** Hirshhorn Museum and Sculpture Garden, Smithsonian Institution, Washington, DC. Gift of Joseph H. Hirshhorn, 1972. Photo: Lee Stalsworth. Art © Judd Foundation/Licensed by VAGA, New York, NY; **22.14** The Newark Museum/Art Resource, NY. Art © The George and Helen Segal Foundation/Licensed by VAGA, New York, NY; **22.15** © The Cleveland Museum of Art, 2007. Purchase with a grant from The National Endowment for the Arts, matched by gifts from members of the Cleveland Society for Contemporary Art, 1974.53. Courtesy of the artist and Nancy Hoffman Gallery, New York; **22.16** Courtesy of Joseph Kosuth. © 2008 Joseph Kosuth/ARS, NY; **22.17** © Miriam Schapiro. Courtesy the artist; **22.18** Image © Board of Trustees, National Gallery of Art, Washington, Gift of Arthur M. Bullowa, in honor of the 50th Anniversary of the National Gallery of Art. 1991.143.2 © Estate of Alice Neel. Courtesy Robert Miller Gallery, New York; **22.19** © Derek Croucher/Corbis; **22.20** Collection Walker Art Center, Minneapolis. T.B. Walker Acquisition Fund, 1992. Courtesy of the artist and Paula Cooper Gallery, New York; **22.21** © Art Resource, NY. © Ansel Kiefer; **22.22** Courtesy the artist and Mary Boone Gallery, New York; **22.23** The Broad Art Foundation, Santa Monica. Photo credit: Zindman/Fremont. © 2008 The Estate of Jean-Michel Basquiat /ADAGP, Paris /ARS, New York; **22.24** The Broad Art Foundation, Santa Monica. © 2008 Susan Rothenberg/ARS, NY; **22.25** Courtesy the artist and Matthew Marks Gallery, New York; **22.26** © Jenny Holzer, Photo: Thomas Holder. © 2008 Jenny Holzer/ARS, NY; **22.27** Courtesy the Estate of David Wojnarowicz and P.P.O.W. Gallery, New York; **22.28** Courtesy the artist and Bernice Steinbaum Gallery, Miami, FL; **22.29** Photo courtesy of Jack Shainman Gallery, New York; **22.30** Courtesy of Canal St. Communications. Photo Adriane Friere; **22.31** Courtesy the artist Cai Guo-Qiang; **22.32** Courtesy Hosfelt Gallery, San Francisco. © Jim Campbell; **22.33** Courtesy the artist; **22.34** Collection of the artist. Photo: Allan Finkelman. Art © Louise Bourgeois/Licensed by VAGA, New York, NY. Art © Louise Bourgeois/Licensed by VAGA, New York, NY; **22.35** Courtesy of the artist. © Bill Viola. Photo Kira Perov; **22.36** Courtesy of Stephen Friedman Gallery, London and James Cohan Gallery, New York; **22.37** Courtesy Blum & Poe, Los Angeles; **22.38** Courtesy Marian Goodman Gallery Paris; **22.39** Courtesy Alexander & Bonin Gallery; **22.40** The Museum of Contemporary Art, Los Angeles. # 2000.69. Courtesy the artist and Marian Goodman Gallery, New York; **22.41** Courtesy Usha Mirchandani, The Fine Art Resource, Bombay. Contact info on the website: http://www.fineartresourceindia.com.

p. 538 © 1991 Hans Namuth Estate, Courtesy Center for Creative Photography, The University of Arizona, Tucson
p. 544 © www.corbis.com/Corbis
p. 551 National Portrait Gallery, Smithsonian Institution/Art Resource, NY. © Estate of Alice Neel. Courtesy Robert Miller Gallery, New York
p. 559 left & right © Guerrilla Girls

INDEX

All references are to page numbers.
Numbers in **boldface** indicate an illustration on that page.